RAND McNALLY

THE NEW
COSMOPOLITAN
WORLD ATLAS

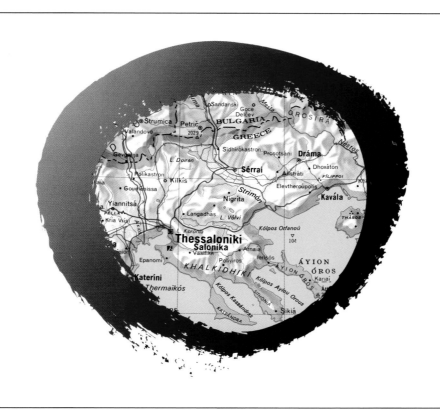

THE NEW COSMOPOLITAN WORLD ATLAS

RAND McNALLY

CHICAGO · NEW YORK · SAN FRANCISCO

CONTENTS

The New Cosmopolitan World Atlas

Cartography

Michael W. Dobson, V. Patrick Healy, Timothy J. Carter,
Winifred V. Farbman, Susan K. Hudson, Robert K. Argersinger,
Ronald F. Peters.

Editorial and Design

Jon M. Leverenz, Elizabeth Fagan Adelman, Laura C. Schmidt,
Vito M. DePinto, Corasue Nicholas, Jerry M. Sullivan (writer).

The New Cosmopolitan World Atlas
Copyright © 1992 by Rand McNally & Company.

1993 Revised Edition

All rights reserved. No part of this publication may be
reproduced, stored in a retrieval system, or transmitted,
in any form or by any means–electronic, mechanical,
photocopied, recorded, or other–without the prior written
permission of Rand McNally & Company.

Printed in the United States of America.

Library of Congress Cataloging-in-Publication Data

Rand McNally and Company.
    The new cosmopolitan world atlas / [cartography,
Michael W. Dobson . . . [et al.]. -- 1993 rev. ed.
        p.   cm.
    Includes index.
    ISBN 0-528-83553-X
    1. Atlases.   I. Dobson, Michael W.   II. Title.   III. Title:
Cosmopolitan world atlas.
G1021.R35 1993 <G&M>   93-15335
912--dc20   ,   CIP
                                                  MAP

THIS FRAGILE EARTH

EARTH IN BALANCE
The Fragile Biosphere

*T*he most lasting value of humanity's exploration of space may be the clear picture it has given us of our own home, the earth. It has been said that the environmental movement began when astronauts brought back the first pictures of the earth taken from the moon. Suddenly we realized that the earth of our tradition-bound imaginations—a vast globe filled with remote reaches scarcely touched by humanity—was really just a tiny ball floating in empty space.

Since those first voyages, spaceships from the earth have explored the rest of the solar system. They have brought us pictures of worlds stranger than our most outlandish ideas. And they have shown us that of all the worlds that swing in their orbits around the sun, only the earth has life.

Even here, life is confined to a thin layer that covers the planet like a coat of paint. This is the *biosphere,* the sphere of life.

The continuous movement of energy, minerals, air, and water through the biosphere connects every part of it with every other part. Clouds, for example, carry the water vapor from the oceans to the hearts of the continents. Ocean currents carry the warmth of tropical sunlight to cold northern regions. Winds blow the nutrient-rich dust from the Great Plains to places far from the United States. A seabird in one part of the world sweeps down on a fish and captures some of the energy its prey gained while feeding in the waters of another part of

The Miracle of the Biosphere
Life clings to the surface of the earth. The interior of our planet is a fiery caldron, a place of temperatures and pressures beyond endurance for any living thing. Just a few miles above our heads, the airless cold of outer space creates an environment as dead as the surface of the moon. Yet here in the biosphere, life has thrived for billions of years. In all that time, the earth has stayed warm enough to keep everything from freezing, and cool enough to keep the oceans from boiling away. As far as we know, there is no other place like this in the universe.

The variety of life in the biosphere is immense. Each species is unique—and therefore precious. Koalas live in Australia, spending their lives in the eucalyptus trees whose leaves are their only food. Destruction of their habitat has made them a rare species.

the world.

The raw materials this complex global system needs—minerals, water, air—come from the earth, but the operation of the system depends on a constant flow of energy from the sun. The movement of currents in the oceans and winds in the atmosphere is created by solar power.

The *hydrologic cycle* that bathes the earth in life-giving rain is another gift of the sun. Solar energy evaporates water from oceans, from lakes and rivers, from the leaves of plants, and from the land itself. This moisture rises, condenses into clouds, and then falls as rain and snow.

The energy that feeds living things also comes from the sun. Green plants have evolved the means to capture a fraction of the sun's radiant energy through the process called *photosynthesis. Chlorophyll,* the pigment that makes green plants green, converts light to chemical energy by breaking down molecules of carbon dioxide from the air and water absorbed from the earth and remaking them as molecules of a simple sugar called *glucose.* Modified in countless ways, this sugar both builds the plant and feeds life on earth.

The only waste product of photosynthesis is oxygen. The constant infusion of oxygen into the atmosphere by green plants balances the consumption of this vital element by animals through respiration and maintains the balance of gases in the atmosphere.

Ecologists call green plants *producers* because they produce energy. Animals and plants without chlorophyll are called *consumers.* They depend on the energy produced by green plants. Both plants and animals live in communities where there is intensive interaction and complex interdependence between species. The term *ecosystem* describes a collection of interdependent producers and consumers. Ecosystems are the basic building blocks of the biosphere. All species live in ecosystems.

Water, air, and minerals are endlessly recycled through ecosystems, but the movement of energy is a one-way trip. Plants use much of the energy they capture as fuel for their own physiologies. Herbivorous animals from mice to elephants use much of the energy they consume carrying on their lives. Only a small amount remains to sustain the carnivores who live by consuming the plant-eating animals.

Human beings have become the most successful species in the history of life on earth largely because of our ability to bend natural processes to fit our own needs and wants. A wheat field is a simplified version of a natural ecosystem. It has only one kind of plant rather than hundreds and only one major herbivore: us. With the domestic animals that supply us with meat, milk, eggs, and hides, we take the role of carnivore, harvesting herbivores from our position at the top of the food chain.

Above: The diversity of life on earth is almost beyond comprehension. This lily is one of about 250,000 different kinds of flowering plants. The dragonfly is one of more than a million species of insects.

Right: Energy flows through the biosphere, from the sun to algae in the sea, from algae to small crustaceans, from crustaceans to small fish, from small fish to salmon, and from salmon to brown bear.

Left: The diversity of human beings and their cultures is one of our strengths as a species. It allows us to live in many different places in many different ways. But we must remember that we need to share the biosphere with all living things.

As human populations have grown and spread, we have modified a substantial portion of the earth's land areas to fit our needs. Plowed fields and pasturelands have replaced forests and grasslands. Our once-scattered settlements have grown into huge urban concentrations covering thousands of square miles.

Our intrusions into natural systems have become so massive that they are interfering with the operations of the processes that sustain life on earth. The difficult environmental problems we face arise from this fact. And the search for solutions to these problems is really the search for ways to sustain human life without disrupting the processes that sustain all life.

On pages I•4 through I•9, we will be looking at the processes that sustain the biosphere and some of the ways we humans have remade the earth. Pages I•10 through I•17 will focus on major environmental problems created by our interference with natural processes and look at some attempts to deal with these problems. Pages I•18 through I•32 look at each of the continents, telling of the most severe environmental problems each continent faces and of the work being done to try to solve them.

Food and Water from the Sun

The sun's energy pulls water from the sea and drops it on the mountains, where gravity takes over to return it to the sea. The sun's radiant energy is transformed by plants to chemical energy. The converted energy then feeds grasshoppers and the meadowlarks that eat them. The same energy sustains the zebra and supports the lion that preys on that zebra. This way, the sun's energy circulates through the biosphere.

I•3

The Restless Earth

The face of the moon is pocked with ancient craters, records of meteor impacts suffered when the solar system was young. They dominate a surface that has not changed in billions of years.

The ancient history of the earth is much harder to read, because on our planet, the crust is in constant motion; the surface is continuously changing. About two hundred million years ago, when dinosaurs were the dominant land animals, the continents were clustered in a single, enormous land mass geologists call Pangaea (Greek for "all land"). Then North America and Europe, South America and Africa began to split along a widening crack that eventually grew into the Atlantic Ocean. Antarctica drifted south toward the pole and India drifted north. Eventually, India collided with Asia, producing the gigantic uplift called the Himalayas. Fossils in the rocks at the top of Mount Everest, the highest place on earth, reveal that the rock was originally part of the seafloor.

The hard rocks of the earth's crust float on a super-heated layer of soft rock. The crust is broken into six large plates and several smaller ones. Driven by forces deep in the earth, these plates are in constant motion. In the middle of the Atlantic, the Eurasian and American plates are pulling apart. Lava flows up through the widening crack between the plates, creating islands like Iceland.

In California, the Pacific Plate and the American Plate are sliding past each other, and the friction of their passing creates many earthquakes. In the western Pacific, the Pacific Plate is sliding under the Eurasian Plate and raising volcanoes like Japan's Mount Fuji.

The history of the earth is a story of 4.6 billion years of processes like these. It is a story of mountain ranges raised up and eroded away. Of continents and oceans changing shape, size, and location. Of minerals rising from the earth's interior to the surface.

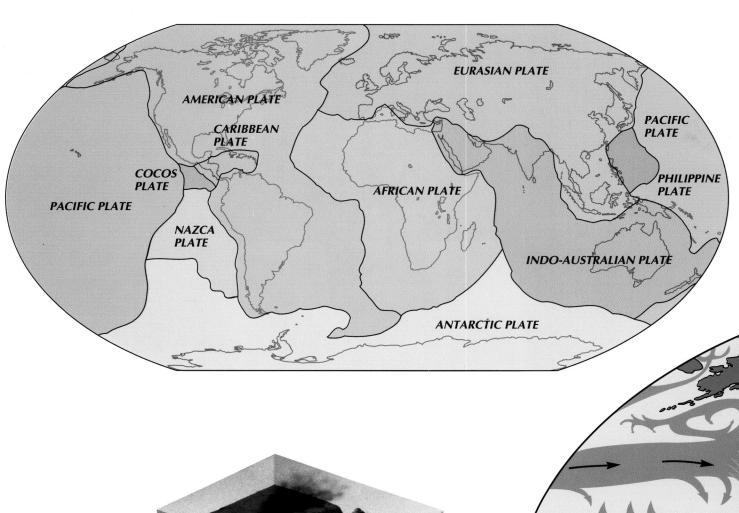

The earth's crust is thinner over midoceanic regions than over the continents. This allows molten magma from the mantle to force its way to the surface and form ridges and new crust. Growth at the midoceanic ridges slowly forces the plates apart. As they spread, their outer edges collide with other plates. One plate is forced beneath the other in a subduction zone, and its crust is melted back into the mantle.

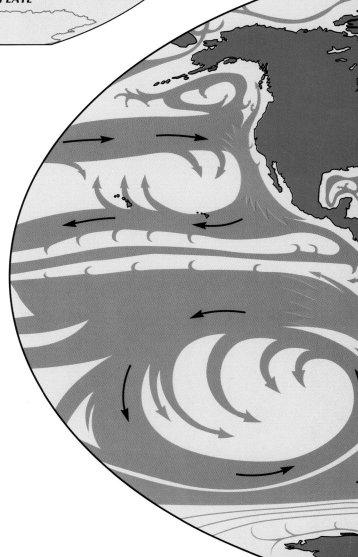

The ocean current called the Gulf Stream carries warm water from the American tropics to the northwest coast of Europe. Westerly winds blow across the warm water and then onto the continent. Because of the Gulf Stream, British farmers can grow wheat at latitudes that, in Canada, grow polar bears.

The waters of the world ocean are in constant motion, too. Water near the surface flows in well-established currents that are like rivers within the ocean. The rotation of the earth on its axis creates a force called *Coriolis force* that bends these currents into giant circles called *gyres.* In the Northern Hemisphere, these gyres flow clockwise. In the Southern Hemisphere, they flow counterclockwise. You can see the same sort of circulation—also caused by Coriolis force—around the drain in your bathtub.

The deep waters flow too. Cold water from the poles flows toward the equator. This cold water is heavy and rich in mineral nutrients. In a few locations, conditions are right for this water to rise to the surface. The minerals make these upwelling zones rich in life. One such zone, off the coast of Peru, provides one-seventh of the world's total catch of ocean fish.

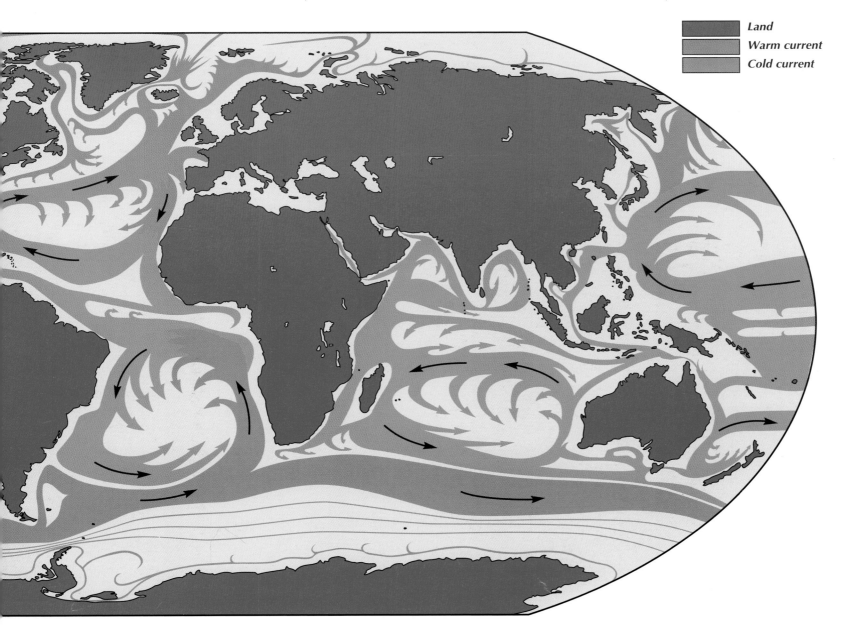

Land
Warm current
Cold current

EARTH IN BALANCE
The Green Mantle

One of the maps on these pages shows the pattern of climates around the world. The other shows the distribution of vegetation types that would exist if humans did not intervene. Notice how similar they are. The fit is not exact, but we can see that tundra vegetation grows in polar climates. The evergreen forests of northern Eurasia and North America appear in moist climates with cold winters and cool summers. The steppes of central Asia and the short-grass prairies of North America grow in cool climates with dry summers. The rain forests of South America, Africa, and Asia are found in hot, wet climates near the equator. Climate is the single most important factor in determining where plants can grow. And vegetation is a major factor determining where animals—including human beings—can live.

We use the word *biome* to describe these divisions of the earth's vegetation and the ani-

winds that used to carry ships from Europe west across the Atlantic to Central and South America. In the temperate zones, the prevailing winds blow from west to east. When the Spanish sent gold from their American colonies back to Europe, the ships skirted Florida and then turned north to catch the westerlies that would blow them home to Spain.

Prevailing winds have a major impact on cli-

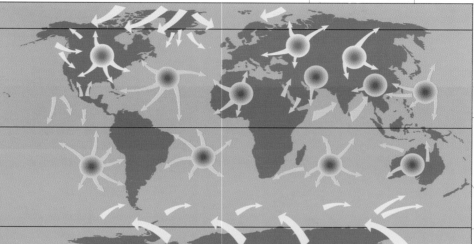

Cold air ⟶   **Warm air** ⟶

Cold winters and warm dry summers in the temperate zone create grasslands like the steppes of central Asia or this prairie in North America's Great Plains.

mals that depend on that vegetation. Thus the tropical forest biome includes both the trees and the monkeys that live in them.

The earth's atmosphere is an ocean of gases with currents that span the globe. The sun drives these currents, and their continuing patterns shape global climate.

Winds flow down a pressure gradient, from areas of high atmospheric pressure to areas of low pressure. Along the equator air pressure is generally low. Air flows in and, heated by the sun, rises. Rising air cools. Its moisture condenses and falls as rain. Equatorial regions receive a constant heavy flow of energy from the sun, and their climates tend to be warm and wet all year.

Around the tropics—about 23 degrees north and south of the equator—is a belt of continuing high pressure where air sinks and creates a hot, dry climate. Notice the cluster of deserts along the tropics. The Sahara and Kalahari in Africa, the deserts of Australia and Arabia are all at those latitudes.

North and south of the tropics, in the temperate zones, we find changeable climates and enough rainfall to support rich forests and grasslands. Near the poles, high pressure areas again dominate, and rain and snow are scarce. The tundra is a very cold desert.

Between the tropics, the prevailing winds blow from east to west. These are the trade

The lush green of this forest in Oregon is the product of a climate with mild winters, cool summers, and precipitation all year.

mate. Coastal California enjoys mild temperatures year-round because of the winds blowing over the waters of the Pacific Ocean. On the east coast at the same latitudes, westerlies blowing across the continent bring hotter summers and colder winters. In North America, the rain shadow of the Sierra Nevada lies to the east of the range because the prevailing winds are from the west. Deserts cover much of Nevada, Utah, and Arizona.

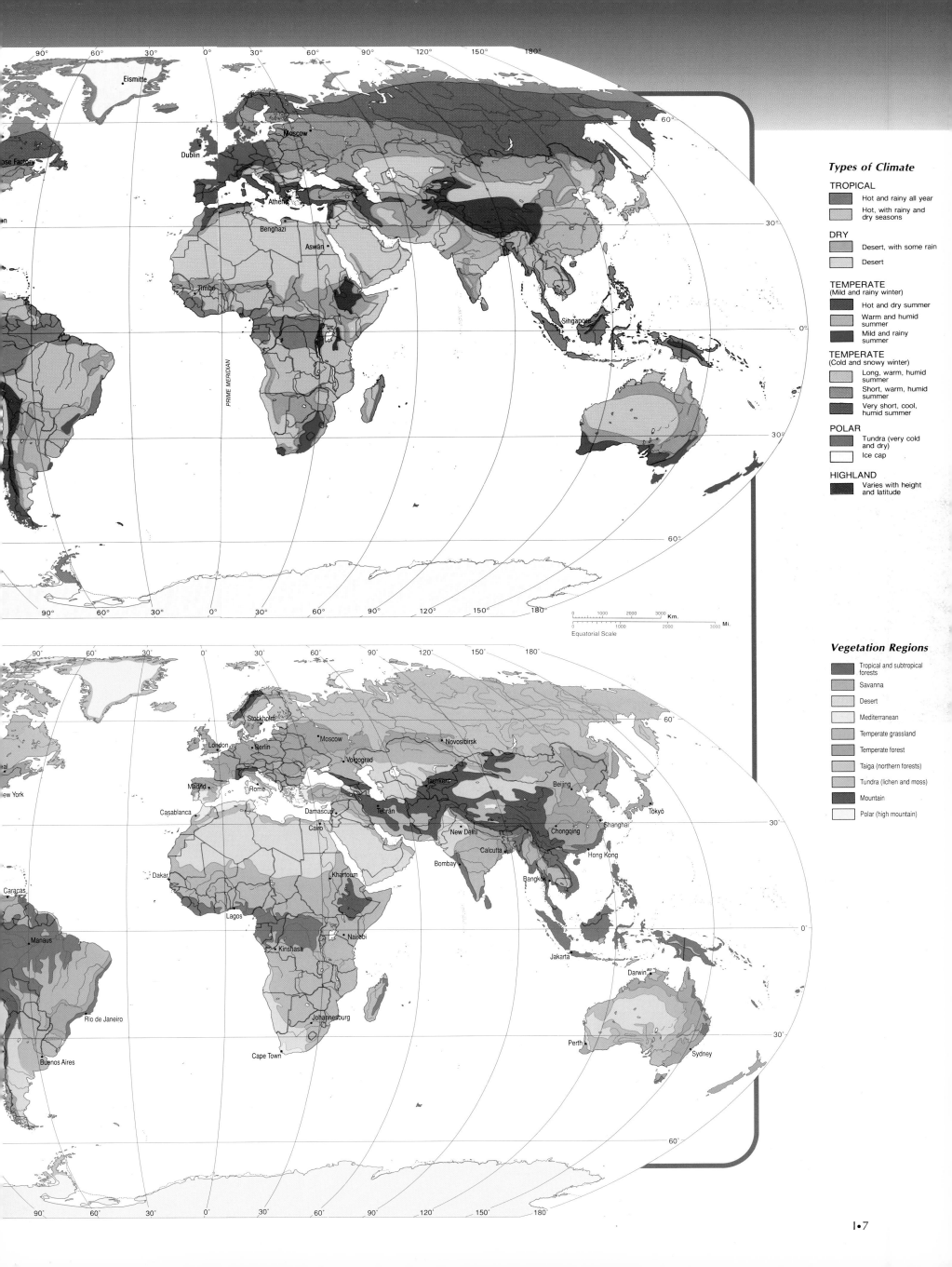

Types of Climate

TROPICAL
- Hot and rainy all year
- Hot, with rainy and dry seasons

DRY
- Desert, with some rain
- Desert

TEMPERATE (Mild and rainy winter)
- Hot and dry summer
- Warm and humid summer
- Mild and rainy summer

TEMPERATE (Cold and snowy winter)
- Long, warm, humid summer
- Short, warm, humid summer
- Very short, cool, humid summer

POLAR
- Tundra (very cold and dry)
- Ice cap

HIGHLAND
- Varies with height and latitude

0   1000   2000   3000   Km.
0   1000   2000   3000   Mi.
Equatorial Scale

Vegetation Regions
- Tropical and subtropical forests
- Savanna
- Desert
- Mediterranean
- Temperate grassland
- Temperate forest
- Taiga (northern forests)
- Tundra (lichen and moss)
- Mountain
- Polar (high mountain)

EARTH IN BALANCE
The Dominant Species

Farming with tractors, with oxen, or by hand, the world's people have turned more than 2 billion acres of our earth into cropland.

More than 40 percent of the world's people now live in towns and cities, and estimates are that by the year 2010, more than half of humanity will be urban.

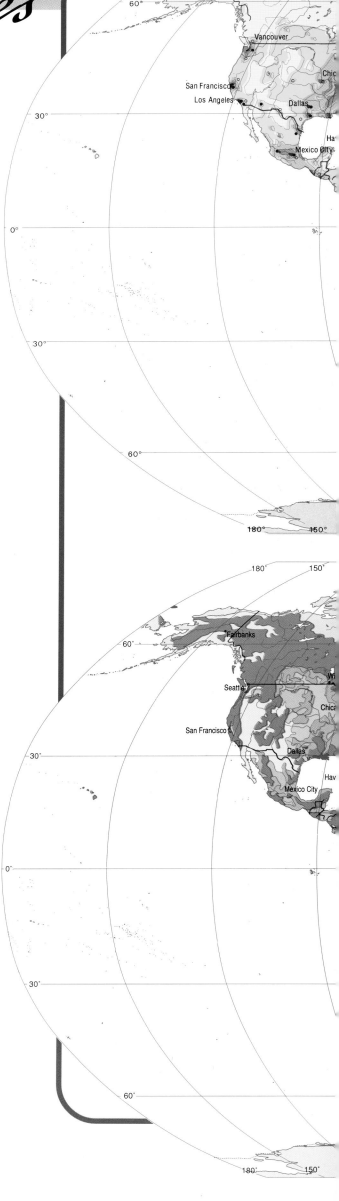

*H*uman beings are unique in the history of life on earth. Today, we say that dinosaurs once dominated the earth. But the species known as dinosaurs were a huge group of animals with many different variations and modes of life. No single species has ever dominated the biosphere the way we do. We are the dominant species in practically every land environment on earth, and our technology has put us at the top of the food chain in the world's oceans as well.

We reached this powerful position by being smart, adaptable, and willing to eat almost anything. Other animals have to wait for the slow processes of evolution to open up new habitats for them. We invent what we need, replacing genetic change with the much faster processes of cultural change. It took only a few thousand years for human beings to colonize the entire Western Hemisphere, from the Arctic environments of northern Alaska to the dense rain forests of the Amazon. The restless intelligence of humanity created the clothing, tools, houses, boats, and other equipment we needed to thrive in almost any environment. We sought out the local varieties of plants and animals suitable for domestication and remade the landscape to fit our needs.

Of all our inventions, none is more important than agriculture. It was discovered independently in several places in the world, and it provided the basis for the development of civilization. Farmers and herdsmen could produce enough food to feed potters, masons, weavers, and eventually, priests, artists, astronomers, and politicians. Modern agriculture has enabled us to feed concentrated human populations, some of which have grown big enough to show up as urban regions on even small-scale maps.

Agriculture also has had a bigger impact on the surface of our planet than any other human activity. Look at the map of world environments on these pages. Millions of square miles of land that were once forests or grasslands are now plowed fields and pastures. Much of North America, Europe, and Asia—especially southern Asia—has been almost completely remade by farmers. Native species of plants and animals have been drastically reduced in numbers—in some cases driven to extinction—by the replacement of their habitats with croplands and pastures.

If you compare the maps on these pages with the vegetation and climate maps on the preceding pages, you will discover the unsurprising fact that human populations are concentrated in temperate and tropical regions with moderate to heavy rainfall. These are areas that were covered with forests or grasslands before humans began remaking the landscape. They are, by and large, the areas that are the most habitable, with the most productive farmland. The only completely uninhabited regions of the earth are those lands perpetually covered with ice, the most arid deserts, or mountains too rugged and inhospitable to offer any space for humans to live.

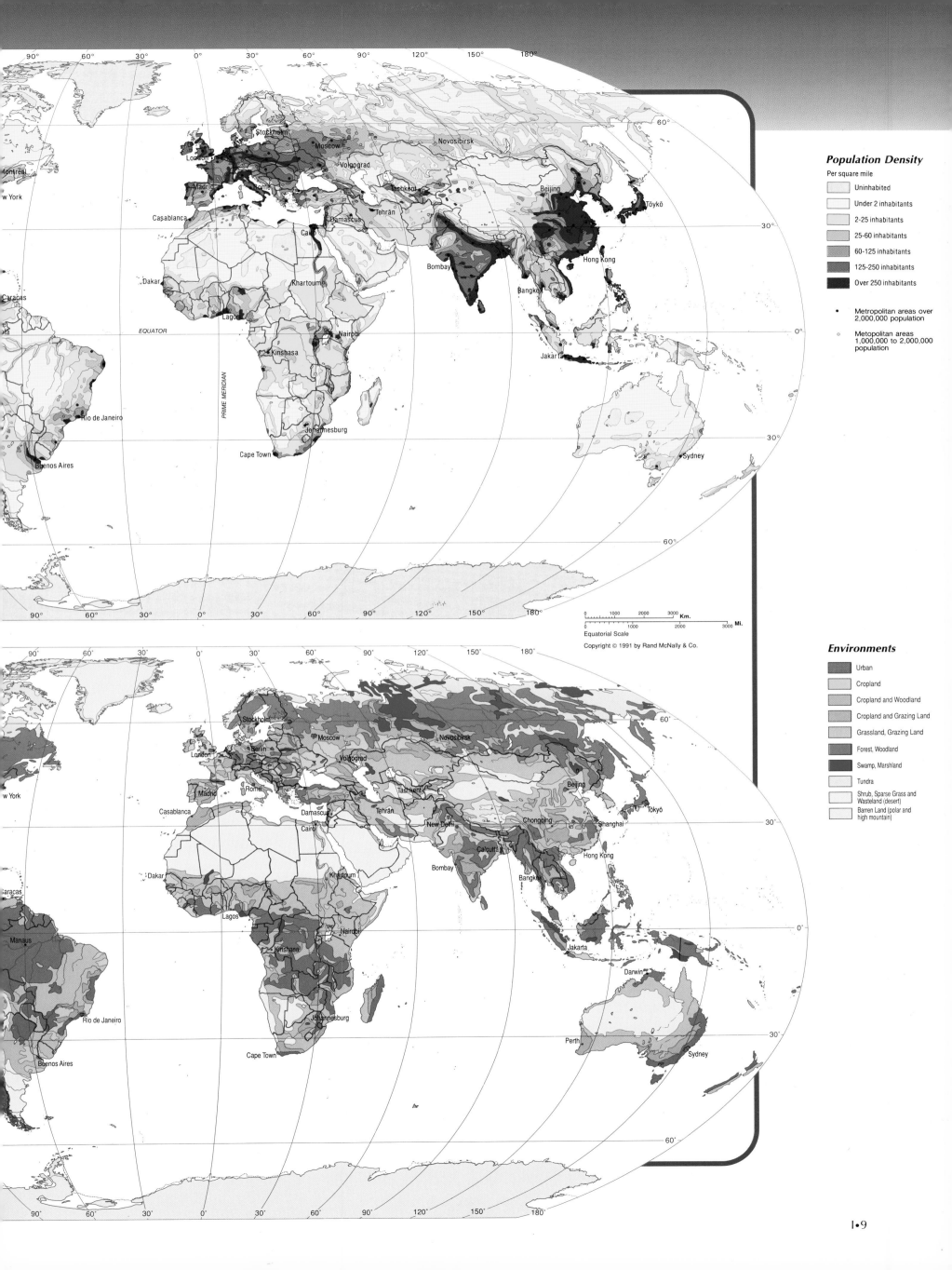

Population Density

Per square mile

	Uninhabited
	Under 2 inhabitants
	2-25 inhabitants
	25-60 inhabitants
	60-125 inhabitants
	125-250 inhabitants
	Over 250 inhabitants

● Metropolitan areas over 2,000,000 population

○ Metopolitan areas 1,000,000 to 2,000,000 population

0   1000   2000   3000   Km.
0   1000   2000   3000   Mi.
Equatorial Scale

Copyright © 1991 by Rand McNally & Co.

Environments

	Urban
	Cropland
	Cropland and Woodland
	Cropland and Grazing Land
	Grassland, Grazing Land
	Forest, Woodland
	Swamp, Marshland
	Tundra
	Shrub, Sparse Grass and Wasteland (desert)
	Barren Land (polar and high mountain)

I•9

*T*he soil is filled with living things. Some of these—insects, spiders, centipedes—are large enough to see. Many others—algae, bacteria, nematodes—are visible only through a microscope. The air is not a living system. It is a mixture of gases. But the proportions of the gases in the mix are maintained by living things. Both earth and air are affected by the actions of human beings. Both are under stress created by our misuse of them.

Most of the organisms that live in the soil get their energy by consuming the remains of plants and animals. Their work releases the nutrients held in the remains, making them available for new growth. All soils are subject to erosion by rain and wind. In a balanced ecosystem, life in the soil compensates for these losses by moving deeper into the subsoil.

Balanced, sustainable systems of agriculture imitate natural systems. Good systems employ crop rotation and fertilizers to replace the nutrients lost in the harvest. They use contour plowing, strip cropping, and other methods to reduce erosion to sustainable levels. With the help of these methods, farmers are also able to keep use of chemical pesticides to a minimum.

Continuing research is developing productive and ecologically sensible ways to grow food. Unfortunately, these methods are not being used on most of the world's cultivated land. Massive erosion reduces fertility, and the heavy use of pesticides releases large amounts of these chemicals into the environment, endangering people and wildlife.

Contour plowing means letting the land dictate the direction of furrows. By plowing across the slope rather than up and down, the farmer creates barriers to erosion that hold both soil and water in place.

Farming Methods Make a Difference

The diagram below shows poor agricultural methods. Spray irrigation loses more water to evaporation and runoff than it supplies to crops. Excessive irrigation also leaves salt deposits in the soil. Crop dusting with aircraft releases large amounts of pesticides into the environment, creating a hazard for wildlife and humans. Plowing up and down slopes rather than across them increases erosion, lowers soil fertility, and muddies streams as well.

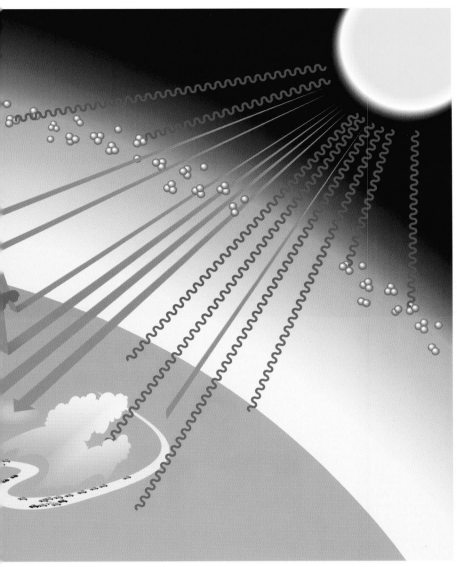

These giant wind generators in California produce electricity without burning fossil fuels and without posing the kind of environmental dangers created by nuclear power. Holding off the greenhouse effect will require more use of renewable, non-polluting sources of energy such as these.

Hazards to the Ozone Layer
Carbon dioxide from the burning of coal and oil and from the massive burning of tropical forests accounts for 56 percent of the greenhouse gases released into the air. Chlorofluorocarbons (CFCs) account for another 23 per- *cent. The chlorine in these compounds—and in other chemicals—is also a major cause of ozone depletion. The amount of carbon dioxide (CO_2) in the air has been rising at an increasing rate since the beginning of the industrial revolution.*

Irrigating arid land creates other problems. Most irrigation methods lose to evaporation up to two-thirds of the water they use. The fresh water used for irrigation carries tiny amounts of salt. The salt accumulates in irrigated fields and in time, renders them unfit for agriculture. More efficient methods of irrigation would not only save water, they would also slow salinization and make soil usable longer.

The atmosphere is under two kinds of stresses. One type is readily visible; the other kind is hidden, subtle, and ultimately, far more dangerous. The visible type of stress is the pollution that creates the pall of dirty brown smog that hangs over many of the world's cities. The hidden, subtle, and more dangerous stresses are *ozone depletion* and the *greenhouse effect.*

Most of the world's free oxygen exists in molecules containing two atoms. The chemical formula is O_2. But high above the earth is a layer of the atmosphere where *ozone*, a form of oxygen whose molecules have three atoms (O_3), is common. Ozone has the ability to absorb ultraviolet radiation. The *ozone layer* is a sort of shield that protects the biosphere from a portion of the sun's energy that is very harmful

to living things. Without the ozone layer, the ability of the biosphere to support life would be reduced, and humans would suffer a dramatic increase in dangerous skin cancers.

The principal threat to the ozone layer is a group of gases called *chlorofluorocarbons* (CFCs), which are used in refrigerators, air conditioners, and some aerosol sprays. These gases break up ozone molecules, destroying the protective barrier. International agreements signed by the major producers of CFCs now call for the elimination of these gases by the turn of the century.

Chlorofluorocarbons play a role in the greenhouse effect too, but the most important gas in that process is CO_2. Our massive use of fossil fuels—oil and coal—is releasing large amounts of carbon into the atmosphere. The carbon is

combined with oxygen to make carbon dioxide, a gas that holds the sun's heat in the atmosphere just as the glass roof of a greenhouse holds heat.

The amount of CO_2 in our atmosphere has been growing, and the rate of growth is increasing. If the earth does get warmer, major agricultural areas—such as the American Midwest—could be struck by severe and continuing droughts. Melting of polar ice caps could raise sea levels enough to flood coastal areas. Significant reductions in our use of fossil fuels will be needed to combat the greenhouse effect.

The human imagination knows no more potent symbol than water. Our religions, our myths, our stories are filled with symbolic springs, cool flowing streams, gentle rains that revive the earth. Water is life.

Yet in the contemporary world, water is not treated wisely. We dump our wastes in it. We use it heedlessly, as if the world had a limitless supply. Even the vast oceans are being stripped of resources and fouled with wastes. Three-fourths of the fresh water we use is devoted to irrigating crops, yet our irrigation methods are so wasteful that most of it never reaches the plants for which it is intended.

Some farmers are now using an irrigation method called *trickle-drip*. This pumps water through hoses or pipes in the fields, and these pipes and hoses apply very small amounts of water to the soil directly over the plant roots. The method provides a double benefit: it saves water, and it reduces the deposition of salt in the soil.

Household use of water accounts for only a small fraction of our water use worldwide—although it makes up a larger proportion in the industrial countries. Wastewater from households is, however, a very serious problem. In most of the world, sewage is dumped untreated into the nearest river, lake, or harbor.

Industrial wastes are also an enormous strain on our freshwater resources. In many respects, they are worse than sewage, because sewage is a natural product that can be attacked by bacteria and eventually reduced to its constituent elements. Industrial wastes include metals—nickel, cadmium, mercury, lead—and other substances that cannot be rendered harmless by natural processes. Once in the water, they stay there.

The world's oceans seem so large that it is hard to imagine how we could harm them. But much of the open sea is virtually the equivalent of a desert; a shortage of mineral nutrients—phosphorus, nitrogen, potassium, and others—limits the growth of the algae that form the base of the food chain. This in turn limits the numbers of animals farther up the chain.

Most of the life in the world's oceans is in shallow water near the shore. Here sunlight and nutrients flowing from the land combine to make a rich environment that supports thousands of species of living things. Some of the animals of the open sea spend the early parts of their lives in these rich offshore locations.

Mangroves dominate thousands of miles of shoreline in tropical regions. These shrubby

Sewage-treatment plants like this one in Austin, Texas, use natural bacterial processes to remove human wastes from water before it is returned to rivers or lakes.

Dirtying the Fresh Water

We misuse fresh water in two major ways: We waste it, and we poison it. We waste it with dams that impound large lakes in arid regions where evaporation takes much of the water. We use more water for irrigation than for any other purpose, but only 25 percent of the water reaches the roots of crops. Arsenic and other poisons leach from mine tailings into streams and ground water. In many cases, wastewater from factories is returned to streams in a highly polluted state, and rivers are routinely used as dumps for toxic byproducts. Many cities dump raw sewage into the nearest river.

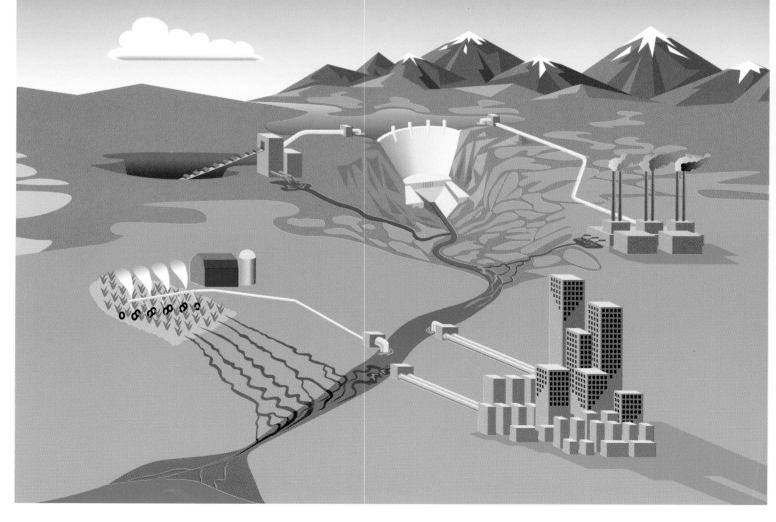

trees provide a shelter from storms for a variety of aquatic life. Offshore, coral reefs create one of the most diverse environments on earth. Along temperate shores, salt marshes teem with life. Estuaries, where fresh and salt water mix, are equally fecund.

The threats to these marine environments come from several sources. Dumping of municipal wastes offshore is a major contributor of pollution. Oil tankers are another source. The big, accidental spills get all the publicity, but ordinary operations such as the cleaning of empty tanks actually account for more oil dumped into the oceans than do the accidental spills. Shoreline development also obliterates hundreds of miles of delicate environments every year.

In both near-shore and open-sea environments, overfishing is a major problem. The annual catch of many important food fish is dropping as the animals become more scarce. Huge floating factories, some of them dragging nets several miles long, capture every living thing in their path: fish, dolphins, sea turtles, even birds.

The plight of whales also calls our attention to our overexploitation of the oceans. Several

Workers scour the beaches of Prince William Sound near Valdez, Alaska, the site of the largest accidental oil spill in United States history. Cleanups are expensive; this one cost $1.3 billion. Looking for better ways to prevent such spills would pay off more in the long run.

Fouling the Salt Water
Most of the life in the oceans is near shore in the shallow waters of the continental shelves. Coral reefs, mangrove swamps, and salt marshes are rich in life and are often nurseries for the young of animals of the open sea. Shoreline development can destroy these habitats, and waste dumping can poison them. Offshore oil drilling and spills from oil tankers pollute the seas. Deliberate spills by oil tankers flushing out tanks actually dump more oil than accidental spills. Overfishing has driven some whales nearly to extinction, and huge trawlers pulling enormous nets catch all the ocean life in their path.

species have been hunted nearly to extinction. International agreements have reduced hunting, but existing agreements could use strengthening. Saving these marine mammals, and commercially important fish species as well, will require a major diplomatic effort to bring all nations into compliance.

Protecting both fresh and salt waters from waste dumping is equally urgent. A beginning has been made on this problem through international agreements limiting dumping of oil, toxics, and industrial and municipal waste, but more remains to be done.

Perhaps the most important change will have to take place in our minds. We need to remember our ancient images of water as life and stop thinking of it as a convenient place to put our garbage.

Plant and Animal Life

Evolution is a process that happens in ecosystems. A constant interplay of complex forces—relations between competitors, between predators and prey, between mutually dependent species, between living things and nonliving factors such as climate—both sustains the ecosystem and creates the selection pressure that gives rise to new species.

Diversity begets diversity. The presence of large numbers of species promotes ever finer divisions of available resources. In the evergreen forests of Canada and the northern United States, the tiny, bright-colored insect-eating birds called wood warblers demonstrate the process. Four species of the genus Dendroica divide tall trees into distinct zones for feeding and nesting. Magnolia warblers nest and feed within fifteen feet of the ground. Black-throated green warblers concentrate in the area between

reclaim the land. The forest ecosystem has been so badly damaged it cannot bounce back.

The demands of human beings are putting all of nature under stress. In the entire North Temperate Zone, in Europe, Asia, and North America, only the area centered on Yellowstone Park in Wyoming can still be considered a functioning ecosystem. Elsewhere, the parks and preserves, while they do provide a measure of protection for many species, are too small and too closely pressed by human populations to function naturally.

Now the destruction of natural areas that has already had such a powerful effect on the North Temperate Zone is spreading to the tropics. Tropical forests, the oldest and richest ecosystems on earth, are being turned into farms and pastures at a dizzying rate. One recent estimate suggests that an area twice the size of Austria is cleared every year.

Usually the best thing we can do for nature is leave it alone. This pine forest in Grand Teton National Park was burned a few years before this picture was taken. Left alone, the forest can restore itself with new growth.

fifteen and forty feet. Blackburnian warblers nest and feed between forty and fifty-five feet, while Cape May warblers concentrate in the tree tops, above fifty-five feet.

Simplicity also begets simplicity. Remove a species, and the effects of the loss ripple through the ecosystem like the waves that radiate from a pebble thrown into the water. When a plant goes extinct, the specialized insects that fed on that plant go with it. A decline in the numbers and variety of insects in the system affects birds, shrews, toads, lizards, and other insect eaters. A decline in these species harms hawks, herons, snakes, and other predators.

Remove enough species, and the whole system may collapse. We cut tropical forests for farmland and pasture. If the farms and pastures are abandoned, often the forest does not

Kill the forest, and you also kill the thousands of species of plants and animals that live in the forest. Tropical forests cover only about 7 percent of the earth, but they harbor half of the earth's species of plants and animals. If the destruction continues, we may lose a million different forms of life by the year 2000.

Most of the world's endangered species—both plants and animals—are on the brink of extinction because their habitats have been destroyed. But some species are threatened in other ways. As many as seventy thousand African elephants are ruthlessly slaughtered each year for their ivory. Rhinos are killed for their horns. Leopards and cheetahs provide pelts worth thousands of dollars each. Parrots by the millions are captured in the wild and sold by the pet trade.

The scope of our destruction of nature is so immense that it is hard to know where to start dealing with it. Stopping the trade in endangered species is the easy part. International agreements already exist, notably the Convention on International Trade in Endangered Species of Wild Fauna and Flora (CITES). Over one hundred countries are now signatories to this convention. CITES is successful only when true international cooperation supports it. Enforcement in the developing nations where the animals come from has to be combined with enforcement in the richer nations that provide the markets.

The more profound problem is the destruction of whole biomes, the loss of the ecosystems that support all life—including human life. Our challenge—in the face of growing human populations—is to satisfy our needs without taking up all the space available on this planet. We need to think about both housing patterns and farming practices to search for ways to get the most out of every acre we use.

We also need to draw on the wisdom of the people who have learned to gain a livelihood from tropical lands in nondestructive ways. The Indians of the Amazon, the Dayaks of Borneo, and many other cultures have a profound knowledge of the ecological processes that sustain the natural systems of their homelands. It will take a combination of their knowledge and the insights of science to develop ways to enjoy the bounty of the forest without destroying the source of that bounty.

Stripping Away Plant Life

Our attack on nature proceeds on several fronts. We take the timber we need with massive clearcuts that remove every tree and thereby create soil erosion and stream pollution. We drain and fill wetlands, destroying the specialized habitats of many plants and animals. We scatter pollutants in the air and water, often harming plants and animals thousands of miles away. And, increasingly, as our populations grow, we simply do not leave nature any space.

A busload of tourists watch a leopard at a game preserve in Kenya. The rise of *ecotourism* has helped many Third World nations pay for preserves where wildlife can be protected.

Hyacinth Macaw

Sperm Whale

Snow Leopard

Elephant

Golden Lion Tamarin

Rhinoceros

Threatening Animal Life

Most of the damage we have visited upon wildlife has been caused by destruction of natural habitats. But some species are undergoing an even more direct assault. We kill whales for their meat and oil. We kill elephants for their ivory tusks and rhinos for their horns. Snow leopards are victims of vanity as they become coats. Parrots are captured from the wild to be locked in cages. Because the slaughter of these animals does not stem from a larger and tougher-to-solve issue, such as habitat destruction, solutions should be easier to find.

Human Life

H uman numbers grew very slowly through most of our history. Births and deaths remained more or less in balance. Our best estimate of world population in A.D. 1 is 150 million. By about 1650, the total was up to 500 million. And then, the explosion began.

By 1850, there were 1.2 billion people in the world. By 1950, that number had doubled to 2.5 billion. By 1990, human numbers had doubled again, to 5.3 billion. It is likely that another three billion will be added to world population by the year 2025.

This explosion is not fueled by an increase in birth rates. People have not been having any more children than they used to have. The critical difference is a major decline in death rates. More food, better sanitation, better housing, and better health care combined to extend the average life span and dramatically lower infant mortality.

But then in Europe, Japan, and North America—the industrialized countries where the benefits of a higher standard of living were spread widely through the population—birth rates began to go down. Instead of having six or eight babies in her lifetime, the average woman had two. Europe, Japan, the United States, and Canada have essentially achieved zero population growth. In some countries—Sweden, Denmark, Germany, Austria, Hungary—population has actually been declining. Demographers speak of the industrial countries as having completed the demographic transition, of having once again balanced birth rates and death rates.

The situation in the Third World is quite different. There, improved health care has lowered death rates, especially among children, but birth rates have remained high. Growth rates of 2 to 3 percent are common, which means that numbers will double in less than twenty-five years.

The countries with the high growth rates are also the countries least able to cope with the social, economic, and environmental consequences of such growth. Think of a country desperately trying to train enough teachers and build enough schools to educate its children when every year the first grade class grows by 3 percent.

Rates of growth have been slowing down in recent years, however, even in the countries with the fastest population growth. And several countries have initiated successful population control programs that offer hope for the future.

The programs that work emphasize the fact that population control cannot be separated from other factors in the lives of people. The decision to have many children is usually rooted in traditional cultural attitudes, but it is also rational and sensible in terms of the life-style many people lead. Infant mortality has been reduced, but it is still higher in the Third World than in the industrialized countries, so having several children gives a family a better chance of raising some of them to adulthood. Children also begin to contribute economically to their families at an early age. By the time they reach puberty, they are likely to be earning more than the cost of their subsistence. Finally, in the absence of Social Security or extensive private pension plans, children are the only way to ensure a comfortable old age.

Successful population control programs—

such as those in Sri Lanka and some of the Indian states—address the problems of poverty as well as teach mothers how to use contraceptive devices. They teach infant and child care and provide immunizations and other health-care assistance so women can feel confident that their babies will live.

The status of women in society also plays a very significant role in the success of family-planning efforts. In cultures where women are subservient to men, where education and the possibility of economic independence are mas-

culine monopolies, it is very difficult to carry out successful population-control programs. In cultures where women have some control over their lives, they generally respond favorably to the opportunity to limit their childbearing.

The long-term question is whether the countries of the Third World will be able to make the demographic transition already accomplished in industrialized countries. Countries that have successfully lowered their birth rates are generally also countries where economic growth has made a difference in the lives of large numbers

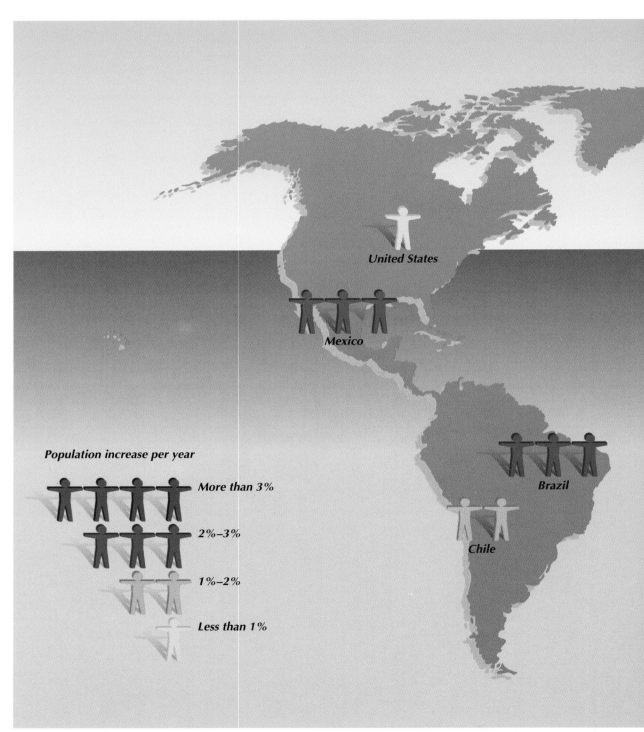

United States

Mexico

Population increase per year

More than 3%

2%–3%

1%–2%

Less than 1%

Brazil

Chile

Crowding Human Life
This map shows very clearly the relationship between economic status and population growth. The industrialized countries, with strong economies—such as France and the United States—show little or no population growth. Chile, a country that is in the middle rank of nations economically, has slightly faster growth. The countries with high growth rates are all among the world's poorer nations. China has managed to cut its growth with the help of an aggressive campaign to limit family size. Countries with high growth rates have young populations who must pass through their child-bearing years before growth will come to a stop.

of people. Continuing development and improvement in the lives of ordinary people must be a major part of population-control efforts.

If population control requires, however, that China's one billion inhabitants and India's 800 million inhabitants consume as much of the earth's resources per person as present-day North Americans or Europeans, then population control is unobtainable. The strain on the biosphere would be so great that the processes that sustain life—including human life—would break down.

That is why our search for sustainable forms of development must be intensified. We need to bend natural processes without breaking them. We need to imitate the actions of nature rather than trying to impose our own vision of how things ought to be done. In agriculture and industry, in the decisions we make about how we want to use the earth, we need to recognize that our grandchildren will someday need to take their living from the same earth that supports us today.

The sprawl of suburban growth around our cities is swallowing up both farmland and natural areas.

France
Russia
Iraq
India
China
Nigeria
Zaire
Madagascar
South Africa

These women in a village in Bangladesh are learning to raise healthy babies as part of a population-control project.

RESTORING THE BALANCE
Europe

A thousand years ago, much of Europe was wilderness. Human populations were small, and ancient forests covered most of the land. And then humans began to expand into these forests, converting woodlands to wheat fields, establishing towns on wilderness rivers. By the end of the Middle Ages, so much forest had been cut that some settlements experienced a shortage of firewood and began mining coal as a substitute fuel. Coal became the fuel that powered the steam engines that powered the Industrial Revolution—perhaps the biggest change in human life since the discovery of agriculture. The power of steam also provided energy for railroads and ships that made travel faster and more reliable.

The Industrial Revolution began in England in the late 18th century, and by 1840, England had become the first nation in which most of the people lived in towns. The rest of Europe followed. Today, nearly three-fourths of all Europeans live in cities; only in a couple of eastern European nations does the majority live in rural areas. In Great Britain, more than 90 percent of the population is urban. Industry dominates European economies. In Germany and France, almost half the work force is employed in industry.

Rural areas are occupied by farms that tend to be small compared to those in the United States. Less than 2 percent of Great Britain's work force is employed in agriculture. In

France, the largest producer and exporter of farm products in western Europe, only 9 percent of the work force is in agriculture.

Centuries of occupation have altered nearly all the natural landscape of the continent. Europe in its natural state survives only in the far north and in a few isolated—mostly mountainous—areas in the east. Even such seemingly wild areas as Germany's Black Forest are actually carefully tended gardens watched over by foresters who literally know every tree.

But those carefully tended woodland gardens are now being threatened by a by-product of the Industrial Revolution called *acid rain.* When we burn coal or oil, the sulphur and nitrogen in these fuels combine with oxygen and escape

Urban	Cropland & Woodland	Grassland, Grazing Land	Swamp, Marshland	Shrub, Sparse Grass, Wasteland (pattern)	Oasis
Cropland	Cropland & Grazing Land	Forest, Woodland	Tundra	Barren Land	

©1991 Rand McNally & Co.

Large populations and heavy industry create scenes like this one in Europe. Here a Bulgarian shepherd tends his flock in the shadow of a giant industrial complex.

Almost three-fourths of Europe's people live in cities. Among the most beautiful of these is Nice on France's Mediterranean coast. Unfortunately, the large numbers of people living near that fragile sea are creating pollution problems. The nations of the Mediterranean are now working together on those problems.

into the air as sulphur dioxide and nitrogen oxide. In the atmosphere, chemical changes convert these oxides to sulfuric and nitric acid. Some of these acids fall to earth as dry particles. Most fall with rain and snow.

Rainfall is naturally acidic, but in industrialized regions, concentrations as much as one hundred times more acid than natural rainfall may occur. The effects are profound. Forty-three percent of the conifers in Switzerland's central alpine region are dead or dying. At least four thousand lakes in Sweden are so heavily acidified that no fish survive in them. Every year, Norway experiences some rainfall that is as acidic as lemon juice.

Who Can Stop the Rain?

Controlling the emissions that create acid rain is difficult and expensive, and the fragmentation of Europe into many countries creates additional problems. Who should pay for emission controls— the countries producing the emissions or the countries suffering from them? Until recently, the division of Europe into two blocs compounded the difficulties.

However, major efforts are now underway. The countries belonging to the European Community have agreed to cut sulfur dioxide emissions from power plants by 60 percent by 2003 and nitrogen oxides by 40 percent by 1998. Twenty-one other nations have agreed to somewhat less stringent standards. There is reason to hope that the problem can be resolved.

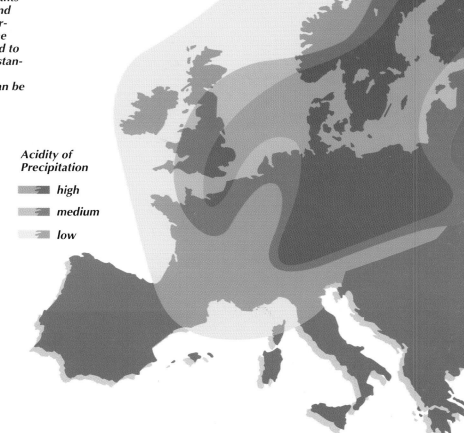

Acidity of Precipitation

- high
- medium
- low

The map shows where acid rain falls in Europe. Regions with acidic bedrock such as Germany and Scandinavia are especially vulnerable. In Germany's Black Forest (left), as many as half the trees are damaged.

RESTORING THE BALANCE
Asia

A sia is a land of superlatives. It is the largest continent in both area and population. It contains the world's highest (Mount Everest) and lowest (the Dead Sea) points. The rain forests at its southern edge are some of the wettest places on earth; the deserts of Arabia are some of the driest. Those same deserts are among the hottest places on earth, and Siberia is one of the coldest.

At the northern edge of the continent, along the shores of the Arctic Ocean, tundra dominates the land. South of that is a broad belt of evergreen forest called *taiga*. Human settlements are widely scattered in these northern regions, and vast expanses of wilderness still exist. However, large development schemes in this region are now having a major impact.

South of the taiga, a narrow belt of grasslands called *steppe* runs east and west across the continent. Some areas here have been converted to wheat fields; others support herds of cattle, horses, sheep, and goats. In the heart of the continent are large, sparsely populated deserts and short-grass steppes.

In eastern China, where deciduous forests were once the dominant vegetation, there exists some of the most intensely used land in the

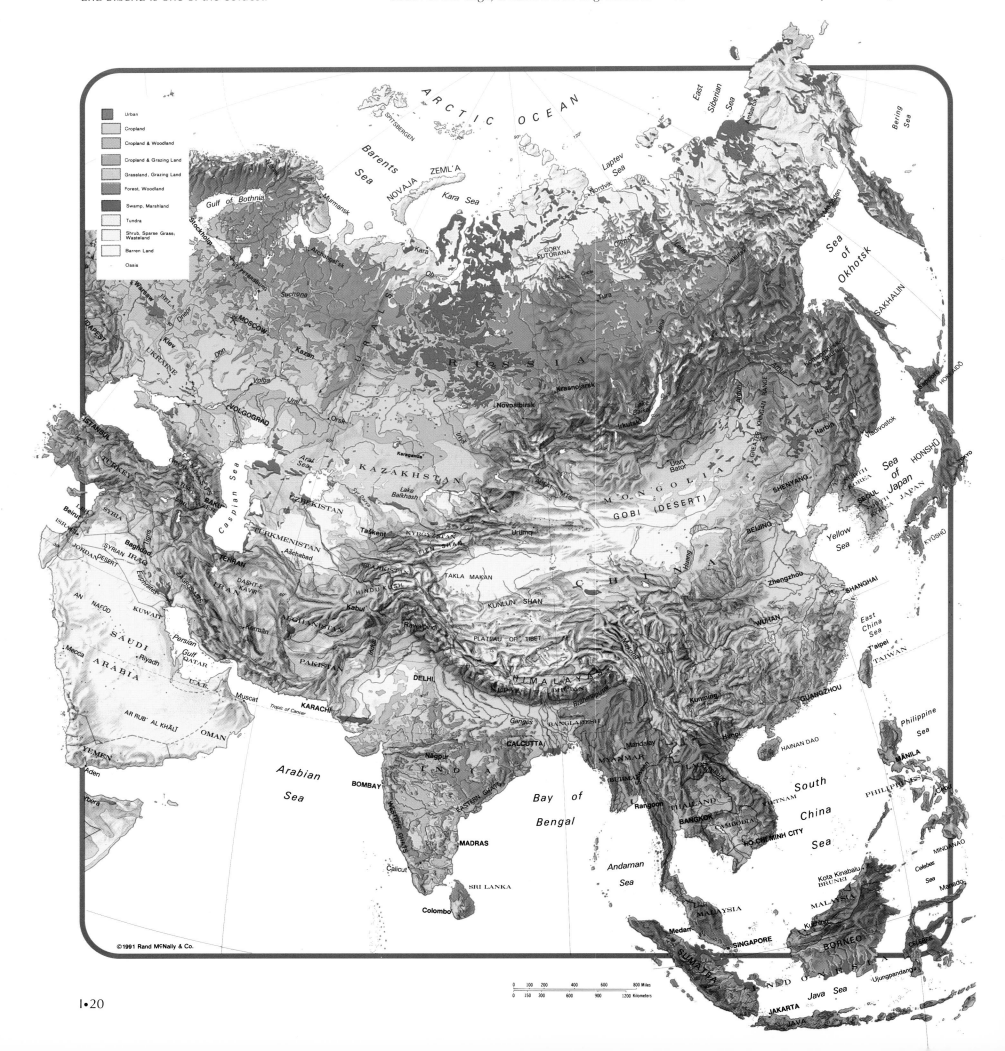

Legend:
- Urban
- Cropland
- Cropland & Woodland
- Cropland & Grazing Land
- Grassland, Grazing Land
- Forest, Woodland
- Swamp, Marshland
- Tundra
- Shrub, Sparse Grass, Wasteland
- Barren Land
- Oasis

©1991 Rand McNally & Co.

world. China has a billion mouths to feed, and only about 10 percent of its land is arable, so maximum yields must be produced from every available acre.

Some portions of India are as thickly populated as eastern China, as are some regions in Southeast Asia. Rich tropical forest is the natural vegetation of much of Southeast Asia and the islands of Indonesia. In recent years, however, millions of acres of this forest have been cut—some for timber, some to clear land for agriculture, some to provide firewood.

The cutting of these forests is a major contributor to one of Asia's most serious environmental problems: soil erosion. Asia is losing twenty-five billion tons of topsoil every year. This is twenty-five times the rate of erosion in the United States.

The problem is visible in its starkest form on the slopes of the Himalayas. Stripped of their protective forests, the soils of these slopes slide downhill, carried along by rushing waters. Springs on the mountainsides dry up because so much of the rainwater flows away rather than soaking into the ground. Rivers that once ran clear become choked with silt. The useful life of dams is drastically shortened as silt deposits deepen behind them. Instead of a steady, reli-

Nearly twenty million people live in the vast sprawl of Tokyo-Yokohama, Japan. Japan's overall population density is among the highest in the world.

These hillside terraces in Nepal are an effective way to increase the amount of arable land and a traditional way to control erosion, but they do require heavy, continuing labor to build and maintain.

able flow, the rivers oscillate between extremes. Catastrophic floods follow rainy seasons, while beds dry up completely in dry seasons. Major rivers such as the Ganges, the Brahmaputra, the Irriwaddy, the Salween, and the Mekong no longer supply regular amounts of irrigation water.

The people of Asia, with help from their governments and from private organizations, are planting millions of trees every year. The trees will protect the soil and provide fuel and wood for the future.

Protecting the Soil

The nations of southern Asia have undertaken major reforestation efforts to fight erosion and the loss of water resources. India alone plants more than three million acres of trees every year. Despite these efforts, India is still losing forest.

The challenge is to provide food, fuel, and land to large and growing populations without destroying the soil that supports human life. Everything from better farming methods to more efficient stoves can contribute to reducing the problem. Thus far, the most successful efforts have been those that involve local people both in the reforestation efforts and in the decisions about how to use their forest resources.

RESTORING THE BALANCE
Africa

A frica inspires myths of Eden. Humanity can trace its beginnings to the ancient savannas of the Rift Valley in East Africa. There, too, is a richness of wildlife unique in the world. In Eurasia and North America, mass extinctions at the end of the Ice Age wiped out many species of large mammals. The antelopes, elephants, zebras, lions, and giraffes of Africa survived that wave of extinctions and are now living reminders of the world that shaped our earliest ancestors.

Deserts dominate much of Africa. In the north, the Sahara, the largest desert on earth, covers 3.5 million square miles. With the Kalahari and the Namib in the south, a full third of the continent is covered by bare sand and sparse scrub.

Along the southern edge of the Sahara, the climate grows gradually more moist. In the region called the Sudan, grasslands and savannas replace the deserts. The people of Africa have long used this land both for pasture and for growing crops such as millet. In recent years, some of this land has been planted in peanuts and other crops grown primarily for export rather than for local consumption.

Farther south, as the climate grows wetter, trees become more common and forests dominate the land. The forest becomes richer and denser near the equator and becomes a region of rain forest in and around the Congo River Basin. South of the basin, drier conditions support more grasslands, deserts, and open woodlands.

Until very recently, most of Africa had been only lightly touched by human activity. The deserts have very small, scattered populations. Large portions of them are totally uninhabited. Even outside the desert areas, population density over most of the continent averages less than ten persons per square mile—about the same density as the states of Nevada and North Dakota. The people of the continent are concentrated in areas whose climate and soils make them particularly attractive for human settlement.

For centuries, the small populations of farmers and herdsmen in Africa's Sudan, or Sahel,

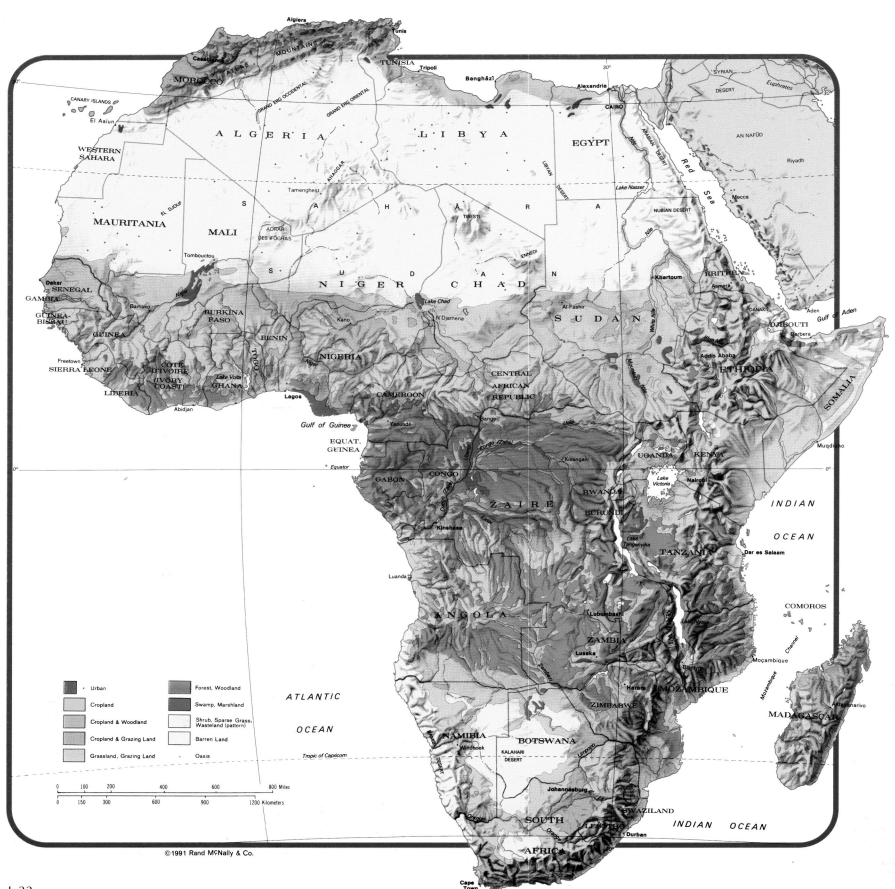

Urban
Cropland
Cropland & Woodland
Cropland & Grazing Land
Grassland, Grazing Land
Forest, Woodland
Swamp, Marshland
Shrub, Sparse Grass, Wasteland (pattern)
Barren Land
Oasis

©1991 Rand M⊃Nally & Co.

Far left: Africa's cities are growing almost 5 percent a year, but two-thirds of the continent's people still live in rural villages like this one in Zimbabwe.

Left: Africa's herds of large animals are among the living wonders of the world. Preserving them in the face of growing human populations is one of the world's more difficult problems.

made a living from the harsh land. They moved their herds periodically; they rotated crops; they let land lie fallow—sometimes for as long as twenty years—to allow it to regain fertility. In recent years, population growth and the conversion of land to crops grown for export have forced people to abandon the traditional ways. Now, drought and overexploitation have stripped the land of its plant cover and turned more than 160 million acres of land into desert. Stripping land of its vegetation actually makes the climate drier, so deserts feed on themselves. The process is called *desertification*, and people in Africa are suffering as it continues.

Garden or Desert?

Africans, on their own or with the help of international agencies, have found ways to reverse desertification through practices such as agroforestry. Shelter belts of trees protect and enrich the soil, provide a source of fuel, and turn back the advancing desert.

Simple stone fences, built by hand, can impound water

from infrequent rains. In Burkina Faso, such structures have increased crop yields by 50 percent. Projects like these must be done on a much larger scale to be truly effective, but their success in small-scale projects shows what can be done.

existing deserts

areas threatened with desertification

This Senegalese farmer cannot plant a crop because drought has turned his land into a desert. He is working his team of oxen to keep them in practice while waiting and hoping for the rains to come.

RESTORING THE BALANCE
Oceania

Strewn across the South Pacific are thousands of islands, ranging in size from Australia—so big, it is considered a continent—to tiny dots of land in remote waters. These islands—commonly grouped together as Oceania—have been isolated from larger land forms for thousands of years. The isolation of Oceania began to crumble, however, when the Polynesians advanced across the Pacific. It ended only two centuries ago when the British began to settle first Australia, and then New Zealand.

Most of the interior of Australia is very dry. Forests, savannas, and grasslands dominate the northern, eastern, and southern coastal regions. As rainfall decreases inland, short grass and desert scrub replace these richer terrains. Most of Australia's cropland and urban areas are along the coasts. The grasslands of the interior are mainly used as grazing land for over 150 million sheep, a flock that produces 30 percent of the world's wool.

When English settlement began in New Zealand, all of North Island and over half of South Island were forested. Timber and other forest products are still very important to New Zealand's economy. Sheep are there, too; a national flock of sixty-four million animals.

The smaller islands of the Pacific range from coral atolls such as the Gilberts, where the highest point is less than fifteen feet above sea level, to mountainous lands of volcanic origin such as Tahiti.

There is a biological boundary in Indonesia. West of it are Borneo, Java, and Sumatra with their typically Asian plants and animals. East of it are Celebes, New Guinea, and Australia with a unique flora and fauna developed through millions of years of isolation.

English settlers in Oceania found it a world almost unimaginably strange. On Australia's broad grasslands kangaroos replaced the familiar sheep and cattle of home. New Zealand had no mammals at all outside of two species of bats, and its birds included the world's only flightless parrot and the world's only flightless songbird.

The newcomers immediately set about

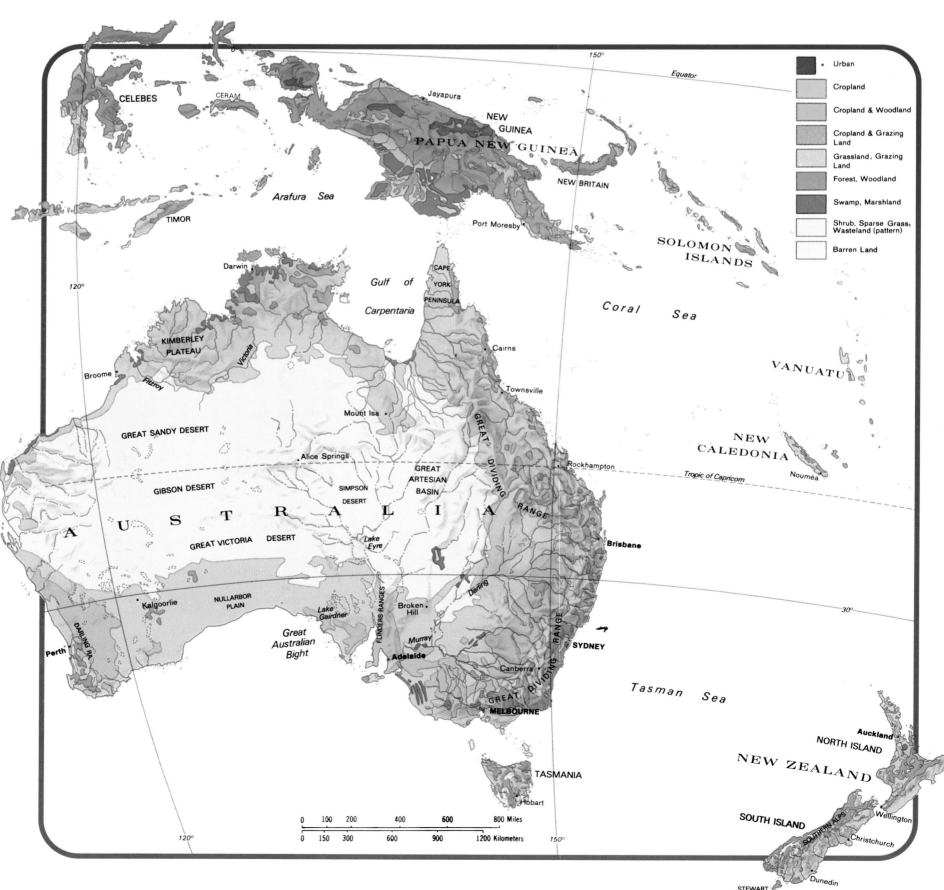

Legend:
- Urban
- Cropland
- Cropland & Woodland
- Cropland & Grazing Land
- Grassland, Grazing Land
- Forest, Woodland
- Swamp, Marshland
- Shrub, Sparse Grass, Wasteland (pattern)
- Barren Land

remaking nature in the new lands. They imported rabbits, red deer, Canada geese, and hosts of other birds. When rabbits became pests in New Zealand, weasels and ferrets were brought in to control them.

The imports—whether competitors or predators—had catastrophic effects on the native species. Australia has lost eighteen species of native mammals in the past two hundred years.

Above: The dry interior of Australia supports very sparse vegetation and very few people. Sheep can be grazed on this sort of land in small numbers.

Left: This beach in Sydney attracts large numbers of Australians. Nearly all of the population of the country lives near the coast, more than 20 percent in the city of Sydney alone.

Domestic cats eliminated New Zealand's flightless songbird within a year of its discovery, and its flightless parrot is barely hanging on in the face of predation by weasels and competition for food from both red deer and sheep. Red deer became such pests that New Zealand's government at one time offered to buy ammunition for anyone willing to shoot them.

Island ecosystems tend to have few species. Many have no land predators and a shortage of competitors for scarce resources. This makes them very vulnerable to disturbances from outside. Animals that have never faced competition or predation are likely to go extinct before they can learn to adapt to the introduction of alien species.

Leaving Nature Alone

The governments of Oceania are faced with a huge task of damage control. They have begun with strict controls on imports of exotic animals to prevent a repeat of the mistakes of the past. A variety of programs are under way to protect native species from the exotics already there. In New Zealand, the kakapo, the flightless parrot, is surviving on a preserve where continued trapping keeps out predators and competitors. Transfer to an off-shore island, a measure already protecting kiwis, may provide a long-term answer. Continuing efforts to control exotics involve hunting, trapping, and even the injection of birth control drugs into females.

This is not a lizard. It is a tuatara, the sole survivor of an ancient order of reptiles. It is threatened by exotic species in New Zealand.

The arrows mark some of the exotic species imported into New Zealand since 1840. The native bat and laughing owl are now extinct; fewer than one hundred kakapos survive.

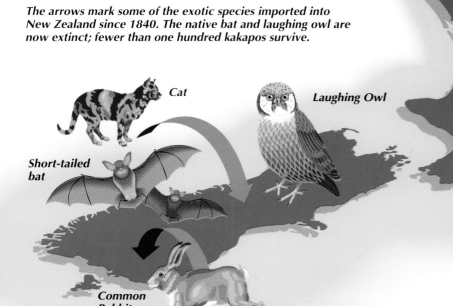

Cat

Laughing Owl

Short-tailed bat

Common Rabbit

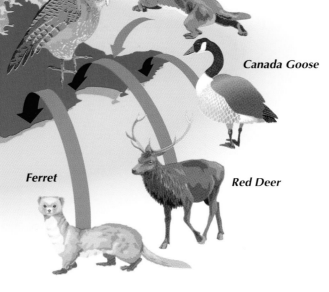

Kakapo

Weasel

Canada Goose

Ferret

Red Deer

RESTORING THE BALANCE
Polar Regions

The South Pole lies in the middle of a continent, hundreds of miles from the nearest shore. The North Pole is in the middle of the Arctic Ocean. Nearly all of Antarctica is buried under an ice cap up to two miles thick. Greenland has a similar cap, but other Arctic lands are ice-free in the summer months.

Antarctica's largest land animal is a tiny insect. The ice-free lands in the Arctic have a well-developed fauna, with grazing animals like caribou and musk-oxen and carnivores like grizzly bears and wolves.

Antarctica has no people. The closest thing to human habitations on this inhospitable continent are the scientific stations established by various nations in recent years. The Arctic has

been peopled for millennia. The Inuit (or Eskimo), various Indian tribes, the Lapps of northern Scandinavia—all have contrived ways to make a sustained living from the harsh lands of the north.

For all these differences, the earth's polar regions have much in common. They are both very cold and very dark for much of the year. Since the sun is the source of the energy that makes ecosystems work, polar ecosystems are characterized by low productivity. Each year, an acre of tundra produces about 1 percent of the plant material produced by an acre of rich, temperate-zone forests. The caribou herds of Alaska and Canada must range over thousands of square miles to find good grazing. North of the Brooks Range on the Alaskan tundra, it takes

one hundred square miles to support one grizzly bear.

A lack of precipitation contributes to this low productivity. Arctic lands average less than two inches of rain and snow a year. Amazingly, the ice-free dry valleys of Antarctica have had no precipitation in two million years.

When polar ecosystems are damaged, recovery is a long, slow process. Tracks left by trucks and other vehicles driving across the Alaskan tundra during World War II are still visible half a century later. With little rain to cleanse the atmosphere, air pollution lingers, too.

There are riches in the sea. Essential minerals are abundant. The seas around Antarctica abound in *krill*, a small relative of the shrimp that is the principal food of penguins, albatross-

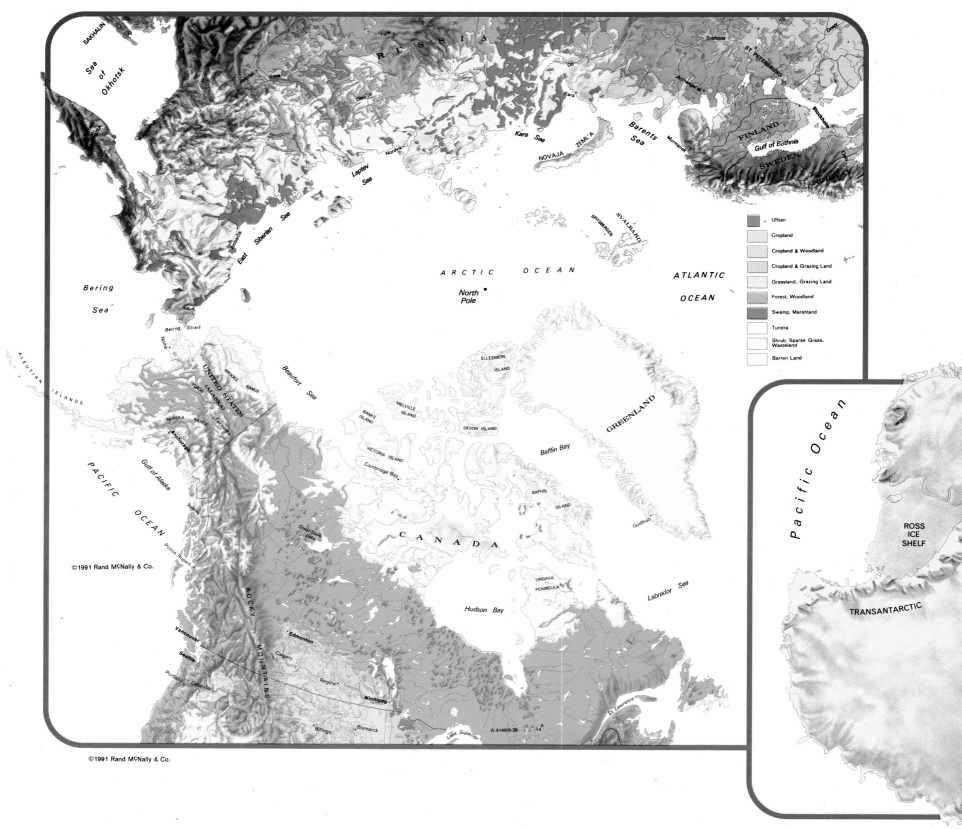

Urban
Cropland
Cropland & Woodland
Cropland & Grazing Land
Grassland, Grazing Land
Forest, Woodland
Swamp, Marshland
Tundra
Shrub, Sparse Grass, Wasteland
Barren Land

©1991 Rand McNally & Co.

©1991 Rand McNally & Co.

es, seals, and whales. The shallower waters of the Arctic Ocean yield about 10 percent of the world's annual catch of fish. The Inuit have traditionally drawn much of their subsistence from seals, walruses, and other creatures of the sea. This abundance can be deceiving, however. If a disaster such as an oil spill seriously affected the krill, all the animals that feed on this one small creature would be harmed.

Many are calling for intensive development of the polar regions. When we contemplate such development, we must keep in mind the fragility of polar ecosystems.

The Lapps of Scandinavia follow their reindeer herds across the tundra. By drawing food, clothing, and other necessities from the herds, the Lapps sustain their way of life in the Arctic without damaging the ecosystem.

These penguins feed at sea, but they come ashore on Antarctica to nest. They are among the few animals to inhabit the continent at the South Pole.

The Vulnerable Wilderness

Arctic haze hangs in the air around Prudhoe Bay, Alaska. It is pollution from the oil fields, and in the cold, dry climate, it is a sort of permanent smog. Conditions are even worse near Russian nickel smelters on the Kola Peninsula.

Protection of the poles requires a major international effort. The eight countries with lands in the Arctic met in 1989 to begin such an effort. Fishing rights, mining, and industry are among the issues these nations will have to deal with. Twenty-nine nations have signed a protection agreement for Antarctica, but the most hopeful sign is that some countries are now backing the idea of making the continent a preserve.

🔺🔺 **Mineral deposits**

🔺 **Coal deposits**

〜 **Possible gas and oil deposits**

This map shows some of the mineral resources of Antarctica. The presence of these minerals is tempting many nations to consider development of this fragile region. Damage from mining or oil drilling could have catastrophic effects.

Trash left behind at a research station in Antarctica will be preserved indefinitely in the cold, dry climate. The results of any human action at the poles may endure virtually forever.

Most of South America lies between the tropics. At the northern end of the continent, grasslands called *llanos* dominate the lowlands east of the Andes. South of the llanos is the vast Amazon River Basin, containing the world's largest tropical forest.

South of the Amazon Basin, the forest becomes more open; grasslands again become prominent parts of the landscape. In Argentina, the lush grassland called the *pampa* gives way to drier grass and scrub vegetation in Patagonia to the south.

When Francisco Pizarro entered South America in 1532, he found a high civilization dominating the Andes Mountains, the spine of the continent. Building on the foundation of a thousand years of Andean culture, the Incas had consolidated an empire that extended from present-day Chile to Colombia. When Francisco de Orellana and his followers became the first Europeans to descend the Amazon in 1540, they found the riverbank lined with settlements.

Things have changed since those days. Now, Peru and Bolivia are two of the poorest countries on the continent. The Indian population of the Amazon Basin is dropping, and indigenous culture may soon be extinct. Today, the richest countries in South America have extractive economies. Suriname with its bauxite mines and Venezuela with its oil wells have the highest per capita incomes on the continent.

In the last few hundred years, settlement in South America has mainly been concentrated in a few favored areas such as the Atlantic highlands of Brazil and the pampa of Argentina. Recently, however, the rapid increase in population and the hopes of South American nations for major economic growth have stimulated invasions of the sparsely peopled parts of the continent. Tropical forests are falling at a terrifying rate. South America has already lost a third of its wet tropical forest. In the mountains, too,

Urban
Cropland
Cropland & Woodland
Cropland & Grazing Land
Grassland, Grazing Land
Forest, Woodland
Swamp, Marshland
Shrub, Sparse Grass, Wasteland
Barren Land

0 100 200 400 600 800 Miles
0 150 300 600 900 1200 Kilometers

©1991 Rand McNally & Co.

Hope shines in the bright greens of these seedlings planted in a forest-restoration project. Careful husbandry is needed to restore the forest after clearing.

The effects of deforestation show plainly in the heavily eroded soil of this cleared rain forest. With nutrients leached away by heavy rains, the soil can no longer support the forest that once grew here.

vast regions of forest have been felled to clear land for the production of coffee, cacao, and coca.

Farms and cattle ranches on the cleared land are seldom successful because tropical forest soils lose their fertility quickly when the tree cover is removed. Despite the conversion of hundreds of thousands of acres from forest to pasture, for example, the Amazon regions of Brazil still have to import much of their beef. Fueled by government subsidies, however, the Amazon land rush continues to destroy the forest and drive thousands of species to extinction.

A coalition of Indians and rubber tappers called the Forest People is now trying to convince the people of Brazil that there is a better way. The Forest People have a knowledge—built up over generations—of how the forest works. Their ways of farming and extraction adapt natural processes to allow a sustained use of the rain forest.

A fisherman spreads his net on Lake Titicaca just as his ancestors did a thousand years ago. The Andean highlands were home to the great Inca civilization.

The skyline of the Andes is rugged and snowcapped even at the equator. The high plains in the foreground are the habitat of such grazing animals as the guanaco.

Preserving the Rain Forest

The assault on the forest includes wasteful logging methods that destroy more trees than they harvest. Bulldozers clear land for farms. Fires set to burn away dead wood spread to uncleared parts of the forest, destroying whole species of plants and animals.

The cleared land is planted in grasses for cattle or plowed for crops. Both have very low rates of success. Only one of the many cattle ranches built with government subsidies in the Brazilian Amazon has ever shown a profit. And when the pastures and fields are abandoned, the forest is often unable to reclaim the land.

RESTORING THE BALANCE
North America

A t the turn of the twentieth century, Phoenix, Arizona, was a dusty little town with only 5,000 inhabitants. Today, nearly 2 million people live in the Phoenix metropolitan area. Dallas, Texas, jumped from 42,000 to 2.7 million in the same span of time.

The boomtown is a familiar story in North America. A flood of settlers from every part of the world has spread across the continent in the past two centuries. Sprawling metropolises have sprung up in the wilderness. Whole biomes have been plowed up and turned into cornfields. The face of the continent has been irrevocably changed.

Even the remote tundra at the northern end of North America has been invaded by oil fields and miners. The taiga, the broad belt of evergreen forest that extends from Alaska across Canada and the northern United States to Maine and the maritime provinces, has been hit by logging and by massive industrial projects like Canada's nickel-smelting operations at Sudbury, Ontario.

The hardwood forests of the eastern United States and southern Canada were once so dense that people said a squirrel could travel from the Atlantic Coast to the Mississippi without ever touching ground. Today, the only remaining extensive tracts of this forest are in the more rugged portions of the Appalachian Mountains. Elsewhere, the landscape is dominated by cities and farms, and the forest has been reduced to

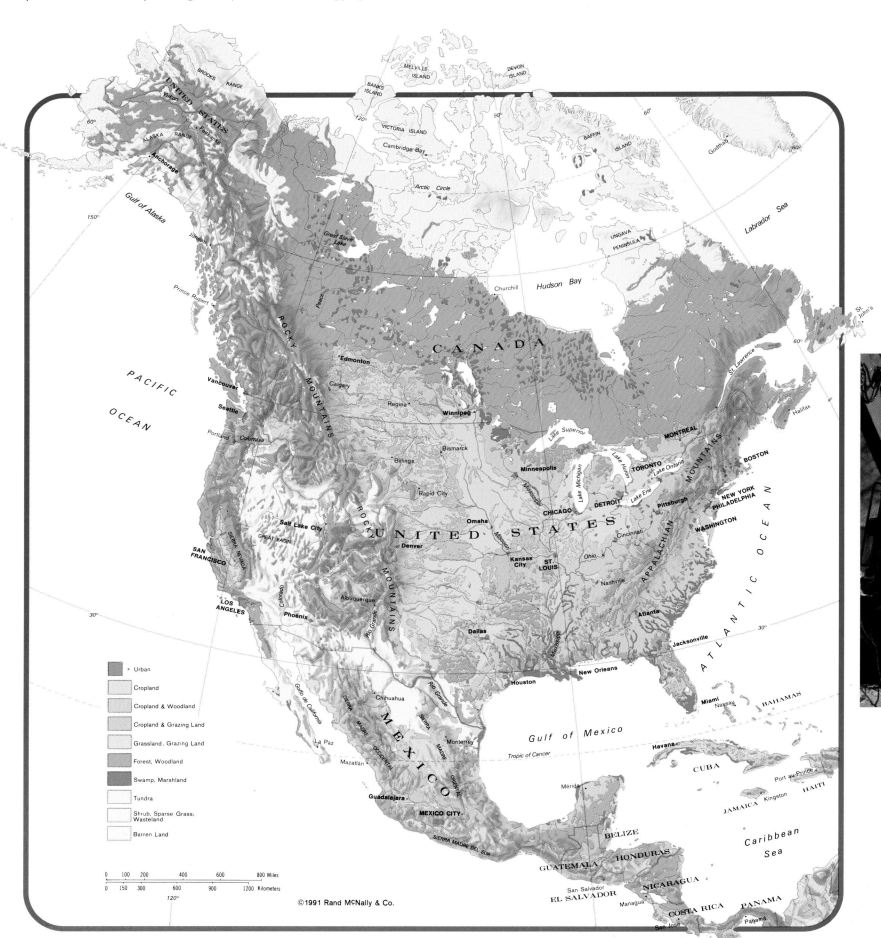

Urban

Cropland

Cropland & Woodland

Cropland & Grazing Land

Grassland, Grazing Land

Forest, Woodland

Swamp, Marshland

Tundra

Shrub, Sparse Grass, Wasteland

Barren Land

©1991 Rand McNally & Co.

North America's once-vast wilderness is now confined to preserves such as Grand Teton National Park in Wyoming where the peak of Mt. Moran rises over the Snake River.

The huge circles of green in these barley and potato fields in Colorado are created by rotating sprinklers that irrigate the fields. Much of what was once grassland in North America is now cropland such as this.

scattered patches.

The tall-grass prairie that once extended from western Indiana to Nebraska and from Saskatchewan to Texas has almost completely disappeared. The rich soils the prairies built through several millenia of growth are now covered with corn, soybean, and wheat fields. On the short-grass prairies of the high plains, cattle have replaced the native buffalo as the main grazing animal.

In the arid lands of the southwestern United States and northern Mexico, huge dams provide irrigation water for vast fruit and vegetable farms that now spread over hundreds of thousands of acres of what was once desert.

In southern Mexico and Central America, ruins of ancient civilizations recall a time when large human populations had a major effect on the landscape. The forests of these regions have reclaimed lands that once provided corn, beans, and peppers for the Mayans, but in recent years, the forests have begun to fall again. Increasing populations and the development of large-scale farming and ranching for world markets are remaking this region as thoroughly as the settlers of a century ago remade the midwestern United States.

Urbanization and industrialization have also had a powerful effect. Mexico City may be the largest city in the world. Monterrey in northern Mexico joins the manufacturing cities of the United States and Canada as a major world center of industry.

Cleaning Up

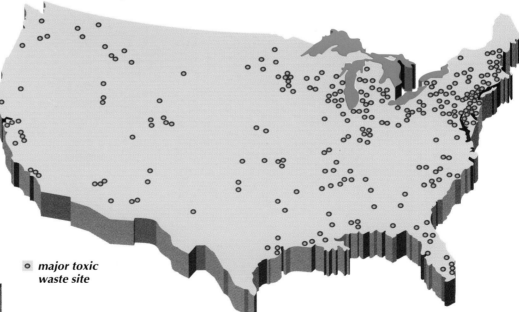

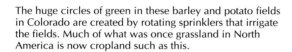

o **major toxic waste site**

Wastes have always been a part of manufacturing. Heavy metals such as lead and cadmium and toxic organic compounds are by-products of many industrial processes.

During much of the history of industry in America, these toxic chemicals were dumped in the cheapest way possible. **Leaks from dumps are now contaminating drinking water and poisoning soils all over the country.**

In 1980, the United States Congress voted to tax the chemical industry to create the Superfund to pay for a cleanup. **The job is now under way, but it will be many years before it is finished. For the future, the answer lies in redesigning production processes so they will not generate toxics.**

Above, left: Cleanup begins on a toxic-waste dump targeted by the Superfund project. Note the protective clothing on the worker in the picture.

Left: Toxics carelessly dumped in leaking drums can contaminate both drinking water and the soil itself.

This elementary school was designed to use solar energy for a large part of its heat. New designs in houses and public building can cut energy use as much as two-thirds.

Almost all the cars on this freeway are carrying one person. In many American households, getting to work and back uses more energy than any other activity. Any serious attempt to cut America's energy use will have to address this problem.

Energy Use or Abuse?

United Kingdom

France

United States

Japan

China

Egypt

India

Venezuela

Nigeria

Brazil

Papua New Guinea

Argentina

South Africa

Australia

Each barrel 🛢 equals one hundred kilograms of oil equivalent per capita

Historically, energy has been cheap in the United States, and Americans have responded to those low prices by using more energy than any other people on earth.

America produces 30 percent of the gases that are thought to be creating the greenhouse effect, and most of that comes from consumption of coal and oil.

We have at least begun to deal with the problem. Since the Arab oil embargo of 1973, the overall economy has been growing four times as fast as energy use.

Household energy use has declined. The United States will need to continue the search for ways to reduce overall energy use and for ways to switch to non-polluting, renewable sources before energy problems can be solved.

Photograph credits

Pages 1-2,3 Koalas: John Cancalosi/Tom Stack & Associates. Children: John Isaac/UNICEF. Lily & dragonfly: John Gerlach/Tom Stack & Associates. Brown bear: John Shaw/Tom Stack & Associates. Polar bear: Mark Newman/Tom Stack & Associates. *1-4,5* England: David M. Dennis/Tom Stack & Associates. *1-6,7* Oregon forest: Milton Rand/Tom Stack & Associates. Prairie: Brian Parker/Tom Stack & Associates. *1-8,9* Nepalese woman: CARE photo by Rudolph von Bernuth. Gary, Indiana: AP/Wide World Photos. *1-10,11* North Dakota: John Running. Wind generators: Kevin Shafer/Tom Stack & Associates. *1-12,13* Treatment plant: Byron Augustin/Tom Stack & Associates. Cleanup: AP/Wide World Photos. *1-14,15* Pines: Diana L. Stratton/Tom Stack & Associates. Leopard: Jeff Foott/Tom Stack & Associates. *1-16,17* Family planning: CARE photo by Rudolph von Bernuth. Subdivision: Gary Milburn/Tom Stack & Associates. Bulgaria: AP/Wide World Photos. Black Forest: Spencer Swanger/Tom Stack & Associates. Nice, France: David C. London/Tom Stack & Associates. *1-20,21* Tokyo: Sheryl S. McNee/Tom Stack & Associates. Planting tree: CARE photo by Rudolph von Bernuth. Nepal: CARE photo by Rudolph von Bernuth. *1-22,23* Zebra & wildebeest: Jeff Foott/Tom Stack & Associates. Zimbabwe: Rod Allin/Tom Stack & Associates. Senegal: Clyde McNair/AID. *1-24,25* Outback: Greg Vaughn/Tom Stack & Associates. Sydney beach: Greg Vaughn/Tom Stack & Associates. Tuatara: John Cancalosi/Tom Stack & Associates. *1-26,27* Penguins: Anna E. Zuckerman/Tom Stack & Associates. Trash: Jack Stein Grove/Tom Stack & Associates. Lapps: Warren & Genny Garst/Tom Stack & Associates. *1-28,29* Andes: Gary Milburn/Tom Stack & Associates. Lake Titicaca: Gary Milburn/Tom Stack & Associates. Colombia: Clyde McNair/AID. Seedlings: Chip & Jill Isenhart/Tom Stack & Associates. *1-30,31* Mount Moran: Gerald & Buff Corsi/Tom Stack & Associates. Fields: Shattil/Rozinski/Tom Stack & Associates. Leakage: Gary Milburn/Tom Stack & Associates. Cleanup: Gary Milburn/Tom Stack & Associates. *1-32,33* Freeway: Jack Swenson/Tom Stack & Associates. School: Stewart M. Green/Tom Stack & Associates.

USING THE ATLAS

MAPS AND ATLASES

Satellite images of the world (figure 1) constantly give us views of the shape and size of the earth. It is hard, therefore, to imagine how difficult it once was to ascertain the look of our planet. Yet from early history we have evidence of humans trying to work out what the world actually looked like.

Twenty-five hundred years ago, on a tiny clay tablet the size of a hand, the Babylonians inscribed the earth as a flat disk (figure 2) with Babylon at the center. The section of the Cantino map of 1502 (figure 3) is an example of a *portolan* chart used by mariners to chart the newly discovered Americas. Handsome and useful maps have been produced by many cultures. The Mexican map drawn in 1583 marks hills with wavy lines and roads with footprints between parallel lines (figure 4). The methods and materials used to create these maps were dependent upon the technology available, and their accuracy suffered considerably. A modern topographic map (figure 5), as well as those in this atlas, shows the detail and accuracy that cartographers are now able to achieve. They benefit from our ever-increasing technology, including satellite imagery and computer assisted cartography.

In 1589 Gerardus Mercator used the word *atlas* to describe a collection of maps. Atlases now bring together not only a variety of maps but an assortment of tables and other reference material as well. They have become a unique and indispensable reference for graphically defining the world and answering the question *where*. Only on a map can the countries, cities, roads, rivers, and lakes covering a vast area be simultaneously viewed in their relative locations. Routes between places can be traced, trips planned, boundaries of neighboring states and countries examined, distances between places measured, the meandering of rivers and streams and the sizes of lakes visualized—and remote places imagined.

FIGURE 1

FIGURE 4

FIGURE 2

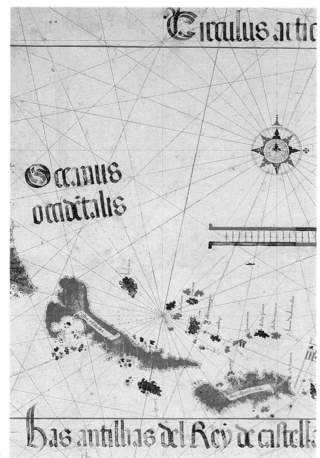

FIGURE 3

FIGURE 5

SEQUENCE OF THE MAPS

The world is made up of seven major landmasses: the continents of Europe, Asia, Africa, Antarctica, Australia, South America, and North America (figure 6). The maps in this atlas follow this continental sequence. To allow for the inclusion of detail, each continent is broken down into a series of maps, and this grouping is arranged so that as consecutive pages are turned, a continuous successive part of the continent is shown. Larger-scale maps are used for regions of greater detail (having many cities, for example) or for areas of global significance.

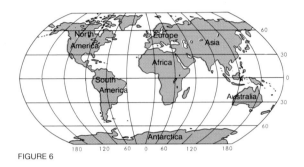

FIGURE 6

GETTING THE INFORMATION

An atlas can be used for many purposes, from planning a trip to finding hot spots in the news and supplementing world knowledge. To realize the potential of an atlas the user must be able to:

1. Find places on the maps
2. Measure distances
3. Determine directions
4. Understand map symbols

FINDING PLACES

One of the most common and important tasks facilitated by an atlas is finding the location of a place in the world. A river's name in a book, a city mentioned in the news, or a vacation spot may prompt your need to know where the place is located. The illustrations and text below explain how to find Yangon (Rangoon), Burma.

1. Look up the place-name in the index at the back of the atlas. Yangon, Burma can be found on the map on page 38, and it can be located on the map by the letter-number key *B2* (figure 7).

Yancey, co., N.C., U.S.	**f10**	140
Yanceyville, N.C., U.S.	**A3**	140
Yanchang, China	**D9**	30
Yancheng, China	**B9**	34
Yandoon, Burma	**F3**	40
Yangjiang, China	**G9**	30
Yangon (Rangoon), Burma	**B2**	38
Yangquan, China	**D9**	30
Yangtze see Chang, stm., China	**E10**	30
Yangzhou, China	**C8**	34
Yanji, China	**C12**	30
Yankton, S.D., U.S.	**E8**	148
Yankton, co., S.D., U.S.	**D8**	148
Yanqi, China	**C4**	30
Yantai (Chefoo), China	**D11**	30
Yantic, stm., Ct., U.S.	**C7**	114
Yapen, Pulau, i., Indon.	**F10**	38
Yaqui, stm., Mex.	**C5**	90
Yaraka, Austl.	**D8**	68

FIGURE 7

2. Turn to the map of Southeastern Asia found on page 38. Note that the letters *A* through *H* and the numbers *1* through *11* appear in the margins of the map.

3. To find Yangon, on the map, place your left index finger on *B* and your right index finger on *2*. Move your left finger across the map and your right finger down the map. Your fingers will meet in the area in which Yangon is located (figure 8).

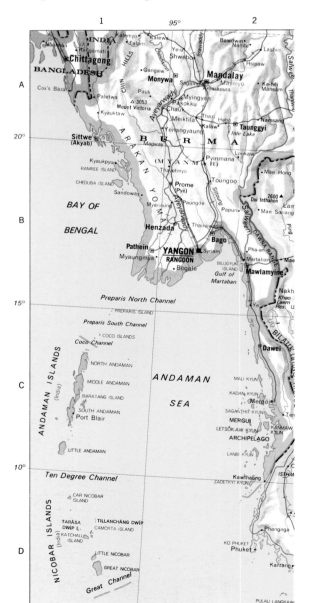

FIGURE 8

MEASURING DISTANCES

In planning trips, determining the distance between two places is essential, and an atlas can help in travel preparation. For instance, to determine the approximate distance between Paris and Rouen, France, follow these three steps:

1. Lay a slip of paper on the map on page 14 so that its edge touches the two cities. Adjust the paper so one corner touches Rouen. Mark the paper directly at the spot where Paris is located (figure 9).

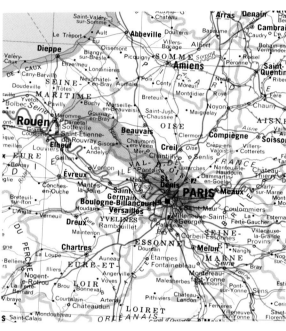

FIGURE 9

2. Place the paper along the scale of miles beneath the map. Position the corner at 0 and line up the edge of the paper along the scale. The pencil mark on the paper indicates Rouen is between 50 and 100 miles from Paris (figure 10).

3. To find the exact distance, move the paper to the left so that the pencil mark is at 100 on the scale. The corner of the paper stands on the fourth 5-mile unit on the scale. This means that the two towns are 50 plus 20, or 70 miles apart (figure 11).

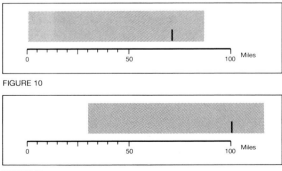

FIGURE 10

FIGURE 11

DETERMINING DIRECTION

Most of the maps in the atlas are drawn so that when oriented for normal reading, north is at the top of the map, south is at the bottom, west is at the left, and east is at the right. Most maps have a series of lines drawn across them–the lines of *latitude* and *longitude*. Lines of latitude, or *parallels* of latitude, are drawn east and west. Lines of longitude, or *meridians* of longitude, are drawn north and south (figure 12).

Parallels and meridians appear as either curved or straight lines. For example, in the section of the map of Europe (figure 13) the parallels of latitude appear as curved lines. The meridians of longitude are straight lines that come together toward the top of the map. Latitude and longitude lines help locate places on maps. Parallels of latitude are numbered in degrees north and south of the *Equator*. Meridians of longitude are numbered in degrees east and west of a line called the *Prime Meridian*, running through Greenwich, England, near London. Any place on earth can be located by the latitude and longitude lines running through it.

To determine directions or locations on the map, you must use the parallels and meridians. For example, suppose you want to know which is farther north, Bergen, Norway, or Stockholm, Sweden. The map in figure 13 shows that Stockholm is south of the 60° parallel of latitude and Bergen is north of it. Bergen is farther north than Stockholm. By looking at the meridians of longitude, you can determine which city is farther east. Bergen is approximately 5° east of the 0° meridian (Prime Meridian), and Stockholm is almost 20° east of it. Stockholm is farther east than Bergen.

UNDERSTANDING MAP SYMBOLS

In a very real sense, the whole map is a symbol, representing the world or a part of it. It is a reduced representation of the earth; each of the world's features–cities, rivers, etc.–is represented on the map by a symbol. Map symbols may take the form of points, such as dots or squares (often used for cities, capital cities, or points of interest), or lines (roads, railroads, rivers). Symbols may also occupy an area, showing extent of coverage (terrain, forests, deserts). They seldom look like the feature they represent and therefore must be identified and interpreted. For instance, the maps in this atlas define political units by a colored line depicting their boundaries. Neither the colors nor the boundary lines are actually found on the surface of the earth, but because countries and states are such important political components of the world, strong symbols are used to represent them. The Map Symbols page in this atlas identifies the symbols used on the maps.

FIGURE 12

FIGURE 13

World Time Zones

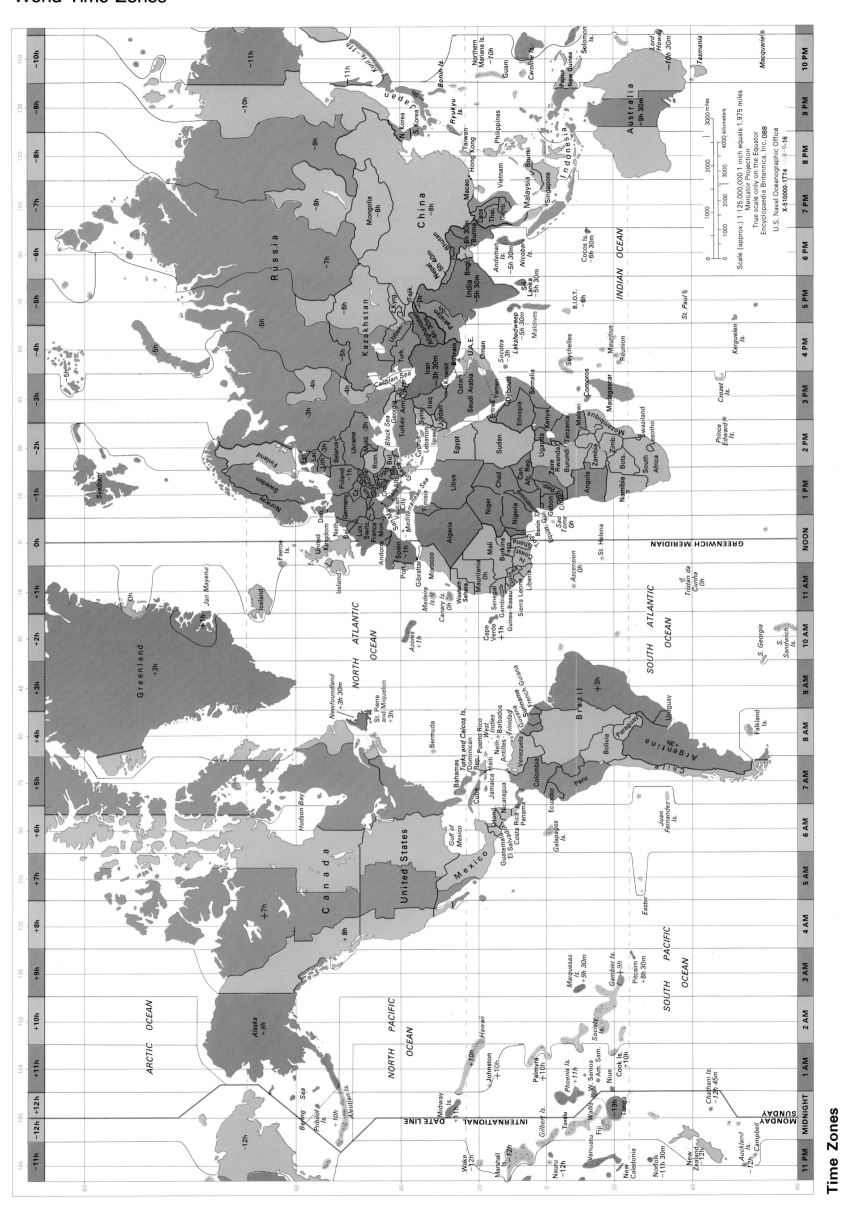

Time Zones

Standard time zone of even-numbered hours from Greenwich time

Standard time zone of odd-numbered hours from Greenwich time

Time varies from the standard time zone by half an hour

Time varies from the standard time zone by other than half an hour

| h m | hours, minutes |

The standard time zone system, fixed by international agreement and by law in each country, is based on a theoretical division of the globe into 24 zones of 15° longitude each. The mid-meridian of each zone fixes the hour for the entire zone. The zero time zone extends 7½° east and 7½° west of the Greenwich meridian, 0° longitude. Since the earth rotates toward the east, time zones to the west of Greenwich are earlier, to the east, later. Plus and minus hours at the top of the map are added to or subtracted from local time to find Greenwich time. Local standard time can be determined for any area in the world by adding one hour for each time zone counted in an easterly direction from

one's own, or by subtracting one hour for each zone counted in a westerly direction. To separate one day from the next, the 180th meridian has been designated as the international date line. On both sides of the line the time of day is the same, but west of the line it is one day later than it is to the east. Countries that adhere to the international zone system adopt the zone applicable to their location. Some countries, however, establish time zones based on political boundaries, or adopt the time zone of a neighboring unit. For all or part of the year some countries also advance their time by one hour, thereby utilizing more daylight hours each day.

Scale (approx.) 1:125,000,000 1 inch equals 1,975 miles
Mercator Projection
True scale only on the Equator
Encyclopaedia Britannica, Inc. 088
U.S. Naval Oceanographic Office
X-510000-1T74   -8-9-16

Map Symbols and Index Map

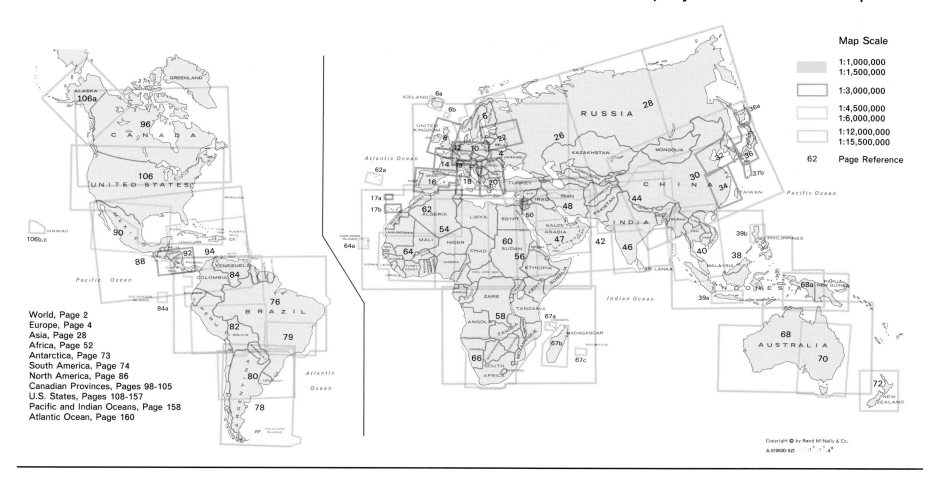

Map Scale

▨	1:1,000,000
	1:1,500,000
▢	1:3,000,000
	1:4,500,000
▢	1:6,000,000
	1:12,000,000
	1:15,500,000
62	Page Reference

World, Page 2
Europe, Page 4
Asia, Page 28
Africa, Page 52
Antarctica, Page 73
South America, Page 74
North America, Page 86
Canadian Provinces, Pages 98-105
U.S. States, Pages 108-157
Pacific and Indian Oceans, Page 158
Atlantic Ocean, Page 160

Copyright © by Rand McNally & Co.
A-519500-921

World Maps Symbols

Inhabited Localities

The size of type indicates the relative economic
and political importance of the locality

Écommoy	Lisieux	**Rouen**
Trouville	**Orléans**	**PARIS**
Bi'r Safājah °	Oasis	

Alternate Names

MOSKVA
MOSCOW
English or second official language
names are shown in reduced size
lettering

Basel
Bâle

Volgograd
(Stalingrad)
Historical or other alternates in
the local language are shown in
parentheses

▨ Urban Area (Area of continuous industrial,
commercial, and residential development)

Capitals of Political Units

BUDAPEST Independent Nation

Cayenne Dependency
(Colony, protectorate, etc.)

Recife State, Province, County, Oblast, etc.

Political Boundaries

International (First-order political unit)

▦▦▦	Demarcated and Undemarcated
—·—·—	Disputed de jure
▦▦▦	Indefinite or Undefined
————	Demarcation Line

Internal

▬▬	State, Province, etc. (Second-order political unit)
MURCIA	Historical Region (No boundaries indicated)
GALAPAGOS (Ecuador)	Administering Country

Transportation

———	Primary Road
———	Secondary Road
---------	Minor Road, Trail
—+—+—	Railway
Canal du Midi	Navigable Canal
	Bridge
—)---(—	Tunnel
TO MALMÖ	Ferry

Hydrographic Features

〰	Shoreline
〰	Undefined or Fluctuating Shoreline
Amur	River, Stream
	Intermittent Stream
	Rapids, Falls
	Irrigation or Drainage Canal
	Reef
The Everglades	Swamp
RIMO GLACIER	Glacier
L. Victoria	Lake, Reservoir
Tuz Gölü	Salt Lake
	Intermittent Lake, Reservoir
	Dry Lake Bed
(395)	Lake Surface Elevation

Topographic Features

Matterhorn △ 4478	Elevation Above Sea Level
76 ▽	Elevation Below Sea Level
Mount Cook ▲ 3764	Highest Elevation in Country
133 ▼	Lowest Elevation in Country
Khyber Pass ≍ 1067	Mountain Pass

Elevations are given in meters.
The highest and lowest elevations in a
continent are underlined

	Sand Area
	Lava
	Salt Flat

State, Province Maps Symbols

✪	Capital		---------	International Boundary
○	County Seat		---------	State, Province Boundary
▲	Military Installation		---------	County Boundary
△	Point of Interest		———	Railroad
+	Mountain Peak		———	Road
				Urban Area

1

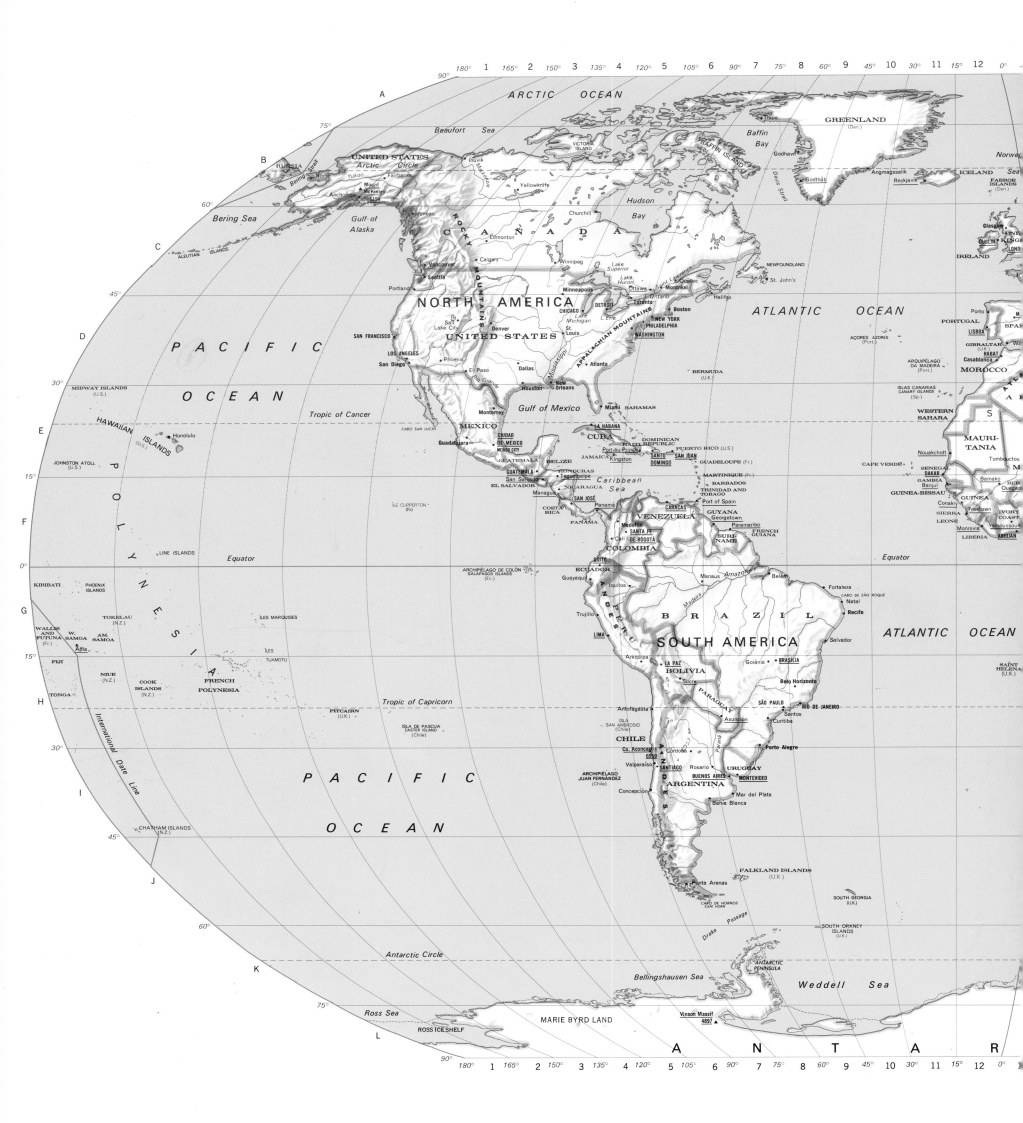

ARCTIC OCEAN

GREENLAND (Den.)

Beaufort Sea

Baffin Bay

Thule

Godhavn

Angmagssalik

ICELAND

FAEROE ISLANDS (Den.)

Norweg

RUSSIA

Bering Strait

UNITED STATES

Arctic Circle

Yukon

Mount McKinley 6194

Nome

Fairbanks

Anchorage

Inuvik

Mackenzie

VICTORIA ISLAND

BAFFIN ISLAND

Godthåb

Reykjavik

Glasgow

IRELAND

DUBLIN

UNI KING

LOND

Juneau

Bering Sea

Gulf of Alaska

CANADA

Edmonton

Calgary

Yellowknife

Churchill

Hudson Bay

Newfoundland

St. John's

Norwer Sea

ALEUTIAN ISLANDS

Vancouver

Seattle

Winnipeg

Lake Superior

Lake Huron

Saint Lawrence

Quebec

Ottawa

Montreal

Halifax

ATLANTIC OCEAN

Porto

PORTUGAL

M

Portland

ROCKY MOUNTAINS

Minneapolis

NORTH AMERICA

CHICAGO

Lake Michigan

DETROIT

Toronto

Ontario

Erie

Boston

NEW YORK

PHILADELPHIA

WASHINGTON

AÇORES AZORES (Port.)

LISBOA

SPA

We

GIBRALTAR (U.K.)

RABAT

PACIFIC

OCEAN

San Francisco

LOS ANGELES

San Diego

UNITED STATES

Salt Lake City

Denver

Phoenix

El Paso

Dallas

St. Louis

Atlanta

APPALACHIAN MOUNTAINS

Mississippi

Rio Grande

New Orleans

Houston

BERMUDA (U.K.)

ARQUIPÉLAGO DA MADEIRA (Port.)

Casablanca

MOROCCO

MIDWAY ISLANDS (U.S.)

Tropic of Cancer

CABO SAN LUCAS

Monterrey

Gulf of Mexico

Miami

BAHAMAS

ISLAS CANARIAS CANARY ISLANDS (Sp.)

WESTERN SAHARA

S

HAWAIIAN ISLANDS

Honolulu

MEXICO

Guadalajara

CIUDAD DE MÉXICO

MEXICO CITY

LA HABANA

CUBA

DOMINICAN REPUBLIC

Port-au-Prince

HAITI

PUERTO RICO (U.S.)

SANTO DOMINGO

SAN JUAN

GUADELOUPE (Fr.)

CAPE VERDE

Nouakchott

MAURI-TANIA

ATL

A

Tombouctou

M

JOHNSTON ATOLL (U.S.)

GUATEMALA

GUATEMALA

San Salvador

EL SALVADOR

BELIZE

HONDURAS

Tegucigalpa

Managua

NICARAGUA

JAMAICA

Kingston

Caribbean Sea

MARTINIQUE (Fr.)

BARBADOS

TRINIDAD AND TOBAGO

Port of Spain

SENEGAL

DAKAR

GAMBIA

Banjul

GUINEA-BISSAU

GUINEA

Conakry

SIERRA LEONE

Freetown

Bamako

BUR

Ouagad

IVORY COAST

Yamoussou

ABIDJAN

LIBERIA

Monrovia

P

ÎLE CLIPPERTON (Fr.)

COSTA RICA

PANAMA

SAN JOSÉ

Panamá

CARACAS

VENEZUELA

Medellín

SANTA FE DE BOGOTÁ

Cali

COLOMBIA

GUYANA

Georgetown

Paramaribo

SURI-NAME

FRENCH GUIANA

O

L

Y

N

E

S

I

A

KIRIBATI

PHOENIX ISLANDS

LINE ISLANDS

Equator

ARCHIPIÉLAGO DE COLÓN GALÁPAGOS ISLANDS (Ec.)

QUITO

ECUADOR

Guayaquil

Iquitos

Manaus

Amazon

Belém

Fortaleza

CABO DE SÃO ROQUE

Natal

Recife

Equator

WALLIS AND FUTUNA (Fr.)

W. SAMOA

Apia

TOKELAU (N.Z.)

AM. SAMOA

ÎLES MARQUISES

Trujillo

ANDES

PERU

B   R   A   Z   I   L

SOUTH AMERICA

Madeira

Salvador

ATLANTIC OCEAN

SAINT HELENA (U.K.)

FIJI

NIUE (N.Z.)

COOK ISLANDS (N.Z.)

FRENCH POLYNESIA

ÎLES TUAMOTU

LIMA

Arequipa

LA PAZ

BOLIVIA

Sucre

Goiânia

BRASÍLIA

Belo Horizonte

TONGA

Tropic of Capricorn

PITCAIRN (U.K.)

ISLA DE PASCUA EASTER ISLAND (Chile)

Antofagasta

ISLA SAN AMBROSIO (Chile)

PARAGUAY

Asunción

SÃO PAULO

Santos

Curitiba

RIO DE JANEIRO

CHILE

Co. Aconcagua 6959

Córdoba

Paraná

Porto Alegre

CHATHAM ISLANDS (N.Z.)

PACIFIC OCEAN

ARCHIPIÉLAGO JUAN FERNÁNDEZ (Chile)

Valparaíso

SANTIAGO

Rosario

ARGENTINA

Concepción

BUENOS AIRES

URUGUAY

MONTEVIDEO

Mar del Plata

Bahía Blanca

International Date Line

FALKLAND ISLANDS (U.K.)

SOUTH GEORGIA (U.K.)

Punta Arenas

CABO DE HORNOS CAPE HORN

Drake Passage

SOUTH ORKNEY ISLANDS (U.K.)

Antarctic Circle

Bellingshausen Sea

ANTARCTIC PENINSULA

Weddell Sea

Ross Sea

MARIE BYRD LAND

Vinson Massif 4897

ROSS ICE SHELF

ANTAR

14 _30°_ 15 _45°_ 16 _60°_ 17 _75°_ 18 _90°_ 19 _105°_ 20 _120°_ 21 _135°_ 22 _150°_ 23 _165°_ 24 _180°_

_90°_

ARCTIC OCEAN

ZEML'A FRANCA-IOSIFA
NOVAJA ZEML'A
Barents Sea (Nor.)
ALBARD
Hammerfest
Narvik
Murmansk
Vorkuta
Dikson
more Laptevych
NOVOSIBIRSKIJE OSTROVA

A

_75°_

SWEDEN FINLAND
Latvskoje ozero
HELSINKI
STOCKHOLM EST.
SANKT-PETERBURG ST. PETERSBURG
Niznij Novgorod
Perm'
Jekaterinburg
Čel'abinsk
Omsk
Noril'sk
Chatanga
Tiksi
Verchojansk
Arctic Circle
Anadyr

B

_60°_

KØBENHAVN
BERLIN POLAND
BELARUS
WARSZAWA
MOSKVA
UKRAINE
KIJEV
Samara
Volgograd
Karaganda
Novosibirsk
Krasnojarsk
Irkutsk
Čita
Ulaanbaatar
Ochotsk
Sea of Okhotsk
Nikolajevsk
Chabarovsk
Petropavlovsk-Kamčatskij
Bering Sea
ALEUTIAN IS. (U.S.)

C

_45°_

ALPS
KAZAKHSTAN
A   S   I   A
Aral'skoje more
ozero Balchaš
ALTAJ
MONGOLIA
GOBI
Hohhot
Harbin
OSTROV SACHALIN
Vladivostok
Sapporo
KURIL'SKIJE OSTROVA

D

_30°_

more
Black Sea
TURKEY
ARMENIJA
BAKU
UZBEKISTAN
TAŠKENT
KYRG.
TIEN SHAN
Ürümqi
CHINA
BEIJING PEKING
Shenyang
N. KOREA
P'YONGYANG
S. KOREA
SEOUL Pusan
JAPAN
Sendai
TŌKYŌ
HONSHŪ

Mediterranean Sea
SYRIA
LEB.
IRAQ
IRAN
Ešfahān
TURKMENISTAN
TADŽ.
AFGHANISTAN
KĀBOL
Islāmābād
Rāwalpindi
Lahore
HIMALAYAS
Lhasa
Lanzhou
Xi'an
Chengdu
Chongqing
Wuhan
Nanjing
SHANGHAI
Changsha
Yellow Sea
Dalian
Qingdao
Fukuoka
ŌSAKA

E

_15°_

LIBYA
EGYPT
AL-QĀHIRAH
CAIRO
AR-RIYĀḌ
QATAR
UNITED ARAB EMIRATES
KUWAIT
Karāchi
DELHI
New Delhi
Kāthmāndu NEPAL
Mount Everest 8848
BHUTAN BNGL.
BURMA
Kunming
Guangzhou
HONG KONG (U.K.)
T'AIPEI
TAIWAN
NANSEI-SHOTŌ
OGASAWARA-GUNTŌ (Japan)

PACIFIC
OCEAN

WAKE ISLAND (U.S.)

SAUDI ARABIA
Makkah
OMAN
Maşqaţ
Ahmadābād
INDIA
Tropic of Cancer
CALCUTTA
DHAKA
HA NOI
South China Sea
Philippine Sea
NORTHERN MARIANA ISLANDS (U.S.)

F

_0°_

NIGER CHAD
AL-KHARŢŪM
SUDAN
YEMEN
Şan'ā'
Aden
GEES GWARDAFUY
Arabian Sea
BOMBAY
Hyderābād
Madras
Bay of Bengal
ANDAMAN ISLANDS (India)
THAILAND
KRUNG THEP
BANGKOK
CAMB.
Phnum Pénh
VIETNAM
Thanh Pho Ho Chi Minh
MANILA
PHILIPPINES
Davao
GUAM (U.S.)
PALAU (U.S.)
MICRONESIA
MARSHALL ISLANDS

NIGERIA
N'Djamena
CEN. AFR. REP.
Bangui
DJIBOUTI
ADIS ABEBA
ETHIOPIA
SOMALIA
Bangalore
Cochin
SRI LANKA
COLOMBO
MALDIVES
NICOBAR ISLANDS (India)
MALAYSIA
KUALA LUMPUR
SINGAPORE
BRUNEI
FEDERATED STATES OF MICRONESIA
Equator
KIRIBATI

G

_15°_

ATORIAL GUINEA
Libreville
GABON
CONGO
Yaoundé
Douala
ZAIRE
Brazzaville
KINSHASA
UGANDA
KAMPALA
RWANDA
BURUNDI
Bujumbura
Kilimanjaro 5895
KENYA
NAIROBI
Lake Rudolf
Lake Victoria
Mombasa
Zanzibar
TANZANIA
Dodoma
DAR ES SALAAM
SEYCHELLES
BRITISH INDIAN OCEAN TERRITORY
Medan
SUMATERA
Palembang
BORNEO
Banjarmasin
KALIMANTAN
SULAWESI
Ujungpandang
INDONESIA
JAKARTA
Surabaya
JAWA
TIMOR
PAPUA NEW GUINEA
Mount Wilhelm 4509
NEW GUINEA
Port Moresby
NAURU
TUVALU
SOLOMON ISLANDS
MELANESIA

ANGOLA
LUANDA
Lobito
Lubumbashi
ZAMBIA
Lusaka
Lake Nyasa
Lake Tanganyika
COCOS ISLANDS (Austl.)
CHRISTMAS ISLAND (Austl.)
CAPE YORK
Darwin
Gulf of Carpentaria
Cairns
Coral Sea
VANUATU
NEW CALEDONIA (Fr.)
Nouméa
Suva
FIJI

INDIAN
OCEAN

H

_15°_

NAMIBIA
Windhoek
(S. Afr.)
BOTSWANA
Gaborone
ZIMBABWE
Harare
MOZAMBIQUE
Lilongwe
MALAWI
Zambezi
MADAGASCAR
ANTANANARIVO
MAURITIUS
RÉUNION (Fr.)
Mozambique Channel
Tropic of Capricorn
Alice Springs
AUSTRALIA
Rockhampton
NORFOLK ISLAND (Austl.)

SOUTH AFRICA
Johannesburg
PRETORIA
MAPUTO
SWAZILAND
LESOTHO
Durban
Port Elizabeth
CAPE TOWN
CAPE AGULHAS
Perth
Adelaide
Canberra
Sydney
Mount Kosciusko 2228
Melbourne
Tasman Sea
NORTH ISLAND
Auckland
NEW ZEALAND
Wellington

I

_30°_

ÎLES KERGUÉLEN (Fr.)
TASMANIA
Hobart
SOUTH ISLAND
Christchurch

SOUTHERN

_45°_

OCEAN

J

_60°_

Antarctic Circle

K

ENDERBY LAND
WILKES LAND

_75°_

L

C   T   I   C   A
Copyright © by Rand McNally & Co.
Map prepared by Rand McNally & Co.
A-510000-264.

14 _30°_ 15 _45°_ 16 _60°_ 17 _75°_ 18 _90°_ 19 _105°_ 20 _120°_ 21 _135°_ 22 _150°_ 23 _165°_ 24 _180°_

Kilometers | 0 | 1000 | 2000 | 3000 Km.
Statute Miles | 0 | 1000 | 2000 | 3000 Mi.

One centimeter represents 750 kilometers.
One inch represents approximately 1200 miles.
Robinson Projection
Scale 1:75,000,000

3

Kilometers 0 200 400 600 Km.

Statute Miles 0 200 400 600 Mi.

Scale 1:12,000,000
One centimeter represents 120 kilometers.
One inch represents approximately 190 miles.
Miller Oblated Stereographic Projection

5

a

1 24° 2 22° 3 20° 4 18° 5 16° 6 14° 7

GREENLAND SEA

Denmark Strait

Arctic Circle

A

ICELAND
ÍSLAND

66°

Húnaflói

Reykjavík

ATLANTIC

OCEAN

b

8
**FAEROE ISLANDS
FØROYAR**
(Denmark)

**NORWEGIAN
SEA**

282

Tórshavn

ATLANTIC

OCEAN

104

NORTH

SEA

TO LERWICK

TO NEWCASTLE

TO NEWCASTLE

TO HARWICH

**NORWEGIAN

SEA**

Arctic Circle

Trondheim

Ålesund

Bergen

Stavanger

Kristiansand

Oslo

Skagerrak

Göteborg
Gothenburg

Kattegat

Ålborg

Randers

Århus

Esbjerg

**KØBENHAVN
COPENHAGEN**

**DENMARK
DANMARK

GERMANY
DEUTSCHLAND**

Kiel

Östersund

Sundsvall

Gävle

Borlänge

Karlstad

Västerås

Uppsala

Örebro

STOCKHOLM

Norrköping

Linköping

Jönköping

Växjö

Kalmar

Halmstad

Helsingborg

Lund

Malmö

Kristianstad

Karlskrona

**BALTIC

SEA**

GOTLAND

ÖLAND

6

Copyright © by Rand McNally & Co.
A-554490-264

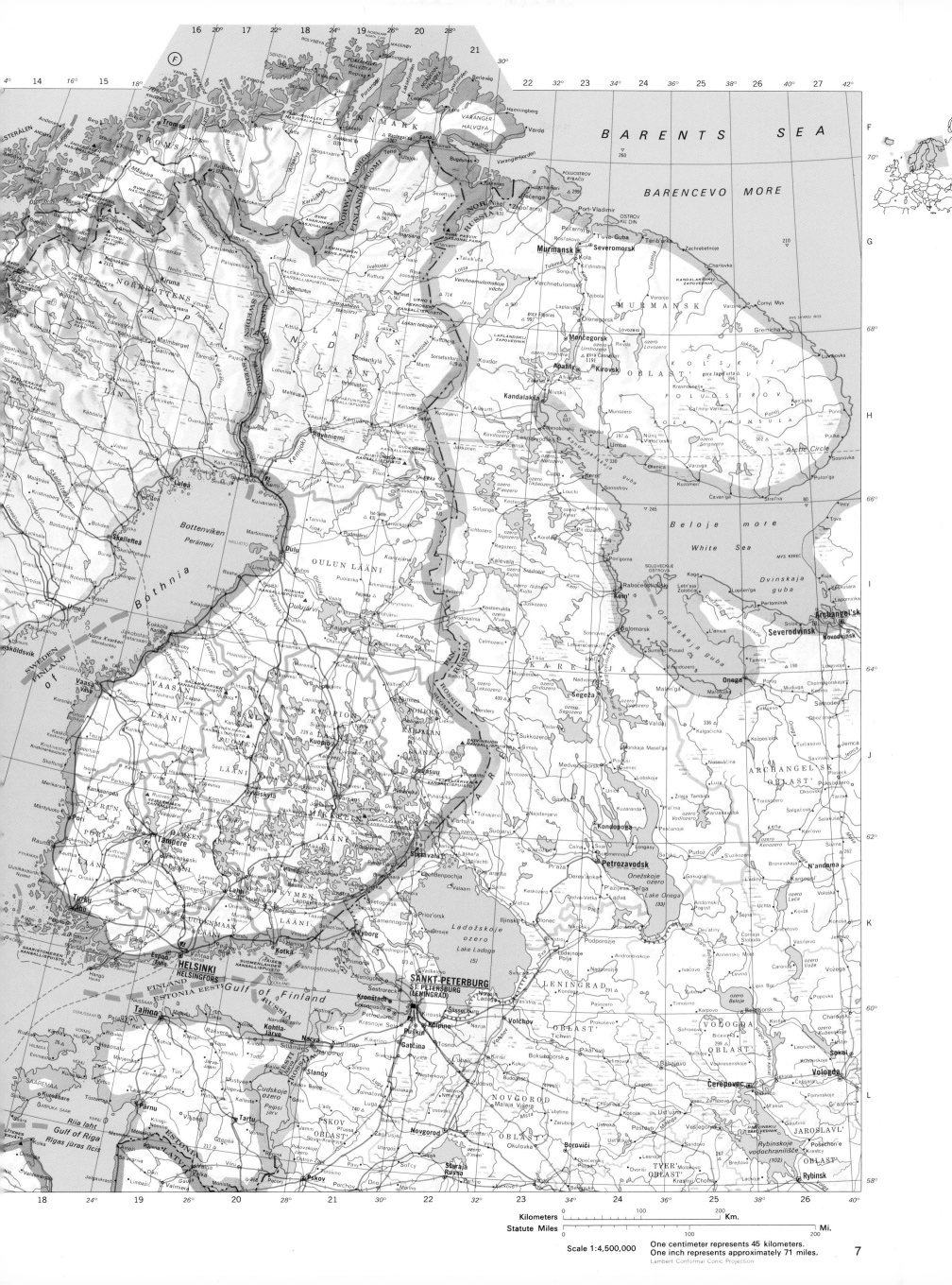

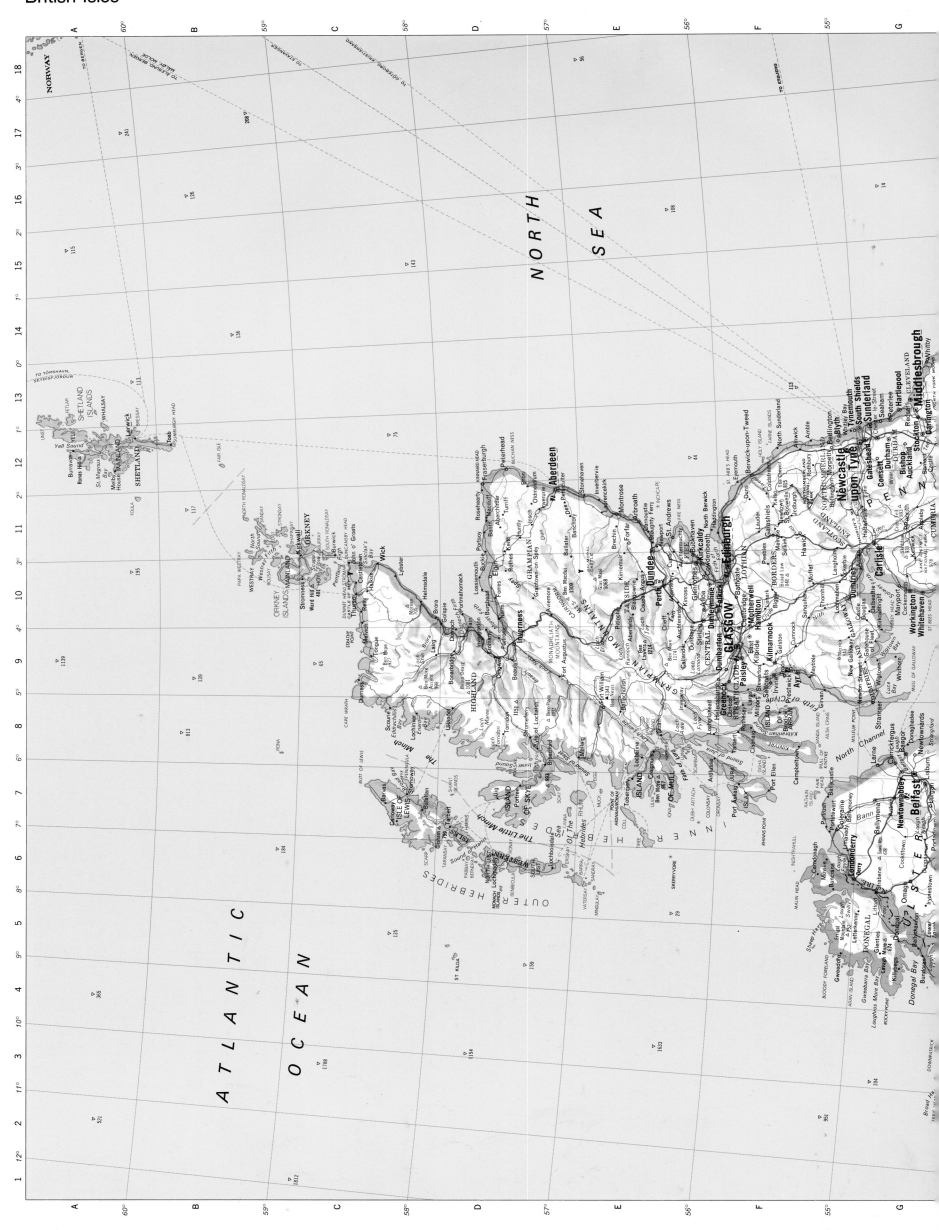

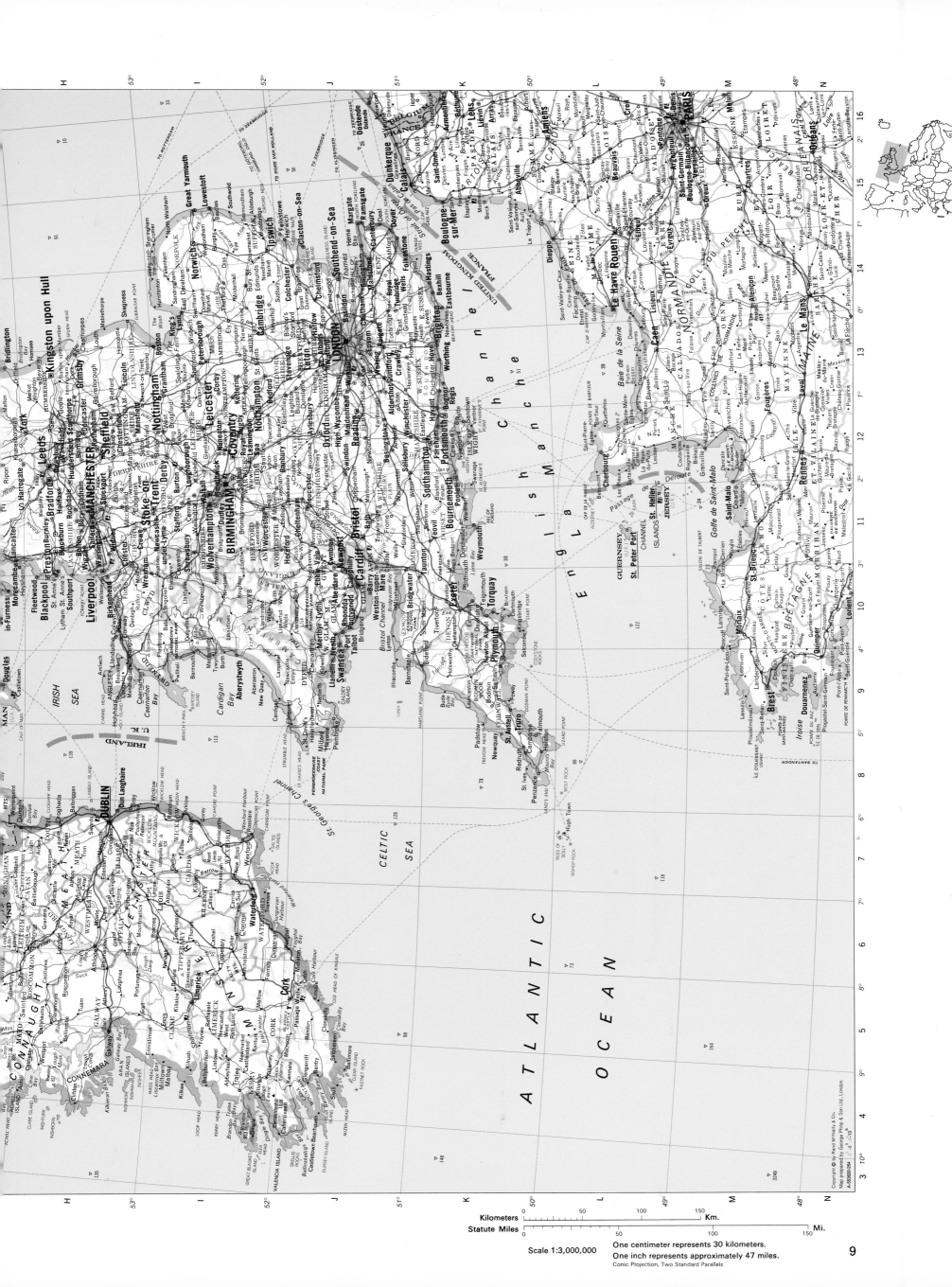

Kilometers

Statute Miles

One centimeter represents 30 kilometers.
One inch represents approximately 47 miles.
Scale 1:3,000,000
Conic Projection, Two Standard Parallels

Kilometers
Statute Miles

Scale 1:3,000,000
One centimeter represents 30 kilometers.
One inch represents approximately 47 miles.
Conic Projection, Two Standard Parallels.

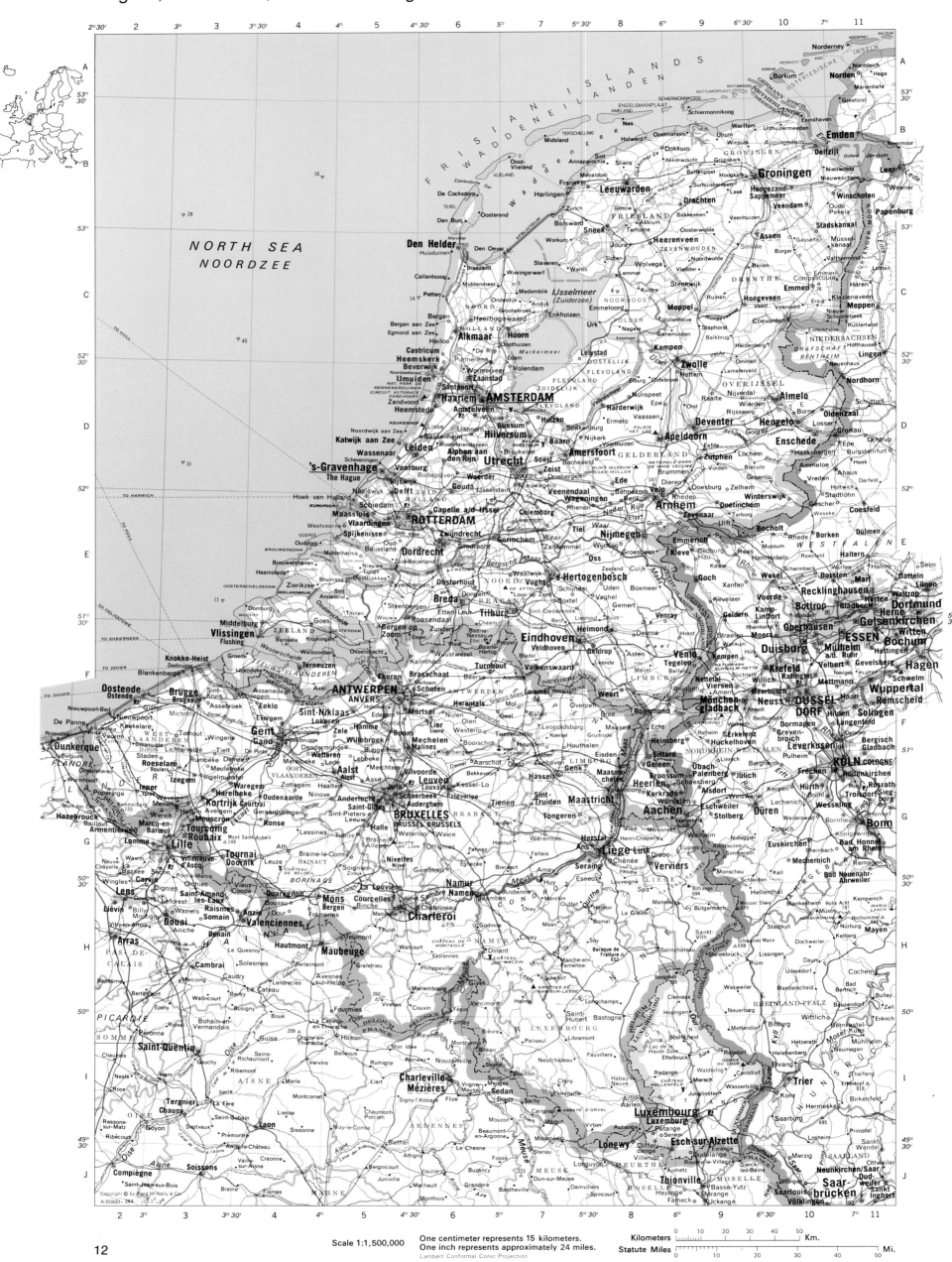

Scale 1:1,500,000
One centimeter represents 15 kilometers.
One inch represents approximately 24 miles.
Lambert Conformal Conic Projection

Kilometers
Statute Miles

Copyright © by Rand McNally & Co.
A-558601- 264

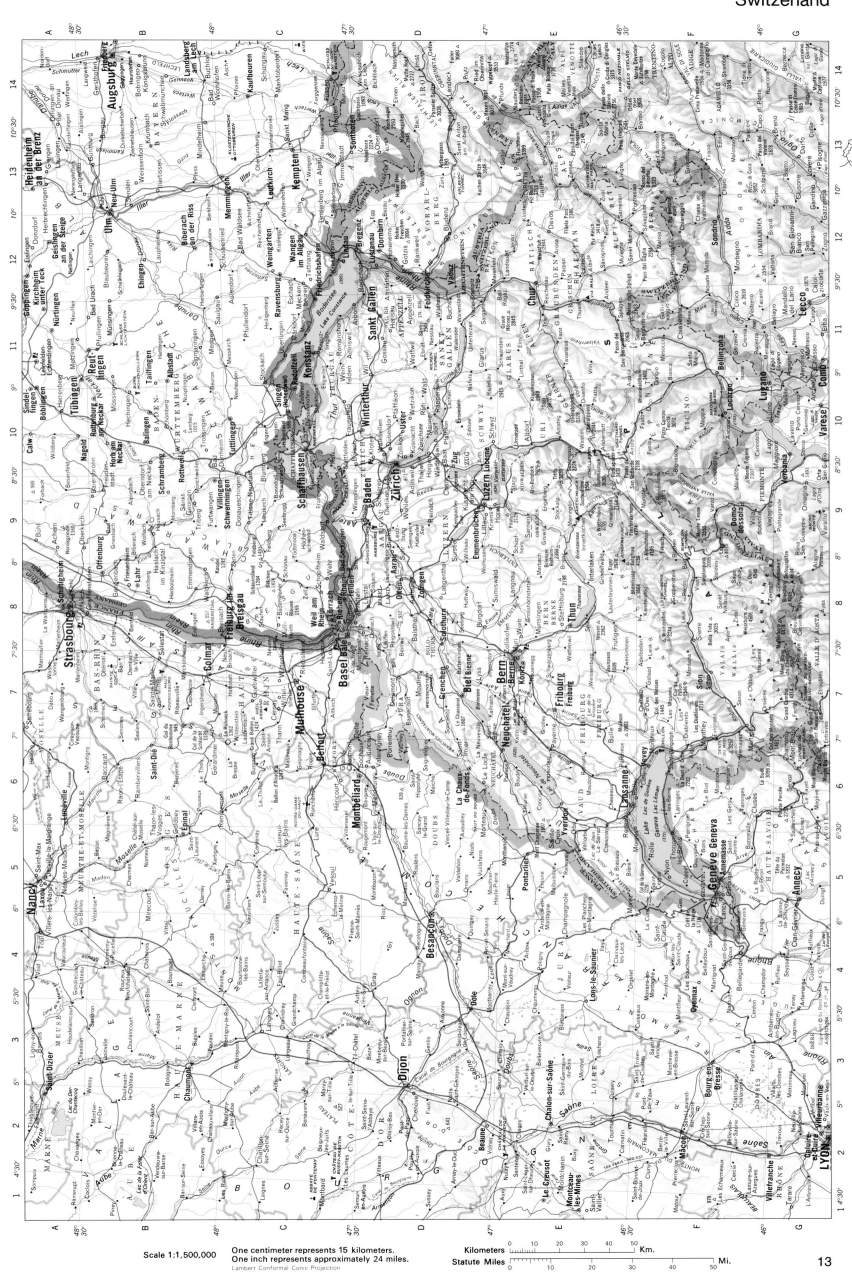

Scale 1:1,500,000

One centimeter represents 15 kilometers.
One inch represents approximately 24 miles.

Lambert Conformal Conic Projection

Kilometers

Statute Miles

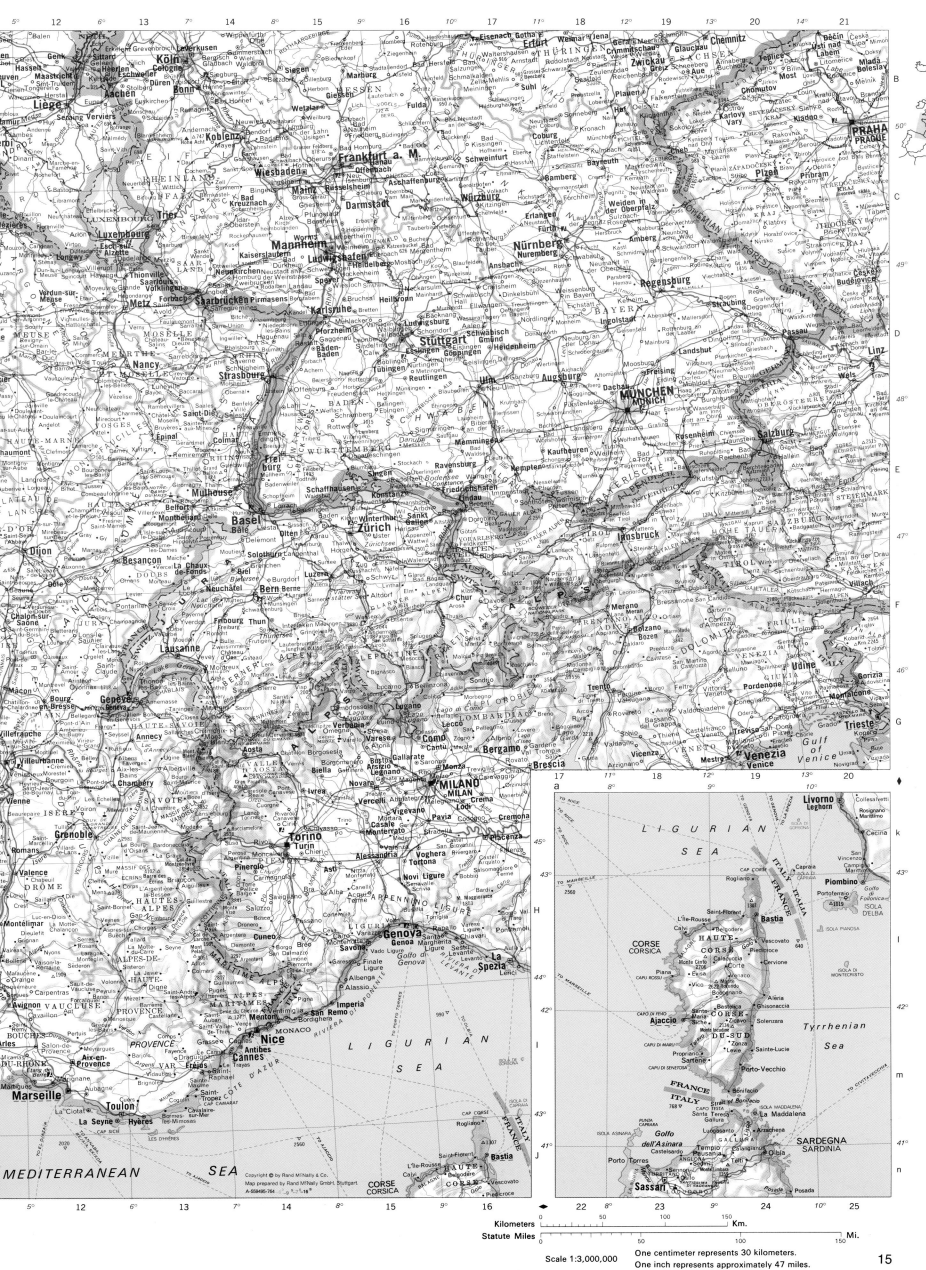

Copyright © by Rand McNally & Co.
Map prepared by Rand McNally GmbH, Stuttgart.
A-559495-764
A-559495-16

Kilometers

Statute Miles

One centimeter represents 30 kilometers.
One inch represents approximately 47 miles.

Scale 1:3,000,000

Lambert Conformal Conic Projection

15

Spain and Portugal

Bay of Biscay

ATLANTIC

OCEAN

CABO ORTEGAL
CABO PRIOR
El Ferrol del Caudillo
La Coruña
CABO TOURIÑAN
Santiago de Compostela
GALICIA
Pontevedra
Vigo
Orense

ATLANTIC OCEAN

Porto
Vila Nova de Gaia
Coimbra

BEIRA
BAIXA

ESTREMADURA

LISBOA LISBON
Setúbal

ALENTEJO

ALGARVE
CABO DE SÃO VICENTE
CAPE ST. VINCENT
Lagos
Faro

Santander
Oviedo
Gijón
ASTURIAS
CANTABRICA
Donostia
San Sebastian
Bilbao
EUSKAL
HERRIKO
Vitoria Gasteiz
BURGOS
LA RIOJA
Logroño
León
Burgos
SORIA
Palencia
Valladolid
CASTILLA
LEON
Zamora
Salamanca
Segovia
Ávila
MADRID
MADRID
Guadalajara
Alcalá de Henares
Toledo
Talavera de la Reina
Aranjuez
CASTILLA LA MANCHA
Cáceres
EXTREMADURA
Mérida
Badajoz
Ciudad Real
Puertollano
Valdepeñas
Albacete
SIERRA MORENA
Córdoba
Sevilla
Seville
ANDALUCIA
Jaén
Úbeda
Linares
Huelva
Jerez de la Frontera
Cádiz
San Fernando
Málaga
Granada
SISTEMAS
BETICOS
Almería
Gibraltar (U.K.)
La Línea
Algeciras
Strait of Gibraltar
ALBORÁN SEA

Tanger
Tangier
Ceuta
Tétouan
MOROCCO
AL-MAGREB
RIF
Melilla (Sp.)
Nador
Al-Hoceima

Copyright © by Rand McNally & Co.
Map prepared by Rand McNally GmbH, Stuttgart.
A-559900-264

16

MEDITERRANEAN SEA

Golfe du Lion

ILLES BALEARS
BALEARIC ISLANDS

MENORCA
MINORCA

MALLORCA
MAJORCA

EIVISSA
IBIZA

FORMENTERA

a

ARQUIPÉLAGO DA MADEIRA
MADEIRA ISLANDS
(Portugal)

MADEIRA

Funchal

ILHAS DESERTAS

ATLANTIC OCEAN

© R. MCN.

b

ISLAS CANARIAS
CANARY ISLANDS
(Spain)

LA PALMA

TENERIFE

Santa Cruz de Tenerife

GOMERA

GRAN CANARIA

Las Palmas de
Gran Canaria

HIERRO
FERRO

LANZAROTE

FUERTEVENTURA

ATLANTIC OCEAN

WESTERN SAHARA

© R. MCN.

ALGERIA
ALGÉRIE

Wahran
Oran

Kilometers

Statute Miles

Km.

Mi.

One centimeter represents 30 kilometers.
One inch represents approximately 47 miles.

Scale 1:3,000,000

Conic Projection, Two Standard Parallels

17

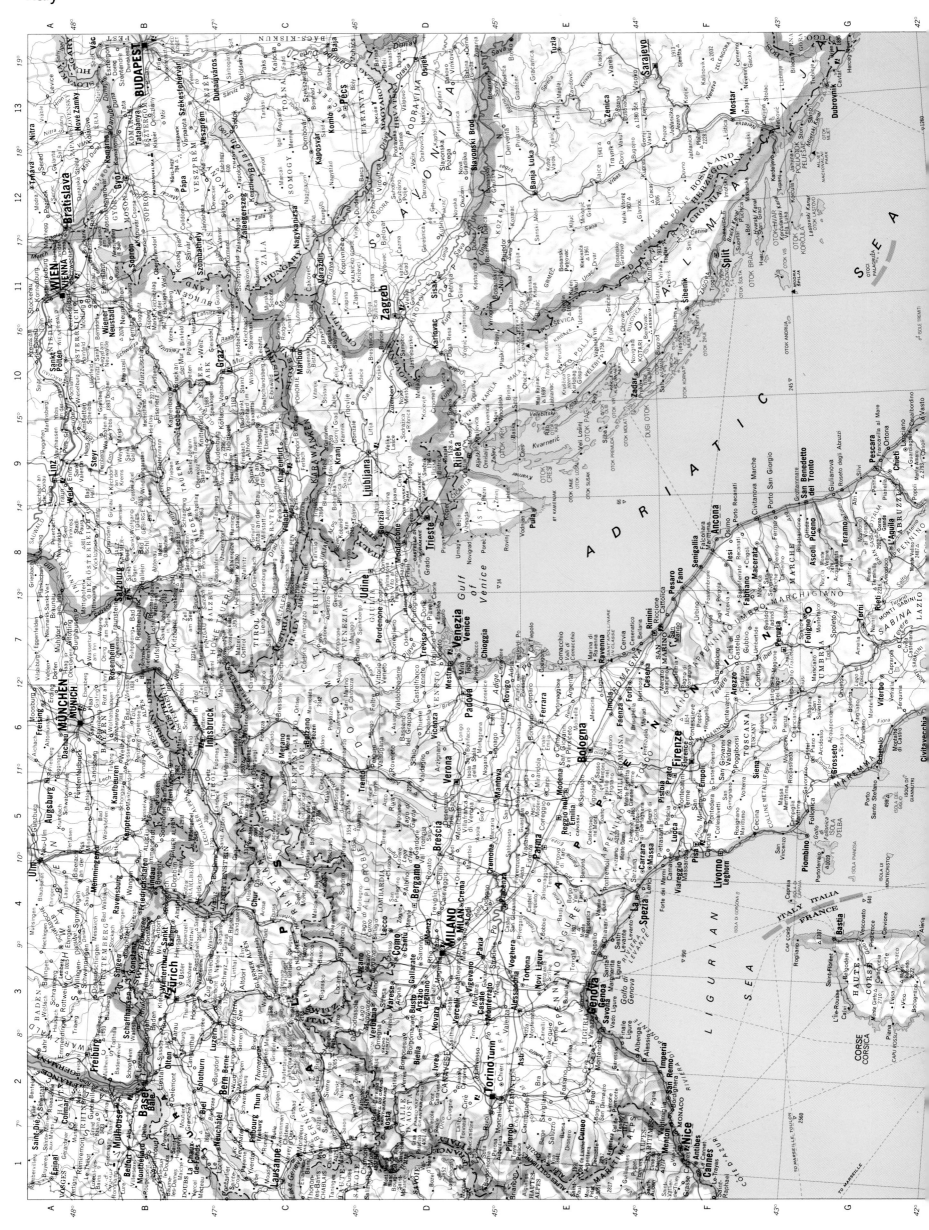

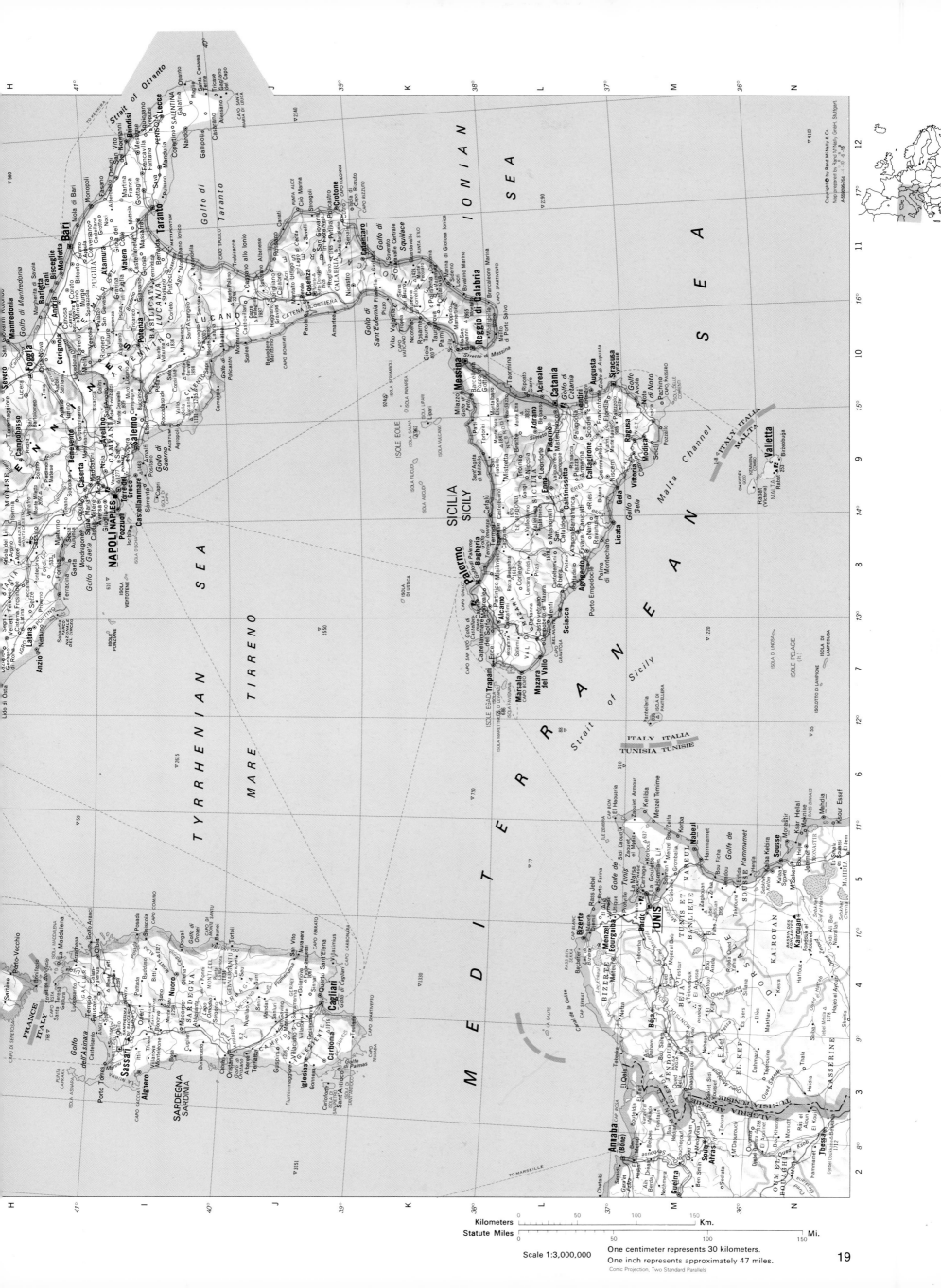

Kilometers
0   50   100   Km.   150

Statute Miles
0   50   100   Mi.   150

Scale 1:3,000,000
One centimeter represents 30 kilometers.
One inch represents approximately 47 miles.
Conic Projection, Two Standard Parallels

Kilometers
Statute Miles

Scale 1:3,000,000

One centimeter represents 30 kilometers.
One inch represents approximately 47 miles.
Conic Projection, Two Standard Parallels

Kilometers

Statute Miles

Scale 1:3,000,000 One centimeter represents 30 kilometers.
One inch represents approximately 47 miles.
Lambert Conformal Conic Projection

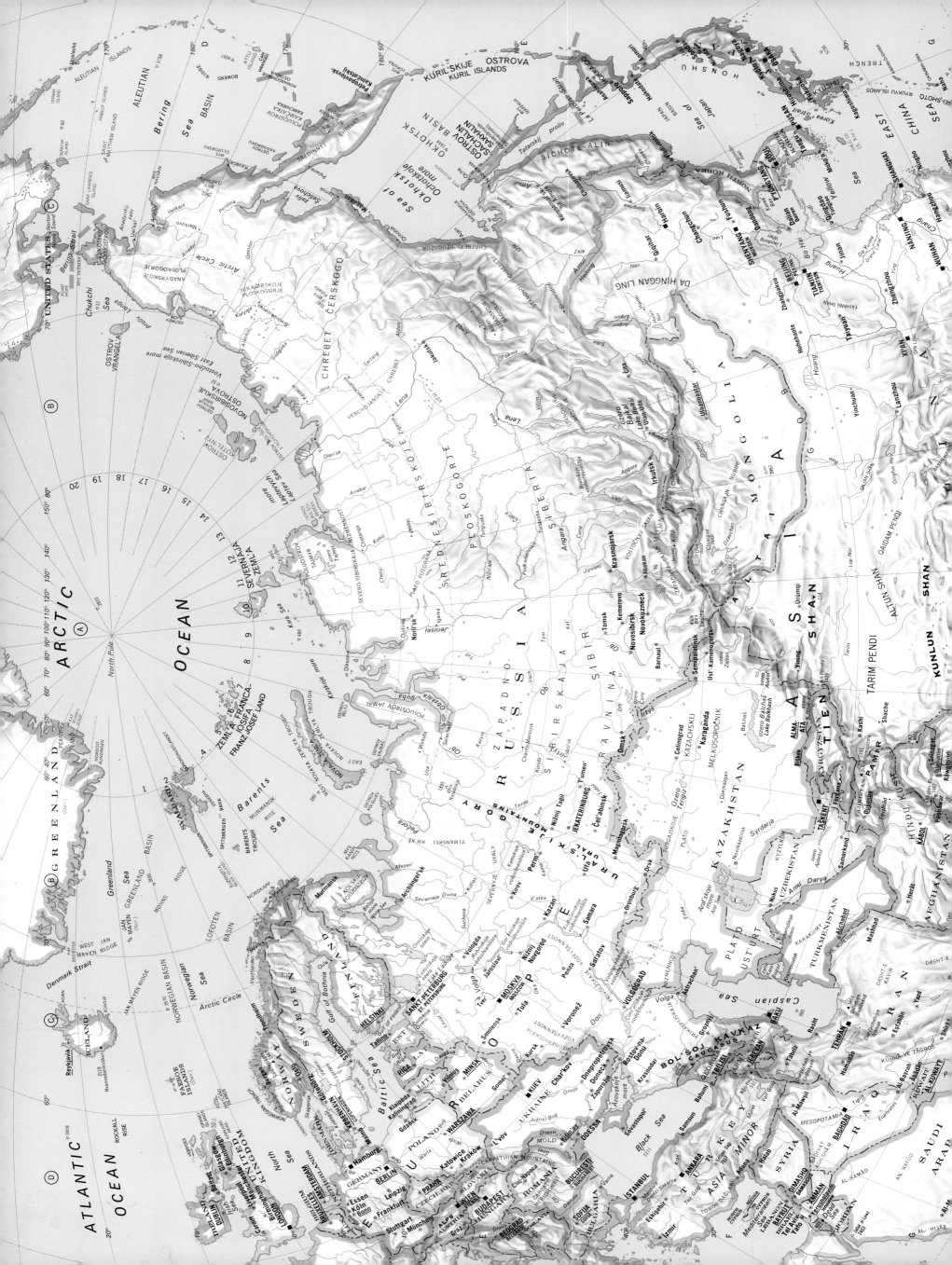

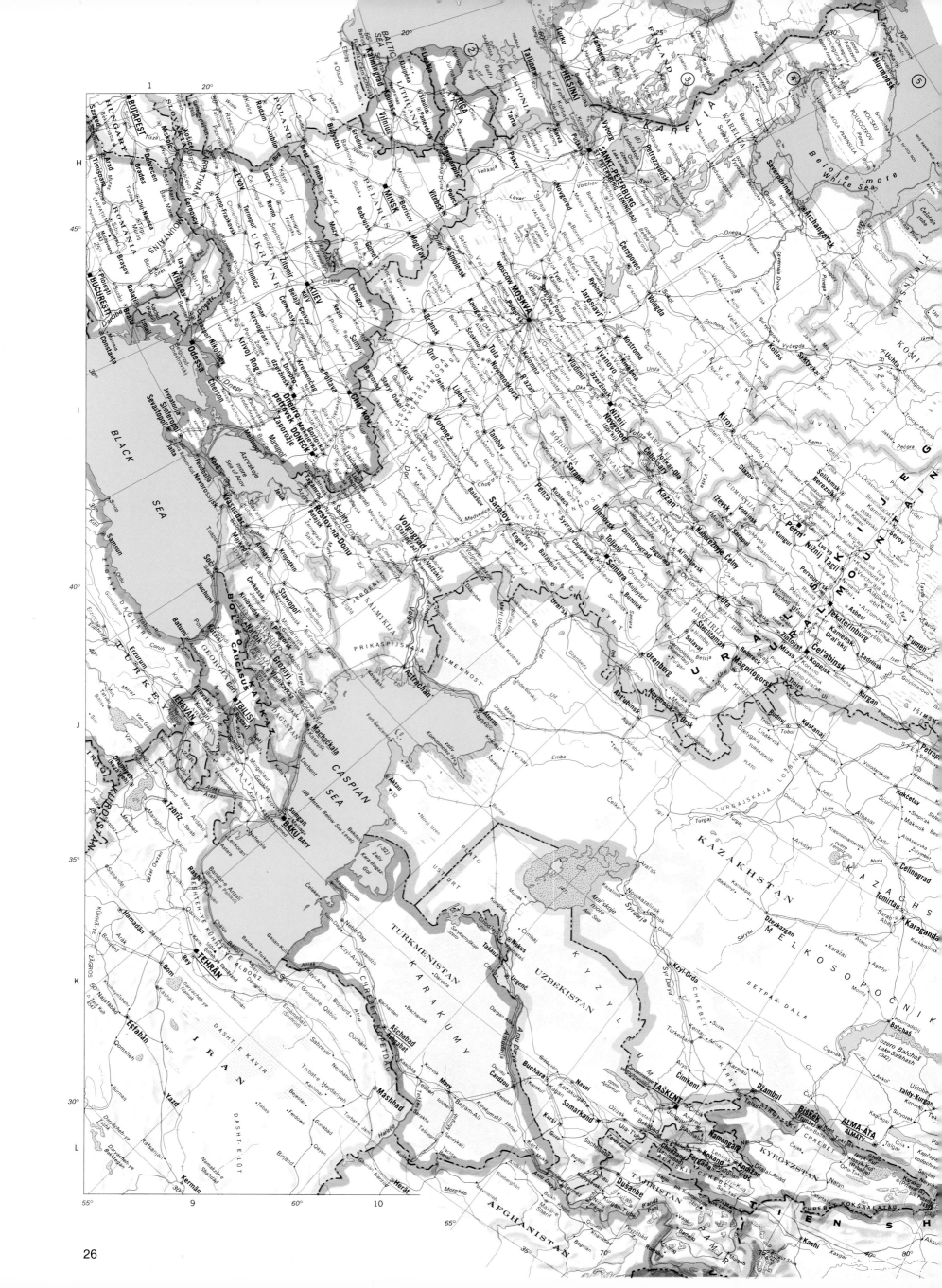

BARENTS SEA

KARSKOJE MORE

KARA SEA

MORE LAPTEVYCH

LAPTEV SEA

NOVAJA ZEMLJA

SEVERNAJA ZEMLJA

OSTROV KOMSOMOLEC
OSTROV PIONER
OSTROV OKTJABR'SKOJ REVOLUCII
OSTROV BOL'ŠEVIK

MYS ARKTIČESKIJ

POLUOSTROV JAMAL

POLUOSTROV GYDANSKIJ

POLUOSTROV TAJMYR

GORY BYRRANGA

SEVERO - SIBIRSKAJA NIZMENNOST

Arctic Circle

Vorkuta

Noril'sk

ZAPADNO

JAMALO NENECKIJ

NENECKIJ

TUNDRA

Surgut

Chanty-Mansijsk

ZAPADNO - SIBIRSKAJA RAVNINA

RUSSIA

PLATO PUTORANA
△ 1701 gora Kamen'

SREDNE - SIBIR'SKOJE

JAKUTIJA

PLOSKOGORJE

Jenisej

Dudinka

Igarka

Turuchansk

Tomsk

Novosibirsk

Anžero-Sudžensk

Ačinsk

Krasnojarsk

Kansk

Bratsk

STANOVOJE NAGORJE

Kemerovo
Leninsk-Kuzneckij
Belovo
Prokopjevsk
Kiselevsk
Novokuzneck

Pavlodar

Barnaul

Bijsk

Abakan

CHAKASIJA

VOSTOČNYJ SAJAN

Lena

STANOVOY MOUNTAINS

Semipalatinsk

Rubcovsk

ZAPADNYJ SAJAN

BURJATIJA

Ust'-Kamenogorsk

ALTAJ

SAJANY SAJAN MOUNTAINS

TUVA

TANNU-OLA

Čeremchovo
Usolje-Sibirskoje
Angarsk
Irkutsk

ozero Bajkal
Lake Baikal

Ulan-Ude

Čita

△ 4506 gora Belucha

MONGOL-ALTAJN NURUU

JABLONOVYJ CHREBET

CHREBET TARBAGATAJ

CHINA

XINJIANG SINKIANG UYGUR ZIZHIQU

CHANGAJN NURUU

MONGOLIA

Suchbaatar

Darchan

CHINA

Yining

Ulaanbaatar

Copyright © by Rand McNally & Co.
Map prepared by Esselte Map Service AB, Stockholm.

A-579594-264

Kilometers 0 200 400 600 Km.
Statute Miles 0 200 400 600 Mi.

Scale 1:12,000,000
One centimeter represents 120 kilometers.
One inch represents approximately 190 miles.
Lambert Conformal Conic Projection

27

Kilometers
Statute Miles

Scale 1:12,000,000

One centimeter represents 120 kilometers.
One inch represents approximately 190 miles.
Lambert Conformal Conic Projection

Copyright © by Rand M?Nally & Co.
Map prepared by Esselte Map Service AB. Stockholm.
A-579395-264

China, Japan, and Korea

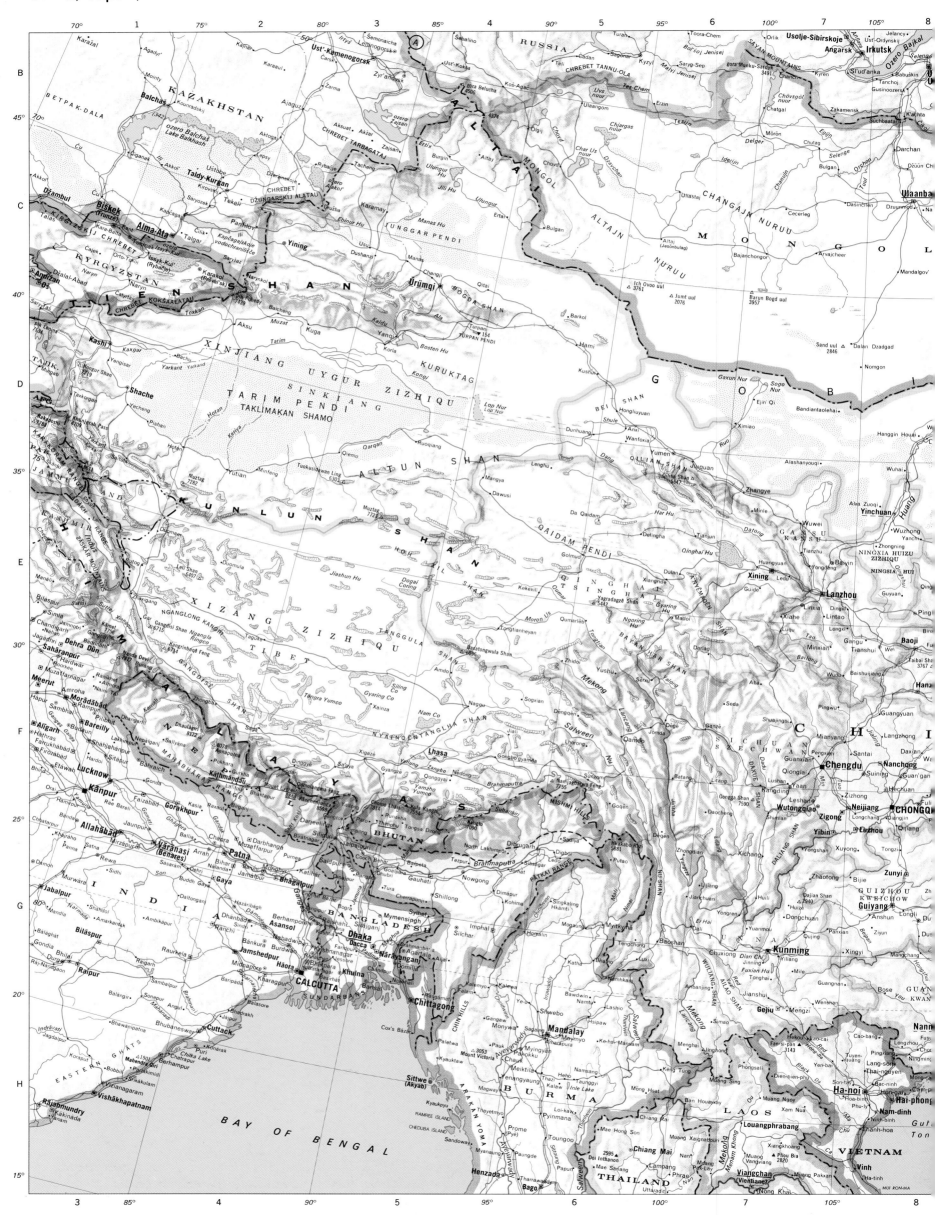

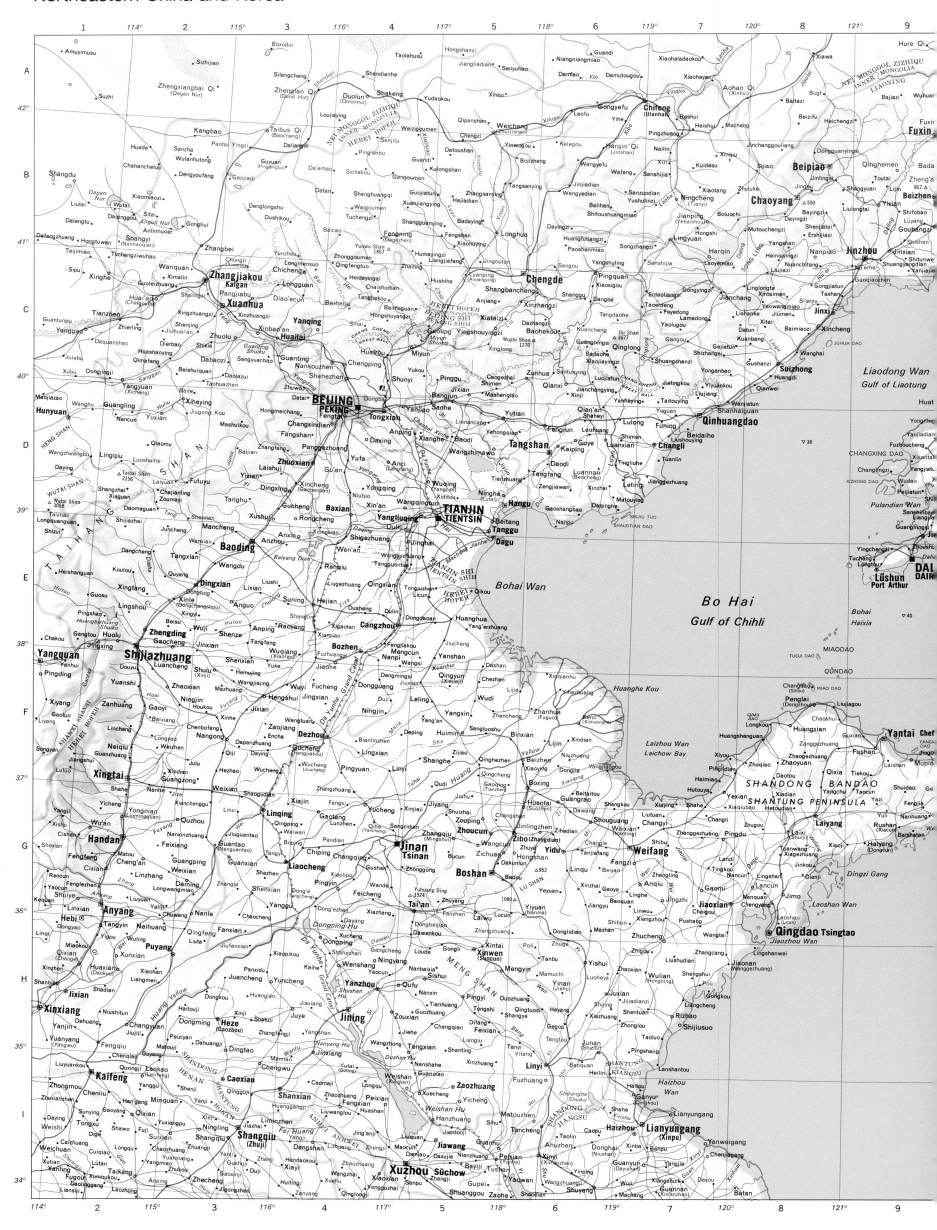

Scale 1:3,000,000

One centimeter represents 30 kilometers.
One inch represents approximately 47 miles.

Lambert Conformal Conic Projection

Kilometers
0   50   100   150 Km.

Statute Miles
0   50   100   150 Mi.

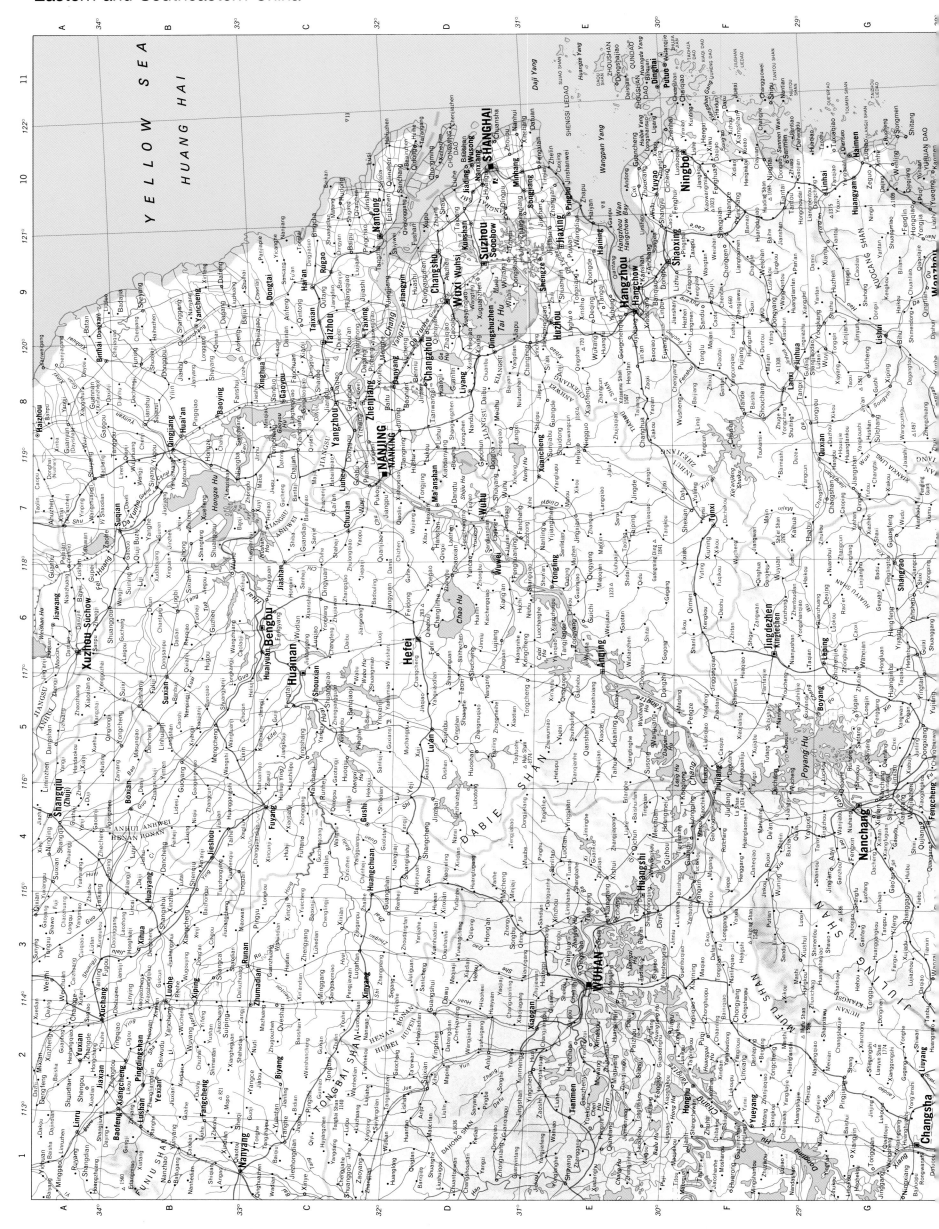

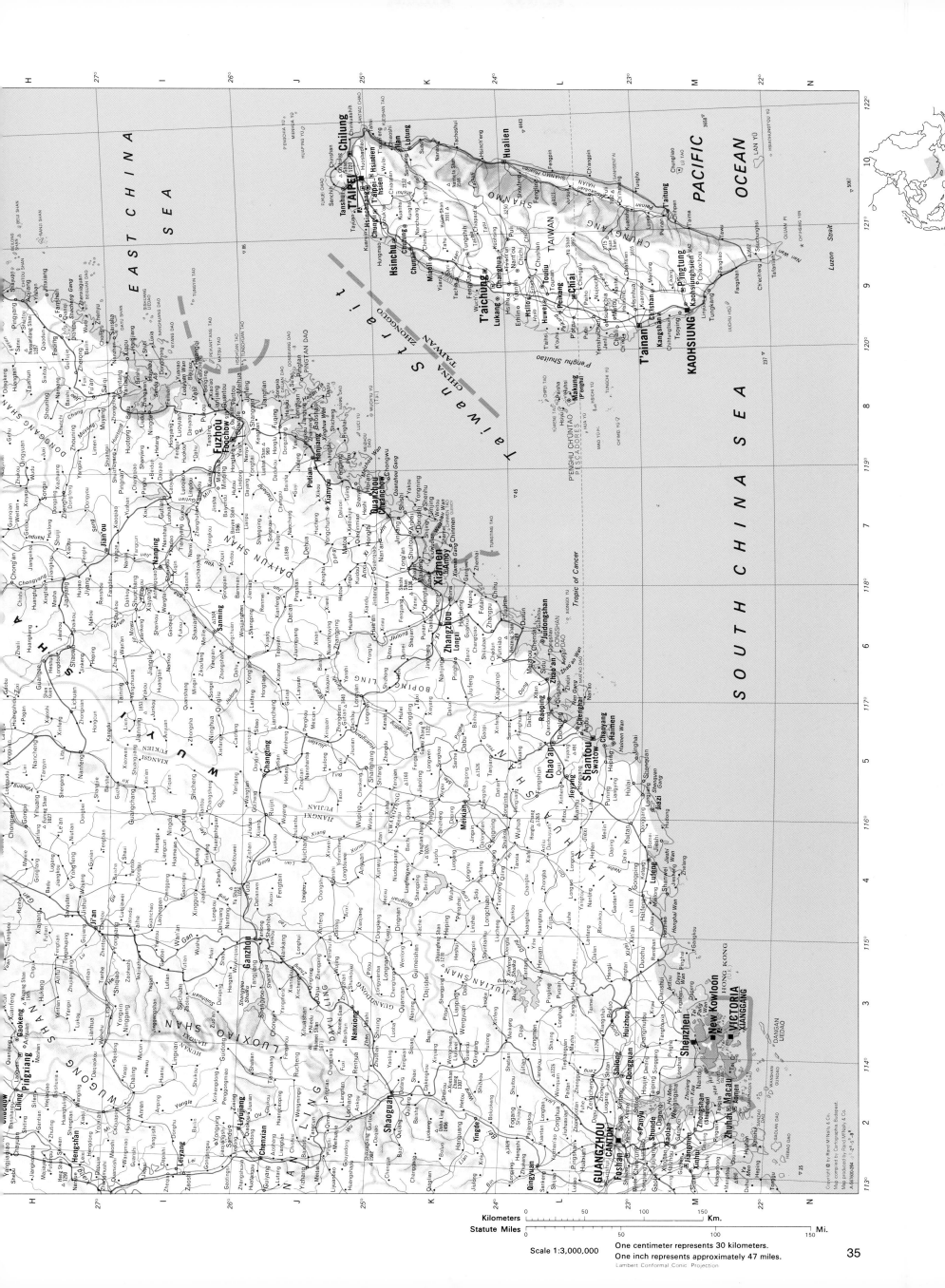

Kilometers

Statute Miles

One centimeter represents 30 kilometers.
One inch represents approximately 47 miles.

Scale 1:3,000,000

Lambert Conformal Conic Projection

35

Japan

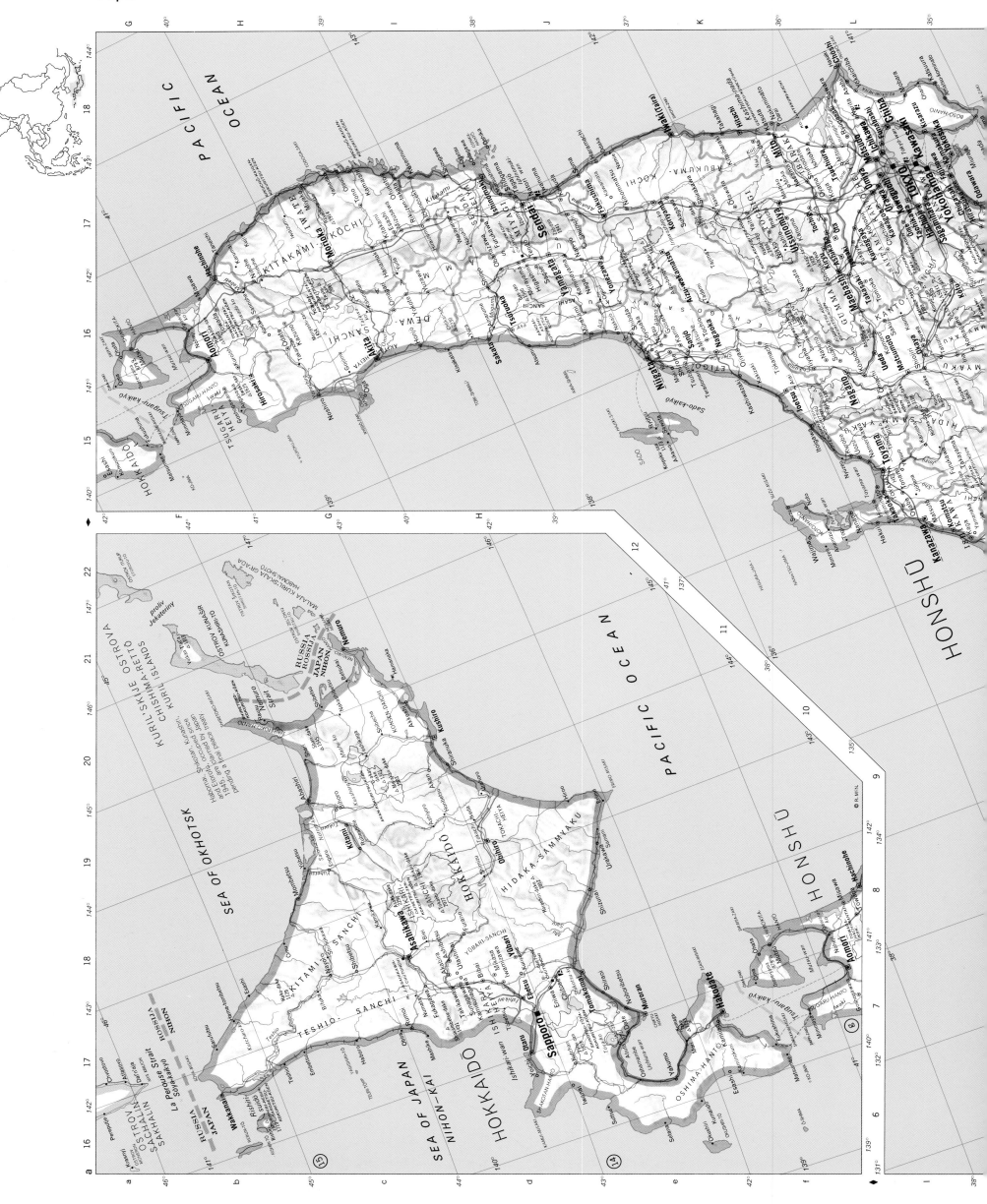

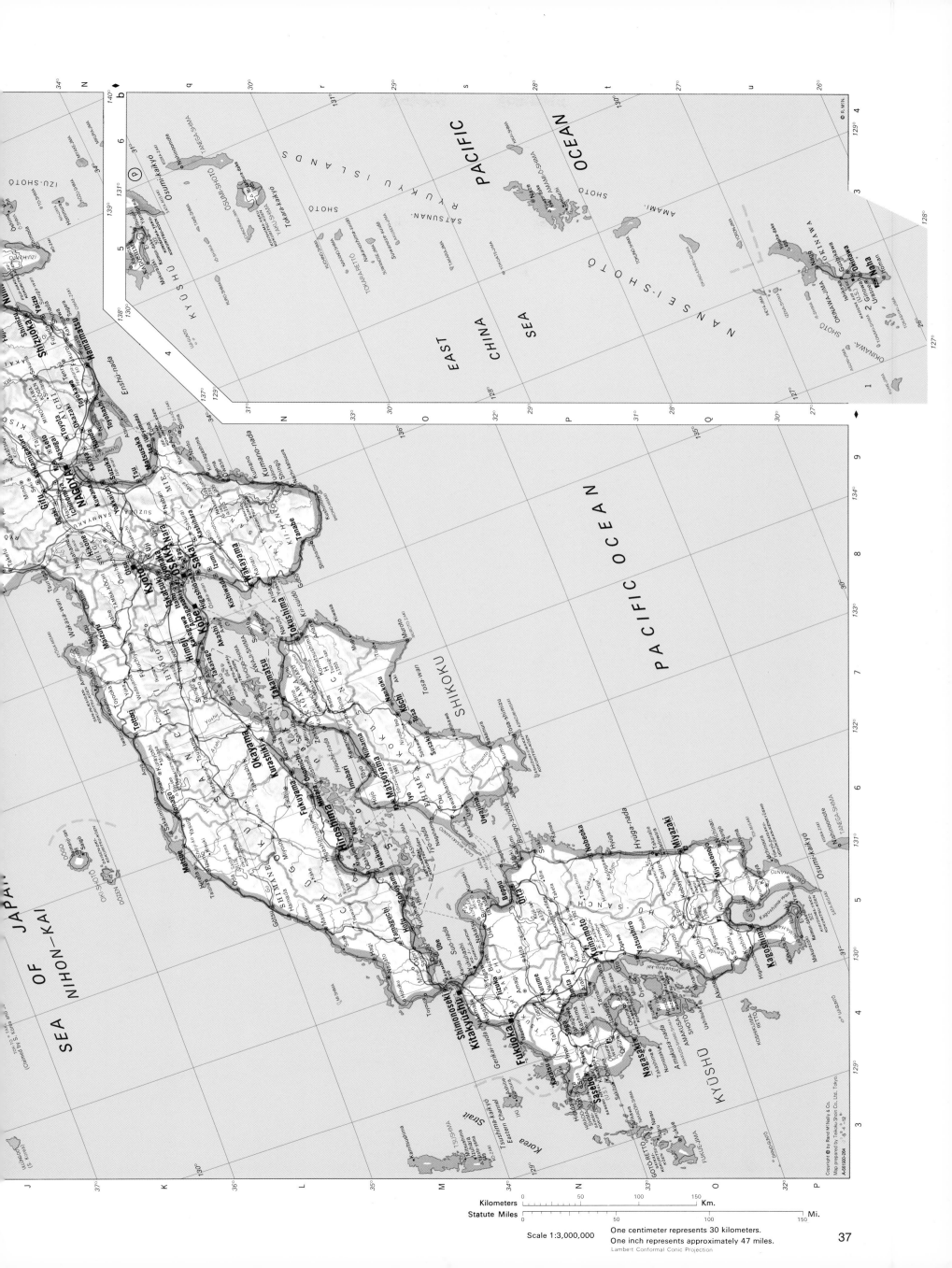

SEA OF JAPAN
NIHON-KAI

PACIFIC OCEAN

EAST CHINA SEA

PACIFIC OCEAN

RYUKYU ISLANDS
NANSEI-SHOTO

KYŪSHŪ
SHIKOKU
OKINAWA
Naha

NAGOYA
KYOTO
OSAKA
KOBE
Hiroshima
Matsuyama
Kōchi
Takamatsu
Okayama
Kurashiki
Fukuyama
Tottori
Matsue
Shimonoseki
Kitakyūshū
Fukuoka
Nagasaki
Sasebo
Kumamoto
Miyazaki
Kagoshima
Beppu
Ōita
Nobeoka

Kilometers
Statute Miles

Scale 1:3,000,000
One centimeter represents 30 kilometers.
One inch represents approximately 47 miles.
Lambert Conformal Conic Projection

Copyright © by Rand McNally & Co.
Map prepared by Teikoku-Shoin Co., Ltd., Tokyo
A-66/900-384   -S⁴-4 -12°

Southeastern Asia

TAIWAN

Tropic of Cancer

Luzon Strait

Bashi Channel

Balintang Channel

BABUYAN ISLANDS

BATAN ISLANDS

LUZON

PHILIPPINES

MINDORO

SAMAR

MANILA
Quezon City

PANAY

Iloilo

Bacolod

Cebu

NEGROS

Cagayan de Oro

MINDANAO

Davao

Zamboanga

Moro Gulf

Davao Gulf

General Santos

SULU ARCHIPELAGO

CELEBES SEA

KEPULAUAN TALAUD

KEPULAUAN NANUSA

PALAU BELAU (T.T.P.I.)

Manado

MINAHASA

HALMAHERA

Gorontalo

LAUT MALUKU MOLUCCA SEA

PACIFIC OCEAN

BIAK

PAPUA NEW GUINEA

Jayapura (Sukarnapura)

PEGUNUNGAN VAN REES

Puncak Jaya

Puncak Trikora

PEGUNUNGAN MAOKE

NEW GUINEA

Gulf of Papua

BURU

SERAM CERAM

Ambon

LAUT SERAM CERAM SEA

KEPULAUAN OBI

KEPULAUAN SULA

KEPULAUAN BANGGAI

SULAWESI CELEBES

Ujungpandang

LAUT BANDA BANDA SEA

KEPULAUAN KAI

KEPULAUAN ARU

PULAU YOS SUDARSO

KEPULAUAN TANIMBAR

KEPULAUAN BABAR

ARAFURA SEA

AUSTRALIA

FLORES

TIMOR

Dili

Kupang

Laut Sawu Savu Sea

SUMBA

TIMOR SEA

Torres Strait

CAPE YORK PENINSULA

Jawa (Java) inset

LAUT JAWA / JAVA SEA

KEPULAUAN KARIMUNJAWA

MADURA

JAKARTA

Bogor

BANDUNG

Cirebon

Pekalongan

Semarang

Surakarta

SURABAYA

Yogyakarta

Malang

Kediri

Probolinggo

Banyuwangi

BALI

JAWA JAVA

JAWA BARAT

JAWA TENGAH

JAWA TIMUR

INDIAN OCEAN

Scale 1:6,000,000

Luzon inset

ILOCOS NORTE

Aparri

Laoag

San Nicolas

KALINGA-APAYAO

CAGAYAN

Vigan

Tuguegarao

ISABELA

MOUNTAIN

CORDILLERA CENTRAL

SIERRA MADRE

Solano

Baguio

Dagupan

LA UNION

BENGUET

NUEVA VIZCAYA

QUIRINO

AURORA

PHILIPPINE SEA

TARLAC

Tarlac

Cabanatuan

LUZON

ZAMBALES

Angeles

San Fernando

Olongapo

Orani

Malolos

Meycauayan

Quezon City

BATAAN

BATANGAS

MANILA

Pasig

Cavite

Santa Cruz

LAGUNA

Lipa

San Pablo

Lucena

Batangas

LUBANG ISLANDS

MINDORO

Calapan

MARINDUQUE

MASBATE

ROMBLON

Daet

Naga

Iriga

Tabaco

Legaspi

Sorsogon

CAMARINES

CATANDUANES ISLAND

Virac

Scale 1:6,000,000

Km.
Mi.

Scale 1:12,000,000

Kilometers
Statute Miles

One centimeter represents 120 kilometers.
One inch represents approximately 190 miles.
Lambert Conformal Conic Projection

39

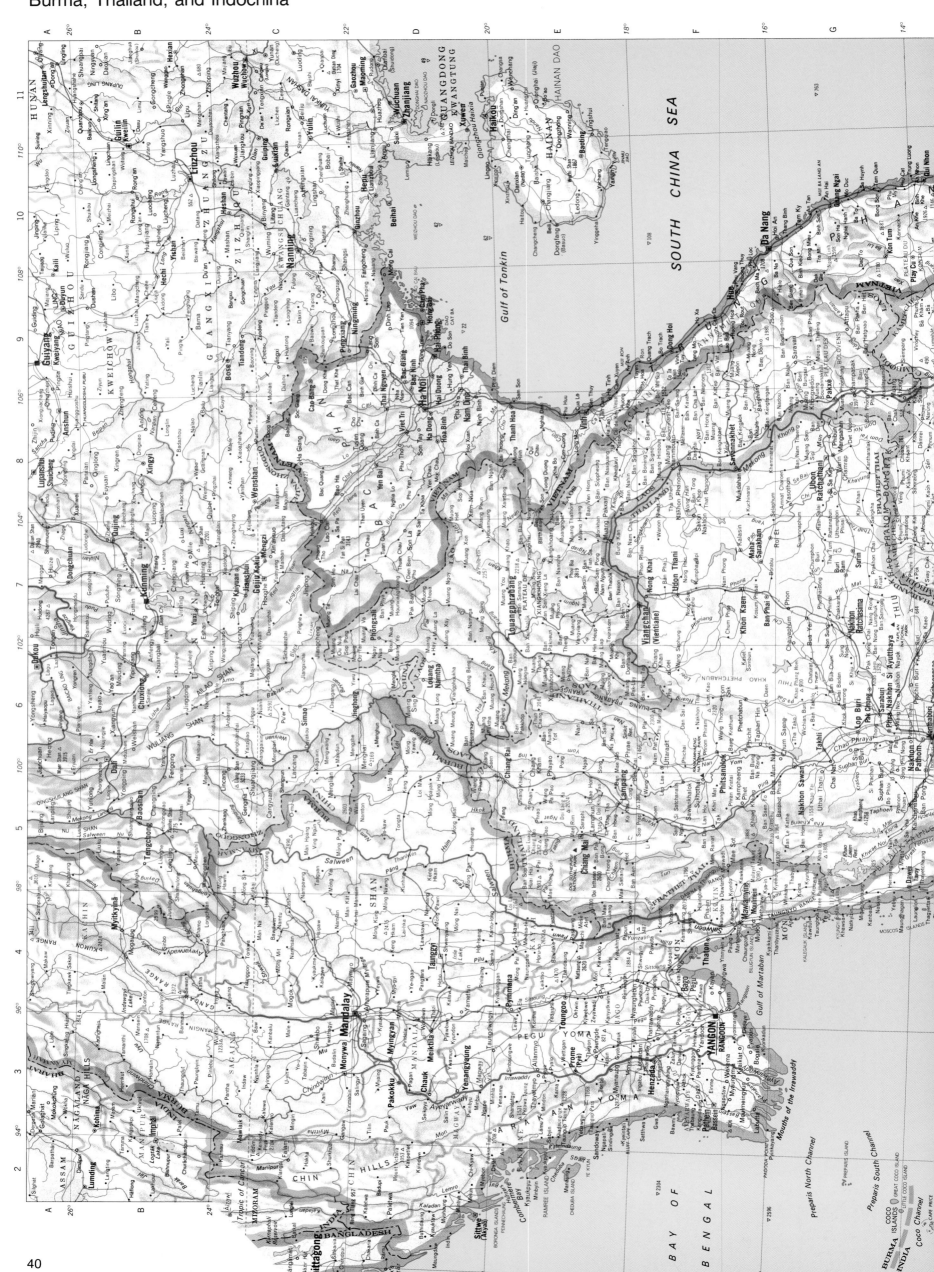

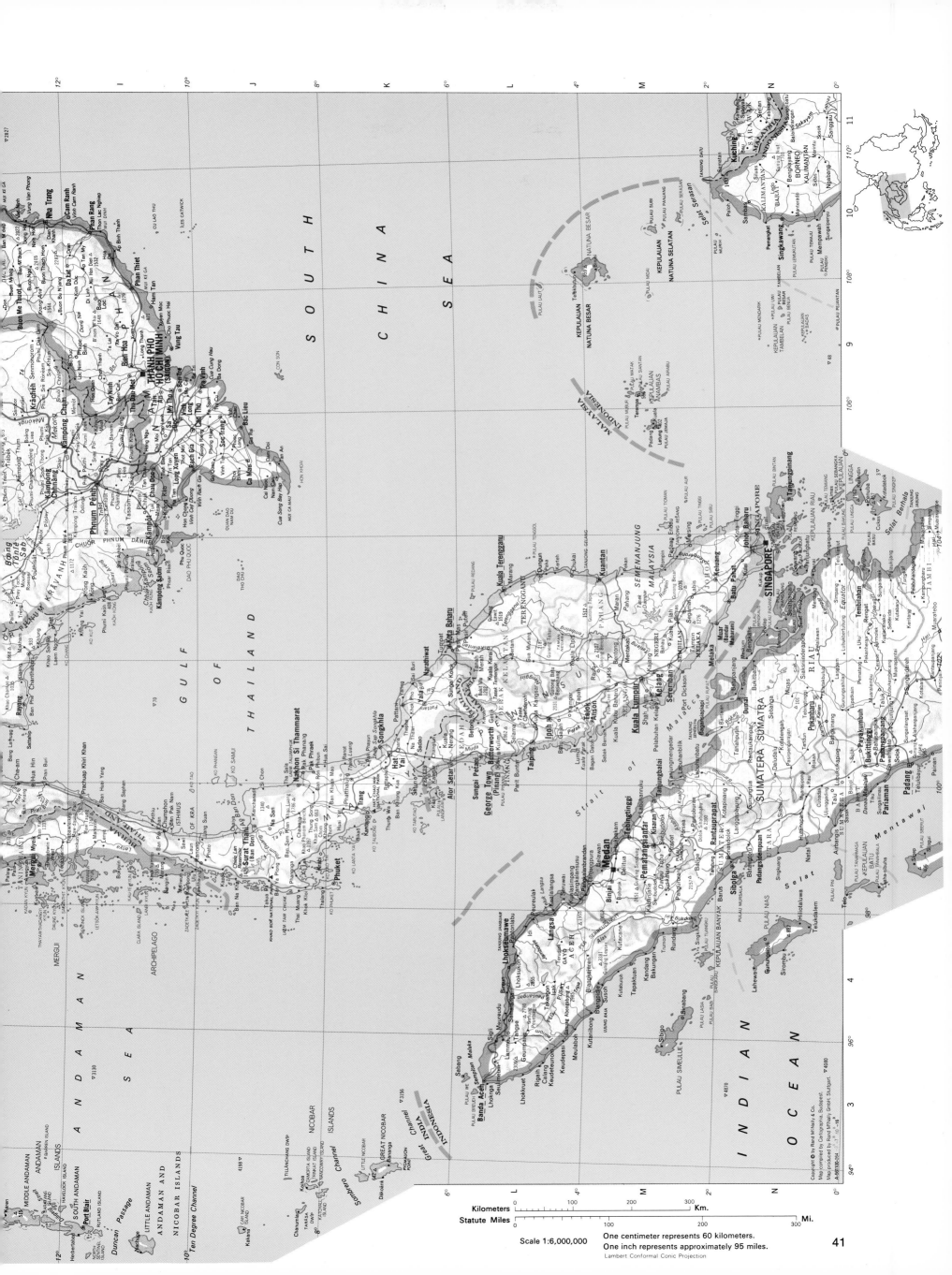

Scale 1:6,000,000

One centimeter represents 60 kilometers.
One inch represents approximately 95 miles.

Lambert Conformal Conic Projection

41

Kilometers
Statute Miles

Scale 1:12,000,000
One centimeter represents 120 kilometers.
One inch represents approximately 190 miles.
Lambert Conformal Conic Projection

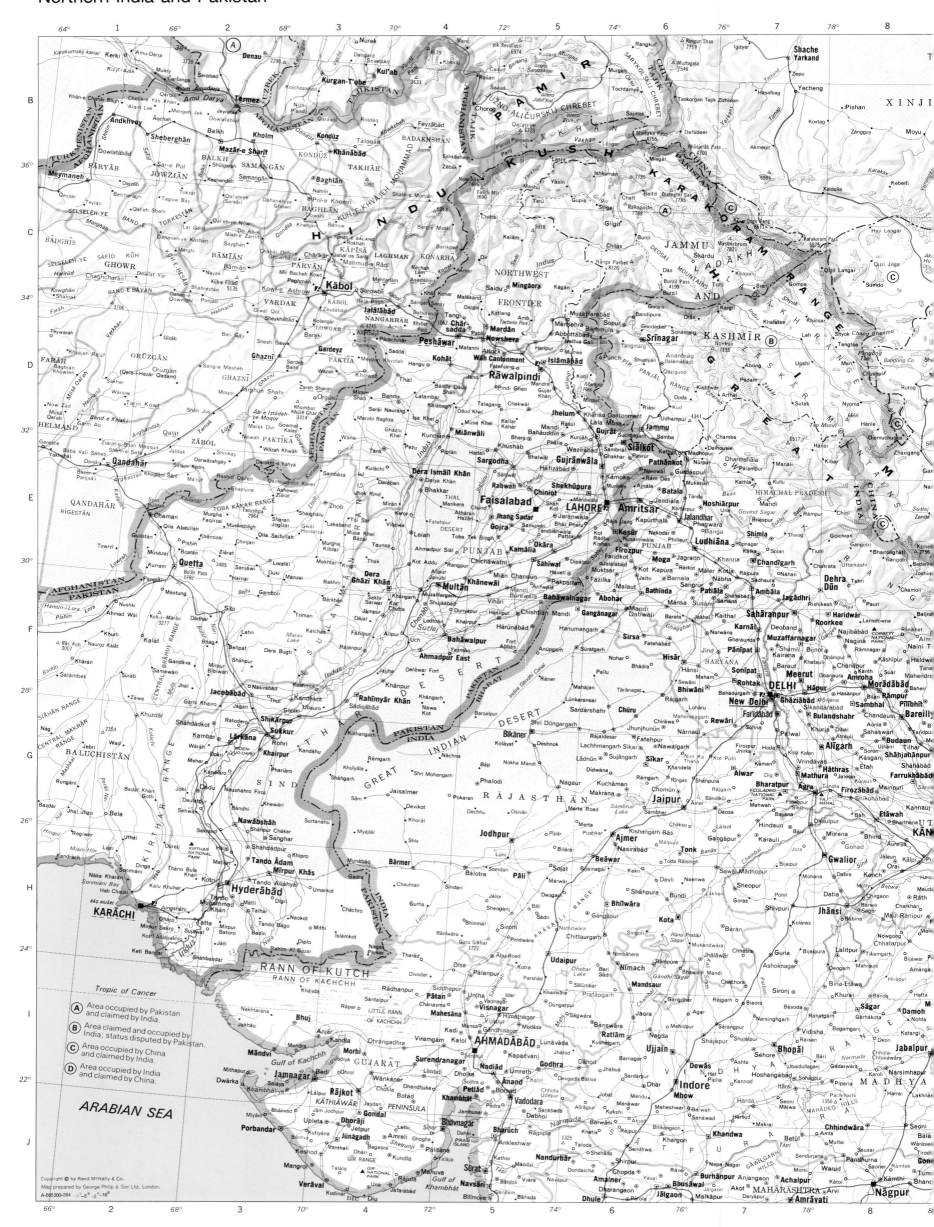

A Area occupied by Pakistan and claimed by India.

B Area claimed and occupied by India; status disputed by Pakistan.

C Area occupied by China and claimed by India.

D Area occupied by India and claimed by China.

Copyright © by Rand McNally & Co.
Map prepared by George Philip & Son Ltd., London.
A-565200-264

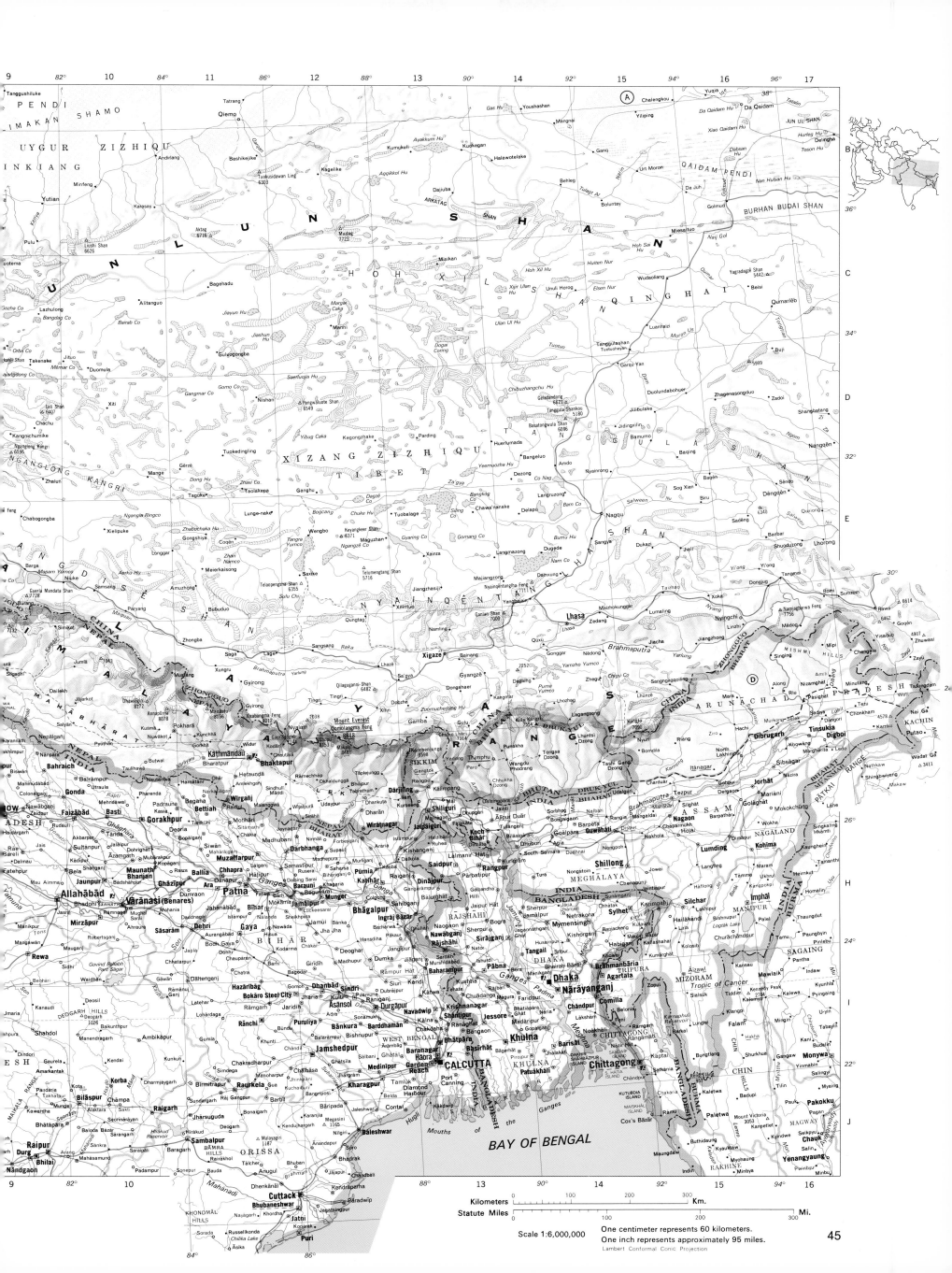

Southern India and Sri Lanka

Copyright © by Rand McNally & Co.
Map prepared by George Philip & Son Ltd., London.
A-565300-264

Kilometers
Statute Miles

One centimeter represents 60 kilometers.
One inch represents approximately 95 miles.

Scale 1:6,000,000
Lambert Conformal Conic Projection

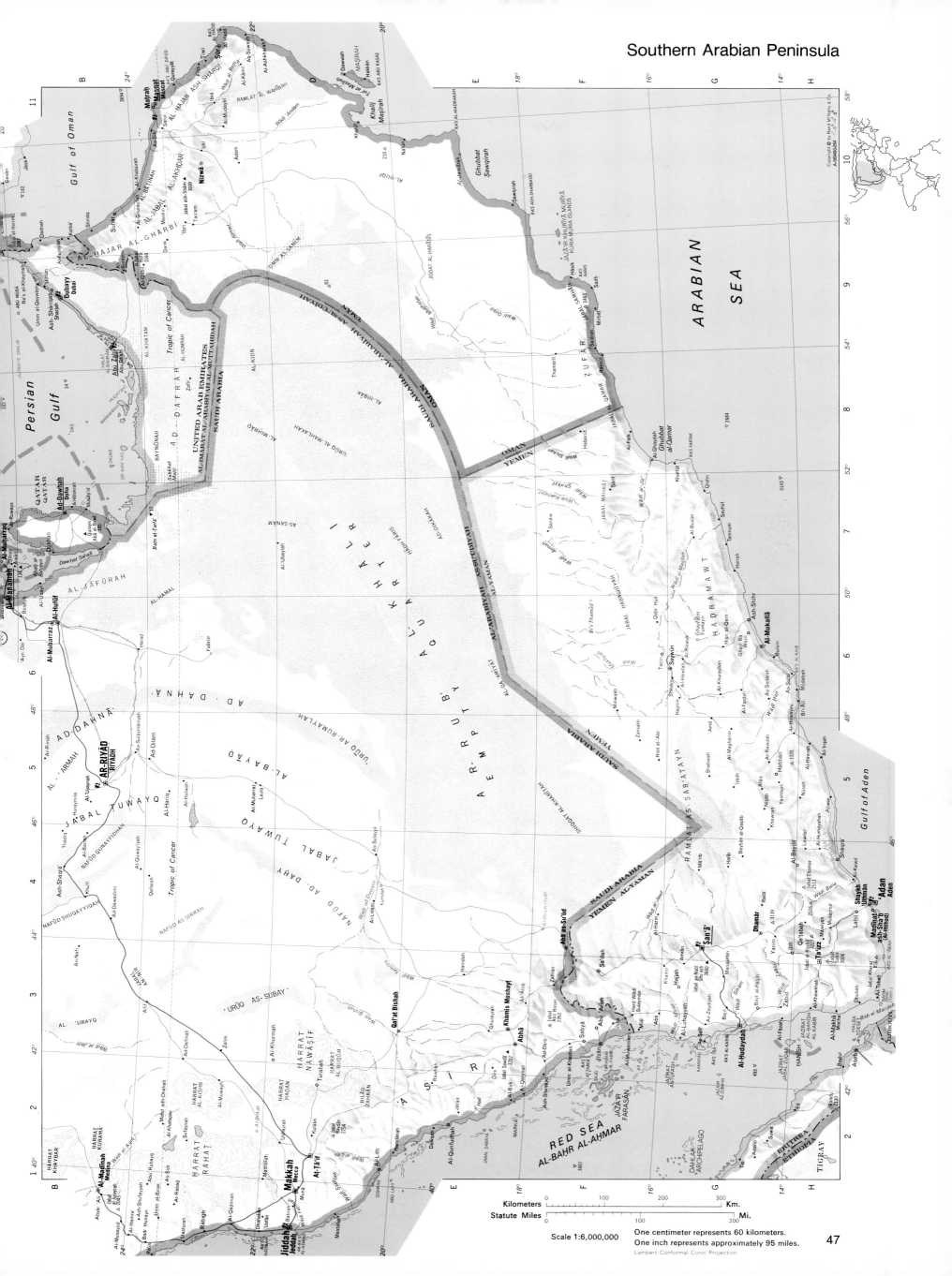

Southern Arabian Peninsula

47

Kilometers
Statute Miles

Scale 1:6,000,000

One centimeter represents 60 kilometers.
One inch represents approximately 95 miles.

Lambert Conformal Conic Projection

0   100   200   300 Km.
0   100   Mi.

Copyright © by Rand McNally & Co.
A-569490034

The Middle East

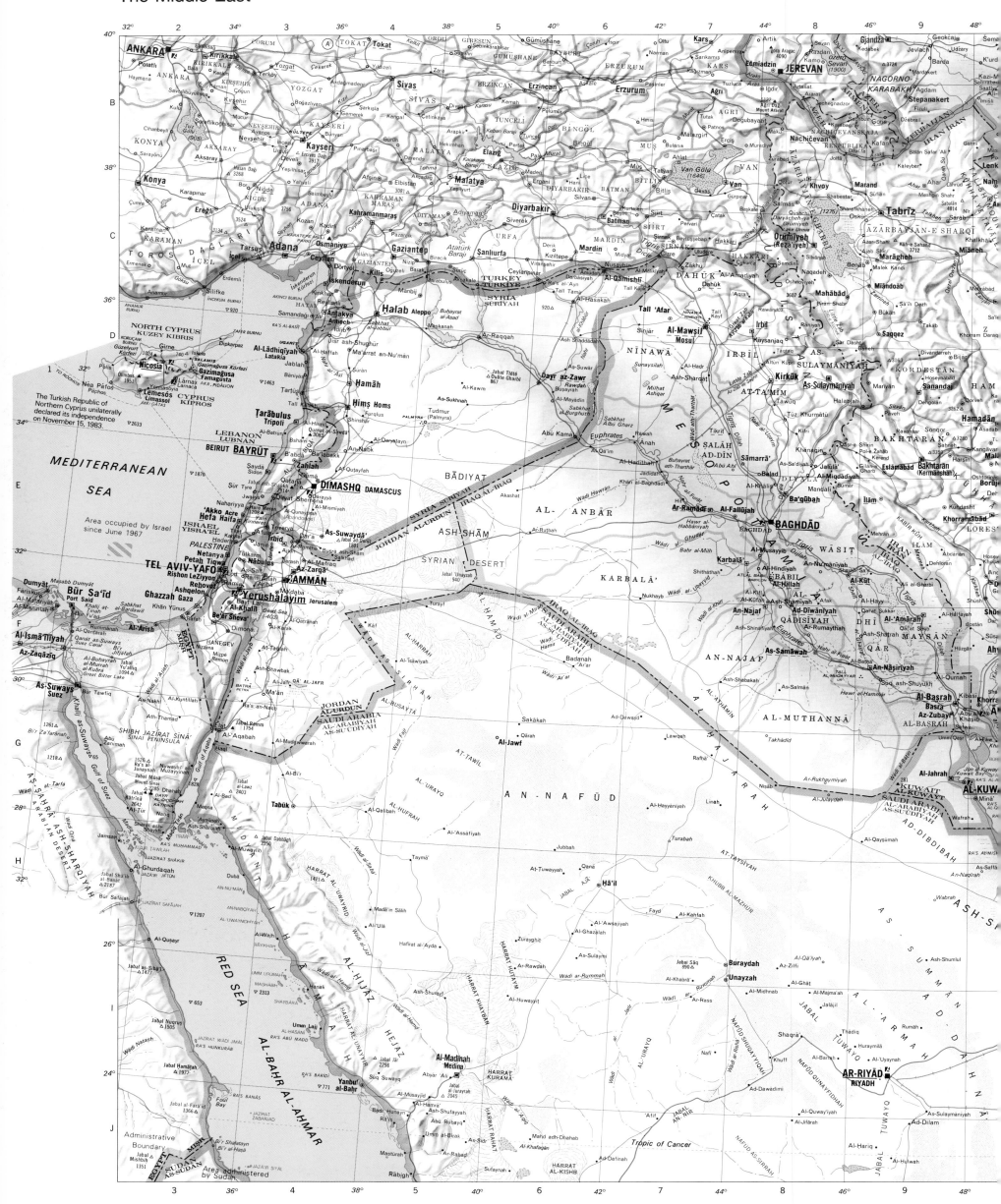

48

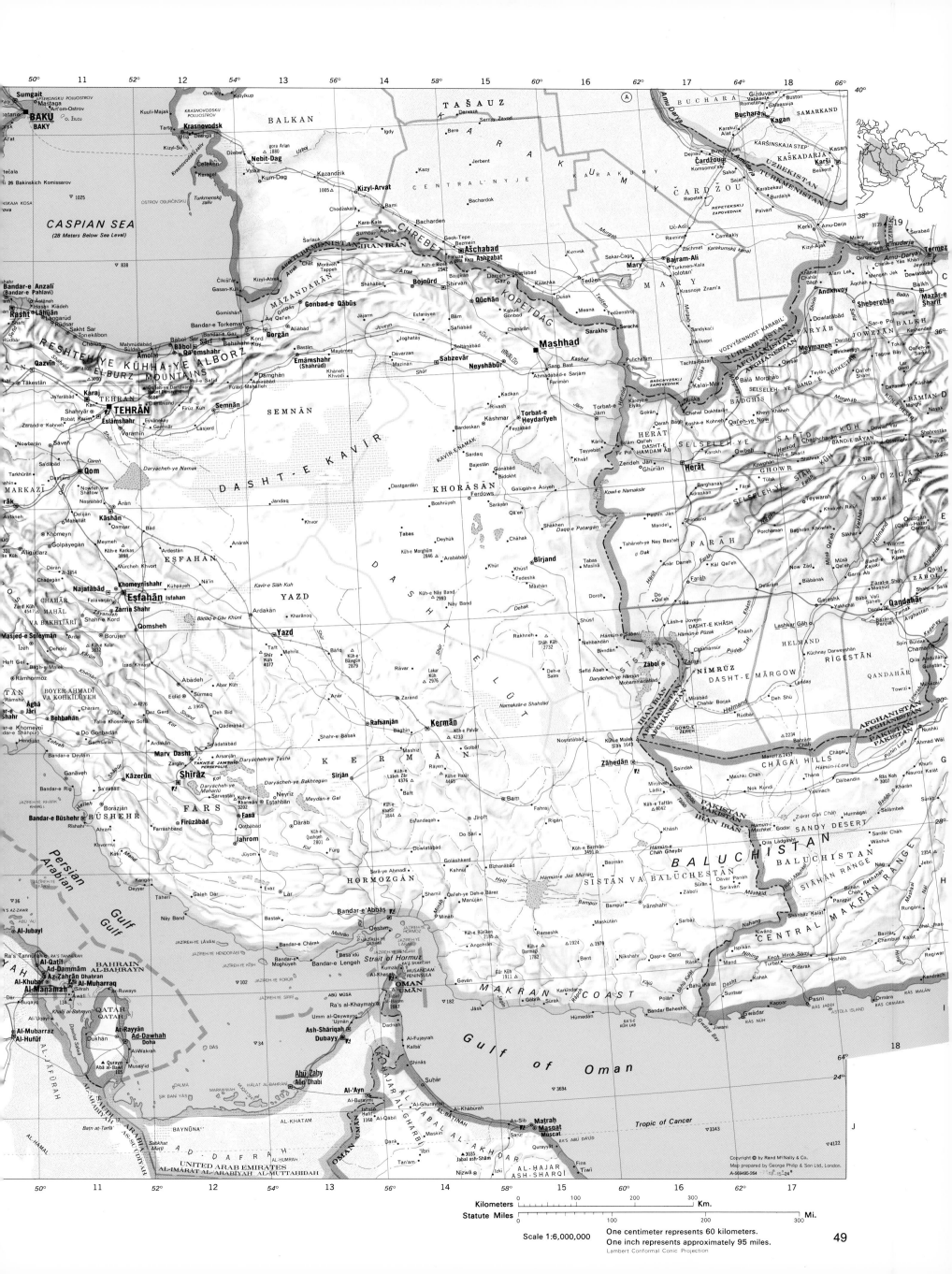

Israel and Southern Lebanon

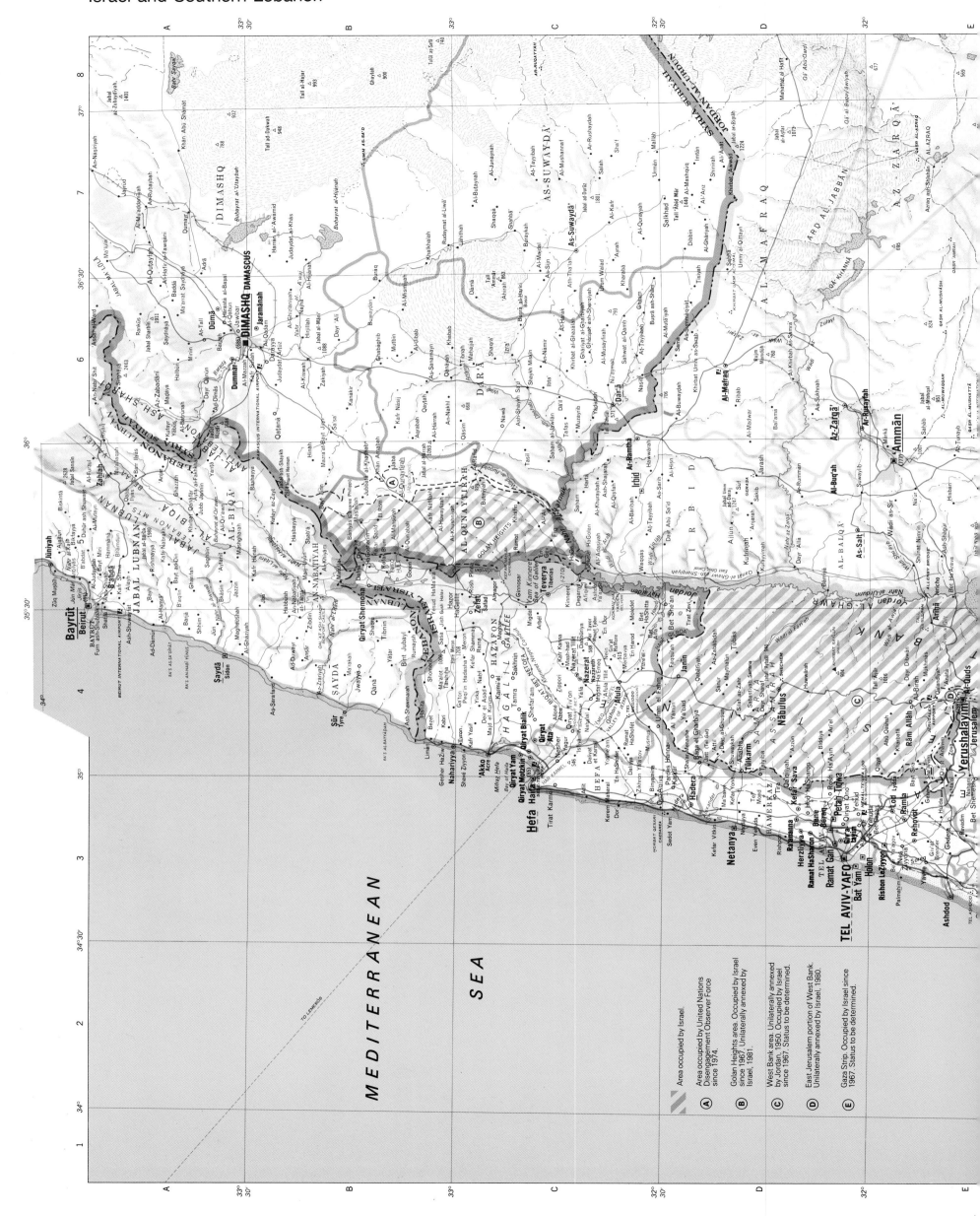

Area occupied by Israel.

(A) Area occupied by United Nations Disengagement Observer Force since 1974.

(B) Golan Heights area. Occupied by Israel since 1967. Unilaterally annexed by Israel, 1981.

(C) West Bank area. Unilaterally annexed by Jordan, 1950. Occupied by Israel since 1967. Status to be determined.

(D) East Jerusalem portion of West Bank. Unilaterally annexed by Israel, 1980.

(E) Gaza Strip. Occupied by Israel since 1967. Status to be determined.

Scale 1:1,000,000

One centimeter represents 10 kilometers.
One inch represents approximately 16 miles.

Lambert Conformal Conic Projection

51

Copyright © by Rand McNally & Co.
Map prepared by Esselte Map Service AB, Stockholm.
A-589491-264

MEDITERRANEAN SEA

ALGERIA

LIBYA

TARABULUS TRIPOLITANIA

FAZZAN FEZZAN

SAHARA

EGYPT

TUNISIA

ITALY

GREECE

TURKEY

NORTH CYPRUS
CYPRUS

NIGER

CHAD

SUDAN

SAHEL

NIGERIA

CAMEROON

CENTRAL AFRICAN REPUBLIC

ZAIRE

CONGO

GABON

EQUAT. GUINEA

SAO TOME AND PRINCIPE

Gulf of Guinea

Bight of Benin

Bight of Biafra

Kilometers
Statute Miles

Scale 1:12,000,000   One centimeter represents 120 kilometers.
One inch represents approximately 190 miles.
Miller Oblated Stereographic Projection

55

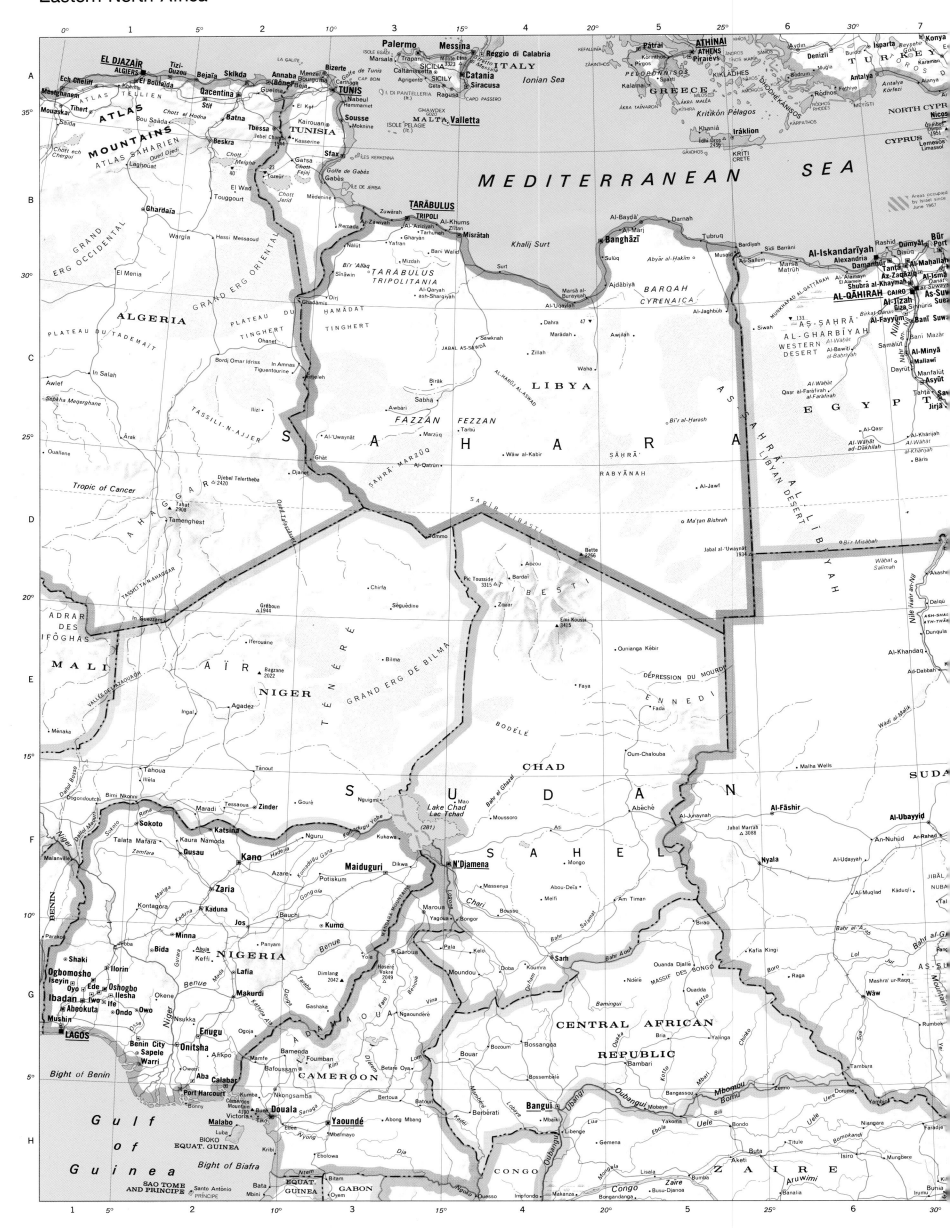

Southern Africa

SAO TOME AND PRINCIPE

PRINCIPE · Santo António

SÃO TOMÉ · São Tomé

G. ANNOBÓN (Equat. Gui.)

EQUATORIAL GUINEA

Bata

Mbini · Oyem

Bitam

Médouneu

Mitzic

Makokou

Ouesso

CAMEROON

Ntem

Impfondo

Makanza

Lisala

Bumba

Zaïre

Congo

Busu-Djanoa

Banalia

Aruwimi

Lindi

Bafwasende

Fort Portal

Lake Albert

Libreville

Kango

Njolé

Boué

Owando

Ogooué

GABON

Lambaréné

Lastoursville

Ewo

Alima

Mossaka

Lukolela

Ikela

Lomela

Katako

Kabalo

Rutshuru

Lake Edward

CAP LOPEZ

Port Gentil

Sindara

Koulamoutou

Franceville

Moanda

Gamboma

Bolobo

Inongo

Lac Mai-Ndombe

Lac Tumba

Boende

Tshuapa

Bokungu

Lomami

Punia

Kasese

Lake George

Omboué

Fougamou

Mouila

Ndendé

Makabana

Sibiti

Zanaga

Pangala

Djambala

Nioki

Fimi

Kutu

Oshwe

Lukénie

Dekese

Kole

Lodja

Bena-Dibele

Kibombo

Kindu

Pangi

Elila

Lualaba

Bukavu

Kalima

Kigoma

BURUNDI

Bujumbura

Iguéla

Mayumba

Kayes

Dolisie

Kibangou

Madingou

Brazzaville

Tshela

Mushie

Kwango

Bandundu

KINSHASA (LEOPOLDVILLE)

Masi-Manimba

Idiofa

Lusanga

Mweka

Lubefu

Lusambo

Lubao

Kongolo

Kabambare

Uvira

MONTS MITUMBA

Lac Kivu

Kalole

RWANDA

Kigali

Butare

Setté Cama

Tchibanga

Mbinda

Mossendjo

Pointe-Noire

CABINDA (Angola)

Cabinda

Banana

Soyo

Boma

Matadi

Nóqui

M'banza Congo

Maquela do Zombo

Cuango

Feshi

Tshikapa

Dibaya

Kananga (Luluabourg)

Mbuji-Mayi (Bakwanga)

Kabinda

Kabalo

Luvua

Manono

Mitwaba

Lake Upemba

Pweto

Lake Mweru

Kongolo

Kasenga

CHUTES DE LIVINGSTONE

Congo

Zaïre

Mbanza-Ngungu

Madimba

Kenge

Popokabaka

Kasongo-Lunda

Kahemba

Chitato

Luiza

Kaniama

Kabongo

Bukama

Sandoa

Kamina

Lac Upemba

Kilwa

Lake Mweru Wantipa

N'zeto

Nova Caipemba

Uíge

Negage

Camabatela

Marimba

Kasongo

Luremo

Caúngula

Luanguela

Camissombo

Kapanga

Lubudi

KATANGA

Tenke

Kasenga

Lake Bangweulu

Luanda

PONTA DAS PALMEIRINHAS

Caxito

Catete

Ndalatando

Dondo

Muxima

Malanje

Cacólo

Muconda

Dilolo

Malonga

Kolwezi

Likasi (Jadotville)

Lac Tshangalele

Kipushi

Mansa

Chililabombwe (Bancroft)

Mufulira

Sakania

Chingola

Kitwe

Ndola

Luanshya

BARRA DO CUANZA

Cambundi-Catembo

Cuanza

Saurimo

Chiluage

Cazombo

Calunda

Mwinilunga

Solwezi

Kasempa

Serenje

ZAMBIA

Porto Amboim

Gabela

ANGOLA

Kuito

Cuíto

Munhango

Luena

Luena

Lungué-Bungo

Balovale

Lukulu

Kabwe (Broken Hill)

Sumbe

Waku Kundo

Camacupa

Zambezi

Cuanza

Lumbala N'guimbo

Mussuma

Kalabo

Mumbwa

Kafue

Feira

Zumbo

CABO DE SANTA MARIA

Lobito

Benguela

Serra Môco 2620

Caála

Huambo (Nova Lisboa)

Chitembo

Luanguing

Mongu

Kaoma

Lusaka

Mazabuka

Zambezi

Kariba

Fing

Ganda

Caconda

Cuíto

Cangombe

Cuando

Senanga

Kalomo

Choma

Lake Kariba

Lucira

Kuvango

Menongue

Mavinga

Neriquinha

Utembo

Kwando

Sesheke

Chinhoyi

Bindura

Hara (Salis

Bibala

Lubango

Capelongo

Cassinga

Caiundo

Utembo

Kazungula

Livingstone

Hwange

Kadoma

Namibe

Cunene

Humbe

Xangongo

Ondjiva

Cuangar

Dirico

CAPRIVI ZIPFEL

VICTORIA FALLS

Chegutu

Tombua

PONTA DA MARCA

Foz do Cunene

Kunene

Chitado

Ondangwa

Okavango

Shakawe

Liuyani

MABABE DEPRESSION

MAKABE

ZIMBABWE

Kwekwe

Rehoboth

OVAMBOLAND

Etosha Pan

Namutoni

Tsumeb

OKAVANGO DELTA

Maun

Shangani

Gwai

Gweru

Mvuma

Shurugwi

KAOKO VELD

CAPE FRIA

Sesfontein

Okaukuejo

Grootfontein

KAUKAU VELD

Lake Ngami

Boteti

Lake Xau

Makgadikgadi

Plumtree

Bulawayo

Zvishavane

Masvingo

Ugab 2574 Brandberg

Omaruru

Otavi

Otjiwarongo

Tsau

Toteng

Ghanzi

BOTSWANA

Francistown

Gwanda

West Nicholson

Mwenezi

Karibib

Usakos

Okahandja

Epiko

Gobabis

Old Tati

Shashe

Tuli

Messina

VENDA

Thohoyandou

Swakopmund

Walvisbaai (S. Afr.)

DAMARALAND

Windhoek

Swakop

Kuiseb

Rehoboth

KALAHARI

Tshwaane

Serowe

Palapye

Lotsane

Mahalatswe

Limpopo

Louis Trichardt

Pietersburg

Tsumis Park

NAMIBIA

Tropic of Capricorn

HOLLANDSBIRD ISLAND

Mariental

Maltahöhe

Gibeon

DESERT

Lehututu

Tshane

Molepolole

Mochudi

Khakhea

Kanye

Gaborone

Lobatse

Mmabatho

Zeerust

Rustenburg

Mafikeng

BOPHUTHATSWANA

Thabazimbi

Nylstroom

Warmbad

Marble Hall

Lydenburg

Belfast

Nelspruit

Wittbank

GREAT NAMAQUALAND

Koes

Tshabong

Molopo

Vryburg

Mmabatho

Krugersdorp

JOHANNESBURG

Pretoria

Springs

Benoni

Bethal

Mar

Mbabane

SWAZILAND

Lüderitz

Aus

Bethanien

Seeheim

Aroab

Askham

Kuruman

BOPHUTHATSWANA

Potchefstroom

Klerksdorp

Germiston

Vereeniging

Vanderbijlpark

Heilbron

Vrede

Ermelo

Standerton

Piet Retief

Lavumisa

HUNSERGES

Fish

Karasburg

Karasburg

Sishen

Upington

Hotazel

Makwassie

Odendaalsrus

Kroonstad

Welkom

Virginia

Bethlehem

Newcastle

Volksrust

Utrecht

Wyheid

Dundee

Lake Saint Lu

ZUL

Oranjemund

Alexander Bay

Orange Oranje

Pofadder

Warmbad

Kakamas

Prieska

Modder

Kimberley

Warrenton

Jagersfontein

Fauresmith

Ficksburg

Bloemfontein

Maseru

Wepener

LESOTHO

Nesuthi 3446

Thabana Ntlenyana 3482

Greytown

Matatiele

Kokstad

Harding

Pietermaritzb

Durban

Port Shepstone

Port Nolloth

Okiep

Springbok

Garies

BUSHMAN LAND

Grootvloer

Kenhardt

Hopetown

Philippolis

Smithfield

Aliwal North

Colesberg

Barkly East

Maclear

Umzimkulu

Port Edward

Paarl

Kaapstad

BUSHMAN LAND

Verneukpan

Brandvlei

Carnarvon

Britstown

De Aar

Noupoort

Middelburg

Cradock

Queenstown

King William's Town

CISKEI

East London Oos-Londen

Calvinia

Klawer

Williston

Sutherland

NIEUWVELDBERGE

2504 Kompasberg

Beaufort West

Graaff-Reinet

Somerset East

Grahamstown

Kirkwood

Port Alfred

TRANSKEI

Umtata

Port Saint Johns

Lambert's Bay

Clanwilliam

Piketberg

Tulbagh

SOUTH AFRICA

Victoria West

GREAT KARROO

Oudtshoorn

Uitenhage

Port Elizabeth

CAPE SAINT FRANCIS

Saldanha

Malmesbury

Wellington

Worcester

Montagu

Swellendam

Humansdorp

Cape Town

Paarl

Stellenbosch

Simon's Town

CAPE OF GOOD HOPE

LITTLE KARROO

GROOT SWARTBERGE

Riversdale

Mosselbaai

Knysna

Hermanus

Bredasdorp

CAPE AGULHAS

ATLANTIC OCEAN

58

KENYA

Mount Elgon
2²0021
Mbale
Marsabit
Maralal
Eldoret
Kitale
Nanyuki
Meru
Kirinyaga
5199
Mado Gashi
Garissa
Kakamega
Nakuru
Kericho
Naivasha
Thika
Kitui
Bura
Kolbio
Kisii
Narok
Nairobi
Machakos
Konza
Buur Gaabo
Magadi
Makindu

SOMALIA   Shabeelle
Afmadow
Lach Dera
Afmadow
Jilib
Jamaame
Kismayoo   Jumboo
PATE ISLAND
Lamu
Kipini
Malindi

TANZANIA

SERENGETI PLAIN
Lake Eyasi
Shinyanga
Singida
MASAI STEPPE
Dodoma
Manyoni
Iringa
Mikumi
Arusha
Kilimanjaro
5895
4565
Moshi
Same
Voi
Tsavo   Galana

Mombasa
Korogwe
Wete   PEMBA
Tanga
Pangani
Zanzibar
ZANZIBAR
Bagamoyo
Dar es Salaam
MAFIA ISLAND
Kilindoni

Morogoro
Kilosa
Sao Hill
Mahenge
Utete
Kilwa Kivinje
Njombe
Liwale
Songea
Matandu
Nachingwea
Masasi
Tunduru

Lindi
Mikindani
Mtwara
CABO DELGADO
Palma
Mocímboa da Praia

MALAWI

Lake Nyasa
(474)
Maniamba
Lichinga
Lake Malawi
Marrupa
Blantyre
Zomba
Spittwa 3002
Mulanje

MOZAMBIQUE

Ibo
Quissanga
Pemba
Montepuez
Maua
Namapa
Lúrio
Nacala
Moçambique
Nampula
Mogincual
Quinga
Angoche
ILHA ANGOCHE
Moma
Pebane

Quelimane
Marromeu
Inhaminga
Chinde
MOZAMBIQUE
Dondo
Beira
Nova Sofala

Nova Mambone
Bartolomeu Dias
PONTA SÃO SEBASTIÃO
ILHA DO BAZARUTO
Vilanculos
Inhambane
PONTA DA BARRA FALSA
Massinga
Morrumbene
Maxixe
PONTA DA BARRA
Inharrime
Funhalouro
Manjacaze
Xai-Xai
INHACA

INDIAN OCEAN

Equator   0°

SEYCHELLES
PRASLIN ISLAND   LA DIGUE
SILHOUETTE   **Victoria**
MAHÉ ISLAND   5°

AMIRANTE ISLANDS (Sey.)   ÎLE DESROCHES (Sey.)   PLATTE ISLAND (Sey.)

ALPHONSE ISLAND (Sey.)   COETIVY ISLAND (Sey.)   C

PROVIDENCE ISLAND (Sey.)
ALDABRA ISLAND (Sey.)   COSMOLEDO I. (Sey.)   SAINT PIERRE ISLAND (Sey.)   CERF ISLAND (Sey.)
ASSUMPTION ISLAND (Sey.)   ASTOVE ISLAND (Sey.)   FARQUHAR GROUP (Sey.)   10°

AGALEGA ISLANDS (Mauritius)

ÎLES GLORIEUSES (Reunion)
CAP D'AMBRE
CAP SAINT-SÉBASTIEN
Antsiranana
NOSY MITSIO
NOSY BE
Hell-Ville   Ambilobe
Vohimarina
MASSIF DU TSARATANANA
Maromokotro 2876
Ambanja

COMOROS
Moroni   NJAZIDJA
Fomboni   Mutsamudu
MWALI   NZWANI
ARCHIPEL DES COMORES
MAYOTTE (Fr.)
Dzaoudzi

NOSY LAVA
Analalava
Baie de Narinda
Antsohihy
Andapa
Sambava
Doany
Analanana
Antalaha

Helodranon' i Mahajamba
Befandriana
Soía
PRESQU' ÎLE DE MASOALA
Maroantsetra   CAP EST
Mahajanga
Lac Kinkony
Port-Berge
Mandritsara
Mananara
Marovoay
Mampikony
Soalala
Tsaratanana
ÎLE TROMELIN (Reunion)
ÎLE CHESTERFIELD (Reunion)
Maevatanana
Andriamena
NOSY BORAHA
Besalampy
Ambodifototra
Fenoarivo Atsinanana
ÎLE JUAN DE NOVA (Reunion)
Tamboharano
Morafenobe
Lac Alaotra
Ambatondrazaka
Maintirano
Ankazobe
Toamasina
NOSY BARREN
Tsiroanomandidy
Antananarivo
Ankavandra
Vohibinany
MADAGASCAR
Belo
Miandrivazo
Ambatolampy
Vatomandry
Tsaribihina
ANKARATRA
Mahanoro
Morondava
Mahabo
Malaimbandy
Antsirabe
Ambositra
Nosy Varika
Mandabe
Manja
Mananjary
Morombe
Ambalavao
Fianarantsoa
Bekopaka
Ankazoabo
Pic Boby 2658
Ihosy
Manakara
Toliara
Betroka
Farafangana
Betioky
Vangaindrano
Midongy Sud
Ampanihy
Bekily
Androka
Tsihombe   Ambovombe
Faradofay
CAP SAINTE-MARIE

MAURITIUS
Port Louis
Curepipe   Mahébourg   20°
Le Port
Saint-Paul
Saint-Denis
RÉUNION (Fr.)
Saint-Pierre
MASCARENE ISLANDS

BASSAS DA INDIA (Reunion)
CAP SAINT-VINCENT
ILE EUROPA (Reunion)

Tropic of Capricorn   F

25°

INDIAN OCEAN

G

Copyright © by Rand McNally & Co.
Map prepared by Esselte Map Service AB, Stockholm.
A-589200-264

Scale 1:12,000,000   One centimeter represents 120 kilometers.
One inch represents approximately 190 miles.
Miller Oblated Stereographic Projection

Kilometers   0   200   400   600   Km.
Statute Miles   0   200   400   600   Mi.

Egypt and Sudan

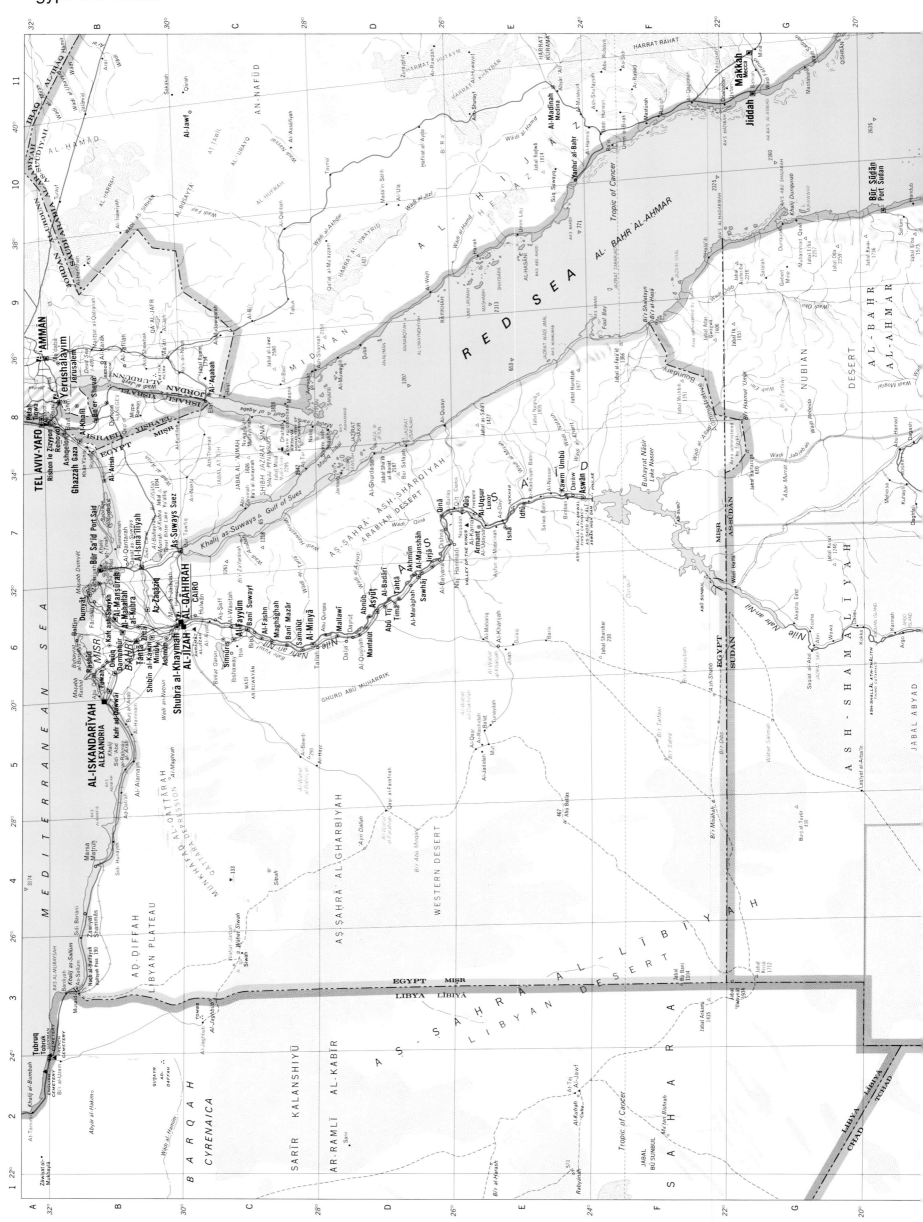

60

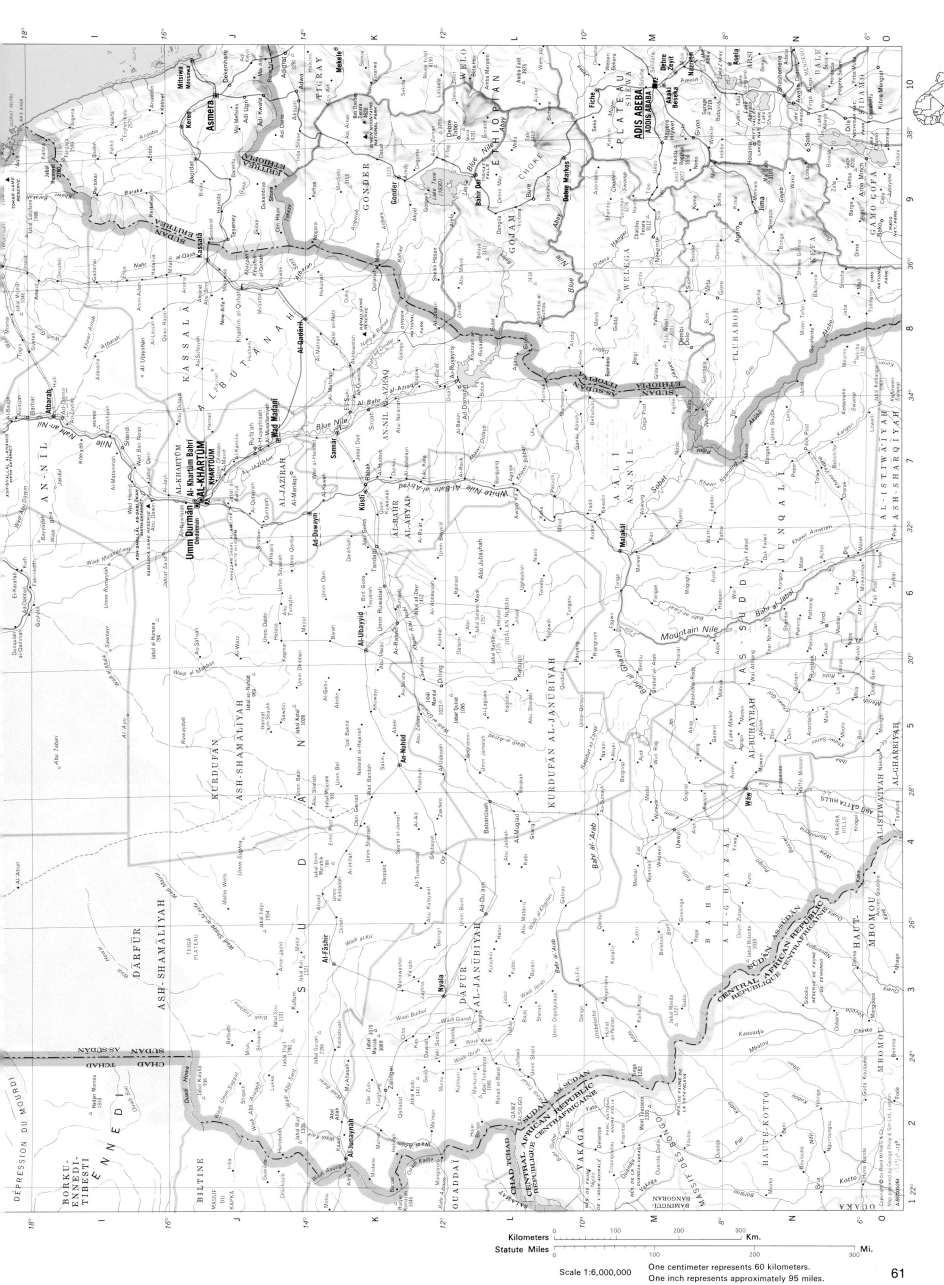

Kilometers 0   100   200   300   Km.
Statute Miles 0   100   200   300   Mi.

Scale 1:6,000,000

One centimeter represents 60 kilometers.
One inch represents approximately 95 miles.

Lambert Azimuthal Equal-Area Projection

61

Copyright by Rand McNally & Co.
Made in U.S.A.
A-570202-364
© George Philip & Son Ltd. London

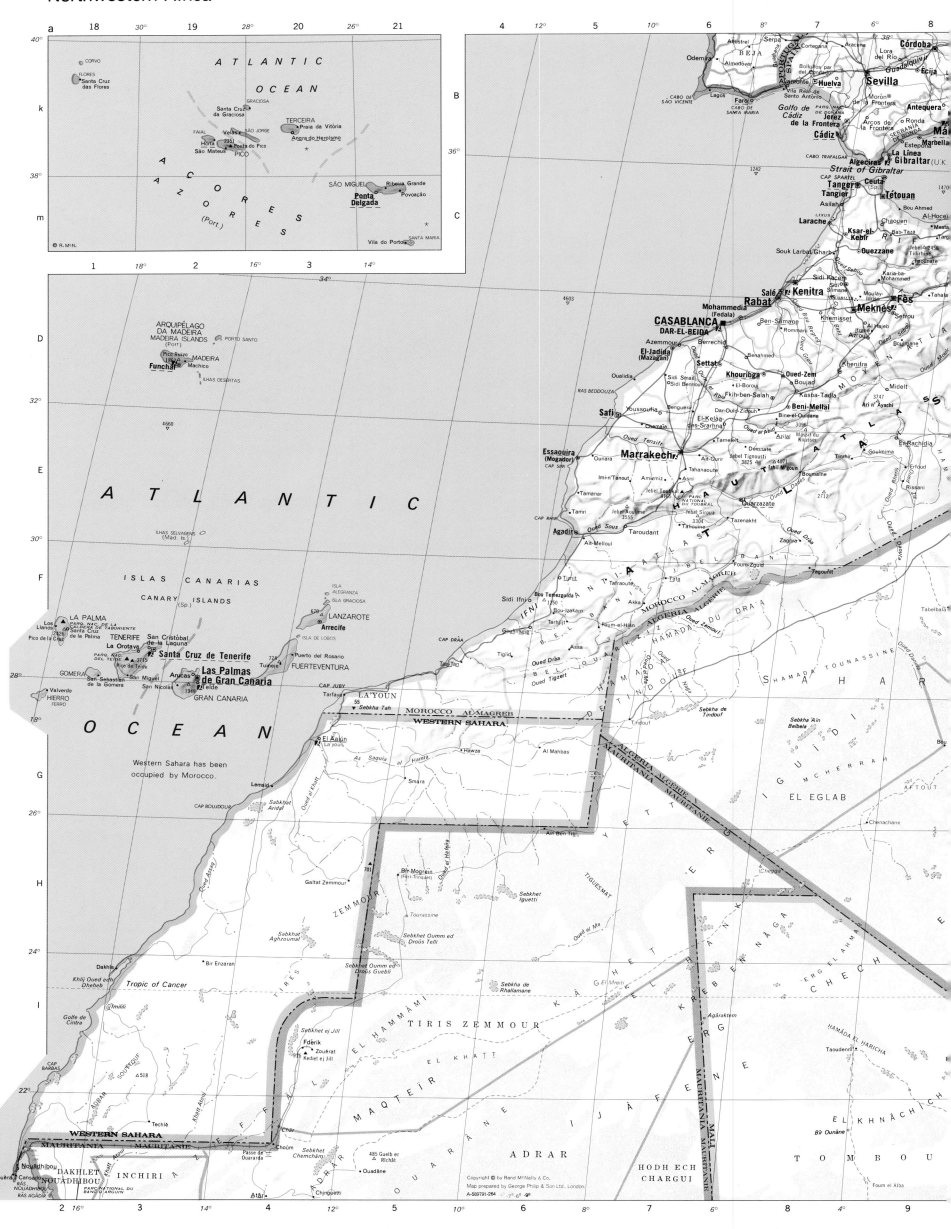

ATLANTIC
OCEAN

CORVO

FLORES
Santa Cruz
das Flores

GRACIOSA
Santa Cruz
da Graciosa

TERCEIRA
Praia da Vitória
Angra do Heroísmo

FAIAL   Velas   SÃO JORGE
Horta   2351   Ponta do Pico
São Mateus   PICO

A   Z   O   R   E   S

SÃO MIGUEL   Ribeira Grande
Ponta
Delgada   Povoação

(Port.)

SANTA MARIA
Vila do Porto

© R. MIN.

ATLANTIC

OCEAN

ARQUIPÉLAGO
DA MADEIRA
MADEIRA ISLANDS
(Port.)   PORTO SANTO

Pico Ruivo
1862   MADEIRA   Machico
Funchal
ILHAS DESERTAS

4660

ILHAS SELVAGENS
(Mad. Is.)

ATLANTIC

ISLAS CANARIAS

CANARY ISLANDS (Sp.)

ISLA
ALEGRANZA
ISLA GRACIOSA

LA PALMA
Los   PARQ. NAC. DE LA
Llanos   CALDERA DE TABURIENTE
2426   LANZAROTE
Santa Cruz   Arrecife
Pico de la Cruz   de la Palma
La Orotava   TENERIFE   San Cristóbal
de la Laguna   ISLA DE LOBOS
PARQ. NAC.   Santa Cruz de Tenerife
DEL TEIDE   3715   Puerto del Rosario
Pico de Teide   724   FUERTEVENTURA
GOMERA   San Miguel   Tuineje
San-Sebastián   Arucas   Las Palmas
de la Gomera   San Nicolás   de Gran Canaria
Valverde   1949   Telde
HIERRO   GRAN CANARIA
FERRO   CAP JUBY

OCEAN

Western Sahara has been
occupied by Morocco.

Tropic of Cancer

CORDOBA
Odemira   BEJA   Cortegana   Aracena   Écija
Almodôvar   Guadalquivir
Bollullos par
del Condado   La Palma
CABO DE   del Condado   del Río
SÃO VICENTE   Lagos   Faro   Vila Real de   Huelva   Sevilla
CABO DE   Santo António
Golfo de   PARQ. NAC.   Morón
SANTA MARIA   Cádiz   DE DOÑANA   Antequera
Arcos de   Ronda
la Frontera
Jerez   SERRANIA
de la Frontera   DE RONDA   Estep   Marbella
CABO TRAFALGAR   Cádiz   La Línea
Algeciras   Gibraltar (U.K.)
CAP SPARTEL   Ceuta (Sp.)   Strait of Gibraltar
1242   Tanger   Tétouan
Tangier   RIF
Asilah   Bou Ahmed   Al-Hoceï
Larache   LIXUS   Chaouen
Ksar-el-   Bab-Taza   Mesta
Kébir   Tidirhine   Tirounate
Souk Larbat Gharb   Jebel 2456
Ouezzane
Sidi Kacem   Tahala
Kenitra   Moulay   Idriss   Fès
Salé   Idriss
Mohammedia   Rabat   Khemisset   Meknès   Sefrou
(Fedala)
CASABLANCA   Ben-Slimane   El Hajeb
DAR-EL-BEIDA   Romman   Iffane   Azrou
Berrechid   Benahmed   MOYEN   Boulemane
El-Jadida   Azemmour   Khenifra
(Mazagan)   Settat   Midelt
Khouribga   Oued-Zem   3747
Oualidia   Sidi Smail   El-Boroúj   Boujad   Ari n' Ayachi
RAS BEDDOUZA   Sidi Bennour   Kasba-Tadla   ATLAS
Benguerir   Beni-Mellal   El-Rachidia
Youssoufia   Dar-Ould-Zidouh   Bine-el-Ouidane
Safi   El-Kelaa-   Azilal   Goulmima
des-Srarhna   3096
Chemaia   Tamelelt   Demnate   Tinrhir
Essaouira   Aït-Ourir   Jebel Tignousti   Erfoud
(Mogador)   Ounara   3825   HAUT   Jebel M'goun
CAP SIM   Marrakech   Tahanaoute   4071   Rissani
Imi-n'Tanout   Amizmiz   Jebel Toubkal   Boumaine
Tamanar   Asni   4165   Jebel   Goulmima
Tamri   Jebel Aoulime   Siroua   2712
CAP RHIR   3555   3304   Tazenakht
Agadir   Taroudant   Ouarzazate
Aït-Melloul   Oued Sous   ANTI   ATLAS   Oued Rheris
Tiznit   Tata   Zagora   Oued Draa
Tafraoute   Foum-Zguid   Tagounite
Sidi Ifni   Bou Temezguida   Tabelbala
IFNI   Akka   MOROCCO   Foum-el-Hisn
Tarhjit   Bou-Izakarn   ALGERIA   ALGÉRIE
Goulimine   Oued Zemoul   HAMADA DU DRÂA
CAP DRÂA   Assa   Oued Zemoul
Tan-Tan   Tiglid   Oued Drâa
Oued Tigzert   SHAMADA TOUNASSINE   SAHARA
Sebkha 'Aïn
LA'YOUN   Belbela
55   Sebkha de
Sebkha Tah   Tindouf   IGUÎDI   AFTOUT
MOROCCO   AL-MAGREB   Tindouf   McHERRAH
WESTERN SAHARA   EL EGLAB
El Aaiún   ALGERIA   ALGÉRIE
La'youn   MAURITANIA   MAURITANIE   Chenachane
Lemsid   Hawza
Smara   Al Mahbas
Al Mahbas
Aïn Ben Tili
CAP BOUJDOUR   Sebkhet
Aridal   Chegga
Bir Mogrein
701   (Fort-Trinquet)   Oued el Hfeira   Sebkhet
Galtat Zemmour   Iguetti   TIGUESMAT
ZEMMOUR   Tourassine
Oued Abaug   Sebkhet Oumm ed
Sebkhet   Droús Telli   Oued el Ma
Aghzoumal   Sebkhet Oumm ed
Dakhla   Bir Enzaran   Droús Guebli   Sebkha de
Khlij Oued edh   Rhallamane
Dheheb   El Mreïti
Ilmilili   TIRIS ZEMMOUR   Agâraktem
Golfe de   Sebkhet ej Jill
Cintra   Fdérik   EL KHATT
Zouérat   Taoudenni
CAP   975   Kediet ej Jill
BARBAS   MAQTEÏR   HAMÂDA EL HARICHA
SOUTTOUF   △518
Techlé   Châr   HODH ECH
Passe de   CHARGUI
WESTERN SAHARA   Ouararda   485 Guelb er
Schoúm   Rîchât
MAURITANIA   MAURITANIE   Oudâne
La Gouéra   Cansado   Sebkhet   ADRAR   Bîr Oûnâne
Chemcham   Foum el Alba
DAKHLET   Atâr   TOMBOU
NOUÂDHIBOU   Chinguetti   HODH ECH
INCHIRI   PARC NATIONAL DU   CHARGUI
RÂS NOUÂDHIBOU   BANC D'ARGUIN   Khatt Atoui
RAS AGADIR

Copyright © by Rand McNally & Co.
Map prepared by George Philip & Son Ltd. London.
A-589791-264

62

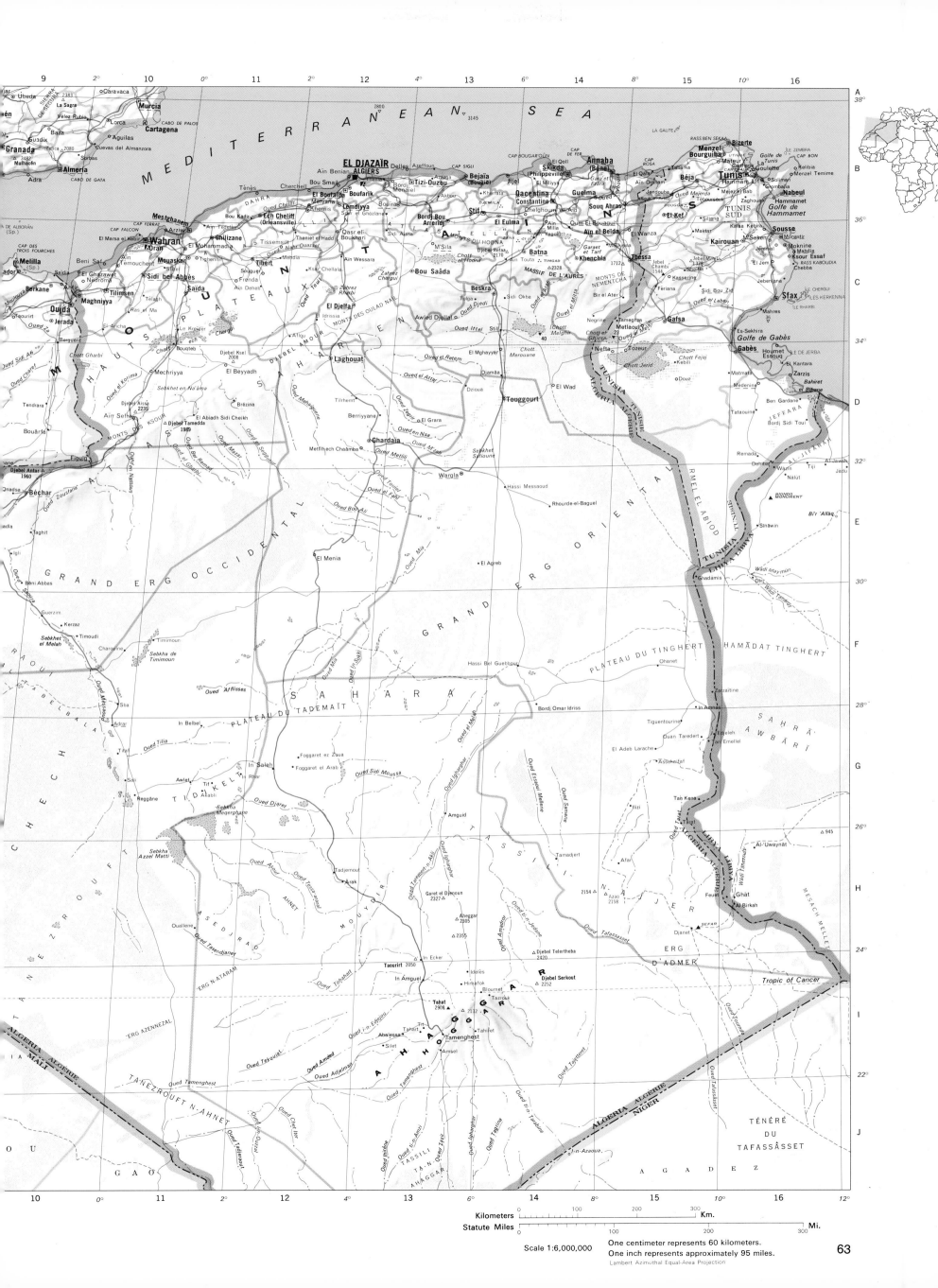

MEDITERRANEAN SEA

EL DJAZAÏR
ALGIERS

TUNIS

GRAND ERG OCCIDENTAL

GRAND ERG ORIENTAL

SAHARA

PLATEAU DU TADEMAÏT

TROPIC OF CANCER

TÉNÉRÉ
DU
TAFASSÂSSET

One centimeter represents 60 kilometers.
One inch represents approximately 95 miles.

Scale 1:6,000,000

Lambert Azimuthal Equal-Area Projection

63

West Africa

Southern Africa and Madagascar

ATLANTIC

OCEAN

Copyright © by Rand McNally & Co.
Map prepared by George Philip & Son Ltd. London.
A-589292-264

Kilometers
0   100   200   300   Km.

Statute Miles
0   100   200   300   Mi.

Scale 1:6,000,000
One centimeter represents 60 kilometers.
One inch represents approximately 95 miles.
Lambert Azimuthal Equal-Area Projection

66

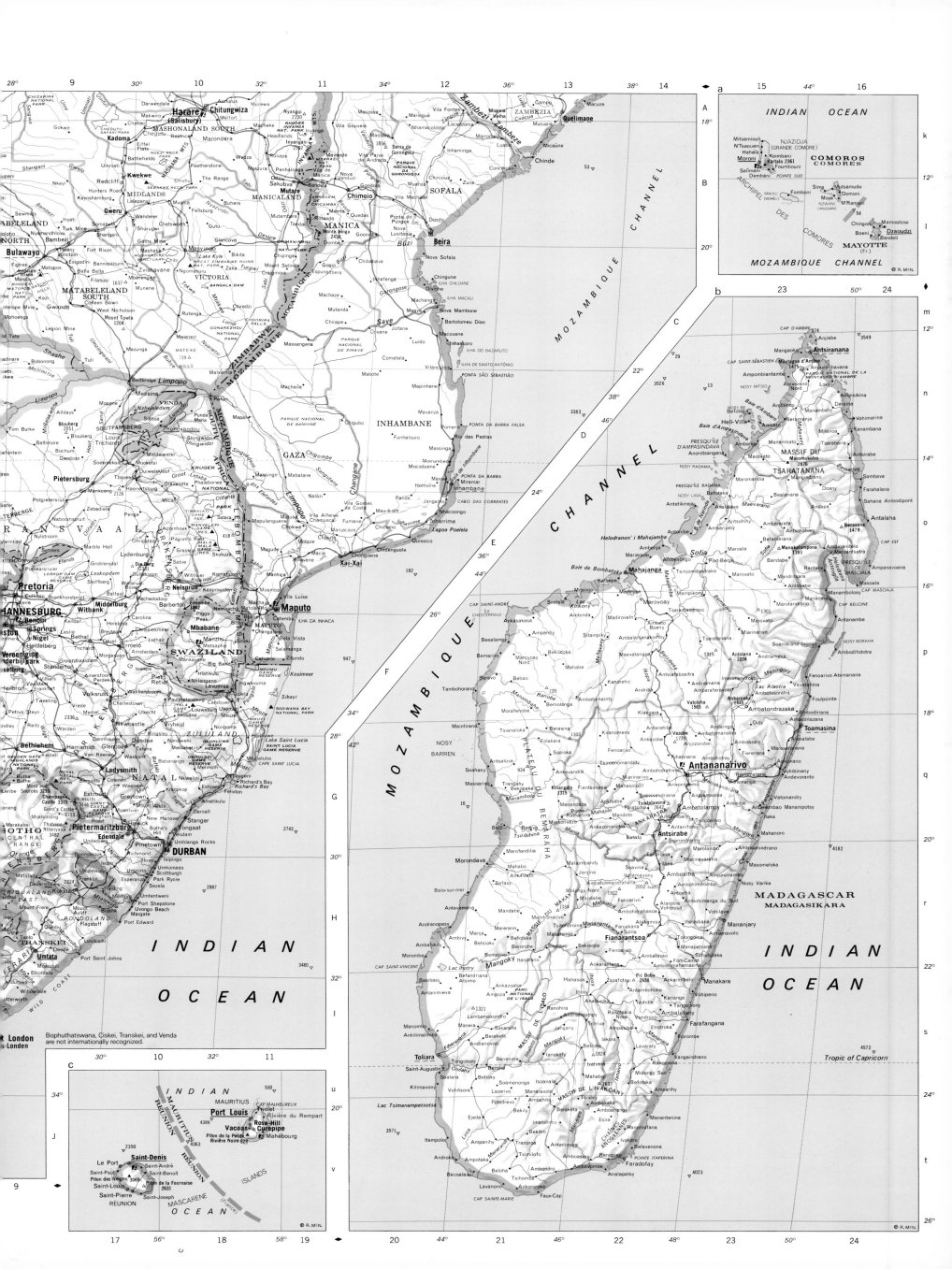

Australia

Inset map (upper left):

PACIFIC OCEAN

PULAU WAIGEO
Equator
KEPULAUAN SCHOUTEN
Sorong
Manokwari
Selat Dampier
JAZIRAH DOBERAI
PULAU NUMFOOR
BIAK
PULAU YAPEN
TANJUNG D'URVILLE
NINIGO GROUP
HERMIT ISLANDS
MUSSAU ISLAND
0 100 200 300 Km.
0 100 200 Mi.
SALAWATI
Teluk Berau
Teluk Cenderawasih
Jayapura (Sukarnapura)
ADMIRALTY ISLANDS
PULAU MISOOL
Faktak
Mamberamo
PEGUNUNGAN VAN REES
Aitape
Wewak
MANUS ISLAND
EMIRAU ISLAND
NEW HANOVER
Kavieng
NEW IRELAND
SERAM
Bula
Kaimana
PEGUNUNGAN MAOKE
Sepik
Madang
KARKAR ISLAND
Rabaul
KEPULAUAN BANDA
PULAU ADI
Puncak Jaya 5030m
Puncak Trikora 4750m
Ramu
WITU ISLANDS
UMBOI ISLAND
Talasea
KEPULAUAN KAI
KAI KECIL
Dobo
PULAU WOKAM
NEW GUINEA
Bismarck Range
Mt. Wilhelm 4509m
Mt. Giluwe 4368m
Lae
Huon Gulf
Morobe
NEW BRITAIN
KEPULAUAN ARU
PULAU KOBROOR
PULAU TRANGAN
PAPUA NEW GUINEA
Fly
Digul
Mt. Ilawun 2574 m
KIRIWINA ISLANDS
KEPULAUAN SELARU
PULAU YAMDENA
PULAU YOS SUDARSO
Merauke
Gulf of Papua
Popondetta
OWEN STANLEY RANGE
MUYUA ISLAND
D'ENTRECASTEAUX ISLANDS
Arafura Sea
TANJUNG VALS
Torres Strait
Port Moresby
MELVILLE ISLAND
COBOURG PEN.
CROKER ISLAND
MOA ISLAND
CAPE YORK
GREAT BARRIER REEF
Samarai
WESSEL ISLANDS
Gulf of Carpentaria
CAPE YORK PEN.
Coral Sea
Van Diemen Gulf
Darwin
BATHURST ISLAND
AUSTRALIA
A-592200-264-1-1-1-2
©1979 R·McN.

INDONESIA

Right portion (upper):

Laut Sawu
Savu Sea
TIMOR
Soe
Kupang
PULAU SEMAU
PULAU ROTI
Timor Sea
Arafura
HIBERNIA REEF
ASHMORE ISLANDS
CARTIER ISLANDS (Austl.)
MELVILLE ISLAND
CAPE CROKER
COBOURG PENINSULA
Van Diemen Gulf
BATHURST ISLAND
Darwin
Humpty Doo
ARNHEM L
POINT BLAZE
Rum Jungle
Jabir
BROWSE ISLAND
CAPE LONDONDERRY
Admiralty Gulf
Joseph Bonaparte Gulf
Clarence Strait
Beagle Gulf
Pine Creek
Katherine
ADÈLE ISLAND
BONAPARTE ARCHIPELAGO
York Sound
Owens Channel
Daly
BEAGLE REEF
COLLIER BAY
Drysdale
Wyndham
Kununurra
Victoria
Daly Waters
BUCCANEER ARCHIPELAGO
CAPE LEVEQUE
KIMBERLEY PLATEAU
KING LEOPOLD RANGES
Lake Argyle
DURACK RANGES
River Downs
Victoria
King Sound
Derby
Mount Ord 937
Fitzroy Crossing
Halls Creek
Ord
Wave Hill
Newcastle Waters
Lake Woods

Main map:

INDIAN OCEAN

ROWLEY SHOALS
Broome
CAPE LATOUCHE TREVILLE
La Grange
NORTHERN
TANAMI
TERRITORY
Lake Gregory
DESERT
EIGHTY MILE BEACH
Goldsworthy
Shay Gap
GREAT SANDY DESERT
Lake White
Barrow
Port Hedland
De Grey
Lake Wills
MONTE BELLO ISLANDS
DAMPIER ARCHIPELAGO
Dampier
Roebourne
Marble Bar
Lake Mackay
BARROW ISLAND
Karratha
Nullagine
Lake Dora
Lake Auld
MUIRON ISLANDS
Fortescue
Wittenoom
NORTH WEST CAPE
Onslow
Pannawonica
HAMERSLEY RANGE
Mount Brockman 1132
Mount Bruce 1235
Lake Disappointment
Mount Leisler 897
Mount Liebig 1524
Mount Zeil 1511
MACDONNELL RANGES
Exmouth
Exmouth Gulf
Tom Price
Mount Meharry 1251
Paraburdoo
Newman
Savory
WESTERN
GIBSON DESERT
Lake Macdonald
Sp
POINT CLOATES
Ashburton
Mount Olga 1069
Lake Neale
CAPE CUVIER
Lake Macleod
Mount Augustus 1105
906 Mount Essendon
AUST
Tropic of Capricorn
105°
Lyons
Peak Hill
Mount Aloysius 1085
Ayers Rock 867
Mount Cockburn 1138
Mount Woodroffe 1440
Geographe Channel
Carnarvon
Gascoyne
ROBINSON RANGE
Lake Carnegie
Lake Gillen
BERNIER ISLAND
DORRE ISLAND
Shark Bay
Wooramel
Meekatharra
Lake Wells
Naturaliste Channel
DIRK HARTOG ISLAND
Denham
Murchison
Nannine
Wiluna
AUSTRALIA
GREAT VICTORIA DESERT
Lake Maurice
SOU
STEEP POINT
Cue
Lake Austin
Sandstone
Agnew
Yeo Lake
Kalbarri
Mount Magnet
Mount Redcliffe 562
Laverton
Lake Minigwal
Northampton
Yalgoo
Léonora
Malcolm
Lake Carey
Maralinga
Ooldea
Mullewa
Pindar
Lake Ballard
Lake Raeside
HOUTMAN ABROLHOS
Geraldton
Mongers Lake
Menzies
Three Springs
Lake Barlee
GREEN HEAD
Dongara
Lake Moore
Dalwallinu
Moora
Bonnie Rock
Bencubbin
Bullfinch
Kalgoorlie
Boulder
Coolgardie
Zanthus
Rawlinna
Forrest
Deakin
NULLARBOR PLAIN
Haig
CAPE ADIEU
SAINT PETER ISLA
Wanneroo
Northam
Merredin
Southern Cross
Lake Lefroy
Perth
Fremantle
DARLING RANGE
York
Beverley
Kellerberrin
Lake Cowan
Norseman
Eyre
Pinjarra
Brookton
Hyden
Lake Johnston
Lake Dundas
POINT CULVER
Bunbury
Collie
Narrogin
Wagin
Newdegate
Ravensthorpe
Geographe Bay
Busselton
Bridgetown
Nyabing
Gnowangerup
Hopetoun
Esperance Bay
CAPE ARID
Great Australian Bight
INVEST
CAPE NATURALISTE
Augusta
Manjimup
Bluff Knoll 1096
Mount Barker
Esperance
ARCHIPELAGO OF THE RECHERCHE
HOOD POINT
CAPE LEEUWIN
Pemberton
Denmark
Albany
CAPE VANCOUVER
POINT D'ENTRECASTEAUX
WEST CAPE HOWE
King George Sound

SOUTHERN OCE

Copyright © by Rand McNally & Co.
Map prepared by Esselte Map Service AB, Stockholm
A-590200-264

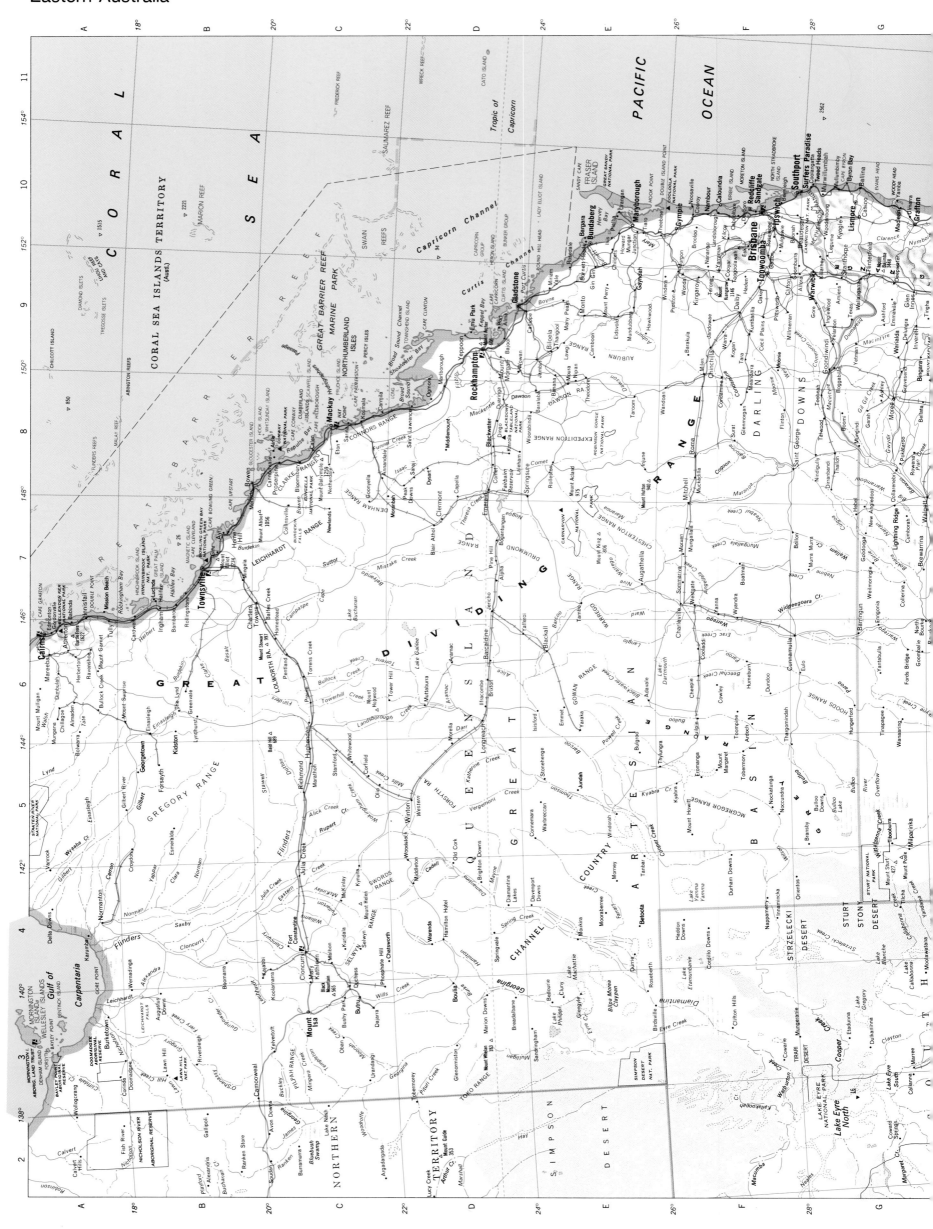

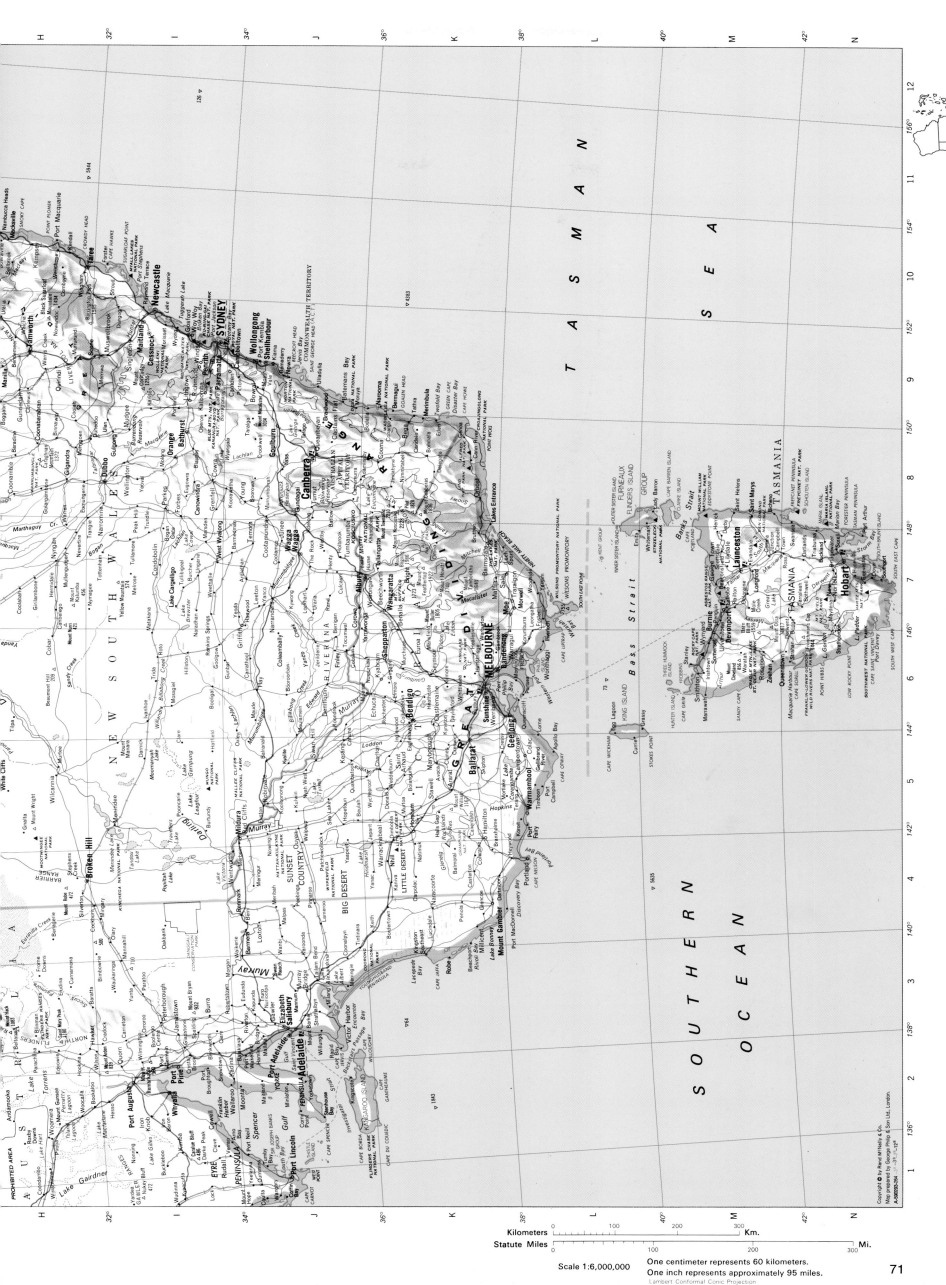

Kilometers
Statute Miles

Scale 1:6,000,000
One centimeter represents 60 kilometers.
One inch represents approximately 95 miles.
Lambert Conformal Conic Projection

New Zealand

Copyright © by Rand McNally & Co.
A-591600-286

Scale 1:6,000,000
One centimeter represents 60 kilometers.
One inch represents approximately 95 miles.
Lambert Conformal Conic Projection

Kilometers

Statute Miles

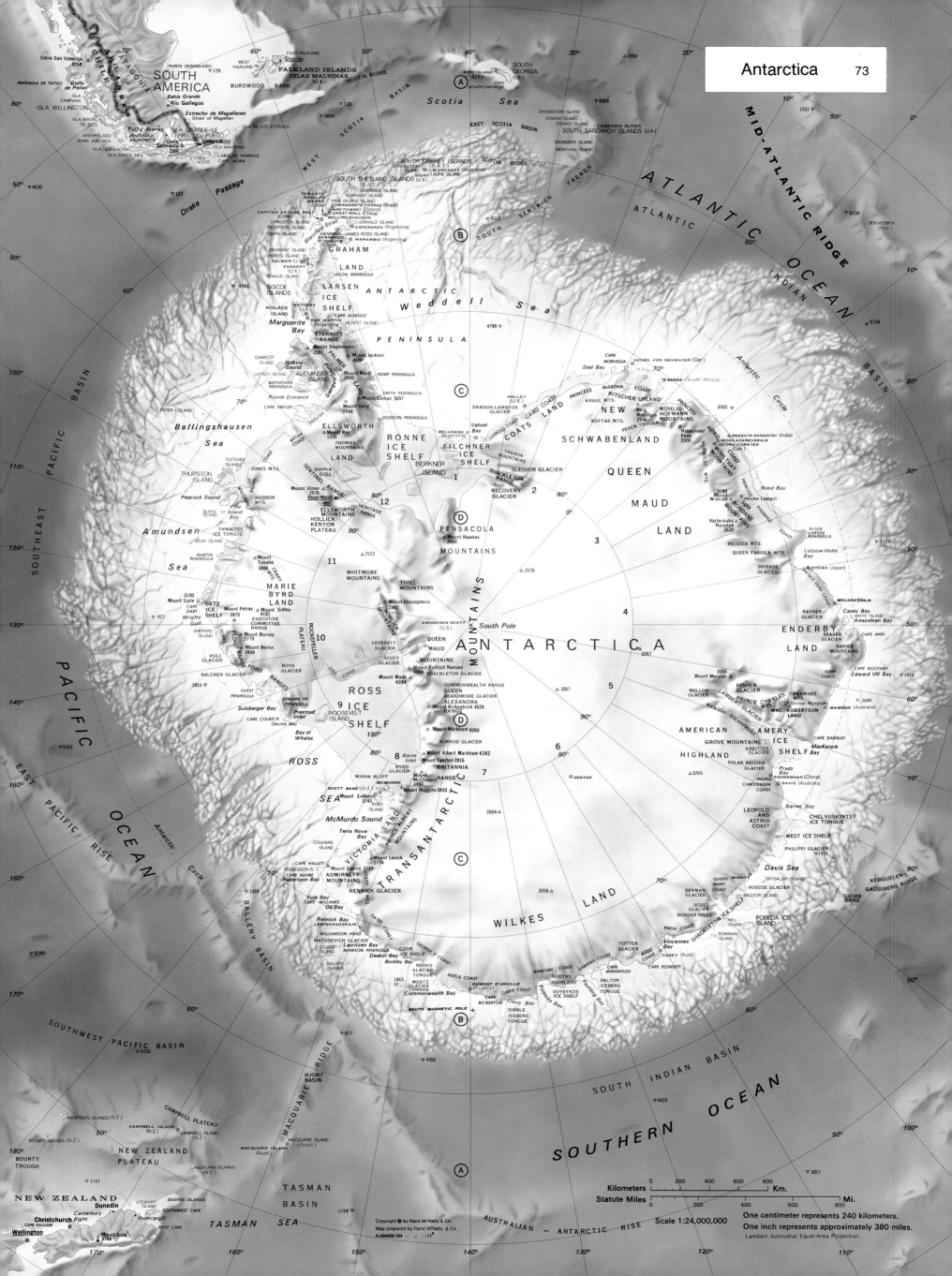

One centimeter represents 240 kilometers.
One inch represents approximately 380 miles.

Scale 1:24,000,000

Lambert Azimuthal Equal-Area Projection

Copyright © by Rand McNally & Co.
Map prepared by Rand McNally & Co.

A-594000-764
-11

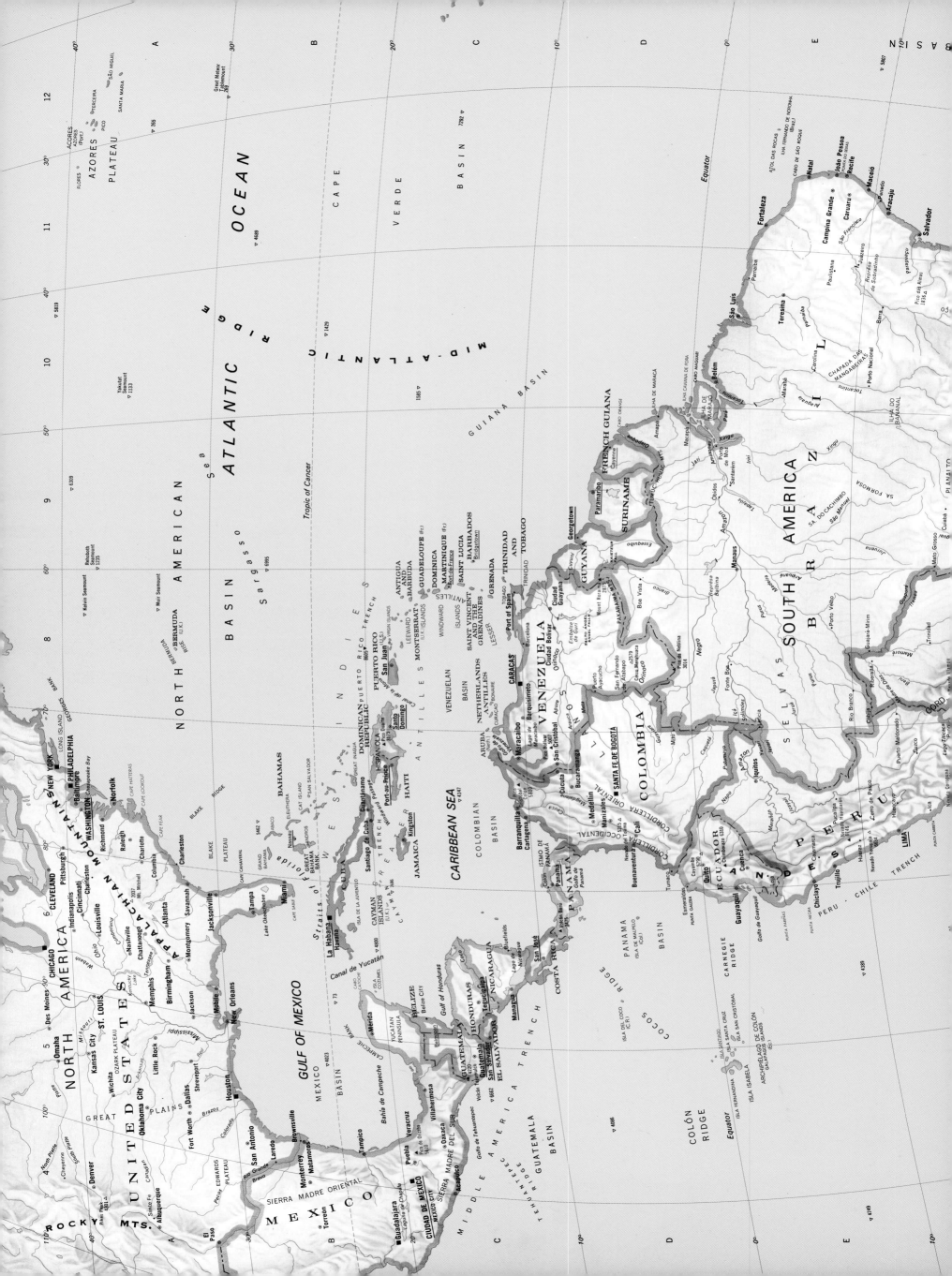

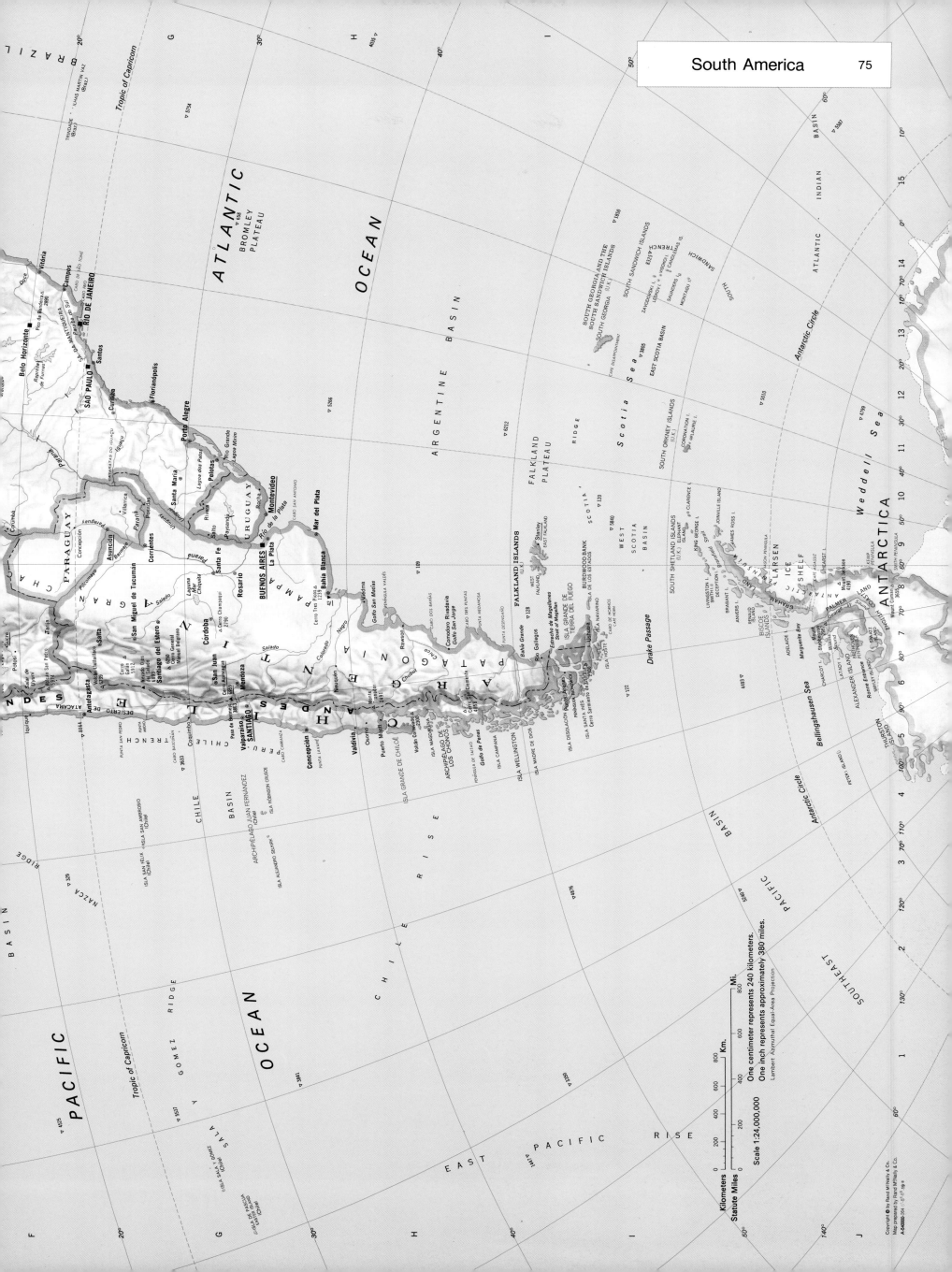

Northern South America

CARIBBEAN SEA

PACIFIC OCEAN

NICARAGUA

COSTA RICA

PANAMA

VENEZUELA

COLOMBIA

ECUADOR

PERU

BOLIVIA

AMAZONAS

SELVA

RONDÔNIA

ACRE

CHILE

ARGENTINA

LESSER ANTILLES

NETHERLANDS ANTILLES

ARUBA (Neth.)

CARACAS

Bogotá (SANTA FE DE BOGOTA)

Quito

LIMA

La Paz

Sucre

Medellín

Cali

Guayaquil

Copyright © by Rand McNally & Co.
Map prepared by Esselte Map Service AB, Stockholm.
A-549100-264

Kilometers

Statute Miles

Scale 1:12,000,000

One centimeter represents 120 kilometers.
One inch represents approximately 190 miles.

Oblique Conic Conformal Projection

76

A

B

ATLANTIC   OCEAN

BARBADOS
etown

TOGO

Charity
Georgetown
Garden of
Eden
Bartica
Kwakoegron
Rockstone
Wismar

New Amsterdam
Nieuw Nickerie
Totness
Overwacht
Paramaribo
Nieuw Amsterdam
Moengo
Paranam
Albina
Saint-Laurent-du-Maroni
Saint-Élie
Simamary

Brokopondo
Stuwmeer

SURINAME

Cayenne
ÎLE DU DIABLE

FRENCH
GUIANA

Juliana Top
1230

Tapanahony

Saül
830

Matoury
Regina
Saint-Georges
Oiapoque

ACARAI MTS.
TUMUC-HUMAC MTS.

AMAPÁ

Serra do Navio

Cunani
Calçoene
Amapá

ILHA DE MARACÁ

C

Oriximiná
Óbidos
Alenquer
Monte Alegre

Macapá
ILHA CAVIANA DE FORA
ILHA MEXIANA
ILHA JANAUCU
ILHA DO CURUÁ
ILHA BAILIQUE

CABO ORANGE

Mazagão
Mexiana
Canal do Norte
CABO MAGUARI

Equator   0°

Amazon
Amazonas
Parintins
Maués
Santarém
Faro
ILHA
GRANDE
DO GURUPÁ
Gurupá
Breves
Portel
Porto de
Moz
ILHA DA
LAGUNA
Corrinhas
Cametá

Belém
Abaetetuba
Bragança
Marapanim
Carutapera

São Bento
Viana
Pinheiro
Canurupu
Camiranga

São Luís
Rosário
Alcântara

Parnaíba
Tutóia

D

PARÁ

Altamira

Tocantins
Tucuruí
Represa
de
Tucuruí

Monção
Pindaré

MARANHÃO
Bacabal
Pedreiras
Barra
do Corda

Codó

Ipu
Pedro II
União
Sobral
Camocim
Acaraú
Marangueta
Baturité

Fortaleza
Aracati
Quixadá

ATOL DAS ROCAS
ILHA FERNANDO
DE NORONHA
(Brazil)

Marabá
São João
do Araguaia
SERRA DOS CARAJÁS
Carajás

Imperatriz
Araguatins
Tocantinópolis

Grajaú

Carolina
Riachão
Balsas

Loreto
Benedito Leite
Colinas
Mirador
Barras
Caxias
Teresina

Amarante
Floriano
Represa Boa
Esperança
Oeiras

Crateús
Senador
Pompeu
Jaguaribe
Russas
Macau
Areia Branca
CABO DE SÃO ROQUE
Natal

E   5°

SERRA DO CACHIMBO

Xingu
Fresco
Gradaús
Conceição do Araguaia

Araguaína
Araguacema

CEARÁ
PIAUÍ
Picos
Iguatu
Crato
Juazeiro
do Norte
Cajazeiras
Sousa
Caicó
Currais Novos
RIO GRANDE DO NORTE

SERRA DOS APIACÁS

Itaituba

Miracema do Tocantins
Tocantínia

Alto Parnaíba
Santa Filomena
Gilbués

São Raimundo Nonato
Paulistana
Remanso
Represa de
Sobradinho
Petrolina
Juazeiro

Patos
Campina Grande
PARAÍBA
Flores
Sertânia
Pesqueira
Garanhuns
Arcoverde
PERNAMBUCO

João Pessoa
PONTA DO SEIXAS
Goiana
Olinda
Recife
Jaboatão
Caruaru
Palmares
Barreiros
Porto de Pedras

E

BRAZIL

TOCANTINS

ILHA
DO
BANANAL

Pium
Cristalândia
Porto Nacional
Gurupi
Natividade
Dianópolis

Paranã
Arraias
Posse
São Domingos

Barreiras

Corrente
Bom Jesus
da Lapa
Santo Antônio de Jesus

Xique-Xique
Barra
Juazeiro
Senhor
do Bonfim
Jacobina
Tucano

Paulo
Afonso
União dos Palmares
ALAGOAS
Rio Largo
Arapiraca
Maceió
Propriá
SERGIPE
Coripe
Perpéd

Aracaju
São Cristóvão

F   10°

MATO GROSSO
Diamantino
Rosário Oeste
PLANALTO DO
MATO GROSSO
Cuiabá
Barão
de Melgaço
Poxoréu
Rondonópolis

SERRA DO RONCADOR
Rio das Mortes
SERRA DOURADA

GOIÁS
Aruanã
Pilar de Goiás
Goiás
Pirenópolis

BAHIA
Barreiras
Lençóis
Mucugê
Paramirim
Pico das
Almas
1836
Carinhanha
Guanambi

Feira de Santana
Alagoinhas
Santo Amaro
Candeias
Salvador
ILHA DE TINHARÉ
Valença
Nazaré

F

SERRA DO TOMBADOR
Utiariti

MATO GROSSO
Barra do Garças
Alto Araguaia
Mineiros

SERRA DO CAIAPÓ

Rio Verde
Jataí

Anápolis
Brasília
Luziânia
Silvânia
Goiânia

PLANALTO
CENTRAL

São Francisco
Januária
Monte Azul
Pirapora
Araçuaí
Minas Novas
Diamantina

Vitória
da Conquista
Itapetinga

Ibicaraí
Ilhéus
Itabuna

G   15°

Corumbá
Porto Esperança
Cáceres

Pantanal
de São
Lourenço

Aquidauana

MATO GROSSO
DO SUL
Campo Grande
Três Lagoas

SERRA DO ESPINHAÇO
Grão Mogol

MINAS GERAIS
Corinto
Curvelo
Pará de Minas
Sete
Lagoas
Belo
Horizonte
Divinópolis
Lavras

Pardo
Pedra Azul
Jequitinhonha
Almenara
Canavieiras
Belmonte
Porto Seguro
Prado
Alcobaça
Caravelas
ILHA CASSUMBA

Governador
Valadares
ESPÍRITO
SANTO
Colatina
São Mateus

H   20°

Puerto
Suárez

Represa de
Ilha Solteira
Três Lagoas
São Simão

Uberlândia
Uberaba
Araxá
Franca

Patos de Minas
Patrocínio

Itabira
Ouro
Preto
Barbacena
Juiz de Fora

Nanuque

Aimorés
Caratinga
Itabira

Vitória
Vila Velha
Cachoeiro de
Itapemirim

SÃO PAULO
Presidente Prudente
Araçatuba
Marília
Bauru
Araraquara
São Carlos
Ribeirão
Preto
Limeira
Piracicaba
Campinas
Jundiaí
Sorocaba
SÃO PAULO
Santos
São Vicente

Poços de
Caldas
Pouso Alegre
São José
dos Campos
Nova
Iguaçu
Niterói
RIO DE JANEIRO
Petrópolis
Volta
Redonda
Campos
CABO FRIO
Tropic of Capricorn

(H)

Southern South America

Kilometers

Statute Miles

Scale 1:12,000,000
One centimeter represents 120 kilometers.
One inch represents approximately 190 miles.
Oblique Conic Conformal Projection

Copyright © by Rand McNally & Co.
Map prepared by Esselte Map Service AB, Stockholm.
A-549200-264

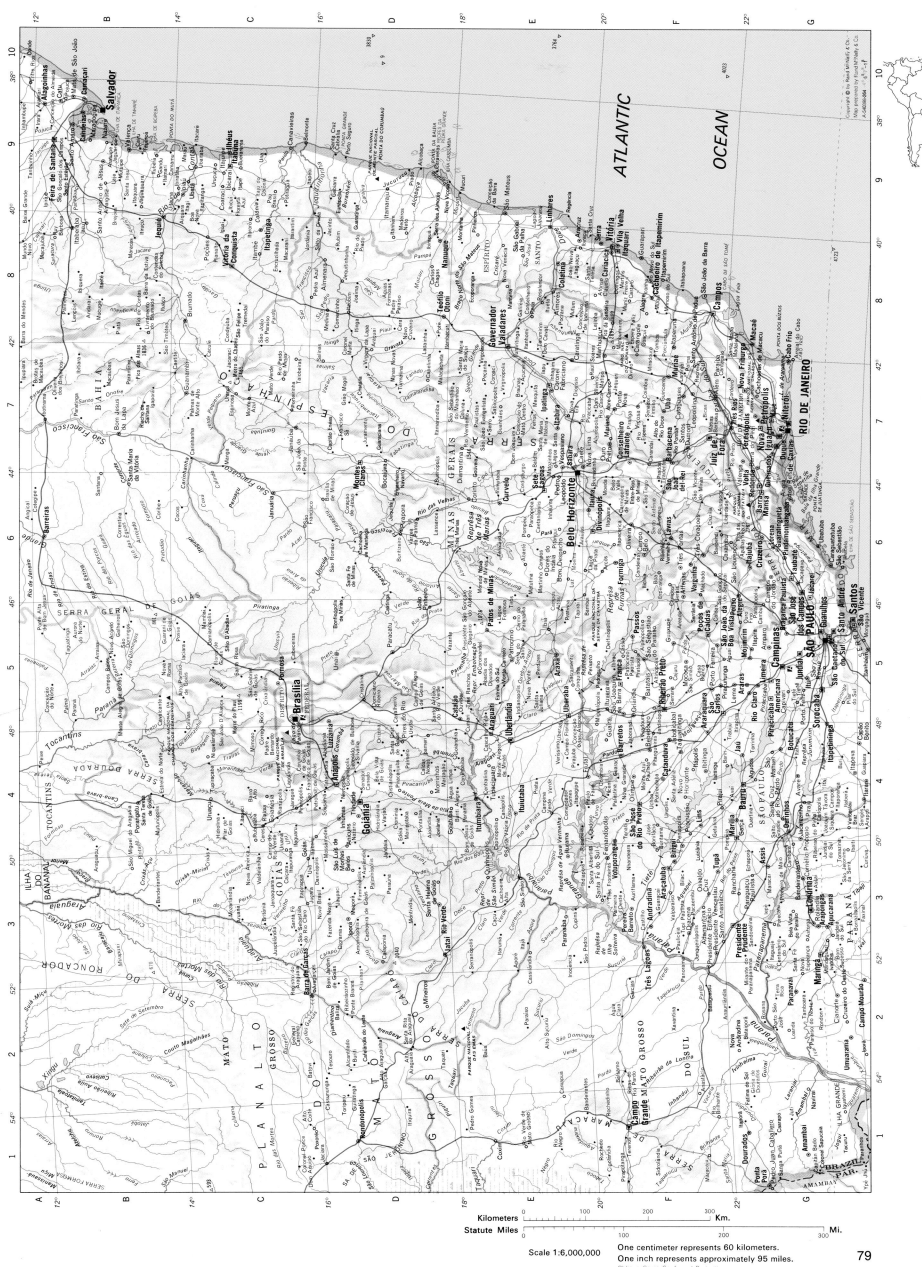

ATLANTIC OCEAN

RIO DE JANEIRO

SÃO PAULO

Copyright © by Rand McNally & Co.
Map prepared by Rand McNally & Co.
A-5403964

Kilometers
0   100   200   300   Km.

Statute Miles
0   100   200   300   Mi.

Scale 1:6,000,000

One centimeter represents 60 kilometers.
One inch represents approximately 95 miles.

Oblique Conic Conformal Projection

One centimeter represents 60 kilometers.
One inch represents approximately 95 miles.
Scale 1:6,000,000
Oblique Conic Conformal Projection

81

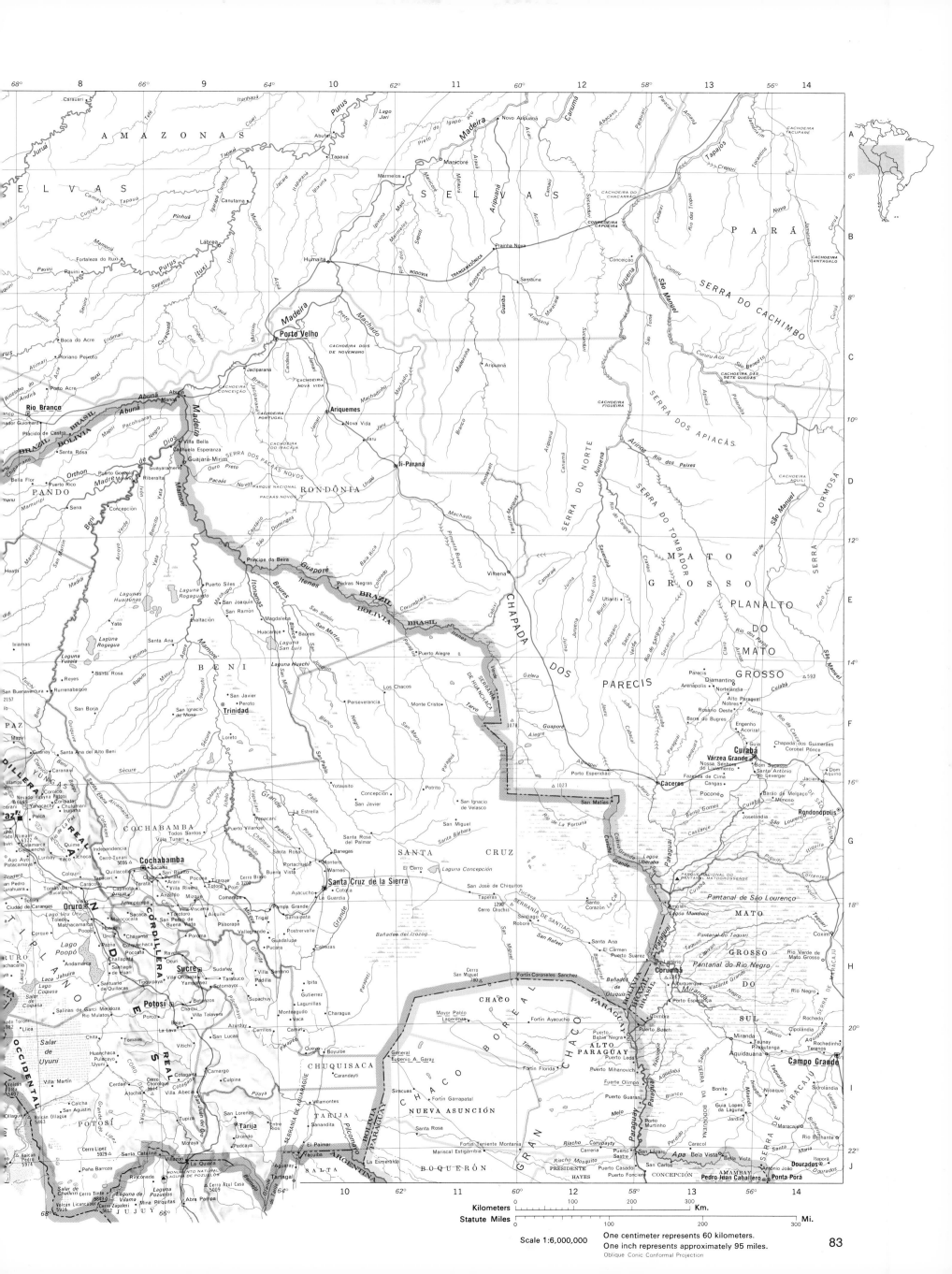

Kilometers

Statute Miles

Scale 1:6,000,000

One centimeter represents 60 kilometers.
One inch represents approximately 95 miles.
Oblique Conic Conformal Projection

Colombia, Ecuador, Venezuela, and Guyana

ATLANTIC

OCEAN

NETHERLANDS   ANTILLES
NEDERLANDSE   ANTILLEN
CURAÇAO   BONAIRE
Kralendijk

L E S S E R   A N T I L L E S

ISLAS LAS AVES
(Ven.)

▽ 1742

Victoria
Saint George's
GRENADA

CARRIACOU

emstad

Puerto
Cumarebo
Pintu
PUNTA ZAMURO

San Juan de los Cayos
Tocuyo de la Costa
Chichiriviche
TUCACAS
PUNTA TUCACAS

ISLAS LOS ROQUES
(Ven.)

ISLA LA ORCHILA
(Ven.)

ISLA BLANQUILLA
(Ven.)

ISLA LOS HERMANOS
(Ven.)

▽ 570

ISLAG LOS TESTIGOS
(Ven.)

TOBAGO
Speyside
Scarborough
TRINIDAD
AND
TOBAGO

▽ 1902

ISLA LA TORTUGA
(Ven.)

NUEVA
ESPARTA
ISLA DE
MARGARITA
Boca de Pozo
Punta de Piedras
ISLA CUBAGUA
LA COCHE

Porlamar
La Asunción

▽ 1379

PUNTA DE ARAYA
Araya

▽ 1353

Golfo de Cariaco
Carúpano

DRAGON'S MOUTHS
GALERA POINT

Juangriego

Port of Spain
TRINIDAD

San Fernando
Point Fortin
Princes Town
SIPARIA
GALEOTA POINT

PARQ. NAC.
PARQ. NAC. HENRI
Maiquetía   PITIER   EL ÁVILA

Puerto
Cabello

CARACAS

Guarenas
Petare

Los Teques

MIRANDA

Guatire

Cúpira
Río Chico
El Guapo

Barcelona
Puerto la Cruz
Pozuelos

Cumaná
Cumanacoa
Caripe
Caripito
Cariaco

SUCRE

PENÍNSULA
DE PARIA
Macuro
Río Caribe
Yaguaraparo
El Pilar
Güiria

Gulf of Paria

PLEUREUX
Caicara de Maturín

Maturín

San Felipe
Maracay
Valencia
CARABOBO
ARAGUA
La Victoria

Barquisimeto
Acarigua

San Carlos
Tinaco
Las Vegas

COJEDES

El Sombrero
Las Mercedes

MONAGAS

DELTA
ORINOCO

DELTA AMACURO

Boca
Grande

ISLA TOBEJUBA

CORDERO ISLAND

Mabaruma
Morawhanna

BARIMA-WAINI
Matthews Ridge
Marlborough
Anna Regina

POMEROON-SUPENAAM

GEORGETOWN

Calabozo
San Juan
de los Morros
Valle de
la Pascua
El Socorro

GUÁRICO

El Calvario

ANZOÁTEGUI

El Tigre
San Tomé
San José
de Guanipa

Temblador

Barrancas
Tucupita
Sacupana
Curiapo

Amacuro

BOLÍVAR

Ciudad Guayana
Soledad

Ciudad
Bolívar
Upata
El Pao

Embalse
de Guri

El Manteco

El Dorado

Tumeremo

El Callao

ESSEQUIBO ISLANDS-
WEST DEMERARA

DEMERARA-MAHAICA
MAHAICA-BERBICE

Paradise
Mahaicony Village
Fort Wellington
Rosignol
Rosehall
New Amsterdam

CUYUNI-
MAZARUNI

VENEZUELA
COLOMBIA

San Fernando de Atabapo

Puerto Ayacucho

Cerro Guanay
2300

Cerro Yaví
2441

Cerro Campanero
2100

Cerro Guaiquinima
2100

SALTO ÁNGEL
ANGEL FALLS
2950

LA GRAN
SABANA

Auyán Tepuy

Mount Roraima
2875

UPPER
DEMERARA-
BERBICE

Corriverton

Linden
Ituni

NICKERIE
Wageningen
Nickerie
CORONIE

PAKARAIMA   MOUNTAINS

POTARO-
SIPARUNI

KAIETEUR
FALL

SIPALIWINI

Corentyne
Corantijn

WILHELMINA
GEB.

AMAZONAS

Cerro Marahuaca
2579

Cerro Duida
2400

SIERRA   PARIMA

Cuchivero

KANUKU
MOUNTAINS

UPPER
TAKUTU-
UPPER
ESSEQUIBO

EAST BERBICE-
CORENTYNE

KAYSER
GEBERGTE

Cerro Uquia
2500

Boa Vista

Lethem

KAMOA
MOUNTAINS

ACARAI   MOUNTAINS

SURINAME

GUYANA

VENEZUELA
BRAZIL

San Felipe
San Carlos de Río Negro
Santa Rosa
de Amanadona
Cucuí

Cerro Avispa
2112

Pico Tamacuari
2340

Pico
da Neblina
3014

RORAIMA

São José de Anauá

ILHA
PEDRO II

PARQUE NACIONAL DO
PICO DA NEBLINA

Equator

PARÁ

Negro

Tapurucuara

Barcelos

Carvoeiro
Moura

Represa
Balbina

AMAZONAS

Japurá

Maraã

PARQUE NACIONAL DO JAÚ

Cachoeira
das Ilhas

Lago do
Erepecuru

Amazon

Içá

Fonte Boa

Tefé

Manacapuru

Manaús

Amazon

PARÁ

Jutaí

Juruá

Solimões

Coari

Madeira

PARQUE NACIONAL
DA AMAZÔNIA

Kilometers   0   100   200   300   Km.
Statute Miles   0   100   200   300   Mi.

Scale 1:6,000,000   One centimeter represents 60 kilometers.
One inch represents approximately 95 miles.
Oblique Conic Conformal Projection

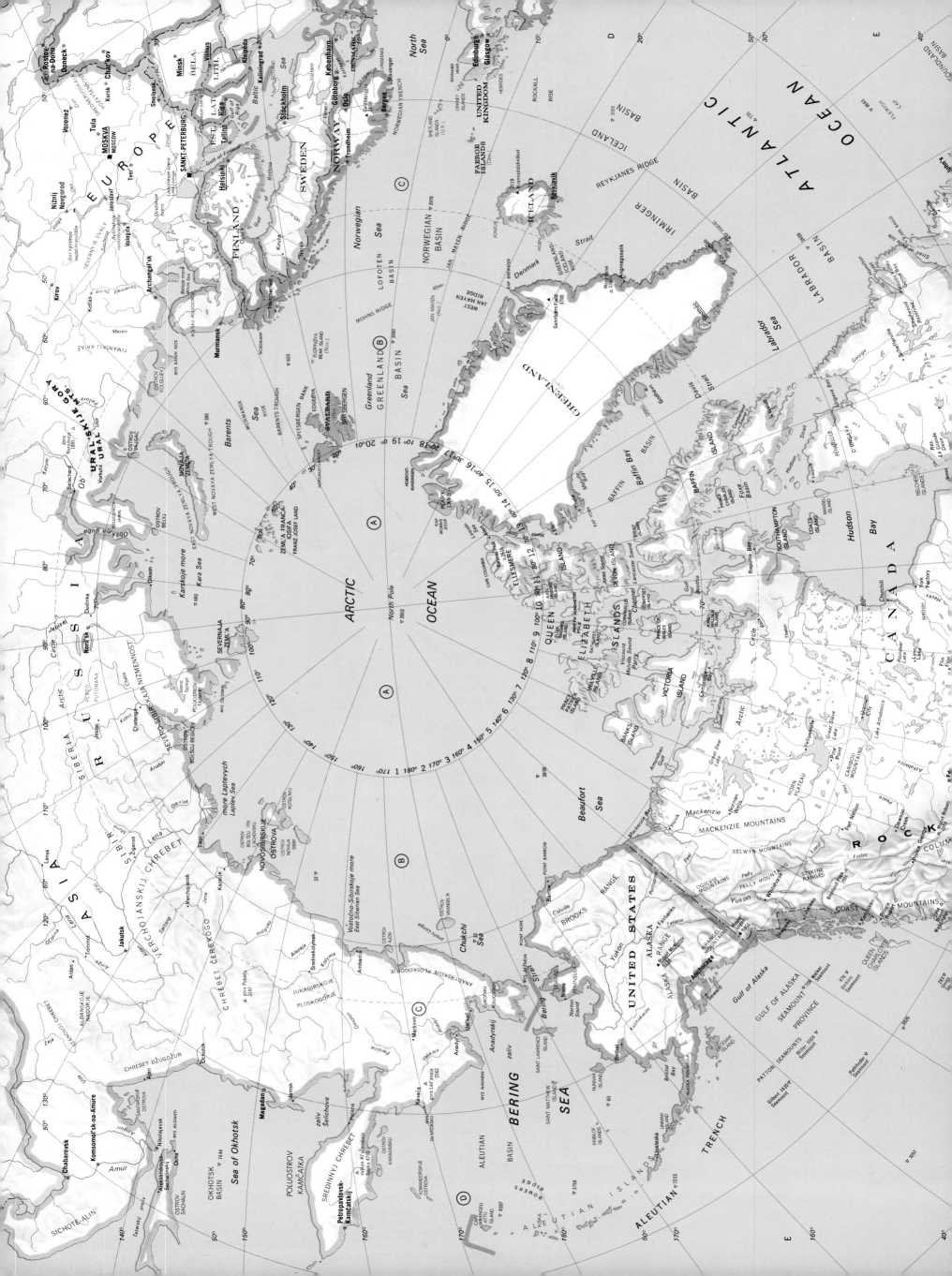

Mexico

Copyright © by Rand McNally & Co.
Map prepared by Rand McNally & Co.
A-531600-264 -13¹

Kilometers

Statute Miles

Scale 1:6,000,000
One centimeter represents 60 kilometers.
One inch represents approximately 95 miles.
Lambert Conformal Conic Projection

Copyright © by Rand McNally & Co.
Map prepared by Rand McNally & Co.
A-533600-264

GUANAJA

9 85° 10 84° 11 83° 12 82° 13 81° 14 80° 15

A

de Guaimoreto
Santa Rosa de Aguán
CABO CAMARÓN
PUNTA PATUCA
CAYOS CAJONES
Limón
Triona
Laguna de Brus
△22
CAYOS BECERRO
105
CAYO DE SERRANILLA (Colombia)

Cerro Payas
1128
Laguna de Ibans
CAYOS VIVORILLO
△40
CAYOS COCOROCUMA

COLÓN
Paya
Brus Laguna
Laguntara

Cerro Piñas
335
ban
△1326

LA MOSQUITIA
Laguna de Waranta
Laguna de Tansin

Dulce Nombre de Culmí
GRACIAS A DIOS
Puerto Lempira
Laguna Rotunta
CABO FALSO
ARRECIFES DE LA MEDIA LUNA
△356

NCHO
Wampú
MONTAÑAS DE COLÓN
CABO GRACIAS A DIOS
Cabo Gracias a Dios

Valencia
Coco
ARRECIFE EDINBURGH
△87

San Ramón
Waspam
Bilwaskarma
Edinburgh Channel

Raiti
Coco
Ulang
MISKITOS REEF
QUITASUEÑO
CAYO DE SERRANA

Bocay
△1132
Waspuk
Likus
PUNTA GORDA
CAYOS MISKITOS
△5

Wawa
Wawa
105

Yablis
Laguna Pahara
Channel

Bonanza
La Rosita
Kukalaya
Laguna de Krukira
105

Siuna
Bambana
47
△1755
CAYOS DE RONCADOR

Yaoya
Laguna de Wounta
Wounta
△534

Tungla
Prinzapolka
△3292

Prinzapolka
ISLA DE PROVIDENCIA

La Cruz de Río Grande
25

ZELAYA
La Barra
C A R I B B E A N

MATAGALPA
Kurinwás
SAN ANDRÉS Y PROVIDENCIA (Colombia)

Rama
ISLA DE SAN ANDRÉS
San Andrés

BOACO
Santo Domingo
Siquia
Laguna de Perlas
CAYOS DEL ESTE SUDESTE

Mico
PUNTA SET NET
PUNTA DE PERLAS

Camoapa
Comalapa
Muelle de los Bueyes
Rama
Escondido
El Bluff

Juigalpa
Rama Sandino
Bluefields
Bahía de Bluefields
ISLA DEL VENADO

CAYOS DE ALBUQUERQUE
3174

ISLAS DEL MAÍZ (Nic.)

S E A

PUNTA MONO

Lago de Nicaragua
Punta Gorda

ISLA DE OMETEPE
Punta Gorda

Bahía de Punta Gorda
2633

RÍO SAN JUAN
San Carlos

El Castillo de La Concepción

Cárdenas
San Juan del Norte

Colorado

Los Chiles
1481

NICARAGUA
COSTA RICA
3381
2116

Upala
Caño Negro

ALAJUELA
PARQUE NACIONAL TORTUGUERO

HEREDIA
Puerto Viejo

Puerto Limón

SAN JOSÉ
Alajuela
Heredia

CARTAGO
Puerto Limón

Punta Cahuita

Punta Mona

LIMÓN
PUNTA MANZANILLO

Portobelo
Nombre de Dios

△47

ARCHIPIÉLAGO DE BOCAS DEL TORO
Colón
PANAMÁ

BOCAS DEL TORO
Bahía de Almirante
Panamá

Golfo de los Mosquitos

COLÓN
Lago Alajuela

Bahía de Coronado
PANAMÁ
La Chorrera
Panamá

PUNTARENAS
Bahía de Panamá

CHIRIQUÍ
David
VERAGUAS
HERRERA
LOS SANTOS

Golfo de Chiriquí
Golfo de Panamá

Kilometers   50   100   150 Km.
Statute Miles   0   50   100   150 Mi.

Scale 1:3,000,000
One centimeter represents 30 kilometers.
One inch represents approximately 47 miles.
Lambert Conformal Conic Projection

93

Caribbean Region

GULF OF MEXICO

UNITED STATES
FLORIDA

West Palm Beach
Fort Myers
Hollywood
Hialeah
MIAMI
Miami Beach
Coral Gables
Fort Lauderdale

Palm Beach
Lake Worth
Delray Beach
Boca Raton
Pompano Beach

West End
GRAND BAHAMA
Freeport

LITTLE ABACO
ABACO
Marsh Harbour

Everglades
National Park

Key Largo

Naples
The

Homestead
Key Largo

BAHAMA

Nassau
NEW PROVIDENCE

ELEUTHERA
Governor's Harbour

Nicholl's Town
ANDROS
Andros Town

Adelaide
Rock Sound

Arthur's Town
CAT ISLAND

Straits of Florida

Key West

FLORIDA KEYS

LA HABANA
HAVANA

San Antonio
de los Baños
San José
de las Lajas
Matanzas
Cárdenas
Jovellanos

Artemisa
Guanajay
Candelaria
Los Palacios
Güines

La Esperanza
Sagua la Grande

Minas de Matahambre
Pinar del Río

Mantua
Guane

Golfo de
Guanahacabibes

CUBA

Santa Clara
Placetas
Cienfuegos

Camagüey

Las Tunas
Holguín
Bayamo
Manzanillo

Palma Soriano
Santiago de Cuba
Guantánamo

SIERRA MAESTRA

YUCATAN
MEXICO

Cancún
MÉRIDA

Cozumel

QUINTANA
ROO

YUCATAN PENINSULA
PENÍNSULA DE YUCATÁN

CAYMAN ISLANDS
(U.K.)

George Town
GRAND CAYMAN

JAMAICA

Montego Bay
Kingston
Spanish Town

GREATER

GULF OF
HONDURAS

Gulf of
Honduras

La Ceiba

HONDURAS

Tegucigalpa

NICARAGUA

Managua
Granada

COSTA RICA

San José

PACIFIC

OCEAN

LA MOSQUITIA

CORDILLERA

León

Bluefields

Lago
de Nicaragua

CARIBBEAN

SAN ANDRÉS
Y PROVIDENCIA
(Col.)

San Andrés

Barranquilla
Santa Ma
Cartagena

Colón
Panamá

PANAMA

Golfo de los
Mosquitos

Copyright by Rand McNally & Co.
Map prepared by Rand McNally & Co.
A-530100-264

Canada

Alberta

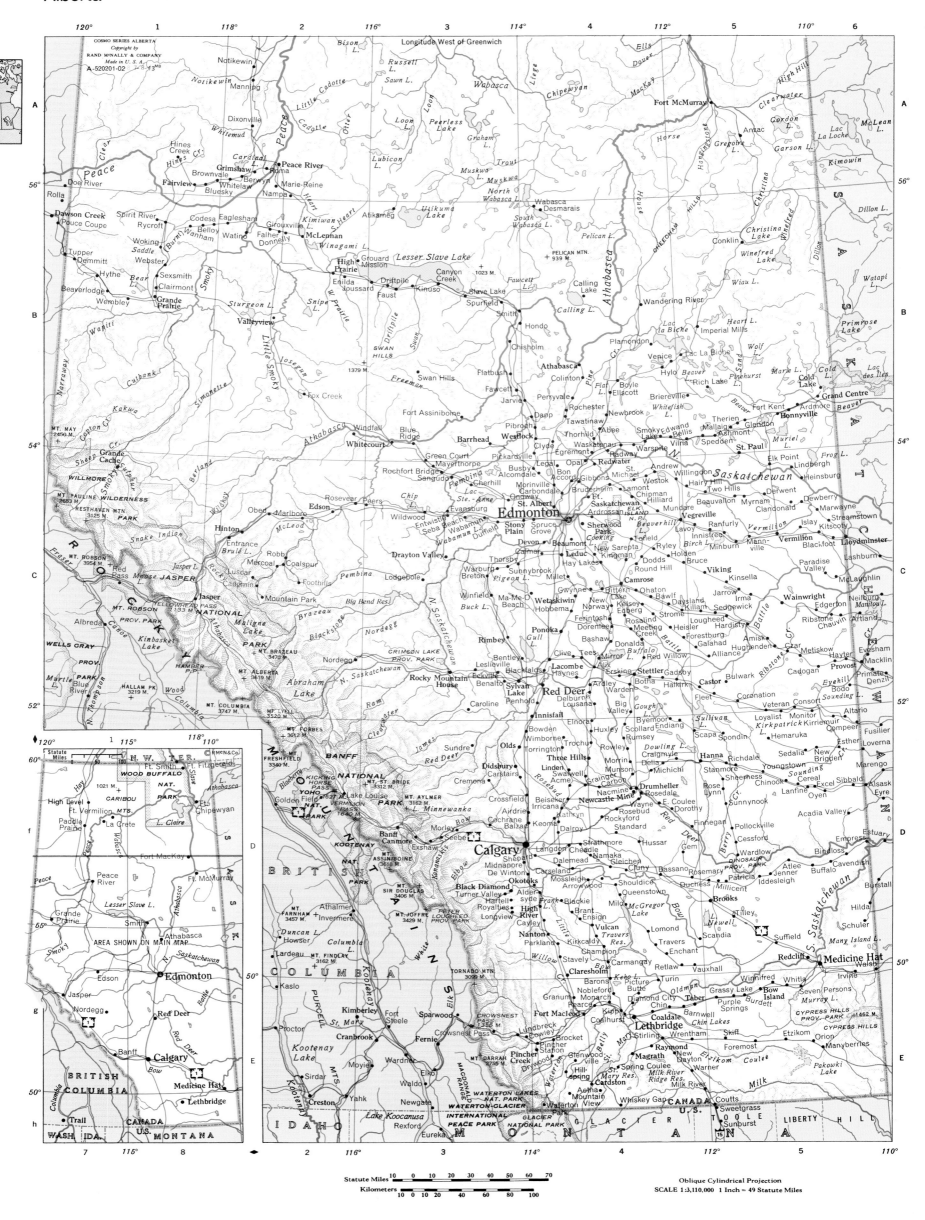

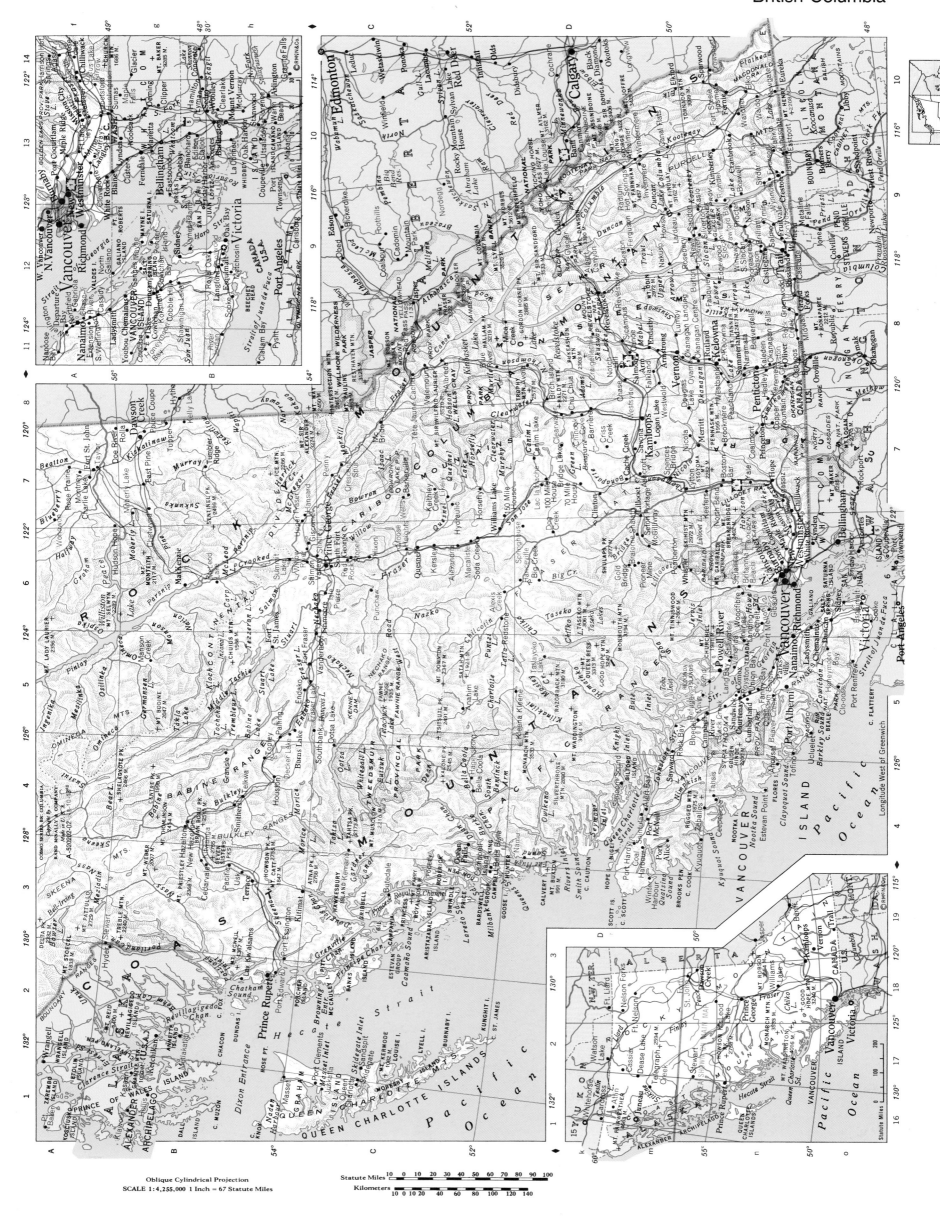

Oblique Cylindrical Projection
SCALE 1:4,255,000 1 Inch = 67 Statute Miles

Statute Miles 10 0 10 20 30 40 50 60 70 80 90 100

Kilometers 10 0 10 20 40 60 80 100 120 140

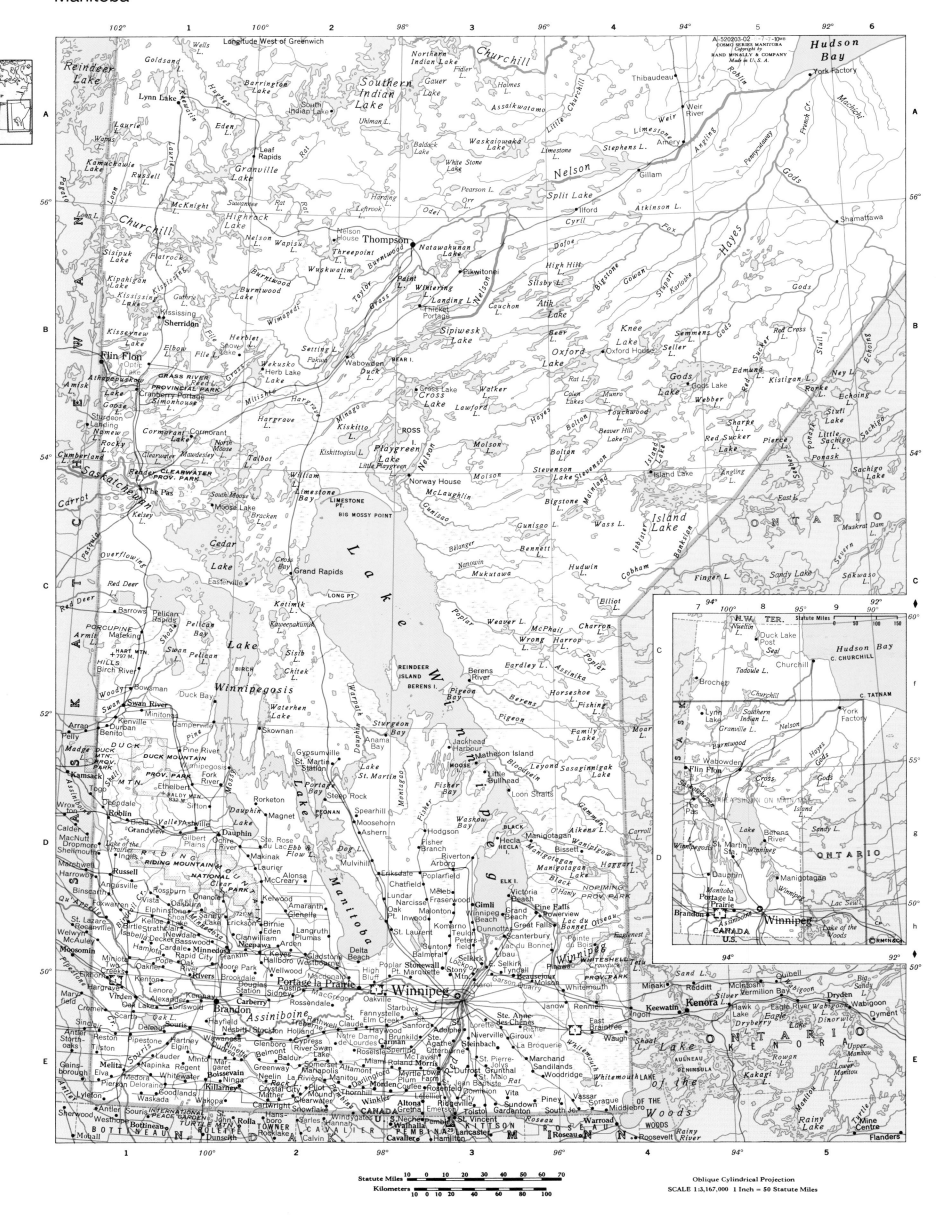

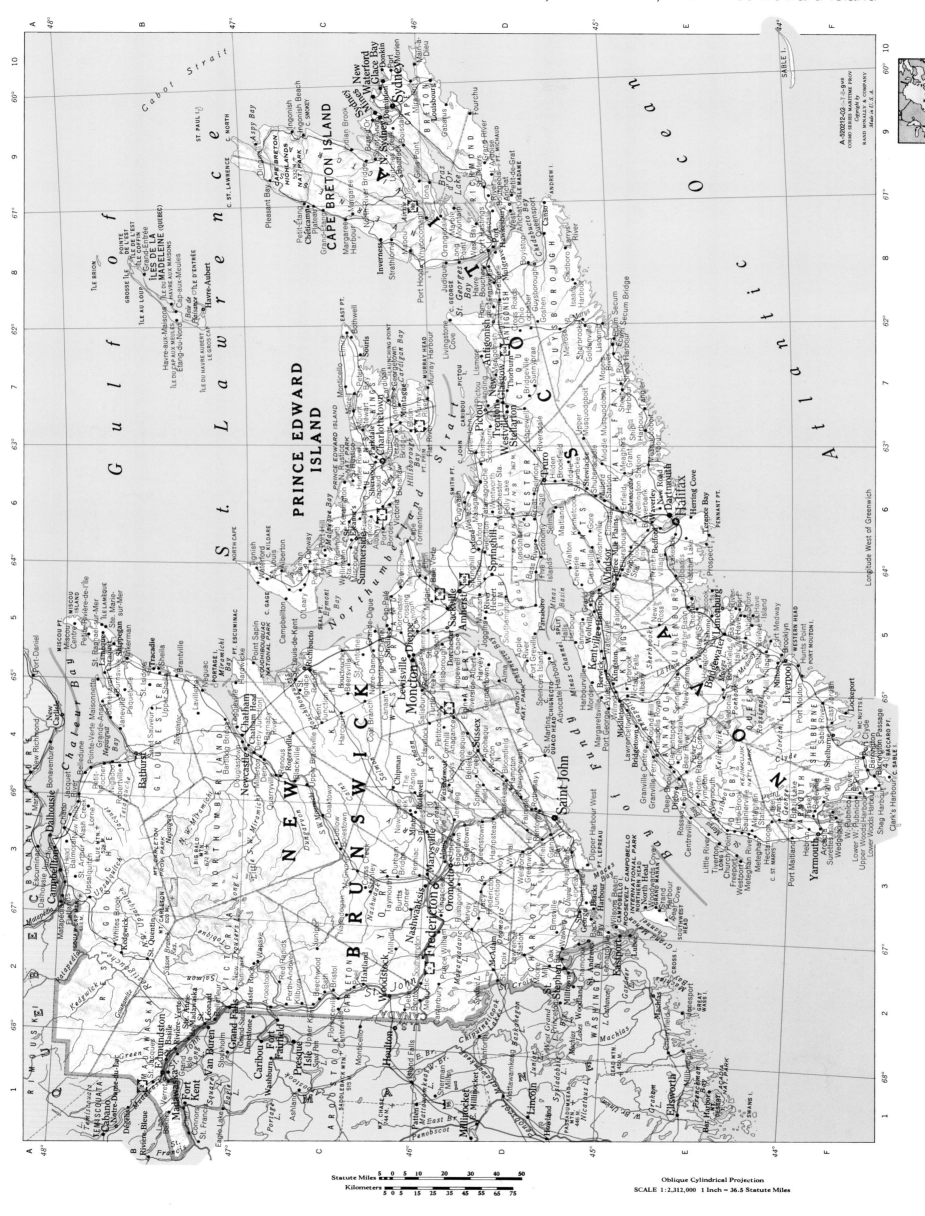

Oblique Cylindrical Projection
SCALE 1:2,312,000   1 Inch = 36.5 Statute Miles

Newfoundland

Oblique Cylindrical Projection
SCALE 1:2,226,000   1 Inch = 35 Statute Miles

Statute Miles 5 0 5 10   20   30   40   50
Kilometers 5 0 5 15 25 35 45 55 65 75

Quebec

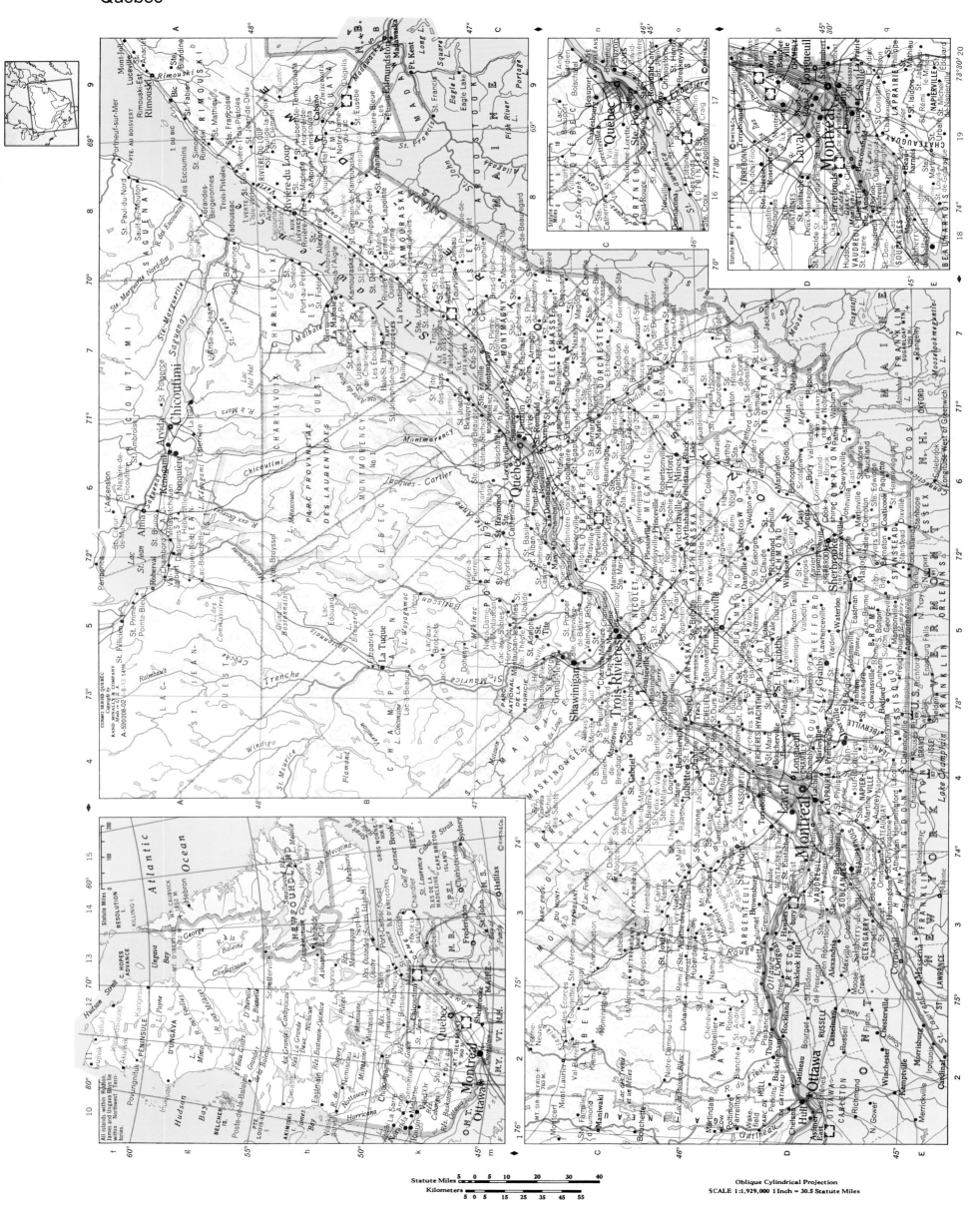

Saskatchewan

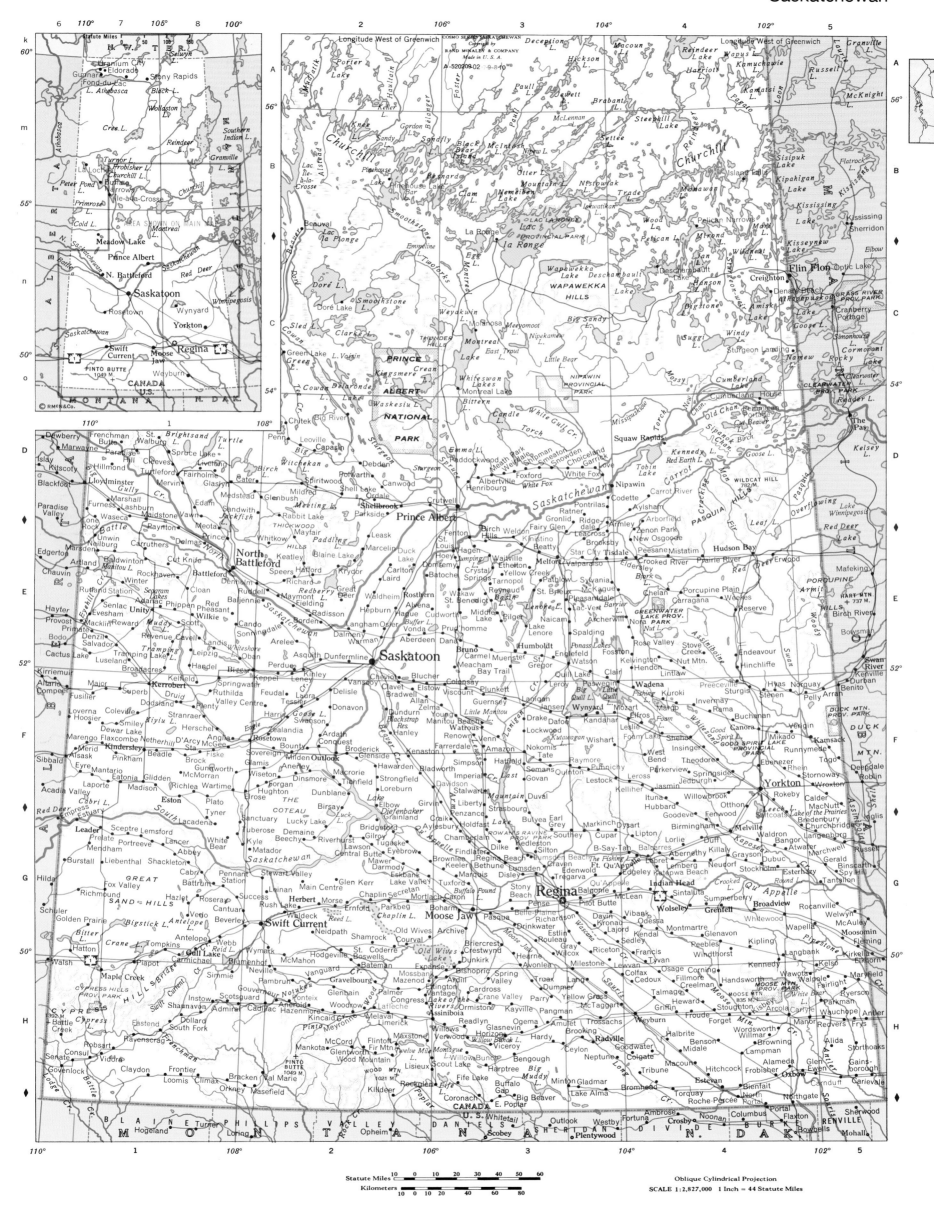

United States of America

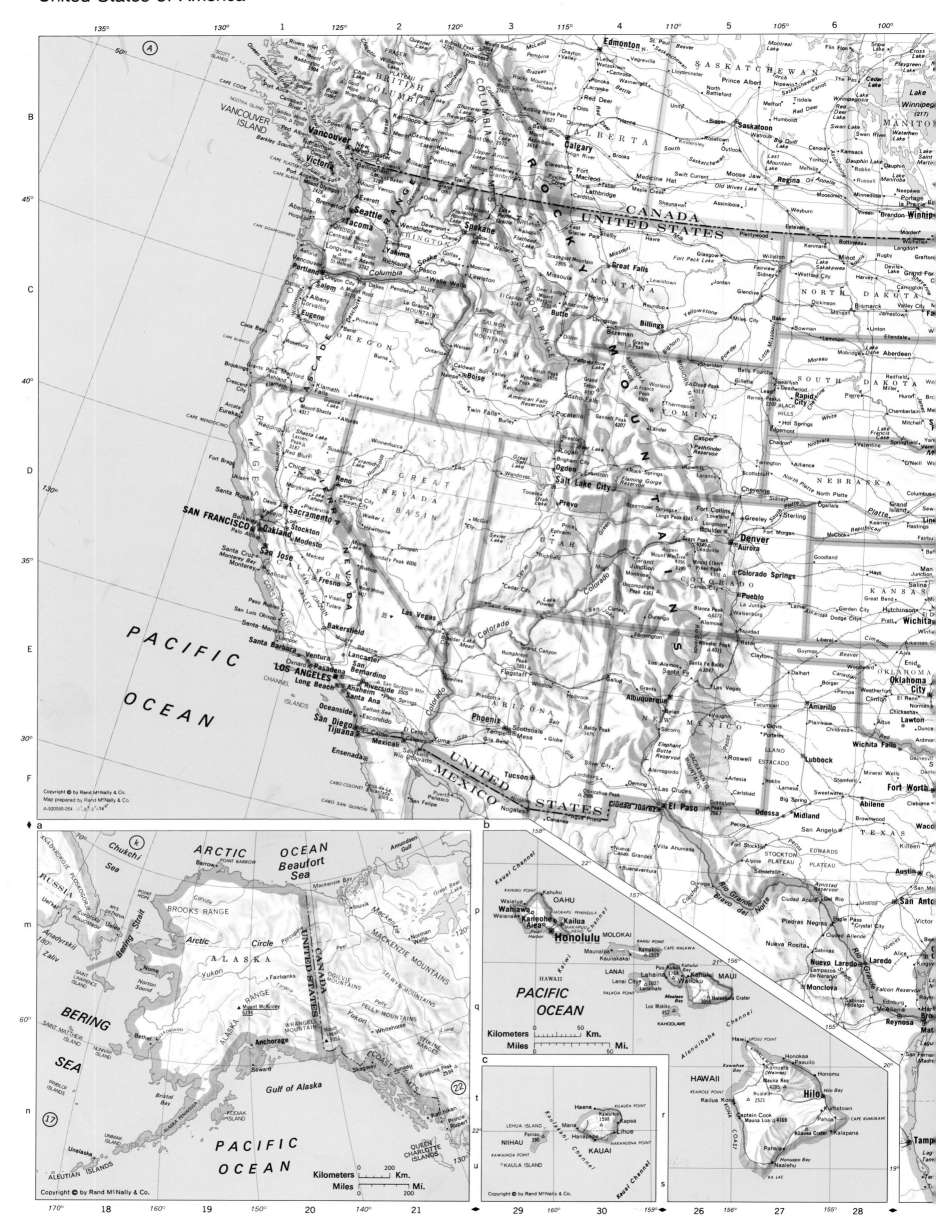

GULF OF

MEXICO

ATLANTIC

OCEAN

CARIBBEAN SEA

WEST INDIES

BERMUDA (U.K.)

BAHAMA

HISPANIOLA

DOMINICAN REPUBLIC

CUBA

Havana

Santo Domingo

Port-au-Prince

Tropic of Cancer

Kilometers 0 200 400 600 Km.

Statute Miles 0 200 400 600 Mi.

Scale 1:12,000,000   One centimeter represents 120 kilometers.
One inch represents approximately 190 miles.
Albers Conical Equal-Area Projection

Alabama

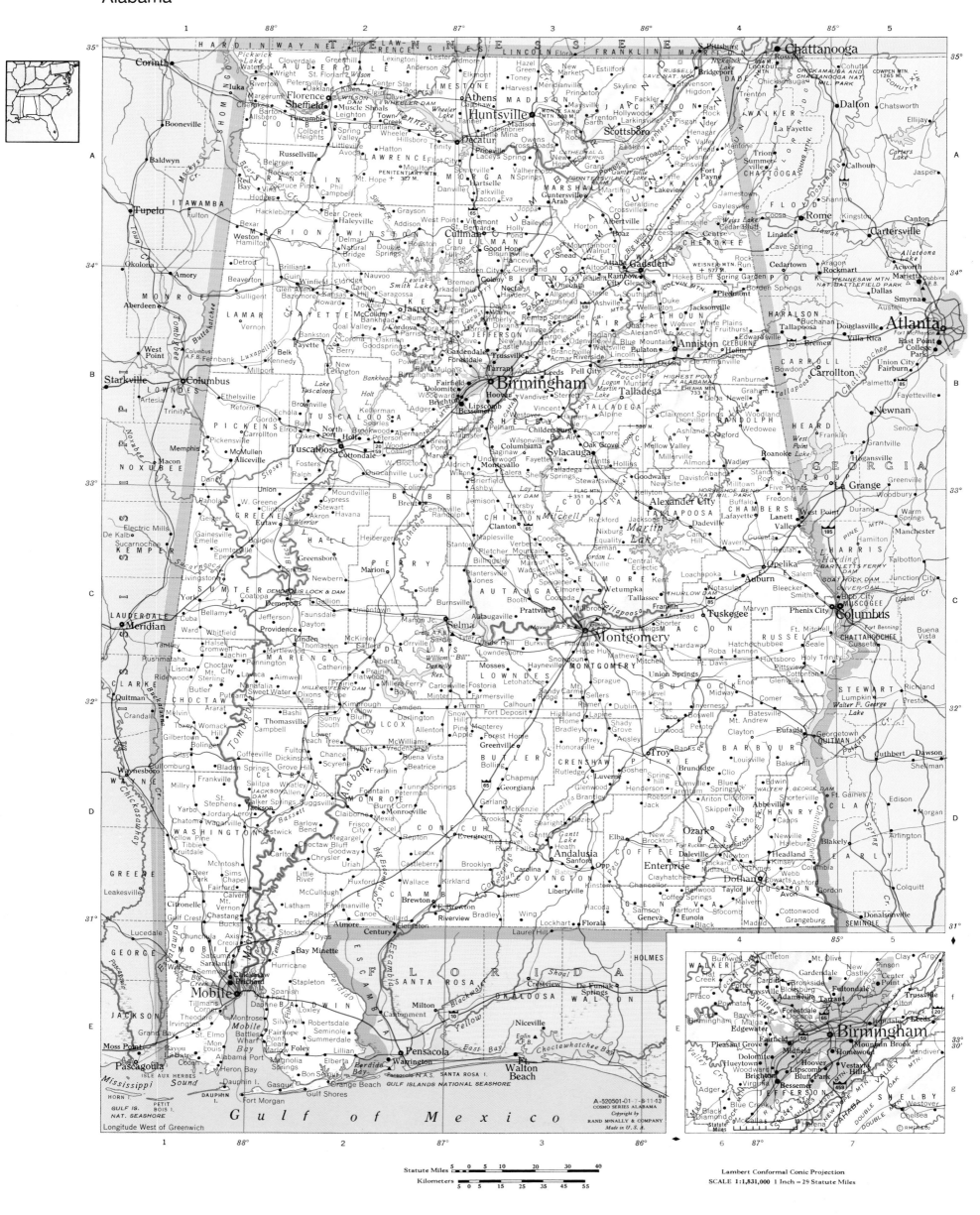

Statute Miles

Kilometers

Lambert Conformal Conic Projection
SCALE 1:1,831,000   1 Inch = 29 Statute Miles

Alaska

Arctic Ocean

Pacific Ocean

Bering Sea

Beaufort Sea

Chukchi Sea

Bristol Bay

Gulf of Alaska

BROOKS RANGE

ALASKA RANGE

COAST MOUNTAINS

KORYAK MOUNTAINS

BRITISH COLUMBIA

CANADA

UNITED STATES

RUSSIA

ALEXANDER ARCHIPELAGO

ALEUTIAN ISLANDS

ALASKA PENINSULA

SEWARD PENINSULA

KENAI PENINSULA

CHUKCHI PENINSULA

ANADYR RANGE

YUKON

KUSKOKWIM

Anchorage

Fairbanks

Juneau

Nome

Sitka

Kodiak

Barrow

Prince Rupert

Whitehorse

Ketchikan

DENALI NAT. PARK

GATES OF THE ARCTIC NAT. PARK

WRANGELL-ST. ELIAS NAT. PARK

KENAI FJORDS NAT. PARK

KATMAI NAT. PARK

LAKE CLARK NAT. PARK

GLACIER BAY NAT. PARK

KLONDIKE GOLD RUSH NAT. HIST. PARK

MT. McKINLEY 6194 M. HIGHEST IN NORTH AMERICA

OSTROV VRANGELYA (WRANGEL I.)

NUNIVAK ISLAND

ST. LAWRENCE ISLAND

PRIBILOF ISLANDS

QUEEN CHARLOTTE ISLANDS

PRINCE OF WALES

KODIAK I.

Cook Inlet

Norton Sound

Bristol Bay

Hecate Strait

Dixon Entrance

Statute Miles 50 25 0 50 100 150 200 250

Kilometers 50 0 100 200 300

Polyconic Projection
SCALE 1:12,000,000   1 Inch = 189 Statute Miles

A-509502-01-5-16. COSMO SERIES ALASKA. Copyright by RAND McNALLY & COMPANY Made in U.S.A.

Arizona

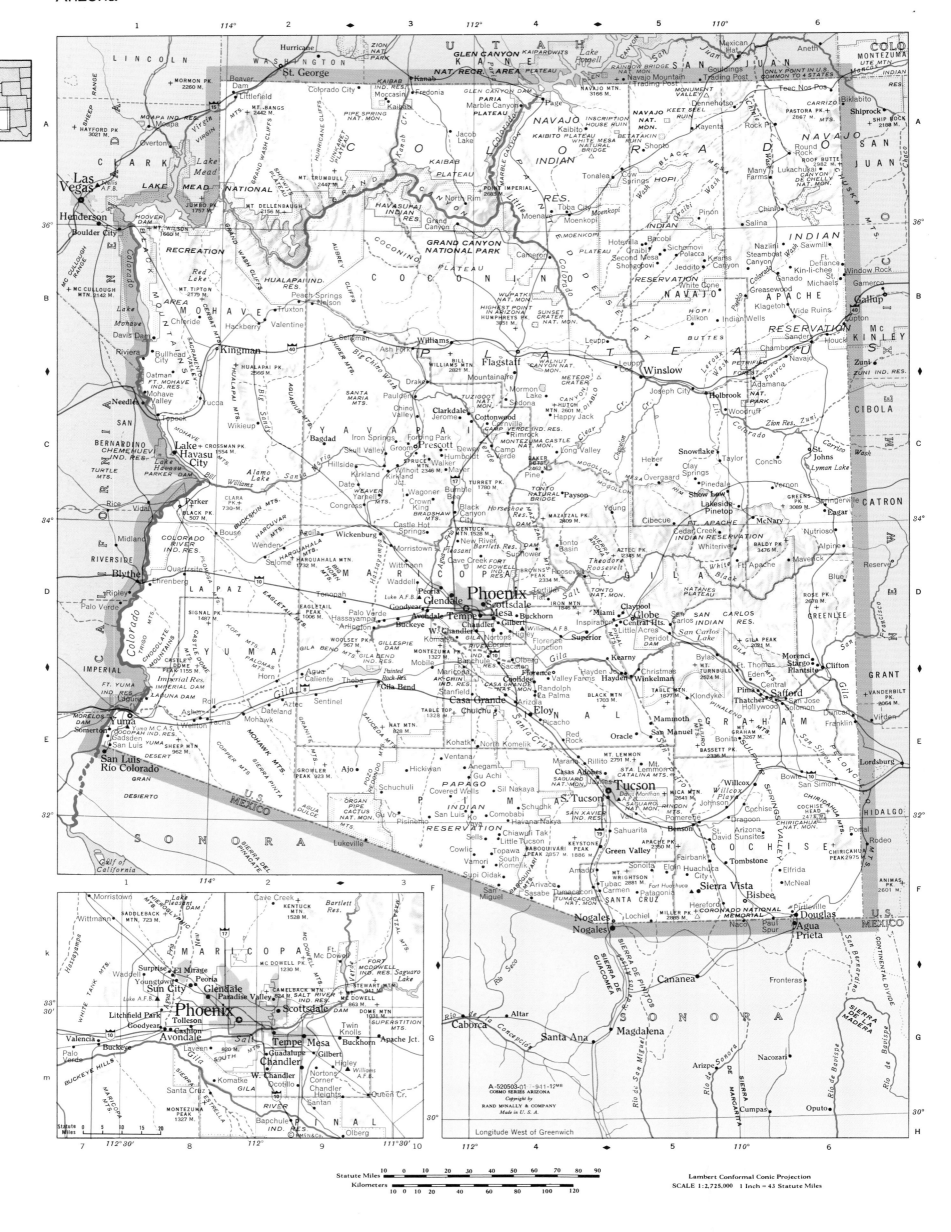

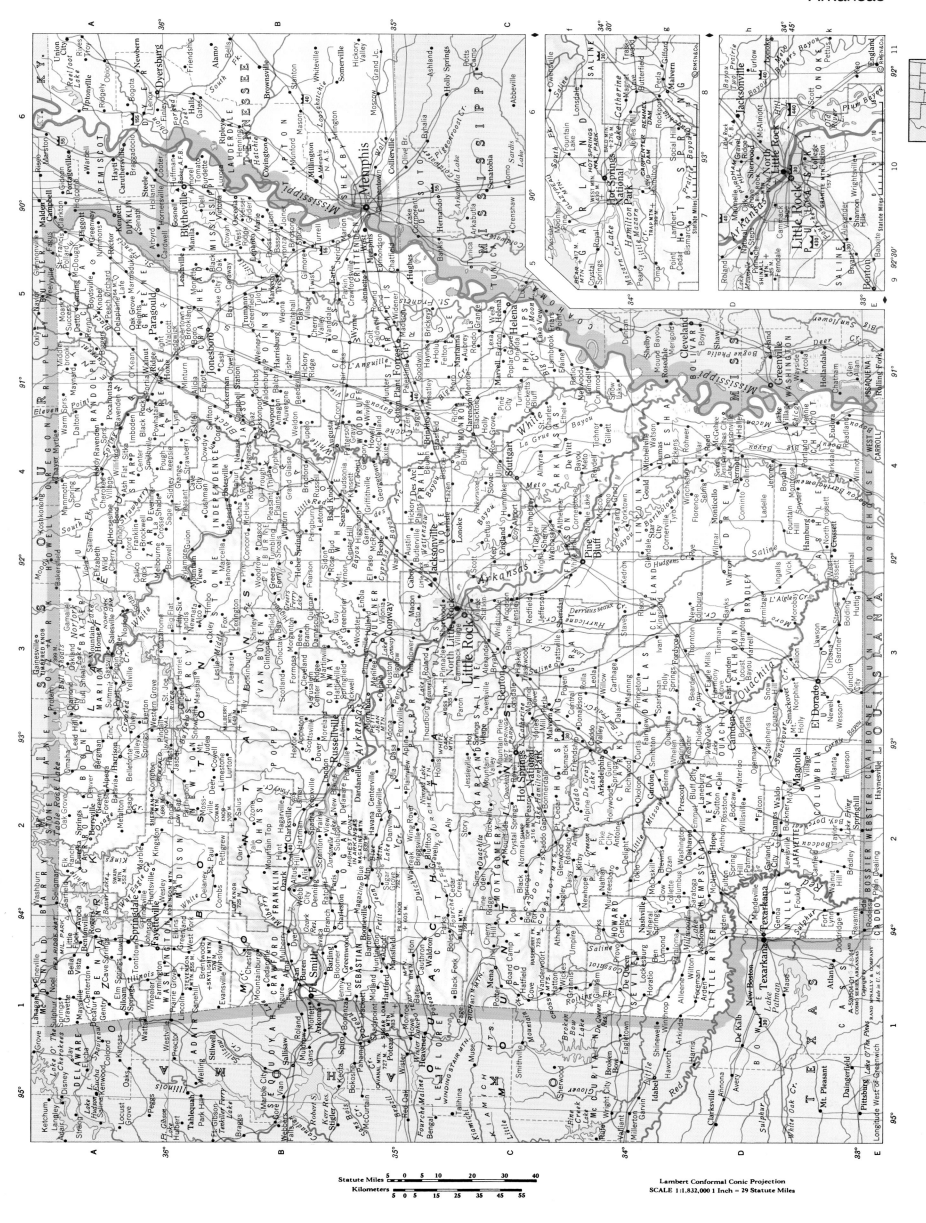

Statute Miles 5 0 5 10 20 30 40
Kilometers 5 0 5 15 25 35 45 55

Lambert Conformal Conic Projection
SCALE 1:1,832,000 1 Inch = 29 Statute Miles

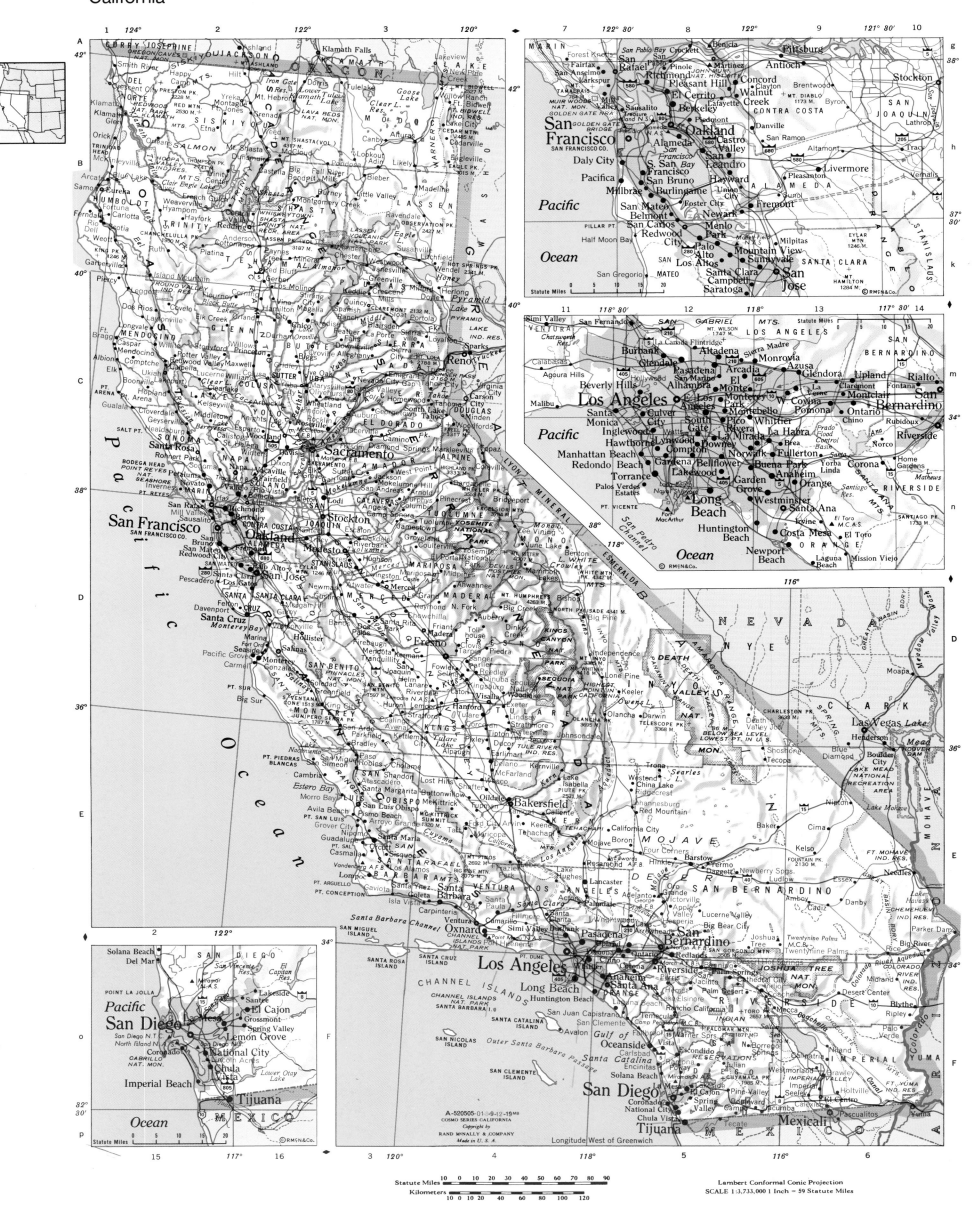

California

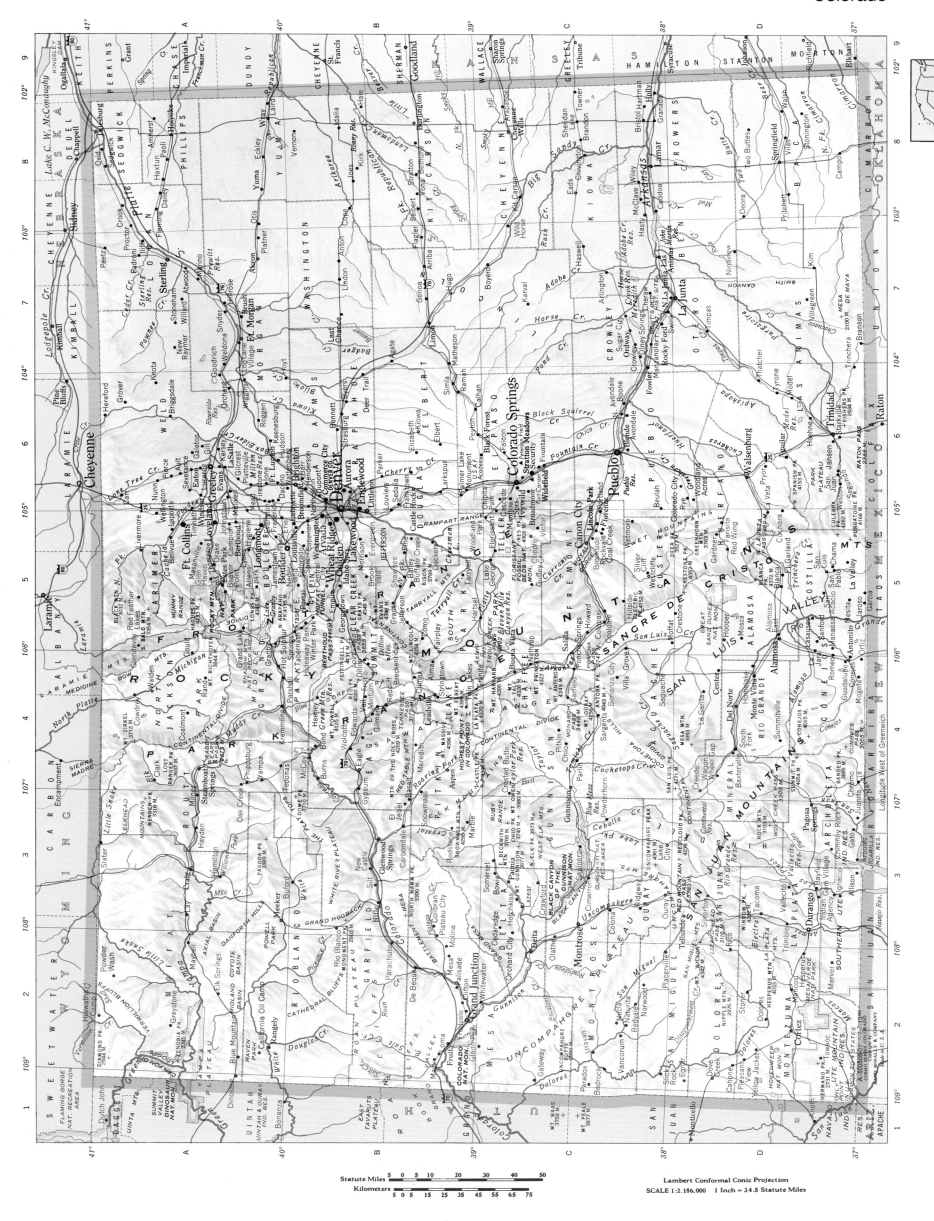

Statute Miles 5 0 5 10 20 30 40 50
Kilometers 5 0 5 15 25 35 45 55 65 75

Lambert Conformal Conic Projection
SCALE 1:2.186.000   1 Inch = 34.5 Statute Miles

Connecticut

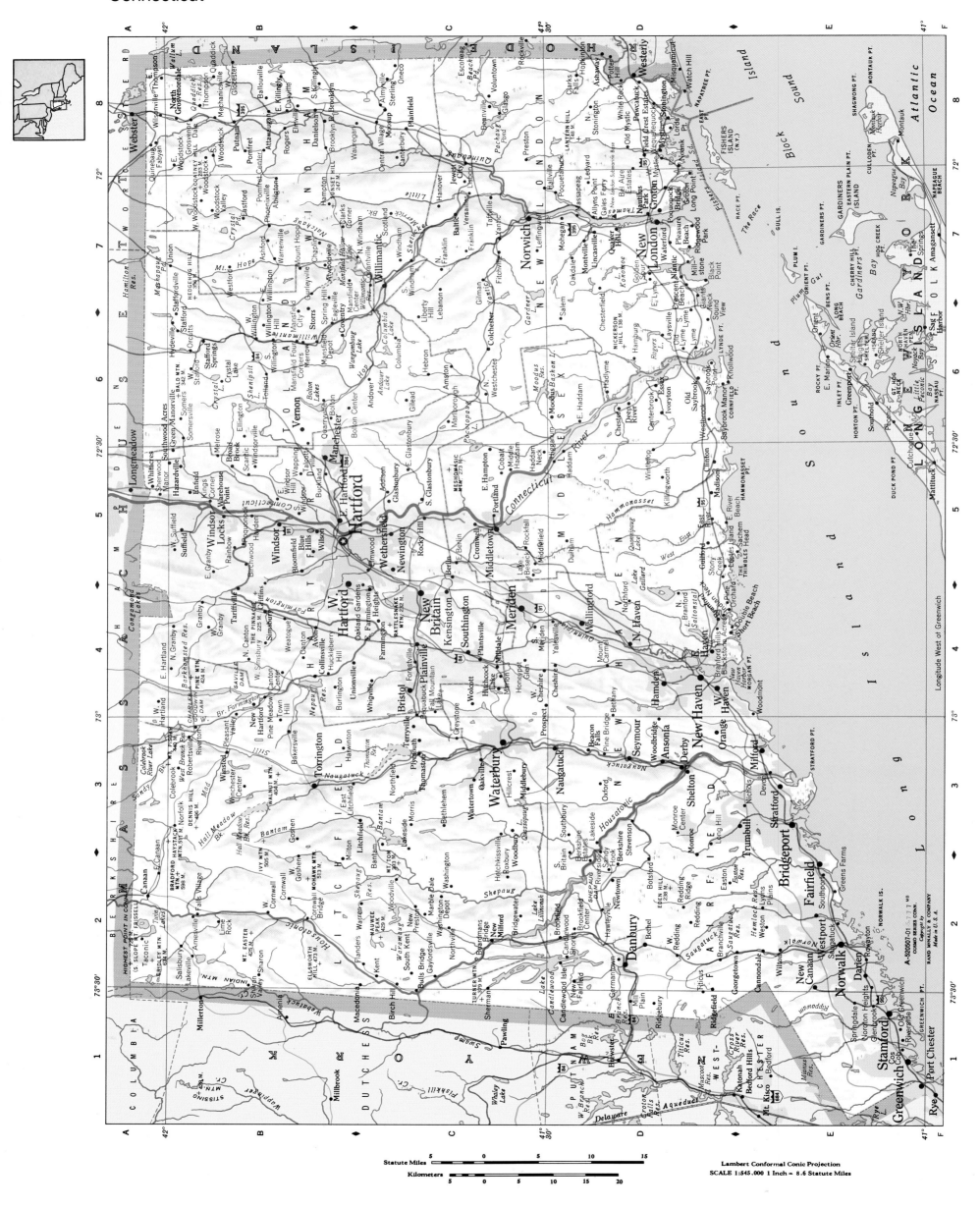

Statute Miles

Kilometers

Lambert Conformal Conic Projection
SCALE 1:545,000   1 Inch = 8.6 Statute Miles

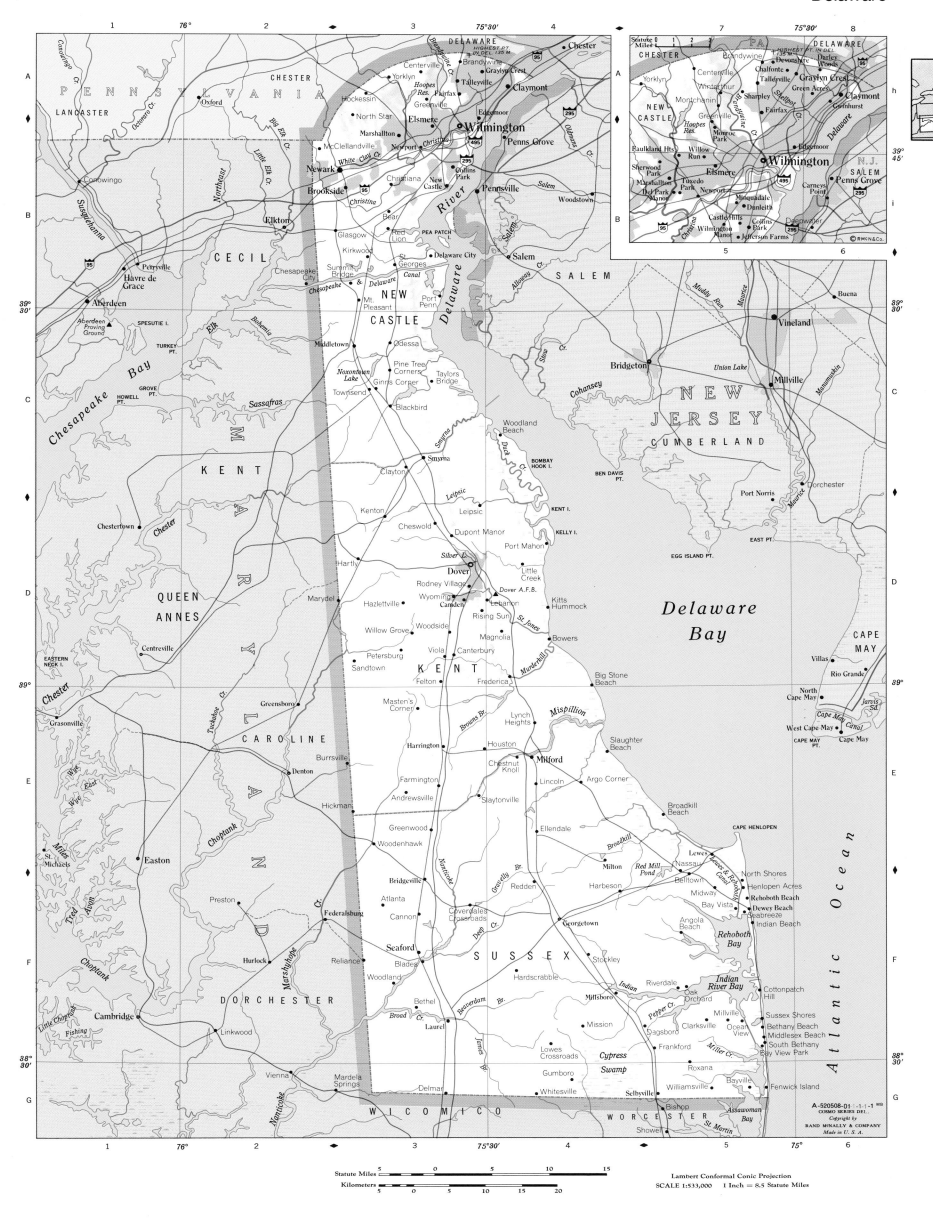

Lambert Conformal Conic Projection
SCALE 1:533,000   1 Inch = 8.5 Statute Miles

A-520508-01 1-1-1-1 MB
COSMO SERIES DEL.
Copyright by
RAND McNALLY & COMPANY
Made in U. S. A.

Florida

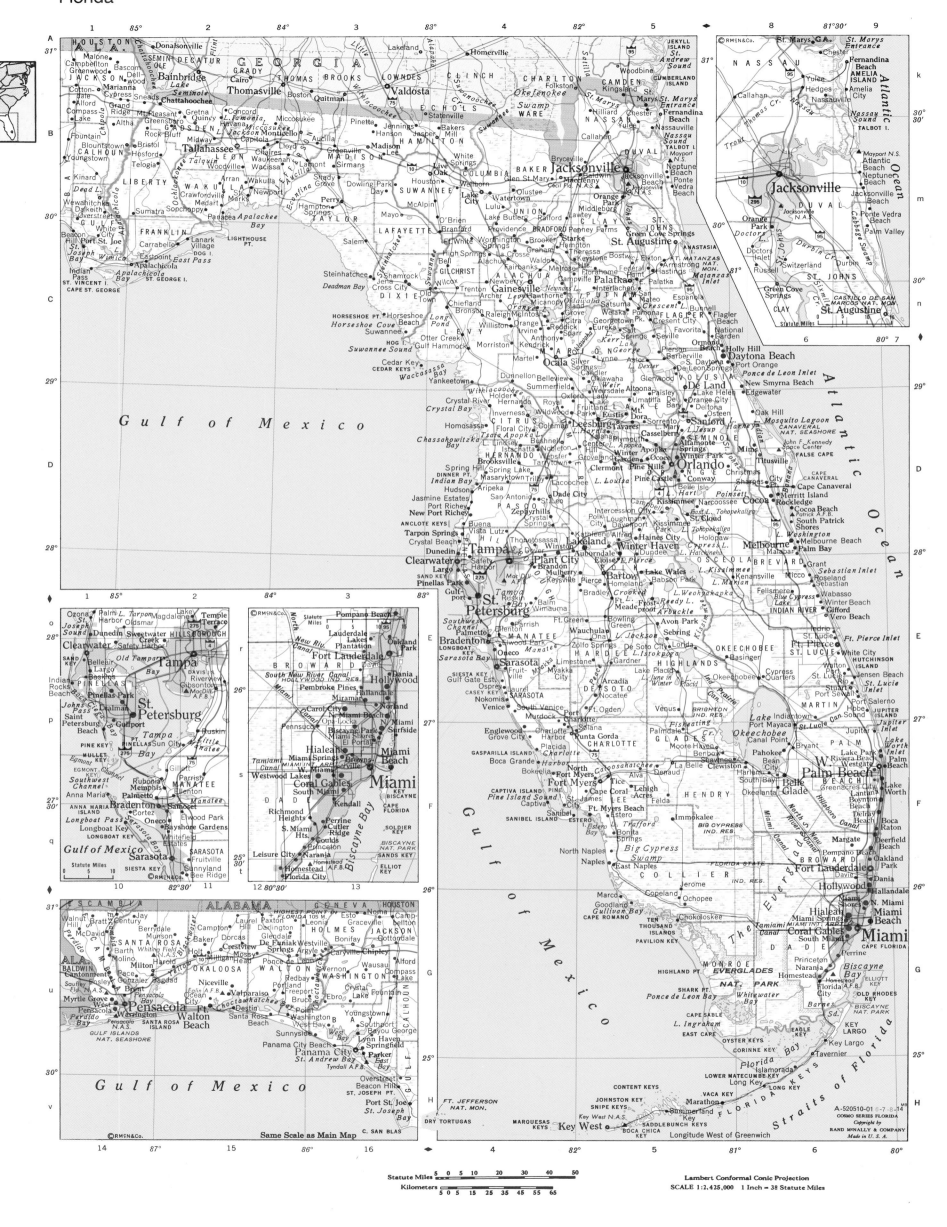

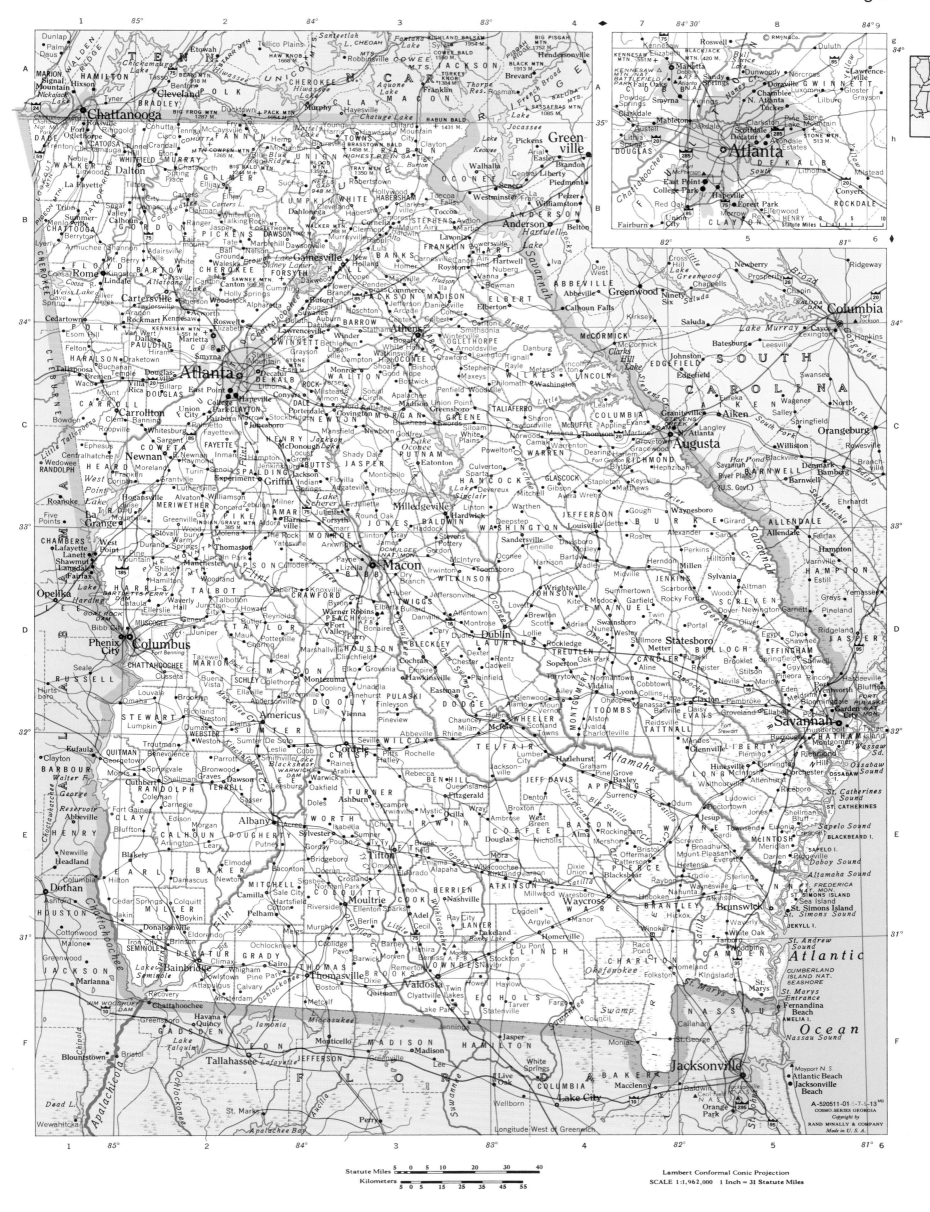

Statute Miles
5 0 5 10 20 30 40
Kilometers
5 0 5 15 25 35 45 55

Lambert Conformal Conic Projection
SCALE 1:1,962,000 1 Inch = 31 Statute Miles

A-520511-01 -7-5-13
COSMO-SERIES GEORGIA
Copyright by
RAND McNALLY & COMPANY
Made in U. S. A.

Hawaii

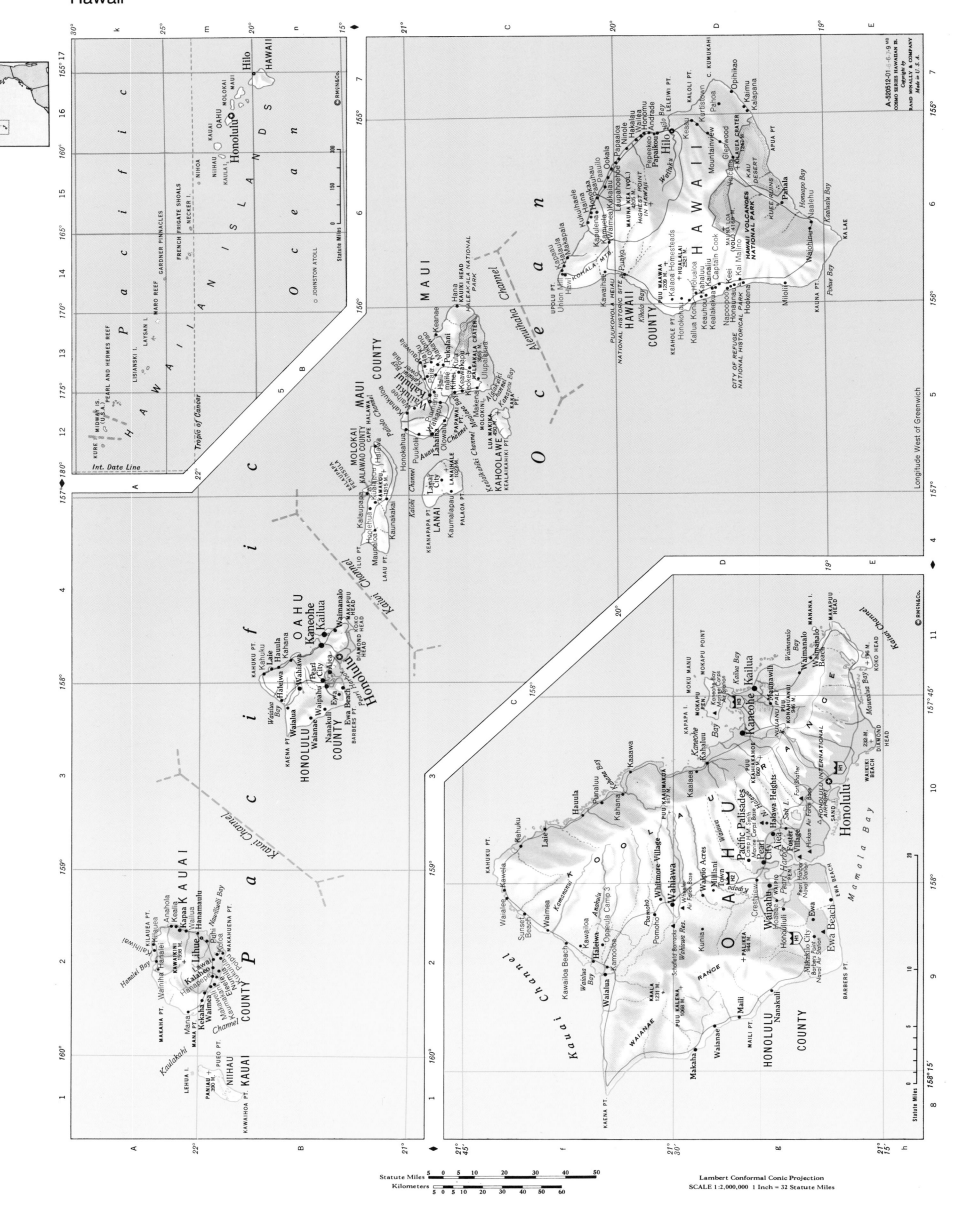

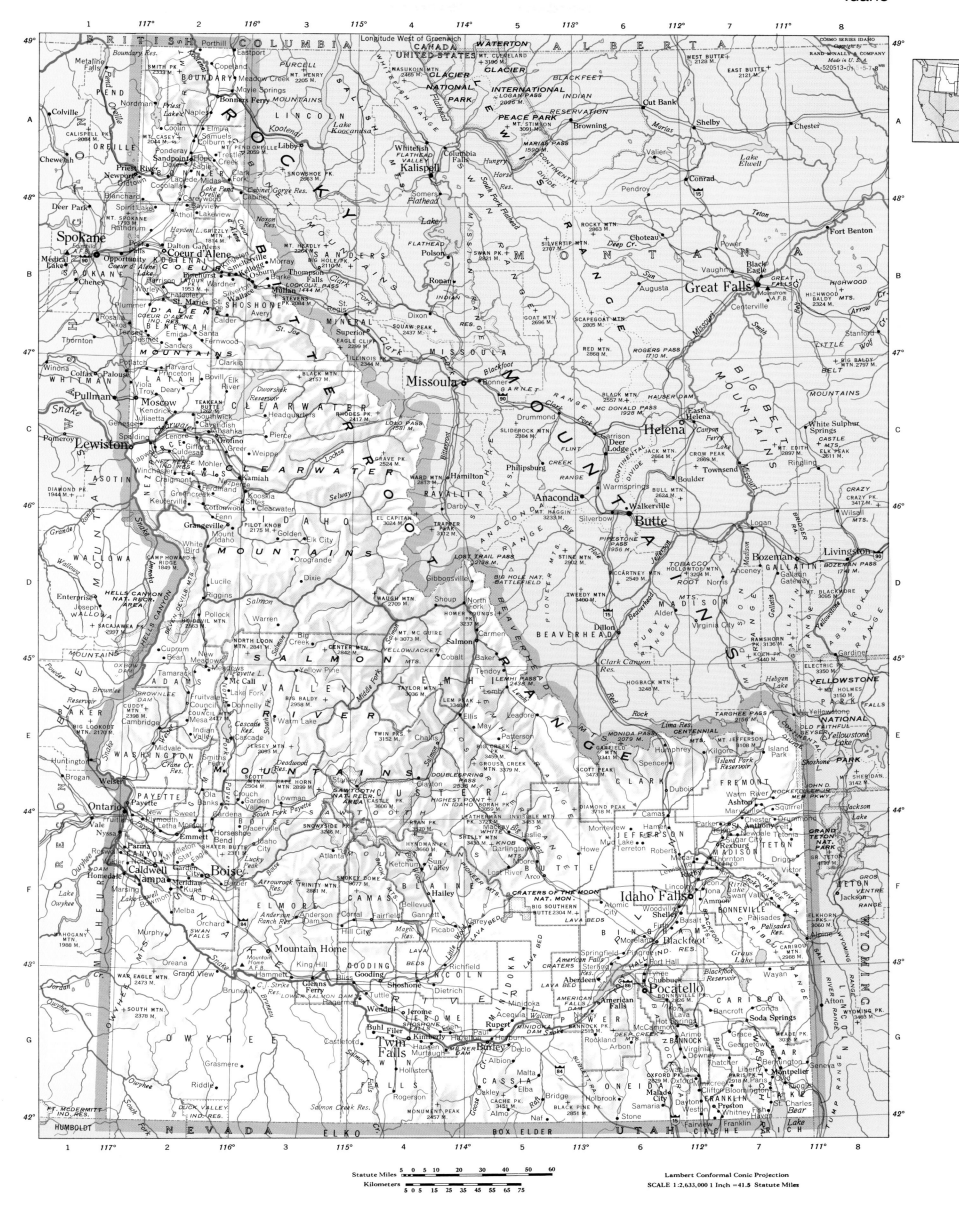

Statute Miles 5 0 5 10 20 30 40 50 60

Kilometers 5 0 5 15 25 35 45 55 65 75

Lambert Conformal Conic Projection
SCALE 1:2,633,000 1 Inch = 41.5 Statute Miles

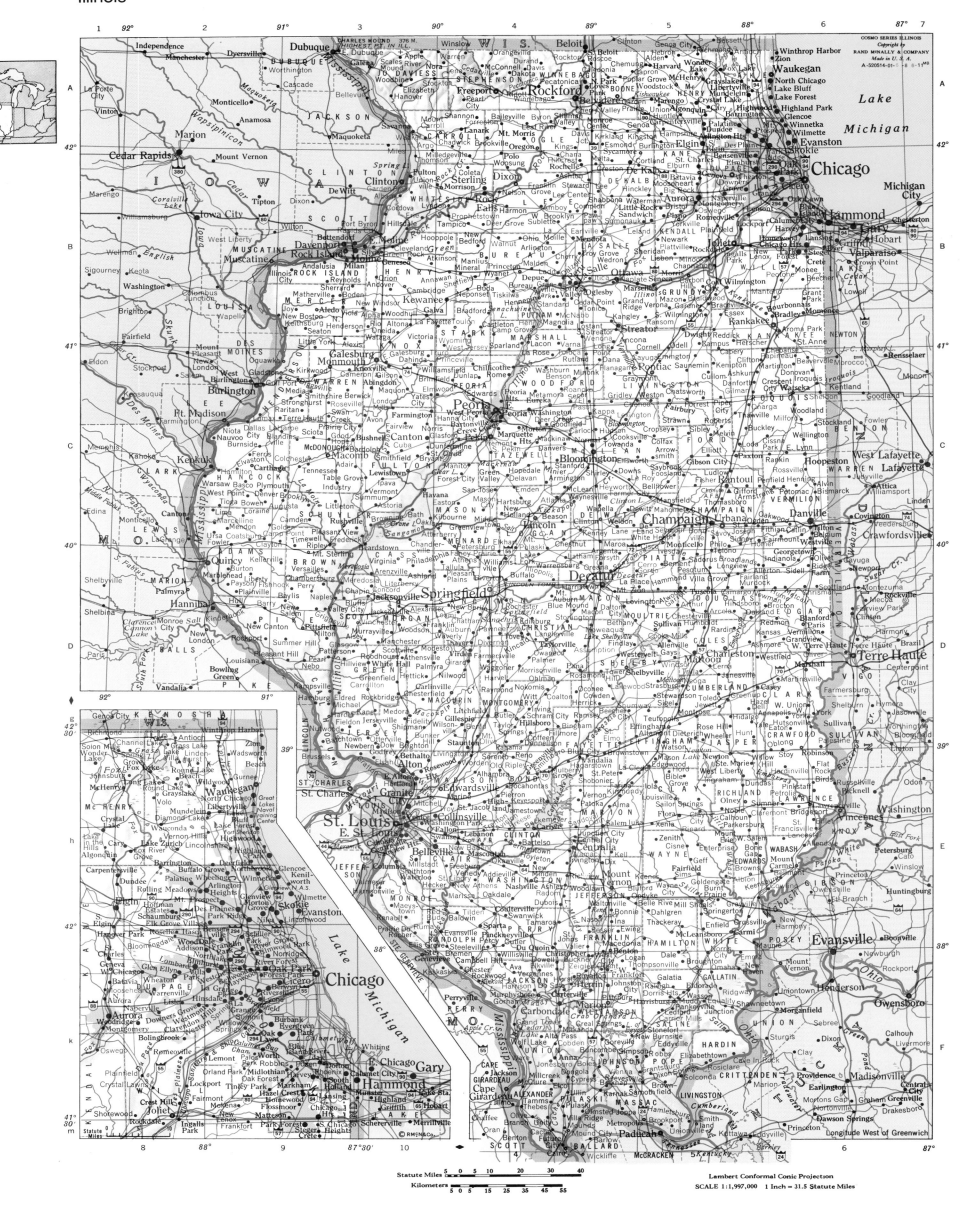

Illustration

Illinois

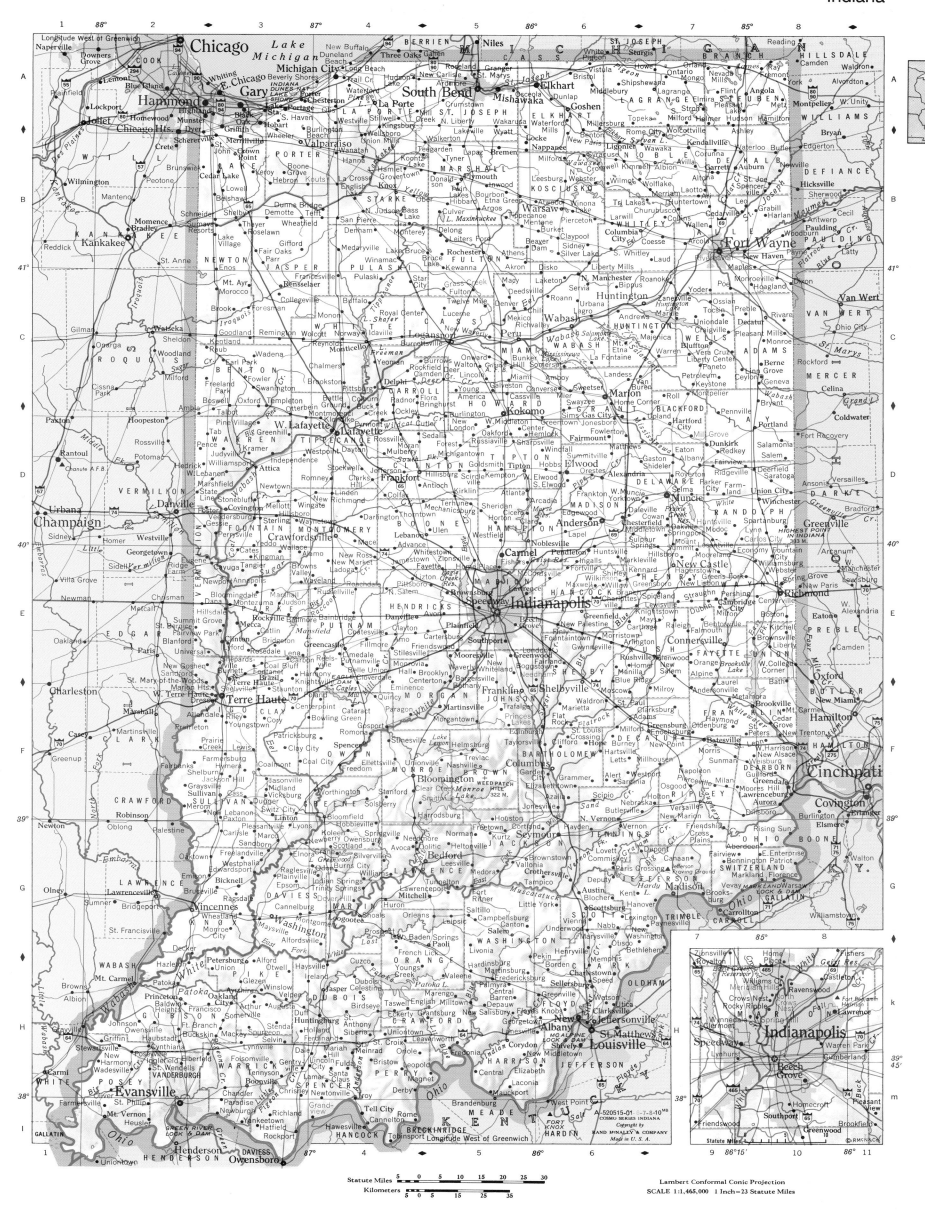

Indiana

Statute Miles 5 0 5 10 15 20 25 30
Kilometers 5 0 5 10 15 25 35

Lambert Conformal Conic Projection
SCALE 1:1,465,000 1 Inch = 23 Statute Miles

A-520515-01 6-7-8-10 MB
COSMO Series Indiana
Copyright by
RAND McNALLY & COMPANY
Made in U.S.A.

121

Iowa

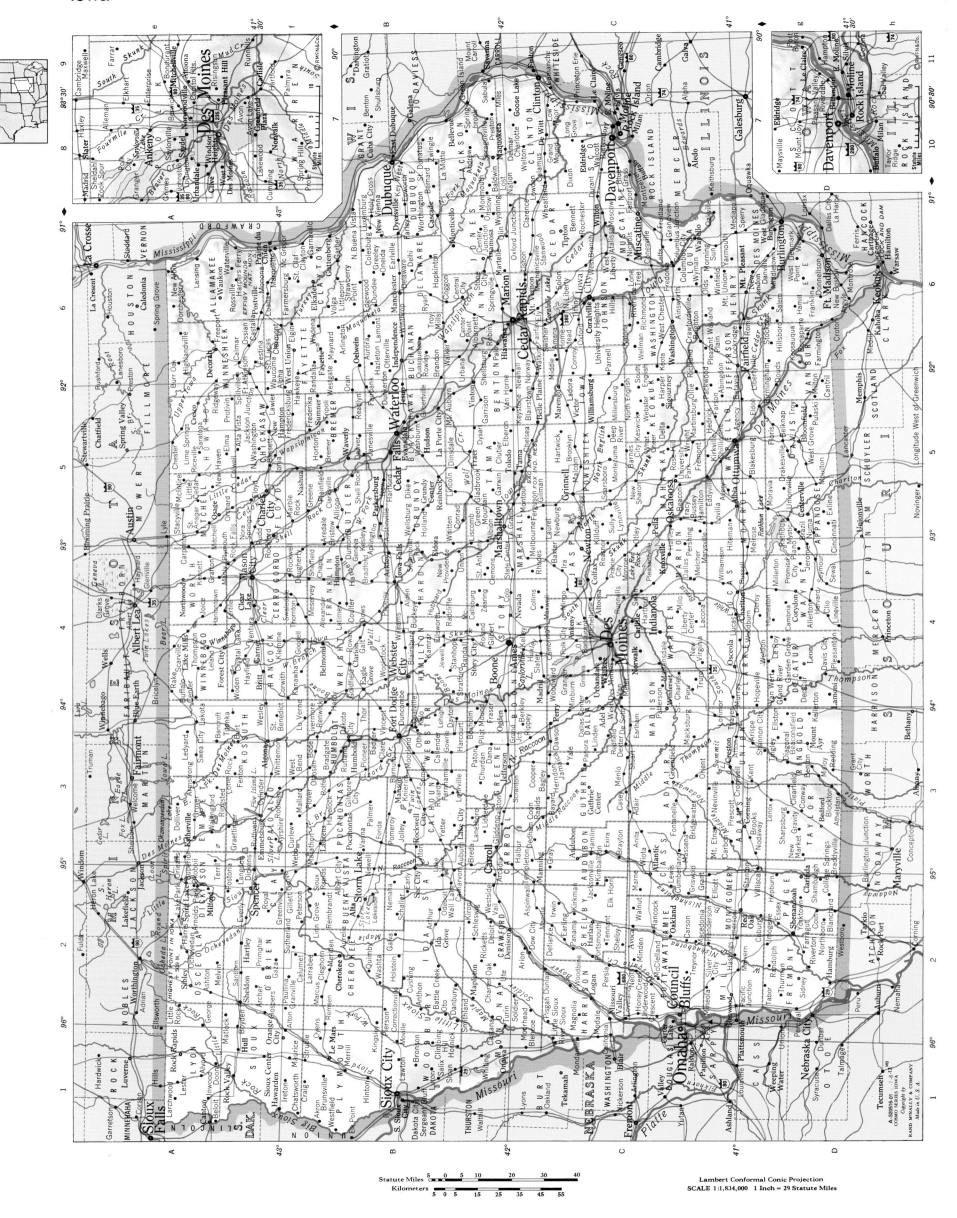

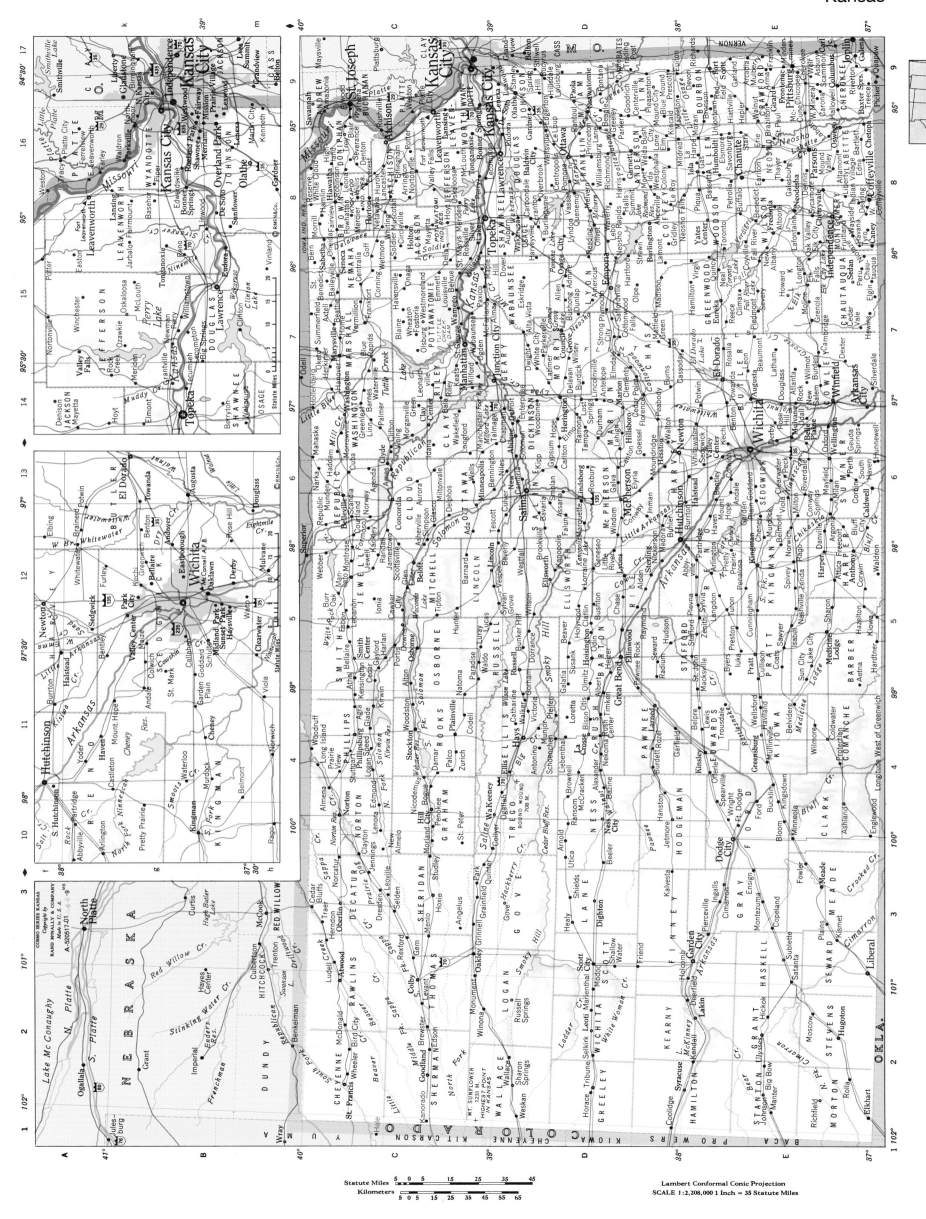

Kentucky

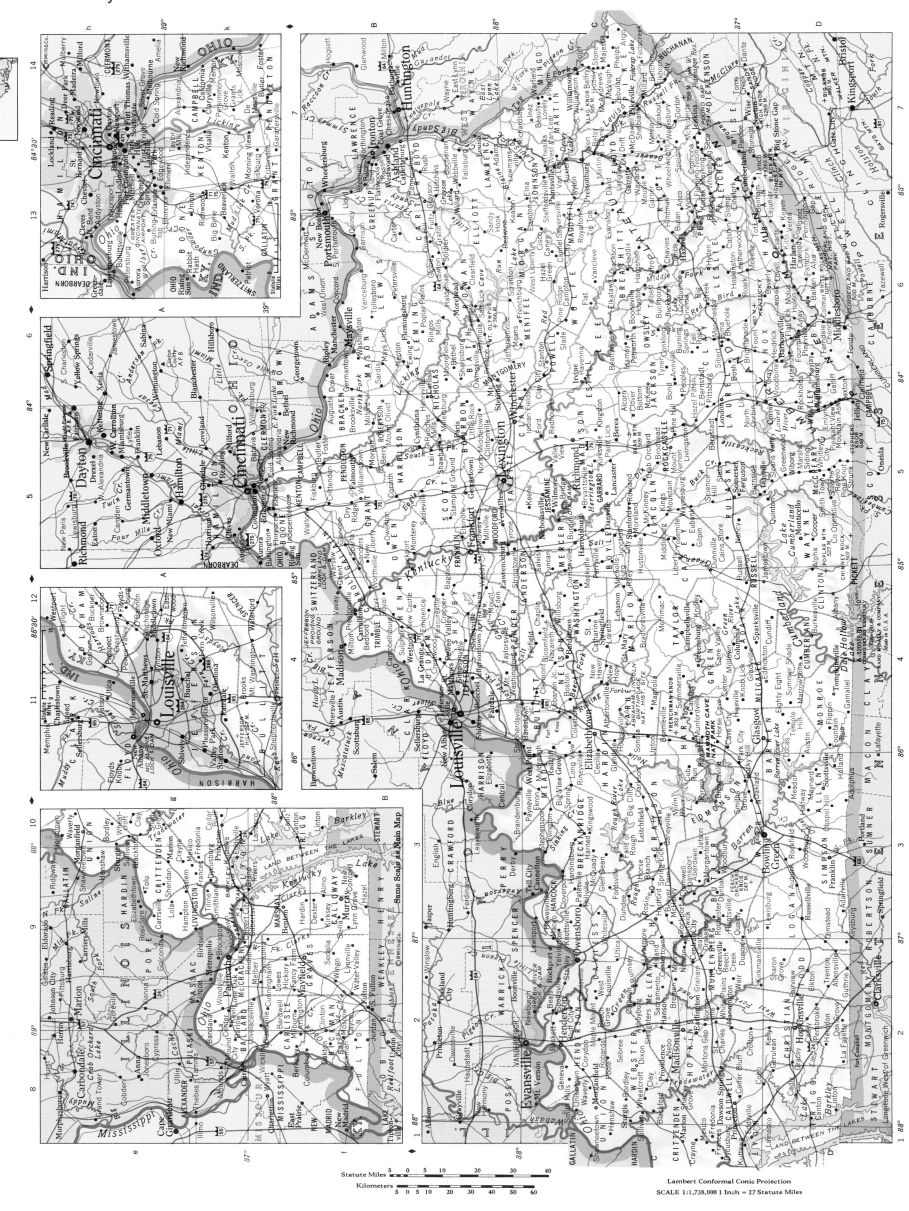

Statute Miles 5 0 5 10 20 30 40
Kilometers 5 0 5 10 20 30 40 50 60

Lambert Conformal Conic Projection
SCALE 1:1,738,000 1 Inch = 27 Statute Miles

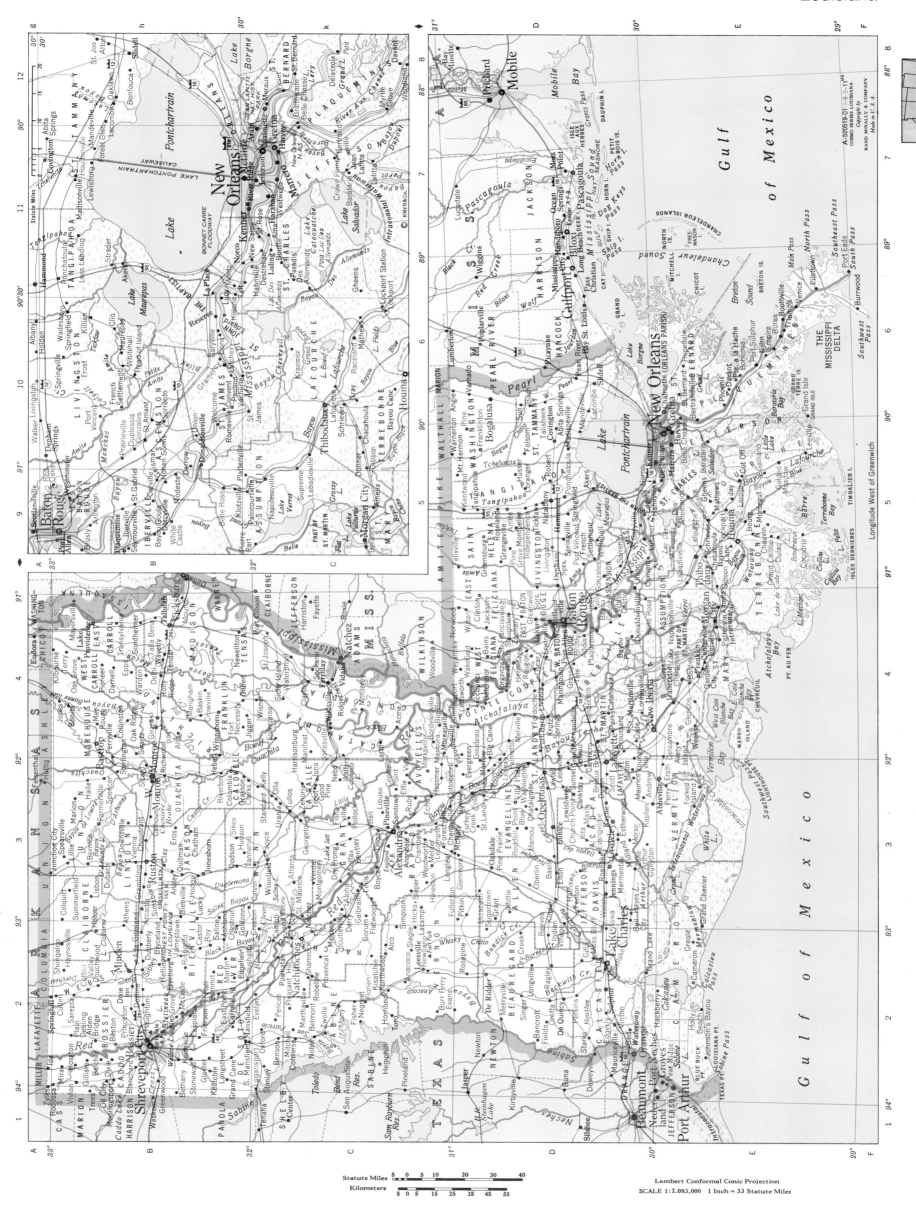

Louisiana

Gulf of Mexico

Gulf of Mexico

Statute Miles

Kilometers

Lambert Conformal Conic Projection
SCALE 1:2,083,000   1 Inch = 33 Statute Miles

Maine

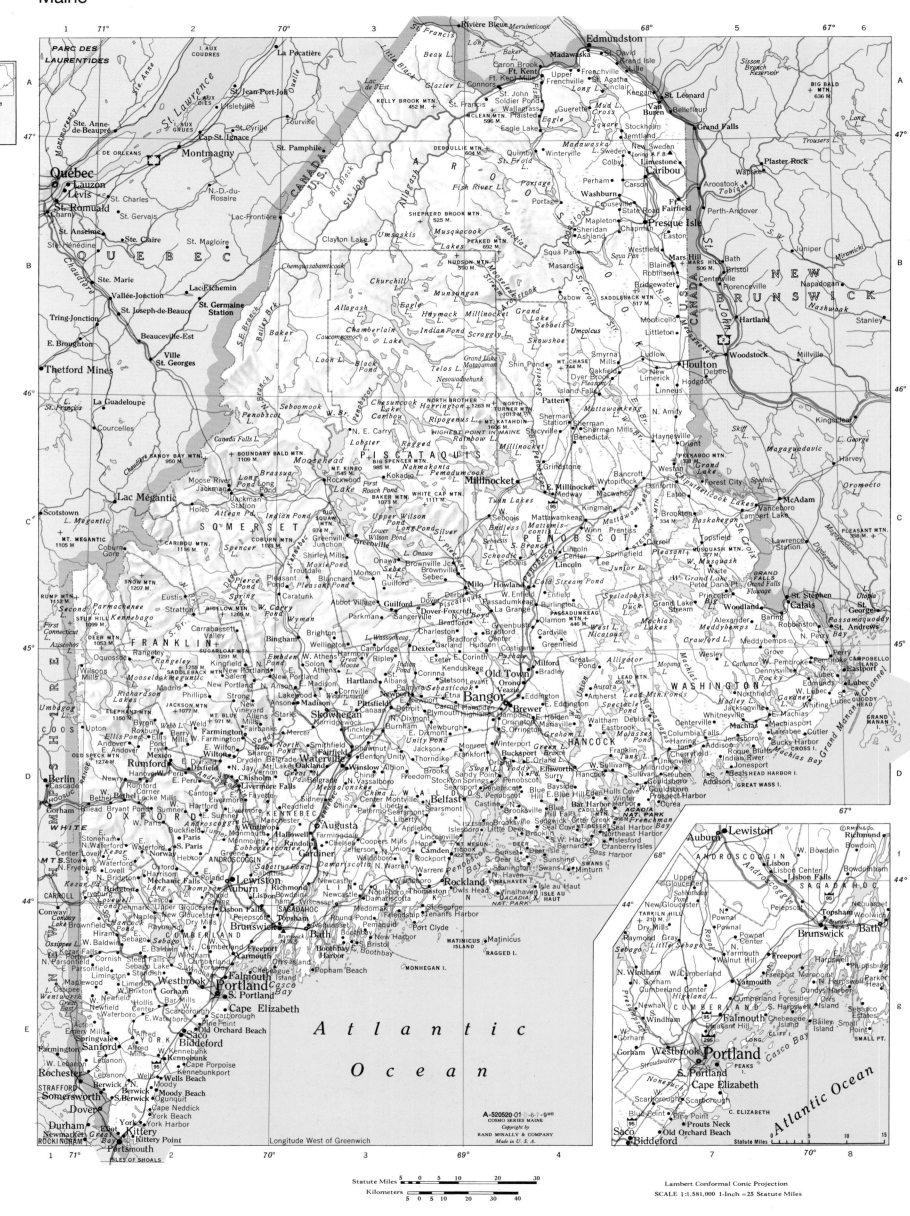

Statute Miles

Kilometers

A-520520-01 -6-7-9MB
COSMO SERIES MAINE
Copyright by
RAND M^cNALLY & COMPANY
Made in U.S.A.

Longitude West of Greenwich

Lambert Conformal Conic Projection
SCALE 1:1,581,000 1-Inch =25 Statute Miles

®RM^cN&Co.

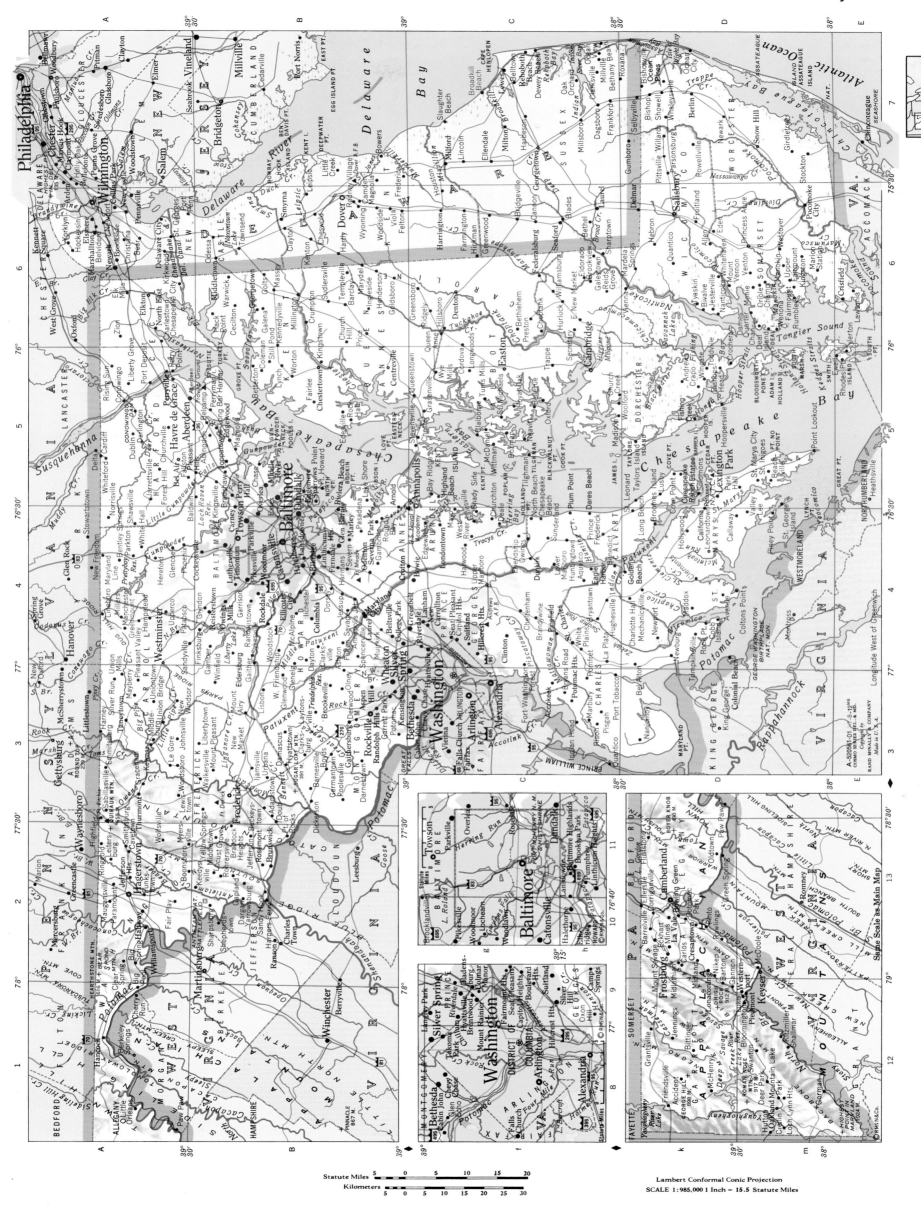

Statute Miles
Kilometers

Lambert Conformal Conic Projection
SCALE 1:985,000 1 Inch = 15.5 Statute Miles

Massachusetts

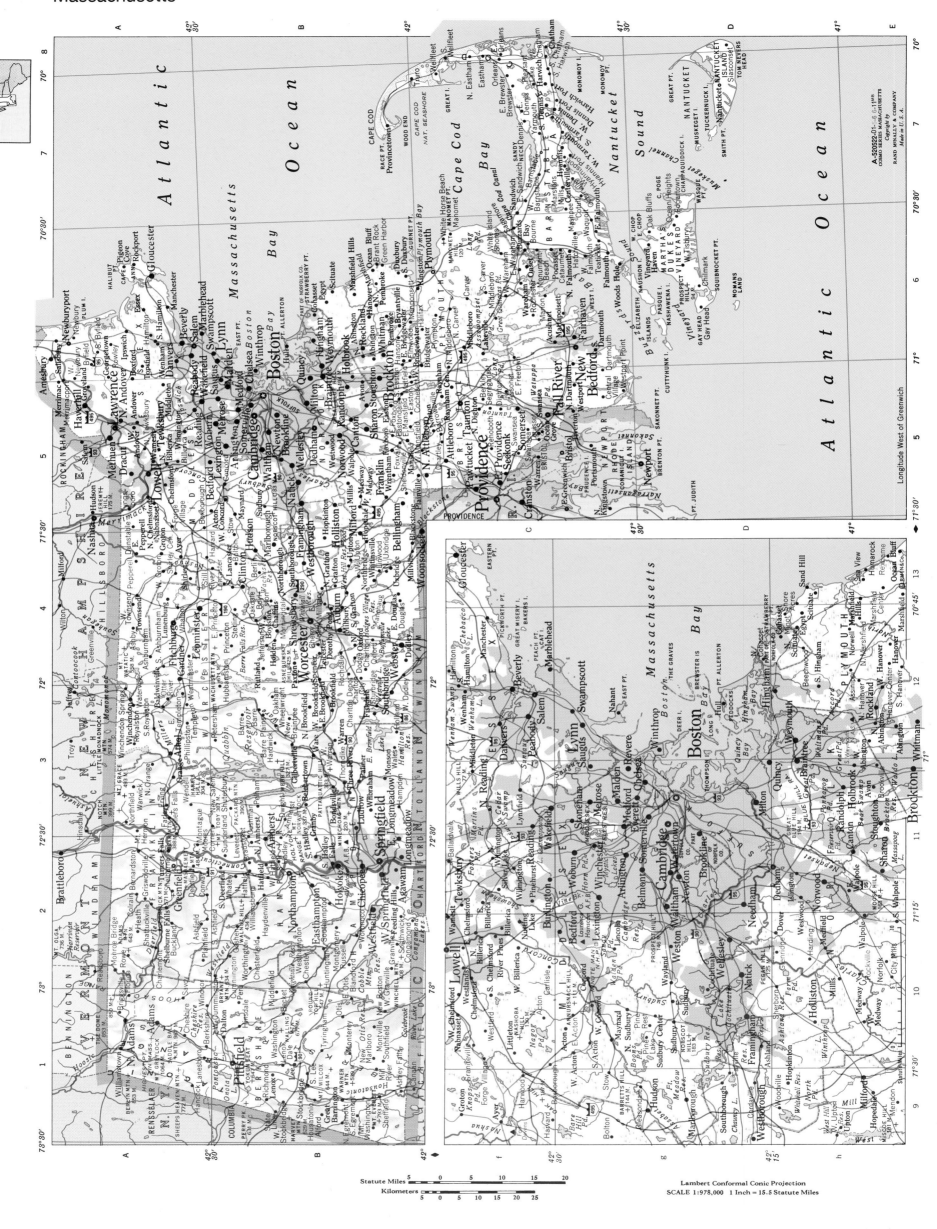

Statute Miles
Kilometers

Lambert Conformal Conic Projection
SCALE 1:978,000   1 Inch = 15.5 Statute Miles

128

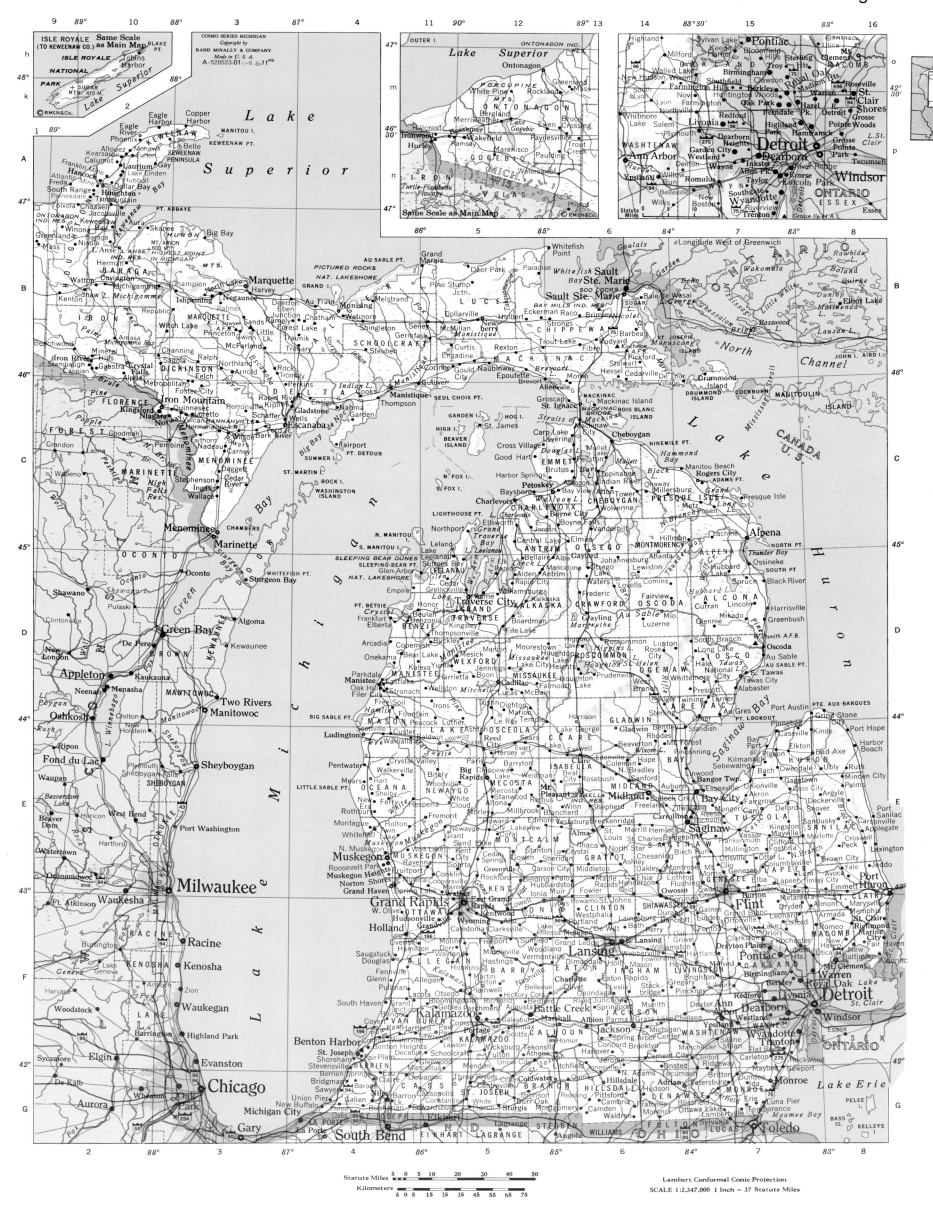

Lambert Conformal Conic Projection
SCALE 1:2,347,000 1 Inch = 37 Statute Miles

Minnesota

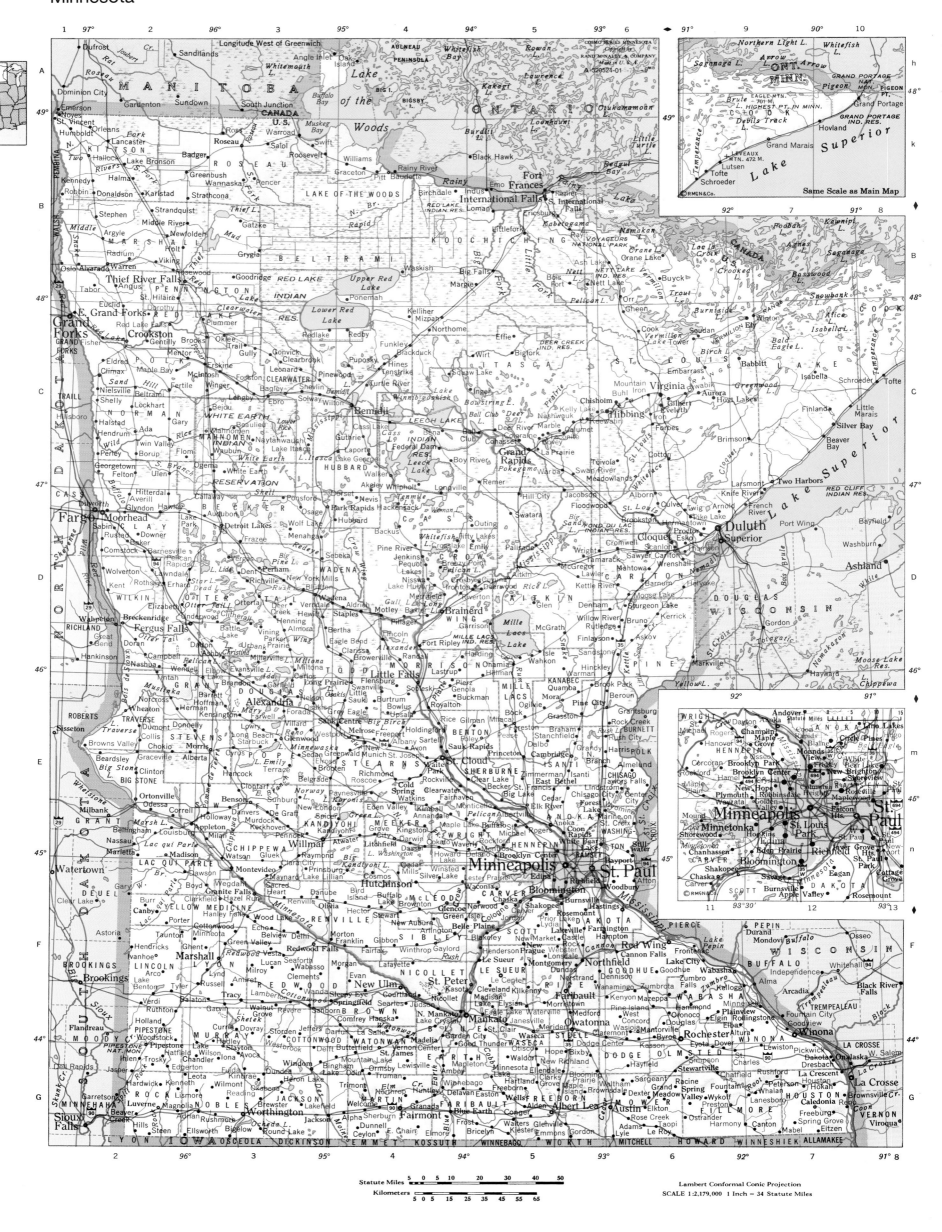

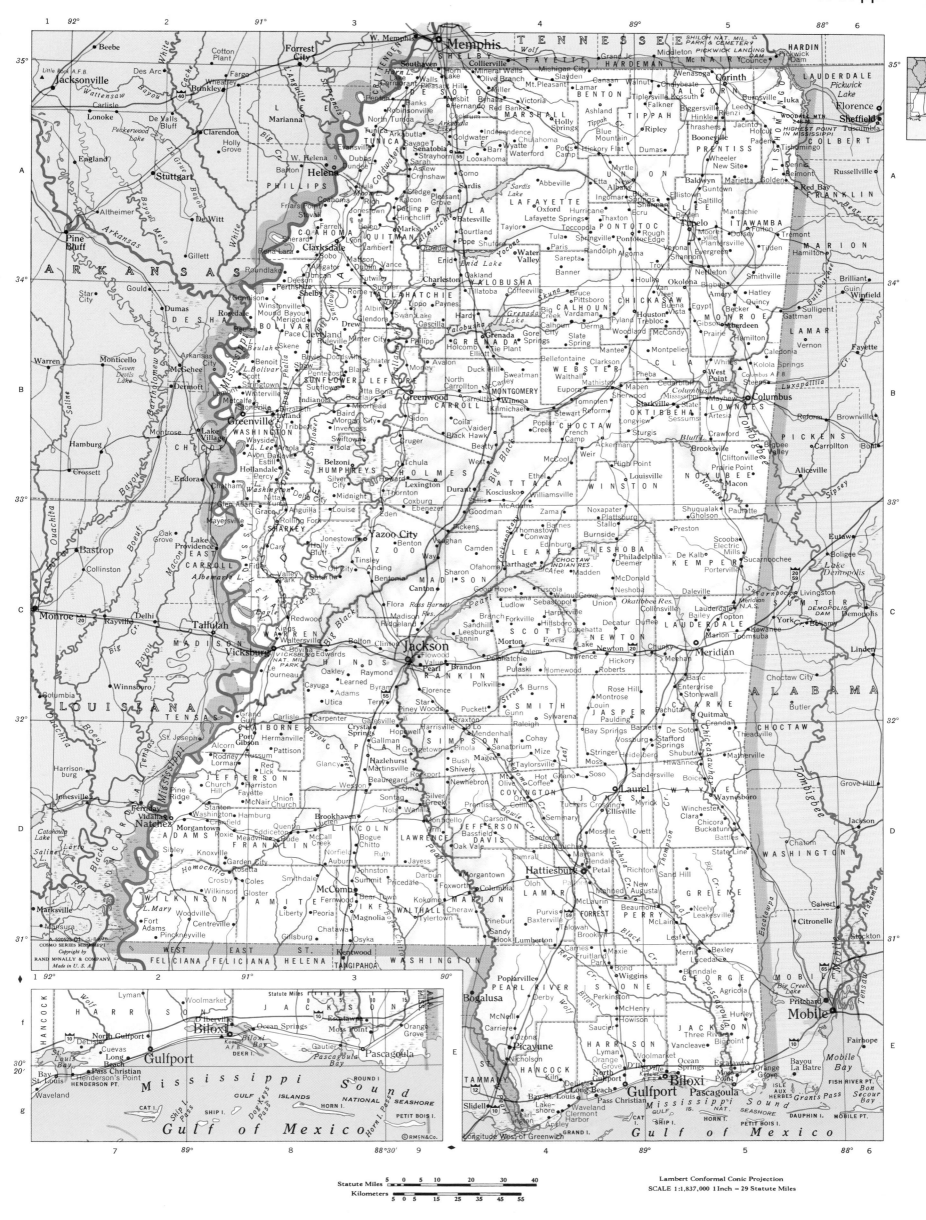

Lambert Conformal Conic Projection
SCALE 1:1,837,000 1 Inch = 29 Statute Miles

Statute Miles 5 0 5 10 20 30 40
Kilometers 5 0 5 15 25 35 45 55

Missouri

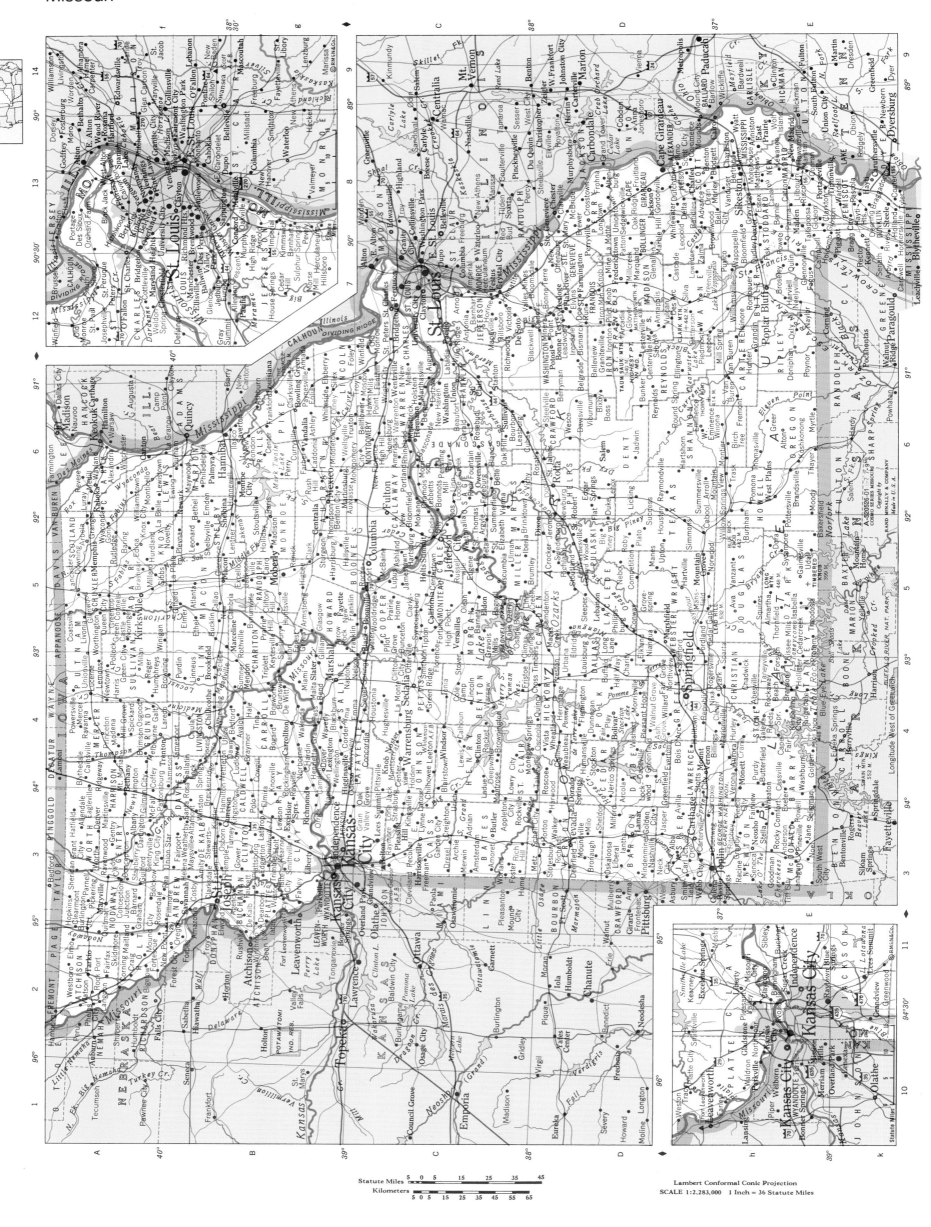

Statute Miles 5 0 5 15 25 35 45
Kilometers 5 0 5 15 25 35 45 55 65

Lambert Conformal Conic Projection
SCALE 1:2,283,000   1 Inch = 36 Statute Miles

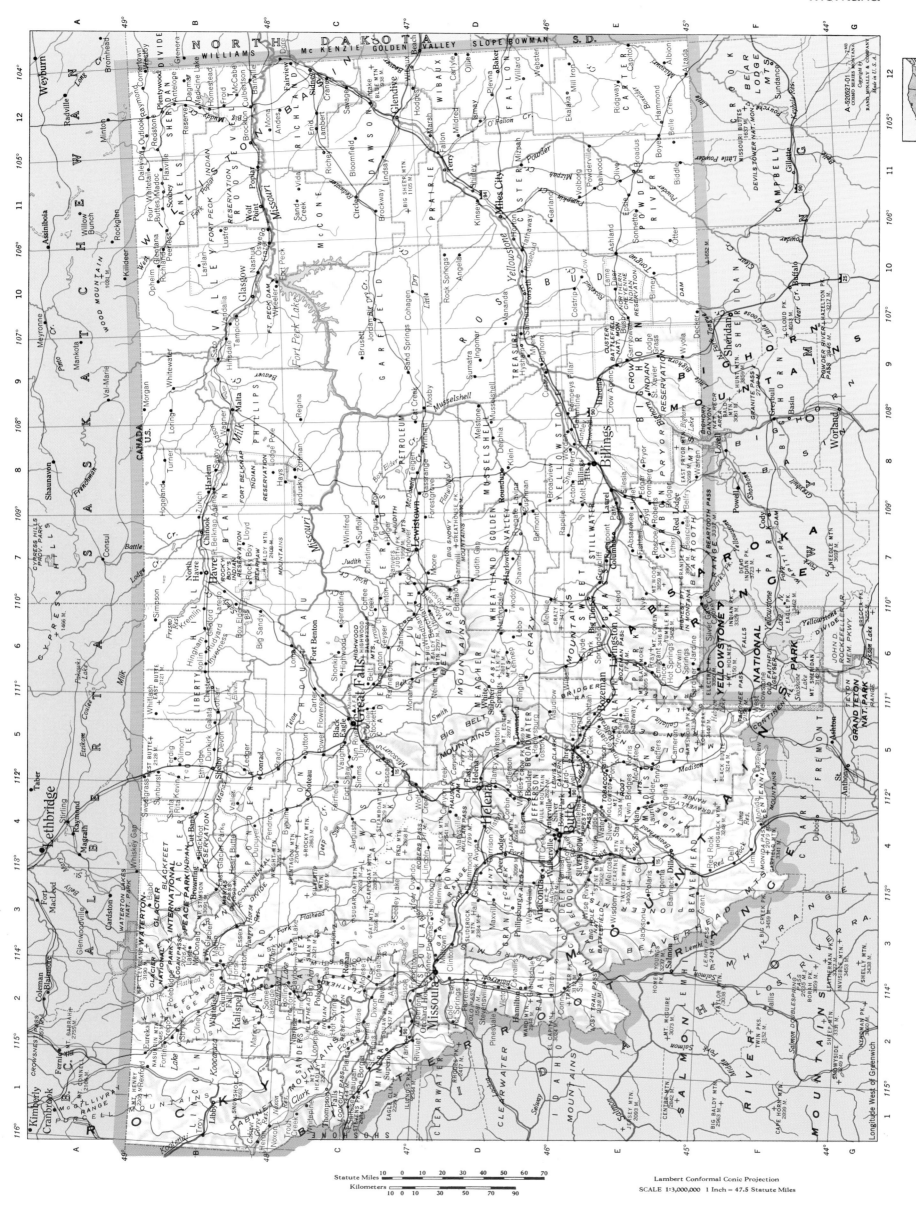

Statute Miles 10 0 10 20 30 40 50 60 70
Kilometers 10 0 10 30 50 70 90

Lambert Conformal Conic Projection
SCALE 1:3,000,000   1 Inch = 47.5 Statute Miles

Nebraska

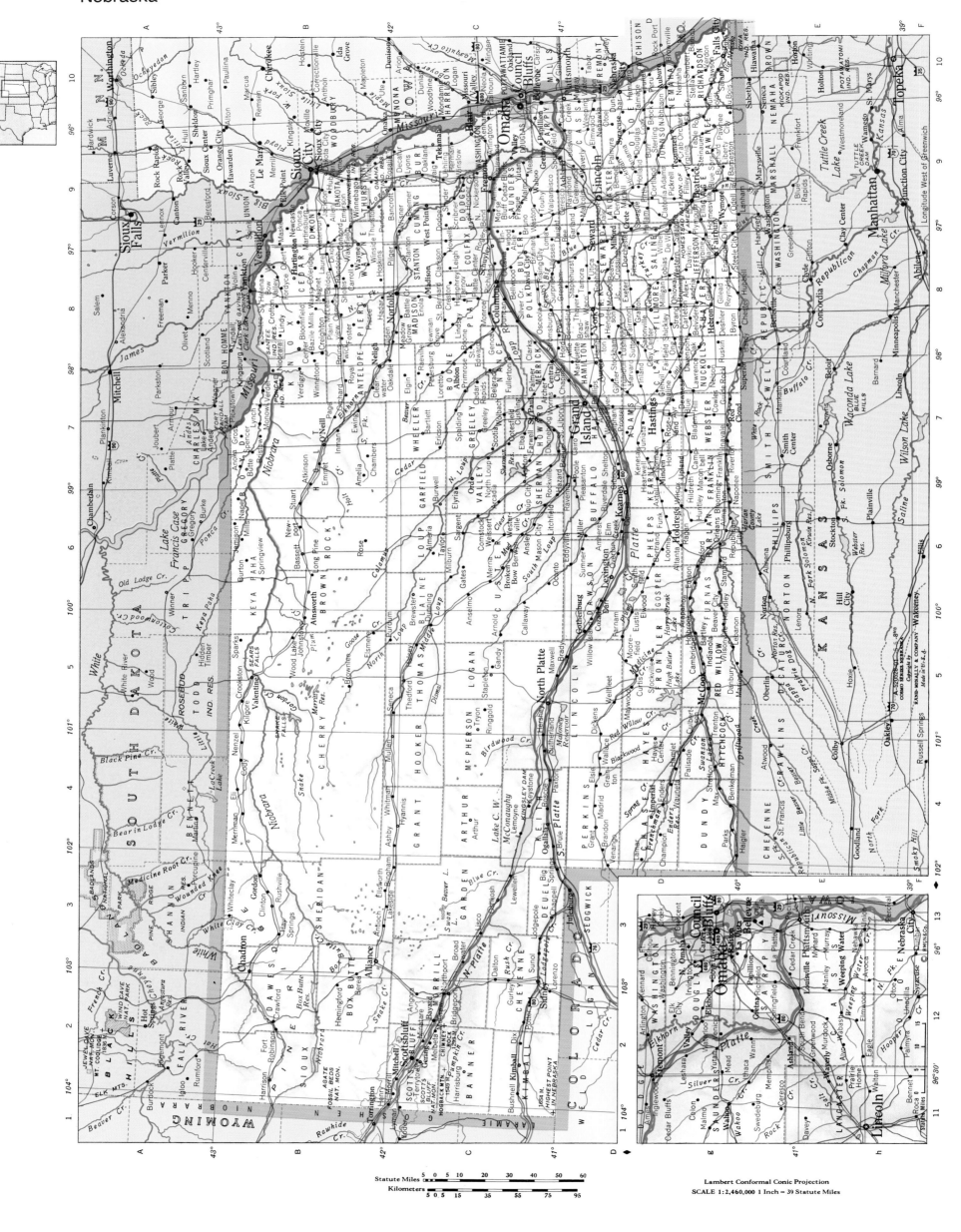

Statute Miles 5 0 5 10 20 30 40 50 60

Kilometers 5 0 5 15 35 55 75 95

Lambert Conformal Conic Projection
SCALE 1:2,460,000 1 Inch = 39 Statute Miles

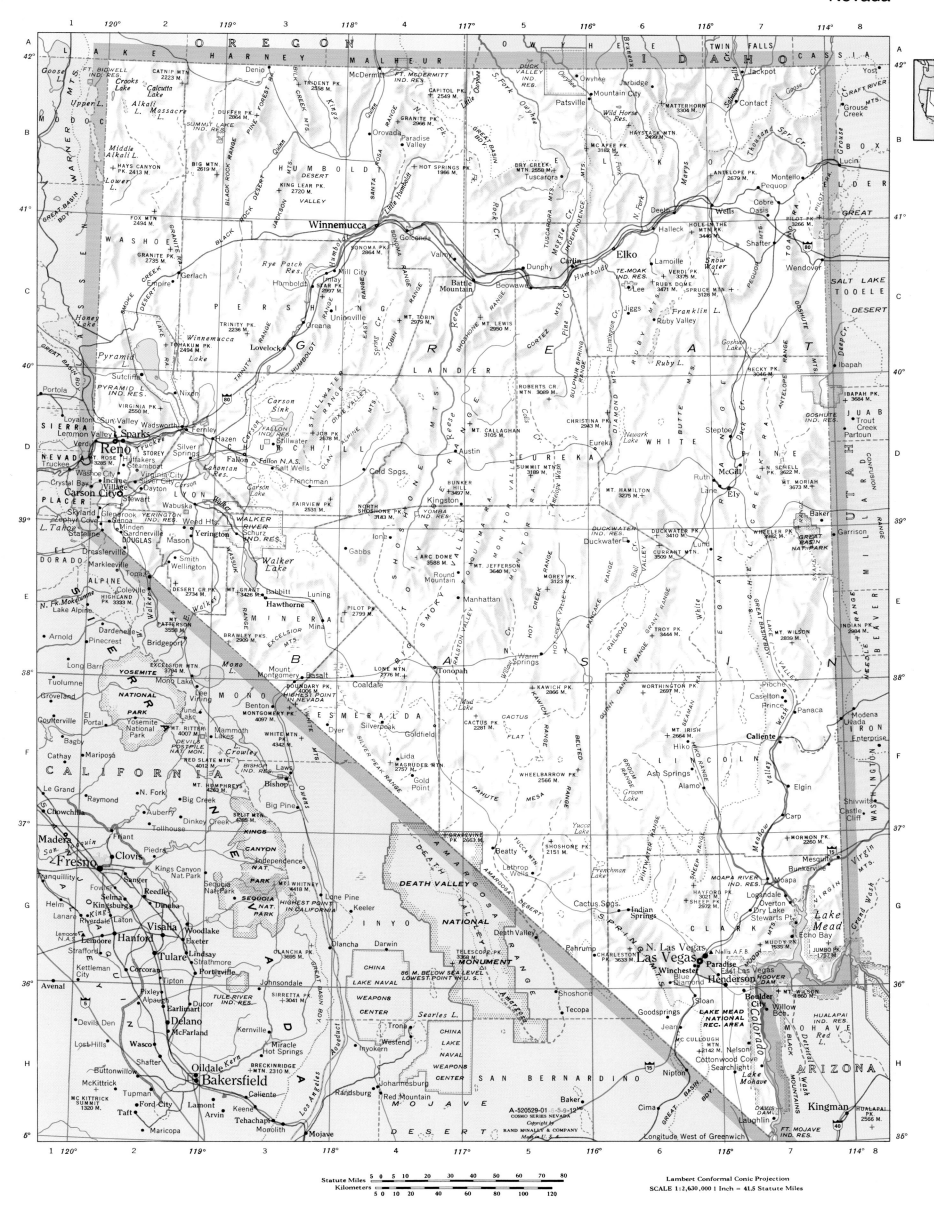

Statute Miles
Kilometers

Lambert Conformal Conic Projection
SCALE 1:2,630,000 1 Inch = 41.5 Statute Miles

New Hampshire

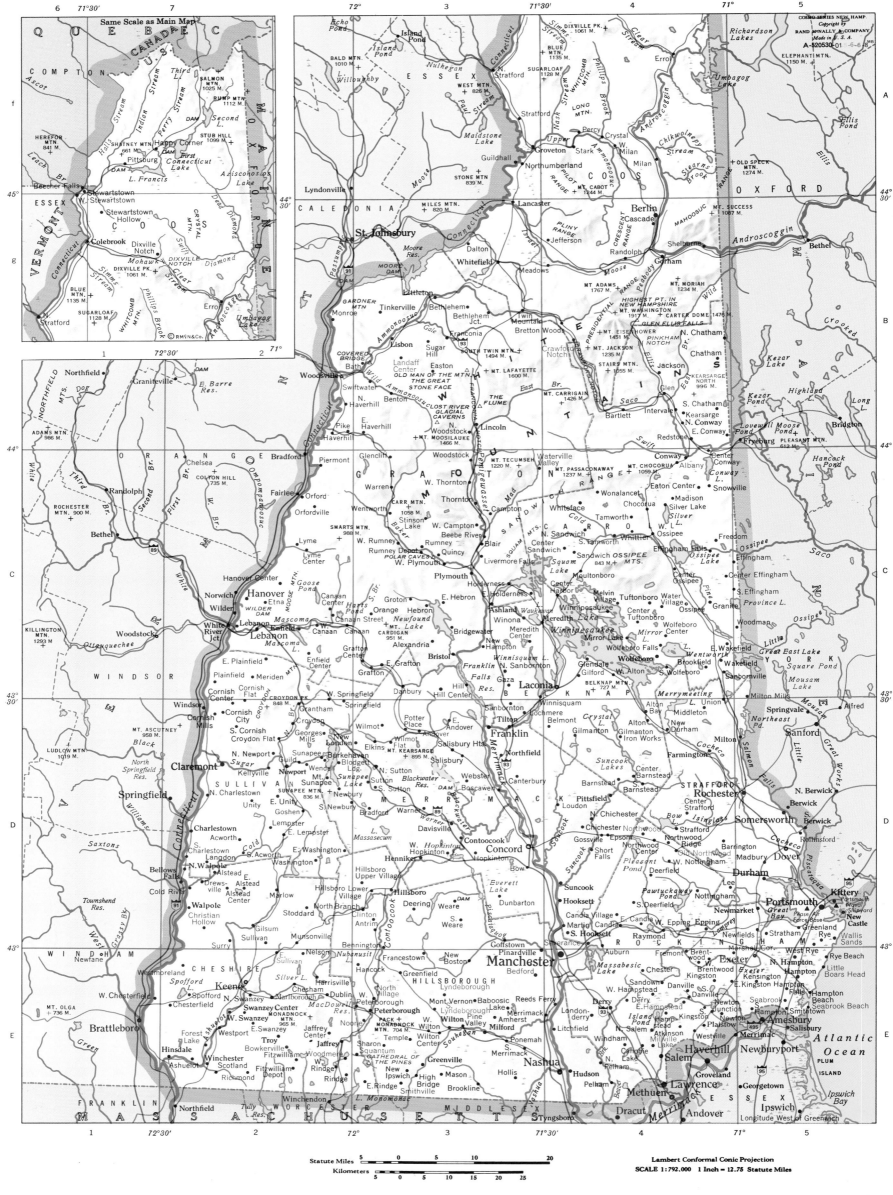

COSMO SERIES NEW HAMP.
Copyright by
RAND M⸱NALLY & COMPANY
Made in U.S.A.
A-520530-01 -6-6

Same Scale as Main Map

Statute Miles

Kilometers

Lambert Conformal Conic Projection
SCALE 1:792,000 1 Inch = 12.75 Statute Miles

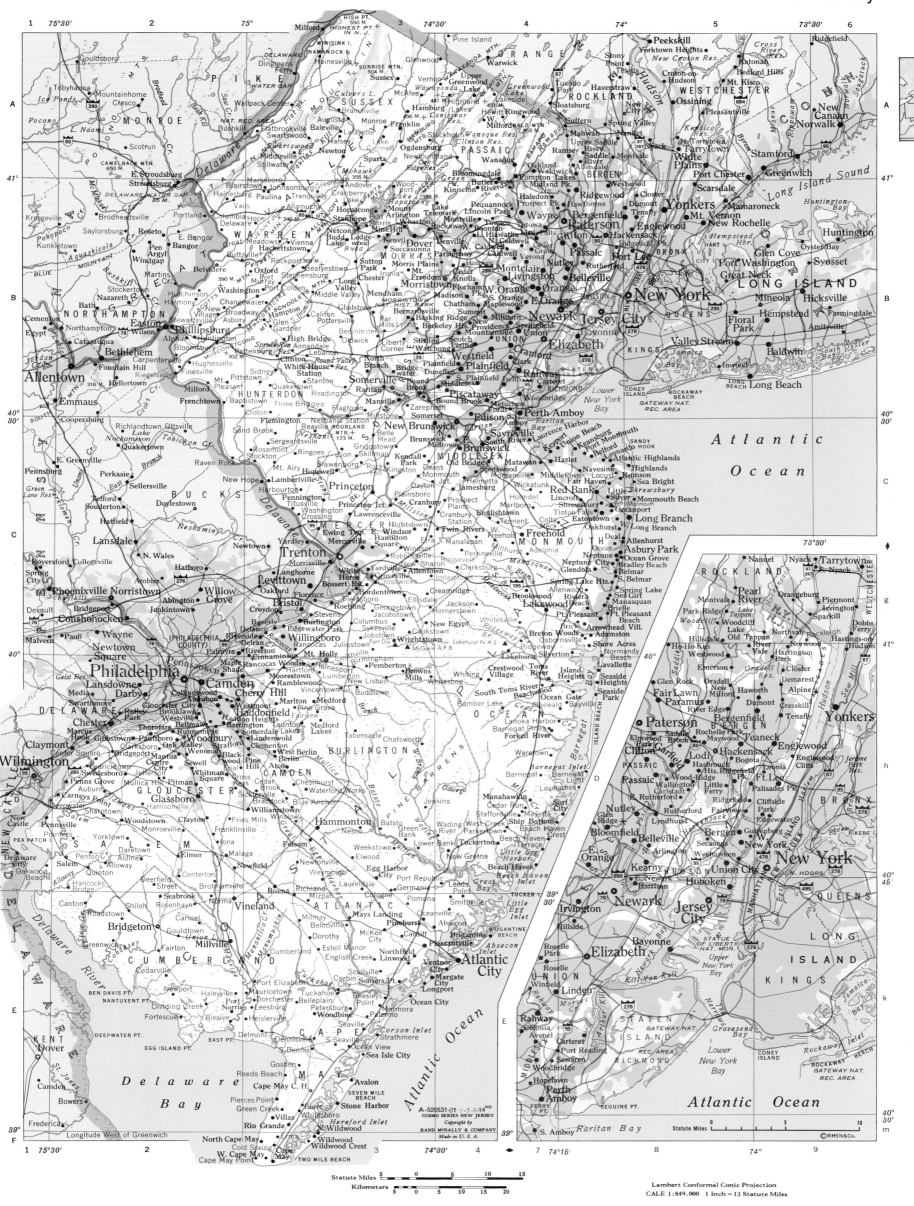

New Jersey

137

New Mexico

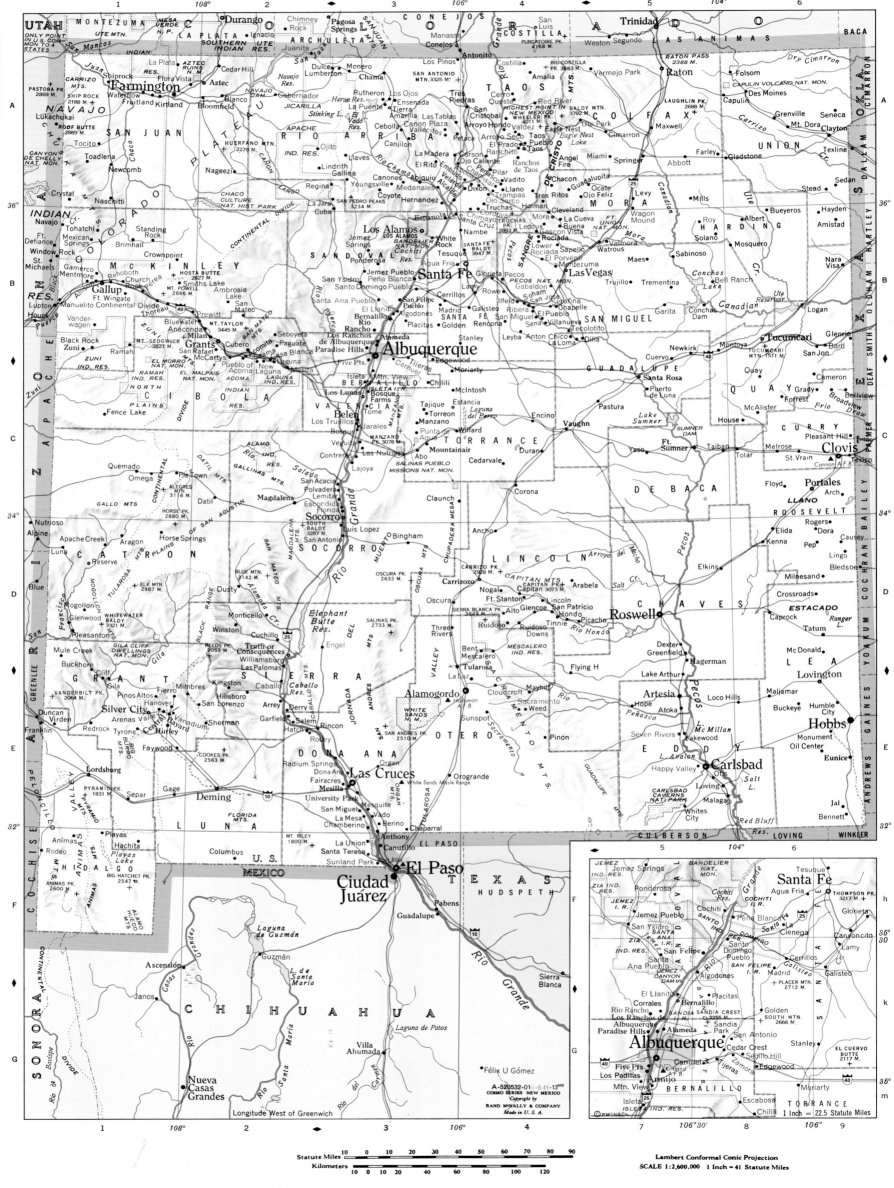

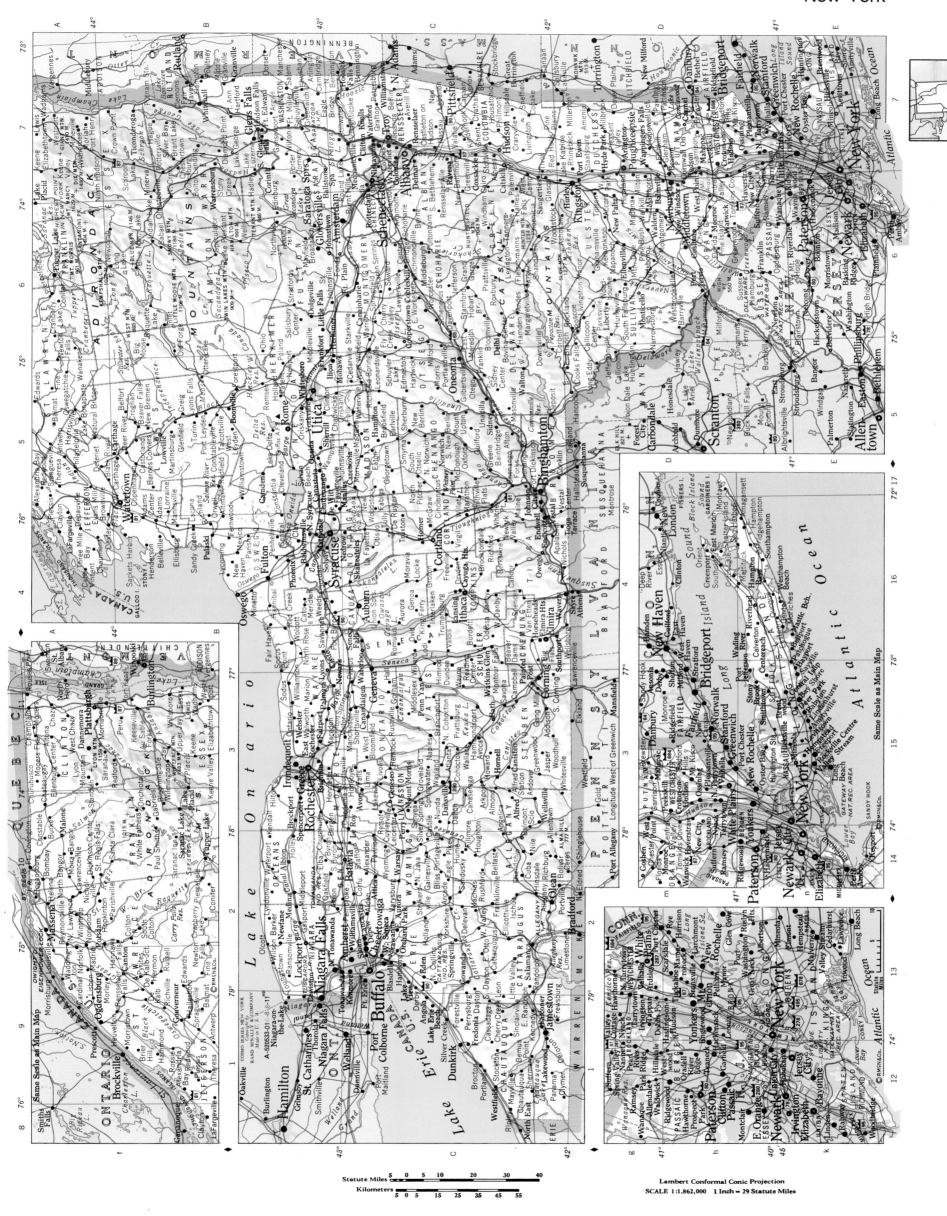

Statute Miles 5 0 5 10 20 30 40
Kilometers 5 0 15 25 35 45 55

Lambert Conformal Conic Projection
SCALE 1:1,862,000   1 Inch = 29 Statute Miles

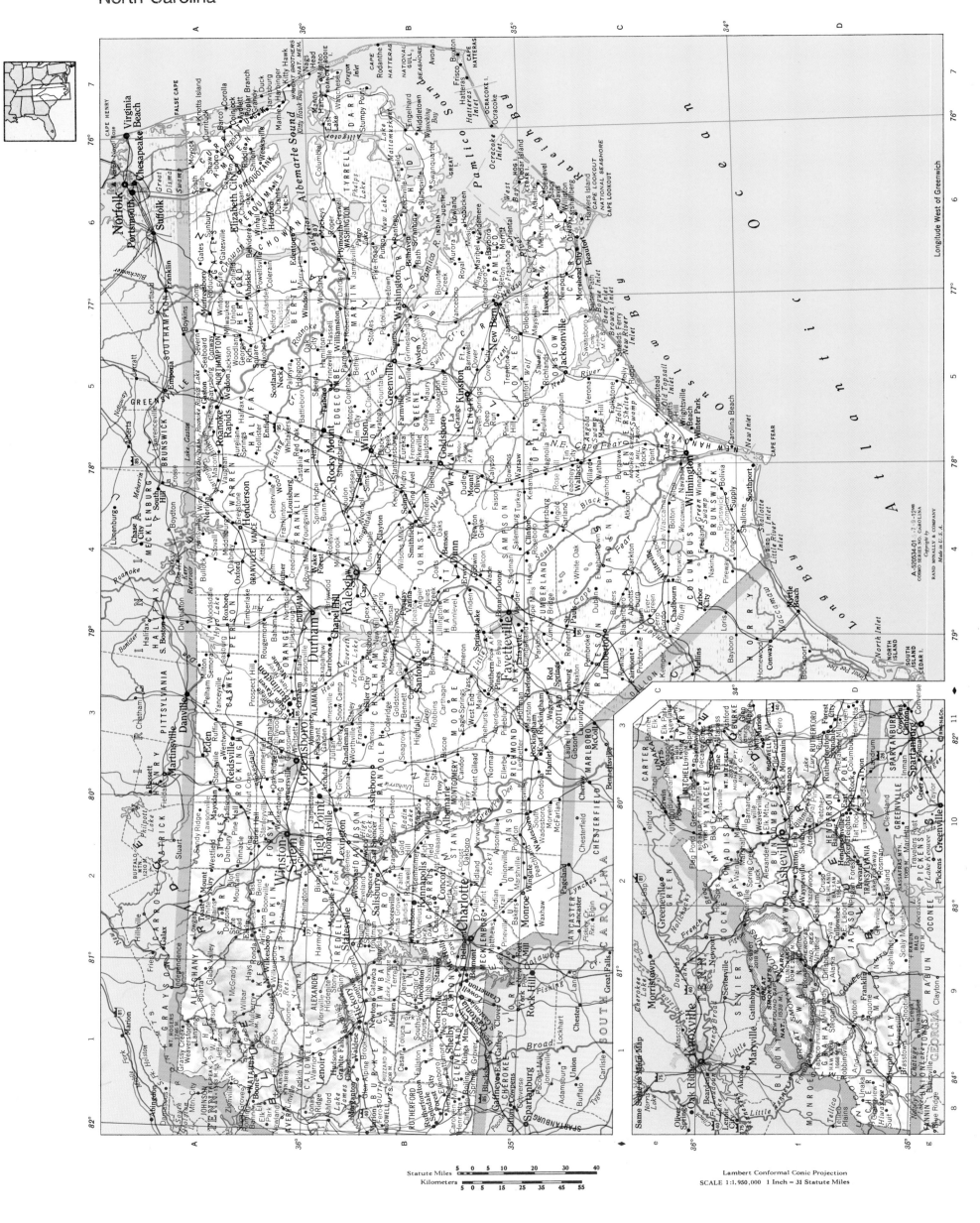

North Carolina

Lambert Conformal Conic Projection
SCALE 1:1,950,000   1 Inch = 31 Statute Miles

Statute Miles
Kilometers

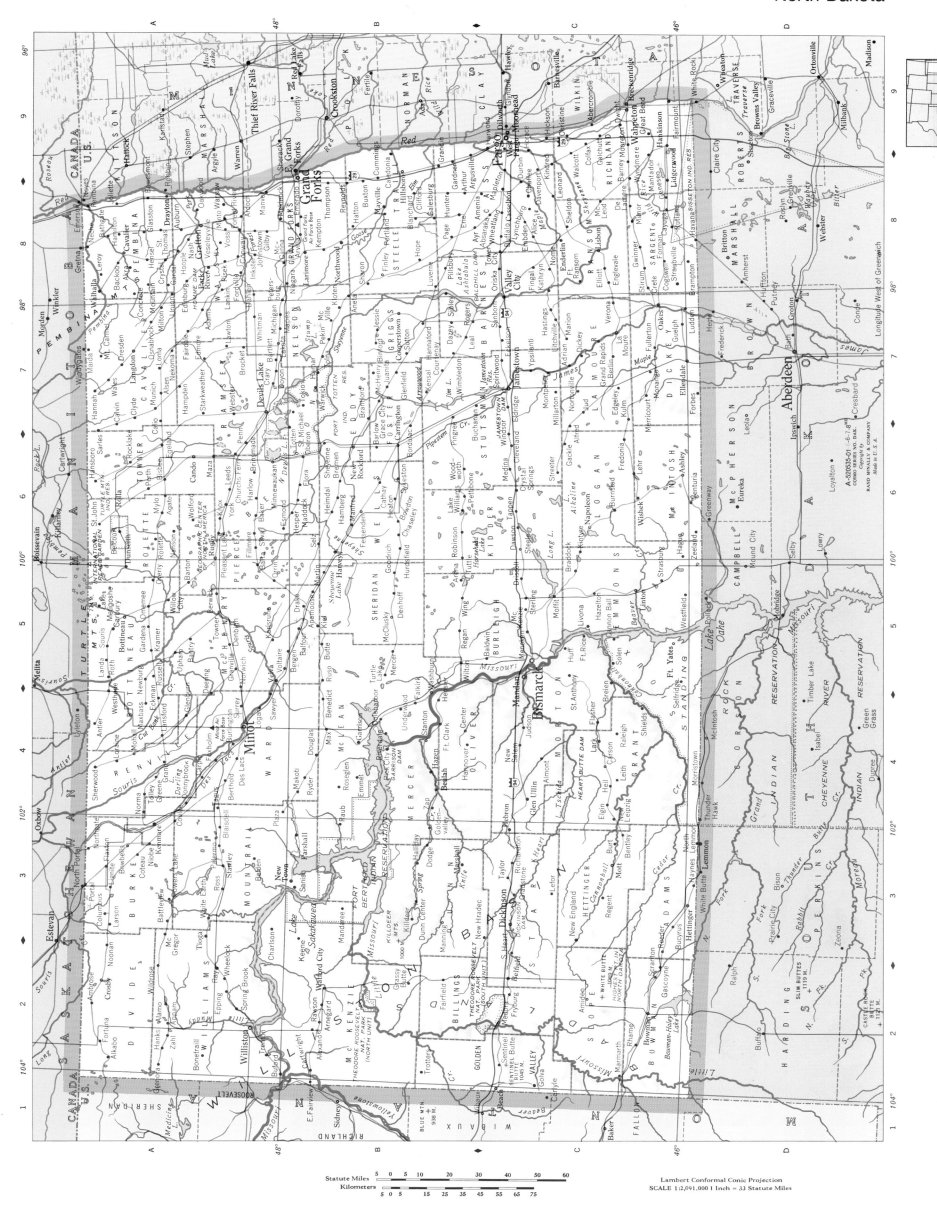

Statute Miles 5 0 5 10 20 30 40 50 60

Kilometers 5 0 5 15 25 35 45 55 65 75

Lambert Conformal Conic Projection
SCALE 1:2,091,000 1 Inch = 33 Statute Miles

Ohio

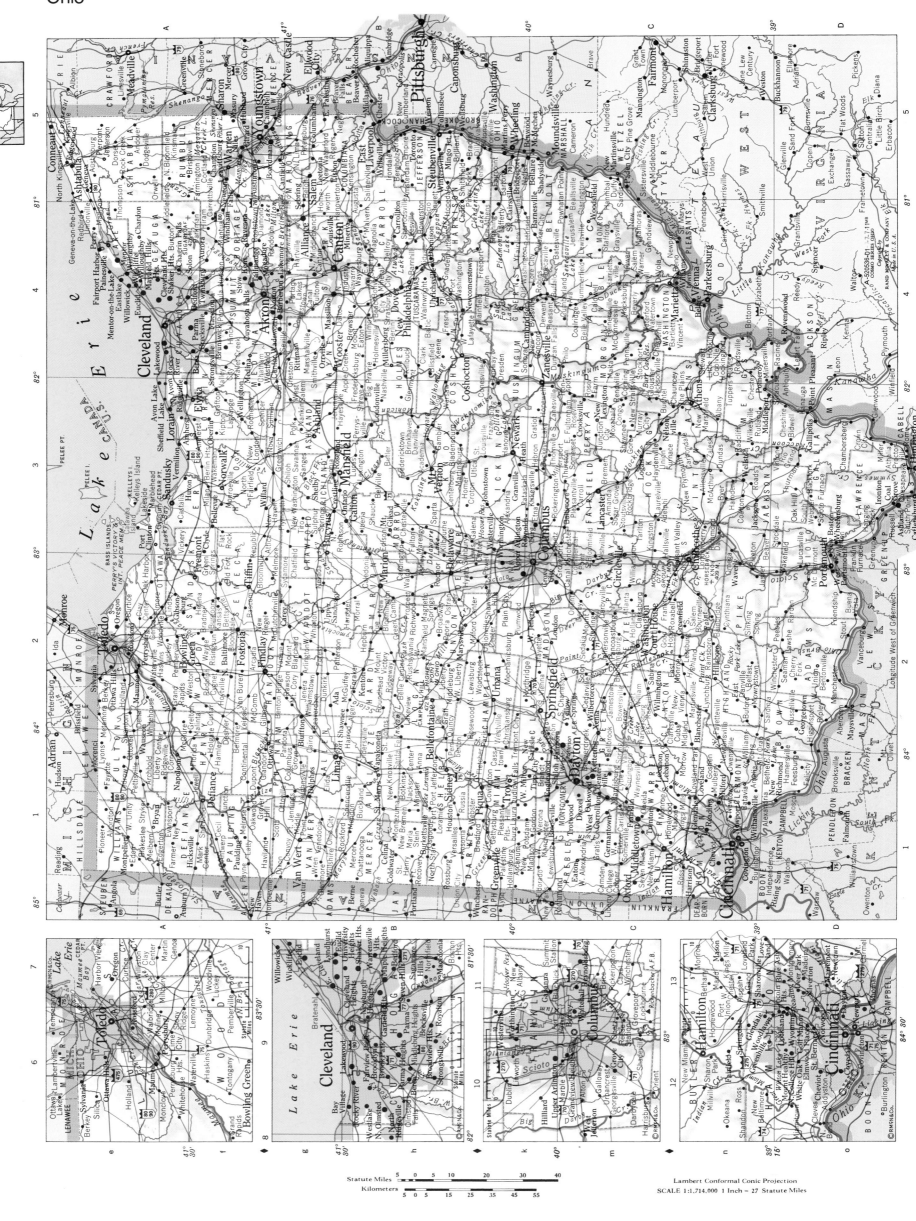

Statute Miles
5 0 5 10 20 30 40
Kilometers
5 0 15 25 45 55

Lambert Conformal Conic Projection
SCALE 1:1,714,000 1 Inch = 27 Statute Miles

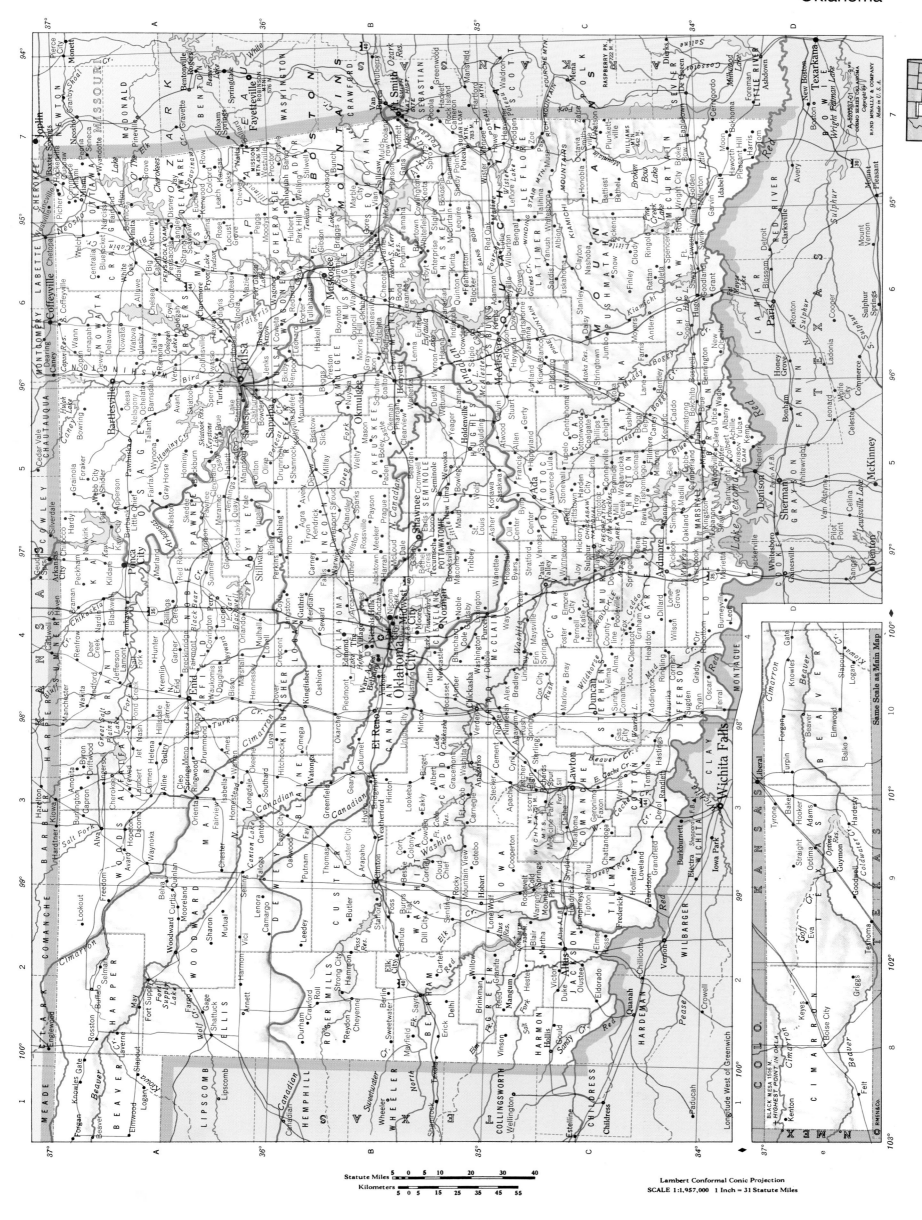

Oklahoma

Lambert Conformal Conic Projection
SCALE 1:1,957,000 1 Inch = 31 Statute Miles

143

Oregon

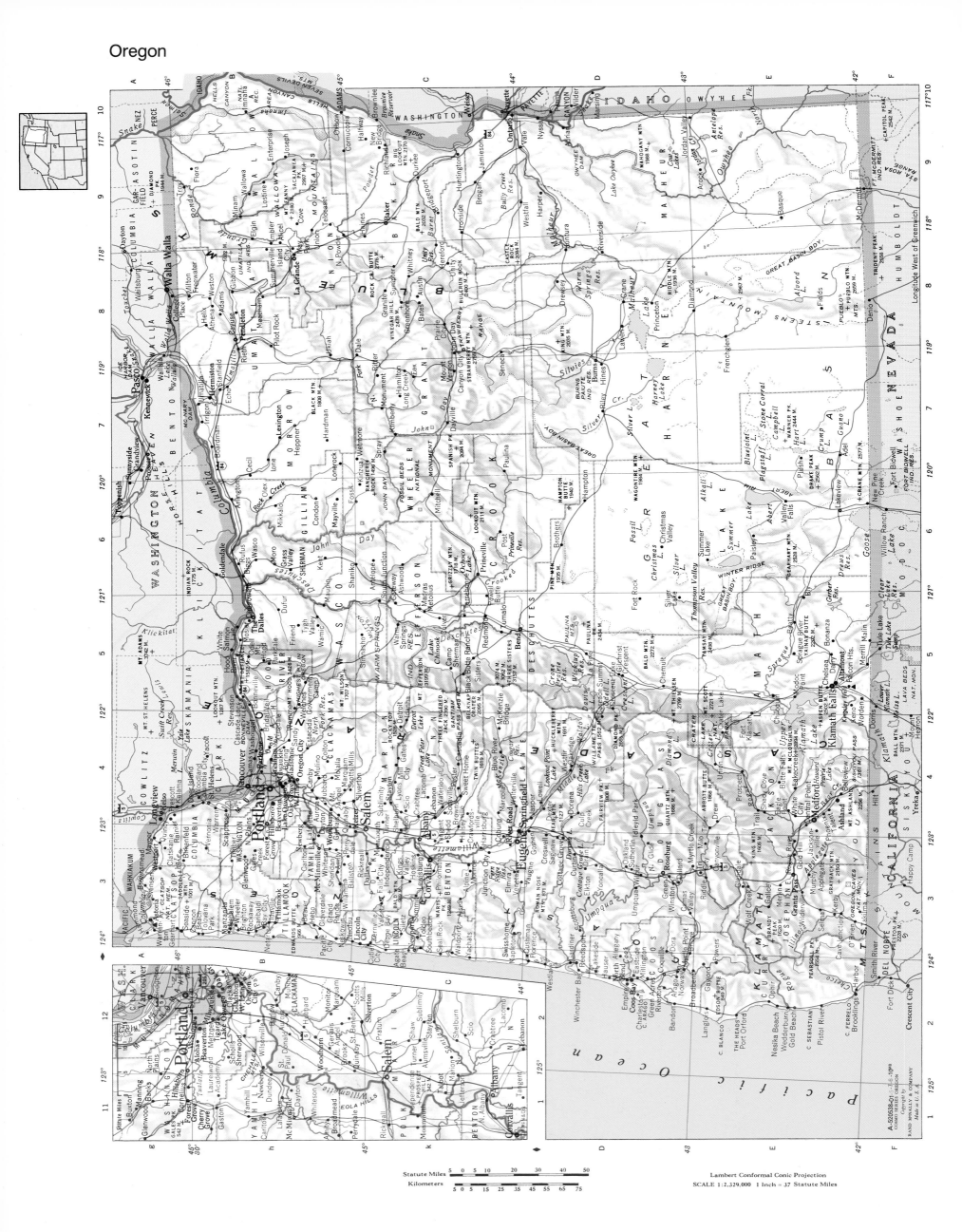

Statute Miles
Kilometers

Lambert Conformal Conic Projection
SCALE 1:2,329,000   1 Inch = 37 Statute Miles

Statute Miles 5 0 5 10 20 30
Kilometers 5 0 15 25 35 45

Lambert Conformal Conic Projection
SCALE 1:1,593,000 1 Inch = 25 Statute Miles

Rhode Island

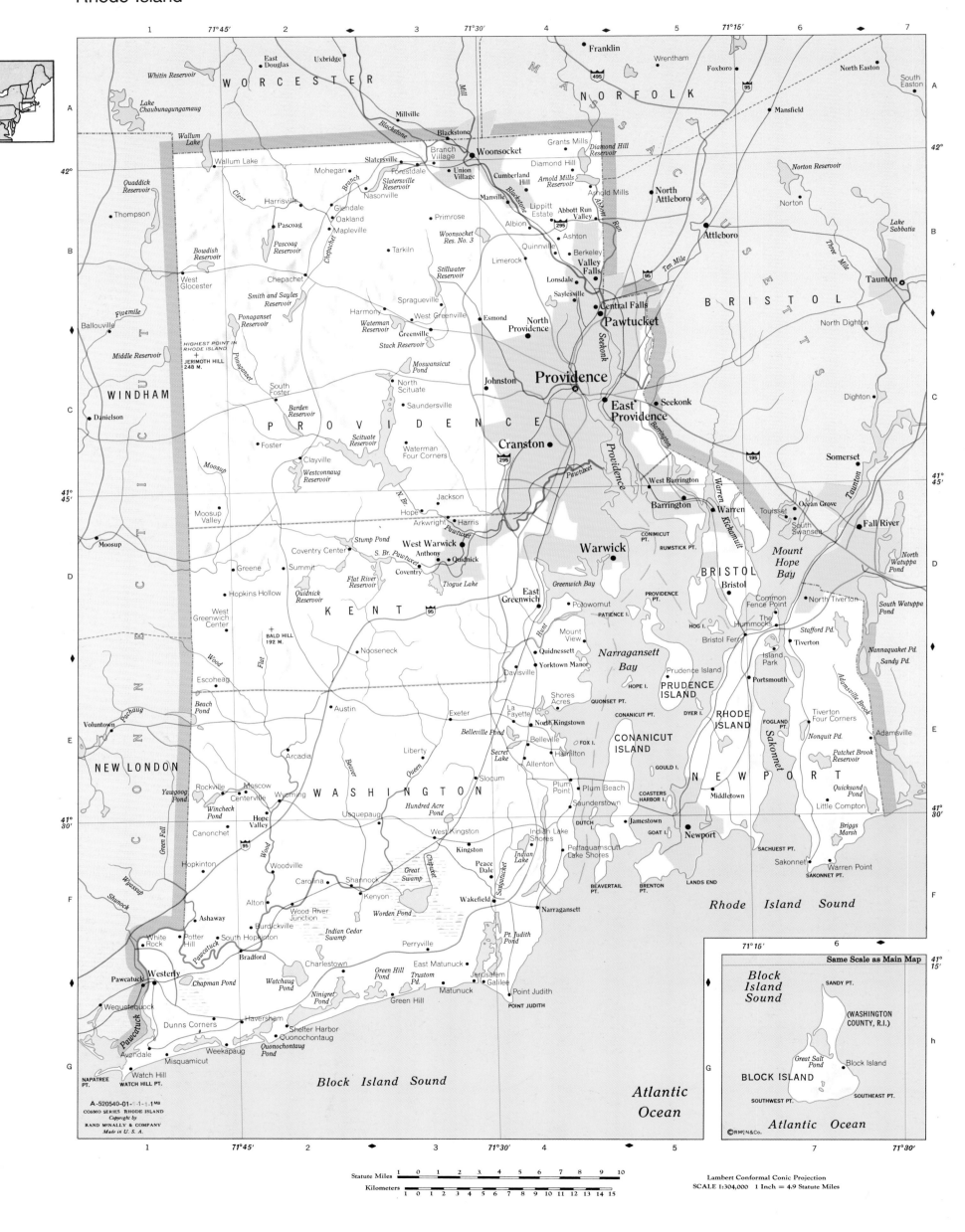

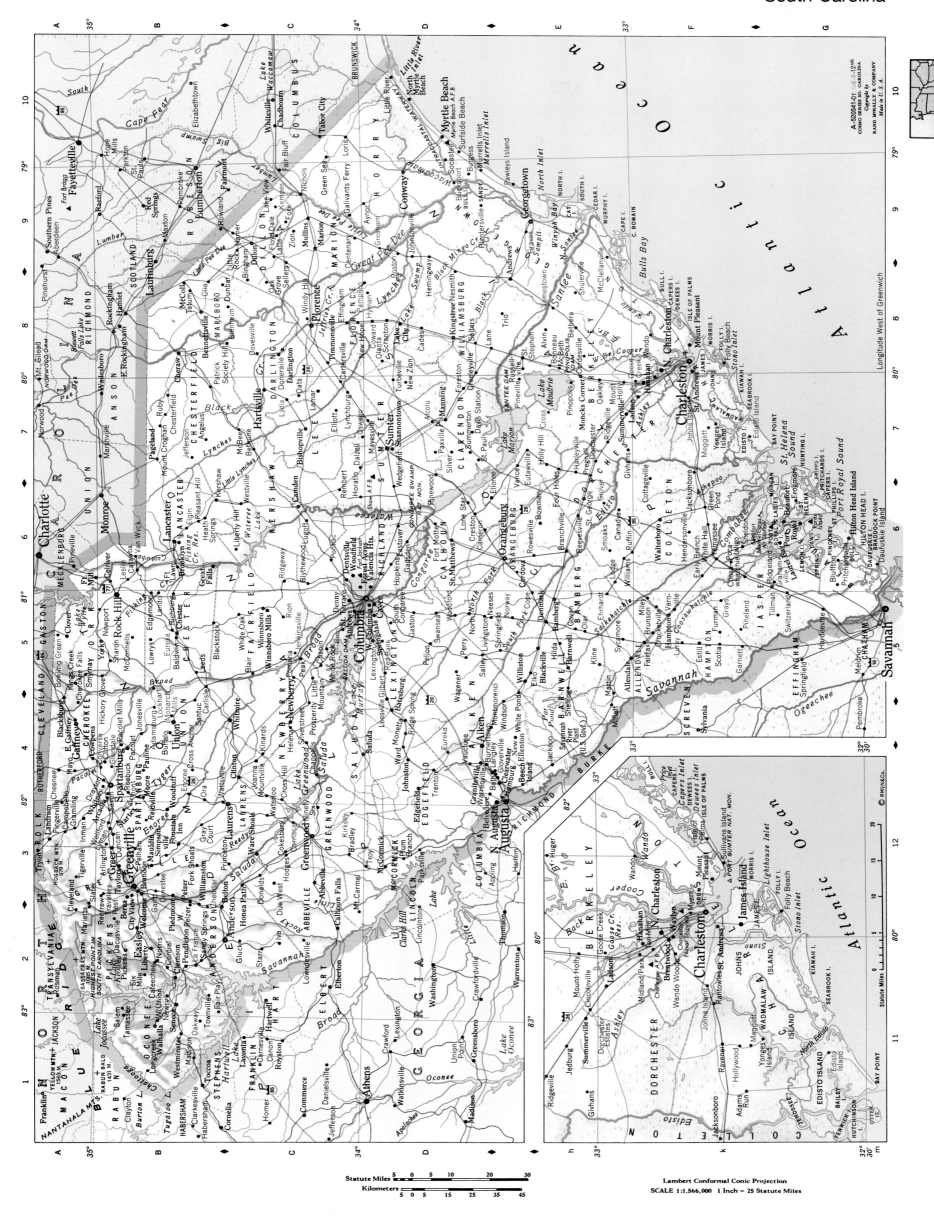

South Carolina

Lambert Conformal Conic Projection
SCALE 1:1,566,000 1 Inch = 25 Statute Miles

Statute Miles
Kilometers

147

South Dakota

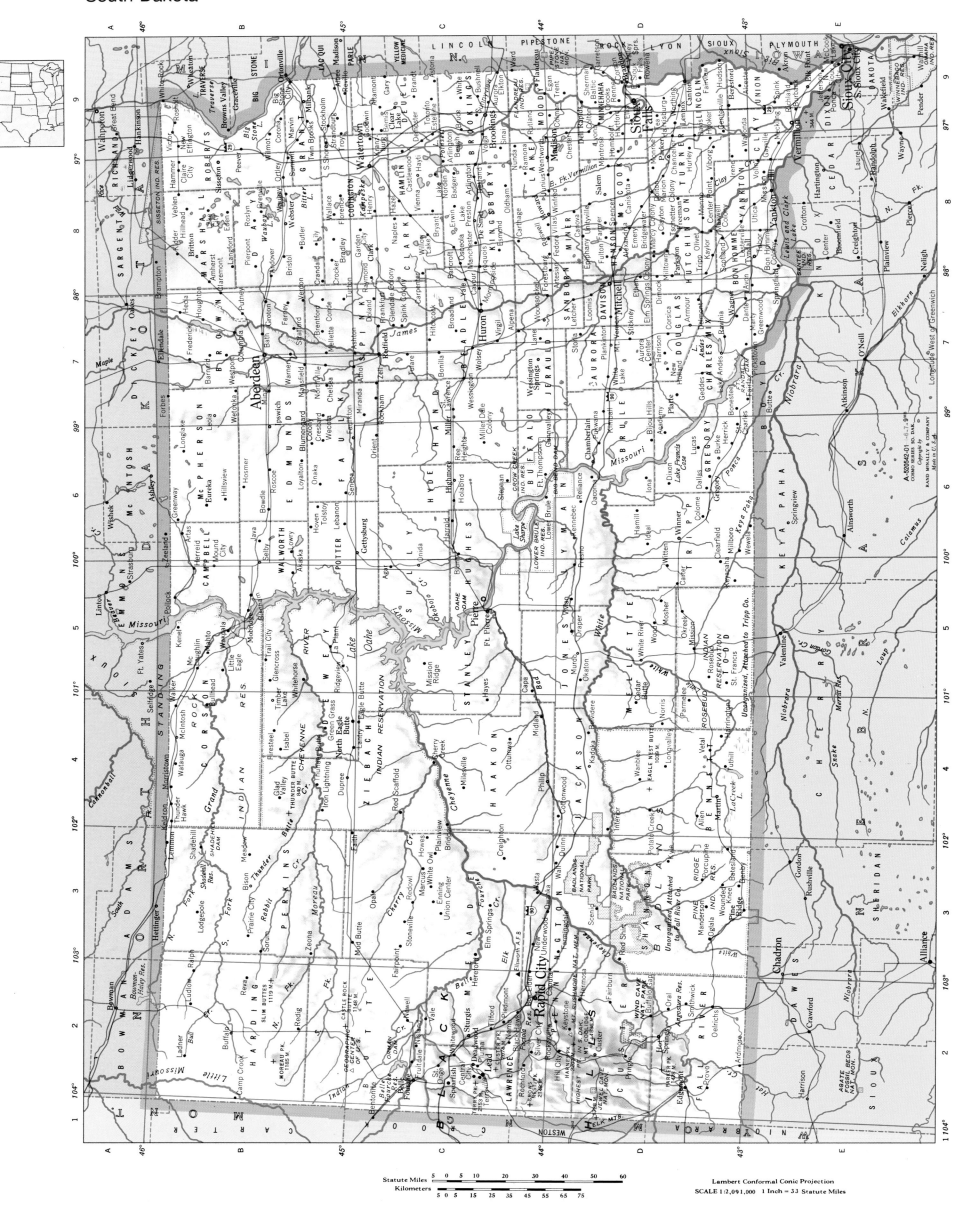

Statute Miles 5 0 5 10   20   30   40   50   60
Kilometers 5 0 5 15   25   35   45   55 65   75

Lambert Conformal Conic Projection
SCALE 1:2,091,000   1 Inch = 33 Statute Miles

148

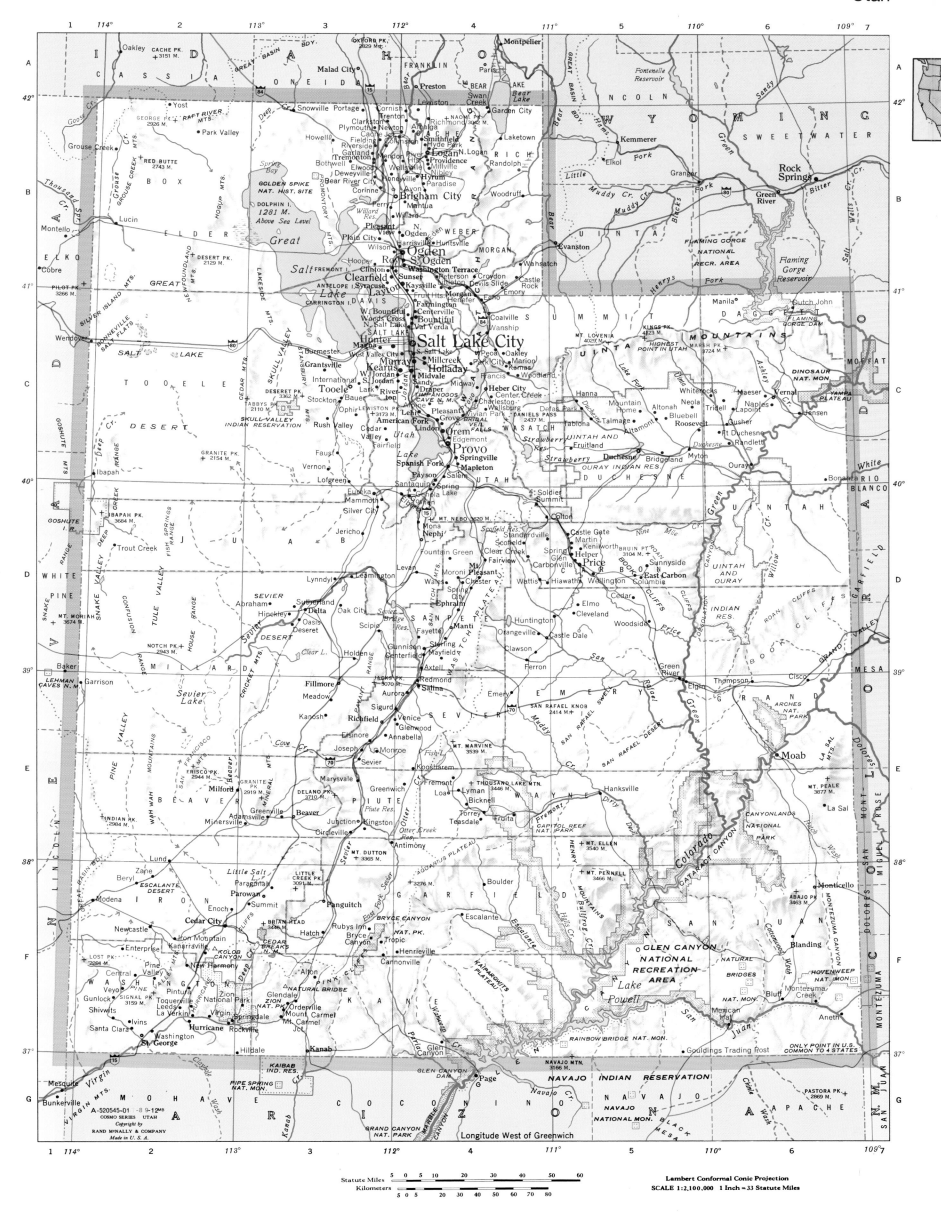

Statute Miles 5 0 5 10 20 30 40 50 60
Kilometers 5 0 5 10 20 30 40 50 60 70 80

Lambert Conformal Conic Projection
SCALE 1:2,100,000   1 Inch = 33 Statute Miles

A-520545-01 -8 9-12MB
COSMO SERIES UTAH
Copyright by
RAND McNALLY & COMPANY
Made in U.S.A.

Longitude West of Greenwich

Vermont

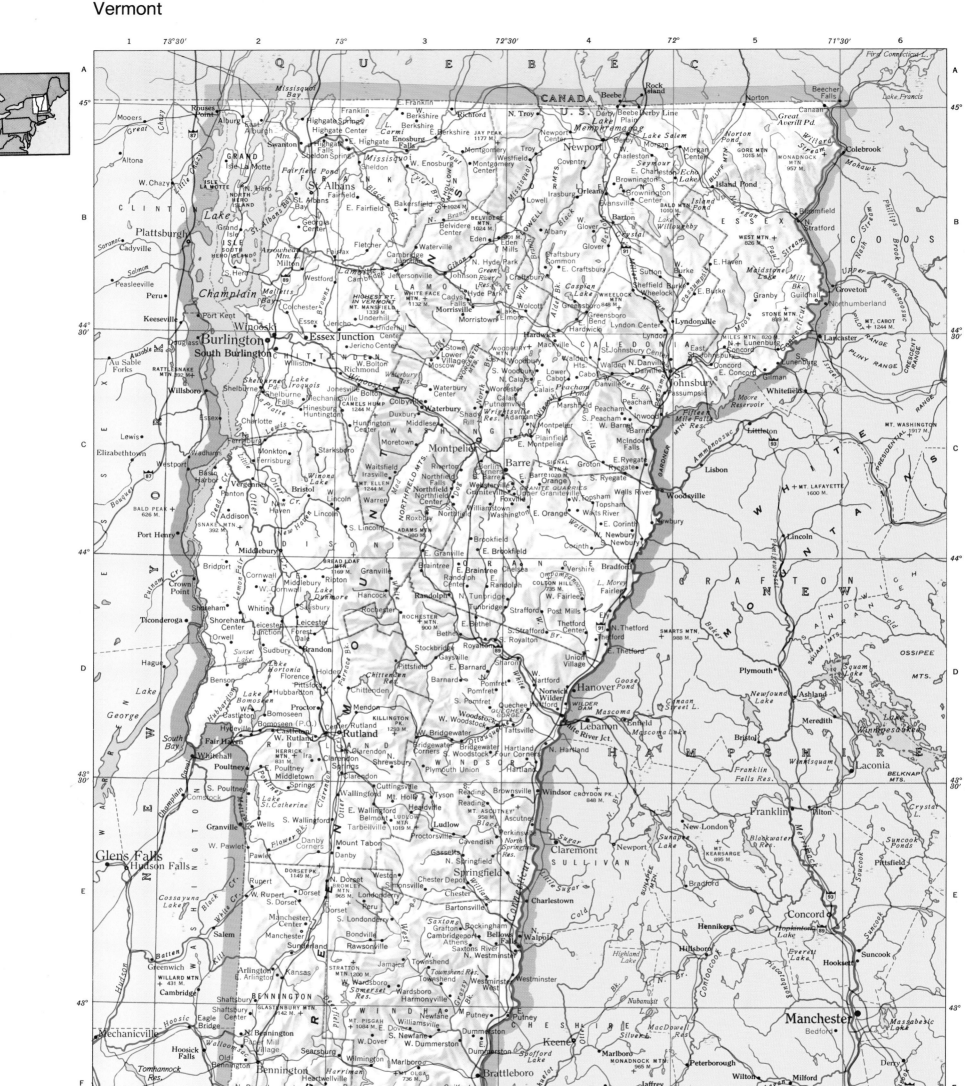

Statute Miles

Kilometers

Lambert Conformal Conic Projection
SCALE 1:903,000 1 Inch = 14.25 Statute Miles

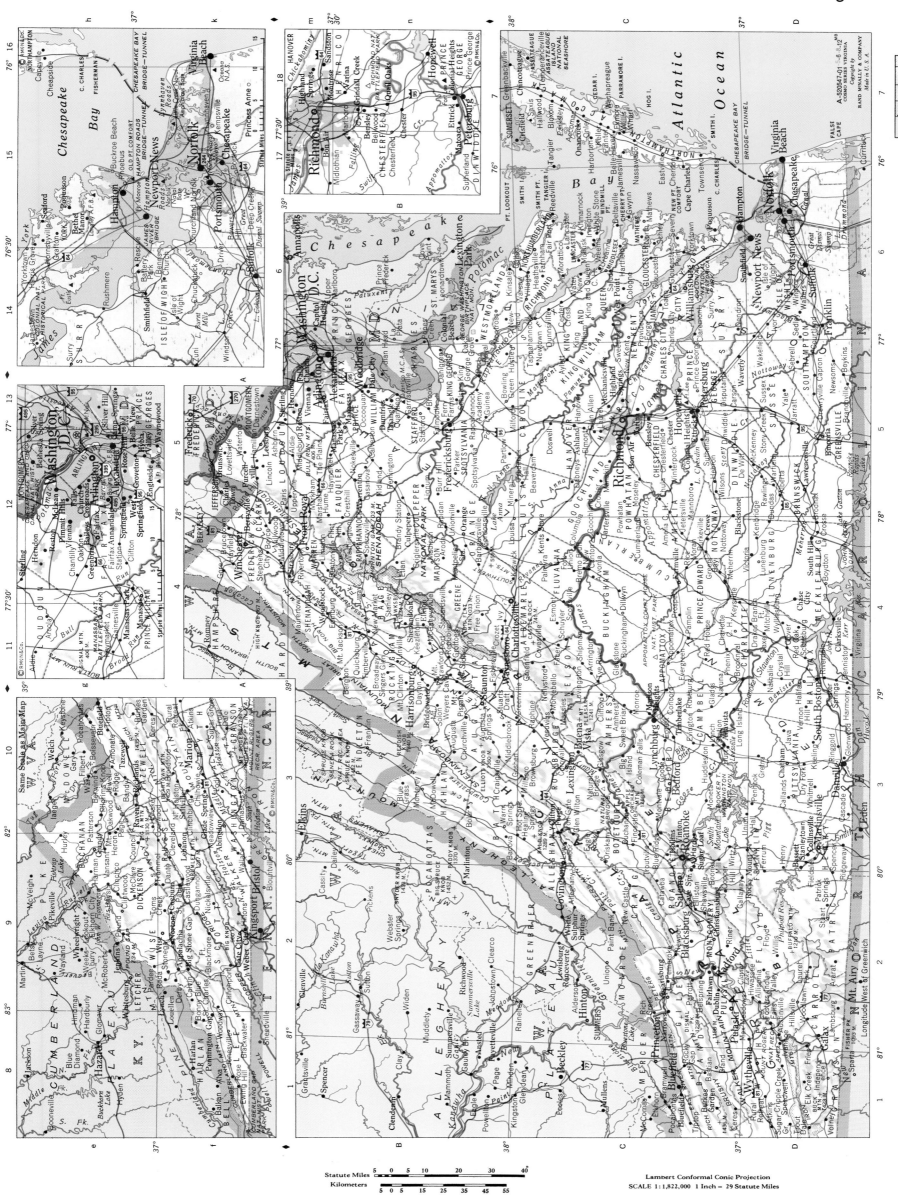

Virginia

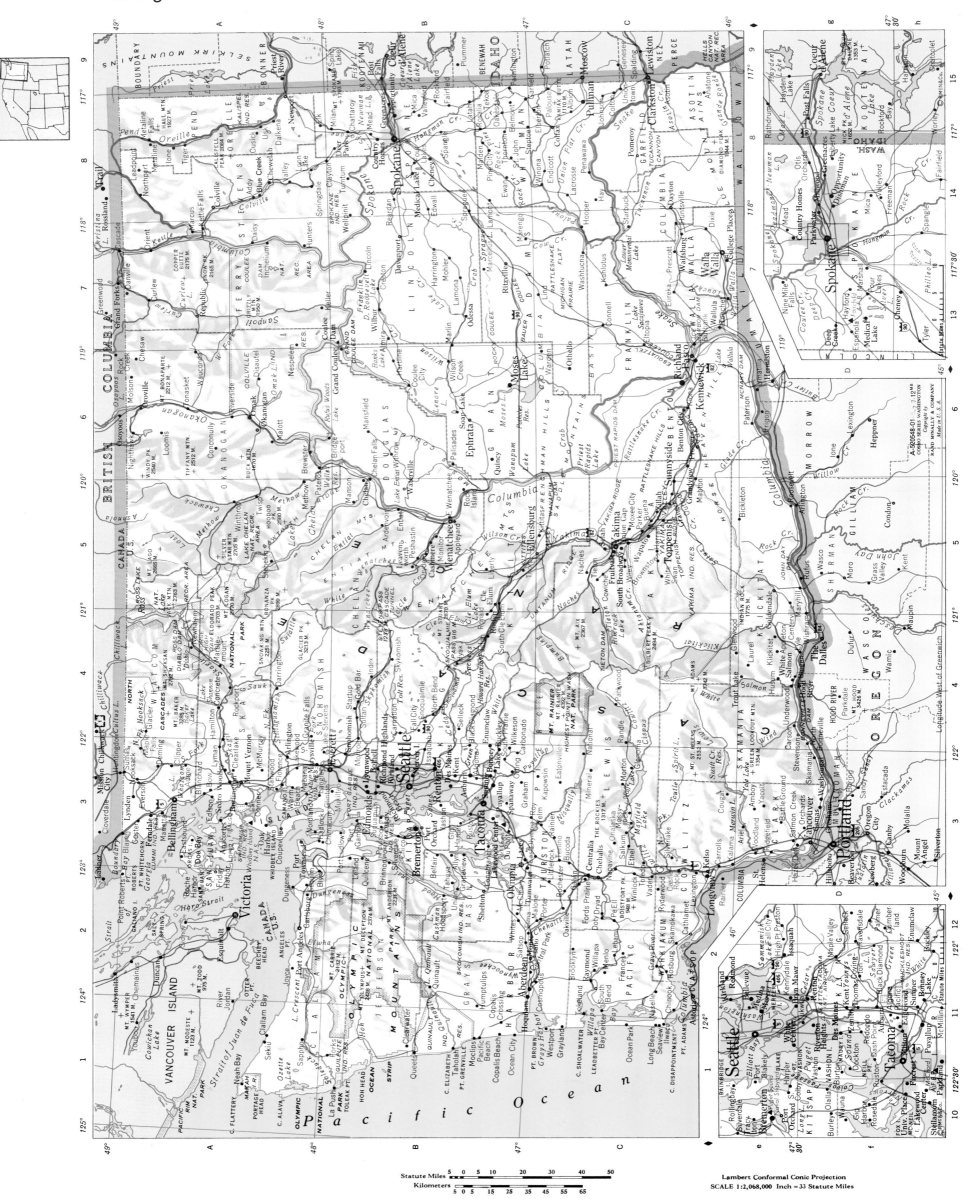

Statute Miles
Kilometers

Lambert Conformal Conic Projection
SCALE 1:2,068,000 Inch = 33 Statute Miles

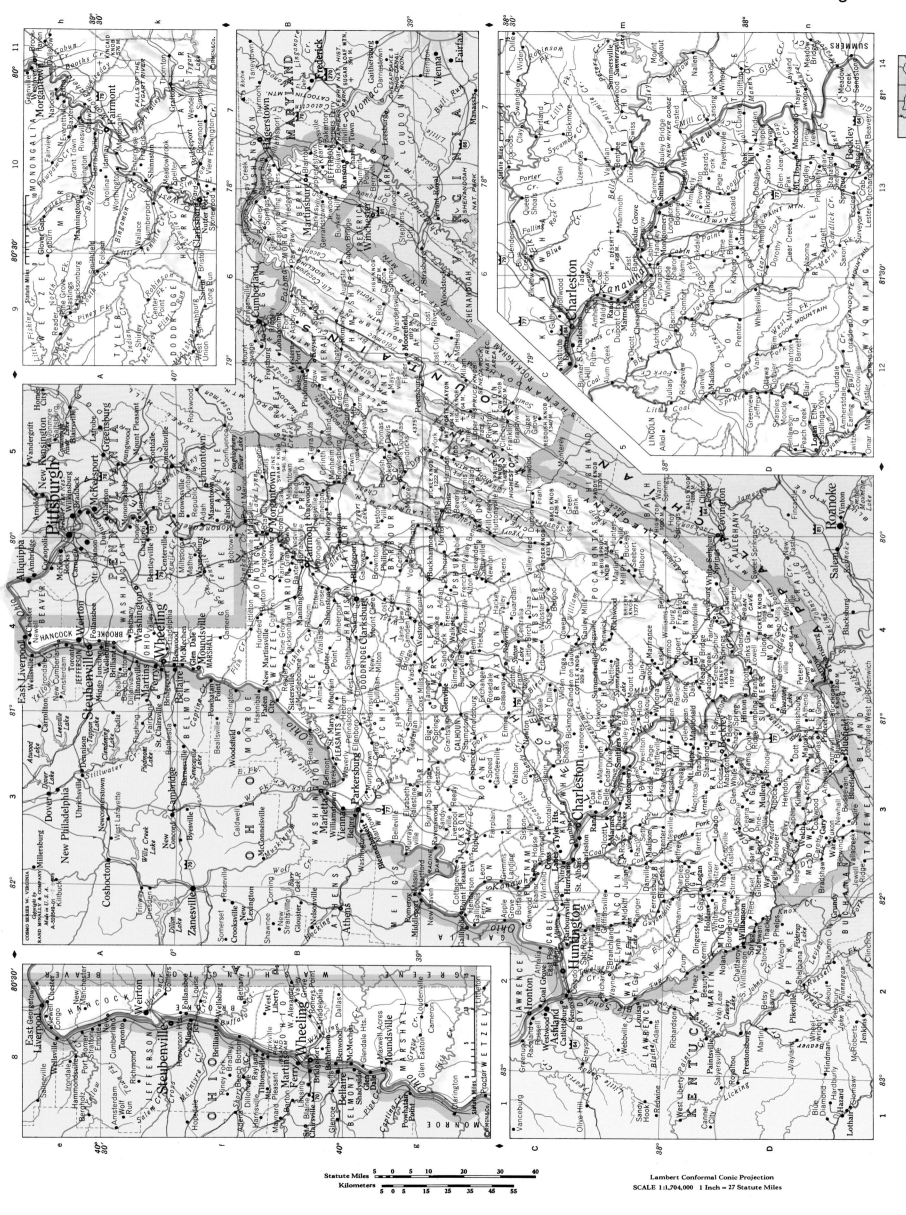

West Virginia

Statute Miles 5 0 10 20 30 40

Kilometers 5 0 15 30 45 55

Lambert Conformal Conic Projection
SCALE 1:1,704,000 1 Inch = 27 Statute Miles

155

Wisconsin

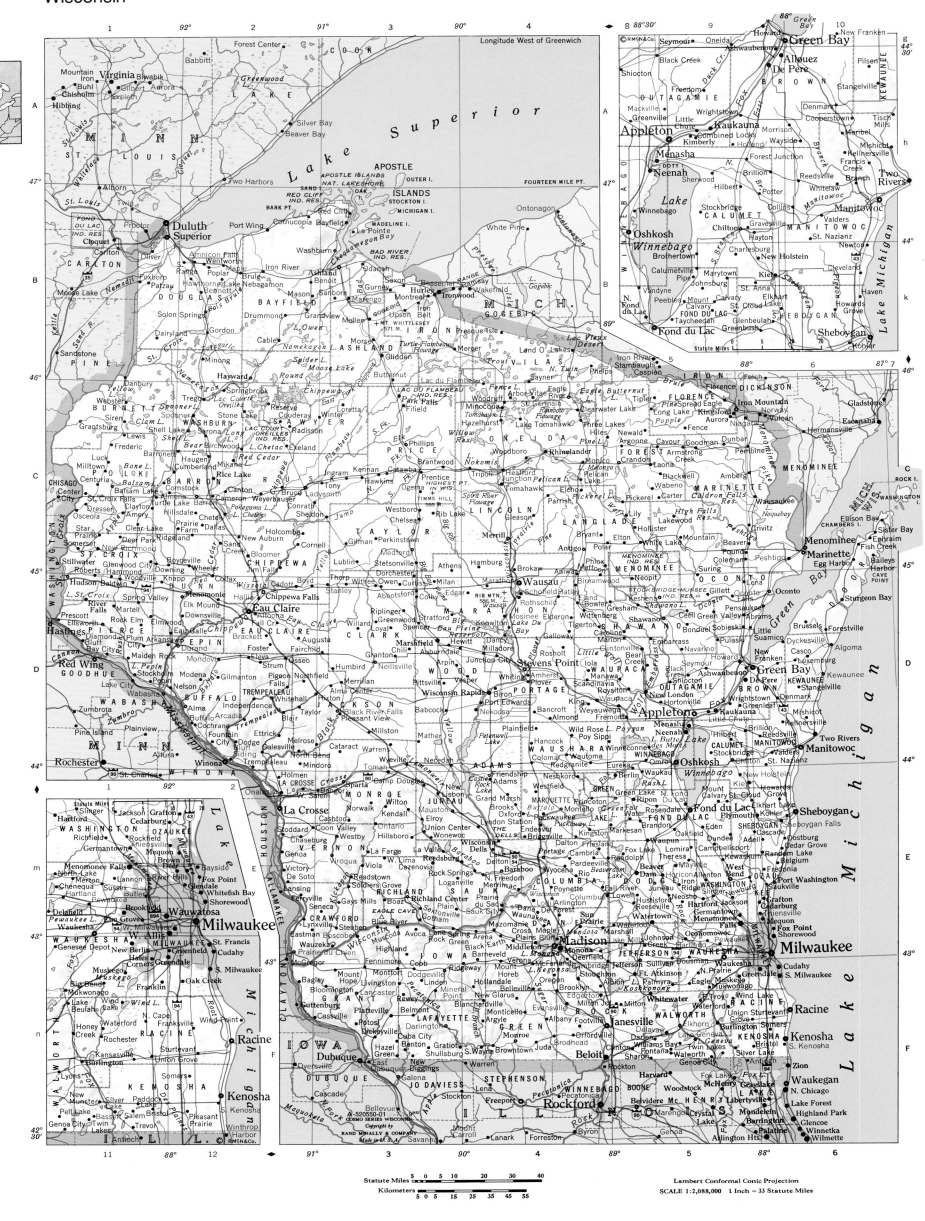

Longitude West of Greenwich

Lambert Conformal Conic Projection
SCALE 1:2,088,000 1 Inch = 33 Statute Miles

Statute Miles
Kilometers

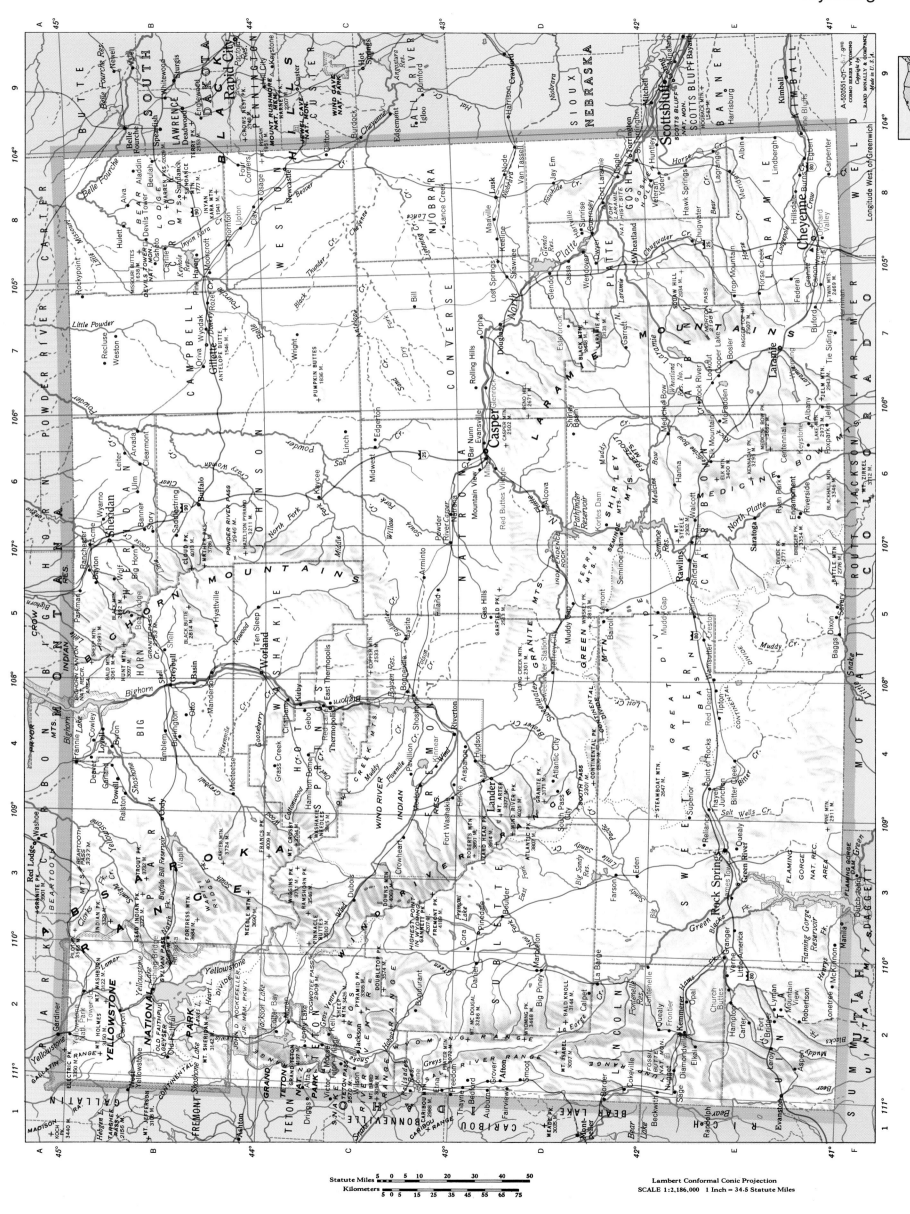

Statute Miles 5 0 5 10   20   30   40   50
Kilometers 5 0 5 15 25 35 45 55 65 75

Lambert Conformal Conic Projection
SCALE 1:2,186,000   1 Inch = 34.5 Statute Miles

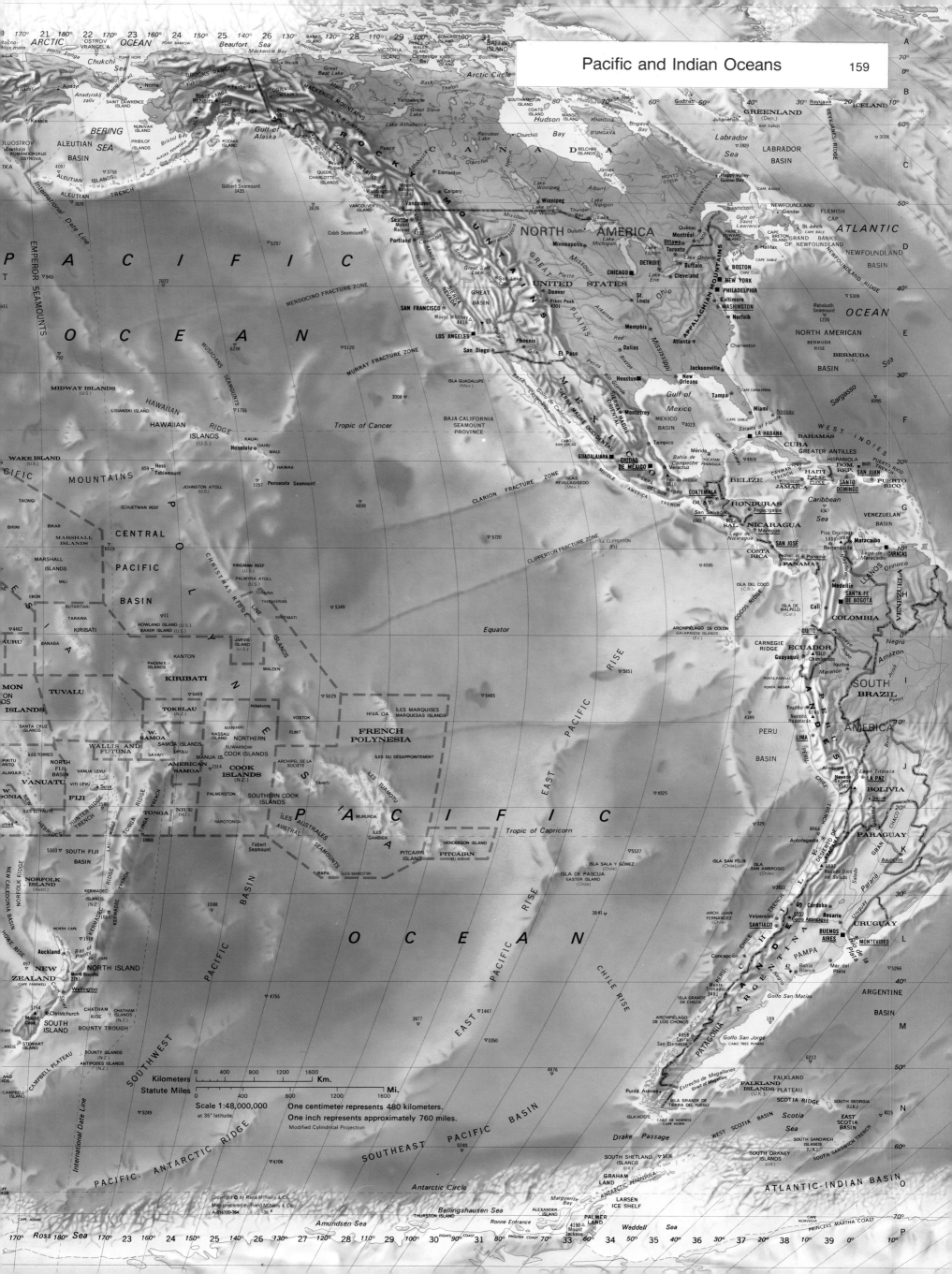

Scale 1:48,000,000
at 35° latitude

One centimeter represents 480 kilometers.
One inch represents approximately 760 miles.

Modified Cylindrical Projection

Kilometers
Statute Miles

Copyright © by Rand McNally & Co.
Map prepared by Rand McNally & Co.
A-513700-764

Index to World Reference Maps

Introduction to the Index

This universal index includes in a single alphabetical list approximately 69,000 names of features that appear on the reference maps. Each name is followed by the name of the country or continent in which it is located, a map-reference key and a page reference.

Names The names of cities appear in the index in regular type. The names of all other features appear in *italics*, followed by descriptive terms (hill, mtn., state) to indicate their nature.

Names that appear in shortened versions on the maps due to space limitations are spelled out in full in the index. The portions of these names omitted from the maps are enclosed in brackets — for example, Acapulco [de Juárez].

Abbreviations of names on the maps have been standardized as much as possible. Names that are abbreviated on the maps are generally spelled out in full in the index.

Country names and names of features that extend beyond the boundaries of one country are followed by the name of the continent in which each is located. Country designations follow the names of all other places in the index. The locations of places in the United States, Canada, and the United Kingdom are further defined by abbreviations that indicate the state, province, or political division in which each is located.

All abbreviations used in the index are defined in the List of Abbreviations below.

Alphabetization Names are alphabetized in the order of the letters of the English alphabet. Spanish *ll* and *ch*, for example, are not treated as distinct letters. Furthermore, diacritical marks are disregarded in alphabetization — German or Scandinavian *ä* or *ö* are treated as *a* or *o*.

The names of physical features may appear inverted, since they are always alphabetized under the proper, not the generic, part of the name, thus: 'Gibraltar, Strait of'. Otherwise every entry, whether consisting of one word or more, is alphabetized as a single continuous entity. 'Lakeland', for example, appears after 'La Crosse' and before 'La Salle'. Names beginning with articles (Le Havre, Den Helder, Al Mansūrah) are not inverted. Names beginning 'St.', 'Ste.' and 'Sainte' are alphabetized as though spelled 'Saint'.

In the case of identical names, towns are listed first, then political divisions, then physical features. Entries that are completely identical are listed alphabetically by country name.

Map-Reference Keys and Page References The map-reference keys and page references are found in the last two columns of each entry.

Each map-reference key consists of a letter and number. The letters appear along the sides of the maps. Lowercase letters indicate reference to inset maps. Numbers appear across the tops and bottoms of the maps.

Map reference keys for point features, such as cities and mountain peaks, indicate the locations of the symbols. For extensive areal features, such as countries or mountain ranges, locations are given for the approximate centers of the features. Those for linear features, such as canals and rivers, are given for the locations of the names.

The page number generally refers to the main map for the country in which the feature is located. Page references to two-page maps always refer to the left-hand page.

List of Abbreviations

Afg.	Afghanistan	C.V.	Cape Verde	Jam.	Jamaica	N. Ire., U.K.	Northern Ireland, U.K.	Sri L.	Sri Lanka
Afr.	Africa	Cyp.	Cyprus	Jord.	Jordan			*state*	state, republic, canton
Ak., U.S.	Alaska, U.S.	Czech.	Czech Republic	Kaz.	Kazakhstan	N.J., U.S.	New Jersey, U.S.		
Al., U.S.	Alabama, U.S.	D.C., U.S.	District of Columbia, U.S.	Kir.	Kiribati	N. Kor.	North Korea	St. Hel.	St. Helena
Alb.	Albania			Ks., U.S.	Kansas, U.S.	N.M., U.S.	New Mexico, U.S.	St. K./N	St. Kitts and Nevis
Alg.	Algeria	De., U.S.	Delaware, U.S.	Kuw.	Kuwait	N. Mar. Is.	Northern Mariana Islands	St. Luc.	St. Lucia
Alta., Can.	Alberta, Can.	Den.	Denmark	Ky., U.S.	Kentucky, U.S.			*stm.*	stream (river, creek)
Am. Sam.	American Samoa	*dep.*	dependency, colony	Kyrg.	Kyrgyzstan	Nmb.	Namibia	S. Tom./P.	Sao Tome and Principe
anch.	anchorage	*depr.*	depression	*l.*	lake, pond	Nor.	Norway		
And.	Andorra	*dept.*	department, district	La., U.S.	Louisiana, U.S.	Norf. I.	Norfolk Island	St. P./M.	St. Pierre and Miquelon
Ang.	Angola	*des.*	desert	Lat.	Latvia	N.S., Can.	Nova Scotia, Can.		
Ant.	Antarctica	Dji.	Djibouti	Leb.	Lebanon	Nv., U.S.	Nevada, U.S.	*strt.*	strait, channel, sound
Antig.	Antigua and Barbuda	Dom.	Dominica	Leso.	Lesotho	N.W. Ter., Can.	Northwest Territories, Can.		
		Dom. Rep.	Dominican Republic	Lib.	Liberia			St. Vin.	St. Vincent and the Grenadines
Ar., U.S.	Arkansas, U.S.	Ec.	Ecuador	Liech.	Liechtenstein	N.Y., U.S.	New York, U.S.		
Arg.	Argentina	El Sal.	El Salvador	Lith.	Lithuania	N.Z.	New Zealand	Sud.	Sudan
Arm.	Armenia	Eng., U.K.	England, U.K.	Lux.	Luxembourg	Oc.	Oceania	Sur.	Suriname
Aus.	Austria	Eq. Gui.	Equatorial Guinea	Ma., U.S.	Massachusetts, U.S.	Oh., U.S.	Ohio, U.S.	*sw.*	swamp, marsh
Austl.	Australia	Erit.	Eritrea			Ok., U.S.	Oklahoma, U.S.	Swaz.	Swaziland
Az., U.S.	Arizona, U.S.	*est.*	estuary	Mac.	Macedonia	Ont., Can.	Ontario, Can.	Swe.	Sweden
Azer.	Azerbaijan	Est.	Estonia	Madag.	Madagascar	Or., U.S.	Oregon, U.S.	Switz.	Switzerland
b.	bay, gulf, inlet, lagoon	Eth.	Ethiopia	Malay.	Malaysia	Pa., U.S.	Pennsylvania, U.S.	Tai.	Taiwan
		Eur.	Europe	Mald.	Maldives	Pak.	Pakistan	Taj.	Tajikistan
Bah.	Bahamas	Faer. Is.	Faeroe Islands	Man., Can.	Manitoba, Can.	Pan.	Panama	Tan.	Tanzania
Bahr.	Bahrain	Falk. Is.	Falkland Islands	Marsh. Is.	Marshall Islands	Pap. N. Gui.	Papua New Guinea	T./C. Is.	Turks and Caicos Islands
Barb.	Barbados	Fin.	Finland	Mart.	Martinique	Para.	Paraguay		
B.A.T.	British Antarctic Territory	Fl., U.S.	Florida, U.S.	Maur.	Mauritania	P.E.I., Can.	Prince Edward Island, Can.	*ter.*	territory
		for.	forest, moor	May.	Mayotte			Thai.	Thailand
B.C., Can.	British Columbia, Can.	Fr.	France	Md., U.S.	Maryland, U.S.	*pen.*	peninsula	Tn., U.S.	Tennessee, U.S.
		Fr. Gu.	French Guiana	Me., U.S.	Maine, U.S.	Phil.	Philippines	Tok.	Tokelau
Bdi.	Burundi	Fr. Poly.	French Polynesia	Mex.	Mexico	Pit.	Pitcairn	Trin.	Trinidad and Tobago
Bel.	Belgium	F.S.A.T.	French Southern and Antarctic Territory	Mi., U.S.	Michigan, U.S.	*pl.*	plain, flat		
Bela.	Belarus			Micron.	Federated States of Micronesia	*plat.*	plateau, highland	Tun.	Tunisia
Ber.	Bermuda					Pol.	Poland	Tur.	Turkey
Bhu.	Bhutan	Ga., U.S.	Georgia, U.S.	Mid. Is.	Midway Islands	Port.	Portugal	Turk.	Turkmenistan
B.I.O.T.	British Indian Ocean Territory	Gam.	Gambia	*mil.*	military installation	P.R.	Puerto Rico	Tx., U.S.	Texas, U.S.
		Geor.	Georgia	Mn., U.S.	Minnesota, U.S.	*prov.*	province, region	U.A.E.	United Arab Emirates
Bngl.	Bangladesh	Ger.	Germany	Mo., U.S.	Missouri, U.S.	Que., Can.	Quebec, Can.		
Bol.	Bolivia	Gib.	Gibraltar	Mol.	Moldova	*reg.*	physical region	Ug.	Uganda
Boph.	Bophuthatswana	Grc.	Greece	Mon.	Monaco	*res.*	reservoir	U.K.	United Kingdom
Bos.	Bosnia and Herzegovina	Gren.	Grenada	Mong.	Mongolia	Reu.	Reunion	Ukr.	Ukraine
		Grnld.	Greenland	Monts.	Montserrat	*rf.*	reef, shoal	Ur.	Uruguay
Bots.	Botswana	Guad.	Guadeloupe	Mor.	Morocco	R.I., U.S.	Rhode Island, U.S.	U.S.	United States
Braz.	Brazil	Guat.	Guatemala	Moz.	Mozambique	Rom.	Romania	Ut., U.S.	Utah, U.S.
Bru.	Brunei	Gui.	Guinea	Mrts.	Mauritius	Rw.	Rwanda	Uzb.	Uzbekistan
Br. Vir. Is.	British Virgin Islands	Gui.-B.	Guinea-Bissau	Ms., U.S.	Mississippi, U.S.	S.A.	South America	Va., U.S.	Virginia, U.S.
Bul.	Bulgaria	Guy.	Guyana	Mt., U.S.	Montana, U.S.	S. Afr.	South Africa	*val.*	valley, watercourse
Burkina	Burkina Faso	Hi., U.S.	Hawaii, U.S.	*mth.*	river mouth or channel	Sask., Can.	Saskatchewan, Can.	Vat.	Vatican City
c.	cape, point	*hist.*	historic site, ruins					Ven.	Venezuela
Ca., U.S.	California, U.S.	*hist. reg.*	historic region	*mtn.*	mountain	Sau. Ar.	Saudi Arabia	Viet.	Vietnam
Cam.	Cameroon	H.K.	Hong Kong	*mts.*	mountains	S.C., U.S.	South Carolina, U.S.	V.I.U.S.	Virgin Islands (U.S.)
Camb.	Cambodia	Hond.	Honduras	Mwi.	Malawi	*sci.*	scientific station	*vol.*	volcano
Can.	Canada	Hung.	Hungary	N.A.	North America	Scot., U.K.	Scotland, U.K.	Vt., U.S.	Vermont, U.S.
Cay. Is.	Cayman Islands	*i.*	island	N.B., Can.	New Brunswick, Can.	S.D., U.S.	South Dakota, U.S.	Wa., U.S.	Washington, U.S.
Cen. Afr. Rep.	Central African Republic	Ia., U.S.	Iowa, U.S.			Sen.	Senegal	Wal./F.	Wallis and Futuna
		I.C.	Ivory Coast	N.C., U.S.	North Carolina, U.S.	Sey.	Seychelles	Wi., U.S.	Wisconsin, U.S.
Christ. I.	Christmas Island	Ice.	Iceland	N. Cal.	New Caledonia	Sing.	Singapore	W. Sah.	Western Sahara
clf.	cliff, escarpment	*ice*	ice feature, glacier	N. Cyp.	North Cyprus	S. Geor.	South Georgia	W. Sam.	Western Samoa
co.	county, parish	Id., U.S.	Idaho, U.S.	N.D., U.S.	North Dakota, U.S.	S. Kor.	South Korea	*wtfl.*	waterfall
Co., U.S.	Colorado, U.S.	Il., U.S.	Illinois, U.S.	Ne., U.S.	Nebraska, U.S.	S.L.	Sierra Leone	W.V., U.S.	West Virginia, U.S.
Col.	Colombia	In., U.S.	Indiana, U.S.	Neth.	Netherlands	Slo.	Slovenia	Wy., U.S.	Wyoming, U.S.
Com.	Comoros	Indon.	Indonesia	Neth. Ant.	Netherlands Antilles	Slov.	Slovakia	Yugo.	Yugoslavia
cont.	continent	I. of Man	Isle of Man	Newf., Can.	Newfoundland, Can.	S. Mar.	San Marino	Yukon, Can.	Yukon Territory, Can.
C.R.	Costa Rica	Ire.	Ireland	N.H., U.S.	New Hampshire, U.S.	Sol. Is.	Solomon Islands		
crat.	crater	*is.*	islands			Som.	Somalia	Zam.	Zambia
Cro.	Croatia	Isr.	Israel	Nic.	Nicaragua	Sp. N. Afr.	Spanish North Africa	Zimb.	Zimbabwe
Ct., U.S.	Connecticut, U.S.	Isr. Occ.	Israeli Occupied Territories	Nig.	Nigeria				
ctry.	country								

Index

A

Name — Map Ref. — Page

Akranes, Ice. B2 6a
Akritas, Ákra, c., Grc. M5 20
Akron, Al., U.S. C2 108
Akron, Co., U.S. A7 113
Akron, In., U.S. B5 121
Akron, Ia., U.S. B1 122
Akron, Mi., U.S. E7 129
Akron, N.Y., U.S. B2 139
Akron, Oh., U.S. A4 142
Akron, Pa., U.S. F9 145
Aksaray, Tur. B3 48
Aksarka, Russia D5 28
Akşehir, Tur. H14 4
Aksu, China C3 30
Aksuat, Kaz. H8 28
Aksum, Eth. J10 60
Aktau, Kaz. I8 26
Aktogaj, Kaz. H7 28
Akt'ubinsk, Kaz. G9 26
Akūbū (Akobo), stm., Afr. G7 56
Akulivik, Que., Can. f11 104
Akune, Japan O5 36
Akureyri, Ice. B4 6a
Akutan, Ak., U.S. E6 109
Akwanga, Nig. G14 64
Akwaya, Cam. H14 64
Akyel, Eth. K9 60
Akžar, Kaz. H8 28
Ala, stm., China C4 30
Alabama, state, U.S. C3 108
Alabama, stm., Al., U.S. D2 108
Alabama Port, Al., U.S. E1 108
Alabaster, Al., U.S. B3 108
Al-'Abbāsīyah, Sud. K6 60
Āl-'Ābis, Sau. Ar. E3 47
Alacant, Spain G11 16
Alachua, Fl., U.S. C4 116
Alachua, co., Fl., U.S. C4 116
Alacrán, Arrecife, rf., Mex. F15 90
Alacranes, Presa, res., Cuba C4 94
Alagoa Grande, Braz. E11 76
Alagoinhas, Braz. B9 79
Alagón, Spain D10 16
Al-Aḥmadī, Kuw. G10 48
Alaior, Spain F16 16
Al-Ait, Sud. K4 60
Alajskij chrebet, mts., Asia J12 26
Alajuela, C.R. G10 92
Alajuela, prov., C.R. G10 92
Alajuela, Lago, res., Pan. H15 92
Alakamisy, Madag. r22 67b
Alakanuk, Ak., U.S. C7 109
Alakol', ozero, l., Kaz. H8 28
Alalakeiki Channel, strt., Hi., U.S. C5 118
Al-'Alamayn, Egypt B5 60
Alalaú, stm., Braz. H12 84
Al-'Amādīyah, Iraq C7 48
Alamance, co., N.C., U.S. B3 140
Al-'Amārah, Iraq F9 48
Alameda, Sask., Can. H4 105
Alameda, Ca., U.S. h8 112
Alameda, N.M., U.S. B3 138
Alameda, co., Ca., U.S. D3 112
Alameda Naval Air Station, mil., Ca., U.S. h8 112
Alamein see Al-'Alamayn, Egypt B5 60
Alamito Creek, stm., Tx., U.S. p12 150
Alamo, Ga., U.S. D4 117
Alamo, Nv., U.S. F6 135
Alamo, Tn., U.S. B2 149
Alamo, Tx., U.S. F3 150
Alamogordo, N.M., U.S. E4 138
Alamo Heights, Tx., U.S. E3 150
Alamo Hueco Mountains, mts., N.M., U.S. F1 138
Alamo Indian Reservation, N.M., U.S. C2 138
Alamo Lake, res., Az., U.S. C2 110
Alamor, Ec. J2 84
Álamos, Mex. D5 90
Álamos, stm., Mex. C9 90
Alamosa, Co., U.S. D5 113
Alamosa, co., Co., U.S. D5 113
Alamosa, stm., Co., U.S. D4 113
Alamosa Creek, stm., N.M., U.S. D2 138
Alamosa East, Co., U.S. D5 113
Álamos de Márquez, Mex. C8 90
Åland (Ahvenanmaa), is., Fin. K16 6
Åland Islands see Åland, is., Fin. K16 6
Alanje, Pan. I12 92
Alanson, Mi., U.S. C6 129
Alanya, Tur. H14 4
Alaotra, Lac, l., Madag. p23 67b
Alapaha, Ga., U.S. E3 117
Alapaha, stm., U.S. E3 117
Alapajevsk, Russia F10 26
Al-'Aqabah, Jord. I4 50
Alarcón, Embalse de, res., Spain F9 16
Al-'Arīsh, Egypt B7 60
Alarobia Vohiposa, Madag. r22 67b
Alaşehir, Tur. K12 20
Alashanyouqi, China C7 30
Alaska, state, U.S. C9 109
Alaska, Gulf of, b., Ak., U.S. D10 109
Alaska Peninsula, pen., Ak., U.S. D8 109
Alaska Range, mts., Ak., U.S. C9 109
Alassio, Italy E3 18
Al'at, Azer. B10 48
Alat, Uzb. B17 48
Al-'Athāmīn, mts., Asia F7 48
Alatna, stm., Ak., U.S. B9 109
Al-'Atrūn, Sud. H4 60
Alatyr', Russia G7 26
Alausí, Ec. I3 84
Alava, Cape, c., Wa., U.S. A1 154
Alawa, Nig. F13 64
Al-'Ayn, U.A.E. I13 48
Al-'Ayyāṭ, Egypt C6 60
Alazeja, stm., Russia C22 28
Al-'Azīzīyah, Libya B3 56
Alba, Italy E3 18
Alba, Mo., U.S. D3 132
Alba, co., Rom. C7 20
Albacete, Spain G10 16
Al-Badārī, Egypt D6 60
Alba Iulia, Rom. C7 20
Al-Ballāş, Egypt D7 60
Al-Balyanā, Egypt D6 60
Alban, Fr. I9 14
Albania (Shqipëri), ctry., Eur. G12 4
Albano Laziale, Italy H7 18
Albany, Austl. G3 68
Albany, P.E.I., Can. C6 101
Albany, Ga., U.S. E2 117
Albany, Il., U.S. B3 120
Albany, In., U.S. D7 121
Albany, Ky., U.S. D4 124
Albany, La., U.S. g10 125
Albany, Mn., U.S. E4 130
Albany, Mo., U.S. A3 132
Albany, N.Y., U.S. C7 139
Albany, Oh., U.S. C3 142
Albany, Or., U.S. C3 144
Albany, Tx., U.S. C3 150
Albany, Vt., U.S. B4 152
Albany, Wi., U.S. F4 156
Albany, Wy., U.S. E6 157
Albany, co., N.Y., U.S. C6 139
Albany, co., Wy., U.S. E7 157
Albany, stm., Ont., Can. o18 103
Al-Baq'ah, Jord. D5 50
Albardón, Arg. F4 80
Al-Barrah, Sau. Ar. B4 47
Al-Barun, Sud. L7 60
Al-Başrah (Basra), Iraq F9 48
Al-Batrūn, Leb. D3 48
Al-Bauga, Sud. H7 60
Al-Bawīṭī, Egypt C5 60
Al-Bayḍā', Libya B5 56
Al-Bayḍā', Yemen G4 47
Albemarle, N.C., U.S. B2 140
Albemarle, co., Va., U.S. C4 153
Albemarle Lake, l., Ms., U.S. C2 131
Albemarle Sound, strt., N.C., U.S. A6 140
Albenga, Italy E3 18
Alberdi, Para. D9 80
Alberga Creek, stm., Austl. E6 68
Albert, Fr. B9 14
Albert, Ks., U.S. D4 123
Albert, Lake, l., Afr. A6 58
Alberta, Al., U.S. C2 108
Alberta, Va., U.S. D5 153
Alberta, prov., Can. C4 98
Alberta, Mount, mtn., Alta., Can. C2 98
Albert City, Ia., U.S. B3 122
Albert Edward Bay, b., N.W. Ter., Can. C12 96
Alberti, Arg. H8 80
Al'bertin, Bela. H8 22
Albertinia, S. Afr. J5 66
Albertkanaal (Canal Albert), Bel. G8 12
Albert Lea, Mn., U.S. G5 130
Albert Markham, Mount, mtn., Ant. D8 73
Albert Nile, stm., Ug. H7 56
Alberton, P.E.I., Can. C5 101
Alberton, Mt., U.S. C2 133
Albertson, N.Y., U.S. k13 139
Albertville, Sask., Can. D3 105
Albertville, Fr. G13 14
Albertville, Al., U.S. A3 108
Albertville, Mn., U.S. E5 130
Albi, Fr. I9 14
Albia, Ia., U.S. C5 122
Albin, Wy., U.S. E8 157
Albina, Sur. B8 76
Albino, Italy D4 18
Albion, Ca., U.S. C2 112
Albion, Id., U.S. G5 119
Albion, Il., U.S. E5 120
Albion, In., U.S. B7 121
Albion, Ia., U.S. B5 122
Albion, Me., U.S. D3 126
Albion, Mi., U.S. F6 129
Albion, Ne., U.S. C7 134
Albion, N.Y., U.S. B2 139
Albion, Pa., U.S. C1 145
Albion, R.I., U.S. B4 146
Albion, Wa., U.S. C8 154
Al-Biqā' (Bekaa Valley), val., Leb. A6 50
Al-Birk, Sau. Ar. E2 47
Alborán, Isla de, i., Spain J8 16
Alborán Sea I8 16
Ålborg, Den. M11 6
Alborn, Mn., U.S. D6 130
Alborz, Reshteh-ye Kūhhā-ye (Elburz Mountains), mts., Iran C12 48
Albrightsville, Pa., U.S. D10 145
Albū Gharz, Sabkhat, l., Asia D6 48
Albuñol, Spain I8 16
Albuquerque, Braz. H13 82
Albuquerque, N.M., U.S. B3 138
Albuquerque, Cayos de, is., Col. H4 94
Al-Buraymī, U.A.E. B9 47
Alburg, Vt., U.S. B2 152
Alburnett, Ia., U.S. B6 122
Alburtis, Pa., U.S. F10 145
Albury, Austl. K7 70
Al-Buṭaynah, Syria C7 50
Alca, Peru F5 82
Alcalá de Guadaira, Spain H6 16
Alcalá de Henares, Spain E8 16
Alcalde, N.M., U.S. A3 138
Alcamachi, stm., Bol. G8 82
Alcamo, Italy L7 18
Alcanar, Spain E12 16
Alcañiz, Spain D11 16
Alcântara, Braz. D10 76
Alcántara, Spain F5 16
Alcántara, Embalse de, res., Spain F5 16
Alcantarilla, Spain H10 16
Alcantilado, Braz. D2 79
Alcaudete, Spain H7 16
Alcázar de San Juan, Spain F8 16
Alcester, S.D., U.S. D9 148
Alčevsk, Ukr. H5 26
Alcira (Gigena), Arg. G6 80
Alcoa, Tn., U.S. D10 149
Alcobaça, Braz. D9 79
Alcobaça, Port. F3 16
Alcobaça, stm., Braz. D9 79
Alcoi, Spain G11 16
Alcolu, S.C., U.S. D7 147
Alcomdale, Alta., Can. C4 98
Alcona, co., Mi., U.S. D7 129
Alcorn, co., Ms., U.S. A5 131
Alcorta, Arg. G8 80
Alcoutim, Port. H4 16
Alcova, Wy., U.S. D6 157
Alcovy, stm., Ga., U.S. C3 117
Alda, Ne., U.S. D7 134
Aldabra Island, i., Sey. C9 58
Aldama, Mex. C7 90
Aldama, Mex. F10 90
Aldan, Russia F17 28
Aldan, stm., Russia F18 28
Aldanskoje nagorje, plat., Russia F17 28
Aldeburgh, Eng., U.K. I15 8
Alden, Il., U.S. A5 120
Alden, Ia., U.S. B4 122
Alden, Ks., U.S. D5 123
Alden, Mi., U.S. D5 129
Alden, Mn., U.S. G5 130
Alden, N.Y., U.S. C2 139
Alden, Pa., U.S. D9 145
Alder, Mt., U.S. E4 133
Alder Brook, stm., Vt., U.S. B4 152
Alderney, i., Guernsey L11 8
Aldershot, Eng., U.K. J13 8
Alderson, Ok., U.S. C6 143
Alderson, W.V., U.S. D4 155
Aldersyde, Alta., Can. D4 98
Aldora, Ga., U.S. C2 117
Aldrich, Al., U.S. B3 108
Aledo, Il., U.S. B3 120
Alefa, Eth. L9 60
Aleg, Maur. C3 64
Alegre, Braz. F8 79
Alegre, stm., Braz. F12 82
Alegres Mountain, mtn., N.M., U.S. C2 138
Alegrete, Braz. E11 80
Alejandro Roca, Arg. G7 80
Alejandro Selkirk, Isla, i., Chile H6 74
Alejo Ledesma, Arg. G7 80
Alejsk, Russia G8 28
Aleknagik, Ak., U.S. D8 109
Aleksandrija, Ukr. H4 26
Aleksandro-Nevskij, Russia H23 22
Aleksandrov, Russia E21 22
Aleksandrov Gaj, Russia G7 26
Aleksandrovsk-Sachalinskij, Russia G20 28
Aleksejevka, Kaz. G12 26
Aleksejevka, Russia G5 26
Aleksejevsk, Russia F13 28
Aleksin, Russia G20 22
Aleksinac, Yugo. F5 20
Alemania, Arg. D6 80
Além Paraíba, Braz. F7 79
Alençon, Fr. D7 14
Alenquer, Braz. D8 76
Alentejo, hist. reg., Port. G3 16
Alenuihaha Channel, strt., Hi., U.S. C5 118
Aleppo see Halab, Syria C4 48
Aléria, Fr. I24 15a
Alert, N.W. Ter., Can. A13 86
Alert Bay, B.C., Can. D4 99
Alès, Fr. H11 14
Alessandria, Italy E3 18
Ålesund, Nor. J10 6
Aletschhorn, mtn., Switz. F9 13
Aleutian Islands, is., Ak., U.S. E3 109
Aleutian Range, mts., Ak., U.S. D9 109
Aleutian Trench D3 86
Alevina, mys, c., Russia F22 28
Alex, Ok., U.S. C4 143
Alexander, Man., Can. E1 100
Alexander, Ar., U.S. C3 111
Alexander, Ga., U.S. C5 117
Alexander, Il., U.S. D3 120
Alexander, N.D., U.S. B2 141
Alexander, co., Il., U.S. F4 120
Alexander, co., N.C., U.S. B1 140
Alexander, Lake, l., Mn., U.S. D4 130
Alexander Archipelago, is., Ak., U.S. D12 109
Alexander Bay, S. Afr. G3 66
Alexander City, Al., U.S. C4 108
Alexander Island, i., Ant. C12 73
Alexander Mills, N.C., U.S. B1 140
Alexandra, N.Z. F2 72
Alexandra, stm., Austl. B4 70
Alexandra Falls, wtfl, N.W. Ter., Can. D9 96
Alexandretta, Gulf of see İskenderun Körfezi, b., Tur. H15 4
Alexandretta see İskenderun, Tur. C4 48
Alexandria, B.C., Can. C6 99
Alexandria, Ont., Can. B10 103
Alexandria, Rom. F9 20
Alexandria, Al., U.S. B4 108
Alexandria, In., U.S. D6 121
Alexandria, Ky., U.S. B5 124
Alexandria, La., U.S. C3 125
Alexandria, Mn., U.S. E3 130
Alexandria, Mo., U.S. A6 132
Alexandria, Ne., U.S. D8 134
Alexandria, N.H., U.S. C3 136
Alexandria, S.D., U.S. D8 148
Alexandria, Tn., U.S. A5 149
Alexandria, Va., U.S. B5 153
Alexandria see Al-Iskandarīyah, Egypt B5 60
Alexandria Bay, N.Y., U.S. A5 139
Alexandrina, Lake, l., Austl. J3 70
Alexandroúpolis, Grc. I9 20
Alexis, Il., U.S. B3 120
Alexis Creek, B.C., Can. C6 99
Alfalfa, co., Ok., U.S. A3 143
Alfaro, Spain C10 16
Al-Fāshir, Sud. K3 60
Al-Fashn, Egypt C6 60
Al-Fāw, Iraq G10 48
Al-Fayyūm, Egypt C6 60
Alfeld, Ger. D9 10
Alfenas, Braz. F6 79
Al-Fifi, Sud. L3 60
Alfiós, stm., Grc. L5 20
Alföld, pl., Hung. H20 10
Alford, Fl., U.S. B1 116
Alfred, Ont., Can. B10 103
Alfred, Me., U.S. E2 126
Alfred, N.Y., U.S. C3 139
Alga, Kaz. H9 26
Ålgård, Nor. L9 6
Al-Garef, Sud. K8 60
Algarrobal, Chile E3 80
Algarrobo, Arg. J7 80
Algarrobo, Arg. F4 80
Algarrobo, Chile G3 80
Algarrobo del Águila, Arg. I5 80
Algarve, hist. reg., Port. H3 16
Algasovo, Russia H24 22
Al-Gebir, Sud. K5 60
Algeciras, Col. F5 84
Algeciras, Spain I6 16
Algemesí, Spain F11 16
Algena, Erit. I10 60
Alger, Oh., U.S. B2 142
Alger, co., Mi., U.S. B4 129
Algeria (Algérie), ctry., Afr. C7 54
Al-Ghāṭ, Sau. Ar. H8 48
Al-Ghawr, val., Asia D5 50
Al-Ghayḍah, Yemen F8 47
Al-Ghazālah, Sau. Ar. H6 48
Alghero, Italy I3 18
Al-Ghurayfah, Oman B10 47
Al-Ghurdaqah, Egypt D7 60
Algiers see El Djazaïr, Alg. B12 62
Alginet, Spain F11 16
Algodón, stm., Peru I6 84
Algodones, N.M., U.S. B3 138
Algoma, Ms., U.S. A4 131
Algoma, Wi., U.S. D6 156
Algona, Ia., U.S. A3 122
Algona, Wa., U.S. B3 154
Algonac, Mi., U.S. F8 129
Algonquin, Ont., Can. C9 103
Algonquin, Il., U.S. A5 120
Algonquin Provincial Park, Ont., Can. B6 103
Algood, Tn., U.S. C8 149
Algorta, Spain B8 16
Algorta, Ur. G10 80
Al-Ḥadīthah, Iraq D7 48
Al-Ḥadīthah, Sau. Ar. E8 50
Al-Ḥajarah, reg., Asia F8 48
Al Hajeb, Mor. D8 62
Al-Ḥamād, pl., Sau. Ar. E5 48
Alhama de Murcia, Spain H10 16
Alhambra, Ca., U.S. m12 112
Alhambra, Il., U.S. E4 120
Al-Ḥammām, Egypt B5 60
Al-Ḥamrā', Sau. Ar. C1 47
Al-Ḥarīq, Sau. Ar. C5 47
Al-Harūj al-Aswad, hills, Libya C4 56
Al-Ḥasakah, Syria C6 48
Alhaurín el Grande, Spain I7 16
Al-Ḥawātah, Sud. K8 60
Al-Ḥawrah, Yemen H5 47
Al-Ḥawṭah, Yemen G6 47
Al-Ḥayy, Iraq E9 48
Al-Ḥayyānīyah, Sau. Ar. G7 48
Al-Ḥayz, Egypt C5 60
Al-Ḥijāz, reg., Sau. Ar. I5 48
Al-Ḥillah, Iraq E8 48
Al-Ḥillah, Sud. K4 60
Al-Hirmil, Leb. D4 48
Al-Ḥiṣn, Jord. D5 50
Al Hoceïma, Mor. A6 54
Al Hoceïma, Baie d', b., Afr. J8 16
Alhucemas, Peñón de, i., Sp. N. Afr. J8 16
Al-Ḥudaydah, Yemen G3 47
Al-Hufūf, Sau. Ar. B6 47
Al-Ḥulwah, Sau. Ar. J9 48
Al-Ḥumayshah, Yemen H4 47
Al-Ḥuṣayḥiṣah, Sud. J7 60
Al-Ḥuwaylizah, Isr. Occ. B5 50
Al-Ḥuwayyiṭ, Sau. Ar. I6 48
'Alīābād, Iran C13 48
Aliaga, Spain E11 16
Aliákmon, stm., Grc. I6 20
Aliákmonos, Tekhnití Límni, res., Grc. I5 20
'Alī al-Gharbī, Iraq E9 48
Alībāg, India C2 46
Ali-Bajramly, Azer. B10 48
Alibej, ozero, l., Ukr. D14 20
Alibunar, Yugo. D4 20
Alice, Ciskei I8 66
Alice, Tx., U.S. F3 150
Alicedale, S. Afr. I8 66
Alice Lake, l., Mn., U.S. C7 130
Alice Springs, Austl. D6 68
Alice Town, Bah. B5 94
Aliceville, Al., U.S. B1 108
Alicia, Ar., U.S. B4 111
Alida, Sask., Can. H5 105
Alīgarh, India G8 44
Alīgūdarz, Iran E10 48
Alijos, Islas, is., Mex. E2 90
Al-Ikhwān, is., Yemen G5 42
Aline, Ok., U.S. A3 143
Aliquippa, Pa., U.S. E1 145
Al-'Irāq, Jord. F5 50
Al-'Īsāwīyah, Sau. Ar. F4 48
Al-Iskandarīyah (Alexandria), Egypt B5 60
Al-Ismā'īlīyah, Egypt B7 60
Aliwal North, S. Afr. H8 66
Alix, Alta., Can. C4 98
Alix, Ar., U.S. B2 111
Al-Jabalayn, Sud. K7 60
Al-Jadīdah, Egypt E5 60
Al-Jafr, Jord. H6 50
Al-Jaghbūb, Libya C3 60
Al-Jawf, Libya E2 60
Al-Jawf, Sau. Ar. G5 48
Al-Jaylī, Sud. I7 60
Al-Jazīrah, reg., Sud. J7 60
Aljezur, Port. H3 16
Al-Jīfārah, Sau. Ar. J8 48
Al-Jifārah (Jeffara), pl., Afr. D16 62
Al-Jīzah, Egypt B6 60
Al-Jubayl, Sau. Ar. H10 48
Al-Jubayn, Sud. K8 60
Al-Judayyidah, Jord. E5 50
Al-Julaydah, well, Asia G8 48
Al-Junaynah, Sud. K2 60
Aljustrel, Port. H3 16
Al-Kafr, Syria C7 50
Alkali Lake, l., Nv., U.S. B2 135
Alkali Lake, l., Or., U.S. E6 144
Alkaline Lake, l., N.D., U.S. C6 141
Al-Kāmil, Oman C11 47
Al-Karabah, Sud. H7 60
Al-Karak, Jord. F5 50
Al-Karnak, Egypt E7 60
Al-Kawah, Sud. K7 60
Al-Khabrā', Sau. Ar. H7 48
Al-Khābūrah, Oman C10 47
Al-Khalīl (Hebron), Isr. Occ. E4 50
Al-Khālis, Iraq E8 48
Al-Khandaq, Sud. H6 60
Al-Khārijah, Egypt E6 60
Al-Kharṭūm (Khartoum), Sud. J7 60
Al-Kharṭūm Baḥrī, Sud. J7 60
Al-Khaṣab, Oman A10 47
Al-Khubar, Sau. Ar. A7 47
Al-Khums, Libya B3 56
Al-Khuraybah, Sau. Ar. C5 50
Al-Khuraybah, Yemen G6 47
Al-Khurmah, Sau. Ar. D3 47
Al-Kidn, reg., Asia C9 47
Alkmaar, Neth. C6 12
Alkol, W.V., U.S. m12 155
Al-Kuntillah, Egypt B8 60
Al-Kūt, Iraq E8 48
Al-Kuwayt, Kuw. G9 48
Allada, Benin H11 64
Al-Lādhiqīyah (Latakia), Syria D3 48
Allagash, stm., Me., U.S. B3 126
Allagash Lake, l., Me., U.S. B3 126
Al-Lagowa, Sud. L5 60
Allahābād, India H9 44
Allakaket, Ak., U.S. B9 109
Allamakee, co., Ia., U.S. A6 122
Allamuchy Mountain, mtn., N.J., U.S. B3 137
Allan, Sask., Can. F2 105
Allanche, Fr. G9 14
Allanmyo, Burma E3 40
'Allāq, Bi'r, well, Libya E16 62
Allardt, Tn., U.S. C9 149
Allatoona Lake, res., Ga., U.S. B2 117
Al-Layyah, Sud. I8 60
Alldays, S. Afr. D9 66
Alleene, Ar., U.S. D1 111
Allegan, Mi., U.S. F5 129
Allegan, co., Mi., U.S. F5 129
Allegany, N.Y., U.S. C2 139
Allegany, co., Md., U.S. k13 127
Allegany, co., N.Y., U.S. C2 139
Allegany Indian Reservation, N.Y., U.S. C2 139
Alleghany, co., N.C., U.S. A1 140
Alleghany, co., Va., U.S. C2 153
Allegheny, co., Pa., U.S. E2 145
Allegheny, stm., U.S. E2 145
Allegheny Front, mtn., W.V., U.S. B5 155
Allegheny Mountain, mts., U.S. B3 153
Allegheny Plateau, plat., U.S. E1 145
Allegheny Reservoir, res., U.S. B4 145
Alleman, Ia., U.S. e8 122
Allemands, Bayou Des, stm., La., U.S. k11 125
Allemands, Lac Des, l., La., U.S. E5 125
Allen, Arg. J5 80
Allen, Ks., U.S. D7 123
Allen, Ky., U.S. C7 124
Allen, Md., U.S. D6 127
Allen, Ne., U.S. B9 134
Allen, Ok., U.S. C5 143
Allen, S.D., U.S. D4 148
Allen, Tx., U.S. C4 150
Allen, Tx., U.S. m10 150
Allen, co., In., U.S. B7 121
Allen, co., Ks., U.S. E8 123
Allen, co., Ky., U.S. D3 124
Allen, co., La., U.S. D3 125
Allen, co., Oh., U.S. B1 142
Allen, Mount, mtn., Ak., U.S. C11 109
Allendale, Il., U.S. E6 120
Allendale, In., U.S. F3 121
Allendale, N.J., U.S. A4 137
Allendale, S.C., U.S. E5 147
Allendale, co., S.C., U.S. F5 147
Allende, Mex. C9 90
Allenford, Ont., Can. C3 103
Allenhurst, Ga., U.S. E5 117
Allen Park, Mi., U.S. p15 129
Allens Mills, Me., U.S. D2 126
Allenspark, Co., U.S. A5 113
Allenstein see Olsztyn, Pol. B20 10
Allensville, Ky., U.S. D2 124
Allenton, Mo., U.S. f12 132
Allenton, R.I., U.S. E4 146
Allenton, Wi., U.S. E5 156
Allentown, Ga., U.S. D3 117
Allentown, N.J., U.S. C3 137
Allentown, Pa., U.S. E11 145
Allentsteig, Aus. G15 10
Allenwood, N.J., U.S. C4 137
Alleppey, India H4 46
Aller, stm., Ger. C9 10
Allerton, Il., U.S. D6 120
Allerton, Ia., U.S. D4 122
Allerton, Point, c., Ma., U.S. B6 128
Allgäu, reg., Ger. H10 10
Allgäuer Alpen, mts., Eur. E17 14
Allgood, Al., U.S. B3 108
Alliance, Alta., Can. C5 98
Alliance, Ne., U.S. B3 134
Alliance, N.C., U.S. B6 140
Alliance, Oh., U.S. B4 142
Al-Lidām, Sau. Ar. D4 47
Allier, dept., Fr. F9 14
Allier, stm., Fr. F10 14
Alligator, Ms., U.S. A3 131
Alligator, stm., N.C., U.S. B6 140
Alligator Lake, l., Me., U.S. D4 126
Allison, Ia., U.S. B5 122
Allison, Pa., U.S. G2 145
Allison Park, Pa., U.S. h14 145
Alliston [Beeton Tecumseth and Tottenham], Ont., Can. C5 103
Al-Lith, Sau. Ar. D2 47
Alloa, Scot., U.K. E10 8
Allons, Tn., U.S. C8 149
Allora, Austl. G9 70
Allouez, Wi., U.S. h9 156
Alloway, N.J., U.S. D2 137
Alloway Creek, stm., N.J., U.S. D2 137
Allport, Ar., U.S. C4 111
Al-Luḥayyah, Yemen G3 47
Allumette Lake, l., Can. B7 103
Allyn, Wa., U.S. B3 154
Alma, N.B., Can. D5 101
Alma, Ont., Can. D4 103
Alma, Que., Can. A6 104
Alma, Ar., U.S. B1 111
Alma, Co., U.S. B4 113
Alma, Ga., U.S. E4 117
Alma, Il., U.S. E5 120
Alma, Ks., U.S. C7 123
Alma, Mi., U.S. E6 129
Alma, Mo., U.S. B4 132
Alma, Ne., U.S. D6 134
Alma, Wi., U.S. D2 156
Alma-Ata (Almaty), Kaz. I13 26
Alma Center, Wi., U.S. D3 156
Almada, Port. G2 16
Almadén, Spain G7 16
Al-Madīnah (Medina), Sau. Ar. B1 47
Al-Mafāzah, Sud. K8 60
Al-Mafraq, Jord. D6 50
Almafuerte, Arg. G6 80
Almagro, Spain G8 16
Al-Maḥallah al-Kubrā, Egypt B6 60
Al-Mahārīq, Egypt E6 60
Al Mahbas, W. Sah. G6 62
Alma Hill, hill, N.Y., U.S. C2 139
Al-Majma'ah, Sau. Ar. I8 48
Al-Makhā' (Mocha), Yemen H3 47
Almalyk, Uzb. I11 26
Al-Manāmah, Bahr. H11 48
Almanor, Lake, l., Ca., U.S. B3 112
Almansa, Spain G10 16
Al-Manshāh, Egypt D6 60
Al-Manṣūrah, Egypt B6 60
Al-Manzilah, Egypt F1 48
Almanzor, mtn., Spain E6 16
Al-Marāghah, Egypt D6 60
Al-Marj, Libya B5 56
Almas, Pico das, mtn., Braz. B8 79
Al-Masīd, Sud. J7 60
Almassora, Spain F11 16
Al-Matammah, Sud. I7 60
Al-Maṭarīyah, Egypt B7 60
Al-Matnah, Sud. K8 60
Almaville, Tn., U.S. B5 149
Al-Mawṣil (Mosul), Iraq C7 48
Al-Mayādīn, Syria D6 48
Al-Mazār, Jord. F5 50
Al-Mazra'ah, Jord. F5 50
Almeida, Port. E5 16
Almeirim, Port. F3 16
Almelo, Neth. D10 12
Almelund, Mn., U.S. E6 130
Almena, Ks., U.S. C4 123
Almena, Wi., U.S. C1 156
Almenara, Braz. D8 79
Almendralejo, Spain G5 16
Almería, Spain I9 16
Almería, Golfo de, b., Spain I9 16
Al'metjevsk, Russia G8 26
Al-Midhnab, Sau. Ar. I8 48
Al-Minyā, Egypt C6 60
Almira, Wa., U.S. B7 154
Almirante, Pan. C1 84
Almirante, Bahía de, b., Pan. H12 92
Almirante Latorre, Chile E3 80
Al-Mismīyah, Syria B6 50
Almo, Id., U.S. G5 119
Almodôvar, Port. H3 16
Almolonga, Guat. C3 92
Almon, Ga., U.S. C3 117
Almond, Wi., U.S. D4 156
Almont, Mi., U.S. F7 129
Almont, N.D., U.S. C4 141
Almonte, Ont., Can. B8 103
Almonte, Spain H5 16
Almora, India F8 44
Al-Mubarraz, Sau. Ar. C5 47
Al-Mubarraz, Sau. Ar. B6 47
Al-Mudawwarah, Jord. G3 48
Al-Muglad, Sud. L4 60
Al-Muharraq, Bahr. H11 48
Al-Mukallā, Yemen G6 47
Almuñécar, Spain I8 16
Al-Musallamīyah, Sud. J7 60
Al-Musayfirah, Syria C6 50
Al-Musayjid, Sau. Ar. B1 47
Al-Mutayn, Leb. A5 50
Al-Muwayh, Sau. Ar. C2 47
Al-Muwaylih, Sau. Ar. H3 48
Almyra, Ar., U.S. C4 111
Alnwick, Eng., U.K. F12 8
Aloândia, Braz. D4 79
Aloha, Or., U.S. h12 144
Alojā, Lat. D7 22
Alonsa, Man., Can. D2 100
Alor, Pulau, i., Indon. G7 38
Alor Setar, Malay. K6 40
Alosno, Spain H4 16
Alost (Aalst), Bel. G5 12
Alpachiri, Arg. I7 80
Alpaugh, Ca., U.S. E4 112
Alpena, Ar., U.S. A2 111
Alpena, Mi., U.S. C7 129
Alpena, S.D., U.S. C7 148
Alpena, co., Mi., U.S. D7 129
Alpes-de-Haute-Provence, dept., Fr. H13 14
Alpes Maritimes, dept., Fr. I14 14
Alpha, Austl. D7 70
Alpha, Il., U.S. B3 120
Alpha, N.J., U.S. B2 137
Alpharetta, Ga., U.S. B2 117
Alpine, Al., U.S. B3 108
Alpine, Az., U.S. D6 110
Alpine, Ar., U.S. C2 111
Alpine, N.J., U.S. h9 137
Alpine, Tn., U.S. C8 149
Alpine, Tx., U.S. D1 150
Alpine, Ut., U.S. C4 151
Alpine, Wy., U.S. C1 157
Alpine, co., Ca., U.S. C4 112
Alpine National Park, Austl. K7 70
Alpinópolis, Braz. F5 79
Alpoca, W.V., U.S. D3 155
Alps, mts., Eur. F10 4
Al-Qābil, Oman C9 47
Al-Qaḍārif, Sud. J8 60
Al-Qaḍīmah, Sau. Ar. C1 47

Name | Map Ref. | Page

Al-Qāhirah (Cairo), Egypt B6 60
Al-Qahmah, Sau. Ar. E2 47
Al-Qalībah, Sau. Ar. G4 48
Al-Qāmishlī, Syria C6 48
Al-Qanṭarah, Egypt B7 60
Al-Qaryah ash-Sharqīyah, Libya B3 56
Al-Qaṣr, Egypt E5 60
Al-Qaṣr, Jord. F5 50
Al-Qaṭīf, Sau. Ar. A7 47
Al-Qaṭrānah, Jord. F6 50
Al-Qaṭrūn, Libya D3 56
Al-Qayṣūmah, Sau. Ar. G9 48
Al-Qiṣfah, Jord. C5 50
Al-Quds see Yerushalayim, Isr. E4 50
Al-Qunayṭirah, Syria B5 50
Al-Qunfudhah, Sau. Ar. E2 47
Al-Qurnah, Iraq F9 48
Al-Quṣaymah, Egypt G2 50
Al-Quṣayr, Egypt D8 60
Al-Qūṣīyah, Egypt D6 60
Al-Quṭayfah, Syria A7 50
Al-Quṭaynah, Sud. J7 60
Al-Quwayʻīyah, Sau. Ar. B4 47
Al-Quwayṣ, Sud. K8 60
Alsace, hist. reg., Fr. D14 14
Alsask, Sask., Can. F1 105
Alsea, Or., U.S. C3 144
Alsen, N.D., U.S. A7 141
Alsey, Il., U.S. D3 120
Alsfeld, Ger. E9 10
Alsina, Arg. G9 80
Alstead, N.H., U.S. D2 136
Alstead, stm., Sask., Can. B2 105
Alstead Center, N.H., U.S. D2 136
Alston, Ga., U.S. D4 117
Alsunga, Lat. E4 22
Alta, Ia., U.S. B2 122
Alta, Wy., U.S. C1 157
Altadena, Ca., U.S. m12 112
Alta Gracia, Arg. F6 80
Altagracia, Nic. F9 92
Altagracia, Ven. B7 84
Altagracia de Orituco, Ven. C9 84
Altai, mts., Asia H16 26
Altaj (Jesönbulag), Mong. B6 30
Altaj, state, Russia G15 26
Altamaha, stm., Ga., U.S. E4 117
Altamaha Sound, strt., Ga., U.S. E5 117
Altamira, Braz. D8 76
Altamira, Chile C4 80
Altamira, C.R. G10 92
Altamont, Man., Can. E2 100
Altamont, Il., U.S. D5 120
Altamont, Ks., U.S. E8 123
Altamont, Mo., U.S. B3 132
Altamont, N.Y., U.S. C6 139
Altamont, Or., U.S. E5 144
Altamont, Tn., U.S. D8 149
Altamonte Springs, Fl., U.S. D5 116
Altamura, Italy I11 18
Altamura, Isla, i., Mex. E5 90
Altar, Mex. B4 90
Altar, stm., Mex. B4 90
Altar, Desierto de, des., Mex. B3 90
Altar de Los Sacrificios, hist., Guat. I14 90
Altario, Alta., Can. D5 98
Altata, Mex. E6 90
Alta Verapaz, dept., Guat. B4 92
Alta Vista, Ia., U.S. A5 122
Alta Vista, Ks., U.S. D7 123
Altavista, Va., U.S. C3 153
Altay, China B4 30
Altdorf, Switz. E10 13
Altenburg, Ger. E12 10
Altenburg, Mo., U.S. D8 132
Altha, Fl., U.S. B1 116
Altheimer, Ar., U.S. C4 111
Althofen, Aus. I14 10
Altinópolis, Braz. F5 79
Altiplano, plat., S.A. H7 82
Altkirch, Fr. E14 14
Altmark, hist. reg., Ger. C11 10
Altmühl, stm., Ger. F10 10
Alto, Ga., U.S. B3 117
Alto, N.M., U.S. D4 138
Alto, Tx., U.S. D5 150
Alto Araguaia, Braz. D2 79
Alto Cedro, Cuba D7 94
Alto Coité, Braz. C1 79
Alto del Carmen, Chile E3 80
Alto do Rio Doce, Braz. F7 79
Alto Garças, Braz. D2 79
Altomünster, Ger. G11 10
Alton, Al., U.S. B3 108
Alton, Il., U.S. E3 120
Alton, Ia., U.S. B2 122
Alton, Ks., U.S. C5 123
Alton, La., U.S. h12 125
Alton, Mo., U.S. E6 132
Alton, N.H., U.S. D4 136
Altona, Man., Can. E3 100
Altona, Il., U.S. B3 120
Altona, In., U.S. B7 121
Alton Bay, N.H., U.S. D4 136
Altoona, Al., U.S. A3 108
Altoona, Fl., U.S. D5 116
Altoona, Ia., U.S. C4 122
Altoona, Ks., U.S. E8 123
Altoona, Pa., U.S. E5 145
Altoona, Wi., U.S. D2 156
Alto Paraguai, Braz. F13 82
Alto Paraguay, dept., Para. I12 82
Alto Paraíso de Goiás, Braz. C5 79
Alto Paraná, dept., Para. C11 80
Alto Parnaíba, Braz. E9 76
Alto Pass, Il., U.S. F4 120
Alto Purús, stm., Peru D6 82
Alto Río Senguer, Arg. F2 78
Alto Sucuriú, Braz. E2 79
Altötting, Ger. G12 10
Alto Yurua, stm., Peru C5 82
Altro, Ky., U.S. C6 124
Altstätten, Switz. D12 13
Altuchovo, Russia I17 22
Altunoluk, Tur. J10 20
Altun Shan, mts., China D4 30
Altura, Mn., U.S. F7 130
Alturas, Ca., U.S. B3 112
Altus, Ar., U.S. B2 111
Altus, Ok., U.S. C2 143
Altus Air Force Base, mil., Ok., U.S. C2 143
Altus Reservoir, res., Ok., U.S. C2 143
Al-ʻUbaylah, Sau. Ar. D7 47
Al-Ubayyid, Sud. K6 60
Al-ʻUdaysāt, Egypt E7 60
Al-Udayyah, Sud. K5 60
Aluk, Sud. M4 60
Alūksne, Lat. D10 22
Al-ʻUlā, Sau. Ar. H4 48
Alum Bank, Pa., U.S. F4 145
Alum Creek, W.V., U.S. m12 155
Alum Creek, stm., Oh., U.S. k11 142
Aluminé, Lago, l., Arg. J3 80
Al-ʻUqaylah, Libya B4 56
Al-ʻUqayr, Sau. Ar. B7 47
Al-Uqṣur (Luxor), Egypt E7 60
Al-ʻUwaynāt, Libya C3 56
Al-ʻUyaynah, Sau. Ar. B5 47
Alva, Fl., U.S. F5 116
Alva, Ok., U.S. A3 143
Alva, Wy., U.S. B8 157
Alvarado, Mex. H12 90
Alvarado, Mn., U.S. B2 130
Alvarado, Tx., U.S. C4 150
Alvarães, Braz. I10 84
Álvaro Obregón, Presa, res., Mex. D5 90
Alvdal, Nor. J12 6
Alvear, Arg. E10 80
Alvena, Sask., Can. E2 105
Alvernia, Mount, hill, Bah. B7 94
Alvesta, Swe. M14 6
Alvin, Il., U.S. C6 120
Alvin, Tx., U.S. E5 150
Alvinópolis, Braz. F7 79
Alvinston, Ont., Can. E3 103
Alvito, Port. G4 16
Älvkarleby, Swe. K15 6
Alvo, Ne., U.S. h12 134
Alvord, Ia., U.S. A1 122
Alvord, Tx., U.S. C4 150
Alvord Lake, l., Or., U.S. E8 144
Älvros, Swe. J14 6
Älvsborgs Län, co., Swe. L13 6
Al-Wajh, Sau. Ar. H4 48
Al-Wakrah, Qatar I11 48
Alwar, India G7 44
Al-Wāsiṭah, Egypt C6 60
Al-Wazz, Sud. J6 60
Alxa Zuoqi, China D8 30
Alytus, Lith. G7 22
Alzamaj, Russia F11 28
Alzira (Alcira), Spain F11 16
Ama, La., U.S. k11 125
Amacuro, stm., S.A. C12 84
Amadeus, Lake, l., Austl. D6 68
Amadjuak Lake, l., N.W. Ter., Can. C18 96
Amador, co., Ca., U.S. C3 112
Amagansett, N.Y., U.S. n16 139
Amagasaki, Japan M10 36
Amagi, Japan N5 36
Amagon, Ar., U.S. B4 111
Amagunze, Nig. H13 64
Amahai, Indon. F8 38
Amaichá del Valle, Arg. D6 80
Amajac, stm., Mex. G10 90
Amaka, stm., Nic. C9 92
Amakusa-shotō, is., Japan O5 36
Amakusa-Shimo-shima, i., Japan O5 36
Åmål, Swe. L13 6
Amalfi, Col. D5 84
Amalfi, Italy I9 18
Amalga, Ut., U.S. B4 151
Amalia, N.M., U.S. A4 138
Amaliás, Grc. L5 20
Amambaí, Braz. G1 79
Amambaí, stm., Braz. G1 79
Amambay, dept., Para. B10 80
Amami-Ō-shima, i., Japan s4 37b
Amami-shotō, is., Japan t3 37b
Amana, Ia., U.S. C6 122
Amanã, stm., Braz. J14 84
Amana, stm., Ven. J13 94
Amanã, Lago, l., Braz. I10 84
Amanda, Oh., U.S. C3 142
Amapá, Braz. D9 74
Amapá, Braz. C8 76
Amapala, Hond. D7 92
Amapala, Punta de, c., El Sal. D7 92
Amarante, Braz. E10 76
Amaranth, Man., Can. D2 100
Amarapura, Burma D4 40
ʻAmārat Abū Sinn, Sud. J8 60
Amares, Port. D3 16
Amargosa, Braz. B9 79
Amargosa, stm., U.S. D5 112
Amargosa Desert, des., U.S. G5 135
Amargosa Range, mts., U.S. G5 135
Amarillo, Tx., U.S. B2 150
ʻAmar Jadīd, Sud. J3 60
Amarkantak, India G3 30
Amarnāth, India C2 46
Amasa, Mi., U.S. B2 129
Amasya, Tur. G15 4
Amataurá, Braz. I8 84
Amatignak Island, i., Ak., U.S. E4 109
Amatikulu, S. Afr. G10 66
Amatique, Bahía de, b., N.A. B6 92
Amatitlán, Guat. C4 92
Amatitlán, Lago de, l., Guat. C4 92
Amazon (Solimões) (Amazonas), stm., S.A. D7 76
Amazonas, state, Braz. H10 84
Amazonas, dept., Col. H7 84
Amazonas, dept., Peru A2 82
Amazonas, ter., Ven. F9 84
Amazonia, Mo., U.S. B3 132
Ambakaka, Madag. t22 67b
Ambāla, India E7 44
Ambalanjanakomby, Madag. p22 67b
Ambalavao, Madag. r22 67b
Amba Maryam, Eth. L10 60
Ambanja, Madag. n23 67b
Ambar, Peru D3 82
Ambararata, Madag. o23 67b
Ambarčik, Russia D24 28
Ambargasta, Salinas de, pl., Arg. E6 80
Ambarnyj, Russia I23 6
Ambato, Ec. H3 84
Ambatofinandrahana, Madag. r22 67b
Ambatolampy, Madag. q22 67b
Ambatondrazaka, Madag. p23 67b
Ámbelos, Ákra, c., Grc. J7 20
Ambenja, Madag. o22 67b
Amber, Ok., U.S. B4 143
Amberg, Ger. F11 10
Amberg, Wi., U.S. C6 156
Ambergris Cay, i., Belize H16 90
Ambérieu-en-Bugey, Fr. G12 14
Ambert, Fr. G10 14
Ambevongo, Madag. o22 67b
Ambia, In., U.S. D2 121
Ambikāpur, India I10 44
Ambilobe, Madag. n23 67b
Ambinanindrano, Madag. r23 67b
Ambivy, Madag. r21 67b
Ambler, Ak., U.S. B8 109
Ambler, Pa., U.S. F11 145
Ambo, Peru D3 82
Amboahangy, Madag. t22 67b
Ambodifototra, Madag. p23 67b
Ambodiriana, Madag. p23 67b
Ambohidray, Madag. q23 67b
Ambohimahamasina, Madag. r22 67b
Amboise, Fr. E7 14
Ambon, Indon. F8 38
Ambondro, Madag. t21 67b
Ambositra, Madag. r22 67b
Ambovombe, Madag. t22 67b
Amboy, Il., U.S. B4 120
Amboy, In., U.S. C6 121
Amboy, Mn., U.S. G4 130
Amboy, Wa., U.S. D3 154
Ambre, Cap d', c., Madag. m23 67b
Ambridge, Pa., U.S. E1 145
Ambrières, Fr. D6 14
Ambriz, Ang. C2 58
Ambrose, Ga., U.S. E4 117
Ambunti, Pap. N. Gui. F11 38
Amchitka Island, i., Ak., U.S. E3 109
Amchitka Pass, strt., Ak., U.S. E4 109
ʻAmd, Yemen G6 47
Amderma, Russia D10 26
Amdo, China E5 30
Ameagle, W.V., U.S. D3 155
Ameca, Mex. G7 90
Ameca, stm., Mex. G7 90
Amecameca [de Juárez], Mex. H10 90
Ameghino, Arg. H7 80
Ameland, i., Neth. B8 12
Amelia, Italy G7 18
Amelia, La., U.S. E4 125
Amelia, Oh., U.S. C1 142
Amelia, co., Va., U.S. C4 153
Amelia Court House, Va., U.S. C5 153
Amelia Island, i., Fl., U.S. k9 116
Amenia, N.Y., U.S. D7 139
Amenia, N.D., U.S. B8 141
Āmer, India G6 44
American, stm., Ca., U.S. C3 112
American, South Fork, stm., Ca., U.S. C3 112
Americana, Braz. G5 79
American Falls, Id., U.S. G6 119
American Falls Dam, Id., U.S. G6 119
American Falls Reservoir, res., Id., U.S. F5 119
American Fork, Ut., U.S. C4 151
American Highland, plat., Ant. C5 73
American Samoa, dep., Oc. G1 2
Americus, Ga., U.S. D2 117
Americus, Ks., U.S. D7 123
Amersfoort, Neth. D7 12
Amersfoort, S. Afr. F9 66
Amery, Wi., U.S. C1 156
Amery Ice Shelf, Ant. B5 73
Ames, Ia., U.S. B4 122
Ames, Ok., U.S. A3 143
Amesbury, Ma., U.S. A6 128
Ámfissa, Grc. K6 20
Amga, Russia E18 28
Amga, stm., Russia E18 28
Amguema, stm., Russia D27 28
Amguid, Alg. G13 62
Amgun', stm., Russia G19 28
Amherst, N.S., Can. D5 101
Amherst, Ma., U.S. B2 128
Amherst, Ne., U.S. D6 134
Amherst, N.H., U.S. E3 136
Amherst, N.Y., U.S. C2 139
Amherst, Oh., U.S. A3 142
Amherst, S.D., U.S. B8 148
Amherst, Tx., U.S. B1 150
Amherst, Va., U.S. C3 153
Amherst, Wi., U.S. D4 156
Amherst, co., Va., U.S. C3 153
Amherstburg, Ont., Can. E1 103
Amherstdale, W.V., U.S. n12 155
Amiens, Fr. C9 14
Amili, China F16 44
Amīndīvi Islands, is., India G2 46
Aminga, Arg. E5 80
Aminuis, Nmb. D4 66
Amirante Islands, is., Sey. C10 58
Amisk, Alta., Can. C5 98
Amisk Lake, l., Sask., Can. C4 105
Amistad, Parque Internacional de la, C.R. H11 92
Amistad National Recreation Area, Tx., U.S. E2 150
Amite, La., U.S. D5 125
Amite, co., Ms., U.S. D3 131
Amite, stm., La., U.S. D5 125
Amity, Ar., U.S. C2 111
Amity, Or., U.S. B3 144
Amityville, N.Y., U.S. E7 139
Amizmiz, Mor. E6 62
Amlia Island, i., Ak., U.S. E5 109
ʻAmm-Adām, Sud. I9 60
ʻAmmān, Jord. E5 50
Ammarnäs, Swe. I15 6
Ammon, Id., U.S. F7 119
Ammonoosuc, stm., N.H., U.S. B3 136
Amne Machin Shan see A'nyêmaqên Shan, mts., China D6 30
Amnok-kang (Yalu), stm., Asia C13 32
Amo, In., U.S. E4 121
Amo, stm., Asia G13 44
Āmol, Iran C12 48
Amolar, Braz. H13 82
Amonate, Va., U.S. e10 153
Amoret, Mo., U.S. C3 132
Amorgós, i., Grc. M9 20
Amorinópolis, Braz. D3 79
Amory, Ms., U.S. B5 131
Amos, Que., Can. k11 104
Amoy see Xiamen, China K7 34
Ampanihy, Madag. t21 67b
Amparihy, Madag. s22 67b
Amparo, Braz. G5 79
Ampato, Nevado, mtn., Peru F6 82
Amper, Nig. G14 64
Ampombiantambo, Madag. n23 67b
Amposta, Spain E12 16
Ampotaka, Madag. t21 67b
ʻAmrān, Yemen G3 47
Amrāvati, India J7 44
Amreli, India J4 44
Amritsar, India E6 44
Amroha, India F8 44
Amsel, Alg. I13 62
Åmsele, Swe. I16 6
Amsteg, Switz. E10 13
Amsterdam, Neth. D6 12
Amsterdam, S. Afr. F10 66
Amsterdam, Ga., U.S. F2 117
Amsterdam, Mo., U.S. C3 132
Amsterdam, Mt., U.S. E5 133
Amsterdam, N.Y., U.S. C6 139
Amsterdam, Oh., U.S. B5 142
Amsterdam, Île, i., F.S.A.T. L11 158
Amsterdam-Rijnkanaal, Neth. E7 12
Amstetten, Aus. G14 10
Amston, Ct., U.S. C6 114
Am Timan, Chad F5 56
Amubri, C.R. H12 92
Amu-Darja, Turk. C18 48
Amu Darya (Amudarja), stm., Asia B2 44
Amukta Pass, strt., Ak., U.S. E5 109
Amundsen Gulf, b., N.W. Ter., Can. B8 96
Amundsen-Scott, sci., Ant. D10 73
Amundsen Sea, Ant. C11 73
Amuntai, Indon. F6 38
Amur (Heilong), stm., Asia B14 30
Amurrio, Spain I3 14
Amuzhong, China E11 44
Amvrakikós Kólpos, b., Grc. K4 20
Amy, Ar., U.S. D3 111
Anabar, stm., Russia C14 28
Anaco, Ven. C10 84
Anacoco, La., U.S. C2 125
Anacoco, Bayou, stm., La., U.S. D2 125
Anaconda, Mt., U.S. D4 133
Anaconda, N.M., U.S. B2 138
Anaconda Range, mts., Mt., U.S. E3 133
Anacortes, Wa., U.S. A3 154
Anacostia, stm., U.S. C4 127
Anacostia, Northwest Branch, stm., Md., U.S. B3 127
Anadarko, Ok., U.S. B3 143
Anadyr', Russia E27 28
Anadyr', stm., Russia E26 28
Anadyrskij zaliv, b., Russia E28 28
Anadyrskoje ploskogorje, plat., Russia D26 28
Anagance, N.B., Can. D4 101
Anagni, Italy H8 18
ʻĀnah, Iraq D6 48
Anaheim, Ca., U.S. F5 112
Anahim Lake, B.C., Can. C5 99
Anahola, Hi., U.S. A2 118
Anáhuac, Mex. D9 90
Anáhuac, Mex. C6 90
Anahuac, Tx., U.S. E5 150
Anahulu, stm., Hi., U.S. f9 118
Ānai Mudi, mtn., India G4 46
Analalava, Madag. o22 67b
Analapatsy, Madag. t22 67b
Anamã, Braz. I12 84
Anamã, Lago, l., Braz. I12 84
Anama Bay, Man., Can. D2 100
Ana María, Golfo de, b., Cuba D5 94
Anambas, Kepulauan, is., Indon. M9 40
Anamoose, N.D., U.S. B5 141
Anamosa, Ia., U.S. B6 122
Anamu, stm., Braz. G14 84
Anamur, Tur. C2 48
Ānand, India I5 44
Anandale, La., U.S. C3 125
Ananea, Peru F7 82
Ananjev, Ukr. B13 20
Anantapur, India E4 46
Anantnāg (Islāmābād), India D6 44
Anápolis, Braz. D4 79
Anār, Iran F13 48
Anārak, Iran E12 48
Anār Darreh, Afg. E16 48
Anastácio, Braz. F1 79
Anastasia Island, i., Fl., U.S. C5 116
ʻAnātā, Isr. Occ. E4 50
Añatuya, Arg. E7 80
Anauá, stm., Braz. G12 84
Anaurilândia, Braz. G2 79
Anavilhanas, Arquipélago das, is., Braz. I12 84
Anawalt, W.V., U.S. D3 155
Anbanjing, China C6 40
Anbu, China L5 34
Anbyŏn, N. Kor. D15 32
Ancash, dept., Peru C3 82
Ancaster, Ont., Can. D5 103
Ancasti, Arg. E6 80
Ancasti, Sierra de, mts., Arg. E6 80
Ancha, Sierra de, mts., Az., U.S. D4 110
Anchang, China E9 34
Anchorage, Ak., U.S. C10 109
Anchorage, Ky., U.S. g11 124
Anchorena, Arg. H6 80
Anchor Point, Ak., U.S. D9 109
Anchor Point, c., Ak., U.S. h15 109
Anci (Langfang), China D4 32
Ancien Goubéré, Cen. Afr. Rep. O4 60
Ancienne-Lorette, Que., Can. C6 104
Anciferovo, Russia C17 22
Anclote Keys, is., Fl., U.S. D4 116
Anco, Ky., U.S. C6 124
Ancón, Peru D3 82
Ancona, Italy F8 18
Ancón de Sardinas, Bahía de, b., S.A. G3 84
Ancoraimes, Bol. F7 82
Ancud, Chile E2 78
Ancud, Golfo de, b., Chile E2 78
Anda, China B12 30
Andacollo, Arg. I3 80
Andacollo, Chile F3 80
Andahuaylas, Peru E5 82
Andale, Ks., U.S. E6 123
Andalgalá, Arg. D5 80
Åndalsnes, Nor. J10 6
Andalucía, prov., Spain H7 16
Andalucía, hist. reg., Spain H7 16
Andalusia, Al., U.S. D3 108
Andalusia, Il., U.S. B3 120
Andaman Islands, is., India H2 40
Andaman Sea, Asia I3 40
Andamarca, Bol. H8 82
Andamarca, Peru H5 82
Andamooka, Austl. H2 70
Andapa, Madag. o23 67b
Andaraí, Braz. B8 79
Andaray, Peru F5 82
Andeer, Switz. E11 13
Andelot, Fr. D12 14
Andenes, Nor. G15 6
Andéranboukane, Mali D11 64
Andermatt, Switz. E10 13
Andernach, Ger. E7 10
Anderson, Al., U.S. A2 108
Anderson, Ak., U.S. C10 109
Anderson, Ca., U.S. B2 112
Anderson, In., U.S. D6 121
Anderson, Mo., U.S. E3 132
Anderson, S.C., U.S. B2 147
Anderson, Tn., U.S. B8 149
Anderson, Tx., U.S. D4 150
Anderson, co., Ks., U.S. D8 123
Anderson, co., Ky., U.S. C4 124
Anderson, co., S.C., U.S. B2 147
Anderson, co., Tn., U.S. C9 149
Anderson, co., Tx., U.S. D5 150
Anderson, stm., N.W. Ter., Can. C7 96
Anderson, stm., In., U.S. H4 121
Anderson, Mount, mtn., Wa., U.S. B2 154
Anderson Ranch Reservoir, res., Id., U.S. F3 119
Andersonville, Ga., U.S. D2 117
Andersonville, In., U.S. F7 121
Andes, Col. E5 84
Andes, mts., S.A. G8 74
Andes, Lake, l., S.D., U.S. D7 148
Andevoranto, Madag. q23 67b
Andhra Pradesh, state, India D5 46
Andikíthira, i., Grc. N7 20
Andimákhia, Grc. M11 20
Andīmeshk, Iran E10 48
Andirá, stm., Braz. I14 84
Andirá, Riozinho do, stm., Braz. C8 82
Andirlang, China B10 44
Ándissa, Grc. J9 20
Andižan, Uzb. I12 26
Andkhvoy, Afg. B1 44
Andoas, Peru I4 84
Andong, S. Kor. G16 32
Andorra, And. C13 16
Andorra, ctry., Eur. G8 4
Andover, Ct., U.S. C6 114
Andover, Il., U.S. B3 120
Andover, Ks., U.S. g12 123
Andover, Me., U.S. D2 126
Andover, Ma., U.S. A5 128
Andover, Mn., U.S. m12 130
Andover, N.H., U.S. D3 136
Andover, N.Y., U.S. C3 139
Andover, Oh., U.S. A5 142
Andover, S.D., U.S. B8 148
Andover Lake, res., Ct., U.S. C6 114
Andøya, i., Nor. G14 6
Andrade, Hi., U.S. D6 118
Andradina, Braz. F3 79
Andranopasy, Madag. r20 67b
Andranovory, Madag. s21 67b
Andreanof Islands, is., Ak., U.S. E4 109
Andreapol', Russia E15 22
Andrejevo, Russia F24 22
Andréville, Que., Can. B8 104
Andrew, Alta., Can. C4 98
Andrew, Ia., U.S. B7 122
Andrew, co., Mo., U.S. B3 132
Andrew Island, i., N.S., Can. D9 101
Andrews, In., U.S. C6 121
Andrews, N.C., U.S. f9 140
Andrews, S.C., U.S. E8 147
Andrews, Tx., U.S. C1 150
Andrews, co., Tx., U.S. C1 150
Andrews Air Force Base, mil., Md., U.S. C4 127
Andria, Italy H11 18
Andriamena, Madag. p22 67b
Andriandampy, Madag. s21 67b
Andrijevica, Yugo. G3 20
Androka, Madag. t21 67b
Ándros, Grc. L8 20
Andros, i., Bah. B6 94
Ándros, i., Grc. L8 20
Androscoggin, co., Me., U.S. D2 126
Androscoggin, stm., Me., U.S. D2 126
Androscoggin Lake, l., Me., U.S. D2 126
Andros Town, Bah. B6 94
Āndrott Island, i., India G2 46
Andrychów, Pol. F19 10
Andújar, Spain G7 16
Anécho, Togo H10 64
Anegada, i., Br. Vir. Is. E12 94
Anegada Passage, strt., N.A. E13 94
Añelo, Arg. J4 80
Aneroid, Sask., Can. H2 105
Aneta, N.D., U.S. B8 141
Aneth, Ut., U.S. F6 151
Aneto, Pico de, mtn., Spain C12 16
Anfeng, China C9 34
Anfeng, China B9 34
Anfengqiao, China I7 34
Anfu, China H3 34
Angamos, Punta, c., Chile B3 80
Ang'angxi, China B11 30
Angao, China B1 34
Angara, stm., Russia F17 26
Angara-Débou, Benin F11 64
Angarbaka, Sud. M3 60
Angarsk, Russia G12 28
Angastaco, Arg. C5 80
Angatuba, Braz. G4 79
Ángel, Salto (Angel Falls), wtfl, Ven. E11 84
Ángel de la Guarda, Isla, i., Mex. C3 90
Angeles, Phil. n19 39b
Angeles Point, c., Wa., U.S. A2 154
Angel Falls see Ángel, Salto, wtfl, Ven. E11 84
Angelica, N.Y., U.S. C2 139
Angelina, co., Tx., U.S. D5 150
Angels Camp, Ca., U.S. C3 112
Angereb, stm., Afr. K9 60
Angermünde, Ger. B14 10
Angers, Fr. E6 14
Angerville, Fr. D9 14
Angical, Braz. B6 79
Angicos, Braz. E11 76
Angier, N.C., U.S. B4 140
Angkor Wat, hist., Camb. H7 40
Ăngk Tasaôm, Camb. I8 40
Angle Inlet, Mn., U.S. A3 130
Anglesey, i., Wales, U.K. H9 8
Angleton, Tx., U.S. E5 150
Angling Lake, l., Man., Can. C5 100
Angmagssalik, Grnld. C16 86
Angoche, Moz. E7 58
Angoche, Ilha, i., Moz. E7 58
Angol, Chile I2 80
Angola, In., U.S. A8 121
Angola, N.Y., U.S. C1 139
Angola, ctry., Afr. D3 58
Angola Swamp, sw., N.C., U.S. C5 140
Angoon, Ak., U.S. D13 109
Angora see Ankara, Tur. B2 48
Angoram, Pap. N. Gui. F11 38
Angostura, Mex. E5 90
Angostura, Presa de la, res., Mex. I13 90
Angostura Reservoir, res., S.D., U.S. D2 148
Angoulême, Fr. G7 14
Angoumois, hist. reg., Fr. G6 14
Angra dos Reis, Braz. G6 79
Angren, Uzb. I12 26
Angualasto, Arg. F4 80
Anguciana, Cerro, mtn., C.R. I11 92
Anguilla, Ms., U.S. C3 131
Anguilla, dep., N.A. E13 94
Anguilla Cays, is., Bah. C5 94
Anguille, Cape, c., Newf., Can. E2 102
Anguo, China E3 32
Angusville, Man., Can. D1 100
Anhai, China K7 34
Anhui (Anhwei), prov., China E10 30
Aniak, Ak., U.S. C8 109
Aniche, Fr. H3 12
Anicuns, Braz. D4 79
Anié, Togo H10 64
Animas, N.M., U.S. F1 138
Animas, stm., U.S. D3 113
Animas Mountains, mts., N.M., U.S. F1 138
Animas Peak, mtn., N.M., U.S. F2 138
Animas Valley, val., N.M., U.S. F1 138
Anina, Rom. D5 20
Anita, Ia., U.S. C3 122
Anita, Pa., U.S. D4 145
Aniva, zaliv, b., Russia H20 28
Anivorano, Madag. q23 67b
Anjangaon, India B4 46
Anjār, India I4 44
ʻAnjar, Leb. A5 50
Anji, China E8 34
Anjiabe, Madag. n23 67b
Anjiang, China C5 32
Anjou, Que., Can. p19 104
Anjou, hist. reg., Fr. E6 14
Anju, N. Kor. D13 32
Ankang, China E8 30
Ankara, Tur. B2 48
Ankaratra, mts., Madag. q22 67b
Ankarimbelo, Madag. s22 67b
Ankasakasa, Madag. p21 67b
Ankavandra, Madag. q21 67b
Ankazoabo, Madag. s21 67b
Ankazobe, Madag. q22 67b
Ankazomiriotra, Madag. q22 67b
Ankeny, Ia., U.S. C4 122
Ankilimalinika, Madag. s20 67b
Ankisabe, Madag. q22 67b
Ankleshwar, India B2 46
Ankober, Eth. G8 56
Ankou, China J2 34
An'kovo, Russia E22 22
Ankpa, Nig. H13 64
Anliu, China L4 34
Anlu, China D2 34
Ann, Cape, c., Ant. B4 73
Ann, Cape, c., Ma., U.S. A6 128
Anna, Il., U.S. F4 120
Anna, Oh., U.S. B1 142
Anna, Lake, res., Va., U.S. B5 153
Annaba (Bône), Alg. B14 62
Annabella, Ut., U.S. E3 151
Annaberg-Buchholz, Ger. E13 10
An-Nabk, Syria D4 48
An-Nafī, Sau. Ar. B3 47
An-Nafūd, des., Sau. Ar. G6 48
An-Najaf, Iraq F8 48
An-Nakhl, Egypt C7 60

Name — Map Ref. — Page

Anna Maria, Fl., U.S. p10 116
Anna Maria Island, i., Fl., U.S. q10 116
Annamitique, Chaîne, mts., Asia F9 40
Annandale, Austl. C8 70
Annandale, Mn., U.S. E4 130
Annandale, N.J., U.S. B3 137
Annandale, Va., U.S. g12 153
Annapolis, In., U.S. E3 121
Annapolis, Md., U.S. C5 127
Annapolis, Mo., U.S. D7 132
Annapolis, stm., N.S., Can. E4 101
Annapolis Junction, Md., U.S. B4 127
Annapolis Royal, N.S., Can. E4 101
Annapūrna, mtn., Nepal F10 44
Ann Arbor, Mi., U.S. F7 129
Anna Regina, Guy. D13 84
An-Nāṣirīyah, Iraq F9 48
An-Nāṣirīyah, Syria A7 50
Annawan, Il., U.S. B4 120
An-Nawfalāb, Sud. J7 60
Anne Arundel, co., Md., U.S. B4 127
Annecy, Fr. G13 14
Annemasse, Fr. F13 14
Annenskij Most, Russia A20 22
An Nhon, Viet. H10 40
Anniston, Al., U.S. B4 108
Anniston, Mo., U.S. E8 132
Annobón, i., Eq. Gui. B1 58
Annonay, Fr. G11 14
An-Nuhūd, Sud. K5 60
An-Nu'mānīyah, Iraq E8 48
Annursnack Hill, hill, Ma., U.S. g10 128
Annville, Ky., U.S. C6 124
Annville, Pa., U.S. F8 145
Anoka, Mn., U.S. E5 130
Anoka, co., Mn., U.S. E5 130
Anopino, Russia F23 22
Anori, Braz. I12 84
Anorí, Col. D5 84
Anping, China D4 32
Anpu, China D11 40
Anqing, China E6 34
Anqiu, China G7 32
Ansbach, Ger. F10 10
Anse-d'Hainault, Haiti E7 94
Anselmo, Ne., U.S. C6 134
Anserma, Col. E5 84
Anshan, China B10 32
Anshun, China A8 40
Ansina, Ur. F11 80
Ansley, Ms., U.S. E4 131
Ansley, Ne., U.S. C6 134
Anson, Me., U.S. D3 126
Anson, Tx., U.S. C3 150
Anson, co., N.C., U.S. B2 140
Ansŏng, S. Kor. F15 32
Ansongo, Mali D10 64
Ansonia, Ct., U.S. D3 114
Ansonia, Oh., U.S. B1 142
Ansonville, N.C., U.S. B2 140
Ansted, W.V., U.S. C3 155
Anta, Peru E5 82
Antabamba, Peru F5 82
Antakya (Antioch), Tur. C4 48
Antalaha, Madag. o24 67b
Antalovcy, Ukr. G22 10
Antalya, Tur. H14 4
Antalya Körfezi, b., Tur. H14 4
Antambohobe, Madag. s22 67b
Antanambao Manampotsy, Madag. q23 67b
Antananarivo, Madag. q22 67b
Antanetibe, Madag. q22 67b
Antanifotsy, Madag. q22 67b
Antarctica D5 73
Antarctic Peninsula, pen., Ant. B12 73
Antas, Rio das, stm., Braz. E13 80
Antelope, Mt., U.S. B12 133
Antelope, co., Ne., U.S. B7 134
Antelope Butte, mtn., Wy., U.S. B7 157
Antelope Creek, stm., Wy., U.S. C7 157
Antelope Island, i., Ut., U.S. B3 151
Antelope Mine, Zimb. C9 66
Antelope Peak, mtn., Nv., U.S. B7 135
Antelope Range, mts., Nv., U.S. D7 135
Antelope Reservoir, res., Or., U.S. E9 144
Antelope Wash, val., Nv., U.S. D5 135
Antequera, Para. C10 80
Antequera, Spain H7 16
Antero, Mount, mtn., Co., U.S. C4 113
Antero Reservoir, res., Co., U.S. C5 113
Antevamena, Madag. r21 67b
Anthon, Ia., U.S. B2 122
Anthony, Fl., U.S. C4 116
Anthony, Ks., U.S. E5 123
Anthony, N.M., U.S. F3 138
Anthony, R.I., U.S. D3 146
Anthony, Tx., U.S. o11 150
Anthony Creek, stm., W.V., U.S. D4 155
Anti-Atlas, mts., Mor. E6 62
Antibes, Fr. I14 14
Anticosti, Île d', i., Que., Can. k14 104
Antietam Creek, stm., Md., U.S. B2 127
Antietam National Battlefield, hist., Md., U.S. B2 127
Antigo, Wi., U.S. C4 156
Antigonish, N.S., Can. D8 101
Antigua, i., Antig. F14 94
Antigua and Barbuda, ctry., N.A. F14 94
Antigua Guatemala, Guat. C4 92
Antiguo Morelos, Mex. F10 90
Anti-Lebanon see Sharqī, Al-Jabal ash-, mts., Asia A6 50
Antilla, Arg. D6 80
Antilla, Cuba D7 94
Antioch, Ca., U.S. h9 112
Antioch, Il., U.S. A5 120
Antioch see Antakya, Tur. C4 48
Antioquia, Col. D5 84
Antioquia, dept., Col. D5 84
Antipodes Islands, is., N.Z. M21 158
Antizana, vol., Ec. H3 84
Antlers, Ok., U.S. C6 143
Antofagasta, Chile B3 80
Antofagasta, prov., Chile B4 80
Antofagasta de la Sierra, Arg. D5 80
Antofalla, Salar de, pl., Arg. C5 80
Antofalla, Volcán, vol., Arg. C5 80
Antoine, Ar., U.S. C2 111
Antón, Pan. C2 84
Anton, Tx., U.S. C1 150
Anton Chico, N.M., U.S. B4 138
Antongila, Helodrano, b., Madag. o23 67b
Antonia, Mo., U.S. C7 132
Antonina, Braz. C14 80
Antonio Amaro, Mex. E7 90
Antônio Prado, Braz. E13 80
Antonito, Co., U.S. D5 113
Antón Lizardo, Punta, c., Mex. H12 90
Antopol', Bela. I7 22
Antora Peak, mtn., Co., U.S. C4 113
Antou, China I7 34
Antrain, Fr. D5 14
Antrim, N. Ire., U.K. G7 8
Antrim, N.H., U.S. D3 136
Antrim, co., Mi., U.S. C5 129
Antrodoco, Italy G8 18
Antropovo, Russia C26 22
Antsalova, Madag. q21 67b
Antsenavolo, Madag. r23 67b
Antsiafabositra, Madag. p22 67b
Antsirabe, Madag. o23 67b
Antsirabe, Madag. q22 67b
Antsiranana, Madag. n23 67b
Antsla, Est. D9 22
Antsohihy, Madag. o22 67b
Antuševo, Russia B20 22
Antwerp, Oh., U.S. A1 142
Antwerp see Antwerpen, Bel. F5 12
Antwerpen (Anvers), Bel. F5 12
Antwerpen, prov., Bel. F6 12
Anugul, India B8 46
Anuradhapura, Sri L. H6 46
Anvers (Antwerpen), Bel. F5 12
Anvers Island, i., Ant. B12 73
Anxi, China C6 30
Anxi, China J7 34
Anxin, China D3 32
Anyama, I.C. I7 64
Anyang, China G2 32
A'nyêmaqên Shan, mts., China D6 30
Anyi, China G4 34
Anykščiai, Lith. F8 22
Anyuan, China H2 34
Anzac, Alta., Can. A5 98
Anzaldo, Bol. G9 82
Anžero-Sudžensk, Russia F15 26
Anzhen, China D8 34
Anzhou, China E3 32
Anzin, Fr. B10 14
Anzio, Italy H7 18
Anzoátegui, state, Ven. C10 84
Anžu, ostrova, is., Russia B20 28
Aoga-shima, i., Japan E14 30
Aohan Qi (Xinhui), China A7 32
Aoji, N. Kor. A18 32
Aojiang, China H9 34
Aojiao, China L6 34
Aomori, Japan G15 36
Aóös (Vijosë), stm., Eur. J4 20
Aôral, Phnum, mtn., Camb. H8 40
Aosta, Italy D2 18
Aotou, China M3 34
Aouderas, Niger C14 64
Aouk, Bahr, stm., Afr. G5 56
Aoukâr, reg., Maur. B5 64
Aourou, Mali D4 64
Aozou, Chad D4 56
Apa, stm., S.A. B10 80
Apache, Ok., U.S. C3 143
Apache, co., Az., U.S. B6 110
Apache Junction, Az., U.S. m9 110
Apache Peak, mtn., Az., U.S. F5 110
Apalachee, Ga., U.S. C3 117
Apalachee Bay, b., Fl., U.S. B2 116
Apalachicola, Fl., U.S. C2 116
Apalachicola, stm., Fl., U.S. B1 116
Apalachicola Bay, b., Fl., U.S. C2 116
Apalachin, N.Y., U.S. C4 139
Apanas, Laguna de, res., Nic. D9 92
Apaporis, stm., S.A. H7 84
Aparados da Serra, Parque Nacional de, Braz. E13 80
Aparri, Phil. I19 39b
Apaseo El Grande, Mex. G9 90
Apatin, Yugo. D2 20
Apatity, Russia D4 26
Apatzingán de la Constitución, Mex. H8 90
Apaxtla de Castrejón, Mex. H10 90
Apayacu, stm., Peru I6 84
Ape, Lat. D9 22
Apeldoorn, Neth. D8 12
Apennines see Appennino, mts., Italy F7 18
Apex, N.C., U.S. B4 140
Api, mtn., Nepal F9 44
Apía, Col. E5 84
Apia, W. Sam. G1 2
Apiacá, stm., Braz. C13 82
Apiacás, Serra dos, plat., Braz. D13 82
Apiaí, Braz. C14 80
Apiaú, stm., Braz. F12 84
Apishapa, stm., Co., U.S. D6 113
Apison, Tn., U.S. h11 149
Apizaco, Mex. H10 90
Apizolaya, Mex. E8 90
Aplahoué, Benin H10 64
Aplao, Peru G5 82
Aplin, Ar., U.S. C3 111
Aplington, Ia., U.S. B5 122
Apo, Mount, mtn., Phil. D8 38
Apohaqui, N.B., Can. D4 101
Apolakkiá, Grc. M11 20
Apolda, Ger. D11 10
Apolinario Saravia, Arg. C6 80
Apollo, Pa., U.S. E2 145
Apolo, Bol. F7 82
Apón, stm., Ven. B6 84
Aponguao, stm., Ven. E12 84
Apopa, El Sal. D5 92
Apopka, Fl., U.S. D5 116
Apopka, Lake, l., Fl., U.S. D5 116
Aporé, Braz. E2 79
Aporé, stm., Braz. E3 79
Apostle Islands, is., Wi., U.S. A3 156
Apostle Islands National Lakeshore, Wi., U.S. A3 156
Apóstoles, Arg. D11 80
Apostolovo, Ukr. H4 26
Appalachia, Va., U.S. f9 153
Appalachian Mountains, mts., N.A. C11 106
Appanoose, co., Ia., U.S. D5 122
Appennino (Apennines), mts., Italy F7 18
Appenzell, Switz. D11 13
Appenzell-Ausserrhoden, state, Switz. D11 13
Apple, stm., Wi., U.S. C1 156
Apple Creek, Oh., U.S. B4 142
Applegate, Or., U.S. E3 144
Applegate, stm., Or., U.S. E3 144
Apple Grove, W.V., U.S. C2 155
Apple Hill, Ont., Can. B10 103
Apple Orchard Mountain, mtn., Va., U.S. C3 153
Apple River, N.S., Can. D5 101
Apple River, Il., U.S. A3 120
Appleton, Ar., U.S. B3 111
Appleton, Mn., U.S. E2 130
Appleton, Wi., U.S. D5 156
Appleton City, Mo., U.S. C3 132
Apple Valley, Ca., U.S. E5 112
Apple Valley, Mn., U.S. n12 130
Applewood, Co., U.S. *B5 113
Appleyard, Wa., U.S. B5 154
Appling, Ga., U.S. C4 117
Appling, co., Ga., U.S. E4 117
Appomattox, Va., U.S. C4 153
Appomattox, co., Va., U.S. C4 153
Appomattox, stm., Va., U.S. C4 153
Appomattox Court House National Historical Park, Va., U.S. C4 153
Aprelevka, Russia F20 22
Apšeronskij poluostrov, pen., Azer. A11 48
Apsley, Ont., Can. C6 103
Apt, Fr. I12 14
Apua Point, c., Hi., U.S. D6 118
Apuaú, stm., Braz. I12 84
Apucarana, Braz. G3 79
Apure, state, Ven. D8 84
Apure, stm., Ven. D9 84
Apurímac, dept., Peru E5 82
Apurímac, stm., Peru E5 82
Apurito, Ven. D8 84
Aqaba, Gulf of, b. C8 60
'Aqīq, Sud. H10 60
Aquarius Mountains, mts., Az., U.S. C2 110
Aquarius Plateau, plat., Ut., U.S. E4 151
Aquidabã, stm., Braz. I13 82
Aquidabán, stm., Para. B10 80
Aquidauana, Braz. I14 82
Aquidauana, stm., Braz. I14 82
Aquila, Mex. H8 90
Aquila, Switz. E10 13
Aquiles Serdán, Mex. C7 90
Aquiles Serdán, Mex. E11 90
Aquin, Haiti E8 94
Aquio, stm., Col. F9 84
Ara, India H11 44
Arab, Al., U.S. A3 108
'Arab, Bahr al-, stm., Sud. M4 60
Arab, Shatt al-, stm., Asia G10 48
'Arab, Wādī al-, val., Jord. C5 50
'Arabah, Wādī al- (Ha'Arava), val., Asia G4 50
Arabako, prov., Spain C9 16
Arabelo, Ven. E10 84
Arabi, Ga., U.S. E3 117
Arabi, La., U.S. k11 125
Arabian Desert see Sharqīyah, Aṣ-Ṣaḥrā' ash-, des., Egypt D7 60
Arabian Gulf see Persian Gulf, b., Asia H11 48
Arabian Peninsula, pen., Asia G5 24
Arabian Sea H7 24
Araçá, stm., Braz. G11 84
Aracaju, Braz. F11 76
Aracataca, Col. B5 84
Aracati, Braz. D11 76
Araçatuba, Braz. F3 79
Aracena, Spain H5 16
Aracruz, Braz. E8 79
Araçuaí, Braz. D7 79
Araçuaí, stm., Braz. D7 79
Arad, Rom. C5 20
Arad, co., Rom. C5 20
Arada, Hond. C6 92
Arafura Sea I17 158
Aragarças, Braz. C2 79
Arago, Cape, c., Or., U.S. D2 144
Aragon, Ga., U.S. B1 117
Aragon, N.M., U.S. D1 138
Aragón, prov., Spain D10 16
Aragón, stm., Spain C10 16
Aragua, state, Ven. B9 84
Araguacema, Braz. E9 76
Araguaçu, Braz. B4 79
Aragua de Barcelona, Ven. C10 84
Aragua de Maturín, Ven. C11 84
Araguaia, stm., Braz. E9 76
Araguaia, Braço Menor, stm., Braz. B3 79
Araguainha, Braz. D2 79
Araguao, Caño, mth., Ven. C12 84
Araguari, Braz. E4 79
Araguari, stm., Braz. C8 76
Araguari, stm., Braz. E4 79
Araguatins, Braz. E9 76
Arak, Alg. H12 62
Arāk, Iran D10 48
Arakan Yoma, mts., Burma E3 40
Arákhthos, stm., Grc. J4 20
Araks (Aras), stm., Asia B10 48
Aral Sea see Aral'skoje more, Asia H10 26
Aral'sk, Kaz. H10 26
Aral'skoje more (Aral Sea), Asia H10 26
Aramac, Austl. D6 70
Aramac, stm., Austl. D6 70
Aramari, Braz. B9 79
Aramberri, Mex. E10 90
Arampampa, Bol. G8 82
Aramtalla, Sud. N5 60
Ārān, Iran D11 48
Aranda de Duero, Spain D8 16
Arandas, Mex. G8 90
Aranđelovac, Yugo. E4 20
Arandis, Nmb. D2 66
Arani, Bol. G9 82
Aran Islands, is., Ire. H4 8
Aranjuez, Spain E8 16
Aransas, co., Tx., U.S. E4 150
Aransas Bay, b., Tx., U.S. E4 150
Aransas Pass, Tx., U.S. F4 150
Aranyaprathet, Thai. H7 40
Arao, Japan O5 36
Araouane, Mali E6 54
Arapa, Laguna, l., Peru F6 82
Arapaho, Ok., U.S. B3 143
Arapahoe, Co., U.S. C8 113
Arapahoe, Ne., U.S. D6 134
Arapahoe, N.C., U.S. B6 140
Arapahoe, co., Co., U.S. B6 113
Arapey, Ur. F10 80
Arapey Chico, stm., Ur. F10 80
Arapey Grande, stm., Ur. F10 80
Arapiraca, Braz. E11 76
Arapkir, Tur. B5 48
Arapongas, Braz. G3 79
Arapoti, Braz. H4 79
'Ar'ar, Sau. Ar. F6 48
'Ar'ar, Wādī, val., Asia B11 60
Araranguá, Braz. E14 80
Araraquara, Braz. F4 79
Araras, Braz. G5 79
Ararat, Arm. B8 48
Ararat, Austl. K5 70
Ararat, Mount see Ağrı Dağı, mtn., Tur. B8 48
Ararirá, stm., Braz. H10 84
Araruama, Lagoa de, b., Braz. G7 79
Aras (Araks), stm., Asia B10 48
Áratos, Grc. H9 20
Aratuípe, Braz. B9 79
Arauã, stm., Braz. C9 82
Arauá, stm., Braz. A11 82
Arauá, stm., Braz. J10 84
Arauca, Col. D7 84
Arauca, dept., Col. D7 84
Arauca, stm., S.A. D9 84
Araucária, Braz. C14 80
Arauco, Chile I2 80
Arauco, Golfo de, b., Chile I2 80
Araújos, Braz. E6 79
Arauquita, Col. D7 84
Araure, Ven. C8 84
Arāvalli Range, mts., India H5 44
Araxá, Braz. E5 79
Araya, Ven. B10 84
Araya, Punta de, c., Ven. B10 84
Arba Minch, Eth. N9 60
Arboga, Swe. L14 6
Arbois, Fr. F12 14
Arboledas, Arg. I8 80
Arboletes, Col. C4 84
Arbon, Switz. C11 13
Arborfield, Sask., Can. D4 105
Arborg, Man., Can. D3 100
Arbroath, Scot., U.K. E11 8
Arbuckle, Ca., U.S. C2 112
Arbuckle, Lake, l., Fl., U.S. E5 116
Arbuckle Mountains, mts., Ok., U.S. C4 143
Arbuckles, Lake of the, res., Ok., U.S. C5 143
Arbyrd, Mo., U.S. E7 132
Arc, Bayou des, stm., Ar., U.S. B4 111
Arcachon, Fr. H5 14
Arcade, Ca., U.S. *C3 112
Arcade, Ga., U.S. B3 117
Arcade, N.Y., U.S. C2 139
Arcadia, N.S., Can. F3 101
Arcadia, Ca., U.S. m12 112
Arcadia, Fl., U.S. E5 116
Arcadia, In., U.S. D5 121
Arcadia, Ia., U.S. B2 122
Arcadia, Ks., U.S. E9 123
Arcadia, La., U.S. B3 125
Arcadia, Mi., U.S. D4 129
Arcadia, Mo., U.S. D7 132
Arcadia, Ne., U.S. C6 134
Arcadia, Oh., U.S. A2 142
Arcadia, Ok., U.S. B4 143
Arcadia, S.C., U.S. B4 147
Arcadia, Wi., U.S. D2 156
Arcanum, Oh., U.S. C1 142
Arcas, Cayos, is., Mex. G14 90
Arcata, Ca., U.S. B1 112
Arcatao, El Sal. C6 92
Arc Dome, mtn., Nv., U.S. E4 135
Arcelia, Mex. H9 90
Archambault, Lac, l., Que., Can. C3 104
Archangel'sk, Russia E6 26
Archbald, Pa., U.S. m18 145
Archbold, Oh., U.S. A1 142
Archdale, N.C., U.S. B3 140
Archer, Fl., U.S. C4 116
Archer, co., Tx., U.S. C3 150
Archer City, Tx., U.S. C3 150
Archerwill, Sask., Can. E4 105
Arches National Park, Ut., U.S. E6 151
Archidona, Spain H7 16
Archie, Mo., U.S. C3 132
Archipovka, Russia E24 22
Archuleta, co., Co., U.S. D3 113
Arciz, Ukr. C13 20
Arco, Id., U.S. F5 119
Arcola, Sask., Can. H4 105
Arcola, Il., U.S. D5 120
Arcola, Ms., U.S. B3 131
Arcola, Va., U.S. g11 153
Arcos, Braz. F6 79
Arcos de la Frontera, Spain I6 16
Arcot, India F5 46
Arcoverde, Braz. E11 76
Arctic Bay, N.W. Ter., Can. B15 96
Arctic Ocean A1 86
Arctic Red, stm., N.W. Ter., Can. C6 96
Arctowski, sci., Ant. B1 73
Arcturus, Zimb. A10 66
Arda, stm., Eur. H9 20
Ardabīl, Iran B10 48
Ardahan, Tur. G16 4
Ardakān, Iran F12 48
Ardakān, Iran E12 48
Årdalstangen, Nor. K10 6
Ardatov, Russia F26 22
Ardèche, dept., Fr. H11 14
Arden, Man., Can. D2 100
Arden, Ont., Can. C8 103
Arden, Ar., U.S. D1 111
Arden, Mount, mtn., Austl. I2 70
Ardennes, dept., Fr. C11 14
Ardennes, reg., Eur. E5 10
Ardestān, Iran E12 48
Ardila, stm., Eur. G4 16
Ardino, Bul. H9 20
Ardlethan, Austl. J7 70
Ardmore, Alta., Can. B5 98
Ardmore, Al., U.S. A3 108
Ardmore, In., U.S. A5 121
Ardmore, Ok., U.S. C4 143
Ardmore, Pa., U.S. F11 145
Ardmore, Tn., U.S. B5 149
Ardoch, Austl. F6 70
Ardrossan, Alta., Can. C4 98
Ardsley, N.Y., U.S. g13 139
Åre, Swe. J13 6
Areado, Braz. F5 79
Arecibo, P.R. E11 94
Areguá, Para. C10 80
Areia, Ribeirão da, stm., Braz. C6 79
Areia Branca, Braz. D11 76
Arena, Wi., U.S. E4 156
Arena, Point, c., Ca., U.S. C2 112
Arena, Punta, c., Mex. F5 90
Arenac, co., Mi., U.S. D7 129
Arena de la Ventana, Punta, c., Mex. E5 90
Arenal, C.R. G10 92
Arenal, Laguna de, l., C.R. G10 92
Arenal, Volcán, vol., C.R. G10 92
Arenápolis, Braz. F13 82
Arenas, Cayo, i., Mex. F14 90
Arenas Valley, N.M., U.S. E1 138
Arendal, Nor. L11 6
Arendtsville, Pa., U.S. G7 145
Arenillas, Ec. I2 84
Arenys de Mar, Spain D14 16
Arenzville, Il., U.S. D3 120
Arequipa, Peru G6 82
Arequipa, dept., Peru F5 82
Arequito, Arg. G8 80
Arès, Fr. H5 14
Arezzo, Italy F6 18
Argadargada, Austl. C2 70
Arganda, Spain E8 16
Arga-Sala, stm., Russia D13 28
Argelès-Gazost, Fr. I7 14
Argelès-sur-Mer, Fr. J10 14
Argenta, Italy E6 18
Argenta, Il., U.S. D5 120
Argentan, Fr. D6 14
Argentat, Fr. G8 14
Argentera, mtn., Italy E2 18
Argentina, ctry., S.A. C4 78
Argentino, Lago, l., Arg. G2 78
Argenton-Château, Fr. F6 14
Argenton-sur-Creuse, Fr. F8 14
Argeș, co., Rom. E8 20
Argeș, stm., Rom. E9 20
Arghandāb, stm., Afg. D2 44
Argo, Sud. H6 60
Argo, Al., U.S. B3 108
Argo, Ky., U.S. C7 124
Argo Corner, De., U.S. E4 115
Argolikós Kólpos, b., Grc. L6 20
Argonia, Ks., U.S. E6 123
Argonne, Wi., U.S. C5 156
Argonne, reg., Fr. C12 14
Árgos, Grc. L6 20
Argos, In., U.S. B5 121
Argostólion, Grc. K4 20
Arguello, Point, c., Ca., U.S. E3 112
Argun' (Ergun), stm., Asia G16 28
Argusville, N.D., U.S. B9 141
Argyle, N.S., Can. F4 101
Argyle, Ga., U.S. E4 117
Argyle, Mn., U.S. B2 130
Argyle, Mo., U.S. C5 132
Argyle, Wi., U.S. F4 156
Argyle, Lake, res., Austl. C5 68
Århus, Den. M12 6
Ariana, Tun. M5 18
Ariano Irpino, Italy H10 18
Ariari, stm., Col. F6 84
Arias, Arg. G7 80
Ariaú, Braz. I14 84
Aribinda, Burkina D9 64
Arica, Chile H6 82
Arica, Col. I7 84
Arichat, N.S., Can. D8 101
Arichuna, Ven. D9 84
Arid, Cape, c., Austl. F4 68
Ariège, dept., Fr. J8 14
Ariguaní, stm., Col. C6 84
Arīḥā (Jericho), Isr. Occ. E4 50
Arīḥā, Jord. F5 50
Arikaree, stm., U.S. B8 113
Arima, Trin. I14 94
Arimo, Id., U.S. G6 119
Arinos, stm., Braz. D12 82
Ario de Rosales, Mex. H9 90
Ariogala, Lith. F6 22
Ariporo, stm., Col. D7 84
Aripuanã, Braz. C11 82
Aripuanã, stm., Braz. B11 82
Ariquemes, Braz. C10 82
Arisa, stm., Ven. D10 84
'Arīsh, Wādī al-, val., Egypt B7 60
Arismendi, Ven. C8 84
Aristazabal Island, i., B.C., Can. C3 99
Ariton, Al., U.S. D4 108
Arivaca, Az., U.S. F4 110
Arivonimamo, Madag. q22 67b
Arizaro, Salar de, pl., Arg. C5 80
Arizgoiti, Spain B9 16
Arizona, Arg. H6 80
Arizona, state, U.S. C4 110
Arizona Sunsites, Az., U.S. F6 110
Arizpe, Mex. B4 90
Arjay, Ky., U.S. D6 124
Arjeplog, Swe. H15 6
Arjona, Col. B5 84
Arkabutla, Ms., U.S. A3 131
Arkabutla Lake, res., Ms., U.S. A4 131
Arkadelphia, Ar., U.S. C2 111
Arkalyk, Kaz. G11 26
Arkansas, co., Ar., U.S. C4 111
Arkansas, state, U.S. C3 111
Arkansas, stm., U.S. D8 106
Arkansas, Salt Fork, stm., U.S. A3 143
Arkansas City, Ar., U.S. D4 111
Arkansas City, Ks., U.S. E6 123
Arklow, Ire. I7 8
Arkoma, Ok., U.S. B7 143
Arkona, Ont., Can. D3 103
Arkona, Kap, c., Ger. A13 10
Arktičeskij, mys, c., Russia A11 28
Arktičeskogo Instituta, ostrova, is., Russia B14 26
Arkwright, Ga., U.S. D3 117
Arlbergpass, Aus. D13 13
Arlberg-Tunnel, Aus. D13 13
Arlee, Mt., U.S. C2 133
Arles, Fr. I11 14
Arley, Al., U.S. A2 108
Arli, Burkina F10 64
Arlington, Az., U.S. D3 110
Arlington, Ga., U.S. E2 117
Arlington, Il., U.S. B4 120
Arlington, In., U.S. E6 121
Arlington, Ia., U.S. B6 122
Arlington, Ks., U.S. E5 123
Arlington, Ky., U.S. f9 124
Arlington, La., U.S. h9 125
Arlington, Ma., U.S. B5 128
Arlington, Mn., U.S. F4 130
Arlington, Ne., U.S. C9 134
Arlington, N.Y., U.S. D7 139
Arlington, N.C., U.S. A2 140
Arlington, Oh., U.S. B2 142
Arlington, Or., U.S. B6 144
Arlington, S.C., U.S. B3 147
Arlington, S.D., U.S. C8 148
Arlington, Tn., U.S. B2 149
Arlington, Tx., U.S. n9 150
Arlington, Vt., U.S. E2 152
Arlington, Va., U.S. B5 153
Arlington, Wa., U.S. A3 154
Arlington, Wi., U.S. E4 156
Arlington, co., Va., U.S. g12 153
Arlington, Lake, res., Tx., U.S. n9 150
Arlington Heights, Il., U.S. A5 120
Arlit, Niger B13 64
Arm, stm., Sask., Can. F3 105
Arma, Ks., U.S. E9 123
Armada, Mi., U.S. F8 129
Armageddon see Tel Megiddo, hist., Isr. C4 50
Armagh, Que., Can. C7 104
Armagh, N. Ire., U.K. G7 8
Armagnac, hist. reg., Fr. I7 14
Armant, Egypt E7 60
Armavir, Russia H6 26
Armazém, Braz. E14 80
Armenia, Col. E5 84
Armenia, ctry., Asia I6 26
Armeniya see Armenia, ctry., Asia I6 26
Armentières, Fr. B9 14
Armería, Mex. H8 90
Armero, Col. E5 84
Armidale, Austl. H9 70
Armijo, N.M., U.S. k7 138
Armington, Il., U.S. C4 120
Armington, Mt., U.S. C6 133
Armorel, Ar., U.S. B6 111
Armour, S.D., U.S. D7 148
Armstrong, Arg. G8 80
Armstrong, B.C., Can. D8 99
Armstrong, Il., U.S. C6 120
Armstrong, Ia., U.S. A3 122
Armstrong, Mo., U.S. B5 132
Armstrong, co., Pa., U.S. E2 145
Armstrong, co., Tx., U.S. B2 150
Armstrong Creek, stm., W.V., U.S. m13 155
Armuchee, Ga., U.S. B1 117
Arnaudville, La., U.S. D4 125
Arnay-le-Duc, Fr. E11 14
Arnedo, Spain C9 16
Arnegard, N.D., U.S. B2 141
Årnes, Nor. K12 6
Arnett, Ok., U.S. A2 143
Arnett, W.V., U.S. D3 155
Arnhem, Neth. E8 12
Arnhem, Cape, c., Austl. B7 68
Arnhem Land, reg., Austl. B6 68
Árnissa, Grc. I5 20
Arno, stm., Italy F5 18
Arno Bay, Austl. I2 70
Arnold, Ca., U.S. C3 112
Arnold, Md., U.S. B5 127
Arnold, Mn., U.S. D6 130
Arnold, Mo., U.S. C7 132
Arnold, Ne., U.S. C5 134
Arnold, Pa., U.S. h14 145
Arnold Mills, R.I., U.S. B4 146
Arnold Mills Reservoir, res., R.I., U.S. B4 146
Arnold's Cove, Newf., Can. E4 102
Arnolds Park, Ia., U.S. A2 122
Arnoldsville, Ga., U.S. C3 117
Arnprior, Ont., Can. B8 103
Arnsberg, Ger. D8 10
Arnstadt, Ger. E10 10
Arnstein, Ont., Can. B5 103
Aro, stm., Ven. D10 84
Aroa, Ven. B8 84
Aroa, stm., Ven. B8 84
Aroab, Nmb. F4 66
Aroma, Sud. J9 60
Aroma Park, Il., U.S. B6 120
Arona, Italy D3 18
Aroostook, N.B., Can. C2 101
Aroostook, co., Me., U.S. B4 126
Aros, stm., Mex. C5 90
Arosa, Switz. E12 13
Arpin, Wi., U.S. D3 156
Arque, Bol. G8 82
Ar-Rabad, Sau. Ar. K8 47
Ar-Radīsīyah Bahrī, Egypt E7 60

Name	Map Ref.	Page
Awegyun, Burma	H5	40
Awjilah, Libya	C5	56
Awled Djellal, Alg.	C13	62
Awlef, Alg.	G11	62
Aworo Kit, Sud.	L7	60
Axel Heiberg Island, i., N.W. Ter., Can.	B10	86
Axial Basin, Co., U.S.	A2	113
Axim, Ghana	I8	64
Axinim, Braz.	J13	84
Axiós (Vardar), stm., Eur.	I6	20
Axis, Al., U.S.	E1	108
Ax-les-Thermes, Fr.	J8	14
Axson, Ga., U.S.	E4	117
Axtell, Ks., U.S.	C7	123
Axtell, Ne., U.S.	D6	134
Ayabaca, Peru	J3	84
Ayabe, Japan	L10	36
Ayacucho, Arg.	I9	80
Ayacucho, Bol.	G10	82
Ayacucho, Peru	E4	82
Ayacucho, dept., Peru	E4	82
Ayamonte, Spain	H4	16
Ayangba, Nig.	H13	64
Ayapel, Col.	C5	84
Ayarza, Laguna de, l., Guat.	C4	92
Ayaviri, Peru	F6	82
Ayaviri, stm., Peru	F6	82
Ayden, N.C., U.S.	B5	140
Aydın, Tur.	L11	20
Ayer, Ma., U.S.	A4	128
Ayers Cliff, Que., Can.	D5	104
Ayers Rock, mtn., Austl.	E6	68
Ayeyarwady (Irrawaddy), stm., Burma	F3	40
Ayía Paraskeví, Grc.	J10	20
Ayiássos, Grc.	J10	20
Áyion Óros, pen., Grc.	I8	20
Áyios Kírikos, Grc.	L10	20
Áyios Nikólaos, Grc.	N9	20
Ayíou Órous, Kólpos, b., Grc.	I8	20
Ayl, Jord.	H5	50
Aylen Lake, l., Ont., Can.	B7	103
Aylesbury, Sask., Can.	G3	105
Aylesbury, Eng., U.K.	J13	8
Aylesford, N.S., Can.	D5	101
Aylmer, Mount, mtn., Alta., Can.	D3	98
Aylmer East, Que., Can.	D2	104
Aylmer Lake, l., N.W. Ter., Can.	D11	96
Aylmer West, Ont., Can.	E4	103
Aylsham, Sask., Can.	D4	105
ʿAyn Dār, Sau. Ar.	B6	47
Aynor, S.C., U.S.	D9	147
ʿAynūnah, Sau. Ar.	G3	48
Ayo, Peru	F5	82
Ayo Ayo, Bol.	G7	82
Ayod, Sud.	M6	60
Ayom, Sud.	N5	60
'Ayoûn el 'Atroûs, Maur.	C5	64
Ayr, Austl.	B7	70
Ayr, Scot., U.K.	F9	8
Ayr, Ne., U.S.	D7	134
ʿAytā al-Fakhkhār, Leb.	A5	50
Ayton, Ont., Can.	C4	103
Ayu, Kepulauan, is., Indon.	E9	38
Ayutla, Mex.	G7	90
Ayutla de los Libres, Mex.	I10	90
Ayvacık, Tur.	J10	20
Ayvalık, Tur.	J10	20
Azacualpa, Hond.	C8	92
Azacualpa, Hond.	B6	92
Azalia, In., U.S.	F6	121
Azambuja, Port.	F3	16
Āzamgarh, India	G10	44
Azángaro, Peru	F6	82
Azángaro, stm., Peru	F6	82
Azaouagh, Vallée de l', val., Afr.	D11	64
Azapa, Quebrada de, stm., Chile	H6	82
Azar, val., Afr.	C12	64
Azare, Nig.	F15	64
Āz̄ar Shahr, Iran	C8	48
Azazga, Alg.	B13	62
Azeffâl, dunes, Afr.	J4	62
Azeffoun, Alg.	B13	62
Azemmour, Mor.	D6	62
Azerbaijan, ctry., Asia	I7	26
Azerbaydzan see Azerbaijan, ctry., Asia	I7	26
Azezo, Eth.	K9	60
Aziscohos Lake, l., Me., U.S.	C1	126
Azle, Tx., U.S.	n9	150
Azogues, Ec.	I3	84
Azores see Açores, is., Port.	k19	62a
Azoum, Bahr (Wādī ʿAẓūm), val., Afr.	K2	60
Azov, Russia	H5	26
Azov, Sea of see Azovskoje more, Eur.	H5	26
Azovskoje more (Sea of Azov), Eur.	H5	26
Azpeitia, Spain	B9	16
Azraq, Al-Baḥr al- see Blue Nile, stm., Afr.	K8	60
Azrou, Mor.	D8	62
Aztec, N.M., U.S.	A2	138
Aztec Peak, mtn., Az., U.S.	D5	110
Aztec Ruins National Monument, N.M., U.S.	A1	138
Azua, Dom. Rep.	E9	94
Azuaga, Spain	G6	16
Azuay, prov., Ec.	I3	84
Azucena, Arg.	I9	80
Azuero, Península de, pen., Pan.	D2	84
Azul, Arg.	I9	80
Azul, Cerro, mtn., C.R.	H9	92
Azul, Cerro, mtn., Hond.	C6	92
Azur, Côte d', Fr.	I14	14
Azurduy, Bol.	H9	82
Azusa, Ca., U.S.	m13	112
Az-Zabadānī, Syria	A6	50
Aẓ-Ẓahrān (Dhahran), Sau. Ar.	A7	47
Az-Zaqāzīq, Egypt	B6	60
Az-Zarqā', Jord.	D6	50
Az-Zāwiyah, Libya	B3	56
Az-Zaydīyah, Yemen	G3	47
Azzel Matti, Sebkha, pl., Alg.	H11	62
Az-Zilfī, Sau. Ar.	H8	48
Az-Zubayr, Iraq	F9	48
B		
Ba, stm., Viet.	H10	40
Baalbek see Baʿlabakk, Leb.	D4	48
Baar, Switz.	D10	13
Baardheere, Som.	H9	56
Baarle-Hertog (Baerle-Duc), Bel.	F6	12
Baarle-Nassau, Bel.	F6	12
Baba, Ec.	H3	84
Babadağ, Tur.	L12	20
Babahoyo, Ec.	H3	84
Babailiqiao, China	C7	34
Babajevo, Russia	B18	22
Babana, Nig.	F11	64
Babanango, S. Afr.	G10	66
Babanūsah, Sud.	L4	60
Babar, Kepulauan, is., Indon.	G8	38
Babar, Pulau, i., Indon.	G8	38
Babb Creek, stm., Pa., U.S.	C7	145
Babbie, Al., U.S.	D3	108
Babbitt, Mn., U.S.	C7	130
Babbitt, Nv., U.S.	E3	135
Bab el Mandeb see Mandeb, Bab el, strt.	H3	47
Babimost, Pol.	C15	10
Babina Greda, Cro.	D2	20
Babinda, Austl.	A6	70
Babine, stm., B.C., Can.	B4	99
Babine Lake, l., B.C., Can.	B5	99
Babine Range, mts., B.C., Can.	B4	99
Babino, Russia	B14	22
Babino, Russia	B23	22
Babo, Indon.	F9	38
Bābol, Iran	C12	48
Bābol Sar, Iran	C12	48
Baboosic Lake, N.H., U.S.	E3	136
Baboquivari Mountains, mts., Az., U.S.	F4	110
Baboquivari Peak, mtn., Az., U.S.	F4	110
Babson Park, Fl., U.S.	E5	116
Babuškin, Russia	G13	28
Babuyan Islands, is., Phil.	B7	38
Babylon, N.Y., U.S.	n15	139
Babynino, Russia	G18	22
Baca, co., Co., U.S.	D8	113
Bacabal, Braz.	D10	76
Bacadéhuachi, Mex.	C5	90
Bacan, Pulau, i., Indon.	F8	38
Bacău, Rom.	C10	20
Bacău, co., Rom.	C10	20
Bac Can, Viet.	C8	40
Baccarat, Fr.	D13	14
Baccaro Point, c., N.S., Can.	F4	101
Bacerac, Mex.	B5	90
Bac Giang, Viet.	D9	40
Bachaquero, Ven.	C7	84
Bacharden, Turk.	J9	26
Bachi, China	K4	34
Bachiniva, Mex.	C6	90
Bachmutovo, Russia	E17	22
Bachu, China	D2	30
Bachuma, Eth.	N8	60
Back, stm., N.W. Ter., Can.	C13	96
Back, stm., S.C., U.S.	h12	147
Bačka Palanka, Yugo.	D3	20
Bačka Topola, Yugo.	D3	20
Back Bay, N.B., Can.	D3	101
Backbone Mountain, mtn., U.S.	m12	127
Backnang, Ger.	G9	10
Backstairs Passage, strt., Austl.	J2	70
Bac Lieu, Viet.	J8	40
Bac Ninh, Viet.	D9	40
Bacoachi, Mex.	B5	90
Bacobi, Az., U.S.	B5	110
Bacolod, Phil.	C7	38
Bacon, co., Ga., U.S.	E4	117
Baconton, Ga., U.S.	E2	117
Bacoor, Phil.	n19	39b
Bács-Kiskun, co., Hung.	I19	10
Bácum, Mex.	D4	90
Bad, stm., S.D., U.S.	C5	148
Bad, stm., Wi., U.S.	B3	156
Badagara, India	G3	46
Badajia, China	B9	34
Badajós, stm., Braz.	I11	84
Badajós, Lago, l., Braz.	I11	84
Badajoz, Spain	G5	16
Badalona, Spain	D14	16
Bādāmi, India	E3	46
Badanah, Sau. Ar.	F6	48
Badaohao, China	B9	32
Badaohe, China	C10	32
Bad Aussee, Aus.	H13	10
Bad Axe, Mi., U.S.	E8	129
Bad Brückenau, Ger.	E9	10
Baddeck, N.S., Can.	C9	101
Bad Doberan, Ger.	A11	10
Bad Dürkheim, Ger.	F8	10
Bad Dürrenberg, Ger.	D12	10
Badeggi, Nig.	G13	64
Badéguichéri, Niger	D12	64
Bad Ems, Ger.	E7	10
Baden, Ont., Can.	D4	103
Baden, Erit.	I9	60
Baden, Switz.	D9	13
Baden, Pa., U.S.	E1	145
Baden-Baden, Ger.	G8	10
Badenweiler, Ger.	H7	10
Baden-Württemberg, state, Ger.	G8	10
Badgastein, Aus.	H13	10
Badger, Newf., Can.	D3	102
Badger, Ia., U.S.	B3	122
Badger, Mn., U.S.	B2	130
Badger, S.D., U.S.	C8	148
Badger Creek, stm., Co., U.S.	B7	113
Bad Hall, Aus.	G14	10
Bad Harzburg, Ger.	D10	10
Bad Hersfeld, Ger.	E9	10
Bad Homburg [vor der Höhe], Ger.	E8	10
Badin, N.C., U.S.	B2	140
Badin Lake, res., N.C., U.S.	B2	140
Badiraguato, Mex.	E6	90
Bad Kissingen, Ger.	E10	10
Bad Kreuznach, Ger.	F7	10
Badlands, hills, S.D., U.S.	D3	148
Badlands, reg., U.S.	C2	141
Badlands National Park, S.D., U.S.	D3	148
Bad Langensalza, Ger.	D10	10
Bad Lauterberg, Ger.	D10	10
Bad Leonfelden, Aus.	G14	10
Bad Mergentheim, Ger.	F9	10
Bad Muskau, Ger.	D14	10
Bad Nauheim, Ger.	E8	10
Bad Neustadt an der Saale, Ger.	E10	10
Bad Oeynhausen, Ger.	C8	10
Badogo, Mali	F5	64
Bad Oldesloe, Ger.	B10	10
Badou, China	G5	32
Badou, Togo	H10	64
Badoumbé, Mali	E4	64
Bad Pyrmont, Ger.	D9	10
Bad Ragaz, Switz.	D12	13
Bad Reichenhall, Ger.	H12	10
Badr Ḥunayn, Sau. Ar.	C1	47
Bad River Indian Reservation, Wi., U.S.	B3	156
Bad Salzuflen, Ger.	C8	10
Bad Salzungen, Ger.	E10	10
Bad Sankt Leonhard im Lavanttal, Aus.	I14	10
Bad Schwalbach, Ger.	E8	10
Bad Schwartau, Ger.	B10	10
Bad Segeberg, Ger.	B10	10
Bad Tölz, Ger.	H11	10
Badu, China	I8	34
Badulla, Sri L.	I6	46
Badupi, Burma	D2	40
Bad Vöslau, Aus.	H16	10
Bad Waldsee, Ger.	H9	10
Badwater Creek, stm., Wy., U.S.	C5	157
Bad Wildungen, Ger.	D9	10
Baediam, Maur.	D4	64
Baena, Spain	H7	16
Baependi, Braz.	F6	79
Baeza, Ec.	H4	84
Bafatá, Gui.-B.	E2	64
Baffin Bay, b., N.A.	B13	86
Baffin Bay, b., Tx., U.S.	E4	150
Baffin Island, i., N.W. Ter., Can.	C18	96
Bafing, stm., Afr.	F4	54
Bafoulabé, Mali	E4	64
Bafoussam, Cam.	G9	54
Bāfq, Iran	F13	48
Bāft, Iran	G14	48
Bafwasende, Zaire	A5	58
Bagaces, C.R.	G9	92
Bagagem, stm., Braz.	C4	79
Bāgalkot, India	D3	46
Bagansiapiapi, Indon.	M6	40
Bağarası, Tur.	L11	20
Bagawi, Sud.	K8	60
Bagdad, Az., U.S.	C2	110
Bagdad, Fl., U.S.	u14	116
Bagdad, Ky., U.S.	B4	124
Bagdarin, Russia	G14	28
Bagé, Braz.	F11	80
Baggs, Wy., U.S.	E5	157
Baghdād, Iraq	E8	48
Bagheria, Italy	K8	18
Baghlān, Afg.	B3	44
Bagley, Ia., U.S.	C3	122
Bagley, Mn., U.S.	C3	130
Bagley, Wi., U.S.	F2	156
Bagnell Dam, Mo., U.S.	C5	132
Bagnères-de-Bigorre, Fr.	I7	14
Bagnères-de-Luchon, Fr.	J7	14
Bagnols-sur-Cèze, Fr.	H11	14
Bago (Pegu), Burma	F4	40
Bagoé, stm., Afr.	F6	64
Bagrationovsk, Russia	G3	22
Baguio, Phil.	m19	39b
Bagzane, mtn., Niger	C14	64
Bahama, N.C., U.S.	A4	140
Bahamas, ctry., N.A.	D9	88
Bahār, Iran	D10	48
Baharampur, India	H13	44
Bahāwalnagar, Pak.	F5	44
Bahāwalpur, Pak.	F4	44
Bahechuan, China	C12	32
Bahia, state, Braz.	B7	79
Bahía, Islas de la, is., Hond.	A8	92
Bahía Azul, Pan.	H13	92
Bahía Blanca, Arg.	J7	80
Bahía Kino, Mex.	C4	90
Bahir Dar, Eth.	L9	60
Baḥrah, Sau. Ar.	D1	47
Bahraich, India	G9	44
Bahrain (Al-Baḥrayn), ctry., Asia	D5	42
Baḥrayn, Khalīj al-, b., Asia	B7	47
Bāhū Kalāt, Iran	I16	48
Baï, Mali	E8	64
Baia Mare, Rom.	B7	20
Baía Rica, stm., Braz.	E10	82
Baia Sprie, Rom.	B7	20
Baicao, China	B4	32
Baicheng, China	B11	30
Baicheng, China	C3	30
Baie-Comeau, Que., Can.	k13	104
Baie-d'Urfé, Que., Can.	q19	104
Baie-Saint-Paul, Que., Can.	B7	104
Baie Verte, N.B., Can.	C5	101
Baie Verte, Newf., Can.	D3	102
Baigong, China	K5	34
Baihebu, China	C4	32
Baijian, China	D3	32
Baiju, China	B9	34
Baikal, Lake see Bajkal, ozero, l., Russia	G13	28
Bailadores, Ven.	C7	84
Baile, China	D2	32
Baile Átha Cliath see Dublin, Ire.	H7	8
Băile Govora, Rom.	D8	20
Bailén, Spain	G8	16
Băilești, Rom.	E7	20
Bailey, Co., U.S.	B5	113
Bailey, N.C., U.S.	B4	140
Bailey, co., Tx., U.S.	B1	150
Bailey Brook, stm., Me., U.S.	B2	126
Bailey Island, Me., U.S.	g8	126
Bailey Island, i., S.C., U.S.	k11	147
Baileys Crossroads, Va., U.S.	g12	153
Baileys Harbor, Wi., U.S.	C6	156
Baileyton, Al., U.S.	A3	108
Baileyton, Tn., U.S.	C11	149
Baileyville, Il., U.S.	A4	120
Baileyville, Ks., U.S.	C7	123
Bailin, China	H9	34
Bailique, Ilha, i., Braz.	C9	76
Bailleul, Fr.	B9	14
Bailong, stm., China	E7	30
Bailundo, Ang.	D3	58
Baimaguan, China	C4	32
Baimashi, China	F7	34
Baimiaozi, China	C8	32
Bainbridge, Ga., U.S.	F2	117
Bainbridge, In., U.S.	E4	121
Bainbridge, N.Y., U.S.	C5	139
Bainbridge, Oh., U.S.	C2	142
Bainbridge Island, i., Wa., U.S.	e10	154
Bain-de-Bretagne, Fr.	E5	14
Bainiqiao, China	F3	34
Bains-les-Bains, Fr.	D13	14
Bainville, Mt., U.S.	B12	133
Baipu, China	C9	34
Baiquan, China	E11	34
Baird, Tx., U.S.	C3	150
Bairdford, Pa., U.S.	h14	145
Baird Inlet, b., Ak., U.S.	C7	109
Baird Mountains, mts., Ak., U.S.	B7	109
Bairin Zuoqi, China	C10	30
Bairnsdale, Austl.	K7	70
Bairoil, Wy., U.S.	D5	157
Bairuopu, China	G1	34
Baisha, China	E10	40
Baishanji, China	B5	34
Baishatan, China	G9	32
Baishuifan, China	E4	34
Baishuijiang, China	E8	30
Baisogala, Lith.	F6	22
Baitazi, China	A8	32
Baitu, China	D8	34
Baixa Grande, Braz.	A8	79
Baixiang, China	F2	32
Baiyin, China	D7	30
Baizhongpu, China	B3	34
Baja, Hung.	I18	10
Baja, Punta, c., Mex.	C2	90
Baja California, pen., Mex.	C3	90
Baja California Norte, state, Mex.	C2	90
Baja California Sur, state, Mex.	E4	90
Bajada del Agrio, Arg.	J3	80
Bajanaul, Kaz.	G13	26
Bajanchongor, Mong.	B7	30
Bajánsenye, Hung.	I16	10
Baja Verapaz, dept., Guat.	B4	92
Bajdarackaja guba, b., Russia	D11	26
Bajestān, Iran	D15	48
Bajiazi, China	B11	32
Bajimba, Mount, mtn., Austl.	G10	70
Bajkal, ozero (Lake Baikal), l., Russia	G13	28
Bajkal'skoje, Russia	F13	28
Bajmak, Russia	G9	26
Bajo Baudó, Col.	E4	84
Bajo Boquete, Pan.	C1	84
Bajos de Haina, Dom. Rep.	E9	94
Bajram-Ali, Turk.	J10	26
Bakebe, Cam.	I14	64
Bakel, Sen.	D3	64
Baker, Ca., U.S.	E5	112
Baker, Fl., U.S.	u15	116
Baker, La., U.S.	D4	125
Baker, Mt., U.S.	D12	133
Baker, Nv., U.S.	D7	135
Baker, Or., U.S.	C9	144
Baker, co., Fl., U.S.	B4	116
Baker, co., Ga., U.S.	E2	117
Baker, co., Or., U.S.	C9	144
Baker, stm., N.H., U.S.	C3	136
Baker, Mount, mtn., Wa., U.S.	A4	154
Baker Air Force Base, mil., Ar., U.S.	B6	111
Baker Butte, mtn., Az., U.S.	C4	110
Baker Hill, Al., U.S.	D4	108
Baker Island, i., Oc.	H22	158
Baker Island, i., Ak., U.S.	n22	109
Baker Lake, N.W. Ter., Can.	D13	96
Baker Lake, l., N.W. Ter., Can.	D13	96
Baker Lake, l., Me., U.S.	B3	126
Baker Lake, res., Wa., U.S.	A4	154
Baker Mountain, mtn., Me., U.S.	C3	126
Bakers, N.C., U.S.	B2	140
Bakers Bayou, stm., Ar., U.S.	k11	111
Bakersfield, Ca., U.S.	E4	112
Bakersfield, Mo., U.S.	E5	132
Bakersfield, Vt., U.S.	B3	152
Bakers Island, i., Ma., U.S.	f12	128
Bakerstown, Pa., U.S.	h14	145
Bakersville, Ct., U.S.	B3	114
Bakersville, N.C., U.S.	e10	140
Bakerton, W.V., U.S.	B7	155
Bākhtarān (Kermānshāh), Iran	D9	48
Bakhtegān, Daryācheh-ye, l., Iran	G13	48
Bakkagerði, Ice.	B7	6a
Baklanka, Russia	C23	22
Bako, Eth.	O9	60
Bakony, mts., Hung.	H17	10
Bakoy, stm., Afr.	F5	54
Baku (Baky), Azer.	I7	26
Bakun, China	D9	44
Bala, Ont., Can.	B5	103
Bala, Sen.	D3	64
Balâ, Tur.	B2	48
Balabac Strait, strt., Asia	D6	38
Baʿlabakk, Leb.	D4	48
Balabanovo, Russia	F19	22
Balachna, Russia	E26	22
Balad, Iraq	D8	48
Bālāghāt, India	J9	44
Balaguer, Spain	D12	16
Balakirevo, Russia	E21	22
Balaklava, Austl.	J3	70
Balakovo, Russia	G7	26
Balallan, Scot., U.K.	C7	8
Bālā Morghāb, Afg.	D17	48
Balāngīr, India	B7	46
Balašicha, Russia	F20	22
Balašov, Russia	G6	26
Balassagyarmat, Hung.	G19	10
Balāṭ, Egypt	E5	60
Balaton, Mn., U.S.	F3	130
Balaton, l., Hung.	I17	10
Balayan, Phil.	o19	39b
Balbieriškis, Lith.	G6	22
Balbina, Represa, res., Braz.	H13	84
Balbirini, Austl.	C7	68
Balboa, Pan.	I15	92
Balbriggan, Ire.	H7	8
Balcanoona, Austl.	H3	70
Balcarce, Arg.	I9	80
Balcarres, Sask., Can.	G4	105
Balchaš, Kaz.	H12	26
Balchaš, ozero (Lake Balkhash), l., Kaz.	H12	26
Balde, Arg.	G5	80
Bald Eagle Lake, l., Mn., U.S.	m12	130
Bald Eagle Lake, l., Mn., U.S.	C7	130
Bald Hill, hill, R.I., U.S.	D2	146
Baldhill Dam, N.D., U.S.	B7	141
Baldim, Braz.	E7	79
Bald Knob, Ar., U.S.	B4	111
Bald Knob, mtn., Va., U.S.	c3	153
Bald Knob, mtn., W.V., U.S.	C5	155
Bald Knoll, mtn., Wy., U.S.	D2	157
Bald Mountain, mtn., Ct., U.S.	B6	114
Bald Mountain, mtn., N.J., U.S.	A4	137
Bald Mountain, mtn., Or., U.S.	D5	144
Bald Mountain, mtn., Or., U.S.	C9	144
Bald Mountain, mtn., Vt., U.S.	B5	152
Bald Mountain, mtn., Wy., U.S.	B5	157
Bald Mountains, mts., N.C., U.S.	f10	140
Baldone, Lat.	E7	22
Baldur, Man., Can.	E2	100
Baldwin, Fl., U.S.	B5	116
Baldwin, Ga., U.S.	B3	117
Baldwin, Il., U.S.	E4	120
Baldwin, La., U.S.	E4	125
Baldwin, Mi., U.S.	E5	129
Baldwin, Pa., U.S.	k14	145
Baldwin, S.C., U.S.	B5	147
Baldwin, Wi., U.S.	D1	156
Baldwin, co., Al., U.S.	E2	108
Baldwin, co., Ga., U.S.	C3	117
Baldwin City, Ks., U.S.	D8	123
Baldwinsville, N.Y., U.S.	B4	139
Baldwinville, Ma., U.S.	A3	128
Baldwyn, Ms., U.S.	A5	131
Baldy Mountain, mtn., B.C., Can.	D7	99
Baldy Mountain, mtn., Man., Can.	D1	100
Baldy Mountain, mtn., Mt., U.S.	B7	133
Baldy Mountain, mtn., N.M., U.S.	A4	138
Baldy Peak, mtn., Az., U.S.	D6	110
Balearic Islands see Balears, Illes, is., Spain	F15	16
Balears, prov., Spain	F15	16
Balears, Illes (Balearic Islands), is., Spain	F15	16
Baleia, Ponta da, c., Braz.	D9	79
Baleine, Rivière à la, stm., Que., Can.	g13	104
Balej, Russia	G15	28
Baler, Phil.	n19	39b
Bāleshwar, India	J12	44
Baléyara, Niger	E11	64
Balfate, Hond.	B8	92
Balfes Creek, Austl.	C6	70
Balfour, N.C., U.S.	f10	140
Balgonie, Sask., Can.	G3	105
Bali, Laut (Bali Sea), Indon.	G6	38
Bali, Selat, strt., Indon.	G5	38
Balihan, China	B6	32
Balıkesir, Tur.	J11	20
Balikpapan, Indon.	F6	38
Balimo, Pap. N. Gui.	G11	38
Balin, China	B11	30
Balingen, Ger.	G8	10
Balintang Channel, strt., Phil.	B7	38
Baliza, Braz.	D2	79
Balkan Mountains see Stara Planina, mts., Eur.	G8	20
Balkan Peninsula, pen., Eur.	D9	52
Balkbrug, Neth.	C9	12
Balkh, Afg.	B2	44
Balkh, stm., Afg.	B2	44
Balkhash, Lake see Balchaš, ozero, l., Kaz.	H12	26
Ball, La., U.S.	C3	125
Ballachulish, Scot., U.K.	E8	8
Ballangen, Nor.	G15	6
Ballantine, Mt., U.S.	E8	133
Ballarat, Austl.	K5	70
Ballard, co., Ky., U.S.	e8	124
Ballardvale, Ma., U.S.	f11	128
Ball Club Lake, l., Mn., U.S.	C5	130
Ballé, Mali	D5	64
Ballenas, Bahía de, b., Mex.	D3	90
Balleny Islands, is., Ant.	B8	73
Balleroy, Fr.	C6	14
Ballesteros, Arg.	G7	80
Balleza, Mex.	D6	90
Balleza, stm., Mex.	D6	90
Ball Ground, Ga., U.S.	B2	117
Ballia, India	H11	44
Ballina, Austl.	G10	70
Ballina, Ire.	G4	8
Ballinger, Tx., U.S.	D3	150
Ball Mountain Lake, res., Vt., U.S.	E3	152
Ballon, Fr.	M14	8
Ballouville, Ct., U.S.	B8	114
Balls Pyramid, i., Austl.	F11	68
Ballston Spa, N.Y., U.S.	B7	139
Ballwin, Mo., U.S.	f12	132
Bally, Pa., U.S.	F10	145
Balm, Fl., U.S.	E4	116
Balmaceda, Chile	F2	78
Balmoral, Man., Can.	D3	100
Balmoral, N.B., Can.	B3	101
Balmorhea, Tx., U.S.	o13	150
Balmville, N.Y., U.S.	D6	139
Balnearia, Arg.	F7	80
Balonne, stm., Austl.	F8	70
Bālotra, India	H5	44
Balovale, Zam.	D4	58
Baloži, Lat.	E7	22
Balrāmpur, India	G10	44
Balranald, Austl.	J5	70
Balsam, N.C., U.S.	f9	140
Balsam Lake, Wi., U.S.	C1	156
Balsam Lake, l., Ont., Can.	C6	103
Balsam Lake, l., Wi., U.S.	C1	156
Bálsamo, Braz.	F2	79
Balsas, Braz.	E9	76
Balsas, stm., Mex.	H8	90
Balsas, Rio das, stm., Braz.	E9	76
Balsas Sur, Mex.	I10	90
Balsthal, Switz.	D8	13
Balta, Ukr.	H3	26
Balta, N.D., U.S.	A5	141
Baltasar Brum, Ur.	F10	80
Baltic, Ct., U.S.	C7	114
Baltic, Oh., U.S.	B4	142
Baltic, S.D., U.S.	D9	148
Baltic Sea, Eur.	M16	6
Baltijsk, Russia	G2	22
Baltijskaja kosa, spit, Eur.	A19	10
Balṭīm, Egypt	B6	60
Baltimore, Ont., Can.	C6	103
Baltimore, Ire.	J4	8
Baltimore, S. Afr.	D9	66
Baltimore, Md., U.S.	B4	127
Baltimore, Oh., U.S.	C3	142
Baltimore, co., Md., U.S.	B4	127
Baltimore Highlands, Md., U.S.	h11	127
Baluarte, stm., Mex.	F7	90
Balvi, Lat.	D10	22
Balya, Tur.	J11	20
Balykši, Kaz.	H8	26
Balzar, Ec.	H3	84
Bam, Iran	G15	48
Bama, China	B9	40
Bamaga, Austl.	B8	68
Bamako, Mali	E5	64
Bamba, Mali	C9	64
Bambamarca, Peru	B2	82
Bambana, stm., Nic.	D11	92
Bambara Maoundé, Mali	D8	64
Bambari, Cen. Afr. Rep.	G5	56
Bambaroo, Austl.	B7	70
Bamberg, Ger.	F10	10
Bamberg, S.C., U.S.	E5	147
Bamberg, co., S.C., U.S.	E5	147
Bambesi, Eth.	M8	60
Bambezi, Zimb.	C9	66
Bambuí, Braz.	F6	79
Bamburral, stm., S.A.	H12	82
Bam Co, l., China	E14	44
Bamenda, Cam.	I15	64
Bami, Turk.	B14	48
Bamingui, stm., Cen. Afr. Rep.	G4	56
Bampūr, Iran	H16	48
Bamumo, China	D15	44
Ba Na, Viet.	G9	40
Banaba, i., Kir.	I20	158
Banalia, Zaire	A5	58
Banana, Zaire	C2	58
Bananal, Ilha do, i., Braz.	F8	76
Banana River, b., Fl., U.S.	D6	116
Banarlı, Tur.	H11	20
Banās, Ra's, c., Egypt	F8	60
Banat, reg., Eur.	D4	20
Banbuji, China	B5	34
Banco, Punta, c., C.R.	I11	92
Bancroft, Ont., Can.	B7	103
Bancroft, Id., U.S.	G7	119
Bancroft, Ia., U.S.	A3	122
Bancroft, Mi., U.S.	F6	129
Bancroft, Ne., U.S.	B9	134
Bānda, India	H9	44
Banda, Kepulauan, is., Indon.	F8	38
Banda, Laut (Banda Sea), Indon.	G8	38
Banda Aceh, Indon.	L3	40
Bānda Dāūd Shāh, Pak.	D4	44
Banda del Río Salí, Arg.	D6	80
Bandama, stm., I.C.	H7	64
Bandama Blanc, stm., I.C.	G7	64
Bandama Rouge, stm., I.C.	G6	64
Bandana, Ky., U.S.	e9	124
Bandar Beheshtī, Iran	I16	48
Bandar-e ʿAbbās, Iran	H14	48
Bandar-e Anzalī (Bandar-e Pahlavī), Iran	C10	48
Bandar-e Būshehr, Iran	G11	48
Bandar-e Deylam, Iran	F11	48
Bandar-e Khomeynī (Bandar-e Shāhpūr), Iran	F10	48
Bandar-e Lengeh, Iran	H13	48
Bandar-e Māh Shahr, Iran	F10	48
Bandar-e Rīg, Iran	G11	48
Bandar-e Torkeman, Iran	C13	48
Bandar see Machilīpatnam, India	D6	46
Bandar Seri Begawan, Bru.	E5	38
Banded Peak, mtn., Co., U.S.	D4	113
Bandeira, Pico da, mtn., Braz.	F8	79
Bandeirantes, Braz.	B3	79
Bandeirantes, Braz.	E1	79
Bandeirantes, Braz.	G3	79
Bandelier National Monument, N.M., U.S.	B3	138
Bandera, Arg.	E7	80
Bandera, Tx., U.S.	E3	150
Bandera, co., Tx., U.S.	E3	150
Bandera, Alto, mtn., Dom. Rep.	E9	94
Banderas, Bahía de, b., Mex.	G7	90
Bandiagara, Mali	D8	64
Bandiantaolehai, China	C7	30
Bandırma, Tur.	I11	20
Bandon, Ire.	J5	8
Bandon, Or., U.S.	D2	144
Ban Don, Ao, b., Thai.	J5	40
Bandula, Moz.	B11	66
Bandundu, Zaire	B3	58
Bandung, Indon.	j13	39a
Bāneh, Iran	D8	48
Banes, Cuba	D7	94
Banff, Scot., U.K.	D11	8

Name — Map Ref. — Page

Banff National Park, Alta., Can. D2 98
Banfora, Burkina F7 64
Bangalore, India F4 46
Bangaon, India I13 44
Bangassou, Cen. Afr. Rep. H5 56
Banggai, Indon. F7 38
Banggai, Kepulauan, is., Indon. F7 38
Banghāzī, Libya B5 56
Bangil, Indon. j16 39a
Bangjang, Sud. L7 60
Bangjun, China D5 32
Bangka, Pulau, i., Indon. F4 38
Bangkalan, Indon. j16 39a
Bangkok see Krung Thep, Thai. H6 40
Bangladesh, ctry., Asia E13 42
Bang Mun Nak, Thai. F6 40
Bangolo, I.C. H6 64
Bangor, Sask., Can. G4 105
Bangor, N. Ire., U.K. G8 8
Bangor, Wales, U.K. H9 8
Bangor, Me., U.S. D4 126
Bangor, Mi., U.S. F4 129
Bangor, Pa., U.S. E11 145
Bangor, Wi., U.S. E3 156
Bangor Township, Mi., U.S. E7 129
Bangs, Tx., U.S. D3 150
Bangs, Mount, mtn., Az., U.S. A2 110
Bang Saphan, Thai. I5 40
Bangshi, China C10 32
Bangued, Phil. m19 39b
Bangui, Cen. Afr. Rep. H4 56
Bangweulu, Lake, l., Zam. D5 58
Ban Hin Heup, Laos E7 40
Ban Houayxay, Laos D6 40
Bani, Burkina D9 64
Baní, Dom. Rep. E9 94
Bani, stm., Mali E7 64
Baniachang, Bngl. H14 44
Banikoara, Benin F11 64
Banī Mazār, Egypt C6 60
Banister, stm., Va., U.S. D4 153
Banī Suwayf, Egypt C6 60
Banī Walīd, Libya B3 56
Bāniyās, Syria B5 50
Banja Luka, Bos. E12 18
Banjarmasin, Indon. F5 38
Banjin, China C9 34
Banjul (Bathurst), Gam. E1 64
Bankas, Mali D8 64
Bankhead Lake, res., Al., U.S. B2 108
Bankilaré, Niger D10 64
Banks, Al., U.S. D4 108
Banks, Or., U.S. g11 144
Banks, co., Ga., U.S. B3 117
Banks Island, i., B.C., Can. C2 99
Banks Island, i., N.W. Ter., Can. B8 96
Banks Lake, res., Ga., U.S. E3 117
Banks Lake, res., Wa., U.S. B6 154
Banks Peninsula, pen., N.Z. E4 72
Banks Strait, strt., Austl. M8 70
Bankston, Al., U.S. B2 108
Bānkura, India I12 44
Ban Mit, Laos E6 40
Bann, stm., N. Ire., U.K. G7 8
Ban Nahin, Laos E8 40
Ban Namnga, Laos D7 40
Banner, co., Ne., U.S. C2 134
Banner Elk, N.C., U.S. A1 140
Ban Ngam, Laos D8 40
Banning, Ca., U.S. F5 112
Banning, Ga., U.S. C2 117
Bannock, co., Id., U.S. G6 119
Bannockburn, Ont., Can. C7 103
Bannock Peak, mtn., Id., U.S. F6 119
Bannock Range, mts., Id., U.S. G6 119
Bannu, Pak. D4 44
Banon, Fr. H12 14
Baños, Ec. H3 84
Baños, Peru D3 82
Ban Pakneun, Laos E6 40
Ban Pong, Thai. H5 40
Banpu, China A8 34
Banqiao, China E9 34
Banqiaoji, China C5 34
Banquan, China H6 32
Banshi, China J4 34
Banská Bystrica, Slov. G19 10
Banská Štiavnica, Slov. G18 10
Ban Songkhon, Laos F8 40
Bānswāra, India I6 44
Bantam, Ct., U.S. C3 114
Bantam, stm., Ct., U.S. B3 114
Bantam Lake, l., Ct., U.S. C3 114
Ban Thanoun, Laos E6 40
Bantry, Ire. J4 8
Ban Xènkhalôk, Laos E6 40
Banyak, Kepulauan, is., Indon. M4 40
Banyoles, Spain C14 16
Banzare Coast, Ant. B7 73
Banzi, China K6 34
Baode, China D9 30
Baoding, China E3 32
Baofeng, China B2 34
Bao Ha, Viet. C8 40
Baohekou, China C6 32
Baoji, China E8 30
Bao Lac, Viet. I9 40
Baonian, China D8 34
Baoquan, China G7 32
Baoshan, China D10 34
Baoshan, China B5 40
Baoting, China H8 30
Baotou, China C8 30
Baowei, China C9 40
Baoxinji, China C4 34
Baoying, China B8 34
Bāpatla, India E6 46
Bapaume, Fr. B9 14
Bapchule, Az., U.S. D4 110
Baptiste, Ont., Can. B6 103
Bāqa el Gharbīya, Isr. D4 50
Baqên, China E16 44
B'aqlīn, Leb. A5 50
Ba'qūbah, Iraq E8 48
Baquedano, Chile B4 80
Bar, Yugo. G3 20
Baraawe, Som. H9 56
Barabinsk, Russia F7 28
Barabinskaja step', pl., Russia F7 28
Baraboo, Wi., U.S. E4 156
Baraboo, stm., Wi., U.S. E3 156
Baraboulé, Burkina D9 64
Baracaju, stm., Braz. B3 79
Baracaldo, Spain B9 16
Barachit, Erit. J10 60
Baracoa, Cuba D7 94
Baracoa, Hond. B7 92
Baradero, Arg. G9 80
Baradine, Austl. H8 70
Baraga, Mi., U.S. B2 129
Baraga, co., Mi., U.S. B2 129
Baragarh, India B7 46
Bārah, Sud. K6 60
Barahona, Dom. Rep. E9 94
Barak, Tur. C4 48
Baraka, val., Afr. E8 56
Baralaba, Austl. E8 70
Baram, stm., Malay. E5 38
Barama, stm., Guy. D13 84
Baran', Bela. G13 22
Baranagar, India I13 44
Baranoa, Col. B5 84
Baranof Island, i., Ak., U.S. m22 109
Baranoviči, Bela. H9 22
Baranya, co., Hung. J18 10
Barão de Melgaço, Braz. G14 82
Baratang Island, i., India H2 40
Barataria, La., U.S. E5 125
Barataria, Bayou, stm., La., U.S. k11 125
Barataria Bay, b., La., U.S. E6 125
Barat Daya, Kepulauan, is., Indon. G8 38
Bar'atino, Russia G17 22
Barauana, stm., Braz. G12 84
Barauni, India H11 44
Baraut, India F7 44
Baraya, Col. F5 84
Barbacena, Braz. F7 79
Barbacoas, Col. G3 84
Barbados, ctry., N.A. H15 94
Barbar, Sud. H7 60
Barbareta, Isla, i., Hond. A8 92
Barbas, Cap, c., W. Sah. I2 62
Barbastro, Spain C12 16
Barbate de Franco, Spain I6 16
Barbeau Peak, mtn., N.W. Ter., Can. A12 86
Barber, co., Ks., U.S. E5 123
Barberena, Guat. C4 92
Barbers Point, c., Hi., U.S. B3 118
Barbers Point Naval Air Station, mil., Hi., U.S. g9 118
Barberton, S. Afr. E10 66
Barberton, Oh., U.S. A4 142
Barbezieux, Fr. G6 14
Barbil, India I11 44
Barbosa, Col. D5 84
Barbosa, Col. E6 84
Barbour, co., Al., U.S. D4 108
Barbour, co., W.V., U.S. B4 155
Barboursville, W.V., U.S. C2 155
Barbourville, Ky., U.S. D6 124
Barbuda, i., Antig. F14 94
Barby, Ger. D11 10
Barcaldine, Austl. D6 70
Barcău (Berettyó), stm., Eur. B6 20
Barce see Al-Marj, Libya B5 56
Barcellona Pozzo di Gotto, Italy K10 18
Barcelona, Mex. D8 90
Barcelona, Spain D14 16
Barcelona, Ven. B10 84
Barcelos, Braz. H11 84
Barcin, Pol. C17 10
Barco, N.C., U.S. A7 140
Barcoo, stm., Austl. E5 70
Barcroft, Lake, res., Va., U.S. g12 153
Barcs, Hung. J17 10
Barczewo, Pol. B20 10
Barda, Azer. A9 48
Barda del Medio, Arg. J4 80
Bardaï, Chad D4 56
Bardai, Sud. K1 60
Bardawīl, Sabkhat al-, sw., Egypt F2 48
Barddhamān, India I12 44
Bardejov, Slov. F21 10
Barden Reservoir, res., R.I., U.S. C2 146
Bardi, Italy E4 18
Bardīyah, Libya B3 60
Bardo, Tun. M5 18
Bardolph, Il., U.S. C3 120
Bardonecchia, Italy D1 18
Bardstown, Ky., U.S. C4 124
Bardu, Nor. G16 6
Bardufoss, Nor. G16 6
Bardwell, Ky., U.S. f9 124
Bardwell Lake, res., Tx., U.S. C4 150
Bare Hill Pond, l., Ma., U.S. g9 128
Bareilly, India F8 44
Barentin, Fr. C7 14
Barents Sea, Eur. B4 24
Barentu, Erit. J9 60
Barfleur, Fr. C5 14
Barge, Eth. N9 60
Bargersville, In., U.S. E5 121
Bargnop, Sud. M5 60
Barguzin, stm., Russia G14 28
Bar Harbor, Me., U.S. D4 126
Bari, Italy H11 18
Baria, stm., Ven. G9 84
Barichara, Col. D6 84
Barillas, Guat. B3 92
Barīm (Perim), i., Yemen H3 47
Barima, stm., S.A. C12 84
Barima-Waini, prov., Guy. D13 84
Barinas, Ven. C7 84
Barinas, state, Ven. C8 84
Baring, Me., U.S. C5 126
Baring, Mo., U.S. A5 132
Baring, Cape, c., N.W. Ter., Can. B9 96
Barinitas, Ven. C7 84
Bāripada, India J12 44
Bariri, Braz. G4 79
Bārīs, Egypt E6 60
Barisāl, Bngl. I14 44
Barisan, Pegunungan, mts., Indon. F3 38
Barito, stm., Indon. F5 38
Barium Springs, N.C., U.S. B2 140
Barjols, Fr. I13 14
Barkal, Bngl. I15 44
Barker Heights, N.C., U.S. f10 140
Barkhamsted Reservoir, res., Ct., U.S. B3 114
Bark Lake, l., Ont., Can. B7 103
Barkley, Lake, res., U.S. f10 124
Barkley Dam, Ky., U.S. e9 124
Barkley Sound, strt., B.C., Can. E5 99
Barkly East, S. Afr. H8 66
Barkly Tableland, plat., Austl. C7 68
Barkly West, S. Afr. G7 66
Barkmere, Que., Can. C3 104
Barkol, China C5 30
Bark Point, c., Wi., U.S. B2 156
Bark River, Mi., U.S. C3 129
Barksdale Air Force Base, mil., La., U.S. B2 125
Bar-le-Duc, Fr. D12 14
Barlee, Lake, l., Austl. E3 68
Barletta, Italy H11 18
Barling, Ar., U.S. B1 111
Barlow, Ky., U.S. e8 124
Bārmer, India H4 44
Bar Mills, Me., U.S. E2 126
Barnaby River, N.B., Can. C4 101
Barnard, Ks., U.S. C5 123
Barnard, Mo., U.S. A3 132
Barnard, Vt., U.S. D3 152
Barnard Castle, Eng., U.K. G15 8
Barnardsville, N.C., U.S. f10 140
Barnaul, Russia G14 26
Barn Bluff, mtn., Austl. M6 70
Barnegat, N.J., U.S. D4 137
Barnegat Bay, b., N.J., U.S. D4 137
Barnegat Inlet, b., N.J., U.S. D4 137
Barnes, Ks., U.S. C7 123
Barnes, co., N.D., U.S. B7 141
Barnesboro, Pa., U.S. E4 145
Barnes City, Ia., U.S. C5 122
Barnes Creek, stm., La., U.S. D2 125
Barnes Ice Cap, N.W. Ter., Can. B18 96
Barnes Sound, strt., Fl., U.S. G6 116
Barneston, Ne., U.S. D9 134
Barnesville, Ga., U.S. C2 117
Barnesville, Mn., U.S. D2 130
Barnesville, Oh., U.S. C4 142
Barnet, Vt., U.S. C4 152
Barnett, Mo., U.S. C5 132
Barneveld, Wi., U.S. E4 156
Barney, Ga., U.S. F3 117
Barney, N.D., U.S. C8 141
Barnhart, Mo., U.S. C7 132
Barnsdall, Ok., U.S. A5 143
Barnstable, Ma., U.S. C7 128
Barnstable, co., Ma., U.S. C7 128
Barnstaple, Eng., U.K. J9 8
Barnstead, N.H., U.S. D4 136
Barnum, Mn., U.S. D6 130
Bar Nunn, Wy., U.S. D6 157
Barnwell, Alta., Can. E4 98
Barnwell, S.C., U.S. E5 147
Barnwell, co., S.C., U.S. E5 147
Baro, stm., Afr. G8 56
Baroda, Mi., U.S. G4 129
Barons, Alta., Can. E4 98
Barpeta, India G14 44
Barqa, China E9 44
Barqah (Cyrenaica), hist. reg., Libya C2 60
Barque Canada Reef, rf., Asia D5 38
Barques, Pointe aux, c., Mi., U.S. D8 129
Barquisimeto, Ven. B8 84
Barr, Co., U.S. B6 113
Barra, Braz. F10 76
Barra, Ponta da, c., Moz. D12 66
Barraba, Austl. H9 70
Barrackville, W.V., U.S. B4 155
Barra da Estiva, Braz. B8 79
Barra do Bugres, Braz. F13 82
Barra do Corda, Braz. E9 76
Barra do Cuanza, Ang. C2 58
Barra do Garças, Braz. C2 79
Barra do Mendes, Braz. A7 79
Barra do Piraí, Braz. G7 79
Barra do Ribeiro, Braz. F13 80
Barra Falsa, Ponta da, c., Moz. D12 66
Barrafranca, Italy L9 18
Barra Mansa, Braz. G6 79
Barranca, Peru D3 82
Barranca, Peru A3 82
Barrancabermeja, Col. D6 84
Barrancas, Col. B6 84
Barrancas, Ven. C7 84
Barrancas, Ven. C11 84
Barrancas, stm., Arg. I3 80
Barranqueras, Arg. D9 80
Barranquilla, Col. B5 84
Barras, Braz. D10 76
Barre, Ma., U.S. B3 128
Barre, Vt., U.S. C4 152
Barre, Lake, l., La., U.S. E5 125
Barreal, Arg. F4 80
Barre Falls Reservoir, res., Ma., U.S. B4 128
Barreiras, Braz. B6 79
Barreirinha, Braz. I14 84
Barreiro, Port. G2 16
Barreiro, stm., Braz. C2 79
Barreiros, Braz. E11 76
Barren, co., Ky., U.S. D4 124
Barren, stm., Ky., U.S. C3 124
Barren, Nosy, is., Madag. q20 67b
Barren Island, i., Md., U.S. D5 127
Barren Islands, is., Ak., U.S. h15 109
Barren River Lake, res., Ky., U.S. D3 124
Barretos, Braz. F4 79
Barrett, Mn., U.S. E3 130
Barrett, W.V., U.S. D3 155
Barretts Hill, hill, Ma., U.S. g9 128
Barrhead, Alta., Can. B3 98
Barrie, Ont., Can. C5 103
Barrie Island, i., Ont., Can. B2 103
Barrière, B.C., Can. D7 99
Barrier Range, mts., Austl. H4 70
Barrington, N.S., Can. F4 101
Barrington, Il., U.S. A5 120
Barrington, N.H., U.S. D4 136
Barrington, N.J., U.S. D2 137
Barrington, R.I., U.S. D5 146
Barrington, stm., R.I., U.S. C5 146
Barrington Lake, l., Man., Can. A1 100
Barrington Passage, N.S., Can. F4 101
Barringun, Austl. G6 70
Barrita Vieja, Guat. D4 92
Barro Alto, Braz. C4 79
Barron, Wi., U.S. C2 156
Barron, co., Wi., U.S. C2 156
Barron Lake, Mi., U.S. G4 129
Barrow, Arg. J8 80
Barrow, Ak., U.S. A8 109
Barrow, co., Ga., U.S. B3 117
Barrow, Point, c., Ak., U.S. A8 109
Barrow Creek, Austl. D6 68
Barrow-in-Furness, Eng., U.K. G10 8
Barrow Island, i., Austl. D3 68
Barrows, Man., Can. C1 100
Barrow Strait, strt., N.W. Ter., Can. B13 96
Barry, Il., U.S. D2 120
Barry, co., Mi., U.S. F5 129
Barry, co., Mo., U.S. E4 132
Barrys Bay, Ont., Can. B7 103
Barryton, Mi., U.S. E5 129
Bārsi, India C3 46
Barsinghausen, Ger. C9 10
Barstow, Ca., U.S. E5 112
Barstow, Tx., U.S. D1 150
Bar-sur-Aube, Fr. D11 14
Bar-sur-Seine, Fr. D11 14
Bartang, stm., Taj. A5 44
Bartelso, Il., U.S. E4 120
Barthélemy, Deo, Viet. E8 40
Bartholomew, co., In., U.S. F6 121
Bartholomew, Bayou, stm., U.S. D4 111
Bartibog Bridge, N.B., Can. B4 101
Bartica, Guy. D13 84
Bartle Frere, mtn., Austl. A6 70
Bartlesville, Ok., U.S. A6 143
Bartlett, Ks., U.S. E8 123
Bartlett, Ne., U.S. C7 134
Bartlett, N.H., U.S. B4 136
Bartlett, Tn., U.S. B2 149
Bartlett, Tx., U.S. D4 150
Bartlett Reservoir, res., Az., U.S. D4 110
Bartletts Ferry Dam, U.S. C4 108
Bartletts Harbour, Newf., Can. C3 102
Bartley, Ne., U.S. D5 134
Bartolomé de las Casas, Arg. C9 80
Bartolomeu Dias, Moz. C12 66
Barton, Al., U.S. A2 108
Barton, Ar., U.S. C5 111
Barton, Md., U.S. k12 127
Barton, Oh., U.S. B5 142
Barton, Vt., U.S. B4 152
Barton, co., Ks., U.S. D5 123
Barton, co., Mo., U.S. D3 132
Barton, stm., Vt., U.S. B4 152
Bartonsville, Vt., U.S. E3 152
Barton-upon-Humber, Eng., U.K. H13 8
Bartonville, Il., U.S. C4 120
Bartoszyce, Pol. A20 10
Bartow, Fl., U.S. E5 116
Bartow, Ga., U.S. D4 117
Bartow, co., Ga., U.S. B2 117
Barú, Volcán, vol., Pan. I12 92
Baruun-Urt, Mong. B9 30
Barva, Volcán, vol., C.R. G10 92
Barwāni, India I6 44
Barwick, Ga., U.S. F3 117
Barwon, stm., Austl. G8 70
Barybino, Russia F20 22
Baryš, Russia G7 26
Basacato del Este, Eq. Gui. J14 64
Basail, Arg. D9 80
Basalt, Co., U.S. B3 113
Basalt, Id., U.S. F6 119
Basankusu, Zaire A3 58
Basarabi, Rom. E12 20
Basatongwula Shan, mtn., China D14 44
Basavilbaso, Arg. G9 80
Basco, Phil. A7 38
Bascom, Oh., U.S. A2 142
Bascuñán, Cabo, c., Chile G7 74
Basehor, Ks., U.S. k16 123
Basel (Bâle), Switz. C8 13
Basey, Phil. C8 38
Bashan Lake, l., Ct., U.S. D6 114
Bashaw, Alta., Can. C4 98
Bashi, Al., U.S. D2 108
Bashi Channel, strt., Asia G11 30
Basile, La., U.S. D3 125
Basilicata, prov., Italy I11 18
Basin, Mt., U.S. D4 133
Basin, Wy., U.S. B4 157
Basīrhāt, India I13 44
Baskahegan Lake, l., Me., U.S. C5 126
Baskakovka, Russia G17 22
Baskatong, Réservoir, res., Que., Can. k11 104
Baskett, Ky., U.S. C2 124
Baskin, Fl., U.S. p10 116
Basking Ridge, N.J., U.S. B3 137
Baškirija, state, Russia G9 26
Bašmakovo, Russia H26 22
Basoko, Zaire A4 58
Basque Lands see Euskal Herriko, prov., Spain B9 16
Basra see Al-Basrah, Iraq F9 48
Bas-Rhin, dept., Fr. D14 14
Bassano, Alta., Can. D4 98
Bassano del Grappa, Italy D6 18
Bassari, Togo G10 64
Bassas da India, rf., Reu. F7 58
Bassecourt, Switz. D7 13
Bassein, mth., Burma F3 40
Bassein see Pathein, Burma F3 40
Basse-Terre, Guad. F14 94
Basseterre, St. K./N. F13 94
Basse-Terre, i., Guad. F14 94
Bassett, Ar., U.S. B5 111
Bassett, Ne., U.S. B6 134
Bassett, Va., U.S. D3 153
Bassett, Wi., U.S. n11 156
Bassett Creek, stm., Al., U.S. D2 108
Bassett Peak, mtn., Az., U.S. E5 110
Basse-Yutz, Fr. J9 12
Bassfield, Ms., U.S. D4 131
Bass Harbor, Me., U.S. D4 126
Bassikounou, Maur. D7 64
Bassila, Benin G10 64
Bass Islands, is., Oh., U.S. A3 142
Bass Lake, In., U.S. B4 121
Bass River, N.S., Can. D6 101
Bass Strait, strt., Austl. L6 70
Basswood, Man., Can. D1 100
Basswood Lake, l., Mn., U.S. B7 130
Bastah, Jord. H5 50
Bastak, Iran H13 48
Bastelica, Fr. I24 15a
Basti, India G10 44
Bastia, Fr. J16 14
Bastian, Va., U.S. C1 153
Bastimentos, Pan. H12 92
Bastimentos, Isla, i., Pan. H12 92
Bastogne (Bastenaken), Bel. H8 12
Bastrop, La., U.S. B4 125
Bastrop, Tx., U.S. D4 150
Bastrop, co., Tx., U.S. D4 150
Bastuträsk, Swe. I17 6
Basutoland see Lesotho, ctry., Afr. G5 58
Bata, Eq. Gui. A1 58
Bataan Peninsula, pen., Phil. n19 39b
Batabanó, Golfo de, b., Cuba C3 94
Bataguassu, Braz. F2 79
Bataiporã, Braz. G2 79
Batajsk, Russia H5 26
Batala, India E6 44
Batan, China A9 34
Batang, China E6 30
Batangas, Phil. o19 39b
Batan Islands, is., Phil. A7 38
Bátaszék, Hung. I18 10
Batatais, Braz. F5 79
Batavia, Arg. H6 80
Batavia, Il., U.S. B5 120
Batavia, Ia., U.S. D5 122
Batavia, N.Y., U.S. C2 139
Batavia, Oh., U.S. C1 142
Batchelor Bay, b., N.C., U.S. B6 140
Batchtown, Il., U.S. D3 120
Bătdâmbâng, Camb. H7 40
Bateckij, Russia C13 22
Batemans Bay, Austl. J9 70
Bates, Ar., U.S. C1 111
Bates, co., Mo., U.S. C3 132
Batesburg, S.C., U.S. D4 147
Batesland, S.D., U.S. D3 148
Batesville, Ar., U.S. B4 111
Batesville, In., U.S. F7 121
Batesville, Ms., U.S. A4 131
Batesville, Tx., U.S. E3 150
Bath, N.B., Can. C2 101
Bath, Ont., Can. C8 103
Bath, Eng., U.K. J11 8
Bath, Il., U.S. C3 120
Bath, Me., U.S. E3 126
Bath, Mi., U.S. F6 129
Bath, N.H., U.S. B3 136
Bath, N.Y., U.S. C3 139
Bath, Pa., U.S. E11 145
Bath, S.C., U.S. D4 147
Bath, S.D., U.S. B7 148
Bath, co., Ky., U.S. B6 124
Bath, co., Va., U.S. B3 153
Bathinda, India E6 44
Bathsheba, Barb. H15 94
Bathurst, Austl. I8 70
Bathurst, N.B., Can. B4 101
Bathurst, S. Afr. I8 66
Bathurst, Cape, c., N.W. Ter., Can. B7 96
Bathurst see Banjul, Gam. E1 64
Bathurst Inlet, b., N.W. Ter., Can. C11 96
Bathurst Island, i., Austl. B6 68
Bathurst Island, i., N.W. Ter., Can. A12 96
Batia, Benin F10 64
Batié, Burkina G8 64
Bāṭin, Wādī al-, val., Asia G9 48
Batiscan, stm., Que., Can. B5 104
Batkanu, S.L. G3 64
Batlow, Austl. J8 70
Batman, Tur. C6 48
Batna, Alg. C14 62
Baṭn al-Ghūl, Jord. I5 50
Baton Rouge, La., U.S. D4 125
Batouri, Cam. H9 54
Batovi, Braz. C2 79
Baṭrā (Petra), hist., Jord. H4 50
Batsto, stm., N.J., U.S. D3 137
Batten Kill, stm., U.S. E2 152
Battery Park, Va., U.S. k14 153
Batticaloa, Sri L. I6 46
Battiest, Ok., U.S. C7 143
Battle, stm., Can. F10 96
Battle, stm., Can. A4 106
Battleboro, N.C., U.S. A5 140
Battle Creek, Ia., U.S. B2 122
Battle Creek, Mi., U.S. F5 129
Battle Creek, Ne., U.S. C8 134
Battleford, Sask., Can. E1 105
Battle Ground, In., U.S. C4 121
Battle Ground, Wa., U.S. D3 154
Battle Lake, Mn., U.S. D3 130
Battlement Mesa, mtn., Co., U.S. B2 113
Battle Mountain, Nv., U.S. C5 135
Battle Mountain, mtn., Wy., U.S. E5 157
Battles, Ms., U.S. D5 131
Battles Wharf, Al., U.S. E2 108
Battonya, Hung. I21 10
Batu, mtn., Eth. G8 56
Batu, Kepulauan, is., Indon. O5 40
Batumi, Geor. I6 26
Batu Pahat, Malay. N7 40
Baturité, Braz. D11 76
Bat Yam, Isr. D3 50
Baubau, Indon. G7 38
Bauchi, Nig. F14 64
Baud, Fr. E3 14
Baudette, Mn., U.S. B4 130
Baudó, stm., Col. E4 84
Bauer Coulee, val., Wa., U.S. B7 154
Bauld, Cape, c., Newf., Can. C4 102
Baume-les-Dames, Fr. E13 14
Baures, Bol. E10 82
Baures, stm., Bol. E10 82
Bauru, Braz. G4 79
Baús, Braz. E2 79
Bauska, Lat. E7 22
Bautzen, Ger. D14 10
Bauxite, Ar., U.S. C3 111
Bavaria, Ks., U.S. D6 123
Bavaria see Bayern, state, Ger. F11 10
Bavispe, Mex. B5 90
Bavispe, stm., Mex. C5 90
Bavleny, Russia E22 22
Bawdwin, Burma C4 40
Bawku, Ghana F9 64
Bawlf, Alta., Can. C4 98
Baxian, China D4 32
Baxley, Ga., U.S. E4 117
Baxter, Ia., U.S. C4 122
Baxter, Mn., U.S. D4 130
Baxter, Tn., U.S. C8 149
Baxter, W.V., U.S. B4 155
Baxter, co., Ar., U.S. A3 111
Baxter Springs, Ks., U.S. E9 123
Baxterville, Ms., U.S. D4 131
Bay, Ar., U.S. B5 111
Bay, co., Fl., U.S. u16 116
Bay, co., Mi., U.S. E6 129
Bayamo, Cuba D6 94
Bayamón, P.R. E11 94
Bayan Har Shan, mts., China E6 30
Bayano, Lago, res., Pan. C3 84
Bayan Obo, China C9 30
Bayard, Ia., U.S. C3 122
Bayard, Ne., U.S. C2 134
Bayard, N.M., U.S. E1 138
Bayard, W.V., U.S. B5 155
Bayberry, N.Y., U.S. *B4 139
Bayboro, N.C., U.S. B6 140
Bay Bulls, Newf., Can. E5 102
Bayburt, Tur. A6 48
Bay Center, Wa., U.S. C2 154
Bay City, Mi., U.S. E7 129
Bay City, Or., U.S. B3 144
Bay City, Tx., U.S. E5 150
Bay City, Wi., U.S. D1 156
Bay de Verde, Newf., Can. D5 102
Baydhabo, Som. H9 56
Bayerische Alpen, mts., Eur. H11 10
Bayern, state, Ger. F11 10
Bayeux, Fr. C6 14
Bayfield, Ont., Can. D3 103
Bayfield, Co., U.S. D3 113
Bayfield, Wi., U.S. B3 156
Bayfield, co., Wi., U.S. B2 156
Bayiji, China A6 34
Bayingzi, China B8 32
Bay L'Argent, Newf., Can. E4 102
Baylis, Il., U.S. D3 120
Baylor, co., Tx., U.S. C3 150
Bay Mills Indian Reservation, Mi., U.S. B6 129
Bay Minette, Al., U.S. E2 108
Bayombong, Phil. m19 39b
Bayon, Fr. D13 14
Bayonne, Fr. I5 14
Bayonne, N.J., U.S. B4 137
Bayou Bodcau Reservoir, res., La., U.S. B2 125
Bayou Cane, La., U.S. E5 125
Bayou D'Arbonne Lake, res., La., U.S. B3 125
Bayou George, Fl., U.S. u16 116
Bayou Goula, La., U.S. D4 125
Bayou La Batre, Al., U.S. E1 108
Bayou Pigeon, La., U.S. D4 125
Bayovar, Peru A1 82
Bay Point, c., S.C., U.S. G7 147
Bayport, N.S., Can. E5 101
Bay Port, Mi., U.S. E7 129
Bayport, Mn., U.S. E6 130
Bayport, N.Y., U.S. n15 139
Bayreuth, Ger. F11 10
Bay Ridge, Md., U.S. C5 127
Bayrischzell, Ger. H12 10
Bay Roberts, Newf., Can. E5 102
Bayrūt (Beirut), Leb. A5 50
Bays, Lake of, l., Ont., Can. B5 103
Bay Saint Louis, Ms., U.S. E4 131
Bay Shore, N.Y., U.S. E7 139
Bayshore Gardens, Fl., U.S. q10 116
Bayside, Wi., U.S. m12 156
Bays Mountain, mtn., Tn., U.S. C10 149
Bay Springs, Ms., U.S. D4 131
Bayt al-Faqīh, Yemen G3 47
Bayt Jinn, Syria B5 50
Bayt Lahm (Bethlehem), Isr. Occ. E4 50
Bayt Mirī, Leb. A5 50
Baytown, Tx., U.S. E5 150
Bayview, Al., U.S. f7 108
Bayview, Id., U.S. B2 119
Bay View Park, De., U.S. F5 115
Bay Village, Oh., U.S. h9 142
Bayville, De., U.S. G5 115
Bayville, N.J., U.S. D4 137
Bayzo, Niger E12 64
Baza, Spain H9 16
Bazaruto, Ilha do, i., Moz. C12 66
Bazas, Fr. H6 14
Bazdār, Pak. G1 44
Bazi, China K2 34
Bazine, Ks., U.S. D4 123
Be, Nosy, i., Madag. n23 67b
Beach, Il., U.S. h9 120
Beach, N.D., U.S. C1 141
Beachburg, Ont., Can. B8 103
Beach City, Oh., U.S. B4 142
Beach City, Tx., U.S. r15 150
Beach Haven, N.J., U.S. D4 137
Beach Haven Inlet, b., N.J., U.S. D4 137
Beach Pond, res., U.S. C8 114
Beachville, Ont., Can. D4 103
Beachwood, N.J., U.S. D4 137
Beacon, Ia., U.S. C5 122
Beacon, N.Y., U.S. D7 139

Name — Map Ref. — Page

Beacon Falls, Ct., U.S. D3 114
Beaconsfield, Austl. M7 70
Beaconsfield, Que., Can. q19 104
Beadle, co., S.D., U.S. C7 148
Beagle Gulf, b., Austl. B6 68
Beagle Reef, rf., Austl. C4 68
Bealanana, Madag. o23 67b
Beale, Cape, c., B.C., Can. E5 99
Beale Air Force Base, mil., Ca., U.S. C3 112
Beals, Me., U.S. D5 126
Bean Lake, Mo., U.S. B3 132
Bean Station, Tn., U.S. C10 149
Bear, De., U.S. B3 115
Bear, stm., U.S. B3 151
Bear Creek, Al., U.S. A2 108
Bear Creek, Wi., U.S. D5 156
Bear Creek, stm., U.S. E2 123
Bear Creek, stm., Al., U.S. A1 108
Bear Creek, stm., Or., U.S. E4 144
Bear Creek, stm., Wy., U.S. E8 157
Bearden, Ar., U.S. D3 111
Beardmore, Ont., Can. o18 103
Beards Fork, W.V., U.S. m13 155
Beardsley, Mn., U.S. E2 130
Beardstown, Il., U.S. C3 120
Bearfort Mountain, mtn., N.J., U.S. A4 137
Bear Inlet, b., N.C., U.S. C5 140
Bear Island, i., Ant. C11 73
Bear Island see Bjørnøya, i., Sval. B2 24
Bear Lake, Mi., U.S. D4 129
Bear Lake, co., Id., U.S. G7 119
Bear Lake, l., Man., Can. B4 100
Bear Lake, l., U.S. A4 151
Bear Lake, l., Wi., U.S. C2 156
Bear Lodge Mountains, mts., Wy., U.S. B8 157
Bear Mountain, mtn., Ar., U.S. f7 111
Bear Mountain, mtn., Ky., U.S. C5 124
Bear Mountain, mtn., Ma., U.S. A3 128
Bear Mountain, mtn., Or., U.S. D4 144
Béarn, hist. reg., Fr. I6 14
Bearpaw Mountains, mts., Mt., U.S. B7 133
Bear Pond Mountain, mtn., Md., U.S. A2 127
Bear River, N.S., Can. E4 101
Bear River City, Ut., U.S. B3 151
Bear Swamp, sw., Ma., U.S. h11 128
Beartooth Pass, Wy., U.S. B3 157
Beartooth Range, mts., U.S. E7 133
Bear Town, Ms., U.S. D3 131
Beartown Mountain, mtn., Va., U.S. f10 153
Beasain, Spain B9 16
Beas de Segura, Spain G9 16
Beason, Il., U.S. C4 120
Beata, Cabo, c., Dom. Rep. F9 94
Beata, Isla, i., Dom. Rep. F9 94
Beatrice, Al., U.S. D2 108
Beatrice, Ne., U.S. D9 134
Beatrice, Zimb. B10 66
Beattie, Ks., U.S. C7 123
Beatty, Sask., Can. E3 105
Beatty, Nv., U.S. G5 135
Beatty, Or., U.S. E5 144
Beattyville, Ky., U.S. C6 124
Beaucaire, Fr. I11 14
Beauce, reg., Fr. D8 14
Beaudesert, Austl. F10 70
Beaufort, Mo., U.S. C6 132
Beaufort, N.C., U.S. C6 140
Beaufort, S.C., U.S. G6 147
Beaufort, co., N.C., U.S. B5 140
Beaufort, co., S.C., U.S. G6 147
Beaufort Marine Corps Air Station, mil., S.C., U.S. F6 147
Beaufort Sea, N.A. B5 86
Beaufort West, S. Afr. I6 66
Beaugency, Fr. E8 14
Beauharnois, Que., Can. D4 104
Beau Lake, l., Me., U.S. A3 126
Beaumont, Alta., Can. C4 98
Beaumont, Fr. C5 14
Beaumont, Ks., U.S. E7 123
Beaumont, Ms., U.S. D5 131
Beaumont, Tx., U.S. D5 150
Beaumont [Lushes Bight-Beaumont North], Newf., Can. D4 102
Beaumont-sur-Sarthe, Fr. D7 14
Beaune, Fr. E11 14
Beauport, Que., Can. n17 104
Beaupré, Que., Can. B7 104
Beaupréau, Fr. E5 14
Beauregard, Ms., U.S. D3 131
Beauregard, co., La., U.S. D2 125
Beaurepaire, Fr. G12 14
Beausejour, Man., Can. D3 100
Beauty, Ky., U.S. C7 124
Beauvais, Fr. C9 14
Beauval, Sask., Can. B2 105
Beauvoir-sur-Mer, Fr. F4 14
Beaver, Ak., U.S. B10 109
Beaver, Ok., U.S. A1 143
Beaver, Pa., U.S. E1 145
Beaver, Ut., U.S. E3 151
Beaver, W.V., U.S. D3 155
Beaver, co., Ok., U.S. e10 143
Beaver, co., Pa., U.S. E1 145
Beaver, co., Ut., U.S. E2 151
Beaver, stm., Can. F11 96
Beaver, stm., Can. D7 96
Beaver, stm., Can. B2 105
Beaver, stm., Can. A5 106
Beaver, stm., U.S. A2 143
Beaver, stm., N.Y., U.S. B6 139
Beaver, stm., R.I., U.S. E2 146
Beaver, stm., Ut., U.S. E2 151
Beaverbank, N.S., Can. E6 101
Beaver Brook, stm., U.S. E4 136
Beaver City, Ne., U.S. D6 134
Beaver Creek, B.C., Can. E5 99
Beavercreek, Oh., U.S. C1 142
Beaver Creek, stm., U.S. E4 134
Beaver Creek, stm., U.S. C8 157
Beaver Creek, stm., Co., U.S. B7 113
Beaver Creek, stm., Ia., U.S. e8 122
Beaver Creek, stm., Ky., U.S. C7 124
Beaver Creek, stm., Md., U.S. A2 127
Beaver Creek, stm., Mo., U.S. E5 132
Beaver Creek, stm., Mt., U.S. B9 133
Beaver Creek, stm., Ne., U.S. C7 134
Beaver Creek, stm., N.D., U.S. C1 141
Beaver Creek, stm., N.D., U.S. C5 141
Beaver Creek, stm., Ok., U.S. C3 143
Beaver Creek, stm., Tn., U.S. m13 149
Beaver Creek, stm., Wy., U.S. D4 157
Beaver Creek Mountains, mts., Al., U.S. B3 108
Beaver Crossing, Ne., U.S. D8 134
Beaverdale, Pa., U.S. F4 145
Beaver Dam, Ky., U.S. C3 124
Beaver Dam, Wi., U.S. E5 156
Beaverdam Branch, stm., De., U.S. F3 115
Beaverdam Lake, res., Wi., U.S. E5 156
Beaverdell, B.C., Can. E8 99
Beaver Falls, Pa., U.S. E1 145
Beaverhead, co., Mt., U.S. E3 133
Beaverhead, stm., Mt., U.S. E4 133
Beaverhead Mountains, mts., U.S. D5 119
Beaverhill Lake, l., Alta., Can. C4 98
Beaver Hill Lake, l., Man., Can. B4 100
Beaver Island, i., Mi., U.S. C5 129
Beaver Lake, res., Ar., U.S. A2 111
Beaverlodge, Alta., Can. B1 98
Beaver Meadows, Pa., U.S. E10 145
Beaver Ridge, mtn., Tn., U.S. D9 149
Beaver Run Reservoir, res., Pa., U.S. F2 145
Beaver Springs, Pa., U.S. E7 145
Beavertail Point, c., R.I., U.S. F4 146
Beaverton, Al., U.S. B1 108
Beaverton, Mi., U.S. E6 129
Beaverton, Or., U.S. B4 144
Beavertown, Pa., U.S. E7 145
Beaverville, Il., U.S. C6 120
Beāwar, India G6 44
Beazley, Arg. G5 80
Bebedouro, Braz. F4 79
Bebeji, Nig. F14 64
Becal, Mex. G14 90
Bécancour, Que., Can. C5 104
Bécancour, stm., Que., Can. C6 104
Bečej, Yugo. D4 20
Beceni, Rom. D10 20
Becerro, Cayos, is., Hond. B11 92
Béchar, Alg. E9 62
Becharof Lake, l., Ak., U.S. D8 109
Bechater, Tun. L4 18
Bechyně, Czech. F14 10
Beckemeyer, Il., U.S. E4 120
Becker, Mn., U.S. E5 130
Becker, Ms., U.S. B5 131
Becker, co., Mn., U.S. D3 130
Beckham, co., Ok., U.S. B2 143
Beckley, W.V., U.S. D3 155
Beckum, Ger. D8 10
Beckville, Tx., U.S. C5 150
Beckwith Creek, stm., La., U.S. D2 125
Becky Peak, mtn., Nv., U.S. D7 135
Bédarieux, Fr. I10 14
Bedele, Eth. M9 60
Bedford, N.S., Can. E6 101
Bedford, Que., Can. D5 104
Bedford, In., U.S. G5 121
Bedford, Ia., U.S. D3 122
Bedford, Ky., U.S. B4 124
Bedford, Ma., U.S. B5 128
Bedford, N.H., U.S. E3 136
Bedford, Oh., U.S. A4 142
Bedford, Pa., U.S. F4 145
Bedford, Va., U.S. C3 153
Bedford, Wy., U.S. D2 157
Bedford, co., Pa., U.S. G4 145
Bedford, co., Tn., U.S. B5 149
Bedford, co., Va., U.S. C3 153
Bedford Hills, N.Y., U.S. D7 139
Bedfordshire, co., Eng., U.K. I13 8
Bedias, Tx., U.S. D5 150
Bednodemjanovsk, Russia H26 22
Bee, Ne., U.S. C8 134
Bee, co., Tx., U.S. E4 150
Beebe, Que., Can. D5 104
Beebe, Ar., U.S. B4 111
Beebe Plain, Vt., U.S. A4 152
Beebe River, N.H., U.S. C3 136
Bee Branch, Ar., U.S. B3 111
Beech Bluff, Tn., U.S. B3 149
Beech Bottom, W.V., U.S. f8 155
Beech Creek, Ky., U.S. C2 124
Beech Creek, Pa., U.S. D6 145
Beecher, Il., U.S. B6 120
Beecher, Mi., U.S. *E7 129
Beecher City, Il., U.S. D5 120
Beech Fork, stm., Ky., U.S. C4 124
Beech Grove, In., U.S. E5 121
Beech Grove, Ky., U.S. C2 124
Beechgrove, Tn., U.S. B5 149
Beech Island, S.C., U.S. E4 147
Beechwood, N.B., Can. C2 101
Beechworth, Austl. K7 70
Beechy, Sask., Can. G2 105
Beecroft Head, c., Austl. J9 70
Beedeville, Ar., U.S. B4 111
Beef Island, i., Tn., U.S. e8 149
Beeler, Ks., U.S. D3 123
Beemer, Ne., U.S. C9 134
Beenleigh, Austl. F10 70
Bee Ridge, Fl., U.S. q11 116
Beersheba see Be'ér Sheva', Isr. F3 50
Beersheba Springs, Tn., U.S. D8 149
Be'ér Sheva (Beersheba), Isr. F3 50
Beersville, N.B., Can. C4 101
Beesleys Point, N.J., U.S. E3 137
Beestekraal, S. Afr. E8 66
Beethoven Peninsula, pen., Ant. C12 73
Beeton (part of Alliston Beeton Tecumseth and Tottenham), Ont., Can. C5 103
Beeville, Tx., U.S. E4 150
Befale, Zaire A4 58
Befandriana, Madag. o23 67b
Befasy, Madag. r21 67b
Befotaka, Madag. s22 67b
Bega, Austl. K8 70
Bega (Begej), stm., Eur. D5 20
Begej (Bega), stm., Eur. D4 20
Beggs, Ok., U.S. B5 143
Begičevskij, Russia H21 22
Begoml', Bela. G11 22
Begoro, Ghana H9 64
Begunicy, Russia B12 22
Begusarai, India H12 44
Behbahān, Iran F11 48
Behm Canal, strt., Ak., U.S. n24 109
Behshahr, Iran C12 48
Bei, stm., China K2 34
Bei'an, China B12 30
Beida see Al-Bayḍā', Libya B5 56
Beidaihe, China D7 32
Beidun, China I7 34
Beigi, Eth. M8 60
Beihai, China D10 40
Beijing (Peking), China D4 32
Beijing Shi (Peking Shih), China C10 30
Beikan, China C10 34
Beiling, China K4 34
Beinwil, Switz. D8 13
Beipan, stm., China F8 30
Beipiao, China B8 32
Beiqi, China I3 34
Beira, Moz. B12 66
Beira Baixa, hist. reg., Port. F4 16
Beira Litoral, hist. reg., Port. E3 16
Beirne, Ar., U.S. D2 111
Beirut see Bayrūt, Leb. A5 50
Beiseker, Alta., Can. D4 98
Beishan, China B10 40
Bei Shan, mts., China C6 30
Beisu, China D9 32
Beitang, China D5 32
Beitbridge, Zimb. D10 66
Beixinzhen, China D10 34
Beizhen, China B9 32
Beja, Port. G4 16
Béja, Tun. M4 18
Bejaïa (Bougie), Alg. B13 62
Béjar, Spain E6 16
Bejuco, Pan. C3 84
Bejuma, Ven. B8 84
Bekabad, Uzb. I11 26
Bekdaš, Turk. I8 26
Békés, Hung. I21 10
Békés, co., Hung. I20 10
Békéscsaba, Hung. I21 10
Bekilli, Tur. K13 20
Bekily, Madag. t21 67b
Bekitro, Madag. t21 67b
Bekkaria, Alg. N3 18
Bekkevoort, Bel. G6 12
Bekodoka, Madag. p21 67b
Bekoji, Eth. N10 60
Bela, India H9 44
Bela, Pak. G2 44
Belabolo, Sud. M3 60
Bela Crkva, Yugo. E5 20
Bel Air, Md., U.S. A5 127
Belaja, stm., Russia G9 26
Belaja Ber'ozka, Russia I16 22
Belaja Cerkov', Ukr. H4 26
Bel'ajevka, Ukr. C14 20
Bel Alton, Md., U.S. D4 127
Bélanger, stm., Man., Can. C3 100
Bélanger, stm., Sask., Can. B2 105
Bela Palanka, Yugo. F6 20
Belarus, ctry., Eur. E13 4
Belau see Palau, dep., Oc. E9 38
Belavenona, Madag. t22 67b
Bela Vista, Braz. B10 80
Bela Vista, Moz. F11 66
Bela Vista de Goiás, Braz. D4 79
Bela Vista do Paraíso, Braz. G3 79
Belawan, Indon. M5 40
Belbubulo, Sud. M8 60
Bel'c', Mol. H3 26
Belcamp, Md., U.S. B5 127
Bełchatów, Pol. D19 10
Belcher, Ky., U.S. C7 124
Belcherāgh, Afg. C1 44
Belcher Islands, is., N.W. Ter., Can. E17 96
Belchertown, Ma., U.S. B3 128
Belden, Ms., U.S. A5 131
Belden, Ne., U.S. B8 134
Belding, Mi., U.S. E5 129
Beled Weyne, Som. H10 56
Belém, Braz. D9 76
Belén, Arg. D5 80
Belén, Chile H7 82
Belén, Col. D6 84
Belén, Nic. F9 92
Belén, Para. B10 80
Belen, Ms., U.S. A3 131
Belen, N.M., U.S. C3 138
Belén, Ur. F10 80
Belén, stm., Arg. D5 80
Belén de Escobar, Arg. H9 80
Belfair, Wa., U.S. B3 154
Belfast, S. Afr. E10 66
Belfast, N. Ire., U.K. G8 8
Belfast, Me., U.S. D3 126
Belfast, N.Y., U.S. C2 139
Belfast, N.C., U.S. B5 140
Belfast, Tn., U.S. B5 149
Belfield, N.D., U.S. C2 141
Belford, N.J., U.S. C4 137
Belfort, Fr. E13 14
Belfry, Ky., U.S. C7 124
Belfry, Mt., U.S. E8 133
Belgaum, India E3 46
Belgium, Il., U.S. C6 120
Belgium, Wi., U.S. E6 156
Belgium, ctry., Eur. E8 4
Belgorod, Russia G5 26
Belgorod-Dnestrovskij, Ukr. H4 26
Belgrade, Mn., U.S. E3 130
Belgrade, Mo., U.S. D7 132
Belgrade, Mt., U.S. E5 133
Belgrade, Ne., U.S. C7 134
Belgrade see Beograd, Yugo. E4 20
Belgrade Lakes, Me., U.S. D3 126
Belgreen, Al., U.S. A2 108
Belhaven, N.C., U.S. B6 140
Beli Drim, stm., Eur. G4 20
Beli Manastir, Cro. D2 20
Belington, W.V., U.S. B5 155
Belitung, i., Indon. F4 38
Belize, ctry., N.A. I15 90
Belize, stm., Belize I15 90
Belize City, Belize I15 90
Belk, Al., U.S. B2 108
Belknap, co., N.H., U.S. C3 136
Belknap Crater, crat., Or., U.S. C5 144
Belknap Mountain, mtn., N.H., U.S. C4 136
Bell, co., Ky., U.S. D6 124
Bell, co., Tx., U.S. D4 150
Bellac, Fr. F8 14
Bella Coola, B.C., Can. C4 99
Bella Coola, stm., B.C., Can. C4 99
Bella Flor, Bol. D8 82
Bellaire, Ks., U.S. g12 123
Bellaire, Mi., U.S. D5 129
Bellaire, Oh., U.S. C5 142
Bellaire, Tx., U.S. r14 150
Bellamy, Al., U.S. C1 108
Bellary, India E4 46
Bella Unión, Ur. F10 80
Bella Vista, Arg. E9 80
Bella Vista, Arg. D6 80
Bella Vista, Para. B10 80
Bellavista, Peru A1 82
Bellavista, Peru B3 82
Bella Vista, Ar., U.S. A1 111
Bellbrook, Oh., U.S. C1 142
Bell Buckle, Tn., U.S. B5 149
Bell City, La., U.S. D3 125
Bell City, Mo., U.S. D8 132
Bellé, Sen. D3 64
Belle, Mo., U.S. C6 132
Belle, W.V., U.S. C3 155
Belle, stm., La., U.S. k9 125
Belleair, Fl., U.S. p10 116
Belle Bay, b., Newf., Can. E4 102
Belle Center, Oh., U.S. B2 142
Belle Chasse, La., U.S. E5 125
Belle Creek, Mt., U.S. E11 133
Belledune, N.B., Can. B4 101
Bellefleur, N.B., Can. B2 101
Bellefontaine, Ms., U.S. B4 131
Bellefontaine, Oh., U.S. B2 142
Bellefonte, Ar., U.S. A2 111
Bellefonte, Pa., U.S. E6 145
Belle Fourche, S.D., U.S. C2 148
Belle Fourche, stm., U.S. C3 148
Belle Fourche Reservoir, res., S.D., U.S. C2 148
Bellegarde, Fr. F12 14
Belle Glade, Fl., U.S. F6 116
Belle Haven, Va., U.S. C7 153
Belle-Île, i., Fr. E3 14
Belle Isle, Fl., U.S. D5 116
Belle Isle, i., Newf., Can. C4 102
Belle Isle, Strait of, strt., Newf., Can. C3 102
Belleisle Creek, N.B., Can. D4 101
Bellême, Fr. D7 14
Belle Meade, Tn., U.S. g10 149
Belle Mina, Al., U.S. A3 108
Belleoram, Newf., Can. E4 102
Belle-Plaine, Sask., Can. G3 105
Belle Plaine, Ia., U.S. C5 122
Belle Plaine, Ks., U.S. E6 123
Belle Plaine, Mn., U.S. F5 130
Belle Rive, Il., U.S. E5 120
Belle River, Ont., Can. E2 103
Belle Rose, La., U.S. D4 125
Belle Vernon, Pa., U.S. F2 145
Belleview, Fl., U.S. C4 116
Belleview, Fl., U.S. *u14 116
Belleview, Mo., U.S. D7 132
Belle View, Va., U.S. g12 153
Belleville, N.S., Can. F4 101
Belleville, Ont., Can. C7 103
Belleville, Ar., U.S. B2 111
Belleville, Il., U.S. E4 120
Belleville, Ks., U.S. C6 123
Belleville, Mi., U.S. p15 129
Belleville, N.J., U.S. B4 137
Belleville, Pa., U.S. E6 145
Belleville, Wi., U.S. F4 156
Belleville Pond, l., R.I., U.S. E4 146
Belleville-sur-Saône, Fr. F11 14
Bellevue, Id., U.S. F4 119
Bellevue, Ia., U.S. B7 122
Bellevue, Ky., U.S. h13 124
Bellevue, Mi., U.S. F5 129
Bellevue, Ne., U.S. C10 134
Bellevue, Oh., U.S. A3 142
Bellevue, Pa., U.S. F1 145
Bellevue, Wa., U.S. e11 154
Belley, Fr. G12 14
Bellflower, Ca., U.S. n12 112
Bellflower, Il., U.S. C5 120
Bellflower, Mo., U.S. B6 132
Bellingen, Austl. H10 70
Bellingham, Eng., U.K. F11 8
Bellingham, Ma., U.S. B5 128
Bellingham, Wa., U.S. A3 154
Bellingshausen, sci., Ant. B1 73
Bellingshausen Sea, Ant. C11 73
Bellinzona, Switz. F11 13
Bell-Irving, stm., B.C., Can. A3 99
Bellis, Alta., Can. B4 98
Bell Island, i., Newf., Can. C4 102
Bellmawr, N.J., U.S. D2 137
Bellmont, Il., U.S. E6 120
Bellmore, In., U.S. E3 121
Bello, Col. D5 84
Bellot Strait, strt., N.W. Ter., Can. B14 96
Bellows Falls, Vt., U.S. E4 152
Bell Peninsula, pen., N.W. Ter., Can. D16 96
Bellport, N.Y., U.S. n16 139
Bells, Tn., U.S. B2 149
Bells Creek, stm., W.V., U.S. m13 155
Belltown, De., U.S. F5 115
Belluno, Italy C7 18
Bell Ville, Arg. G7 80
Bellville, Ga., U.S. D5 117
Bellville, Oh., U.S. B3 142
Bellville, Tx., U.S. E4 150
Bellvue, Co., U.S. A5 113
Bellwood, Al., U.S. D4 108
Bellwood, Il., U.S. k9 120
Bellwood, Ne., U.S. C8 134
Bellwood, Pa., U.S. E5 145
Bellwood, Va., U.S. n18 153
Belmar, N.J., U.S. C4 137
Belmond, Ia., U.S. B4 122
Belmont, Man., Can. E2 100
Belmont, N.S., Can. D6 101
Belmont, Ont., Can. E3 103
Belmont, S. Afr. G7 66
Belmont, Ca., U.S. h8 112
Belmont, Ma., U.S. g11 128
Belmont, Ms., U.S. A5 131
Belmont, N.H., U.S. D4 136
Belmont, N.Y., U.S. C2 139
Belmont, N.C., U.S. B1 140
Belmont, Vt., U.S. E3 152
Belmont, W.V., U.S. B3 155
Belmont, Wi., U.S. F3 156
Belmont, co., Oh., U.S. C4 142
Belmonte, Braz. C9 79
Belmonte, Port. E4 16
Belmopan, Belize I15 90
Belmullet, Ire. G3 8
Bel-Nor, Mo., U.S. f13 132
Belo, Madag. q21 67b
Beloeil, Que., Can. D4 104
Belogorsk, Russia G17 28
Belo Horizonte, Braz. E7 79
Beloit, Ks., U.S. C5 123
Beloit, Oh., U.S. B5 142
Beloit, Wi., U.S. F4 156
Beloit North, Wi., U.S. *F4 156
Beloje, ozero, l., Russia A20 22
Beloje more (White Sea), Russia D5 26
Belomorsk, Russia E4 26
Belomorsko-Baltijskij kanal, Russia I24 6
Beloomut, Russia G22 22
Beloozersk, Bela. I8 22
Belorečensk, Russia I5 26
Beloreck, Russia G9 26
Belorussia see Belarus, ctry., Eur. E13 4
Belousovo, Russia F19 22
Bel'ov, Russia H19 22
Belo Vale, Braz. F6 79
Belovo, Russia G9 28
Belozʹorsk, Russia A20 22
Belpre, Ks., U.S. E4 123
Belpre, Oh., U.S. C4 142
Belspring, Va., U.S. C2 153
Belt, Mt., U.S. C6 133
Belt Creek, stm., Mt., U.S. C6 133
Belted Range, mts., Nv., U.S. F5 135
Belton, Mo., U.S. C3 132
Belton, S.C., U.S. B3 147
Belton, Tx., U.S. D4 150
Belton Lake, res., Tx., U.S. D4 150
Beltrami, co., Mn., U.S. B3 130
Beltrán, Arg. D6 80
Beltsville, Md., U.S. B4 127
Belucha, gora, mtn., Asia H15 26
Beluchistān, hist. reg., Asia G17 48
Belūr, India G10 42
Belvedere, S.C., U.S. D4 147
Belvès, Fr. H8 14
Belvidere, Il., U.S. A5 120
Belvidere, Ne., U.S. D8 134
Belvidere, N.J., U.S. B2 137
Belvidere Mountain, mtn., Vt., U.S. B3 152
Belview, Mn., U.S. F3 130
Belvís de la Jara, Spain F7 16
Belvue, Ks., U.S. C7 123
Belwood, Ont., Can. D4 103
Belyando, stm., Austl. C7 70
Belyj, Russia F15 22
Belyj, ostrov, i., Russia C12 26
Belyje Berega, Russia H17 22
Belyje Stolby, Russia F20 22
Belyj Gorodok, Russia E20 22
Belyj Luch, stm., Russia D27 22
Belyniči, Bela. H12 22
Belynkoviči, Bela. H15 22
Belzoni, Ms., U.S. B3 131
Bemarivo, Madag. r21 67b
Bemavo, Madag. r21 67b
Bembèrèkè, Benin F11 64
Bement, Il., U.S. D5 120
Bemidji, Mn., U.S. C4 130
Bemidji, Lake, l., Mn., U.S. C4 130
Bemiss, Ga., U.S. F3 117
Benāb, Iran C9 48
Bena-Dibele, Zaire B4 58
Benagerie, Austl. H4 70
Benahmed, Mor. D7 62
Ben'akoni, Bela. G8 22
Benalla, Austl. K6 70
Benalto, Alta., Can. C3 98
Benares see Vārānasi, India H10 44
Ben Arous, Tun. B16 62
Benavente, Spain C6 16
Benavides, Tx., U.S. F3 150
Ben Badis, Alg. K11 16
Benbrook, Tx., U.S. n9 150
Benbrook Lake, res., Tx., U.S. n9 150
Bencubbin, Austl. F3 68
Bend, Or., U.S. C5 144
Bendaja, Lib. H4 64
Ben Davis Point, c., N.J., U.S. E2 137
Bende, Nig. I13 64
Bendeleben, Mount, mtn., Ak., U.S. B7 109
Bendemeer, Austl. H9 70
Bendery, Mol. H3 26
Bendigo, Austl. K6 70
Bendugu, S.L. G4 64
Běne, Lat. E6 22
Bene Beraq, Isr. D3 50
Benedict, Md., U.S. C4 127
Benedict, Ne., U.S. C8 134
Benedito Leite, Braz. E10 76
Benenitra, Madag. s21 67b
Benešov, Czech. F14 10
Benevento, Italy H9 18
Benevolence, Ga., U.S. E2 117
Benewah, co., Id., U.S. B2 119
Benfeld, Fr. D14 14
Bengal, Bay of, b., Asia J14 44
Ben Gardane, Tun. D16 62
Bengbu, China C6 34
Benghazi see Banghāzī, Libya B5 56
Ben Giang, Viet. G9 40
Bengkalis, Indon. N7 40
Bengkulu, Indon. F3 38
Bengough, Sask., Can. H3 105
Benguela, Ang. D2 58
Benguerir, Mor. D7 62
Benham, Ky., U.S. D7 124
Ben Hill, co., Ga., U.S. E3 117
Beni, Zaire A5 58
Beni, dept., Bol. E9 82
Beni, stm., Bol. D9 82
Béni Abbas, Alg. E9 62
Benicarló, Spain E12 16
Benicia, Ca., U.S. C2 112
Benicito, stm., Bol. D9 82
Benima, Cen. Afr. Rep. O2 60
Beni-Mellal, Mor. D7 62
Benin (Bénin), ctry., Afr. G7 54
Benin, Bight of, Afr. G7 54
Benin City, Nig. H12 64
Beni Saf, Alg. J10 16
Benissa, Spain G12 16
Benito, Man., Can. D1 100
Benito Juárez, Arg. I9 80
Benito Juárez, Presa, res., Mex. I12 90
Benjamín Aceval, Para. C10 80
Benjamin Constant, Braz. J7 84
Benjamín Hill, Mex. B4 90
Benjamín Zorrilla, Arg. J6 80
Benkelman, Ne., U.S. D4 134
Benld, Il., U.S. D4 120
Ben Lomond, Ar., U.S. D1 111
Ben Mehidi, Alg. M2 18
Bennet, Ne., U.S. D9 134
Bennett, Co., U.S. B6 113
Bennett, Ia., U.S. C7 122
Bennett, co., S.D., U.S. D4 148
Bennetta, ostrov, i., Russia B21 28
Bennett Creek, stm., Md., U.S. B3 127
Bennettsville, S.C., U.S. B8 147
Bennington, Id., U.S. G7 119
Bennington, Ks., U.S. C6 123
Bennington, Ne., U.S. g12 134
Bennington, N.H., U.S. D3 136
Bennington, Ok., U.S. C5 143
Bennington, Vt., U.S. F2 152
Bennington, co., Vt., U.S. E2 152
Benniu, China D8 34
Benoit, Ms., U.S. B2 131
Benoni, S. Afr. F9 66
Bénoué (Benue), stm., Afr. G9 54
Benque Viejo del Carmen, Belize I15 90
Bensenville, Il., U.S. B6 120
Bensheim, Ger. F8 10
Bensley, Va., U.S. C5 153
Ben-Slimane, Mor. D7 62
Ben Smih, Alg. M2 18
Benson, Sask., Can. H4 105
Benson, Az., U.S. F5 110
Benson, Il., U.S. C4 120
Benson, Mn., U.S. E3 130
Benson, N.C., U.S. B4 140
Benson, co., N.D., U.S. A6 141
Bent, co., Co., U.S. D7 113
Bentinck Island, i., Austl. C7 68
Bentiu, Sud. M5 60
Bentley, Alta., Can. C3 98
Bentley, Ks., U.S. E6 123
Bentley, La., U.S. C3 125
Bentleyville, Pa., U.S. F1 145
Bento Gomes, stm., Braz. G13 82
Bento Gonçalves, Braz. E13 80
Benton, N.B., Can. D2 101
Benton, Ar., U.S. C3 111
Benton, Il., U.S. E5 120
Benton, In., U.S. B6 121
Benton, Ks., U.S. E6 123
Benton, Ky., U.S. f9 124
Benton, La., U.S. B2 125
Benton, Ms., U.S. C3 131
Benton, Mo., U.S. D8 132
Benton, Pa., U.S. D9 145
Benton, Tn., U.S. B7 149
Benton, Wi., U.S. F3 156
Benton, co., Ar., U.S. A1 111
Benton, co., In., U.S. C3 121
Benton, co., Ia., U.S. B5 122
Benton, co., Mn., U.S. E4 130
Benton, co., Ms., U.S. A4 131
Benton, co., Mo., U.S. C4 132
Benton, co., Or., U.S. C3 144
Benton, co., Tn., U.S. A3 149
Benton, co., Wa., U.S. C6 154
Benton City, Wa., U.S. C6 154
Bentong, Malay. M6 40
Benton Harbor, Mi., U.S. F4 129
Benton Heights, Mi., U.S. F4 129
Bentonia, Ms., U.S. C3 131
Bentonville, Ar., U.S. A1 111
Bentonville, Va., U.S. B4 153
Ben Tre, Viet. I9 40
Bentree, W.V., U.S. m13 155
Bent's Old Fort National Historic Site, hist., Co., U.S. C7 113
Benue (Bénoué), stm., Afr. G8 54
Benwood, W.V., U.S. f8 155
Benxi (Penhsi), China B11 32
Benzie, co., Mi., U.S. D4 129
Benzonia, Mi., U.S. D4 129
Beograd (Belgrade), Yugo. E4 20
Beowawe, Nv., U.S. C5 135
Beppu, Japan N6 36
Bequia, i., St. Vin. H14 94
Beramanja, Madag. n23 67b
Berat, Alb. I3 20
Berau, Teluk, b., Indon. F9 38
Beravina, Madag. q21 67b
Berbera, Som. F10 56
Berbérati, Cen. Afr. Rep. H4 56
Berbice, stm., Guy. D14 84
Berchtesgaden, Ger. H13 10
Berd'ansk, Ukr. H5 26
Berdičev, Ukr. H3 26
Berdigest'ach, Russia E17 28
Berdsk, Russia G8 28

Name — Map Ref. — Page

Berea, Ky., U.S. C5 124
Berea, Oh., U.S. A4 142
Berea, S.C., U.S. B3 147
Beregomet, Ukr. A9 20
Beregovo, Ukr. G22 10
Berekua, Dom. G14 94
Berendejevo, Russia E22 22
Berens, stm., Can. C3 100
Berens River, Man., Can. C3 100
Beresford, S.D., U.S. D9 148
Berettyó (Barcău), stm., Eur. B5 20
Berevo, Madag. q21 67b
Berezajka, Russia D16 22
Berezino, Bela. H11 22
Berezino, Bela. G11 22
Berezino, Ukr. C13 20
Berezniki, Russia F9 26
Berg, Nor. G15 6
Berga, Spain C13 16
Bergama, Tur. J11 20
Bergamo, Italy D4 18
Bergantín, Ven. B10 84
Bergara, Spain B9 16
Bergby, Swe. K15 6
Bergen (Mons), Bel. H4 12
Bergen, Ger. C10 10
Bergen, Neth. C6 12
Bergen, Nor. K9 6
Bergen, N.Y., U.S. B3 139
Bergen, co., N.J., U.S. A4 137
Bergen aan Zee, Neth. C6 12
Bergen [auf Rügen], Ger. A13 10
Bergenfield, N.J., U.S. B4 137
Bergen op Zoom, Neth. E5 12
Berger, Mo., U.S. C6 132
Bergerac, Fr. H7 14
Bergholz, Oh., U.S. B5 142
Bergisch, Ger. D7 10
Bergisch Gladbach, Ger. E7 10
Bergland, Mi., U.S. m12 129
Bergman, Ar., U.S. A2 111
Bergoo, W.V., U.S. C4 155
Bergsche Maas, stm., Neth. E6 12
Bergsjö, Swe. K15 6
Bergstrom Air Force Base, mil., Tx., U.S. D4 150
Berguent, Mor. C9 62
Bergues, Fr. B9 14
Berhala, Selat, strt., Indon. O8 40
Beringa, ostrov, i., Russia F25 28
Bering Sea C2 86
Bering Strait, strt. m18 106a
Berino, N.M., U.S. E3 138
Berja, Spain I9 16
Berkane, Mor. C9 62
Berkeley, Ont., Can. C4 103
Berkeley, Ca., U.S. D2 112
Berkeley, Mo., U.S. f13 132
Berkeley, R.I., U.S. B4 146
Berkeley, co., S.C., U.S. E8 147
Berkeley, co., W.V., U.S. B6 155
Berkeley Heights, N.J., U.S. B4 137
Berkeley Springs, W.V., U.S. B6 155
Berkley, Mi., U.S. F7 129
Berkner Island, i., Ant. C1 73
Berks, co., Pa., U.S. F9 145
Berkshire, Vt., U.S. B3 152
Berkshire, co., Eng., U.K. J12 8
Berkshire, co., Ma., U.S. B1 128
Berkshire Hills, hills, Ma., U.S. B1 128
Berlaimont, Fr. B10 14
Berland, stm., Alta., Can. C1 98
Berlin, Ger. C13 10
Berlin, S. Afr. I8 66
Berlin, Ct., U.S. C5 114
Berlin, Ga., U.S. E3 117
Berlin, Md., U.S. D7 127
Berlin, N.H., U.S. B4 136
Berlin, N.J., U.S. D3 137
Berlin, N.Y., U.S. C7 139
Berlin, Oh., U.S. B4 142
Berlin, Pa., U.S. G4 145
Berlin, Wi., U.S. E5 156
Berlin, state, Ger. C13 10
Berlin, Mount, mtn., Ant. C10 73
Berlin Corners, Vt., U.S. C3 152
Berlin Heights, Oh., U.S. A3 142
Berlin Lake, res., Oh., U.S. A4 142
Berlin Mountain, mtn., U.S. A1 128
Bermejillo, Mex. E8 90
Bermejo, Arg. F5 80
Bermejo, stm., Arg. F5 80
Bermejo, stm., S.A. C9 80
Bermejo, Paso del, S.A. G3 80
Bermeo, Spain B9 16
Bermuda, dep., N.A. B12 88
Bern (Berne), Switz. E7 13
Bern, Ks., U.S. C8 123
Bern (Berne), state, Switz. E8 13
Bernalda, Italy I11 18
Bernalillo, N.M., U.S. B3 138
Bernalillo, co., N.M., U.S. C3 138
Bernard, Me., U.S. D4 126
Bernardsville, N.J., U.S. B3 137
Bernasconi, Arg. I7 80
Bernau bei Berlin, Ger. C13 10
Bernay, Fr. C7 14
Bernburg, Ger. D11 10
Berne, In., U.S. C8 121
Berner Alpen, mts., Switz. F7 13
Bernice, La., U.S. B3 125
Bernice, Ok., U.S. A7 143
Bernie, Mo., U.S. E8 132
Bernier Bay, b., N.W. Ter., Can. B15 96
Bernina, mts., Eur. F12 13
Bernina, Passo del, Switz. F13 13
Bernina, Piz, mtn., Eur. F16 14
Bernville, Pa., U.S. F9 145
Beromünster, Switz. H8 10
Berón de Astrada, Arg. D10 80
Beroroha, Madag. r21 67b
Ber'ostovica, Bela. H6 22
Beroun, Czech. F14 10
Berounka, stm., Czech. F13 10
Berovo, Mac. H6 20
Ber'oza, Bela. I7 22
Ber'ozovo, Russia E11 26
Berrechid, Mor. D7 62
Berri, Austl. J4 70
Berrien, co., Ga., U.S. E3 117
Berrien, co., Mi., U.S. F4 129
Berrien Springs, Mi., U.S. G4 129
Berrigan, Austl. J6 70
Berriyyane, Alg. D12 62
Berry, Al., U.S. B2 108
Berry, Ky., U.S. B5 124
Berry, hist. reg., Fr. E9 14
Berry Creek, stm., Alta., Can. D5 98
Berryessa, Lake, res., Ca., U.S. C2 112
Berry Hill, Tn., U.S. g10 149
Berry Islands, is., Bah. B6 94
Berrys Chapel, Tn., U.S. B5 149
Berryton, Ga., U.S. B1 117
Berryville, Ar., U.S. A2 111
Berryville, Va., U.S. A5 153
Beršad', Ukr. A13 20
Berseba, Nmb. F3 66
Bersenbrück, Ger. C7 10
Bertha, Mn., U.S. D3 130
Berthierville, Que., Can. C4 104
Berthold, N.D., U.S. A4 141
Berthoud, Co., U.S. A5 113
Berthoud Pass, Co., U.S. B5 113
Bertie, co., N.C., U.S. A5 140
Bertoua, Cam. H9 54
Bertram, Tx., U.S. D4 150
Bertrand, Mo., U.S. E8 132
Bertrand, Ne., U.S. D6 134
Beruri, Braz. I12 84
Berwick, N.S., Can. D5 101
Berwick, Il., U.S. C3 120
Berwick, Ia., U.S. e8 122
Berwick, La., U.S. E4 125
Berwick, Me., U.S. E2 126
Berwick, Pa., U.S. D9 145
Berwick-upon-Tweed, Eng., U.K. F11 8
Berwind, W.V., U.S. D3 155
Berwyn, Alta., Can. A2 98
Berwyn, Il., U.S. k9 120
Berwyn, Ne., U.S. C6 134
Berwyn, Pa., U.S. o20 145
Besalampy, Madag. p21 67b
Besançon, Fr. E13 14
Besbes, Alg. M2 18
Bešenkoviči, Bela. F12 22
Beskid Mountains, mts., Eur. F20 10
Beskra, Alg. C13 62
Besni, Tur. C4 48
Besor, Naḥal, val., Asia F2 50
Bessarabia, hist. reg., Mol. C12 20
Bessarabka, Ukr. C12 20
Besse, Nig. F12 64
Bessemer, Al., U.S. B3 108
Bessemer, Mi., U.S. n11 129
Bessemer, Pa., U.S. E1 145
Bessemer City, N.C., U.S. B1 140
Bessie, Ok., U.S. B3 143
Best'ach, Russia E17 28
Bestobe, Kaz. G12 26
Betafo, Madag. q22 67b
Betanzos, Bol. H9 82
Betanzos, Spain B3 16
Betaré Oya, Cam. G9 54
Betatakin Ruin, hist., Az., U.S. A5 110
Betbetti, Sud. J3 60
Bete Hor, Eth. L10 60
Bétera, Spain F11 16
Bétérou, Benin G11 64
Bet Guvrin, Isr. E3 50
Bet Ha'arava, Isr. Occ. E5 50
Bethal, S. Afr. F9 66
Bethalto, Il., U.S. E3 120
Bethanien, Nmb. F3 66
Bethany, Ont., Can. C6 103
Bethany, Ct., U.S. D4 114
Bethany, Il., U.S. D5 120
Bethany, Mo., U.S. A3 132
Bethany, Ok., U.S. B4 143
Bethany, W.V., U.S. A4 155
Bethany Beach, De., U.S. F5 115
Bethel, Ak., U.S. C7 109
Bethel, Ct., U.S. D2 114
Bethel, De., U.S. F3 115
Bethel, Ky., U.S. B6 124
Bethel, Me., U.S. D2 126
Bethel, N.C., U.S. B5 140
Bethel, Oh., U.S. D1 142
Bethel, Ok., U.S. C7 143
Bethel, Pa., U.S. F9 145
Bethel, Vt., U.S. D3 152
Bethel Acres, Ok., U.S. B5 143
Bethel Park, Pa., U.S. k14 145
Bethel Springs, Tn., U.S. B3 149
Bethesda, Ar., U.S. B4 111
Bethesda, Md., U.S. C3 127
Bethesda, Oh., U.S. B4 142
Bethlehem, S. Afr. G9 66
Bethlehem, Ct., U.S. C3 114
Bethlehem, Ga., U.S. C3 117
Bethlehem, N.H., U.S. B3 136
Bethlehem, Pa., U.S. E11 145
Bethlehem see Bayt Laḥm, Isr. Occ. E4 50
Bethpage, Tn., U.S. A5 149
Bethune, Sask., Can. G3 105
Béthune, Fr. B9 14
Bethune, Co., U.S. B8 113
Bethune, S.C., U.S. C7 147
Beticos, Sistemas, mts., Spain H8 16
Betijoque, Ven. C7 84
Betioky, Madag. s21 67b
Betlica, Russia G16 22
Betong, Thai. L6 40
Betoota, Austl. E4 70
Betpak-Dala, des., Kaz. H12 26
Betroka, Madag. s22 67b
Bet She'an, Isr. C5 50
Bet Shemesh, Isr. E4 50
Betsiboka, stm., Madag. p22 67b
Betsie, Point, c., Mi., U.S. D4 129
Betsioky, Madag. r21 67b
Betsy Layne, Ky., U.S. C7 124
Bette, mtn., Libya D4 56
Bettendorf, Ia., U.S. C7 122
Bettsville, Oh., U.S. A2 142
Betūl, India J7 44
Betzdorf, Ger. E7 10
Beulah, Al., U.S. C4 108
Beulah, Co., U.S. C6 113
Beulah, Mi., U.S. D4 129
Beulah, Ms., U.S. B3 131
Beulah, N.D., U.S. B4 141
Beulah, Wy., U.S. B8 157
Beulah, Lake, l., Ms., U.S. B3 131
Beulaville, N.C., U.S. C5 140
Bevensen, Ger. B10 10
B. Everett Jordan Lake, res., N.C., U.S. B3 140
Beverley, Austl. F3 68
Beverley, Eng., U.K. H13 8
Beverley Head, c., Newf., Can. D2 102
Beverly, Ks., U.S. C6 123
Beverly, Ma., U.S. A6 128
Beverly, N.J., U.S. C3 137
Beverly, Oh., U.S. C4 142
Beverly, Tn., U.S. m14 149
Beverly, W.V., U.S. C5 155
Beverly Hills, Ca., U.S. m12 112
Beverly Shores, In., U.S. A4 121
Beverwijk, Neth. D6 12
Bewdley, Ont., Can. C6 103
Bexar, co., Tx., U.S. E3 150
Bexley, Oh., U.S. m11 142
Beyçayırı, Tur. I10 20
Beylul, Erit. H3 47
Beypazarı, Tur. G14 4
Beyşehir Gölü, l., Tur. H14 4
Bezaha, Madag. s21 67b
Bežanicy, Russia E12 22
Bezau, Aus. H9 10
Bežeck, Russia D19 22
Bezerra, stm., Braz. B5 79
Béziers, Fr. I10 14
Bezmein, Turk. B15 48
Bhadrak, India J12 44
Bhadrāvati, India F3 46
Bhāg, Pak. F2 44
Bhāgalpur, India H12 44
Bhakkar, Pak. E4 44
Bhakkar, Pak. E4 44
Bhaktapur, Nepal G11 44
Bhamo, Burma B4 40
Bhandāra, India J8 44
Bharatpur, India G7 44
Bharatpur, Nepal G11 44
Bharūch, India J5 44
Bhātāpāra, India B6 46
Bhātpāra, India I13 44
Bhāvnagar, India J5 44
Bhawānipatna, India C7 46
Bhera, Pak. D5 44
Bhilai, India J9 44
Bhīlwāra, India H6 44
Bhind, India G8 44
Bhiwandi, India C2 46
Bhiwāni, India F7 44
Bhongīr, India D5 46
Bhopāl, India I7 44
Bhubaneshwar, India J11 44
Bhuj, India I3 44
Bhusāwal, India J6 44
Bhutan (Druk-Yul), ctry., Asia D13 42
Bia, stm., Afr. H8 64
Biá, stm., Braz. I9 84
Bia, Phou, mtn., Laos E7 40
Biabo, stm., Peru B3 82
Biafra, Bight of, Afr. H8 54
Biak, i., Indon. F10 38
Biała, Pol. E17 10
Biała Podlaska, Pol. C23 10
Biała Rawska, Pol. D20 10
Białogard, Pol. A16 10
Białystok, Pol. B23 10
Bianco, Monte (Mont Blanc), mtn., Eur. G13 14
Biarritz, Fr. I5 14
Biasca, Switz. F10 13
Bibā, Egypt C6 60
Bibai, Japan d16 36a
Bibala, Ang. D2 58
Bibb, co., Al., U.S. C2 108
Bibb, co., Ga., U.S. D3 117
Bibb City, Ga., U.S. D2 117
Biberach an der Riss, Ger. G9 10
Bibiani, Ghana H8 64
Biblián, Ec. I3 84
Bic, Que., Can. A9 104
Bic, Île du, i., Que., Can. A9 104
Bicas, Braz. F7 79
Bicaz, Rom. C10 20
Bičevinka, Russia B20 22
Biche, Lac la, l., Alta., Can. B4 98
Bichena, Eth. L10 60
Bickett Knob, mtn., W.V., U.S. D4 155
Bickle Knob, mtn., W.V., U.S. C5 155
Bicknell, In., U.S. G3 121
Bicknell, Ut., U.S. E4 151
Bicske, Hung. H18 10
Bicudo, stm., Braz. E6 79
Bīd, India C3 46
Bida, Nig. G13 64
Bīdar, India D4 46
Biddeford, Me., U.S. E2 126
Bididan, China C2 34
Bidwell, Mount, mtn., Ca., U.S. B3 112
Bieber, Ca., U.S. B3 112
Biecz, Pol. F21 10
Biedenkopf, Ger. E8 10
Biel (Bienne), Switz. D7 13
Bielawa, Pol. E16 10
Bielefeld, Ger. C8 10
Bielersee, l., Switz. D7 13
Biella, Italy D3 18
Bielsko-Biała, Pol. F19 10
Bielsk Podlaski, Pol. C23 10
Bienfait, Sask., Can. H4 105
Bien Hoa, Viet. I9 40
Bienville, La., U.S. B3 125
Bienville, co., La., U.S. B2 125
Bienville, Lac, l., Que., Can. g12 104
Big, stm., Mo., U.S. c7 132
Biga, Tur. I11 20
Big A Mountain, mtn., Va., U.S. e9 153
Big Arm, Mt., U.S. C2 133
Big Bald, mtn., U.S. f10 140
Big Bald, mtn., Ga., U.S. B2 117
Big Bald Mountain, mtn., N.B., Can. B3 101
Big Baldy, mtn., Id., U.S. E3 119
Big Baldy Mountain, mtn., Mt., U.S. D6 133
Big Bay, Mi., U.S. B3 129
Big Bay De Noc, b., Mi., U.S. C4 129
Big Bayou, stm., Ar., U.S. D4 111
Big Bear City, Ca., U.S. E5 112
Big Beaver, Sask., Can. H3 105
Big Belt Mountains, mts., Mt., U.S. D5 133
Big Bend, Swaz. F10 66
Big Bend, Wi., U.S. n11 156
Big Bend Dam, S.D., U.S. C6 148
Big Bend National Park, Tx., U.S. E1 150
Big Birch Lake, l., Mn., U.S. E4 130
Big Black, stm., Me., U.S. B3 126
Big Black, stm., Ms., U.S. C3 131
Big Blue, stm., In., U.S. E6 121
Big Burro Mountains, mts., N.M., U.S. E1 138
Big Butt, mtn., Tn., U.S. C11 149
Big Cabin, Ok., U.S. A6 143
Big Cabin Creek, stm., Ok., U.S. A6 143
Big Canyon, val., Tx., U.S. D1 150
Big Chino Wash, val., Az., U.S. B3 110
Big Clifty, Ky., U.S. C3 124
Big Coal, stm., W.V., U.S. C3 155
Big Costilla Peak, mtn., N.M., U.S. A4 138
Big Creek, B.C., Can. D6 99
Big Creek, Ca., U.S. D4 112
Big Creek, Ky., U.S. C6 124
Big Creek, W.V., U.S. C2 155
Big Creek, stm., Ar., U.S. C5 111
Big Creek, stm., In., U.S. G7 121
Big Creek, stm., In., U.S. H2 121
Big Creek, stm., Ks., U.S. D4 123
Big Creek, stm., La., U.S. B4 125
Big Creek, stm., Ms., U.S. D5 131
Big Creek, stm., Mo., U.S. C3 132
Big Creek, stm., Tn., U.S. e8 149
Big Creek Lake, res., Al., U.S. E1 108
Big Creek Peak, mtn., Id., U.S. E5 119
Big Cypress Indian Reservation, Fl., U.S. F5 116
Big Cypress Swamp, sw., Fl., U.S. F5 116
Big Darby Creek, stm., Oh., U.S. C2 142
Big Delta, Ak., U.S. C10 109
Big Desert, des., Austl. J4 70
Big Dry Creek, stm., Mt., U.S. C10 133
Big Duke Dam, N.C., U.S. B2 140
Big Eau Pleine, stm., Wi., U.S. D3 156
Big Eau Pleine Reservoir, res., Wi., U.S. D4 156
Big Elk Creek, stm., Md., U.S. A6 127
Bigelow, Ar., U.S. B3 111
Bigelow, Mount, mtn., Me., U.S. C2 126
Big Escambia Creek, stm., U.S. D2 108
Big Falls, Mn., U.S. B5 130
Big Flat Mountain, mtn., Va., U.S. B4 153
Big Flats, N.Y., U.S. C4 139
Bigfork, Mn., U.S. C5 130
Bigfork, Mt., U.S. B2 133
Big Fork, stm., Mn., U.S. B5 130
Big Frog Mountain, mtn., Tn., U.S. D9 149
Biggar, Sask., Can. E1 105
Biggar, Scot., U.K. F10 8
Biggers, Ar., U.S. A5 111
Biggersville, Ms., U.S. A5 131
Biggs, Ca., U.S. C3 112
Biggsville, Il., U.S. C3 120
Big Hatchet Peak, mtn., N.M., U.S. F1 138
Big Hole, stm., Mt., U.S. E4 133
Big Hole National Battlefield, hist., Mt., U.S. E3 133
Big Horn, Wy., U.S. B5 157
Big Horn, co., Mt., U.S. E9 133
Big Horn, co., Wy., U.S. B4 157
Bighorn, stm., U.S. B5 106
Bighorn Canyon National Recreation Area, U.S. F8 133
Bighorn Lake, res., U.S. E8 133
Bighorn Mountains, mts., U.S. B5 157
Big Horn Mountains, mts., Az., U.S. D2 110
Big Island, Va., U.S. C3 153
Big Island, i., N.W. Ter., Can. D18 96
Big Island, i., N.W. Ter., Can. f8 102
Big Kandiyohi Lake, l., Mn., U.S. F4 130
Big Knob, mtn., Pa., U.S. F6 145
Big Knob, mtn., Va., U.S. f9 153
Big Lake, Mn., U.S. E5 130
Big Lake, Tx., U.S. D2 150
Big Lake, l., Me., U.S. C5 126
Biglerville, Pa., U.S. G7 145
Big Lookout Mountain, mtn., Or., U.S. C9 144
Big Lost, stm., Id., U.S. F5 119
Big Mossy Point, c., Man., Can. C2 100
Big Mountain, mtn., Nv., U.S. B2 135
Big Muddy, stm., Il., U.S. F4 120
Big Muddy Creek, stm., Mt., U.S. B12 133
Bignasco, Switz. F10 13
Big Nemaha, stm., Ne., U.S. D10 134
Bignona, Sen. E1 64
Big North Mountain, mts., Va., U.S. B4 153
Big Otter, stm., Va., U.S. C3 153
Big Pine, Ca., U.S. D4 112
Big Pine Creek, stm., In., U.S. D3 121
Big Pine Lake, l., Mn., U.S. D3 130
Big Pine Mountain, mtn., Ca., U.S. E4 112
Big Piney, Wy., U.S. D2 157
Big Piney, stm., Mo., U.S. D5 132
Big Piney Creek, stm., Ar., U.S. B2 111
Big Pipe Creek, stm., Md., U.S. A3 127
Bigpoint, Ms., U.S. E5 131
Big Raccoon Creek, stm., In., U.S. E4 121
Big Rapids, Mi., U.S. E5 129
Big Rib, stm., Wi., U.S. C3 156
Big River, Sask., Can. D2 105
Big River, Ca., U.S. E6 112
Big Rock, Il., U.S. B5 120
Big Rock, Tn., U.S. A4 149
Big Rock Mountain, mtn., Ar., U.S. h10 111
Big Run, Pa., U.S. E4 145
Big Sable Point, c., Mi., U.S. D4 129
Big Sandy, Mt., U.S. B6 133
Big Sandy, Tn., U.S. A3 149
Big Sandy, Tx., U.S. C5 150
Big Sandy, stm., U.S. C2 155
Big Sandy, stm., Az., U.S. C2 110
Big Sandy, stm., Tn., U.S. B3 149
Big Sandy, stm., Wy., U.S. D3 157
Big Sandy Creek, stm., Co., U.S. C8 113
Big Sandy Creek, stm., Mt., U.S. B6 133
Big Sandy Creek, stm., W.V., U.S. C3 155
Big Sandy Lake, l., Mn., U.S. D5 130
Big Sandy Reservoir, res., Wy., U.S. D3 157
Big Satilla Creek, stm., Ga., U.S. E4 117
Big Savage Mountain, mtn., U.S. k12 127
Big Sheep Mountain, mtn., Mt., U.S. C11 133
Big Shiney Mountian, mtn., Pa., U.S. n18 145
Big Sioux, stm., U.S. E9 148
Big Slough, stm., Ga., U.S. F2 117
Big Smoky Valley, val., Nv., U.S. E4 135
Big Snowy Mountains, mts., Mt., U.S. D7 133
Big Southern Butte, mtn., Id., U.S. F5 119
Big South Fork, stm., Ky., U.S. k13 124
Big Spencer Mountain, mtn., Me., U.S. C3 126
Big Spring, Tx., U.S. C2 150
Big Springs, Ne., U.S. C3 134
Big Spruce Knob, mtn., W.V., U.S. C4 155
Big Squaw Mountain, mtn., Me., U.S. C3 126
Big Stone, co., Mn., U.S. E2 130
Bigstone, stm., Man., Can. B4 100
Big Stone City, S.D., U.S. B9 148
Big Stone Gap, Va., U.S. f9 153
Big Stone Lake, l., U.S. E2 130
Big Sunflower, stm., Ms., U.S. B3 131
Big Sur, Ca., U.S. D3 112
Big Thompson, stm., Co., U.S. A5 113
Big Timber, Mt., U.S. E7 133
Big Top, mtn., Tn., U.S. B5 149
Big Trout Lake, l., Ont., Can. n17 103
Biguaçu, Braz. D14 80
Big Valley, Alta., Can. C4 98
Big Walnut Creek, stm., Oh., U.S. m11 142
Big Warrambool, stm., Austl. G8 70
Big Water, Ut., U.S. F4 151
Big Wells, Tx., U.S. E3 150
Big Wills Creek, stm., Al., U.S. A3 108
Bigwood, Ont., Can. A4 103
Big Wood, stm., Id., U.S. F4 119
Bihać, Bos. E10 18
Bihār, India H11 44
Bihār, state, India H11 44
Bihor, co., Rom. B6 20
Bija, stm., Russia G15 26
Bijagós, Arquipélago dos, is., Gui.-B. F1 64
Bījār, Iran D9 48
Bijeljina, Bos. E3 20
Bijelo Polje, Yugo. F3 20
Bijie, China F8 30
Bijou Creek, stm., Co., U.S. B6 113
Bijsk, Russia G9 28
Bīkāner, India F5 44
Bikeqi, China C9 30
Bikin, Russia H18 28
Bikin, stm., Russia H19 28
Bikini, atoll, Marsh. Is. G20 158
Bikoro, Zaire B3 58
Bilac, Braz. F3 79
Bilāspur, India I10 44
Bilauktaung Range, mts., Asia H5 40
Bilbao, Spain B9 16
Bilian, China G9 34
Bilimora, India B2 46
Bilin, Burma F4 40
Bílina, Czech. E13 10
Bilk Creek Mountains, mts., Nv., U.S. B3 135
Billabong Creek, stm., Austl. J6 70
Billerica, Ma., U.S. A5 128
Billings, Mo., U.S. D4 132
Billings, Mt., U.S. E8 133
Billings, Ok., U.S. A4 143
Billings, co., N.D., U.S. C2 141
Billings Heights, Mt., U.S. E8 133
Billingsley, Al., U.S. C3 108
Billom, Fr. G10 14
Bill Williams, stm., Az., U.S. C1 110
Bill Williams Mountain, mtn., Az., U.S. B3 110
Bilma, Niger E9 54
Biloela, Austl. E9 70
Biloxi, Ms., U.S. E5 131
Biloxi, stm., Ms., U.S. E4 131
Biloxi Bay, b., Ms., U.S. f8 131
Biltmore Forest, N.C., U.S. f10 140
Bilugyun Island, i., Burma F4 40
Bilwaskarma, Nic. C11 92
Bim, W.V., U.S. n12 155
Bimbān, Egypt E7 60
Bimbila, Ghana G10 64
Bimini Islands, is., Bah. B5 94
Binche, Bel. H5 12
Bindura, Zimb. E6 58
Binéfar, Spain D12 16
Binford, N.D., U.S. B7 141
Binga, Monte, mtn., Afr. B11 66
Bingamon Creek, stm., W.V., U.S. k10 155
Bingara, Austl. G9 70
Bingen, Ger. F7 10
Bingen, Wa., U.S. D4 154
Binger, Ok., U.S. B3 143
Bingham, Me., U.S. C3 126
Bingham, co., Id., U.S. F6 119
Bingham Lake, Mn., U.S. G3 130
Binghamton, N.Y., U.S. C5 139
Bingöl, Tur. B6 48
Binhai (Dongkan), China A8 34
Binjai, Indon. M5 40
Binscarth, Man., Can. D1 100
Bintan, Pulau, i., Indon. N8 40
Bintang, Gam. E1 64
Bintimani, mtn., S.L. G4 64
Bint Jubayl, Leb. B4 50
Bintulu, Malay. E5 38
Binxian, China D8 30
Binyamina, Isr. C3 50
Binyang, China C10 40
Bin Yauri, Nig. F12 64
Bíobío, prov., Chile I3 80
Bíobío, stm., Chile I2 80
Bíobío, stm., Chile F3 80
Bioko, i., Eq. Gui. J14 64
Bippus, In., U.S. C6 121
Birāk, Libya C3 56
Bi'r al-Uzam, Libya B2 60
Birao, Cen. Afr. Rep. L2 60
Birātnagar, Nepal F4 30
Birch, stm., W.V., U.S. C4 155
Birch Hills, Sask., Can. E3 105
Birch Island, B.C., Can. D8 99
Birch Island, i., Man., Can. C2 100
Birch Lake, l., Mn., U.S. C7 130
Birch River, Man., Can. C1 100
Birch Rock Hill, mtn., Pa., U.S. F3 145
Birch Run, Mi., U.S. E7 129
Birch Tree, Mo., U.S. E6 132
Birchwood, Ct., U.S. B5 114
Birchwood, Tn., U.S. D9 149
Birchwood, Wi., U.S. C2 156
Birchwood City, Md., U.S. *f9 127
Birchy Bay, Newf., Can. D4 102
Bird City, Ks., U.S. C2 123
Bird Creek, stm., Ok., U.S. A6 143
Bird Island, Mn., U.S. F4 130
Bird Island, i., N.C., U.S. D4 140
Bird Island, sci., S. Geor. A1 73
Bird Islet, i., Austl. D11 68
Birdsboro, Pa., U.S. F10 145
Birds Creek, Ont., Can. B7 103
Birdseye, In., U.S. H4 121
Birdsong, Ar., U.S. B5 111
Birdsville, Austl. E3 70
Birdtown, N.C., U.S. f9 140
Birdum, Austl. C6 68
Birdwood Creek, stm., Ne., U.S. C4 134
Birecik, Tur. C4 48
Bir el Ater, Alg. C15 62
Bir Enzaran, W. Sah. I3 62
Birigui, Braz. F3 79
Biril'ussy, Russia F16 26
Bīrjand, Iran E15 48
Birkenhead, Eng., U.K. H10 8
Birkfeld, Aus. H15 10
Bîrlad, Rom. C11 20
Birmingham, Eng., U.K. I12 8
Birmingham, Al., U.S. B3 108
Birmingham, Ia., U.S. D6 122
Birmingham, Mi., U.S. F7 129
Birmingham, Mo., U.S. h11 132
Birmitrapur, India I11 44
Bîr Mogreïn (Fort-Trinquet), Maur. H5 62
Birnamwood, Wi., U.S. D4 156
Birni, Benin F10 64
Birnie, Man., Can. D2 100
Birni Ngaouré, Niger E11 64
Birnin Gwari, Nig. F13 64
Birni Nkonni, Niger E12 64
Birnin Kudu, Nig. F14 64
Birobidžan, Russia H18 28
Biron, Wi., U.S. D4 156
Birrie, stm., Austl. G7 70
Birsay, Sask., Can. F2 105
Birsk, Russia F9 26
Birtle, Man., Can. D1 100
Bir'usa, stm., Russia F17 26
Biržai, Lith. E7 22
Bîrzava, stm., Eur. D5 20
Bisbee, Az., U.S. F6 110
Bisbee, N.D., U.S. A6 141
Biscarrosse, Fr. H5 14
Biscay, Bay of, b., Eur. H3 14
Biscayne, Key, i., Fl., U.S. s13 116
Biscayne Bay, b., Fl., U.S. G6 116
Biscayne National Monument, Fl., U.S. G6 116
Biscayne Park, Fl., U.S. s13 116
Bisceglie, Italy H11 18
Bischofswerda, Ger. D14 10
Biscoe, Ar., U.S. C4 111
Biscoe, N.C., U.S. B3 140
Biscoe Islands, is., Ant. B12 73
Biscucuy, Ven. C8 84
Bisha, Erit. J9 60
Bishkek see Biškek, Kyrg. I12 26
Bisho, Ciskei I8 66
Bishop, Ca., U.S. D4 112
Bishop, Ga., U.S. C3 117
Bishop, Tx., U.S. F4 150
Bishop Auckland, Eng., U.K. G12 8
Bishop's Falls, Newf., Can. D4 102
Bishops Mills, Ont., Can. C9 103
Bishopton, Que., Can. D6 104
Bishopville, S.C., U.S. C7 147
Bishrah, Ma'ṭan, well, Libya F2 60
Biškek (Frunze), Kyrg. I12 26
Bislig, Phil. D8 38
Bismarck, Ar., U.S. C2 111
Bismarck, Il., U.S. C6 120
Bismarck, Mo., U.S. D7 132
Bismarck, N.D., U.S. C5 141
Bismarck Archipelago, is., Pap. N. Gui. k16 68a
Bismarck Range, mts., Pap. N. Gui. m15 68a

Name	Map Ref.	Page
Bismarck Sea, Pap. N. Gui.	I18	158
Bismuna, Laguna, b., Nic.	C11	92
Bison, Ks., U.S.	D4	123
Bison, S.D., U.S.	B3	148
Bison Peak, mtn., Co., U.S.	B5	113
Bissau, Gui.-B.	F3	54
Bissett, Man., Can.	D4	100
Bissikrima, Gui.	F4	64
Bissorã, Gui.-B.	E2	64
Bistineau, Lake, res., La., U.S.	B2	125
Bistriţa, Rom.	B8	20
Bistriţa, stm., Rom.	C10	20
Bistriţa-Năsăud, co., Rom.	B8	20
Bisztynek, Pol.	A20	10
Bitam, Gabon	A2	58
Bitburg, Ger.	F6	10
Bitche, Fr.	C14	14
Bitlis, Tur.	B7	48
Bitola, Mac.	H5	20
Bitonto, Italy	H11	18
Bitter Creek, stm., Wy., U.S.	E4	157
Bitterfeld, Ger.	D12	10
Bitterfontein, S. Afr.	H4	66
Bitter Lake, l., S.D., U.S.	B8	148
Bittern Lake, Alta., Can.	C4	98
Bitterroot, stm., Mt., U.S.	D2	133
Bitterroot Range, mts., U.S.	B3	119
Bitti, Italy	I4	18
Bitung, Indon.	E8	38
Bituruna, Braz.	D13	80
Biwabik, Mn., U.S.	C6	130
Biwa-ko, l., Japan	L11	36
Bixby, Ok., U.S.	B6	143
Biyang, China	C2	34
Bizana, Transkei	H9	66
Bizerte, Tun.	L4	18
Bizkaiko, prov., Spain	B9	16
Bjala Slatina, Bul.	F7	20
Bjelovar, Cro.	D11	18
Bjork Lake, l., Sask., Can.	E4	105
Björna, Swe.	J16	6
Bjørnøya (Bear Island), i., Sval.	B2	24
Bla, Mali	E7	64
Black, Al., U.S.	D4	108
Black (Lixian) (Da), stm., Asia	D8	40
Black, stm., Man., Can.	D4	100
Black, stm., Az., U.S.	D5	110
Black, stm., Ar., U.S.	B4	111
Black, stm., La., U.S.	C4	125
Black, stm., Mi., U.S.	E8	129
Black, stm., N.Y., U.S.	B4	139
Black, stm., N.C., U.S.	C4	140
Black, stm., S.C., U.S.	D8	147
Black, stm., Vt., U.S.	E3	152
Black, stm., Vt., U.S.	B4	152
Black, stm., Wi., U.S.	D3	156
Black, Bayou, stm., La., U.S.	E5	125
Blackall, Austl.	E6	70
Black Bear Creek, stm., Ok., U.S.	A4	143
Blackbeard Island, i., Ga., U.S.	E5	117
Black Bear Island Lake, l., Sask., Can.	B3	105
Blackbird, De., U.S.	C3	115
Blackburn, Mo., U.S.	B4	132
Blackburn, Mount, mtn., Ak., U.S.	C11	109
Black Butte, mtn., Mt., U.S.	F5	133
Black Butte, mtn., Wy., U.S.	B5	157
Black Butte Lake, res., Ca., U.S.	C2	112
Black Canyon, val., Co., U.S.	C3	113
Black Canyon City, Az., U.S.	C3	110
Black Canyon of the Gunnison National Monument, Co., U.S.	C3	113
Black Creek, B.C., Can.	E5	99
Black Creek, N.C., U.S.	B5	140
Black Creek, Wi., U.S.	D5	156
Black Creek, stm., U.S.	B1	138
Black Creek, stm., Ms., U.S.	D4	131
Black Creek, stm., S.C., U.S.	B7	147
Black Diamond, Alta., Can.	D3	98
Black Diamond, Al., U.S.	g6	108
Black Diamond, Wa., U.S.	B4	154
Blackduck, Mn., U.S.	C4	130
Black Duck, stm., Can.	E15	96
Black Eagle, Mt., U.S.	C5	133
Black Earth, Wi., U.S.	E4	156
Blackey, Ky., U.S.	C7	124
Blackfalds, Alta., Can.	C4	98
Blackfeet Indian Reservation, Mt., U.S.	B4	133
Blackfoot, Alta., Can.	C5	98
Blackfoot, Id., U.S.	F6	119
Blackfoot, Mt., U.S.	B4	133
Blackfoot, stm., Mt., U.S.	C3	133
Blackfoot Mountains, mts., Id., U.S.	F7	119
Blackfoot Reservoir, res., Id., U.S.	G7	119
Blackford, co., In., U.S.	D7	121
Black Forest, Co., U.S.	C6	113
Black Forest see Schwarzwald, mts., Ger.	G8	10
Blackhall Mountain, mtn., Wy., U.S.	E6	157
Black Hawk, S.D., U.S.	C2	148
Black Hawk, co., Ia., U.S.	B5	122
Black Hills, mts., U.S.	C2	148
Blackie, Alta., Can.	D4	98
Blackjack Mountain, mtn., Ga., U.S.	h8	117
Black Lake, Que., Can.	C6	104
Black Lake, l., Sask., Can.	m7	105
Black Lake, l., Mi., U.S.	C6	129
Black Lake, l., N.Y., U.S.	f9	139
Black Lake Bayou, stm., La., U.S.	B2	125
Black Lick, Pa., U.S.	F3	145
Blacklick Estates, Oh., U.S.	*m11	142
Black Mesa, mtn., Az., U.S.	A5	110
Black Mesa, mtn., Ok., U.S.	e8	143
Black Mingo Creek, stm., S.C., U.S.	D9	147
Blackmore, Mount, mtn., Mt., U.S.	E6	133
Black Mountain, N.C., U.S.	f10	140
Black Mountain, mtn., U.S.	D7	124
Black Mountain, mtn., Az., U.S.	E4	110
Black Mountain, mtn., Co., U.S.	A5	113
Black Mountain, mtn., Id., U.S.	C3	119
Black Mountain, mtn., Mt., U.S.	D4	133
Black Mountain, mtn., Or., U.S.	B7	144
Black Mountain, mtn., Wy., U.S.	B5	157
Black Mountain, mtn., Wy., U.S.	D7	157
Black Mountains, mts., Az., U.S.	B1	110
Black Oak, Ar., U.S.	B5	111
Black Peak, mtn., Az., U.S.	C1	110
Black Pine Peak, mtn., Id., U.S.	G5	119
Black Pond, l., Me., U.S.	B3	126
Blackpool, Eng., U.K.	H10	8
Black Range, mts., N.M., U.S.	D2	138
Black River, N.Y., U.S.	A5	139
Black River Falls, Wi., U.S.	D3	156
Black Rock, Ar., U.S.	A4	111
Black Rock, N.M., U.S.	B1	138
Black Rock, S. Geor.	G8	78
Black Rock Desert, des., Nv., U.S.	B3	135
Black Rock Range, mts., Nv., U.S.	B3	135
Blacksburg, S.C., U.S.	A4	147
Blacksburg, Va., U.S.	C2	153
Black Sea	G15	4
Blacks Fork, stm., U.S.	E3	157
Blacks Harbour, N.B., Can.	D3	101
Blackshear, Ga., U.S.	E4	117
Blackshear, Lake, res., Ga., U.S.	E2	117
Black Squirrel Creek, stm., Co., U.S.	C6	113
Blackstock, Ont., Can.	C6	103
Blackstone, Ma., U.S.	B4	128
Blackstone, Va., U.S.	C5	153
Blackstone, stm., R.I., U.S.	B4	146
Black Thunder Creek, stm., Wy., U.S.	C8	157
Black Tickle, Newf., Can.	B4	102
Blackville, N.B., Can.	C4	101
Blackville, S.C., U.S.	E5	147
Black Volta (Volta Noire), stm., Afr.	G6	54
Blackwalnut Point, c., Md., U.S.	C5	127
Black Warrior, stm., Al., U.S.	C2	108
Blackwater, Mo., U.S.	C5	132
Blackwater, stm., Ire.	I5	8
Blackwater, stm., Fl., U.S.	u15	116
Blackwater, stm., Md., U.S.	D5	127
Blackwater, stm., N.H., U.S.	D3	136
Blackwater, stm., Va., U.S.	D6	153
Blackwater Reservoir, res., N.H., U.S.	D3	136
Blackwell, Ar., U.S.	B3	111
Blackwell, Ok., U.S.	A4	143
Blackwood, N.J., U.S.	D2	137
Blackwood Creek, stm., Ne., U.S.	D4	134
Bladel, Neth.	F7	12
Bladen, Ne., U.S.	D7	134
Bladen, co., N.C., U.S.	C4	140
Bladenboro, N.C., U.S.	C4	140
Bladensburg, Md., U.S.	f9	127
Blades, De., U.S.	F3	115
Bladgrond, S. Afr.	G4	66
Bladon Springs, Al., U.S.	D1	108
Bladworth, Sask., Can.	F2	105
Blaeberry, stm., B.C., Can.	D2	98
Blagodarnyj, Russia	H6	26
Blagoevgrad, Bul.	G7	20
Blagoveščensk, Russia	G17	28
Blain, Fr.	E5	14
Blaine, Me., U.S.	B5	126
Blaine, Mn., U.S.	m12	130
Blaine, Tn., U.S.	C10	149
Blaine, Wa., U.S.	A3	154
Blaine, co., Id., U.S.	F4	119
Blaine, co., Mt., U.S.	B7	133
Blaine, co., Ne., U.S.	C6	134
Blaine, co., Ok., U.S.	B3	143
Blaine Creek, stm., Ky., U.S.	B7	124
Blaine Lake, Sask., Can.	E2	105
Blair, Ne., U.S.	C9	134
Blair, Ok., U.S.	C2	143
Blair, W.V., U.S.	n12	155
Blair, Wi., U.S.	D2	156
Blair, co., Pa., U.S.	E5	145
Blair Athol, Austl.	D7	70
Blairsburg, Ia., U.S.	B4	122
Blairstown, Ia., U.S.	C5	122
Blairstown, Mo., U.S.	C4	132
Blairsville, Ga., U.S.	B3	117
Blairsville, Pa., U.S.	F3	145
Blake Island, i., Wa., U.S.	e11	154
Blakely, Ga., U.S.	E2	117
Blakely, Pa., U.S.	m18	145
Blake Point, c., Mi., U.S.	h10	129
Blakesburg, Ia., U.S.	D5	122
Blanc, Mont (Monte Bianco), mtn., Eur.	G13	14
Blanca, Co., U.S.	D5	113
Blanca, Bahía, b., Arg.	J7	80
Blanca, Isla, i., Peru	C2	82
Blanca, Punta, c., Chile	C3	80
Blanca, Sierra, mtn., Tx., U.S.	o12	150
Blanca Peak, mtn., Co., U.S.	D5	113
Blancas, Peñas, mts., Nic.	D9	92
Blanchard, Id., U.S.	A2	119
Blanchard, La., U.S.	B2	125
Blanchard, Mi., U.S.	E5	129
Blanchard, Ok., U.S.	B4	143
Blanchard, Pa., U.S.	D6	145
Blanchard, stm., Oh., U.S.	A1	142
Blanchardville, Wi., U.S.	F4	156
Blanche, Lake, l., Austl.	G3	70
Blanchester, Oh., U.S.	C2	142
Blanco, N.M., U.S.	A2	138
Blanco, Tx., U.S.	D3	150
Blanco, co., Tx., U.S.	D3	150
Blanco, stm., Arg.	E4	80
Blanco, stm., Bol.	E10	82
Blanco, stm., Ec.	G3	84
Blanco, Cabo, c., C.R.	H9	92
Blanco, Cape, c., Or., U.S.	E2	144
Bland, Mo., U.S.	C6	132
Bland, Va., U.S.	C1	153
Bland, co., Va., U.S.	C1	153
Blandburg, Pa., U.S.	E5	145
Blandford, Ma., U.S.	B2	128
Blanding, Ut., U.S.	F6	151
Blandinsville, Il., U.S.	C3	120
Blanes, Spain	D14	16
Blanford, In., U.S.	E2	121
Blangy-sur-Bresle, Fr.	C8	14
Blankenberge, Bel.	F3	12
Blankenburg, Ger.	D10	10
Blanquilla, Isla, i., Ven.	B10	84
Blantyre, Mwi.	E7	58
Blarney Castle, hist., Ire.	J5	8
Blasdell, N.Y., U.S.	C2	139
Blatná, Czech.	F13	10
Blaufelden, Ger.	F9	10
Blawnox, Pa., U.S.	k14	145
Blaye-et-Sainte-Luce, Fr.	G6	14
Blayney, Austl.	I8	70
Bleckley, co., Ga., U.S.	D3	117
Bledsoe, co., Tn., U.S.	D8	149
Bleiburg, Aus.	I14	10
Blekinge Län, co., Swe.	M14	6
Blencoe, Ia., U.S.	C1	122
Blende, Co., U.S.	C6	113
Blenheim, Ont., Can.	E3	103
Blenheim, N.Z.	D4	72
Blennerhassett, W.V., U.S.	B3	155
Blessing, Tx., U.S.	E4	150
Bletterans, Fr.	F12	14
Blevins, Ar., U.S.	D2	111
Blind, stm., La., U.S.	h10	125
Blind River, Ont., Can.	A2	103
Bliss, Id., U.S.	G4	119
Blissfield, Mi., U.S.	G7	129
Blitar, Indon.	k16	39a
Blocher, In., U.S.	G6	121
Blocker, Ok., U.S.	B6	143
Block Island, R.I., U.S.	h7	146
Block Island, i., R.I., U.S.	h7	146
Block Island Sound, strt., U.S.	G2	146
Blockton, Ia., U.S.	D3	122
Blodgett, Mo., U.S.	D8	132
Bloemfontein, S. Afr.	G8	66
Bloemhof, S. Afr.	F7	66
Blois, Fr.	E8	14
Blönduós, Ice.	B3	6a
Blood Mountain, mtn., Ga., U.S.	B3	117
Bloodsworth Island, i., Md., U.S.	D5	127
Bloodvein, stm., Can.	D3	100
Bloomdale, Oh., U.S.	A2	142
Bloomer, Ar., U.S.	B1	111
Bloomer, Wi., U.S.	C2	156
Bloomfield, N.B., Can.	D4	101
Bloomfield, Ont., Can.	D7	103
Bloomfield, Ct., U.S.	B5	114
Bloomfield, In., U.S.	F4	121
Bloomfield, Ia., U.S.	D5	122
Bloomfield, Ky., U.S.	C4	124
Bloomfield, Mo., U.S.	E8	132
Bloomfield, Ne., U.S.	B8	134
Bloomfield, N.J., U.S.	h8	137
Bloomfield, N.M., U.S.	A2	138
Bloomfield Hills, Mi., U.S.	o15	129
Bloomingburg, Oh., U.S.	C2	142
Bloomingdale, Ga., U.S.	D5	117
Bloomingdale, Il., U.S.	k8	120
Bloomingdale, In., U.S.	E3	121
Bloomingdale, Mi., U.S.	F5	129
Bloomingdale, N.J., U.S.	A4	137
Bloomingdale, Tn., U.S.	C11	149
Blooming Grove, Tx., U.S.	C4	150
Blooming Prairie, Mn., U.S.	G5	130
Bloomington, Id., U.S.	G7	119
Bloomington, Il., U.S.	C4	120
Bloomington, In., U.S.	F4	121
Bloomington, Mn., U.S.	F5	130
Bloomington, Ne., U.S.	D6	134
Bloomington, Tx., U.S.	E4	150
Bloomington, Wi., U.S.	F3	156
Bloomington, Lake, res., Il., U.S.	C5	120
Bloomsburg, Pa., U.S.	E9	145
Bloomsdale, Mo., U.S.	C7	132
Bloomville, Oh., U.S.	A2	142
Blora, Indon.	j15	39a
Blossburg, Al., U.S.	f7	108
Blossburg, Pa., U.S.	C7	145
Blossom, Tx., U.S.	C5	150
Bloumet, Alg.	I14	62
Blount, co., Al., U.S.	B3	108
Blount, co., Tn., U.S.	D10	149
Blountstown, Fl., U.S.	B1	116
Blountsville, Al., U.S.	A3	108
Blountville, Tn., U.S.	C11	149
Blovice, Czech.	F13	10
Blowering Reservoir, res., Austl.	J8	70
Blowing Rock, N.C., U.S.	A1	140
Bloxom, Va., U.S.	C7	153
Bludenz, Aus.	H9	10
Blue, Ok., U.S.	C5	143
Blue, stm., Co., U.S.	B4	113
Blue, stm., In., U.S.	H5	121
Blue, stm., Mo., U.S.	k10	132
Blue, stm., Ok., U.S.	C5	143
Blue, Bayou, stm., La., U.S.	E5	125
Blue, Mount, mtn., Me., U.S.	D2	126
Blue Ash, Oh., U.S.	o13	142
Blueberry, stm., B.C., Can.	A7	99
Blue Buck Knob, hill, Mo., U.S.	E5	132
Blue Buck Point, c., La., U.S.	E2	125
Blue Creek, Al., U.S.	g6	108
Blue Creek, W.V., U.S.	m13	155
Blue Creek, stm., Ne., U.S.	C3	134
Blue Creek, stm., W.V., U.S.	m13	155
Blue Cypress Lake, l., Fl., U.S.	E6	116
Blue Diamond, Nv., U.S.	G6	135
Blue Earth, Mn., U.S.	G4	130
Blue Earth, co., Mn., U.S.	G4	130
Blue Earth, stm., Mn., U.S.	G4	130
Bluefield, Va., U.S.	C1	153
Bluefield, W.V., U.S.	D3	155
Bluefields, Nic.	E11	92
Bluefields, Bahía de, b., Nic.	F11	92
Blue Grass, Ia., U.S.	C7	122
Blue Hill, Me., U.S.	D4	126
Blue Hill, Ne., U.S.	D7	134
Blue Hill Range, hills, Ma., U.S.	h11	128
Blue Hills, Ct., U.S.	B5	114
Bluehole, Ky., U.S.	C6	124
Blue Island, Il., U.S.	B6	120
Bluejoint Lake, l., Or., U.S.	E7	144
Blue Knob, mtn., Pa., U.S.	F4	145
Blue Lake, Ca., U.S.	B2	112
Blue Mesa Reservoir, res., Co., U.S.	C3	113
Blue Mound, Il., U.S.	D4	120
Blue Mound, Ks., U.S.	D8	123
Blue Mountain, Al., U.S.	B4	108
Blue Mountain, Ar., U.S.	B2	111
Blue Mountain, Ms., U.S.	A4	131
Blue Mountain, mtn., Newf., Can.	C3	102
Blue Mountain, mtn., Ar., U.S.	C1	111
Blue Mountain, mtn., Mt., U.S.	C12	133
Blue Mountain, mtn., N.H., U.S.	A4	136
Blue Mountain, mtn., N.M., U.S.	D2	138
Blue Mountain, mtn., N.Y., U.S.	B6	139
Blue Mountain, mtn., Pa., U.S.	F6	145
Blue Mountain Lake, res., Ar., U.S.	B2	111
Blue Mountain Peak, mtn., Jam.	E6	94
Blue Mountains, mts., U.S.	B3	106
Blue Nile (Al-Baḩr al-Azraq) (Abay), stm., Afr.	F7	56
Blue Point, Me., U.S.	g7	126
Blue Rapids, Ks., U.S.	C7	123
Blue Ridge, Alta., Can.	B3	98
Blue Ridge, Ga., U.S.	B2	117
Blue Ridge, In., U.S.	E6	121
Blue Ridge, Va., U.S.	C3	153
Blue Ridge, mts., U.S.	D10	106
Blue Ridge Lake, res., Ga., U.S.	B2	117
Blue Ridge Summit, Pa., U.S.	G7	145
Blue River, B.C., Can.	C8	99
Blue River, Or., U.S.	C4	144
Blue River, Wi., U.S.	E3	156
Bluesky, Alta., Can.	A1	98
Blue Springs, Al., U.S.	D4	108
Blue Springs, Mo., U.S.	h11	132
Blue Springs, Ne., U.S.	D9	134
Bluestone, stm., W.V., U.S.	D3	155
Bluestone Lake, res., U.S.	D4	155
Bluevale, Ont., Can.	D3	103
Bluewater, N.M., U.S.	B2	138
Bluewell, W.V., U.S.	D3	155
Bluff, N.Z.	G2	72
Bluff, Ut., U.S.	F6	151
Bluff City, Ar., U.S.	D2	111
Bluff City, Il., U.S.	E4	120
Bluff City, Tn., U.S.	C11	149
Bluff Creek, stm., Ks., U.S.	E4	123
Bluff Creek, stm., Ok., U.S.	A4	143
Bluff Lake, res., Ms., U.S.	B5	131
Bluff Mountain, mtn., Vt., U.S.	B5	152
Bluff Park, Al., U.S.	g7	108
Bluffs, Il., U.S.	D3	120
Bluffton, Ga., U.S.	E2	117
Bluffton, In., U.S.	C7	121
Bluffton, Mn., U.S.	D3	130
Bluffton, Oh., U.S.	B2	142
Bluffton, S.C., U.S.	G6	147
Bluford, Il., U.S.	E5	120
Blumberg, Ger.	H8	10
Blumenau, Braz.	D14	80
Blunt, S.D., U.S.	C6	148
Bly, Or., U.S.	E5	144
Blying Sound, strt., Ak., U.S.	h17	109
Blyth, Ont., Can.	D3	103
Blythe, Ca., U.S.	F6	112
Blythe, Ga., U.S.	C4	117
Blytheville, Ar., U.S.	B6	111
Bø, Nor.	G14	6
Bø, Nor.	L11	6
Bo, S.L.	H4	64
Boaco, Nic.	E9	92
Boaco, dept., Nic.	E9	92
Boa Esperança, Braz.	F6	79
Boa Esperança, Reprêsa, res., Braz.	E10	76
Boalsburg, Pa., U.S.	E6	145
Boa Nova, Braz.	C8	79
Boardman, Oh., U.S.	A5	142
Boardman, Or., U.S.	B7	144
Boatman, Austl.	F7	70
Boa Vista, Braz.	F12	84
Boa Vista, i., C.V.	m17	64a
Boavita, Col.	D6	84
Boaz, Al., U.S.	A3	108
Bobai, China	C10	40
Bobbili, India	C7	46
Bobbio, Italy	E4	18
Bobcaygeon, Ont., Can.	C6	103
Böblingen, Ger.	G9	10
Bobo Dioulasso, Burkina	F7	64
Bobolice, Pol.	B16	10
Bobonaza, stm., Ec.	I4	84
Bobonong, Bots.	C9	66
Bobr, Bela.	G12	22
Bobrujsk, Bela.	H12	22
Bobtown, Pa., U.S.	G2	145
Bobures, Ven.	C7	84
Boby, Pic, mtn., Madag.	s22	67b
Boca Brava, Isla, i., Pan.	I12	92
Boca Chica Key, i., Fl., U.S.	H5	116
Boca Ciega Bay, b., Fl., U.S.	p10	116
Boca del Monte, Pan.	I12	92
Boca de Pozo, Ven.	B10	84
Boca do Acre, Braz.	C8	82
Boca Grande, Fl., U.S.	F4	116
Bocaiúva, Braz.	D7	79
Bocanda, I.C.	H7	64
Boca Raton, Fl., U.S.	F6	116
Bocas del Toro, Pan.	C1	84
Bocas del Toro, prov., Pan.	I12	92
Bocas del Toro, Archipiélago de, is., Pan.	H12	92
Bocay, Nic.	C9	92
Bocay, stm., Nic.	C9	92
Bochnia, Pol.	F20	10
Bocholt, Ger.	D6	10
Bochum, Ger.	D7	10
Bochum, S. Afr.	D9	66
Bocón, Caño, stm., Col.	F8	84
Boconó, Ven.	C7	84
Bodajbo, Russia	F14	28
Bodcau Creek, stm., Ar., U.S.	D2	111
Bodcaw, Ar., U.S.	D2	111
Bode, Ia., U.S.	B3	122
Bodega Head, c., Ca., U.S.	C2	112
Bodegraven, Neth.	D6	12
Bodélé, reg., Chad	E4	56
Boden, Swe.	I17	6
Bodensee (Lake Constance), l., Eur.	E16	14
Bodh Gaya, India	E11	42
Bodie Island, i., N.C., U.S.	B7	140
Bodināyakkanūr, India	G4	46
Bodkin Point, c., Md., U.S.	B5	127
Bodo, Alta., Can.	C5	98
Bodø, Nor.	H14	6
Bodoquena, Serra da, plat., Braz.	I13	82
Bodrog, stm., Eur.	A5	20
Bodrum, Tur.	L11	20
Boelus, Ne., U.S.	C7	134
Boende, Zaire	B4	58
Boeo, Capo, c., Italy	L7	18
Boerne, Tx., U.S.	E3	150
Boeuf, stm., La., U.S.	C4	125
Boeuf, Bayou, stm., La., U.S.	D3	125
Boeuf, Lake, l., La., U.S.	k10	125
Bogale, Burma	F3	40
Bogalusa, La., U.S.	D6	125
Bogan, stm., Austl.	H7	70
Bogandé, Burkina	E9	64
Bogard, Mo., U.S.	B4	132
Bogart, Ga., U.S.	C3	117
Bogata, Tx., U.S.	C5	150
Boğazlıyan, Tur.	B3	48
Bogda Shan, mts., China	C4	30
Boger City, N.C., U.S.	B1	140
Boggabri, Austl.	H9	70
Boggstown, In., U.S.	E6	121
Bogo, Phil.	C7	38
Bogol'ubovo, Russia	E23	22
Bogong, Mount, mtn., Austl.	K7	70
Bogor, Indon.	j13	39a
Bogorodick, Russia	H21	22
Bogorodsk, Russia	E26	22
Bogota, N.J., U.S.	h8	137
Bogota, Tn., U.S.	A2	149
Bogotá see Santa Fe de Bogotá, Col.	E5	84
Bogotol, Russia	F9	28
Bogou, Togo	F10	64
Bogra, Bngl.	H13	44
Bogué, Maur.	C2	64
Bogue, Ks., U.S.	C4	123
Bogue Chitto, Ms., U.S.	D3	131
Bogue Chitto, stm., U.S.	D5	125
Bogue Inlet, b., N.C., U.S.	C5	140
Bogue Phalia, stm., Ms., U.S.	B3	131
Boguševsk, Bela.	G13	22
Bo Hai (Gulf of Chihli), b., China	E8	32
Bohai Haixia, strt., China	E9	32
Bohain-en-Vermandois, Fr.	C10	14
Bohan, Bel.	I6	12
Bohemia see Čechy, hist. reg., Czech.	F14	10
Bohemian Forest, mts., Eur.	F12	10
Bohicon, Benin	H11	64
Bohol, i., Phil.	D7	38
Bohol Sea, Phil.	D7	38
Boiaçu, Braz.	H12	84
Boiestown, N.B., Can.	C3	101
Boigu Island, i., Austl.	A8	68
Boiling Springs, N.C., U.S.	B1	140
Boiling Springs, Pa., U.S.	F7	145
Boipeba, Ilha de, i., Braz.	B9	79
Bois, Rio dos, stm., Braz.	E3	79
Bois Blanc Island, i., Mi., U.S.	C6	129
Bois Brule, stm., Wi., U.S.	B2	156
Boischâtel, Que., Can.	C6	104
Boisdale, N.S., Can.	C9	101
Bois D'Arc, Mo., U.S.	D4	132
Bois-des-Filion, Que., Can.	p19	104
Bois de Sioux, stm., Mn., U.S.	E2	130
Boise, Id., U.S.	F2	119
Boise, co., Id., U.S.	F3	119
Boise City, Ok., U.S.	e8	143
Bois Fort, Mn., U.S.	B5	130
Boissevain, Man., Can.	E1	100
Boissevain, Va., U.S.	e10	153
Boistfort Peak, mtn., Wa., U.S.	C2	154
Boisvert, Pointe au, c., Que., Can.	A8	104
Bojayá, stm., Col.	D4	84
Bojeador, Cape, c., Phil.	I19	39b
Bojnūrd, Iran	C14	48
Bojonegoro, Indon.	j15	39a
Boju, Nig.	H13	64
Bojuru, Braz.	F13	80
Bokani, Nig.	G12	64
Bokchito, Ok., U.S.	C5	143
Boké, Gui.	F2	64
Bokeelia, Fl., U.S.	F4	116
Bokhara, stm., Austl.	G7	70
Bokino, Russia	I24	22
Bokolako, Sen.	E3	64
Bokoshe, Ok., U.S.	B7	143
Boksitogorsk, Russia	B16	22
Bokungu, Zaire	B4	58
Bol, Cro.	F11	18
Bolama, Gui.-B.	F2	64
Bolaños, stm., Mex.	F8	90
Bolaños de Calatrava, Spain	G8	16
Bolbec, Fr.	C7	14
Bolchov, Russia	H19	22
Bolckow, Mo., U.S.	A3	132
Boles, Ar., U.S.	C1	111
Bolesławiec, Pol.	D15	10
Boleszkowice, Pol.	C14	10
Boley, Ok., U.S.	B5	143
Bolgatanga, Ghana	F9	64
Bolgrad, Ukr.	D12	20
Boli, China	B13	30
Boli, Sud.	N5	60
Boligee, Al., U.S.	C1	108
Boling, Tx., U.S.	E5	150
Bolingbrook, Il., U.S.	k8	120
Bolinger, Al., U.S.	D1	108
Bolívar, Col.	G4	84
Bolívar, Col.	E4	84
Bolívar, Col.	E4	84
Bolívar, Peru	B3	82
Bolivar, Mo., U.S.	D4	132
Bolivar, N.Y., U.S.	C2	139
Bolivar, Oh., U.S.	B4	142
Bolivar, Tn., U.S.	B3	149
Bolivar, W.V., U.S.	B7	155
Bolívar, state, Ven.	D11	84
Bolívar, prov., Ec.	H3	84
Bolívar, dept., Col.	C5	84
Bolivar, co., Ms., U.S.	B3	131
Bolívar, Cerro, mtn., Ven.	D11	84
Bolivar, Lake, l., Ms., U.S.	B3	131
Bolívar, Pico, mtn., Ven.	C7	84
Bolivia, ctry., S.A.	F8	74
Bollène, Fr.	H11	14
Bollinger, co., Mo., U.S.	D7	132
Bollnäs, Swe.	K15	6
Bollon, Austl.	G7	70
Bollullos par del Condado, Spain	H5	16
Bolobo, Zaire	B3	58
Bolochovo, Russia	G20	22
Bologna, Italy	E6	18
Bolognesi, Peru	B5	82
Bologoje, Russia	D17	22
Bolomba, Zaire	A3	58
Bolonchén de Rejón, Mex.	G15	90
Bolotino, Mol.	B11	20
Bolotnoje, Russia	F14	26
Bolovens, Plateau des, plat., Laos	G9	40
Bol'šaja Balachn'a, stm., Russia	C12	28
Bol'šaja Cheta, stm., Russia	D14	26
Bol'šaja Čuja, stm., Russia	F14	28
Bol'šaja Ižora, Russia	B12	22
Bol'šaja Kuonamka, stm., Russia	D13	28
Bol'šaja Lipovica, Russia	I24	22
Bol'šaja Murta, Russia	F16	26
Bol'šaja Višera, Russia	C15	22
Bol'šakovo, Russia	G4	22
Bolsena, Italy	G6	18
Bolsena, Lago di, l., Italy	G6	18
Bol'šereck, Russia	G23	28
Bol'ševik, Bela.	I13	22
Bol'ševik, Russia	E21	28
Bol'ševik, ostrov, i., Russia	B12	28
Bol'šezemel'skaja Tundra, reg., Russia	D9	26
Bol'šoj An'uj, stm., Russia	D24	28
Bol'šoj Begičev, ostrov, i., Russia	C14	28
Bol'šoje Michajlovskoje, Russia	E21	22
Bol'šoje Polpino, Russia	H17	22
Bol'šoj Jenisej, stm., Russia	G11	28
Bol'šoj Kavkaz (Caucasus), mts.	I6	26
Bol'šoj L'achovskij, ostrov, i., Russia	C20	28
Bol'šoj Tal'cy, Russia	B16	22
Bol'šoj T'uters, ostrov, i., Russia	B10	22
Bol'šoj Uzen', stm., Asia	H7	26
Bolton, Ms., U.S.	C3	131
Bolton, N.C., U.S.	C4	140
Bolton Lakes, l., Ct., U.S.	B6	114
Bolton Landing, N.Y., U.S.	B7	139
Bolu, Tur.	G14	4
Boluntay, China	B15	44
Boluochi, China	B7	32
Bóly, Hung.	J18	10
Bolzano (Bozen), Italy	C6	18
Boma, Zaire	C2	58
Bomaderry, Austl.	J9	70
Bombala, Austl.	K8	70
Bombarral, Port.	F2	16
Bombay, India	C2	46
Bombay Hook Island, i., De., U.S.	C4	115
Bomberai, Semenanjung, pen., Indon.	F9	38
Bom Despacho, Braz.	E6	79
Bomei, China	M4	34
Bom Jardim de Goiás, Braz.	D2	79
Bom Jesus da Lapa, Braz.	B7	79
Bom Jesus de Goiás, Braz.	E4	79
Bomoseen, Vt., U.S.	D2	152
Bomoseen, Lake, l., Vt., U.S.	D2	152
Bom Retiro, Braz.	D14	80
Bom Sucesso, Braz.	G3	79
Bom Sucesso, Braz.	F13	82
Bomu (Mbomou), stm., Afr.	H5	56
Bon, Cap, c., Tun.	L6	18
Bon Accord, Alta., Can.	C4	98
Bon Air, Tn., U.S.	D8	149
Bon Air, Va., U.S.	C5	153
Bonaire, Ga., U.S.	D3	117
Bonaire, i., Neth. Ant.	H10	94
Bonampak, hist., Mex.	I14	90
Bonanza, Nic.	C10	92
Bonanza, Ar., U.S.	B1	111
Bonanza, Or., U.S.	E5	144
Bonanza Peak, mtn., Wa., U.S.	A5	154
Bonao, Dom. Rep.	E9	94
Bonaparte, Ia., U.S.	D6	122
Bonaparte, Mount, mtn., Wa., U.S.	A6	154
Bonaparte Archipelago, is., Austl.	B5	68
Bonaparte Lake, l., B.C., Can.	D7	99
Bon Aqua, Tn., U.S.	B4	149
Bonarbridge, Scot., U.K.	D9	8
Bonarcado, Italy	I3	18
Bonasila Dome, mtn., Ak., U.S.	C7	109
Bonaventure, Que., Can.	A4	101
Bonavista, Newf., Can.	D5	102
Bonavista, Cape, c., Newf., Can.	D5	102
Bonavista Bay, b., Newf., Can.	D5	102
Bond, Ky., U.S.	C5	124

Name — Map Ref. — Page

Bond, Ms., U.S. E4 131
Bond, co., Il., U.S. E4 120
Bondeno, Italy E6 18
Bondo, Zaire H5 56
Bondoukou, I.C. G8 64
Bondsville, Ma., U.S. B3 128
Bonduel, Wi., U.S. D5 156
Bondurant, Ia., U.S. C4 122
Bondurant, Wy., U.S. C2 157
Bondville, Il., U.S. C5 120
Bone, Teluk, b., Indon. F7 38
Bone Gap, Il., U.S. E6 120
Bone Lake, l., Wi., U.S. C1 156
Bonesteel, S.D., U.S. D7 148
Bonete, Cerro, mtn., Arg. D4 80
Bonete Chico, Cerro, mtn., Arg. E4 80
Bonfouca, La., U.S. h12 125
Bonga, Eth. N9 60
Bongak, Sud. N7 60
Bongandanga, Zaire A4 58
Bongo, Massif des, mts., Cen. Afr. Rep. M2 60
Bongor, Chad F4 56
Bongouanou, I.C. H7 64
Bonham, Tx., U.S. C4 150
Bon Homme, co., S.D., U.S. D8 148
Bonhomme, Morne, mtn., Haiti E8 94
Bon Homme Colony, S.D., U.S. E8 148
Bonifacio, Fr. m24 15a
Bonifacio, Strait of, strt., Eur. H4 18
Bonifay, Fl., U.S. u16 116
Bonita, La., U.S. B4 125
Bonita Springs, Fl., U.S. F5 116
Bonito, Braz. I13 82
Bonito, stm., Braz. D3 79
Bonito, Pico, mtn., Hond. B8 92
Bonkoukou, Niger D11 64
Bonn, Ger. E7 10
Bonneau, S.C., U.S. E8 147
Bonneauville, Pa., U.S. G7 145
Bonne Bay (Woody Point), Newf., Can. D3 102
Bonne Bay, b., Newf., Can. D3 102
Bonneia, Eth. O9 60
Bonne Idee, Bayou, stm., La., U.S. B4 125
Bonner, Mt., U.S. D3 133
Bonner, co., Id., U.S. A2 119
Bonners Ferry, Id., U.S. A2 119
Bonner Springs, Ks., U.S. C9 123
Bonnétable, Fr. D7 14
Bonnet Carre Floodway, La., U.S. h11 125
Bonne Terre, Mo., U.S. D7 132
Bonnet Plume, stm., Yukon, Can. C6 96
Bonneval, Fr. D8 14
Bonneville, Fr. F13 14
Bonneville, co., Id., U.S. F7 119
Bonneville Dam, U.S. B4 144
Bonneville Peak, mtn., Id., U.S. F6 119
Bonneville Salt Flats, pl., Ut., U.S. C2 151
Bonney Lake, Wa., U.S. B3 154
Bonnie, Il., U.S. E5 120
Bonnie Doone, N.C., U.S. B4 140
Bonnie Rock, Austl. F3 68
Bonnieville, Ky., U.S. C4 124
Bonnots Mill, Mo., U.S. C6 132
Bonny, Nig. I13 64
Bonny Reservoir, res., Co., U.S. B8 113
Bonnyville, Alta., Can. B5 98
Bono, Ar., U.S. B5 111
Bonorva, Italy I3 18
Bon Secour, Al., U.S. E2 108
Bonsecours, Fr. C8 14
Bonshaw, P.E.I., Can. C6 101
Bonthe, S.L. H3 64
Bontoc, Phil. m19 39b
Bon Wier, Tx., U.S. D6 150
Bonyhád, Hung. I18 10
Booischot, Bel. F6 12
Bookaloo, Austl. H2 70
Book Cliffs, clf, U.S. D6 151
Booker, Tx., U.S. A2 150
Booker T. Washington National Monument, Va., U.S. C3 153
Boola, Gui. G5 64
Boom, Bel. F5 12
Boomarra, Austl. B4 70
Boomer, W.V., U.S. C3 155
Boonah, Austl. G10 70
Boone, Co., U.S. C6 113
Boone, Ia., U.S. B4 122
Boone, N.C., U.S. A1 140
Boone, co., Ar., U.S. A2 111
Boone, co., Il., U.S. A5 120
Boone, co., In., U.S. D4 121
Boone, co., Ia., U.S. B3 122
Boone, co., Ky., U.S. B5 124
Boone, co., Mo., U.S. B5 132
Boone, co., Ne., U.S. C7 134
Boone, co., W.V., U.S. C3 155
Boone, stm., Ia., U.S. B4 122
Boone Lake, res., Tn., U.S. C11 149
Boones Mill, Va., U.S. C3 153
Booneville, Ar., U.S. B2 111
Booneville, Ky., U.S. C6 124
Booneville, Ms., U.S. A5 131
Boonsboro, Md., U.S. A2 127
Boons Pond, l., Ma., U.S. g10 128
Boonton, N.J., U.S. B4 137
Boonville, Ca., U.S. C2 112
Boonville, In., U.S. H3 121
Boonville, Mo., U.S. C5 132
Boonville, N.Y., U.S. B5 139
Boonville, N.C., U.S. A2 140
Boopi, stm., Bol. G8 82
Boorama, Som. G9 56
Boorindal, Austl. H7 70
Boorowa, Austl. J8 70
Boosaaso, Som. F10 56
Booth, Al., U.S. C3 108
Boothbay, Me., U.S. E3 126
Boothbay Harbor, Me., U.S. E3 126
Boothia, Gulf of, b., N.W. Ter., Can. B14 96
Boothia Peninsula, pen., N.W. Ter., Can. B14 96
Booths Creek, stm., W.V., U.S. h11 155
Boothville, La., U.S. E6 125
Booué, Gabon B2 58
Bophuthatswana, ctry., Afr. F7 66
Bopo, Nig. H13 64
Boquerón, Pan. I12 92
Boquerón, dept., Para. B8 80
Boquilla, Presa de la, res., Mex. D7 90
Boquillas del Carmen, Mex. C8 90
Bor, Czech. F12 10
Bor, Russia E27 22
Bor, Sud. N6 60
Bor, Tur. C3 48
Bor, Yugo. E6 20
Boraha, Nosy, i., Madag. p23 67b
Borah Peak, mtn., Id., U.S. E5 119
Borås, Swe. M13 6
Borāzjān, Iran G11 48
Borba, Braz. J13 84
Borba, Port. G4 16
Borda, Cape, c., Austl. J2 70
Bordeaux, Fr. H6 14
Bordelonville, La., U.S. C4 125
Borden, Sask., Can. E2 105
Borden, In., U.S. H6 121
Borden, co., Tx., U.S. C2 150
Borden Peninsula, pen., N.W. Ter., Can. B16 96
Bordentown, N.J., U.S. C3 137
Borderland, W.V., U.S. D2 155
Borders, prov., Scot., U.K. F10 8
Bordertown, Austl. K4 70
Borđeyri, Ice. B3 6a
Bordighera, Italy F2 18
Bordj Bou Arreridj, Alg. B13 62
Bordj Menaïel, Alg. B12 62
Bordj Omar Idriss, Alg. F14 62
Bordj Sidi Toui, Tun. D16 62
Boreda, Eth. N9 60
Borgå (Porvoo), Fin. K19 6
Borger, Tx., U.S. B2 150
Borgholm, Swe. M15 6
Borghorst, Ger. C7 10
Borgne, Lake, b., La., U.S. D6 125
Borgosesia, Italy D3 18
Boring, Or., U.S. B4 144
Borinskoje, Russia I22 22
Borisoglebsk, Russia G6 26
Borisoglebskij, Russia D22 22
Borisov, Bela. G11 22
Borja, Peru J4 84
Borken, Ger. D6 10
Borkoviči, Bela. F11 22
Borkum, i., Ger. B6 10
Borlänge, Swe. K14 6
Bormes-les-Mimosas, Fr. I13 14
Bormio, Italy C5 18
Borna, Ger. D13 10
Borneo (Kalimantan), i., Asia N11 40
Bornholm, i., Den. N14 6
Boro, stm., Sud. M3 60
Borodarou, Benin F11 64
Borodino, Russia F18 22
Borodino, Ukr. C13 20
Borogoncy, Russia E18 28
Boromo, Burkina F8 64
Boron, Ca., U.S. E5 112
Boroviči, Russia C16 22
Borovsk, Russia F19 22
Borovucha, Bela. F11 22
Borrachudo, stm., Braz. E6 79
Borrazópolis, Braz. G3 79
Borrego Springs, Ca., U.S. F5 112
Borriana, Spain F11 16
Borroloola, Austl. C7 68
Borş, Rom. B5 20
Borşa, Rom. B8 20
Borsad, India I5 44
Borsod-Abaúj-Zemplén, co., Hung. G21 10
Borth, Wales, U.K. I9 8
Bort-les-Orgues, Fr. G9 14
Boruca, C.R. H11 92
Borūjen, Iran F11 48
Borūjerd, Iran E10 48
Borz'a, Russia G15 28
Bosa, Italy I3 18
Bosanska Dubica, Bos. D11 18
Bosanska Gradiška, Bos. D12 18
Bosanski Novi, Bos. D11 18
Bosanski Šamac, Bos. D2 20
Bosavi, Mount, mtn., Pap. N. Gui. G11 38
Boscawen, N.H., U.S. D3 136
Boscobel, Wi., U.S. E3 156
Bose, China C9 40
Boshan, China G5 32
Boshoek, S. Afr. E8 66
Boshrūyeh, Iran E14 48
Bosler, Wy., U.S. E7 157
Bosna, stm., Bos. E13 18
Bosna-Hercegovina see Bosnia and Herzegovina, ctry., Eur. E12 18
Bosnia and Herzegovina, ctry., Eur. G11 4
Bosporus see İstanbul Boğazı, strt., Tur. H13 20
Bosque, N.M., U.S. C3 138
Bosque, co., Tx., U.S. D4 150
Bosque Farms, N.M., U.S. C3 138
Boss, Mo., U.S. D6 132
Bossangoa, Cen. Afr. Rep. G4 56
Bossé Bangou, Niger E10 64
Bossembélé, Cen. Afr. Rep. G4 56
Bossert Estates, N.J., U.S. C3 137
Bossier, co., La., U.S. B2 125
Bossier City, La., U.S. B2 125
Bosso, Dallol, val., Niger E11 64
Bosten Hu, l., China C4 30
Boston, Eng., U.K. I13 8
Boston, Ga., U.S. F3 117
Boston, In., U.S. E8 121
Boston, Ky., U.S. C4 124
Boston, Ma., U.S. B5 128
Boston Bay, b., Ma., U.S. B6 128
Boston Heights, Oh., U.S. h9 142
Boston Mountains, mts., Ar., U.S. B2 111
Bostonnais, stm., Que., Can. B5 104
Bostwick, Fl., U.S. C5 116
Bostwick, Ga., U.S. C3 117
Boswarlos, Newf., Can. D2 102
Boswell, B.C., Can. E9 99
Boswell, In., U.S. C3 121
Boswell, Ok., U.S. C6 143
Boswell, Pa., U.S. F3 145
Bosworth, Mo., U.S. B4 132
Botād, India I4 44
Botany Bay, b., Austl. I9 70
Boteti, stm., Bots. C6 66
Botetourt, co., Va., U.S. C3 153
Botha, Alta., Can. C4 98
Botha's Hill, S. Afr. G10 66
Bothaville, S. Afr. F8 66
Bothell, Wa., U.S. B3 154
Bothnia, Gulf of, b., Eur. J17 6
Bothwell, Ont., Can. E3 103
Bothwell, P.E.I., Can. C7 101
Botija, Ilha da, i., Braz. J11 84
Botkins, Oh., U.S. B1 142
Botoşani, Rom. B10 20
Botoşani, co., Rom. B10 20
Botrange, mtn., Bel. H9 12
Botro, I.C. H7 64
Botsford, Ct., U.S. D2 114
Botswana, ctry., Afr. F4 58
Bottenhavet (Selkämeri), b., Eur. K16 6
Bottenviken (Perämeri), b., Eur. I18 6
Bottineau, N.D., U.S. A5 141
Bottineau, co., N.D., U.S. A4 141
Bottrop, Ger. D6 10
Botucatu, Braz. G4 79
Botwood, Newf., Can. D4 102
Bouaflé, I.C. H7 64
Bou Ahmed, Mor. J6 16
Bouaké, I.C. H7 64
Bouandougou, I.C. G7 64
Bouar, Cen. Afr. Rep. G4 56
Bou Arada, Tun. M4 18
Bouârfa, Mor. D10 62
Bouaye, Fr. E5 14
Bou Bernous, Alg. G9 62
Bouchegouf, Alg. M2 18
Boucherville, Que., Can. D4 104
Bouches-du-Rhône, dept., Fr. I12 14
Bouctouche, N.B., Can. C5 101
Boudreaux, Lake, l., La., U.S. E5 125
Boudry, Switz. E6 13
Boufarik, Alg. B12 62
Bou Ficha, Tun. M5 18
Bougainville, i., Pap. N. Gui. I19 158
Bougouni, Mali F6 64
Bougouriba, stm., Burkina F8 64
Bou Hadjar, Alg. M3 18
Bou Hajar, Tun. N5 18
Bouïra, Alg. B12 62
Boujad, Mor. D7 62
Boujdour, Cap, c., W. Sah. G3 62
Bou Kadir, Alg. B11 62
Bou Khadra, Alg. N3 18
Boukombé, Benin F10 64
Boulder, Austl. F4 68
Boulder, Co., U.S. A5 113
Boulder, Mt., U.S. D4 133
Boulder, co., Co., U.S. A5 113
Boulder City, Nv., U.S. H7 135
Boulevard Heights, Md., U.S. f9 127
Bouli, stm., Burkina E9 64
Boulia, Austl. D3 70
Boulogne-Billancourt, Fr. D9 14
Boulogne-sur-Gesse, Fr. I7 14
Boulogne-sur-Mer, Fr. B8 14
Boulouba, Cen. Afr. Rep. N2 60
Boulouli, Mali D5 64
Boulsa, Burkina E9 64
Bouly, Maur. D4 64
Boumalne, Mor. E8 62
Boûmdeïd, Maur. C5 64
Bouna, I.C. G8 64
Boundary, co., Id., U.S. A2 119
Boundary Bald Mountain, mtn., Me., U.S. C2 126
Boundary Bay, b., Wa., U.S. A3 154
Boundary Peak, mtn., Nv., U.S. F3 135
Bound Brook, N.J., U.S. B3 137
Bountiful, Ut., U.S. C4 151
Bounty Islands, is., N.Z. M21 158
Bouqteb, Alg. C11 62
Boura, Mali E7 64
Bourbeuse, stm., Mo., U.S. C6 132
Bourbon, In., U.S. B5 121
Bourbon, Mo., U.S. C6 132
Bourbon, co., Ks., U.S. E9 123
Bourbon, co., Ky., U.S. B5 124
Bourbon-Lancy, Fr. F10 14
Bourbonnais, Il., U.S. B6 120
Bourbonnais, hist. reg., Fr. F9 14
Bourbonne-les-Bains, Fr. E12 14
Bourem, Mali C9 64
Bourg, La., U.S. E5 125
Bourganeuf, Fr. G8 14
Bourg-en-Bresse, Fr. F12 14
Bourges, Fr. E9 14
Bourgogne (Burgundy), hist. reg., Fr. E11 14
Bourgogne, Canal de, Fr. E11 14
Bourgoin, Fr. G12 14
Bourg-Saint-Andéol, Fr. H11 14
Bourg-Saint-Maurice, Fr. G13 14
Bourke, Austl. H6 70
Bourne, Eng., U.K. I13 8
Bourne, Ma., U.S. C6 128
Bournemouth, Eng., U.K. K12 8
Bourzanga, Burkina E9 64
Bou Saâda, Alg. C13 62
Bou Salem, Tun. M3 18
Bouse, Az., U.S. D2 110
Bou Smail, Alg. B12 62
Boussac, Fr. F9 14
Bousso, Chad F4 56
Boussouma, Burkina E9 64
Bouteldja, Alg. M3 18
Boutilimit, Maur. C2 64
Boutte, La., U.S. k11 125
Bouvetøya, i., Ant. A3 73
Bouza, Niger D13 64
Bou Zadjar, Alg. J10 16
Bøverdal, Nor. K11 6
Bovey, Mn., U.S. C5 130
Bovill, Id., U.S. C2 119
Bovina, Tx., U.S. B1 150
Bovril, Arg. F9 80
Bow, N.H., U.S. D3 136
Bow, stm., Alta., Can. D4 98
Bowang, China D7 34
Bowbells, N.D., U.S. A3 141
Bowden, Alta., Can. D4 98
Bowdish Reservoir, res., R.I., U.S. B1 146
Bowdle, S.D., U.S. B6 148
Bowdoinham, Me., U.S. D3 126
Bowdon, Ga., U.S. C1 117
Bowdon, N.D., U.S. B6 141
Bowen, Arg. H5 80
Bowen, Austl. C8 70
Bowen, Il., U.S. C2 120
Bowers, De., U.S. D4 115
Bowersville, Ga., U.S. B3 117
Bowie, Az., U.S. E6 110
Bowie, Md., U.S. C4 127
Bowie, Tx., U.S. C4 150
Bowie, co., Tx., U.S. C5 150
Bowie Creek, stm., Ms., U.S. D4 131
Bow Island, Alta., Can. E5 98
Bow Lake, l., N.H., U.S. D4 136
Bowlegs, Ok., U.S. B5 143
Bowling Green, Fl., U.S. E5 116
Bowling Green, In., U.S. F4 121
Bowling Green, Ky., U.S. D3 124
Bowling Green, Md., U.S. k13 127
Bowling Green, Mo., U.S. B6 132
Bowling Green, Oh., U.S. A2 142
Bowling Green, S.C., U.S. A5 147
Bowling Green, Va., U.S. B5 153
Bowling Green, Cape, c., Austl. B7 70
Bowlus, Mn., U.S. E4 130
Bowman, Ga., U.S. B3 117
Bowman, N.D., U.S. C2 141
Bowman, S.C., U.S. E6 147
Bowman, co., N.D., U.S. C2 141
Bowman Creek, stm., Pa., U.S. m16 145
Bowman-Haley Lake, res., N.D., U.S. C2 141
Bowmanstown, Pa., U.S. E10 145
Bowral, Austl. J9 70
Bowron, stm., B.C., Can. C7 99
Bowser Lake, l., B.C., Can. A3 99
Bowsman, Man., Can. C1 100
Bowstring Lake, l., Mn., U.S. C5 130
Bow Valley, Ne., U.S. B8 134
Box Butte, co., Ne., U.S. B2 134
Box Butte Creek, stm., Ne., U.S. B3 134
Box Butte Reservoir, res., Ne., U.S. B2 134
Box Elder, Mt., U.S. B6 133
Box Elder, S.D., U.S. C2 148
Box Elder, co., Ut., U.S. B2 151
Box Elder Creek, stm., Co., U.S. A6 113
Boxelder Creek, stm., Mt., U.S. E12 133
Box Elder Creek, stm., Mt., U.S. C8 133
Boxford, Ma., U.S. A6 128
Boxholm, Ia., U.S. B3 122
Boxian, China B4 34
Boxmeer, Neth. E8 12
Boxodoi, China A3 32
Boxtel, Neth. E7 12
Boyacá, dept., Col. E6 84
Boyalık, Tur. H12 20
Boyang, China G5 34
Boyce, La., U.S. C3 125
Boyce, Va., U.S. A4 153
Boyceville, Wi., U.S. C1 156
Boyd, Mn., U.S. F3 130
Boyd, Tx., U.S. C4 150
Boyd, Wi., U.S. D2 156
Boyd, co., Ky., U.S. B7 124
Boyd, co., Ne., U.S. B7 134
Boyden, Ia., U.S. A2 122
Boyd Lake, l., Me., U.S. C4 126
Boyd's Cove, Newf., Can. D4 102
Boydton, Va., U.S. D4 153
Boyer, stm., Ia., U.S. C2 122
Boyer Knob, mtn., Md., U.S. k13 127
Boyertown, Pa., U.S. F10 145
Boykin, Ga., U.S. E2 117
Boykins, Va., U.S. D5 153
Boyle, Alta., Can. B4 98
Boyle, Ire. H5 8
Boyle, Ms., U.S. B3 131
Boyle, co., Ky., U.S. C5 124
Boylston, N.S., Can. D8 101
Boylston, Ma., U.S. B4 128
Boyne, stm., Austl. E9 70
Boyne, stm., Ire. H7 8
Boyne City, Mi., U.S. C6 129
Boyne Falls, Mi., U.S. C6 129
Boynton, Ok., U.S. B6 143
Boynton Beach, Fl., U.S. F6 116
Boysen Reservoir, res., Wy., U.S. C4 157
Boys Ranch, Tx., U.S. B1 150
Boys Town, Ne., U.S. g12 134
Boyuibe, Bol. I10 82
Bozel, Fr. G13 14
Bozeman, Mt., U.S. E5 133
Bozeman Pass, Mt., U.S. E6 133
Bozen see Bolzano, Italy C6 18
Bozhen, China E4 32
Bozman, Md., U.S. C5 127
Bozoum, Cen. Afr. Rep. G4 56
Bozovici, Rom. E5 20
Bra, Italy E2 18
Brabant, prov., Bel. G6 12
Brabant Island, i., Ant. B12 73
Brač, Otok, i., Cro. F11 18
Bracciano, Italy G7 18
Bracciano, Lago di, l., Italy G7 18
Bracebridge, Ont., Can. B5 103
Braceville, Il., U.S. B5 120
Bracken, Sask., Can. H1 105
Bracken, co., Ky., U.S. B5 124
Bracken Lake, l., Man., Can. C2 100
Brackenridge, Pa., U.S. h15 145
Brackettville, Tx., U.S. E2 150
Braço do Norte, Braz. E14 80
Brad, Rom. C6 20
Braddock, Pa., U.S. k14 145
Braddock Heights, Md., U.S. B2 127
Braddock Point, c., S.C., U.S. G6 147
Braddyville, Ia., U.S. D2 122
Braden, Tn., U.S. B2 149
Bradenton, Fl., U.S. E4 116
Bradenville, Pa., U.S. F3 145
Bradford, Ar., U.S. B4 111
Bradford, Il., U.S. B4 120
Bradford, N.H., U.S. D3 136
Bradford, Oh., U.S. B1 142
Bradford, Pa., U.S. C4 145
Bradford, R.I., U.S. F2 146
Bradford, Tn., U.S. A3 149
Bradford, Vt., U.S. D4 152
Bradford, co., Fl., U.S. C4 116
Bradford, co., Pa., U.S. C8 145
Bradford Mountain, mtn., Ct., U.S. B2 114
Bradfordsville, Ky., U.S. C4 124
Bradford [West Gwillimbury], Ont., Can. C5 103
Bradfordwoods, Pa., U.S. h13 145
Bradley, Ar., U.S. D2 111
Bradley, Fl., U.S. E5 116
Bradley, Il., U.S. B6 120
Bradley, Me., U.S. D4 126
Bradley, S.D., U.S. B8 148
Bradley, W.V., U.S. D3 155
Bradley, co., Ar., U.S. D3 111
Bradley, co., Tn., U.S. D9 149
Bradley Beach, N.J., U.S. C4 137
Bradner, Oh., U.S. A2 142
Bradshaw, Md., U.S. B5 127
Bradshaw, Ne., U.S. D8 134
Bradshaw, W.V., U.S. D3 155
Bradshaw Mountains, mts., Az., U.S. C3 110
Bradwell, Sask., Can. F2 105
Brady, Mt., U.S. B5 133
Brady, Ne., U.S. C5 134
Brady, Tx., U.S. D3 150
Braeside, Ont., Can. B8 103
Braga, Port. D3 16
Bragado, Arg. H8 80
Bragança, Braz. D9 76
Bragança, Port. D5 16
Bragança Paulista, Braz. G5 79
Braggadocio, Mo., U.S. E8 132
Braggs, Ok., U.S. B6 143
Braham, Mn., U.S. E5 130
Brāhmanbāria, Bngl. I14 44
Brāhmani, stm., India J11 44
Brahmapur, India C8 46
Brahmaputra (Yarlung), stm., Asia G15 44
Braich y Pwll, c., Wales, U.K. I9 8
Braidwood, Austl. J8 70
Braidwood, Il., U.S. B5 120
Brăila, Rom. D11 20
Brăila, co., Rom. D11 20
Brainard, Ne., U.S. C9 134
Braine-l'Alleud (Eigenbrakel), Bel. G5 12
Braine-le-Comte ('s-Gravenbrakel), Bel. G5 12
Brainerd, Mn., U.S. D4 130
Braintree, Ma., U.S. B5 128
Brake, Ger. B8 10
Brakwater, Nmb. D3 66
Bralorne, B.C., Can. D6 99
Braman, Ok., U.S. A4 143
Brampton, Ont., Can. D5 103
Bramsche, Ger. C7 10
Bramwell, W.V., U.S. D3 155
Branch, Newf., Can. E5 102
Branch, Ar., U.S. B2 111
Branch, co., Mi., U.S. G5 129
Branch, stm., R.I., U.S. B3 146
Branch, stm., Wi., U.S. h10 156
Branch Lake, l., Me., U.S. D4 126
Branchland, W.V., U.S. C2 155
Branch Village, R.I., U.S. B3 146
Branchville, Al., U.S. B3 108
Branchville, Ct., U.S. D2 114
Branchville, S.C., U.S. E6 147
Branco, stm., Braz. I13 82
Branco, stm., Braz. C7 82
Branco, stm., Braz. C11 82
Branco, stm., Braz. C9 82
Branco, stm., Braz. C11 82
Branco, stm., Braz. H12 84
Brandberg, mtn., Nmb. C2 66
Brandbu, Nor. K12 6
Brandenburg, Ger. C12 10
Brandenburg, Ky., U.S. C3 124
Brandenburg, state, Ger. C13 10
Brand-Erbisdorf, Ger. E13 10
Brandon, Man., Can. E2 100
Brandon, Fl., U.S. E4 116
Brandon, Ia., U.S. B6 122
Brandon, Mn., U.S. E3 130
Brandon, Ms., U.S. C4 131
Brandon, S.C., U.S. B3 147
Brandon, S.D., U.S. D9 148
Brandon, Vt., U.S. D2 152
Brandon, Wi., U.S. E5 156
Brandsen, Arg. H9 80
Brandsville, Mo., U.S. E6 132
Brandt, S.D., U.S. C9 148
Brandvlei, S. Afr. H5 66
Brandy Peak, mtn., Or., U.S. E3 144
Brandýs nad Labem, Czech. E14 10
Brandy Station, Va., U.S. B5 153
Brandywine, Md., U.S. C4 127
Brandywine, W.V., U.S. C5 155
Brandywine Creek, stm., U.S. A3 115
Branford, Ct., U.S. D4 114
Branford, Fl., U.S. C4 116
Branford Hills, Ct., U.S. D4 114
Braniewo, Pol. A19 10
Branquinho, stm., Braz. A6 82
Bransby, Austl. G5 70
Bransfield Strait, strt., Ant. B12 73
Brańsk, Pol. C22 10
Br'ansk, Russia H17 22
Branson, Mo., U.S. E4 132
Brant, Alta., Can. D4 98
Brantford, Ont., Can. D4 103
Brant Lake, N.Y., U.S. B7 139
Brantley, Al., U.S. D3 108
Brantley, co., Ga., U.S. E4 117
Brant Rock, Ma., U.S. B6 128
Brantville, N.B., Can. B5 101
Branxholme, Austl. K4 70
Bras-d'Or, N.S., Can. C9 101
Bras d'Or Lake, l., N.S., Can. D9 101
Brashear, Mo., U.S. A5 132
Brasiléia, Braz. D7 82
Brasília, Braz. C5 79
Brasília, Parque Nacional de, Braz. C4 79
Brasília de Minas, Braz. D6 79
Braşov, Rom. D9 20
Braşov, co., Rom. D8 20
Brasstown Bald, mtn., Ga., U.S. B3 117
Brassua Lake, res., Me., U.S. C3 126
Břasy, Czech. F13 10
Bratca, Rom. C6 20
Bratenahl, Oh., U.S. g9 142
Bratislava, Slov. G17 10
Bratsk, Russia F12 28
Bratskoje vodochranilišče, res., Russia F18 26
Bratt, Fl., U.S. u14 116
Brattleboro, Vt., U.S. F3 152
Braulio Carrillo, Parque Nacional, C.R. G10 92
Braúnas, Braz. E7 79
Braunau [am Inn], Aus. G13 10
Braunschweig (Brunswick), Ger. C10 10
Brava, i., C.V. m16 64a
Brava, Costa, Spain D15 16
Brava, Laguna, l., Arg. E4 80
Brava, Punta, c., Ur. H10 80
Bravičа, Mol. B12 20
Bravo, Cerro, mtn., Bol. G9 82
Bravo, Cerro, mtn., Peru A2 82
Bravo del Norte (Rio Grande), stm., N.A. F6 106
Brawley, Ca., U.S. F6 112
Brawley Peaks, mts., Nv., U.S. E3 135
Braxton, co., W.V., U.S. C4 155
Bray, Ire. H7 8
Bray, Ok., U.S. C4 143
Braymer, Mo., U.S. B4 132
Brazeau, stm., Alta., Can. C2 98
Brazil, In., U.S. E3 121
Brazil, Tn., U.S. B2 149
Brazil (Brasil), ctry., S.A. F8 76
Brazil Lake, N.S., Can. F4 101
Brazoria, Tx., U.S. r14 150
Brazoria, co., Tx., U.S. E5 150
Brazos, co., Tx., U.S. D4 150
Brazos, stm., Tx., U.S. D4 150
Brazzaville, Congo B3 58
Brčko, Bos. E2 20
Brea, Ca., U.S. n13 112
Breadalbane, Austl. D3 70
Bread Loaf Mountain, mtn., Vt., U.S. D3 152
Breakenridge, Mount, mtn., B.C., Can. E7 99
Breakeyville, Que., Can. o17 104
Brea Pozo, Arg. E7 80
Breathitt, co., Ky., U.S. C6 124
Breaux Bridge, La., U.S. D4 125
Breaza, Rom. D9 20
Brécey, Fr. D5 14
Brechin, Ont., Can. C5 103
Brechin, Scot., U.K. E11 8
Breckenridge, Co., U.S. B4 113
Breckenridge, Mi., U.S. E6 129
Breckenridge, Mn., U.S. D2 130
Breckenridge, Mo., U.S. B4 132
Breckenridge, Ok., U.S. A4 143
Breckenridge, Tx., U.S. C3 150
Breckinridge, co., Ky., U.S. C3 124
Brecksville, Oh., U.S. A4 142
Břeclav, Czech. G16 10
Brecon, Wales, U.K. J10 8
Breda, Neth. E6 12
Breda, Ia., U.S. B3 122
Bredasdorp, S. Afr. J5 66
Bredenbury, Sask., Can. G4 105
Breese, Il., U.S. E4 120
Breezand, Neth. C6 12
Breezy Point, Mn., U.S. D4 130
Bregenz, Aus. H9 10
Bréhal, Fr. D5 14
Breiðafjörður, b., Ice. B2 6a
Brejo, Braz. D10 76
Brejões, Braz. B9 79
Brekken, Nor. J12 6
Brekstad, Nor. J11 6
Bremen, Ger. B8 10
Bremen, Ga., U.S. C1 117
Bremen, In., U.S. B5 121
Bremen, Ky., U.S. C2 124
Bremen, Oh., U.S. C3 142
Bremer, co., Ia., U.S. B5 122
Bremerhaven, Ger. B8 10
Bremerton, Wa., U.S. B3 154
Bremervörde, Ger. B9 10
Bremond, Tx., U.S. D4 150
Brenham, Tx., U.S. D4 150
Brenner Pass, Eur. H11 10
Brent, Al., U.S. C2 108
Brent, Fl., U.S. u14 116
Brenton Point, c., R.I., U.S. F5 146
Brentwood, Ca., U.S. h9 112
Brentwood, Md., U.S. f9 127
Brentwood, Mo., U.S. f13 132
Brentwood, N.H., U.S. E4 136
Brentwood, N.Y., U.S. E7 139
Brentwood, Pa., U.S. k14 145
Brentwood, S.C., U.S. k11 147
Brentwood, Tn., U.S. A5 149
Brescia, Italy D8 18
Breslau see Wrocław, Pol. D17 10
Bresse, reg., Fr. F12 14
Bressuire, Fr. F6 14
Brest, Bela. C23 10
Brest, Fr. D2 14
Bretagne (Brittany), hist. reg., Fr. D3 14
Breteuil, Fr. C9 14
Breteuil-sur-Iton, Fr. D7 14
Breton, Alta., Can. C3 98
Breton Islands, is., La., U.S. E6 125
Breton Sound, strt., La., U.S. E6 125
Brett, Cape, c., N.Z. A5 72
Bretten, Ger. F8 10
Bretton Woods, N.H., U.S. B4 136
Breu, Rio do, stm., Braz. I9 84

Name | Map Ref. | Page

Breukelen, Neth. D7 12
Brevard, N.C., U.S. f10 140
Brevard, co., Fl., U.S. E6 116
Breves, Braz. D8 76
Brevoort Lake, l., Mi., U.S. B6 129
Brewarrina, Austl. G7 70
Brewer, Me., U.S. D4 126
Brewster, Ks., U.S. C2 123
Brewster, Ma., U.S. C7 128
Brewster, Mn., U.S. G3 130
Brewster, N.Y., U.S. D7 139
Brewster, Oh., U.S. B4 142
Brewster, Wa., U.S. A6 154
Brewster, co., Tx., U.S. E1 150
Brewster, Kap, c., Grnld. B17 86
Brewster, Lake, l., Austl. I7 70
Brewster Islands, is., Ma., U.S. g12 128
Brewton, Al., U.S. D2 108
Brewton, Ga., U.S. D4 117
Brežice, Slo. D10 18
Brézina, Alg. D11 62
Breznik, Bul. G6 20
Bria, Cen. Afr. Rep. N1 60
Brian Boru Peak, mtn., B.C., Can. B4 99
Briançon, Fr. H13 14
Brian Head, mtn., Ut., U.S. F3 151
Briare, Fr. E9 14
Bričany, Mol. A11 20
Bricelyn, Mn., U.S. G5 130
Briceville, Tn., U.S. C9 149
Brick [Township], N.J., U.S. C4 137
Bricquebec, Fr. C5 14
Bridal Veil Falls, wtfl, Ut., U.S. C4 151
Bridesville, B.C., Can. E8 99
Bridgeboro, Ga., U.S. E3 117
Bridgehampton, N.Y., U.S. n16 139
Bridgeport, Al., U.S. A4 108
Bridgeport, Ca., U.S. C4 112
Bridgeport, Ct., U.S. E3 114
Bridgeport, Il., U.S. E6 120
Bridgeport, Mi., U.S. E7 129
Bridgeport, Ne., U.S. C2 134
Bridgeport, Oh., U.S. B5 142
Bridgeport, Pa., U.S. o20 145
Bridgeport, Tx., U.S. C4 150
Bridgeport, Wa., U.S. B6 154
Bridgeport, W.V., U.S. B4 155
Bridger, Mt., U.S. E8 133
Bridger Peak, mtn., Wy., U.S. E5 157
Bridger Range, mts., Mt., U.S. E6 133
Bridgeton, In., U.S. E3 121
Bridgeton, Mo., U.S. C7 132
Bridgeton, N.J., U.S. E2 137
Bridgeton, N.C., U.S. B5 140
Bridgetown, Austl. F3 68
Bridgetown, Barb. H15 94
Bridgetown, N.S., Can. E4 101
Bridgeville, N.S., Can. D7 101
Bridgeville, De., U.S. F3 115
Bridgeville, Pa., U.S. k13 145
Bridgewater, Austl. N7 70
Bridgewater, N.S., Can. E5 101
Bridgewater, Ct., U.S. C2 114
Bridgewater, Ia., U.S. C3 122
Bridgewater, Me., U.S. B5 126
Bridgewater, Ma., U.S. C6 128
Bridgewater, N.J., U.S. B3 137
Bridgewater, S.D., U.S. D8 148
Bridgewater, Vt., U.S. D3 152
Bridgewater, Va., U.S. B4 153
Bridgman, Mi., U.S. G4 129
Bridgton, Me., U.S. D2 126
Bridgwater, Eng., U.K. J10 8
Bridport, Vt., U.S. D2 152
Brie, reg., Fr. D10 14
Briec, Fr. D2 14
Brielle, N.J., U.S. C4 137
Brienne-le-Château, Fr. D11 14
Brienz, Switz. E9 13
Brienzersee, l., Switz. E9 13
Brier Creek, stm., Ga., U.S. C5 117
Briercrest, Sask., Can. G3 105
Brierfield, Al., U.S. B3 108
Briery Knob, mtn., W.V., U.S. C4 155
Briey, Fr. C12 14
Brig, Switz. F9 13
Brigantine, N.J., U.S. E4 137
Brigantine Beach, N.J., U.S. E4 137
Brig Bay, Newf., Can. C3 102
Brigden, Ont., Can. E2 103
Briggs Marsh, sw., R.I., U.S. F6 146
Briggsville, Wi., U.S. E4 156
Brigham City, Ut., U.S. B3 151
Brig Harbour Island, i., Newf., Can. A3 102
Bright, Austl. K7 70
Bright, Ont., Can. D4 103
Brighton, Ont., Can. C7 103
Brighton, Eng., U.K. K13 8
Brighton, Al., U.S. B3 108
Brighton, Co., U.S. B6 113
Brighton, Il., U.S. D3 120
Brighton, Ia., U.S. C6 122
Brighton, Mi., U.S. F7 129
Brighton, N.Y., U.S. B3 139
Brighton, Tn., U.S. B2 149
Brighton Downs, Austl. D4 70
Brighton Indian Reservation, Fl., U.S. E5 116
Brignoles, Fr. I13 14
Brikama, Gam. E1 64
Brilhante, stm., Braz. F1 79
Brilliant, B.C., Can. E9 99
Brilliant, Al., U.S. A2 108
Brilliant, Oh., U.S. B5 142
Brillion, Wi., U.S. D5 156
Brilon, Ger. D8 10
Brimfield, Il., U.S. C4 120
Brimhall, N.M., U.S. B1 138
Brimley, Mi., U.S. B6 129
Brindisi, Italy I12 18
Bringhurst, In., U.S. C5 121
Brinje, Cro. D10 18
Brinkley, Ar., U.S. C4 111
Brinnon, Wa., U.S. B3 154
Brinson, Ga., U.S. F2 117
Brion, Île, i., Que., Can. B8 101
Brioude, Fr. G10 14
Briouze, Fr. D6 14
Brisbane, Austl. F10 70
Briscoe, co., Tx., U.S. B2 150
Bristol, N.B., Can. C2 101
Bristol, Eng., U.K. J11 8
Bristol, Co., U.S. C8 113
Bristol, Ct., U.S. C4 114
Bristol, Fl., U.S. B2 116
Bristol, Ga., U.S. E4 117
Bristol, Il., U.S. B5 120
Bristol, In., U.S. A6 121
Bristol, N.H., U.S. C3 136
Bristol, R.I., U.S. D5 146
Bristol, S.D., U.S. B8 148
Bristol, Tn., U.S. C11 149
Bristol, Vt., U.S. C2 152
Bristol, Va., U.S. f9 153
Bristol, Wi., U.S. F5 156
Bristol, co., Ma., U.S. C5 128
Bristol, co., R.I., U.S. D5 146
Bristol Bay, b., Ak., U.S. D7 109
Bristol [Township], Pa., U.S. F12 145
Bristolville, Oh., U.S. A5 142
Bristow, Ne., U.S. B7 134
Bristow, Ok., U.S. B5 143
Britânia, Braz. C3 79
Britannia Beach, B.C., Can. E6 99
British Antarctic Territory, dep., S.A. B1 73
British Columbia, prov., Can. C6 99
British Honduras see Belize, ctry., N.A. I15 90
British Indian Ocean Territory, dep., Afr. J8 24
British Virgin Islands, dep., N.A. E12 94
Brits, S. Afr. E8 66
Britstown, S. Afr. H6 66
Britt, Ia., U.S. A4 122
Brittany see Bretagne, hist. reg., Fr. D3 14
Britton, Mi., U.S. G7 129
Britton, S.D., U.S. B8 148
Brive-la-Gaillarde, Fr. G8 14
Brixton, Austl. D6 70
Brno, Czech. F16 10
Broa, Ensenada de la, b., Cuba C3 94
Broad, stm., Ga., U.S. B4 117
Broad, stm., S.C., U.S. C5 147
Broadalbin, N.Y., U.S. B6 139
Broadbent, Or., U.S. E2 144
Broad Brook, Ct., U.S. B5 114
Broad Creek, stm., De., U.S. F3 115
Broadford, Scot., U.K. D8 8
Broadford, Va., U.S. f10 153
Broadkill, stm., De., U.S. E4 115
Broadkill Beach, De., U.S. E5 115
Broadlands, Il., U.S. D6 120
Broad Run, stm., Va., U.S. g11 153
Broad Sound, strt., Austl. D8 70
Broad Sound Channel, strt., Austl. D9 70
Broadus, Mt., U.S. E11 133
Broadview, Sask., Can. G4 105
Broadview, Mt., U.S. D8 133
Broadview Heights, Oh., U.S. h9 142
Broadwater, Ne., U.S. C3 134
Broadwater, co., Mt., U.S. D5 133
Broadway, N.C., U.S. B3 140
Broadway, Va., U.S. B4 153
Brocēni, Lat. E5 22
Brochet, Man., Can. f7 100
Brock, Sask., Can. F1 105
Brock, Ne., U.S. D10 134
Brocket, N.D., U.S. A7 141
Brockport, N.Y., U.S. B3 139
Brockton, Ma., U.S. B5 128
Brockton, Mt., U.S. B12 133
Brockton Reservoir, res., Ma., U.S. h11 128
Brockville, Ont., Can. C9 103
Brockway, Pa., U.S. D4 145
Brocton, Il., U.S. D6 120
Brocton, N.Y., U.S. C1 139
Broderick, Sask., Can. F2 105
Brodeur Peninsula, pen., N.W. Ter., Can. B15 96
Brodhead, Ky., U.S. C5 124
Brodhead, Wi., U.S. F4 156
Brodheadsville, Pa., U.S. E11 145
Brodnax, Va., U.S. D4 153
Brodnica, Pol. B19 10
Broken Arrow, Ok., U.S. A6 143
Broken Bay, b., Austl. I9 70
Broken Bow, Ne., U.S. C6 134
Broken Bow, Ok., U.S. C7 143
Broken Bow Lake, res., Ok., U.S. C7 143
Broken Hill, Austl. H4 70
Brokopondo, Sur. B8 76
Brokopondo Stuwmeer, res., Sur. C7 76
Brome, Que., Can. D5 104
Brome, Lac, l., Que., Can. D5 104
Bromley Mountain, mtn., Vt., U.S. E3 152
Bromptonville, Que., Can. D6 104
Bronaugh, Mo., U.S. D3 132
Bronnicy, Russia F21 22
Bronnoje, Bela. I13 22
Bronson, Fl., U.S. C4 116
Bronson, Ia., U.S. B1 122
Bronson, Ks., U.S. E8 123
Bronson, Mi., U.S. G5 129
Bronte, Italy L9 18
Bronte, Tx., U.S. D2 150
Bronwood, Ga., U.S. E2 117
Bronx, co., N.Y., U.S. E7 139
Bronxville, N.Y., U.S. h13 139
Brook, In., U.S. C3 121
Brookdale, Man., Can. D2 100
Brooke, co., W.V., U.S. A4 155
Brookfield, N.S., Can. D6 101
Brookfield, Ct., U.S. D2 114
Brookfield, Ga., U.S. E3 117
Brookfield, Il., U.S. k9 120
Brookfield, Ma., U.S. B3 128
Brookfield, Mo., U.S. B4 132
Brookfield, Va., U.S. *B5 153
Brookfield, Wi., U.S. m11 156
Brookfield Center, Ct., U.S. D2 114
Brookford, N.C., U.S. B1 140
Brookhaven, Ms., U.S. D3 131
Brookhaven, W.V., U.S. h11 155
Brookings, Or., U.S. E2 144
Brookings, S.D., U.S. C9 148
Brookings, co., S.D., U.S. C9 148
Brookland, Ar., U.S. B5 111
Brooklandville, Md., U.S. g10 127
Brooklawn, N.J., U.S. D2 137
Brooklet, Ga., U.S. D5 117
Brooklin, Me., U.S. D4 126
Brookline, Ma., U.S. B5 128
Brookline, N.H., U.S. E3 136
Brooklyn, N.S., Can. E5 101
Brooklyn, Al., U.S. D3 108
Brooklyn, Ct., U.S. B8 114
Brooklyn, In., U.S. E5 121
Brooklyn, Ia., U.S. C5 122
Brooklyn, Mi., U.S. F6 129
Brooklyn, Ms., U.S. D4 131
Brooklyn, Oh., U.S. h9 142
Brooklyn, S.C., U.S. B6 147
Brooklyn, Wi., U.S. F4 156
Brooklyn Center, Mn., U.S. E5 130
Brooklyn Park, Md., U.S. h11 127
Brooklyn Park, Mn., U.S. m12 130
Brookneal, Va., U.S. C4 153
Brook Park, Oh., U.S. h9 142
Brookport, Il., U.S. F5 120
Brooks, Alta., Can. D5 98
Brooks, Ky., U.S. g11 124
Brooks, Me., U.S. D3 126
Brooks, Mn., U.S. C2 130
Brooks, Or., U.S. h12 144
Brooks, co., Ga., U.S. F3 117
Brooks, co., Tx., U.S. F3 150
Brooks Air Force Base, mil., Tx., U.S. k7 150
Brookshire, Tx., U.S. E5 150
Brookside, Al., U.S. f7 108
Brookside, Co., U.S. C5 113
Brookside, De., U.S. B3 115
Brooks Peninsula, pen., B.C., Can. D4 99
Brooks Range, mts., Ak., U.S. B9 109
Brookston, In., U.S. C4 121
Brooksville, Fl., U.S. D4 116
Brooksville, Ky., U.S. B5 124
Brooksville, Ms., U.S. B5 131
Brookton, Austl. F3 68
Brookton, Me., U.S. C5 126
Brookvale, Co., U.S. B5 113
Brookville, In., U.S. F8 121
Brookville, Ks., U.S. D6 123
Brookville, Oh., U.S. C1 142
Brookville, Pa., U.S. D3 145
Brookville Lake, res., In., U.S. E7 121
Brookwood, Al., U.S. B2 108
Brookwood, N.J., U.S. C4 137
Broomall, Pa., U.S. p20 145
Broome, Austl. C4 68
Broome, co., N.Y., U.S. C5 139
Broomes Island, Md., U.S. D4 127
Broomfield, Co., U.S. B5 113
Broons, Fr. D4 14
Brooten, Mn., U.S. E3 130
Brora, Scot., U.K. C10 8
Brossard, Que., Can. q20 104
Brotas de Macaúbas, Braz. B7 79
Brou, Fr. D8 14
Broughton, Il., U.S. F5 120
Broughty Ferry, Scot., U.K. E11 8
Broussard, La., U.S. D4 125
Brouwersdam, Neth. E4 12
Brouwershaven, Neth. E4 12
Broward, co., Fl., U.S. F6 116
Browerville, Mn., U.S. D4 130
Brown, co., Il., U.S. D3 120
Brown, co., In., U.S. F5 121
Brown, co., Ks., U.S. C8 123
Brown, co., Mn., U.S. F4 130
Brown, co., Ne., U.S. B6 134
Brown, co., Oh., U.S. D2 142
Brown, co., S.D., U.S. B7 148
Brown, co., Tx., U.S. D3 150
Brown, co., Wi., U.S. D6 156
Brown, Point, c., Wa., U.S. C1 154
Brown City, Mi., U.S. E8 129
Brown Deer, Wi., U.S. m12 156
Brownfield, Tx., U.S. C1 150
Browning, Mo., U.S. A4 132
Browning, Mt., U.S. B3 133
Brownlee, Sask., Can. G2 105
Brownlee Dam, U.S. E2 119
Brownlee Reservoir, res., U.S. C10 144
Browns, Il., U.S. E6 120
Browns, stm., Vt., U.S. B2 152
Brownsboro, Ky., U.S. g11 124
Browns Branch, stm., De., U.S. E3 115
Brownsburg, Que., Can. D3 104
Brownsburg, In., U.S. E5 121
Brownsdale, Mn., U.S. G6 130
Browns Inlet, b., N.C., U.S. C5 140
Browns Mills, N.J., U.S. D3 137
Browns Peak, mtn., Az., U.S. D4 110
Brownstown, Il., U.S. E5 120
Brownstown, In., U.S. G5 121
Brownstown, Pa., U.S. F9 145
Browns Valley, Mn., U.S. E2 130
Brownsville, Fl., U.S. s13 116
Brownsville, In., U.S. E8 121
Brownsville, Ky., U.S. C3 124
Brownsville, Mn., U.S. G7 130
Brownsville, Or., U.S. C4 144
Brownsville, Pa., U.S. F2 145
Brownsville, Tn., U.S. B2 149
Brownsville, Tx., U.S. G4 150
Brownton, Mn., U.S. F4 130
Brownton, W.V., U.S. B4 155
Brownvale, Alta., Can. A2 98
Brownville, Al., U.S. B2 108
Brownville, Me., U.S. C3 126
Brownville, Ne., U.S. D10 134
Brownville, N.Y., U.S. A5 139
Brownville Junction, Me., U.S. C3 126
Brownwood, Mo., U.S. D8 132
Brownwood, Tx., U.S. D3 150
Brownwood, Lake, res., Tx., U.S. D3 150
Browse Island, i., Austl. B4 68
Broxton, Ga., U.S. E4 117
Broža, Bela. I12 22
Bruay-en-Artois, Fr. B9 14
Bruce, Alta., Can. C4 98
Bruce, Ms., U.S. B4 131
Bruce, S.D., U.S. C9 148
Bruce, Wi., U.S. C2 156
Bruce, Mount, mtn., Austl. D3 68
Bruce Crossing, Mi., U.S. m12 129
Brucefield, Ont., Can. D3 103
Bruce National Park, Ont., Can. B3 103
Bruce Peninsula, pen., Ont., Can. B3 103
Bruceton, Tn., U.S. A3 149
Bruceville, In., U.S. G3 121
Bruchsal, Ger. F8 10
Bruck an der Mur, Aus. H15 10
Bruderheim, Alta., Can. C4 98
Bruges (Brugge), Bel. F3 12
Brugg, Switz. D9 13
Brugge (Bruges), Bel. F3 12
Brugge-Gent, Kanaal, Bel. F3 12
Brühl, Ger. E6 10
Bruinisse, Neth. E5 12
Bruin Point, mtn., Ut., U.S. D5 151
Bruja, Cerro, mtn., Pan. H15 92
Brule, Ne., U.S. C4 134
Brule, co., S.D., U.S. D6 148
Brule, stm., U.S. C5 156
Brûlé, Lac, l., Can. F20 96
Brule Lake, l., Mn., U.S. k9 130
Brumadinho, Braz. F6 79
Brumado, Braz. C8 79
Brumath, Fr. D14 14
Brumley Mountain, mtn., Va., U.S. f9 153
Brundidge, Al., U.S. D4 108
Bruneau, Id., U.S. G3 119
Bruneau, stm., U.S. G3 119
Brunei, ctry., Asia E5 38
Brunette Island, i., Newf., Can. E4 102
Bruning, Ne., U.S. D8 134
Brunkild, Man., Can. E3 100
Bruno, Sask., Can. E3 105
Bruno, Ne., U.S. C9 134
Brunson, S.C., U.S. F5 147
Brunswick, Ga., U.S. E5 117
Brunswick, In., U.S. B2 121
Brunswick, Me., U.S. E3 126
Brunswick, Md., U.S. B2 127
Brunswick, Mo., U.S. B4 132
Brunswick, Ne., U.S. B8 134
Brunswick, N.C., U.S. C4 140
Brunswick, Oh., U.S. A4 142
Brunswick, co., N.C., U.S. C4 140
Brunswick, co., Va., U.S. D5 153
Brunswick, Peninsula, pen., Chile G2 78
Brunswick see Braunschweig, Ger. C10 10
Brunswick Naval Air Station, mil., Me., U.S. E3 126
Bruntál, Czech. F17 10
Brus, Laguna de, b., Hond. B10 92
Brush, Co., U.S. A7 113
Brushy Mountain, mtn., Va., U.S. C1 153
Brushy Mountains, mts., N.C., U.S. B1 140
Brus Laguna, Hond. B10 92
Brusly, La., U.S. D4 125
Brusovo, Russia D18 22
Brusque, Braz. D14 80
Brussels, Ont., Can. D3 103
Brussels see Bruxelles, Bel. G5 12
Brusy, Pol. B17 10
Bruthen, Austl. K7 70
Bruxelles (Brussel) (Brussels), Bel. G5 12
Bruyères, Fr. D13 14
Bruzual, Ven. C8 84
Bryan, Oh., U.S. A1 142
Bryan, Tx., U.S. D4 150
Bryan, co., Ga., U.S. D5 117
Bryan, co., Ok., U.S. D5 143
Bryansk see Br'ansk, Russia H17 22
Bryans Road, Md., U.S. C3 127
Bryant, Ar., U.S. C3 111
Bryant, Fl., U.S. F6 116
Bryant, Il., U.S. C3 120
Bryant, In., U.S. C8 121
Bryant, S.D., U.S. C8 148
Bryant Creek, stm., Mo., U.S. E5 132
Bryant Mountain, mtn., Ma., U.S. B2 128
Bryantown, Md., U.S. C4 127
Bryant Pond, Me., U.S. D2 126
Bryantville, Ma., U.S. B6 128
Bryce Canyon National Park, Ut., U.S. F3 151
Bryn Mawr, Wa., U.S. e11 154
Bryson, Tx., U.S. C3 150
Bryson City, N.C., U.S. f9 140
Brzeg, Pol. E17 10
Brzesko, Pol. F20 10
Brzeziny, Pol. D19 10
B-Say-Tah, Sask., Can. G4 105
Bsharrī, Leb. D4 48
Bua Yai, Thai. G7 40
Buba, Gui.-B. F2 64
Bū Bānī, Jabal, mtn., Afr. F3 60
Bubaque, Gui.-B. F2 64
Būbiyān, i., Kuw. G10 48
Bucaramanga, Col. D6 84
Buccaneer Archipelago, is., Austl. C4 68
Buccino, Italy I10 18
Buchanan, Sask., Can. F4 105
Buchanan, Lib. I4 64
Buchanan, Ga., U.S. C1 117
Buchanan, Mi., U.S. G4 129
Buchanan, Tn., U.S. A3 149
Buchanan, Va., U.S. C3 153
Buchanan, co., Ia., U.S. B6 122
Buchanan, co., Mo., U.S. B3 132
Buchanan, co., Va., U.S. e9 153
Buchanan, Lake, l., Austl. C6 70
Buchans, Newf., Can. D3 102
Buchara, Uzb. J10 26
Bucharest see București, Rom. E10 20
Buchholz, Ger. B9 10
Buchloe, Ger. G10 10
Buchs, Switz. D11 13
Buchtel, Oh., U.S. C3 142
Buchy, Fr. C8 14
Buckatunna, Ms., U.S. D5 131
Buck Creek, In., U.S. D4 121
Buck Creek, stm., Ga., U.S. D2 117
Buck Creek, stm., In., U.S. m11 121
Buck Creek, stm., Ky., U.S. C5 124
Bückeburg, Ger. C9 10
Buckeye, Az., U.S. D3 110
Buckeye, W.V., U.S. C4 155
Buckeye Hills, hills, Az., U.S. m7 110
Buckeye Lake, Oh., U.S. C3 142
Buckfield, Me., U.S. D2 126
Buckhannon, W.V., U.S. C4 155
Buckhaven, Scot., U.K. E10 8
Buckhead, Ga., U.S. C3 117
Buck Hill Falls, Pa., U.S. D11 145
Buckhorn, Ky., U.S. C6 124
Buckhorn Knob, mtn., W.V., U.S. D4 155
Buckhorn Lake, res., Ky., U.S. C6 124
Buckie, Scot., U.K. D11 8
Buckingham, Que., Can. D2 104
Buckingham, co., Va., U.S. C4 153
Buckingham Bay, b., Austl. B7 68
Buckinghamshire, co., Eng., U.K. J13 8
Buckland, Que., Can. C7 104
Buckland, Ak., U.S. B7 109
Bucklands, S. Afr. G6 66
Buckley, Il., U.S. C5 120
Buckley, Mi., U.S. D5 129
Buckley, Wa., U.S. B3 154
Buckley, stm., Austl. C3 70
Bucklin, Ks., U.S. E4 123
Bucklin, Mo., U.S. B5 132
Buck Mountain, mtn., Va., U.S. D1 153
Buck Mountain, mtn., Wa., U.S. A6 154
Buckner, Ar., U.S. D2 111
Buckner, Il., U.S. F4 120
Buckner, Ky., U.S. g12 124
Buckner, Mo., U.S. h11 132
Buckow, Ger. C14 10
Bucks, Al., U.S. D1 108
Bucks, co., Pa., U.S. F11 145
Buckskin, In., U.S. H3 121
Buckskin Mountains, mts., Az., U.S. C2 110
Bucksport, Me., U.S. D4 126
Bucksport, S.C., U.S. D9 147
Bucoda, Wa., U.S. C3 154
Bucun, China G5 32
București (Bucharest), Rom. E10 20
Bucyrus, Ks., U.S. D9 123
Bucyrus, Oh., U.S. B3 142
Bud, W.V., U.S. D3 155
Buda, Il., U.S. B4 120
Buda, Tx., U.S. D4 150
Budalin, Burma C3 40
Budapest, Hung. H19 10
Búđardalur, Ice. B3 6a
Budaun, India F8 44
Budd Lake, l., N.J., U.S. B3 137
Buddu, Sud. L3 60
Bude, Ms., U.S. D3 131
Büdingen, Ger. E9 10
Búdir, Ice. B7 6a
Budogošč', Russia B15 22
Bud'onnovsk, Russia I6 26
Budweis see České Budějovice, Czech. G14 10
Buea, Cam. I14 64
Buena, N.J., U.S. D3 137
Buena, Wa., U.S. C5 154
Buena Esperanza, Arg. H6 80
Buena Park, Ca., U.S. n12 112
Buenaventura, Col. F4 84
Buenaventura, Mex. C6 90
Buena Vista, Bol. G10 82
Buena Vista, Para. D10 80
Buena Vista, Co., U.S. C4 113
Buena Vista, Fl., U.S. D4 116
Buena Vista, Ga., U.S. D2 117
Buena Vista, N.M., U.S. B4 138
Buena Vista, Va., U.S. C3 153
Buena Vista, co., Ia., U.S. B2 122
Buendia, Embalse de, res., Spain E9 16
Buenópolis, Braz. D6 79
Buenos Aires, Arg. H9 80
Buenos Aires, Col. F4 84
Buenos Aires, C.R. H11 92
Buenos Aires, prov., Arg. I8 80
Buenos Aires, Lago (Lago General Carrera), l., S.A. F2 78
Buerarema, Braz. C9 79
Buesaco, Col. G4 84
Buffalo, Il., U.S. D4 120
Buffalo, In., U.S. C4 121
Buffalo, Ia., U.S. C7 122
Buffalo, Ks., U.S. E8 123
Buffalo, Mn., U.S. E5 130
Buffalo, Mo., U.S. D4 132
Buffalo, N.Y., U.S. C2 139
Buffalo, N.D., U.S. C8 141
Buffalo, Oh., U.S. C4 142
Buffalo, Ok., U.S. A2 143
Buffalo, S.C., U.S. B4 147
Buffalo, S.D., U.S. B2 148
Buffalo, Tx., U.S. D5 150
Buffalo, W.V., U.S. C3 155
Buffalo, Wi., U.S. D2 156
Buffalo, Wy., U.S. B6 157
Buffalo, co., Ne., U.S. D6 134
Buffalo, co., S.D., U.S. C6 148
Buffalo, co., Wi., U.S. D2 156
Buffalo, stm., Can. E10 96
Buffalo, stm., Ar., U.S. B3 111
Buffalo, stm., Mn., U.S. D2 130
Buffalo, stm., Tn., U.S. B4 149
Buffalo, stm., Wi., U.S. D2 156
Buffalo Bill Reservoir, res., Wy., U.S. B3 157
Buffalo Center, Ia., U.S. A4 122
Buffalo Creek, Co., U.S. B5 113
Buffalo Creek, stm., U.S. f8 155
Buffalo Creek, stm., W.V., U.S. n12 155
Buffalo Creek, stm., W.V., U.S. h10 155
Buffalo Gap, S.D., U.S. D2 148
Buffalo Grove, Il., U.S. h9 120
Buffalo Lake, Mn., U.S. F4 130
Buffalo Lake, l., Alta., Can. C4 98
Buffalo Lake, res., Tx., U.S. B1 150
Buffalo Lake, res., Wi., U.S. E4 156
Buffalo Mountain, mtn., Va., U.S. D2 153
Buffumville Lake, res., Ma., U.S. B4 128
Buford, Ga., U.S. B2 117
Bug, stm., Eur. E12 4
Buga, Col. F4 84
Buga, Nig. G13 64
Bugalagrande, Col. E4 84
Bugeat, Fr. G8 14
Bugojno, Bos. E12 18
Bugry, Russia C18 22
Bugt, China B11 30
Bugt, China A8 32
Bugul'ma, Russia G8 26
Buguruslan, Russia G8 26
Buhera, Zimb. B10 66
Buhl, Al., U.S. B2 108
Buhl, Id., U.S. G4 119
Buhl, Mn., U.S. C6 130
Buhler, Ks., U.S. D6 123
Buhuși, Rom. C10 20
Buies Creek, N.C., U.S. B4 140
Builth Wells, Wales, U.K. I10 8
Buin, Chile G3 80
Buin, Piz, mtn., Eur. E13 13
Buir Nuur, l., Asia B10 30
Buj, Russia C24 22
Bujalance, Spain H7 16
Buji, China D16 44
Bujnaksk, Russia I7 26
Bujumbura, Bdi. B5 58
Bukačača, Russia G15 28
Bukama, Zaire C5 58
Būkān, Iran C9 48
Bukavu, Zaire B5 58
Bukittinggi, Indon. O6 40
Bukovina, hist. reg., Eur. B9 20
Bülach, Switz. C10 13
Bulan, Phil. o20 39b
Bulan, Ky., U.S. C6 124
Bulandshahr, India F7 44
Būlāq, Egypt E6 60
Bulawayo, Zimb. C9 66
Buldibuyo, Peru C3 82
Buldir Island, i., Ak., U.S. E3 109
Bulgan, Mong. B5 30
Bulgan, Mong. B7 30
Bulgaria (Bălgarija), ctry., Eur. G13 4
Bulki, Eth. N9 60
Bulkley, stm., B.C., Can. B4 99
Bulkley Ranges, mts., B.C., Can. B4 99
Bullard, Ga., U.S. D3 117
Bullas, Spain G10 16
Bull Creek, stm., Nv., U.S. E6 135
Bull Creek, stm., S.D., U.S. B2 148
Buller, Mount, mtn., Austl. K7 70
Bullfinch, Austl. F3 68
Bullfrog Creek, stm., Ut., U.S. F5 151
Bullhead, S.D., U.S. B4 148
Bullhead City, Az., U.S. B1 110
Bull Island, i., S.C., U.S. G6 147
Bull Island, i., S.C., U.S. F8 147
Bull Island, i., S.C., U.S. D9 147
Bullitt, co., Ky., U.S. C4 124
Bullittsville, Ky., U.S. h13 124
Bull Mountain, mtn., Mt., U.S. D4 133
Bulloch, co., Ga., U.S. D5 117
Bullock, co., Al., U.S. C4 108
Bullock Creek, Austl. A6 70
Bullock Creek, Mi., U.S. E6 129
Bulloo, stm., Austl. G5 70
Bull Run, stm., Va., U.S. g11 153
Bull Run Mountains, mts., Va., U.S. B5 153
Bullrun Ridge, mtn., Tn., U.S. m13 149
Bullrun Rock, mtn., Or., U.S. C8 144
Bulls Bay, b., S.C., U.S. F8 147
Bulls Gap, Tn., U.S. C10 149
Bull Shoals, Ar., U.S. A3 111
Bull Shoals Lake, res., U.S. A3 111
Bull Sluice Lake, res., Ga., U.S. h8 117
Bully Creek Reservoir, res., Or., U.S. C9 144
Bulnes, Chile I2 80
Bultfontein, S. Afr. G8 66
Bulukumba, Indon. G7 38
Bulyea, Sask., Can. G3 105
Bumba, Zaire A4 58
Bumbuna, S.L. G4 64
Bumping, stm., Wa., U.S. C4 154
Bumpus Mills, Tn., U.S. A4 149
Buna, Tx., U.S. D6 150
Bunbury, Austl. F3 68
Bunceton, Mo., U.S. C5 132
Buncombe, Il., U.S. F5 120
Buncombe, co., N.C., U.S. f10 140
Bundaberg, Austl. E10 70
Bünde, Ger. C8 10
Būndi, India H6 44
Bundick Creek, stm., La., U.S. D2 125
Bungo-suidō, strt., Japan N7 36
Bunia, Zaire A6 58
Bunker, Mo., U.S. D6 132
Bunker Group, is., Austl. D10 70
Bunker Hill, Il., U.S. D4 120
Bunker Hill, In., U.S. C5 121
Bunker Hill, Ks., U.S. D5 123
Bunker Hill, W.V., U.S. B6 155
Bunker Hill, W.V., U.S. m12 155
Bunker Hill, mtn., Nv., U.S. D4 135
Bunkerville, Nv., U.S. G7 135
Bunkie, La., U.S. D3 125
Bunn, N.C., U.S. B4 140
Bunnell, Fl., U.S. C5 116
Bunnlevel, N.C., U.S. B4 140
Buntok, Indon. F5 38
Bünyan, Tur. B3 48
Bunyolo, Spain F11 16
Bunza, Nig. E11 64
Buon Me Thuot, Viet. H10 40
Buor-Chaja, guba, b., Russia C18 28
Buor-Chaja, mys, c., Russia C18 28
Buqayq, Sau. Ar. B6 47
Bura, Kenya B7 58
Buram, Sud. L3 60
Burang, China E3 30
Buranhém, stm., Braz. D9 79

Name	Map Ref.	Page

177

Name | Map Ref. | Page

Copertino, Italy I13 18
Copetonas, Arg. J8 80
Copiah, co., Ms., U.S. D3 131
Copiapó, Chile D3 80
Copiapó, stm., Chile D3 80
Coplay, Pa., U.S. E10 145
Copley, Austl. H3 70
Copparo, Italy E6 18
Copper, stm., Ak., U.S. C11 109
Copperas Cove, Tx., U.S. D4 150
Copper Butte, mtn., Wa., U.S. A7 154
Copper Canyon see Cobre, Barranca del, val., Mex. D6 90
Copper Center, Ak., U.S. C10 109
Copper Harbor, Mi., U.S. A3 129
Copperhill, Tn., U.S. D9 149
Coppermine, N.W. Ter., Can. C9 96
Coppermine, stm., N.W. Ter., Can. C10 96
Copper Mountain, mtn., Wy., U.S. C5 157
Copper Mountains, mts., Az., U.S. E2 110
Copper Ridge, mtn., Tn., U.S. m13 149
Copper Ridge, mtn., Va., U.S. f9 153
Coppet, Switz. F5 13
Coquille, Or., U.S. D2 144
Coquimbo, Chile E3 80
Coquimbo, prov., Chile F3 80
Corabia, Rom. F8 20
Coração de Jesus, Braz. D6 79
Coração de Maria, Braz. B9 79
Coracora, Peru F5 82
Coral, Pa., U.S. F3 145
Coral Gables, Fl., U.S. G6 116
Coral Harbour, N.W. Ter., Can. D16 96
Coralque, stm., Peru G6 82
Coral Sea, Oc. J19 158
Coral Sea Islands Territory, ter., Austl. B9 70
Coralville, Ia., U.S. C6 122
Coralville Lake, res., Ia., U.S. C5 122
Coram, Mt., U.S. B2 133
Corangamite, Lake, l., Austl. L5 70
Coraopolis, Pa., U.S. E1 145
Corato, Italy H11 18
Corbeil-Essonnes, Fr. D9 14
Corbetton, Ont., Can. C4 103
Corbin, Ky., U.S. D5 124
Corcoran, Ca., U.S. D4 112
Corcoran, Mn., U.S. m11 130
Corcovado, Golfo, b., Chile E2 78
Corcovado, Parque Nacional, C.R. I11 92
Corcovado, Volcán, vol., Chile I7 74
Cord, Ar., U.S. B4 111
Cordaville, Ma., U.S. g9 128
Cordeiro, Braz. G7 79
Cordele, Ga., U.S. E3 117
Cordell, Ok., U.S. B3 143
Cordell Hull Lake, res., Tn., U.S. C8 149
Corder, Mo., U.S. B4 132
Cordillera, dept., Para. C10 80
Cordillo Downs, Austl. F4 70
Cordisburgo, Braz. E6 79
Córdoba, Arg. F6 80
Córdoba, Mex. H11 90
Córdoba, Spain H7 16
Córdoba, prov., Arg. F7 80
Córdoba, dept., Col. C5 84
Córdova, Peru F4 82
Cordova, Al., U.S. B2 108
Cordova, Ak., U.S. C10 109
Cordova, Il., U.S. B3 120
Cordova, Md., U.S. C6 127
Cordova, N.M., U.S. A4 138
Cordova, N.C., U.S. C3 140
Cordova, Tn., U.S. B2 149
Cordova Mines, Ont., Can. C7 103
Cordova Peak, mtn., Ak., U.S. C10 109
Corea, Me., U.S. D5 126
Corentyne (Corantijn) (Coeroeni), stm., S.A. E14 84
Corerepe, Mex. E5 90
Corfu see Kérkira, Grc. J3 20
Corfu see Kérkira, i., Grc. J3 20
Coria, Spain F5 16
Coria del Río, Spain H5 16
Coribe, Braz. B6 79
Corigliano Calabro, Italy J11 18
Corinda, Austl. A3 70
Corinna, Me., U.S. D3 126
Corinne, Ut., U.S. B3 151
Corinne Key, i., Fl., U.S. G6 116
Corinth, Ga., U.S. C2 117
Corinth, Ms., U.S. A5 131
Corinth, N.Y., U.S. B7 139
Corinth, W.V., U.S. B5 155
Corinth, Gulf of see Korinthiakós Kólpos, b., Grc. K6 20
Corinth Canal see Korínthou, Dhiórix, Grc. L6 20
Corinth see Kórinthos, Grc. L6 20
Corinto, Braz. E6 79
Corinto, El Sal. D7 92
Corinto, Nic. E7 92
Coripata, Bol. G8 82
Corire, Peru G5 82
Coris, Peru C3 82
Cork, N.B., Can. D3 101
Cork, Ire. J5 8
Cork, co., Ire. I5 8
Corlay, Fr. D3 14
Corleone, Italy L8 18
Çorlu, Tur. H11 20
Cormeilles, Fr. C7 14
Cormorant, Man., Can. B1 100
Cormorant Lake, l., Man., Can. B1 100
Corn, Ok., U.S. B3 143
Cornelia, Ga., U.S. B3 117
Cornélio Procópio, Braz. G3 79
Cornelius, N.C., U.S. B2 140
Cornelius, Or., U.S. g11 144
Cornell, Il., U.S. C5 120
Cornell, Wi., U.S. C2 156
Corner Brook, Newf., Can. D3 102
Cornerstone, Ar., U.S. C4 111
Cornersville, Tn., U.S. B5 149
Corneta, Punta, c., Mex. J11 90
Cornfield Point, c., Ct., U.S. D6 114
Cornhill, N.B., Can. D4 101
Cornie Bayou, stm., U.S. D3 111
Corning, Ar., U.S. A5 111
Corning, Ca., U.S. C2 112
Corning, Ia., U.S. D3 122
Corning, Ks., U.S. C7 123
Corning, N.Y., U.S. C3 139
Corning, Oh., U.S. C3 142
Cornish, Me., U.S. E2 126
Cornish, Ut., U.S. B4 151
Cornish Center, N.H., U.S. D2 136
Cornish Flat, N.H., U.S. D2 136
Cornishville, Ky., U.S. C5 124
Corno Grande, mtn., Italy G8 18
Cornville, Az., U.S. C4 110
Cornwall, Ont., Can. B10 103
Cornwall, Ct., U.S. B2 114
Cornwall, Pa., U.S. F9 145
Cornwall, co., Eng., U.K. K9 8
Cornwallis Island, i., N.W. Ter., Can. A14 96
Cornwall on Hudson, N.Y., U.S. D6 139
Coro, Ven. B8 84
Coro, Golfete de, b., Ven. I10 94
Coroaci, Braz. E7 79
Corocoro, Bol. G7 82
Corocoro Island, i., S.A. C12 84
Coroico, Bol. G8 82
Coroico, stm., Bol. F8 82
Coromandel, Braz. E5 79
Coromandel Coast, India F6 46
Coromandel Peninsula, pen., N.Z. B5 72
Corona, Al., U.S. B2 108
Corona, Ca., U.S. F5 112
Corona, N.M., U.S. C4 138
Corona, S.D., U.S. B9 148
Coronach, Sask., Can. H3 105
Coronado, Mex. F9 90
Coronado, Ca., U.S. F5 112
Coronado, Bahía de, b., C.R. H11 92
Coronado National Memorial, Az., U.S. F5 110
Coronation, Alta., Can. C5 98
Coronation Gulf, b., N.W. Ter., Can. C10 96
Coronation Island, i., Ant. B1 73
Coronation Island, i., Ak., U.S. n22 109
Coronda, Arg. F8 80
Coronel, Chile I2 80
Coronel Bogado, Para. D10 80
Coronel Dorrego, Arg. J8 80
Coronel Du Graty, Arg. D8 80
Coronel Eugenio del Busto, Arg. J6 80
Coronel Fabriciano, Braz. E7 79
Coronel Moldes, Arg. C6 80
Coronel Moldes, Arg. G6 80
Coronel Murta, Braz. D7 79
Coronel Oviedo, Para. C10 80
Coronel Ponce, Braz. C1 79
Coronel Pringles, Arg. I8 80
Coronel Sapucaia, Braz. G1 79
Coronel Suárez, Arg. I8 80
Coronel Vidal, Arg. I10 80
Coronel Vivida, Braz. C12 80
Corongo, Peru C3 82
Coronie, dept., Sur. E14 84
Coropuna, Nevado, mtn., Peru F5 82
Corowa, Austl. K7 70
Corozal, Belize H15 90
Corozal, Col. C5 84
Corozal, Hond. B8 92
Corps, Fr. H12 14
Corpus, Arg. D11 80
Corpus Christi, Tx., U.S. F4 150
Corpus Christi Naval Air Station, mil., Tx., U.S. F4 150
Corque, Bol. H8 82
Corquín, Hond. C6 92
Corral, Chile D2 78
Corral de Almaguer, Spain F8 16
Corral de Bustos, Arg. G7 80
Corralejo, Spain o27 17b
Corrales, N.M., U.S. k7 138
Correctionville, Ia., U.S. B2 122
Correggio, Italy E5 18
Córrego Rico, Braz. C5 79
Corrente, stm., Braz. E3 79
Corrente, stm., Braz. B6 79
Correntes, stm., Braz. D1 79
Correntina, Braz. B6 79
Corrèze, dept., Fr. G8 14
Corrib, Lough, l., Ire. H4 8
Corrientes, Arg. D9 80
Corrientes, prov., Arg. E10 80
Corrientes, stm., Arg. E9 80
Corrientes, stm., S.A. I5 84
Corrientes, Bahía de, b., Cuba D2 94
Corrientes, Cabo, c., Arg. J10 80
Corrientes, Cabo, c., Col. E4 84
Corrientes, Cabo, c., Cuba D2 94
Corrientes, Cabo, c., Mex. G7 90
Corrigan, Tx., U.S. D5 150
Corriganville, Md., U.S. k13 127
Corriverton, Guy. E14 84
Corry, Pa., U.S. C2 145
Corse (Corsica), i., Fr. I24 15a
Corse, Cap, c., Fr. k24 15a
Corse-du-Sud, dept., Fr. m24 15a
Corsica, S.D., U.S. D7 148
Corsica see Corse, i., Fr. I24 15a
Corsicana, Tx., U.S. C4 150
Corson, co., S.D., U.S. B4 148
Corson Inlet, b., N.J., U.S. E3 137
Cortazar, Mex. G9 90
Corte, Fr. I24 15a
Cortegana, Spain H5 16
Cortés, dept., Hond. B6 92
Cortez, Co., U.S. D2 113
Cortez, Fl., U.S. q10 116
Cortez, Sea of 20 California, Golfo de, b., Mex. D4 90
Cortez Mountains, mts., Nv., U.S. C5 135
Cortina d'Ampezzo, Italy C7 18
Cortland, Il., U.S. B5 120
Cortland, In., U.S. G6 121
Cortland, Ne., U.S. D9 134
Cortland, N.Y., U.S. C4 139
Cortland, Oh., U.S. A5 142
Cortland, co., N.Y., U.S. C4 139
Cortona, Italy F6 18
Corubal (Koliba), stm., Afr. F2 64
Çoruh, stm., Asia A6 48
Çorum, Tur. J12 20
Corumbá, Braz. H13 82
Corumbá, stm., Braz. E4 79
Corumbá de Goiás, Braz. C4 79
Corumbaíba, Braz. E4 79
Corumbataí, stm., Braz. C13 80
Corumbaú, Ponta do, c., Braz. D9 79
Corumbiara, stm., Braz. E11 82
Corumo, stm., Ven. D12 84
Corunna, In., U.S. B7 121
Corunna, Mi., U.S. F6 129
Coruripe, Braz. F11 76
Corvallis, Mt., U.S. D2 133
Corvallis, Or., U.S. C3 144
Corwith, Ia., U.S. B4 122
Cory, In., U.S. F3 121
Corydon, In., U.S. H5 121
Corydon, Ia., U.S. D4 122
Corydon, Ky., U.S. C2 124
Coryell, co., Tx., U.S. D4 150
Corzuela, Arg. D8 80
Cosamaloapan [de Carpio], Mex. H12 90
Cosapa, Bol. H7 82
Cosby, Tn., U.S. D10 149
Cosenza, Italy J11 18
Coshocton, Oh., U.S. B4 142
Coshocton, co., Oh., U.S. B4 142
Cosigüina, Punta, c., Nic. E7 92
Cosigüina, Volcán, vol., Nic. E7 92
Cosmoledo Island, i., Sey. C9 58
Cosmopolis, Wa., U.S. C2 154
Cosmos, Mn., U.S. F4 130
Cosne-Cours-sur-Loire, Fr. E9 14
Cospán, Peru B2 82
Cosquín, Arg. F6 80
Cossatot, stm., Ar., U.S. C1 111
Cossatot Mountains, mtn., Ar., U.S. C2 111
Cossonay, Switz. E6 13
Costa Mesa, Ca., U.S. n13 112
Costa Rica, Mex. E6 90
Costa Rica, ctry., N.A. G10 92
Costilla, N.M., U.S. A4 138
Costilla, co., Co., U.S. D5 113
Coswig, Ger. D12 10
Cotabambas, Peru E5 82
Cotabato, Phil. D7 38
Cotacajes, stm., Bol. G8 82
Cotagaita, Bol. I9 82
Cotagaita, stm., Bol. I9 82
Cotahuasi, Peru F5 82
Coteau-Landing, Que., Can. D3 104
Coteaux, Haiti E7 94
Côte-d'Or, dept., Fr. E11 14
Cotegipe, Braz. B6 79
Cotentin, pen., Fr. C5 14
Côtes-d'Armor, dept., Fr. D4 14
Coti, stm., Braz. C9 82
Cotija de la Paz, Mex. H8 90
Cotingo, stm., Braz. E12 84
Cotoca, Bol. G10 82
Cotonou, Benin H11 64
Cotopaxi, Co., U.S. C5 113
Cotopaxi, prov., Ec. H3 84
Cotopaxi, vol., Ec. H3 84
Cotswold Hills, hills, Eng., U.K. J11 8
Cottage Grove, Mn., U.S. n13 130
Cottage Grove, Or., U.S. D3 144
Cottage Grove Reservoir, res., Or., U.S. D3 144
Cottageville, S.C., U.S. F7 147
Cottageville, W.V., U.S. C3 155
Cottam, Ont., Can. E2 103
Cottbus, Ger. D14 10
Cotter, Ar., U.S. A3 111
Cottiennes, Alpes (Alpi Cozie), mts., Eur. E1 18
Cottle, co., Tx., U.S. B2 150
Cottle Knob, mtn., W.V., U.S. C4 155
Cottleville, Mo., U.S. f12 132
Cotton, Ga., U.S. E2 117
Cotton, Mn., U.S. C6 130
Cotton, co., Ok., U.S. C3 143
Cottondale, Al., U.S. B2 108
Cottondale, Fl., U.S. B1 116
Cotton Plant, Ar., U.S. B4 111
Cottonport, La., U.S. C3 125
Cottonton, Al., U.S. C4 108
Cottontown, Tn., U.S. A5 149
Cotton Valley, La., U.S. B2 125
Cottonwood, Al., U.S. D4 108
Cottonwood, Az., U.S. C3 110
Cottonwood, Ca., U.S. B2 112
Cottonwood, Id., U.S. C2 119
Cottonwood, Mn., U.S. F3 130
Cottonwood, Ok., U.S. C5 143
Cottonwood, co., Mn., U.S. F3 130
Cottonwood, stm., Ks., U.S. D7 123
Cottonwood, stm., Mn., U.S. F3 130
Cottonwood Cove, Nv., U.S. H7 135
Cottonwood Creek, stm., Wy., U.S. C4 157
Cottonwood Falls, Ks., U.S. D7 123
Cottonwood Wash, val., Ut., U.S. F6 151
Cotuhé, stm., Col. I7 84
Cotuí, Dom. Rep. E9 94
Cotuit, Ma., U.S. C7 128
Cotulla, Tx., U.S. E3 150
Coudersport, Pa., U.S. C5 145
Cougar Reservoir, res., Or., U.S. C4 144
Couhé, Fr. F7 14
Coulee City, Wa., U.S. B6 154
Coulee Creek, stm., Wa., U.S. g13 154
Coulee Dam, Wa., U.S. B7 154
Coulee Dam National Recreation Area, Wa., U.S. A7 154
Coulommiers, Fr. D10 14
Coulter, Ia., U.S. B4 122
Coulterville, Ca., U.S. D2 112
Coulterville, Il., U.S. E4 120
Counce, Tn., U.S. B3 149
Council, Id., U.S. E2 119
Council Bluffs, Ia., U.S. C2 122
Council Grove, Ks., U.S. D7 123
Council Grove Lake, res., Ks., U.S. D7 123
Council Mountain, mtn., Id., U.S. E2 119
Country Homes, Wa., U.S. B8 154
Countyline, Ok., U.S. C4 143
Coupeville, Wa., U.S. A3 154
Courcelles, Bel. H5 12
Courcelles, Que., Can. D7 104
Courland see Kurzeme, hist. reg., Lat. E5 22
Couronnement, Île du see Coronation Island, i., Ant. B1 73
Courtalain, Fr. D8 14
Courtenay, B.C., Can. E5 99
Courte Oreilles, Lac, l., Wi., U.S. C2 156
Courtland, Ont., Can. E4 103
Courtland, Al., U.S. A2 108
Courtland, Ks., U.S. C6 123
Courtland, Mn., U.S. F4 130
Courtland, Ms., U.S. A4 131
Courtland, Va., U.S. D5 153
Courtrai (Kortrijk), Bel. G3 12
Coushatta, La., U.S. B2 125
Coutances, Fr. C5 14
Couto Magalhães, stm., Braz. B2 79
Coutts, Alta., Can. E5 98
Couvin, Bel. H5 12
Covasna, co., Rom. D9 20
Cove, Ar., U.S. C1 111
Cove, Or., U.S. B9 144
Cove City, N.C., U.S. B5 140
Cove Creek, stm., Ut., U.S. E3 151
Covedale, Oh., U.S. o12 142
Covelo, Ca., U.S. C2 112
Coventry, Eng., U.K. I12 8
Coventry, Ct., U.S. B6 114
Coventry, R.I., U.S. D3 146
Coventry, Vt., U.S. B4 152
Cove Point, Md., U.S. D5 127
Cove Point, c., Md., U.S. D5 127
Coverdales Crossroads, De., U.S. F3 115
Covered Wells, Az., U.S. E3 110
Covert, Mi., U.S. F4 129
Covesville, Va., U.S. C4 153
Covilhã, Port. E4 16
Covina, Ca., U.S. m13 112
Covington, Ga., U.S. C3 117
Covington, In., U.S. D3 121
Covington, Ky., U.S. A5 124
Covington, La., U.S. D5 125
Covington, Mi., U.S. B2 129
Covington, Oh., U.S. B1 142
Covington, Ok., U.S. A4 143
Covington, Pa., U.S. C7 145
Covington, Tn., U.S. B2 149
Covington, Va., U.S. C3 153
Covington, Wa., U.S. f11 154
Covington, co., Al., U.S. D3 108
Covington, co., Ms., U.S. D4 131
Covunco, Arroyo, stm., Arg. J4 80
Cowal, Lake, l., Austl. I7 70
Cowan, In., U.S. D7 121
Cowan, Tn., U.S. B5 149
Cowan, Lake, l., Austl. F4 68
Cowan Knob, mtn., Ar., U.S. B2 111
Cowan Lake, l., Sask., Can. C2 105
Cowansville, Que., Can. D5 104
Coward, S.C., U.S. D8 147
Coward Springs, Austl. G2 70
Cowarie, Austl. F3 70
Cowarts, Al., U.S. D4 108
Cow Creek, stm., Ks., U.S. D5 123
Cow Creek, stm., Wa., U.S. C7 154
Cowden, Il., U.S. D5 120
Cowdenbeath, Scot., U.K. E10 8
Cowee Mountains, mts., N.C., U.S. f9 140
Cowell, Austl. I2 70
Cowen, W.V., U.S. C4 155
Cowen, Mount, mtn., Mt., U.S. E6 133
Coweta, Ok., U.S. B6 143
Coweta, co., Ga., U.S. C2 117
Cowgill, Mo., U.S. B4 132
Cow Head, Newf., Can. D3 102
Cowichan Bay, B.C., Can. g12 99
Cowiche, Wa., U.S. C5 154
Cow Knob, mtn., W.V., U.S. C5 155
Cow Lakes, l., Or., U.S. D9 144
Cowley, Austl. F6 70
Cowley, Alta., Can. E3 98
Cowley, Wy., U.S. B4 157
Cowley, co., Ks., U.S. E7 123
Cowlic, Az., U.S. F4 110
Cowlington, Ok., U.S. B7 143
Cowlitz, co., Wa., U.S. C2 154
Cowlitz, stm., Wa., U.S. C3 154
Cowpasture, stm., Va., U.S. B3 153
Cowpen Mountain, mtn., Ga., U.S. B2 117
Cowpens, S.C., U.S. A4 147
Cowra, Austl. I8 70
Cowskin Creek, stm., Ks., U.S. g11 123
Coxá, stm., Braz. C6 79
Coxim, Braz. E1 79
Coxim, stm., Braz. E1 79
Coxsackie, N.Y., U.S. C7 139
Cox's Bāzār, Bngl. J14 44
Cox's Cove, Newf., Can. D2 102
Coy, Al., U.S. D2 108
Coy, Ar., U.S. C4 111
Coyaguaima, Cerro, mtn., Arg. B5 80
Coyame, Mex. C7 90
Coyanosa Draw, val., Tx., U.S. D1 150
Coya Sur, Chile B4 80
Coyle, Ok., U.S. B4 143
Coyote, N.M., U.S. A3 138
Coyote Basin, Co., U.S. A2 113
Coyuca de Benítez, Mex. I9 90
Coyuca de Catalán, Mex. H9 90
Cozad, Ne., U.S. D6 134
Cozie, Alpi (Alpes Cottiennes), mts., Eur. E2 18
Cozumel, Mex. G16 90
Cozumel, Isla, i., Mex. G16 90
Crab Creek, stm., Wa., U.S. C6 154
Crab Creek, stm., Wa., U.S. B7 154
Crab Orchard, Ky., U.S. C5 124
Crab Orchard, Tn., U.S. D9 149
Crab Orchard, W.V., U.S. n13 155
Crab Orchard Lake, res., Il., U.S. F4 120
Crab Orchard Mountains, mts., Tn., U.S. D9 149
Crabtree, Or., U.S. C4 144
Crabtree, Pa., U.S. F3 145
Crabtree Mills, Que., Can. D4 104
Cracking, stm., Sask., Can. D4 105
Cradock, S. Afr. I7 66
Crafton, Pa., U.S. k13 145
Craftsbury, Vt., U.S. B4 152
Craftsbury Common, Vt., U.S. B4 152
Cragford, Al., U.S. B4 108
Craig, Ak., U.S. D13 109
Craig, Co., U.S. A3 113
Craig, Mo., U.S. A2 132
Craig, Mt., U.S. C5 133
Craig, Ne., U.S. C9 134
Craig, co., Ok., U.S. A6 143
Craig, co., Va., U.S. C2 153
Craig Air Force Base, mil., Al., U.S. C3 108
Craig Creek, stm., Va., U.S. C2 153
Craigellachie, B.C., Can. D8 99
Craighead, co., Ar., U.S. B5 111
Craigmont, Id., U.S. C2 119
Craigmyle, Alta., Can. D4 98
Craignure, Scot., U.K. E8 8
Craigsville, Va., U.S. B3 153
Craigsville, W.V., U.S. C4 155
Craik, Sask., Can. F3 105
Crailsheim, Ger. F10 10
Craiova, Rom. E7 20
Cramerton, N.C., U.S. B1 140
Cranberry Lake, l., N.Y., U.S. A6 139
Cranberry Portage, Man., Can. B1 100
Cranbrook, B.C., Can. E10 99
Crandall, Ga., U.S. B2 117
Crandall, Tx., U.S. n10 150
Crandon, Wi., U.S. C5 156
Crane, Az., U.S. *E1 110
Crane, In., U.S. G4 121
Crane, Mo., U.S. E4 132
Crane, Tx., U.S. D1 150
Crane, co., Tx., U.S. D1 150
Crane Creek, stm., Oh., U.S. e7 142
Crane Creek Reservoir, res., Id., U.S. E2 119
Crane Hill, Al., U.S. A2 108
Crane Lake, Mn., U.S. B6 130
Crane Lake, l., Sask., Can. G1 105
Crane Lake, l., Il., U.S. C3 120
Crane Lake, l., Mn., U.S. B6 130
Crane Mountain, mtn., Or., U.S. E6 144
Crane Prairie Reservoir, res., Or., U.S. D5 144
Crane Valley, Sask., Can. H3 105
Cranfield, Ms., U.S. D2 131
Cranford, N.J., U.S. B4 137
Cranston, R.I., U.S. C4 146
Craon, Fr. E6 14
Craonne, Fr. C10 14
Crapaud, P.E.I., Can. C6 101
Craponne, Fr. G10 14
Crary, N.D., U.S. A7 141
Crasna, Rom. C11 20
Crasna (Kraszna), stm., Eur. B6 20
Crater Lake, Or., U.S. E4 144
Crater Lake, l., Or., U.S. E4 144
Crater Lake National Park, Or., U.S. E4 144
Craters of the Moon National Monument, Id., U.S. F5 119
Crateús, Braz. E10 76
Crauford, Cape, c., N.W. Ter., Can. B16 96
Cravari, stm., Braz. E13 82
Craven, Sask., Can. G3 105
Craven, co., N.C., U.S. B5 140
Cravo Norte, Col. D7 84
Cravo Norte, stm., Col. D7 84
Cravo-Sur, stm., Col. E7 84
Crawford, Co., U.S. C3 113
Crawford, Ga., U.S. C3 117
Crawford, Ms., U.S. B5 131
Crawford, Ne., U.S. B2 134
Crawford, co., Ar., U.S. B1 111
Crawford, co., Ga., U.S. D3 117
Crawford, co., Il., U.S. D6 120
Crawford, co., In., U.S. H4 121
Crawford, co., Ia., U.S. B2 122
Crawford, co., Ks., U.S. E9 123
Crawford, co., Mi., U.S. D6 129
Crawford, co., Mo., U.S. D6 132
Crawford, co., Oh., U.S. B3 142
Crawford, co., Pa., U.S. C1 145
Crawford, co., Wi., U.S. E3 156
Crawford Bay, B.C., Can. E9 99
Crawford Lake, l., Me., U.S. C5 126
Crawford Notch State Park, N.H., U.S. B4 136
Crawfordsville, Ar., U.S. B5 111
Crawfordsville, In., U.S. D4 121
Crawfordsville, Ia., U.S. C6 122
Crawfordville, Fl., U.S. B2 116
Crawfordville, Ga., U.S. C4 117
Crayne, Ky., U.S. e9 124
Crazy Mountains, mts., Mt., U.S. D6 133
Crazy Peak, mtn., Mt., U.S. D6 133
Crazy Woman Creek, stm., Wy., U.S. B6 157
Creal Springs, Il., U.S. F5 120
Crécy-en-Brie, Fr. D9 14
Creede, Co., U.S. D4 113
Creedmoor, N.C., U.S. A4 140
Creek, co., Ok., U.S. B5 143
Creel, Mex. D6 90
Cree Lake, l., Sask., Can. m7 105
Creelman, Sask., Can. H4 105
Creemore, Ont., Can. C4 103
Creighton, Sask., Can. C5 105
Creighton, Mo., U.S. C3 132
Creighton, Ne., U.S. B8 134
Creighton, Pa., U.S. h14 145
Creil, Fr. C9 14
Crema, Italy D4 18
Cremona, Alta., Can. D3 98
Cremona, Italy D5 18
Crenshaw, Ms., U.S. A3 131
Crenshaw, co., Al., U.S. D3 108
Creola, Al., U.S. E1 108
Crepori, stm., Braz. A13 82
Cres, Otok, i., Cro. E9 18
Cresaptown, Md., U.S. k13 127
Cresbard, S.D., U.S. B7 148
Crescent, Ga., U.S. E5 117
Crescent, Mo., U.S. f12 132
Crescent, Ok., U.S. B4 143
Crescent, Or., U.S. D5 144
Crescent, Lake, l., Wa., U.S. A2 154
Crescent City, Ca., U.S. B1 112
Crescent City, Fl., U.S. C5 116
Crescent City, Il., U.S. C6 120
Crescent Lake, l., Fl., U.S. C5 116
Crescent Lake, l., Or., U.S. D5 144
Crescent Range, mtn., N.H., U.S. B4 136
Crescent Springs, Ky., U.S. h13 124
Cresco, Ia., U.S. A5 122
Crespo, Arg. G8 80
Cresskill, N.J., U.S. h9 137
Cresson, Pa., U.S. F4 145
Cressona, Pa., U.S. E9 145
Crested Butte, Co., U.S. C4 113
Crest Hill, Il., U.S. k8 120
Crestline, Oh., U.S. B3 142
Creston, B.C., Can. E9 99
Creston, Il., U.S. B5 120
Creston, Ia., U.S. C3 122
Creston, Ne., U.S. C8 134
Creston, Oh., U.S. B4 142
Creston, Wa., U.S. B7 154
Crestone Peak, mtn., Co., U.S. D5 113
Crestview, Fl., U.S. u15 116
Crestview, Hi., U.S. g10 118
Crestwood, Ky., U.S. B4 124
Crestwood Village, N.J., U.S. D4 137
Creswell, N.C., U.S. B6 140
Creswell, Or., U.S. D3 144
Creswick, Austl. K5 70
Crete, Il., U.S. B6 120
Crete, Ne., U.S. D9 134
Crete see Kríti, i., Grc. N8 20
Crétéville, Tun. M5 18
Creus, Cap de, c., Spain C15 16
Creuse, dept., Fr. F9 14
Creve Coeur, Il., U.S. C4 120
Crevillent, Spain G11 16
Crewe, Eng., U.K. H11 8
Crewe, Va., U.S. C4 153
Crewkerne, Eng., U.K. K11 8
Cricamola, stm., Pan. I13 92
Cricaré, stm., Braz. E8 79
Criciúma, Braz. E14 80
Cricket, N.C., U.S. A1 140
Cricket Mountains, mts., Ut., U.S. E3 151
Cridersville, Oh., U.S. B1 142
Crieff, Scot., U.K. E10 8
Crikvenica, Cro. D9 18
Crimea see Krymskij poluostrov, pen., Ukr. H4 26
Crimmitschau, Ger. E12 10
Crîngeni, Rom. E8 20
Cripple Creek, Co., U.S. C5 113
Cripple Creek, Va., U.S. D1 153
Crisfield, Md., U.S. E6 127
Crisp, co., Ga., U.S. E3 117
Crissiumal, Braz. D11 80
Cristalândia, Braz. F9 76
Cristalina, Braz. D5 79
Cristalino, stm., Braz. B3 79
Cristianópolis, Braz. D4 79
Cristóbal, Pan. C3 84
Cristóbal Colón, Pico, mtn., Col. B6 84
Crișul Alb, stm., Eur. C5 20
Crișul Negru, stm., Eur. C5 20
Crișul Repede (Sebes Körös), stm., Eur. B6 20
Crittenden, Ky., U.S. B5 124
Crittenden, co., Ar., U.S. B5 111
Crittenden, co., Ky., U.S. e9 124
Crivitz, Wi., U.S. C6 156
Crixalândia, Braz. C5 79
Crixás, Braz. C4 79
Crixás-Açu, stm., Braz. B3 79
Crixás-Mirim, stm., Braz. C3 79
Crna Gora, state, Yugo. G2 20
Črnomelj, Slo. D10 18
Croatia, ctry., Eur. F11 4
Crocker, Mo., U.S. D5 132
Crockett, Ca., U.S. g8 112
Crockett, Tx., U.S. D5 150
Crockett, co., Tn., U.S. B2 149
Crockett, co., Tx., U.S. D2 150
Crockett Mills, Tn., U.S. B2 149
Crofton, Ky., U.S. C2 124
Crofton, Md., U.S. B4 127
Crofton, Ne., U.S. B8 134
Croix, Lac la, l., Mn., U.S. B6 130
Croker, Cape, c., Austl. B6 68
Croker, Cape, c., Ont., Can. C4 103
Croker Island, i., Austl. B6 68
Cromarty, Scot., U.K. D9 8
Cromer, Man., Can. E1 100
Cromínia, Braz. D4 79
Cromona, Ky., U.S. C7 124
Cromwell, N.Z. F2 72
Cromwell, Al., U.S. C1 108
Cromwell, Ct., U.S. C5 114
Cromwell, In., U.S. B6 121
Cromwell, Ky., U.S. C3 124
Cromwell, Ok., U.S. B5 143
Crook, Co., U.S. A8 113
Crook, co., Or., U.S. C6 144
Crook, co., Wy., U.S. B8 157
Crooked, stm., Or., U.S. C6 144
Crooked Creek, Ak., U.S. C8 109
Crooked Creek, stm., U.S. E3 123
Crooked Creek, stm., Ar., U.S. A3 111
Crooked Creek, stm., In., U.S. k10 121
Crooked Creek, stm., Pa., U.S. C7 145

Name — Map Ref. — Page

Danville, Ar., U.S. B2 111
Danville, Ca., U.S. h9 112
Danville, Ga., U.S. D3 117
Danville, Il., U.S. C6 120
Danville, In., U.S. E4 121
Danville, Ia., U.S. D6 122
Danville, Ky., U.S. C5 124
Danville, N.H., U.S. E4 136
Danville, Oh., U.S. B3 142
Danville, Pa., U.S. E8 145
Danville, Vt., U.S. C4 152
Danville, Va., U.S. D3 153
Danville, W.V., U.S. C3 155
Danyang, China C8 34
Danzig see Gdańsk, Pol. A18 10
Daocheng, China F7 30
Daolin, China H1 34
Daoukro, I.C. H8 64
Daoulas, Fr. D2 14
Daoura, Oued, val., Afr. F9 62
Dapango, Togo F10 64
Daphne, Al., U.S. E2 108
Dapp, Alta., Can. B4 98
Da Qaidam, China B16 44
Daqing, China D6 32
Daqqāq, Sud. K4 60
Dara, Sen. D2 64
Dar'ā, Syria C6 50
Dārāb, Iran G13 48
Darabani, Rom. A10 20
Daraina, Madag. n23 67b
Darāw, Egypt E7 60
Dārayyā, Syria B6 50
Darbhanga, India G11 44
D'Arbonne, Bayou, stm., La., U.S. B3 125
Darby, Mt., U.S. D2 133
Darby, Pa., U.S. G11 145
Darbydale, Oh., U.S. m10 142
Darchan, Mong. B8 30
Dardanelle, Ar., U.S. B2 111
Dardanelle Lake, res., Ar., U.S. B2 111
Dardanelles see Çanakkale Boğazı, strt., Tur. I10 20
Dardara, Mor. J6 16
Darden, Tn., U.S. B3 149
Dardenne Creek, stm., Mo., U.S. f12 132
Dare, co., N.C., U.S. B7 140
Dar-el-Beida see Casablanca, Mor. D7 62
Darende, Tur. B4 48
Dares Beach, Md., U.S. C4 127
Dar es Salaam, Tan. C7 58
Dargai, Pak. C4 44
Dargan-Ata, Turk. I10 26
Dargaville, N.Z. A4 72
Dargol, Niger E10 64
Darién, Col. F4 84
Darien, Ct., U.S. E2 114
Darien, Ga., U.S. E5 117
Darien, Wi., U.S. F5 156
Darién, Serranía del, mts. C4 84
Dariense, Cordillera, mts., Nic. E9 92
Dariganga, Mong. B9 30
Dārjiling, India G13 44
Darke, co., Oh., U.S. B1 142
Darkesville, W.V., U.S. B6 155
Darlag, China E6 30
Darley Woods, De., U.S. h8 115
Darling, S. Afr. I4 66
Darling, Ms., U.S. A3 131
Darling, stm., Austl. I5 70
Darling, Lake, res., N.D., U.S. A4 141
Darling Downs, reg., Austl. F9 70
Darlingford, Man., Can. E2 100
Darling Range, mts., Austl. F3 68
Darlington, Al., U.S. D2 108
Darlington, In., U.S. D4 121
Darlington, Md., U.S. A5 127
Darlington, S.C., U.S. C8 147
Darlington, Wi., U.S. F3 156
Darlington, co., S.C., U.S. C8 147
Darłowo, Pol. A16 10
Darmstadt, Ger. F8 10
Darnah, Libya B5 56
Darnestown, Md., U.S. B3 127
Darnétal, Fr. C8 14
Darney, Fr. D13 14
Darnley, Cape, c., Ant. B5 73
Darnley Bay, b., N.W. Ter., Can. C8 96
Daroca, Spain D10 16
Dar-Ould-Zidouh, Mor. D7 62
Darou Mousti, Sen. D1 64
Darrah, Mount, mtn., Can. E3 98
Darregueira, Arg. I7 80
Darreh Gaz, Iran C15 48
Darrington, Wa., U.S. A4 154
Darrow, La., U.S. h10 125
Dart, Cape, c., Ant. C10 73
Dartmoor, for., Eng., U.K. K9 8
Dartmouth, N.S., Can. E6 101
Dartmouth, Eng., U.K. K10 8
Dartmouth, Lake, l., Austl. F6 70
Daru, Pap. N. Gui. A8 68
Daru, S.L. H4 64
Daruvar, Cro. D12 18
Darwin, Arg. J6 80
Darwin, Austl. B6 68
Darwin, Mn., U.S. E4 130
Dās, i., U.A.E. B8 47
Dashaping, China F2 34
Dasht, stm., Pak. I16 48
Dashwood, Ont., Can. D3 103
Dasiji, China B4 34
Dašinčilen, Mong. B7 30
Daškovka, Bela. H13 22
Dassel, Mn., U.S. E4 130
Date, Japan e15 36a
Dateland, Az., U.S. E2 110
Datia, India H8 44
Datian, China K5 34
Datil, N.M., U.S. C2 138
Datil Mountains, mts., N.M., U.S. C2 138
D'at'kovo, Russia H17 22
D'atlovo, Bela. H8 22
Datong, China C9 30
Datong, stm., China D7 30
Datoushan, China B5 32
Datto, Ar., U.S. A5 111
Datu, Tanjung, c., Asia M10 40
Daua (Dawa), stm., Afr. H9 56
Daufuskie Island, i., S.C., U.S. G6 147
Daugai, Lith. G7 22
Daugava (Zapadnaja Dvina), stm., Eur. E7 22
Daugavpils, Lat. F9 22
Daule, Ec. G2 84
Daule, Ec. H3 84
Daule, stm., Ec. H2 84
Daun, Ger. E6 10
Dauphin, Man., Can. D1 100
Dauphin, co., Pa., U.S. F8 145
Dauphin, stm., Man., Can. D2 100
Dauphiné, hist. reg., Fr. H12 14
Dauphin Island, Al., U.S. E1 108
Dauphin Island, i., Al., U.S. E1 108
Dauphin Lake, l., Man., Can. D2 100
Daura, Nig. E14 64
Daus, Tn., U.S. D8 149
Dāvangere, India E3 46
Davao, Phil. D8 38
Davao Gulf, b., Phil. D8 38
Dāvar Panāh, Iran H17 48
Davel, S. Afr. F9 66
Daveluyville, Que., Can. C5 104
Davenport, Fl., U.S. D5 116
Davenport, Ia., U.S. C7 122
Davenport, Ne., U.S. D8 134
Davenport, N.D., U.S. C8 141
Davenport, Ok., U.S. B5 143
Davenport, Wa., U.S. B7 154
Davey, Ne., U.S. h11 134
Davey, Port, b., Austl. N6 70
David, Pan. C1 84
David, Ky., U.S. C7 124
David City, Ne., U.S. C8 134
Davidson, N.C., U.S. B2 140
Davidson, Ok., U.S. C2 143
Davidson, co., N.C., U.S. B2 140
Davidson, co., Tn., U.S. A5 149
Davie, Fl., U.S. F6 116
Davie, co., N.C., U.S. B2 140
Daviess, co., In., U.S. G3 121
Daviess, co., Ky., U.S. C2 124
Daviess, co., Mo., U.S. B3 132
Davin, Sask., Can. G3 105
Davinópolis, Braz. C3 79
Davis, Ca., U.S. C3 112
Davis, Il., U.S. A4 120
Davis, N.C., U.S. C6 140
Davis, Ok., U.S. C4 143
Davis, S.D., U.S. D9 148
Davis, W.V., U.S. B5 155
Davis, co., Ia., U.S. D5 122
Davis, co., Ut., U.S. C3 151
Davis, Mount, mtn., Pa., U.S. G3 145
Davisboro, Ga., U.S. D4 117
Davis City, Ia., U.S. D4 122
Davis Creek, stm., W.V., U.S. m12 155
Davis Dam, Az., U.S. B1 110
Davis Dam, U.S. H7 135
Davis Inlet, Newf., Can. g9 102
Davis Islands, is., Fl., U.S. p11 116
Davis Junction, Il., U.S. A4 120
Davis Lake, l., Or., U.S. E5 144
Davis-Monthan Air Force Base, mil., Az., U.S. E5 110
Davis Mountains, mts., Tx., U.S. o12 150
Davison, Mi., U.S. E7 129
Davison, co., S.D., U.S. D7 148
Davis Strait, strt., N.A. C21 96
Daviston, Al., U.S. B4 108
Davisville, R.I., U.S. E4 146
Davlekanovo, Russia G9 26
Davos, Switz. E12 13
Davutlar, Tur. L11 20
Davy, W.V., U.S. D3 155
Dawa (Daua), stm., Afr. H9 56
Dawāsir, Wādī ad-, val., Sau. Ar. D4 47
Dawei (Tavoy), Burma G5 40
Dawes, co., Ne., U.S. B2 134
Dawn, Mo., U.S. B4 132
Dawna Range, mts., Burma F5 40
Dawqah, Sau. Ar. E2 47
Dawrah, Sud. K3 60
Daws Island, i., S.C., U.S. G6 147
Dawson, Yukon, Can. D5 96
Dawson, Ga., U.S. E2 117
Dawson, Mn., U.S. F2 130
Dawson, Ne., U.S. D10 134
Dawson, N.D., U.S. C6 141
Dawson, Tx., U.S. D4 150
Dawson, co., Ga., U.S. B2 117
Dawson, co., Mt., U.S. C11 133
Dawson, co., Ne., U.S. D6 134
Dawson, co., Tx., U.S. C1 150
Dawson, stm., Austl. E8 70
Dawson, Isla, i., Chile G2 78
Dawson, Mount, mtn., B.C., Can. D9 99
Dawson Creek, B.C., Can. B7 99
Dawson Range, mts., Austl. E8 70
Dawson Springs, Ky., U.S. C2 124
Dawsonville, Ga., U.S. B2 117
Dawusi, China D5 30
Dax, Fr. I5 14
Daxian, China E8 30
Daxing, China C4 32
Daxue Shan, mts., China E7 30
Day, co., S.D., U.S. B8 148
Daye, China D1 34
Daying, China D1 32
Daying (Taping), stm., Asia B5 40
Daykin, Ne., U.S. D8 134
Daylesford, Austl. K6 70
Daymān, stm., Ur. F10 80
Daym Zubayr, Sud. N4 60
Dayr Abū Sa'īd, Jord. C5 50
Dayr 'Alī, Syria B6 50
Dayr az-Zawr, Syria D6 48
Dayr Qānūn, Syria A6 50
Dayrūt, Egypt D6 60
Daysland, Alta., Can. C4 98
Dayton, Id., U.S. G6 119
Dayton, In., U.S. D4 121
Dayton, Ia., U.S. B3 122
Dayton, Ky., U.S. h14 124
Dayton, Md., U.S. B4 127
Dayton, Mn., U.S. m12 130
Dayton, Mt., U.S. C2 133
Dayton, Nv., U.S. D2 135
Dayton, N.J., U.S. C3 137
Dayton, Oh., U.S. C1 142
Dayton, Or., U.S. B3 144
Dayton, Tn., U.S. D8 149
Dayton, Tx., U.S. D5 150
Dayton, Va., U.S. B4 153
Dayton, Wa., U.S. C8 154
Dayton, Wy., U.S. B5 157
Daytona Beach, Fl., U.S. C5 116
Dayu, China J3 34
Dayu Ling, mts., China J3 34
Da Yunhe (Grand Canal), China E10 30
Dayville, Ct., U.S. B8 114
Dazey, N.D., U.S. B7 141
Dazui, China E3 34
Dcheïra, Mor. E6 62
De Aar, S. Afr. H7 66
Dead, North Branch, stm., Me., U.S. C2 126
Dead, South Branch, stm., Me., U.S. C2 126
Dead Creek, stm., Vt., U.S. C2 152
Dead Diamond, stm., N.H., U.S. g7 136
Dead Indian Peak, mtn., Wy., U.S. B3 157
Dead Lake, l., Mn., U.S. D3 130
Dead Lakes, l., Fl., U.S. B1 116
Deadman Bay, b., Fl., U.S. C3 116
Deadman Creek, stm., Wa., U.S. g14 154
Deadman's Cay, Bah. C7 94
Dead Sea (Al-Bahr al-Mayyit) (Yam HaMelah), l., Asia F4 50
Deadwood, S.D., U.S. C2 148
Deadwood Reservoir, res., Id., U.S. E3 119
Deaf Smith, co., Tx., U.S. B1 150
Deakin, Austl. F5 68
Deal, Eng., U.K. J15 8
Deal, N.J., U.S. C4 137
Deale, Md., U.S. C4 127
Deal Island, Md., U.S. D6 127
Deal Island, i., Md., U.S. D6 127
Dean, stm., B.C., Can. C4 99
Dean Channel, strt., B.C., Can. C4 99
Deán Funes, Arg. F6 80
Deanville, W.V., U.S. B4 155
Dearborn, Mi., U.S. F7 129
Dearborn, Mo., U.S. B3 132
Dearborn, co., In., U.S. F7 121
Dearborn Heights, Mi., U.S. p15 129
Dearing, Ga., U.S. C4 117
Dearing, Ks., U.S. E8 123
De Armanville, Al., U.S. B4 108
Deary, Id., U.S. C2 119
Dease Arm, b., N.W. Ter., Can. C8 96
Dease Lake, B.C., Can. m16 99
Dease Strait, strt., N.W. Ter., Can. C11 96
Death Valley, val., Ca., U.S. D5 112
Death Valley National Monument, U.S. D5 112
Deatsville, Al., U.S. C3 108
Deauville, Fr. C7 14
Deaver, Wy., U.S. B4 157
De Baca, co., N.M., U.S. C5 138
Debar, Mac. H4 20
De Bary, Fl., U.S. D5 116
Debauch Mountain, mtn., Ak., U.S. C8 109
Debden, Sask., Can. D2 105
Debec, N.B., Can. C2 101
De Beque, Co., U.S. B2 113
Dębica, Pol. E21 10
Dęblin, Pol. D21 10
De Borgia, Mt., U.S. C1 133
Deboullie Mountain, mtn., Me., U.S. B4 126
Debrecen, Hung. H21 10
Debre Markos, Eth. L9 60
Debre May, Eth. L9 60
Debre Tabor, Eth. L10 60
Debre Zebit, Eth. L10 60
Debre Zeyit, Eth. M10 60
Debrzno, Pol. B17 10
De Cade, Lake, l., La., U.S. E5 125
Decatur, Al., U.S. A3 108
Decatur, Ar., U.S. A1 111
Decatur, Ga., U.S. C2 117
Decatur, Il., U.S. D5 120
Decatur, In., U.S. C8 121
Decatur, Mi., U.S. F5 129
Decatur, Ms., U.S. C4 131
Decatur, Ne., U.S. B9 134
Decatur, Tn., U.S. D9 149
Decatur, Tx., U.S. C4 150
Decatur, co., Ga., U.S. F2 117
Decatur, co., In., U.S. F6 121
Decatur, co., Ia., U.S. D4 122
Decatur, co., Ks., U.S. C3 123
Decatur, co., Tn., U.S. B3 149
Decatur, Lake, res., Il., U.S. D5 120
Decaturville, Tn., U.S. B3 149
Decazeville, Fr. H9 14
Deccan, plat., India D5 46
Deception, stm., Bots. C6 66
Deception, Mount, mtn., Wa., U.S. B2 154
Deception Island, i., Ant. B12 73
Decherd, Tn., U.S. B5 149
Děčín, Czech. E14 10
Decize, Fr. F10 14
Decker, Man., Can. D1 100
Decker, In., U.S. G2 121
Decker Lake, B.C., Can. B5 99
Deckers, Co., U.S. B5 113
Deckerville, Mi., U.S. E8 129
Declo, Id., U.S. G5 119
De Cocksdorp, Neth. B6 12
Decorah, Ia., U.S. A6 122
Decota, W.V., U.S. m13 155
Decs, Hung. I18 10
Deda, Rom. C8 20
Dedham, Ia., U.S. C3 122
Dedham, Ma., U.S. B5 128
De Doorns, S. Afr. I4 66
Dédougou, Burkina E8 64
Dedovsk, Russia F20 22
Dee, stm., U.K. H10 8
Dee, stm., Scot., U.K. D11 8
Deep, stm., N.C., U.S. B3 140
Deep Brook, N.S., Can. E4 101
Deep Creek, stm., De., U.S. F3 115
Deep Creek, stm., Mt., U.S. C4 133
Deep Creek, stm., Ut., U.S. B3 151
Deep Creek, stm., Ut., U.S. C2 151
Deep Creek, stm., Ut., U.S. F3 151
Deep Creek, stm., Wa., U.S. g13 154
Deep Creek Lake, res., Md., U.S. K12 127
Deep Creek Mountains, mts., Id., U.S. G6 119
Deep Creek Range, mts., Ut., U.S. D2 151
Deep Fork, stm., Ok., U.S. B5 143
Deep Gap, N.C., U.S. A1 140
Deep Inlet, b., Newf., Can. g10 102
Deep Red Creek, stm., Ok., U.S. C3 143
Deep River, Ont., Can. A7 103
Deep River, Ct., U.S. D6 114
Deep River, Ia., U.S. C5 122
Deepstep, Ga., U.S. C4 117
Deepwater, Mo., U.S. C4 132
Deep Water, W.V., U.S. m13 155
Deer, Ar., U.S. B2 111
Deer Creek, Il., U.S. C4 120
Deer Creek, In., U.S. C5 121
Deer Creek, Mn., U.S. D3 130
Deer Creek, stm., In., U.S. C5 121
Deer Creek, stm., Md., U.S. A5 127
Deer Creek, stm., Ms., U.S. B3 131
Deer Creek, stm., Oh., U.S. C2 142
Deer Creek Indian Reservation, Mn., U.S. C5 130
Deerfield, Il., U.S. h9 120
Deerfield, Ks., U.S. E2 123
Deerfield, Ma., U.S. A2 128
Deerfield, Mi., U.S. G7 129
Deerfield, N.H., U.S. D4 136
Deerfield, Wi., U.S. E4 156
Deerfield, stm., U.S. A2 128
Deerfield Beach, Fl., U.S. F6 116
Deering, Ak., U.S. B7 109
Deering, N.D., U.S. A4 141
Deer Island, pen., Ma., U.S. g12 128
Deer Island, i., Ms., U.S. f8 131
Deer Isle, Me., U.S. D4 126
Deer Isle, i., Me., U.S. D4 126
Deer Lake, Newf., Can. D3 102
Deer Lake, l., Newf., Can. D3 102
Deer Lake, l., Mn., U.S. C5 130
Deer Lodge, Mt., U.S. D4 133
Deer Lodge, co., Mt., U.S. E3 133
Deer Mountain, mtn., Me., U.S. C2 126
Deer Park, Al., U.S. D1 108
Deer Park, Md., U.S. m12 127
Deer Park, N.Y., U.S. n15 139
Deer Park, Oh., U.S. o13 142
Deer Park, Tx., U.S. r14 150
Deer Park, Wa., U.S. B8 154
Deer Peak, mtn., Co., U.S. C5 113
Deer River, Mn., U.S. C5 130
Deer Trail, Co., U.S. B6 113
Deerwood, Mn., U.S. D5 130
Deeth, Nv., U.S. B6 135
Defiance, Ia., U.S. C2 122
Defiance, Mo., U.S. f12 132
Defiance, Oh., U.S. A1 142
Defiance, co., Oh., U.S. A1 142
Defiance, Mount, mtn., Or., U.S. B5 144
De Forest, Wi., U.S. E4 156
De Funiak Springs, Fl., U.S. u15 116
Dêgê, China E6 30
Degeh Bur, Eth. G9 56
Dégelis, Que., Can. B9 104
Degerfors, Swe. L14 6
Deggendorf, Ger. G12 10
Degh, stm., Asia D6 44
Degoma, Eth. K9 60
De Graff, Oh., U.S. B2 142
De Gray Lake, res., Ar., U.S. C2 111
De Grey, stm., Austl. D4 68
Dehalak Deset, i., Erit. E9 56
Deh Bīd, Iran F12 48
Dehibat, Tun. D16 62
Dehiwala-Mount Lavinia, Sri L. I5 46
Deh Kord, Iran E10 48
Dehlorān, Iran E9 48
Dehra Dūn, India E8 44
Dehri, India H11 44
Dehua, China J7 34
Dehui, China C12 30
Dej, Rom. B7 20
Dejnau, Turk. J10 26
De Kalb, Il., U.S. B5 120
De Kalb, Ms., U.S. C5 131
De Kalb, Mo., U.S. B3 132
De Kalb, Tx., U.S. C5 150
De Kalb, co., Al., U.S. A4 108
De Kalb, co., Ga., U.S. C2 117
De Kalb, co., Il., U.S. B5 120
De Kalb, co., In., U.S. B7 121
De Kalb, co., Mo., U.S. B3 132
De Kalb, co., Tn., U.S. D8 149
Dekemhare, Erit. J10 60
Dekese, Zaire B4 58
Dekina, Nig. H13 64
Delacroix, La., U.S. k12 125
Delafield, Wi., U.S. m11 156
De Lamere, N.D., U.S. C8 141
Delanco, N.J., U.S. C3 137
De Land, Fl., U.S. C5 116
De Land, Il., U.S. C5 120
Delano, Ca., U.S. E4 112
Delano, Mn., U.S. E5 130
Delano, Tn., U.S. D9 149
Delano Peak, mtn., Ut., U.S. E3 151
Delaplaine, Ar., U.S. A5 111
Delārām, Afg. E17 48
Delareyville, S. Afr. F7 66
Delaronde Lake, l., Sask., Can. C2 105
Del'atin, Ukr. A8 20
Delavan, Il., U.S. C4 120
Delavan, Ks., U.S. D7 123
Delavan, Wi., U.S. F5 156
Delaware, Ont., Can. E3 103
Delaware, Ar., U.S. B2 111
Delaware, Oh., U.S. B2 142
Delaware, Ok., U.S. A6 143
Delaware, co., In., U.S. D7 121
Delaware, co., Ia., U.S. B6 122
Delaware, co., N.Y., U.S. C5 139
Delaware, co., Oh., U.S. B2 142
Delaware, co., Ok., U.S. A7 143
Delaware, co., Pa., U.S. G11 145
Delaware, state, U.S. D3 115
Delaware, stm., U.S. E2 137
Delaware, stm., Ks., U.S. C8 123
Delaware, East Branch, stm., N.Y., U.S. C5 139
Delaware, West Branch, stm., U.S. C5 139
Delaware Bay, b., U.S. D11 106
Delaware City, De., U.S. B3 115
Delaware Lake, res., Oh., U.S. B3 142
Delaware Mountains, mts., Tx., U.S. o12 150
Delaware Water Gap, Pa., U.S. E11 145
Delaware Water Gap, N.J., U.S. B2 137
Delaware Water Gap National Recreation Area, U.S. B2 137
Delbarton, W.V., U.S. D2 155
Delburne, Alta., Can. C4 98
Delcambre, La., U.S. E4 125
Del Campillo, Arg. H6 80
Del City, Ok., U.S. B4 143
Delco, N.C., U.S. C4 140
Delegate, Austl. K8 70
Délembé, Cen. Afr. Rep. M2 60
Delémont, Switz. D7 13
De Leon, Tx., U.S. C3 150
De Leon Springs, Fl., U.S. C5 116
Delevan, N.Y., U.S. C2 139
Delfinópolis, Braz. F5 79
Delft, Neth. D5 12
Delfzijl, Neth. B10 12
Delgado, El Sal. D5 92
Delgado, Cabo, c., Moz. D8 58
Delhi, India F7 44
Delhi, Ia., U.S. B6 122
Delhi, La., U.S. B4 125
Delhi, N.Y., U.S. C6 139
Delhi, ter., India F7 44
Delia, Alta., Can. D4 98
Delia, Ks., U.S. C8 123
Delicias, Mex. C7 90
Delight, Ar., U.S. C2 111
Delingde, Russia C14 28
Delingha, China D6 30
Delisle, Sask., Can. F2 105
De Lisle, Ms., U.S. E4 131
Delitzsch, Ger. D12 10
Dell, Ar., U.S. B5 111
Dell City, Tx., U.S. o12 150
Delle, Fr. E14 14
Dellenbaugh, Mount, mtn., Az., U.S. A2 110
Delles, Alg. B12 62
Dell Rapids, S.D., U.S. D9 148
Dellslow, W.V., U.S. h11 155
Delmar, Al., U.S. A2 108
Del Mar, Ca., U.S. o15 112
Delmar, De., U.S. G3 115
Delmar, Ia., U.S. C7 122
Delmar, Md., U.S. D6 127
Delmar, N.Y., U.S. C7 139
Delmarva Peninsula, pen., U.S. D11 106
Delmas, Sask., Can. E1 105
Delmenhorst, Ger. B8 10
Delmont, S.D., U.S. D7 148
Del Norte, Co., U.S. D4 113
Del Norte, co., Ca., U.S. B2 112
Deloit, Ia., U.S. B2 122
Delong, In., U.S. B5 121
De-Longa, ostrova, is., Russia B22 28
Deloraine, Austl. M7 70
Deloraine, Man., Can. E1 100
Deloro, Ont., Can. C7 103
Del Park Manor, De., U.S. i7 115
Delphi, In., U.S. C4 121
Delphi see Dhelfoí, hist., Grc. K6 20
Delphos, Ks., U.S. C6 123
Delphos, Oh., U.S. B1 142
Delran, N.J., U.S. C3 137
Delray Beach, Fl., U.S. F6 116
Del Rio, Tx., U.S. E2 150
Delson, Que., Can. q19 104
Delta, Ont., Can. C8 103
Delta, Al., U.S. B4 108
Delta, Co., U.S. C2 113
Delta, Ia., U.S. C5 122
Delta, Mo., U.S. D8 132
Delta, Oh., U.S. A2 142
Delta, Pa., U.S. G9 145
Delta, Ut., U.S. D3 151
Delta, co., Co., U.S. C3 113
Delta, co., Mi., U.S. C3 129
Delta, co., Tx., U.S. C5 150
Delta, reg., Ms., U.S. B3 131
Delta Amacuro, ter., Ven. C12 84
Delta Beach, Man., Can. D2 100
Delta City, Ms., U.S. B3 131
Delta Downs, Austl. A4 70
Delta Junction, Ak., U.S. C10 109
Delta Peak, mtn., B.C., Can. A3 99
Delta Reservoir, res., N.Y., U.S. B5 139
Deltaville, Va., U.S. C6 153
Delton, Mi., U.S. F5 129
Deltona, Fl., U.S. D5 116
Demaine, Sask., Can. G2 105
Dem'ansk, Russia D15 22
Demarest, N.J., U.S. h9 137
Demba, Zaire C4 58
Dembecha, Eth. L9 60
Dembéni, Com. k15 67a
Dembi, Eth. M9 60
Dembi Dolo, Eth. M8 60
Demerara, stm., Guy. D13 84
Demidov, Russia F14 22
Deming, N.M., U.S. E2 138
Deming, Wa., U.S. A3 154
Demini, stm., Braz. H11 84
Demirci, Tur. J12 20
Demirtaş, Tur. I13 20
Demjanka, stm., Russia F6 28
Demjanskoje, Russia F11 26
Demmin, Ger. B13 10
Demnate, Mor. E7 62
Demopolis, Al., U.S. C2 108
Demopolis Lock and Dam, Al., U.S. C2 108
Demorest, Ga., U.S. B3 117
Demorestville, Ont., Can. C7 103
Demotte, In., U.S. B3 121
Dempster, S.D., U.S. C9 148
Denain, Fr. B10 14
Denakil, reg., Afr. F9 56
Denali National Park, Ak., U.S. C9 109
Denare Beach, Sask., Can. C4 105
Denau, Uzb. J11 26
Denbigh, Wales, U.K. H10 8
Dender (Dendre), stm., Bel. G4 12
Dendermonde (Termonde), Bel. F5 12
Dendron, S. Afr. D9 66
Dendron, Va., U.S. C6 153
Deneba, Eth. M10 60
Dengcheng, China B3 34
Dênggên, China E6 30
Dengshahe, China D10 32
Denham, Austl. E2 68
Denham, In., U.S. B4 121
Denham, Mount, mtn., Jam. E6 94
Denham Island, i., Austl. A3 70
Denham Range, mts., Austl. C7 70
Denham Springs, La., U.S. D5 125
Den Helder, Neth. C6 12
Denhoff, N.D., U.S. B5 141
Denholm, Sask., Can. E1 105
Dénia, Spain G12 16
Déniè, Mali F6 64
Deniliquin, Austl. J6 70
Denison, Ia., U.S. B2 122
Denison, Ks., U.S. k14 123
Denison, Tx., U.S. C4 150
Denison Dam, U.S. D5 143
Denizli, Tur. L13 20
Denmark, Austl. F3 68
Denmark, N.S., Can. D6 101
Denmark, Ia., U.S. D6 122
Denmark, S.C., U.S. E5 147
Denmark, Wi., U.S. D6 156
Denmark (Danmark), ctry., Eur. D10 4
Denmark Strait, strt. B4 52
Dennard, Ar., U.S. B3 111
Dennehotso, Az., U.S. A6 110
Denning, Ar., U.S. B2 111
Dennis, Ks., U.S. E8 123
Dennis, Ma., U.S. C7 128
Dennis, Ms., U.S. A5 131
Dennis Hill, mtn., Ct., U.S. B3 114
Dennison, Mn., U.S. F5 130
Dennison, Oh., U.S. B4 142
Dennis Port, Ma., U.S. C7 128
Denny Terrace, S.C., U.S. C5 147
Denpasar, Indon. G6 38
Dent, Mn., U.S. D3 130
Dent, co., Mo., U.S. D6 132
Denton, Ga., U.S. E4 117
Denton, Ks., U.S. C8 123
Denton, Md., U.S. C6 127
Denton, Mi., U.S. p14 129
Denton, Mt., U.S. C7 133
Denton, Ne., U.S. D9 134
Denton, N.C., U.S. B2 140
Denton, Tx., U.S. C4 150
Denton, co., Tx., U.S. C4 150
D'Entrecasteaux, Point, c., Austl. F3 68
D'Entrecasteaux Islands, is., Pap. N. Gui. A10 68
Dentsville, S.C., U.S. C6 147
Denver, Co., U.S. B6 113
Denver, In., U.S. C5 121
Denver, Ia., U.S. B5 122
Denver, N.C., U.S. B1 140
Denver, Pa., U.S. F9 145
Denver, Tn., U.S. A4 149
Denver, co., Co., U.S. B6 113
Denver City, Tx., U.S. C1 150
Denville, N.J., U.S. B4 137
Denzil, Sask., Can. E1 105
Deoghar, India H12 44
Deolāli, India C2 46
Deoria, India G10 44
Depauw, In., U.S. H5 121
De Pere, Wi., U.S. D5 156
Depew, N.Y., U.S. C2 139
Depew, Ok., U.S. B5 143
Depoe Bay, Or., U.S. C2 144
Depok, Indon. j13 39a
Deport, Tx., U.S. C5 150
Deposit, N.Y., U.S. C5 139
Depue, Il., U.S. B4 120
Deputy, In., U.S. G6 121
Dêqên, China F6 30
De Queen, Ar., U.S. C1 111
De Queen Reservoir, res., Ar., U.S. C1 111
De Quincy, La., U.S. D2 125
Dera, Lach, val., Afr. A8 58
Dera Ghāzi Khān, Pak. E4 44
Dera Ismāīl Khān, Pak. E4 44
Derbent, Russia I7 26
Derby, Austl. M7 70
Derby, N.B., Can. C4 101
Derby, Eng., U.K. I12 8
Derby, Ct., U.S. D3 114
Derby, Ks., U.S. E6 123
Derby, Ms., U.S. E4 131
Derby, N.Y., U.S. C2 139
Derby, Vt., U.S. B4 152
Derby, Va., U.S. f9 153
Derby Junction, N.B., Can. C4 101
Derby Line, Vt., U.S. A4 152
Derbyshire, co., Eng., U.K. H12 8
Derdepoort, S. Afr. E8 66
Derecske, Hung. H21 10
Derev'anka, Russia K24 6
De Ridder, La., U.S. D2 125
Derik, Tur. C6 48
Derma, Ms., U.S. B4 131
Dermott, Ar., U.S. D4 111
Dernieres, Isles, is., La., U.S. E5 125
Déroute, Passage de la, strt., Eur. L11 8
Derriesseaux Creek, stm., Ar., U.S. C3 111
Derry, N.H., U.S. E4 136
Derry, N.M., U.S. E2 138
Derry, Pa., U.S. F3 145
Derry see Londonderry, N. Ire., U.K. F6 8

Easl-Elho

Name	Map Ref.	Page
Easley, S.C., U.S.	B2	147
East, stm., Ct., U.S.	D5	114
East, stm., N.Y., U.S.	k13	139
East, stm., Wi., U.S.	h9	156
Eastaboga, Al., U.S.	B3	108
Eastabuchie, Ms., U.S.	D4	131
East Acton, Ma., U.S.	g10	128
East Alstead, N.H., U.S.	D2	136
East Alton, Il., U.S.	E3	120
East Andover, N.H., U.S.	D3	136
East Angus, Que., Can.	D6	104
East Arlington, Vt., U.S.	E2	152
East Aurora, N.Y., U.S.	C2	139
East Baldwin, Me., U.S.	E2	126
East Bangor, Pa., U.S.	E11	145
East Bank, W.V., U.S.	m13	155
East Barre, Vt., U.S.	C4	152
East Baton Rouge, co., La., U.S.	D4	125
East Bay, b., Fl., U.S.	u16	116
East Bay, b., Tx., U.S.	R15	150
East Beckwith Mountain, mtn., Co., U.S.	C3	113
East Bend, N.C., U.S.	A2	140
East Berbice-Corentyne, prov., Guy.	E13	84
East Berlin, Ct., U.S.	C5	114
East Berlin, Pa., U.S.	G8	145
East Bernard, Tx., U.S.	E4	150
East Bernstadt, Ky., U.S.	C5	124
East Bethel, Mn., U.S.	E5	130
East Bethel, Vt., U.S.	D3	152
East Billerica, Ma., U.S.	f11	128
East Blue Hill, Me., U.S.	D4	126
East Bonne Terre, Mo., U.S.	D7	132
East Boothbay, Me., U.S.	E3	126
Eastborough, Ks., U.S.	g12	123
East Brady, Pa., U.S.	E2	145
East Branch Clarion River Lake, res., Pa., U.S.	C4	145
East Brewton, Al., U.S.	D2	108
East Bridgewater, Ma., U.S.	B6	128
East Brimfield Lake, res., Ma., U.S.	B3	128
East Brookfield, Ma., U.S.	B3	128
East Brooklyn, Ct., U.S.	B8	114
East Broughton, Que., Can.	C6	104
East Brunswick, N.J., U.S.	C4	137
East Burke, Vt., U.S.	B5	152
East Butler, Pa., U.S.	E2	145
East Butte, mtn., Mt., U.S.	B5	133
East Cache Creek, stm., Ok., U.S.	C3	143
East Caicos, i., T./C. Is.	D9	94
East Calais, Vt., U.S.	C4	152
East Camden, Ar., U.S.	D3	111
East Canaan, Ct., U.S.	A2	114
East Candia, N.H., U.S.	D4	136
East Cape, c., N.Z.	B7	72
East Cape, c., Fl., U.S.	G5	116
East Carbon, Ut., U.S.	D5	151
East Carroll, co., La., U.S.	B4	125
East Chain, Mn., U.S.	G3	130
East Chicago, In., U.S.	A3	121
East China Sea, Asia	r3	37b
East Chop, c., Ma., U.S.	D6	128
East Cleveland, Oh., U.S.	g9	142
East Concord, Vt., U.S.	C5	152
East Corinth, Me., U.S.	D3	126
East Cote Blanche Bay, b., La., U.S.	E4	125
East Coulee, Alta., Can.	D4	98
East Dennis, Ma., U.S.	C7	128
East Derry, N.H., U.S.	E4	136
East Detroit, Mi., U.S.	p16	129
East Dorset, Vt., U.S.	E2	152
East Douglas, Ma., U.S.	B4	128
East Dover, Vt., U.S.	F3	152
East Dubuque, Il., U.S.	A3	120
East Dummerston, Vt., U.S.	F3	152
East Eddington, Me., U.S.	D4	126
East Ellijay, Ga., U.S.	B2	117
Eastend, Sask., Can.	H1	105
Easter, Mount, mtn., Ct., U.S.	B2	114
Easter Island see Pascua, Isla de, i., Chile	G4	74
Eastern Bay, b., Md., U.S.	C5	127
Eastern Ghāts, mts., India	F5	46
Eastern Neck Island, i., Md., U.S.	B5	127
Eastern Point, c., Ma., U.S.	f13	128
Easterville, Man., Can.	C2	100
East Fairfield, Vt., U.S.	B3	152
East Fairview, N.D., U.S.	B1	141
East Falkland, i., Falk. Is.	G5	78
East Falmouth, Ma., U.S.	C6	128
East Farmington Heights, Ct., U.S.	C4	114
East Feliciana, co., La., U.S.	D4	125
East Flat Rock, N.C., U.S.	f10	140
Eastford, Ct., U.S.	B7	114
East Fork, stm., Wy., U.S.	D3	157
East Fork Lake, res., Oh., U.S.	C1	142
East Foxboro, Ma., U.S.	B5	128
East Frisian Islands see Ostfriesische Inseln, is., Ger.	B7	10
East Fultonham, Oh., U.S.	C3	142
East Gaffney, S.C., U.S.	A4	147
East Galesburg, Il., U.S.	C3	120
East Glacier Park, Mt., U.S.	B3	133
East Glastonbury, Ct., U.S.	C5	114
East Granby, Ct., U.S.	B5	114
East Grand Forks, Mn., U.S.	C2	130
East Grand Rapids, Mi., U.S.	F5	129
East Greenville, Pa., U.S.	F10	145
East Greenwich, R.I., U.S.	D4	146
East Gwillimbury, Ont., Can.	C5	103
East Haddam, Ct., U.S.	D6	114
Eastham, Ma., U.S.	C8	128
East Hampstead, N.H., U.S.	E4	136
East Hampton, Ct., U.S.	C5	114
Easthampton, Ma., U.S.	B2	128
East Hampton, N.Y., U.S.	n16	139
East Hanover, N.J., U.S.	*B4	137
East Hardwick, Vt., U.S.	B4	152
East Hartford, Ct., U.S.	B5	114
East Hartland, Ct., U.S.	B4	114
East Haven, Ct., U.S.	D4	114
East Haverhill, N.H., U.S.	B3	136
East Helena, Mt., U.S.	D5	133
East Holden, Me., U.S.	D4	126
East Jordan, N.S., Can.	F4	101
East Jordan, Mi., U.S.	C5	129
East Juliette, Ga., U.S.	C3	117
East Kilbride, Scot., U.K.	F9	8
East Killingly, Ct., U.S.	B8	114
East Kingston, N.H., U.S.	E4	136
East Lansing, Mi., U.S.	F6	129
Eastlake, Mi., U.S.	D4	129
Eastlake, Oh., U.S.	A4	142
East Lake, l., Ont., Can.	C5	100
East Lake Tohopekaliga, l., Fl., U.S.	D5	116
Eastland, Tx., U.S.	C3	150
Eastland, co., Tx., U.S.	C3	150
East Lansing, Mi., U.S.	F6	129
East Las Vegas, Nv., U.S.	G6	135
East Laurinburg, N.C., U.S.	C3	140
East Lempster, N.H., U.S.	D2	136
East Liverpool, Oh., U.S.	B5	142
East London (Oos-Londen), S. Afr.	I8	66
East Longmeadow, Ma., U.S.	B2	128
East Los Angeles, Ca., U.S.	m12	112
East Lyme, Ct., U.S.	D7	114
East Lynn, Il., U.S.	C6	120
East Lynn, W.V., U.S.	C2	155
East Lynne, Mo., U.S.	C3	132
East Lynn Lake, res., W.V., U.S.	C2	155
East Machias, Me., U.S.	D5	126
East Madison, Me., U.S.	D3	126
Eastmain-Opinaca, Réservoir, res., Que., Can.	h11	104
Eastman, Que., Can.	D5	104
Eastman, Ga., U.S.	D3	117
Eastman, Wi., U.S.	E2	156
East Marion, N.Y., U.S.	m16	139
East Matunuck, R.I., U.S.	F3	146
East Middlebury, Vt., U.S.	D2	152
East Millbury, Ma., U.S.	B4	128
East Millinocket, Me., U.S.	C4	126
East Moline, Il., U.S.	B3	120
East Montpelier, Vt., U.S.	C4	152
East Naples, Fl., U.S.	F5	116
East Newark, N.J., U.S.	k8	137
East Newnan, Ga., U.S.	C2	117
East Nishnabotna, stm., Ia., U.S.	C2	122
East Norriton, Pa., U.S.	o20	145
East Olympia, Wa., U.S.	C3	154
Easton, Il., U.S.	C4	120
Easton, Ks., U.S.	k15	123
Easton, Me., U.S.	B5	126
Easton, Md., U.S.	C5	127
Easton, Mo., U.S.	B3	132
Easton, Pa., U.S.	E11	145
Easton, Wa., U.S.	B4	154
Easton Reservoir, res., Ct., U.S.	E2	114
East Orange, N.J., U.S.	B4	137
East Orleans, Ma., U.S.	C8	128
Eastover, S.C., U.S.	D6	147
East Palatka, Fl., U.S.	C5	116
East Palestine, Oh., U.S.	B5	142
East Parsonfield, Me., U.S.	E2	126
East Pass, strt., Fl., U.S.	C2	116
East Pea Ridge, W.V., U.S.	C2	155
East Peoria, Il., U.S.	C4	120
East Pepperell, Ma., U.S.	A4	128
East Petersburg, Pa., U.S.	F9	145
East Pittsburgh, Pa., U.S.	k14	145
Eastpoint, Fl., U.S.	C2	116
East Point, Ga., U.S.	C2	117
East Point, c., P.E.I., Can.	C8	101
East Point, c., Ma., U.S.	B6	128
East Point, c., N.J., U.S.	E2	137
Eastport, Newf., Can.	D5	102
Eastport, Me., U.S.	D6	126
Eastport, N.Y., U.S.	n16	139
East Poultney, Vt., U.S.	D2	152
East Prairie, Mo., U.S.	E8	132
East Providence, R.I., U.S.	C4	146
East Pryor Mountain, mtn., Mt., U.S.	E8	133
East Quogue, N.Y., U.S.	n16	139
East Range, mts., Nv., U.S.	C4	135
East Ridge, Tn., U.S.	h11	149
East Rindge, N.H., U.S.	E3	136
East River, Ct., U.S.	D5	114
East River Mountain, mts., U.S.	C1	153
East Rochester, N.Y., U.S.	B3	139
East Rockingham, N.C., U.S.	C3	140
East Rutherford, N.J., U.S.	h8	137
East Saint Johnsbury, Vt., U.S.	C5	152
East Saint Louis, Il., U.S.	E3	120
East Salt Creek, stm., Co., U.S.	B2	113
East Sandwich, Ma., U.S.	C7	128
East Sebago, Me., U.S.	E2	126
East Selkirk, Man., Can.	D3	100
East Siberian Sea see Vostočno-Sibirskoje more, Russia	C23	28
East Sioux Falls, S.D., U.S.	D9	148
Eastsound, Wa., U.S.	A3	154
East Sparta, Oh., U.S.	B4	142
East Spencer, N.C., U.S.	B2	140
East Stroudsburg, Pa., U.S.	D11	145
East Sullivan, Me., U.S.	D4	126
East Sullivan, N.H., U.S.	E2	136
East Swanzey, N.H., U.S.	E2	136
East Tawas, Mi., U.S.	D7	129
East Templeton, Ma., U.S.	A3	128
East Thermopolis, Wy., U.S.	C4	157
East Thompson, Ct., U.S.	A8	114
East Troy, Wi., U.S.	F5	156
East Vestal, N.Y., U.S.	C4	139
East View, W.V., U.S.	k10	155
East Walker, stm., U.S.	E2	135
East Wallingford, Vt., U.S.	E3	152
East Walpole, Ma., U.S.	h11	128
East Wareham, Ma., U.S.	C6	128
East Washington, Pa., U.S.	F1	145
East Waterboro, Me., U.S.	E2	126
East Wenatchee, Wa., U.S.	B5	154
East Wilton, Me., U.S.	D6	126
East Windsor, N.J., U.S.	C3	137
Eastwood, Ky., U.S.	g12	124
East York, Ont., Can.	D5	103
Eaton, Co., U.S.	A6	113
Eaton, In., U.S.	D7	121
Eaton, Oh., U.S.	C1	142
Eaton, co., Mi., U.S.	F6	129
Eatonia, Sask., Can.	F1	105
Eaton Rapids, Mi., U.S.	F6	129
Eatonton, Ga., U.S.	C3	117
Eatontown, N.J., U.S.	C4	137
Eatonville, Wa., U.S.	C3	154
Eau Claire, Mi., U.S.	G4	129
Eau Claire, Wi., U.S.	D2	156
Eau Claire, co., Wi., U.S.	D2	156
Eau Claire, stm., Wi., U.S.	D2	156
Eau Claire, Lac à l', l., Que., Can.	g11	104
Eauze, Fr.	I7	14
Eban, Nig.	G12	64
Ebano, Mex.	F10	90
Ebb and Flow Lake, l., Man., Can.	D2	100
Ebbw Vale, Wales, U.K.	J10	8
Ebenezer, Sask., Can.	F4	105
Eben Junction, Mi., U.S.	B4	129
Ebensburg, Pa., U.S.	F4	145
Ebensee, Aus.	H13	10
Eberbach, Ger.	F8	10
Ebermannstadt, Ger.	F11	10
Eberndorf, Aus.	I14	10
Ebersbach, Ger.	D14	10
Ebersberg, Ger.	G11	10
Eberstein, Aus.	I14	10
Eberswalde, Ger.	C13	10
Ebetsu, Japan	d16	36a
Ebinur Hu, l., China	C3	30
Ebnat, Switz.	D11	13
Eboli, Italy	I10	18
Ebolowa, Cam.	H9	54
Ebony, Nmb.	D2	66
Ebro (Ebre), stm., Spain	E12	16
Ebro, Embalse del, res., Spain	B8	16
Eccles, W.V., U.S.	n13	155
Echaporã, Braz.	G3	79
Ech Cheliff (Orléansville), Alg.	B11	62
Echeconnee Creek, stm., Ga., U.S.	D3	117
Echo, Al., U.S.	D4	108
Echo, La., U.S.	C3	125
Echo, Mn., U.S.	F3	130
Echo, Or., U.S.	B7	144
Echo Bay, Nv., U.S.	G7	135
Echoing Lake, l., Ont., Can.	B5	100
Echo Lake, l., Me., U.S.	D3	126
Echo Lake, l., Vt., U.S.	B5	152
Echols, co., Ga., U.S.	F4	117
Echt, Neth.	F8	12
Echuca, Austl.	K6	70
Écija, Spain	H6	16
Eckernförde, Ger.	A9	10
Eckerty, In., U.S.	H4	121
Eckhart Mines, Md., U.S.	k13	127
Eckley, Co., U.S.	A8	113
Eckville, Alta., Can.	C3	98
Eclectic, Al., U.S.	C3	108
Eclipse Sound, strt., N.W. Ter., Can.	B17	96
Ečmiadzin, Arm.	I6	26
Econfina, stm., Fl., U.S.	B3	116
Economy, N.S., Can.	D6	101
Economy, In., U.S.	E7	121
Economy, Pa., U.S.	*h13	145
Écorces, Rivière aux, stm., Que., Can.	A6	104
Ecorse, Mi., U.S.	p15	129
Écrins, Barre des, mtn., Fr.	H13	14
Ecru, Ms., U.S.	A4	131
Ector, co., Tx., U.S.	D1	150
Ecuador, ctry., S.A.	D3	76
Ecum Secum, N.S., Can.	E7	101
Ecum Secum Bridge, N.S., Can.	E7	101
Ed, Erit.	H2	47
Edam, Sask., Can.	D1	105
Edam, Neth.	C7	12
Edberg, Alta., Can.	C4	98
Edcouch, Tx., U.S.	F4	150
Eddiceton, Ms., U.S.	D3	131
Eddy, co., N.M., U.S.	E5	138
Eddy, co., N.D., U.S.	B7	141
Eddystone, Pa., U.S.	p20	145
Eddystone Point, c., Austl.	M8	70
Eddyville, Ia., U.S.	C5	122
Eddyville, Ky., U.S.	e9	124
Eddyville, Ne., U.S.	C6	134
Ede, Nig.	H12	64
Edéa, Cam.	H9	54
Edéia, Braz.	D4	79
Edelény, Hung.	G20	10
Eden, Austl.	K8	70
Eden, Man., Can.	D2	100
Eden, Az., U.S.	E6	110
Eden, Ga., U.S.	D5	117
Eden, Id., U.S.	G4	119
Eden, Md., U.S.	D6	127
Eden, N.Y., U.S.	C2	139
Eden, N.C., U.S.	A3	140
Eden, S.D., U.S.	B8	148
Eden, Tx., U.S.	D3	150
Eden, Ut., U.S.	B4	151
Eden, Wi., U.S.	E5	156
Eden, Wy., U.S.	D3	157
Edenburg, S. Afr.	G7	66
Eden Hill, hill, Ct., U.S.	D2	114
Eden Prairie, Mn., U.S.	n12	130
Edenton, N.C., U.S.	A6	140
Eden Valley, Mn., U.S.	E4	130
Edenville, S. Afr.	F8	66
Edenville, Mi., U.S.	E6	129
Edenwold, Sask., Can.	G3	105
Edeowie, Austl.	H3	70
Eder, stm., Ger.	D8	10
Edfu see Idfū, Egypt	E7	60
Edgar, Ne., U.S.	D8	134
Edgar, Wi., U.S.	D4	156
Edgar, co., Il., U.S.	D6	120
Edgard, La., U.S.	D5	125
Edgar Springs, Mo., U.S.	D6	132
Edgartown, Ma., U.S.	D6	128
Edgecombe, co., N.C., U.S.	B5	140
Edgecumbe, Cape, c., Ak., U.S.	m21	109
Edgefield, S.C., U.S.	D4	147
Edgefield, co., S.C., U.S.	D4	147
Edgeley, N.D., U.S.	C7	141
Edgemere, Md., U.S.	B5	127
Edgemont, S.D., U.S.	D2	148
Edgemoor, De., U.S.	A3	115
Edgemoor, S.C., U.S.	B5	147
Edgemoor, Tn., U.S.	m13	149
Edgeøya, i., Sval.	B3	24
Edgerly, La., U.S.	D2	125
Edgerton, Alta., Can.	C5	98
Edgerton, Ks., U.S.	D8	123
Edgerton, Mn., U.S.	G2	130
Edgerton, Mo., U.S.	B3	132
Edgerton, Oh., U.S.	A1	142
Edgerton, Wi., U.S.	F4	156
Edgerton, Wy., U.S.	C6	157
Edgewater, Al., U.S.	f7	108
Edgewater, Fl., U.S.	D6	116
Edgewater, Md., U.S.	C4	127
Edgewater, N.J., U.S.	h9	137
Edgewater Park, N.J., U.S.	C3	137
Edgewood, B.C., Can.	E8	99
Edgewood, Il., U.S.	E5	120
Edgewood, In., U.S.	D6	121
Edgewood, Ia., U.S.	B6	122
Edgewood, Ky., U.S.	h13	124
Edgewood, Md., U.S.	B5	127
Edgewood, N.M., U.S.	B3	138
Edgewood, Oh., U.S.	A5	142
Edgewood, Pa., U.S.	k14	145
Edgewood, Wa., U.S.	f11	154
Edgeworth, Pa., U.S.	h13	145
Édhessa, Grc.	I6	20
Edina, Mn., U.S.	F5	130
Edina, Mo., U.S.	A5	132
Edinboro, Pa., U.S.	C1	145
Edinburg, Il., U.S.	D4	120
Edinburg, N.D., U.S.	A8	141
Edinburg, Tx., U.S.	F3	150
Edinburg, Va., U.S.	B4	153
Edinburgh, Scot., U.K.	F10	8
Edinburgh, In., U.S.	F6	121
Edinburgh, Arrecife, rf., Nic.	C12	92
Edinburgh Channel, strt., Nic.	C12	92
Edincik, Tur.	I11	20
Edirne, Tur.	H10	20
Edison, Ga., U.S.	E2	117
Edison, Ne., U.S.	D6	134
Edison, N.J., U.S.	B4	137
Edison, Wa., U.S.	A3	154
Edisto, stm., S.C., U.S.	E6	147
Edisto, North Fork, stm., S.C., U.S.	D5	147
Edisto, South Fork, stm., S.C., U.S.	E5	147
Edisto Island, i., S.C., U.S.	F7	147
Edith, Mount, mtn., Mt., U.S.	D5	133
Edjeleh, Alg.	G15	62
Edmond, Ok., U.S.	B4	143
Edmonds, Wa., U.S.	B3	154
Edmondson, Ar., U.S.	B5	111
Edmondson Heights, Md., U.S.	*g10	127
Edmonson, co., Ky., U.S.	C3	124
Edmonton, Austl.	A6	70
Edmonton, Alta., Can.	C4	98
Edmonton, Ky., U.S.	D4	124
Edmore, Mi., U.S.	E5	129
Edmore, N.D., U.S.	A7	141
Edmunds, co., S.D., U.S.	B6	148
Edmundston, N.B., Can.	B1	101
Edna, Ks., U.S.	E8	123
Edna, Tx., U.S.	E4	150
Edolo, Italy	C5	18
Edon, Oh., U.S.	A1	142
Édouard, Lac, l., Que., Can.	B5	104
Edremit, Tur.	J11	20
Edsbro, Swe.	L16	6
Edsbyn, Swe.	K14	6
Edson, Alta., Can.	C2	98
Edson Butte, mtn., Or., U.S.	E2	144
Eduardo Castex, Arg.	H6	80
Edward, Lake, l., Afr.	B5	58
Edwards, Co., U.S.	B4	113
Edwards, Il., U.S.	C4	120
Edwards, Ms., U.S.	C3	131
Edwards, co., Il., U.S.	E5	120
Edwards, co., Ks., U.S.	E4	123
Edwards, co., Tx., U.S.	E2	150
Edwards Air Force Base, mil., Ca., U.S.	E5	112
Edwardsburg, Mi., U.S.	G4	129
Edwards Butte, mtn., Or., U.S.	B3	144
Edwards Plateau, plat., Tx., U.S.	D2	150
Edwardsport, In., U.S.	G3	121
Edwardsville, Al., U.S.	B4	108
Edwardsville, Il., U.S.	E4	120
Edwardsville, Ks., U.S.	k16	123
Edwardsville, Pa., U.S.	n17	145
Edward VII Peninsula, pen., Ant.	C9	73
Edwin, Al., U.S.	D4	108
Eek, Ak., U.S.	C7	109
Eeklo, Bel.	F4	12
Eel, stm., Ca., U.S.	B2	112
Eel, stm., In., U.S.	F3	121
Eel, stm., In., U.S.	C6	121
Effigy Mounds National Monument, Ia., U.S.	A6	122
Effingham, Il., U.S.	D5	120
Effingham, Ks., U.S.	C8	123
Effingham, co., Ga., U.S.	D5	117
Effingham, co., Il., U.S.	D5	120
Efland, N.C., U.S.	A3	140
Ega, stm., Spain	C9	16
Egadi, Isole, is., Italy	L7	18
Egan, S.D., U.S.	D9	148
Egaña, Arg.	I9	80
Egan Range, mts., Nv., U.S.	E7	135
Eganville, Ont., Can.	B7	103
Egegik, Ak., U.S.	D8	109
Egeland, N.D., U.S.	A6	141
Eger, Hung.	H20	10
Eger see Cheb, Czech.	E12	10
Egersund, Nor.	L10	6
Eggenburg, Aus.	G15	10
Egg Harbor City, N.J., U.S.	D3	137
Egg Island Point, c., N.J., U.S.	E2	137
Egilsstaðir, Ice.	B6	6a
Eglin Air Force Base, mil., Fl., U.S.	u15	116
Egmont, Mount, mtn., N.Z.	C4	72
Egmont Bay, b., P.E.I., Can.	C5	101
Egmont Channel, strt., Fl., U.S.	p10	116
Egmont Key, i., Fl., U.S.	p10	116
Egremont, Alta., Can.	B4	98
Éguas, Rio das, stm., Braz.	B6	79
Egypt, Ar., U.S.	B5	111
Egypt, Ga., U.S.	D5	117
Egypt, Ma., U.S.	B6	128
Egypt (Miṣr), ctry., Afr.	C7	56
Egypt, Lake of, res., Il., U.S.	F5	120
Ehrenberg, Az., U.S.	D1	110
Ehrhardt, S.C., U.S.	E5	147
Eibar, Spain	B9	16
Eichstätt, Ger.	G11	10
Eidsvåg, Nor.	J11	6
Eidsvold, Austl.	E9	70
Eielson Air Force Base, mil., Ak., U.S.	C10	109
Eifel, mts., Ger.	E6	10
Eiger, mtn., Switz.	E9	13
Eight Degree Channel, strt., Asia	I2	46
Eightmile Creek, stm., Ks., U.S.	h12	123
Eights Coast, Ant.	C11	73
Eighty Eight, Ky., U.S.	D4	124
Eighty Mile Beach, Austl.	C4	68
Eildon, Austl.	K6	70
Eildon, Lake, res., Austl.	K6	70
Eilenburg, Ger.	D12	10
Einasleigh, Austl.	B6	70
Einasleigh, stm., Austl.	A5	70
Einbeck, Ger.	D9	10
Eindhoven, Neth.	F7	12
Einsiedeln, Switz.	D10	13
Eiru, stm., Braz.	B6	82
Eirunepé, Braz.	B7	82
Eisden, Bel.	G8	12
Eisenach, Ger.	E10	10
Eisenberg, Ger.	E11	10
Eisenerz, Aus.	H14	10
Eisenhower, Mount, mtn., N.H., U.S.	B4	136
Eisenhüttenstadt, Ger.	C14	10
Eisenkappel, Aus.	I14	10
Eisenstadt, Aus.	H16	10
Eišiškės, Lith.	G8	22
Eisleben, Ger.	D11	10
Eitorf, Ger.	E7	10
Eivissa, Spain	G13	16
Eivissa (Ibiza), i., Spain	G13	16
Ejea de los Caballeros, Spain	C10	16
Ejeda, Madag.	t21	67b
Ejido, Ven.	C7	84
Ejido Jaboncillos, Mex.	C8	90
Ejin Qi, China	C7	30
Ejutla de Crespo, Mex.	I11	90
Ekalaka, Mt., U.S.	E12	133
Eket, Nig.	I13	64
Ekibastuz, Kaz.	G7	28
Ekpoma, Nig.	H13	64
Eksjö, Swe.	M14	6
Ela, Burma	E4	40
El Aaiún (La'youn), W. Sah.	G4	62
El Abiadh Sidi Cheikh, Alg.	D11	62
El Adeb Larache, Alg.	G15	62
El Adelanto, Guat.	C5	92
El Agreb, Alg.	E13	62
El Aguilar, Arg.	B6	80
Elaine, Ar., U.S.	C5	111
El Alamein see Al-'Alamayn, Egypt	B5	60
El Alia, Tun.	L5	18
El Alto, Arg.	E6	80
El Alto, Peru	J2	84
El Amparo de Apure, Ven.	D7	84
Elamville, Al., U.S.	D4	108
Elandsvlei, S. Afr.	I4	66
El Angel, Ec.	G4	84
El Aouinet, Alg.	N2	18
El Arahal, Spain	H6	16
El Arco, Mex.	C3	90
El Aricha, Alg.	C10	62
El Aroussa, Tun.	M4	18
Elat, Isr.	I3	50
El Ávila, Parque Nacional, Ven.	B9	84
Elâzığ, Tur.	B5	48
Elba, Al., U.S.	D3	108
Elba, Ne., U.S.	C7	134
Elba, Isola d', i., Italy	G5	18
El Banco, Col.	C6	84
El Barco de Valdeorras, Spain	C5	16
Elbasan, Alb.	H4	20
El Baúl, Ven.	C8	84
El Baúl, Cerro, mtn., Mex.	I12	90
El Baúl, Cerro, mtn., Mex.	I9	90
Elbe (Labe), stm., Eur.	B9	10
Elberfeld, In., U.S.	H3	121
Elberon, Ia., U.S.	B5	122
Elbert, Co., U.S.	B6	113
Elbert, co., Co., U.S.	B6	113
Elbert, co., Ga., U.S.	B4	117
Elbert, Mount, mtn., Co., U.S.	B4	113
Elberta, Al., U.S.	E2	108
Elberta, Ga., U.S.	D3	117
Elberta, Mi., U.S.	D4	129
Elberton, Ga., U.S.	B4	117
Elbeuf, Fr.	C8	14
El Beyyadh, Alg.	D11	62
Elbing, Ks., U.S.	f12	123
Elbistan, Tur.	B4	48
Elbląg (Elbing), Pol.	A19	10
El Bluff, Nic.	F11	92
El-Borouj, Mor.	D7	62
El Boulaïda, Alg.	B12	62
Elbow, Sask., Can.	F2	105
Elbow, stm., Alta., Can.	D3	98
Elbow Cay, i., Bah.	C4	94
Elbow Lake, Mn., U.S.	E3	130
El'brus, gora, mtn., Russia	I6	26
Elbrus, Mount see El'brus, gora, mtn., Russia	I6	26
Elburn, Il., U.S.	B5	120
El Cabezo, Arrecife, rf., Mex.	H12	90
El Caburé, Arg.	D7	80
El Caimanero, Laguna, b., Mex.	F6	90
El Cajon, Ca., U.S.	F5	112
El Cajón, Embalse, res., Hond.	B7	92
El Calafate, Arg.	G2	78
El Callao, Ven.	D12	84
El Calvario, Col.	E6	84
El Calvario, Ven.	C9	84
El Campo, Tx., U.S.	E4	150
El Capitan, mtn., Mt., U.S.	D2	133
El Capitan Reservoir, res., Ca., U.S.	o16	112
El Carmen, Arg.	C6	80
El Cármen, Bol.	H12	82
El Carmen, Col.	C6	84
El Carmen, Peru	E3	82
El Carmen, stm., Mex.	B6	90
El Carmen de Bolívar, Col.	C5	84
El Carricito, Mex.	C8	90
El Carril, Arg.	C6	80
El Castillo de La Concepción, Nic.	F10	92
El Cedral, Guat.	A4	92
El Cedrito, Mex.	C9	90
El Centro, Ca., U.S.	F6	112
El Cerrito, Col.	F4	84
El Cerrito, Ca., U.S.	h8	112
El Cerro, Bol.	G11	82
El Chile, Montaña, mtn., Hond.	C8	92
Elcho, Wi., U.S.	C4	156
El Chorrillo, Arg.	G5	80
El Cocuy, Col.	D6	84
El Colorado, Arg.	D9	80
El Cóndor, Cerro, mtn., Arg.	D4	80
El Congo, El Sal.	D5	92
El Corazón, Ec.	H3	84
El Corpus, Hond.	D7	92
El Coyote, stm., Mex.	B3	90
El Cozón, Mex.	B3	90
El Cuco, El Sal.	D6	92
El Cuervo, Laguna, l., Mex.	C7	90
El Cuervo Butte, mtn., N.M., U.S.	k9	138
Elda, Spain	G11	16
El Dátil, Mex.	B3	90
Eldersburg, Md., U.S.	B4	127
Eldersley, Sask., Can.	E4	105
El Desemboque, Mex.	C3	90
El Desemboque, Mex.	B3	90
El'dikan, Russia	E19	28
El Diviso, Col.	G3	84
El Djazaïr (Algiers), Alg.	B12	62
El Djelfa, Alg.	C12	62
Eldon, P.E.I., Can.	C7	101
Eldon, Ia., U.S.	D5	122
Eldon, Mo., U.S.	C5	132
Eldora, Ia., U.S.	B4	122
Eldorado, Arg.	D11	80
Eldorado, Braz.	C14	80
Eldorado, Ont., Can.	C7	103
El Dorado, Mex.	E6	90
El Dorado, Ar., U.S.	D3	111
Eldorado, Ga., U.S.	E3	117
Eldorado, Il., U.S.	F5	120
El Dorado, Ks., U.S.	E7	123
Eldorado, Oh., U.S.	C1	142
Eldorado, Ok., U.S.	C2	143
Eldorado, Tx., U.S.	D2	150
El Dorado, Ven.	D12	84
El Dorado, co., Ca., U.S.	C3	112
Eldorado Peak, mtn., Wa., U.S.	A4	154
Eldorado Springs, Co., U.S.	B5	113
El Dorado Springs, Mo., U.S.	D3	132
Eldorendo, Ga., U.S.	E2	117
Eldoret, Kenya	A7	58
Eldred, Il., U.S.	D3	120
Eldred, Pa., U.S.	C5	145
Eldridge, Al., U.S.	B2	108
Eldridge, Ia., U.S.	C7	122
Eleanor, W.V., U.S.	C3	155
Electra, Tx., U.S.	C3	150
Electra Lake, res., Co., U.S.	D3	113
Electric Peak, mtn., Co., U.S.	C5	113
Electric Peak, mtn., Mt., U.S.	E6	133
Elefante, Isla del see Elephant Island, i., Ant.	B1	73
Elefantes, Rio dos (Olifants), stm., Afr.	E11	66
Elei, Wādī, val., Afr.	G8	60
Eleja, Lat.	E6	22
Elektrogorsk, Russia	F21	22
Elektrostal', Russia	F21	22
El Encanto, Col.	H6	84
El Encanto, Guat.	I15	90
Elephant Butte Reservoir, res., N.M., U.S.	D2	138
Elephant Island, i., Ant.	K9	74
Elephant Mountain, mtn., Me., U.S.	D2	126
El Estor, Guat.	B5	92
El Eulma, Alg.	B13	62
Eleuthera, i., Bah.	B6	94
Eleuthera Point, c., Bah.	B6	94
Eleva, Wi., U.S.	D2	156
Eleven Mile Canyon Reservoir, res., Co., U.S.	C5	113
Eleven Point, stm., U.S.	A4	111
Elevsís, Grc.	K7	20
El Fahs, Tun.	M4	18
El Ferrol del Caudillo, Spain	B3	16
Elfrida, Az., U.S.	F6	110
Elfros, Sask., Can.	F4	105
El Fuerte, Mex.	D5	90
El Galpón, Arg.	C6	80
El Ghazawet, Alg.	C10	62
Elgin, Man., Can.	E1	100
Elgin, N.B., Can.	D4	101
Elgin, Scot., U.K.	D10	8
Elgin, Al., U.S.	A2	108
Elgin, Il., U.S.	A5	120
Elgin, Ia., U.S.	B6	122
Elgin, Ks., U.S.	E7	123
Elgin, Mn., U.S.	F6	130
Elgin, Ne., U.S.	C7	134
Elgin, N.D., U.S.	C4	141
Elgin, Ok., U.S.	C3	143
Elgin, Or., U.S.	B9	144
Elgin, S.C., U.S.	B6	147
Elgin, Tx., U.S.	D4	150
El Golfete, l., Guat.	B6	92
Elgon, Mount, mtn., Afr.	A6	58
El Grara, Alg.	D13	62
El Grove, Spain	C3	16
El Guaje, Mex.	D8	90
El Guaje, Laguna, l., Mex.	C8	90
El Guamo, Col.	B5	84
El Guapo, Ven.	B10	84
El Guayabo de Abajo, Mex.	D6	90
El Hadjar, Alg.	M2	18
El Hank, clf, Afr.	D5	54
El Haouaria, Tun.	L6	18
Elhovo, Bul.	G10	20

Elhu-Esca

Name | Map Ref. | Page

El Huecú, Arg. I3 80
El Huisache, Mex. F9 90
Elida, N.M., U.S. D6 138
Elida, Oh., U.S. B1 142
El Ídolo, Isla, i., Mex. G11 90
El Idrissia, Alg. C12 62
Elim, Ak., U.S. C7 109
El Infiernillo, Canal, strt., Mex. C3 90
Eliot, Me., U.S. E2 126
Élisabethville see Lubumbashi, Zaire D5 58
Elisenvaara, Russia K21 6
Elista, Russia H6 26
Elizabeth, Austl. J3 70
Elizabeth, Co., U.S. B6 113
Elizabeth, Il., U.S. A3 120
Elizabeth, In., U.S. H6 121
Elizabeth, La., U.S. D3 125
Elizabeth, Mn., U.S. D2 130
Elizabeth, Ms., U.S. B3 131
Elizabeth, N.J., U.S. B4 137
Elizabeth, W.V., U.S. B3 155
Elizabeth, Cape, c., Wa., U.S. B1 154
Elizabeth City, N.C., U.S. A6 140
Elizabeth Islands, is., Ma., U.S. D6 128
Elizabethton, Tn., U.S. C11 149
Elizabethtown, Il., U.S. F5 120
Elizabethtown, In., U.S. F6 121
Elizabethtown, Ky., U.S. C4 124
Elizabethtown, N.Y., U.S. A7 139
Elizabethtown, N.C., U.S. C4 140
Elizabethtown, Pa., U.S. F8 145
Elizabethville, Pa., U.S. E8 145
El-Jadida (Mazagan), Mor. D6 62
El Jaralito, Mex. D7 90
El Jebel, Co., U.S. B3 113
El-Jebha, Mor. J7 16
El Jem, Tun. N5 18
El Jícaro, stm., Nic. D8 92
Ełk, Pol. B22 10
Elk, co., Ks., U.S. E7 123
Elk, co., Pa., U.S. D4 145
Elk, stm., B.C., Can. D10 99
Elk, stm., U.S. A2 108
Elk, stm., Co., U.S. A4 113
Elk, stm., Ks., U.S. E7 123
Elk, stm., W.V., U.S. C3 155
Elk, stm., Wi., U.S. C3 156
Elkader, Ia., U.S. B6 122
El Kantara, Tun. D16 62
El-Karafab, Sud. H6 60
Elk City, Id., U.S. D3 119
Elk City, Ks., U.S. E8 123
Elk City, Ok., U.S. B2 143
Elk City Lake, res., Ks., U.S. E7 123
Elk Creek, Ne., U.S. D9 134
Elk Creek, stm., Ok., U.S. B2 143
Elk Creek, stm., S.D., U.S. C3 148
El Kef, Tun. M3 18
El-Kelâa-des-Srarhna, Mor. D7 62
El Kerma, Alg. J11 16
Elk Falls, Ks., U.S. E7 123
Elkford, B.C., Can. D10 99
Elk Garden, W.V., U.S. B5 155
Elk Grove, Ca., U.S. C3 112
Elk Grove Village, Il., U.S. h9 120
Elkhart, Il., U.S. C4 120
Elkhart, In., U.S. A6 121
Elkhart, Ia., U.S. e8 122
Elkhart, Ks., U.S. E2 123
Elkhart, Tx., U.S. D5 150
Elkhart, co., In., U.S. A6 121
Elkhart, stm., In., U.S. B6 121
Elkhart Lake, Wi., U.S. E5 156
Elkhead Mountains, mts., Co., U.S. A3 113
Elkhorn, Man., Can. E1 100
Elk Horn, Ia., U.S. C2 122
Elkhorn, Ne., U.S. g12 134
Elkhorn, Wi., U.S. F5 156
Elkhorn, stm., Ne., U.S. B7 134
Elkhorn, North Fork, stm., Ne., U.S. B8 134
Elkhorn, South Fork, stm., Ne., U.S. B7 134
Elkhorn City, Ky., U.S. C7 124
Elkhorn Peaks, mts., Id., U.S. F7 119
Elkin, N.C., U.S. A2 140
Elkins, Ar., U.S. A1 111
Elkins, W.V., U.S. C5 155
Elkland, Pa., U.S. C7 145
Elk Mills, Md., U.S. A6 127
Elkmont, Al., U.S. A3 108
Elk Mound, Wi., U.S. D2 156
Elk Mountain, Wy., U.S. E6 157
Elk Mountain, mtn., N.M., U.S. D1 138
Elk Mountain, mtn., Wy., U.S. E6 157
Elk Mountains, mts., U.S. D1 148
Elk Mountains, mts., Co., U.S. B3 113
Elko, B.C., Can. E10 99
Elko, Ga., U.S. D3 117
Elko, Nv., U.S. C6 135
Elko, co., Nv., U.S. B6 135
El Kouif, Alg. N3 18
Elk Park, N.C., U.S. A1 140
Elk Peak, mtn., Mt., U.S. D6 133
Elk Point, Alta., Can. C5 98
Elk Point, S.D., U.S. E9 148
Elk Rapids, Mi., U.S. D5 129
El Krib, Tun. M4 18
Elkridge, Md., U.S. B4 127
Elkridge, W.V., U.S. m13 155
Elk River, Id., U.S. C2 119
Elk River, Mn., U.S. E5 130
Elkton, Ky., U.S. D2 124
Elkton, Md., U.S. A6 127
Elkton, Mi., U.S. E7 129
Elkton, S.D., U.S. C9 148
Elkton, Tn., U.S. B5 149
Elkton, Va., U.S. B4 153
Elkview, W.V., U.S. m13 155
Elkville, Il., U.S. F4 120
Ellabell, Ga., U.S. D5 117
Ellaville, Ga., U.S. D2 117
Ellef Ringnes Island, i., N.W. Ter., Can. B9 86
Ellen, Mount, mtn., Ut., U.S. E5 151
Ellen, Mount, mtn., Vt., U.S. C3 152
Ellenboro, N.C., U.S. B1 140
Ellenboro, W.V., U.S. B3 155
Ellendale, De., U.S. E4 115
Ellendale, Mn., U.S. G5 130
Ellendale, N.D., U.S. C7 141
Ellensburg, Wa., U.S. C5 154
Ellenton, Fl., U.S. E4 116
Ellenton, Ga., U.S. E3 117
Ellenville, N.Y., U.S. D6 139
Ellenwood, Ga., U.S. h8 117
Ellerbe, N.C., U.S. B3 140
Ellershouse, N.S., Can. E6 101
Ellerslie, Ga., U.S. D2 117
Ellerslie, Md., U.S. k13 127
Ellès, Tun. N4 18
Ellesmere Island, i., N.W. Ter., Can. A11 86
Ellettsville, In., U.S. F4 121
Ellice, stm., N.W. Ter., Can. C12 96
Ellice Islands see Tuvalu, ctry., Oc. G24 2
Ellichpur see Achalpur, India J7 44
Ellicott City, Md., U.S. B4 127
Ellijay, Ga., U.S. B2 117
El Limón de Teachi, Mex. E6 90
Ellington, Ct., U.S. B6 114
Ellington, Mo., U.S. D7 132
Ellinwood, Ks., U.S. D5 123
Elliot, S. Afr. H8 66
Elliotdale, Transkei H9 66
Elliot Lake, Ont., Can. A2 103
Elliott, Il., U.S. C5 120
Elliott, Ia., U.S. C2 122
Elliott, Ms., U.S. B4 131
Elliott, S.C., U.S. C7 147
Elliott, co., Ky., U.S. B6 124
Elliott Bay, b., Wa., U.S. e11 154
Elliott Key, i., Fl., U.S. G6 116
Elliott Knob, mtn., Va., U.S. B3 153
Ellis, Ks., U.S. D4 123
Ellis, S.D., U.S. D9 148
Ellis, co., Ks., U.S. D4 123
Ellis, co., Ok., U.S. A2 143
Ellis, co., Tx., U.S. C4 150
Ellis, stm., N.H., U.S. B4 136
Ellis Grove, Il., U.S. E4 120
Ellison Bay, Wi., U.S. C6 156
Ellis Pond, l., Me., U.S. D2 126
Ellisras, S. Afr. D8 66
Elliston, Newf., Can. D5 102
Elliston, Mt., U.S. D4 133
Elliston, Va., U.S. C2 153
Ellisville, Ms., U.S. D4 131
Ellisville, Mo., U.S. f12 132
Elloree, S.C., U.S. D6 147
Ellore see Elūru, India F11 42
Ellport, Pa., U.S. E1 145
Ellsinore, Mo., U.S. E7 132
Ellsworth, Il., U.S. C5 120
Ellsworth, Ia., U.S. B4 122
Ellsworth, Ks., U.S. D5 123
Ellsworth, Me., U.S. D4 126
Ellsworth, Mi., U.S. C5 129
Ellsworth, Mn., U.S. G2 130
Ellsworth, Pa., U.S. F1 145
Ellsworth, Wi., U.S. D1 156
Ellsworth, co., Ks., U.S. D5 123
Ellsworth Air Force Base, mil., S.D., U.S. C2 148
Ellsworth Hill, mtn., Ct., U.S. B2 114
Ellsworth Land, reg., Ant. C12 73
Ellsworth Mountains, mts., Ant. C12 73
Ellwangen, Ger. G10 10
Ellwood City, Pa., U.S. E1 145
Elm, Switz. E11 13
Elm, stm., N.D., U.S. B8 141
Elm, stm., S.D., U.S. B7 148
Elma, Ia., U.S. A5 122
Elma, Wa., U.S. C2 154
El Mahdia, Tun. C16 62
El Malah, Alg. J10 16
El Maneadero, Mex. B1 90
El Manteco, Ven. D11 84
El Marsa el Kebir, Alg. C10 62
Elm City, N.C., U.S. B5 140
Elm Creek, Man., Can. E2 100
Elm Creek, Ne., U.S. D6 134
Elm Creek, stm., Mn., U.S. G4 130
El Médano, Mex. E4 90
Elmendorf, Tx., U.S. k7 150
Elmendorf Air Force Base, mil., Ak., U.S. C10 109
El Menia, Alg. E12 62
Elmer, N.J., U.S. D2 137
El Mghayyar, Alg. D13 62
Elm Grove, Wi., U.S. m11 156
Elmhurst, Il., U.S. B6 120
Elmhurst, Pa., U.S. D10 145
El Milagro, Arg. F6 80
El Miliyya, Alg. B14 62
Elmina, Ghana I9 64
Elmira, P.E.I., Can. C7 101
Elmira, N.Y., U.S. C4 139
Elmira, Or., U.S. C3 144
El Mirage, Az., U.S. k8 110
Elmira Heights, N.Y., U.S. C4 139
Elmo, Mo., U.S. A2 132
Elmo, Mt., U.S. C2 133
Elmo, Ut., U.S. D5 151
El Mochito, Hond. C6 92
El Mohammadia, Alg. C11 62
El Molinillo, Spain F7 16
Elmont, Ks., U.S. k14 123
Elmont, N.Y., U.S. k13 139
Elmont, Va., U.S. C5 153
El Monte, Chile G3 80
El Monte, Ca., U.S. m12 112
Elmora, Pa., U.S. E4 145
Elmore, Austl. K6 70
Elmore, Al., U.S. C3 108
Elmore, Mn., U.S. G4 130
Elmore, Oh., U.S. A2 142
Elmore, co., Al., U.S. C3 108
Elmore, co., Id., U.S. F3 119
Elmore City, Ok., U.S. C4 143
El Morro National Monument, N.M., U.S. B1 138
Elmsdale, N.S., Can. E6 101
Elmshorn, Ger. B9 10
Elm Springs, Ar., U.S. A1 111
Elm Springs Colony, S.D., U.S. D8 148
Elmsville, N.B., Can. D3 101
El Multe, Mex. I14 90
Elmvale, Ont., Can. C5 103
Elmville, Ct., U.S. B8 114
Elmwood, Ont., Can. C3 103
Elmwood, Il., U.S. C3 120
Elmwood, Ne., U.S. D9 134
Elmwood, Wi., U.S. D1 156
Elmwood Park, Il., U.S. k9 120
Elmwood Park, N.J., U.S. h8 137
Elmwood Place, Oh., U.S. o13 142
Elne, Fr. J9 14
El Negrito, Hond. B7 92
El Nihuil, Arg. H4 80
El Nopal, Cerro, mtn., Mex. C6 90
Elnora, Alta., Can. D4 98
Elnora, In., U.S. G3 121
El Ocote, Cerro, mtn., Mex. E6 90
Eloise, Fl., U.S. E5 116
Elon College, N.C., U.S. A3 140
Elora, Ont., Can. D4 103
Elora, Tn., U.S. B5 149
El Oro, prov., Ec. I3 84
Elortondo, Arg. G8 80
Elorza, Ven. D8 84
Eloy, Az., U.S. E4 110
Eloy Alfaro, Ec. I3 84
El Pacayal, Mex. J13 90
El Palmar, Bol. I10 82
El Palmar, Ven. D12 84
El Palqui, Chile F3 80
El Pao, Ven. C11 84
El Pao, Ven. C8 84
El Paraíso, Hond. C8 92
El Paraíso, dept., Hond. C8 92
El Paso, Spain o23 17b
El Paso, Ar., U.S. B3 111
El Paso, Il., U.S. C4 120
El Paso, Tx., U.S. o11 150
El Paso, co., Co., U.S. C6 113
El Paso, co., Tx., U.S. o11 150
El Peñuelo, Mex. E9 90
El Perú, Ven. D12 84
Elphinstone, Man., Can. D1 100
El Pilar, Ven. B11 84
El Piñón, Col. B5 84
El Pintado, Arg. C8 80
El Piquete, Arg. C8 80
El Pital, Cerro, mtn., N.A. C5 92
El Portal, Ca., U.S. D4 112
El Portal, Fl., U.S. s13 116
El Port de Pollença, Spain F15 16
El Porvenir, Peru C2 82
El Porvenir, N.M., U.S. B4 138
El Prado, N.M., U.S. A4 138
El Prat de Llobregat, Spain D14 16
El Progreso, Guat. C5 92
El Progreso, Hond. B7 92
El Progreso, dept., Guat. C4 92
El Puerto de Santa María, Spain I5 16
El Puesto, Arg. D5 80
El Qala, Alg. B15 62
El Qoll, Alg. B14 62
El Quebrachal, Arg. C6 80
El Quelite, Mex. F6 90
Elqui, stm., Chile E3 80
Elrama, Pa., U.S. F2 145
El Rastro, Ven. C9 84
El Real de Santa María, Pan. C4 84
El Reno, Ok., U.S. B4 143
El Rey, Parque Nacional, Arg. C6 80
El Rito, N.M., U.S. A3 138
El Roble, Mesa, mtn., Mex. B2 90
Elrod, Al., U.S. B2 108
El Rom, Isr. Occ. B5 50
El Rosarito, Mex. C2 90
Elrose, Sask., Can. F1 105
Elroy, Wi., U.S. E3 156
Elsa, Yukon, Can. D5 96
Elsa, Tx., U.S. F3 150
Elsah, Il., U.S. E3 120
El Salado, Chile D3 80
El Salitre, Ec. H3 84
El Salto, Mex. F7 90
El Salvador, ctry., N.A. D6 92
El Samán de Apure, Ven. D8 84
El Sauz, Mex. C6 90
El Sauzal, Mex. B1 90
Elsberry, Mo., U.S. B7 132
El Seibo, Dom. Rep. E10 94
Elsie, Mi., U.S. E6 129
Elsie, Ne., U.S. D4 134
Elsinore, Ut., U.S. E3 151
Elsmere, De., U.S. B3 115
Elsmere, Ky., U.S. B5 124
El Socorro, Ven. C10 84
El Sombrero, Ven. C9 84
Elst, Neth. E8 12
Elsterwerda, Ger. D13 10
Elstow, Sask., Can. F2 105
El Sueco, Mex. C6 90
El Tagarete, Cerro, mtn., Mex. D7 90
El Tajín, hist., Mex. G11 90
El Tala, Arg. D6 80
El Tamarindo, El Sal. D7 92
El Tambo, Col. G4 84
El Tarf, Alg. M3 18
El Tecuán, Mex. E6 90
El Tigre, Ven. C10 84
El Tigre, Isla, i., Hond. D7 92
Eltmann, Ger. F10 10
El Tocuyo, Ven. C8 84
El Tofo, Chile E3 80
Elton, La., U.S. D3 125
Eltopia, Wa., U.S. C7 154
El Toro, Ca., U.S. n13 112
El Toro Marine Corps Air Station, mil., Ca., U.S. n13 112
El Tránsito, Chile E3 80
El Tránsito, El Sal. D6 92
El Trébol, Arg. G8 80
El Triunfo, Hond. D7 92
El Triunfo, Mex. F4 90
El Triunfo, Cerro, mtn., Mex. B2 92
El Triunfo de la Cruz, Hond. B7 92
El Tunal, Arg. C6 80
El Turbio, Arg. G2 78
Elūru, India D6 46
Elva, Man., Can. E1 100
Elva, Est. C9 22
El Vado Reservoir, res., N.M., U.S. A3 138
El Valle, Pan. C2 84
Elvas, Port. G4 16
El Vendrell, Spain D13 16
El Viejo, Nic. E7 92
El Vigía, Ven. C7 84
El Vigía, Cerro, mtn., Mex. G7 90
Elvins, Mo., U.S. D7 132
Elvira, Arg. H9 80
El Volcán, Chile G3 80
El Wad, Alg. D14 62
El Wanza, Alg. C15 62
Elwell, Lake, res., Mt., U.S. B5 133
Elwha, stm., Wa., U.S. A2 154
Elwood, In., U.S. D6 121
Elwood, Ks., U.S. C9 123
Elwood, Ne., U.S. D6 134
Elwood, N.J., U.S. D3 137
Elwood, Ut., U.S. B3 151
Elwood Park, Fl., U.S. E4 116
Elx, Spain G11 16
Ely, Ia., U.S. C6 122
Ely, Mn., U.S. C7 130
Ely, Nv., U.S. D7 135
El Yagual, Ven. D8 84
Elyria, Oh., U.S. A3 142
Elysburg, Pa., U.S. E8 145
Elysian, Mn., U.S. F5 130
Emāmshahr (Shāhrūd), Iran C13 48
Emanuel, co., Ga., U.S. D4 117
Emas, Parque Nacional das, Braz. E2 79
Emba, Kaz. H9 26
Emba, stm., Kaz. H9 26
Embarcación, Arg. B6 80
Embarras, stm., Il., U.S. E6 120
Embarrass, Wi., U.S. D5 156
Embarrass, stm., Wi., U.S. D5 156
Embden Pond, l., Me., U.S. D3 126
Embreeville, Tn., U.S. C11 149
Embro, Ont., Can. D4 103
Embrun, Fr. H13 14
Emden, Ger. B7 10
Emden, Il., U.S. C4 120
Emerado, N.D., U.S. B8 141
Emerald, Austl. D8 70
Emerson, Man., Can. E3 100
Emerson, Ar., U.S. D2 111
Emerson, Ga., U.S. B2 117
Emerson, Ia., U.S. C2 122
Emerson, Ne., U.S. B9 134
Emerson, N.J., U.S. h8 137
Emery, S.D., U.S. D8 148
Emery, Ut., U.S. E4 151
Emery, co., Ut., U.S. E5 151
Emery Mills, Me., U.S. E2 126
Emet, Tur. J13 20
Emida, Id., U.S. B2 119
Emiliano Zapata, Mex. I14 90
Emiliano Zapata, Bahía, b., Mex. H16 90
Emilia-Romagna, prov., Italy E6 18
Emily, Mn., U.S. D5 130
Emily, Lake, l., Mn., U.S. E3 130
Emine, nos, c., Bul. G11 20
Eminence, In., U.S. F4 121
Eminence, Ky., U.S. B4 124
Eminence, Mo., U.S. D6 132
Emlembe, mtn., Afr. E10 66
Emlenton, Pa., U.S. D2 145
Emlyn, Ky., U.S. D5 124
Emma, Mo., U.S. C4 132
Emma Lake, l., Sask., Can. D3 105
Emmaus, Pa., U.S. E11 145
Emmaville, Austl. G9 70
Emmeline Lake, l., Sask., Can. C2 105
Emmeloord, Neth. C8 12
Emmen, Neth. C10 12
Emmenbrücke, Switz. D9 13
Emmendingen, Ger. G7 10
Emmer-Compascuum, Neth. C11 12
Emmerich, Ger. D6 10
Emmet, Ar., U.S. D2 111
Emmet, co., Ia., U.S. A3 122
Emmet, co., Mi., U.S. C6 129
Emmetsburg, Ia., U.S. A3 122
Emmett, Id., U.S. F2 119
Emmett, Ks., U.S. C7 123
Emmiganūru, India E4 46
Emmitsburg, Md., U.S. A3 127
Emmonak, Ak., U.S. C7 109
Emmons, Mn., U.S. G5 130
Emmons, co., N.D., U.S. C5 141
Emory, Tx., U.S. E5 150
Emory Peak, mtn., Tx., U.S. E1 150
Empalme, Mex. D4 90
Empangeni, S. Afr. G10 66
Empedrado, Arg. D9 80
Empedrado, Chile H2 80
Empire, Al., U.S. B2 108
Empire, Co., U.S. B5 113
Empire, Ga., U.S. D3 117
Empire, La., U.S. E6 125
Empire, Mi., U.S. D4 129
Empire, Nv., U.S. C2 135
Empoli, Italy F5 18
Emporia, Ks., U.S. D7 123
Emporia, Va., U.S. D5 153
Emporium, Pa., U.S. D5 145
Empress, Alta., Can. D5 98
Empty Quarter see Ar-Rub' al-Khālī, des., Asia E5 47
Ems, stm., Eur. C7 10
Emsdale, Ont., Can. B5 103
Emsdetten, Ger. C7 10
Emsworth, Pa., U.S. h13 145
Emure-Ekiti, Nig. H12 64
En (Inn), stm., Eur. F17 14
Encampment, Wy., U.S. E6 157
Encantado, Braz. E13 80
Encarnación, Para. D11 80
Enchant, Alta., Can. D4 98
Encinal, Tx., U.S. E3 150
Encinitas, Ca., U.S. F5 112
Encino, N.M., U.S. C4 138
Encino, Tx., U.S. F3 150
Encontrados, Ven. C6 84
Encounter Bay, b., Austl. J3 70
Encruzilhada, Braz. C8 79
Encruzilhada do Sul, Braz. F12 80
Encs, Hung. G21 10
Endako, B.C., Can. B5 99
Endako, stm., B.C., Can. B5 99
Ende, Indon. G7 38
Endeavor, Wi., U.S. E4 156
Endeavour, Sask., Can. E4 105
Endeavour Strait, strt., Austl. B8 68
Enderby, B.C., Can. D8 99
Enderby Land, reg., Ant. B4 73
Enderlin, N.D., U.S. C8 141
Enders Reservoir, res., Ne., U.S. D4 134
Endiang, Alta., Can. D4 98
Endicott, Ne., U.S. D8 134
Endicott, N.Y., U.S. C4 139
Endicott, Wa., U.S. C8 154
Endicott Mountains, mts., Ak., U.S. B9 109
Endimari, stm., Braz. C8 82
Endless Lake, l., Me., U.S. C4 126
Endola, Nmb. A2 66
Endwell, N.Y., U.S. C4 139
Ene, stm., Peru D4 82
Enewetak, atoll, Marsh. Is. G20 158
Enez, Tur. I10 20
Enfida, Tun. M5 18
Enfield, N.S., Can. E6 101
Enfield (Thompsonville), Ct., U.S. B5 114
Enfield, Il., U.S. E5 120
Enfield, Me., U.S. C4 126
Enfield, N.H., U.S. C2 136
Enfield, N.C., U.S. A5 140
Enfield Center, N.H., U.S. C2 136
Engadine, Mi., U.S. B5 129
Engaño, Cabo, c., Dom. Rep. E10 94
Engcobo, Transkei H9 66
'En Gedi, Isr. F4 50
Engelberg, Switz. E9 13
Engelhard, N.C., U.S. B7 140
Engel's, Russia G7 26
Engenho, Braz. F13 82
'En Gev, Isr. C5 50
Enggano, Pulau, i., Indon. G3 38
England, Ar., U.S. C4 111
England, ter., U.K. I12 8
England Air Force Base, mil., La., U.S. C3 125
Englee, Newf., Can. C3 102
Englefeld, Sask., Can. E3 105
Englefield, Cape, c., N.W. Ter., Can. C15 96
Engleside, Va., U.S. g12 153
Englewood, Co., U.S. B6 113
Englewood, Fl., U.S. F4 116
Englewood, N.J., U.S. B5 137
Englewood, Oh., U.S. C1 142
Englewood, Tn., U.S. D9 149
Englewood Cliffs, N.J., U.S. h9 137
English, In., U.S. H5 121
English Bay, Ak., U.S. h16 109
English Channel (La Manche), strt., Eur. K12 8
English Coast, Ant. C12 73
Englishtown, N.J., U.S. C4 137
Énguera, Spain G11 16
Engure, Lat. D6 22
Engwilen, Switz. C11 13
'En Harod, Isr. C4 50
Enid, Ok., U.S. A4 143
Enid Lake, res., Ms., U.S. A4 131
Enigma, Ga., U.S. E3 117
Enilda, Alta., Can. B2 98
eNjesuthi, mtn., Afr. G9 66
Enka, N.C., U.S. f10 140
Enkhuizen, Neth. C7 12
Enmedio, Cerro de, mtn., Mex. H9 90
Enna, Italy L9 18
Ennedi, plat., Chad E5 56
Ennis, Mt., U.S. E5 133
Ennis, Tx., U.S. C4 150
Enniskillen, N. Ire., U.K. G6 8
Enns, Aus. G14 10
Enns, stm., Aus. G14 10
Enoch, Ut., U.S. F2 151
Enola, Ar., U.S. B3 111
Enola, Pa., U.S. F8 145
Enon, Oh., U.S. *C2 142
Enoree, S.C., U.S. B4 147
Enoree, stm., S.C., U.S. B3 147
Enosburg Falls, Vt., U.S. B3 152
Enrique Urien, Arg. D8 80
Enriquillo, Dom. Rep. F9 94
Enriquillo, Lago, l., Dom. Rep. E9 94
Enschede, Neth. D10 12
Ensenada, Arg. H10 80
Ensenada, Mex. B1 90
Ensenada, N.M., U.S. A3 138
Enshi, China E8 30
Ensign, Alta., Can. D4 98
Ensign, Ks., U.S. E3 123
Ensley, Fl., U.S. u14 116
Entebbe, Ug. A6 58
Enterprise, Ont., Can. C8 103
Enterprise, Guy. D13 84
Enterprise, Al., U.S. D4 108
Enterprise, Ks., U.S. D6 123
Enterprise, Ms., U.S. C5 131
Enterprise, Or., U.S. B9 144
Enterprise, Ut., U.S. F2 151
Enterprise, W.V., U.S. B4 155
Entiat, Wa., U.S. B5 154
Entiat, stm., Wa., U.S. B5 154
Entiat, Lake, l., Wa., U.S. B5 154
Entiat Mountains, mts., Wa., U.S. B5 154
Entrance, Alta., Can. C2 98
Entre Rios, Bol. I9 82
Entre Rios, Braz. A9 79
Entre Ríos, prov., Arg. F9 80
Entre Ríos, Cordillera, mts., Hond. C9 92
Entre-Rios de Minas, Braz. F6 79
Entroncamento, Port. F3 16
Entwistle, Alta., Can. C3 98
Enugu, Nig. H13 64
Enumclaw, Wa., U.S. B4 154
Envalira, Port d', Eur. C13 16
Envermeu, Fr. C8 14
Envigado, Col. D5 84
Enville, Tn., U.S. B3 149
Envira, Braz. B6 82
Envira, stm., Braz. B6 82
Eo, stm., Spain B4 16
Eola Hills, hills, Or., U.S. h11 144
Eolia, Mo., U.S. B6 132
Eolie, Isole, is., Italy K9 18
Epe, Nig. H11 64
Epecuén, Lago, l., Arg. I7 80
Épéhy, Fr. H3 12
Épernay, Fr. C10 14
Epes, Al., U.S. C1 108
Ephesus, Ga., U.S. C1 117
Ephesus, hist., Tur. L11 20
Ephraim, Ut., U.S. D4 151
Ephrata, Pa., U.S. F9 145
Ephrata, Wa., U.S. B6 154
Épinal, Fr. D13 14
Epirus see Ípeiros, hist. reg., Grc. J4 20
Epokiro, Nmb. C4 66
Epping, Eng., U.K. J14 8
Epping, N.H., U.S. D4 136
Epps, La., U.S. B4 125
Epsom, Eng., U.K. J13 8
Epsom, N.H., U.S. D4 136
Epukiro, stm., Afr. C5 66
Epworth, Ia., U.S. B7 122
Eqlīd, Iran F12 48
Equality, Al., U.S. C3 108
Equality, Il., U.S. F5 120
Equatorial Guinea, ctry., Afr. H8 54
Erath, La., U.S. E3 125
Erath, co., Tx., U.S. C3 150
Erba, Italy D4 18
Erbacon, W.V., U.S. C4 155
Erciş, Tur. B7 48
Erciyes Dağı, mtn., Tur. B3 48
Érd, Hung. H18 10
Erdaoliangzi, China C7 32
Erdene, Mong. C9 30
Erding, Ger. G11 10
Erebato, stm., Ven. E10 84
Erebus, Mount, mtn., Ant. C8 73
Ereğli, Tur. C3 48
Erenhot, China C9 30
Erepecuru, Lago do, l., Braz. H14 84
Eressós, Grc. J9 20
Erétria, Grc. K7 20
Erexim, Braz. D12 80
Erfoud, Mor. E8 62
Erft, stm., Ger. D6 10
Erfurt, Ger. E11 10
Erges (Erjas), stm., Eur. F5 16
Ērgļi, Lat. E8 22
Ergun (Argun'), stm., Asia A11 30
Er Hai, l., China B6 40
Erhard, Mn., U.S. D2 130
Erhlin, Tai. L9 34
Erial, N.J., U.S. D2 137
Eriba, Sud. I9 60
Erice, Italy K7 18
Erick, Ok., U.S. B2 143
Erickson, B.C., Can. E9 99
Erickson, Man., Can. D2 100
Ericson, Ne., U.S. C7 134
Erie, Co., U.S. A5 113
Erie, Il., U.S. B3 120
Erie, Ks., U.S. E8 123
Erie, Mi., U.S. G7 129
Erie, N.D., U.S. B8 141
Erie, Pa., U.S. B1 145
Erie, co., N.Y., U.S. C2 139
Erie, co., Oh., U.S. A3 142
Erie, co., Pa., U.S. C1 145
Erie, Lake, l., N.A. C10 106
Erieau, Ont., Can. E3 103
Erie Canal, N.Y., U.S. B5 139
Eriksdale, Man., Can. D2 100
Erimo-misaki, c., Japan f18 36a
Erin, Ont., Can. D4 103
Erin, Tn., U.S. A4 149
Eritrea, ctry., Afr. E8 56
Erjas (Erges), stm., Eur. F5 16
Erjiazhen, China C10 34
Erkelenz, Ger. D6 10
Erkowit, Sud. H9 60
Erlangen, Ger. F11 10
Erlanger, Ky., U.S. A5 124
Erling, Lake, res., Ar., U.S. D2 111
Erma, N.J., U.S. F3 137
Ermelo, Neth. D8 12
Ermelo, S. Afr. F9 66
Ermenek, Tur. C2 48
Ermoúpolis, Grc. L8 20
Erne, Lower Lough, l., N. Ire., U.K. G6 8
Erne, Upper Lough, l., Eur. G6 8
Ernée, Fr. D6 14
Ernfold, Sask., Can. G2 105
Erode, India G4 46
Eromanga, Austl. F5 70
Erongo, Nmb. C2 66
Erota, Erit. I9 60
Er-Rachidia, Mor. E8 62
Errol, N.H., U.S. A4 136
Erskine, Alta., Can. C4 98
Erskine, Mn., U.S. C3 130
Erstein, Fr. D14 14
Ertai, China B5 30
Ertil', Russia J23 22
Ertix (Irtyš), stm., Asia H9 28
Ertuğrul, Tur. J11 20
Erudina, Austl. H3 70
Eruwa, Nig. H11 64
Erval, Braz. G12 80
Erval d'Oeste, Braz. D13 80
Erwin, N.C., U.S. B4 140
Erwin, Tn., U.S. C11 149
Erwinville, La., U.S. D4 125
Erwood, Sask., Can. E4 105
Eryuan, China A5 40
Erzgebirge (Krušné hory), mts., Eur. E13 10
Erzin, Russia G17 26
Erzincan, Tur. B5 48
Erzurum, Tur. B6 48
Esa'ala, Pap. N. Gui. A10 68
Esashi, Japan F15 36
Esashi, Japan H16 36
Esbjerg, Den. N11 6
Esbon, Ks., U.S. C5 123
Esca, stm., Spain J5 14
Escalante, Ut., U.S. F4 151
Escalante, stm., Ut., U.S. F4 151
Escalante, stm., Ven. C7 84
Escalante Creek, stm., Co., U.S. C2 113
Escalante Desert, des., Ut., U.S. F2 151
Escalón, Mex. D7 90
Escalon, Ca., U.S. D3 112
Escambia, co., Al., U.S. D2 108
Escambia, co., Fl., U.S. u14 116
Escambia, stm., Fl., U.S. u14 116
Escanaba, Mi., U.S. C3 129
Escanaba, stm., Mi., U.S. B3 129
Escárcega, Mex. H14 90
Escarpada Point, c., Phil. I20 39b

Name	Map Ref.	Page
Fortine, Mt., U.S.	B2	133
Fortín Florida, Para.	I12	82
Fortín Garrapatal, Para.	I11	82
Fortín Teniente Montanía, Para.	B9	80
Fortín Uno, Arg.	J6	80
Fort Jackson, mil., S.C., U.S.	C6	147
Fort Jefferson National Monument, Fl., U.S.	H4	116
Fort Jones, Ca., U.S.	B2	112
Fort Kent, Alta., Can.	B5	98
Fort Kent, Me., U.S.	A4	126
Fort Kent Mills, Me., U.S.	A4	126
Fort Knox, mil., Ky., U.S.	B4	124
Fort-Lamy see N'Djamena, Chad	F4	56
Fort Laramie, Wy., U.S.	D8	157
Fort Laramie National Historic Site, hist., Wy., U.S.	D8	157
Fort Lauderdale, Fl., U.S.	F6	116
Fort Lawn, S.C., U.S.	B6	147
Fort Leavenworth, mil., Ks., U.S.	C9	123
Fort Lee, N.J., U.S.	B5	137
Fort Lee, mil., Va., U.S.	C5	153
Fort Leonard Wood, mil., Mo., U.S.	D5	132
Fort Lewis, mil., Wa., U.S.	B3	154
Fort Liard, N.W. Ter., Can.	D8	96
Fort-Liberté, Haiti	E9	94
Fort Loramie, Oh., U.S.	B1	142
Fort Loudon, Pa., U.S.	G6	145
Fort Loudoun Lake, res., Tn., U.S.	D9	149
Fort Lupton, Co., U.S.	A6	113
Fort MacArthur, mil., Ca., U.S.	n12	112
Fort MacKay, Alta., Can.	f8	98
Fort Macleod, Alta., Can.	E4	98
Fort Madison, Ia., U.S.	D6	122
Fort Matanzas National Monument, Fl., U.S.	C5	116
Fort McClellan, mil., Al., U.S.	B4	108
Fort McDermitt Indian Reservation, U.S.	B4	135
Fort McDowell, Az., U.S.	k9	110
Fort McDowell Indian Reservation, Az., U.S.	D4	110
Fort McHenry National Monument And Historic Shrine, Md., U.S.	g11	127
Fort McMurray, Alta., Can.	A5	98
Fort McPherson, N.W. Ter., Can.	C6	96
Fort Meade, Fl., U.S.	E5	116
Fort Meade, mil., Md., U.S.	B4	127
Fort Meadow Reservoir, res., Ma., U.S.	g9	128
Fort Mill, S.C., U.S.	A6	147
Fort Mitchell, Al., U.S.	C4	108
Fort Mitchell, Ky., U.S.	h13	124
Fort Mojave Indian Reservation, U.S.	C1	110
Fort Monmouth, mil., N.J., U.S.	C4	137
Fort Monroe, mil., Va., U.S.	h15	153
Fort Morgan, Co., U.S.	A7	113
Fort Myer, mil., Va., U.S.	g12	153
Fort Myers, Fl., U.S.	F5	116
Fort Myers Beach, Fl., U.S.	F5	116
Fort Nelson, B.C., Can.	m18	99
Fort Norman, N.W. Ter., Can.	D7	96
Fort Ogden, Fl., U.S.	E5	116
Fort Oglethorpe, Ga., U.S.	B1	117
Fort Ord, mil., Ca., U.S.	D3	112
Fort Payne, Al., U.S.	A4	108
Fort Peck, Mt., U.S.	B10	133
Fort Peck Dam, Mt., U.S.	B10	133
Fort Peck Indian Reservation, Mt., U.S.	B11	133
Fort Peck Lake, res., Mt., U.S.	C9	133
Fort Pierce, Fl., U.S.	E6	116
Fort Pierce Inlet, b., Fl., U.S.	E6	116
Fort Pierre, S.D., U.S.	C5	148
Fort Plain, N.Y., U.S.	C6	139
Fort Polk, mil., La., U.S.	C2	125
Fort Portal, Ug.	A6	58
Fort Providence, N.W. Ter., Can.	D9	96
Fort Qu'Appelle, Sask., Can.	G4	105
Fort Randall Dam, S.D., U.S.	D7	148
Fort Ransom, N.D., U.S.	C8	141
Fort Recovery, Oh., U.S.	B1	142
Fort Resolution, N.W. Ter., Can.	D10	96
Fortress Mountain, mtn., Wy., U.S.	B3	157
Fort Richardson, mil., Ak., U.S.	C10	109
Fort Riley, mil., Ks., U.S.	C7	123
Fort Ritchie, mil., Md., U.S.	A3	127
Fort Rucker, mil., Al., U.S.	D4	108
Fort Saint James, B.C., Can.	B5	99
Fort Saint John, B.C., Can.	A7	99
Fort Sam Houston, mil., Tx., U.S.	k7	150
Fort Saskatchewan, Alta., Can.	C4	98
Fort Scott, Ks., U.S.	E9	123
Fort-Ševčenko, Kaz.	I8	26
Fort Severn, Ont., Can.	n18	103
Fort Shafter, mil., Hi., U.S.	g10	118
Fort Shaw, Mt., U.S.	C5	133
Fort Shawnee, Oh., U.S.	B1	142
Fort Sheridan, mil., Il., U.S.	h9	120
Fort Sill, mil., Ok., U.S.	C3	143
Fort Simpson, N.W. Ter., Can.	D8	96
Fort Smith, N.W. Ter., Can.	D10	96
Fort Smith, Ar., U.S.	B1	111
Fort Stanton, N.M., U.S.	D4	138
Fort Steele, B.C., Can.	E10	99
Fort Stewart, mil., Ga., U.S.	D5	117
Fort Stockton, Tx., U.S.	D1	150
Fort Sumner, N.M., U.S.	C5	138
Fort Sumter National Monument, S.C., U.S.	k12	147
Fort Supply, Ok., U.S.	A2	143
Fort Supply Lake, res., Ok., U.S.	A2	143
Fort Thomas, Az., U.S.	D6	110
Fort Thomas, Ky., U.S.	h14	124
Fort Thompson, S.D., U.S.	C6	148
Fort Totten, N.D., U.S.	B7	141
Fort Totten Indian Reservation, N.D., U.S.	B7	141
Fort Towson, Ok., U.S.	C6	143
Fortuna, Arg.	H6	80
Fortuna, C.R.	G10	92
Fortuna, Ca., U.S.	B1	112
Fortuna, Mo., U.S.	C5	132
Fortuna, Río de la, stm., Bol.	G12	82
Fortune, Newf., Can.	E4	102
Fortune Bay, b., Newf., Can.	E4	102
Fortune Harbour, Newf., Can.	D4	102
Fort Union National Monument, N.M., U.S.	B5	138
Fort Valley, Ga., U.S.	D3	117
Fort Vermilion, Alta., Can.	f7	98
Fortville, In., U.S.	E6	121
Fort Wainwright, mil., Ak., U.S.	C10	109
Fort Walton Beach, Fl., U.S.	u15	116
Fort Washakie, Wy., U.S.	C4	157
Fort Washington, Pa., U.S.	o21	145
Fort Washington Forest, Md., U.S.	C4	127
Fort Wayne, In., U.S.	B7	121
Fort Wellington, Guy.	D14	84
Fort William, Scot., U.K.	E8	8
Fort Wingate, N.M., U.S.	B1	138
Fort Worth, Tx., U.S.	C4	150
Fort Wright, Ky., U.S.	h13	124
Fort Yates, N.D., U.S.	C5	141
Forty Fort, Pa., U.S.	D10	145
Fort Yukon, Ak., U.S.	B10	109
Fort Yuma Indian Reservation, Ca., U.S.	F6	112
Foshan, China	L2	34
Fossano, Italy	E2	18
Fossil, Or., U.S.	B6	144
Fossil Butte National Monument, Wy., U.S.	E2	157
Fossil Lake, l., Or., U.S.	D6	144
Foss Reservoir, res., Ok., U.S.	B2	143
Fosston, Sask., Can.	E4	105
Fosston, Mn., U.S.	C3	130
Foster, Austl.	L7	70
Foster, Mo., U.S.	C3	132
Foster, Or., U.S.	C4	144
Foster, co., N.D., U.S.	B6	141
Foster Brook, Pa., U.S.	C4	145
Foster City, Ca., U.S.	h8	112
Foster City, Mi., U.S.	C3	129
Fosters, Al., U.S.	B2	108
Fosters Pond, l., Ma., U.S.	f11	128
Foster Village, Hi., U.S.	g10	118
Fosterville, Tn., U.S.	B5	149
Fostoria, Al., U.S.	C3	108
Fostoria, Ia., U.S.	A2	122
Fostoria, Mi., U.S.	E7	129
Fostoria, Oh., U.S.	A2	142
Fouesnant, Fr.	E2	14
Fougamou, Gabon	B2	58
Fougères, Fr.	D5	14
Fouke, Ar., U.S.	D2	111
Foul Bay, b., Egypt	J3	48
Foulpointe, Madag.	p23	67b
Foulwind, Cape, c., N.Z.	D3	72
Foumban, Cam.	G9	54
Foumbouni, Com.	k15	67a
Foum-el-Hisn, Mor.	F6	62
Foum-Zguid, Mor.	E7	62
Foundiougne, Sen.	D1	64
Fountain, Al., U.S.	D2	108
Fountain, Co., U.S.	C6	113
Fountain, Fl., U.S.	B1	116
Fountain, Mn., U.S.	G6	130
Fountain, N.C., U.S.	B5	140
Fountain, co., In., U.S.	D3	121
Fountain City, In., U.S.	E8	121
Fountain City, Wi., U.S.	D2	156
Fountain Creek, stm., Co., U.S.	C6	113
Fountain Green, Ut., U.S.	D4	151
Fountain Hill, Ar., U.S.	D4	111
Fountain Hill, Pa., U.S.	E11	145
Fountain Inn, S.C., U.S.	B3	147
Fountain Lake, Ar., U.S.	f8	111
Fountain Peak, mtn., Ca., U.S.	E6	112
Fountain Place, La., U.S.	*D4	125
Fountain Run, Ky., U.S.	D4	124
Fountaintown, In., U.S.	E6	121
Fourche Creek, stm., Ar., U.S.	k10	111
Fourche LaFave, stm., Ar., U.S.	C2	111
Fourche Maline, stm., Ok., U.S.	C6	143
Fourche Mountain, mtn., Ar., U.S.	C2	111
Fouriesburg, S. Afr.	G9	66
Four Lakes, Wa., U.S.	B8	154
Fourmies, Fr.	B11	14
Fourmile, Ky., U.S.	D6	124
Fourmile Creek, stm., Ia., U.S.	e8	122
Four Mountains, Islands of, is., Ak., U.S.	E6	109
Fournier, Ont., Can.	B10	103
Four Oaks, N.C., U.S.	B4	140
Fouta Djalon, reg., Gui.	F3	64
Foux, Cap à, c., Haiti	E8	94
Foveaux Strait, strt., N.Z.	G1	72
Fowler, Ca., U.S.	D4	112
Fowler, Co., U.S.	C6	113
Fowler, Il., U.S.	C2	120
Fowler, In., U.S.	C3	121
Fowler, Ks., U.S.	E3	123
Fowler, Mi., U.S.	E6	129
Fowlerton, In., U.S.	D6	121
Fowlerville, Mi., U.S.	F6	129
Fowlkes, Tn., U.S.	B2	149
Fowlstown, Ga., U.S.	F2	117
Fowman, Iran	C10	48
Fox, Ar., U.S.	B3	111
Fox, Ok., U.S.	C4	143
Fox, stm., Man., Can.	B4	100
Fox, stm., U.S.	B5	120
Fox, stm., U.S.	A6	132
Fox, stm., Mi., U.S.	B4	129
Fox, stm., Wi., U.S.	D5	156
Foxboro, Ont., Can.	C7	103
Foxboro, Ma., U.S.	B5	128
Fox Creek, Alta., Can.	B2	98
Foxe Basin, b., N.W. Ter., Can.	C17	96
Foxe Channel, strt., N.W. Ter., Can.	D16	96
Foxe Peninsula, pen., N.W. Ter., Can.	D17	96
Fox Harbour, Newf., Can.	E5	102
Fox Island, i., R.I., U.S.	E4	146
Fox Island, i., Wa., U.S.	f10	154
Fox Islands, is., Ak., U.S.	E6	109
Fox Lake, Il., U.S.	A5	120
Fox Lake, Wi., U.S.	E5	156
Fox Lake, l., Il., U.S.	h8	120
Fox Mountain, mtn., Nv., U.S.	B2	135
Foxpark, Wy., U.S.	E6	157
Fox Point, Wi., U.S.	E6	156
Fox River Grove, Il., U.S.	h8	120
Fox Valley, Sask., Can.	G1	105
Foxville, Vt., U.S.	C4	152
Foxwarren, Man., Can.	D1	100
Foxworth, Ms., U.S.	D4	131
Foyle, Lough, b., Eur.	F6	8
Foz do Cunene, Ang.	E2	58
Foz do Iguaçu, Braz.	C11	80
Foz do Jordão, Braz.	C6	82
Foz Giraldo, Port.	E4	16
Foziling, China	D5	34
Frackville, Pa., U.S.	E9	145
Fraga, Arg.	G6	80
Fraile Muerto, Ur.	G11	80
Framingham, Ma., U.S.	B5	128
Frampol, Pol.	E22	10
Franca, Braz.	F5	79
Franca-Iosifa, Zeml'a (Franz Josef Land), is., Russia	A6	24
Francavilla Fontana, Italy	I12	18
France, ctry., Eur.	F8	4
Francestown, N.H., U.S.	E3	136
Francés Viejo, Cabo, c., Dom. Rep.	E10	94
Francesville, In., U.S.	C4	121
Franceville, Gabon	B2	58
Franche-Comté, hist. reg., Fr.	F12	14
Francia, Ur.	G10	80
Francis, Sask., Can.	G4	105
Francis, Ok., U.S.	C5	143
Francis, Ut., U.S.	C4	151
Francis, Lake, l., N.H., U.S.	f7	136
Francis Case, Lake, res., S.D., U.S.	D6	148
Francisco, In., U.S.	H3	121
Francisco Beltrão, Braz.	D12	80
Francisco I. Madero, Mex.	E8	90
Francisco I. Madero, Mex.	E7	90
Francisco Morazán, dept., Hond.	C7	92
Francisco Murguía, Mex.	E8	90
Francisco Sá, Braz.	D7	79
Francis Creek, Wi., U.S.	h10	156
Francistown, Bots.	C8	66
Francofonte, Italy	L9	18
François, Newf., Can.	E3	102
Franconia, N.H., U.S.	B3	136
Franconia Notch, N.H., U.S.	B3	136
Francs Peak, mtn., Wy., U.S.	C3	157
Frangy, Fr.	F12	14
Frankenmuth, Mi., U.S.	E7	129
Frankford, Ont., Can.	C7	103
Frankford, De., U.S.	F5	115
Frankford, Mo., U.S.	B6	132
Frankford, W.V., U.S.	D4	155
Frankfort, S. Afr.	I8	66
Frankfort, S. Afr.	F9	66
Frankfort, Il., U.S.	m9	120
Frankfort, In., U.S.	D4	121
Frankfort, Ks., U.S.	C7	123
Frankfort, Ky., U.S.	B5	124
Frankfort, Me., U.S.	D4	126
Frankfort, Mi., U.S.	D4	129
Frankfort, N.Y., U.S.	B5	139
Frankfort, Oh., U.S.	C2	142
Frankfort, S.D., U.S.	C7	148
Frankfurt am Main, Ger.	E8	10
Frankfurt an der Oder, Ger.	C14	10
Franklin, Man., Can.	D2	100
Franklin, Al., U.S.	D2	108
Franklin, Az., U.S.	E6	110
Franklin, Ar., U.S.	A4	111
Franklin, Ga., U.S.	C1	117
Franklin, Id., U.S.	G7	119
Franklin, Il., U.S.	D3	120
Franklin, In., U.S.	F5	121
Franklin, Ks., U.S.	E9	123
Franklin, Ky., U.S.	D3	124
Franklin, La., U.S.	E4	125
Franklin, Me., U.S.	D4	126
Franklin, Ma., U.S.	B5	128
Franklin, Mn., U.S.	F4	130
Franklin, Mo., U.S.	B5	132
Franklin, Ne., U.S.	D7	134
Franklin, N.H., U.S.	D3	136
Franklin, N.J., U.S.	A3	137
Franklin, N.C., U.S.	f9	140
Franklin, Oh., U.S.	C1	142
Franklin, Pa., U.S.	D2	145
Franklin, Tn., U.S.	B5	149
Franklin, Tx., U.S.	D4	150
Franklin, Va., U.S.	D6	153
Franklin, W.V., U.S.	C5	155
Franklin, Wi., U.S.	n11	156
Franklin, co., Al., U.S.	A2	108
Franklin, co., Ar., U.S.	B2	111
Franklin, co., Fl., U.S.	C2	116
Franklin, co., Ga., U.S.	B3	117
Franklin, co., Id., U.S.	G7	119
Franklin, co., Il., U.S.	E4	120
Franklin, co., In., U.S.	F7	121
Franklin, co., Ia., U.S.	B4	122
Franklin, co., Ks., U.S.	D8	123
Franklin, co., Ky., U.S.	B5	124
Franklin, co., La., U.S.	B4	125
Franklin, co., Me., U.S.	C2	126
Franklin, co., Ma., U.S.	A2	128
Franklin, co., Ms., U.S.	D3	131
Franklin, co., Mo., U.S.	C6	132
Franklin, co., Ne., U.S.	D7	134
Franklin, co., N.Y., U.S.	f10	139
Franklin, co., N.C., U.S.	A4	140
Franklin, co., Oh., U.S.	B2	142
Franklin, co., Pa., U.S.	G6	145
Franklin, co., Tn., U.S.	B5	149
Franklin, co., Tx., U.S.	C5	150
Franklin, co., Vt., U.S.	B2	152
Franklin, co., Va., U.S.	D3	153
Franklin, co., Wa., U.S.	C6	154
Franklin, Point, c., Ak., U.S.	A8	109
Franklin Bay, b., N.W. Ter., Can.	C7	96
Franklin D. Roosevelt Lake, res., Wa., U.S.	B7	154
Franklin Falls Reservoir, res., N.H., U.S.	C3	136
Franklin Grove, Il., U.S.	B4	120
Franklin Harbor, b., Austl.	I2	70
Franklin Island, i., Ont., Can.	B4	103
Franklin Lake, l., Nv., U.S.	C6	135
Franklin Mine, Mi., U.S.	A2	129
Franklin Mountains, mts., N.W. Ter., Can.	D8	96
Franklin Park, Il., U.S.	k9	120
Franklin Park, Pa., U.S.	*h13	145
Franklin Strait, strt., N.W. Ter., Can.	B13	96
Franklinton, La., U.S.	D5	125
Franklinton, N.C., U.S.	A4	140
Franklinville, N.J., U.S.	D2	137
Franklinville, N.Y., U.S.	C2	139
Franklinville, N.C., U.S.	B3	140
Frankston, Tx., U.S.	C5	150
Franksville, Wi., U.S.	n12	156
Frankton, In., U.S.	D6	121
Franktown, Co., U.S.	B6	113
Frankville, N.S., Can.	D8	101
Frankville, Al., U.S.	D1	108
Frannie, Wy., U.S.	B4	157
Franz Josef Land see Franca Iosifa, Zeml'a, is., Russia	A6	24
Frascati, Italy	H7	18
Fraser, Co., U.S.	B5	113
Fraser, stm., B.C., Can.	E7	99
Fraser, stm., Newf., Can.	g9	102
Fraser, Mount, mtn., Can.	C8	99
Fraserburg, S. Afr.	H5	66
Fraser Island, i., Austl.	E10	70
Fraser Lake, B.C., Can.	B5	99
Fraser Plateau, plat., B.C., Can.	D6	99
Fraserwood, Man., Can.	D3	100
Frauenfeld, Switz.	C10	13
Fray Bentos, Ur.	G9	80
Fray Luis Beltrán, Arg.	J6	80
Fray Marcos, Ur.	H11	80
Frazee, Mn., U.S.	D3	130
Frazer, Mt., U.S.	B10	133
Frazeysburg, Oh., U.S.	B3	142
Frazier Park, Ca., U.S.	E4	112
Fr'azino, Russia	F21	22
Frederic, Mi., U.S.	D6	129
Frederic, Wi., U.S.	C1	156
Frederica, De., U.S.	D4	115
Fredericia, Den.	N11	6
Frederick, Co., U.S.	A6	113
Frederick, Md., U.S.	B3	127
Frederick, Ok., U.S.	C2	143
Frederick, S.D., U.S.	B7	148
Frederick, co., Md., U.S.	B3	127
Frederick, co., Va., U.S.	A4	153
Frederick Reef, rf., Austl.	C11	70
Fredericksburg, In., U.S.	H5	121
Fredericksburg, Ia., U.S.	B5	122
Fredericksburg, Oh., U.S.	B4	142
Fredericksburg, Pa., U.S.	F9	145
Fredericksburg, Tx., U.S.	D3	150
Fredericksburg, Va., U.S.	B5	153
Frederick Sound, strt., Ak., U.S.	m23	109
Fredericktown, Mo., U.S.	D7	132
Fredericktown, Oh., U.S.	B3	142
Fredericktown, Pa., U.S.	F1	145
Frederico Westphalen, Braz.	D12	80
Fredericton, N.B., Can.	D3	101
Fredericton Junction, N.B., Can.	D3	101
Frederikshavn, Den.	M12	6
Frederiksted, V.I.U.S.	F12	94
Frederik Willem IV Vallen, wtfl, Sur.	F14	84
Fredonia, Col.	E5	84
Fredonia, Az., U.S.	A3	110
Fredonia, Ia., U.S.	C6	122
Fredonia, Ks., U.S.	E8	123
Fredonia, Ky., U.S.	C1	124
Fredonia, N.Y., U.S.	C1	139
Fredonia, Pa., U.S.	D1	145
Fredonia, Wi., U.S.	E6	156
Fredrikstad, Nor.	L12	6
Freeborn, Mn., U.S.	G5	130
Freeborn, co., Mn., U.S.	G5	130
Freeburg, Il., U.S.	E4	120
Freeburg, Mo., U.S.	C6	132
Freeburg, Pa., U.S.	E8	145
Freedom, In., U.S.	F4	121
Freedom, N.H., U.S.	C4	136
Freedom, Ok., U.S.	A2	143
Freedom, Pa., U.S.	E1	145
Freedom, Wi., U.S.	h9	156
Freedom, Wy., U.S.	D2	157
Freehold, N.J., U.S.	C4	137
Freeland, Mi., U.S.	E6	129
Freeland, Pa., U.S.	D10	145
Freelandville, In., U.S.	G3	121
Freel Peak, mtn., Ca., U.S.	C4	112
Freels, Cape, c., Newf., Can.	D5	102
Freels, Cape, c., Newf., Can.	E5	102
Freeman, Mo., U.S.	C3	132
Freeman, S.D., U.S.	D8	148
Freeman, Lake, l., In., U.S.	C4	121
Freemansburg, Pa., U.S.	E11	145
Freemanville, Al., U.S.	D2	108
Freemason Island, i., La., U.S.	E7	125
Freeport, Bah.	A5	94
Freeport, N.S., Can.	E3	101
Freeport, Fl., U.S.	u15	116
Freeport, Il., U.S.	A4	120
Freeport, Me., U.S.	E2	126
Freeport, Mi., U.S.	F5	129
Freeport, Mn., U.S.	E4	130
Freeport, N.Y., U.S.	n15	139
Freeport, Pa., U.S.	E2	145
Freeport, Tx., U.S.	E5	150
Freer, Tx., U.S.	F3	150
Freestone, co., Tx., U.S.	D4	150
Freetown, P.E.I., Can.	C6	101
Freetown, S.L.	G3	64
Freetown, In., U.S.	G5	121
Freezeout Mountains, mts., Wy., U.S.	D6	157
Fregenal de la Sierra, Spain	G5	16
Freiberg, Ger.	E13	10
Freiburg [im Breisgau], Ger.	H7	10
Freirina, Chile	E3	80
Freising, Ger.	G11	10
Freistadt, Aus.	G14	10
Freital, Ger.	D13	10
Fréjus, Fr.	I13	14
Fremantle, Austl.	F3	68
Fremont, Ca., U.S.	D2	112
Fremont, In., U.S.	A8	121
Fremont, Ia., U.S.	C5	122
Fremont, Mi., U.S.	E5	129
Fremont, Mo., U.S.	E6	132
Fremont, Ne., U.S.	C9	134
Fremont, N.H., U.S.	E4	136
Fremont, N.C., U.S.	B5	140
Fremont, Oh., U.S.	A2	142
Fremont, Ut., U.S.	E4	151
Fremont, Wi., U.S.	D5	156
Fremont, co., Co., U.S.	C5	113
Fremont, co., Id., U.S.	E7	119
Fremont, co., Ia., U.S.	D2	122
Fremont, co., Wy., U.S.	C4	157
Fremont, stm., Ut., U.S.	E4	151
Fremont Island, i., Ut., U.S.	B3	151
Fremont Lake, l., Wy., U.S.	D3	157
Fremont Peak, mtn., Wy., U.S.	C3	157
French Broad, stm., U.S.	D10	149
Frenchburg, Ky., U.S.	C6	124
French Camp, Ms., U.S.	B4	131
French Creek, stm., Pa., U.S.	C2	145
French Frigate Shoals, rf., Hi., U.S.	m14	118
French Guiana (Guyane français), dep., S.A.	C8	76
French Gulch, Ca., U.S.	B2	112
French Island, i., Austl.	L6	70
French Lick, In., U.S.	G4	121
Frenchman Bay, b., Me., U.S.	D4	126
Frenchman Butte, Sask., Can.	D1	105
Frenchman Creek, stm., U.S.	D4	134
Frenchman Hills, hills, Wa., U.S.	C6	154
Frenchman Knob, mtn., Ky., U.S.	C4	124
Frenchman Lake, l., Nv., U.S.	G6	135
Frenchmans Cap, mtn., Austl.	N6	70
Frenchman's Cove, Newf., Can.	D2	102
Frenchman's Cove, Newf., Can.	E4	102
French Polynesia, dep., Oc.	H3	2
French River, Mn., U.S.	D7	130
French Settlement, La., U.S.	D5	125
French Southern and Antarctic Territories, dep., Afr.	M10	158
Frenchtown, Mt., U.S.	C2	133
Frenchtown, N.J., U.S.	B2	137
French Village, N.S., Can.	E6	101
Frenchville, Me., U.S.	A4	126
Frenda, Alg.	C11	62
Fresco, stm., Braz.	E8	76
Freshfield, Mount, mtn., Can.	D2	98
Fresne-Saint-Mamès, Fr.	E12	14
Fresnes-en-Woëvre, Fr.	C12	14
Fresnillo, Mex.	F8	90
Fresno, Col.	E5	84
Fresno, Ca., U.S.	D4	112
Fresno, co., Ca., U.S.	D4	112
Fresno Reservoir, res., Mt., U.S.	B6	133
Frewsburg, N.Y., U.S.	C1	139
Freycinet Peninsula, pen., Austl.	N8	70
Freyre, Arg.	F7	80
Fria, Cape, c., Nmb.	E2	58
Friant, Ca., U.S.	D4	112
Friars Point, Ms., U.S.	A3	131
Frías, Arg.	E6	80
Frías, Peru	A2	82
Fribourg (Freiburg), Switz.	E7	13
Fribourg (Freiburg), state, Switz.	E7	13
Friday Harbor, Wa., U.S.	A2	154
Fridley, Mn., U.S.	m12	130
Fridtjof Nansen, Mount, mtn., Ant.	D9	73
Friedberg, Aus.	H16	10
Friedberg, Ger.	E8	10
Friedberg, Ger.	G10	10
Friedland, Ger.	B13	10
Friedrichshafen, Ger.	H9	10
Friedrichsort, Ger.	A10	10
Friedrichstadt, Ger.	A9	10
Friend, Ne., U.S.	D8	134
Friendship, Ar., U.S.	C3	111
Friendship, Me., U.S.	E3	126
Friendship, N.Y., U.S.	C2	139
Friendship, Oh., U.S.	D2	142
Friendship, Tn., U.S.	B2	149
Friendship, Wi., U.S.	E4	156
Friendsville, Md., U.S.	k12	127
Friendsville, Tn., U.S.	D9	149
Friendswood, Tx., U.S.	r14	150
Fries, Va., U.S.	D2	153
Friesach, Aus.	I14	10
Friesland, prov., Neth.	B8	12
Friguia, Gui.	E4	64
Frio, co., Tx., U.S.	E3	150
Frío, stm., N.A.	G10	92
Frio, stm., Tx., U.S.	E3	150
Frio, Cabo, c., Braz.	G7	79
Frio Draw, val., U.S.	C6	138
Friona, Tx., U.S.	B1	150
Fripps Island, i., S.C., U.S.	G7	147
Frisco, Co., U.S.	B4	113
Frisco, N.C., U.S.	B7	140
Frisco City, Al., U.S.	D2	108
Frisco Peak, mtn., Ut., U.S.	E2	151
Frisian Islands, is., Eur.	E9	4
Frissell, Mount, mtn., U.S.	A2	114
Fritch, Tx., U.S.	B2	150
Friuli-Venezia-Giulia, prov., Italy	C7	18
Friza, proliv, strt., Russia	H21	28
Frobisher, Sask., Can.	H4	105
Frobisher Bay, b., N.W. Ter., Can.	D19	96
Frobisher Lake, l., Sask., Can.	m7	105
Frohna, Mo., U.S.	D8	132
Frohnleiten, Aus.	H15	10
Froid, Mt., U.S.	B12	133
Frolovo, Russia	H6	26
Fromberg, Mt., U.S.	E8	133
Frombork, Pol.	A19	10
Frome, stm., Austl.	G3	70
Frome, Lake, l., Austl.	H3	70
Frontenac, Ks., U.S.	E9	123
Frontenac, Mn., U.S.	F6	130
Frontera, Mex.	H13	90
Frontera, Mex.	D9	90
Frontier, Sask., Can.	H1	105
Frontier, Wy., U.S.	E2	157
Frontier, co., Ne., U.S.	D5	134
Frontino, Col.	D4	84
Frontino, Páramo, mtn., Col.	D4	84
Front Range, mts., Co., U.S.	A5	113
Front Royal, Va., U.S.	B4	153
Frosinone, Italy	H8	18
Frost, Tx., U.S.	C4	150
Frostburg, Md., U.S.	k13	127
Frostproof, Fl., U.S.	E5	116
Frøya, i., Nor.	J11	6
Fruges, Fr.	B9	14
Fruita, Co., U.S.	B2	113
Fruitdale, Al., U.S.	D1	108
Fruit Heights, Ut., U.S.	B4	151
Fruithurst, Al., U.S.	B4	108
Fruitland, Id., U.S.	F2	119
Fruitland, Ia., U.S.	C6	122
Fruitland, Md., U.S.	D6	127
Fruitland, N.M., U.S.	A1	138
Fruitland, Tn., U.S.	B3	149
Fruitland Park, Fl., U.S.	D5	116
Fruitport, Mi., U.S.	E4	129
Fruitvale, B.C., Can.	E9	99
Fruitvale, Co., U.S.	B2	113
Fruitvale, Id., U.S.	E2	119
Fruitvale, Wa., U.S.	C5	154
Fruitville, Fl., U.S.	E4	116
Frunze see Biškek, Kyrg.	I12	26
Frunzovka, Ukr.	B13	20
Frutal, Braz.	F4	79
Frutigen, Switz.	E8	13
Frýdek-Místek, Czech.	F18	10
Fryeburg, Me., U.S.	D2	126
Fuchang, China	E2	34
Fuchū, Japan	M8	36
Fuchun, stm., China	F8	34
Fuding, China	H9	34
Fuego, Volcán de, vol., Guat.	C4	92
Fuencaliente de la Palma, Spain	o23	17b
Fuensalida, Spain	E7	16
Fuente de Cantos, Spain	G5	16
Fuente de Oro, Col.	F6	84
Fuentesaúco, Spain	D6	16
Fuerte, stm., Mex.	D5	90
Fuerte Olimpo, Para.	I13	82
Fuerteventura, i., Spain	o26	17b
Fufeng, China	E8	30
Fuhe, China	L2	34
Fuhu, China	F7	34
Fuji, Japan	L13	36
Fujian (Fukien), prov., China	F10	30
Fujieda, Japan	M13	36
Fujin, China	B13	30
Fujinomiya, Japan	L13	36
Fuji-san (Fujiyama), vol., Japan	L13	36
Fujisawa, Japan	L14	36
Fujiyama see Fuji-san, vol., Japan	L13	36
Fuji-yoshida, Japan	L13	36
Fukagawa, Japan	d17	36a
Fukou, China	I6	34
Fukuchiyama, Japan	L10	36
Fukue-jima, i., Japan	O3	36
Fukui, Japan	K11	36
Fukuoka, Japan	N5	36
Fukushima, Japan	J15	36
Fukuyama, Japan	M8	36
Fulacunda, Gui.-B.	F2	64
Fūlādī, Kūh-e, mtn., Afg.	C2	44
Fulda, Ger.	E9	10
Fulda, In., U.S.	H4	121
Fulda, Mn., U.S.	G3	130
Fulda, stm., Ger.	D9	10
Fulechang, China	B8	40
Fuling, China	F8	30
Fullarton, Ont., Can.	D3	103
Fullerton, Ca., U.S.	n13	112
Fullerton, Ne., U.S.	C8	134
Fullerton, N.D., U.S.	C7	141
Fulpmes, Aus.	H11	10
Fulshear, Tx., U.S.	r14	150
Fulton, Al., U.S.	D2	108
Fulton, Ar., U.S.	D2	111
Fulton, Il., U.S.	B3	120
Fulton, In., U.S.	C5	121
Fulton, Ks., U.S.	D9	123
Fulton, Ky., U.S.	f9	124
Fulton, Md., U.S.	B4	127
Fulton, Mi., U.S.	A2	129
Fulton, Ms., U.S.	A5	131
Fulton, Mo., U.S.	C6	132
Fulton, N.Y., U.S.	B4	139
Fulton, co., Ar., U.S.	A4	111
Fulton, co., Ga., U.S.	C2	117
Fulton, co., Il., U.S.	C3	120
Fulton, co., In., U.S.	B5	121
Fulton, co., Ky., U.S.	f8	124
Fulton, co., N.Y., U.S.	B6	139
Fulton, co., Oh., U.S.	A1	142
Fulton, co., Pa., U.S.	G5	145
Fultondale, Al., U.S.	f7	108
Fultz, Ky., U.S.	B6	124
Fumay, Fr.	C11	14
Fumel, Fr.	H7	14
Fumintun, China	A14	32
Funabashi, Japan	L14	36
Funchal, Port.	m21	17a
Fundación, Col.	B5	84
Fundy, Bay of, b., Can.	D4	101

Name — Map Ref. — Page

Fundy National Park, N.B., Can. D4 101
Funhalouro, Moz. D12 66
Funing, China B8 34
Funk, Ne., U.S. D6 134
Funkstown, Md., U.S. A2 127
Funtua, Nig. F13 64
Funza, Col. E5 84
Fuqikou, China F6 34
Fuquay-Varina, N.C., U.S. B4 140
Furano, Japan d17 36a
Fūrg, Iran G13 48
Furman, Al., U.S. C3 108
Furmanov, Russia D24 22
Furnace Brook, stm., Vt., U.S. D3 152
Furnas, co., Ne., U.S. D6 134
Furnas, Represa de, res., Braz. F5 79
Furneaux Group, is., Austl. L8 70
Furnes (Veurne), Bel. F2 12
Furness, Sask., Can. D1 105
Furqlus, Syria D4 48
Fürstenfeldbruck, Ger. G11 10
Fürstenwalde, Ger. C14 10
Fürth, Ger. F10 10
Furth im Wald, Ger. F12 10
Furudal, Swe. K14 6
Furukawa, Japan K12 36
Furukawa, Japan I15 36
Fury and Hecla Strait, strt., N.W. Ter., Can. C15 96
Fusagasugá, Col. E5 84
Fushan, China D9 34
Fushuigang, China D2 34
Fushun, China B11 32
Fusui, China G8 30
Futianpu, China H1 34
Future City, Il., U.S. F4 120
Futuyu, China D2 32
Fuwah, Egypt B6 60
Fuxi, China J2 34
Fuxian, China D8 30
Fuxian (Wafangdian), China D10 32
Fuxian Hu, l., China B7 40
Fuxin, China A9 32
Fuyang, China C4 34
Fuyu, China B11 30
Fuzhai, China F9 34
Fuzhou, China G5 34
Fuzhou (Foochow), China I8 34
Fuzhuang, China I6 32
Fyffe, Al., U.S. A4 108
Fyn, i., Den. N12 6

G

Gaalkacyo, Som. G10 56
Gaastra, Mi., U.S. B2 129
Gabarus, N.S., Can. D9 101
Gabas, stm., Fr. I6 14
Gabbs, Nv., U.S. E4 135
Gabela, Ang. D2 58
Gabès, Tun. D16 62
Gabès, Golfe de, b., Tun. C16 62
Gabiarra, Braz. D9 79
Gabir, Sud. M3 60
Gabon, ctry., Afr. B2 58
Gaborone, Bots. E7 66
Gabriel Strait, strt., N.W. Ter., Can. D19 96
Gabriola, B.C., Can. f12 99
Gabrovo, Bul. G9 20
Gacé, Fr. D7 14
Gachetá, Col. E6 84
Gachsārān, Iran F11 48
Gackle, N.D., U.S. C6 141
Gadag, India E3 46
Gadamai, Sud. I9 60
Gäddede, Swe. I14 6
Gadilovići, Bela. H13 22
Gadsby, Alta., Can. C4 98
Gadsden, Al., U.S. A3 108
Gadsden, Az., U.S. E1 110
Gadsden, Tn., U.S. B3 149
Gadsden, co., Fl., U.S. B2 116
Gaeta, Italy H8 18
Gaeta, Golfo di, b., Italy H8 18
Gaffney, S.C., U.S. A4 147
Gafour, Tun. M4 18
Gafsa, Tun. C15 62
Gagarin, Russia F18 22
Gage, Ok., U.S. A2 143
Gage, co., Ne., U.S. D9 134
Gagetown, N.B., Can. D3 101
Gagetown, Mi., U.S. E7 129
Gaggenau, Ger. G8 10
Gaghamni, Sud. L5 60
Gagnoa, I.C. H7 64
Gagra, Geor. I6 26
Gahanna, Oh., U.S. k11 142
Gaibandha, Bngl. H13 44
Gaillac, Fr. I8 14
Gaillard, Lake, l., Ct., U.S. D5 114
Gaillon, Fr. C8 14
Gaines, Mi., U.S. F7 129
Gaines, co., Tx., U.S. C1 150
Gainesboro, Tn., U.S. C8 149
Gaines Creek, stm., Ok., U.S. C6 143
Gainesville, Al., U.S. C1 108
Gainesville, Fl., U.S. C4 116
Gainesville, Ga., U.S. B3 117
Gainesville, Mo., U.S. E5 132
Gainesville, Tx., U.S. C4 150
Gainesville, Va., U.S. g11 153
Gainsborough, Sask., Can. H5 105
Gairdner, Lake, l., Austl. F7 68
Gaital, Cerro, mtn., Pan. I14 92
Gaithersburg, Md., U.S. B3 127
Gaixian, China C10 32
Gajny, Russia E8 26
Gajutino, Russia C21 22
Gajvoron, Ukr. A13 20
Galaassija, Uzb. B18 48
Galahad, Alta., Can. C5 98
Galán, Cerro, mtn., Arg. G8 74
Galán, Cerro, mtn., Arg. C5 80
Galapagos Islands see Colón, Archipiélago de, is., Ec. m15 84a
Galashiels, Scot., U.K. F11 8
Galați, Rom. D12 20
Galați, co., Rom. D11 20
Galatia, Il., U.S. F5 120
Galatina, Italy I13 18
Galax, Va., U.S. D2 153
Gáldar, Spain o25 17b
Galdhøpiggen, mtn., Nor. K11 6
Galeana, Mex. B6 90
Galeana, Mex. E9 90
Galela, Indon. E8 38
Galena, Ak., U.S. C8 109
Galena, Il., U.S. A3 120
Galena, Ks., U.S. E9 123
Galena, Mo., U.S. E4 132
Galeota Point, c., Trin. I14 94
Galera, stm., Braz. F12 82
Galera, Punta, c., Ec. G2 84
Galera Point, c., Trin. I14 94
Galesburg, Il., U.S. C3 120
Galesburg, Ks., U.S. E8 123
Galesburg, Mi., U.S. F5 129
Galesburg, N.D., U.S. B8 141
Gales Ferry, Ct., U.S. D7 114
Galesville, Md., U.S. C4 127
Galesville, Wi., U.S. D2 156
Galeton, Co., U.S. A6 113
Galeton, Pa., U.S. C6 145
Galheiros, Braz. B5 79
Galiano Island, i., B.C., Can. E6 99
Galič, Russia C25 22
Galicia, prov., Spain C3 16
Galicia, hist. reg., Eur. F12 4
Galien, Mi., U.S. G4 129
Galilee, R.I., U.S. F3 146
Galilee, Lake, l., Austl. D6 70
Galilee, Sea of see Kinneret, Yam, l., Isr. C5 50
Galiléia, Braz. E8 79
Galion, Oh., U.S. B3 142
Galisteo Creek, stm., N.M., U.S. k8 138
Galiuro Mountains, mts., Az., U.S. E5 110
Gallant, Al., U.S. B3 108
Gallarate, Italy D3 18
Gallatin, Mo., U.S. B4 132
Gallatin, Tn., U.S. A5 149
Gallatin, co., Il., U.S. F5 120
Gallatin, co., Ky., U.S. B5 124
Gallatin, co., Mt., U.S. E5 133
Gallatin, stm., Mt., U.S. E5 133
Gallatin Gateway, Mt., U.S. E5 133
Gallatin Range, mts., Mt., U.S. E5 133
Gallaway, Tn., U.S. B2 149
Galle, Sri L. I6 46
Gallia, co., Oh., U.S. D3 142
Galliano, La., U.S. E5 125
Galliate, Italy D3 18
Gallina, N.M., U.S. A3 138
Gallinas, Punta, c., Col. A7 84
Gallinas Mountains, mts., N.M., U.S. C2 138
Gallion, Al., U.S. C2 108
Gallipoli, Austl. B2 70
Gallipoli, Italy I12 18
Gallipoli see Gelibolu, Tur. I10 20
Gallipoli Peninsula see Gelibolu Yarımadası, pen., Tur. I10 20
Gallipolis, Oh., U.S. D3 142
Gallipolis Ferry, W.V., U.S. C2 155
Gallitzin, Pa., U.S. F4 145
Gällivare, Swe. H17 6
Gallo Mountains, mts., N.M., U.S. C1 138
Galloo Island, i., N.Y., U.S. B4 139
Galloway, W.V., U.S. B4 155
Galloway, Mull of, c., Scot., U.K. G9 8
Gallup, N.M., U.S. B1 138
Galougo, Mali E4 64
Galt, Ca., U.S. C3 112
Galt, Mo., U.S. A4 132
Galtat Zemmour, W. Sah. H4 62
Galty Mountains, mts., Ire. I5 8
Galva, Il., U.S. B3 120
Galva, Ia., U.S. B2 122
Galva, Ks., U.S. D6 123
Galvarino, Chile J2 80
Galveston, In., U.S. C5 121
Galveston, Tx., U.S. E5 150
Galveston, co., Tx., U.S. E5 150
Galveston Bay, b., Tx., U.S. E5 150
Galveston Island, i., Tx., U.S. E5 150
Gálvez, Arg. G8 80
Galway, Ire. H4 8
Galway, co., Ire. H5 8
Galway Bay, b., Ire. H4 8
Gamagōri, Japan M12 36
Gamaliel, Ar., U.S. A3 111
Gamaliel, Ky., U.S. D4 124
Gamarra, Col. C6 84
Gambaga, Ghana F9 64
Gambela, Eth. M8 60
Gambell, Ak., U.S. C5 109
Gambia, ctry., Afr. F3 54
Gambia (Gambie), stm., Afr. F3 54
Gambi Aṭrash, Sud. L7 60
Gambier, Oh., U.S. B3 142
Gambier, Îles, is., Fr. Poly. K26 158
Gambo, Newf., Can. D4 102
Gamboa, Pan. C3 84
Gamboma, Congo B3 58
Gambrills, Md., U.S. B4 127
Gamerco, N.M., U.S. B1 138
Gamoep, S. Afr. G4 66
Gamon, Sen. E3 64
Gan, stm., China A11 30
Gan, stm., China G4 34
Ganado, Az., U.S. B6 110
Ganado, Tx., U.S. E4 150
Gananoque, Ont., Can. C8 103
Ganāveh, Iran G11 48
Gancevići, Bela. I9 22
Gand (Gent), Bel. F4 12
Ganda, Ang. D2 58
Gandak (Nārāyani), stm., Asia G11 44
Gander, Newf., Can. D4 102
Gander, stm., Newf., Can. D4 102
Ganderkesee, Ger. B8 10
Gander Lake, l., Newf., Can. D4 102
Gāndhi Sāgar, res., India H6 44
Gandi, Nig. E12 64
Gandia, Spain G11 16
Gandu, Braz. B9 79
Ganfang, China G3 34
Gangānagar, India F5 44
Gangāpur, India G7 44
Gangaw, Burma C3 40
Gangdisê Shan, mts., China E9 44
Ganges, B.C., Can. g12 99
Ganges, Fr. I10 14
Ganges (Ganga) (Padma), stm., Asia I13 44
Ganghu, China D12 44
Gangi, Italy L9 18
Gangkou, China F4 34
Gang Mills, N.Y., U.S. C3 139
Gangotri, India E8 44
Gangotri, India E8 44
Gangou, China C7 32
Gangoumen, China B4 32
Gangtok, India G13 44
Gangu, China E8 30
Gannett Peak, mtn., Wy., U.S. C3 157
Gannvalley, S.D., U.S. C7 148
Ganq, China B15 44
Gans, Ok., U.S. B7 143
Gansu (Kansu), prov., China D7 30
Gantt, Al., U.S. D3 108
Gantt, S.C., U.S. B3 147
Gantt Lake, res., Al., U.S. D3 108
Ganxi, China G7 34
Ganzê, China E7 30
Ganzhou, China J3 34
Ganzo Azul, Peru C4 82
Gao, Mali C9 64
Gaobu, China H6 34
Gaocun, China F10 32
Gaohe, China M1 34
Gaokeng, China H2 34
Gaoling, China C5 32
Gaona, Arg. C6 80
Gaoqiaozhen, China C9 32
Gaoshan, China J8 34
Gaotan, China E6 34
Gaotingsi, China I1 34
Gaoua, Burkina F8 64
Gaoxinji, China A4 34
Gaoya, China G6 32
Gaoyou, China C8 34
Gaoyou Hu, l., China C8 34
Gap, Fr. H13 14
Gap, Pa., U.S. G9 145
Gap Mills, W.V., U.S. D4 155
Gar, China E3 30
Garachiné, Pan. C3 84
Garagoa, Col. E6 84
Garanhuns, Braz. E11 76
Garara, Pap. N. Gui. A9 68
Garber, Ok., U.S. A4 143
Garberville, Ca., U.S. B2 112
Garça, Braz. G4 79
Garças, Rio das, stm., Braz. C2 79
García, Mex. C5 90
García de Sola, Embalse de, res., Spain F6 16
Garcias, Braz. F2 79
Gard, dept., Fr. I11 14
Garda, Italy D5 18
Garda, Lago di, l., Italy D5 18
Gardelegen, Ger. C11 10
Garden, co., Ne., U.S. C3 134
Gardena, Ca., U.S. n12 112
Garden City, Al., U.S. A3 108
Garden City, Ga., U.S. D5 117
Garden City, Id., U.S. F2 119
Garden City, In., U.S. F6 121
Garden City, Ks., U.S. E3 123
Garden City, Mi., U.S. p15 129
Garden City, Mn., U.S. F4 130
Garden City, Mo., U.S. C3 132
Garden City, S.D., U.S. C8 148
Gardendale, Al., U.S. B3 108
Garden Grove, Ca., U.S. n13 112
Garden Grove, Ia., U.S. D4 122
Garden Island, i., Mi., U.S. C5 129
Garden Plain, Ks., U.S. E6 123
Garden Prairie, Il., U.S. A5 120
Garden Reach, India I13 44
Gardenton, Man., Can. E3 100
Garden Valley, Id., U.S. E3 119
Gardey, Arg. I9 80
Gardeyz, Afg. D3 44
Gardi, Ga., U.S. E5 117
Gardiner, Me., U.S. D3 126
Gardiner, Mt., U.S. E6 133
Gardiner, Or., U.S. D2 144
Gardiners Island, i., N.Y., U.S. m16 139
Gardner, Ar., U.S. D3 111
Gardner, Il., U.S. B5 120
Gardner, Ks., U.S. D9 123
Gardner, Ma., U.S. A4 128
Gardner, N.D., U.S. B9 141
Gardner, Tn., U.S. A3 149
Gardner Canal, strt., B.C., Can. C3 99
Gardner Lake, l., Ct., U.S. C6 114
Gardner Lake, l., Me., U.S. D5 126
Gardner Mountain, mtn., N.H., U.S. B3 136
Gardner Pinnacles, Hi., U.S. k14 118
Gardnerville, Nv., U.S. E2 135
Gardone Val Trompia, Italy D5 18
Garešnica, Cro. D11 18
Garfield, Ar., U.S. A2 111
Garfield, Ga., U.S. D4 117
Garfield, Ks., U.S. D4 123
Garfield, N.J., U.S. h8 137
Garfield, N.M., U.S. E2 138
Garfield, Wa., U.S. B8 154
Garfield, co., Co., U.S. B2 113
Garfield, co., Mt., U.S. C9 133
Garfield, co., Ne., U.S. C6 134
Garfield, co., Ok., U.S. A4 143
Garfield, co., Ut., U.S. F4 151
Garfield, co., Wa., U.S. C8 154
Garfield Heights, Oh., U.S. h9 142
Garfield Mountain, mtn., Mt., U.S. F4 133
Garfield Peak, mtn., Wy., U.S. D5 157
Gargouna, Mali D10 64
Gargždai, Lith. F4 22
Garibaldi, Braz. E13 80
Garibaldi, Or., U.S. B3 144
Garibaldi, Mount, mtn., B.C., Can. E6 99
Garies, S. Afr. H4 66
Garissa, Kenya B7 58
Garita Palmera, El Sal. D4 92
Garko, Nig. F14 64
Garland, Ar., U.S. D2 111
Garland, Ks., U.S. E9 123
Garland, Ne., U.S. D9 134
Garland, N.C., U.S. C4 140
Garland, Tn., U.S. B2 149
Garland, Tx., U.S. n10 150
Garland, Ut., U.S. B3 151
Garland, co., Ar., U.S. C2 111
Garlasco, Italy D3 18
Garliava, Lith. G6 22
Garlin, Fr. I6 14
Garm, Taj. J12 26
Garmisch-Partenkirchen, Ger. H11 10
Garnavillo, Ia., U.S. B6 122
Garner, Ar., U.S. B4 111
Garner, Ia., U.S. A4 122
Garner, Ky., U.S. C7 124
Garner, N.C., U.S. B4 140
Garnet Range, mts., Mt., U.S. D3 133
Garnett, Ks., U.S. D8 123
Garnish, Newf., Can. E4 102
Garonne, stm., Eur. H6 14
Garoua, Cam. G9 54
Garrard, co., Ky., U.S. C5 124
Garretson, S.D., U.S. D9 148
Garrett, In., U.S. B7 121
Garrett, Ky., U.S. C7 124
Garrett, co., Md., U.S. k12 127
Garrett Park, Md., U.S. B3 127
Garrettsville, Oh., U.S. A4 142
Garrick, Sask., Can. D3 105
Garrison, Ia., U.S. B5 122
Garrison, Ky., U.S. B6 124
Garrison, Md., U.S. B4 127
Garrison, N.Y., U.S. D7 139
Garrison, N.D., U.S. B4 141
Garrison, Tx., U.S. D5 150
Garrison Dam, N.D., U.S. B4 141
Garrovillas, Spain F5 16
Garry Lake, l., N.W. Ter., Can. C12 96
Garson Quarry, Man., Can. D3 100
Garth, Al., U.S. A3 108
Garthby Station (Beaulac), Que., Can. D6 104
Garub, Nmb. F3 66
Garut, Indon. j13 39a
Garvin, co., Ok., U.S. C4 143
Garwin, Ia., U.S. B5 122
Garwolin, Pol. D21 10
Garwood, Tx., U.S. E4 150
Gary, In., U.S. A3 121
Gary, S.D., U.S. C9 148
Gary, W.V., U.S. D3 155
Garyarsa, China E9 44
Garysburg, N.C., U.S. A5 140
Garyville, La., U.S. D5 125
Garza, Arg. E7 80
Garza, co., Tx., U.S. C2 150
Garza-Little Elm Reservoir, res., Tx., U.S. C4 150
Garzón, Col. F5 84
Garzón, Ur. H11 80
Gas, Ks., U.S. E8 123
Gas City, In., U.S. D6 121
Gascogne, hist. reg., Fr. H6 14
Gasconade, Mo., U.S. C6 132
Gasconade, co., Mo., U.S. C6 132
Gasconade, stm., Mo., U.S. C6 132
Gasconade, Osage Fork, stm., Mo., U.S. D5 132
Gascoyne, stm., Austl. E2 68
Gash (Nahr al-Qāsh), stm., Afr. F8 56
Gashaka, Nig. G9 54
Gas Hills, Wy., U.S. D5 157
Gaspar, Braz. D14 80
Gasparilla Island, i., Fl., U.S. F4 116
Gaspé, Que., Can. k14 104
Gaspésie, Péninsule de la, pen., Que., Can. k13 104
Gasport, N.Y., U.S. B2 139
Gassaway, W.V., U.S. C4 155
Gassville, Ar., U.S. A3 111
Gaston, In., U.S. D7 121
Gaston, N.C., U.S. A5 140
Gaston, Or., U.S. h11 144
Gaston, S.C., U.S. D5 147
Gaston, co., N.C., U.S. B1 140
Gaston, Lake, res., U.S. A5 140
Gaston Dam, N.C., U.S. A5 140
Gastonia, N.C., U.S. B1 140
Gastre, Arg. E3 78
Gata, Cabo de, c., Spain I9 16
Gátas, Akrotírion, c., Cyp. D2 48
Gatčina, Russia B13 22
Gate City, Va., U.S. f9 153
Gates, N.Y., U.S. *B3 139
Gates, N.C., U.S. A6 140
Gates, Or., U.S. C4 144
Gates, Tn., U.S. B2 149
Gates, co., N.C., U.S. A6 140
Gateshead, Eng., U.K. G12 8
Gates of the Arctic National Park, Ak., U.S. B9 109
Gatesville, N.C., U.S. A6 140
Gatesville, Tx., U.S. D4 150
Gateway, Co., U.S. C2 113
Gatineau, Que., Can. D2 104
Gatineau, stm., Que., Can. D2 104
Gatineau, Parc de la, Que., Can. D2 104
Gatliff, Ky., U.S. D5 124
Gatlinburg, Tn., U.S. D10 149
Gattinara, Italy D3 18
Gatton, Austl. F10 70
Gatún, Esclusas de, Pan. H15 92
Gatún, Lago, res., Pan. H15 92
Gauley, stm., W.V., U.S. C3 155
Gauley Bridge, W.V., U.S. C3 155
Gaurīśaṅgkar, mtn., Asia G12 44
Gause, Tx., U.S. D4 150
Gautier, Ms., U.S. f8 131
Gauting, Ger. G11 10
Gavà, Spain D14 16
Gávdhos, i., Grc. O8 20
Gavião, stm., Braz. C8 79
Gavins Point Dam, U.S. B8 134
Gävle, Swe. K15 6
Gävleborgs Län, co., Swe. K15 6
Gavrilov-Jam, Russia D22 22
Gavrilov Posad, Russia E23 22
Gawler, Austl. J3 70
Gawler Ranges, mts., Austl. F7 68
Gaxun Nur, l., China C7 30
Gay, Ga., U.S. C2 117
Gaya, India H11 44
Gay Head, c., Ma., U.S. D6 128
Gaylesville, Al., U.S. A4 108
Gaylord, Ks., U.S. C5 123
Gaylord, Mi., U.S. C6 129
Gaylord, Mn., U.S. F4 130
Gaylordsville, Ct., U.S. C2 114
Gayndah, Austl. E9 70
Gays, Il., U.S. D5 120
Gays Mills, Wi., U.S. E3 156
Gaysville, Vt., U.S. D3 152
Gayville, S.D., U.S. E8 148
Gaza see Ghazzah, Isr. Occ. F3 48
Gaza Strip, hist. reg., Isr. Occ. F2 50
Gaziantep, Tur. C4 48
Gazimağusa (Famagusta), N. Cyp. D2 48
Gbangbatok, S.L. H3 64
Gbanhala, stm., Afr. G5 64
Gbarnga, Lib. H5 64
Gbongan, Nig. H12 64
Gcoverega, Bots. B7 66
Gdańsk (Danzig), Pol. A18 10
Gdańsk, Gulf of, b., Eur. A19 10
Gdov, Russia C10 22
Gdyel, Alg. J11 16
Gdynia, Pol. A18 10
Gearhart, Or., U.S. A3 144
Gearhart Mountain, mtn., Or., U.S. E6 144
Geary, N.B., Can. D3 101
Geary, Ok., U.S. B3 143
Geary, co., Ks., U.S. D7 123
Geauga, co., Oh., U.S. A4 142
Geba, stm., Afr. F4 54
Gebeit Mine, Sud. G9 60
Gebze, Tur. I13 20
Gecha, Eth. N8 60
Geddes, S.D., U.S. D7 148
Gedera, Isr. E3 50
Gediz, Tur. J13 20
Gedo, Eth. M9 60
Gedun, China H7 34
Geel, Bel. F7 12
Geelong, Austl. L6 70
Geesthacht, Ger. B10 10
Geeveston, Austl. N7 70
Geff, Il., U.S. E5 120
Gegong, China E6 34
Geiger, Al., U.S. C1 108
Geilo, Nor. K11 6
Geiranger, Nor. J10 6
Geislingen, Ger. G9 10
Geistown, Pa., U.S. F4 145
Geist Reservoir, res., In., U.S. E6 121
Geithain, Ger. D12 10
Gejiatun, China C7 32
Gejiu (Kokiu), China C7 40
Gela, Italy L9 18
Gelderland, prov., Neth. D8 12
Geldermalsen, Neth. E7 12
Geldrop, Neth. F8 12
Gelenbe, Tur. J11 20
Gelert, Ont., Can. C6 103
Gelgaudiškis, Lith. F6 22
Gelibolu, Tur. I10 20
Gelibolu Yarımadası (Gallipoli Peninsula), pen., Tur. I10 20
Gelsenkirchen, Ger. D7 10
Geltsa, Eth. N9 60
Gem, Ks., U.S. C3 123
Gem, co., Id., U.S. E2 119
Gemena, Zaire H4 56
Gemlik, Tur. I13 20
Gemsbok National Park, Bots. E5 66
Gemünden, Ger. E9 10
Gem Village, Co., U.S. D3 113
Gen, stm., China A11 30
Genale (Jubba), stm., Afr. G9 56
Gençay, Fr. F7 14
General, stm., C.R. H11 92
General Acha, Arg. I6 80
General Alvear, Arg. I8 80
General Alvear, Arg. H5 80
General Aquino, Para. C10 80
General Arenales, Arg. H8 80
General Belgrano, Arg. H9 80
General Bravo, Mex. E10 90
General Cabrera, Arg. G7 80
General Campos, Arg. F9 80
General Carneiro, Braz. C2 79
General Carrera, Lago (Lago Buenos Aires), l., S.A. F2 78
General Cepeda, Mex. E9 90
General Conesa, Arg. I10 80
General Daniel Cerri, Arg. J7 80
General Elizardo Aquino, Para. D10 80
General Enrique Martínez, Ur. G12 80
General Enrique Mosconi, Arg. B7 80
General Escobedo, Mex. E7 90
General Eugenio A. Garay, Para. C10 80
General Eugenio A. Garay, Para. I10 82
General Galarza, Arg. G9 80
General Güemes, Arg. C6 80
General Guido, Arg. I10 80
General José de San Martín, Arg. D9 80
General Juan José Ríos, Mex. E5 90
General Juan Madariaga, Arg. I10 80
General La Madrid, Arg. I8 80
General Lavalle, Arg. I10 80
General Leonidas Plaza Gutiérrez, Ec. I3 84
General Levalle, Arg. H7 80
General Manuel Belgrano, Cerro, mtn., Arg. E5 80
General O'Brien, Arg. H8 80
General Paz, Arg. H9 80
General Pico, Arg. H7 80
General Pinedo, Arg. D8 80
General Pinto, Arg. H8 80
General Pizarro, Arg. C6 80
General Roca, Arg. J5 80
General San Martín, Arg. H9 80
General San Martín, Arg. I7 80
General Santos, Phil. D8 38
General Terán, Mex. E10 90
General Viamonte (Los Toldos), Arg. H8 80
General Villegas, Arg. H7 80
Genesee, Id., U.S. C2 119
Genesee, Mi., U.S. E7 129
Genesee, co., Mi., U.S. E7 129
Genesee, co., N.Y., U.S. B2 139
Genesee, stm., N.Y., U.S. C2 139
Genesee Depot, Wi., U.S. n11 156
Geneseo, Il., U.S. B3 120
Geneseo, Ks., U.S. D5 123
Geneseo, N.Y., U.S. C3 139
Geneseo, N.D., U.S. C8 141
Geneva, Al., U.S. D4 108
Geneva, Ga., U.S. D2 117
Geneva, Il., U.S. B5 120
Geneva, In., U.S. C8 121
Geneva, Ky., U.S. C2 124
Geneva, Ne., U.S. D8 134
Geneva, N.Y., U.S. C4 139
Geneva, Oh., U.S. A5 142
Geneva, co., Al., U.S. D4 108
Geneva, Lake, l., Eur. F13 14
Geneva, Lake, l., Wi., U.S. F5 156
Geneva see Genève, Switz. F13 14
Geneva-on-the-Lake, Oh., U.S. A5 142
Genève (Geneva), Switz. F5 13
Genève, state, Switz. F5 13
Gengma, China C5 40
Genk, Bel. G8 12
Genlis, Fr. E12 14
Genoa, Ar., U.S. D2 111
Genoa, Co., U.S. B7 113
Genoa, Il., U.S. A5 120
Genoa, Ne., U.S. C8 134
Genoa, Nv., U.S. D2 135
Genoa, Oh., U.S. A2 142
Genoa City, Wi., U.S. F5 156
Genoa see Genova, Italy E3 18
Genola, Ut., U.S. D4 151
Genova (Genoa), Italy E3 18
Genova, Golfo di, b., Italy E3 18
Genrijetty, ostrov, i., Russia B23 28
Gent (Gand), Bel. F4 12
Genthin, Ger. C12 10
Gentry, Ar., U.S. A1 111
Gentry, co., Mo., U.S. A3 132
Gentryville, In., U.S. H3 121
Geographe Bay, b., Austl. F3 68
Geographe Channel, strt., Austl. D2 68
Geokčaj, Azer. I7 26
Geok-Tepe, Turk. B14 48
George, S. Afr. I6 66
George, Ia., U.S. A2 122
George, co., Ms., U.S. E5 131
George, stm., Que., Can. g13 104
George, Cape, c., N.S., Can. D8 101
George, Lake, l., Austl. J8 70
George, Lake, l., N.S., Can. E3 101
George, Lake, l., Ug. B6 58
George, Lake, l., Fl., U.S. C5 116
George, Lake, l., N.Y., U.S. B7 139
George Air Force Base, mil., Ca., U.S. E5 112
George B. Stevenson Reservoir, res., Pa., U.S. D6 145
George Hill, mtn., Md., U.S. k12 127
George Peak, mtn., Ut., U.S. B2 151
Georges Bank E13 86
Georges Mills, N.H., U.S. D2 136
George Town, Austl. M7 70
Georgetown, P.E.I., Can. C7 101
George Town, Cay. Is. E4 94
Georgetown, Gam. E2 64
Georgetown, Guy. D13 84
George Town (Pinang), Malay. L6 40
Georgetown, St. Vin. H14 94
Georgetown, Ar., U.S. B4 111
Georgetown, Ca., U.S. C3 112
Georgetown, Co., U.S. B5 113
Georgetown, Ct., U.S. D2 114
Georgetown, De., U.S. F4 115
Georgetown, Fl., U.S. C5 116
Georgetown, Ga., U.S. E1 117
Georgetown, Id., U.S. G7 119
Georgetown, Il., U.S. D6 120
Georgetown, In., U.S. H6 121
Georgetown, Ky., U.S. B5 124
Georgetown, La., U.S. C3 125
Georgetown, Ma., U.S. A6 128
Georgetown, Ms., U.S. D3 131
Georgetown, Oh., U.S. D2 142
Georgetown, S.C., U.S. E9 147
Georgetown, Tx., U.S. D4 150
Georgetown, co., S.C., U.S. E9 147
George V Coast, Ant. B7 73
George VI Sound, strt., Ant. C12 73
George Washington Birthplace National Monument, Va., U.S. B6 153
George Washington Carver National Monument, Mo., U.S. E3 132
George West, Tx., U.S. E3 150
Georgia, ctry., Asia I6 26
Georgia, state, U.S. D3 117
Georgiana, Al., U.S. D3 108
Georgian Bay, b., Ont., Can. B3 103
Georgijevsk, Russia I6 26
Georgina, stm., Austl. D3 70
Gera, Ger. E12 10
Geral, Serra, clf, Braz. D14 80
Gerald, Sask., Can. G5 105
Gerald, Mo., U.S. C6 132
Geral de Goiás, Serra, clf, Braz. B5 79
Geraldine, Al., U.S. A4 108
Geraldine, Mt., U.S. C6 133
Geraldton, Austl. E2 68
Geraldton, Ont., Can. o18 103
Gérardmer, Fr. D13 14
Gerber, Ca., U.S. B2 112
Gerber Reservoir, res., Or., U.S. E5 144
Gerdine, Mount, mtn., Ak., U.S. C9 109

Gere-Gori

Name — Map Ref. — Page

Gereshk, Afg. E1 44
Gering, Ne., U.S. C2 134
Gerlach, Nv., U.S. C2 135
Gerlachovský štít, mtn., Slov. F20 10
Germantown, N.B., Can. D5 101
Germantown, Il., U.S. E4 120
Germantown, Ky., U.S. B6 124
Germantown, Md., U.S. B3 127
Germantown, Oh., U.S. C1 142
Germantown, Tn., U.S. B2 149
Germantown, Wi., U.S. E5 156
Germany (Deutschland), ctry., Eur. E9 4
Germiston, S. Afr. F9 66
Gernika-Lumo (Guernica y Luno), Spain B9 16
Geronimo, Ok., U.S. C3 143
Gerrardstown, W.V., U.S. B6 155
Gers, dept., Fr. I7 14
Gerufa, Bots. B8 66
Gervais, Or., U.S. B4 144
Gêrzê, China D11 44
Gesher HaZiw, Isr. B4 50
Getafe, Spain E8 16
Gettysburg, Oh., U.S. B1 142
Gettysburg, Pa., U.S. G7 145
Gettysburg, S.D., U.S. C6 148
Getulina, Braz. F4 79
Getúlio Vargas, Braz. D12 80
Geuda Springs, Ks., U.S. E6 123
Gevgelija, Mac. H6 20
Gévora, stm., Eur. F4 16
Gex, Fr. F13 14
Geyikli, Tur. J10 20
Geyser, Mt., U.S. C6 133
Geyserville, Ca., U.S. C2 112
Ghaapplato, plat., Afr. F7 66
Ghadāmis, Libya E15 62
Ghāghara, stm., Asia G10 44
Ghana, ctry., Afr. G6 54
Ghanzi, Bots. C5 66
Ghanzi, dept., Bots. D6 66
Gharbi, Oued el, val., Alg. D11 62
Gharbīyah, Aṣ-Ṣaḥrā' al- (Western Desert), des., Egypt D4 60
Ghardaïa, Alg. D12 62
Ghardimaou, Tun. M3 18
Gharig, Sud. L4 60
Gharyān, Libya B3 56
Ghaṣm, Syria C6 50
Ghāt, Libya H16 62
Ghātāl, India I12 44
Għawdex (Gozo), i., Malta M9 18
Ghawr ash-Sharqīyah, Qanāt al- (East Ghor Canal), Jord. D5 50
Ghayth, Wādī, val., Jord. G5 50
Ghazāl, Baḥr al-, stm., Sud. M5 60
Ghazal, Bahr el, val., Chad F4 56
Ghāziābād, India F7 44
Ghāzīpur, India H10 44
Ghazlūna, Pak. E2 44
Ghaznī, Afg. D3 44
Ghazzah (Gaza), Isr. Occ. F3 48
Ghedi, Italy D5 18
Gheen, Mn., U.S. C6 130
Ghent, Ky., U.S. B4 124
Ghent, Mn., U.S. F3 130
Ghent see Gent, Bel. F4 12
Gheorghe Gheorghiu-Dej, Rom. C10 20
Gheorgheni, Rom. C9 20
Gherla, Rom. B7 20
Ghilizane, Alg. C11 62
Ghisonaccia, Fr. I24 15a
Ghudāf, Wādī al-, val., Iraq E7 48
Ghūriān, Afg. D16 48
Giant Mountain, mtn., N.Y., U.S. A7 139
Giant's Castle, mtn., Afr. G9 66
Giants Neck, Ct., U.S. D7 114
Giarre, Italy L10 18
Gibara, Cuba D6 94
Gibbon, Mn., U.S. F4 130
Gibbon, Ne., U.S. D7 134
Gibbons, Alta., Can. C4 98
Gibbonsville, Id., U.S. D5 119
Gibbstown, N.J., U.S. D2 137
Gibeon, Nmb. E3 66
Gibraleón, Spain H5 16
Gibraltar, Gib. I6 16
Gibraltar, dep., Eur. H6 4
Gibraltar, Strait of (Estrecho de Gibraltar), strt. J6 16
Gibsland, La., U.S. B2 125
Gibson, Ga., U.S. C4 117
Gibson, La., U.S. E5 125
Gibson, N.C., U.S. C3 140
Gibson, Tn., U.S. B3 149
Gibson, co., In., U.S. H2 121
Gibson, co., Tn., U.S. A3 149
Gibsonburg, Oh., U.S. A2 142
Gibson City, Il., U.S. C5 120
Gibson Desert, des., Austl. D5 68
Gibsonia, Pa., U.S. h14 145
Gibson Island, i., Md., U.S. B5 127
Gibsons, B.C., Can. E6 99
Gibsonton, Fl., U.S. p11 116
Gibsonville, N.C., U.S. A3 140
Gidami, Eth. M8 60
Gidda, Eth. M8 60
Giddings, Tx., U.S. D4 150
Gideon, Mo., U.S. E8 132
Gidole, Eth. O9 60
Gidrotorf, Russia E26 22
Gien, Fr. E9 14
Giessen, Ger. E8 10
Gifford, Ar., U.S. g8 111
Gifford, Fl., U.S. E6 116
Gifford, Il., U.S. C5 120
Gifhorn, Ger. C10 10
Gifu, Japan L11 36
Giganta, Sierra de la, mts., Mex. E4 90
Gigante, Col. F5 84
Gig Harbor, Wa., U.S. B3 154
Gihon, stm., Vt., U.S. B3 152
Gijón, Spain B6 16
Gila, N.M., U.S. E1 138
Gila, co., Az., U.S. D5 110
Gila, stm., U.S. E4 106
Gila Bend, Az., U.S. E3 110
Gila Bend Indian Reservation, Az., U.S. D3 110
Gila Bend Mountains, mts., Az., U.S. D2 110
Gila Cliff Dwellings National Monument, N.M., U.S. D1 138
Gila Mountains, mts., Az., U.S. D6 110
Gila Peak, mtn., Az., U.S. D6 110
Gila River Indian Reservation, Az., U.S. D4 110
Gilbert, Az., U.S. D4 110
Gilbert, Ia., U.S. B4 122
Gilbert, La., U.S. B4 125
Gilbert, Mn., U.S. C6 130
Gilbert, S.C., U.S. D5 147
Gilbert, W.V., U.S. D3 155
Gilbert, stm., Austl. A4 70
Gilbert, stm., Newf., Can. B3 102
Gilbertown, Al., U.S. D1 108
Gilbert Peak, mtn., Wa., U.S. C4 154
Gilbert Plains, Man., Can. D1 100
Gilbertsville, Ky., U.S. f9 124
Gilbertsville, Pa., U.S. F10 145
Gilbertville, Ia., U.S. B5 122
Gilbertville, Ma., U.S. B3 128
Gilboa', Haré, hills, Asia D4 50
Gilbués, Braz. E9 76
Gilby, N.D., U.S. A8 141
Gilchrist, Or., U.S. D5 144
Gilchrist, co., Fl., U.S. C4 116
Gilcrest, Co., U.S. A6 113
Gildford, Mt., U.S. B6 133
Giles, co., Tn., U.S. B4 149
Giles, co., Va., U.S. C2 153
Gilford, N.H., U.S. C4 136
Gilford Island, i., B.C., Can. D4 99
Gilgandra, Austl. H8 70
Gilgit, Pak. C6 44
Gilgit, stm., Pak. B5 44
Gill, Co., U.S. A6 113
Gillam, Man., Can. A4 100
Gilles, Lake, l., Austl. I2 70
Gillespie, Il., U.S. D4 120
Gillespie, co., Tx., U.S. D3 150
Gillespie Dam, Az., U.S. D3 110
Gillett, Ar., U.S. C4 111
Gillett, Wi., U.S. D5 156
Gillette, Wy., U.S. B7 157
Gillham, Ar., U.S. C1 111
Gilliam, Mo., U.S. B4 132
Gilliam, co., Or., U.S. B6 144
Gilman, Co., U.S. B4 113
Gilman, Il., U.S. C5 120
Gilman, Ia., U.S. C5 122
Gilman, Mn., U.S. E5 130
Gilman, Vt., U.S. C5 152
Gilman, Wi., U.S. C3 156
Gilman City, Mo., U.S. A4 132
Gilmanton, N.H., U.S. D4 136
Gilmanton Iron Works, N.H., U.S. D4 136
Gilmer, Tx., U.S. C5 150
Gilmer, co., Ga., U.S. B2 117
Gilmer, co., W.V., U.S. C4 155
Gilmore, Ar., U.S. B5 111
Gilmore City, Ia., U.S. B3 122
Gilpin, co., Co., U.S. B5 113
Gilroy, Ca., U.S. D3 112
Gilson, Il., U.S. C3 120
Gilsum, N.H., U.S. D2 136
Gilt Edge, Tn., U.S. B2 149
Giltner, Ne., U.S. D7 134
Giluwe, Mount, mtn., Pap. N. Gui. m15 68a
Gimbi, Eth. M8 60
Gimie, Mount, mtn., St. Luc. H14 94
Gimli, Man., Can. D3 100
Gimoly, Russia J23 6
Gimont, Fr. I7 14
Gin Gin, Austl. E9 70
Ginir, Eth. G9 56
Ginosa, Italy I11 18
Gioia del Colle, Italy I11 18
Gioia Tauro, Italy K10 18
Gipuzkoako, prov., Spain B9 16
Girard, Ga., U.S. C5 117
Girard, Il., U.S. D4 120
Girard, Ks., U.S. E9 123
Girard, Oh., U.S. A5 142
Girard, Pa., U.S. B1 145
Girardot, Col. E5 84
Girardville, Pa., U.S. E9 145
Girbovu, Rom. E7 20
Girdletree, Md., U.S. D7 127
Girgarre, Austl. K6 70
Girīdīh, India H12 44
Girne, N. Cyp. D2 48
Giromagny, Fr. E13 14
Girón, Ec. I3 84
Girona, Spain D14 16
Gironde, dept., Fr. G6 14
Gironde, est., Fr. G6 14
Giroux, Man., Can. E3 100
Girouxville, Alta., Can. B2 98
Giru, Austl. B7 70
Giruá, Braz. E11 80
Girvas, Russia J23 6
Gisborne, N.Z. C7 72
Giscome, B.C., Can. B6 99
Gisenyi, Rw. B5 58
Gisors, Fr. C8 14
Giswil, Switz. E9 13
Gitega, Bdi. B5 58
Giugliano [in Campania], Italy I9 18
Giulianova, Italy G8 18
Giurgiu, Rom. F9 20
Giv'atayim, Isr. D3 50
Givet, Fr. B11 14
Givors, Fr. G11 14
Givry, Fr. F11 14
Giyon, Eth. M9 60
Giza see Al-Jīzah, Egypt B6 60
Gīzāb, Afg. D2 44
Gižduvan, Uzb. I10 26
Gizen, Sud. L8 60
Gižiginskaja guba, b., Russia E23 28
Giżycko, Pol. A21 10
Gjandža, Azer. I7 26
Gjirokastër, Alb. I4 20
Gjoa Haven, N.W. Ter., Can. C13 96
Gjøvik, Nor. K12 6
Gjuhëzës, Kep i, c., Alb. I3 20
Glace Bay, N.S., Can. C10 101
Glacier, Wa., U.S. A4 154
Glacier, co., Mt., U.S. B3 133
Glacier Bay, b., Ak., U.S. k21 109
Glacier Bay National Park, Ak., U.S. D12 109
Glacier National Park, B.C., Can. D9 99
Glacier National Park, Mt., U.S. B2 133
Glacier Peak, mtn., Wa., U.S. A4 154
Gladbach see Mönchengladbach, Ger. D6 10
Gladbeck, Ger. D6 10
Gladbrook, Ia., U.S. B5 122
Glade, Ks., U.S. C4 123
Glade Creek, stm., Wa., U.S. C6 154
Glade Creek, stm., W.V., U.S. n14 155
Glade Creek, stm., W.V., U.S. n13 155
Glade Park, Co., U.S. B2 113
Glades, co., Fl., U.S. F5 116
Glade Spring, Va., U.S. f10 153
Gladeville, Tn., U.S. A5 149
Gladewater, Tx., U.S. C5 150
Gladmar, Sask., Can. H3 105
Gladstone, Austl. D9 70
Gladstone, Austl. I3 70
Gladstone, Man., Can. D2 100
Gladstone, Il., U.S. C3 120
Gladstone, Mi., U.S. C4 129
Gladstone, Mo., U.S. h10 132
Gladstone, N.J., U.S. B3 137
Gladstone, N.D., U.S. C3 141
Gladstone, Or., U.S. B4 144
Gladwin, Mi., U.S. E6 129
Gladwin, co., Mi., U.S. D6 129
Gladys, Va., U.S. C3 153
Glåma, stm., Nor. K12 6
Glandorf, Oh., U.S. A1 142
Glarner Alpen, mts., Switz. E10 13
Glarus, Switz. D11 13
Glarus, state, Switz. E11 13
Glasco, Ks., U.S. C6 123
Glasco, N.Y., U.S. C7 139
Glascock, co., Ga., U.S. C4 117
Glasford, Il., U.S. C4 120
Glasgow, Scot., U.K. F9 8
Glasgow, Ky., U.S. C4 124
Glasgow, Mo., U.S. B5 132
Glasgow, Mt., U.S. B10 133
Glasgow, Va., U.S. C3 153
Glasgow, W.V., U.S. m13 155
Glaslyn, Sask., Can. D1 105
Glassboro, N.J., U.S. D2 137
Glasscock, co., Tx., U.S. D2 150
Glass Mountains, mts., Tx., U.S. D1 150
Glassport, Pa., U.S. F2 145
Glastenbury Mountain, mtn., Vt., U.S. F2 152
Glastonbury, Ct., U.S. C5 114
Glattfelden, Switz. C10 13
Glauchau, Ger. E12 10
Glaževo, Russia B15 22
Glazier Lake, l., Me., U.S. A3 126
Glazov, Russia F8 26
Glazunovka, Russia I19 22
Glazypeau Mountain, mtn., Ar., U.S. f7 111
Gleason, Tn., U.S. A3 149
Gleichen, Alta., Can. D4 98
Gleisdorf, Aus. H15 10
Glen, N.H., U.S. B4 136
Glen Allan, Ms., U.S. B2 131
Glen Allen, Al., U.S. B2 108
Glen Allen, Va., U.S. C5 153
Glen Alpine, N.C., U.S. B1 140
Glenavon, Sask., Can. G4 105
Glenbeulah, Wi., U.S. k9 156
Glenboro, Man., Can. E2 100
Glenbrook, Nv., U.S. D2 135
Glenburn, N.D., U.S. A4 141
Glen Burnie, Md., U.S. B4 127
Glen Canyon, val., U.S. G4 151
Glen Canyon Dam, Az., U.S. A4 110
Glen Canyon National Recreation Area, U.S. F5 151
Glencoe, Austl. K4 70
Glencoe, Ont., Can. E3 103
Glencoe, Al., U.S. B4 108
Glencoe, Il., U.S. A6 120
Glencoe, Ky., U.S. B5 124
Glencoe, Mn., U.S. F4 130
Glencoe, Mo., U.S. f12 132
Glencoe, Ok., U.S. A5 143
Glen Cove, N.Y., U.S. h13 139
Glendale, Az., U.S. D3 110
Glendale, Ca., U.S. m12 112
Glendale, Ky., U.S. C4 124
Glendale, Ms., U.S. D4 131
Glendale, Oh., U.S. C1 142
Glendale, Or., U.S. E3 144
Glendale, R.I., U.S. B2 146
Glendale, S.C., U.S. B4 147
Glendale, Ut., U.S. F3 151
Glen Dale, W.V., U.S. B4 155
Glendale, Wi., U.S. m12 156
Glendale Colony, S.D., U.S. C7 148
Glendale Heights, W.V., U.S. g8 155
Glendive, Mt., U.S. C12 133
Glendo, Wy., U.S. D7 157
Glendola, N.J., U.S. C4 137
Glendon, Alta., Can. B5 98
Glendora, Ca., U.S. m13 112
Glendora, Ms., U.S. B3 131
Glendo Reservoir, res., Wy., U.S. D8 157
Glen Elder, Ks., U.S. C5 123
Glenelg, Md., U.S. B4 127
Glenella, Man., Can. D2 100
Glen Ellis Falls, wtfl, N.H., U.S. B4 136
Glen Ellyn, Il., U.S. k8 120
Glen Ewen, Sask., Can. H4 105
Glenfield, N.D., U.S. B7 141
Glen Gardner, N.J., U.S. B3 137
Glenham, N.Y., U.S. D7 139
Glenham, S.D., U.S. B5 148
Glen Haven, Co., U.S. A5 113
Glen Innes, Austl. G9 70
Glen Jean, W.V., U.S. D3 155
Glen Lake, l., Mi., U.S. D5 129
Glen Lyon, Pa., U.S. D9 145
Glenmora, La., U.S. D3 125
Glenmorgan, Austl. F8 70
Glenn, co., Ca., U.S. C2 112
Glennallen, Ak., U.S. f19 109
Glenns Ferry, Id., U.S. G3 119
Glennville, Ga., U.S. E5 117
Glenolden, Pa., U.S. p20 145
Glenoma, Wa., U.S. C3 154
Glenormiston, Austl. D3 70
Glenpool, Ok., U.S. B5 143
Glen Raven, N.C., U.S. A3 140
Glenreagh, Austl. H10 70
Glen Ridge, N.J., U.S. h8 137
Glen Robertson, Ont., Can. B10 103
Glen Rock, N.J., U.S. h8 137
Glen Rock, Pa., U.S. G8 145
Glenrock, Wy., U.S. D7 157
Glen Rose, Tx., U.S. C4 150
Glen Saint Mary, Fl., U.S. B4 116
Glens Falls, N.Y., U.S. B7 139
Glenside, Sask., Can. F2 105
Glenside, Pa., U.S. F11 145
Glenties, Ire. G5 8
Glentworth, Sask., Can. H2 105
Glen Ullin, N.D., U.S. C4 141
Glenview, Il., U.S. h9 120
Glenview Naval Air Station, mil., Il., U.S. h9 120
Glenvil, Ne., U.S. D7 134
Glenville, Mn., U.S. G5 130
Glenville, N.C., U.S. f9 140
Glenville, W.V., U.S. C4 155
Glen White, W.V., U.S. D3 155
Glen Wilton, Va., U.S. C3 153
Glenwood, Newf., Can. D4 102
Glenwood, Al., U.S. D3 108
Glenwood, Ar., U.S. C2 111
Glenwood, Fl., U.S. C5 116
Glenwood, Ga., U.S. D4 117
Glenwood, In., U.S. E7 121
Glenwood, Ia., U.S. C2 122
Glenwood, Mn., U.S. E3 130
Glenwood, Mo., U.S. A5 132
Glenwood, N.M., U.S. D1 138
Glenwood, Ut., U.S. E4 151
Glenwood, Va., U.S. D3 153
Glenwood, Wa., U.S. C4 154
Glenwood City, Wi., U.S. C1 156
Glenwood Springs, Co., U.S. B3 113
Glenwoodville, Alta., Can. E4 98
Glidden, Sask., Can. F1 105
Glidden, Ia., U.S. B3 122
Glidden, Wi., U.S. B3 156
Glide, Or., U.S. D3 144
Glinka, Russia G15 22
Gliwice (Gleiwitz), Pol. E18 10
Globe, Az., U.S. D5 110
Globe, Ky., U.S. B6 124
Gloggnitz, Aus. H15 10
Głogów, Pol. D16 10
Glória de Dourados, Braz. G1 79
Glorieta, N.M., U.S. B4 138
Glorieuses, Îles, is., Reu. D9 58
Gloster, Ms., U.S. D2 131
Gloucester, Austl. H9 70
Gloucester, Ont., Can. h12 103
Gloucester, Eng., U.K. J11 8
Gloucester, Ma., U.S. A6 128
Gloucester, Va., U.S. C6 153
Gloucester, co., N.J., U.S. D2 137
Gloucester, co., Va., U.S. C6 153
Gloucester City, N.J., U.S. D2 137
Gloucester Island, i., Austl. C8 70
Gloucester Point, Va., U.S. C6 153
Gloucestershire, co., Eng., U.K. J11 8
Glouster, Oh., U.S. C3 142
Glover, Vt., U.S. B4 152
Glover Island, i., Newf., Can. D3 102
Glovers Reef, rf., Belize I16 90
Gloversville, N.Y., U.S. B6 139
Glovertown, Newf., Can. D4 102
Gloverville, S.C., U.S. E4 147
Głowno, Pol. D19 10
Głubczyce, Pol. E17 10
Glubokoje, Bela. F10 22
Głuchołazy, Pol. E17 10
Gluck, S.C., U.S. C2 147
Glückstadt, Ger. B9 10
Gluša, Bela. H11 22
Glusk, Bela. I11 22
Glybokaja, Ukr. A9 20
Glyndon, Md., U.S. B4 127
Glyndon, Mn., U.S. D2 130
Glynn, co., Ga., U.S. E5 117
Gmünd, Aus. G15 10
Gmünd, Aus. I13 10
Gmunden, Aus. H13 10
Gnadenhutten, Oh., U.S. B4 142
Gnalta, Austl. H5 70
Gnezdovo, Russia G14 22
Gniew, Pol. B18 10
Gniewkowo, Pol. C18 10
Gniezno, Pol. C17 10
Gnjilane, Yugo. G5 20
Gnowangerup, Austl. F3 68
Goa, state, India E2 46
Goalen Head, c., Austl. K9 70
Goālpāra, India G14 44
Goan, Mali E7 64
Goascorán, Hond. D7 92
Goascorán, stm., N.A. D7 92
Goat Island, i., R.I., U.S. F5 146
Goat Mountain, mtn., Mt., U.S. C3 133
Goat Rock Dam, U.S. C4 108
Goba, Eth. G9 56
Gobabis, Nmb. D4 66
Gobabis, dept., Nmb. D4 66
Gobernador Gregores, Arg. F2 78
Gobernador Ingeniero Valentín Virasoro, Arg. E10 80
Gobernador Juan E. Martínez, Arg. E9 80
Gobernador Racedo, Arg. F8 80
Gobi, des., Asia C7 30
Gobles, Mi., U.S. F5 129
Gobō, Japan N10 36
Goce Delčev, Bul. H7 20
Goch, Ger. D6 10
Gochas, Nmb. E4 66
Godāvari, stm., India D6 46
Goddard, Ks., U.S. E6 123
Goderich, Ont., Can. D3 103
Goderville, Fr. C7 14
Godfrey, Ga., U.S. C3 117
Godfrey, Il., U.S. E3 120
Godhavn, Grnld. C14 86
Godhra, India I5 44
Godinne, Bel. H6 12
Godley, Tx., U.S. n9 150
Godoy Cruz, Arg. G4 80
Gods, stm., Man., Can. A5 100
Gods Lake, l., Man., Can. B4 100
Gods Mercy, Bay of, b., N.W. Ter., Can. D15 96
Godthåb, Grnld. C14 86
Godwin Austen see K2, mtn., Asia C7 44
Goehner, Ne., U.S. D8 134
Goélands, Lac aux, l., Que., Can. g8 102
Goes, Neth. E4 12
Goessel, Ks., U.S. D6 123
Goff, Ks., U.S. C8 123
Goff Creek, stm., Ok., U.S. e9 143
Goffstown, N.H., U.S. D3 136
Gogebic, co., Mi., U.S. n12 129
Gogebic, Lake, l., Mi., U.S. m12 129
Gogebic Range, hills, U.S. B3 156
Gogland, ostrov, i., Russia A10 22
Gogonou, Benin F11 64
Gohad, India G8 44
Gohitafla, I.C. H7 64
Goiana, Braz. E12 76
Goianápolis, Braz. D4 79
Goiandira, Braz. E4 79
Goianésia, Braz. C4 79
Goiânia, Braz. D4 79
Goiás, Braz. C3 79
Goiás, state, Braz. B4 79
Goiatuba, Braz. E4 79
Goio-Erê, Braz. C12 80
Gôio-Erê, stm., Braz. B12 80
Goito, Italy D5 18
Gojō, Japan M10 36
Gokāk, India D3 46
Gol, Nor. K11 6
Golāghāt, India G15 44
Golan Heights, clf, Isr. Occ. C5 50
Golbāf, Iran G14 48
Golconda, Il., U.S. F5 120
Golconda, Nv., U.S. C4 135
Gölcük, Tur. J11 20
Gołdap, Pol. A22 10
Gold Bar, Wa., U.S. B4 154
Gold Beach, Or., U.S. E2 144
Goldboro, N.S., Can. D8 101
Gold Coast, Ghana I9 64
Golden, B.C., Can. D9 99
Golden, Co., U.S. B5 113
Golden, Il., U.S. C2 120
Golden, Ms., U.S. A5 131
Golden Beach, Md., U.S. D4 127
Golden City, Mo., U.S. D3 132
Goldendale, Wa., U.S. D5 154
Golden Gate Bridge, Ca., U.S. h7 112
Golden Gate National Recreation Area, Ca., U.S. h7 112
Golden Hinde, mtn., B.C., Can. E5 99
Golden Lake, Ont., Can. B7 103
Golden Meadow, La., U.S. E5 125
Golden Prairie, Sask., Can. G1 105
Golden Spike National Historic Site, hist., Ut., U.S. B3 151
Golden Valley, Mn., U.S. n12 130
Goldenvalley, N.D., U.S. B3 141
Golden Valley, co., Mt., U.S. D7 133
Golden Valley, co., N.D., U.S. B2 141
Goldfield, Ia., U.S. B4 122
Goldfield, Nv., U.S. F4 135
Gold Hill, N.C., U.S. B2 140
Gold Hill, Or., U.S. E3 144
Goldonna, La., U.S. B3 125
Goldsboro, N.C., U.S. B5 140
Goldsby, Ok., U.S. B4 143
Goldsmith, In., U.S. D5 121
Goldsworthy, Austl. D3 68
Goldthwaite, Tx., U.S. D3 150
Golela, S. Afr. F10 66
Goleniów, Pol. B14 10
Goleta, Ca., U.S. E4 112
Golfito, C.R. I11 92
Golf Manor, Oh., U.S. o13 142
Golfo de Santa Clara, Mex. B2 90
Goliad, Tx., U.S. E4 150
Goliad, co., Tx., U.S. E4 150
Golicyno, Russia F19 22
Golmud, China D5 30
Golo, stm., Fr. I24 15a
Golovanevsk, Ukr. A14 20
Golovin, Ak., U.S. C7 109
Golpāyegān, Iran E11 48
Goltry, Ok., U.S. A3 143
Golva, N.D., U.S. C2 141
Golynki, Russia G14 22
Golyšmanovo, Russia F11 26
Goma, Zaire B5 58
Gomel', Bela. I14 22
Gomera, i., Spain o23 17b
Gómez Farías, Mex. C6 90
Gómez Palacio, Mex. E8 90
Gómez Plata, Col. D5 84
Gonābād, Iran D15 48
Gonaïves, Haiti E8 94
Gonâve, Golfe de la, b., Haiti E8 94
Gonâve, Île de la, i., Haiti E8 94
Gonbad-e Qābūs, Iran C13 48
Gonda, India G9 44
Gondal, India J4 44
Gondarbal, India D6 44
Gonder, Eth. K9 60
Gondia, India J9 44
Gondrecourt-le-Château, Fr. D12 14
Gönen, Tur. I11 20
Gongbo'gyamda, China F5 30
Gongchenqiao, China E9 34
Gongchuan, China I6 34
Gongdian, China G5 34
Gongga Shan, mtn., China F7 30
Gongkou, China H7 32
Gongola, stm., Nig. F9 54
Gongpinyu, China I1 34
Gongxian, China E9 30
Gongyingzi, China C7 32
Goñi, Ur. G10 80
Goniądz, Pol. B22 10
Gonvick, Mn., U.S. C3 130
Gonzales, Ca., U.S. D3 112
Gonzales, La., U.S. D5 125
Gonzales, Tx., U.S. E4 150
Gonzales, co., Tx., U.S. E4 150
González, Mex. F10 90
Gonzalez, Fl., U.S. u14 116
González, Riacho, stm., Para. B9 80
González Chaves, Arg. J8 80
González Moreno, Arg. H7 80
Gonzanamá, Ec. J3 84
Goochland, Va., U.S. C5 153
Goochland, co., Va., U.S. C5 153
Goode, Mount, mtn., Ak., U.S. g18 109
Goodell, Ia., U.S. B4 122
Gooderham, Ont., Can. C6 103
Goodeve, Sask., Can. F4 105
Goodfellow Air Force Base, mil., Tx., U.S. D2 150
Goodfield, Il., U.S. C4 120
Good Hope, S. Afr. H5 66
Good Hope, Al., U.S. A3 108
Good Hope, Ga., U.S. C3 117
Good Hope, Il., U.S. C3 120
Good Hope, Cape of, c., S. Afr. J4 66
Good Hope Mountain, mtn., B.C., Can. D5 99
Goodhue, Mn., U.S. F6 130
Goodhue, co., Mn., U.S. F6 130
Gooding, Id., U.S. G4 119
Gooding, co., Id., U.S. F4 119
Goodland, Fl., U.S. G5 116
Goodland, In., U.S. C3 121
Goodland, Ks., U.S. C2 123
Goodlands, Man., Can. E1 100
Goodlettsville, Tn., U.S. g10 149
Goodman, Ms., U.S. C4 131
Goodman, Mo., U.S. E3 132
Goodman, Wi., U.S. C5 156
Goodnews Bay, Ak., U.S. D7 109
Good Pine, La., U.S. C3 125
Goodrich, N.D., U.S. B5 141
Goodsprings, Al., U.S. B2 108
Goodsprings, Nv., U.S. H6 135
Good Thunder, Mn., U.S. F4 130
Goodview, Mn., U.S. F7 130
Goodwater, Al., U.S. B3 108
Goodway, Al., U.S. D2 108
Goodwell, Ok., U.S. e9 143
Goodwin, Ar., U.S. C4 111
Goodwin, S.D., U.S. C9 148
Goodyear, Az., U.S. D3 110
Goolgowi, Austl. I6 70
Goombalie, Austl. G6 70
Goondiwindi, Austl. G9 70
Goose, stm., Newf., Can. h9 102
Goose, stm., N.D., U.S. B8 141
Goose Bay, b., Newf., Can. B1 102
Goose Bay see Happy Valley-Goose Bay, Newf., Can. B1 102
Gooseberry Creek, stm., Wy., U.S. B4 157
Goose Creek, S.C., U.S. F7 147
Goose Creek, stm., U.S. G5 119
Goose Creek, stm., Ne., U.S. B5 134
Goose Creek, stm., Va., U.S. C3 153
Goose Creek Reservoir, res., S.C., U.S. k11 147
Goose Lake, Ia., U.S. C7 122
Goose Lake, l., U.S. B3 112
Goose Pond, l., N.H., U.S. C2 136
Gooty, India E4 46
Gopichettipālaiyam, India G4 46
Goppenstein, Switz. F8 13
Göppingen, Ger. G9 10
Goqên, China F6 30
Góra, Pol. D16 10
Goradit, Eth. L10 60
Gorakhpur, India G10 44
Gor'any, Bela. F12 22
Goražde, Bos. F2 20
Gorbatov, Russia E26 22
Gorbatovka, Russia E26 22
Gorboviči, Bela. H13 22
Gorčucha, Russia D26 22
Gorda, Punta, c., Chile H6 82
Gorda, Punta, c., Cuba C3 94
Gorda, Punta, c., Nic. C11 92
Gorda, Punta, c., Nic. F11 92
Gordo, Al., U.S. B2 108
Gordon, Al., U.S. D4 108
Gordon, Ga., U.S. D3 117
Gordon, Ne., U.S. B3 134
Gordon, Wi., U.S. B2 156
Gordon, co., Ga., U.S. B2 117
Gordon, Lake, res., Austl. N7 70
Gordon Creek, stm., Ne., U.S. B5 134
Gordonsville, Tn., U.S. C8 149
Gordonsville, Va., U.S. B4 153
Gordonvale, Austl. A6 70
Gordonville, Mo., U.S. D8 132
Gore, N.S., Can. D6 101
Gore, Eth. M8 60
Gore, N.Z. G2 72
Gore, Ok., U.S. B6 143
Gore Bay, Ont., Can. B2 103
Gore Mountain, mtn., Vt., U.S. B5 152
Gore Point, c., Austl. A3 70
Gore Point, c., Ak., U.S. h16 109
Gore Range, mts., Co., U.S. B4 113
Goreville, Il., U.S. F5 120
Gorgān, Iran C13 48
Gorgas, Al., U.S. B2 108
Gorge High Dam, Wa., U.S. A4 154
Gorgona, Isla, i., Col. F3 84
Gorgor, Peru D3 82
Gorgora, Eth. K9 60
Gorham, Il., U.S. F4 120
Gorham, Ks., U.S. D4 123
Gorham, Me., U.S. E2 126
Gorham, N.H., U.S. B4 136
Gorham, N.Y., U.S. C3 139
Gori, Geor. I6 26
Goricy, Russia D19 22
Gorinchem, Neth. E7 12
Goris, Arm. B9 48
Gorizia, Italy D8 18

Name | Map Ref. | Page

Gorj, co., Rom. E7 20
Gorkhā, Nepal F11 44
Gorki, Bela. G13 22
Gor'kovskoje vodochranilišče, res., Russia D26 22
Gorky see Nižnij Novgorod, Russia E27 22
Gorlice, Pol. F21 10
Görlitz, Ger. D14 10
Gorlovka, Ukr. H5 26
Gorlovo, Russia H22 22
Gorman, Tx., U.S. C3 150
Gormania, W.V., U.S. B5 155
Gorn'ackij, Russia D10 26
Gorn'ak, Russia H22 22
Gornji Milanovac, Yugo. E4 20
Gorno-Altajsk, Russia G9 28
Gornozavodsk, Russia H20 28
Gorochovec, Russia E25 22
Gorodec, Russia E26 22
Gorodec, Russia C12 22
Gorodeja, Bela. H9 22
Gorodenka, Ukr. A9 20
Gorodišče, Bela. H9 22
Gorodišče, Bela. H12 22
Gorodkovka, Ukr. A12 20
Gorodok, Bela. F12 22
Goroka, Pap. N. Gui. G12 38
Gorontalo, Indon. E7 38
Gorouol, stm., Afr. D10 64
Gorrie, Ont., Can. D3 103
Gorutuba, stm., Braz. C7 79
Gorzów Wielkopolski (Landsberg an der Warthe), Pol. C15 10
Gosford, Austl. I9 70
Goshabi, Sud. I6 60
Goshen, N.S., Can. D8 101
Goshen, Al., U.S. D3 108
Goshen, Ct., U.S. B3 114
Goshen, In., U.S. A6 121
Goshen, Ky., U.S. g11 124
Goshen, N.H., U.S. D2 136
Goshen, N.Y., U.S. D6 139
Goshen, Oh., U.S. C1 142
Goshen, Ut., U.S. D4 151
Goshen, Va., U.S. C3 153
Goshen, co., Wy., U.S. D8 157
Goshen Hole, Wy., U.S. D8 157
Goshute Indian Reservation, U.S. D7 135
Goshute Lake, l., Nv., U.S. C7 135
Goshute Mountains, mts., Nv., U.S. C7 135
Goslar, Ger. D10 10
Gosnell, Ar., U.S. B6 111
Gosper, co., Ne., U.S. D6 134
Gosport, In., U.S. F4 121
Gossas, Sen. D1 64
Gossi, Mali D9 64
Gossville, N.H., U.S. D4 136
Gostivar, Mac. H4 20
Gostyń, Pol. D17 10
Gostynin, Pol. C19 10
Göta älv, stm., Swe. M13 6
Gotebo, Ok., U.S. B3 143
Göteborg (Gothenburg), Swe. M12 6
Göteborgs och Bohus län, co., Swe. L12 6
Gotemba, Japan L13 36
Gotešty, Mol. C12 20
Gotha, Ger. E10 10
Gotham, Wi., U.S. E3 156
Gothenburg, Ne., U.S. D5 134
Gothenburg see Göteborg, Swe. M12 6
Gothèye, Niger E10 64
Gotland, i., Swe. M16 6
Gotlands Län, co., Swe. M16 6
Gotō-rettō, is., Japan O3 36
Göttingen, Ger. D9 10
Gouarec, Fr. D3 14
Gouda, Neth. D6 12
Goudge, Arg. H4 80
Goudiry, Sen. D3 64
Gough, Ga., U.S. C4 117
Gough Island, i., St. Hel. M6 52
Gouin, Réservoir, res., Que., Can. k12 104
Goulburn, Austl. J8 70
Goulburn Islands, is., Austl. B6 68
Gould, Ar., U.S. D4 111
Gould, Ok., U.S. C2 143
Goulding, Fl., U.S. u14 116
Gould Island, i., R.I., U.S. E5 146
Goulds, Fl., U.S. s13 116
Gouldsboro, Me., U.S. D4 126
Goulimime, Mor. F5 62
Gounamitz, stm., N.B., Can. B2 101
Goundam, Mali C8 64
Gourdon, Fr. H8 14
Gouré, Niger E15 64
Gourin, Fr. D3 14
Gourma Rharous, Mali C9 64
Gournay-en-Bray, Fr. C8 14
Gouveia, Braz. E7 79
Gouverneur, N.Y., U.S. f9 139
Gouyadong, China J1 34
Govan, Sask., Can. F3 105
Gove, Ks., U.S. D3 123
Gove, co., Ks., U.S. D3 123
Govena, mys, c., Russia F25 28
Governador Valadares, Braz. E8 79
Government Camp, Or., U.S. B5 144
Governor's Harbour, Bah. B6 94
Govind Ballabh Pant Sāgar, res., India H10 44
Govind Sāgar, res., India E7 44
Gowanda, N.Y., U.S. C2 139
Gowan Range, mts., Austl. E6 70
Gowen, Mi., U.S. E5 129
Gowen, Ok., U.S. C6 143
Gower, Mo., U.S. B3 132
Gowmal (Gumal), stm., Asia D3 44
Gowrie, Ia., U.S. B3 122
Goya, Arg. E9 80
Gozo see Ghawdex, i., Malta M9 18
Graaff-Reinet, S. Afr. I7 66
Grabill, In., U.S. B8 121
Grabo, I.C. I6 64
Grabowiec, Pol. E23 10
Gračanica, Bos. E2 20
Grace, Id., U.S. G7 119
Grace, Ms., U.S. C3 131
Grace, Mount, mtn., Ma., U.S. A3 128
Grace City, N.D., U.S. B7 141
Gracemont, Ok., U.S. B3 143
Graceville, Fl., U.S. u16 116
Graceville, Mn., U.S. E2 130
Gracewood, Ga., U.S. C4 117
Gracey, Ky., U.S. D2 124
Gracias, Hond. C6 92
Gracias a Dios, dept., Hond. B10 92
Gracias a Dios, Cabo, c., N.A. B11 92
Gradačac, Bos. E2 20
Gradaús, Braz. E8 76
Grado, Italy D8 18
Grady, Ar., U.S. C4 111
Grady, N.M., U.S. C6 138
Grady, co., Ga., U.S. F2 117
Grady, co., Ok., U.S. C4 143
Graettinger, Ia., U.S. A3 122
Grafenau, Ger. G13 10
Gräfenhainichen, Ger. D12 10
Grafing [bei München], Ger. G11 10
Graford, Tx., U.S. C3 150
Grafton, Austl. G10 70
Grafton, Ont., Can. D6 103
Grafton, Il., U.S. E3 120
Grafton, Ia., U.S. A4 122
Grafton, Ma., U.S. B4 128
Grafton, Ne., U.S. D8 134
Grafton, N.H., U.S. C3 136
Grafton, N.D., U.S. A8 141
Grafton, Oh., U.S. A3 142
Grafton, Vt., U.S. E3 152
Grafton, Va., U.S. h15 153
Grafton, W.V., U.S. B4 155
Grafton, Wi., U.S. E6 156
Grafton, co., N.H., U.S. C3 136
Grafton, Cape, c., Austl. A6 70
Graham, Ky., U.S. C2 124
Graham, Mo., U.S. A2 132
Graham, N.C., U.S. A3 140
Graham, Ok., U.S. C4 143
Graham, Tx., U.S. C3 150
Graham, co., Az., U.S. E5 110
Graham, co., Ks., U.S. C4 123
Graham, co., N.C., U.S. f9 140
Graham, Lake, res., Tx., U.S. C3 150
Graham, Mount, mtn., Az., U.S. E6 110
Graham Creek, stm., In., U.S. G6 121
Graham Island, i., B.C., Can. C1 99
Graham Lake, l., Me., U.S. D4 126
Graham Land, reg., Ant. B12 73
Graham Moore, Cape, c., N.W. Ter., Can. B17 96
Graham Moore Bay, b., N.W. Ter., Can. A12 96
Grahamstown, S. Afr. I8 66
Grahamsville, N.Y., U.S. D6 139
Grahn, Ky., U.S. B6 124
Grain Coast, Lib. I5 64
Grainfield, Ks., U.S. C3 123
Grainger, co., Tn., U.S. C10 149
Grain Valley, Mo., U.S. B3 132
Grajaú, Braz. E9 76
Grajaú, stm., Braz. D9 76
Grajewo, Pol. B22 10
Gramada, Bul. F6 20
Gramado, Braz. E13 80
Gramalote, Col. D6 84
Grambling, La., U.S. B3 125
Gramercy, La., U.S. h10 125
Gramilla, Arg. D6 80
Gramling, S.C., U.S. A3 147
Grammer, In., U.S. F6 121
Grammichele, Italy L9 18
Grampian, prov., Scot., U.K. D11 8
Grampian Mountains, mts., Scot., U.K. E9 8
Grampians National Park, Austl. K5 70
Granada, Col. F6 84
Granada, Nic. F9 92
Granada, Spain H8 16
Granada, Co., U.S. C8 113
Granada, Mn., U.S. G4 130
Granada, dept., Nic. F8 92
Granadilla de Abona, Spain o24 17b
Granbury, Tx., U.S. C4 150
Granby, Que., Can. D5 104
Granby, Co., U.S. A5 113
Granby, Ct., U.S. B4 114
Granby, Ma., U.S. B2 128
Granby, Mo., U.S. E3 132
Granby, Lake, res., Co., U.S. A5 113
Gran Canaria, i., Spain o25 17b
Gran Chaco, pl., S.A. C8 80
Grand, co., Co., U.S. A4 113
Grand, co., Ut., U.S. E6 151
Grand, stm., Ont., Can. D4 103
Grand, stm., Mi., U.S. E5 129
Grand, stm., Mo., U.S. A3 132
Grand, stm., Oh., U.S. A4 142
Grand, stm., S.D., U.S. B4 148
Grand, North Fork, stm., U.S. B2 148
Grand, South Fork, stm., S.D., U.S. B3 148
Grand Bahama, i., Bah. A5 94
Grand Bank, Newf., Can. E4 102
Grand Banks of Newfoundland E14 86
Grand-Bassam, I.C. I8 64
Grand Bay, N.B., Can. D3 101
Grand Bay, Al., U.S. E1 108
Grand Bayou, stm., La., U.S. h9 125
Grand Bayou, stm., La., U.S. k10 125
Grand Bend, Ont., Can. D3 103
Grand Blanc, Mi., U.S. F7 129
Grand Bruit, Newf., Can. E2 102
Grand Caillou, La., U.S. E5 125
Grand Canal, Ire. H6 8
Grand Canal see Da Yunhe, China E10 30
Grand Canyon, Az., U.S. A3 110
Grand Canyon, val., Az., U.S. A3 110
Grand Canyon National Park, Az., U.S. B3 110
Grand Cayman, i., Cay. Is. E4 94
Grand Centre, Alta., Can. B5 98
Grand Cess, Lib. I5 64
Grand Chenier, La., U.S. E3 125
Grand Codroy, stm., Newf., Can. E2 102
Grand Combin, mtn., Switz. G7 13
Grand Coteau, La., U.S. D3 125
Grand Coulee, Wa., U.S. B6 154
Grand Coulee Dam, Wa., U.S. B6 154
Grand-Couronne, Fr. C8 14
Grande, stm., Arg. I4 80
Grande, stm., Arg. C6 80
Grande, stm., Bol. G9 82
Grande, stm., Braz. F10 76
Grande, stm., Braz. E3 79
Grande, stm., Chile F3 80
Grande, stm., Nic. E8 92
Grande, stm., Pan. I14 92
Grande, stm., Peru F4 82
Grande, Arroyo, stm., Ur. G10 80
Grande, Bahía, Arg. G3 78
Grande, Boca, mth., Ven. C12 84
Grande, Cerro, mtn., Mex. C6 90
Grande, Cerro, mtn., Mex. G8 90
Grande, Corixa, stm., S.A. G7 76
Grande, Corixa (Curiche Grande), sw., S.A. G12 82
Grande, Cuchilla, mtn., Ur. G11 80
Grande, Ilha, i., Braz. G6 79
Grande, Ilha, i., Braz. B11 80
Grande, Ponta, c., Braz. D9 79
Grande, Punta, c., Chile A3 80
Grande, Rio (Bravo del Norte), stm., N.A. F7 106
Grande-Anse, N.B., Can. B4 101
Grande Cache, Alta., Can. C1 98
Grande Cayemite, i., Haiti E8 94
Grande Ecore, La., U.S. C2 125
Grande de Lipez, stm., Bol. I8 82
Grande de Manacapuru, Lago, l., Braz. I12 84
Grande de Matagalpa, stm., Nic. D11 92
Grande de Santiago, stm., Mex. G7 90
Grande de Tarija, stm., S.A. J9 82
Grande de Térraba, stm., C.R. I11 92
Grande-Digue, N.B., Can. C5 101
Grande do Gurupá, Ilha, i., Braz. D8 76
Grand-Entrée, Que., Can. B8 101
Grande Prairie, Alta., Can. B1 98
Grand Erg de Bilma, des., Niger E9 54
Grand Erg Occidental, des., Alg. E11 62
Grand Erg Oriental, des., Alg. E14 62
Grande rivière de la Baleine, stm., Que., Can. g11 104
Grande Ronde, stm., U.S. C8 154
Grandes, Salinas, pl., Arg. B6 80
Grandes, Salinas, pl., Arg. F6 80
Grandes-Bergeronnes, Que., Can. A8 104
Grand-Étang, N.S., Can. C8 101
Grande-Terre, i., Guad. F14 94
Grand Falls (Grand-Sault), N.B., Can. B2 101
Grandfalls, Tx., U.S. D1 150
Grand Falls, wtfl, Me., U.S. C5 126
Grand Falls [-Windsor], Newf., Can. D4 102
Grandfather Mountain, mtn., N.C., U.S. A1 140
Grandfield, Ok., U.S. C3 143
Grand Forks, B.C., Can. E8 99
Grand Forks, N.D., U.S. B8 141
Grand Forks, co., N.D., U.S. B8 141
Grand Forks Air Force Base, mil., N.D., U.S. B8 141
Grand Gorge, N.Y., U.S. C6 139
Grand Harbour, N.B., Can. E3 101
Grand Haven, Mi., U.S. E4 129
Grand Hers, stm., Fr. I8 14
Grand Hogback, mtn., Co., U.S. B3 113
Grandiči, Bela. H6 22
Grandin, Mo., U.S. E7 132
Grandin, N.D., U.S. B9 141
Grand Island, Ne., U.S. D7 134
Grand Island, i., La., U.S. D6 125
Grand Island, i., Mi., U.S. B4 129
Grand Isle, La., U.S. E6 125
Grand Isle, Me., U.S. A4 126
Grand Isle, Vt., U.S. B2 152
Grand Isle, co., Vt., U.S. B2 152
Grand Isle, i., La., U.S. E6 125
Grand Junction, Co., U.S. B2 113
Grand Junction, Ia., U.S. B3 122
Grand Junction, Tn., U.S. B2 149
Grand lac Bostonnais, l., Que., Can. B5 104
Grand-Lahou, I.C. I7 64
Grand Lake, Co., U.S. A5 113
Grand Lake, l., N.B., Can. D3 101
Grand Lake, l., Newf., Can. D3 102
Grand Lake, l., Newf., Can. B1 102
Grand Lake, l., La., U.S. E3 125
Grand Lake, l., La., U.S. E6 125
Grand Lake, l., Mi., U.S. C7 129
Grand Lake, l., Oh., U.S. B1 142
Grand Lake Matagamon, l., Me., U.S. B4 126
Grand Lake Seboeis, l., Me., U.S. B4 126
Grand Lake Stream, Me., U.S. C5 126
Grand Ledge, Mi., U.S. F6 129
Grand Manan Island, i., N.B., Can. E3 101
Grand Marais, Mi., U.S. B5 129
Grand Marais, Mn., U.S. k9 130
Grand Marsh, Wi., U.S. E4 156
Grand Meadow, Mn., U.S. G6 130
Grand-Mère, Que., Can. C5 104
Grand Mesa, mtn., Co., U.S. C2 113
Grand Mound, Ia., U.S. C7 122
Grand-Popo, Benin H10 64
Grand Portage, Mn., U.S. k10 130
Grand Portage Indian Reservation, Mn., U.S. k10 130
Grand Portage National Monument, Mn., U.S. h10 130
Grand Prairie, Tx., U.S. n10 150
Grand Pré, N.S., Can. D5 101
Grand Rapids, Mi., U.S. F5 129
Grand Rapids, Mn., U.S. C5 130
Grand Rapids, Oh., U.S. f6 142
Grand Ridge, Fl., U.S. B1 116
Grand Ridge, Il., U.S. B5 120
Grandrieu, Bel. H5 12
Grand River, N.S., Can. D9 101
Grand Rivers, Ky., U.S. f9 124
Grand Ronde, Or., U.S. B3 144
Grand-Saint-Bernard, Col du, Eur. G7 13
Grand-Saint-Bernard, Tunnel du, Eur. G14 14
Grand Saline, Tx., U.S. C5 150
Grand Terre Islands, is., La., U.S. E6 125
Grand Teton, mtn., Wy., U.S. C2 157
Grand Teton National Park, Wy., U.S. C2 157
Grand Tower, Il., U.S. F4 120
Grand Traverse, co., Mi., U.S. D5 129
Grand Traverse Bay, b., Mi., U.S. C5 129
Grand Traverse Bay, East Arm, b., Mi., U.S. D5 129
Grand Traverse Bay, West Arm, b., Mi., U.S. D5 129
Grand Turk, T./C. Is. D9 94
Grand Valley, Ont., Can. D4 103
Grand Valley, val., U.S. B2 113
Grandview, Man., Can. D1 100
Grand View, Id., U.S. G2 119
Grandview, In., U.S. I4 121
Grandview, Ia., U.S. C6 122
Grandview, Mo., U.S. C3 132
Grandview, Tn., U.S. D9 149
Grandview, Wa., U.S. C6 154
Grandview Heights, Oh., U.S. m10 142
Grandville, Mi., U.S. F5 129
Grand Wash Cliffs, clf, Az., U.S. B2 110
Grandy, Mn., U.S. E5 130
Grandy, N.C., U.S. A7 140
Graneros, Chile H3 80
Granger, In., U.S. A5 121
Granger, Ia., U.S. C4 122
Granger, Tx., U.S. D4 150
Granger, Wa., U.S. C5 154
Granger, Wy., U.S. E3 157
Grangeville, Id., U.S. D2 119
Gran Guardia, Arg. C9 80
Granisle, B.C., Can. B4 99
Granite, Ok., U.S. C2 143
Granite, co., Mt., U.S. D3 133
Granite Canon, Wy., U.S. E7 157
Granite City, Il., U.S. E3 120
Granite Falls, Mn., U.S. F3 130
Granite Falls, N.C., U.S. B1 140
Granite Falls, Wa., U.S. A4 154
Granite Lake, res., Newf., Can. D3 102
Granite Mountain, mtn., Ak., U.S. B7 109
Granite Mountains, mts., Az., U.S. E2 110
Granite Mountains, mts., Wy., U.S. D5 157
Granite Pass, Wy., U.S. B5 157
Granite Peak, mtn., Mt., U.S. E7 133
Granite Peak, mtn., Nv., U.S. C2 135
Granite Peak, mtn., Nv., U.S. B4 135
Granite Peak, mtn., Ut., U.S. E3 151
Granite Peak, mtn., Ut., U.S. C2 151
Granite Peak, mtn., Wy., U.S. D4 157
Granite Quarry, N.C., U.S. B2 140
Granite Range, mts., Nv., U.S. C2 135
Graniteville, Ma., U.S. f10 128
Graniteville, S.C., U.S. D4 147
Graniteville, Vt., U.S. C4 152
Grannis, Ar., U.S. C1 111
Granollers, Spain D14 16
Gran Pajonal, mts., Peru D4 82
Gran Paradiso, mtn., Italy D2 18
Gran Sasso d'Italia, mts., Italy G8 18
Grant, Al., U.S. A3 108
Grant, Fl., U.S. E6 116
Grant, Mi., U.S. E5 129
Grant, Ne., U.S. D4 134
Grant, Ok., U.S. D6 143
Grant, co., Ar., U.S. C3 111
Grant, co., In., U.S. D6 121
Grant, co., Ks., U.S. E2 123
Grant, co., Ky., U.S. B5 124
Grant, co., La., U.S. C3 125
Grant, co., Mn., U.S. E2 130
Grant, co., Ne., U.S. C4 134
Grant, co., N.M., U.S. E1 138
Grant, co., N.D., U.S. C4 141
Grant, co., Ok., U.S. A4 143
Grant, co., Or., U.S. C7 144
Grant, co., S.D., U.S. B8 148
Grant, co., Wa., U.S. B6 154
Grant, co., W.V., U.S. B5 155
Grant, co., Wi., U.S. F3 156
Grant, Mount, mtn., Nv., U.S. E3 135
Gran Tarajal, Spain o26 17b
Grant City, Mo., U.S. A3 132
Grantham, N.H., U.S. D2 136
Granton, Ont., Can. D3 103
Granton, Wi., U.S. D3 156
Grant Park, Il., U.S. B6 120
Grant Range, mts., Nv., U.S. E6 135
Grants, N.M., U.S. B2 138
Grantsboro, N.C., U.S. B6 140
Grantsburg, In., U.S. H5 121
Grantsburg, Wi., U.S. C1 156
Grantsdale, Mt., U.S. D2 133
Grants Pass, Or., U.S. E3 144
Grantsville, Md., U.S. k12 127
Grantsville, Ut., U.S. C3 151
Grantsville, W.V., U.S. C3 155
Grant Town, W.V., U.S. B4 155
Grantville, Ga., U.S. C2 117
Grantville, Ks., U.S. k14 123
Granum, Alta., Can. E4 98
Granville, Fr. D5 14
Granville, Il., U.S. B4 120
Granville, Ia., U.S. B2 122
Granville, N.Y., U.S. B7 139
Granville, N.D., U.S. A5 141
Granville, Oh., U.S. B3 142
Granville, Vt., U.S. D3 152
Granville, W.V., U.S. h11 155
Granville, co., N.C., U.S. A4 140
Granville Centre, N.S., Can. E4 101
Granville Ferry, N.S., Can. E4 101
Granville Lake, l., Man., Can. A1 100
Granvin, Nor. K10 6
Grão Mogol, Braz. D7 79
Grapeland, Tx., U.S. D5 150
Grapeview, Wa., U.S. B3 154
Grapevine, Tx., U.S. C4 150
Grapevine Lake, res., Tx., U.S. n9 150
Grapevine Peak, mtn., Nv., U.S. G4 135
Grasmere, S. Afr. F8 66
Grasonville, Md., U.S. C5 127
Grass, stm., Man., Can. B2 100
Grass, stm., N.Y., U.S. f9 139
Grass Creek, In., U.S. C5 121
Grasse, Fr. I13 14
Grassflat, Pa., U.S. D5 145
Grass Lake, Il., U.S. h8 120
Grass Lake, Mi., U.S. F6 129
Grass Lake, l., Il., U.S. h8 120
Grassrange, Mt., U.S. C8 133
Grass Valley, Ca., U.S. C3 112
Grassy, Austl. M6 70
Grassy Brook, stm., Vt., U.S. E3 152
Grassy Lake, Alta., Can. E5 98
Grassy Lake, l., La., U.S. k9 125
Grates Cove, Newf., Can. D5 102
Grates Point, c., Newf., Can. D5 102
Gratiot, co., Mi., U.S. E6 129
Gratis, Oh., U.S. C1 142
Gratz, Pa., U.S. E8 145
Graubünden (Grischun), state, Switz. E11 13
Gravatá, Braz. E11 76
Gravatá, stm., Braz. D7 79
Grave Creek, stm., W.V., U.S. g8 155
Gravelines, Fr. B9 14
Gravell Point, c., N.W. Ter., Can. C17 96
Gravelly, Ar., U.S. C2 111
Gravelly Branch, stm., De., U.S. F4 115
Gravelly Range, mts., Mt., U.S. E4 133
Gravel Ridge, Ar., U.S. h10 111
Gravenhurst, Ont., Can. C5 103
Grave Peak, mtn., Id., U.S. C4 119
Graves, co., Ky., U.S. f9 124
Gravette, Ar., U.S. A1 111
Gravina in Puglia, Italy I11 18
Gravity, Ia., U.S. D3 122
Gray, Sask., Can. G3 105
Gray, Fr. E12 14
Gray, Ga., U.S. C3 117
Gray, Ky., U.S. D5 124
Gray, La., U.S. k10 125
Gray, Me., U.S. g7 126
Gray, co., Ks., U.S. E3 123
Gray, co., Tx., U.S. B2 150
Grayback Mountain, mtn., Or., U.S. E3 144
Gray Court, S.C., U.S. B3 147
Grayland, Wa., U.S. C1 154
Grayling, Ak., U.S. C7 109
Grayling, Mi., U.S. D6 129
Graylyn Crest, De., U.S. A3 115
Grays Harbor, co., Wa., U.S. B2 154
Grays Harbor, b., Wa., U.S. C1 154
Grayslake, Il., U.S. A5 120
Grays Lake, sw., Id., U.S. F7 119
Grayson, Sask., Can. G4 105
Grayson, Al., U.S. A2 108
Grayson, Ga., U.S. C3 117
Grayson, Ky., U.S. B7 124
Grayson, La., U.S. B3 125
Grayson, co., Ky., U.S. C3 124
Grayson, co., Tx., U.S. C4 150
Grayson, co., Va., U.S. D1 153
Grayson Lake, res., Ky., U.S. B7 124
Grays Peak, mtn., Co., U.S. B5 113
Grays River, Wa., U.S. C2 154
Gray Summit, Mo., U.S. g12 132
Graysville, Al., U.S. f7 108
Graysville, Tn., U.S. D8 149
Grayville, Il., U.S. E5 120
Graz, Aus. H15 10
Grazalema, Spain I6 16
Gr'azi, Russia I22 22
Gr'aznoje, Russia G22 22
Gr'azovec, Russia C23 22
Greasewood, Az., U.S. B6 110
Great Artesian Basin, Austl. E5 70
Great Australian Bight, Austl. F5 68
Great Averill Pond, l., Vt., U.S. B5 152
Great Barrier Island, i., N.Z. B5 72
Great Barrier Reef, rf., Austl. C9 68
Great Barrier Reef Marine Park, Austl. C9 68
Great Barrington, Ma., U.S. B1 128
Great Basin, U.S. C3 106
Great Basin National Park, Nv., U.S. E7 135
Great Bay, b., N.H., U.S. D5 136
Great Bay, b., N.J., U.S. D4 137
Great Bear Lake, l., N.W. Ter., Can. C8 96
Great Bend, Ks., U.S. D5 123
Great Bend, N.D., U.S. C9 141
Great Bend, Pa., U.S. C10 145
Great Blue Hill, hill, Ma., U.S. B5 128
Great Britain, i., U.K. E7 4
Great Burnt Lake, l., Newf., Can. D3 102
Great Cacapon, W.V., U.S. B6 155
Great Captain Island, i., Ct., U.S. F1 114
Great Channel, strt., Asia K3 40
Great Dismal Swamp, sw., U.S. D6 153
Great Divide Basin, Wy., U.S. E4 157
Great Dividing Range, mts., Austl. E9 68
Great Duck Island, i., Ont., Can. B2 103
Great East Lake, l., U.S. C5 136
Great Egg Harbor, stm., N.J., U.S. D3 137
Greater Antilles, is., N.A. D7 94
Greater Cincinnati Airport, Ky., U.S. h13 124
Greater Khingan Range see Da Hinggan Ling, mts., China B11 30
Greater Sunda Islands, is., Asia F5 38
Great Exuma, i., Bah. C7 94
Great Falls, Man., Can. D3 100
Great Falls, Mt., U.S. C5 133
Great Falls, S.C., U.S. B6 147
Great Falls, wtfl, Md., U.S. B3 127
Great Falls Dam, Tn., U.S. D6 149
Great Guana Cay, i., Bah. B6 94
Greathouse Peak, mtn., Mt., U.S. D7 133
Great Inagua, i., Bah. D8 94
Great Indian Desert (Thar Desert), des., Asia G4 44
Great Island, spit, Ma., U.S. C7 128
Great Island, i., N.C., U.S. B6 140
Great Karroo, plat., S. Afr. I6 66
Great Lake, l., Austl. M7 70
Great Lakes Naval Training Center, mil., Il., U.S. h9 120
Great Miami, stm., U.S. C1 142
Great Misery Island, i., Ma., U.S. f12 128
Great Moose Lake, l., Me., U.S. D3 126
Great Namaqualand, hist. reg., Nmb. E3 66
Great Neck, N.Y., U.S. h13 139
Great Nicobar, i., India K2 40
Great North Mountain, mtn., U.S. C6 155
Great Palm Island, i., Austl. B7 70
Great Pee Dee, stm., U.S. D9 147
Great Plain of the Koukdjuak, pl., N.W. Ter., Can. C18 96
Great Plains, pl., N.A. E9 86
Great Point, c., Ma., U.S. D7 128
Great Pond, l., Me., U.S. D3 126
Great Pond, l., Ma., U.S. h12 128
Great Pond, l., Ma., U.S. h11 128
Great Quittacas Pond, l., Ma., U.S. C6 128
Great Ruaha, stm., Tan. C7 58
Great Sacandaga Lake, l., N.Y., U.S. C6 139
Great Saint Bernard Pass see Grand-Saint-Bernard, Col du, Eur. G7 13
Great Salt Lake, l., Ut., U.S. B3 151
Great Salt Lake Desert, des., Ut., U.S. C2 151
Great Salt Plains Lake, res., Ok., U.S. A3 143
Great Salt Pond, b., R.I., U.S. h7 146
Great Sand Dunes National Monument, Co., U.S. D5 113
Great Sand Hills, hills, Sask., Can. G1 105
Great Sandy Desert, des., Austl. D4 68
Great Scarcies (Kolenté), stm., Afr. G3 64
Great Seneca Creek, stm., Md., U.S. B3 127
Great Slave Lake, l., N.W. Ter., Can. D10 96
Great Smoky Mountains, mts., U.S. B8 149
Great Smoky Mountains National Park, U.S. B8 149
Great Swamp, sw., R.I., U.S. F3 146
Great Valley, val., U.S. C2 153
Great Victoria Desert, des., Austl. E5 68
Great Village, N.S., Can. D6 101
Great Wall, sci., Ant. B1 73
Great Wall see Chang Cheng, hist., China C4 32
Great Wass Island, i., Me., U.S. D5 126
Great Yarmouth, Eng., U.K. I15 8
Great Zab (Büyükzap) (Az-Zāb al-Kabīr), stm., Asia C7 48
Gréboun, mtn., Niger A14 64
Grecia, C.R. G10 92
Greco, Ur. G10 80
Greece, N.Y., U.S. B3 139
Greece (Ellás), ctry., Eur. H12 4
Greeley, Co., U.S. A6 113
Greeley, Ia., U.S. B6 122
Greeley, Ks., U.S. D8 123
Greeley, Ne., U.S. C7 134
Greeley, Pa., U.S. D12 145
Greeley, co., Ks., U.S. D2 123
Greeley, co., Ne., U.S. C7 134
Greeleyville, S.C., U.S. D8 147
Green, Ks., U.S. C6 123
Green, Or., U.S. D3 144
Green, co., Ky., U.S. C4 124
Green, co., Wi., U.S. F4 156
Green, stm., N.B., Can. B1 101
Green, stm., U.S. D5 106
Green, stm., U.S. A1 113
Green, stm., U.S. F3 152
Green, stm., Il., U.S. B4 120
Green, stm., Ky., U.S. C2 124
Green, stm., Wa., U.S. B3 154
Green Acres, De., U.S. h8 115

Name — Map Ref. — Page

Greenacres, Wa., U.S. B8 154
Greenacres City, Fl., U.S. F6 116
Greenback, Tn., U.S. D9 149
Greenbackville, Va., U.S. C7 153
Green Bank, W.V., U.S. C5 155
Green Bay, Wi., U.S. D6 156
Green Bay, b., U.S. D3 129
Greenbelt, Md., U.S. C4 127
Greenbriar, Va., U.S. g12 153
Greenbrier, Al., U.S. A3 108
Greenbrier, Ar., U.S. B3 111
Green Brier, Tn., U.S. A5 149
Greenbrier, co., W.V., U.S. D4 155
Greenbrier, stm., W.V., U.S. D4 155
Greenbush, Me., U.S. C4 126
Greenbush, Mn., U.S. B2 130
Greencastle, In., U.S. E4 121
Green Castle, Mo., U.S. A5 132
Greencastle, Pa., U.S. G6 145
Green City, Mo., U.S. A5 132
Green Court, Alta., Can. B3 98
Green Cove Springs, Fl., U.S. C5 116
Green Creek, N.J., U.S. E3 137
Greendale, In., U.S. F8 121
Greendale, Wi., U.S. F6 156
Greene, Ia., U.S. B5 122
Greene, Me., U.S. D2 126
Greene, N.Y., U.S. C5 139
Greene, co., Al., U.S. C1 108
Greene, co., Ar., U.S. A5 111
Greene, co., Ga., U.S. C3 117
Greene, co., Il., U.S. D3 120
Greene, co., In., U.S. F4 121
Greene, co., Ia., U.S. B3 122
Greene, co., Ms., U.S. D5 131
Greene, co., Mo., U.S. D4 132
Greene, co., N.Y., U.S. C6 139
Greene, co., N.C., U.S. B5 140
Greene, co., Oh., U.S. C2 142
Greene, co., Pa., U.S. G1 145
Greene, co., Tn., U.S. C11 149
Greene, co., Va., U.S. B4 153
Greeneville, Tn., U.S. C11 149
Green Fall, stm., U.S. F1 146
Greenfield, Ar., U.S. B5 111
Greenfield, Ca., U.S. D3 112
Greenfield, Il., U.S. D3 120
Greenfield, In., U.S. E6 121
Greenfield, Ia., U.S. C3 122
Greenfield, Ma., U.S. A2 128
Greenfield, Mo., U.S. D4 132
Greenfield, N.H., U.S. E3 136
Greenfield, N.M., U.S. D5 138
Greenfield, Oh., U.S. C2 142
Greenfield, Ok., U.S. B3 143
Greenfield, Tn., U.S. A3 149
Greenfield, Wi., U.S. n12 156
Greenfield Plaza, Ia., U.S. e8 122
Green Forest, Ar., U.S. A2 111
Green Harbor, Ma., U.S. B6 128
Green Head, c., Austl. F2 68
Greenhill, Al., U.S. A2 108
Green Hill Pond, l., R.I., U.S. G3 146
Greenhills, Oh., U.S. n12 142
Greenhorn Creek, stm., Co., U.S. D6 113
Green Lake, Sask., Can. C2 105
Green Lake, Wi., U.S. E5 156
Green Lake, co., Wi., U.S. E4 156
Green Lake, l., Me., U.S. D4 126
Green Lake, l., Wi., U.S. E5 156
Greenland, Ar., U.S. B1 111
Greenland, Mi., U.S. B1 129
Greenland, N.H., U.S. D5 136
Greenland (Kalaallit Nunaat), dep., N.A. B15 86
Greenland Sea B20 86
Greenleaf, Ks., U.S. C7 123
Greenleaf, Wi., U.S. D5 156
Greenlee, co., Az., U.S. D6 110
Green Lookout Mountain, mtn., Wa., U.S. D3 154
Greenmount, Md., U.S. A4 127
Green Mountain, Ia., U.S. B5 122
Green Mountain, mtn., Wy., U.S. D5 157
Green Mountain Reservoir, res., Co., U.S. B4 113
Green Mountains, mts., Vt., U.S. F2 152
Greenock, Pa., U.S. F2 145
Green Peter Lake, res., Or., U.S. C4 144
Green Pond, Al., U.S. B2 108
Green Pond, l., N.J., U.S. A4 137
Green Pond Mountain, mtn., N.J., U.S. B3 137
Greenport, N.Y., U.S. m16 139
Green Ridge, Mo., U.S. C4 132
Green River, Ut., U.S. E5 151
Green River, Wy., U.S. E3 157
Green River Lake, res., Ky., U.S. C4 124
Green River Lock and Dam, U.S. I2 121
Green River Reservoir, res., Vt., U.S. B3 152
Green Rock, Il., U.S. B3 120
Greensboro, Al., U.S. C2 108
Greensboro, Fl., U.S. B2 116
Greensboro, Ga., U.S. C3 117
Greensboro, In., U.S. E7 121
Greensboro, Md., U.S. C6 127
Greensboro, N.C., U.S. A3 140
Greensboro, Vt., U.S. B4 152
Greensboro Bend, Vt., U.S. B4 152
Greensburg, In., U.S. F7 121
Greensburg, Ks., U.S. E4 123
Greensburg, Ky., U.S. C4 124
Greensburg, La., U.S. D5 125
Greensburg, Pa., U.S. F2 145
Greens Fork, In., U.S. E7 121
Greens Peak, mtn., Az., U.S. C6 110
Greenspond, Newf., Can. D5 102
Green Spring, W.V., U.S. B6 155
Green Springs, Oh., U.S. A2 142
Greensville, co., Va., U.S. D5 153
Green Swamp, sw., N.C., U.S. C4 140
Greentop, Mo., U.S. A5 132
Greentown, In., U.S. D6 121
Greenup, Il., U.S. D5 120
Greenup, Ky., U.S. B7 124
Greenup, co., Ky., U.S. B7 124
Greenvale, Austl. B6 70
Green Valley, Az., U.S. F5 110
Green Valley, Il., U.S. C4 120
Green Valley, val., Tx., U.S. p13 150
Greenview, Il., U.S. C4 120
Greenview, W.V., U.S. n12 155
Greenville, Lib. I5 64
Greenville, Al., U.S. D3 108
Greenville, Ca., U.S. B3 112
Greenville, De., U.S. A3 115
Greenville, Fl., U.S. B3 116
Greenville, Ga., U.S. C2 117
Greenville, Il., U.S. E4 120
Greenville, In., U.S. H6 121
Greenville, Ky., U.S. C2 124
Greenville, Me., U.S. C3 126
Greenville, Mi., U.S. E5 129
Greenville, Ms., U.S. B2 131
Greenville, Mo., U.S. D7 132
Greenville, N.H., U.S. E3 136
Greenville, N.C., U.S. B5 140
Greenville, Oh., U.S. B1 142
Greenville, Pa., U.S. D1 145
Greenville, R.I., U.S. C3 146
Greenville, S.C., U.S. B3 147
Greenville, Tx., U.S. C4 150
Greenville, Va., U.S. B3 153
Greenville, co., S.C., U.S. B3 147
Greenville Creek, stm., Oh., U.S. B1 142
Greenville Junction, Me., U.S. C3 126
Greenway, Ar., U.S. A5 111
Greenwich, Ct., U.S. E1 114
Greenwich, N.Y., U.S. B7 139
Greenwich, Oh., U.S. A3 142
Greenwich Bay, b., R.I., U.S. D4 146
Greenwich Hill, N.B., Can. D3 101
Greenwich Point, c., Ct., U.S. E1 114
Greenwood, B.C., Can. E8 99
Greenwood, Ar., U.S. B1 111
Greenwood, De., U.S. E3 115
Greenwood, Fl., U.S. B1 116
Greenwood, In., U.S. E5 121
Greenwood, La., U.S. B2 125
Greenwood, Ms., U.S. B3 131
Greenwood, Mo., U.S. k11 132
Greenwood, Ne., U.S. D9 134
Greenwood, Pa., U.S. E5 145
Greenwood, S.C., U.S. C3 147
Greenwood, S.D., U.S. E7 148
Greenwood, Wi., U.S. D3 156
Greenwood, co., Ks., U.S. E7 123
Greenwood, co., S.C., U.S. C3 147
Greenwood, Lake, res., In., U.S. G4 121
Greenwood, Lake, res., S.C., U.S. C4 147
Greenwood Lake, N.Y., U.S. D6 139
Greenwood Lake, l., U.S. A4 137
Greenwood Lake, l., Mn., U.S. C7 130
Greer, S.C., U.S. B3 147
Greer, co., Ok., U.S. C2 143
Greers Ferry, Ar., U.S. B3 111
Greers Ferry Lake, res., Ar., U.S. B3 111
Greeson, Lake, res., Ar., U.S. C2 111
Gregg, co., Tx., U.S. C5 150
Gregoire Lake, l., Alta., Can. A5 98
Gregório, stm., Braz. B6 82
Gregory, Ar., U.S. B4 111
Gregory, Mi., U.S. F6 129
Gregory, S.D., U.S. D6 148
Gregory, co., S.D., U.S. D6 148
Gregory, stm., Austl. B3 70
Gregory, Lake, l., Austl. G3 70
Gregory Bald, mtn., U.S. D10 149
Gregory Range, mts., Austl. B5 70
Greifswald, Ger. A13 10
Greilickville, Mi., U.S. D5 129
Greiz, Ger. E12 10
Grem'ačinsk, Russia F9 26
Grenada, Ca., U.S. B2 112
Grenada, Ms., U.S. B4 131
Grenada, co., Ms., U.S. B4 131
Grenada, ctry., N.A. H14 94
Grenada Lake, res., Ms., U.S. B4 131
Grenadines, is., N.A. H14 94
Grenchen, Switz. D7 13
Grenfell, Austl. I8 70
Grenfell, Sask., Can. G4 105
Grenoble, Fr. G12 14
Grenola, Ks., U.S. E7 123
Grenora, N.D., U.S. A2 141
Grenville, Que., Can. D3 104
Grenville, Cape, c., Austl. B8 68
Grenville, Point, c., Wa., U.S. B1 154
Gréoux-les-Bains, Fr. I12 14
Gresham, Ne., U.S. C8 134
Gresham, Or., U.S. B4 144
Gresham, Wi., U.S. D5 156
Gresik, Indon. j16 39a
Gresten, Aus. G15 10
Gretna, Man., Can. E3 100
Gretna, Fl., U.S. B2 116
Gretna, La., U.S. E5 125
Gretna, Ne., U.S. C9 134
Gretna, Va., U.S. D3 153
Greven, Ger. C7 10
Grevená, Grc. I5 20
Grevenbroich, Ger. D6 10
Grey, stm., Newf., Can. E3 102
Greybull, Wy., U.S. B4 157
Greybull, stm., Wy., U.S. B4 157
Grey Eagle, Mn., U.S. E4 130
Greylock, Mount, mtn., Ma., U.S. A1 128
Greymouth, N.Z. E3 72
Grey Range, mts., Austl. G5 70
Greys, stm., Wy., U.S. C2 157
Greytown, S. Afr. G10 66
Gribanovskij, Russia G6 26
Gridley, Ca., U.S. C3 112
Gridley, Il., U.S. C5 120
Gridley, Ks., U.S. D8 123
Gridley Mountain, mtn., Ct., U.S. A2 114
Griesbach, Ger. G13 10
Griesheim, Ger. F8 10
Griffin, Sask., Can. H4 105
Griffin, Ga., U.S. C2 117
Griffin, In., U.S. H2 121
Griffiss Air Force Base, mil., N.Y., U.S. B5 139
Griffith, Austl. J7 70
Griffith, In., U.S. A3 121
Griffith Island, i., Ont., Can. C4 103
Griffithsville, W.V., U.S. C3 155
Griffithville, Ar., U.S. B4 111
Grifton, N.C., U.S. B5 140
Griggs, co., N.D., U.S. B7 141
Griggsville, Il., U.S. D3 120
Grignan, Fr. H11 14
Grigoriopol', Mol. B13 20
Grijalva, stm., Mex. I13 90
Grijalva (Cuilco), stm., N.A. B3 92
Grijpskerk, Neth. B9 12
Grim, Cape, c., Austl. M6 70
Grimes, Al., U.S. D4 108
Grimes, Ia., U.S. C4 122
Grimes, co., Tx., U.S. D4 150
Grimesland, N.C., U.S. B5 140
Grimma, Ger. D12 10
Grimsby, Ont., Can. D5 103
Grimsby, Eng., U.K. H13 8
Grimselpass, Switz. E9 13
Grimshaw, Alta., Can. A2 98
Grimsley, Tn., U.S. C9 149
Grímsstaðir, Ice. B5 6a
Grimstad, Nor. L11 6
Grímsvötn, mtn., Ice. B5 6a
Grin'ava, Ukr. B8 20
Grindall Creek, Va., U.S. n18 153
Grindelwald, Switz. E9 13
Grinnell, Ia., U.S. C5 122
Grinnell, Ks., U.S. C3 123
Grinnell Peninsula, pen., N.W. Ter., Can. A13 96
Gris-Nez, Cap, c., Fr. B8 14
Grissom Air Force Base, mil., In., U.S. C5 121
Griswold, Man., Can. E1 100
Griswold, Ia., U.S. C2 122
Grizzly Bear Mountain, mtn., N.W. Ter., Can. C8 96
Grizzly Mountain, mtn., Id., U.S. B2 119
Grizzly Mountain, mtn., Or., U.S. C6 144
Grizzly Mountain, mtn., Wa., U.S. A7 154
Groais Island, i., Newf., Can. C4 102
Grobiņa, Lat. E4 22
Groblersdal, S. Afr. E9 66
Groblershoop, S. Afr. G5 66
Grodków, Pol. E17 10
Grodno, Bela. H6 22
Grodzisk Mazowiecki, Pol. C20 10
Groede, Neth. F4 12
Groenlo, Neth. D10 12
Groesbeck, Tx., U.S. D4 150
Groesbeek, Neth. E8 12
Groix, Fr. E3 14
Grójec, Pol. D20 10
Grombalia, Tun. M5 18
Gronau, Ger. C7 10
Groningen, Neth. B10 12
Groningen, prov., Neth. B10 12
Gronlid, Sask., Can. D3 105
Groom, Tx., U.S. B2 150
Groom Lake, l., Nv., U.S. F6 135
Groom Range, mts., Nv., U.S. F6 135
Groot-Brakrivier, S. Afr. J5 66
Groote Eylandt, i., Austl. B7 68
Grootfontein, Nmb. B4 66
Groot Karasberge, mts., Nmb. F4 66
Groot-Kei, stm., Afr. I9 66
Groot Laagte, stm., Afr. C5 66
Groot-Marico, S. Afr. E8 66
Groot-Vis, stm., Afr. I8 66
Gros-Mécatina, Île du, i., Que., Can. C2 102
Gros Morne, mtn., Newf., Can. D3 102
Gros Morne National Park, Newf., Can. D3 102
Grosse Île, i., Que., Can. B8 101
Grosse Isle Naval Air Station, mil., Mi., U.S. p15 129
Grossenhain, Ger. D13 10
Grosse Pointe, Mi., U.S. *p16 129
Grosse Pointe Park, Mi., U.S. p16 129
Grosse Pointe Woods, Mi., U.S. p16 129
Grosse Tete, La., U.S. D4 125
Grosseto, Italy G6 18
Gross-Gerau, Ger. F8 10
Grossglockner, mtn., Aus. H12 10
Grosshöchstetten, Switz. E8 13
Grossmont, Ca., U.S. o16 112
Grossräschen, Ger. D14 10
Grosvenor Dale, Ct., U.S. B8 114
Gros Ventre, stm., Wy., U.S. C2 157
Gros Ventre Range, mts., Wy., U.S. C2 157
Groton, Ct., U.S. D7 114
Groton, Ma., U.S. A4 128
Groton, N.H., U.S. C3 136
Groton, N.Y., U.S. C4 139
Groton, S.D., U.S. B7 148
Groton, Vt., U.S. C4 152
Groton Long Point, Ct., U.S. D7 114
Grottaglie, Italy I12 18
Grottoes, Va., U.S. B4 153
Grouard Mission, Alta., Can. B2 98
Grouse Creek, stm., Ks., U.S. E7 123
Grouse Creek, stm., Ut., U.S. B2 151
Grouse Creek Mountain, mtn., Id., U.S. E5 119
Grouse Creek Mountains, mts., Ut., U.S. B2 151
Grovania, Ga., U.S. D3 117
Grove, Ok., U.S. A7 143
Grove City, Fl., U.S. F4 116
Grove City, Mn., U.S. E4 130
Grove City, Oh., U.S. C2 142
Grove City, Pa., U.S. D1 145
Grove Hill, Al., U.S. D2 108
Groveland, Fl., U.S. D5 116
Groveland, Ga., U.S. D5 117
Groveland, Ma., U.S. A5 128
Grove Point, c., Md., U.S. B5 127
Groveport, Oh., U.S. C3 142
Grover, Co., U.S. A6 113
Grover, N.C., U.S. B1 140
Grover, Wy., U.S. D2 157
Grover City, Ca., U.S. E3 112
Grover Hill, Oh., U.S. A1 142
Groves, Tx., U.S. E6 150
Grovespring, Mo., U.S. D5 132
Groveton, N.H., U.S. A3 136
Groveton, Tx., U.S. D5 150
Groveton, Va., U.S. g12 153
Groveton Gardens, Va., U.S. *B5 153
Grovetown, Ga., U.S. C4 117
Groveville, N.J., U.S. C3 137
Growler Peak, mtn., Az., U.S. E2 110
Groznyj, Russia I7 26
Grubbs, Ar., U.S. B4 111
Grudziądz, Pol. B18 10
Gruetli-Laager, Tn., U.S. D8 149
Gruitrode, Bel. F8 12
Grulla, Tx., U.S. F3 150
Grünau, Nmb. F4 66
Grünau [im Almtal], Aus. H13 10
Grundy, Va., U.S. e9 153
Grundy, co., Il., U.S. B5 120
Grundy, co., Ia., U.S. B5 122
Grundy, co., Mo., U.S. A4 132
Grundy, co., Tn., U.S. D8 149
Grundy Center, Ia., U.S. B5 122
Grunthal, Man., Can. E3 100
Gruver, Tx., U.S. A2 150
Gruziya see Georgia, ctry., Asia I6 26
Grybów, Pol. F20 10
Gryfice, Pol. B15 10
Gstaad, Switz. F7 13
Guabito, Pan. H12 92
Guacanayabo, Golfo de, b., Cuba D6 94
Guacara, Ven. B9 84
Guacarí, Col. F4 84
Gu Achi, Az., U.S. E3 110
Guachiría, stm., Col. E7 84
Guachochi, Mex. D6 90
Guaçuí, Braz. F8 79
Guadalajara, Mex. G8 90
Guadalajara, Spain E8 16
Guadalcanal, i., Sol.Is. I20 158
Guadalén, stm., Spain G8 16
Guadalén, Embalse de, res., Spain G8 16
Guadalmena, stm., Spain G9 16
Guadalquivir, stm., Spain H6 16
Guadalupe, Bol. H9 82
Guadalupe, Col. F5 84
Guadalupe, C.R. H10 92
Guadalupe, Mex. E9 90
Guadalupe, Mex. F8 90
Guadalupe, Peru B2 82
Guadalupe, Az., U.S. m9 110
Guadalupe, Ca., U.S. E3 112
Guadalupe, Co., U.S. D4 113
Guadalupe, co., N.M., U.S. C5 138
Guadalupe, co., Tx., U.S. E4 150
Guadalupe [Bravos], Mex. B6 90
Guadalupe Mountains, mts., U.S. E5 138
Guadalupe Mountains National Park, Tx., U.S. o12 150
Guadalupe Peak, mtn., Tx., U.S. o12 150
Guadalupe Victoria, Mex. E7 90
Guadalupita, N.M., U.S. A4 138
Guadarrama, Sierra de, mts., Spain E7 16
Guadeloupe, dep., N.A. F14 94
Guadeloupe Passage, strt., N.A. F14 94
Guadiana, stm., Eur. H4 16
Guadix, Spain H8 16
Guaíba, Braz. F13 80
Guaíba, est., Braz. F13 80
Guaihe, China B1 34
Guaimaca, Hond. C8 92
Guaimoreto, Laguna de, b., Hond. B9 92
Guainía, dept., Col. F8 84
Guainía, stm., S.A. F9 84
Guaiquinima, Cerro, mtn., Ven. E11 84
Guaíra, Braz. F4 79
Guaíra, Braz. C11 80
Guairá, dept., Para. C10 80
Guáitara, stm., Col. G4 84
Guajaba, Cayo, i., Cuba D6 94
Guajará-Mirim, Braz. D9 82
Gualaca, Pan. C1 84
Gualaceo, Ec. I3 84
Gualala, Ca., U.S. C2 112
Gualán, Guat. B5 92
Gualaquiza, Ec. I3 84
Gualdo Tadino, Italy F7 18
Gualeguay, Arg. G9 80
Gualeguay, stm., Arg. G9 80
Gualeguaychú, Arg. G9 80
Gualicho, Salina del, pl., Arg. E3 78
Guam, dep., Oc. F22 2
Guamal, Col. C5 84
Guamal, Col. F6 84
Guaminí, Arg. I7 80
Guamo, Col. E5 84
Guamote, Ec. H3 84
Guamúchil, Mex. E5 90
Guamués, stm., Col. G4 84
Guanacaste, prov., C.R. G9 92
Guanacaste, Cordillera de, mts., C.R. G9 92
Guanacaste, Parque Nacional, C.R. G9 92
Guanacaure, Cerro, mtn., Hond. D7 92
Guanaceví, Mex. E7 90
Guanache, stm., Peru B4 82
Guanahacabibes, Golfo de, b., Cuba C2 94
Guanaja, Hond. A9 92
Guanaja, Isla de, i., Hond. A9 92
Guanajay, Cuba C3 94
Guanajuato, Mex. G9 90
Guanajuato, state, Mex. G9 90
Guanambi, Braz. C7 79
Guanaparo, Caño, stm., Ven. C8 84
Guañape, Islas, is., Peru C2 82
Guanare, Ven. C8 84
Guanare, stm., Ven. C8 84
Guanarito, Ven. C8 84
Guanay, Bol. F8 82
Guanay, Cerro, mtn., Ven. E9 84
Guanbuqiao, China F3 34
Guandacol, Arg. E4 80
Guandanghu, China E2 34
Guandian, China C7 34
Guane, Cuba C2 94
Guang'an, China E8 30
Guangde, China E8 34
Guangdong (Kwangtung), prov., China G9 30
Guanghua, China E9 30
Guangnan, China G8 30
Guangrao, China F6 32
Guangxi Zhuangzu Zizhiqu (Kwangsi Chuang), prov., China G8 30
Guangyuan, China E8 30
Guangzhou (Canton), China L2 34
Guanhães, Braz. E7 79
Guanipa, stm., Ven. C11 84
Guankou, China E4 34
Guano, Ec. H3 84
Guano Lake, l., Or., U.S. E7 144
Guanqian, China E6 34
Guanqiaopu, China D1 34
Guanta, Ven. B10 84
Guantánamo, Cuba D7 94
Guantao (Nanguantao), China G3 32
Guantou, China G9 34
Guanxian, China E7 30
Guanyintang, China D1 34
Guanzhuang, China F2 32
Guanzhuang, China C3 34
Guapí, Col. F4 84
Guapiara, Braz. H4 79
Guápiles, C.R. G11 92
Guaporé, Braz. E13 80
Guaporé (Itenes), stm., S.A. E10 82
Guaqui, Bol. G7 82
Guará, stm., Braz. B6 79
Guarabira, Braz. E11 76
Guaraçaí, Braz. F3 79
Guaraci, Braz. F4 79
Guaraciana, Braz. D7 79
Guaramirim, Braz. D14 80
Guaranda, Ec. H3 84
Guaraniaçu, Braz. C12 80
Guarani das Missões, Braz. E11 80
Guarani de Goiás, Braz. B5 79
Guarapari, Braz. F8 79
Guarapuava, Braz. C13 80
Guaraqueçaba, Braz. C14 80
Guararé, Pan. D2 84
Guaratinguetá, Braz. G6 79
Guaratuba, Braz. C14 80
Guarda, Port. E4 16
Guardafui, Cape see Caseyr, c., Som. F11 56
Guardavalle, Italy K11 18
Guardia Escolta, Arg. E7 80
Guardiagrele, Italy G9 18
Guardo, Spain C7 16
Guareña, Spain G5 16
Guarenas, Ven. B9 84
Guariba, stm., Braz. C11 82
Guarico, Ven. C8 84
Guárico, state, Ven. C9 84
Guárico, stm., Ven. C9 84
Guárico, Embalse del, res., Ven. C9 84
Guariquito, stm., Ven. D9 84
Guarizama, Hond. C8 92
Guarulhos, Braz. G5 79
Guasare, stm., Ven. B6 84
Guasave, Mex. E5 90
Guasdualito, Ven. D7 84
Guasipati, Ven. D12 84
Guastalla, Italy E5 18
Guastatoya, Guat. C4 92
Guatajiagua, El Sal. D6 92
Guatemala, Guat. C4 92
Guatemala, dept., Guat. C4 92
Guatemala, ctry., N.A. E6 88
Guateque, Col. E6 84
Guatimozín, Arg. G7 80
Guatopo, Parque Nacional, Ven. C9 84
Guatraché, Arg. I7 80
Guaviare, ter., Col. F6 84
Guaviare, stm., Col. F8 84
Guaxupé, Braz. F5 79
Guayabal, Cuba D6 94
Guayabal, Ven. C9 84
Guayabero, stm., Col. F6 84
Guayacán, Chile E3 80
Guayama, P.R. F11 94
Guayambre, stm., Hond. C8 92
Guayape, Hond. C8 92
Guayape, stm., Hond. C9 92
Guayapo, stm., Ven. E9 84
Guayaquil, Ec. I32 158
Guayaquil, Golfo de, b., S.A. I2 84
Guayaramerín, Bol. D9 82
Guayas, prov., Ec. H2 84
Guayas, stm., Col. G5 84
Guayas, stm., Ec. I3 84
Guayatayoc, Laguna de, l., Arg. B6 80
Guaycora, Mex. C5 90
Guaymas, Mex. D4 90
Guayquiraró, stm., Arg. F9 80
Guayuriba, stm., Col. F6 84
Guazacapán, Guat. C4 92
Guazapares, Mex. D5 90
Guazárachi, Mex. D6 90
Guba, Eth. L8 60
Gubacha, Russia F9 26
Gubbio, Italy F7 18
Guben, Ger. D14 10
Gubin, Pol. D14 10
Gubkin, Russia G5 26
Gucheng, China C7 34
Gūdalūr, India H4 46
Gudermes, Russia I7 26
Gudianzi, China D5 34
Gudiyāttam, India F5 46
Gūdūr, India E5 46
Guebwiller, Fr. E14 14
Güejar, stm., Col. F6 84
Guelma, Alg. B14 62
Guelph, Ont., Can. D4 103
Guéméné-sur-Scorff, Fr. D3 14
Guené, Benin F11 64
Guérande, Fr. E4 14
Guercif, Mor. C9 62
Güere, stm., Ven. C10 84
Guéréda, Chad J2 60
Guéret, Fr. F8 14
Guernsey, Sask., Can. F3 105
Guernsey, Wy., U.S. D8 157
Guernsey, co., Oh., U.S. B4 142
Guernsey, dep., Eur. F7 .4
Guerrero, Mex. C6 90
Guerrero, state, Mex. I9 90
Guerzim, Alg. F10 62
Guessou-Sud, Benin F11 64
Gueydan, La., U.S. D3 125
Gugang, China G2 34
Guge, mtn., Eth. N9 60
Guia, Braz. F13 82
Guía de Isora, Spain o24 17b
Guia Lopes da Laguna, Braz. I13 82
Guibes, Nmb. F3 66
Güicán, Col. D6 84
Guichen, Fr. E5 14
Guichón, Ur. G10 80
Guidan Roumji, Niger E13 64
Guide, China D7 30
Guide Rock, Ne., U.S. D7 134
Guidigri, Niger E14 64
Guidimouni, Niger E14 64
Guiding, China A9 40
Guifujie, China H9 34
Guiglo, I.C. H6 64
Güija, Lago de, l., N.A. C5 92
Guild, N.H., U.S. D2 136
Guildford, Eng., U.K. J13 8
Guilford, Ct., U.S. D5 114
Guilford, Me., U.S. C3 126
Guilford, Vt., U.S. F3 152
Guilford, co., N.C., U.S. A3 140
Guilin (Kweilin), China B11 40
Guillaumes, Fr. H13 14
Güimar, Spain o24 17b
Guimarães, Port. D3 16
Guin, Al., U.S. B2 108
Guinea (Guinée), ctry., Afr. F4 54
Guinea, Gulf of, b., Afr. H7 52
Guinea-Bissau (Guiné-Bissau), ctry., Afr. F3 54
Güines, Cuba C3 94
Guînes, Fr. B8 14
Guingamp, Fr. D3 14
Güinope, Hond. D8 92
Guiones, Punta, c., C.R. H9 92
Guiping, China C11 40
Guir, Hammada du, des., Afr. E9 62
Guir, Oued, val., Afr. E9 62
Güira de Melena, Cuba C3 94
Guiraí, stm., Braz. G2 79
Guiratinga, Braz. D2 79
Güiria, Ven. B11 84
Guiricema, Braz. F7 79
Guise, Fr. C10 14
Güisisil, mtn., Nic. E8 92
Guist Creek, stm., Ky., U.S. B4 124
Guita Koulouba, Cen. Afr. Rep. O2 60
Guitou, China K2 34
Guîtres, Fr. G6 14
Guiuan, Phil. C8 38
Guixi, China G6 34
Guixian, China C10 40
Guiyang (Kweiyang), China A9 40
Güiza, stm., Col. G3 84
Guizhou (Kweichow), prov., China F8 30
Gujarāt, state, India I4 44
Gujrānwāla, Pak. D6 44
Gujrāt, Pak. D6 44
Gulbarga, India D4 46
Gulbene, Lat. D9 22
Guledagudda, India D3 46
Guleitou, China L6 34
Gulf, co., Fl., U.S. C1 116
Gulf Gate Estates, Fl., U.S. E4 116
Gulf Hammock, Fl., U.S. C4 116
Gulf Islands National Seashore, U.S. E5 131
Gulfport, Fl., U.S. E4 116
Gulf Port, Il., U.S. C2 120
Gulfport, Ms., U.S. E4 131
Gulf Shores, Al., U.S. E2 108
Gulgong, Austl. I8 70
Gulistān, Pak. E2 44
Gulistan, Uzb. I11 26
Gulkana, Ak., U.S. C10 109
Gull Island, i., N.C., U.S. B7 140
Gullivan Bay, b., Fl., U.S. G5 116
Gull Lake, Sask., Can. G1 105
Gull Lake, l., Alta., Can. C4 98
Gull Lake, l., Mn., U.S. D4 130
Güllük, Tur. L11 20
Gulnam, Sud. N5 60
Gülpınar, Tur. J10 20
Guluy, Erit. J9 60
Gumal (Gowmal), stm., Asia D3 44
Gumare, Bots. B6 66
Gumboro, De., U.S. G4 115
Gumiao, China C2 34
Gummersbach, Ger. D7 10
Gummi, Nig. E12 64
Gum Spring Mountain, mtn., Tn., U.S. D8 149
Gum Springs, Ar., U.S. C2 111
Gum Swamp Creek, stm., Ga., U.S. D3 117
Gümüşhane, Tur. A5 48
Guna, India H7 44
Gundagai, Austl. J8 70
Gungu, Zaire C3 58
Gunisao, stm., Man., Can. C3 100
Gunisao Lake, l., Man., Can. C3 100
Gunnbjørn Fjeld, mtn., Grnld. C17 86
Gunnedah, Austl. H9 70
Gunnison, Co., U.S. C4 113
Gunnison, Ms., U.S. B3 131
Gunnison, Ut., U.S. D4 151
Gunnison, co., Co., U.S. C3 113
Gunnison, stm., Co., U.S. C2 113

Name	Map Ref.	Page

Gunnison, Mount, mtn., Co., U.S. C3 113
Gunpowder Creek, stm., Ky., U.S. k13 124
Gunpowder Neck, c., Md., U.S. B5 127
Gunpowder River, b., Md., U.S. B5 127
Guntakal, India E4 46
Gunter Air Force Base, mil., Al., U.S. C3 108
Guntersville, Al., U.S. A3 108
Guntersville Dam, Al., U.S. A3 108
Guntersville Lake, res., Al., U.S. A3 108
Gunton, Man., Can. D3 100
Guntown, Ms., U.S. A5 131
Guntūr, India D6 46
Gunungsitoli, Indon. N4 40
Gunzenhausen, Ger. F10 10
Guolutan, China C4 34
Guozhuang, China H5 32
Gupei, China I5 32
Guraferda, Eth. N8 60
Gura-Galbena, Mol. C12 20
Gurara, stm., Nig. G13 64
Gurdāspur, India D6 44
Gurdon, Ar., U.S. D2 111
Güre, Tur. K13 20
Gurgueia, stm., Braz. E10 76
Guri, Embalse de, res., Ven. D11 84
Gurjevsk, Russia G3 22
Gurjevsk, Russia G15 26
Gurley, Al., U.S. A3 108
Gurley, Ne., U.S. C3 134
Gurnee, Il., U.S. h9 120
Gurnet Point, c., Ma., U.S. B6 128
Gurupá, Braz. D8 76
Gurupi, Braz. F9 76
Gurupi, stm., Braz. D9 76
Gusau, Nig. E13 64
Gus'-Chrustal'nyj, Russia F23 22
Gusev, Russia G5 22
Gusevskij, Russia F23 22
Gushanzi, China C8 32
Gushi, China C4 34
Gushikawa, Japan u2 37b
Gusino, Russia G14 22
Gusinoozersk, Russia G13 28
Guspini, Italy J3 18
Gustavus, Ak., U.S. D12 109
Gustine, Ca., U.S. D3 112
Güstrow, Ger. B12 10
Gus'-Železnyj, Russia F24 22
Gütersloh, Ger. D8 10
Guthrie, Ky., U.S. D2 124
Guthrie, Ok., U.S. B4 143
Guthrie, W.V., U.S. m12 155
Guthrie, co., Ia., U.S. C3 122
Guthrie Center, Ia., U.S. C3 122
Gutian, China I7 34
Gutierrez, Bol. H10 82
Gutiérrez Zamora, Mex. G11 90
Guttenberg, Ia., U.S. B6 122
Guttenberg, N.J., U.S. h8 137
Gutu, Zimb. B10 66
Gu Vo, Az., U.S. E3 110
Guwāhāti, India G14 44
Guxian, China F9 32
Guxiansi, China C5 34
Guy, Ar., U.S. B3 111
Guyana, ctry., S.A. B7 76
Guyandotte, stm., W.V., U.S. C2 155
Guyandotte Mountain, mtn., W.V., U.S. n12 155
Guyi, China J7 34
Guymon, Ok., U.S. e9 143
Guyot, Mount, mtn., U.S. D10 149
Guyra, Austl. H9 70
Guys, Tn., U.S. B3 149
Guysborough, N.S., Can. D8 101
Guyton, Ga., U.S. D5 117
Guyuan, China D8 30
Guzar, Uzb. J11 26
Guzhu, China I5 34
Guzmán, Mex. B6 90
Guzmán, Laguna, l., Mex. B6 90
Gvardejsk, Russia G4 22
Gvozdec, Ukr. A9 20
Gwa, Burma F3 40
Gwadabawa, Nig. E12 64
Gwādar, Pak. I17 48
Gwai, Zimb. B8 66
Gwāl Haidarzai, Pak. E3 44
Gwalior, India G8 44
Gwanda, Zimb. C9 66
Gwandu, Nig. E12 64
Gwātar Bay, b., Asia I16 48
Gwent, co., Wales, U.K. J11 8
Gweru, Zimb. B9 66
Gweta, Bots. C7 66
Gwinhurst, De., U.S. h8 115
Gwinn, Mi., U.S. B3 129
Gwinner, N.D., U.S. C8 141
Gwinnett, co., Ga., U.S. C2 117
Gwydyr Bay, b., Ak., U.S. A10 109
Gwynedd, co., Wales, U.K. H9 8
Gwynn, Va., U.S. C6 153
Gwynne, Alta., Can. C4 98
Gwynneville, In., U.S. E6 121
Gwynns Falls, stm., Md., U.S. g10 127
Gy, Fr. E12 14
Gyangzê, China F4 30
Gyaring Co, l., China E13 44
Gyaring Hu, l., China E6 30
Gydanskaja guba, b., Russia C13 26
Gydanskij poluostrov, pen., Russia C13 26
Gyirong, China F11 44
Gympie, Austl. F10 70
Gyobingauk, Burma E3 40
Gyoma, Hung. I20 10
Gyöngyös, Hung. H19 10
Győr, Hung. H17 10
Győr-Moson-Sopron, co., Hung. H17 10
Gypsum, Co., U.S. B4 113
Gypsum, Ks., U.S. D6 123
Gypsum Point, c., N.W. Ter., Can. D10 96
Gypsumville, Man., Can. D2 100
Gyula, Hung. I21 10

H

Haag in Oberbayern, Ger. G12 10
Haakon, co., S.D., U.S. C4 148
Haalenberg, Nmb. F2 66
Haaltert, Bel. G5 12
Haapajärvi, Fin. J19 6
Haapamäki, Fin. J19 6
Haapsalu, Est. C6 22
Ha'Arava (Wādī al-'Arabah), val., Asia G4 50
Ha'Arava (Wādī al-Jayb), val., Asia H4 50
Haarlem, Neth. D6 12
Ḥabarūt, Yemen F8 47
Ḥabbān, Yemen G5 47
Habbūsh, Leb. B4 50
Habermehl Peak, mtn., Ant. C3 73
Habersham, co., Ga., U.S. B3 117
Habiganj, Bngl. H14 44
Habomai-shotō see Malaja Kuril'skaja Gr'ada, is., Russia d21 36a
Hachijō-jima, i., Japan E14 30
Hachinohe, Japan G16 36
Hachiōji, Japan L14 36
Hacienda Miravalles, C.R. G9 92
Hacienda Murciélago, C.R. G9 92
Hackberry, La., U.S. E2 125
Hackberry Creek, stm., Ks., U.S. D3 123
Hackensack, N.J., U.S. B4 137
Hackensack, stm., N.J., U.S. h8 137
Hacker Valley, W.V., U.S. C4 155
Hackett, Ar., U.S. B1 111
Hackettstown, N.J., U.S. B3 137
Hackleburg, Al., U.S. A2 108
Hack Point, Md., U.S. B6 127
Hadalīya, Sud. I9 60
Hadar, Ne., U.S. B8 134
Hadd, Ra's al-, c., Oman C11 47
Haddam, Ct., U.S. D5 114
Haddam, Ks., U.S. C6 123
Haddington, Scot., U.K. F11 8
Haddix, Ky., U.S. C6 124
Haddock, Ga., U.S. C3 117
Haddonfield, N.J., U.S. D2 137
Haddon Heights, N.J., U.S. D2 137
Hadejia, Nig. E14 64
Hadejia, stm., Nig. E14 64
Ḥadera, Isr. D3 50
Ḥadera, stm., Asia D3 50
Hadley, Ma., U.S. B2 128
Hadley, N.Y., U.S. B7 139
Hadley Bay, b., N.W. Ter., Can. B11 96
Hadley Lake, l., Me., U.S. D5 126
Hadlock, Wa., U.S. A3 154
Hadlyme, Ct., U.S. D6 114
Ha Dong, Viet. D8 40
Ḥaḍramawt, reg., Yemen G6 47
Haeju, N. Kor. E13 32
Haenam, S. Kor. I14 32
Hafford, Sask., Can. E2 105
Haffouz, Tun. N4 18
Ḥafīrat al-'Ayda, Sau. Ar. H5 48
Hafnarfjördur, Ice. B3 6a
Haft Gel, Iran F10 48
Hafun, Ras, c., Som. F11 56
Hagan, Ga., U.S. D5 117
Hagarville, Ar., U.S. B2 111
Hagemeister Island, i., Ak., U.S. D7 109
Hagen, Ger. D7 10
Hagensborg, B.C., Can. C4 99
Hagere Hiywet, Eth. M9 60
Hagere Selam, Eth. N10 60
Hagerman, Id., U.S. G4 119
Hagerman, N.M., U.S. D5 138
Hagerstown, In., U.S. E7 121
Hagerstown, Md., U.S. A2 127
Hagetmau, Fr. I6 14
Haggin, Mount, mtn., Mt., U.S. D3 133
Ha Giang, Viet. C8 40
Hagondange, Fr. C13 14
Hague, Sask., Can. E2 105
Hague, N.D., U.S. C6 141
Hague, Cap de la, c., Fr. C5 14
Haguenau, Fr. D14 14
Hagues Peak, mtn., Co., U.S. A5 113
Ha90 Ha90, Baie des, b., Que., Can. C2 102
Hahaïa, Com. k15 67a
Hahira, Ga., U.S. F3 117
Hahnville, La., U.S. E5 125
Haian Shanmo, mts., Tai. L10 34
Haicheng, China C10 32
Haïdra, Tun. N3 18
Hai Duong, Viet. D9 40
Haifa see Hefa, Isr. C4 50
Haifeng, China M4 34
Haig, Austl. F5 68
Haigler, Ne., U.S. D4 134
Haikang (Leizhou), China D11 40
Haikou, China D11 40
Haiku, Hi., U.S. C5 118
Ḥā'il, Sau. Ar. H6 48
Hailākāndi, India H15 44
Hailar, China B10 30
Hailar, stm., China B11 30
Hailey, Id., U.S. F4 119
Haileybury, Ont., Can. p20 103
Haileyville, Ok., U.S. C6 143
Hailong (Meihekou), China A13 32
Hailun, China B12 30
Haimen, China G10 34
Haimen, China L5 34
Hainan, prov., China H8 30
Hainan Dao, i., China E10 40
Hainaut, prov., Bel. G4 12
Hainaut, hist. reg., Eur. H4 12
Haines, Ak., U.S. D12 109
Haines, Or., U.S. C9 144
Haines City, Fl., U.S. D5 116
Haines Falls, N.Y., U.S. C6 139
Haines Junction, Yukon, Can. D5 96
Hainesport, N.J., U.S. D3 137
Hainfeld, Aus. G15 10
Hai Phong, Viet. D9 40
Hairy Hill, Alta., Can. C5 98
Haiti (Haïti), ctry., N.A. E8 94
Haitou, China I7 32
Haiyaopu, China A6 40
Haizhou, China A8 34
Hajdú-Bihar, co., Hung. H21 10
Hajdúböszörmény, Hung. H21 10
Hajdúnánás, Hung. H21 10
Hajeb el Ayoun, Tun. N4 18
Haji Langar, China C8 44
Hājīpur, India H11 44
Ḥajjah, Yemen G3 47
Hajnówka, Pol. C23 10
Hakalau, Hi., U.S. D6 118
Ḥakīm, Abyār al-, well, Libya B2 60
Hakkâri, Tur. C7 48
Hakodate, Japan f15 36a
Hakui, Japan K11 36
Ḥalab (Aleppo), Syria C4 48
Halabjah, Iraq D8 48
Halachó, Mex. G14 90
Ḥalā'ib, Egypt F9 60
Halaula, Hi., U.S. C6 118
Halawa, Cape, c., Hi., U.S. B5 118
Halawa Heights, Hi., U.S. g10 118
Halawotelake, China B14 44
Halberstadt, Ger. D11 10
Halbrite, Sask., Can. H4 105
Halbur, Ia., U.S. C3 122
Haldeman, Ky., U.S. B6 124
Haldimand, Ont., Can. E5 103
Haldwāni, India F8 44
Hale, Mi., U.S. D7 129
Hale, Mo., U.S. B4 132
Hale, co., Al., U.S. C2 108
Hale, co., Tx., U.S. B2 150
Haleakala Crater, crat., Hi., U.S. C5 118
Haleakala National Park, Hi., U.S. C6 118
Hale Center, Tx., U.S. B2 150
Haleiwa, Hi., U.S. B3 118
Hales Corners, Wi., U.S. n11 156
Halethorpe, Md., U.S. B4 127
Haleyville, Al., U.S. A2 108
Half Moon Bay, Ca., U.S. k8 112
Halfway, Md., U.S. A2 127
Half Way, Mo., U.S. D4 132
Halfway, Or., U.S. C9 144
Haliburton, Ont., Can. B6 103
Halibut Point, c., Ma., U.S. A6 128
Halifax, Austl. B7 70
Halifax, N.S., Can. E6 101
Halifax, Ma., U.S. C6 128
Halifax, N.C., U.S. A5 140
Halifax, Pa., U.S. F8 145
Halifax, Va., U.S. D4 153
Halifax, co., N.C., U.S. A5 140
Halifax, co., Va., U.S. D4 153
Halifax Bay, b., Austl. B7 70
Haliimaile, Hi., U.S. C5 118
Halkirk, Alta., Can. C4 98
Hall, Mt., U.S. D3 133
Hall, co., Ga., U.S. B3 117
Hall, co., Ne., U.S. D7 134
Hall, co., Tx., U.S. B2 150
Hallam, Ne., U.S. D9 134
Hallam Peak, mtn., B.C., Can. C8 99
Hallandale, Fl., U.S. G6 116
Hallands Län, co., Swe. M13 6
Halla-san, mtn., S. Kor. E12 30
Halle (Hal), Bel. G5 12
Halle, Ger. D11 10
Hallein, Aus. H13 10
Hallettsville, Tx., U.S. E4 150
Halley, Ar., U.S. D4 111
Halliday, N.D., U.S. B3 141
Hallie, Wi., U.S. D2 156
Hall in Tirol, Aus. H11 10
Hall Island, i., Ak., U.S. C5 109
Hall Meadow Brook, stm., Ct., U.S. B3 114
Hall Meadow Brook Reservoir, res., Ct., U.S. B3 114
Hall Mountain, mtn., Wa., U.S. A8 154
Hällnäs, Swe. I16 6
Hallock, Mn., U.S. B2 130
Hallowell, Ks., U.S. E9 123
Hallowell, Me., U.S. D3 126
Hall Peninsula, pen., N.W. Ter., Can. D19 96
Halls, Tn., U.S. B2 149
Hallsberg, Swe. L14 6
Hallsboro, N.C., U.S. C4 140
Halls Creek, Austl. C5 68
Halls Creek, stm., Ut., U.S. F5 151
Halls Crossroads, Tn., U.S. m14 149
Halls Harbour, N.S., Can. D5 101
Halls Stream, stm., N.H., U.S. f7 136
Hallstavik, Swe. K16 6
Hallstead, Pa., U.S. C10 145
Hallsville, Mo., U.S. B5 132
Hallsville, Tx., U.S. C5 150
Hall Top, mtn., Tn., U.S. D10 149
Halltown, Mo., U.S. D4 132
Hallwood, Va., U.S. C7 153
Halma, Bel. H7 12
Halmahera, i., Indon. E8 38
Halmahera, Laut (Halmahera Sea), Indon. F8 38
Halmstad, Swe. M13 6
Halsell, Al., U.S. C1 108
Halsey, Ne., U.S. C5 134
Halsey, Or., U.S. C3 144
Hälsingborg see Helsingborg, Swe. M13 6
Halstad, Mn., U.S. C2 130
Halstead, Ks., U.S. E6 123
Haltern, Ger. D7 10
Haltiatunturi, mtn., Eur. G17 6
Halton Hills, Ont., Can. D5 103
Hamad, Sud. J7 60
Hamada, Japan M7 36
Hamadān, Iran D10 48
Ḥamāh, Syria D4 48
Hamale, Ghana F8 64
Hamamatsu, Japan M12 36
Hamar, Nor. K12 6
Ḥamāṭah, Jabal, mtn., Egypt I3 48
Hamblen, co., Tn., U.S. C10 149
Hamburg, Ger. B9 10
Hamburg, Ar., U.S. D4 111
Hamburg, Ia., U.S. D2 122
Hamburg, N.J., U.S. A3 137
Hamburg, N.Y., U.S. C2 139
Hamburg, Pa., U.S. E10 145
Hamburg Mountains, mts., N.J., U.S. A3 137
Ḥamdānah, Sau. Ar. E2 47
Hamden, Ct., U.S. D4 114
Hamden, Oh., U.S. C3 142
Hämeen lääni, prov., Fin. K19 6
Hämeenlinna, Fin. K19 6
Hamel, Mn., U.S. m11 130
Hameln, Ger. C9 10
Hamer, S.C., U.S. C9 147
Hamersley Range, mts., Austl. D3 68
Hamersley Range National Park, Austl. D3 68
Hamersville, Oh., U.S. D2 142
Hamhŭng, N. Kor. D15 32
Hami, China C5 30
Hamill, S.D., U.S. D6 148
Hamilton, Austl. K5 70
Hamilton, Ber. B12 88
Hamilton, Ont., Can. D5 103
Hamilton, N.Z. B5 72
Hamilton, Scot., U.K. F9 8
Hamilton, Al., U.S. A2 108
Hamilton, Ga., U.S. D2 117
Hamilton, Il., U.S. C2 120
Hamilton, In., U.S. A8 121
Hamilton, Ks., U.S. E7 123
Hamilton, Ma., U.S. A6 128
Hamilton, Mi., U.S. F4 129
Hamilton, Ms., U.S. B5 131
Hamilton, Mo., U.S. B3 132
Hamilton, Mt., U.S. D2 133
Hamilton, N.Y., U.S. C5 139
Hamilton, N.C., U.S. B5 140
Hamilton, Oh., U.S. C1 142
Hamilton, Tx., U.S. D3 150
Hamilton, Va., U.S. A5 153
Hamilton, Wa., U.S. A4 154
Hamilton, co., Fl., U.S. B3 116
Hamilton, co., Il., U.S. E5 120
Hamilton, co., In., U.S. D5 121
Hamilton, co., Ia., U.S. B4 122
Hamilton, co., Ks., U.S. E2 123
Hamilton, co., Ne., U.S. D7 134
Hamilton, co., N.Y., U.S. B6 139
Hamilton, co., Oh., U.S. C1 142
Hamilton, co., Tn., U.S. D8 149
Hamilton, co., Tx., U.S. D3 150
Hamilton, stm., Austl. D4 70
Hamilton, Lake, res., Ar., U.S. C2 111
Hamilton, Mount, mtn., Ak., U.S. C8 109
Hamilton, Mount, mtn., Ca., U.S. k9 112
Hamilton, Mount, mtn., Nv., U.S. D6 135
Hamilton City, Ca., U.S. C2 112
Hamilton Dome, Wy., U.S. C4 157
Hamilton Hotel, Austl. D4 70
Hamilton Inlet, b., Newf., Can. A2 102
Hamilton Mountain, mtn., N.Y., U.S. B6 139
Hamilton Reservoir, res., Ma., U.S. B3 128
Hamilton Sound, strt., Newf., Can. D4 102
Hamilton Square, N.J., U.S. C3 137
Hamina, Fin. K20 6
Hamiota, Man., Can. D1 100
Ḥāmir, Wādī, val., Asia F7 48
Hamīrpur, India H9 44
Hamler, Oh., U.S. A1 142
Hamlet, In., U.S. B4 121
Hamlet, N.C., U.S. C3 140
Hamlet, Mount, mtn., Ak., U.S. B6 109
Hamlin, Pa., U.S. D11 145
Hamlin, Tx., U.S. C2 150
Hamlin, W.V., U.S. C2 155
Hamlin, co., S.D., U.S. C8 148
Hamlin Lake, l., Mi., U.S. D4 129
Hamm, Ger. D7 10
Hammamet, Alg. N2 18
Hammamet, Tun. M5 18
Hammamet, Golfe de, b., Tun. M5 18
Hammam Lif, Tun. M5 18
Ḥammār, Hawr al-, l., Iraq F9 48
Hamme, Bel. F5 12
Hammerdal, Swe. J14 6
Hammerfest, Nor. F18 6
Hammett, Id., U.S. G3 119
Hammon, Ok., U.S. B2 143
Hammonasset, stm., Ct., U.S. D5 114
Hammonasset Point, c., Ct., U.S. E5 114
Hammond, Il., U.S. D5 120
Hammond, In., U.S. A2 121
Hammond, La., U.S. D5 125
Hammond, Or., U.S. A3 144
Hammond, Wi., U.S. D1 156
Hammond Bay, b., Mi., U.S. C6 129
Hammondsport, N.Y., U.S. C3 139
Hammonton, N.J., U.S. D3 137
Ham-Nord, Que., Can. D6 104
Hamoyet, Jabal, mtn., Afr. I10 60
Hampden, Newf., Can. D3 102
Hampden, Me., U.S. D4 126
Hampden, Ma., U.S. B3 128
Hampden, N.D., U.S. A7 141
Hampden, co., Ma., U.S. B2 128
Hampden Highlands, Me., U.S. D4 126
Hampshire, Il., U.S. A5 120
Hampshire, Tn., U.S. B4 149
Hampshire, co., Eng., U.K. J12 8
Hampshire, co., Ma., U.S. B2 128
Hampshire, co., W.V., U.S. B6 155
Hampstead, N.B., Can. D3 101
Hampstead, Md., U.S. A4 127
Hampstead, N.H., U.S. E4 136
Hampstead, N.C., U.S. C5 140
Hampton, N.B., Can. D4 101
Hampton, Ar., U.S. D3 111
Hampton, Ct., U.S. B7 114
Hampton, Ga., U.S. C2 117
Hampton, Ia., U.S. B4 122
Hampton, Mn., U.S. F5 130
Hampton, Ne., U.S. D8 134
Hampton, N.H., U.S. E5 136
Hampton, N.J., U.S. B3 137
Hampton, S.C., U.S. F5 147
Hampton, Tn., U.S. C11 149
Hampton, Va., U.S. C6 153
Hampton, co., S.C., U.S. F5 147
Hampton Bays, N.Y., U.S. n16 139
Hampton Beach, N.H., U.S. E5 136
Hampton Butte, mtn., Or., U.S. D6 144
Hampton Falls, N.H., U.S. E5 136
Hampton Roads, Va., U.S. k15 153
Hampton Roads Bridge-Tunnel, Va., U.S. k15 153
Hamra, As Saquia al, val., W. Sah. G4 62
Hams Fork, stm., Wy., U.S. E2 157
Hamtramck, Mi., U.S. p15 129
Hamyang, S. Kor. H15 32
Han, stm., China E9 30
Hana, Hi., U.S. C6 118
Hanahan, S.C., U.S. F7 147
Hanalei, Hi., U.S. A2 118
Hanalei Bay, b., Hi., U.S. A2 118
Hanamaki, Japan H16 36
Hanamaulu, Hi., U.S. B2 118
Hanapepe, Hi., U.S. B2 118
Hanau, Ger. E8 10
Hanbury, stm., N.W. Ter., Can. D11 96
Hanceville, B.C., Can. D6 99
Hanceville, Al., U.S. A3 108
Hancheng, China D9 30
Hancock, Ia., U.S. C2 122
Hancock, Me., U.S. D4 126
Hancock, Md., U.S. A1 127
Hancock, Mi., U.S. A2 129
Hancock, Mn., U.S. E3 130
Hancock, N.H., U.S. E3 136
Hancock, N.Y., U.S. D5 139
Hancock, Vt., U.S. D3 152
Hancock, Wi., U.S. D4 156
Hancock, co., Ga., U.S. C3 117
Hancock, co., Il., U.S. C2 120
Hancock, co., In., U.S. E6 121
Hancock, co., Ia., U.S. A4 122
Hancock, co., Ky., U.S. C3 124
Hancock, co., Me., U.S. D4 126
Hancock, co., Ms., U.S. E4 131
Hancock, co., Oh., U.S. A2 142
Hancock, co., Tn., U.S. C10 149
Hancock, co., W.V., U.S. A4 155
Hancock Pond, l., Me., U.S. E2 126
Hancocks Bridge, N.J., U.S. D2 137
Hand, co., S.D., U.S. C6 148
Handa, Japan M11 36
Handa, Som. F11 56
Handan, China G2 32
Handley, W.V., U.S. m13 155
Handub, Sud. H9 60
HaNegev (Negev Desert), reg., Isr. G3 50
Hanford, Ca., U.S. D4 112
Han'gang, China I2 32
Han-gang, stm., Asia F14 32
Hangchow see Hangzhou, China E9 34
Hanggin Houqi, China C8 30
Hanggin Qi, China D8 30
Hangman Creek, stm., Wa., U.S. B8 154
Hangö (Hanko), Fin. L18 6
Hangu, China D5 32
Hangu, Pak. D4 44
Hangzhou (Hangchow), China E9 34
Hangzhou Wan (Hangchow Bay), b., China E10 34
Hani, Tur. B6 48
Ḥanīsh, is., Yemen H3 47
Ḥanita, Isr. B4 50
Hanjiang, China J8 34
Hankey, S. Afr. I7 66
Hankinson, N.D., U.S. C9 141
Hanko see Hangö, Fin. D12 4
Hankow see Wuhan, China E3 34
Hanksville, Ut., U.S. E5 151
Hanley, Sask., Can. F2 105
Hanna, Alta., Can. D5 98
Hanna, In., U.S. B4 121
Hanna, Wy., U.S. E6 157
Hanna City, Il., U.S. C4 120
Hannaford, N.D., U.S. B7 141
Hannahville Indian Reservation, Mi., U.S. C3 129
Hannibal, Mo., U.S. B6 132
Hannibal, Oh., U.S. C5 142
Hannover, Ger. C9 10
Ha Noi, Viet. D8 40
Hanover, Ont., Can. C3 103
Hanover, Ct., U.S. C7 114
Hanover, Il., U.S. A3 120
Hanover, In., U.S. G7 121
Hanover, Ks., U.S. C7 123
Hanover, Me., U.S. D2 126
Hanover, Ma., U.S. B6 128
Hanover, Mi., U.S. F6 129
Hanover, Mn., U.S. m11 130
Hanover, N.H., U.S. C2 136
Hanover, N.M., U.S. E1 138
Hanover, Oh., U.S. B3 142
Hanover, Pa., U.S. G8 145
Hanover, Va., U.S. C5 153
Hanover, co., Va., U.S. C5 153
Hanover Center, Ma., U.S. h12 128
Hanover see Hannover, Ger. C9 10
Hanover Park, Il., U.S. k8 120
Hansen, Id., U.S. G4 119
Hansford, co., Tx., U.S. A2 150
Hānsi, India F6 44
Hanska, Mn., U.S. F4 130
Hanson, Ky., U.S. C2 124
Hanson, Ma., U.S. B6 128
Hanson, co., S.D., U.S. D8 148
Hanston, Ks., U.S. D4 123
Hant's Harbour, Newf., Can. D5 102
Hantsport, N.S., Can. D5 101
Hanumangarh, India F6 44
Hanušovice, Czech. E16 10
Hanwood, Austl. J7 70
Hanzhong, China E8 30
Hanzhuang, China I5 32
Haohekou, China G1 34
Hāora, India I13 44
Hapeville, Ga., U.S. C2 117
Happy, Tx., U.S. B2 150
Happy Jack, Az., U.S. C4 110
Happy Valley, N.M., U.S. E5 138
Happy Valley-Goose Bay, Newf., Can. B1 102
Hāpur, India F7 44
Haquira, Peru F5 82
Haraḍ, Sau. Ar. B6 47
Harad, Jabal al-, mtn., Jord. I5 50
Harahan, La., U.S. k11 125
Haralson, co., Ga., U.S. C1 117
Harare (Salisbury), Zimb. A10 66
Harash, Bi'r al-, well, Libya E2 60
Harbeson, De., U.S. F4 115
Harbin, China B12 30
Harbinger, N.C., U.S. A7 140
Harbor, Or., U.S. E2 144
Harbor Beach, Mi., U.S. E8 129
Harborcreek, Pa., U.S. B2 145
Harbor Springs, Mi., U.S. C6 129
Harborton, Va., U.S. C7 153
Harbour Breton, Newf., Can. E4 102
Harbour Grace, Newf., Can. E5 102
Harbour Mille, Newf., Can. E4 102
Harbourville, N.S., Can. D5 101
Harcourt, N.B., Can. C4 101
Harcourt, Ia., U.S. B3 122
Harcuvar Mountains, mts., Az., U.S. D2 110
Harda, India I7 44
Hardangerfjorden, Nor. K10 6
Hardaway, Al., U.S. C4 108
Hardee, co., Fl., U.S. E5 116
Hardeeville, S.C., U.S. G5 147
Hardeman, co., Tn., U.S. B2 149
Hardeman, co., Tx., U.S. B3 150
Harderwijk, Neth. D8 12
Hardesty, Ok., U.S. e9 143
Hardin, Il., U.S. D3 120
Hardin, Ky., U.S. f9 124
Hardin, Mo., U.S. B4 132
Hardin, Mt., U.S. E9 133
Hardin, co., Il., U.S. F5 120
Hardin, co., Ia., U.S. B4 122
Hardin, co., Ky., U.S. C4 124
Hardin, co., Oh., U.S. B2 142
Hardin, co., Tn., U.S. B3 149
Hardin, co., Tx., U.S. D5 150
Harding, S. Afr. H9 66
Harding, co., N.M., U.S. B5 138
Harding, co., S.D., U.S. B2 148
Harding, Lake, res., U.S. C4 108
Hardinsburg, In., U.S. H5 121
Hardinsburg, Ky., U.S. C3 124
Hardisty, Alta., Can. C5 98
Hardoi, India G9 44
Hardshell, Ky., U.S. C6 124
Hardtner, Ks., U.S. E5 123
Hardwick, Ga., U.S. C3 117
Hardwick, Vt., U.S. B4 152
Hardwicke, N.B., Can. B5 101
Hardwood Ridge, mtn., Pa., U.S. D11 145
Hardy, Ar., U.S. A4 111
Hardy, Ne., U.S. D8 134
Hardy, co., W.V., U.S. B6 155
Hardy Lake, res., In., U.S. G6 121
Hare Bay, Newf., Can. D4 102
Hare Bay, b., Newf., Can. C4 102
Harer, Eth. G9 56
Hareto, Eth. M9 60
Harford, co., Md., U.S. A5 127
Hargeysa, Som. G9 56
Harghita, co., Rom. C9 20
Hargill, Tx., U.S. F3 150
Har Hu, l., China D6 30
Hari, stm., Indon. F3 38
Haria, Spain n27 17b
Haridwār, India F8 44
Harihar, India E3 46
Haringvliet, strt., Neth. E5 12
Harīrūd (Tedžen), stm., Asia C16 48
Harkers Island, N.C., U.S. C6 140
Harlan, In., U.S. B8 121
Harlan, Ia., U.S. C2 122
Harlan, Ky., U.S. D6 124
Harlan, co., Ky., U.S. D6 124
Harlan, co., Ne., U.S. D6 134
Harlan County Lake, res., Ne., U.S. E6 134
Harlem, Fl., U.S. F6 116
Harlem, Ga., U.S. C4 117
Harlem, Mt., U.S. B8 133
Harleyville, S.C., U.S. E7 147
Harlingen, Neth. B7 12
Harlingen, Tx., U.S. F4 150
Harlowton, Mt., U.S. D7 133
Harman, Va., U.S. e9 153
Harmanli, Bul. H9 20
Harmon, co., Ok., U.S. C2 143
Harmon Creek, stm., W.V., U.S. f8 155
Harmony, In., U.S. E3 121
Harmony, Me., U.S. D3 126
Harmony, Mn., U.S. G6 130
Harmony, N.C., U.S. B2 140
Harmony, Pa., U.S. E1 145
Harmony, R.I., U.S. B3 146
Harmony Grove, Ar., U.S. D3 111
Harned, Ky., U.S. C3 124
Harnett, co., N.C., U.S. B4 140
Harney, co., Or., U.S. D7 144
Harney, Lake, l., Fl., U.S. D5 116
Harney Lake, l., Or., U.S. D7 144
Harney Peak, mtn., S.D., U.S. D2 148
Härnösand, Swe. J15 6
Haro, Spain C9 16
Haro, Cabo, c., Mex. D4 90
Haro Strait, strt., Wa., U.S. A2 154
Harper, Lib. I6 64
Harper, Ks., U.S. E5 123
Harper, Wa., U.S. e10 154
Harper, co., Ks., U.S. E5 123
Harper, co., Ok., U.S. A2 143
Harper, Mount, mtn., Ak., U.S. C11 109
Harpers Ferry, Ia., U.S. A6 122
Harpers Ferry, W.V., U.S. B7 155
Harpers Ferry National Historical Park, W.V., U.S. B7 155
Harpersville, Al., U.S. B3 108
Harperville, Ms., U.S. C4 131
Harpeth, stm., Tn., U.S. A5 149
Harqin Qi (Jinshan), China B6 32
Harquahala Mountain, mtn., Az., U.S. D2 110

Name | Map Ref. | Page

Herstal, Bel. G8 12
Hertford, N.C., U.S. A6 140
Hertford, co., N.C., U.S. A5 140
Hertfordshire, co., Eng., U.K. J13 8
Hervey Bay, b., Austl. E10 70
Herzberg, Ger. D13 10
Herzberg [am Harz], Ger. D10 10
Herzliyya, Isr. D3 50
Hesdin, Fr. B9 14
Heshangqiao, China A2 34
Heshi, China J7 34
Heshuijian, China E5 34
Hesperia, Ca., U.S. E5 112
Hesperia, Mi., U.S. E4 129
Hesperus, Co., U.S. D2 113
Hesperus Mountain, mtn., Co., U.S. D2 113
Hessen, state, Ger. E9 10
Hessmer, La., U.S. C3 125
Hesston, Ks., U.S. D6 123
Hetang, China I8 34
Hetou, China K2 34
Hettick, Il., U.S. D3 120
Hettinger, N.D., U.S. D3 141
Hettinger, co., N.D., U.S. C3 141
Hettstedt, Ger. D11 10
Hetupu, China E5 34
Heves, Hung. H20 10
Heves, co., Hung. H20 10
Hevron, Nahal, val., Asia F3 50
Hewitt, Mn., U.S. D3 130
Hewitt, Tx., U.S. D4 150
Hewitt, Wi., U.S. D3 156
Hexi, China K6 34
Hexian, China G9 30
Heyang, China H6 32
Heyburn, Id., U.S. G5 119
Heywood, Austl. L4 70
Heyworth, Il., U.S. C5 120
Heze (Caozhou), China H3 32
Hezhen, China F9 34
Hialeah, Fl., U.S. G6 116
Hiattville, Ks., U.S. E9 123
Hiawassee, Ga., U.S. B3 117
Hiawatha, Ia., U.S. B6 122
Hiawatha, Ks., U.S. C8 123
Hibbing, Mn., U.S. C6 130
Hibbs, Point, c., Austl. N6 70
Hibernia Reef, rf., Austl. B4 68
Hickam Air Force Base, mil., Hi., U.S. g10 118
Hickman, De., U.S. E3 115
Hickman, Ky., U.S. f8 124
Hickman, Ne., U.S. D9 134
Hickman, co., Ky., U.S. f8 124
Hickman, co., Tn., U.S. B4 149
Hickman's Harbour, Newf., Can. D5 102
Hickory, Ky., U.S. f9 124
Hickory, Ms., U.S. C4 131
Hickory, N.C., U.S. B1 140
Hickory, co., Mo., U.S. D4 132
Hickory Flat, Ms., U.S. A4 131
Hickory Plains, Ar., U.S. C4 111
Hickory Ridge, Ar., U.S. B5 111
Hickory Valley, Tn., U.S. B2 149
Hicks, Point, c., Austl. K8 70
Hickson, Ont., Can. D4 103
Hicksville, N.Y., U.S. E7 139
Hicksville, Oh., U.S. A1 142
Hico, Tx., U.S. D3 150
Hico, W.V., U.S. C3 155
Hidalgo, Mex. D10 90
Hidalgo, Mex. E9 90
Hidalgo, Mex. E10 90
Hidalgo, Mex. F8 90
Hidalgo, Tx., U.S. F3 150
Hidalgo, state, Mex. G10 90
Hidalgo, co., N.M., U.S. F1 138
Hidalgo, co., Tx., U.S. F3 150
Hidalgo del Parral, Mex. D7 90
Hida-sammyaku, mts., Japan K12 36
Hiddenite, N.C., U.S. B1 140
Hidrolândia, Braz. D4 79
Hidrolina, Braz. C4 79
Hieflau, Aus. H14 10
Hieroglyphic Mountains, mts., Az., U.S. k8 110
Hierro (Ferro), i., Spain p22 17b
Higashine, Japan I15 36
Higashiōsaka, Japan M10 36
Higbee, Mo., U.S. B5 132
Higdon, Al., U.S. A4 108
Higganum, Ct., U.S. D5 114
Higgins Lake, Mi., U.S. D6 129
Higgins Lake, l., Mi., U.S. D6 129
Higgins Millpond, res., Md., U.S. C6 127
Higginson, Ar., U.S. B4 111
Higginsville, Mo., U.S. B4 132
High Bluff, Man., Can. D2 100
High Bridge, N.J., U.S. B3 137
High Falls Reservoir, res., Wi., U.S. C5 156
Highfield, Md., U.S. A3 127
Highgate, Ont., Can. E3 103
Highgate Falls, Vt., U.S. B2 152
High Hill, Mo., U.S. C6 132
High Island, Tx., U.S. E5 150
High Island, i., Mi., U.S. C5 129
High Knob, mtn., U.S. A4 153
High Knob, mtn., W.V., U.S. C5 155
Highland, Il., U.S. E4 120
Highland, In., U.S. A3 121
Highland, Ks., U.S. C8 123
Highland, Mi., U.S. o14 129
Highland, N.Y., U.S. D7 139
Highland, Wi., U.S. E3 156
Highland, prov., Scot., U.K. D8 8
Highland, co., Oh., U.S. C2 142
Highland, co., Va., U.S. B3 153
Highland Grove, Ont., Can. B6 103
Highland Home, Al., U.S. D3 108
Highland Lake, l., Me., U.S. g7 126
Highland Lakes, N.J., U.S. A4 137
Highland Park, Il., U.S. A6 120
Highland Park, Mi., U.S. p15 129
Highland Park, Tx., U.S. n10 150
Highland Peak, mtn., Ca., U.S. C4 112
Highland Point, c., Fl., U.S. G5 116
Highlands, N.J., U.S. C5 137
Highlands, N.C., U.S. f9 140
Highlands, Tx., U.S. r14 150
Highlands, co., Fl., U.S. E5 116
Highland Springs, Va., U.S. C5 153
High Level, Alta., Can. F7 98
Highmore, S.D., U.S. C6 148
High Point, N.C., U.S. B2 140
High Point, Wa., U.S. e12 154
High Prairie, Alta., Can. B2 98
High Ridge, Mo., U.S. g12 132
High River, Alta., Can. D4 98
High Rock, mtn., Md., U.S. k12 127
Highrock Lake, l., Man., Can. B1 100
High Rock Lake, res., N.C., U.S. B2 140
High Shoals, Ga., U.S. C3 117
High Shoals, N.C., U.S. B1 140
High Spire, Pa., U.S. F8 145
High Springs, Fl., U.S. C4 116
High Top, mtn., W.V., U.S. C5 155
Hightstown, N.J., U.S. C3 137
Highwood, Il., U.S. A6 120
Highwood, Mt., U.S. C6 133
Highwood Baldy, mtn., Mt., U.S. C6 133
Highwood Mountains, mts., Mt., U.S. C6 133
High Wycombe, Eng., U.K. J13 8
Higley, Az., U.S. D4 110
Higuera de Abuya, Mex. E6 90
Higuera de Zaragoza, Mex. E5 90
Higuerote, Punta, c., P.R. E11 94
Higüey, Dom. Rep. E10 94
Higuito, stm., Hond. C6 92
Hiiumaa, i., Est. C5 22
Hiko, Nv., U.S. F6 135
Hikone, Japan L11 36
Hiko Range, mts., Nv., U.S. F6 135
Hilbert, Wi., U.S. D5 156
Hilda, Alta., Can. D5 98
Hilda, S.C., U.S. E5 147
Hildale, Ut., U.S. F3 151
Hildburghausen, Ger. E10 10
Hilden, N.S., Can. D6 101
Hildesheim, Ger. C9 10
Hildreth, Ne., U.S. D6 134
Hill, N.H., U.S. C3 136
Hill, co., Mt., U.S. B6 133
Hill, co., Tx., U.S. D4 150
Hillaby, Mount, mtn., Barb. H15 94
Hill Bank, Belize I15 90
Hill City, Ga., U.S. B2 117
Hill City, Ks., U.S. C4 123
Hill City, Mn., U.S. D5 130
Hill City, S.D., U.S. D2 148
Hillcrest, Il., U.S. B4 120
Hillcrest, Mi., U.S. n11 129
Hillcrest Heights, Md., U.S. C4 127
Hilli, Bngl. H13 44
Hilliard, Alta., Can. C4 98
Hilliard, Fl., U.S. B5 116
Hilliard, Oh., U.S. k10 142
Hillier, Ont., Can. D7 103
Hillisburg, In., U.S. D5 121
Hill Lake, l., Ar., U.S. h10 111
Hillman, Mi., U.S. C7 129
Hillrose, Co., U.S. A7 113
Hills, Ia., U.S. C6 122
Hills, Mn., U.S. G2 130
Hillsboro, Al., U.S. A2 108
Hillsboro, Ga., U.S. C3 117
Hillsboro, Il., U.S. D4 120
Hillsboro, In., U.S. D3 121
Hillsboro, Ks., U.S. D6 123
Hillsboro, Ms., U.S. C4 131
Hillsboro, Mo., U.S. C7 132
Hillsboro, N.H., U.S. D3 136
Hillsboro, N.M., U.S. E2 138
Hillsboro, N.D., U.S. B8 141
Hillsboro, Oh., U.S. C2 142
Hillsboro, Or., U.S. B4 144
Hillsboro, Tn., U.S. D8 149
Hillsboro, Tx., U.S. C4 150
Hillsboro, Wi., U.S. E3 156
Hillsboro Canal, Fl., U.S. F6 116
Hillsborough, N.B., Can. D5 101
Hillsborough, N.C., U.S. A3 140
Hillsborough, co., Fl., U.S. E4 116
Hillsborough, co., N.H., U.S. E3 136
Hillsborough, Cape, c., Austl. C8 70
Hillsborough Bay, b., P.E.I., Can. C6 101
Hillsborough Lower Village, N.H., U.S. D3 136
Hillsborough Upper Village, N.H., U.S. D3 136
Hillsburgh, Ont., Can. D4 103
Hills Creek Lake, res., Or., U.S. D4 144
Hillsdale, Ont., Can. C5 103
Hillsdale, Il., U.S. B3 120
Hillsdale, In., U.S. E3 121
Hillsdale, Ks., U.S. D9 123
Hillsdale, Mi., U.S. G6 129
Hillsdale, N.J., U.S. g8 137
Hillsdale, Wy., U.S. E8 157
Hillsdale, co., Mi., U.S. G6 129
Hillside, N.J., U.S. k8 137
Hillspring, Alta., Can. E4 98
Hillston, Austl. I6 70
Hillsville, Pa., U.S. D1 145
Hillsville, Va., U.S. D2 153
Hilltonia, Ga., U.S. D5 117
Hillview, Il., U.S. D3 120
Hilo, Hi., U.S. D6 118
Hilo Bay, b., Hi., U.S. D6 118
Hilton, N.Y., U.S. B3 139
Hilton Head Island, S.C., U.S. G6 147
Hilton Head Island, i., S.C., U.S. G6 147
Hilversum, Neth. D7 12
Hima, Ky., U.S. C6 124
Himāchal Pradesh, state, India E7 44
Himalayas, mts., Asia F11 44
Himeji, Japan M9 36
Himi, Japan K11 36
Himş (Homs), Syria D4 48
Hinche, Haiti E8 94
Hinchinbrook Island, i., Austl. B7 70
Hinchinbrook Island, i., Ak., U.S. g18 109
Hinch Mountain, mtn., Tn., U.S. D9 149
Hinckley, Il., U.S. B5 120
Hinckley, Me., U.S. D3 126
Hinckley, Mn., U.S. D6 130
Hinckley, Oh., U.S. A4 142
Hinckley, Ut., U.S. D3 151
Hinckley Reservoir, res., N.Y., U.S. B5 139
Hindaun, India G7 44
Hindman, Ky., U.S. C7 124
Hindmarsh, Lake, l., Austl. K4 70
Hinds, co., Ms., U.S. C3 131
Hindsboro, Il., U.S. D5 120
Hinds Lake, l., Newf., Can. D3 102
Hindu Kush, mts., Asia B4 44
Hindupur, India F4 46
Hines, Or., U.S. D7 144
Hinesburg, Vt., U.S. C2 152
Hines Creek, Alta., Can. A1 98
Hineston, La., U.S. C3 125
Hinesville, Ga., U.S. E5 117
Hinganghāt, India B5 46
Hingham, Ma., U.S. B6 128
Hingham, Mt., U.S. B6 133
Hingham Bay, b., Ma., U.S. g12 128
Hingol, stm., Pak. H1 44
Hingoli, India C4 46
Hınıs, Tur. B6 48
Hinkle, Ms., U.S. A5 131
Hinkley, Ca., U.S. E5 112
Hinnøya, i., Nor. G14 6
Hinojosa del Duque, Spain G6 16
Hinsdale, Il., U.S. k9 120
Hinsdale, Ma., U.S. B1 128
Hinsdale, Mt., U.S. B9 133
Hinsdale, N.H., U.S. E2 136
Hinsdale, N.Y., U.S. C2 139
Hinsdale, co., Co., U.S. D3 113
Hinterrhein, stm., Switz. E11 13
Hinton, Alta., Can. C2 98
Hinton, Ia., U.S. B1 122
Hinton, Ok., U.S. B3 143
Hinton, W.V., U.S. D4 155
Hipólito, Mex. E9 90
Hipólito Yrigoyen, Arg. G5 80
Hirado, Japan N4 36
Hīrākud Reservoir, res., India B7 46
Hiram, Ga., U.S. C2 117
Hiram, Me., U.S. E2 126
Hiram, Oh., U.S. A4 142
Hirata, Japan L7 36
Hiratsuka, Japan L14 36
Hirhafok, Alg. I13 62
Hirjillah, Syria B6 50
Hirosaki, Japan G15 36
Hiroshima, Japan M7 36
Hirson, Fr. C11 14
Hisār, India F7 44
Hisbān, Jord. E5 50
Hiseville, Ky., U.S. C4 124
Hişn al-Qarn, Yemen G6 47
Hispaniola, i., N.A. E9 94
Hita, Japan N5 36
Hitachi, Japan K15 36
Hitchcock, Sask., Can. H4 105
Hitchcock, S.D., U.S. C7 148
Hitchcock, Tx., U.S. r14 150
Hitchcock, co., Ne., U.S. D4 134
Hitchcock Lake, Ct., U.S. C4 114
Hitchins, Ky., U.S. B7 124
Hitoyoshi, Japan O5 36
Hitra, i., Nor. J11 6
Hiva Oa, i., Fr. Poly. I26 158
Hiwannee, Ms., U.S. D5 131
Hiwassee, stm., Tn., U.S. D9 149
Hiwassee Lake, res., N.C., U.S. f8 140
Hixon, B.C., Can. C6 99
Hixton, Wi., U.S. D3 156
Hkakabo Razi, mtn., Burma F6 30
Hkok (Kok), stm., Asia D5 40
Hlatikulu, Swaz. F10 66
Hlegu, Burma F4 40
Hlinsko, Czech. F15 10
Hlobane, S. Afr. F10 66
Hlohovec, Slov. G17 10
Hluboká nad Vltavou, Czech. F14 10
Hlučín, Czech. F18 10
Hmawbi, Burma F4 40
Ho, Ghana H10 64
Hoa Binh, Viet. D8 40
Hoagland, In., U.S. C8 121
Hoback, stm., Wy., U.S. C2 157
Hobart, Austl. N7 70
Hobart, In., U.S. A3 121
Hobart, Ok., U.S. B2 143
Hobbema, Alta., Can. C4 98
Hobbs, In., U.S. D6 121
Hobbs, N.M., U.S. E6 138
Hobe Sound, Fl., U.S. E6 116
Hobgood, N.C., U.S. A5 140
Hobo, Col. F5 84
Hoboken, Bel. F5 12
Hoboken, Ga., U.S. E4 117
Hoboken, N.J., U.S. k8 137
Hobson, Mt., U.S. D7 133
Hobucken, N.C., U.S. B6 140
Hobyo, Som. G10 56
Hochalmspitze, mtn., Aus. H13 10
Hochkönig, mtn., Aus. H13 10
Höchstadt an der Aisch, Ger. F10 10
Hockenheim, Ger. F8 10
Hockessin, De., U.S. A3 115
Hocking, co., Oh., U.S. C3 142
Hocking, stm., Oh., U.S. C3 142
Hockley, Tx., U.S. q14 150
Hockley, co., Tx., U.S. C1 150
Hodeida see Al-Ḩudaydah, Yemen G3 47
Hodgdon, Me., U.S. B5 126
Hodge, La., U.S. B3 125
Hodgeman, co., Ks., U.S. D4 123
Hodgen, Ok., U.S. C7 143
Hodgenville, Ky., U.S. C4 124
Hodges, Al., U.S. A2 108
Hodges Village Reservoir, res., Ma., U.S. B4 128
Hodgeville, Sask., Can. G2 105
Hodgson, Man., Can. D3 100
Hódmezővásárhely, Hung. I20 10
Hodna, Chott el, l., Alg. C13 62
Hodonín, Czech. G17 10
Hoehne, Co., U.S. D6 113
Hoek van Holland, Neth. E5 12
Hoeryŏng, N. Kor. A17 32
Hoey, Sask., Can. E3 105
Hoeyang, N. Kor. E15 32
Hof, Ger. E11 10
Hof, Ice. B6 6a
Hoffman, Mn., U.S. E3 130
Hoffman, N.C., U.S. B3 140
Hoffman Estates, Il., U.S. h8 120
Hofmeyr, S. Afr. H7 66
Höfn, Ice. B6 6a
Hofors, Swe. K15 6
Hōfu, Japan M6 36
Hofuf see Al-Hufūf, Sau. Ar. I10 48
Hogansville, Ga., U.S. C2 117
Hogback Mountain, mtn., Mt., U.S. F4 133
Hogback Mountain, mtn., Ne., U.S. C2 134
Hogback Mountain, mtn., S.C., U.S. A3 147
Hoggar see Ahaggar, mts., Alg. I13 62
Hog Island, i., Fl., U.S. C3 116
Hog Island, i., Mi., U.S. C5 129
Hog Island, i., N.C., U.S. B6 140
Hog Island, i., R.I., U.S. D5 146
Hog Island, i., Va., U.S. C7 153
Högsby, Swe. M15 6
Hogup Mountains, mts., Ut., U.S. B2 151
Hoh, stm., Wa., U.S. B1 154
Hohenau, Para. D11 80
Hohenau an der March, Aus. G16 10
Hohenlimburg, Ger. D7 10
Hohenthurn, Aus. I13 10
Hohenwald, Tn., U.S. B4 149
Hoher Dachstein, mtn., Aus. H13 10
Hohe Tauern, mts., Aus. H12 10
Hoh Head, c., Wa., U.S. B1 154
Hohhot, China C9 30
Hohoe, Ghana H10 64
Ho-Ho-Kus, N.J., U.S. h8 137
Hoh Xil Shan, mts., China C13 44
Hoi An, Viet. G10 40
Hoisington, Ks., U.S. D5 123
Hojāi, India G15 44
Hokah, Mn., U.S. G7 130
Hoke, co., N.C., U.S. B3 140
Hokes Bluff, Al., U.S. B4 108
Hokitika, N.Z. E3 72
Hokkaidō, i., Japan d17 36a
Holbrook, Austl. J7 70
Holbrook, Az., U.S. C5 110
Holbrook, Id., U.S. G6 119
Holbrook, Ma., U.S. B5 128
Holbrook, Ne., U.S. D5 134
Holcomb, Ks., U.S. E3 123
Holcomb, Ms., U.S. B4 131
Holcomb, Mo., U.S. E7 132
Holcombe, Wi., U.S. C2 156
Holden, Alta., Can. C4 98
Holden, La., U.S. g10 125
Holden, Ma., U.S. B4 128
Holden, Mo., U.S. C4 132
Holden, Ut., U.S. D3 151
Holden, W.V., U.S. D2 155
Holdenville, Ok., U.S. B5 143
Holder, Fl., U.S. D4 116
Holderness, N.H., U.S. C3 136
Holdfast, Sask., Can. G3 105
Holdingford, Mn., U.S. E4 130
Holdrege, Ne., U.S. D6 134
Hole in the Mountain Peak, mtn., Nv., U.S. C6 135
Holgate, Oh., U.S. A1 142
Holguín, Cuba D6 94
Holíč, Slov. G17 10
Hollabrunn, Aus. G16 10
Holladay, Ut., U.S. C4 151
Holland, Man., Can. E2 100
Holland, In., U.S. H3 121
Holland, Ia., U.S. B5 122
Holland, Ky., U.S. D3 124
Holland, Mi., U.S. F4 129
Holland, Mo., U.S. E8 132
Holland, Ne., U.S. D9 134
Holland, N.Y., U.S. C2 139
Holland, Oh., U.S. A2 142
Holland, Tx., U.S. D4 150
Hollandale, Ms., U.S. B3 131
Holland Centre, Ont., Can. C4 103
Holland Island, i., Md., U.S. D5 127
Holland see Netherlands, ctry., Eur. E9 4
Holland Point, c., Md., U.S. C4 127
Hollandsbird Island, i., S. Afr. E2 66
Hollandsch Diep, strt., Neth. E5 12
Holland Straits, strt., Md., U.S. D5 127
Holley, N.Y., U.S. B2 139
Holliday, Tx., U.S. C3 150
Hollidaysburg, Pa., U.S. F5 145
Hollins, Al., U.S. B3 108
Hollins, Va., U.S. C3 153
Hollis, N.H., U.S. E3 136
Hollis, Ok., U.S. C2 143
Hollis Center, Me., U.S. E2 126
Hollister, Ca., U.S. D3 112
Hollister, Id., U.S. G4 119
Hollister, Mo., U.S. E4 132
Hollister, N.C., U.S. A5 140
Holliston, Ma., U.S. B5 128
Holloman Air Force Base, mil., N.M., U.S. E3 138
Hollow Rock, Tn., U.S. A3 149
Hollowtop Mountain, mtn., Mt., U.S. E4 133
Hollsopple, Pa., U.S. F4 145
Holly, Co., U.S. C8 113
Holly, Mi., U.S. F7 129
Holly Bluff, Ms., U.S. C3 131
Holly Grove, Ar., U.S. C4 111
Holly Hill, Fl., U.S. C5 116
Holly Hill, S.C., U.S. E7 147
Holly Pond, Al., U.S. A3 108
Holly Ridge, N.C., U.S. C5 140
Holly Shelter Swamp, sw., N.C., U.S. C5 140
Holly Springs, Ga., U.S. B2 117
Holly Springs, Ms., U.S. A4 131
Holly Springs, N.C., U.S. B4 140
Hollywood, Al., U.S. A4 108
Hollywood, Az., U.S. E6 110
Hollywood (part of Los Angeles), Ca., U.S. m12 112
Hollywood, Fl., U.S. F6 116
Hollywood, Ga., U.S. B3 117
Hollywood, Md., U.S. D4 127
Hollywood, S.C., U.S. k11 147
Hollywood Indian Reservation, Fl., U.S. r3 116
Hollywood Park, Tx., U.S. h7 150
Holman, N.W. Ter., Can. B9 96
Holman, N.M., U.S. A4 138
Holmen, Wi., U.S. E2 156
Holmes, co., Fl., U.S. u16 116
Holmes, co., Ms., U.S. B3 131
Holmes, co., Oh., U.S. B4 142
Holmes, Mount, mtn., Wy., U.S. B2 157
Holmestrand, Nor. L12 6
Holmesville, Ne., U.S. D9 134
Holmia, Guy. E13 84
Holod, Rom. C6 20
Holoit, Punta, c., Mex. G15 90
Holon, Isr. D3 50
Holoog, Nmb. F3 66
Holstebro, Den. M11 6
Holstein, Ont., Can. C4 103
Holstein, Ia., U.S. B2 122
Holstein, Ne., U.S. D7 134
Holston, stm., Tn., U.S. C11 149
Holston, Middle Fork, stm., Va., U.S. f10 153
Holston High Knob, mtn., Tn., U.S. C11 149
Holt, Al., U.S. B2 108
Holt, Fl., U.S. u15 116
Holt, Mi., U.S. F6 129
Holt, Mo., U.S. B3 132
Holt, co., Mo., U.S. A2 132
Holt, co., Ne., U.S. B7 134
Holt Creek, stm., Ne., U.S. B6 134
Holt Knob, mtn., Tn., U.S. g10 149
Holt Lake, res., Al., U.S. B2 108
Holton, In., U.S. F7 121
Holton, Ks., U.S. C8 123
Holton, Mi., U.S. E4 129
Holtville, Al., U.S. C3 108
Holtville, Ca., U.S. F6 112
Holualoa, Hi., U.S. D6 118
Holy Cross, Ak., U.S. C8 109
Holy Cross, Ia., U.S. B7 122
Holy Cross, Mountain of the, mtn., Co., U.S. B4 113
Holyoke, Co., U.S. A8 113
Holyoke, Ma., U.S. B2 128
Holyoke Range, hills, Ma., U.S. B2 128
Holyrood, Ks., U.S. D5 123
Holy Trinity, Al., U.S. C4 108
Holzkirchen, Ger. H11 10
Holzminden, Ger. D9 10
Homalin, Burma B3 40
Homathko, stm., B.C., Can. D5 99
Homberg, Ger. D9 10
Hombori Tondo, mtn., Mali D9 64
Hombre Muerto, Salar del, pl., Arg. C5 80
Homburg, Ger. F7 10
Homburg see Bad Homburg vor der Höhe, Ger. E8 10
Home, Ks., U.S. C7 123
Home Corner, In., U.S. C6 121
Homecroft, In., U.S. m10 121
Homedale, Id., U.S. F2 119
Home Gardens, Ca., U.S. n14 112
Home Hill, Austl. B7 70
Homelake, Co., U.S. D4 113
Homeland, Fl., U.S. E5 116
Homeland, Ga., U.S. F4 117
Home Place, In., U.S. E5 121
Homer, Ak., U.S. D9 109
Homer, Ga., U.S. B3 117
Homer, Il., U.S. C6 120
Homer, In., U.S. E6 121
Homer, La., U.S. B2 125
Homer, Mi., U.S. F6 129
Homer, Ne., U.S. B9 134
Homer, N.Y., U.S. C4 139
Homer City, Pa., U.S. E3 145
Homerville, Ga., U.S. E4 117
Homer Youngs Peak, mtn., Mt., U.S. E3 133
Homestead, Fl., U.S. G6 116
Homestead, Ia., U.S. C6 122
Homestead, Pa., U.S. k14 145
Homestead Air Force Base, mil., Fl., U.S. G6 116
Homestead National Monument of America, Ne., U.S. D9 134
Homewood, Al., U.S. g7 108
Homewood, Ca., U.S. C3 112
Homewood, Il., U.S. B6 120
Homewood, Oh., U.S. C1 142
Hominy, Ok., U.S. A5 143
Hominy Creek, stm., Ok., U.S. A5 143
Homme Dam, N.D., U.S. A8 141
Homochitto, stm., Ms., U.S. D2 131
Homosassa, Fl., U.S. D4 116
Homs see Al-Khums, Libya B3 56
Homs see Himş, Syria D4 48
Honaker, Va., U.S. e10 153
Honan see Henan, prov., China E9 30
Honaunau, Hi., U.S. D6 118
Honaz, Tur. L13 20
Honda, Col. E5 84
Honda, Bahía, b., Col. A7 84
Hondeklipbaai, S. Afr. H3 66
Hondo, N.M., U.S. D4 138
Hondo, Tx., U.S. E3 150
Hondo, stm., N.A. H15 90
Hondo, Rio, stm., N.M., U.S. D4 138
Hondsrug, hills, Neth. C10 12
Honduras, ctry., N.A. B8 92
Honduras, Cabo de, c., Hond. A8 92
Honduras, Gulf of, b., N.A. E7 88
Honduras, Port, b., Belize A6 92
Honea Path, S.C., U.S. C3 147
Hønefoss, Nor. K12 6
Honeoye Falls, N.Y., U.S. C3 139
Honesdale, Pa., U.S. C11 145
Honey Brook, Pa., U.S. F10 145
Honey Creek, Wi., U.S. n11 156
Honey Grove, Tx., U.S. C5 150
Honey Lake, l., Ca., U.S. B3 112
Honeymoon Bay, B.C., Can. E5 99
Honeypot Glen, Ct., U.S. C4 114
Honeyville, Ut., U.S. B3 151
Honfleur, Fr. C7 14
Hon Gai, Viet. D9 40
Hong'an, China D3 34
Honga River, b., Md., U.S. D5 127
Hongch'ŏn, S. Kor. F15 32
Hongcun, China H5 34
Honghu, China F2 34
Hongjiang, China F8 30
Hong Kong, dep., Asia G9 30
Honglai, China J7 34
Hongliuyuan, China C6 30
Honglu, China J8 34
Hongmendu, China A7 40
Hong Ngu, Viet. I8 40
Hong see Red, stm., Asia C8 40
Hongshi, China B7 32
Hongshui, stm., China C10 40
Hongshuyangzi, China C4 32
Hongsŏng, S. Kor. G14 32
Hongtong, China D9 30
Hongwŏn, N. Kor. C15 32
Hongxingqiao, China E8 34
Hongyang, China L5 34
Hongze Hu, l., China B7 34
Honiara, Sol.Is. I19 158
Honobia, Ok., U.S. C7 143
Honokaa, Hi., U.S. C6 118
Honokahua, Hi., U.S. B5 118
Honokohau, Hi., U.S. D6 118
Honolulu, Hi., U.S. B4 118
Honolulu, co., Hi., U.S. B3 118
Honolulu International Airport, Hi., U.S. g10 118
Honomu, Hi., U.S. D6 118
Honouliuli, Hi., U.S. g9 118
Hon Quan, Viet. I9 40
Honshū, i., Japan K13 36
Honuapo Bay, b., Hi., U.S. D6 118
Hood, co., Tx., U.S. C4 150
Hood, Mount, mtn., Or., U.S. B5 144
Hood Canal, b., Wa., U.S. B2 154
Hoodoo Peak, mtn., Wa., U.S. A5 154
Hood Point, c., Austl. F3 68
Hood River, Or., U.S. B5 144
Hood River, co., Or., U.S. B5 144
Hoodsport, Wa., U.S. B2 154
Hoods Range, mts., Austl. G6 70
Hooker, Ok., U.S. e9 143
Hooker, co., Ne., U.S. C4 134
Hookerton, N.C., U.S. B5 140
Hookina, Austl. H3 70
Hook Island, i., Austl. C8 70
Hooks, Tx., U.S. C5 150
Hooksett, N.H., U.S. D4 136
Hoolehua, Hi., U.S. B4 118
Hoonah, Ak., U.S. D12 109
Hoopa Valley Indian Reservation, Ca., U.S. B2 112
Hooper, Co., U.S. D5 113
Hooper, Ne., U.S. C9 134
Hooper, Ut., U.S. B3 151
Hooper Bay, Ak., U.S. C6 109
Hooper Creek, stm., Ne., U.S. h12 134
Hooper Islands, is., Md., U.S. D5 127
Hooper Strait, strt., Md., U.S. D5 127
Hoopes Reservoir, res., De., U.S. A3 115
Hoopeston, Il., U.S. C6 120
Hoople, N.D., U.S. A8 141
Hoosac Range, mts., U.S. A1 128
Hoosic, stm., U.S. C7 139
Hoosick Falls, N.Y., U.S. C7 139
Hoosuc Range, mts., U.S. D1 126
Hoover, Al., U.S. B3 108
Hoover Dam, U.S. G7 135
Hoover Reservoir, res., Oh., U.S. B3 142
Hooverson Heights, W.V., U.S. f8 155
Hooversville, Pa., U.S. F4 145
Hopatcong, N.J., U.S. B3 137
Hopatcong, Lake, l., N.J., U.S. A3 137
Hope, B.C., Can. E7 99
Hope, Ak., U.S. C10 109
Hope, Ar., U.S. D2 111
Hope, In., U.S. F6 121
Hope, Ks., U.S. D6 123
Hope, Mn., U.S. G5 130
Hope, N.M., U.S. E5 138
Hope, N.D., U.S. B8 141
Hope, R.I., U.S. D3 146
Hope, Point, c., Ak., U.S. B6 109
Hopedale, Newf., Can. g9 102
Hopedale, Il., U.S. C4 120
Hopedale, La., U.S. E6 125
Hopedale, Ma., U.S. B4 128
Hopedale, Oh., U.S. B5 142
Hopefield, S. Afr. I4 66
Hope Hull, Al., U.S. C3 108
Hope Island, i., R.I., U.S. E5 146
Hopelchén, Mex. H15 90
Hope Mills, N.C., U.S. C4 140
Hopes Advance, Cap, c., Que., Can. f13 104
Hopetoun, Austl. F4 68
Hopetoun, Austl. J5 70
Hopetown, S. Afr. G7 66
Hope Valley, R.I., U.S. E2 146
Hopewell, N.S., Can. D7 101
Hopewell, N.J., U.S. C3 137
Hopewell, Oh., U.S. C3 142
Hopewell, Va., U.S. C5 153
Hopewell Cape, N.B., Can. D5 101
Hopewell Junction, N.Y., U.S. D7 139
Hopi Buttes, mtn., Az., U.S. B5 110
Hopi Indian Reservation, Az., U.S. A5 110
Hopkins, Mi., U.S. F5 129
Hopkins, Mn., U.S. n12 130
Hopkins, Mo., U.S. A3 132
Hopkins, S.C., U.S. D6 147
Hopkins, co., Ky., U.S. C2 124
Hopkins, co., Tx., U.S. C5 150
Hopkinsville, Ky., U.S. D2 124
Hopkinton, Ia., U.S. B6 122
Hopkinton, Ma., U.S. B4 128
Hopkinton, N.H., U.S. D3 136
Hopkinton, R.I., U.S. F1 146
Hopkinton Lake, res., N.H., U.S. D3 136
Hopland, Ca., U.S. C2 112

Name	Map Ref.	Page
Iaçu, Braz.	B8	79
Iaeger, W.V., U.S.	D3	155
Ialomiţa, co., Rom.	E11	20
Ialomiţa, stm., Rom.	E11	20
Iamonia, Lake, l., Fl., U.S.	B2	116
Ianakafy, Madag.	s21	67b
Iantha, Mo., U.S.	D3	132
Iapó, stm., Braz.	C13	80
Iapu, Braz.	E7	79
Iaşi, Rom.	B11	20
Iaşi, co., Rom.	B11	20
Iatt, Lake, res., La., U.S.	C3	125
Iauaretê, Braz.	G8	84
Ibadan, Nig.	H11	64
Ibagué, Col.	E5	84
Ibaiti, Braz.	G3	79
Ibans, Laguna de, b., Hond.	B10	92
Ibapah Peak, mtn., Ut., U.S.	D2	151
Ibarra, Ec.	G3	84
Ibarreta, Arg.	C9	80
Ibb, Yemen	G4	47
Ibbenbüren, Ger.	C7	10
Iberia, Mo., U.S.	C5	132
Iberia, co., La., U.S.	E4	125
Ibérica, Península, pen., Eur.	E6	52
Ibérico, Sistema, mts., Spain	D9	16
Iberville, Que., Can.	D4	104
Iberville, La., U.S.	D4	125
Iberville, co., La., U.S.	D4	125
Iberville, Mont d' (Mount Caubvick), mtn., Can.	g14	104
Ibeto, Nig.	F12	64
Ibiá, Braz.	E5	79
Ibicaraí, Braz.	C9	79
Ibiçuí, Braz.	C9	79
Ibicuí, stm., Braz.	E10	80
Ibicuy, Arg.	G9	80
Ibiquera, Braz.	B8	79
Ibiraci, Braz.	F5	79
Ibiraçu, Braz.	E8	79
Ibirama, Braz.	D14	80
Ibirapuã, Braz.	D8	79
Ibirapuitã, stm., Braz.	F11	80
Ibirataia, Braz.	C9	79
Ibirubá, Braz.	E12	80
Ibitiara, Braz.	B7	79
Ibitinga, Braz.	F4	79
Ibo, Moz.	D8	58
Ibotirama, Braz.	B7	79
ʿIbrī, Oman	C10	47
Ibshawāy, Egypt	C6	60
Ibusuki, Japan	P5	36
Ica, Peru	F4	82
Ica, dept., Peru	F4	82
Ica, stm., Peru	F4	82
Içá (Putumayo), stm., S.A.	I8	84
Icabarú, stm., Ven.	E11	84
Icamaquã, stm., Braz.	E11	80
Içana, Braz.	G9	84
Içana (Isana), stm., S.A.	G9	84
Icaño, Arg.	E6	80
Icaño, Arg.	E7	80
Ice Harbor Dam, Wa., U.S.	C7	154
İçel, Tur.	C3	48
Iceland (Ísland), ctry., Eur.	B4	4
Icém, Braz.	F4	79
Ichaikaronji, India	D3	46
Ichikawa, Japan	L14	36
Ichilo, stm., Bol.	G9	82
Ichinomiya, Japan	L11	36
Ichinoseki, Japan	I16	36
Ichkeul, Lac, l., Tun.	L4	18
Ichoa, stm., Bol.	F9	82
Ichoca, Bol.	G8	82
Ich'on, N. Kor.	E14	32
Ich'ŏn, S. Kor.	F15	32
Icicle Creek, stm., Wa., U.S.	B5	154
Ičinskaja Sopka, vulkan, vol., Russia	F23	28
Icó, Braz.	E11	76
Iconha, Braz.	F8	79
Icy Cape, c., Ak., U.S.	A7	109
Icy Strait, strt., Ak., U.S.	k22	109
Ida, La., U.S.	A2	125
Ida, Mi., U.S.	G7	129
Ida, co., Ia., U.S.	B2	122
Ida, Lake, l., Mn., U.S.	D3	130
Idabel, Ok., U.S.	D7	143
Ida Grove, Ia., U.S.	B2	122
Idah, Nig.	H13	64
Idaho, co., Id., U.S.	D3	119
Idaho, state, U.S.	E3	119
Idaho City, Id., U.S.	F3	119
Idaho Falls, Id., U.S.	F6	119
Idaho Springs, Co., U.S.	B5	113
Idalia, Co., U.S.	B8	113
Idalou, Tx., U.S.	C2	150
Idamay, W.V., U.S.	k10	155
Idana, Ks., U.S.	C6	123
Idanha, Or., U.S.	C4	144
Idanre, Nig.	H12	64
Idāppādi, India	G4	46
Idar-Oberstein, Ger.	F7	10
Idaville, In., U.S.	C4	121
Ideal, Ga., U.S.	D2	117
Idelès, Alg.	I13	62
Ider, Al., U.S.	A4	108
Idfū, Egypt	E7	60
Ídhi Óros, mtn., Grc.	N8	20
Ídhra, i., Grc.	L7	20
Idi, Indon.	L4	40
Idiofa, Zaire	C3	58
Idlewild, Tn., U.S.	A3	149
Idleyld Park, Or., U.S.	D3	144
Idlib, Syria	D4	48
Idre, Swe.	K13	6
Idrica, Russia	E11	22
Idrija, Slo.	C9	18
Idutywa, Transkei	I9	66
Iecava, Lat.	E7	22
Iepê, Braz.	G3	79
Ieper (Ypres), Bel.	G2	12
Ierisós, Grc.	I7	20
Ife, Nig.	H12	64
Iferouâne, Niger	B14	64
Ifni, hist. reg., Mor.	F5	62
Ifôghas, Adrar des, mts., Afr.	E7	54
Ifon-Oshogbo, Nig.	H12	64
Igal, Hung.	I17	10
Iganna, Nig.	H11	64
Igaporã, Braz.	B7	79
Igara Paraná, stm., Col.	H6	84
Igarka, Russia	D9	28
Igbasa-Odo, Nig.	H11	64
Iğdır, Tur.	B8	48
Igharghar, Oued, val., Afr.	J14	62
Igizyar, China	A7	44
Iglesia, Arg.	F4	80
Iglesias, Italy	J3	18
Igli, Alg.	E9	62
Igloolik, N.W. Ter., Can.	C16	96
Ignacej, Mol.	B12	20
Ignacio, Co., U.S.	D3	113
Ignacio Zaragoza, Mex.	C6	90
Ignalina, Lith.	F9	22
İğneada, Tur.	H11	20
Iguaçu, stm., S.A.	C12	80
Iguaçu, Cataratas do (Iguassu Falls), wtfl, S.A.	C11	80
Iguaí, Braz.	C8	79
Iguala, Mex.	H10	90
Igualada, Spain	D13	16
Iguana, stm., Ven.	C10	84
Iguape, Braz.	C15	80
Iguassu Falls see Iguaçu, Cataratas 99do, wtfl, S.A.	C11	80
Iguatemi, Braz.	G1	79
Iguatemi, stm., Braz.	G1	79
Iguatu, Braz.	E11	76
Iguazú, Parque Nacional, S.A.	C11	80
Iguéla, Gabon	B1	58
Iguîdi, 'Erg, dunes, Afr.	C5	54
Igžej, Russia	G12	28
Iheya-shima, i., Japan	t2	37b
Ihiala, Nig.	I13	64
Ihosy, Madag.	s22	67b
Ihtiman, Bul.	G7	20
Iida, Japan	L12	36
Iisaku, Est.	B10	22
Ii-shima, i., Japan	F12	30
Iiyama, Japan	K13	36
Iizuka, Japan	N5	36
Ijâfene, des., Afr.	D5	54
Ijaji, Eth.	M9	60
Ijebu-Igbo, Nig.	H12	64
IJmuiden, Neth.	D6	12
IJssel, stm., Neth.	C8	12
IJsselmeer (Zuiderzee), Neth.	C7	12
IJsselstein, Neth.	D7	12
Ijuí, Braz.	E12	80
Ijuí, stm., Braz.	E11	80
Ikalamavony, Madag.	r22	67b
Ikang, Nig.	I14	64
Ikaría, i., Grc.	L10	20
Ikeja, Nig.	H11	64
Ikela, Zaire	B4	58
Ikirun, Nig.	H12	64
Ikot Ekpene, Nig.	I13	64
Ikša, Russia	E20	22
Ila, Ga., U.S.	B3	117
Ilabaya, Peru	G6	82
Ilagan, Phil.	m19	39b
Ilaka, Madag.	q23	67b
Īlām, Iran	E9	48
Ilām, Nepal	G12	44
Ilan, Tai.	K10	34
Ilanskij, Russia	F17	26
Ilanz, Switz.	E11	13
Ilaro, Nig.	H11	64
Iława, Pol.	B19	10
Ilbenge, Russia	E16	28
Ilchester, Md., U.S.	B4	127
Ilderton, Ont., Can.	D3	103
Île-à-la-Crosse, Sask., Can.	m7	105
Île-à-la-Crosse, Lac, l., Sask., Can.	B2	105
Ilebo, Zaire	B4	58
Île-de-France, hist. reg., Fr.	C9	14
Ilek, stm., Asia	G8	26
Île-Perrot, Que., Can.	q19	104
Ilesha, Nig.	H12	64
Ilesha Ibarida, Nig.	G11	64
Ilford, Man., Can.	A4	100
Ilfov, co., Rom.	E10	20
Ilfracombe, Austl.	D6	70
Ilhabela, Braz.	G6	79
Ilha Grande, Baía da, b., Braz.	G6	79
Ilha Solteira, Reprêsa de, res., Braz.	F3	79
Ilhéus, Braz.	C9	79
Ili, stm., Asia	H12	26
Iliamna Lake, l., Ak., U.S.	D8	109
Iliamna Volcano, vol., Ak., U.S.	C9	109
Ilicínia, Braz.	F6	79
Iliff, Co., U.S.	A7	113
Iligan, Phil.	D7	38
Ilimsk, Russia	F12	28
Ilinza, mtn., Ec.	H3	84
Ilion, N.Y., U.S.	B5	139
Ilio Point, c., Hi., U.S.	B4	118
Ilizi, Alg.	G15	62
Iljinskij, Russia	K23	6
Iljinskij, Russia	H20	28
Iljinskoje, Russia	E20	22
Iljinskoje, Russia	D21	22
Iljinskoje-Chovanskoje, Russia	E22	22
Ilkal, India	E4	46
Il'kino, Russia	F24	22
Illampu, Nevado, mtn., Bol.	F7	82
Illapel, Chile	F3	80
Ille-et-Vilaine, dept., Fr.	D5	14
Illéla, Niger	D12	64
Iller, stm., Ger.	H10	10
Illescas, Mex.	F8	90
Illescas, Spain	E8	16
Illiers, Fr.	D8	14
Illimani, Nevado, mtn., Bol.	G8	82
Illimo, Peru	B2	82
Illinois, state, U.S.	C4	120
Illinois, stm., U.S.	A7	143
Illinois, stm., Il., U.S.	B5	120
Illinois, stm., Or., U.S.	E3	144
Illinois City, Il., U.S.	B3	120
Illinois Peak, mtn., Id., U.S.	B3	119
Illiopolis, Il., U.S.	D4	120
Illmo, Mo., U.S.	D8	132
Il'men', ozero, l., Russia	C14	22
Ilmenau, Ger.	E10	10
Ilo, Peru	G6	82
Ilobasco, El Sal.	D6	92
Iloilo, Phil.	C7	38
Ilopango, Lago de, l., El Sal.	D5	92
Ilora, Nig.	H11	64
Ilorin, Nig.	G12	64
Ilūkste, Lat.	F9	22
Ilwaco, Wa., U.S.	C1	154
Ilwaki, Indon.	G8	38
Imabari, Japan	M8	36
Imabu, stm., Braz.	H14	84
Imandra, ozero, l., Russia	H23	6
Imari, Japan	N4	36
Imaruí, Braz.	E14	80
Imaruí, Lagoa do, b., Braz.	E14	80
Imatra, Fin.	K21	6
Imbabura, prov., Ec.	G3	84
Imbituba, Braz.	E14	80
Imbituva, Braz.	C13	80
Imbler, Or., U.S.	B9	144
Imboden, Ar., U.S.	A4	111
Imeni Babuškina, Russia	B26	22
Imeni 0206 Bakinskich Komissarov, Azer.	B10	48
Imeni C'urupy, Russia	F21	22
Imeni Vorovskogo, Russia	F24	22
Imeni Žel'abova, Russia	C19	22
Imerimandroso, Madag.	p23	67b
Imi, Eth.	G9	56
Imías, Cuba	D7	94
Imilac, Chile	C4	80
Imi-n'Tanout, Mor.	E6	62
Imišli, Azer.	B10	48
Imjin-gang, stm., Asia	F14	32
Imlay, Nv., U.S.	C3	135
Imlay City, Mi., U.S.	E7	129
Immingham Dock, Eng., U.K.	H13	8
Immokalee, Fl., U.S.	F5	116
Imnaha, stm., Or., U.S.	B10	144
Imola, Italy	E6	18
Imotski, Cro.	F12	18
Imperatriz, Braz.	E9	76
Imperia, Italy	F3	18
Imperial, Sask., Can.	F3	105
Imperial, Peru	E3	82
Imperial, Ca., U.S.	F6	112
Imperial, Mo., U.S.	C7	132
Imperial, Ne., U.S.	D4	134
Imperial, Pa., U.S.	k13	145
Imperial, Tx., U.S.	D1	150
Imperial, co., Ca., U.S.	F6	112
Imperial, stm., Chile	J2	80
Imperial Beach, Ca., U.S.	o15	112
Imperial Dam, U.S.	E1	110
Imperial Mills, Alta., Can.	B5	98
Imperial Reservoir, res., U.S.	E1	110
Imperial Valley, val., Ca., U.S.	F6	112
Impfondo, Congo	A3	58
Imphāl, India	H15	44
Impilachti, Russia	K22	6
Imsil, S. Kor.	H15	32
Imuris, Mex.	B4	90
Ina, Japan	L12	36
Ina, Il., U.S.	E5	120
Inambari, stm., Peru	E7	82
In Amguel, Alg.	I13	62
In Amnas, Alg.	F15	62
Iñapari, Peru	D7	82
In'aptuk, gora, mtn., Russia	F14	28
Inari, Fin.	G20	6
Inarijärvi, l., Fin.	G20	6
Inauini, stm., Braz.	C8	82
Inavale, Ne., U.S.	D7	134
Inawashiro-ko, l., Japan	J15	36
In Belbel, Alg.	G11	62
Inca, Spain	F14	16
Inca de Oro, Chile	D4	80
Incaguasi, Chile	E3	80
İncesu, Tur.	B3	48
Inchelium, Wa., U.S.	A7	154
Inch'ŏn, S. Kor.	F14	32
Incline Village, Nv., U.S.	D2	135
Incomáti (Komati), stm., Afr.	E11	66
Indaiá, stm., Braz.	E6	79
Inda Silase, Eth.	J10	60
Indaw, Burma	C3	40
Indé, Mex.	E7	90
Independence, Ca., U.S.	D4	112
Independence, In., U.S.	D3	121
Independence, Ia., U.S.	B6	122
Independence, Ks., U.S.	E8	123
Independence, Ky., U.S.	B5	124
Independence, La., U.S.	D5	125
Independence, Ms., U.S.	A4	131
Independence, Mo., U.S.	B3	132
Independence, Or., U.S.	C3	144
Independence, Va., U.S.	D1	153
Independence, Wi., U.S.	D2	156
Independence, co., Ar., U.S.	B4	111
Independence, stm., N.Y., U.S.	B5	139
Independence Mountains, mts., Nv., U.S.	C5	135
Independence National Historical Park, Pa., U.S.	p21	145
Independence Rock, mtn., Wy., U.S.	D5	157
Independencia, Bol.	G8	82
Independencia, Isla, i., Peru	F3	82
India (Bhārat), ctry., Asia	E10	42
Indiahoma, Ok., U.S.	C3	143
Indian, stm., Ont., Can.	B7	103
Indian, stm., De., U.S.	F4	115
Indian, stm., Mi., U.S.	B4	129
Indian, stm., N.Y., U.S.	A5	139
Indiana, Pa., U.S.	E3	145
Indiana, co., Pa., U.S.	E3	145
Indiana, state, U.S.	E5	121
Indiana Dunes National Lakeshore, In., U.S.	A3	121
Indianapolis, In., U.S.	E5	121
Indian Bay, b., Fl., U.S.	D4	116
Indian Brook, N.S., Can.	C9	101
Indian Cedar Swamp, sw., R.I., U.S.	F2	146
Indian Church, Belize	I15	90
Indian Creek, stm., In., U.S.	H5	121
Indian Creek, stm., Md., U.S.	C4	127
Indian Creek, stm., Oh., U.S.	C1	142
Indian Creek, stm., S.D., U.S.	B2	148
Indian Creek, stm., Tn., U.S.	B3	149
Indian Creek, stm., W.V., U.S.	k9	155
Indian Creek, stm., W.V., U.S.	D4	155
Indian Grave Mountain, hill, Ga., U.S.	C2	117
Indian Head, Sask., Can.	G4	105
Indian Head, Md., U.S.	C3	127
Indian Island, i., N.C., U.S.	B6	140
Indian Lake, l., Mi., U.S.	C4	129
Indian Lake, l., N.Y., U.S.	B6	139
Indian Lake, l., Oh., U.S.	B2	142
Indian Lake, l., R.I., U.S.	F4	146
Indian Mound, Tn., U.S.	A4	149
Indian Mound Beach, Ma., U.S.	*C6	128
Indian Mountain, mtn., Ct., U.S.	B2	114
Indian Neck, Ct., U.S.	D4	114
Indian Ocean	J11	158
Indianola, Il., U.S.	D6	120
Indianola, Ia., U.S.	C4	122
Indianola, Ms., U.S.	B3	131
Indianola, Ne., U.S.	D5	134
Indianópolis, Braz.	E5	79
Indian Peak, mtn., Ut., U.S.	E2	151
Indian Peak, mtn., Wy., U.S.	B3	157
Indian Pond, l., Me., U.S.	B3	126
Indian Pond, l., Me., U.S.	C3	126
Indian Pond, l., Me., U.S.	D3	126
Indian Prairie Canal, Fl., U.S.	E5	116
Indian River, Ont., Can.	C6	103
Indian River, Mi., U.S.	C6	129
Indian River, co., Fl., U.S.	E6	116
Indian River, b., Fl., U.S.	D6	116
Indian River Bay, b., De., U.S.	F5	115
Indian Rock, mtn., Wa., U.S.	D5	154
Indian Rocks Beach, Fl., U.S.	p10	116
Indian Springs, Ga., U.S.	C3	117
Indian Springs, Nv., U.S.	G6	135
Indian Stream, stm., N.H., U.S.	f7	136
Indiantown, Fl., U.S.	E6	116
Indian Trail, N.C., U.S.	B2	140
Indian Village, Ks., U.S.	E8	123
Indian Village, La., U.S.	D3	125
Indiaporã, Braz.	E3	79
Indibir, Eth.	M9	60
Indigirka, stm., Russia	D21	28
Indio, Ca., U.S.	F5	112
Indio, stm., Nic.	F10	92
Indio, stm., Pan.	H14	92
Indira Gandhi Canal, India	F5	44
Indispensable Reefs, rf., Sol.Is.	B12	68
Indochina, reg., Asia	H11	24
Indonesia, ctry., Asia	G7	38
Indore, India	I6	44
Indragiri, stm., Indon.	O7	40
Indrāvati, stm., India	C6	46
Indre, dept., Fr.	F8	14
Indre-et-Loire, dept., Fr.	E7	14
Indrio, Fl., U.S.	E6	116
Indura, Bela.	H6	22
Indus, stm., Asia	H2	44
Industry, Il., U.S.	C3	120
Indwe, S. Afr.	H8	66
İnece, Tur.	H11	20
In Ecker, Alg.	H13	62
İnegöl, Tur.	I13	20
Inez, Ky., U.S.	C7	124
Inez, Tx., U.S.	E4	150
Inferior, Laguna, b., Mex.	I12	90
Infiernillo, Presa del, res., Mex.	H9	90
Ingal, Niger	C13	64
Ingalls, In., U.S.	E6	121
Ingalls, Ks., U.S.	E3	123
Ingalls Park, Il., U.S.	B5	120
Ingelheim, Ger.	F8	10
Ingelmunster, Bel.	G3	12
Ingende, Zaire	B3	58
Ingeniero Luiggi, Arg.	H6	80
Ingeniero Luis A. Huergo, Arg.	J5	80
Ingeniero White, Arg.	J7	80
Ingenio La Esperanza, Arg.	C6	80
Ingenio Santa Ana, Arg.	D6	80
Ingersoll, Ont., Can.	D4	103
Ingham, Austl.	B7	70
Ingham, co., Mi., U.S.	F6	129
Ingleside, Tx., U.S.	F4	150
Inglewood, Austl.	G9	70
Inglewood, Ca., U.S.	n12	112
Inglewood, Ne., U.S.	C9	134
Inglis, Man., Can.	D1	100
Ingoda, stm., Russia	G14	28
Ingoldsby, Ont., Can.	C6	103
Ingolstadt, Ger.	G11	10
Ingomar, Ms., U.S.	A4	131
Ingonish, N.S., Can.	C9	101
Ingonish Beach, N.S., Can.	C9	101
Ingraham, Lake, l., Fl., U.S.	G5	116
Ingrāj Bāzār, India	H13	44
Ingram, Pa., U.S.	k13	145
Ingram, Tx., U.S.	D3	150
In Guezzam, Alg.	B12	64
Ingwiller, Fr.	D14	14
Inhaca, Ilha da, i., Moz.	F11	66
Inhafenga, Moz.	C11	66
Inhambane, Moz.	D12	66
Inhambupe, Braz.	A9	79
Inhaminga, Moz.	B12	66
Inhanduí, stm., Braz.	F1	79
Inhapim, Braz.	E7	79
Inharrime, Moz.	E12	66
Inhaúma, Braz.	E6	79
Inhumas, Braz.	D4	79
Inimutaba, Braz.	E6	79
Inírida, stm., Col.	F8	84
Inisa, Nig.	H12	64
Inishmore, i., Ire.	H4	8
Injibara, Eth.	L9	60
Injune, Austl.	E8	70
Inkerman, N.B., Can.	B5	101
Inkom, Id., U.S.	G6	119
Inkster, Mi., U.S.	p15	129
Inkster, N.D., U.S.	A8	141
Inland Sea see Seto-naikai, Japan	M7	36
Inle Lake, l., Burma	D4	40
Inman, Ga., U.S.	C2	117
Inman, Ks., U.S.	D6	123
Inman, Ne., U.S.	B7	134
Inman, S.C., U.S.	A3	147
Inn (En), stm., Eur.	D20	14
Innamincka, Austl.	F4	70
Inner Channel, strt., Belize	I15	90
Inner Hebrides, is., Scot., U.K.	E7	8
Inner Mongolia see Nei Monggol Zizhiqu, prov., China	C10	30
Innertkirchen, Switz.	E9	13
Innisfail, Austl.	A7	70
Innisfail, Alta., Can.	C4	98
Innisfree, Alta., Can.	C5	98
Innsbruck, Aus.	H11	10
Innviertel, reg., Aus.	G13	10
Inocência, Braz.	E3	79
Inola, Ok., U.S.	A6	143
Inongo, Zaire	B3	58
Inowrocław, Pol.	C18	10
In Rhar, Alg.	G11	62
In Salah, Alg.	G12	62
Inscription House Ruin, hist., Az., U.S.	A5	110
Ińsko, Pol.	B15	10
Institute, W.V., U.S.	m12	155
Inta, Russia	D10	26
Intendente Alvear, Arg.	H7	80
İntepe, Tur.	I10	20
Intercession City, Fl., U.S.	D5	116
Interlachen, Fl., U.S.	C5	116
Interlaken, Switz.	E8	13
Interlândia, Braz.	D4	79
International Falls, Mn., U.S.	B5	130
Intervale, N.H., U.S.	B4	136
Inthanon, Doi, mtn., Thai.	E5	40
Intibucá, Hond.	C6	92
Intibucá, dept., Hond.	C6	92
Intipucá, El Sal.	D6	92
Intiyaco, Arg.	E8	80
Intracoastal Waterway, U.S.	E4	125
Intuto, Peru	I5	84
Inukjuak, Que., Can.	g11	104
Inuvik, N.W. Ter., Can.	C6	96
Inuya, stm., Peru	D5	82
Invercargill, N.Z.	G2	72
Inverell, Austl.	G9	70
Invergordon, Scot., U.K.	D9	8
Inver Grove Heights, Mn., U.S.	n12	130
Invermay, Sask., Can.	F4	105
Invermere, B.C., Can.	D9	99
Inverness, Que., Can.	C6	104
Inverness, Scot., U.K.	D9	8
Inverness, Ca., U.S.	C2	112
Inverness, Fl., U.S.	D4	116
Inverness, Ms., U.S.	B3	131
Inverness, Mt., U.S.	B6	133
Investigator Group, is., Austl.	F6	68
Investigator Strait, strt., Austl.	J2	70
Invisible Mountain, mtn., Id., U.S.	F5	119
Inwood, Man., Can.	D3	100
Inwood, Ont., Can.	E3	103
Inwood, In., U.S.	B5	121
Inwood, Ia., U.S.	A1	122
Inwood, N.Y., U.S.	k13	139
Inwood, W.V., U.S.	B6	155
Inyangani, mtn., Zimb.	B11	66
Inyan Kara Creek, stm., Wy., U.S.	B8	157
Inyan Kara Mountain, mtn., Wy., U.S.	B8	157
Inyantue, Zimb.	B8	66
Inyati, Zimb.	B9	66
Inyo, co., Ca., U.S.	D5	112
Inyo, Mount, mtn., Ca., U.S.	D5	112
Inyo Mountains, mts., Ca., U.S.	D4	112
Inywa, Burma	C4	40
Inza, Russia	G7	26
Inzana Lake, l., B.C., Can.	B5	99
Inžavino, Russia	I25	22
Ioánnina, Grc.	J4	20
Iō-jima (Iwo Jima), i., Japan	F18	158
Iola, Ks., U.S.	E8	123
Iola, Wi., U.S.	D4	156
Iolotan', Turk.	J10	26
Iona, N.S., Can.	D9	101
Iona, Id., U.S.	F7	119
Iona, Mn., U.S.	G3	130
Ione, Ca., U.S.	C3	112
Ione, Or., U.S.	B7	144
Ione, Wa., U.S.	A8	154
Ionia, Ia., U.S.	A5	122
Ionia, Mi., U.S.	F5	129
Ionia, co., Mi., U.S.	F5	129
Ionian Islands see Iónioi Nísoi, is., Grc.	K4	20
Ionian Sea, Eur.	H11	4
Iónioi Nísoi, is., Grc.	K4	20
Íos, i., Grc.	M9	20
Iosco, co., Mi., U.S.	D7	129
Iosegun, stm., Alta., Can.	B2	98
Iota, La., U.S.	D3	125
Iowa, La., U.S.	D2	125
Iowa, co., Ia., U.S.	C5	122
Iowa, co., Wi., U.S.	E3	156
Iowa, state, U.S.	C4	122
Iowa, stm., Ia., U.S.	C6	122
Iowa, West Branch, stm., Ia., U.S.	B4	122
Iowa City, Ia., U.S.	C6	122
Iowa Falls, Ia., U.S.	B4	122
Iowa Indian Reservation, U.S.	C8	123
Iowa Lake, l., U.S.	A3	122
Iowa Park, Tx., U.S.	C3	150
Ipameri, Braz.	D4	79
Ipatinga, Braz.	E7	79
Ipava, Il., U.S.	C3	120
Ípeiros, hist. reg., Grc.	J4	20
Ipel' (Ipoly), stm., Eur.	G19	10
Iphigenia Bay, b., Ak., U.S.	n22	109
Ipiales, Col.	G4	84
Ipiaú, Braz.	C9	79
Ipirá, Braz.	B9	79
Ipiranga, Braz.	C13	80
Ipita, Bol.	H10	82
Ipixuna, stm., Braz.	B5	82
Ipixuna, stm., Braz.	B10	82
Ipixuna, stm., Braz.	B10	82
Ipoh, Malay.	L6	40
Ipoly (Ipel'), stm., Eur.	G18	10
Iporá, Braz.	D3	79
Iporã, Braz.	G2	79
Ipoti-Ekiti, Nig.	H12	64
Ipswich, Austl.	F10	70
Ipswich, Eng., U.K.	I15	8
Ipswich, Ma., U.S.	A6	128
Ipswich, S.D., U.S.	B6	148
Ipswich, stm., Ma., U.S.	A5	128
Ipu, Braz.	D10	76
Ipupiara, Braz.	A7	79
Iqaluit, N.W. Ter., Can.	D19	96
Iquique, Chile	G7	74
Iquique, Chile	I6	82
Iquitos, Peru	I6	84
Iraan, Tx., U.S.	D2	150
Iracajá, Cachoeira do, wtfl, Braz.	D9	82
Iraí, Braz.	D12	80
Iráklion, Grc.	N9	20
Iran (Īrān), ctry., Asia	C5	42
Iran, Pegunungan, mts., Asia	E5	38
Īrānshahr, Iran	H16	48
Irapa, Ven.	B11	84
Irapuato, Mex.	G9	90
Iraq (Al-ʿIrāq), ctry., Asia	C3	42
Irará, Braz.	B9	79
Irasburg, Vt., U.S.	B4	152
Irati, Braz.	C13	80
Irazú, Volcán, vol., C.R.	H11	92
Irbeni väin (Irbes jūras šaurums), strt., Eur.	D5	22
Irbes jūras šaurums (Irbeni väin), strt., Eur.	D5	22
Irbid, Jord.	C5	50
Irbīl, Iraq	C8	48
Irbit, Russia	F10	26
Iredell, co., N.C., U.S.	B2	140
Ireland, In., U.S.	H3	121
Ireland (Éire), ctry., Eur.	E6	4
Irene, S. Afr.	E9	66
Irene, S.D., U.S.	D8	148
Ireng (Maú), stm., S.A.	E13	84
Ireton, Ia., U.S.	B1	122
Irgiz, Kaz.	H10	26
Iri, S. Kor.	H14	32
Iriba, Chad	J2	60
Irîgui, reg., Afr.	C7	64
Iringa, Tan.	C7	58
Irion, co., Tx., U.S.	D2	150
Iriona, Hond.	B9	92
Iriri, stm., Braz.	D8	76
Irish, Mount, mtn., Nv., U.S.	F6	135
Irish Sea, Eur.	H8	8
Irkutsk, Russia	G12	28
Irma, Alta., Can.	C5	98
Irmo, S.C., U.S.	C5	147
Iron, co., Mi., U.S.	B2	129
Iron, co., Mo., U.S.	D7	132
Iron, co., Ut., U.S.	F2	151
Iron, co., Wi., U.S.	B3	156
Iron Belt, Wi., U.S.	B3	156
Iron City, Ga., U.S.	E2	117
Iron City, Tn., U.S.	B4	149
Irondale, Al., U.S.	f7	108
Irondale, Mo., U.S.	D7	132
Irondequoit, N.Y., U.S.	B3	139
Iron Gate, Va., U.S.	C3	153
Iron Gate, val., Eur.	E6	20
Iron Gate Reservoir, res., Eur.	E6	20
Iron Gate Reservoir, res., Ca., U.S.	B2	112
Ironia, N.J., U.S.	B3	137
Iron Knob, Austl.	I2	70
Iron Mountain, Mi., U.S.	C2	129
Iron Mountain, Mo., U.S.	D7	132
Iron Mountain, mtn., Az., U.S.	D4	110
Iron Mountains, mts., U.S.	D1	153
Iron Range, Austl.	B8	68
Iron Ridge, Wi., U.S.	E5	156
Iron River, Mi., U.S.	B2	129
Iron River, Wi., U.S.	B2	156
Ironton, Mn., U.S.	D5	130
Ironton, Mo., U.S.	D7	132
Ironton, Oh., U.S.	D3	142
Ironwood, Mi., U.S.	n11	129
Iroquois, Ont., Can.	C9	103
Iroquois, S.D., U.S.	C8	148
Iroquois, co., Il., U.S.	C6	120
Iroquois, stm., U.S.	C6	120
Iroquois, Lake, l., Vt., U.S.	B2	152
Iroquois Falls, Ont., Can.	o19	103
Irrawaddy see Ayeyarwady, stm., Burma	F3	40
Irricana, Alta., Can.	D4	98
Irrigon, Or., U.S.	B7	144
Iršava, Ukr.	A7	20
Irtyš (Ertix), stm., Asia	E11	26
Irtyš (Ertix), stm., Asia	A3	30
Irtyšsk, Kaz.	G13	26
Irumu, Zaire	A5	58
Irún, Spain	B10	16
Irupana, Bol.	G8	82
Irurzun, Spain	C10	16
Irú Tepuy, mtn., Ven.	E12	84
Irvine, Alta., Can.	E5	98
Irvine, Scot., U.K.	F9	8
Irvine, Ca., U.S.	n13	112
Irvine, Ky., U.S.	C6	124
Irving, Il., U.S.	D4	120
Irving, Tx., U.S.	n10	150
Irvington, Al., U.S.	E1	108
Irvington, Il., U.S.	E4	120
Irvington, Ky., U.S.	C3	124
Irvington, Ne., U.S.	g12	134
Irvington, N.J., U.S.	k8	137
Irvington, N.Y., U.S.	g13	139
Irvington, Va., U.S.	C6	153
Irvona, Pa., U.S.	E4	145
Irwin, Id., U.S.	F7	119
Irwin, Ia., U.S.	C2	122
Irwin, Pa., U.S.	F2	145
Irwin, co., Ga., U.S.	E3	117
Irwinton, Ga., U.S.	D3	117
Irwinville, Ga., U.S.	E3	117
Isaac, stm., Austl.	D8	70
Isaac Lake, l., B.C., Can.	C7	99
Isabel, Ks., U.S.	E5	123
Isabel, S.D., U.S.	B4	148
Isabel, Mount, mtn., Wy., U.S.	D2	157
Isabela, Phil.	D7	38
Isabela, Cabo, c., Dom. Rep.	E9	94
Isabela, Isla, i., Mex.	G7	90
Isabelia, Cordillera, mts., Nic.	D9	92
Isabella, Ga., U.S.	E3	117
Isabella, Mo., U.S.	E5	132
Isabella, Tn., U.S.	D9	149
Isabella, co., Mi., U.S.	E6	129
Isabella Indian Reservation, Mi., U.S.	E6	129

Name | Map Ref. | Page

Jay, Me., U.S. D2 126
Jay, Ok., U.S. A7 143
Jay, co., In., U.S. D7 121
Jaya, Puncak, mtn., Indon. F10 38
Jayanca, Peru B2 82
Jayapura (Sukarnapura), Indon. F11 38
Jayb, Wādī al- (Ha'Arava), val., Asia H4 50
Jay Peak, mtn., Vt., U.S. B3 152
Jaypur, India C7 46
Jayton, Tx., U.S. C2 150
Jaželbicy, Russia C15 22
J. B. Thomas, Lake, res., Tx., U.S. C2 150
Jean, Nv., U.S. H6 135
Jeanerette, La., U.S. E4 125
Jean Lafitte, La., U.S. k11 125
Jean Lafitte National Historical Park, La., U.S. k12 125
Jeannette, Pa., U.S. F2 145
Jebba, Nig. G12 64
Jebeniana, Tun. C16 62
Jeberos, Peru A3 82
Jechegnadzor, Arm. B8 48
Jedburg, Mo., U.S. f12 132
Jeddore Lake, res., Newf., Can. D3 102
Jędrzejów, Pol. E20 10
Jefawa, Sud. L2 60
Jeff, Ky., U.S. C6 124
Jeffara (Al-Jifārah), pl., Afr. D16 62
Jeff Davis, co., Ga., U.S. E4 117
Jeff Davis, co., Tx., U.S. o12 150
Jeffers, Mn., U.S. F3 130
Jeffers, Mt., U.S. E5 133
Jefferson, Al., U.S. C2 108
Jefferson, Ar., U.S. C3 111
Jefferson, Co., U.S. B5 113
Jefferson, Ga., U.S. B3 117
Jefferson, In., U.S. D4 121
Jefferson, Ia., U.S. B3 122
Jefferson, La., U.S. k11 125
Jefferson, Me., U.S. D3 126
Jefferson, Ma., U.S. B4 128
Jefferson, N.H., U.S. B4 136
Jefferson, N.C., U.S. A1 140
Jefferson, Oh., U.S. A5 142
Jefferson, Or., U.S. C3 144
Jefferson, S.C., U.S. B7 147
Jefferson, S.D., U.S. E9 148
Jefferson, Tx., U.S. C5 150
Jefferson, Wi., U.S. E5 156
Jefferson, co., Al., U.S. B3 108
Jefferson, co., Ar., U.S. C3 111
Jefferson, co., Co., U.S. B5 113
Jefferson, co., Fl., U.S. B3 116
Jefferson, co., Ga., U.S. C4 117
Jefferson, co., Id., U.S. F6 119
Jefferson, co., Il., U.S. E5 120
Jefferson, co., In., U.S. G6 121
Jefferson, co., Ia., U.S. C5 122
Jefferson, co., Ks., U.S. C8 123
Jefferson, co., Ky., U.S. B4 124
Jefferson, co., La., U.S. E5 125
Jefferson, co., Ms., U.S. D2 131
Jefferson, co., Mo., U.S. C7 132
Jefferson, co., Mt., U.S. D4 133
Jefferson, co., Ne., U.S. D8 134
Jefferson, co., N.Y., U.S. A5 139
Jefferson, co., Oh., U.S. B5 142
Jefferson, co., Ok., U.S. C4 143
Jefferson, co., Or., U.S. C5 144
Jefferson, co., Pa., U.S. D3 145
Jefferson, co., Tn., U.S. C10 149
Jefferson, co., Tx., U.S. E5 150
Jefferson, co., Wa., U.S. B1 154
Jefferson, co., W.V., U.S. B7 155
Jefferson, co., Wi., U.S. E5 156
Jefferson, stm., Mt., U.S. E5 133
Jefferson, Mount, mtn., Id., U.S. E7 119
Jefferson, Mount, mtn., Nv., U.S. E5 135
Jefferson, Mount, mtn., Or., U.S. C5 144
Jefferson City, Mo., U.S. C5 132
Jefferson City, Mt., U.S. D5 133
Jefferson City, Tn., U.S. C10 149
Jefferson Davis, co., La., U.S. D3 125
Jefferson Davis, co., Ms., U.S. D4 131
Jefferson Farms, De., U.S. i7 115
Jefferson Heights, Md., U.S. A2 127
Jefferson Hill, hill, Ky., U.S. g11 124
Jefferson Proving Ground, mil., In., U.S. G7 121
Jeffersontown, Ky., U.S. B4 124
Jeffersonville, Ga., U.S. D3 117
Jeffersonville, In., U.S. H6 121
Jeffersonville, Ky., U.S. C6 124
Jeffersonville, Oh., U.S. C2 142
Jeffersonville, Vt., U.S. B3 152
Jeffrey, W.V., U.S. D3 155
Jeffrey City, Wy., U.S. D5 157
Jeffries Creek, stm., S.C., U.S. C8 147
Jefimovskij, Russia L24 6
Jefremov, Russia G5 26
Jega, Nig. E12 64
Jegenstorf, Switz. D8 13
Jegorjevsk, Russia F22 22
Jehossee Island, i., S.C., U.S. k11 147
Jejsk, Russia H5 26
Jēkabpils, Lat. E8 22
Jekaterinburg, Russia F10 26
Jekateriny, proliv, strt., Russia I21 28
Jekimoviči, Russia G16 22
Jekyll Island, i., Ga., U.S. E5 117
Jelabuga, Russia F8 26
Jelancy, Russia G13 28
Jel'cy, Russia E16 22
Jelec, Russia I21 22
Jelenia Góra (Hirschberg), Pol. E15 10
Jelenskij, Russia H18 22
Jelgava, Lat. E6 22
Jelizarovo, Russia C27 22
Jelizavety, mys, c., Russia G20 28
Jelizovo, Bela. H12 22
Jellico, Tn., U.S. C9 149
Jelm Mountain, mtn., Wy., U.S. E7 157
Jel'n'a, Russia G16 22
Jelnat', Russia D25 22
Jeloguj, stm., Russia E15 26
Jelšava, Slov. G20 10
Jemanželinsk, Russia G10 26
Jember, Indon. G5 38
Jemca, Russia J27 6
Jemez, stm., N.M., U.S. k7 138
Jemez Canyon Dam, N.M., U.S. k7 138
Jemez Indian Reservation, N.M., U.S. h7 138
Jemez Pueblo, N.M., U.S. B3 138
Jemez Springs, N.M., U.S. B3 138
Jemison, Al., U.S. C3 108
Jemmal, Tun. N5 18
Jemseg, N.B., Can. D3 101
Jena, Ger. E11 10
Jena, La., U.S. C3 125
Jenašimskij Polkan, gora, mtn., Russia F16 26
Jenbach, Aus. H11 10
Jendouba (Souk el Arba), Tun. M3 18
Jenisej (Yenisey), stm., Russia D15 26
Jenisejsk, Russia F10 28
Jenisejskij kr'až, mts., Russia F16 26
Jenisejskij zaliv, b., Russia C8 28
Jenkins, Ky., U.S. C7 124
Jenkins, Mn., U.S. D4 130
Jenkins, co., Ga., U.S. D5 117
Jenkinsburg, Ga., U.S. C2 117
Jenkintown, Pa., U.S. o21 145
Jenks, Ok., U.S. A6 143
Jenner, Alta., Can. D5 98
Jenners, Pa., U.S. F3 145
Jennersdorf, Aus. I16 10
Jennette, Ar., U.S. B5 111
Jennie, Ar., U.S. D4 111
Jennings, Fl., U.S. B3 116
Jennings, Ks., U.S. C3 123
Jennings, La., U.S. D3 125
Jennings, Mo., U.S. f13 132
Jennings, Ok., U.S. A5 143
Jennings, co., In., U.S. G6 121
Jenny Jump Mountain, mtn., N.J., U.S. B3 137
Jenny Lind, Ar., U.S. B1 111
Jensen, Ut., U.S. C6 151
Jensen Beach, Fl., U.S. E6 116
Jeparit, Austl. K4 70
Jepelacio, Peru B3 82
Jepifan', Russia H21 22
Jeptha Knob, hill, Ky., U.S. B4 124
Jequeri, Braz. F7 79
Jequetepeque, stm., Peru B2 82
Jequié, Braz. B8 79
Jequitaí, Braz. D6 79
Jequitinhonha, Braz. D8 79
Jequitinhonha, stm., Braz. D9 79
Jerada, Mor. C9 62
Jeradou, Tun. M5 18
Jerauld, co., S.D., U.S. C7 148
Jerba, Île de, i., Tun. D16 62
Jerécuaro, Mex. G9 90
Jérémie, Haiti E7 94
Jeremoabo, Braz. F11 76
Jerevan, Arm. I6 26
Jerez de García Salinas, Mex. F8 90
Jerez de la Frontera, Spain I5 16
Jerez de los Caballeros, Spain G5 16
Jergeni, hills, Russia H6 26
Jericho, Ar., U.S. B5 111
Jericho, Vt., U.S. B3 152
Jericho see Arīḥā, Isr. Occ. E4 50
Jericó, Col. E5 84
Jerico Springs, Mo., U.S. D4 132
Jerid, Chott, sw., Tun. D15 62
Jerilderie, Austl. J6 70
Jerimoth Hill, hill, R.I., U.S. C1 146
Jermiš', Russia G25 22
Jermolajevo, Russia E19 4
Jermolino, Russia F19 22
Jermyn, Pa., U.S. C10 145
Jeroaquara, Braz. C3 79
Jerofej Pavlovič, Russia G16 28
Jerome, Az., U.S. C3 110
Jerome, Fl., U.S. F5 116
Jerome, Id., U.S. G4 119
Jerome, Mo., U.S. D6 132
Jerome, Pa., U.S. F4 145
Jerome, co., Id., U.S. G4 119
Jeromesville, Oh., U.S. B3 142
Jersey, Ga., U.S. C3 117
Jersey, co., Il., U.S. D3 120
Jersey, dep., Eur. F7 4
Jersey City, N.J., U.S. B4 137
Jersey Mountain, mtn., Id., U.S. E3 119
Jersey Shore, Pa., U.S. D7 145
Jersey Village, Tx., U.S. r14 150
Jerseyville, Il., U.S. D3 120
Jeršov, Russia G7 26
Jerusalem, Ar., U.S. B3 111
Jerusalem see Yerushalayim, Isr. E4 50
Jervis, Cape, c., Austl. J3 70
Jervis Bay, b., Austl. J9 70
Jervis Inlet, b., B.C., Can. D6 99
Jesenice, Czech. E13 10
Jesi, Italy F8 18
Jesil', Kaz. G11 26
Jessamine, co., Ky., U.S. C5 124
Jessentuki, Russia I6 26
Jessieville, Ar., U.S. C2 111
Jessore, Bngl. I13 44
Jessup, Md., U.S. B4 127
Jessup, Pa., U.S. m18 145
Jesup, Ga., U.S. E5 117
Jesup, Ia., U.S. B5 122
Jesup, Lake, l., Fl., U.S. D5 116
Jesús, Para. D11 80
Jésus, Île, i., Que., Can. p19 104
Jesús Carranza, Mex. I12 90
Jesús de Otoro, Hond. C7 92
Jesús María, Arg. F6 80
Jesús María, Mex. E6 90
Jesús María, stm., Mex. F7 90
Jesús Menéndez, Cuba D6 94
Jet, Ok., U.S. A3 143
Jetmore, Ks., U.S. D4 123
Jetpur, India J4 44
Jette, Bel. G5 12
Jeumont, Fr. B11 14
Jever, Ger. B7 10
Jevlach, Azer. I7 26
Jevpatorija, Ukr. H4 26
Jevrej, state, Russia H18 28
Jewel Cave National Monument, S.D., U.S. D2 148
Jewell, Ia., U.S. B4 122
Jewell, Ks., U.S. C5 123
Jewell, co., Ks., U.S. C5 123
Jewell Ridge, Va., U.S. e10 153
Jewett, Oh., U.S. B4 142
Jewett, Tx., U.S. D4 150
Jewett City, Ct., U.S. C8 114
Jewett Lake, l., Sask., Can. A3 105
Jezerce, mtn., Alb. G3 20
Jezerišče, Bela. F12 22
Jeziorany, Pol. B20 10
Jhābua, India I6 44
Jhālāwār, India H7 44
Jhal Jhao, Pak. G1 44
Jhang Sadar, Pak. E5 44
Jhānsi, India H8 44
Jharia, India I12 44
Jhārsuguda, India B8 46
Jhelum, Pak. D5 44
Jhelum, stm., Asia E5 44
Jhok Rind, Pak. E4 44
Jhunjhunūn, India F6 44
Jiaban, China B9 40
Jiading, China D10 34
Jiāganj, India H13 44
Jiakou, China E8 34
Jiali, China E5 30
Jialing, stm., China E8 30
Jialou, China C2 34
Jiamusi, China B13 30
Ji'an, China H3 34
Jianchang, China B12 32
Jianchuan, China A5 40
Jiangbeixu, China I4 34
Jiangbianzhai, China C6 40
Jiangcun, China G6 34
Jiangdihe, China B6 40
Jiangduo, China C9 34
Jianggezhuang, China D7 32
Jiangji, China C4 34
Jiangjin, China F8 30
Jiangkou, China G9 30
Jiangkou, China H7 34
Jiangkouji, China C5 34
Jiangliadian, China A5 32
Jiangmen, China M2 34
Jiangsu (Kiangsu), prov., China E10 30
Jiangtun, China B10 32
Jiangxi (Kiangsi), prov., China F10 30
Jiangxiang, China C6 34
Jiangyin, China D9 34
Jiangzhasiji, China E13 44
Jianli, China F1 34
Jianning, China I5 34
Jian'ou, China H7 34
Jianshan, China F9 34
Jianshui, China C7 40
Jiantouji, China I5 32
Jiaohe, China C12 30
Jiaomei, China K6 34
Jiaoshanhe, China F1 34
Jiaoxian, China G7 32
Jiaozuo, China D9 30
Jiashan, China C7 34
Jiashun Hu, l., China C12 44
Jiawang, China A6 34
Jiaxian, China B2 34
Jiaxing, China E9 34
Jiayu, China F2 34
Jiazi, China M5 34
Jibiya, Nig. E13 64
Jiboa, stm., El Sal. D5 92
Jicarilla Apache Indian Reservation, N.M., U.S. A2 138
Jicarón, Isla, i., Pan. D2 84
Jicatuyo, stm., Hond. C6 92
Jiddah (Jeddah), Sau. Ar. D1 47
Jidingxilin, China D15 44
Jiedong, China I2 34
Jiehe, China H5 32
Jieji, China B7 34
Jiepai, China E8 34
Jiesheng, China M4 34
Jieshou, China B4 34
Jieshou, China B8 34
Jieyang, China L5 34
Jieznas, Lith. G7 22
Jigongzhen, China A4 34
Jiguaní, Cuba D6 94
Jiguanshan, China A12 32
Jigüey, Bahía de, b., Cuba C5 94
Jihlava, Czech. F15 10
Jijel, Alg. B13 62
Jijiadianzi, China H6 32
Jikawo, Eth. M7 60
Jikawo, stm., Afr. M8 60
Jilib, Som. A8 58
Jili Hu, l., China B4 30
Jilin, China C12 30
Jilin (Kirin), prov., China C12 30
Jill, Kediet ej, mtn., Maur. I4 62
Jima, Eth. N9 60
Jimbolia, Rom. D4 20
Jiménez, Mex. D7 90
Jiménez, Mex. C9 90
Jiménez del Téul, Mex. F7 90
Jim Hogg, co., Tx., U.S. F3 150
Jim Lake, res., N.D., U.S. B7 141
Jimo, China G8 32
Jim Thorpe, Pa., U.S. E10 145
Jim Wells, co., Tx., U.S. F3 150
Jin (Gam), stm., Asia C8 40
Jināḥ, Egypt E6 60
Jinan (Tsinan), China G4 32
Jinbang, China J7 34
Jincheng, China D9 30
Jīnd, India F7 44
Jindřichův Hradec, Czech. F15 10
Jingangtou, China H2 34
Jingcheng, China K6 34
Jingdezhen (Kingtechen), China F6 34
Jinggang, China G1 34
Jinggangshan (Ciping), China I3 34
Jinghai, China E4 32
Jinghaiwei, China G10 32
Jinghong, China C6 40
Jingning, China H8 34
Jingoutun, China B5 32
Jingxi, China C9 40
Jingxian, China F4 32
Jingyu, China A14 32
Jingzhi, China G7 32
Jinhua, China F8 34
Jining, China C9 30
Jining, China H4 32
Jinja, Ug. A6 58
Jinjiang, China A6 40
Jinjing, China G2 34
Jinkeng, China H6 34
Jinkou, China G8 32
Jinlingzhen, China G6 32
Jinning, China B7 40
Jinotega, Nic. D8 92
Jinotega, dept., Nic. D9 92
Jinotepe, Nic. F8 92
Jinping, China A10 40
Jinrui, China H3 34
Jinsha, stm., China F6 30
Jinshan, China E10 34
Jinshi, China F9 30
Jintian, China H3 34
Jinxi, China C8 32
Jinxian, China D9 32
Jinyun, China G9 34
Jinzhaizhen, China D4 34
Jinzhou (Chinchou), China B9 32
Ji-Paraná, Braz. D11 82
Jipijapa, Ec. H2 84
Jiquilisco, El Sal. D6 92
Jiquilisco, Bahía de, b., El Sal. D6 92
Jiquiriçá, stm., Braz. B8 79
Jirāfī, Wādī al- (Naḥal Paran), val. I3 50
Jirbān, Sud. L6 60
Jirjā, Egypt D6 60
Jirkov, Czech. E13 10
Jīroft, Iran G14 48
Jisr ash-Shughūr, Syria D4 48
Jitan, China K4 34
Jitaúna, Braz. C9 79
Jiu, stm., Rom. F7 20
Jiubao, China J4 34
Jiucheng, China E5 32
Jiuguan, China F9 32
Jiuhu, China F5 32
Jiuhuaxian, China L2 34
Jiujiang, China F4 34
Jiukou, China E1 34
Jiulian Shan, mts., China K3 34
Jiuling Shan, mts., China G3 34
Jiulong, China K1 34
Jiumianyang, China E2 34
Jiuningyang, China J6 34
Jiuquan, China D6 30
Jiushangshui, China B3 34
Jiutai, China C12 30
Jiuxian, China B2 34
Jiuxiangcheng, China B3 34
Jixi, China B13 30
Jixian, China H2 32
Jixian, China C5 32
Jixingji, China C5 34
Jiyang, China G5 32
Jīzān, Sau. Ar. F3 47
Joaçaba, Braz. D13 80
Joaíma, Braz. D8 79
Joanna, S.C., U.S. C4 147
João Neiva, Braz. E8 79
João Pessoa, Braz. E12 76
João Pinheiro, Braz. D5 79
Joaquim Távora, Braz. G4 79
Joaquín V. González, Arg. C6 80
Job Peak, mtn., Nv., U.S. D3 135
Jocassee, Lake, res., U.S. B1 147
Jocolí, Arg. G4 80
Jocón, Hond. B8 92
Jocoro, El Sal. D6 92
Jocotán, Guat. C5 92
Jódar, Spain H8 16
Jo Daviess, co., Il., U.S. A3 120
Jodhpur, India G5 44
Jodie, W.V., U.S. m13 155
Joe Batt's Arm [-Barr'd Islands-Shoal Bay], Newf., Can. D4 102
Joensuu, Fin. J21 6
Joes Brook, stm., Vt., U.S. C4 152
Joes Creek, stm., W.V., U.S. m12 155
Joetsu, Japan J13 36
Joffre, Mount, mtn., Can. D3 98
Jõgeva, Est. C9 22
Jog Falls, wtfl, India E3 46
Joggins, N.S., Can. D5 101
Jogui, stm., Braz. G1 79
Johannesburg, S. Afr. F9 66
John, Cape, c., N.S., Can. D6 101
John Day, Or., U.S. C8 144
John Day, stm., Or., U.S. B6 144
John Day, North Fork, stm., Or., U.S. C7 144
John Day Dam, U.S. D5 154
John Day Fossil Beds National Monument, Or., U.S. C6 144
John F. Kennedy Space Center, sci., Fl., U.S. D6 116
John H. Kerr Dam, Va., U.S. D4 153
John H. Kerr Reservoir, res., U.S. D4 153
John Martin Reservoir, res., Co., U.S. C7 113
John Muir National Historical Site, hist., Ca., U.S. h8 112
John o' Groats, Scot., U.K. C10 8
John Redmond Reservoir, res., Ks., U.S. D8 123
Johnsburg, Il., U.S. h8 120
John Sevier, Tn., U.S. m14 149
Johns Island, S.C., U.S. F7 147
Johns Island, i., S.C., U.S. F7 147
Johnson, Ar., U.S. A1 111
Johnson, Ks., U.S. E2 123
Johnson, Ne., U.S. D10 134
Johnson, Vt., U.S. B3 152
Johnson, co., Ar., U.S. B2 111
Johnson, co., Ga., U.S. D4 117
Johnson, co., Il., U.S. F5 120
Johnson, co., In., U.S. F5 121
Johnson, co., Ia., U.S. C6 122
Johnson, co., Ks., U.S. D9 123
Johnson, co., Ky., U.S. C7 124
Johnson, co., Mo., U.S. C4 132
Johnson, co., Ne., U.S. D9 134
Johnson, co., Tn., U.S. C12 149
Johnson, co., Tx., U.S. C4 150
Johnson, co., Wy., U.S. B6 157
Johnsonburg, Pa., U.S. D4 145
Johnson City, N.Y., U.S. C5 139
Johnson City, Tn., U.S. C11 149
Johnson City, Tx., U.S. D3 150
Johnson Creek, Wi., U.S. E5 156
Johnsonville, S.C., U.S. D9 147
Johns Pass, strt., Fl., U.S. p10 116
Johnston, Ia., U.S. e8 122
Johnston, R.I., U.S. C4 146
Johnston, S.C., U.S. D4 147
Johnston, co., N.C., U.S. B4 140
Johnston, co., Ok., U.S. C5 143
Johnston Atoll, atoll, Oc. G23 158
Johnston City, Il., U.S. F5 120
Johnstone Strait, strt., B.C., Can. D4 99
Johnston Key, i., Fl., U.S. H5 116
Johnstown, Co., U.S. A6 113
Johnstown, N.Y., U.S. B6 139
Johnstown, Oh., U.S. B3 142
Johnstown, Pa., U.S. F4 145
Johnsville, Md., U.S. A3 127
John W. Flannagan Reservoir, res., Va., U.S. e9 153
Johor Baharu, Malay. N7 40
Joice, Ia., U.S. A4 122
Joigny, Fr. E10 14
Joiner, Ar., U.S. B5 111
Joinvile, Braz. D14 80
Joinville, Fr. D12 14
Joinville Island, i., Ant. B1 73
Jokkmokk, Swe. H16 6
Jolārpettai, India F5 46
Jolfā, Iran B8 48
Joliet, Il., U.S. B5 120
Joliet, Mt., U.S. E8 133
Joliette, Que., Can. C4 104
Jolo, Phil. D7 38
Jomda, China E6 30
Jonava, Lith. F7 22
Jones, Al., U.S. C3 108
Jones, Ok., U.S. B4 143
Jones, co., Ga., U.S. C3 117
Jones, co., Ia., U.S. B6 122
Jones, co., Ms., U.S. D4 131
Jones, co., N.C., U.S. B5 140
Jones, co., S.D., U.S. D5 148
Jones, co., Tx., U.S. C3 150
Jonesboro, Ar., U.S. B5 111
Jonesboro, Ga., U.S. C2 117
Jonesboro, Il., U.S. F4 120
Jonesboro, In., U.S. D6 121
Jonesboro, La., U.S. B3 125
Jonesboro, Me., U.S. D5 126
Jonesborough, Tn., U.S. C11 149
Jonesburg, Mo., U.S. C6 132
Jones Creek, Tx., U.S. s14 150
Jones Mill, Ar., U.S. C3 111
Jonesport, Me., U.S. D5 126
Jones Sound, strt., N.W. Ter., Can. A15 96
Jonestown, Ms., U.S. C3 131
Jonestown, Ms., U.S. A3 131
Jonestown, Pa., U.S. F9 145
Jonesville, In., U.S. F6 121
Jonesville, La., U.S. C4 125
Jonesville, Mi., U.S. G6 129
Jonesville, N.C., U.S. A2 140
Jonesville, S.C., U.S. B4 147
Jonesville, Vt., U.S. C3 152
Jonesville, Va., U.S. f8 153
Joniškėlis, Lith. E7 22
Joniškis, Lith. E6 22
Jönköping, Swe. M14 6
Jonquière, Que., Can. A6 104
Jonuta, Mex. H13 90
Joplin, Mo., U.S. D3 132
Joplin, Mt., U.S. B6 133
Joppa, Al., U.S. A3 108
Joppa, Il., U.S. F5 120
Joppatowne, Md., U.S. B5 127
Jordan, Al., U.S. D1 108
Jordan, Mn., U.S. F5 130
Jordan, Mt., U.S. C10 133
Jordan, N.Y., U.S. B4 139
Jordan (Al-Urdun), ctry., Asia C2 42
Jordan (Nahr al-Urdunn) (HaYarden), stm., Asia E5 50
Jordan, stm., Ut., U.S. C4 151
Jordan Creek, stm., U.S. E9 144
Jordânia, Braz. C8 79
Jordan Lake, l., N.S., Can. E4 101
Jordan Lake, res., Al., U.S. C3 108
Jordanów, Pol. F19 10
Jordan Valley, Or., U.S. D9 144
Jordão, stm., Braz. C13 80
Jordet, Nor. K13 6
Jorhāt, India G16 44
Jornado del Muerto, des., N.M., U.S. D3 138
Jos, Nig. G14 64
José Batlle y Ordóñez, Ur. G11 80
José Bonifácio, Braz. F4 79
José Francisco Vergara, Chile B4 80
Joselândia, Braz. G13 82
José Pedro Varela, Ur. G11 80
Joseph, Or., U.S. B9 144
Joseph, Lac, l., Newf., Can. h8 102
Joseph Bonaparte Gulf, b., Austl. B5 68
Joseph City, Az., U.S. C5 110
Josephine, co., Or., U.S. E3 144
Josephville, Mo., U.S. f12 132
Joshua, Tx., U.S. n9 150
Joshua Tree, Ca., U.S. E5 112
Joshua Tree National Monument, Ca., U.S. F6 112
Joškar-Ola, Russia F7 26
Josselin, Fr. E4 14
Joubertina, S. Afr. I6 66
Jourdanton, Tx., U.S. E3 150
Joussard, Alta., Can. B3 98
Jovellanos, Cuba C4 94
Joviânia, Braz. D4 79
Jowhar, Som. H10 56
Joy, Il., U.S. B3 120
Joyce, La., U.S. C3 125
Józefów, Pol. C21 10
J. Percy Priest Lake, res., Tn., U.S. A5 149
Juab, co., Ut., U.S. D2 151
Juami, stm., Braz. H9 84
Juan Aldama, Mex. E8 90
Juan B. Arruabarrena, Arg. F9 80
Juan Bautista Alberdi, Arg. D6 80
Juan de Fuca, Strait of, strt., N.A. A1 154
Juan de Mena, Para. C10 80
Juan de Nova, Île, i., Reu. E8 58
Juan E. Barra, Arg. I8 80
Juan Eugenio, Mex. E8 90
Juan Fernández, Archipiélago, is., Chile C1 78
Juangriego, Ven. B11 84
Juan Guerra, Peru B3 82
Juan Jorba, Arg. G6 80
Juan José Castelli, Arg. C8 80
Juán José Perez, Bol. F7 82
Juanjuí, Peru B3 82
Juan L. Lacaze, Ur. H10 80
Juan N. Fernández, Arg. J9 80
Juan Viñas, C.R. H11 92
Juárez, Mex. D9 90
Juárez, Mex. B5 90
Juárez, Sierra de, mts., Mex. B2 90
Juárez see Ciudad Juárez, Mex. B6 90
Juatinga, Ponta de, c., Braz. G6 79
Juàzeiro, Braz. E10 76
Juazeiro do Norte, Braz. E11 76
Jūbā, Sud. H7 56
Juba, stm., Braz. F12 82
Jūbāl, Maḍīq, strt., Egypt D7 60
Jubal, Strait of see Jūbāl, Maḍīq, strt., Egypt D7 60
Jubaysho, Eth. O9 60
Jubayt, Sud. H9 60
Jubba (Genale), stm., Afr. H9 56
Jubbah, Sau. Ar. G6 48
Jubones, stm., Ec. I3 84
Juby, Cap, c., Mor. G4 62
Júcar (Xúquer), stm., Spain F10 16
Juçara, Braz. C3 79
Júcaro, Cuba D5 94
Juchipila, Mex. G8 90
Juchitán de Zaragoza, Mex. I12 90
Juchnov, Russia G18 22
Juchoviči, Bela. E11 22
Jucuapa, El Sal. D6 92
Jucurucu, stm., Braz. D9 79
Jud, N.D., U.S. C7 141
Juda, Wi., U.S. F4 156
Judaea, hist. reg., Asia E4 50
Judas, Punta, c., C.R. H10 92
Judenburg, Aus. H14 10
Judique, N.S., Can. D8 101
Judith, stm., Mt., U.S. C7 133
Judith, Point, c., R.I., U.S. G4 115
Judith Basin, co., Mt., U.S. C6 133
Judith Gap, Mt., U.S. D7 133
Judith Island, i., N.C., U.S. B6 140
Judith Mountains, mts., Mt., U.S. C7 133
Judith Peak, mtn., Mt., U.S. C7 133
Judson, Mn., U.S. F4 130
Judson, N.D., U.S. C4 141
Judsonia, Ar., U.S. B4 111
Juexi, China F10 34
Jufari, stm., Braz. H11 84
Jugon, Fr. D4 14
Juḥā, Sau. Ar. F3 47
Juidongshan, China L6 34
Juigalpa, Nic. E9 92
Juína, stm., Braz. E12 82
Juiz de Fora, Braz. F7 79
Jujuy, prov., Arg. B5 80
Jukagirskoje ploskogorje, plat., Russia D23 28
Julesburg, Co., U.S. A8 113
Juli, Peru G7 82
Juliaca, Peru F6 82
Julia Creek, Austl. C4 70
Juliaetta, Id., U.S. C2 119
Julian, Ca., U.S. F5 112
Julian, W.V., U.S. C3 155
Julianakanaal, Neth. F8 12
Julian Alps, mts., Eur. C8 18
Juliana Top, mtn., Sur. F14 84
Julianehåb, Grnld. C15 86
Jülich, Ger. E6 10
Juliette, Ga., U.S. C3 117
Julimes, Mex. C7 90
Júlio de Castilhos, Braz. E12 80
Julu, China F3 32
Juma, Russia I23 6
Jumay, Volcán, vol., Guat. C5 92
Jumbilla, Peru A3 82
Jumboo, Som. B8 58
Jumbo Peak, mtn., Nv., U.S. G7 135
Jumentos Cays, is., Bah. C7 94
Jumet, Bel. H5 12
Jumilla, Spain G10 16
Jump, stm., Wi., U.S. C3 156
Jump, North Fork, stm., Wi., U.S. C3 156
Jump, South Fork, stm., Wi., U.S. C3 156
Jumping Branch, W.V., U.S. D4 155
Jumping Lake, l., Sask., Can. E3 105
Jūnāgadh, India J4 44
Junaynah, Ra's al-, mtn., Egypt G2 48
Junction, Il., U.S. F5 120
Junction, Tx., U.S. D3 150
Junction City, Ar., U.S. D3 111
Junction City, Ga., U.S. D2 117
Junction City, Il., U.S. E4 120
Junction City, Ks., U.S. C7 123
Junction City, Ky., U.S. C5 124
Junction City, La., U.S. A3 125
Junction City, Oh., U.S. C3 142
Junction City, Or., U.S. C3 144
Junction City, Wi., U.S. D4 156
Jundiaí, Braz. G5 79
Jundiaí do Sul, Braz. G3 79
Juneau, Ak., U.S. D13 109
Juneau, Wi., U.S. E5 156
Juneau, co., Wi., U.S. E3 156
Junee, Austl. J7 70
June in Winter, Lake, l., Fl., U.S. E5 116

Name — Map Ref. — Page

Katmai, Mount, mtn., Ak., U.S. D9 109
Katmai National Park, Ak., U.S. D9 109
Kātmāndu see Kāthmāndau, Nepal G11 44
Katoomba, Austl. I9 70
Katoúna, Grc. K5 20
Katowice, Pol. E19 10
Kātrīnā, Jabal, mtn., Egypt C7 60
Katsepe, Madag. o22 67b
Katsina, Nig. E13 64
Katsina Ala, Nig. H14 64
Katsina Ala, stm., Afr. G8 54
Katsuta, Japan K15 36
Katsuura, Japan L15 36
Katsuyama, Japan K11 36
Kattakurgan, Uzb. J11 26
Kattaviá, Grc. N11 20
Kattegat, strt., Eur. M12 6
Katun', stm., Russia G9 28
Katunki, Russia E26 22
Kātwa, India I13 44
Katwijk aan Zee, Neth. D5 12
Katy, Tx., U.S. r14 150
Katyn, Russia G14 22
Kauai, co., Hi., U.S. B1 118
Kauai, i., Hi., U.S. A2 118
Kauai Channel, strt., Hi., U.S. B3 118
Kau Desert, des., Hi., U.S. D6 118
Kaufbeuren, Ger. H10 10
Kaufman, Tx., U.S. C4 150
Kaufman, co., Tx., U.S. C4 150
Kauiki Head, c., Hi., U.S. C6 118
Kaukauna, Wi., U.S. D5 156
Kaukau Veld, plat., Afr. B5 66
Kaula Island, i., Hi., U.S. m15 118
Kaulakahi Channel, strt., Hi., U.S. A2 118
Kauliranta, Fin. H18 6
Kaumakani, Hi., U.S. B2 118
Kaumalapau, Hi., U.S. C5 118
Kaunakakai, Hi., U.S. B4 118
Kauna Point, c., Hi., U.S. D6 118
Kaunas, Lith. G6 22
Kaura Namoda, Nig. E13 64
Kauru, Nig. F14 64
Kaušany, Mol. C13 20
Kaustinen, Fin. J18 6
Kautokeino, Nor. G18 6
Kavacık, Tur. J12 20
Kavajë, Alb. H3 20
Kavála, Grc. I8 20
Kavalerovo, Russia I19 28
Kāvali, India E5 46
Kavaratti Island, i., India G2 46
Kāveri, stm., India G5 46
Kāveri Falls, wtfl, India F4 46
Kaverino, Russia G24 22
Kavieng, Pap. N. Gui. k17 68a
Kavimba, Bots. B7 66
Kavīr, Dasht-e, des., Iran D13 48
Kawagoe, Japan L14 36
Kawaguchi, Japan L14 36
Kawaihae, Hi., U.S. C6 118
Kawaihoa Point, c., Hi., U.S. B1 118
Kawaikini, mtn., Hi., U.S. A2 118
Kawailoa, Hi., U.S. f9 118
Kawailoa Beach, Hi., U.S. f9 118
Kawambwa, Zam. C5 58
Kawara Débé, Niger E11 64
Kawasaki, Japan L14 36
Kaw City, Ok., U.S. A5 143
Kawdut, Burma G4 40
Kaweenakumik Lake, l., Man., Can. C2 100
Kawela, Hi., U.S. f9 118
Kawich Peak, mtn., Nv., U.S. F5 135
Kawich Range, mts., Nv., U.S. F5 135
Kaw Lake, res., Ok., U.S. A5 143
Kawludo, Burma E4 40
Kawm Umbū, Egypt E7 60
Kawthaung, Burma J5 40
Kaxgar, stm., China D2 30
Kay, co., Ok., U.S. A4 143
Kaya, Burkina E9 64
Kayan, Burma F4 40
Kayan, stm., Indon. E6 38
Kāyankulam, India H4 46
Kaycee, Wy., U.S. C6 157
Kayenta, Az., U.S. A5 110
Kayes, Congo B2 58
Kayes, Mali D4 64
Kayford, W.V., U.S. C3 155
Kayjay, Ky., U.S. D6 124
Kaylor, S.D., U.S. D8 148
Kayser Gebergte, mts., Sur. F14 84
Kayseri, Tur. B3 48
Kaysville, Ut., U.S. B4 151
Kayville, Sask., Can. H3 105
Kazachskij melkosopočnik, hills, Kaz. H12 26
Kazachstan see Kazakhstan, ctry., Asia H11 26
Kazačinskoje, Russia F16 26
Kazakhstan, ctry., Asia H11 26
Kazaki, Russia I21 22
Kazaklija, Mol. C12 20
Kazakstan see Kazakhstan, ctry., Asia H11 26
Kazalinsk, Kaz. H10 26
Kazan', Russia F7 26
Kazan, stm., N.W. Ter., Can. D13 96
Kazandžik, Turk. J9 26
Kazanlâk, Bul. G9 20
Kazanovka, Russia H21 22
Kazbek, gora, mtn. I6 26
Kāzerūn, Iran G11 48
Kazi-Magomed, Azer. I7 26
Kazimierza Wielka, Pol. E20 10
Kazincbarcika, Hung. G20 10
Kazinka, Russia I22 22
Kazlų Rūda, Lith. G6 22
Kazungula, Zam. A7 66
Kazym, stm., Russia E5 28
Kazyr, stm., Russia G17 26
Kcynia, Pol. B17 10
Kdyně, Czech. F13 10
Kéa, i., Grc. L8 20
Keaau, Hi., U.S. D6 118
Keahiakahoe, Puu, mtn., Hi., U.S. g10 118
Keahole Point, c., Hi., U.S. D5 118
Kealaikahiki Channel, strt., Hi., U.S. C5 118
Kealaikahiki Point, c., Hi., U.S. C5 118
Kealakekua, Hi., U.S. D6 118
Kealia, Hi., U.S. A2 118
Keams Canyon, Az., U.S. B5 110
Keanae, Hi., U.S. C5 118
Keanapapa Point, c., Hi., U.S. C4 118
Keansburg, N.J., U.S. C4 137
Kearney, Ont., Can. B5 103
Kearney, Mo., U.S. B3 132
Kearney, Ne., U.S. D6 134
Kearney, co., Ne., U.S. D7 134
Kearneysville, W.V., U.S. B7 155
Kearns, Ut., U.S. C4 151
Kearny, Az., U.S. D5 110
Kearny, N.J., U.S. h8 137
Kearny, co., Ks., U.S. D2 123
Kearsarge, N.H., U.S. B4 136
Kearsarge, Mount, mtn., N.H., U.S. D3 136
Kearsarge North, mtn., N.H., U.S. B4 136
Keatchie, La., U.S. B2 125
Keaton, Ky., U.S. C7 124
Keats, Ks., U.S. C7 123
Keauhou, Hi., U.S. D6 118
Kebeiti, China B8 44
Kébémer, Sen. D1 64
Kebili, Tun. D15 62
Kebnekaise, mtn., Swe. H16 6
Kebri Dehar, Eth. G9 56
Kecel, Hung. I19 10
Kech, stm., Pak. H17 48
Kecskemét, Hung. I19 10
Kėdainiai, Lith. F7 22
Kedges Straits, strt., Md., U.S. D5 127
Kedgwick, N.B., Can. B2 101
Kediri, Indon. j16 39a
Kédougou, Sen. E3 64
Kędzierzyn Kozle, Pol. E18 10
Keedysville, Md., U.S. B2 127
Keegan, Me., U.S. A5 126
Keego Harbor, Mi., U.S. o15 129
Keei, Hi., U.S. D6 118
Keele Peak, mtn., Yukon, Can. D6 96
Keeling Islands see Cocos Islands, dep., Oc. K10 24
Keels, Newf., Can. D5 102
Keene, Ont., Can. C6 103
Keene, Ky., U.S. C5 124
Keene, N.H., U.S. E2 136
Keene, Tx., U.S. n9 150
Keenesburg, Co., U.S. A6 113
Keeney Knob, mtn., W.V., U.S. D4 155
Keensburg, Il., U.S. E6 120
Keerbergen, Bel. F6 12
Keeseville, N.Y., U.S. f11 139
Keesler Air Force Base, mil., Ms., U.S. E5 131
Keetmanshoop, Nmb. F4 66
Keet Seel Ruin, hist., Az., U.S. A5 110
Keewatin, Ont., Can. E4 100
Keewatin, Mn., U.S. C5 130
Keewatin, stm., Man., Can. A1 100
Keezletown, Va., U.S. B4 153
Kefallinía, i., Grc. K4 20
Kefar Blum, Isr. B5 50
Kefar 'Ezyon, Isr. Occ. E4 50
Kefar Naḥum (Capernaum), hist., Isr. C5 50
Kefar Sava, Isr. D3 50
Keffi, Nig. G13 64
Keffin Hausa, Nig. E14 64
Keflavík, Ice. B2 6a
Keftya, Eth. K9 60
Ke Ga, Mui, c., Viet. H10 40
Kegonsa, Lake, l., Wi., U.S. F4 156
Kegums, Lat. E7 22
Kehra, Est. B8 22
Ke-hsi Mānsām, Burma D4 40
Keila, Est. B7 22
Keimoes, S. Afr. G5 66
Keiser, Ar., U.S. B5 111
Keith, Scot., U.K. D11 8
Keith, co., Ne., U.S. C4 134
Keith Arm, b., N.W. Ter., Can. C8 96
Keithsburg, Il., U.S. B3 120
Keizer, Or., U.S. C3 144
Kejimkujik National Park, N.S., Can. E4 101
Kekaha, Hi., U.S. B2 118
Kékes, mtn., Hung. H20 10
Kekexili, China B5 30
Kelafo, Eth. G9 56
Kelang, Malay. M6 40
Kelantan, stm., Malay. L7 40
Kelegou, China B6 32
Kelibia, Tun. M6 18
Kell, Il., U.S. E5 120
Keller, Tx., U.S. n9 150
Keller, Va., U.S. C7 153
Keller, Wa., U.S. A7 154
Kellerberrin, Austl. F3 68
Kellerman, Al., U.S. B2 108
Kellerton, Ia., U.S. D3 122
Kellett, Cape, c., N.W. Ter., Can. B7 96
Kelley, Ia., U.S. C4 122
Kelleys Island, i., Oh., U.S. A3 142
Kelliher, Sask., Can. F4 105
Kelliher, Mn., U.S. C4 130
Kellnersville, Wi., U.S. D6 156
Kellogg, Id., U.S. B2 119
Kellogg, Ia., U.S. C5 122
Kellogg, Mn., U.S. F6 130
Kelly, Wy., U.S. C2 157
Kelly Air Force Base, mil., Tx., U.S. k7 150
Kelly Brook Mountain, mtn., Me., U.S. A3 126
Kelly Island, i., De., U.S. D4 115
Kelly Lake, B.C., Can. B7 99
Kellyton, Al., U.S. C3 108
Kellyville, N.H., U.S. D2 136
Kellyville, Ok., U.S. B5 143
Kelmė, Lith. F5 22
Kel'mency, Ukr. A10 20
Kelmet, Erit. I10 60
Kelo, Chad G4 56
Kelolokan, Indon. E6 38
Kelowna, B.C., Can. E8 99
Kelsey Lake, l., Man., Can. C1 100
Kelseyville, Ca., U.S. C2 112
Kelso, Mo., U.S. D8 132
Kelso, Wa., U.S. C3 154
Keluang, Malay. M7 40
Kelvington, Sask., Can. E4 105
Kelwood, Man., Can. D2 100
Kem', Russia E4 26
Kemalpaşa, Tur. K11 20
Kemano, B.C., Can. C4 99
Kemer Barajı, res., Tur. L12 20
Kemerovo, Russia F9 28
Kemi, Fin. I19 6
Kemijärvi, Fin. H20 6
Kemijoki, stm., Fin. H19 6
Kemmerer, Wy., U.S. E2 157
Kemnath, Ger. F11 10
Kemnay, Man., Can. E1 100
Kemp, Tx., U.S. C4 150
Kemp, Lake, res., Tx., U.S. C3 150
Kemparana, Mali E7 64
Kempele, Fin. I19 6
Kempen, Ger. D6 10
Kemper, co., Ms., U.S. C5 131
Kemps Bay, Bah. B6 94
Kempsey, Austl. H10 70
Kempshall Mountain, mtn., N.Y., U.S. A6 139
Kempten [Allgäu], Ger. H10 10
Kempton, Il., U.S. C5 120
Kempton, In., U.S. D5 121
Kemptville, Ont., Can. B9 103
Kenai, Ak., U.S. C9 109
Kenai Fjords National Park, Ak., U.S. D10 109
Kenai Mountains, mts., Ak., U.S. h16 109
Kenai Peninsula, pen., Ak., U.S. h16 109
Kenansville, Fl., U.S. E6 116
Kenansville, N.C., U.S. C5 140
Kenaston, Sask., Can. F2 105
Kenbridge, Va., U.S. D4 153
Kendal, Sask., Can. G4 105
Kendal, S. Afr. F9 66
Kendall, Fl., U.S. s13 116
Kendall, Ks., U.S. E2 123
Kendall, Wi., U.S. E3 156
Kendall, co., Il., U.S. B5 120
Kendall, co., Tx., U.S. E3 150
Kendall, Cape, c., N.W. Ter., Can. D15 96
Kendall Park, N.J., U.S. C3 137
Kendallville, In., U.S. B7 121
Kendari, Indon. F7 38
Kendrāparha, India J12 44
Kendrick, Id., U.S. C2 119
Kenduskeag, Me., U.S. D4 126
Kenedy, Tx., U.S. E4 150
Kenedy, co., Tx., U.S. F4 150
Kenel, S.D., U.S. B5 148
Kenema, S.L. H4 64
Kenesaw, Ne., U.S. D7 134
Kenge, Zaire B3 58
Kengtian, China J8 34
Kēng Tung, Burma D5 40
Kenhardt, S. Afr. G5 66
Kenilworth, Il., U.S. h9 120
Kenilworth, Ut., U.S. D5 151
Kenitra, Mor. C7 62
Kenly, N.C., U.S. B4 140
Kenmare, N.D., U.S. A3 141
Kenmore, N.Y., U.S. C2 139
Kenna, W.V., U.S. C3 155
Kennaday Peak, mtn., Wy., U.S. E6 157
Kennard, In., U.S. E6 121
Kennard, Ne., U.S. C9 134
Kennebago Lake, l., Me., U.S. C2 126
Kennebec, S.D., U.S. D5 148
Kennebec, co., Me., U.S. D3 126
Kennebec, stm., Me., U.S. D3 126
Kennebunk, Me., U.S. E2 126
Kennebunkport, Me., U.S. E2 126
Kennedy, Sask., Can. G4 105
Kennedy, Al., U.S. B2 108
Kennedy, Mn., U.S. B2 130
Kennedy, Zimb. B8 66
Kennedy, Mount, mtn., Yukon, Can. D5 96
Kennedy Entrance, strt., Ak., U.S. D9 109
Kenner, La., U.S. E5 125
Kennesaw, Ga., U.S. B2 117
Kennesaw Mountain, mtn., Ga., U.S. C2 117
Kennesaw Mountain National Battlefield Park, Ga., U.S. h7 117
Kennetcook, N.S., Can. D6 101
Kennett, Mo., U.S. E7 132
Kennett Square, Pa., U.S. G10 145
Kennewick, Wa., U.S. C6 154
Kenn Reef, rf., Austl. D11 68
Kennydale, Wa., U.S. e11 154
Keno, Or., U.S. E5 144
Kénogami, Lac, l., Que., Can. A6 104
Kenora, Ont., Can. o16 103
Kenosha, Wi., U.S. F6 156
Kenosha, co., Wi., U.S. F5 156
Kenova, W.V., U.S. C2 155
Kensal, N.D., U.S. B7 141
Kensett, Ar., U.S. B4 111
Kensett, Ia., U.S. A4 122
Kensico Reservoir, res., N.Y., U.S. g13 139
Kensington, P.E.I., Can. C6 101
Kensington, Ct., U.S. C4 114
Kensington, Ks., U.S. C4 123
Kensington, Md., U.S. B3 127
Kensington, Mn., U.S. E3 130
Kensington, N.H., U.S. E5 136
Kent, S.L. G3 64
Kent, Al., U.S. C4 108
Kent, Ct., U.S. C2 114
Kent, Oh., U.S. A4 142
Kent, Wa., U.S. B3 154
Kent, co., Eng., U.K. J14 8
Kent, co., De., U.S. D3 115
Kent, co., Md., U.S. B5 127
Kent, co., Mi., U.S. E5 129
Kent, co., R.I., U.S. D2 146
Kent, co., Tx., U.S. C2 150
Kentau, Kaz. I11 26
Kent Bridge, Ont., Can. E2 103
Kent City, Mi., U.S. E5 129
Kent Group, is., Austl. L7 70
Kent Island, i., De., U.S. D4 115
Kent Island, i., Md., U.S. C5 127
Kent Junction, N.B., Can. C4 101
Kentland, In., U.S. C3 121
Kenton, Man., Can. E1 100
Kenton, De., U.S. D3 115
Kenton, Ky., U.S. k14 124
Kenton, Oh., U.S. B2 142
Kenton, Tn., U.S. A2 149
Kenton, co., Ky., U.S. B5 124
Kent Peninsula, pen., N.W. Ter., Can. C11 96
Kent Point, c., Md., U.S. C5 127
Kentucky, state, U.S. C4 124
Kentucky, stm., Ky., U.S. B5 124
Kentucky, Middle Fork, stm., Ky., U.S. C6 124
Kentucky, North Fork, stm., Ky., U.S. C6 124
Kentucky, South Fork, stm., Ky., U.S. C6 124
Kentucky Dam, Ky., U.S. e9 124
Kentucky Lake, res., U.S. D9 106
Kentucky Ridge, mtn., Ky., U.S. D6 124
Kentville, N.S., Can. D5 101
Kentwood, La., U.S. D5 125
Kentwood, Mi., U.S. F5 129
Kenvil, N.J., U.S. B3 137
Kenville, Man., Can. D1 100
Kenvir, Ky., U.S. D6 124
Kenya, ctry., Afr. B7 58
Kenya, Mount see Kirinyaga, mtn., Kenya B7 58
Kenyon, Mn., U.S. F6 130
Kenyon, R.I., U.S. F2 146
Keo, Ar., U.S. C3 111
Keokea, Hi., U.S. C5 118
Keokuk, Ia., U.S. D6 122
Keokuk, co., Ia., U.S. C5 122
Keokuk Lock and Dam, U.S. D6 122
Keoma, Alta., Can. D4 98
Keo Neua, Col de, Asia E8 40
Keosauqua, Ia., U.S. D6 122
Keota, Ia., U.S. C6 122
Keota, Ok., U.S. B7 143
Keowee, Lake, res., S.C., U.S. B2 147
Kępice, Pol. A16 10
Kępno, Pol. D17 10
Keppel Bay, b., Austl. D9 70
Kequan, China G2 32
Kerala, state, India G4 46
Kerang, Austl. J5 70
Kerby, Or., U.S. E3 144
Kerč', Ukr. H5 26
Keremeos, B.C., Can. E8 99
Keren, Erit. J10 60
Kerend, Iran D9 48
Kerens, Tx., U.S. C4 150
Keret', ozero, l., Russia I23 6
Kerewan, Gam. E1 64
Kerguélen, Îles, is., F.S.A.T. M10 158
Kerhonkson, N.Y., U.S. D6 139
Kericho, Kenya B7 58
Keri Kera, Sud. K7 60
Kerinci, Gunung, mtn., Indon. F3 38
Keriya, stm., China B9 44
Kerkebet, Erit. I9 60
Kerkenna, Îles, is., Tun. C16 62
Kerkhoven, Mn., U.S. E3 130
Kerki, Turk. J11 26
Kérkira (Corfu), Grc. J3 20
Kérkira, i., Grc. J3 20
Kerkrade, Neth. G9 12
Kermadec Islands, is., N.Z. K22 158
Kermān, Iran F14 48
Kerman, Ca., U.S. D3 112
Kermit, Tx., U.S. D1 150
Kermit, W.V., U.S. D2 155
Kermode, Mount, mtn., B.C., Can. C2 99
Kern, co., Ca., U.S. E4 112
Kern, stm., Ca., U.S. E4 112
Kernersville, N.C., U.S. A2 140
Kernville, Ca., U.S. E4 112
Kérou, Benin F11 64
Kerpinen', Mol. C12 20
Kerr, co., Tx., U.S. D3 150
Kerr, Lake, l., Fl., U.S. C5 116
Kerrobert, Sask., Can. F1 105
Kerrville, Tx., U.S. D3 150
Kerry, co., Ire. I4 8
Kersey, Co., U.S. A6 113
Kersey, Pa., U.S. D4 145
Kershaw, S.C., U.S. B6 147
Kershaw, co., S.C., U.S. C6 147
Kerulen (Cherlen) (Herlen), stm., Asia B10 30
Kerzaz, Alg. F10 62
Kerzers, Switz. E7 13
Keşan, Tur. I10 20
Kesennuma, Japan I16 36
Keshena, Wi., U.S. D5 156
Keshod, India J4 44
Keskin, Tur. B2 48
Keski-Suomen lääni, prov., Fin. J19 6
Keskozero, Russia K23 6
Kes'ma, Russia C20 22
Kesova Gora, Russia D20 22
Kesra, Tun. N4 18
Kesten'ga, Russia I22 6
Keswick, Ia., U.S. C5 122
Keszthely, Hung. I17 10
Ket', stm., Russia F8 28
Keta, Ghana I10 64
Keta, ozero, l., Russia D10 28
Ketama, Mor. K7 16
Ketang, China M4 34
Ketchikan, Ak., U.S. D13 109
Ketchum, Id., U.S. F4 119
Ketchum, Ok., U.S. A6 143
Kete Krachi, Ghana H9 64
Kétou, Benin H11 64
Kętrzyn (Rastenburg), Pol. A21 10
Kettering, Eng., U.K. I13 8
Kettering, Oh., U.S. C1 142
Kettle, stm., Mn., U.S. D6 130
Kettle Creek, stm., Pa., U.S. D6 145
Kettle Creek Lake, res., Pa., U.S. D6 145
Kettle Falls, Wa., U.S. A7 154
Kettleman City, Ca., U.S. E4 112
Kettle River, Mn., U.S. D6 130
Keuka Lake, l., N.Y., U.S. C3 139
Kevil, Ky., U.S. e9 124
Kevin, Mt., U.S. B5 133
Kew, T./C. Is. D8 94
Kewanee, Il., U.S. B4 120
Kewanee, Mo., U.S. E8 132
Kewanna, In., U.S. B5 121
Kewaskum, Wi., U.S. E5 156
Kewaunee, Wi., U.S. D6 156
Kewaunee, co., Wi., U.S. D6 156
Keweenaw, co., Mi., U.S. A2 129
Keweenaw Bay, b., Mi., U.S. B2 129
Keweenaw Peninsula, pen., Mi., U.S. A3 129
Keweenaw Point, c., Mi., U.S. A3 129
Keya Paha, co., Ne., U.S. B6 134
Keya Paha, stm., U.S. A5 134
Keyes, Ok., U.S. e8 143
Keyesport, Il., U.S. E4 120
Keyhole Reservoir, res., Wy., U.S. B8 157
Key Largo, Fl., U.S. G6 116
Keymar, Md., U.S. A3 127
Keyport, N.J., U.S. C4 137
Keyser, W.V., U.S. B6 155
Keystone, In., U.S. C7 121
Keystone, Ia., U.S. C5 122
Keystone, S.D., U.S. D2 148
Keystone, W.V., U.S. D3 155
Keystone Heights, Fl., U.S. C4 116
Keystone Lake, res., Ok., U.S. A5 143
Keystone Peak, mtn., Az., U.S. F4 110
Keysville, Ga., U.S. C4 117
Keysville, Va., U.S. C4 153
Keytesville, Mo., U.S. B5 132
Key West, Fl., U.S. H5 116
Key West, Ia., U.S. B7 122
Key West Naval Air Station, mil., Fl., U.S. H5 116
Kezar Falls, Me., U.S. E2 126
Kezar Lake, l., Me., U.S. D2 126
Kezar Pond, l., Me., U.S. D2 126
Kežmarok, Slov. F20 10
Kgalagadi, dept., Bots. E5 66
Kgatleng, dept., Bots. E8 66
Khābūr, Nahr al-, stm., Asia D6 48
Khadki (Kirkee), India C2 46
Khairpur, Pak. G3 44
Khajrāho, India H8 44
Khakhea, Bots. E6 66
Khalkhalah, Syria B7 50
Khalkidhikí, hist. reg., Grc. I7 20
Khalkís, Grc. K7 20
Khalūf, Oman D11 47
Khambhāliya, India I3 44
Khambhāt, India I5 44
Khambhāt, Gulf of, b., India J5 44
Khāmgaon, India B4 46
Khamir, Yemen F3 47
Khamīs Mushayț, Sau. Ar. E3 47
Khamkeut, Laos E8 40
Khammam, India D6 46
Khānābād, Afg. B3 44
Khān al-Baghdādī, Iraq E7 48
Khānaqīn, Iraq D8 48
Khancoban, Austl. K8 70
Khandwa, India J7 44
Khānewāl, Pak. E4 44
Khāngarh, Pak. F4 44
Khaniá, Grc. N8 20
Khānpur, Pak. F4 44
Khān Yūnus, Isr. Occ. F2 50
Kharagpur, India I12 44
Kharānoq, Iran E13 48
Kharg Island see Khārk, Jazīreh-ye, i., Iran G11 48
Khargon, India J6 44
Khārān Cantonment, Pak. D5 44
Khārk, Jazīreh-ye, i., Iran G11 48
Kharkov see Char'kov, Ukr. E15 4
Khartoum see Al-Kharṭūm, Sud. J7 60
Khartoum North see Al-Kharṭūm Baḥrī, Sud. J7 60
Khartum see Al-Kharṭūm, Sud. J7 60
Khasebake, Bots. C7 66
Khāsh, Afg. F17 48
Khāsh, Iran G16 48
Khashm al-Qirbah, Sud. J8 60
Khatt, Oued al, val., W. Sah. G4 62
Khawsa, Burma G4 40
Khemis, Alg. B12 62
Khemmarat, Thai. F8 40
Khenchla, Alg. C14 62
Khenifra, Mor. D8 62
Kherrata, Alg. B13 62
Khíos, Grc. K10 20
Khíos, i., Grc. K10 20
Khirbat 'Awwād, Syria D7 50
Khlong Thom, Thai. K5 40
Kholm, Afg. B2 44
Khomeyn, Iran E11 48
Khomeynīshahr, Iran E11 48
Khomodimo, Bots. D6 66
Khon Kaen, Thai. F7 40
Khóra, Grc. L5 20
Khorramābād, Iran E10 48
Khorramshahr, Iran F10 48
Khossanto, Sen. E4 64
Khouribga, Mor. D7 62
Khowst, Afg. D3 44
Khuff, Sau. Ar. B4 47
Khugaung, Burma A5 40
Khuis, Bots. F5 66
Khu Khan, Thai. G8 40
Khulna, Bngl. I13 44
Khūnjerāb Pass, Asia B6 44
Khurai, India H8 44
Khurīyā Murīyā, Jazā'ir, is., Oman F10 47
Khurja, India F7 44
Khuzdār, Pak. G2 44
Khvāf, Iran D16 48
Khvor, Iran E13 48
Khvormūj, Iran G11 48
Khvoy, Iran B8 48
Khwae Noi, stm., Thai. G5 40
Khyber Pass, Asia C4 44
Kiama, Austl. J9 70
Kiamichi, stm., Ok., U.S. C6 143
Kiamika, stm., Que., Can. C2 104
Kiana, Ak., U.S. B7 109
Kiangarow, Mount, mtn., Austl. F9 70
Kiangsi see Jiangxi, prov., China F10 30
Kiangsu see Jiangsu, prov., China E10 30
Kiawah Island, i., S.C., U.S. F7 147
Kibangou, Congo B2 58
Kibombo, Zaire B5 58
Kibre Mengist, Eth. O10 60
Kičevo, Mac. H4 20
Kickamuit, stm., R.I., U.S. D5 146
Kickany, Mol. C13 20
Kickapoo, stm., Wi., U.S. E3 156
Kickapoo, Lake, res., Tx., U.S. C3 150
Kickapoo Creek, stm., Il., U.S. C4 120
Kickapoo Indian Reservation, Ks., U.S. C8 123
Kicking Horse Pass, Can. D2 98
Kicman', Ukr. A9 20
Kidal, Mali B10 64
Kidder, Mo., U.S. B3 132
Kidder, S.D., U.S. B8 148
Kidder, co., N.D., U.S. C6 141
Kidira, Sen. D3 64
Kiefer, Ok., U.S. B5 143
Kiel, Ger. A10 10
Kiel, Wi., U.S. E5 156
Kiel Canal see Nord-Ostsee-Kanal, Ger. A9 10
Kielce, Pol. E20 10
Kieler Bucht, b., Ger. A10 10
Kiester, Mn., U.S. G5 130
Kiev see Kijev, Ukr. G4 26
Kiffa, Maur. C4 64
Kifisiá, Grc. K7 20
Kifrī, Iraq D8 48
Kigali, Rw. B6 58
Kigille, Sud. M8 60
Kigoma, Tan. B5 58
Kihei, Hi., U.S. C5 118
Kihniö, Fin. J18 6
Kihnu, i., Est. C7 22
Kiholo Bay, b., Hi., U.S. D5 118
Kii-suidō, strt., Japan N9 36
Kijev (Kiev), Ukr. G4 26
Kijevskoje vodochranilišče, res., Ukr. G4 26
Kikerino, Russia B12 22
Kikinda, Yugo. D4 20
Kikládhes (Cyclades), is., Grc. L9 20
Kikori, Pap. N. Gui. G11 38
Kikwit, Zaire C3 58
Kila, Mt., U.S. B2 133
Kilambé, Cerro, mtn., Nic. D9 92
Kilauea, Hi., U.S. A2 118
Kilauea Crater, crat., Hi., U.S. D6 118
Kilauea Point, c., Hi., U.S. A2 118
Kilbourne, Il., U.S. C4 120
Kilbourne, La., U.S. B4 125
Kilburn, N.B., Can. C2 101
Kilchu, N. Kor. C17 32
Kilcoy, Austl. F10 70
Kildare, Ire. H7 8
Kildare, co., Ire. H7 8
Kil'din, ostrov, i., Russia G24 6
Kil'dinstroj, Russia G23 6
Kilgore, Tx., U.S. C5 150
Kilibo, Benin G11 64
Kilija, Ukr. D13 20
Kilikollūr, India H4 46
Kilimanjaro, mtn., Tan. B7 58
Kilimavony, Madag. s20 67b
Kilingi-Nõmme, Est. C7 22
Kilis, Tur. C4 48
Kilkenny, Ire. I6 8
Kilkenny, Mn., U.S. F5 130
Kilkenny, co., Ire. I6 8
Kilkís, Grc. H6 20
Killaloe, Ire. I5 8
Killaloe Station, Ont., Can. B7 103
Killaly, Sask., Can. G4 105
Killam, Alta., Can. C5 98
Killarney, Man., Can. E2 100
Killarney, Ire. I4 8
Killarney Provincial Park, Ont., Can. A3 103
Killbuck, Oh., U.S. B4 142
Killdeer, N.D., U.S. B3 141
Killdeer Mountains, mts., N.D., U.S. B3 141
Killeen, Tx., U.S. D4 150
Killen, Al., U.S. A2 108
Killian, La., U.S. h10 125
Killik, stm., Ak., U.S. B9 109
Killington Peak, mtn., Vt., U.S. D3 152
Killinkoski, Fin. J18 6
Killona, La., U.S. h11 125
Kilmarnock, Scot., U.K. F9 8
Kilmarnock, Va., U.S. C6 153
Kilmichael, Ms., U.S. B4 131
Kiln, Ms., U.S. E4 131
Kilomines, Zaire A6 58
Kilosa, Tan. C7 58
Kilpisjärvi, Fin. G17 6
Kilrush, Ire. I4 8
Kilttān Island, i., India G2 46
Kilwa, Zaire C5 58
Kim, stm., Cam. G9 54
Kimba, Austl. I2 70
Kimball, Mn., U.S. E4 130
Kimball, Ne., U.S. C2 134
Kimball, S.D., U.S. D7 148
Kimball, W.V., U.S. D3 155
Kimball, co., Ne., U.S. C2 134
Kimball, Mount, mtn., Ak., U.S. C11 109
Kimballton, Ia., U.S. C2 122
Kimberley, B.C., Can. E9 99
Kimberley, S. Afr. G7 66
Kimberley Plateau, plat., Austl. C5 68

Name — Map Ref. — Page

Kimberling City, Mo., U.S. E4 132
Kimberlin Heights, Tn., U.S. n14 149
Kimberly, Al., U.S. B3 108
Kimberly, Id., U.S. G4 119
Kimberly, W.V., U.S. m13 155
Kimberly, Wi., U.S. h9 156
Kimble, co., Tx., U.S. D3 150
Kimbrough, Al., U.S. C2 108
Kimch'aek (Sŏngjin), N. Kor. C17 32
Kimch'ŏn, S. Kor. G16 32
Kimito (Kemiö), Fin. K18 6
Kimiwan Lake, l., Alta., Can. B2 98
Kimje, S. Kor. H14 32
Kimmell, In., U.S. B6 121
Kimovsk, Russia H21 22
Kimry, Russia E20 22
Kinabalu, Gunong, mtn., Malay. D6 38
Kinbasket Lake, res., B.C., Can. D8 99
Kinburn, Ont., Can. B8 103
Kincaid, Sask., Can. H2 105
Kincaid, Il., U.S. D4 120
Kincaid, Ks., U.S. D8 123
Kincaid, W.V., U.S. m13 155
Kincaid, Lake, res., Il., U.S. D4 120
Kincaid Knob, mtn., W.V., U.S. k11 155
Kincardine, Ont., Can. C3 103
Kinchafoonee Creek, stm., Ga., U.S. E2 117
Kincheloe Air Force Base, mil., Mi., U.S. B6 129
Kindberg, Aus. H15 10
Kinde, Mi., U.S. E8 129
Kinder, La., U.S. D3 125
Kinderhook, Il., U.S. D2 120
Kinderhook, N.Y., U.S. C7 139
Kindersley, Sask., Can. F1 105
Kindia, Gui. F3 64
Kindred, N.D., U.S. C9 141
Kindu, Zaire B5 58
Kinel', Russia G8 26
Kineo, Mount, mtn., Me., U.S. C3 126
Kinešma, Russia D25 22
King, N.C., U.S. A2 140
King, Wi., U.S. D4 156
King, co., Tx., U.S. C2 150
King, co., Wa., U.S. B3 154
King and Queen, co., Va., U.S. C6 153
Kingaroy, Austl. F9 70
King City, Ca., U.S. D3 112
King City, Mo., U.S. A3 132
King Cove, Ak., U.S. E7 109
Kingfield, Me., U.S. D2 126
Kingfisher, Ok., U.S. B4 143
Kingfisher, co., Ok., U.S. B3 143
King George, Va., U.S. B5 153
King George, co., Va., U.S. B5 153
King George Island, i., Ant. B1 73
King George Islands, is., N.W. Ter., Can. E17 96
King Hill, Id., U.S. F3 119
Kingisepp, Russia B11 22
King Island, i., Austl. L6 70
King Island, i., B.C., Can. C4 99
King Lear Peak, mtn., Nv., U.S. B3 135
King Leopold Ranges, mts., Austl. C5 68
Kingman, Alta., Can. C4 98
Kingman, Az., U.S. B1 110
Kingman, In., U.S. E3 121
Kingman, Ks., U.S. E5 123
Kingman, Me., U.S. C4 126
Kingman, co., Ks., U.S. E5 123
Kingman Reef, rf., Oc. H23 158
King Mountain, mtn., Ok., U.S. C2 143
King Mountain, mtn., Or., U.S. E3 144
King Mountain, mtn., Or., U.S. D8 144
King of Prussia, Pa., U.S. F11 145
King Peak, mtn., Ca., U.S. B1 112
Kings, Il., U.S. A4 120
Kings, Ms., U.S. C3 131
Kings, co., Ca., U.S. D4 112
Kings, co., N.Y., U.S. E7 139
Kings, stm., Ar., U.S. A2 111
Kings, stm., Ca., U.S. D4 112
Kings, stm., Nv., U.S. B3 135
King Salmon, Ak., U.S. D8 109
Kingsburg, Ca., U.S. D4 112
Kingsbury, In., U.S. A4 121
Kingsbury, co., S.D., U.S. C8 148
Kings Canyon National Park, Ca., U.S. D4 112
Kingsclear, N.B., Can. D3 101
Kingscote, Austl. J2 70
Kingsdown, Ks., U.S. E4 123
Kingsey-Falls, Que., Can. D5 104
Kingsford, Mi., U.S. C2 129
Kingsgate, B.C., Can. E9 99
Kingsland, Ar., U.S. D3 111
Kingsland, Ga., U.S. F5 117
Kingsland, Tx., U.S. D3 150
Kingsley, Ia., U.S. B2 122
Kingsley, Mi., U.S. D5 129
Kingsley Dam, Ne., U.S. C4 134
King's Lynn, Eng., U.K. I14 8
Kings Mills, Oh., U.S. C1 142
Kings Mountain, N.C., U.S. B1 140
King Solomon's Mines see Mikhrot Shelomo Hamelekh, hist., Isr. I3 50
King Sound, strt., Austl. C4 68
Kings Park West, Va., U.S. *B5 153
Kings Peak, mtn., Ut., U.S. C5 151
Kings Point, Newf., Can. D3 102
Kingsport, Tn., U.S. C11 149
Kingston, Ont., Can. C8 103
Kingston, Jam. E6 94
Kingston, N.Z. F2 72
Kingston, Ar., U.S. A2 111
Kingston, Ga., U.S. B2 117
Kingston, Id., U.S. B2 119
Kingston, Il., U.S. A5 120
Kingston, Ky., U.S. C5 124
Kingston, Ma., U.S. C6 128
Kingston, Mi., U.S. E7 129
Kingston, Mo., U.S. B3 132
Kingston, N.H., U.S. E4 136
Kingston, N.J., U.S. C3 137
Kingston, N.Y., U.S. D6 139
Kingston, Oh., U.S. C3 142
Kingston, Ok., U.S. D5 143
Kingston, Pa., U.S. D10 145
Kingston, R.I., U.S. F3 146
Kingston, Tn., U.S. D9 149
Kingston, Wi., U.S. E4 156
Kingston Southeast, Austl. K3 70
Kingston Springs, Tn., U.S. A4 149
Kingston upon Hull, Eng., U.K. H13 8
Kingstown, St. Vin. H14 94
Kingstown, Md., U.S. B5 127
Kingstree, S.C., U.S. D8 147
Kingsville, Ont., Can. E2 103
Kingsville, Md., U.S. B5 127
Kingsville, Mo., U.S. C3 132
Kingsville (North Kingsville), Oh., U.S. A5 142
Kingsville, Tx., U.S. F4 150
Kingsville Naval Air Station, mil., Tx., U.S. F4 150
Kingswood, Ky., U.S. C3 124
King William, co., Va., U.S. C5 153
King William Island, i., N.W. Ter., Can. C13 96
King William's Town, S. Afr. I8 66
Kingwood, Tx., U.S. q14 150
Kingwood, W.V., U.S. B5 155
Kinistino, Sask., Can. E3 105
Kinkaid Lake, res., Il., U.S. F4 120
Kinkony, Lac, l., Madag. p21 67b
Kinkora, P.E.I., Can. C6 101
Kinley, Sask., Can. E2 105
Kin-li-chee, Az., U.S. B6 110
Kinloch, Mo., U.S. f13 132
Kinmount, Ont., Can. C6 103
Kinmundy, Il., U.S. E5 120
Kinnaird Head, c., Scot., U.K. D11 8
Kinnear, Wy., U.S. C4 157
Kinnelon, N.J., U.S. B4 137
Kinneret, Yam (Sea of Galilee), l., Isr. C5 50
Kinney, co., Tx., U.S. E2 150
Kinross, P.E.I., Can. C7 101
Kinsale, Va., U.S. B6 153
Kinsale, Old Head of, c., Ire. J5 8
Kinsella, Alta., Can. C5 98
Kinsey, Al., U.S. D4 108
Kinshasa (Léopoldville), Zaire B3 58
Kinsley, Ks., U.S. E4 123
Kinsman, Oh., U.S. A5 142
Kinston, Al., U.S. D3 108
Kinston, N.C., U.S. B5 140
Kinta, Ok., U.S. B6 143
Kintampo, Ghana G9 64
Kintyre, pen., Scot., U.K. F8 8
Kintyre, Mull of, c., Scot., U.K. F8 8
Kinuso, Alta., Can. B3 98
Kinyeti, mtn., Sud. H7 56
Kinzua, Or., U.S. C6 144
Kiosk, Ont., Can. A6 103
Kiowa, Co., U.S. B6 113
Kiowa, Ks., U.S. E5 123
Kiowa, Ok., U.S. C6 143
Kiowa, co., Co., U.S. C8 113
Kiowa, co., Ks., U.S. E4 123
Kiowa, co., Ok., U.S. C2 143
Kiowa Creek, stm., Co., U.S. B6 113
Kiowa Creek, stm., Ok., U.S. A1 143
Kipapa Stream, stm., Hi., U.S. g9 118
Kipengere Range, mts., Tan. C6 58
Kiperčeny, Mol. B12 20
Kipling, Sask., Can. G4 105
Kipling, Mi., U.S. C3 129
Kipnuk, Ak., U.S. C7 109
Kipp, Ks., U.S. D6 123
Kipushi, Zaire D5 58
Kirane, Mali D4 64
Kirazlı, Tur. I10 20
Kirby, Ar., U.S. C2 111
Kirby, Wy., U.S. C4 157
Kirbyville, Tx., U.S. D6 150
Kirchberg, Ger. F9 10
Kirchheim, Ger. G10 10
Kirchheimbolanden, Ger. F8 10
Kirchmöser, Ger. C12 10
Kirchschlag in der Buckligen Welt, Aus. H16 10
Kirejevsk, Russia H20 22
Kirenga, stm., Russia F13 28
Kirensk, Russia F13 28
Kirghizia see Kyrgyzstan, ctry., Asia I13 26
Kirgizskij chrebet, mts., Asia I12 26
Kiri, Zaire B3 58
Kiribati, ctry., Oc. F24 2
Kırıkhan, Tur. C4 48
Kırıkkale, Tur. B2 48
Kirillov, Russia B21 22
Kirillovskoje, Russia A12 22
Kirin see Jilin, China C12 30
Kirin see Jilin, prov., China C12 30
Kirinyaga, mtn., Kenya B7 58
Kiriši, Russia B15 22
Kiriwina Islands, is., Pap. N. Gui. A10 68
Kirk, Co., U.S. B8 113
Kırkağaç, Tur. J11 20
Kirkcaldy, Scot., U.K. E10 8
Kirkcudbright, Scot., U.K. G9 8
Kirkenes, Nor. G22 6
Kirkersville, Oh., U.S. C3 142
Kirkfield, Ont., Can. C5 103
Kirkjubæjarklaustur, Ice. C4 6a
Kirkland, Al., U.S. D2 108
Kirkland, Il., U.S. A5 120
Kirkland, Wa., U.S. B3 154
Kirkland Lake, Ont., Can. o19 103
Kırklareli, Tur. H11 20
Kirklin, In., U.S. D5 121
Kirkpatrick, Mount, mtn., Ant. D8 73
Kirksey, Ky., U.S. f9 124
Kirksville, Ky., U.S. C5 124
Kirksville, Mo., U.S. A5 132
Kirkton, Ont., Can. D3 103
Kirkūk, Iraq D8 48
Kirkwall, Scot., U.K. C11 8
Kirkwood, S. Afr. I7 66
Kirkwood, De., U.S. B3 115
Kirkwood, Il., U.S. C3 120
Kirkwood, Mo., U.S. f13 132
Kiron, Ia., U.S. B2 122
Kirov, Russia G17 22
Kirov, Russia F7 26
Kirovakan, Arm. I6 26
Kirovgrad, Russia F10 26
Kirovograd, Ukr. H4 26
Kirovsk, Bela. H12 22
Kirovsk, Russia B14 22
Kirovsk, Russia D4 26
Kirovskij, Azer. I7 26
Kirovskij, Kaz. I13 26
Kirs, Russia F8 26
Kirsanov, Russia I25 22
Kırşehir, Tur. B3 48
Kīrthar Range, mts., Pak. G2 44
Kirtland, N.M., U.S. A1 138
Kirtland Air Force Base, mil., N.M., U.S. k7 138
Kiruna, Swe. H17 6
Kirwin, Ks., U.S. C4 123
Kirwin Reservoir, res., Ks., U.S. C4 123
Kiryū, Japan K14 36
Kiržač, Russia E21 22
Kisa, Swe. M14 6
Kisangani (Stanleyville), Zaire A5 58
Kisarazu, Japan L14 36
K.I. Sawyer Air Force Base, mil., Mi., U.S. B3 129
Kisbey, Sask., Can. H4 105
Kisel'ovsk, Russia G9 28
Kishanganj, India G12 44
Kishangarh Bās, India G6 44
Kishi, Nig. G11 64
Kishiwada, Japan M10 36
Kishorganj, Bngl. H14 44
Kishwaukee, stm., Il., U.S. A5 120
Kisii, Kenya B6 58
Kišin'ov, Mol. B12 20
Kisiwa Creek, stm., Ks., U.S. g11 123
Kiska Island, i., Ak., U.S. E3 109
Kiskittogisu Lake, l., Man., Can. B2 100
Kiskunfélegyháza, Hung. I19 10
Kiskunhalas, Hung. I19 10
Kiskunmajsa, Hung. I19 10
Kislovodsk, Russia I6 26
Kismaayo, Som. B8 58
Kismet, Ks., U.S. E3 123
Kiso-sammyaku, mts., Japan L12 36
Kissee Mills, Mo., U.S. E4 132
Kissidougou, Gui. G4 64
Kissimmee, Fl., U.S. D5 116
Kissimmee, stm., Fl., U.S. E5 116
Kissimmee, Lake, l., Fl., U.S. E5 116
Kissimmee Park, Fl., U.S. D5 116
Kississing Lake, l., Man., Can. B1 100
Kistler, W.V., U.S. D3 155
Kisújszállás, Hung. H20 10
Kisumu, Kenya B6 58
Kisvárda, Hung. G22 10
Kita, Mali E5 64
Kita-Daitō-jima, i., Japan F13 30
Kitaibaraki, Japan K15 36
Kitakata, Japan J14 36
Kitakyūshū, Japan N5 36
Kitale, Kenya A7 58
Kitami, Japan d18 36a
Kitami-sanchi, mts., Japan c17 36a
Kit Carson, Co., U.S. C8 113
Kit Carson, co., Co., U.S. B8 113
Kitchener, Ont., Can. D4 103
Kite, Ga., U.S. D4 117
Kiteiyab, Sud. I7 60
Kíthira, Grc. M7 20
Kíthira, i., Grc. M6 20
Kíthnos, i., Grc. L8 20
Kitimat, B.C., Can. B3 99
Kitsap, co., Wa., U.S. B3 154
Kitscoty, Alta., Can. C5 98
Kittanning, Pa., U.S. E2 145
Kittatinny Mountain, mtn., U.S. B2 137
Kittery, Me., U.S. E2 126
Kittery Point, Me., U.S. E2 126
Kittilä, Fin. H19 6
Kittitas, Wa., U.S. C5 154
Kittitas, co., Wa., U.S. B4 154
Kittitas Valley, val., Wa., U.S. B5 154
Kitts, Ky., U.S. D6 124
Kitts Hummock, De., U.S. D4 115
Kittson, co., Mn., U.S. B2 130
Kitty Hawk, N.C., U.S. A7 140
Kitty Hawk Bay, b., N.C., U.S. A7 140
Kitui, Kenya B7 58
Kitwanga, B.C., Can. B3 99
Kitwe, Zam. D5 58
Kitwitwi, Nmb. A4 66
Kitzbühel, Aus. H12 10
Kitzingen, Ger. F10 10
Kiukiang see Jiujiang, China F4 34
Kivalina, Ak., U.S. B7 109
Kiviõli, Est. B9 22
Kivu, Lac, l., Afr. B5 58
Kıyıköy, Tur. H12 20
Kizel, Russia F9 26
Kızıl, stm., Tur. A2 48
Kızıltepe, Tur. C6 48
Kizl'ar, Russia I7 26
Kizyl-Arvat, Turk. J9 26
Kizyl-Atrek, Turk. J8 26
Kizyl-Su, Turk. B12 48
Kjustendil, Bul. G6 20
Kladanj, Bos. E2 20
Kladno, Czech. E14 10
Klagenfurt, Aus. I14 10
Klagetoh, Az., U.S. B6 110
Klaipėda (Memel), Lith. F4 22
Klaksvík, Faer. Is. D8 6b
Klamath, Ca., U.S. B1 112
Klamath, co., Or., U.S. E5 144
Klamath, stm., U.S. B2 112
Klamath Falls, Or., U.S. E5 144
Klamath Glen, Ca., U.S. B2 112
Klamath Mountains, mts., U.S. E2 144
Klangpi, Burma C2 40
Klarälven, stm., Eur. K13 6
Kl'asticy, Bela. F11 22
Klatovy, Czech. F13 10
Klawer, S. Afr. H4 66
Klawock, Ak., U.S. D13 109
Kl'az'ma, stm., Russia E25 22
Kleberg, co., Tx., U.S. F4 150
Kleck, Bela. H9 22
Kleena Kleene, B.C., Can. D5 99
Klemme, Ia., U.S. A4 122
Klerksdorp, S. Afr. F8 66
Klet', mtn., Czech. G14 10
Kletn'a, Russia H16 22
Kleve, Ger. D6 10
Kličev, Bela. H12 22
Klickitat, Wa., U.S. D4 154
Klickitat, co., Wa., U.S. D4 154
Klickitat, stm., Wa., U.S. C4 154
Klimoviči, Bela. H14 22
Klimovo, Russia I15 22
Klimovsk, Russia F20 22
Klin, Russia E19 22
Klincy, Russia I15 22
Klipplaat, S. Afr. I7 66
Kliškovcy, Ukr. A10 20
Kłobuck, Pol. E18 10
Kłodzko, Pol. E16 10
Klondike, hist. reg., Yukon, Can. D5 96
Klondike Gold Rush National Historical Park, Ak., U.S. k22 109
Klosterneuburg, Aus. G16 10
Klosters, Switz. E12 13
Kloten, Switz. D10 13
Klötze, Ger. C11 10
Klotzville, La., U.S. h9 125
Klouto, Togo H10 64
Kluane Lake, l., Yukon, Can. D5 96
Kl'učevskaja Sopka, vulkan, vol., Russia F24 28
Kl'uči, Russia F24 28
Kluczbork, Pol. E18 10
Klukwan, Ak., U.S. k22 109
Klutina Lake, l., Ak., U.S. g19 109
Knapp, Wi., U.S. D1 156
Knapp Creek, stm., W.V., U.S. C5 155
Knäred, Swe. M13 6
Kn'ažji Gory, Russia E18 22
Knee Lake, l., Man., Can. B4 100
Knevicy, Russia D15 22
Kneža, Bul. F8 20
Knić, Yugo. F4 20
Knife, stm., N.D., U.S. B3 141
Knife River, Mn., U.S. D7 130
Knifley, Ky., U.S. C4 124
Knightdale, N.C., U.S. B4 140
Knight Inlet, b., B.C., Can. D5 99
Knight Island, i., Ak., U.S. g18 109
Knights Landing, Ca., U.S. C3 112
Knightstown, In., U.S. E6 121
Knightsville, In., U.S. E3 121
Knightville Reservoir, res., Ma., U.S. B2 128
Knin, Cro. E11 18
Knittelfeld, Aus. H14 10
Knob Creek, stm., Ky., U.S. g11 124
Knobel, Ar., U.S. A5 111
Knobly Mountain, mtn., W.V., U.S. B5 155
Knob Noster, Mo., U.S. C4 132
Knokke-Heist, Bel. F3 12
Knollwood, Ct., U.S. D6 114
Knollwood, W.V., U.S. m12 155
Knops Pond, l., Ma., U.S. f9 128
Knott, co., Ky., U.S. C6 124
Knotts Island, N.C., U.S. A7 140
Knottsville, Ky., U.S. C3 124
Knox, In., U.S. B4 121
Knox, Pa., U.S. D2 145
Knox, co., Il., U.S. B3 120
Knox, co., In., U.S. G3 121
Knox, co., Ky., U.S. D6 124
Knox, co., Me., U.S. D4 126
Knox, co., Mo., U.S. A5 132
Knox, co., Ne., U.S. B8 134
Knox, co., Oh., U.S. B3 142
Knox, co., Tn., U.S. C10 149
Knox, co., Tx., U.S. C3 150
Knox, Cape, c., B.C., Can. B1 99
Knox City, Mo., U.S. A5 132
Knox City, Tx., U.S. C3 150
Knox Coast, Ant. B6 73
Knoxville, Ar., U.S. B2 111
Knoxville, Ga., U.S. D3 117
Knoxville, Il., U.S. C3 120
Knoxville, Ia., U.S. C4 122
Knoxville, Tn., U.S. D10 149
Knysna, S. Afr. J6 66
Knyszyn, Pol. B22 10
Kobar Sink, depr., Eth. F9 56
Kobayashi, Japan P5 36
Kōbe, Japan M10 36
København (Copenhagen), Den. N13 6
Koblenz, Ger. E7 10
Koboža, Russia C18 22
Kobrin, Bela. I7 22
Kobrinskoje, Russia B13 22
Kobuk, stm., Ak., U.S. B8 109
Kobuk Valley National Park, Ak., U.S. B8 109
Kobylin, Pol. D17 10
Kočani, Mac. H6 20
Kočečum, stm., Russia D12 28
Kočetovka, Russia I23 22
Kočevje, Slo. D9 18
Kōch'ang, S. Kor. H14 32
Kochanovo, Bela. G13 22
Koch Bihār, India G13 44
Kōchi, Japan N8 36
Kochma, Russia E24 22
Koch Peak, mtn., Mt., U.S. E5 133
Kodaikānal, India G4 46
Kodak, Ky., U.S. C6 124
Kodāri, Nepal G11 44
Kodiak, Ak., U.S. D9 109
Kodiak Island, i., Ak., U.S. D9 109
Kodino, Russia J26 6
Kodok, Sud. M7 60
Kodyma, Ukr. A13 20
Koekelare, Bel. F2 12
Koersel, Bel. F7 12
Koes, Nmb. E4 66
Kofa Mountains, mts., Az., U.S. D2 110
Köflach, Aus. H15 10
Koforidua, Ghana H9 64
Kōfu, Japan L13 36
Koga, Japan K14 36
Kogaluk, stm., Newf., Can. g9 102
Kogan, Austl. F9 70
Køge, Den. N13 6
Kogoni, Mali D6 64
Kohala Mountains, mts., Hi., U.S. C6 118
Kohāt, Pak. D4 44
Kohila, Est. B7 22
Kohīma, India H16 44
Kohler, Wi., U.S. E6 156
Kohtla-Järve, Est. B10 22
Kohŭng, S. Kor. I15 32
Kohunlich, hist., Mex. H15 90
Koidu, S.L. G4 64
Koigi, Est. C8 22
Koimbani, Com. k15 67a
Kojgorodok, Russia E8 26
Kojŏ, N. Kor. E15 32
Kok (Hkok), stm., Asia D5 40
Kokand, Uzb. I12 26
Kokanee Glacier Provincial Park, B.C., Can. E9 99
Kokčetav, Kaz. G11 26
Koki, Sen. D2 64
Kokka, Sud. G6 60
Kokkola (Karleby), Fin. J18 6
Koknese, Lat. E8 22
Koko, Nig. F12 64
Kokoda, Pap. N. Gui. A9 68
Koko Head, c., Hi., U.S. B4 118
Kokolik, stm., Ak., U.S. B7 109
Kokomo, Hi., U.S. C5 118
Kokomo, In., U.S. D5 121
Kokomo, Ms., U.S. D3 131
Kokong, Bots. E6 66
Koko Nor see Qinghai Hu, l., China D7 30
Kokopo, Pap. N. Gui. k17 68a
Kokorevka, Russia I17 22
Kokosing, stm., Oh., U.S. B3 142
Kokšaalatau, chrebet, mts., Asia I13 26
Koksan, N. Kor. E14 32
Koksilah, B.C., Can. g12 99
Koksŏng, S. Kor. H15 32
Kokstad, S. Afr. H9 66
Kola, Russia G23 6
Kolahun, Lib. G4 64
Kola Peninsula see Kol'skij poluostrov, pen., Russia D5 26
Kolār, India F5 46
Kolār Gold Fields, India F5 46
Kolárovo, Slov. H18 10
Kolbasna, Mol. B13 20
Kolbio, Kenya B8 58
Kolchozabad, Taj. B3 44
Kol'čugino, Russia E22 22
Kolda, Sen. E2 64
Kolenté (Great Scarcies), stm., Afr. G3 64
Kolgujev, ostrov, i., Russia D7 26
Kolhāpur, India D3 46
Kolia, I.C. G6 64
Koliba (Corubal), stm., Afr. E3 64
Koliganek, Ak., U.S. D8 109
Kolimbine, stm., Afr. D4 64
Kolín, Czech. E15 10
Kolka, Lat. D5 22
Kolkasrags, c., Lat. D5 22
Kollegāl, India F4 46
Köln (Cologne), Ger. E6 10
Kolno, Pol. B21 10
Kolo, Niger E11 64
Koło, Pol. C18 10
Koloa, Hi., U.S. B2 118
Kolob Canyon, val., Ut., U.S. F2 151
Kolobovo, Russia E24 22
Kołobrzeg, Pol. A15 10
Kolodn'a, Russia G15 22
Kologriv, Russia C27 22
Koloko, Burkina F7 64
Kolola Springs, Ms., U.S. B5 131
Kolomna, Russia F21 22
Kolomyja, Ukr. H3 26
Kol'osnoje, Ukr. C13 20
Kolpaševo, Russia F8 28
Kolpino, Russia B13 22
Kolpny, Russia I20 22
Kol'skij poluostrov (Kola Peninsula), pen., Russia D5 26
Kol'ubakino, Russia F19 22
Kolwezi, Zaire D5 58
Kolyma, stm., Russia D23 28
Kolymskaja nizmennost', pl., Russia D22 28
Koma, Eth. M9 60
Komadugu Gana, stm., Nig. F9 54
Komadugu Yobe, stm., Afr. F9 54
Komandorskije ostrova, is., Russia F25 28
Komariči, Russia I17 22
Komarniki, Ukr. F23 10
Komarno, Man., Can. D3 100
Komárno, Slov. H18 10
Komárom, Hung. H18 10
Komárom-Esztergom, co., Hung. H18 10
Komarovo, Russia C16 22
Komati (Incomáti), stm., Afr. E10 66
Komatipoort, S. Afr. E10 66
Komatke, Az., U.S. D3 110
Komatsu, Japan K11 36
Komatsushima, Japan M9 36
Kombone, Cam. I14 64
Komi, state, Russia E8 26
Komin Yanga, Burkina F10 64
Komló, Hung. I18 10
Kommunizma, pik, mtn., Taj. J12 26
Komodo, Pulau, i., Indon. G6 38
Komoé, stm., Afr. G6 54
Komotiní, Grc. H9 20
Komrat, Mol. C12 20
Komsomolec, Kaz. G10 26
Komsomolec, ostrov, i., Russia A17 26
Komsomolec, zaliv, b., Kaz. H8 26
Komsomol'sk, Russia D23 22
Komsomol'sk, Turk. B17 48
Komsomol'sk-na-Amure, Russia G19 28
Komsomol'skoj Pravdy, ostrova, is., Russia B13 28
Kona, Mali D8 64
Konahuanui, Puu, mtn., Hi., U.S. g10 118
Konakovo, Russia E19 22
Konakpınar, Tur. J11 20
Konar, stm., Asia C4 44
Konārak, India K12 44
Konawa, Ok., U.S. C5 143
Konceba, Ukr. A13 20
Konch, India H8 44
Konda, stm., Russia E5 28
Kondoa, Tan. B7 58
Kondopoga, Russia E4 26
Kondratjevo, Russia A11 22
Kondrovo, Russia G18 22
Kondūz, Afg. B3 44
Konfara, Gui. F5 64
Kông, stm., Asia H9 40
Kongcheng, China D6 34
Kongfang, China H5 34
Kongju, S. Kor. G15 32
Konglong, China F4 34
Kongolo, Zaire C5 58
Kongor, Sud. N6 60
Kongsvinger, Nor. K13 6
Kongur Shan, mtn., China D2 30
Kongzhen, China D8 34
Konice, Czech. F16 10
Königswinter, Ger. E7 10
Konin, Pol. C18 10
Köniz, Switz. E7 13
Konjic, Bos. F1 20
Könkämäälven, stm., Eur. G17 6
Kon'-Kolodez', Russia I22 22
Konkouré, stm., Gui. F3 64
Konnur, India D3 46
Konomoc, Lake, res., Ct., U.S. D7 114
Konoša, Russia E6 26
Konotop, Ukr. G4 26
Kon'ovo, Russia J26 6
Konqi, stm., China C4 30
Końskie, Pol. D20 10
Konstantinovka, Ukr. H5 26
Konstantinovskij, Russia D22 22
Konstanz, Ger. H9 10
Kontagora, Nig. F12 64
Kontejevo, Russia C24 22
Kontich, Bel. F5 12
Kontiomäki, Fin. I21 6
Kon Tum, Viet. G10 40
Kontum, Plateau du, plat., Viet. H10 40
Konya, Tur. C2 48
Konza, Kenya B7 58
Konžakovskij Kamen', gora, mtn., Russia F9 26
Koochiching, co., Mn., U.S. B4 130
Koolamarra, Austl. C4 70
Koolau Range, mts., Hi., U.S. f10 118
Kooloonong, Austl. J5 70
Koondrook, Austl. J6 70
Koontz Lake, In., U.S. B5 121
Koosharem, Ut., U.S. E4 151
Kooskia, Id., U.S. C3 119
Koossa, Gui. G5 64
Kootenai, co., Id., U.S. B2 119
Kootenay Lake, l., B.C., Can. E9 99
Kootenay National Park, B.C., Can. D9 99
Kootjieskolk, S. Afr. H5 66
Kopargaon, India C3 46
Kópasker, Ice. A5 6a
Kopcevići, Bela. I11 22
Kopejsk, Russia F10 26
Koper, Slo. D8 18
Kopetdag, chrebet, mts., Asia C15 48
Koppal, India E4 46
Kopparbergs Län, co., Swe. K14 6
Koppel, Pa., U.S. E1 145
Koprivnica, Cro. C11 18
Kopt'ovo, Russia E23 22
Kopyl', Bela. H10 22
Kopys', Bela. G13 22
Korab, mts., Eur. H4 20
Korablino, Russia H23 22
Kor'akskaja Sopka, vulkan, vol., Russia G23 28
Korāput, India C7 46
Korba, Tun. M5 18
Korbach, Ger. D8 10
Korbous, Tun. M5 18
Korçë, Alb. I4 20
Korčula, Otok, i., Cro. G12 18
Kord Kūy, Iran C13 48
Korea, North, ctry., Asia C12 30
Korea, South, ctry., Asia D12 30
Korea Bay, b., Asia E11 32
Korea Strait, strt., Asia I16 32
Korekozevo, Russia G19 22
Koreliči, Bela. H9 22
Korfovskij, Russia H19 28
Korgus, Sud. H7 60
Korhogo, I.C. G7 64
Korinthiakós Kólpos, b., Grc. K6 20
Kórinthos (Corinth), Grc. L6 20
Korínthou, Dhiórix, Grc. L6 20
Kōriyama, Japan J15 36
Korkino, Russia G10 26
Korla, China C4 30
Kornešty, Mol. B11 20
Korneuburg, Aus. G16 10
Koro, Mali D8 64
Korogwe, Tan. C7 58
Koroit, Austl. L5 70
Korol'ovo, Ukr. A7 20
Koróni, Grc. M5 20
Koronis, Lake, l., Mn., U.S. E4 130
Koronowo, Pol. B17 10
Körös, stm., Hung. I21 10
Korosten', Ukr. G3 26
Korotovo, Russia C20 22
Korovin Volcano, vol., Ak., U.S. E5 109
Korpilahti, Fin. J19 6
Korpo (Korppoo), Fin. K17 6
Korsakov, Russia H20 28
Korsør, Den. N12 6
Korsze, Pol. A21 10

Litt-Lota

Name | Map Ref. | Page

Little Egg Harbor, b., N.J., U.S. D4 137
Little Egg Inlet, b., N.J., U.S. E4 137
Little Exuma, i., Bah. C7 94
Little Falls, Mn., U.S. E4 130
Little Falls, N.J., U.S. B4 137
Little Falls, N.Y., U.S. B6 139
Little Ferry, N.J., U.S. h8 137
Littlefield, Tx., U.S. C1 150
Little Fishing Creek, stm., W.V., U.S. h9 155
Littlefork, Mn., U.S. B5 130
Little Fork, stm., Mn., U.S. B5 130
Little Frog Mountain, mtn., Tn., U.S. D9 149
Little Goose Creek, stm., Wy., U.S. B6 157
Little Gunpowder Falls, stm., Md., U.S. A4 127
Little Hocking, Oh., U.S. C4 142
Little Humboldt, stm., Nv., U.S. B4 135
Little Humboldt, North Fork, stm., Nv., U.S. B4 135
Little Humboldt, South Fork, stm., Nv., U.S. B5 135
Little Inagua, i., Bah. D8 94
Little Kanawha, stm., W.V., U.S. C4 155
Little Kanawha, West Fork, stm., W.V., U.S. B3 155
Little Lake, Mi., U.S. B3 129
Little Lake, l., La., U.S. E5 125
Little Lynches, stm., S.C., U.S. C7 147
Little Manatee, stm., Fl., U.S. p11 116
Little Mazarn Creek, stm., Ar., U.S. g7 111
Little Mecatina, stm., Can. h9 102
Little Mexico, Tx., U.S. D1 150
Little Miami, stm., Oh., U.S. C1 142
Little Miami, East Fork, stm., Oh., U.S. C1 142
Little Miami, Todd Fork, stm., Oh., U.S. C1 142
Little Missouri, stm., U.S. B6 106
Little Missouri, stm., Ar., U.S. D2 111
Little Moose Mountain, mtn., N.Y., U.S. B6 139
Little Muddy, stm., Il., U.S. E4 120
Little Muddy, stm., N.D., U.S. A2 141
Little Nicobar, i., India K2 40
Little Osage, stm., U.S. E9 123
Little Otter Creek, stm., Vt., U.S. C2 152
Little Owyhee, stm., U.S. B5 135
Little Pee Dee, stm., S.C., U.S. C9 147
Little Pigeon Creek, stm., In., U.S. I3 121
Little Pipe Creek, stm., Md., U.S. A3 127
Little Powder, stm., U.S. F11 133
Little Rann of Kachchh, pl., India I4 44
Little Red, stm., Ar., U.S. B4 111
Little Red, Middle Fork, stm., Ar., U.S. B3 111
Little River, N.S., Can. E3 101
Little River, Ks., U.S. D5 123
Little River, S.C., U.S. D10 147
Little River, co., Ar., U.S. D1 111
Little River Inlet, b., S.C., U.S. D10 147
Little Rock, Ar., U.S. C3 111
Little Rock, Ia., U.S. A2 122
Little Rock, S.C., U.S. C9 147
Littlerock, Wa., U.S. C2 154
Little Rock, stm., U.S. A1 122
Little Rock Air Force Base, mil., Ar., U.S. C3 111
Little Sable Point, c., Mi., U.S. E4 129
Little Saint Bernard Pass see Petit-Saint-Bernard, Col du, Eur. G13 14
Little Salt Lake, l., Ut., U.S. F3 151
Little Sand Creek, stm., Mn., U.S. D6 130
Little Sandy, stm., Ky., U.S. B6 124
Little Sandy Creek, stm., Wy., U.S. D3 157
Little Scarcies, stm., Afr. G4 54
Little Sebago Lake, l., Me., U.S. g7 126
Little Silver, N.J., U.S. C4 137
Little Sioux, Ia., U.S. C1 122
Little Sioux, stm., U.S. B2 122
Little Sioux, West Fork, stm., Ia., U.S. B2 122
Little Smoky, stm., Alta., Can. B2 98
Little Snake, stm., U.S. A2 113
Little Spokane, stm., Wa., U.S. B8 154
Littlestown, Pa., U.S. G7 145
Little Tallapoosa, stm., U.S. B4 108
Little Tenmile Creek, stm., W.V., U.S. k10 155
Little Tennessee, stm., U.S. D9 149
Littleton, Co., U.S. B6 113
Littleton, Me., U.S. B5 126
Littleton, Ma., U.S. f10 128
Littleton, N.H., U.S. B3 136
Littleton, N.C., U.S. A5 140
Little Valley, N.Y., U.S. C2 139
Littleville, Al., U.S. A2 108
Little Wabash, stm., Il., U.S. E5 120
Little Walnut, stm., Ks., U.S. g13 123
Little West Fork, stm., Tn., U.S. A4 149
Little White, stm., S.D., U.S. D5 148
Little Wolf, stm., Wi., U.S. D4 156
Little Wood, stm., Id., U.S. F4 119
Little York, Il., U.S. B3 120
Little York, In., U.S. G6 121
Little Zab (Zāb-e Kūchek) (Az-Zāb aṣ-Ṣaghīr), stm., Asia D7 48
Litvínov, Czech. E13 10
Liuchen, China C11 40
Liucheng, China B10 40
Liucura, Chile J3 80
Liudaogou, China B15 32
Liufangling, China E3 34
Liuguan, China F2 34
Liuhe, China A13 32
Liuhe, China C7 34
Liujia, China B9 40
Liujiadu, China C9 34
Liujiahe, China C2 34
Liuku, China B5 40
Liulongtai, China B8 32
Liuquan, China I5 32
Liurenba, China F3 34
Liushilipu, China C4 34
Liushuigou, China D1 34
Liutai, China B1 32
Liuwanglou, China I4 32
Liuyang, China G2 34
Liuyuan, China G2 32
Liuzhou, China B10 40
Liuzhuang, China B9 34
Līvāni, Lat. E9 22
Livelong, Sask., Can. D1 105
Live Oak, Ca., U.S. C3 112
Live Oak, Fl., U.S. B4 116
Live Oak, co., Tx., U.S. E3 150
Livermore, Ca., U.S. h9 112
Livermore, Ia., U.S. B3 122
Livermore, Ky., U.S. C2 124
Livermore, Me., U.S. D2 126
Livermore, Mount, mtn., Tx., U.S. o12 150
Livermore Falls, Me., U.S. D2 126
Liverpool, N.S., Can. E5 101
Liverpool, Eng., U.K. H11 8
Liverpool, Pa., U.S. E7 145
Livingston, Guat. B6 92
Livingston, Al., U.S. C1 108
Livingston, Ca., U.S. D3 112
Livingston, Il., U.S. E4 120
Livingston, Ky., U.S. C5 124
Livingston, La., U.S. D5 125
Livingston, Mt., U.S. E6 133
Livingston, N.J., U.S. B4 137
Livingston, Tn., U.S. C8 149
Livingston, Tx., U.S. D5 150
Livingston, Wi., U.S. F3 156
Livingston, co., Il., U.S. C5 120
Livingston, co., Ky., U.S. e9 124
Livingston, co., La., U.S. D5 125
Livingston, co., Mi., U.S. F7 129
Livingston, co., Mo., U.S. B4 132
Livingston, co., N.Y., U.S. C3 139
Livingston, Lake, res., Tx., U.S. D5 150
Livingstone, Zam. A7 66
Livingstone, Chutes de, wtfl, Afr. B2 58
Livingstone Cove, N.S., Can. D8 101
Livingstone Falls see Livingstone, Chutes de, wtfl, Afr. B2 58
Livingstone Mountains, mts., N.Z. F2 72
Livingstonia, Mwi. D6 58
Livingston Island, i., Ant. B12 73
Livingston Manor, N.Y., U.S. D6 139
Livno, Bos. F12 18
Livny, Russia I20 22
Livonia, La., U.S. D4 125
Livonia, Mi., U.S. F7 129
Livonia, N.Y., U.S. C3 139
Livorno (Leghorn), Italy F5 18
Livramento do Brumado, Braz. B8 79
Lixi, China F3 34
Lixian, China E3 32
Lixing, China B8 34
Liyang, China D8 34
Liyuanbao, China J1 34
Liyujiang, China J2 34
Lizard Creek, stm., Ia., U.S. B3 122
Lizard Head Pass, Co., U.S. D3 113
Lizard Head Peak, mtn., Wy., U.S. D3 157
Lizard Point, c., Eng., U.K. L8 8
Lizella, Ga., U.S. D3 117
Lizhu, China F9 34
Lizton, In., U.S. E4 121
Ljubija, Bos. E11 18
Ljubljana, Slo. C9 18
Ljubuški, Bos. F12 18
Ljungby, Swe. M13 6
Ljusdal, Swe. K15 6
Llaima, Volcán, vol., Chile J3 80
Llamara, Salar de, pl., Chile I7 82
Llancanelo, Laguna, l., Arg. H4 80
Llandrindod Wells, Wales, U.K. I10 8
Llangefni, Wales, U.K. H9 8
Llangollen, Wales, U.K. I10 8
Llanidloes, Wales, U.K. I10 8
Llano, N.M., U.S. A4 138
Llano, Tx., U.S. D3 150
Llano, co., Tx., U.S. D3 150
Llano, stm., Tx., U.S. D3 150
Llanos, pl., S.A. E7 84
Llanwrtyd Wells, Wales, U.K. I10 8
Llata, Peru C3 82
Lleida, Spain D12 16
Llera de Canales, Mex. F10 90
Lleulleu, Lago, l., Chile J2 80
Llica, Bol. H7 82
Llico, Chile H2 80
Lliria, Spain F11 16
Llorona, Punta, c., C.R. I11 92
Lloyd, Ky., U.S. B7 124
Lloydminster, Alta., Can. C5 98
Lloydminster (Alta. and Sask.), Sask., Can. D1 105
Lloyds, stm., Newf., Can. D3 102
Llucmajor, Spain F14 16
Llullaillaco, Volcán, vol., S.A. A3 80
Llusco, Peru F5 82
Lluta, stm., Chile H7 82
Lo (Panlong), stm., Asia C8 40
Loa, Ut., U.S. E4 151
Loa, stm., Chile I7 82
Loachapoka, Al., U.S. C4 108
Loami, Il., U.S. D4 120
Loanda, Braz. G2 79
Loange (Luangue), stm., Afr. C3 58
Lobanovo, Russia H21 22
Lobatse, Bots. E7 66
Lobaye, stm., Cen. Afr. Rep. H4 56
Lobelville, Tn., U.S. B4 149
Lobería, Arg. J9 80
Lobito, Ang. D2 58
Lobitos, Peru J2 84
Lobn'a, Russia E20 22
Lobos, Arg. H9 80
Lobos, Cay, i., Bah. C6 94
Lobos, Isla, i., Mex. D4 90
Lobos, Punta, c., Chile I6 82
Lobos de Afuera, Islas, is., Peru B1 82
Lobos de Tierra, Isla, i., Peru B1 82
Lobster Lake, l., Me., U.S. C3 126
Locarno, Switz. F10 13
Lochearn, Md., U.S. g10 127
Loches, Fr. E8 14
Loch Lomond, Va., U.S. *B5 153
Loch Lynn Heights, Md., U.S. m12 127
Lochmaben, Scot., U.K. F10 8
Lochmere, N.H., U.S. D3 136
Loch Raven Reservoir, res., Md., U.S. B4 127
Lochsa, stm., Id., U.S. C3 119
Lock, Austl. I1 70
Locke Mills, Me., U.S. D2 126
Lockeport, N.S., Can. F4 101
Lockerbie, Scot., U.K. F10 8
Lockesburg, Ar., U.S. D1 111
Lockhart, Austl. J7 70
Lockhart, Al., U.S. D3 108
Lockhart, Tx., U.S. E4 150
Lock Haven, Pa., U.S. D7 145
Lockland, Oh., U.S. o13 142
Lockney, Tx., U.S. B2 150
Löcknitz, Ger. B14 10
Lockport, Man., Can. D3 100
Lockport, Il., U.S. B5 120
Lockport, La., U.S. E5 125
Lockport, N.Y., U.S. B2 139
Lockridge, Ia., U.S. C6 122
Lockwood, Mo., U.S. D4 132
Lockwood, Mt., U.S. E8 133
Loc Ninh, Viet. I9 40
Loco Hills, N.M., U.S. E6 138
Locri, Italy K11 18
Locroja, Peru E4 82
Locumba, Peru G6 82
Locumba, stm., Peru G6 82
Locust, N.C., U.S. B2 140
Locust Bayou, Ar., U.S. D3 111
Locust Creek, stm., Mo., U.S. B4 132
Locust Fork, stm., Al., U.S. B3 108
Locust Grove, Ga., U.S. C2 117
Locust Grove, Md., U.S. B2 127
Locust Grove, Ok., U.S. A6 143
Lod (Lydda), Isr. E3 50
Loda, Il., U.S. C5 120
Lodejnoje Pole, Russia A16 22
Lodève, Fr. I10 14
Lodge, Newf., Can. B4 102
Lodge Grass, Mt., U.S. E9 133
Lodgepole, Alta., Can. C3 98
Lodge Pole, Mt., U.S. B8 133
Lodgepole, Ne., U.S. C3 134
Lodgepole Creek, stm., U.S. C3 134
Lodi, Italy D4 18
Lodi, Ca., U.S. C3 112
Lodi, N.J., U.S. h8 137
Lodi, Oh., U.S. A3 142
Lodi, Wi., U.S. E4 156
Lodja, Zaire B4 58
Lodore, Canyon of, val., Co., U.S. A2 113
Lodwar, Kenya H8 56
Łódź, Pol. D19 10
Loei, Thai. F6 40
Loeriesfontein, S. Afr. H4 66
Lofa, stm., Afr. G4 54
Lofoten, is., Nor. G13 6
Loga, Niger E11 64
Logan, Il., U.S. F5 120
Logan, Ia., U.S. C2 122
Logan, Ks., U.S. C4 123
Logan, Mt., U.S. E5 133
Logan, N.M., U.S. B6 138
Logan, N.D., U.S. A4 141
Logan, Oh., U.S. C3 142
Logan, Ut., U.S. B4 151
Logan, W.V., U.S. D3 155
Logan, co., Ar., U.S. B2 111
Logan, co., Co., U.S. A7 113
Logan, co., Il., U.S. C4 120
Logan, co., Ks., U.S. D2 123
Logan, co., Ky., U.S. D3 124
Logan, co., Ne., U.S. C5 134
Logan, co., N.D., U.S. C6 141
Logan, co., Oh., U.S. B2 142
Logan, co., Ok., U.S. B4 143
Logan, co., W.V., U.S. D3 155
Logan, Mount, mtn., Yukon, Can. D4 96
Logan, Mount, mtn., Wa., U.S. A5 154
Logan Creek, stm., Ne., U.S. B9 134
Logandale, Nv., U.S. G7 135
Logan Lake, B.C., Can. D7 99
Logan Martin Lake, res., Al., U.S. B3 108
Logan Pass, Mt., U.S. B2 133
Logansport, In., U.S. C5 121
Logansport, La., U.S. C2 125
Loganville, Ga., U.S. C3 117
Loganville, Pa., U.S. G8 145
Loggieville, N.B., Can. B4 101
Log Lane Village, Co., U.S. A7 113
Logojsk, Bela. G10 22
Logone, stm., Afr. F4 56
Logroño, Spain C9 16
Løgstør, Den. M11 6
Lohiniva, Fin. H19 6
Lohit, stm., Asia G16 44
Lohja, Fin. K19 6
Lohne, Ger. C8 10
Lohr, Ger. E9 10
Lohrville, Ia., U.S. B3 122
Loi, stm., Asia D6 40
Loi-kaw, Burma E4 40
Loimaa, Fin. K18 6
Loire, dept., Fr. G11 14
Loire, stm., Fr. E5 14
Loire-Atlantique, dept., Fr. E5 14
Loiret, dept., Fr. D9 14
Loir-et-Cher, dept., Fr. E8 14
Loitz, Ger. B13 10
Loja, Ec. E7 74
Loja, Ec. I3 84
Loja, Ec. J12 86
Loja, Spain H7 16
Loja, prov., Ec. J3 84
Lokandu, Zaire B5 58
Lokan tekojärvi, res., Fin. H20 6
Lokbatan, Azer. A10 48
Lokka, Fin. H20 6
Løkken, Den. M11 6
Lokn'a, Russia E13 22
Loko, Nig. G13 64
Lokoja, Nig. H13 64
Lokolama, Zaire B3 58
Lokossa, Benin H10 64
Lokot', Russia I17 22
Lol, Sud. N5 60
Lol, stm., Sud. M4 60
Lola, Gui. H5 64
Lola, Ky., U.S. e9 124
Lola, Mount, mtn., Ca., U.S. C3 112
Lolo, Mt., U.S. D2 133
Lolo Pass, U.S. C4 119
Lolotique, El Sal. D6 92
Lom, Bul. F7 20
Lom, Russia D22 22
Lom, stm., Afr. G9 54
Loma, Eth. N9 60
Loma, Co., U.S. B2 113
Loma, Mt., U.S. C6 133
Lomas de Zamora, Arg. H9 80
Lomax, Al., U.S. C3 108
Lomax, Il., U.S. C2 120
Lombard, Il., U.S. k8 120
Lombardia, prov., Italy D4 18
Lomblen, Pulau, i., Indon. G7 38
Lombok, i., Indon. G6 38
Lomé, Togo H10 64
Lomela, Zaire B4 58
Lometa, Tx., U.S. D3 150
Lomira, Wi., U.S. E5 156
Lo Miranda, Chile H3 80
Lommel, Bel. F7 12
Lomond, Alta., Can. D4 98
Lomond, Loch, l., Scot., U.K. E9 8
Lomonosov, Russia B12 22
Lomonosovskij, Kaz. G11 26
Lompoc, Ca., U.S. E3 112
Lom Sak, Thai. F6 40
Łomża, Pol. B22 10
Lonaconing, Md., U.S. k13 127
Loncoche, Chile D2 78
Loncopué, Arg. J3 80
Londesborough, Ont., Can. D3 103
Londinières, Fr. C8 14
London, Ont., Can. E3 103
London, Eng., U.K. J13 8
London, Ar., U.S. B2 111
London, Ky., U.S. C5 124
London, Oh., U.S. C2 142
Londonderry, N.S., Can. D6 101
Londonderry (Derry), N. Ire., U.K. F6 8
Londonderry, N.H., U.S. E4 136
Londonderry, Vt., U.S. E3 152
Londonderry, Cape, c., Austl. B5 68
London Mills, Il., U.S. C3 120
Londontown, Md., U.S. C4 127
Londres, Arg. D5 80
Londrina, Braz. G3 79
Lone Grove, Ok., U.S. C4 143
Lone Jack, Mo., U.S. C3 132
Lone Mountain, Tn., U.S. C10 149
Lone Mountain, mtn., Nv., U.S. E4 135
Lone Oak, Ky., U.S. e9 124
Lone Oak, Tx., U.S. C5 150
Lone Pine, Ca., U.S. D4 112
Lone Rock, Sask., Can. D1 105
Lone Rock, Wi., U.S. E3 156
Lone Tree, Ia., U.S. C6 122
Lone Tree Creek, stm., Co., U.S. A6 113
Lone Wolf, Ok., U.S. C2 143
Long, co., Ga., U.S. E5 117
Longa, stm., Ang. D2 58
Longa, proliv, strt., Russia C27 28
Long'an, China B10 40
Longaví, Chile H3 80
Long Bar Harbor, Md., U.S. B5 127
Long Beach, Ca., U.S. F4 112
Long Beach, In., U.S. A4 121
Long Beach, Md., U.S. D5 127
Long Beach, Ms., U.S. g7 131
Long Beach, N.Y., U.S. E7 139
Long Beach, Wa., U.S. C1 154
Long Beach Naval Shipyard, mil., Ca., U.S. n12 112
Longboat Key, Fl., U.S. q10 116
Longboat Key, i., Fl., U.S. E4 116
Longboat Pass, strt., Fl., U.S. q10 116
Long Branch, N.J., U.S. C5 137
Longbranch, Wa., U.S. B3 154
Long Cay, i., Bah. C7 94
Longchang, China F8 30
Longchuan, China K4 34
Longchuan (Shweli), stm., Asia B4 40
Long Creek Mountain, mtn., Wy., U.S. D5 157
Longcun, China L4 34
Longdale, Ok., U.S. A3 143
Longdou, China H6 34
Longeau, Fr. E12 14
Longford, Austl. L7 70
Longford, Ont., Can. C5 103
Longford, co., Ire. H6 8
Long Grove, Ia., U.S. C7 122
Long Harbour [-Mount Arlington Heights], Newf., Can. E5 102
Longhua, China B5 32
Long Island, Ks., U.S. C4 123
Long Island, i., Austl. D8 70
Long Island, i., Bah. C7 94
Long Island, i., N.S., Can. E3 101
Long Island, i., Me., U.S. g7 126
Long Island, i., Ma., U.S. g12 128
Long Island, i., N.Y., U.S. E7 139
Long Island Sound, strt., U.S. E7 139
Longitudinal, Valle, val., Chile H3 80
Longjiang, China B11 30
Longjin, China G5 34
Longka, China D8 44
Longkangji, China B5 34
Long Key, i., Fl., U.S. H6 116
Longkou, China D11 30
Longkou, China I4 34
Long Lake, Il., U.S. h8 120
Long Lake, l., Me., U.S. A4 126
Long Lake, l., Me., U.S. D2 126
Long Lake, l., Mi., U.S. D5 129
Long Lake, l., Mi., U.S. C7 129
Long Lake, l., Mn., U.S. D4 130
Long Lake, l., N.Y., U.S. B6 139
Long Lake, l., N.D., U.S. C6 141
Long Lake, l., Wa., U.S. f10 154
Long Lake, l., Wi., U.S. C2 156
Longleaf, La., U.S. C3 125
Longli, China F8 30
Longling, China B5 40
Longmeadow, Ma., U.S. B2 128
Longmensuo, China C3 32
Longming, China C9 40
Longmont, Co., U.S. A5 113
Long Mountain, mtn., Mo., U.S. E5 132
Long Mountain, mtn., N.H., U.S. A4 136
Longnan, China K3 34
Longnawan, Indon. E5 38
Longny, Fr. M14 8
Long Pine, Ne., U.S. B6 134
Long Point, N.S., Can. D8 101
Long Point, Ont., Can. E4 103
Long Point, Il., U.S. B5 120
Long Point, c., Man., Can. C2 100
Long Point, c., Newf., Can. D2 102
Long Point, pen., Ont., Can. E4 103
Long Pond, l., Me., U.S. C3 126
Long Pond, l., Me., U.S. C2 126
Long Pond, l., Ma., U.S. C6 128
Long Pond, l., Ma., U.S. C6 128
Long Pond, res., Fl., U.S. C4 116
Longport, N.J., U.S. E3 137
Long Prairie, Mn., U.S. E4 130
Longquan, China G8 34
Longquanguan, China E1 32
Long Range Mountains, mts., Newf., Can. D3 102
Longreach, Austl. D6 70
Longshansuo, China E10 34
Longsheng, China B11 40
Longs Peak, mtn., Co., U.S. A5 113
Longtian, China J8 34
Longton, Ks., U.S. E7 123
Longtoupu, China H2 34
Longueuil, Que., Can. D4 104
Longuyon, Fr. C12 14
Long Valley, N.J., U.S. B3 137
Longview, Alta., Can. D3 98
Long View, Ky., U.S. C4 124
Longview, Ms., U.S. B5 131
Long View, N.C., U.S. B1 140
Longview, Tx., U.S. C5 150
Longview, Wa., U.S. C3 154
Longwangmiao, China G3 32
Longwy, Fr. C12 14
Longxi, China E7 30
Long Xuyen, Viet. I8 40
Longyan, China J6 34
Longyuanba, China K3 34
Longzhou, China C9 40
Lonigo, Italy D6 18
Löningen, Ger. C7 10
Lonoke, Ar., U.S. C4 111
Lonoke, co., Ar., U.S. C4 111
Lonsdale, Ont., Can. C7 103
Lonsdale, Ar., U.S. C3 111
Lonsdale, Mn., U.S. F5 130
Lonsdale, R.I., U.S. B4 146
Lons-le-Saunier, Fr. F12 14
Lonton, Burma B4 40
Lontra, Ribeirão da, stm., Braz. F2 79
Loogootee, In., U.S. G4 121
Lookout, Ky., U.S. C7 124
Lookout, W.V., U.S. C4 155
Lookout, Cape, c., N.C., U.S. C6 140
Lookout, Point, c., Mi., U.S. d7 129
Lookout Mountain, Tn., U.S. h11 149
Lookout Mountain, mtn., U.S. D8 149
Lookout Mountain, mtn., Or., U.S. C6 144
Lookout Pass, U.S. B3 119
Lookout Point Lake, res., Or., U.S. D4 144
Loomis, Ne., U.S. D6 134
Loomis, Wa., U.S. A6 154
Loon Bay, Newf., Can. D4 102
Loon Lake, Wa., U.S. A8 154
Loon Lake, l., Me., U.S. B3 126
Loon op Zand, Neth. E7 12
Loop, Tx., U.S. C1 150
Loop Creek, stm., W.V., U.S. m13 155
Loosahatchie, stm., Tn., U.S. B2 149
Loose Creek, Mo., U.S. C6 132
Lop, China B9 44
Lopar'ovo, Russia C25 22
Lopatina, gora, mtn., Russia G20 28
Lopatka, mys, c., Russia G23 28
Lop Buri, Thai. G6 40
López, Mex. D7 90
Lopez, Cap, c., Gabon B1 58
Lopez Island, i., Wa., U.S. A3 154
Lop Nur (Lop Nor), l., China C5 30
Łopuszno, Pol. E20 10
Lora, stm., Ven. C6 84
Lora, Hāmūn-i-, l., Asia F1 44
Lora del Río, Spain H6 16
Lorado, W.V., U.S. D3 155
Lorain, Oh., U.S. A3 142
Lorain, co., Oh., U.S. A3 142
Loraine, Il., U.S. C2 120
Loraine, Tx., U.S. C2 150
Loramie, Lake, res., Oh., U.S. B1 142
Loranger, La., U.S. D5 125
Lorca, Spain H10 16
Lord Howe Island, i., Austl. F11 68
Lordsburg, N.M., U.S. E1 138
Loreauville, La., U.S. D4 125
Loreburn, Sask., Can. F2 105
Loreley, Ger. E7 10
Lorena, Braz. G6 79
Lorentz, W.V., U.S. B4 155
Lorenzo, Tx., U.S. C2 150
Lorenzo Geyres (Queguay), Ur. G10 80
Loreto, Arg. D10 80
Loreto, Bol. F9 82
Loreto, Braz. E9 76
Loreto, Mex. D4 90
Loreto, Mex. F9 90
Loreto, Para. B10 80
Loreto, dept., Peru I5 84
Loreto Mocagua, Col. I7 84
Lorette, Man., Can. E3 100
Loretteville, Que., Can. C6 104
Loretto, Ky., U.S. C4 124
Loretto, Mi., U.S. C3 129
Loretto, Pa., U.S. F4 145
Loretto, Tn., U.S. B4 149
Lorica, Col. C5 84
Lorida, Fl., U.S. E5 116
Lorient, Fr. E3 14
L'Orignal, Ont., Can. B10 103
Lorimor, Ia., U.S. C3 122
Loring Air Force Base, mil., Me., U.S. B5 126
Loriol, Fr. H11 14
Loris, S.C., U.S. C10 147
Lorman, Ms., U.S. D2 131
Lorne, Austl. L5 70
Lorne, N.B., Can. B3 101
Lorneville, Ont., Can. C5 103
Lörrach, Ger. H7 10
Lorraine, Ks., U.S. D5 123
Lorraine, hist. reg., Fr. D13 14
Lorris, Fr. E9 14
Losada, stm., Col. F5 84
Los Alamos, Ca., U.S. E3 112
Los Alamos, N.M., U.S. B3 138
Los Alamos, co., N.M., U.S. B3 138
Los Aldamas, Mex. D10 90
Los Altos, Ca., U.S. k8 112
Los Amates, Guat. B5 92
Los Americanos, Barra, i., Mex. E11 90
Los Andes, Chile G3 80
Los Ángeles, Chile I2 80
Los Angeles, Ca., U.S. E4 112
Los Angeles, co., Ca., U.S. E4 112
Los Angeles Aqueduct, Ca., U.S. E4 112
Losantville, In., U.S. D7 121
Los Banos, Ca., U.S. D3 112
Los Berros, Arg. F4 80
Los Blancos, Arg. B7 80
Los Bolones, Cerro, mtn., Mex. I13 90
Los Cerrillos, Arg. F6 80
Los Chacos, Bol. F10 82
Los Chiles, C.R. F10 92
Los Conquistadores, Arg. F9 80
Los Cristianos, Spain o24 17b
Los Esclavos, stm., Guat. D4 92
Los Frentones, Arg. D8 80
Los Fresnos, Tx., U.S. F4 150
Los Gatos, Ca., U.S. D2 112
Los Hermanos, Islas, is., Ven. B10 84
Łosice, Pol. C22 10
Los Juríes, Arg. E7 80
Los Lagos, Chile D2 78
Los Llanos de Aridane, Spain o23 17b
Los Lunas, N.M., U.S. C3 138
Los Maribios, Cordillera, mts., Nic. E8 92
Los Micos, Laguna de, b., Hond. B7 92
Los Mochis, Mex. E5 90
Los Molinos, Ca., U.S. B2 112
Lošnica, Bela. G11 22
Los Ojos, N.M., U.S. A3 138
Los Padillas, N.M., U.S. m7 138
Los Palacios, Arg. E4 80
Los Palacios, Cuba C3 94
Los Palacios y Villafranca, Spain H6 16
Los Pinos, stm., Co., U.S. D3 113
Los Quirquinchos, Arg. G8 80
Los Ranchos de Albuquerque, N.M., U.S. B3 138
Los Ríos, prov., Ec. H3 84
Los Rodríguez, Mex. D9 90
Los Roques, Islas, is., Ven. B9 84
Los Santos, prov., Pan. J14 92
Los Santos de Maimona, Spain G5 16
Los Sauces, Chile I2 80
Los Sauces, Spain o23 17b
Lossiemouth, Scot., U.K. D10 8
Lost, stm., In., U.S. G4 121
Lost, stm., Wa., U.S. A5 154
Lost, stm., W.V., U.S. B6 155
Lostant, Il., U.S. B4 120
Los Taques, Ven. B7 84
Lost Creek, W.V., U.S. B4 155
Lost Creek, stm., Ar., U.S. C3 111
Lost Creek, stm., Wy., U.S. D4 157
Los Telares, Arg. E7 80
Los Teques, Ven. B9 84
Los Testigos, Islas, is., Ven. B11 84
Lost Hills, Ca., U.S. E4 112
Lost Nation, Ia., U.S. C7 122
Lost Peak, mtn., Ut., U.S. F2 151
Lost Ranger Peak, mtn., Co., U.S. A4 113
Lost River Glacial Caverns, N.H., U.S. B3 136
Lost River Range, mts., Id., U.S. E5 119
Los Trujillos, N.M., U.S. C3 138
Lost Springs, Ks., U.S. D7 123
Lost Trail Pass, U.S. D5 119
Losuia, Pap. N. Gui. A10 68
Los Vidrios, Mex. B3 90
Los Vilos, Chile F3 80
Lot, dept., Fr. H8 14
Lot, stm., Fr. H7 14
Lota, Chile I2 80
Lotawana, Lake, res., Mo., U.S. k11 132

Name — Map Ref. — Page

Lotbinière, Que., Can. C6 104
Lot-et-Garonne, dept., Fr. H7 14
Lothair, S. Afr. F10 66
Lothian, prov., Scot., U.K. F10 8
Lotsane, stm., Bots. D8 66
Lott, Tx., U.S. D4 150
Lotung, Tai. K10 34
Louang Namtha, Laos D6 40
Louangphrabang, Laos E7 40
Louann, Ar., U.S. D3 111
Louchi, Russia D4 26
Loudéac, Fr. D4 14
Loudon, Tn., U.S. D9 149
Loudon, co., Tn., U.S. D9 149
Loudonville, Oh., U.S. B3 142
Loudoun, co., Va., U.S. A5 153
Loudun, Fr. E7 14
Loué, Fr. D6 14
Louga, Sen. D1 64
Louge, Arg. I8 80
Lougheed, Alta., Can. C5 98
Loughman, Fl., U.S. D5 116
Louhans, Fr. F12 14
Louin, Ms., U.S. C4 131
Louisa, Ky., U.S. B7 124
Louisa, Va., U.S. B4 153
Louisa, co., Ia., U.S. C6 122
Louisa, co., Va., U.S. C5 153
Louisa, Lake, l., Fl., U.S. D5 116
Louisbourg, N.S., Can. D10 101
Louisburg, Ks., U.S. D9 123
Louisburg, N.C., U.S. A4 140
Louisdale, N.S., Can. D8 101
Louise, Ga., U.S. C2 117
Louise, Ms., U.S. C3 131
Louise, Tx., U.S. E4 150
Louise, Lake, l., Ak., U.S. f18 109
Louise Island, i., B.C., Can. C2 99
Louiseville, Que., Can. C5 104
Louisiade Archipelago, is., Pap. N. Gui. B10 68
Louisiana, Mo., U.S. B6 132
Louisiana, state, U.S. C3 125
Louisiana Point, c., La., U.S. E2 125
Louis Trichardt, S. Afr. D9 66
Louisville, Al., U.S. D4 108
Louisville, Co., U.S. B5 113
Louisville, Ga., U.S. C4 117
Louisville, Il., U.S. E5 120
Louisville, Ks., U.S. C7 123
Louisville, Ky., U.S. B4 124
Louisville, Ms., U.S. B4 131
Louisville, Ne., U.S. D9 134
Louisville, Oh., U.S. B4 142
Louisville, Tn., U.S. D9 149
Louis-XIV, Pointe, c., Que., Can. h11 104
Loujiaying, China A4 32
Loup, co., Ne., U.S. C6 134
Loup, stm., Ne., U.S. C8 134
Loup, Rivière du, stm., Que., Can. B8 104
Loup, Rivière du, stm., Que., Can. C4 104
Loup City, Ne., U.S. C7 134
Lourdes, Newf., Can. D2 102
Lourdes, Fr. I6 14
Lourenço Marques see Maputo, Moz. E11 66
Lousana, Alta., Can. C4 98
Louta, Burkina E8 64
Louth, co., Ire. H7 8
Loutre, Bayou de, stm., La., U.S. B3 125
Louvain (Leuven), Bel. G6 12
Louvale, Ga., U.S. D2 117
Louviers, Fr. C8 14
Louviers, Co., U.S. B6 113
Lovat', stm., Russia D14 22
Love, Sask., Can. D3 105
Love, co., Ok., U.S. D4 143
Loveč, Bul. F8 20
Lovelaceville, Ky., U.S. f9 124
Lovelady, Tx., U.S. D5 150
Loveland, Co., U.S. A5 113
Loveland, Oh., U.S. n13 142
Loveland Park, Oh., U.S. C1 142
Loveland Pass, Co., U.S. B5 113
Lovell, Me., U.S. D2 126
Lovell, Wy., U.S. B4 157
Lovelock, Nv., U.S. C3 135
Lovely, Ky., U.S. C7 124
Lovenia, Mount, mtn., Ut., U.S. C5 151
Love Point, c., Md., U.S. B5 127
Lovere, Italy D5 18
Loves Park, Il., U.S. A4 120
Lovettsville, Va., U.S. A5 153
Lovewell Pond, l., Me., U.S. D2 126
Lovick, Al., U.S. f7 108
Lovilia, Ia., U.S. C5 122
Loving, N.M., U.S. E5 138
Loving, co., Tx., U.S. D1 150
Lovingston, Va., U.S. C4 153
Lovington, Il., U.S. D5 120
Lovington, Ia., U.S. e8 122
Lovington, N.M., U.S. E6 138
Lovosice, Czech. E14 10
Lovozero, Russia G24 6
Lovozero, ozero, l., Russia H24 6
Lövstabruk, Swe. K15 6
Low, Cape, c., N.W. Ter., Can. D15 96
Lowden, Ia., U.S. C7 122
Lowe Farm, Man., Can. E3 100
Lowell, Ar., U.S. A1 111
Lowell, In., U.S. B3 121
Lowell, Ma., U.S. A5 128
Lowell, Mi., U.S. F5 129
Lowell, N.C., U.S. B1 140
Lowell, Oh., U.S. C4 142
Lowell, Or., U.S. D4 144
Lowell, Vt., U.S. B4 152
Lowell, Wi., U.S. E5 156
Lowell, Lake, res., Id., U.S. F2 119
Lowelli, Sud. O7 60
Lowell Mountains, mts., Vt., U.S. B4 152
Lowellville, Oh., U.S. A5 142
Löwenberg, Ger. C13 10
Lower Arrow Lake, res., B.C., Can. E8 99
Lower Brule, S.D., U.S. C6 148
Lower Brule Indian Reservation, S.D., U.S. C6 148
Lower California see Baja California, pen., Mex. C3 90
Lower East Pubnico, N.S., Can. F4 101
Lower Hutt, N.Z. D5 72
Lower Island Cove, Newf., Can. D5 102
Lower Klamath Lake, l., Ca., U.S. B3 112
Lower Matecumbe Key, i., Fl., U.S. H6 116
Lower Monumental Lake, res., Wa., U.S. C7 154
Lower New York Bay, b., N.J., U.S. B4 137
Lower Otay Lake, res., Ca., U.S. o16 112
Lower Paia, Hi., U.S. C5 118
Lower Peach Tree, Al., U.S. D2 108
Lower Red Lake, l., Mn., U.S. C3 130
Lower Rice Lake, l., Mn., U.S. C3 130
Lower Salmon Dam, Id., U.S. G4 119
Lower Saxony see Niedersachsen, state, Ger. C8 10
Lower Village, Vt., U.S. C3 152
Lower West Pubnico, N.S., Can. F4 101
Lower Wilson Pond, l., Me., U.S. C3 126
Lower Woods Harbour, N.S., Can. F4 101
Lowes, Ky., U.S. f9 124
Lowestoft, Eng., U.K. I15 8
Łowicz, Pol. C19 10
Lowmansville, Ky., U.S. C7 124
Low Moor, Ia., U.S. C7 122
Lowmoor, Va., U.S. C3 153
Lowndes, co., Al., U.S. C3 108
Lowndes, co., Ga., U.S. F3 117
Lowndes, co., Ms., U.S. B5 131
Lowndesboro, Al., U.S. C3 108
Lowrah (Pishīn Lora), stm., Asia G18 48
Low Rocky Point, c., Austl. N6 70
Lowry Air Force Base, mil., Co., U.S. B6 113
Lowry City, Mo., U.S. C4 132
Lowville, N.Y., U.S. B5 139
Loxley, Al., U.S. E2 108
Loxton, Austl. J4 70
Loxton, S. Afr. H6 66
Loyal, Wi., U.S. D3 156
Loyall, Ky., U.S. D6 124
Loyalsock Creek, stm., Pa., U.S. D8 145
Loyalton, Ca., U.S. C3 112
Lozère, dept., Fr. H10 14
Loznica, Yugo. E3 20
Lualaba, stm., Zaire B5 58
Lua Makika, crat., Hi., U.S. C5 118
Lu'an, China D5 34
Luan, stm., China C10 30
Luanda, Ang. C2 58
Luando, stm., Ang. D3 58
Luang, Thale, b., Thai. K6 40
Luang Prabang Range, mts., Asia E6 40
Luangue (Loange), stm., Afr. C3 58
Luanguinga, stm., Afr. D4 58
Luangwa, stm., Afr. D6 58
Luanhaizi, China C15 44
Luanshishan, China A11 32
Luanshya, Zam. D5 58
Luán Toro, Arg. I6 80
Luapula, stm., Afr. D5 58
Luau, Ang. D4 58
Luba, Eq. Gui. H8 54
Lubaantun, hist., Belize I15 90
L'uban', Bela. I10 22
Lubań, Pol. D15 10
L'uban', Russia B14 22
Lubāna, Lat. E9 22
Lubango, Ang. D2 58
Lubao, China L1 34
L'ubašovka, Ukr. B14 20
Lubawa, Pol. B19 10
Lübbenau, Ger. D13 10
Lubbock, Tx., U.S. C2 150
Lubbock, co., Tx., U.S. C2 150
L'ubča, Bela. H9 22
Lubec, Me., U.S. D6 126
Lübeck, Ger. B10 10
Lubefu, Zaire B4 58
L'ubercy, Russia F20 22
L'ubim, Russia C23 22
Lubin, Pol. D16 10
Lublin, Pol. D22 10
Lubliniec, Pol. E18 10
Lubnān, Jabal (Lebanon Mountains), mts., Leb. A5 50
L'ubnica, Russia D15 22
Lubny, Ukr. G4 26
L'ubochna, Russia H17 22
Luboń, Pol. C16 10
L'ubotin, Ukr. H5 26
Lubraniec, Pol. C18 10
Lubsko, Pol. D14 10
Lubudi, Zaire C5 58
Lubumbashi (Élisabethville), Zaire D5 58
Lubutu, Zaire B5 58
L'ubytino, Russia C16 22
Lübz, Ger. B12 10
Lucama, N.C., U.S. B4 140
Lucan, Ont., Can. D3 103
Lucanas, Peru F4 82
Lucania, Mount, mtn., Yukon, Can. D4 96
Lucas, Ia., U.S. C4 122
Lucas, Ks., U.S. C5 123
Lucas, Oh., U.S. B3 142
Lucas, co., Ia., U.S. C4 122
Lucas, co., Oh., U.S. A2 142
Lucas González, Arg. G9 80
Lucasville, Oh., U.S. D3 142
Lucca, Italy F5 18
Luce, co., Mi., U.S. B5 129
Lucedale, Ms., U.S. E5 131
Lucena, Phil. o19 39b
Lucena, Spain H7 16
Lučenec, Slov. G19 10
Lucera, Italy H10 18
Lucerne, Ca., U.S. C2 112
Lucerne, Co., U.S. A6 113
Lucerne, In., U.S. C5 121
Lucerne, Lake see Vierwaldstätter See, l., Switz. D9 13
Lucerne see Luzern, Switz. D9 13
Lucernemines, Pa., U.S. E3 145
Lucerne Valley, Ca., U.S. E5 112
Luceville, Que., Can. A9 104
Luch, stm., Russia E25 22
Lucheng, China B9 40
Luchovicy, Russia G22 22
Lüchow, Ger. C11 10
Luchow see Luzhou, China F8 30
Luchuan, China C11 40
Luci, China F8 34
Lucie, stm., Sur. F14 84
Lucile, Id., U.S. D2 119
Lucindale, Austl. K4 70
Lucira, Ang. D2 58
Luck, Ukr. G3 26
Luck, Wi., U.S. C1 156
Luckau, Ger. D13 10
Luckenwalde, Ger. C13 10
Luckey, Oh., U.S. A2 142
Luckhoff, S. Afr. G7 66
Lucknow, Ont., Can. D3 103
Lucknow, India G9 44
Lucky, La., U.S. B3 125
Lucky Lake, Sask., Can. G2 105
Lucky Peak Lake, res., Id., U.S. F3 119
Luçon, Fr. F5 14
Lucun, China G6 32
Lucy, La., U.S. h10 125
Lucy, Tn., U.S. B2 149
Lüda see Dalian, China E9 32
Lüdenscheid, Ger. D7 10
Lüderitz, Nmb. F2 66
Ludhiāna, India E6 44
Lüdinghausen, Ger. D7 10
Ludington, Mi., U.S. E4 129
L'udinovo, Russia H17 22
L'udkovo, Russia G17 22
Ludlow, N.B., Can. C3 101
Ludlow, Il., U.S. C5 120
Ludlow, Ky., U.S. h13 124
Ludlow, Ma., U.S. B3 128
Ludlow, Ms., U.S. C4 131
Ludlow, Pa., U.S. C4 145
Ludlow, Vt., U.S. E3 152
Ludlow Mountain, mtn., Vt., U.S. E3 152
Ludowici, Ga., U.S. E5 117
Ludvika, Swe. K14 6
Ludwigsburg, Ger. G9 10
Ludwigsfelde, Ger. C13 10
Ludwigshafen, Ger. F8 10
Ludwigslust, Ger. B11 10
Ludza, Lat. E10 22
Luebo, Zaire C4 58
Luena, Ang. D3 58
Luena, Zaire C5 58
Luena, stm., Ang. D4 58
Luepa, Ven. E12 84
Lufeng, China M4 34
Lufeng, China B7 40
Lufkin, Tx., U.S. D5 150
Luga, Russia C12 22
Lugano, Switz. F10 13
Lugano, Lago di, l., Eur. C4 18
Lugansk (Vorošilovgrad), Ukr. H5 26
Lugenda, stm., Moz. D7 58
Lugnaquillia Mountain, mtn., Ire. I7 8
Lugo, Italy E6 18
Lugo, Spain B4 16
Lugoff, S.C., U.S. C6 147
Lugoj, Rom. D5 20
Lühedian, China C3 34
Luik (Liège), Bel. G8 12
Luino, Italy C3 18
Luishia, Zaire D5 58
Luis Lopez, N.M., U.S. D3 138
Luiza, Zaire C4 58
Luiziânia, Braz. F3 79
Luján, Arg. G4 80
Luján, Arg. G6 80
Lujiao, China F1 34
Lukachukai, Az., U.S. A6 110
Lukang, Tai. K9 34
Lukanga Swamp, sw., Zam. D5 58
Luke Air Force Base, mil., Az., U.S. D3 110
Luknovo, Russia E25 22
Lukolela, Zaire B3 58
Lukou, China H3 34
Lukoupu, China F2 34
Łuków, Pol. D22 10
Lukulu, Zam. D4 58
Lula, Ga., U.S. B3 117
Lula, Ms., U.S. A3 131
Luleå, Swe. I18 6
Lüleburgaz, Tur. H11 20
Lules, Arg. D6 80
Luliang, China B7 40
Lüliang Shan, mts., China D9 30
Luling, La., U.S. k11 125
Luling, Tx., U.S. E4 150
Lulinang, China F15 44
Lumbala N'guimbo, Ang. D4 58
Lumber, stm., U.S. C9 147
Lumber City, Ga., U.S. E4 117
Lumberport, W.V., U.S. B4 155
Lumberton, Ms., U.S. D4 131
Lumberton, N.J., U.S. D3 137
Lumberton, N.M., U.S. A3 138
Lumberton, N.C., U.S. C3 140
Lumberton, Tx., U.S. D5 150
Lumbres, Fr. B9 14
Lumby, B.C., Can. D8 99
Lumding, India H15 44
Lummi Indian Reservation, Wa., U.S. A3 154
Lumpkin, Ga., U.S. D2 117
Lumpkin, co., Ga., U.S. B2 117
Lumsden, Newf., Can. D5 102
Lumsden, Sask., Can. G3 105
Lumut, Malay. L6 40
Luna, N.M., U.S. D1 138
Luna, co., N.M., U.S. E2 138
Luna, stm., Braz. J12 84
Luna Pier, Mi., U.S. G7 129
Lūnāvāda, India I5 44
Lund, Swe. N13 6
Lund, Nv., U.S. E6 135
Lundale, W.V., U.S. n12 155
Lundar, Man., Can. D2 100
Lundazi, Zam. D6 58
Lundbreck, Alta., Can. E3 98
Lundi, stm., Zimb. C10 66
Lüneburg, Ger. B10 10
Lüneburger Heide, reg., Ger. B10 10
Lunel, Fr. I11 14
Lünen, Ger. D7 10
Lunenburg, N.S., Can. E5 101
Lunenburg, Ma., U.S. A4 128
Lunenburg, Vt., U.S. C5 152
Lunenburg, co., Va., U.S. D4 153
Lunéville, Fr. D13 14
Lunga, stm., Zam. D5 58
Lunge'nake, China E11 44
Lungi, S.L. G3 64
Lunguè-Bungo, stm., Afr. D4 58
Lunin, Bela. I9 22
Luninec, Bela. I9 22
Lunjiao, China M2 34
Lunno, Bela. H7 22
Luo, stm., China E9 30
Luochanghe, China D6 34
Luoci, China B7 40
Luofang, China H4 34
Luogang, China K4 34
Luohe, China B3 34
Luoheya, China H6 32
Luoji, China C6 34
Luokeng, China K2 34
Luoqiao, China I8 34
Luoshuihe, China D2 32
Luotuodian, China C2 34
Luoyang, China E9 30
Lupala, Nmb. A4 66
Lupani, Zimb. B8 66
Lupeni, Rom. D7 20
Luqu, China E7 30
Luray, Ks., U.S. C5 123
Luray, Va., U.S. B4 153
Lure, Fr. E13 14
Lure, Lake, res., N.C., U.S. f10 140
Luremo, Ang. C3 58
Luribay, Bol. G8 82
Lurín, Peru E3 82
Lúrio, Moz. D8 58
Lúrio, stm., Moz. D7 58
Lusaka, Zam. E5 58
Lusambo, Zaire B4 58
Lusanga, Zaire B3 58
Lusby, Md., U.S. D5 127
Luseland, Sask., Can. E1 105
Lushan, China E7 30
Lu Shan, mtn., China F10 30
Lushanguanliju, China F4 34
Lushnje, Alb. I3 20
Lushoto, Tan. B7 58
Lushui, China A5 40
Lüshun (Port Arthur), China E9 32
Lüsi, China C10 34
Lusignan, Fr. F7 14
L'usino, Bela. I9 22
Lusk, Wy., U.S. D8 157
Lūt, Dasht-e, des., Iran E15 48
Lutai, China B4 34
Lutang, China J1 34
Lutcher, La., U.S. D5 125
Luther, Mi., U.S. D5 129
Luther, Ok., U.S. B4 143
Luthersville, Ga., U.S. C2 117
Lutherville-Timonium, Md., U.S. B4 127
Lutian, China I3 34
Luton, Eng., U.K. J13 8
Lutong, Malay. E5 38
Lutou, China C1 34
Lutsen, Mn., U.S. k9 130
Luttrell, Tn., U.S. C10 149
Lutts, Tn., U.S. B4 149
Lutz, Fl., U.S. D4 116
Lützow-Holm Bay, b., Ant. B8 73
Lutzputs, S. Afr. G5 66
Lutzville, S. Afr. H4 66
Luuq, Som. H9 56
Luverne, Al., U.S. D3 108
Lu Verne, Ia., U.S. B3 122
Luverne, Mn., U.S. G2 130
Luvuvhu, stm., Afr. D10 66
Luxapallila Creek, stm., U.S. B5 131
Luxembourg (Luxemburg), Lux. I9 12
Luxembourg, prov., Bel. I7 12
Luxembourg, ctry., Eur. F9 4
Luxemburg, Ia., U.S. B6 122
Luxemburg, Wi., U.S. D6 156
Luxeuil-les-Bains, Fr. E13 14
Luxi (Mangshi), China B5 40
Lüxia, China I9 34
Luxomni, Ga., U.S. h8 117
Luxora, Ar., U.S. B6 111
Luxor see Al-Uqṣur, Egypt E7 60
Lüyang, China B9 32
Luz, Braz. E6 79
Luza, Russia E7 26
Luzarches, Fr. C9 14
Luzern, Switz. D9 13
Luzern, state, Switz. D9 13
Luzerne, Mi., U.S. D6 129
Luzerne, Pa., U.S. n17 145
Luzerne, co., Pa., U.S. D9 145
Luzhou, China F8 30
Luziânia, Braz. D5 79
Lužnice, stm., Eur. G14 10
Luzon, i., Phil. n19 39b
Luzon Strait, strt., Asia N9 34
Luzy, Fr. F10 14
L'vov, Ukr. H2 26
L'vovskij, Russia F20 22
Lwówek, Pol. C16 10
Lybster, Scot., U.K. C10 8
Lyčkovo, Russia D15 22
Lycksele, Swe. I16 6
Lycoming, co., Pa., U.S. D7 145
Lycoming Creek, stm., Pa., U.S. D7 145
Lydenburg, S. Afr. E10 66
Lydia, S.C., U.S. C7 147
Lyell, Mount, mtn., Can. D2 98
Lyell Island, i., B.C., Can. C2 99
Lyerly, Ga., U.S. B1 117
Lyford, In., U.S. E3 121
Lyford, Tx., U.S. F4 150
Lykens, Pa., U.S. E8 145
Lykošino, Russia C16 22
Lyle, Mn., U.S. G6 130
Lyle, Wa., U.S. D4 154
Lyles, Tn., U.S. B4 149
Lyleton, Man., Can. E1 100
Lyman, Ms., U.S. E4 131
Lyman, Ne., U.S. C1 134
Lyman, S.C., U.S. B3 147
Lyman, Wa., U.S. A3 154
Lyman, Wy., U.S. E2 157
Lyman, co., S.D., U.S. D6 148
Lyman Lake, res., Az., U.S. C6 110
Lyme, Ct., U.S. D6 114
Lyme, N.H., U.S. C2 136
Lyme Center, N.H., U.S. C2 136
Lyme Regis, Eng., U.K. K11 8
Łyna (Lava), stm., Eur. G3 22
Lynch, Ky., U.S. D7 124
Lynch, Ne., U.S. B7 134
Lynchburg, Oh., U.S. C2 142
Lynchburg, S.C., U.S. C7 147
Lynchburg, Tn., U.S. B5 149
Lynchburg, Va., U.S. C3 153
Lynches, stm., S.C., U.S. D8 147
Lynch Heights, De., U.S. E4 115
Lynch Station, Va., U.S. C3 153
Lynd, Mn., U.S. F3 130
Lynden, Wa., U.S. A3 154
Lynde Point, c., Ct., U.S. D6 114
Lyndhurst, Austl. H3 70
Lyndhurst, Ont., Can. C8 103
Lyndhurst, N.J., U.S. h8 137
Lyndhurst, Oh., U.S. g9 142
Lyndon, Il., U.S. B4 120
Lyndon, Ks., U.S. D8 123
Lyndon, Ky., U.S. g11 124
Lyndon, Vt., U.S. B4 152
Lyndon B. Johnson National Historical Site, hist., Tx., U.S. D3 150
Lyndon B. Johnson Space Center, sci., Tx., U.S. r14 150
Lyndon Center, Vt., U.S. B4 152
Lyndon Station, Wi., U.S. E4 156
Lyndonville, N.Y., U.S. B2 139
Lyndonville, Vt., U.S. B4 152
Lyndora, Pa., U.S. E2 145
Lyngdal, Nor. L10 6
Lyngen, Nor. G17 6
Lyngør, Nor. L11 6
Lynn, Al., U.S. A2 108
Lynn, Ar., U.S. A4 111
Lynn, In., U.S. D8 121
Lynn, Ma., U.S. B6 128
Lynn, co., Tx., U.S. C2 150
Lynn, Lake, res., W.V., U.S. B5 155
Lynn Canal, b., Ak., U.S. k22 109
Lynne, Fl., U.S. C5 116
Lynne Acres, Md., U.S. *B4 127
Lynnfield, Ma., U.S. f11 128
Lynn Garden, Tn., U.S. A9 149
Lynn Garden, Tn., U.S. C11 149
Lynn Grove, Ky., U.S. f9 124
Lynn Haven, Fl., U.S. u16 116
Lynnhaven Roads, b., Va., U.S. k15 153
Lynnville, In., U.S. H3 121
Lynnville, Ia., U.S. C5 122
Lynnville, Tn., U.S. B4 149
Lynnwood, Wa., U.S. B3 154
Lyntupy, Bela. F9 22
Lynwood, Ca., U.S. n12 112
Lyon, Fr. G11 14
Lyon, Ms., U.S. A3 131
Lyon, co., Ia., U.S. A1 122
Lyon, co., Ks., U.S. D7 123
Lyon, co., Ky., U.S. C1 124
Lyon, co., Mn., U.S. F3 130
Lyon, co., Nv., U.S. D2 135
Lyon Creek, stm., Ks., U.S. D7 123
Lyon Mountain, N.Y., U.S. f11 139
Lyon Mountain, mtn., N.Y., U.S. f11 139
Lyonnais, Monts du, mts., Fr. G11 14
Lyons, Co., U.S. A5 113
Lyons, Ga., U.S. D4 117
Lyons, Il., U.S. k9 120
Lyons, In., U.S. G3 121
Lyons, Ks., U.S. D5 123
Lyons, Mi., U.S. F6 129
Lyons, Ne., U.S. C9 134
Lyons, N.Y., U.S. B3 139
Lyons, Oh., U.S. A1 142
Lyons, Or., U.S. C4 144
Lyons, S.D., U.S. D9 148
Lyons, Wi., U.S. n11 156
Lyons, stm., Austl. D3 68
Lyons Plains, Ct., U.S. E2 114
Lys (Leie), stm., Eur. B9 14
Lysite, Wy., U.S. C5 157
Lyster Station, Que., Can. C6 104
Lys'va, Russia F9 26
Lytle, Tx., U.S. E3 150
Lytton, B.C., Can. D7 99
Lytton, Ia., U.S. B3 122

M

Ma, stm., Asia D8 40
Maalaea Bay, b., Hi., U.S. C5 118
Ma'alot-Tarshiha, Isr. B4 50
Ma'ān, Jord. H5 50
Ma'anshan, China D7 34
Maardu, Est. B8 22
Ma'arrat an-Nu'mān, Syria D4 48
Maas (Meuse), stm., Eur. D5 10
Maaseik, Bel. F8 12
Maasmechelen, Bel. G8 12
Maastricht, Neth. G8 12
Maave, Moz. C12 66
Maba, China C7 34
Mababe Depression, depr., Bots. B7 66
Mabank, Tx., U.S. C4 150
Mabaruma, Guy. C13 84
Mabel, Mn., U.S. G7 130
Mabeleapodi, Bots. C6 66
Maben, Ms., U.S. B4 131
Mabeul, Tun. M5 18
Mableton, Ga., U.S. h7 117
Mabou, N.S., Can. C8 101
Mabrūk, Sud. M5 60
Mabscott, W.V., U.S. D3 155
Mabton, Wa., U.S. C5 154
Mabuasehube Game Reserve, Bots. E6 66
Mabuguai, China F1 34
Macachín, Arg. I7 80
Macaé, Braz. G8 79
Macajuba, Braz. B8 79
Macalister, stm., Austl. K6 70
Macalister, Mount, mtn., Austl. J8 70
Macão, Port. F3 16
Macapá, Braz. C8 76
Macará, Ec. J3 84
Macarani, Braz. C8 79
Macareo, Caño, mth., Ven. C12 84
Macas, Ec. I3 84
Macau, Braz. E11 76
Macau (Aomen), Macau M2 34
Macau, dep., Asia G9 30
Macauã, stm., Braz. C7 82
Macaúbas, Braz. B7 79
Macaya, Pic, mtn., Haiti E7 94
Maccan, N.S., Can. D5 101
MacClenny, Fl., U.S. B4 116
Macclesfield, Eng., U.K. H11 8
MacClesfield, N.C., U.S. B5 140
Macdhui, Ben, mtn., Afr. H8 66
MacDill Air Force Base, mil., Fl., U.S. E4 116
Macdonald, Man., Can. D2 100
Macdonald, W.V., U.S. D3 155
Macdonald Range, mts., B.C., Can. E10 99
MacDonnell Ranges, mts., Austl. D6 68
MacDowell Reservoir, res., N.H., U.S. E2 136
Macduff, Scot., U.K. D11 8
Macdui, Ben, mtn., Scot., U.K. D10 8
Mace, In., U.S. D4 121
Macedon, N.Y., U.S. B3 139
Macedonia, Ia., U.S. C2 122
Macedonia, Oh., U.S. A4 142
Macedonia, hist. reg., Eur. H6 20
Macedonia (Makedonija), ctry., Eur. H5 20
Maceió, Braz. E11 76
Macenta, Gui. G5 64
Maceo, Col. D5 84
Maceo, Ky., U.S. C3 124
Macerata, Italy F8 18
Maces Bay, b., N.B., Can. D3 101
Macfarlane, Lake, l., Austl. H2 70
MacGregor, Man., Can. E2 100
Machacamarca, Bol. H8 82
Machachi, Ec. H3 84
Machačkala, Russia I7 26
Machadinho, stm., Braz. C10 82
Machado, Braz. F6 79
Machado, stm., Braz. C10 82
Machagai, Arg. D8 80
Machakos, Kenya B7 58
Machala, Ec. I3 84
Machalí, Chile H3 80
Machaneng, Bots. D8 66
Machang, China A7 32
Machangfu, China B7 40
Machaquilá, stm., Guat. A5 92
Machattie, Lake, l., Austl. E3 70
Machecoul, Fr. E5 14
Machias, Me., U.S. D5 126
Machias, N.Y., U.S. C2 139
Machias, stm., Me., U.S. D5 126
Machias, stm., Me., U.S. B4 126
Machias Bay, b., Me., U.S. D5 126
Machias Lakes, l., Me., U.S. C5 126
Machiasport, Me., U.S. D5 126
Machico, Port. m21 17a
Machilīpatnam (Bandar), India D6 46
Machiques, Ven. B6 84
Macho, Arroyo del, val., N.M., U.S. C4 138
Machupicchu, Peru E5 82
Machupicchu, hist., Peru E5 82
Machupo, stm., Bol. E9 82
Machynlleth, Wales, U.K. I10 8
Maciá, Arg. G9 80
Macintyre, stm., Austl. G8 70
Mack, Co., U.S. B2 113
Mackay, Austl. C8 70
Mackay, Id., U.S. F5 119
MacKay, stm., Alta., Can. A4 98
Mackay, Lake, l., Austl. D5 68
MacKenzie, B.C., Can. B6 99
Mackenzie, Guy. D13 84
Mackenzie, stm., N.W. Ter., Can. C6 96
Mackenzie Bay, b., Can. C5 96
Mackenzie Mountains, mts., Can. D7 96
Mackinac, co., Mi., U.S. B5 129
Mackinac, Straits of, strt., Mi., U.S. C6 129
Mackinac Bridge, Mi., U.S. C6 129
Mackinac Island, Mi., U.S. C6 129
Mackinac Island, i., Mi., U.S. C6 129
Mackinaw, Il., U.S. C4 120
Mackinaw, stm., Il., U.S. C4 120
Mackinaw City, Mi., U.S. C6 129
Mackinnon Road, Kenya B7 58
Macklin, Sask., Can. E1 105
Macks Creek, Mo., U.S. D5 132
Macksville, Austl. H10 70
Macksville, Ks., U.S. E5 123
Macksville, Ky., U.S. C4 124
Maclean, Austl. G10 70
Macleod, Lake, l., Austl. D2 68
Maclovio Herrera, Mex. C7 90
Macmillan, stm., Yukon, Can. D6 96
MacNutt, Sask., Can. F5 105
Macomb, Il., U.S. C3 120
Macomb, co., Mi., U.S. F8 129
Macomer, Italy I3 18
Mâcon, Fr. F11 14
Macon, Ar., U.S. C3 111
Macon, Ga., U.S. D3 117
Macon, Il., U.S. D5 120
Macon, Ms., U.S. B5 131
Macon, Mo., U.S. B5 132
Macon, Tn., U.S. B2 149
Macon, co., Al., U.S. C4 108
Macon, co., Ga., U.S. D2 117
Macon, co., Il., U.S. D4 120
Macon, co., Mo., U.S. B5 132

Maco-Mani

Name — Map Ref. — Page

Macon, co., N.C., U.S. f9 140
Macon, co., Tn., U.S. A5 149
Macon, Bayou, stm., U.S. B4 125
Macorís, Cabo, c., Dom. Rep. E9 94
Macoun, Sask., Can. H4 105
Macoupin, co., Il., U.S. D4 120
Macoupin Creek, stm., Il., U.S. D3 120
Macquarie, stm., Austl. M7 70
Macquarie, stm., Austl. H7 70
Macquarie Harbour, b., Austl. N6 70
Macquarie Island, i., Austl. A8 73
Mac. Robertson Land, reg., Ant. B5 73
Macroom, Ire. J5 8
Macrorie, Sask., Can. F2 105
MacTier, Ont., Can. B5 103
Macucuau, stm., Braz. H12 84
Macuelizo, Hond. B6 92
Macujer, Col. G6 84
Macungie, Pa., U.S. E10 145
Macunqiao, China B5 34
Macuro, Ven. B12 84
Macusani, Peru F6 82
Macuspana, Mex. I13 90
Macusse, Ang. A5 66
Macy, In., U.S. C5 121
Macy, Ne., U.S. B9 134
Mad, stm., Ca., U.S. B2 112
Mad, stm., Ct., U.S. B3 114
Mad, stm., N.H., U.S. C3 136
Mad, stm., Oh., U.S. C2 142
Mad, stm., Vt., U.S. C3 152
Ma'dabā, Jord. E5 50
Madagascar (Madagasikara), ctry., Afr. E9 58
Madā'in Ṣāliḥ, Sau. Ar. H4 48
Madame, Isle, i., N.S., Can. D9 101
Madanapalle, India F5 46
Madang, Pap. N. Gui. m16 68a
Mādārīpur, Bngl. I14 44
Madawaska, Ont., Can. B7 103
Madawaska, Me., U.S. A4 126
Madawaska, stm., Can. B9 104
Madawaska, stm., Ont., Can. B7 103
Madawaska Lake, l., Me., U.S. A4 126
Maddaloni, Italy H9 18
Madden, Ms., U.S. C4 131
Maddock, N.D., U.S. B6 141
Madeira, Oh., U.S. o13 142
Madeira, i., Port. m21 17a
Madeira, stm., S.A. E6 76
Madeira, Arquipélago da, is., Port. m21 17a
Madeirinha, stm., Braz. C11 82
Madeirinha, Paraná, mth., Braz. I13 84
M'adel', Bela. G9 22
Mädelegabel, mtn., Eur. E17 14
Madeleine, Îles de la, is., Que., Can. B8 101
Madelia, Mn., U.S. F4 130
Madeline Island, i., Wi., U.S. B3 156
Maden, Tur. B5 48
Madera, Mex. C5 90
Madera, Ca., U.S. D3 112
Madera, Pa., U.S. E5 145
Madera, co., Ca., U.S. D4 112
Maderas, Volcán, vol., Nic. F9 92
Madhubani, India G12 44
Madhya Pradesh, state, India I8 44
Madibogo, S. Afr. F7 66
Madidi, stm., Bol. E8 82
Madill, Ok., U.S. C5 143
Madimba, Zaire B3 58
Madina do Boé, Gui.-B. F2 64
Madinani, I.C. G6 64
Madīnat ash-Sha'b (Al-Ittihad), Yemen H4 47
Madingou, Congo B2 58
Madirobe, Madag. p22 67b
Madison, Al., U.S. A3 108
Madison, Ar., U.S. B5 111
Madison, Ct., U.S. D5 114
Madison, Fl., U.S. B3 116
Madison, Ga., U.S. C3 117
Madison, Il., U.S. E3 120
Madison, In., U.S. G7 121
Madison, Ks., U.S. D7 123
Madison, Me., U.S. D3 126
Madison, Mn., U.S. E2 130
Madison, Ms., U.S. C3 131
Madison, Mo., U.S. B5 132
Madison, Ne., U.S. C8 134
Madison, N.H., U.S. C4 136
Madison, N.J., U.S. B4 137
Madison, N.C., U.S. A3 140
Madison, Oh., U.S. A4 142
Madison, S.D., U.S. D8 148
Madison, Va., U.S. B4 153
Madison, W.V., U.S. C3 155
Madison, Wi., U.S. E4 156
Madison, co., Al., U.S. A3 108
Madison, co., Ar., U.S. B2 111
Madison, co., Fl., U.S. B3 116
Madison, co., Ga., U.S. B3 117
Madison, co., Id., U.S. F7 119
Madison, co., Il., U.S. E4 120
Madison, co., In., U.S. D6 121
Madison, co., Ia., U.S. C3 122
Madison, co., Ky., U.S. C5 124
Madison, co., La., U.S. B4 125
Madison, co., Ms., U.S. C4 131
Madison, co., Mo., U.S. D7 132
Madison, co., Mt., U.S. E5 133
Madison, co., Ne., U.S. C8 134
Madison, co., N.Y., U.S. C5 139
Madison, co., N.C., U.S. f10 140
Madison, co., Oh., U.S. C2 142
Madison, co., Tn., U.S. B3 149
Madison, co., Tx., U.S. D5 150
Madison, co., Va., U.S. B4 153
Madison, stm., Mt., U.S. E5 133
Madison Heights, Mi., U.S. o15 129
Madison Heights, Va., U.S. C3 153
Madison Lake, Mn., U.S. F5 130
Madison Range, mts., Mt., U.S. E5 133
Madisonville, Ky., U.S. C2 124
Madisonville, La., U.S. D5 125
Madisonville, Tn., U.S. D9 149
Madisonville, Tx., U.S. D5 150
Madiun, Indon. j15 39a
Madoc, Ont., Can. C7 103
Madoi, China E6 30
Madol, Sud. M4 60
Madona, Lat. E9 22
Madougou, Mali D8 64
Madrakah, Sau. Ar. D1 47
Madrakah, Ra's al-, c., Oman E10 47
Madras, India G11 42
Madras, Or., U.S. C5 144
Madras see Tamil Nādu, state, India G5 46
Madre, Laguna, b., Mex. E11 90
Madre, Laguna, b., Tx., U.S. F4 150
Madre, Sierra, mts., Phil. m20 39b
Madre de Chiapas, Sierra, mts., N.A. B2 92
Madre de Dios, dept., Peru D6 82
Madre de Dios, stm., S.A. D8 82
Madre de Dios, Isla, i., Chile A12 73
Madre de Dios, Isla, i., Chile J7 74
Madre del Sur, Sierra, mts., Mex. I10 90
Madre Occidental, Sierra, mts., Mex. E6 90
Madre Oriental, Sierra, mts., Mex. F9 90
Madre Vieja, stm., Guat. C3 92
Madrid, Col. E5 84
Madrid, Spain E8 16
Madrid, Al., U.S. D4 108
Madrid, Ia., U.S. C4 122
Madrid, Ne., U.S. D4 134
Madrid, N.Y., U.S. f9 139
Madrid, prov., Spain E8 16
Madridejos, Spain F8 16
Madriz, dept., Nic. D8 92
Madura, i., Indon. j16 39a
Madurai, India H5 46
Maebashi, Japan K14 36
Mae Hong Son, Thai. E4 40
Mae Klong, stm., Thai. G5 40
Maengsan, N. Kor. D14 32
Mae Sariang, Thai. E4 40
Maeser, Ut., U.S. C6 151
Mae Sot, Thai. F5 40
Maestra, Sierra, mts., Cuba D6 94
Maevatanana, Madag. p22 67b
Mafeking, Man., Can. C1 100
Mafeteng, Leso. G8 66
Maffra, Austl. K7 70
Mafia Island, i., Tan. C7 58
Mafikeng, Boph. G5 58
Mafikeng, S. Afr. E7 66
Mafra, Braz. D14 80
Magadan, Russia F22 28
Magadi, Kenya B7 58
Magalia, Ca., U.S. C3 112
Magallanes, Phil. o20 39b
Magallanes, Estrecho de (Strait of Magellan), strt., S.A. G3 78
Magangué, Col. C5 84
Magazine, Ar., U.S. B2 111
Magazine Mountain, mtn., Ar., U.S. B2 111
Magburaka, S.L. G4 64
Magdagači, Russia G17 28
Magdalena, Arg. H10 80
Magdalena, Bol. E9 82
Magdalena, Mex. G8 90
Magdalena, Peru B3 82
Magdalena, N.M., U.S. C2 138
Magdalena, dept., Col. B5 84
Magdalena, stm., Col. C5 84
Magdalena, stm., Mex. B4 90
Magdalena, Bahía, b., Mex. E3 90
Magdalena, Isla, i., Chile E2 78
Magdalena, Isla, i., Mex. E3 90
Magdalena, Punta, c., Col. F4 84
Magdalena de Kino, Mex. B4 90
Magdalena Mountains, mts., N.M., U.S. D2 138
Magdeburg, Ger. C11 10
Magee, Ms., U.S. D4 131
Magelang, Indon. j15 39a
Magellan, Strait of see Magallanes, Estrecho de, strt., S.A. G3 78
Magenta, Italy D3 18
Maggia, Switz. F10 13
Maggie Creek, stm., Nv., U.S. C5 135
Maggiore, Lago, l., Eur. C3 18
Maghāghah, Egypt C6 60
Maghama, Maur. D3 64
Maghniyya, Alg. C10 62
Magic Reservoir, res., Id., U.S. F4 119
Magione, Italy F7 18
Maglaj, Bos. E2 20
Magna, Ut., U.S. C3 151
Magness, Ar., U.S. B4 111
Magnetawan, Ont., Can. B5 103
Magnetawan, stm., Ont., Can. B4 103
Magnet Cove, Ar., U.S. C3 111
Magnitogorsk, Russia G9 26
Magnolia, Ar., U.S. D2 111
Magnolia, De., U.S. D4 115
Magnolia, Il., U.S. B4 120
Magnolia, Ia., U.S. C2 122
Magnolia, Ky., U.S. C4 124
Magnolia, Mn., U.S. G2 130
Magnolia, Ms., U.S. D3 131
Magnolia, N.C., U.S. C4 140
Magnolia, Oh., U.S. B4 142
Magnolia, Tx., U.S. D5 150
Magnolia Springs, Al., U.S. E2 108
Magoffin, co., Ky., U.S. C6 124
Magog, Que., Can. D5 104
Magothy River, b., Md., U.S. B4 127
Magozal, Mex. G11 90
Magpie, stm., Que., Can. h8 102
Magrath, Alta., Can. E4 98
Magruder Mountain, mtn., Nv., U.S. F4 135
Maguari, Cabo, c., Braz. D9 76
Maguzhan, China E13 44
Magway, Burma D3 40
Mahābād, Iran C8 48
Mahābaleshwar, India F9 42
Mahabe, Madag. p21 67b
Mahābhārat Lek, mts., Nepal F10 44
Mahabo, Madag. s22 67b
Mahabo, Madag. r21 67b
Mahaica-Berbice, prov., Guy. D14 84
Mahaicony Village, Guy. D14 84
Mahajamba, Helodranon' i, b., Madag. o22 67b
Mahajanga, Madag. o22 67b
Mahākālī (Sārda), stm., Asia F9 44
Mahakam, stm., Indon. E6 38
Mahalatswe, Bots. D8 66
Mahallāt, Iran E11 48
Mahanoro, Madag. q23 67b
Mahanoy City, Pa., U.S. E9 145
Mahārāshtra, state, India C3 46
Maha Sarakham, Thai. F7 40
Mahaska, co., Ia., U.S. C5 122
Mahasoa, Madag. s22 67b
Mahasolo, Madag. q22 67b
Mahates, Col. B5 84
Mahatsinjo, Madag. r21 67b
Mahaṭṭat al-Hafīf, Jord. D8 50
Mahbūbnagar, India D4 46
Mahd adh-Dhahab, Sau. Ar. C2 47
Mahdia, Tun. N6 18
Mahe, India G3 46
Mahébourg, Mrts. v18 67c
Mahé Island, i., Sey. B11 58
Mahendra Giri, mtn., India C8 46
Mahesāna, India I5 44
Mahia Peninsula, pen., N.Z. C7 72
Mahned, Ms., U.S. D4 131
Mahnomen, Mn., U.S. C3 130
Mahnomen, co., Mn., U.S. C3 130
Mahoba, India H8 44
Mahogany Mountain, mtn., Or., U.S. D9 144
Mahomet, Il., U.S. C5 120
Mahone Bay, N.S., Can. E5 101
Mahoning, co., Oh., U.S. B5 142
Mahoning, stm., U.S. A5 142
Mahoosuc Range, mts., N.H., U.S. B4 136
Mahopac, N.Y., U.S. D7 139
Mahres, Tun. C16 62
Mahtowa, Mn., U.S. D6 130
Mahuva, India B1 46
Mahwah, N.J., U.S. A4 137
Mai Aini, Erit. J10 60
Maicao, Col. B6 84
Maîche, Fr. E13 14
Maici, stm., Braz. B11 82
Maicuru, stm., Braz. D8 76
Maiden, N.C., U.S. B1 140
Maidenhead, Eng., U.K. J13 8
Maidstone, Sask., Can. D1 105
Maidstone, Eng., U.K. J14 8
Maidstone Lake, l., Vt., U.S. B5 152
Maidsville, W.V., U.S. B5 155
Maiduguri, Nig. F9 54
Maienfeld, Switz. D12 13
Maigatari, Nig. E14 64
Maignelay, Fr. C9 14
Maili, Hi., U.S. g9 118
Maili Point, c., Hi., U.S. g9 118
Maillezais, Fr. F6 14
Mai Mefales, Erit. J10 60
Main, stm., Ger. F9 10
Main-à-Dieu, N.S., Can. C10 101
Main Channel, strt., Ont., Can. B3 103
Mai-Ndombe, Lac, l., Zaire B3 58
Maine, N.Y., U.S. C4 139
Maine, hist. reg., Fr. D6 14
Maine, state, U.S. C3 126
Maine, Gulf of, b., N.A. C13 106
Maine-et-Loire, dept., Fr. E6 14
Mainhardt, Ger. F9 10
Mainland, i., Scot., U.K. B10 8
Mainland, i., Scot., U.K. A12 8
Main Pass, strt., La., U.S. E6 125
Mainpuri, India G8 44
Maintenon, Fr. D8 14
Maintirano, Madag. q21 67b
Main Topsail, mtn., Newf., Can. D3 102
Mainz, Ger. E8 10
Maio, i., C.V. m17 64a
Maipo, stm., Chile G3 80
Maipo, Volcán, vol., S.A. H4 80
Maipú, Arg. I10 80
Maipú, Arg. G4 80
Maipú, Chile G3 80
Maiquetía, Ven. B9 84
Mairipotaba, Braz. D4 79
Maisonnette, N.B., Can. B4 101
Maitengwe, Bots. C8 66
Maitengwe, stm., Afr. C8 66
Maitland, Austl. J2 70
Maitland, Austl. I9 70
Maitland, N.S., Can. D6 101
Maitland, Ont., Can. C9 103
Maitland, Mo., U.S. A2 132
Maíz, stm., Nic. F10 92
Maíz, Islas del, is., Nic. E11 92
Maize, Ks., U.S. g12 123
Maizuru, Japan L10 36
Maja, stm., Russia F18 28
Majagual, Col. C5 84
Majaki, Ukr. C14 20
Majari, stm., Braz. F12 84
Majé, Braz. G7 79
Majestic, Ky., U.S. C7 124
Maji, Eth. N8 60
Majia, China C7 34
Majie, China B7 40
Majja, Russia E18 28
Majkain, Kaz. G13 26
Majkop, Russia I6 26
Major, Sask., Can. F1 105
Major, co., Ok., U.S. A3 143
Majorca see Mallorca, i., Spain F15 16
Maka, Sen. E2 64
Makabana, Congo B2 58
Makaha, Hi., U.S. g9 118
Makaha Point, c., Hi., U.S. A2 118
Makah Indian Reservation, Wa., U.S. A1 154
Makahuena Point, c., Hi., U.S. B2 118
Makakilo City, Hi., U.S. g9 118
Makalamabedi, Bots. C6 66
Makallé, Arg. D9 80
Makalu, mtn., Asia G12 44
Makanda, Il., U.S. F4 120
Makanza, Zaire A3 58
Makapala, Hi., U.S. C6 118
Makapuu Head, c., Hi., U.S. B4 118
Makarjev, Russia D26 22
Makarov, Russia H20 28
Makarska, Cro. F12 18
Makasar, Selat (Makassar Strait), strt., Indon. F6 38
Makassar Strait see Makasar, Selat, strt., Indon. F6 38
Makat, Kaz. H8 26
Makawao, Hi., U.S. C5 118
Makaweli, Hi., U.S. B2 118
Makedonija see Macedonia, ctry., Eur. H5 20
Makejevka, Ukr. H5 26
Makeni, S.L. G3 64
Makgadikgadi, pl., Bots. C7 66
Makgadikgadi Pans Game Reserve, Bots. C7 66
Makhfar al-Quwayrah, Jord. I4 50
Makhfar Ramn, Jord. I4 50
Makhrūq, Wādī al-, val., Asia F7 50
Makindu, Kenya B7 58
Makinsk, Kaz. G12 26
M'akiševo, Russia E11 22
M'akit, Russia E22 28
Makkah (Mecca), Sau. Ar. D1 47
Makkovik, Newf., Can. g10 102
Makó, Hung. I20 10
Makokou, Gabon A2 58
Makoti, N.D., U.S. B4 141
Makoua, Congo A3 58
Makrāna, India G6 44
Makran Coast, Asia I16 48
M'aksa, Russia C21 22
Maksaticha, Russia D18 22
Makthar, Tun. N4 18
Mākū, Iran B8 48
Makumbi, Zaire C4 58
Makung (P'enghu), Tai. L8 34
Makurdi, Nig. H14 64
Makushin Volcano, vol., Ak., U.S. E6 109
Makwassie, S. Afr. F8 66
Mal, Maur. C3 64
Mala, Peru E3 82
Mala, stm., Peru E3 82
Mala, Punta, c., Pan. D3 84
Malabang, Phil. D7 38
Malabar, Fl., U.S. D6 116
Malabar Coast, India F3 46
Malabo, Eq. Gui. J14 64
Malacacheta, Braz. D7 79
Malacca, Strait of, strt., Asia M6 40
Malacky, Slov. G17 10
Malad City, Id., U.S. G6 119
Málaga, Col. D6 84
Málaga, Spain I7 16
Malaga, N.J., U.S. D2 137
Malaga, N.M., U.S. E5 138
Malagash, N.S., Can. D6 101
Malagasy Republic see Madagascar, ctry., Afr. E9 58
Malagón, Spain F8 16
Malaimbandy, Madag. r21 67b
Malaja Kuril'skaja Gr'ada (Habomai-Shotō), is., Russia d21 36a
Malaja Višera, Russia C15 22
Malakāl, Sud. M6 60
Malakoff, Tx., U.S. C4 150
Malambo, Col. B5 84
Malān, Burma B4 40
Malang, Indon. j16 39a
Malanggwā, Nepal G11 44
Malanje, Ang. C3 58
Malanville, Benin F11 64
Malanzán, Arg. F5 80
Mälaren, l., Swe. L15 6
Malargüe, Arg. H4 80
Malartic, Que., Can. k11 104
Malaspina Glacier, Ak., U.S. D11 109
Malatya, Tur. B5 48
Malaut, India E6 44
Malawi, ctry., Afr. D6 58
Malawi, Lake see Nyasa, Lake, l., Afr. D6 58
Malaybalay, Phil. D8 38
Malāyer, Iran D10 48
Malay Peninsula, pen., Asia K6 40
Malay Reef, rf., Austl. A8 70
Malaysia, ctry., Asia E3 38
Malazgirt, Tur. B7 48
Malbaie, stm., Que., Can. B7 104
Malbork, Pol. A19 10
Malbrán, Arg. E7 80
Malcolm, Austl. E4 68
Malcolm, Ne., U.S. D9 134
Malcom, Ia., U.S. C5 122
Maldegem, Bel. F3 12
Malden, Il., U.S. B4 120
Malden, Ma., U.S. B5 128
Malden, Mo., U.S. E8 132
Malden, W.V., U.S. m12 155
Maldive Islands, is., Mald. I2 46
Maldives, ctry., Asia I8 24
Maldonado, Ur. H11 80
Malé, Italy C5 18
Male', Mald. I8 24
Maléa, Ákra, c., Grc. M7 20
Mālegaon, India B3 46
Malek, Sud. N6 60
Malek Siāh, Kūh-e, mtn., Asia G16 48
Malema, Moz. D7 58
Malen'ga, Russia J25 6
Māler Kotla, India E6 44
Malesherbes, Fr. D9 14
Malestroit, Fr. E4 14
Malha Wells, Sud. J4 60
Malheur, co., Or., U.S. D9 144
Malheur, stm., Or., U.S. D9 144
Malheur Lake, l., Or., U.S. D8 144
Mali, ctry., Afr. E6 54
Mali, stm., Burma A4 40
Malibu, Ca., U.S. m11 112
Malik, Wādī al-, val., Sud. I6 60
Mali Kyun, i., Burma H5 40
Malin, Or., U.S. E5 144
Malinalco, hist., Mex. H10 90
Malinaltepec, Mex. I10 90
Malines (Mechelen), Bel. F5 12
Malin Head, c., Ire. F6 8
Maliwun, Burma I5 40
Maljamar, N.M., U.S. E6 138
Malka, Russia G23 28
Malkāpur, India B4 46
Malkara, Tur. I10 20
Mallāh, Syria C7 50
Mallaig, Alta., Can. B5 98
Mallaig, Scot., U.K. D8 8
Mallala, Austl. J3 70
Mallaoua, Niger E14 64
Mallard, Ia., U.S. B3 122
Mallawī, Egypt D6 60
Mallet, Braz. C13 80
Malletts Bay, b., Vt., U.S. B2 152
Malligasta, Arg. E5 80
Mallnitz, Aus. I13 10
Mallorca, i., Spain F15 16
Mallow, Ire. I5 8
Malmédy, Bel. H9 12
Malmesbury, S. Afr. I4 66
Malmö, Swe. N13 6
Malmo, Ne., U.S. C9 134
Malmöhus Län, co., Swe. N13 6
Malmstrom Air Force Base, mil., Mt., U.S. C5 133
Maloarchangel'sk, Russia I19 22
Maloja, Switz. F12 13
Malojaroslavec, Russia F19 22
Maloje Kozino, Russia E26 22
Maloje Skuratovo, Russia H20 22
Malolos, Phil. n19 39b
Malone, Fl., U.S. B1 116
Malone, N.Y., U.S. f10 139
Malone, Wa., U.S. C2 154
Maloney Reservoir, res., Ne., U.S. C5 134
Malonga, Zaire D4 58
Małopolska, reg., Pol. E21 10
Malošujka, Russia E5 26
Malott, Wa., U.S. A6 154
Måløy, Nor. K9 6
Malpaisillo, Nic. E8 92
Malpas, Austl. J4 70
Malpelo, Isla de, i., Col. C2 76
Malpeque Bay, b., P.E.I., Can. C6 101
Malta, Lat. E10 22
Malta, Id., U.S. G5 119
Malta, Il., U.S. B5 120
Malta, Mt., U.S. B9 133
Malta, Oh., U.S. C4 142
Malta, ctry., Eur. H10 4
Malta, i., Malta N9 18
Malta Bend, Mo., U.S. B4 132
Malta Channel, strt., Eur. M9 18
Maltahöhe, Nmb. E3 66
Maltepe, Tur. I11 20
Maluku (Moluccas), is., Indon. F8 38
Maluku, Laut (Molucca Sea), Indon. F7 38
Malumfashi, Nig. F13 64
Malvern, Al., U.S. D4 108
Malvern, Ar., U.S. C3 111
Malvern, Ia., U.S. D2 122
Malvern, Oh., U.S. B4 142
Malvern, Pa., U.S. o19 145
Malverne, N.Y., U.S. k13 139
Malvinas, Arg. E9 80
Malwal, Sud. M6 60
Malý Dunaj, stm., Slov. H17 10
Malyj, ostrov, i., Russia A11 22
Malyj An'uj, stm., Russia D24 28
Malyj Jenisej, stm., Russia G11 28
Malyj Kavkaz, mts., Asia I6 26
Malyj Tajmyr, ostrov, i., Russia B13 28
Malyj T'uters, ostrov, i., Russia B9 22
Malyj Uzen', stm., Asia H7 26
Malyševo, Russia D18 22
Mamala Bay, b., Hi., U.S. g10 118
Mamara, Peru F5 82
Mamaroneck, N.Y., U.S. h13 139
Mambaí, Braz. C5 79
Mamberamo, stm., Indon. F10 38
Mambéré, stm., Cen. Afr. Rep. H4 56
Ma-Me-O Beach, Alta., Can. C4 98
Mamers, Fr. D7 14
Mamfe, Cam. G8 54
Mamiá, Lago, l., Braz. J11 84
Mamiña, Chile I7 82
Mammoth, Az., U.S. E5 110
Mammoth, W.V., U.S. C3 155
Mammoth Cave National Park, Ky., U.S. C4 124
Mammoth Lakes, Ca., U.S. D4 112
Mammoth Spring, Ar., U.S. A4 111
Mamonovo, Russia G2 22
Mamoré, stm., S.A. D9 82
Mamori, Lago, l., Braz. I12 84
Mamoriá, stm., Braz. B8 82
Mamou, Gui. F3 64
Mamou, La., U.S. D3 125
Mamoutzou, May. I16 67a
Mampikony, Madag. p22 67b
Mamry, Jezioro, l., Pol. A21 10
Mamuchi, China H6 32
Ma'mūn, Sud. K2 60
Mamuno, Bots. D5 66
Mamuru, stm., Braz. I14 84
Man, I.C. H6 64
Man, W.V., U.S. D3 155
Mana, stm., Fr. Gu. B8 76
Manabí, prov., Ec. H2 84
Manacacías, stm., Col. F6 84
Manacapuru, Braz. I12 84
Manacor, Spain F15 16
Manado, Indon. E7 38
Managua, Nic. E8 92
Managua, dept., Nic. E8 92
Managua, Lago de, l., Nic. E8 92
Manahawkin, N.J., U.S. D4 137
Manakara, Madag. s23 67b
Manakin, Va., U.S. C5 153
Manāli, India C10 42
Manama see Al-Manāmah, Bahr. H11 48
Manambato, Madag. n23 67b
Manambolosy, Madag. p23 67b
Mánamo, Caño, mth., Ven. C11 84
Manana Island, i., Hi., U.S. g11 118
Mananara, Madag. p23 67b
Mananjary, Madag. r23 67b
Manantenina, Madag. t22 67b
Manantico Creek, stm., N.J., U.S. E3 137
Manapiare, stm., Ven. E9 84
Manapire, stm., Ven. C9 84
Mana Point, c., Hi., U.S. A2 118
Manaquiri, Lago, l., Braz. I12 84
Manaravolo, Madag. s21 67b
Manas, China C4 30
Manās, stm., Asia G14 44
Manas Hu, l., China B4 30
Manāslu, mtn., Nepal F11 44
Manasquan, N.J., U.S. C4 137
Manasquan, stm., N.J., U.S. C4 137
Manassa, Co., U.S. D5 113
Manassas, Ga., U.S. D4 117
Manassas, Va., U.S. B5 153
Manassas National Battlefield Park, Va., U.S. g11 153
Manassas Park, Va., U.S. B5 153
Manatee, co., Fl., U.S. E4 116
Manatee, stm., Fl., U.S. E4 116
Manatí, Col. B5 84
Manatí, P.R. E11 94
Manaung, Burma E2 40
Manaus, Braz. I12 84
Manawa, Wi., U.S. D5 156
Manbij, Syria C4 48
Mancelona, Mi., U.S. D5 129
Manchac, Bayou, stm., La., U.S. h10 125
Mancha Real, Spain H8 16
Manchaug, Ma., U.S. B4 128
Manche, dept., Fr. C5 14
Manchester, Eng., U.K. H11 8
Manchester, Ct., U.S. B5 114
Manchester, Ga., U.S. D2 117
Manchester, Il., U.S. D3 120
Manchester, Ia., U.S. B6 122
Manchester, Ky., U.S. C6 124
Manchester, Me., U.S. D3 126
Manchester, Md., U.S. A4 127
Manchester, Ma., U.S. A6 128
Manchester, Mi., U.S. F6 129
Manchester, Mo., U.S. f12 132
Manchester, N.H., U.S. E4 136
Manchester, N.Y., U.S. C3 139
Manchester, Oh., U.S. D2 142
Manchester, Pa., U.S. F8 145
Manchester, Tn., U.S. B5 149
Manchester, Vt., U.S. E2 152
Manchester Center, Vt., U.S. E2 152
Manchón, Guat. C2 92
Manchuria, hist. reg., China B12 30
Máncora, Peru J2 84
Mancos, Co., U.S. D2 113
Mancos, stm., U.S. D2 113
Mandabe, Madag. r21 67b
Mandaguari, Braz. G3 79
Mandal, Nor. L10 6
Mandala, Puncak, mtn., Indon. F11 38
Mandalay, Burma C4 40
Mandalgov', Mong. B8 30
Mandalī, Iraq E8 48
Mandan, N.D., U.S. C5 141
Mandara Mountains, mts., Afr. F9 54
Mandaree, N.D., U.S. B3 141
Mandas, Italy J4 18
Mandeb, Bab el, strt. H3 47
Mandel, Afg. E16 48
Manderson, S.D., U.S. D3 148
Manderson, Wy., U.S. B5 157
Mandeville, Jam. E6 94
Mandeville, Ar., U.S. D2 111
Mandeville, La., U.S. D5 125
Mandi, India E7 44
Mandiana, Gui. F5 64
Mandimba, Moz. D7 58
Mandioli, Pulau, i., Indon. F8 38
Mandioré, Lagoa, l., S.A. H13 82
Mandla, India A6 46
Mandoto, Madag. q22 67b
Mandouri, Togo F10 64
Mandra, Pak. D5 44
Mandritsara, Madag. o23 67b
Mandronarivo, Madag. r21 67b
Mandsaur, India H6 44
Manduria, Italy I12 18
Māndvi, India I3 44
Mandya, India F4 46
Manfalūt, Egypt D6 60
Manfredonia, Italy H10 18
Manfredonia, Golfo di, b., Italy H11 18
Manga, Braz. C7 79
Manga, Burkina F9 64
Mangabeiras, Chapada das, hills, Braz. F9 76
Mangalagiri, India D6 46
Mangalore, India F3 46
Mangaoka, Madag. n23 67b
Mangchang, China F8 30
Mange, China D10 44
Mange, S.L. G3 64
Mangham, La., U.S. B4 125
Manglares, Cabo, c., Col. G3 84
Mangochi, Mwi. D7 58
Mangoky, stm., Madag. r21 67b
Mangole, Pulau, i., Indon. F8 38
Mangoupa, Cen. Afr. Rep. O3 60
Mangrol, India J4 44
Mangrove Cay, i., Bah. B6 94
Mangueira, Lagoa, b., Braz. G12 80
Mangueirinha, Braz. C12 80
Mangulile, Hond. B8 92
Mangum, Ok., U.S. C2 143
Mangya, China D5 30
Manhattan, Ks., U.S. C7 123
Manhattan, Mt., U.S. E5 133
Manhattan Beach, Ca., U.S. n12 112
Manhattan Island, i., N.Y., U.S. h13 139
Manheim, Pa., U.S. F9 145
Manhuaçu, Braz. F7 79
Manhuaçu, stm., Braz. E8 79
Manhumirim, Braz. F8 79
Maniago, Italy C7 18
Maniamba, Moz. D7 58
Manicoré, Braz. A11 82
Manicoré, stm., Braz. B11 82
Manicouagan, Réservoir, res., Que., Can. h13 104
Manignan, I.C. F6 64
Manigotagan, Man., Can. D3 100
Manila, Phil. n19 39b

Name	Map Ref.	Page

Name | Map Ref. | Page

Meandarra, Austl. F8 70
Meander Creek Reservoir, res., Oh., U.S. A5 142
Means, Ky., U.S. C6 124
Mears, Mi., U.S. E4 129
Meath, co., Ire. H7 8
Meath, hist. reg., Ire. H6 8
Meath Park, Sask., Can. D3 105
Meaux, Fr. D9 14
Mebane, N.C., U.S. A3 140
Mecaya, stm., Col. G5 84
Mecca, Ca., U.S. F5 112
Mecca, In., U.S. E3 121
Mecca see Makkah, Sau. Ar. D1 47
Mechanic Falls, Me., U.S. D2 126
Mechanicsburg, In., U.S. D5 121
Mechanicsburg, Oh., U.S. B2 142
Mechanicsburg, Pa., U.S. F7 145
Mechanicsville, Ia., U.S. C6 122
Mechanicsville, Md., U.S. D4 127
Mechanicsville, Va., U.S. C5 153
Mechanicville, N.Y., U.S. C7 139
Mechant, Lake, l., La., U.S. E4 125
Mechelen (Malines), Bel. F5 12
Mechita, Arg. H8 80
Mechra Safsaf, Mor. K9 16
Mechriyya, Alg. D10 62
Mechroha, Alg. M2 18
Mecklenburg, co., N.C., U.S. B2 140
Mecklenburg, co., Va., U.S. D4 153
Mecklenburg, hist. reg., Ger. B12 10
Mecklenburger Bucht, b., Ger. A11 10
Mecklenburg-Vorpommern, state, Ger. B12 10
Meckling, S.D., U.S. E8 148
Mecosta, Mi., U.S. E5 129
Mecosta, co., Mi., U.S. E5 129
Meda, Port. E4 16
Medan, Indon. M5 40
Medanales, N.M., U.S. A3 138
Médanos, Arg. J7 80
Medanosa, Punta, c., Arg. F3 78
Medaryville, In., U.S. B4 121
Meddybumps Lake, l., Me., U.S. C5 126
Mede, Italy D3 18
Medeiros Neto, Braz. D8 79
Medellín, Col. D5 84
Médenine, Tun. D16 62
Mederdra, Maur. C2 64
Medfield, Ma., U.S. h10 128
Medford, Ma., U.S. B5 128
Medford, Mn., U.S. F5 130
Medford, N.J., U.S. D3 137
Medford, Ok., U.S. A4 143
Medford, Or., U.S. E4 144
Medford, Wi., U.S. C3 156
Medford Lakes, N.J., U.S. D3 137
Medgidia, Rom. E12 20
Media, Pa., U.S. G11 145
Mediapolis, Ia., U.S. C6 122
Mediaş, Rom. C8 20
Medical Lake, Wa., U.S. B8 154
Medicina, Italy E6 18
Medicine Bow, Wy., U.S. E6 157
Medicine Bow, stm., Wy., U.S. E6 157
Medicine Bow Mountains, mts., U.S. E6 157
Medicine Bow Peak, mtn., Wy., U.S. E6 157
Medicine Creek, stm., Mo., U.S. B4 132
Medicine Creek, stm., Ne., U.S. D5 134
Medicine Hat, Alta., Can. D5 98
Medicine Lake, Mt., U.S. B12 133
Medicine Lodge, Ks., U.S. E5 123
Medicine Lodge, stm., U.S. E4 123
Medicine Park, Ok., U.S. C3 143
Medina, Braz. D8 79
Medina, N.Y., U.S. B2 139
Medina, N.D., U.S. C6 141
Medina, Oh., U.S. A4 142
Medina, Tn., U.S. B3 149
Medina, Wa., U.S. e11 154
Medina, co., Oh., U.S. A4 142
Medina, co., Tx., U.S. E3 150
Medina, stm., Tx., U.S. k7 150
Medina see Al-Madīnah, Sau. Ar. B1 47
Medina del Campo, Spain D7 16
Medininkai, Lith. G8 22
Medinīpur, India I12 44
Medio, Punta, c., Chile D3 80
Mediterranean Sea E9 52
Medjerda, Monts de la, mts., Afr. M3 18
Mednogorsk, Russia G9 26
Mednoje, Russia E18 22
Mednyj, ostrov, i., Russia G25 28
Médoc, reg., Fr. G6 14
Medora, Man., Can. E1 100
Medora, Il., U.S. D3 120
Medora, In., U.S. G5 121
Medora, N.D., U.S. C2 141
Médouneu, Gabon A2 58
Medstead, Sask., Can. D1 105
Meductic, N.B., Can. D2 101
Medveda, Yugo. G5 20
Medvedevskoje, Russia C18 22
Medvedica, stm., Russia G6 26
Medvežjegorsk, Russia E4 26
Medveži ostrova, is., Russia C24 28
Medway, Me., U.S. C4 126
Medway, Ma., U.S. B5 128
Medway, stm., N.S., Can. E5 101
Medyn', Russia G18 22
Meekatharra, Austl. E3 68
Meeker, Co., U.S. A3 113
Meeker, Ok., U.S. B5 143
Meeker, co., Mn., U.S. E4 130
Meelpaeg Lake, res., Newf., Can. D3 102
Meer, Bel. F6 12
Meerane, Ger. E12 10
Meerut, India F7 44
Meeteetse, Wy., U.S. B4 157
Meeting Creek, Alta., Can. C4 98
Mega, Eth. H8 56
Mégantic, Lac, l., Que., Can. D7 104
Mégantic, Mont, mtn., Que., Can. D6 104
Mégara, Grc. K7 20
Megargel, Al., U.S. D2 108
Meggett, S.C., U.S. F7 147
Meghālaya, state, India H14 44
Meghna, stm., Bngl. H14 44
Megunticook, Mount, mtn., Me., U.S. D3 126
Mehadia, Rom. E6 20
Mehar, Pak. G2 44
Mehdia, Alg. C11 62
Mehedinţi, co., Rom. E6 20
Meherrin, stm., U.S. A4 140
Mehlville, Mo., U.S. f13 132
Mehrān, Iran E9 48
Meia Ponte, Rio da, stm., Braz. D4 79
Meigs, Ga., U.S. E2 117
Meigs, co., Oh., U.S. C3 142
Meigs, co., Tn., U.S. D9 149
Meiktila, Burma D3 40
Meilie, China I6 34
Meiningen, Ger. E10 10
Meiringen, Switz. E9 13
Meissen, Ger. D13 10
Meixian, China K5 34
Meiyino, Sud. N8 60
Meizhai, China B10 40
Mejerda, Oued (Oued Medjerda), stm., Afr. M4 18
Mejez el Bab, Tun. M4 18
Mejicanos, El Sal. D5 92
Mejillones, Chile B3 80
Mejillones, Península, pen., Chile B3 80
Mejillones del Sur, Bahía de, b., Chile B3 80
Mékambo, Gabon A2 58
Mekele, Eth. K10 60
Mekinock, N.D., U.S. A8 141
Meknès, Mor. D8 62
Mekong, stm., Asia H8 40
Mekoryuk, Ak., U.S. C6 109
Mékrou, stm., Afr. F7 54
Melado, stm., Chile H3 80
Melaka, Malay. M7 40
Melanesia, is., Oc. I19 158
Melba, Id., U.S. F2 119
Melber, Ky., U.S. f9 124
Melbeta, Ne., U.S. C2 134
Melbourne, Austl. K6 70
Melbourne, Ont., Can. E3 103
Melbourne, Ar., U.S. A4 111
Melbourne, Fl., U.S. D6 116
Melbourne, Ia., U.S. C4 122
Melbourne, Ky., U.S. h14 124
Melbourne Beach, Fl., U.S. D6 116
Melby House, Scot., U.K. A12 8
Melcher, Ia., U.S. C4 122
Melchor Múzquiz, Mex. D9 90
Meldorf, Ger. A9 10
Meldrim, Ga., U.S. D5 117
Melechovo, Russia E24 22
Melegnano, Italy D4 18
Melenki, Russia F24 22
Meleuz, Russia G9 26
Mélèzes, Rivière aux, stm., Que., Can. g12 104
Melfi, Chad F4 56
Melfi, Italy H10 18
Melfort, Sask., Can. E3 105
Melgaço, Port. C3 16
Melgar, Col. E5 84
Melghir, Chott, l., Alg. C14 62
Melhus, Nor. J12 6
Meli, stm., Afr. G4 64
Meliane, Oued, stm., Tun. M5 18
Melide, Switz. G10 13
Melilla, Sp. N. Afr. C9 62
Melincué, Arg. G8 80
Melipilla, Chile G3 80
Melita, Man., Can. E1 100
Melitopol', Ukr. F15 4
Mellègue, Oued, stm., Afr. M3 18
Mellen, Wi., U.S. B3 156
Mellette, S.D., U.S. B7 148
Mellette, co., S.D., U.S. D5 148
Mellott, In., U.S. D3 121
Mellwood, Ar., U.S. C5 111
Mel'nica-Podol'skaja, Ukr. A10 20
Mělník, Czech. E14 10
Melo, Ur. G11 80
Melo, stm., Para. I12 82
Melocheville, Que., Can. q19 104
Melong, Cam. I14 64
Melos see Mílos, i., Grc. M8 20
Melrose, N.B., Can. C6 101
Melrose, N.S., Can. D7 101
Melrose, Ct., U.S. B5 114
Melrose, Fl., U.S. C4 116
Melrose, Ma., U.S. B5 128
Melrose, Mn., U.S. E4 130
Melrose, N.M., U.S. C6 138
Melrose, Wi., U.S. D2 156
Melstone, Mt., U.S. D9 133
Melton Hill Lake, res., Tn., U.S. D9 149
Melton Mowbray, Eng., U.K. I13 8
Melúa, Col. F6 84
Melun, Burma D2 40
Melun, Fr. D9 14
Melvern, Ks., U.S. D8 123
Melvern Lake, res., Ks., U.S. D8 123
Melville, Sask., Can. G4 105
Melville, La., U.S. D4 125
Melville, Lake, l., Newf., Can. B2 102
Melville Bugt, b., Grnld. B13 86
Melville Island, i., Austl. B6 68
Melville Island, i., N.W. Ter., Can. B8 86
Melville Peninsula, pen., N.W. Ter., Can. C16 96
Melville Sound, strt., N.W. Ter., Can. C11 96
Melvin, Al., U.S. D1 108
Melvin, Il., U.S. C5 120
Melvin, Ia., U.S. A2 122
Melvin, Ky., U.S. C7 124
Melvin, Lough, l., Eur. G5 8
Melvin Village, N.H., U.S. C4 136
Melyana, Alg. B12 62
Melzo, Italy D4 18
Memel, S. Afr. F9 66
Memel see Nemunas, stm., Eur. F6 22
Memmingen, Ger. H10 10
Memo, stm., Ven. C9 84
Mémót, Camb. I9 40
Mempawah, Indon. N10 40
Memphis, Fl., U.S. p10 116
Memphis, In., U.S. H6 121
Memphis, Mi., U.S. F8 129
Memphis, Mo., U.S. A5 132
Memphis, Ne., U.S. g12 134
Memphis, Tn., U.S. B1 149
Memphis, Tx., U.S. B2 150
Memphis Naval Air Station, mil., Tn., U.S. B2 149
Memramcook, N.B., Can. C5 101
Mena, Ar., U.S. C1 111
Menahga, Mn., U.S. D3 130
Ménaka, Mali D11 64
Menaldum, Neth. B8 12
Menan, Id., U.S. F7 119
Menands, N.Y., U.S. C7 139
Menard, Tx., U.S. D3 150
Menard, co., Il., U.S. C4 120
Menard, co., Tx., U.S. D3 150
Menasha, Wi., U.S. D5 156
Menawashei, Sud. K3 60
Mendawai, stm., Indon. F5 38
Mende, Fr. H10 14
Menden, Ger. D7 10
Mendenhall, Ms., U.S. D4 131
Mendes, Ga., U.S. E5 117
Méndez, Mex. E10 90
Mendham, Sask., Can. G1 105
Mendham, N.J., U.S. B3 137
Mendi, Eth. M8 60
Mendi, Pap. N. Gui. G11 38
Mendocino, Ca., U.S. C2 112
Mendocino, co., Ca., U.S. C2 112
Mendon, Il., U.S. C2 120
Mendon, Ma., U.S. h9 128
Mendon, Mi., U.S. F5 129
Mendon, Mo., U.S. B4 132
Mendon, Oh., U.S. B1 142
Mendon, Ut., U.S. B4 151
Mendota, Ca., U.S. D3 112
Mendota, Il., U.S. B4 120
Mendota, Lake, l., Wi., U.S. E4 156
Mendoza, Arg. G4 80
Mendoza, Peru B3 82
Mendoza, prov., Arg. H4 80
Mendoza, stm., Arg. G4 80
Ménéac, Fr. D4 14
Mene de Mauroa, Ven. B7 84
Mene Grande, Ven. C7 84
Menemen, Tur. K11 20
Menen (Menin), Bel. G3 12
Menfi, Italy L7 18
Mengcheng, China E10 30
Menggala, Indon. F4 38
Menggu, China A7 40
Menghai, China C6 40
Mengla, China D6 40
Mengzhi, China B5 40
Mengzi, China C7 40
Menifee, Ar., U.S. B3 111
Menifee, co., Ky., U.S. C6 124
Menindee, Austl. I5 70
Menindee Lake, l., Austl. I5 70
Menlo, Ga., U.S. B1 117
Menlo, Ia., U.S. C3 122
Menlo, Wa., U.S. C2 154
Menlo Park, Ca., U.S. k8 112
Menno, S.D., U.S. D8 148
Menominee, Mi., U.S. C3 129
Menominee, co., Mi., U.S. C3 129
Menominee, co., Wi., U.S. C5 156
Menominee, stm., U.S. C6 156
Menominee Indian Reservation, Wi., U.S. C5 156
Menomonee, stm., Wi., U.S. m11 156
Menomonee Falls, Wi., U.S. E5 156
Menomonie, Wi., U.S. D2 156
Menongue, Ang. D3 58
Menorca, i., Spain F16 16
Mens, Fr. H12 14
Mentawai, Kepulauan, is., Indon. F2 38
Mentawai, Selat, strt., Indon. F3 38
Mentmore, N.M., U.S. B1 138
Menton, Fr. I14 14
Mentone, Al., U.S. A4 108
Mentone, In., U.S. B5 121
Mentor, Ky., U.S. k14 124
Mentor, Oh., U.S. A4 142
Mentor, Tn., U.S. n13 149
Mentor-on-the-Lake, Oh., U.S. A4 142
Menzel Bourguiba, Tun. L4 18
Menzel Bou Zelfa, Tun. M5 18
Menzel Djemil, Tun. L4 18
Menzel Temime, Tun. M5 18
Menzies, Austl. E4 68
Menzies, Mount, mtn., Ant. C5 73
Meoqui, Mex. C7 90
Meota, Sask., Can. D1 105
Meppel, Neth. C9 12
Meppen, Ger. C7 10
Meqerghane, Sebkha, pl., Alg. G11 62
Mequon, Wi., U.S. E6 156
Mer, Fr. E8 14
Meramec, stm., Mo., U.S. C7 132
Merano (Meran), Italy C6 18
Merasheen Island, i., Newf., Can. E4 102
Merate, Italy D4 18
Merauke, Indon. G11 38
Meraux, La., U.S. k12 125
Mercaderes, Col. G4 84
Mercāra, India F3 46
Merced, Ca., U.S. D3 112
Merced, co., Ca., U.S. D3 112
Merced, stm., Ca., U.S. D3 112
Mercedario, Cerro, mtn., Arg. F3 80
Mercedes, Arg. H9 80
Mercedes, Arg. E9 80
Mercedes, Arg. G6 80
Mercedes, Tx., U.S. F4 150
Mercedes, Ur. G9 80
Mercer, Mo., U.S. A4 132
Mercer, N.D., U.S. B5 141
Mercer, Pa., U.S. D1 145
Mercer, Tn., U.S. B2 149
Mercer, Wi., U.S. B3 156
Mercer, co., Il., U.S. B3 120
Mercer, co., Ky., U.S. C5 124
Mercer, co., Mo., U.S. A4 132
Mercer, co., N.J., U.S. C3 137
Mercer, co., N.D., U.S. B4 141
Mercer, co., Oh., U.S. B1 142
Mercer, co., Pa., U.S. D1 145
Mercer, co., W.V., U.S. D3 155
Mercer Island, Wa., U.S. B3 154
Mercer Island, i., Wa., U.S. e11 154
Mercersburg, Pa., U.S. G6 145
Mercerville, N.J., U.S. C3 137
Merchtem, Bel. G5 12
Mercier, Que., Can. D4 104
Mercy, Cape, c., N.W. Ter., Can. D20 96
Meredith, N.H., U.S. C3 136
Meredith, Lake, l., Co., U.S. C7 113
Meredith, Lake, res., Tx., U.S. B2 150
Meredith Center, N.H., U.S. C3 136
Meredosia, Il., U.S. D3 120
Meredosia Lake, l., Il., U.S. D3 120
Mereeg, Som. H10 56
Merenkurkku (Norra Kvarken), strt., Eur. J17 6
Merevari, stm., Ven. E10 84
Merewa, Eth. N9 60
Mergui (Myeik), Burma H5 40
Mergui Archipelago, is., Burma H5 40
Meriç (Marica) (Évros), stm., Eur. H10 20
Mérida, Mex. G15 90
Mérida, Spain G5 16
Mérida, Ven. C7 84
Mérida, state, Ven. C7 84
Mérida, Cordillera de, mts., Ven. C7 84
Meriden, Ct., U.S. C4 114
Meriden, Ks., U.S. C8 123
Meriden, N.H., U.S. C2 136
Meriden, Wy., U.S. E8 157
Meridian, Ga., U.S. E5 117
Meridian, Id., U.S. F2 119
Meridian, Ms., U.S. C5 131
Meridian, Pa., U.S. E2 145
Meridian, Tx., U.S. D4 150
Meridian Hills, In., U.S. k10 121
Meridian Naval Air Station, mil., Ms., U.S. C5 131
Meridianville, Al., U.S. A3 108
Mérignac, Fr. H6 14
Merigold, Ms., U.S. B3 131
Merigomish, N.S., Can. D7 101
Merimbula, Austl. K8 70
Merín, Laguna (Lagoa Mirim), b., S.A. G12 80
Merino, Co., U.S. A7 113
Merinos, Ur. G10 80
Meriwether, co., Ga., U.S. C2 117
Merkel, Tx., U.S. C2 150
Merkendorf, Ger. F10 10
Merkinė, Lith. G7 22
Merkulovići, Bela. I13 22
Merlin, Ont., Can. E2 103
Merlin, Or., U.S. E3 144
Merlo, Arg. G6 80
Mermentau, La., U.S. D3 125
Mermentau, stm., La., U.S. E3 125
Merna, Ne., U.S. C6 134
Mernye, Hung. I17 10
Merom, In., U.S. F2 121
Meron, Hare, mtn., Isr. C4 50
Merredin, Austl. F3 68
Merriam, Ks., U.S. k16 123
Merrick, co., Ne., U.S. C7 134
Merrick Brook, stm., Ct., U.S. C7 114
Merrickville, Ont., Can. C9 103
Merrifield, Mn., U.S. D4 130
Merrill, Ia., U.S. B1 122
Merrill, Mi., U.S. E6 129
Merrill, Or., U.S. E5 144
Merrill, Wi., U.S. C4 156
Merrillan, Wi., U.S. D3 156
Merrillville, In., U.S. B3 121
Merrimac, Ma., U.S. A5 128
Merrimac, Wi., U.S. E4 156
Merrimack, N.H., U.S. E4 136
Merrimack, co., N.H., U.S. D3 136
Merrimack, stm., U.S. A5 128
Merriman, Ne., U.S. B4 134
Merritt, B.C., Can. D7 99
Merritt Island, Fl., U.S. D6 116
Merritt Reservoir, res., Ne., U.S. B5 134
Merriwa, Austl. I9 70
Mer Rouge, La., U.S. B4 125
Merrymeeting Lake, l., N.H., U.S. D4 136
Merryville, La., U.S. D2 125
Mersch, Lux. I9 12
Merseburg, Ger. D11 10
Mersey, stm., Austl. M7 70
Mershon, Ga., U.S. E4 117
Mersing, Malay. M7 40
Mērsrags, Lat. D6 22
Merthyr Tydfil, Wales, U.K. J10 8
Mértola, Port. H4 16
Merton, Wi., U.S. m11 156
Mertzon, Tx., U.S. D2 150
Méru, Fr. C9 14
Meru, Kenya A7 58
Meru, Mount, mtn., Tan. B7 58
Mervin, Sask., Can. D1 105
Merwin Lake, res., Wa., U.S. C3 154
Méry, Fr. D10 14
Merzig, Ger. F6 10
Mesa, Az., U.S. D4 110
Mesa, Co., U.S. B2 113
Mesa, co., Co., U.S. C2 113
Mesa, stm., Spain D10 16
Mesabi Range, hills, Mn., U.S. C6 130
Mesagne, Italy I12 18
Mesa Mountain, mtn., Co., U.S. D4 113
Mesa Verde National Park, Co., U.S. D2 113
Mescalero, N.M., U.S. D4 138
Mescalero Indian Reservation, N.M., U.S. D4 138
Meschede, Ger. D8 10
Meščovsk, Russia G18 22
Mesena, Ga., U.S. C4 117
Meservey, Ia., U.S. B4 122
Mesfinto, Eth. K9 60
Meshgīn Shahr, Iran B9 48
Meshomasic Mountain, mtn., Ct., U.S. C5 114
Mesick, Mi., U.S. D5 129
Mesilla, N.M., U.S. E3 138
Mesita, N.M., U.S. C2 138
Meskiana, Alg. C14 62
Meslay-du-Maine, Fr. E6 14
Mesocco, Switz. F11 13
Mesolóngion, Grc. K5 20
Mesopotamia, hist. reg., Asia D8 48
Mesquita, Braz. E7 79
Mesquite, Nv., U.S. G7 135
Mesquite, N.M., U.S. E3 138
Mesquite, Tx., U.S. n10 150
Messalo, stm., Moz. D7 58
Messalonskee Lake, l., Me., U.S. D3 126
Messina, Italy K10 18
Messina, S. Afr. D10 66
Messina, Stretto di, strt., Italy K10 18
Messíni, Grc. L6 20
Messiniakós Kólpos, b., Grc. M6 20
Messojacha, stm., Russia D13 26
Mestá, Grc. K9 20
Mesta (Néstos), stm., Eur. H7 20
Mestasa, Mor. C8 62
Mestghanem, Alg. C11 62
Mestre, Italy D7 18
Meta, Mo., U.S. C5 132
Meta, dept., Col. F6 84
Meta, stm., S.A. D9 84
Métabetchouan, Que., Can. A6 104
Métabetchouane, stm., Que., Can. A5 104
Meta Incognita Peninsula, pen., N.W. Ter., Can. D19 96
Metairie, La., U.S. k11 125
Metaline, Wa., U.S. A8 154
Metaline Falls, Wa., U.S. A8 154
Metamora, Il., U.S. C4 120
Metamora, In., U.S. F7 121
Metamora, Mi., U.S. F7 129
Metamora, Oh., U.S. A2 142
Metán, Arg. C6 80
Metapán, El Sal. C5 92
Meta Pond, l., Newf., Can. D4 102
Metcalf, Ga., U.S. F3 117
Metcalf, Il., U.S. D6 120
Metcalfe, Ont., Can. B9 103
Metcalfe, Ms., U.S. B2 131
Metcalfe, co., Ky., U.S. C4 124
Metedeconk, North Branch, stm., N.J., U.S. C4 137
Metedeconk, South Branch, stm., N.J., U.S. C3 137
Meteghan, N.S., Can. E3 101
Meteghan River, N.S., Can. E3 101
Meteghan Station, N.S., Can. E3 101
Metema, Eth. K9 60
Meteor Crater, crat., Az., U.S. C4 110
Methóni, Grc. M5 20
Methow, stm., Wa., U.S. A5 154
Methuen, Ma., U.S. A5 128
Metiskow, Alta., Can. C5 98
Metković, Cro. F12 18
Metlakatla, Ak., U.S. D13 109
Metlaoui, Tun. C15 62
Metlatonoc, Mex. I10 90
Meto, Bayou, stm., Ar., U.S. C4 111
Metolius, Or., U.S. C5 144
Metonga, Lake, l., Wi., U.S. C5 156
Metropolis, Il., U.S. F5 120
Metsematluku, Bots. E7 66
Mettawee, stm., U.S. E2 152
Metter, Ga., U.S. D4 117
Mettmann, Ger. D6 10
Mettuppālaiyam, India G4 46
Mettūr, India G4 46
Metu, Eth. M8 60
Metuchen, N.J., U.S. B4 137
Metulla, Isr. B5 50
Metz, Fr. C13 14
Metzger, Or., U.S. h12 144
Meulan, Fr. C8 14
Meureudu, Indon. L4 40
Meurthe, stm., Fr. D13 14
Meurthe-et-Moselle, dept., Fr. D13 14
Meuse, dept., Fr. D12 14
Meuse (Maas), stm., Eur. E5 10
Meuselwitz, Ger. D12 10
Mexia, Al., U.S. D2 108
Mexia, Tx., U.S. D4 150
Mexia, Lake, res., Tx., U.S. D4 150
Mexiana, Ilha, i., Braz. D9 76
Mexicali, Mex. A2 90
Mexican Springs, N.M., U.S. B1 138
Mexico, In., U.S. C5 121
Mexico, Me., U.S. D2 126
Mexico, Mo., U.S. B6 132
Mexico, N.Y., U.S. B4 139
México, state, Mex. H10 90
Mexico (México), ctry., N.A. F9 90
Mexico, Gulf of, b., N.A. C6 88
Mexico City see Ciudad de México, Mex. H10 90
Meximieux, Fr. G12 14
Meycauayan, Phil. n19 39b
Meyersdale, Pa., U.S. G3 145
Meyisti, i., Grc. H13 4
Meymac, Fr. G9 14
Meymaneh, Afg. C1 44
Meymeh, stm., Asia E9 48
Meyrargues, Fr. I12 14
Meẓada, Ḥorvot (Masada), hist., Isr. F4 50
Mezapa, Hond. B7 92
Mezcala, Mex. I10 90
Mezcalapa, stm., Mex. I13 90
Meždurečensk, Russia G9 28
Mèze, Fr. I10 14
Mezen', Russia D6 26
Mezen', stm., Russia D6 26
Mežgorje, Ukr. A7 20
Mézin, Fr. H7 14
Mezinovskij, Russia F23 22
Mezőberény, Hung. I21 10
Mezőcsát, Hung. H20 10
Mezőkovácsháza, Hung. I20 10
Mezőkövesd, Hung. H20 10
Mezőtúr, Hung. H20 10
Mezquital, Mex. F7 90
Mezquital, stm., Mex. F7 90
Mglin, Russia H15 22
M'goun, Irhil, mtn., Mor. E7 62
Mhow, India I6 44
Miahuatlán de Porfirio Díaz, Mex. I11 90
Miajadas, Spain F6 16
Miami, Man., Can. E2 100
Miami, Az., U.S. D5 110
Miami, Fl., U.S. G6 116
Miami, In., U.S. C5 121
Miami, N.M., U.S. A5 138
Miami, Ok., U.S. A7 143
Miami, Tx., U.S. B2 150
Miami, W.V., U.S. m13 155
Miami, co., In., U.S. C5 121
Miami, co., Ks., U.S. D9 123
Miami, co., Oh., U.S. B1 142
Miami Beach, Fl., U.S. G6 116
Miami Canal, Fl., U.S. F6 116
Miami International Airport, Fl., U.S. G6 116
Miamisburg, Oh., U.S. C1 142
Miami Shores, Fl., U.S. G6 116
Miami Springs, Fl., U.S. G6 116
Miamitown, Oh., U.S. o12 142
Miāndoāb, Iran C9 48
Miandrivazo, Madag. q21 67b
Miāneh, Iran C9 48
Miangas, Pulau, i., Indon. D8 38
Mianhu, China L5 34
Mianus Reservoir, res., U.S. E1 114
Miānwāli, Pak. D4 44
Mianyang, China E7 30
Mianyang, China E2 34
Miaoli, Tai. K9 34
Miarinavaratra, Madag. r22 67b
Miass, Russia G10 26
Miastko, Pol. A17 10
Mica Creek, B.C., Can. C8 99
Mica Mountain, mtn., Az., U.S. E5 110
Micanopy, Fl., U.S. C4 116
Micaúne, Moz. B13 66
Micco, Fl., U.S. E6 116
Miccosukee, Lake, res., Fl., U.S. B2 116
Michajlov, Russia G22 22
Michajlovka, Russia G6 26
Michanoviči, Bela. H10 22
Michaud, Point, c., N.S., Can. D9 101
Michelson, Mount, mtn., Ak., U.S. B11 109
Miches, Dom. Rep. E10 94
Michichi, Alta., Can. D4 98
Michie, Tn., U.S. B3 149
Michigamme, Mi., U.S. B2 129
Michigamme, Lake, l., Mi., U.S. B2 129
Michigamme Reservoir, res., Mi., U.S. B2 129
Michigan, N.D., U.S. A7 141
Michigan, state, U.S. E6 129
Michigan, stm., Co., U.S. A4 113
Michigan, Lake, l., U.S. C9 106
Michigan Center, Mi., U.S. F6 129
Michigan City, In., U.S. A4 121
Michigan City, Ms., U.S. A4 131
Michigan Island, i., Wi., U.S. B3 156
Michigan Prairie, reg., Wa., U.S. C7 154
Michigantown, In., U.S. D5 121
Michnevo, Russia F20 22
Michoacán, state, Mex. H9 90
Mico, stm., Nic. E10 92
Mico, Montañas del, mts., Guat. B6 92
Micro, N.C., U.S. B4 140
Micronesia, is., Oc. G19 158
Micronesia, Federated States of, ctry., Oc. H19 158
Mičurinsk, Russia I23 22
Midale, Sask., Can. H4 105
Midar, Mor. C9 62
Mid-Atlantic Ridge F9 160
Middelburg, Neth. E4 12
Middelburg, S. Afr. H7 66
Middelburg, S. Afr. E9 66
Middelfart, Den. N11 6
Middelharnis, Neth. E5 12
Middelpos, S. Afr. H5 66
Middelwater, S. Afr. D10 66
Middenmeer, Neth. C7 12
Middle, Ia., U.S. C6 122
Middle, stm., Ia., U.S. C3 122
Middle, stm., Mn., U.S. B2 130
Middle America Trench H10 86
Middle Andaman, i., India H2 40
Middleboro (Middleborough Center), Ma., U.S. C6 128
Middlebourne, W.V., U.S. B4 155
Middlebranch, Oh., U.S. B4 142
Middlebro, Man., Can. E4 100
Middlebrook, Va., U.S. B3 153
Middleburg, Fl., U.S. B5 116
Middleburg, Ky., U.S. C5 124
Middleburg, Pa., U.S. E7 145
Middleburg, Va., U.S. B5 153
Middleburgh, N.Y., U.S. C6 139
Middleburg Heights, Oh., U.S. h9 142
Middlebury, Ct., U.S. C3 114
Middlebury, In., U.S. A6 121
Middlebury, Vt., U.S. C2 152
Middle Caicos, i., T./C. Is. D9 94
Middlefield, Ct., U.S. C5 114
Middlefield, Oh., U.S. A4 142
Middle Haddam, Ct., U.S. C5 114
Middle Island Creek, stm., W.V., U.S. B3 155
Middle Lake, Sask., Can. E3 105
Middle Loup, stm., Ne., U.S. C5 134
Middle Musquodoboit, N.S., Can. D6 101
Middle Nodaway, stm., Ia., U.S. C3 122
Middle Park, val., Co., U.S. A4 113
Middle Patuxent, stm., Md., U.S. B4 127
Middle Point, Oh., U.S. B1 142
Middleport, N.Y., U.S. B2 139

Name	Map Ref.	Page
Middleport, Oh., U.S.	C3	142
Middle Raccoon, stm., Ia., U.S.	C3	122
Middle River, Md., U.S.	B5	127
Middle River, Mn., U.S.	B2	130
Middlesboro, Ky., U.S.	D6	124
Middlesbrough, Eng., U.K.	G12	8
Middlesex, Belize	I15	90
Middlesex, N.J., U.S.	B4	137
Middlesex, N.C., U.S.	B4	140
Middlesex, Vt., U.S.	C3	152
Middlesex, co., Ct., U.S.	D5	114
Middlesex, co., Ma., U.S.	A5	128
Middlesex, co., N.J., U.S.	C4	137
Middlesex, co., Va., U.S.	C6	153
Middlesex Fells Reservation, Ma., U.S.	g11	128
Middle Stewiacke, N.S., Can.	D6	101
Middleton, N.S., Can.	E4	101
Middleton, Id., U.S.	F2	119
Middleton, Ma., U.S.	A5	128
Middleton, Mi., U.S.	E6	129
Middleton, N.H., U.S.	D4	136
Middleton, Tn., U.S.	B3	149
Middleton, Wi., U.S.	E4	156
Middletown, Ca., U.S.	C2	112
Middletown, Ct., U.S.	C5	114
Middletown, De., U.S.	C3	115
Middletown, Il., U.S.	C4	120
Middletown, In., U.S.	D6	121
Middletown, Ia., U.S.	D6	122
Middletown, Ky., U.S.	g11	124
Middletown, Md., U.S.	B2	127
Middletown, Mo., U.S.	B6	132
Middletown, N.J., U.S.	C4	137
Middletown, N.Y., U.S.	D6	139
Middletown, Oh., U.S.	C1	142
Middletown, Pa., U.S.	F8	145
Middletown, R.I., U.S.	E5	146
Middletown, Va., U.S.	A4	153
Middletown Springs, Vt., U.S.	E2	152
Middleville, Mi., U.S.	F5	129
Midelt, Mor.	D8	62
Midfield, Al., U.S.	g7	108
Midgic, N.B., Can.	D5	101
Mid Glamorgan, co., Wales, U.K.	J10	8
Midhurst, Ont., Can.	C5	103
Midi, Canal du, Fr.	I9	14
Midi de Bigorre, Pic du, mtn., Fr.	J7	14
Midkiff, W.V., U.S.	C2	155
Midland, Ont., Can.	C5	103
Midland, Ar., U.S.	B1	111
Midland, In., U.S.	F3	121
Midland, La., U.S.	D3	125
Midland, Md., U.S.	k13	127
Midland, Mi., U.S.	E6	129
Midland, N.C., U.S.	B2	140
Midland, Pa., U.S.	E1	145
Midland, S.D., U.S.	C4	148
Midland, Tx., U.S.	D1	150
Midland, co., Mi., U.S.	E6	129
Midland, co., Tx., U.S.	D1	150
Midland Basin, Co., U.S.	A2	113
Midland City, Al., U.S.	D4	108
Midland Park, Ks., U.S.	g12	123
Midland Park, N.J., U.S.	B4	137
Midland Park, S.C., U.S.	k11	147
Midlothian, Il., U.S.	k9	120
Midlothian, Md., U.S.	k13	127
Midlothian, Tx., U.S.	C4	150
Midlothian, Va., U.S.	m17	153
Midnight, Ms., U.S.	B3	131
Midongy Sud, Madag.	s22	67b
Miduzhen, China	B6	40
Midvale, Id., U.S.	E2	119
Midvale, Oh., U.S.	B4	142
Midvale, Ut., U.S.	C4	151
Midville, Ga., U.S.	D4	117
Midway, B.C., Can.	E8	99
Midway, Al., U.S.	C4	108
Midway, De., U.S.	F5	115
Midway, Fl., U.S.	B2	116
Midway, Ky., U.S.	B5	124
Midway, Pa., U.S.	G7	145
Midway, Tn., U.S.	C11	149
Midway, Ut., U.S.	C4	151
Midway Islands, dep., Oc.	E1	2
Midway Range, mts., B.C., Can.	E8	99
Midwest, Wy., U.S.	C6	157
Midwest City, Ok., U.S.	B4	143
Midyat, Tur.	C6	48
Midžor (Midžur), mtn., Eur.	F6	20
Miechów, Pol.	E20	10
Międzychód, Pol.	C15	10
Międzyrzec Podlaski, Pol.	C22	10
Międzyrzecz, Pol.	C15	10
Miélan, Fr.	I7	14
Mielec, Pol.	E21	10
Mier, Mex.	D10	90
Mier, In., U.S.	C6	121
Miercurea-Ciuc, Rom.	C9	20
Mieres, Spain	B6	16
Mier y Noriega, Mex.	F9	90
Miesbach, Ger.	H11	10
Mifflin, Pa., U.S.	E7	145
Mifflin, co., Pa., U.S.	E6	145
Mifflinburg, Pa., U.S.	E7	145
Mifflintown, Pa., U.S.	E7	145
Mifflinville, Pa., U.S.	D9	145
Migdal, Isr.	C5	50
Migennes, Fr.	E10	14
Miguel Alemán, Presa, res., Mex.	H11	90
Miguel Auza, Mex.	E8	90
Miguel de la Borda, Pan.	H14	92
Miguel Hidalgo, Presa, res., Mex.	D5	90
Miguelópolis, Braz.	F4	79
Miguel Riglos, Arg.	I7	80
Mihajlovgrad, Bul.	F7	20
Mihara, Japan	M8	36
Mijdahah, Yemen	G6	47
Mikado, Sask., Can.	F4	105
Mikana, Wi., U.S.	C2	156
Mikaševiči, Bela.	I10	22
Mikhrot Shelomo Hamelekh (Timna') (King Solomon's Mines), hist., Isr.	I3	50
Mikkeli, Fin.	K20	6
Mikkelin lääni, prov., Fin.	J20	6
Mikołajki, Pol.	B21	10
Mikołów, Pol.	E18	10
Míkonos, Grc.	L9	20
Mikun', Russia	E8	26
Milaca, Mn., U.S.	E5	130
Milagro, Ec.	I3	84
Milam, co., Tx., U.S.	D4	150
Milan, Ga., U.S.	D3	117
Milan, Il., U.S.	B3	120
Milan, In., U.S.	F7	121
Milan, Ks., U.S.	E6	123
Milan, Mi., U.S.	F7	129
Milan, Mn., U.S.	E3	130
Milan, Mo., U.S.	A4	132
Milan, N.H., U.S.	A4	136
Milan, N.M., U.S.	B2	138
Milan, Oh., U.S.	A3	142
Milan, Tn., U.S.	B3	149
Milan see Milano, Italy	D4	18
Milano (Milan), Italy	D4	18
Milanoa, Madag.	n23	67b
Milazzo, Italy	K10	18
Milbank, S.D., U.S.	B9	148
Milbridge, Me., U.S.	D5	126
Milburn, Ky., U.S.	f9	124
Milburn, Ok., U.S.	C5	143
Milden, Sask., Can.	F2	105
Mildmay, Ont., Can.	C3	103
Mildred, Pa., U.S.	D9	145
Mildura, Austl.	J5	70
Mile, China	B7	40
Miles, Austl.	F9	70
Miles, Ia., U.S.	B7	122
Miles, Tx., U.S.	D2	150
Milesburg, Pa., U.S.	E6	145
Miles City, Mt., U.S.	D11	133
Miles Mountain, mtn., Vt., U.S.	C5	152
Milestone, Sask., Can.	G3	105
Milevsko, Czech.	F14	10
Milford, Ct., U.S.	E3	114
Milford, De., U.S.	E4	115
Milford, Il., U.S.	C6	120
Milford, In., U.S.	B6	121
Milford, Ia., U.S.	A2	122
Milford, Ks., U.S.	C7	123
Milford, Me., U.S.	D4	126
Milford, Ma., U.S.	B4	128
Milford, Mi., U.S.	F7	129
Milford, Ne., U.S.	D8	134
Milford, N.H., U.S.	E3	136
Milford, N.J., U.S.	B2	137
Milford, Oh., U.S.	C1	142
Milford, Pa., U.S.	D12	145
Milford, Ut., U.S.	E2	151
Milford, Va., U.S.	B5	153
Milford Center, Oh., U.S.	B2	142
Milford Haven, Wales, U.K.	J8	8
Milford Lake, res., Ks., U.S.	C6	123
Milford Station, N.S., Can.	D6	101
Milh, Bahr al-, l., Iraq	E7	48
Milicz, Pol.	D17	10
Mililani Town, Hi., U.S.	g9	118
Milk Creek, stm., Co., U.S.	A3	113
Mil'kovo, Russia	G23	28
Milk River, Alta., Can.	E4	98
Mill, stm., Ma., U.S.	h9	128
Milladore, Wi., U.S.	D4	156
Millard, co., Ut., U.S.	D2	151
Millau, Fr.	H10	14
Millbank, Ont., Can.	D4	103
Millboro, Va., U.S.	C3	153
Millbrae, Ca., U.S.	h8	112
Millbrook, Ont., Can.	C6	103
Millbrook, Al., U.S.	C3	108
Millbrook, N.Y., U.S.	D7	139
Mill Brook, stm., Vt., U.S.	B5	152
Millburn, N.J., U.S.	B4	137
Millbury, Ma., U.S.	B4	128
Millbury, Oh., U.S.	e7	142
Mill City, Or., U.S.	C4	144
Mill Creek, In., U.S.	A4	121
Mill Creek, Ok., U.S.	C5	143
Millcreek, Ut., U.S.	C4	151
Mill Creek, W.V., U.S.	C5	155
Mill Creek, stm., In., U.S.	F4	121
Mill Creek, stm., Ks., U.S.	C7	123
Mill Creek, stm., Ks., U.S.	C6	123
Mill Creek, stm., N.J., U.S.	D4	137
Mill Creek, stm., Oh., U.S.	B2	142
Mill Creek, stm., Tn., U.S.	g10	149
Mill Creek, stm., W.V., U.S.	C3	155
Mill Creek, stm., W.V., U.S.	m13	155
Millcreek Township, Pa., U.S.	B1	145
Milldale, Ct., U.S.	C4	114
Milledgeville, Ga., U.S.	C3	117
Milledgeville, Il., U.S.	B4	120
Milledgeville, Tn., U.S.	B3	149
Mille Îles, Rivière des, stm., Que., Can.	p19	104
Mille Lacs, co., Mn., U.S.	E5	130
Mille Lacs Indian Reservation, Mn., U.S.	D5	130
Mille Lacs Lake, l., Mn., U.S.	D5	130
Millen, Ga., U.S.	D5	117
Miller, Ne., U.S.	D6	134
Miller, S.D., U.S.	C7	148
Miller, co., Ar., U.S.	D2	111
Miller, co., Ga., U.S.	E2	117
Miller, co., Mo., U.S.	C5	132
Miller, Mount, mtn., Ak., U.S.	C11	109
Miller Creek, stm., De., U.S.	F5	115
Millerovo, Russia	H6	26
Miller Peak, mtn., Az., U.S.	F5	110
Miller Run, stm., Vt., U.S.	B4	152
Millers, stm., Ma., U.S.	A3	128
Millersburg, In., U.S.	A6	121
Millersburg, Ky., U.S.	B5	124
Millersburg, Oh., U.S.	B4	142
Millersburg, Pa., U.S.	E8	145
Millers Falls, Ma., U.S.	A3	128
Millers Ferry, Al., U.S.	C2	108
Millers Ferry Dam, Al., U.S.	C2	108
Millersport, Oh., U.S.	C3	142
Millerstown, Pa., U.S.	E7	145
Millersville, Pa., U.S.	F9	145
Millerton, N.B., Can.	C4	101
Millerton, N.Y., U.S.	D7	139
Millerton, Ok., U.S.	D6	143
Millertown, Newf., Can.	D3	102
Millerville, Al., U.S.	B4	108
Millet, Alta., Can.	C4	98
Millevaches, Plateau de, plat., Fr.	G9	14
Mill Grove, In., U.S.	D7	121
Mill Hall, Pa., U.S.	D7	145
Millheim, Pa., U.S.	E7	145
Millhousen, In., U.S.	F7	121
Millicent, Austl.	K4	70
Milligan, Fl., U.S.	u15	116
Milligan, Ne., U.S.	D8	134
Milliken, Co., U.S.	A6	113
Millington, Mi., U.S.	E7	129
Millington, Or., U.S.	D2	144
Millington, Tn., U.S.	B2	149
Millinocket, Me., U.S.	C4	126
Millinocket Lake, l., Me., U.S.	B4	126
Millinocket Lake, l., Me., U.S.	C4	126
Millis, Ma., U.S.	B5	128
Millmerran, Austl.	F9	70
Millport, Al., U.S.	B1	108
Mill Run, Pa., U.S.	G3	145
Millry, Al., U.S.	D1	108
Mills, Wy., U.S.	D6	157
Mills, co., Ia., U.S.	C2	122
Mills, co., Tx., U.S.	D3	150
Millsboro, De., U.S.	F4	115
Millsboro, Pa., U.S.	G1	145
Mill Shoals, Il., U.S.	E5	120
Mill Spring, Mo., U.S.	D7	132
Millstadt, Il., U.S.	E3	120
Millstatt, Aus.	I13	10
Millstone, stm., N.J., U.S.	C4	137
Millstream Chichester Range National Park, Austl.	D3	68
Milltown, In., U.S.	H5	121
Milltown, Ky., U.S.	C4	124
Milltown, Mt., U.S.	D3	133
Milltown, N.J., U.S.	C4	137
Milltown, Wi., U.S.	C1	156
Milltown [-Head of Bay d'Espoir], Newf., Can.	E4	102
Millvale, Pa., U.S.	k14	145
Mill Valley, Ca., U.S.	D2	112
Mill Village, N.S., Can.	E5	101
Millville, N.B., Can.	C2	101
Millville, De., U.S.	F5	115
Millville, Ky., U.S.	B5	124
Millville, Ma., U.S.	B4	128
Millville, N.J., U.S.	E2	137
Millville, Oh., U.S.	n12	142
Millville, Pa., U.S.	D9	145
Millville, Ut., U.S.	B4	151
Millville, W.V., U.S.	B7	155
Millville Lake, N.H., U.S.	E4	136
Millwood, Ga., U.S.	E4	117
Millwood, Va., U.S.	A4	153
Millwood, Wa., U.S.	g14	154
Millwood Lake, res., Ar., U.S.	D1	111
Milne Bay, b., Pap. N. Gui.	B10	68
Milner, Co., U.S.	A3	113
Milner, Ga., U.S.	C2	117
Milner Dam, Id., U.S.	G5	119
Milnor, N.D., U.S.	C8	141
Milo, Alta., Can.	D4	98
Milo, Ia., U.S.	C4	122
Milo, Me., U.S.	C4	126
Milo, Or., U.S.	E3	144
Milos, Grc.	M8	20
Milos, i., Grc.	M8	20
Miloslavskoje, Russia	H22	22
Milparinka, Austl.	G4	70
Milpitas, Ca., U.S.	k9	112
Milroy, In., U.S.	F7	121
Milroy, Mn., U.S.	F3	130
Milroy, Pa., U.S.	E6	145
Milstead, Al., U.S.	C4	108
Milstead, Ga., U.S.	C3	117
Miltenberg, Ger.	F9	10
Milton, Ont., Can.	D5	103
Milton, N.Z.	G2	72
Milton, De., U.S.	E4	115
Milton, Fl., U.S.	u14	116
Milton, Il., U.S.	D3	120
Milton, In., U.S.	E7	121
Milton, Ia., U.S.	D5	122
Milton, Ky., U.S.	B4	124
Milton, La., U.S.	D3	125
Milton, Ma., U.S.	B5	128
Milton, N.H., U.S.	D5	136
Milton, N.Y., U.S.	D7	139
Milton, N.D., U.S.	A7	141
Milton, Pa., U.S.	D8	145
Milton, Vt., U.S.	B2	152
Milton, Wa., U.S.	f11	154
Milton, W.V., U.S.	C2	155
Milton, Wi., U.S.	F5	156
Milton, Lake, l., Oh., U.S.	A4	142
Miltona, Mn., U.S.	D3	130
Miltona, Lake, l., Mn., U.S.	D3	130
Milton-Freewater, Or., U.S.	B8	144
Milton Mills, N.H., U.S.	C5	136
Milton Reservoir, res., Co., U.S.	A6	113
Miltonvale, Ks., U.S.	C6	123
Milverton, Ont., Can.	D4	103
Milwaukee, Wi., U.S.	E6	156
Milwaukee, co., Wi., U.S.	E6	156
Milwaukee, stm., Wi., U.S.	m12	156
Milwaukie, Or., U.S.	B4	144
Mim, Ghana	H8	64
Mimoso, Braz.	C4	79
Mimoso, Braz.	G14	82
Mimoso do Sul, Braz.	F8	79
Mims, Fl., U.S.	D6	116
Min, stm., China	E7	30
Min, stm., China	I7	34
Mina, Nv., U.S.	E3	135
Mīnāb, Iran	H14	48
Mina El Limón, Nic.	E8	92
Minahasa, pen., Indon.	E7	38
Minamata, Japan	O5	36
Minami-Daitō-jima, i., Japan	F13	30
Mina Pirquitas, Arg.	B5	80
Minas, Cuba	D6	94
Minas, Ur.	H11	80
Minas, Sierra de las, mts., Guat.	B5	92
Minas Basin, b., N.S., Can.	D5	101
Minas Channel, strt., N.S., Can.	D5	101
Minas de Barroterán, Mex.	D9	90
Minas de Corrales, Ur.	F11	80
Minas de Matahambre, Cuba	C3	94
Minas de Oro, Hond.	C7	92
Minas Gerais, state, Braz.	E6	79
Minas Novas, Braz.	D7	79
Minatare, Ne., U.S.	C2	134
Minatitlán, Mex.	I12	90
Minbu, Burma	D3	40
Minburn, Alta., Can.	C5	98
Minburn, Ia., U.S.	C3	122
Minco, Ok., U.S.	B4	143
Mindanao, i., Phil.	D8	38
Mindelo, C.V.	k16	64a
Mindemoya, Ont., Can.	B2	103
Minden, Ont., Can.	C6	103
Minden, Ger.	C8	10
Minden, Ia., U.S.	C2	122
Minden, La., U.S.	B2	125
Minden, Ne., U.S.	D7	134
Minden, Nv., U.S.	E2	135
Minden, W.V., U.S.	D3	155
Mindenmines, Mo., U.S.	D3	132
Mindon, Burma	E3	40
Mindoro, i., Phil.	C7	38
Mindoro Strait, strt., Phil.	C7	38
Mine Centre, Ont., Can.	E5	100
Minechoag Mountain, hill, Ma., U.S.	B3	128
Mine Hill, N.J., U.S.	B3	137
Mineiros, Braz.	D2	79
Mineola, N.Y., U.S.	E7	139
Mineola, Tx., U.S.	C5	150
Miner, Mo., U.S.	E8	132
Miner, co., S.D., U.S.	D8	148
Mineral, Il., U.S.	B4	120
Mineral, Va., U.S.	B5	153
Mineral, Wa., U.S.	C3	154
Mineral, co., Co., U.S.	D4	113
Mineral, co., Mt., U.S.	C1	133
Mineral, co., Nv., U.S.	E3	135
Mineral, co., W.V., U.S.	B6	155
Mineral City, Oh., U.S.	B4	142
Mineral de Cucharas, Mex.	F7	90
Mineral Mountains, mts., Ut., U.S.	E3	151
Mineral'nyje Vody, Russia	I6	26
Mineral Point, Mo., U.S.	D7	132
Mineral Point, Wi., U.S.	F3	156
Mineral Springs, Ar., U.S.	D2	111
Mineral Wells, Ms., U.S.	A4	131
Mineral Wells, Tx., U.S.	C3	150
Minersville, Pa., U.S.	E9	145
Minersville, Ut., U.S.	E3	151
Minerva, Oh., U.S.	B4	142
Minervino Murge, Italy	H11	18
Minetto, N.Y., U.S.	B4	139
Mineville, N.Y., U.S.	A7	139
Minfeng, China	D3	30
Mingečaur, Azer.	I7	26
Mingela, Austl.	B7	70
Minggang, China	C3	34
Mingo, Ia., U.S.	C4	122
Mingo, co., W.V., U.S.	D2	155
Mingo Junction, Oh., U.S.	B5	142
Minhang, China	D10	34
Minhla, Burma	F3	40
Minho, hist. reg., Port.	D3	16
Minho (Miño), stm., Eur.	D3	16
Minhou, China	I8	34
Minicoy Island, i., India	H2	46
Minidoka, co., Id., U.S.	G5	119
Minidoka Dam, Id., U.S.	G5	119
Minier, Il., U.S.	C4	120
Mīnīn, Syria	A6	50
Miniota, Man., Can.	D1	100
Minipi Lake, l., Newf., Can.	h9	102
Minisink Island, i., N.J., U.S.	A3	137
Minitonas, Man., Can.	C1	100
Minjar, Russia	F9	26
Min'kovo, Russia	B26	22
Minlaton, Austl.	J2	70
Minle, China	D7	30
Minna, Nig.	G13	64
Minneapolis, Ks., U.S.	C6	123
Minneapolis, Mn., U.S.	F5	130
Minnedosa, Man., Can.	D2	100
Minnedosa, stm., Man., Can.	D1	100
Minnehaha, co., S.D., U.S.	D9	148
Minneola, Ks., U.S.	E3	123
Minneota, Mn., U.S.	F3	130
Minnesota, state, U.S.	E4	130
Minnesota, stm., Mn., U.S.	F2	130
Minnesota Lake, Mn., U.S.	G5	130
Minnetonka, Mn., U.S.	n12	130
Minnetonka, Lake, l., Mn., U.S.	n11	130
Minnewaska, Lake, l., Mn., U.S.	E3	130
Minnewaukan, N.D., U.S.	A6	141
Mino, Japan	L11	36
Miño (Minho), stm., Eur.	D3	16
Minocqua, Wi., U.S.	C4	156
Minonk, Il., U.S.	C4	120
Minooka, Il., U.S.	B5	120
Minor Hill, Tn., U.S.	B4	149
Minot, Ma., U.S.	h12	128
Minot, N.D., U.S.	A4	141
Minot Air Force Base, mil., N.D., U.S.	A4	141
Minquadale, De., U.S.	i7	115
Minsk, Bela.	H10	22
Mińsk Mazowiecki, Pol.	C21	10
Minster, Oh., U.S.	B1	142
Mintaka Pass, Asia	B6	44
Minter City, Ms., U.S.	B3	131
Mint Hill, N.C., U.S.	B2	140
Minto, Man., Can.	E1	100
Minto, N.B., Can.	C3	101
Minto, Ak., U.S.	C10	109
Minto, N.D., U.S.	A8	141
Minto, Mount, mtn., Ant.	C8	73
Minto Inlet, b., N.W. Ter., Can.	B9	96
Minton, Sask., Can.	H3	105
Minturn, Ar., U.S.	B4	111
Minturn, Co., U.S.	B4	113
Minturno, Italy	H8	18
Minusinsk, Russia	G10	28
Minute Man National Historical Park, Ma., U.S.	g10	128
Minxian, China	E7	30
Minya see Al-Minyā, Egypt	C6	60
Minya Konka see Gongga Shan, mtn., China	F7	30
Mio, Mi., U.S.	D6	129
Miory, Bela.	F10	22
Mir, Bela.	H9	22
Mira, Port.	E3	16
Mira, stm., Col.	G3	84
Mirabel, Que., Can.	D3	104
Miracema do Tocantins, Braz.	E9	76
Mirador, Braz.	E10	76
Miradouro, Braz.	F7	79
Miraflores, Arg.	E6	80
Miraflores, Col.	E6	84
Miraflores, Col.	G6	84
Miraflores, Esclusas de, Pan.	I15	92
Mira Gut, N.S., Can.	C10	101
Mīrah, Wādī al-, val., Asia	B11	60
Miraj, India	D3	46
Miramar, Arg.	J10	80
Miramar, Arg.	F7	80
Miramar, C.R.	G10	92
Miramar, Fl., U.S.	s13	116
Miramar Naval Air Station, mil., Ca., U.S.	F5	112
Miramas, Fr.	I12	14
Miramichi Bay, b., N.B., Can.	B5	101
Miranda, Braz.	I13	82
Miranda, Col.	F4	84
Miranda, state, Ven.	B9	84
Miranda, stm., Braz.	H13	82
Miranda de Ebro, Spain	C9	16
Miranda do Douro, Port.	D5	16
Mirande, Fr.	I7	14
Mirandela, Port.	D4	16
Mirandola, Italy	E6	18
Mirante do Paranapanema, Braz.	G3	79
Mirapuxi, stm., Braz.	B3	79
Mira Taglio, Italy	D7	18
Miravalles, Volcán, vol., C.R.	G9	92
Mirbāt, Oman	F9	47
Mirebeau-sur-Bèze, Fr.	E12	14
Mirecourt, Fr.	D13	14
Miri, Malay.	E5	38
Miriam Vale, Austl.	E9	70
Mirim, Lagoa, b., S.A.	H9	74
Mirim, Lagoa (Laguna Merín), b., S.A.	G12	80
Miriñay, stm., Arg.	E10	80
Miritiparanā, stm., Col.	H7	84
Mīrjāveh, Iran	G16	48
Mirnyj, Russia	E14	28
Mirnyy, sci., Ant.	B6	73
Mirow, Ger.	B12	10
Mīrpur, Pak.	D5	44
Mīrpur Khās, Pak.	H3	44
Mirria, Niger	E14	64
Mirror, Alta., Can.	C4	98
Mirror Lake, N.H., U.S.	C4	136
Mirror Lake, l., N.H., U.S.	C4	136
Mirzāpur, India	H10	44
Misāhah, Bi'r, well, Egypt	F4	60
Misantla, Mex.	H11	90
Miscoe Hill, hill, Ma., U.S.	h9	128
Miscou Centre, N.B., Can.	B5	101
Miscouche, P.E.I., Can.	C6	101
Miscou Island, i., N.B., Can.	B5	101
Miscou Point, c., N.B., Can.	A5	101
Misenheimer, N.C., U.S.	B2	140
Mishagua, stm., Peru	D5	82
Mishan, China	B13	30
Mishawaka, In., U.S.	A5	121
Mishbih, Jabal, mtn., Egypt	J3	48
Misheguk Mountain, mtn., Ak., U.S.	B7	109
Mishicot, Wi., U.S.	D6	156
Misikan, China	C13	44
Misilmeri, Italy	K8	18
Misiones, prov., Arg.	D11	80
Misiones, dept., Para.	D10	80
Misión San Francisco de Laishí, Arg.	D9	80
Misión San Vicente, Mex.	B1	90
Miskī, Sud.	J3	60
Miskito Channel, strt., Nic.	C11	92
Miskitos, Cayos, is., Nic.	C12	92
Miskitos Reef, rf., Nic.	C12	92
Miskolc, Hung.	G20	10
Mislata, Spain	A10	62
Misool, Pulau, i., Indon.	F9	38
Mispillion, stm., De., U.S.	E4	115
Misrātah, Libya	B4	56
Missaukee, co., Mi., U.S.	D5	129
Missaukee, Lake, l., Mi., U.S.	D5	129
Mission, Ks., U.S.	m16	123
Mission, S.D., U.S.	D5	148
Mission, Tx., U.S.	F3	150
Mission Hill, S.D., U.S.	E8	148
Mission Mountain, mtn., Ok., U.S.	A7	145
Mission Range, mts., Mt., U.S.	C3	133
Mission Viejo, Ca., U.S.	n13	112
Missisquoi, stm., Vt., U.S.	B3	152
Missisquoi Bay, b., Vt., U.S.	A2	152
Mississauga, Ont., Can.	D5	103
Mississinewa, stm., U.S.	D7	121
Mississinewa Lake, res., In., U.S.	C6	121
Mississippi, co., Ar., U.S.	B5	111
Mississippi, co., Mo., U.S.	E8	132
Mississippi, state, U.S.	C4	131
Mississippi, stm., U.S.	E8	106
Mississippi Delta, La., U.S.	E6	125
Mississippi Lake, l., Ont., Can.	B8	103
Mississippi Sound, strt., U.S.	E5	131
Mississippi State, Ms., U.S.	B5	131
Missoula, Mt., U.S.	D2	133
Missoula, co., Mt., U.S.	D2	133
Missouri, state, U.S.	C5	132
Missouri, stm., U.S.	C7	106
Missouri Buttes, mtn., Wy., U.S.	B8	157
Missouri City, Mo., U.S.	h11	132
Missouri City, Tx., U.S.	r14	150
Missouri Valley, Ia., U.S.	C2	122
Mistaken Point, c., Newf., Can.	E5	102
Mistassini, Que., Can.	h12	104
Mistassini, Lac, l., Que., Can.	h12	104
Mistastin Lake, l., Newf., Can.	g9	102
Mistatim, Sask., Can.	E4	105
Mistelbach, Aus.	G16	10
Misterbianco, Italy	L10	18
Misterei, Sud.	K2	60
Misti, Volcán, vol., Peru	G6	82
Mistretta, Italy	L9	18
Mita, Punta, c., Mex.	G7	90
Mitchell, Austl.	F7	70
Mitchell, Ont., Can.	D3	103
Mitchell, Ga., U.S.	C4	117
Mitchell, Il., U.S.	E3	120
Mitchell, In., U.S.	G5	121
Mitchell, Ne., U.S.	C2	134
Mitchell, S.D., U.S.	D7	148
Mitchell, co., Ga., U.S.	E2	117
Mitchell, co., Ia., U.S.	A5	122
Mitchell, co., Ks., U.S.	C5	123
Mitchell, co., N.C., U.S.	e10	140
Mitchell, co., Tx., U.S.	C2	150
Mitchell, stm., Austl.	K7	70
Mitchell, Lake, l., Mi., U.S.	D5	129
Mitchell, Lake, res., Al., U.S.	C3	108
Mitchell, Mount, mtn., N.C., U.S.	f10	140
Mitchell Island, i., La., U.S.	E6	125
Mitchellsburg, Ky., U.S.	C5	124
Mitchellville, Ar., U.S.	D4	111
Mitchellville, Ia., U.S.	C4	122
Mitchellville, Tn., U.S.	A5	149
Mitilíni, Grc.	J10	20
Mitkof Island, i., Ak., U.S.	m23	109
Mitla, hist., Mex.	I11	90
Mito, Japan	K15	36
Mitsamiouli, Com.	k15	67a
Mitsinjo, Madag.	p21	67b
Mitsio, Nosy, i., Madag.	n23	67b
Mitsiwa (Massawa), Erit.	J10	60
Mittellandkanal, Ger.	C9	10
Mittenwald, Ger.	H11	10
Mittersill, Aus.	H12	10
Mitú, Col.	G7	84
Mitumba, Monts, mts., Zaire	B5	58
Mitwaba, Zaire	C5	58
Mitzic, Gabon	A2	58
Miura, Japan	L14	36
Mixco Viejo, hist., Guat.	C4	92
Miyake-jima, i., Japan	M14	36
Miyako, Japan	H16	36
Miyakonojō, Japan	P6	36
Miyazaki, Japan	P6	36
Miyazu, Japan	L10	36
Miyun, China	C4	32
Mizan Teferi, Eth.	N8	60
Mizdah, Libya	B3	56
Mize, Ms., U.S.	D4	131
Mizen Head, c., Ire.	J4	8
Mizoram, state, India	I15	44
Mizpah, N.J., U.S.	E3	137
Mizpah Creek, stm., Mt., U.S.	E11	133
Mizpé Ramon, Isr.	G3	50
Mizque, Bol.	G9	82
Mizque, stm., Bol.	H9	82
Mjøsa, l., Nor.	K12	6
Mladá Boleslav, Czech.	E14	10
Mladenovac, Yugo.	E4	20
Mlanje Peak see Sapitwa, mtn., Mwi.	E7	58
Mława, Pol.	B20	10
Mmabatho, Boph.	E7	66
Mmadinare, Bots.	C8	66
Mo, Nor.	H14	6
Mo, stm., Afr.	G10	64
Moa, stm., Afr.	G4	54
Moa, stm., Braz.	B5	82
Moab, Ut., U.S.	E6	151
Moaco, stm., Braz.	C7	82
Moa Island, i., Austl.	B8	68
Moama, Austl.	K6	70
Moanda, Gabon	B2	58
Moapa, Nv., U.S.	G7	135
Moapa River Indian Reservation, Nv., U.S.	G7	135
Moark, Ar., U.S.	A5	111
Mobara, Japan	L15	36
Mobaye, Cen. Afr. Rep.	H5	56
Moberly, Mo., U.S.	B5	132
Moberly Lake, B.C., Can.	B7	99
Mobile, Newf., Can.	E5	102
Mobile, Al., U.S.	E1	108
Mobile, co., Al., U.S.	E1	108
Mobile, stm., Al., U.S.	E1	108
Mobile Bay, b., Al., U.S.	E1	113
Mobridge, S.D., U.S.	B5	148
Moca, Dom. Rep.	E9	94
Mocal, stm., N.A.	C6	92
Moçambique, Moz.	E8	58
Mocanal, Spain	p23	17b
Mocanaqua, Pa., U.S.	D9	145
Moccasin, Az., U.S.	A3	110
Moccasin, Mt., U.S.	C7	133
Mocha, Isla, i., Chile	J2	80
Mocha see Al-Makhā', Yemen	H3	47
Moche, stm., Peru	C2	82
Moche, hist., Peru	C2	82
Mochudi, Bots.	E8	66
Mocímboa da Praia, Moz.	D8	58
Mocksville, N.C., U.S.	B2	140
Moclips, Wa., U.S.	B1	154
Môco, Serra, mtn., Ang.	D3	58
Mococa, Braz.	G4	84
Mococa, Braz.	F5	79
Mocoduene, Moz.	D12	66
Mocoretá, Arg.	F10	80
Mocorito, Mex.	E6	90
Moctezuma, Mex.	C5	90
Moctezuma, stm., Mex.	C5	90
Moctezuma, stm., Mex.	G10	90
Mocuba, Moz.	E7	58
Modale, Ia., U.S.	C2	122
Modane, Fr.	G13	14
Modderrivier, S. Afr.	G7	66
Model Reservoir, res., Co., U.S.	D6	113
Modena, Italy	E5	18
Modena, N.Y., U.S.	D6	139
Modesto, Ca., U.S.	D3	112
Modesto, Il., U.S.	D4	120
Modica, Italy	M9	18
Mödling, Aus.	G16	10
Modoc, In., U.S.	D7	121
Modoc, co., Ca., U.S.	B3	112
Moe, Austl.	L7	70
Moeda, Braz.	F6	79
Moema, Braz.	E6	79
Moengo, Sur.	B8	76
Moenkopi, Az., U.S.	A4	110
Moenkopi Plateau, plat., Az., U.S.	B4	110
Moenkopi Wash, val., Az., U.S.	A5	110
Moers, Ger.	D6	10

Name — Map Ref. — Page

Moffat, co., Co., U.S. A2 113
Moffat Tunnel, Co., U.S. B5 113
Moffett, Ok., U.S. B7 143
Moffett Field Naval Air Station, mil., Ca., U.S. k8 112
Moffit, N.D., U.S. C5 141
Moga, India E6 44
Mogadiscio see Muqdisho, Som. H10 56
Mogadishu see Muqdisho, Som. H10 56
Mogadore, Oh., U.S. A4 142
Mogán, Spain p25 17b
Mogapinyana, Bots. D8 66
Mogaung, Burma B4 40
Mogil'ov, Bela. H13 22
Mogil'ov-Podol'skij, Ukr. H3 26
Mogincual, Moz. E8 58
Mogliano Veneto, Italy D7 18
Mogoča, Russia G15 28
Mogogh, Sud. M6 60
Mogok, Burma C4 40
Mogollon Mesa, mtn., Az., U.S. C4 110
Mogollon Mountains, mts., N.M., U.S. D1 138
Mogollon Rim, clf, Az., U.S. C5 110
Mogote, Co., U.S. D4 113
Mogotes, Col. D6 84
Mogotón, mtn., N.A. D8 92
Moguer, Spain H5 16
Mogzon, Russia G14 28
Mohács, Hung. J18 10
Mohall, N.D., U.S. A4 141
Mohammedia (Fedala), Mor. D7 62
Mohave, co., Az., U.S. B1 110
Mohave, Lake, res., U.S. H7 135
Mohave Mountains, mts., Az., U.S. C1 110
Mohave Valley, Az., U.S. C1 110
Mohawk, Mi., U.S. A2 129
Mohawk, N.Y., U.S. C5 139
Mohawk, stm., N.H., U.S. g7 136
Mohawk, stm., N.Y., U.S. C6 139
Mohawk Lake, l., N.J., U.S. A3 137
Mohawk Mountain, mtn., Ct., U.S. B2 114
Mohawk Mountains, mts., Az., U.S. E2 110
Mohe, China A11 30
Mohican, stm., Oh., U.S. B3 142
Mohican, Black Fork, stm., Oh., U.S. B3 142
Mohican, Clear Fork, stm., Oh., U.S. B3 142
Mohnton, Pa., U.S. F10 145
Moho, stm., Belize A6 92
Moinești, Rom. C10 20
Mointy, Kaz. H12 26
Moiporá, Braz. D3 79
Mõisaküla, Est. C8 22
Moisés Ville, Arg. F8 80
Moisie, Que., Can. h8 102
Moissac, Fr. H8 14
Moitaco, Ven. C10 84
Mojana, Brazo, mth., Col. C5 84
Mojave, Ca., U.S. E4 112
Mojave, stm., Ca., U.S. E5 112
Mojave Desert, des., Ca., U.S. E5 112
Mojicuaçu, stm., Braz. F5 79
Mojimirim, Braz. G5 79
Mojjero, stm., Russia D12 28
Mojo, Eth. M10 60
Mokāma, India H11 44
Mokane, Mo., U.S. C6 132
Mokapu Peninsula, pen., Hi., U.S. g10 118
Mokapu Point, c., Hi., U.S. g11 118
Mokelumne, stm., Ca., U.S. C3 112
Mokelumne Hill, Ca., U.S. C3 112
Mokena, Il., U.S. k9 120
Moknine, Tun. N5 18
Mokp'o, S. Kor. I14 32
Mokrisset, Mor. K6 16
Mokša, stm., Russia G24 22
Moku Manu, i., Hi., U.S. g11 118
Mokwa, Nig. G12 64
Mol, Bel. F7 12
Mola di Bari, Italy H12 18
Molalla, Or., U.S. B4 144
Molasses Pond, l., Me., U.S. D4 126
Moldau see Vltava, stm., Czech. F14 10
Moldavia, hist. reg., Rom. B11 20
Molde, Nor. J10 6
Moldova, ctry., Eur. F13 4
Moldoveanu, Vîrful, mtn., Rom. D8 20
Môle, Cap du, c., Haiti E8 94
Molena, Ga., U.S. C2 117
Molepolole, Bots. E7 66
Molėtai, Lith. F8 22
Molfetta, Italy H11 18
Molina, Chile H3 80
Molina de Segura, Spain G10 16
Moline, Il., U.S. B3 120
Moline, Ks., U.S. E7 123
Moline, Mi., U.S. F5 129
Molino, Fl., U.S. u14 116
Molinos, Arg. C5 80
Molins de Rei, Spain D14 16
Molise, prov., Italy H9 18
Mollendo, Peru G5 82
Mollepata, Peru E5 82
Mölln, Ger. B10 10
Mölndal, Swe. M13 6
Moločnoje, Russia B22 22
Molodečno, Bela. G9 22
Mologa, stm., Russia C19 22
Molokai, i., Hi., U.S. B5 118
Molokini, i., Hi., U.S. C5 118
Molong, Austl. I8 70
Molopo, stm., Afr. F5 66
Molotov see Perm', Russia F9 26
Molou, Chad K1 60
Molsheim, Fr. D14 14
Molson, stm., Man., Can. C3 100
Molson Lake, l., Man., Can. B3 100
Molteno, S. Afr. H8 66
Molucca Sea see Maluku, Laut, Indon. F7 38
Moluccas see Maluku, is., Indon. F8 38
Molus, Ky., U.S. D6 124
Moma, Moz. E7 58
Moma, stm., Russia D20 28
Momanga, Nmb. B5 66
Mombachito, Cerro, mtn., Nic. E9 92
Mombacho, Volcán, vol., Nic. F9 92
Mombasa, Kenya B7 58
Mombetsu, Japan c18 36a
Momence, Il., U.S. B6 120
Momotombo, Volcán, vol., Nic. E8 92
Mompós, Col. C5 84
Mona, Ut., U.S. D4 151
Mona, Canal de la, strt., N.A. E11 94
Mona, Isla de, i., P.R. E11 94
Mona, Punta, c., C.R. H12 92
Monaca, Pa., U.S. E1 145
Monaco, Mon. I14 14
Monaco, ctry., Eur. G9 4
Monadnock, Mount, mtn., N.H., U.S. E2 136
Monadnock Mountain, mtn., Vt., U.S. B5 152
Monagas, state, Ven. C11 84
Monaghan, co., Ire. G6 8
Monagrillo, Pan. D2 84
Monahans, Tx., U.S. D1 150
Monarch, Alta., Can. E4 98
Monarch, Mt., U.S. C6 133
Monarch Mills, S.C., U.S. B4 147
Monarch Pass, Co., U.S. C4 113
Monashee Mountains, mts., B.C., Can. D8 99
Monastir, Tun. N5 18
Monastir see Bitola, Mac. H5 20
Monastyrščina, Russia G14 22
Moncalieri, Italy D2 18
Monção, Braz. D9 76
Mončegorsk, Russia D4 26
Mönchengladbach, Ger. D6 10
Moncks Corner, S.C., U.S. E7 147
Monclo, W.V., U.S. D3 155
Monclova, Mex. D9 90
Moncontour, Fr. D4 14
Moncoutant, Fr. F6 14
Moncton, N.B., Can. C5 101
Moncure, N.C., U.S. B3 140
Mondaí, Braz. D12 80
Mondamin, Ia., U.S. C1 122
Monday, stm., Para. C11 80
Mondoro, Mali D9 64
Mondoubleau, Fr. E7 14
Mondovi, Wi., U.S. D2 156
Mondragone, Italy H8 18
Monee, Il., U.S. B6 120
Moneron, ostrov, i., Russia a16 36a
Monessen, Pa., U.S. F2 145
Monesterio, Spain G5 16
Monett, Mo., U.S. E4 132
Monette, Ar., U.S. B5 111
Monfalcone, Italy D8 18
Monflanquin, Fr. H7 14
Monforte, Port. F4 16
Monforte de Lemos, Spain C4 16
Monfort Heights, Oh., U.S. *o12 142
Mongaguá, Braz. H5 79
Mongalla, Sud. G7 56
Mong Cai, Viet. D9 40
Mongers Lake, l., Austl. E3 68
Möng Hsat, Burma D5 40
Möng Mit, Burma C4 40
Mongo, Chad F4 56
Mongo, In., U.S. A7 121
Mongo, stm., Afr. G4 64
Mongol Altajn nuruu, mts., Asia H16 26
Mongolia (Mongol Ard Uls), ctry., Asia B8 30
Mongororo, Chad K2 60
Möng Pai, Burma E4 40
Mongu, Zam. E4 58
Möng Yawng, Burma D6 40
Monhegan Island, i., Me., U.S. E3 126
Monheim, Ger. G10 10
Monida Pass, U.S. E6 119
Monino, Russia F21 22
Moniquirá, Col. E6 84
Monistrol-sur-Loire, Fr. G11 14
Moniteau, co., Mo., U.S. C5 132
Monitor, Alta., Can. D5 98
Monitor Range, mts., Nv., U.S. E5 135
Monitor Valley, val., Nv., U.S. D5 135
Monkey River, Belize A6 92
Mońki, Pol. B22 10
Monkira, Austl. E4 70
Monkton, Ont., Can. D3 103
Monkton, Vt., U.S. C2 152
Mon Louis, Al., U.S. E1 108
Monmouth, Il., U.S. C3 120
Monmouth, Me., U.S. D2 126
Monmouth, Or., U.S. C3 144
Monmouth, co., N.J., U.S. C4 137
Monmouth Beach, N.J., U.S. C5 137
Monmouth Junction, N.J., U.S. C3 137
Monmouth Mountain, mtn., B.C., Can. D6 99
Mono, co., Ca., U.S. D4 112
Mono, stm., Afr. G7 54
Mono, Caño, stm., Col. E8 84
Mono, Punta, c., Nic. F11 92
Monocacy, stm., Md., U.S. B3 127
Mono Lake, l., Ca., U.S. D4 112
Monomonac, Lake, l., U.S. E3 136
Monomoy Island, i., Ma., U.S. C7 128
Monomoy Point, c., Ma., U.S. C7 128
Monon, In., U.S. C4 121
Monona, Ia., U.S. A6 122
Monona, Wi., U.S. E4 156
Monona, co., Ia., U.S. B1 122
Monona, Lake, l., Wi., U.S. E4 156
Monongah, W.V., U.S. B4 155
Monongahela, Pa., U.S. F2 145
Monongahela, stm., U.S. G2 145
Monongalia, co., W.V., U.S. B4 155
Monopoli, Italy I12 18
Monòver, Spain G11 16
Monreale, Italy K8 18
Monroe, Ar., U.S. C4 111
Monroe, Ct., U.S. D3 114
Monroe, Ga., U.S. C3 117
Monroe, In., U.S. C8 121
Monroe, Ia., U.S. C4 122
Monroe, La., U.S. B3 125
Monroe, Mi., U.S. G7 129
Monroe, Ne., U.S. C8 134
Monroe, N.H., U.S. B2 136
Monroe, N.Y., U.S. D6 139
Monroe, N.C., U.S. C2 140
Monroe, Oh., U.S. C1 142
Monroe, Ok., U.S. C7 143
Monroe, Or., U.S. C3 144
Monroe, S.D., U.S. D8 148
Monroe, Ut., U.S. E3 151
Monroe, Va., U.S. C3 153
Monroe, Wa., U.S. B4 154
Monroe, Wi., U.S. F4 156
Monroe, co., Al., U.S. D2 108
Monroe, co., Ar., U.S. C4 111
Monroe, co., Fl., U.S. G5 116
Monroe, co., Ga., U.S. D3 117
Monroe, co., Il., U.S. E3 120
Monroe, co., In., U.S. F4 121
Monroe, co., Ia., U.S. D5 122
Monroe, co., Ky., U.S. D4 124
Monroe, co., Mi., U.S. G7 129
Monroe, co., Ms., U.S. B5 131
Monroe, co., Mo., U.S. B5 132
Monroe, co., N.Y., U.S. B3 139
Monroe, co., Oh., U.S. C4 142
Monroe, co., Pa., U.S. D11 145
Monroe, co., Tn., U.S. D9 149
Monroe, co., W.V., U.S. D4 155
Monroe, co., Wi., U.S. E3 156
Monroe Center, Ct., U.S. D3 114
Monroe Center, Il., U.S. A5 120
Monroe City, In., U.S. G3 121
Monroe City, Mo., U.S. B6 132
Monroe Lake, res., In., U.S. F5 121
Monroe Park, De., U.S. h7 115
Monroeville, Al., U.S. D2 108
Monroeville, In., U.S. C8 121
Monroeville, Oh., U.S. A3 142
Monroeville, Pa., U.S. k14 145
Monrovia, Lib. H4 64
Monrovia, Ca., U.S. m13 112
Monrovia, In., U.S. E5 121
Mons (Bergen), Bel. H4 12
Monsefú, Peru B2 82
Monselice, Italy D6 18
Monson, Me., U.S. C3 126
Monson, Ma., U.S. B3 128
Montabaur, Ger. E7 10
Montagnana, Italy D6 18
Montagu, S. Afr. I5 66
Montague, P.E.I., Can. C7 101
Montague, Ca., U.S. B2 112
Montague, Mi., U.S. E4 129
Montague, co., Tx., U.S. C4 150
Montague, Isla, i., Mex. B2 90
Montague Island, i., Ak., U.S. D10 109
Montague Peak, mtn., Ak., U.S. g18 109
Montague Strait, strt., Ak., U.S. h18 109
Montagu Island, i., S. Geor. A2 73
Montaigu, Fr. F5 14
Montalcino, Italy F6 18
Montalegre, Port. D4 16
Mont Alto, Pa., U.S. G6 145
Montana, Switz. F7 13
Montana, state, U.S. D7 133
Montandon, Pa., U.S. E8 145
Montargis, Fr. D9 14
Montauban, Fr. H8 14
Montbard, Fr. E11 14
Montbarrey, Fr. E12 14
Montbéliard, Fr. E13 14
Mont Belvieu, Tx., U.S. E5 150
Mont Blanc, Tunnel du, Eur. G6 13
Montbrison, Fr. G11 14
Montbron, Fr. G7 14
Montcalm, co., Mi., U.S. E5 129
Montceau [-les-Mines], Fr. F11 14
Montchanin, Fr. F11 14
Montchanin, De., U.S. h7 115
Montclair, Ca., U.S. m13 112
Montclair, N.J., U.S. B4 137
Mont Clare, Pa., U.S. o19 145
Montcoal, W.V., U.S. D3 155
Mont-de-Marsan, Fr. I6 14
Montdidier, Fr. C9 14
Monte, Laguna del, l., Arg. I7 80
Monteagle, Tn., U.S. D8 149
Monteagudo, Bol. H10 82
Monte Albán, hist., Mex. I11 90
Monte Alegre, Braz. D8 76
Monte Alegre de Goiás, Braz. B5 79
Monte Alegre de Minas, Braz. E4 79
Monte Azul, Braz. C7 79
Monte Azul Paulista, Braz. F4 79
Montebello, Que., Can. D3 104
Montebello, Ca., U.S. m12 112
Monte Bello Islands, is., Austl. D3 68
Monte Buey, Arg. G7 80
Montecarlo, Arg. D11 80
Monte Caseros, Arg. F10 80
Montecassino, Abbazia di, Italy H8 18
Montecatini-Terme, Italy F5 18
Montecillos, Cordillera de, mts., Hond. C7 92
Monte Comán, Arg. H5 80
Monte Cristi, Dom. Rep. E9 94
Montecristi, Ec. H2 84
Monte Cristo, Bol. F11 82
Monte Escobedo, Mex. F8 90
Montego Bay, Jam. E6 94
Monte Grande, Chile F3 80
Montegut, La., U.S. E5 125
Montelíbano, Col. C5 84
Montélimar, Fr. H11 14
Montelindo, stm., Para. B9 80
Montellano, Spain H6 16
Montello, Nv., U.S. B7 135
Montello, Wi., U.S. E4 156
Monte Maíz, Arg. G7 80
Montemorelos, Mex. E10 90
Montemor-o-Novo, Port. G3 16
Montemor-o-Velho, Port. E3 16
Montendre, Fr. G6 14
Montenegro, Braz. E13 80
Montenegro see Crna Gora, state, Yugo. G2 20
Monte Pascoal, Parque Nacional de, Braz. D9 79
Monte Patria, Chile F3 80
Montepuez, Moz. D7 58
Montepulciano, Italy F6 18
Monte Quemado, Arg. C7 80
Montereau-Faut-Yonne, Fr. D9 14
Monterey, Ca., U.S. D3 112
Monterey, In., U.S. B4 121
Monterey, Ky., U.S. B5 124
Monterey, Tn., U.S. C8 149
Monterey, Va., U.S. B3 153
Monterey, co., Ca., U.S. D3 112
Monterey Bay, b., Ca., U.S. D2 112
Monterey Park, Ca., U.S. m12 112
Montería, Col. C5 84
Montero, Bol. G10 82
Monteros, Arg. D6 80
Monterotondo, Italy G7 18
Monterrey, Mex. E9 90
Montesano, Italy I10 18
Montesano, Wa., U.S. C2 154
Monte Sano Mountain, mtn., Al., U.S. A3 108
Monte Sant'Angelo, Italy H10 18
Montesarchio, Italy H9 18
Montes Claros, Braz. F10 74
Montes Claros, Braz. D7 79
Montevallo, Al., U.S. B3 108
Montevarchi, Italy F6 18
Montevideo, Mn., U.S. F3 130
Montevideo, Ur. H10 80
Monte Vista, Co., U.S. D4 113
Montezuma, Ga., U.S. D2 117
Montezuma, In., U.S. E3 121
Montezuma, Ia., U.S. C5 122
Montezuma, Ks., U.S. E3 123
Montezuma, N.M., U.S. B4 138
Montezuma, co., Co., U.S. D2 113
Montezuma Canyon, val., Ut., U.S. F6 151
Montezuma Castle National Monument, Az., U.S. C4 110
Montezuma Creek, Ut., U.S. F6 151
Montezuma Peak, mtn., Az., U.S. D3 110
Montfort, Fr. D5 14
Montfort, Wi., U.S. F3 156
Montgomery, Al., U.S. C3 108
Montgomery, Ga., U.S. E5 117
Montgomery, Il., U.S. B5 120
Montgomery, In., U.S. G3 121
Montgomery, La., U.S. C3 125
Montgomery, Mi., U.S. G6 129
Montgomery, Mn., U.S. F5 130
Montgomery, N.Y., U.S. D6 139
Montgomery, Oh., U.S. o13 142
Montgomery, Pa., U.S. D8 145
Montgomery, Vt., U.S. B3 152
Montgomery, W.V., U.S. C3 155
Montgomery, co., Al., U.S. C3 108
Montgomery, co., Ar., U.S. C2 111
Montgomery, co., Ga., U.S. D4 117
Montgomery, co., Il., U.S. D4 120
Montgomery, co., In., U.S. D4 121
Montgomery, co., Ia., U.S. C2 122
Montgomery, co., Ks., U.S. E8 123
Montgomery, co., Ky., U.S. B6 124
Montgomery, co., Md., U.S. B3 127
Montgomery, co., Ms., U.S. B4 131
Montgomery, co., Mo., U.S. C6 132
Montgomery, co., N.Y., U.S. C6 139
Montgomery, co., N.C., U.S. B3 140
Montgomery, co., Oh., U.S. C1 142
Montgomery, co., Pa., U.S. F11 145
Montgomery, co., Tn., U.S. A4 149
Montgomery, co., Tx., U.S. D5 150
Montgomery, co., Va., U.S. C2 153
Montgomery Center, Vt., U.S. B3 152
Montgomery City, Mo., U.S. C6 132
Montgomery Creek, Ca., U.S. B3 112
Monthermé, Fr. C11 14
Monthey, Switz. F6 13
Monthois, Fr. C11 14
Monticello, P.E.I., Can. C7 101
Monticello, Ar., U.S. D4 111
Monticello, Fl., U.S. B3 116
Monticello, Ga., U.S. C3 117
Monticello, Il., U.S. C5 120
Monticello, In., U.S. C4 121
Monticello, Ia., U.S. B6 122
Monticello, Ky., U.S. D5 124
Monticello, Me., U.S. B5 126
Monticello, Mn., U.S. E5 130
Monticello, Ms., U.S. D3 131
Monticello, N.Y., U.S. D6 139
Monticello, Ut., U.S. F6 151
Monticello, Wi., U.S. F4 156
Montichiari, Italy D5 18
Montier, Mo., U.S. D6 132
Montignac, Fr. G8 14
Montigny-le-Roi, Fr. D12 14
Montigny-sur-Aube, Fr. E11 14
Montijo, Pan. D2 84
Montijo, Port. G3 16
Montijo, Spain G5 16
Montijo, Golfo de, b., Pan. D2 84
Montilla, Spain H7 16
Montividiu, Braz. D3 79
Montivilliers, Fr. C7 14
Mont-Joli, Que., Can. A9 104
Mont-Laurier, Que., Can. C2 104
Mont-Louis, Fr. J9 14
Montluçon, Fr. F9 14
Montluel, Fr. G12 14
Montmagny, Que., Can. C7 104
Montmartre, Sask., Can. G4 105
Montmédy, Fr. C12 14
Montmirail, Fr. D10 14
Montmorenci, In., U.S. D3 121
Montmorenci, S.C., U.S. D4 147
Montmorency, co., Mi., U.S. C6 129
Montmorillon, Fr. F7 14
Monto, Austl. E9 70
Montoro, Spain G7 16
Montour, Ia., U.S. C5 122
Montour, co., Pa., U.S. D8 145
Montour Falls, N.Y., U.S. C4 139
Montoursville, Pa., U.S. D8 145
Montpelier, Id., U.S. G7 119
Montpelier, In., U.S. C7 121
Montpelier, Ia., U.S. C7 122
Montpelier, Oh., U.S. A1 142
Montpelier, Vt., U.S. C3 152
Montpellier, Que., Can. D2 104
Montpellier, Fr. I10 14
Montpon-Ménesterol, Fr. G7 14
Montréal, Que., Can. D4 104
Montreal, Wi., U.S. B3 156
Montréal, Île de, i., Que., Can. q19 104
Montreal Lake, l., Sask., Can. C3 105
Montréal-Nord, Que., Can. p19 104
Montreat, N.C., U.S. f10 140
Montreuil, Fr. B8 14
Montreux, Switz. F6 13
Montrevel [-en-Bresse], Fr. F12 14
Mont-Rolland, Que., Can. D3 104
Montrose, B.C., Can. E9 99
Montrose, Scot., U.K. E11 8
Montrose, Al., U.S. E2 108
Montrose, Ar., U.S. D4 111
Montrose, Co., U.S. C3 113
Montrose, Ga., U.S. D3 117
Montrose, Il., U.S. D5 120
Montrose, Ia., U.S. D6 122
Montrose, Mi., U.S. E7 129
Montrose, Mo., U.S. C4 132
Montrose, Pa., U.S. C10 145
Montrose, S.D., U.S. D8 148
Montrose, Va., U.S. m18 153
Montrose, co., Co., U.S. C2 113
Montross, Va., U.S. B6 153
Mont-Royal, Que., Can. p19 104
Mont-Saint-Michel see Le Mont-Saint-Michel, Fr. D5 14
Montserrat, Mo., U.S. C4 132
Montserrat, dep., N.A. F13 94
Mont-Tremblant, Parc Provincial du, Que., Can. C3 104
Montvale, N.J., U.S. A4 137
Montvale, Va., U.S. C3 153
Mont Vernon, N.H., U.S. E3 136
Montville, Ct., U.S. D7 114
Montville, N.J., U.S. B4 137
Montz, La., U.S. h11 125
Monument, Co., U.S. B6 113
Monument, N.M., U.S. E6 138
Monument Beach, Ma., U.S. C6 128
Monument Peak, mtn., Co., U.S. B3 113
Monument Peak, mtn., Id., U.S. G4 119
Monument Valley, val., Az., U.S. A5 110
Monywa, Burma C3 40
Monza, Italy D4 18
Monzón, Peru C3 82
Monzón, Spain D12 16
Moodus, Ct., U.S. D6 114
Moodus Reservoir, res., Ct., U.S. C6 114
Moody, Me., U.S. E2 126
Moody, Tx., U.S. D4 150
Moody, co., S.D., U.S. C9 148
Moody Air Force Base, mil., Ga., U.S. F3 117
Mooirivier, S. Afr. G9 66
Mookane, Bots. E7 66
Moolawatana, Austl. G3 70
Moonie, stm., Austl. F8 70
Moon Lake, l., Ms., U.S. A3 131
Moon Run, Pa., U.S. k13 145
Moonta, Austl. J2 70
Moora, Austl. F3 68
Moorcroft, Wy., U.S. B8 157
Moore, Id., U.S. F5 119
Moore, Mt., U.S. D7 133
Moore, Ok., U.S. B4 143
Moore, co., N.C., U.S. B3 140
Moore, co., Tn., U.S. B5 149
Moore, co., Tx., U.S. B2 150
Moore, Lake, l., Austl. E3 68
Moore Dam, U.S. B3 136
Moorefield, Ont., Can. D4 103
Moorefield, Ky., U.S. B6 124
Moorefield, W.V., U.S. B6 155
Moore Haven, Fl., U.S. F5 116
Mooreland, In., U.S. E7 121
Mooreland, Ok., U.S. A2 143
Moore Mill, N.B., Can. D2 101
Moore Reservoir, res., U.S. B3 136
Mooresburg, Tn., U.S. C10 149
Moores Creek National Military Park, N.C., U.S. C4 140
Moores Hill, In., U.S. F7 121
Moorestown, N.J., U.S. D3 137
Mooresville, In., U.S. E5 121
Mooresville, N.C., U.S. B2 140
Mooreton, N.D., U.S. C9 141
Mooreville, Ms., U.S. A5 131
Moorhead, Ia., U.S. C2 122
Moorhead, Mn., U.S. D2 130
Moorhead, Ms., U.S. B3 131
Mooringsport, La., U.S. B2 125
Moorland, Ia., U.S. B3 122
Moorman, Ky., U.S. C2 124
Moornanyah Lake, l., Austl. I5 70
Moorreesburg, S. Afr. I4 66
Moosburg, Ger. G11 10
Moose, Wy., U.S. C2 157
Moose, stm., N.H., U.S. B4 136
Moose, stm., N.Y., U.S. B5 139
Moose, stm., Vt., U.S. B5 152
Moose Creek, Ont., Can. B10 103
Moosehead Lake, l., Me., U.S. C3 126
Mooseheart, Il., U.S. B5 120
Moose Hill, hill, Ma., U.S. h11 128
Moosehorn, Man., Can. D2 100
Moose Jaw, Sask., Can. G3 105
Moose Jaw, stm., Sask., Can. G3 105
Moose Lake, Man., Can. C1 100
Moose Lake, Mn., U.S. D6 130
Moose Lake, l., B.C., Can. C1 98
Moose Lake, l., Wi., U.S. B2 156
Mooseleuk Stream, stm., Me., U.S. B4 126
Mooselookmeguntic Lake, l., Me., U.S. D2 126
Moose Mountain, mtn., Sask., Can. H4 105
Moose Mountain, mtn., N.H., U.S. C2 136
Moose Mountain Creek, stm., Sask., Can. H4 105
Moose Mountain Provincial Park, Sask., Can. H4 105
Moose River, Me., U.S. C2 126
Moosic, Pa., U.S. m18 145
Moosilauke, Mount, mtn., N.H., U.S. B3 136
Moosomin, Sask., Can. G5 105
Moosonee, Ont., Can. o19 103
Moosup, Ct., U.S. C8 114
Moosup, stm., U.S. C1 146
Mopane, S. Afr. D9 66
Mopang Lake, l., Me., U.S. D5 126
Mopipi, Bots. C7 66
Mopti, Mali D7 64
Moquegua, Peru G6 82
Moquegua, dept., Peru G6 82
Mór, Hung. H18 10
Mora, Spain F8 16
Mora, Swe. K14 6
Mora, Mn., U.S. E5 130
Mora, N.M., U.S. B4 138
Mora, co., N.M., U.S. A5 138
Mora, stm., N.M., U.S. B5 138
Morādābād, India F8 44
Morada Nova de Minas, Braz. E6 79
Moradel, Montaña de, mtn., Hond. B8 92
Mora de Rubielos, Spain E11 16
Morafenobe, Madag. p21 67b
Mórahalom, Hung. I19 10
Mor'akovskij Zaton, Russia F14 26
Moraleda, Canal, strt., Chile E2 78
Morales, Guat. B6 92
Morales, Peru B3 82
Morales, Laguna, b., Mex. F11 90
Moran, Ks., U.S. E8 123
Morant Bay, Jam. F6 94
Morant Cays, is., Jam. F7 94
Morant Point, c., Jam. F6 94
Moratalla, Spain G10 16
Morattico, Va., U.S. C6 153
Moratuwa, Sri L. I5 46
Morava, hist. reg., Czech. F17 10
Morava (March), stm., Eur. G16 10
Moravia, C.R. H11 92
Moravia, Ia., U.S. D5 122
Moravia, N.Y., U.S. C4 139
Moravia see Morava, hist. reg., Czech. F17 10
Morawhanna, Guy. C13 84
Moraya, Bol. I9 82
Moray Firth, est., Scot., U.K. D10 8
Morazán, Guat. C4 92
Morazán, Hond. B7 92
Morbegno, Italy C4 18
Morbi, India I4 44
Morbihan, dept., Fr. E4 14
Morcenx, Fr. H6 14
Morden, Man., Can. E2 100
Morden, N.S., Can. D5 101
Mordovija, state, Russia G6 26
Mordovo, Russia I23 22
Mordves, Russia G21 22
Moreau, stm., S.D., U.S. B3 148
Moreau, North Fork, stm., S.D., U.S. B2 148
Moreau, South Fork, stm., S.D., U.S. B2 148
Moreau Peak, mtn., S.D., U.S. B2 148
Moreauville, La., U.S. C4 125
Moree, Austl. G8 70
Morée, Fr. E8 14
Morehead, Ky., U.S. B6 124
Morehead City, N.C., U.S. C6 140
Morehouse, Mo., U.S. E8 132
Morehouse, co., La., U.S. B4 125
Moreland, Ar., U.S. B3 111
Moreland, Ga., U.S. C2 117
Moreland, Id., U.S. F6 119
Morelia, Mex. H9 90
Morell, P.E.I., Can. C7 101
Morelos, Mex. D6 90
Morelos, state, Mex. H10 90
Moremi Wildlife Reserve, Bots. B6 66
Morena, India G8 44
Morena, Sierra, mts., Spain G6 16
Morenci, Az., U.S. D6 110
Morenci, Mi., U.S. G6 129
Moreno, Bahía, b., Chile B3 80
Møre og Romsdal, co., Nor. J10 6
Moresby Island, i., B.C., Can. C2 99
Mores Island, i., Bah. A6 94
Moresnet, Bel. G8 12
Moreton Island, i., Austl. F10 70
Moretown, Vt., U.S. C3 152
Moreuil, Fr. C9 14
Morewood, Ont., Can. B9 103
Morey, Lake, l., Vt., U.S. D4 152
Morey Peak, mtn., Nv., U.S. E5 135
Morez, Fr. F13 14
Morgan, Ga., U.S. E2 117
Morgan, Mn., U.S. F4 130
Morgan, Ut., U.S. B4 151
Morgan, co., Al., U.S. A3 108
Morgan, co., Co., U.S. A7 113
Morgan, co., Ga., U.S. C3 117
Morgan, co., Il., U.S. D3 120
Morgan, co., In., U.S. F5 121
Morgan, co., Ky., U.S. C6 124
Morgan, co., Mo., U.S. C5 132
Morgan, co., Oh., U.S. C4 142
Morgan, co., Tn., U.S. C9 149
Morgan, co., Ut., U.S. B4 151
Morgan, co., W.V., U.S. B6 155
Morgan Center, Vt., U.S. B5 152
Morgan City, La., U.S. E4 125
Morganfield, Ky., U.S. C2 124
Morgan Hill, Ca., U.S. D3 112
Morgan Island, i., S.C., U.S. G6 147
Morganito, Ven. E9 84
Morgan Point, c., Ct., U.S. E4 114
Morganton, Ga., U.S. B2 117
Morganton, N.C., U.S. B1 140
Morgantown, In., U.S. F5 121
Morgantown, Ky., U.S. C3 124
Morgantown, Ms., U.S. D2 131
Morgantown, Ms., U.S. D4 131
Morgantown, Pa., U.S. F10 145
Morgantown, Tn., U.S. D8 149
Morgantown, W.V., U.S. B5 155
Morganville, Ks., U.S. C6 123
Morganville, N.J., U.S. C4 137

Name	Map Ref.	Page
Morganza, La., U.S.	D4	125
Morgenzon, S. Afr.	F9	66
Morghāb (Murgab), stm., Asia	B16	48
Moriah, Mount, mtn., Nv., U.S.	D7	135
Moriah, Mount, mtn., N.H., U.S.	B4	136
Moriarty, N.M., U.S.	C3	138
Moribaya, Gui.	G5	64
Morice Lake, l., B.C., Can.	B4	99
Morichal Largo, stm., Ven.	C11	84
Moriki, Nig.	E13	64
Moringen, Ger.	D9	10
Morino, Russia	D13	22
Morinville, Alta., Can.	C4	98
Morioka, Japan	H16	36
Morisset, Austl.	I9	70
Morkiny Gory, Russia	D19	22
Morkoka, stm., Russia	D14	28
Morlaix, Fr.	D3	14
Morland, Ks., U.S.	C3	123
Morley, Mi., U.S.	E5	129
Morley, Mo., U.S.	D8	132
Mormal', Bela.	I12	22
Mormon Lake, Az., U.S.	C4	110
Mormon Peak, mtn., Nv., U.S.	G7	135
Morney, Austl.	E4	70
Morningdale, Ma., U.S.	B4	128
Morningside, S.D., U.S.	C7	148
Morning Sun, Ia., U.S.	C6	122
Mornington, Austl.	L6	70
Mornington, Isla, i., Chile	F1	78
Mornington Island, i., Austl.	A3	70
Morning View, Ky., U.S.	k14	124
Moro, Ar., U.S.	C5	111
Moro, Or., U.S.	B6	144
Moro, stm., Afr.	H4	64
Morobe, Pap. N. Gui.	m16	68a
Morocco, In., U.S.	C3	121
Morocco (Al-Magreb), ctry., Afr.	B5	54
Morococala, Bol.	H8	82
Morococha, Peru	D3	82
Moro Creek, stm., Ar., U.S.	D3	111
Morogoro, Tan.	C7	58
Moro Gulf, b., Phil.	D7	38
Moroleón, Mex.	G9	90
Morombe, Madag.	r20	67b
Morón, Arg.	H9	80
Morón, Cuba	C5	94
Mörön, Mong.	B7	30
Morón, Ven.	B8	84
Morona, stm., Peru	I4	84
Morona-Santiago, prov., Ec.	I3	84
Morondava, Madag.	r21	67b
Morón de la Frontera, Spain	H6	16
Moroni, Com.	k15	67a
Moroni, Ut., U.S.	D4	151
Morotai, i., Indon.	E8	38
Morozovsk, Russia	H6	26
Morpeth, Ont., Can.	E3	103
Morrill, Ks., U.S.	C8	123
Morrill, Ne., U.S.	C2	134
Morrill, co., Ne., U.S.	C2	134
Morrilton, Ar., U.S.	B3	111
Morrin, Alta., Can.	D4	98
Morrinhos, Braz.	D4	79
Morrinsville, N.Z.	B5	72
Morris, Man., Can.	E3	100
Morris, Al., U.S.	B3	108
Morris, Ga., U.S.	E2	117
Morris, Il., U.S.	B5	120
Morris, In., U.S.	F7	121
Morris, Mn., U.S.	E3	130
Morris, Ok., U.S.	B6	143
Morris, co., Ks., U.S.	D7	123
Morris, co., N.J., U.S.	B3	137
Morris, co., Tx., U.S.	C5	150
Morris, Mount, mtn., N.Y., U.S.	A6	139
Morrisburg, Ont., Can.	C9	103
Morrisdale, Pa., U.S.	E5	145
Morris Island, i., S.C., U.S.	F8	147
Morris Jesup, Kap, c., Grnld.	A16	86
Morrison, Arg.	G7	80
Morrison, Co., U.S.	B5	113
Morrison, Il., U.S.	B4	120
Morrison, Mo., U.S.	C6	132
Morrison, Ok., U.S.	A4	143
Morrison, Tn., U.S.	D8	149
Morrison, co., Mn., U.S.	D4	130
Morrison City, Tn., U.S.	C11	149
Morrisonville, Il., U.S.	D4	120
Morrisonville, N.Y., U.S.	f11	139
Morris Plains, N.J., U.S.	B4	137
Morristown, Az., U.S.	D3	110
Morristown, In., U.S.	E6	121
Morristown, Mn., U.S.	F5	130
Morristown, N.J., U.S.	B4	137
Morristown, Tn., U.S.	C10	149
Morristown National Historical Park, N.J., U.S.	B3	137
Morrisville, Mo., U.S.	D4	132
Morrisville, N.Y., U.S.	C5	139
Morrisville, Pa., U.S.	F12	145
Morrisville, Vt., U.S.	B3	152
Morrito, Nic.	F9	92
Morro, Ec.	I2	84
Morro, Punta, c., Mex.	H14	90
Morro Bay, Ca., U.S.	E3	112
Morro del Jable, Spain	o26	17b
Morro do Chapéu, Braz.	F10	76
Morropón, Peru	A1	82
Morrosquillo, Golfo de, b., Col.	C5	84
Morrow, Ga., U.S.	C2	117
Morrow, La., U.S.	D3	125
Morrow, Oh., U.S.	C1	142
Morrow, co., Oh., U.S.	B3	142
Morrow, co., Or., U.S.	B7	144
Morrowville, Ks., U.S.	C6	123
Morrumbene, Moz.	D12	66
Moršansk, Russia	H24	22
Morse, Sask., Can.	G2	105
Morse, La., U.S.	D3	125
Morse Bluff, Ne., U.S.	C9	134
Morse Mill, Mo., U.S.	g12	132
Morse Reservoir, res., In., U.S.	D5	121
Morses Creek, stm., N.J., U.S.	k8	137
Mortagne, Fr.	D7	14
Mortagne-sur-Sèvre, Fr.	E6	14
Mortain, Fr.	D6	14
Mortara, Italy	D3	18
Morteau, Fr.	E13	14
Morteros, Arg.	F7	80
Mortes, Rio das, stm., Braz.	B3	79
Mortesoro, Sud.	L8	60
Mortlach, Sask., Can.	G2	105
Mortlake, Austl.	L5	70
Morton, Il., U.S.	C4	120
Morton, Mn., U.S.	F4	130
Morton, Ms., U.S.	C4	131
Morton, Tx., U.S.	C1	150
Morton, Wa., U.S.	C3	154
Morton, co., Ks., U.S.	E2	123
Morton, co., N.D., U.S.	C4	141
Morton Grove, Il., U.S.	h9	120
Morton Pass, Wy., U.S.	E7	157
Mortons Gap, Ky., U.S.	C2	124
Moruya, Austl.	J9	70
Morven, Austl.	F7	70
Morven, Ga., U.S.	F3	117
Morven, N.C., U.S.	C2	140
Morwell, Austl.	L7	70
Morženga, Russia	B23	22
Mosal'sk, Russia	G17	22
Mosby, Mo., U.S.	h11	132
Moščnyj, ostrov, i., Russia	A10	22
Moscow, Ar., U.S.	C4	111
Moscow, Id., U.S.	C2	119
Moscow, Ia., U.S.	C6	122
Moscow, Ks., U.S.	E2	123
Moscow, Pa., U.S.	m18	145
Moscow, Tn., U.S.	B2	149
Moscow, Vt., U.S.	C3	152
Moscow Mills, Mo., U.S.	C7	132
Moscow see Moskva, Russia	F20	22
Mosel (Moselle), stm., Eur.	C13	14
Moselle, Ms., U.S.	D4	131
Moselle, dept., Fr.	D13	14
Moselle (Mosel), stm., Eur.	D13	14
Mosers River, N.S., Can.	E7	101
Moses Coulee, val., Wa., U.S.	B6	154
Moses Lake, Wa., U.S.	B6	154
Moses Lake, l., Wa., U.S.	B6	154
Mosetse, Bots.	C8	66
Moshanpu, China	F1	34
Moshaweng, stm., Afr.	F6	66
Mosheim, Tn., U.S.	C11	149
Mosherville, N.S., Can.	D6	101
Moshi, Tan.	B7	58
Mosina, Pol.	C16	10
Mosinee, Wi., U.S.	D4	156
Mosjøen, Nor.	I13	6
Moskva (Moscow), Russia	F20	22
Moskva, stm., Russia	F21	22
Moskvy, kanal imeni, Russia	E20	22
Mošok, Russia	F24	22
Mosolovo, Russia	G23	22
Mosomane, Bots.	E8	66
Mosonmagyaróvár, Hung.	H17	10
Mosopa, Bots.	E7	66
Mosquera, Col.	F3	84
Mosquero, N.M., U.S.	B6	138
Mosquito, Punta, c., Pan.	C4	84
Mosquito, Riacho, stm., Para.	B9	80
Mosquito Creek, stm., Ia., U.S.	C2	122
Mosquito Creek Lake, res., Oh., U.S.	A5	142
Mosquito Lagoon, b., Fl., U.S.	D6	116
Mosquitos, Costa de, hist. reg., Nic.	D11	92
Mosquitos, Golfo de los, b., Pan.	H13	92
Moss, Nor.	L12	6
Moss, Ms., U.S.	D4	131
Moss, Tn., U.S.	C8	149
Mossaka, Congo	B3	58
Mossâmedes, Braz.	D3	79
Mossbank, Sask., Can.	H3	105
Moss Bluff, La., U.S.	D2	125
Mosselbaai, S. Afr.	J6	66
Mossendjo, Congo	B2	58
Mossleigh, Alta., Can.	D4	98
Moss Mountain, mtn., Ar., U.S.	C3	111
Mossoró, Braz.	E11	76
Moss Point, Ms., U.S.	E5	131
Moss Vale, Austl.	J9	70
Mossyrock, Wa., U.S.	C3	154
Most, Czech.	E13	10
Mosta, Russia	E25	22
Mostar, Bos.	F12	18
Mostardas, Braz.	F13	80
Mostiska, Ukr.	F23	10
Mostok, Bela.	H13	22
Mosty, Bela.	H7	22
Mosul see Al-Mawṣil, Iraq	C7	48
Moswansicut Pond, l., R.I., U.S.	C3	146
Mota, Eth.	L9	60
Motagua, stm., N.A.	B6	92
Motala, Swe.	L14	6
Motatán, Ven.	C7	84
Motherwell, Scot., U.K.	F9	8
Motihāri, India	G11	44
Motley, Mn., U.S.	D4	130
Motley, co., Tx., U.S.	B2	150
Motloutse, Bots.	C8	66
Motozintla de Mendoza, Mex.	J13	90
Motril, Spain	I8	16
Motru, Rom.	E7	20
Mott, N.D., U.S.	C3	141
Mottola, Italy	I12	18
Motueka, N.Z.	D4	72
Motul [de Felipe Carrillo Puerto], Mex.	G15	90
Motupe, Peru	B2	82
Mouaskar, Alg.	C11	62
Mouchoir Passage, strt., N.A.	D9	94
Moudjéria, Maur.	C3	64
Moudon, Switz.	E6	13
Mouila, Gabon	B2	58
Mouit, Maur.	C3	64
Mouka, Cen. Afr. Rep.	N1	60
Moulamein, Austl.	J6	70
Moulay-Idriss, Mor.	C8	62
Moulins, Fr.	F10	14
Moulins-la-Marche, Fr.	D7	14
Moulmeingyun, Burma	F3	40
Moulmein see Mawlamyine, Burma	F4	40
Moulouya, Oued, stm., Mor.	C9	62
Moulton, Al., U.S.	A2	108
Moulton, Ia., U.S.	D5	122
Moultonboro, N.H., U.S.	C4	136
Moultrie, Ga., U.S.	E3	117
Moultrie, co., Il., U.S.	D5	120
Moultrie, Lake, res., S.C., U.S.	E7	147
Mound, Mn., U.S.	n11	130
Mound Bayou, Ms., U.S.	B3	131
Mound City, Il., U.S.	F4	120
Mound City, Ks., U.S.	D9	123
Mound City, Mo., U.S.	A2	132
Mound City, S.D., U.S.	B5	148
Mound City Group National Monument, Oh., U.S.	C2	142
Moundou, Chad	G4	56
Moundridge, Ks., U.S.	D6	123
Mounds, Il., U.S.	F4	120
Mounds, Ok., U.S.	B5	143
Mounds View, Mn., U.S.	m12	130
Moundsville, W.V., U.S.	B4	155
Mound Valley, Ks., U.S.	E8	123
Moundville, Al., U.S.	C2	108
Mounlapamôk, Laos	G8	40
Mountain, N.D., U.S.	A8	141
Mountainair, N.M., U.S.	C3	138
Mountainaire, Az., U.S.	B4	110
Mountainboro, Al., U.S.	A3	108
Mountain Brook, Al., U.S.	g7	108
Mountainburg, Ar., U.S.	B1	111
Mountain City, Ga., U.S.	B3	117
Mountain City, Nv., U.S.	B6	135
Mountain City, Tn., U.S.	C12	149
Mountain Fork, stm., U.S.	C7	143
Mountain Grove, Ont., Can.	C8	103
Mountain Grove, Mo., U.S.	D5	132
Mountain Home, Ar., U.S.	A3	111
Mountain Home, Id., U.S.	F3	119
Mountainhome, Pa., U.S.	D11	145
Mountain Home Air Force Base, mil., Id., U.S.	F3	119
Mountain Iron, Mn., U.S.	C6	130
Mountain Lake, Mn., U.S.	G4	130
Mountain Lake Park, Md., U.S.	m12	127
Mountain Nile (Baḥr al-Jabal), stm., Sud.	M6	60
Mountain Park, Ok., U.S.	C3	143
Mountain Pine, Ar., U.S.	C2	111
Mountainside, N.J., U.S.	B4	137
Mountain Valley, Ar., U.S.	C2	111
Mountain View, Alta., Can.	E4	98
Mountain View, Ar., U.S.	B3	111
Mountain View, Ca., U.S.	k8	112
Mountainview, Hi., U.S.	D6	118
Mountain View, Mo., U.S.	D6	132
Mountain View, N.M., U.S.	C3	138
Mountain View, Ok., U.S.	B3	143
Mountain View, Wy., U.S.	E2	157
Mountain View, Wy., U.S.	D6	157
Mountain Village, Ak., U.S.	C7	109
Mount Airy, Ga., U.S.	B3	117
Mount Airy, Md., U.S.	B3	127
Mount Airy, N.C., U.S.	A2	140
Mount Albert, Ont., Can.	C5	103
Mount Alida, S. Afr.	G10	66
Mount Angel, Or., U.S.	B4	144
Mount Arlington, N.J., U.S.	B3	137
Mount Auburn, Il., U.S.	D4	120
Mount Ayr, In., U.S.	C3	121
Mount Ayr, Ia., U.S.	D3	122
Mount Barker, Austl.	F3	68
Mount Barker, Austl.	J3	70
Mount Berry, Ga., U.S.	B1	117
Mount Calvary, Wi., U.S.	E5	156
Mount Carmel, Al., U.S.	C3	108
Mount Carmel, Il., U.S.	E6	120
Mount Carmel, Oh., U.S.	o13	142
Mount Carmel, Pa., U.S.	E9	145
Mount Carmel [-Mitchell's Brook-Saint Catherine's], Newf., Can.	E5	102
Mount Carroll, Il., U.S.	A4	120
Mount Clare, W.V., U.S.	B4	155
Mount Clemens, Mi., U.S.	F8	129
Mount Crawford, Va., U.S.	B4	153
Mount Desert Island, i., Me., U.S.	D4	126
Mount Dora, Fl., U.S.	D5	116
Mount Eden, Ky., U.S.	B4	124
Mount Elgin, Ont., Can.	E4	103
Mount Enterprise, Tx., U.S.	D5	150
Mount Forest, Ont., Can.	D4	103
Mount Freedom, N.J., U.S.	B3	137
Mount Gambier, Austl.	K4	70
Mount Garnet, Austl.	A6	70
Mount Gay, W.V., U.S.	D2	155
Mount Gilead, N.C., U.S.	B3	140
Mount Gilead, Oh., U.S.	B3	142
Mount Hagen, Pap. N. Gui.	G11	38
Mount Healthy, Oh., U.S.	o12	142
Mount Holly, Ar., U.S.	D3	111
Mount Holly, N.J., U.S.	D3	137
Mount Holly, N.C., U.S.	B1	140
Mount Holly, Vt., U.S.	E3	152
Mount Holly Springs, Pa., U.S.	F7	145
Mount Hope, Austl.	J1	70
Mount Hope, Al., U.S.	A2	108
Mount Hope, Ks., U.S.	E6	123
Mount Hope, W.V., U.S.	D3	155
Mount Hope, stm., Ct., U.S.	B7	114
Mount Hope Bay, b., U.S.	D6	146
Mount Horeb, Wi., U.S.	E4	156
Mount Ida, Ar., U.S.	C2	111
Mount Isa, Austl.	C3	70
Mount Jackson, Va., U.S.	B4	153
Mount Jewett, Pa., U.S.	C4	145
Mount Joy, Ia., U.S.	h10	122
Mount Joy, Pa., U.S.	F9	145
Mount Juliet, Tn., U.S.	A5	149
Mount Kisco, N.Y., U.S.	D7	139
Mount Lebanon, Pa., U.S.	F1	145
Mount Lemmon, Az., U.S.	E5	110
Mount Lookout, W.V., U.S.	C4	155
Mount Magnet, Austl.	E3	68
Mount Manara, Austl.	I5	70
Mount Meigs, Al., U.S.	C3	108
Mount Morgan, Austl.	D9	70
Mount Morris, Il., U.S.	A4	120
Mount Morris, Mi., U.S.	E7	129
Mount Morris, N.Y., U.S.	C3	139
Mount Morris, Pa., U.S.	G1	145
Mount Mulligan, Austl.	A6	70
Mount Olive, Al., U.S.	B3	108
Mount Olive, Il., U.S.	D4	120
Mount Olive, Ms., U.S.	D4	131
Mount Olive, N.C., U.S.	B4	140
Mount Olive, Tn., U.S.	n14	149
Mount Olivet, Ky., U.S.	B5	124
Mount Orab, Oh., U.S.	C2	142
Mount Pearl, Newf., Can.	E5	102
Mount Penn, Pa., U.S.	F10	145
Mount Perry, Austl.	E9	70
Mount Pleasant, Ar., U.S.	B4	111
Mount Pleasant, Ia., U.S.	D6	122
Mount Pleasant, Mi., U.S.	E6	129
Mount Pleasant, Ms., U.S.	A4	131
Mount Pleasant, N.C., U.S.	B2	140
Mount Pleasant, Pa., U.S.	F2	145
Mount Pleasant, S.C., U.S.	F8	147
Mount Pleasant, Tn., U.S.	B4	149
Mount Pleasant, Tx., U.S.	C5	150
Mount Pleasant, Ut., U.S.	D4	151
Mount Pocono, Pa., U.S.	D11	145
Mount Prospect, Il., U.S.	A6	120
Mount Pulaski, Il., U.S.	C4	120
Mountrail, co., N.D., U.S.	A3	141
Mount Rainier, Md., U.S.	f9	127
Mount Rainier National Park, Wa., U.S.	C4	154
Mount Revelstoke National Park, B.C., Can.	D8	99
Mount Rogers National Recreation Area, Va., U.S.	D1	153
Mount Rushmore National Memorial, hist., S.D., U.S.	D2	148
Mount Savage, Md., U.S.	k13	127
Mount Shasta, Ca., U.S.	B2	112
Mount Sidney, Va., U.S.	B4	153
Mount Sterling, Il., U.S.	D3	120
Mount Sterling, Ky., U.S.	B6	124
Mount Sterling, Oh., U.S.	C2	142
Mount Stewart, P.E.I., Can.	C7	101
Mount Stewart, S. Afr.	I7	66
Mount Storm, W.V., U.S.	B5	155
Mount Summit, In., U.S.	D7	121
Mount Sunapee, N.H., U.S.	D2	136
Mount Surprise, Austl.	B6	70
Mount Uniacke, N.S., Can.	E6	101
Mount Union, Pa., U.S.	F6	145
Mount Vernon, Al., U.S.	D1	108
Mount Vernon, Ar., U.S.	B3	111
Mount Vernon, Ga., U.S.	D4	117
Mount Vernon, Il., U.S.	E5	120
Mount Vernon, In., U.S.	I2	121
Mount Vernon, Ia., U.S.	C6	122
Mount Vernon, Ky., U.S.	C5	124
Mount Vernon, Me., U.S.	D3	126
Mount Vernon, Mo., U.S.	D4	132
Mount Vernon, N.Y., U.S.	h13	139
Mount Vernon, Oh., U.S.	B3	142
Mount Vernon, Or., U.S.	C7	144
Mount Vernon, S.D., U.S.	D7	148
Mount Vernon, Tn., U.S.	D9	149
Mount Vernon, Tx., U.S.	C5	150
Mount Vernon, Wa., U.S.	A3	154
Mount Victory, Oh., U.S.	B2	142
Mount View, R.I., U.S.	D4	146
Mountville, Ga., U.S.	C2	117
Mount Washington, Ky., U.S.	B4	124
Mount Wolf, Pa., U.S.	F8	145
Mount Zion, Ga., U.S.	C1	117
Mount Zion, Il., U.S.	D5	120
Moura, Austl.	E8	70
Moura, Braz.	H12	84
Moura, Port.	G4	16
Mourdi, Dépression du, depr., Chad	E5	56
Mourdiah, Mali	D6	64
Mourne Mountains, mts., N. Ire., U.K.	G7	8
Mousie, Ky., U.S.	C7	124
Moussoro, Chad	F4	56
Moutier, Switz.	D7	13
Moûtiers, Fr.	G13	14
Mouzon, Fr.	C12	14
Moville, Ire.	F6	8
Moville, Ia., U.S.	B1	122
Moweaqua, Il., U.S.	D4	120
Mower, co., Mn., U.S.	G6	130
Moxee City, Wa., U.S.	C5	154
Moxie Pond, l., Me., U.S.	C3	126
Moya, Com.	I16	67a
Moya, Peru	E4	82
Moyahua, Mex.	G8	90
Moyamba, S.L.	G3	64
Moyen Atlas, mts., Mor.	D8	62
Moyeuvre-Grande, Fr.	C13	14
Moyie, B.C., Can.	E10	99
Moyie Springs, Id., U.S.	A2	119
Moyobamba, Peru	B3	82
Moyock, N.C., U.S.	A6	140
Moyogalpa, Nic.	F9	92
Moyuta, Volcán, vol., Guat.	C4	92
Možajsk, Russia	F19	22
Mozambique (Moçambique), ctry., Afr.	E7	58
Mozambique Channel, strt., Afr.	E8	58
Mozarlândia, Braz.	C3	79
Mozart, Sask., Can.	F3	105
Mozdok, Russia	I6	26
Mozelle, Ky., U.S.	D6	124
Možga, Russia	F8	26
Mozyr', Bela.	G3	26
Mphoengs, Zimb.	C8	66
Mpika, Zam.	D6	58
Mpraeso, Ghana	H9	64
Mpwapwa, Tan.	C7	58
Mqanduli, Transkei	H9	66
Mrągowo, Pol.	B21	10
M'Ramani, Com.	I16	67a
Mrkopalj, Cro.	D9	18
M'Saken, Tun.	N5	18
M'Sila, Alg.	C13	62
Mšinskaja, Russia	B12	22
Msta, Russia	D17	22
Msta, stm., Russia	C14	22
Mstera, Russia	E24	22
Mstislavl', Bela.	G14	22
Mszczonów, Pol.	D20	10
Mtamvuna, stm., Afr.	H9	66
Mtwara, Tan.	D8	58
Mu, Cerro, mtn., S.A.	C6	84
Muanda, Zaire	C2	58
Muang Hôngsa, Laos	E6	40
Muang Huang, Laos	E7	40
Muang Khammouan, Laos	F8	40
Muang Khi, Laos	E6	40
Muang Không, Laos	G8	40
Muang Khôngxédôn, Laos	G8	40
Muang Long, Laos	D6	40
Muang Ngoy, Laos	D7	40
Muang Ou Nua, Laos	C6	40
Muang Ou Tai, Laos	C6	40
Muang Pak-Lay, Laos	E6	40
Muang Pakxan, Laos	E7	40
Muang Phiang, Laos	E6	40
Muang Phoun, Laos	E7	40
Muang Sing, Laos	D6	40
Muang Souy, Laos	E7	40
Muang Thadua, Laos	E6	40
Muang Vangviang, Laos	E7	40
Muang Vapi, Laos	G8	40
Muang Xaignabouri, Laos	E6	40
Muang Xay, Laos	D6	40
Muang Xépôn, Laos	F9	40
Muang Xon, Laos	D7	40
Muang You, Laos	E7	40
Muar (Bandar Maharani), Malay.	M7	40
Muarasiberut, Indon.	F2	38
Mucajaí, stm., Braz.	F12	84
Muchanovo, Russia	E21	22
Muchinga Mountains, mts., Zam.	D6	58
Muchtolovo, Russia	F26	22
Muckadilla, Austl.	F8	70
Muckalee Creek, stm., Ga., U.S.	D2	117
Mučkapskij, Russia	J25	22
Muckleshoot Indian Reservation, Wa., U.S.	f11	154
Muconda, Ang.	D4	58
Mucuchíes, Ven.	C7	84
Mucugê, Braz.	B8	79
Mucuim, stm., Braz.	B9	82
Muçum, Braz.	E13	80
Mucupia, Moz.	B13	66
Mucupina, Monte, mtn., Hond.	B8	92
Mucur, Tur.	B3	48
Mucuri, Braz.	E9	79
Mucuri, stm., Braz.	E9	79
Mucusso, Ang.	B5	66
Mud, stm., Ky., U.S.	C3	124
Mud, stm., Mn., U.S.	B3	130
Mud, stm., W.V., U.S.	C2	155
Mudan, stm., China	B12	30
Mudanjiang, China	C12	30
Mud Creek, stm., Al., U.S.	g6	108
Mud Creek, stm., Co., U.S.	D8	113
Mud Creek, stm., Ia., U.S.	e9	122
Mud Creek, stm., Ne., U.S.	C6	134
Mud Creek, stm., Ok., U.S.	C4	143
Muddy Boggy Creek, stm., Ok., U.S.	C6	143
Muddy Creek, stm., Co., U.S.	A4	113
Muddy Creek, stm., Ks., U.S.	k14	123
Muddy Creek, stm., Ut., U.S.	E4	151
Muddy Creek, stm., Wy., U.S.	E2	157
Muddy Creek, stm., Wy., U.S.	E5	157
Muddy Creek, stm., Wy., U.S.	C4	157
Muddy Creek, stm., Wy., U.S.	D6	157
Muddy Mountains, mts., Nv., U.S.	G7	135
Muddy Peak, mtn., Nv., U.S.	G7	135
Mudgee, Austl.	I8	70
Mudjuga, Russia	J26	6
Mud Lake, Id., U.S.	F6	119
Mud Lake, l., Me., U.S.	A4	126
Mud Lake, l., Nv., U.S.	F4	135
Mud Lick Creek, stm., Ky., U.S.	k13	124
Mudon, Burma	F4	40
Mudu, China	D9	34
Muelle de los Bueyes, Nic.	E10	92
Muenster, Sask., Can.	E3	105
Muenster, Tx., U.S.	C4	150
Muerto, stm., Arg.	B7	80
Mufulira, Zam.	D5	58
Mu Gia, Deo, Asia	F8	40
Muğla, Tur.	L12	20
Mugron, Fr.	I6	14
Muḥammad, Ra's, c., Egypt	D8	60
Muḥammad Qawl, Sud.	G9	60
Mühlacker, Ger.	G8	10
Mühldorf, Ger.	G12	10
Muhlenberg, co., Ky., U.S.	C2	124
Mühlhausen, Ger.	D10	10
Mühlig-Hofmann Mountains, mts., Ant.	C3	73
Muhu, i., Est.	C6	22
Muhu väin, strt., Est.	C6	22
Muir, Mi., U.S.	E6	129
Muirkirk, Md., U.S.	B4	127
Muiron Islands, is., Austl.	D2	68
Muir Woods National Monument, Ca., U.S.	h7	112
Muisne, Ec.	G2	84
Mujang-ni, S. Kor.	H14	32
Mujezerskij, Russia	J22	6
Mujnak, Uzb.	I9	26
Muju, S. Kor.	G15	32
Mukačevo, Ukr.	H2	26
Mukah, Malay.	E5	38
Mukdahan, Thai.	F8	40
Mukden see Shenyang, China	B11	32
Mukilteo, Wa., U.S.	B3	154
Mukry, Turk.	J11	26
Muktsar, India	E6	44
Mukwonago, Wi., U.S.	F5	156
Mula, Spain	G10	16
Mulanje, Mwi.	E7	58
Mulas, Punta de, c., Cuba	D7	94
Mulatos, Mex.	C5	90
Mulberry, Ar., U.S.	B1	111
Mulberry, Fl., U.S.	E4	116
Mulberry, In., U.S.	D4	121
Mulberry, Ks., U.S.	E9	123
Mulberry, N.C., U.S.	A1	140
Mulberry, Oh., U.S.	C1	142
Mulberry, Tn., U.S.	B5	149
Mulberry, stm., Ar., U.S.	B1	111
Mulberry Fork, stm., Al., U.S.	B3	108
Mulberry Grove, Il., U.S.	E4	120
Mulberry Mountain, mtn., Ar., U.S.	B3	111
Mulchén, Chile	I2	80
Mulde, stm., Ger.	D12	10
Muldraugh, Ky., U.S.	C4	124
Muldrow, Ok., U.S.	B7	143
Mulegé, Mex.	D3	90
Mulegns, Switz.	E12	13
Muleshoe, Tx., U.S.	B1	150
Mulga, Al., U.S.	B3	108
Mulgowie, Austl.	F10	70
Mulgrave, N.S., Can.	D8	101
Mulhacén, mtn., Spain	H8	16
Mulhouse, Fr.	E14	14
Mulino, Or., U.S.	B4	144
Mull, Island of, i., Scot., U.K.	E7	8
Mullan, Id., U.S.	B3	119
Mullan Pass, Mt., U.S.	D4	133
Mullen, Ne., U.S.	B4	134
Mullengudgery, Austl.	H7	70
Mullens, W.V., U.S.	D3	155
Muller, Pegunungan, mts., Indon.	E5	38
Mullet Key, i., Fl., U.S.	p10	116
Mullett Lake, l., Mi., U.S.	C6	129
Mullewa, Austl.	E3	68
Mullica, stm., N.J., U.S.	D3	137
Mullica Hill, N.J., U.S.	D2	137
Mulligan, stm., Austl.	D3	70
Mulliken, Mi., U.S.	F6	129
Mullingar, Ire.	H6	8
Mullins, S.C., U.S.	C9	147
Mullinville, Ks., U.S.	E4	123
Mullumbimby, Austl.	G10	70
Multān, Pak.	E4	44
Multnomah, co., Or., U.S.	B4	144
Mulvane, Ks., U.S.	E6	123
Mulvihill, Man., Can.	D2	100
Mulyah Mountain, mtn., Austl.	H6	70
Mumbwa, Zam.	D5	58
Mummy Range, mts., Co., U.S.	A5	113
Mumu, Sud.	K2	60
Mumungwe, Bots.	C8	66
Mun, stm., Thai.	G8	40
Muna, Mex.	G15	90
Munā, Sau. Ar.	D1	47
Muna, stm., Russia	D15	28
Münchberg, Ger.	E11	10
München (Munich), Ger.	G11	10
München-Gladbach see Mönchengladbach, Ger.	D6	10
Münchenstein, Switz.	C8	13
Munchique, Cerro, mtn., Col.	F4	84
Munch'ŏn, N. Kor.	D15	32
Muncie, In., U.S.	D7	121
Muncy, Pa., U.S.	D8	145
Mundare, Alta., Can.	C4	98
Munday, Tx., U.S.	C3	150
Mundelein, Il., U.S.	A5	120
Münden, Ger.	D9	10
Munden, Ks., U.S.	C6	123
Mundo Novo, Braz.	A8	79
Mundubbera, Austl.	E9	70
Munene, Zimb.	C10	66
Munford, Al., U.S.	B4	108
Munford, Tn., U.S.	B2	149
Munfordville, Ky., U.S.	C4	124
Mungallala, Austl.	F7	70
Mungbere, Zaire	H6	56
Munger, India	H12	44
Mungindi, Austl.	G8	70
Munhall, Pa., U.S.	k14	145
Munhango, Ang.	D3	58
Munich, N.D., U.S.	A7	141
Munich see München, Ger.	G11	10
Munising, Mi., U.S.	B4	129
Munith, Mi., U.S.	F6	129
Muniz Freire, Braz.	F8	79
Munjor, Ks., U.S.	D4	123
Munku-Sardyk, gora, mtn., Asia	G12	28
Munsan, S. Kor.	F14	32
Münsingen, Switz.	E8	13
Munson, Alta., Can.	D4	98
Munsonville, N.H., U.S.	D2	136
Munster, Fr.	D14	14
Munster, Ger.	C10	10
Münster, Ger.	D7	10
Munster, In., U.S.	A2	121
Munster, hist. reg., Ire.	I5	8
Munsungan Lake, l., Me., U.S.	B3	126
Munuscong Lake, l., Mi., U.S.	B6	129
Muong Saiapoun, Laos	E6	40
Muonio, Fin.	H18	6
Muoro, Italy	I4	18
Muqayshiṭ, i., U.A.E.	B8	47
Muqdisho (Mogadishu), Som.	H10	56
Muqi, China	B12	32
Muqui, Braz.	F8	79
Mur (Mura), stm., Eur.	I15	10
Mura (Mur), stm., Eur.	I16	10
Muradiye, Tur.	B7	48
Murakami, Japan	I14	36
Muraši, Russia	F7	26
Murat, stm., Tur.	B5	48
Muravjovo, Russia	E17	22
Murča, Port.	D4	16
Mūrcheh Khvort, Iran	E11	48
Murchison, Austl.	K6	70
Murchison, stm., Austl.	E3	68
Murchison, Mount, mtn., N.Z.	E3	72
Murchison Falls see Kabalega Falls, wtfl, Ug.	H7	56
Murcia, Spain	H10	16
Murcia, prov., Spain	G10	16
Murciélago, Islas, is., C.R.	G9	92
Murderkill, stm., De., U.S.	D4	115
Murdo, S.D., U.S.	D5	148
Murdock, Mn., U.S.	E3	130
Murdock, Ne., U.S.	h12	134
Mureck, Aus.	I15	10
Mureș, co., Rom.	C8	20
Mureș (Maros), stm., Eur.	C5	20
Muret, Fr.	I8	14
Murfreesboro, Ar., U.S.	C2	111
Murfreesboro, N.C., U.S.	A5	140
Murfreesboro, Tn., U.S.	B5	149
Murgab, Taj.	J12	26

Name — Map Ref. — Page

Murgab (Morghāb), stm., Asia B16 48
Murgha Kibzai, Pak. E3 44
Murgon, Austl. F9 70
Muri, Switz. E7 13
Muriaé, Braz. F7 79
Muriaé, stm., Braz. F8 79
Müritz, l., Ger. B12 10
Murmansk, Russia D4 26
Murmino, Russia G23 22
Murnei, Sud. K2 60
Murom, Russia F25 22
Muroran, Japan e15 36a
Muroto, Japan N9 36
Murphy, Ga., U.S. E3 117
Murphy, Id., U.S. F2 119
Murphy, Mo., U.S. g13 132
Murphy, N.C., U.S. f8 140
Murphy, Or., U.S. E3 144
Murphy Island, i., S.C., U.S. E9 147
Murphy Lake, l., B.C., Can. C7 99
Murphys, Ca., U.S. C3 112
Murphysboro, Il., U.S. F4 120
Murphytown, W.V., U.S. B3 155
Murray, Id., U.S. B3 119
Murray, Ia., U.S. C4 122
Murray, Ky., U.S. f9 124
Murray, Ne., U.S. D10 134
Murray, Ut., U.S. C4 151
Murray, co., Ga., U.S. B2 117
Murray, co., Mn., U.S. F3 130
Murray, co., Ok., U.S. C4 143
Murray, stm., Austl. J3 70
Murray, stm., B.C., Can. B7 99
Murray, Lake, l., Pap. N. Gui. G11 38
Murray, Lake, res., Ok., U.S. C4 143
Murray, Lake, res., S.C., U.S. C5 147
Murray Bridge, Austl. J3 70
Murray Harbour, P.E.I., Can. D7 101
Murray Head, c., P.E.I., Can. C7 101
Murray River, P.E.I., Can. C7 101
Murraysburg, S. Afr. H6 66
Murrayville, Ga., U.S. B3 117
Murrayville, Il., U.S. D3 120
Murree, Pak. D5 44
Murrells Inlet, S.C., U.S. D9 147
Murrells Inlet, b., S.C., U.S. D10 147
Murrhardt, Ger. G9 10
Murrī, stm., Col. D4 84
Murrumbidgee, stm., Austl. J6 70
Murrumburrah, Austl. J8 70
Murrurundi, Austl. H9 70
Murska Sobota, Slo. C11 18
Murtajāpur, India B4 46
Murtaugh, Id., U.S. G4 119
Murten, Switz. E7 13
Murtoa, Austl. K5 70
Murtosa, Port. E3 16
Muru, stm., Braz. C6 82
Murud, Gunong, mtn., Malay. E6 38
Murupara, N.Z. C6 72
Murutinga, Braz. I13 84
Murwāra, India I9 44
Murwillumbah, Austl. G10 70
Mürzzuschlag, Aus. H15 10
Muş, Tur. B6 48
Mūsā, Jabal (Mount Sinai), mtn., Egypt C7 60
Musaid, Libya B3 60
Musala, mtn., Bul. G7 20
Musan, N. Kor. A17 32
Musandam Peninsula, pen., Oman A10 47
Mūsā Qal'eh, Afg. D1 44
Musay'īd, Qatar D11 56
Muscatatuck, stm., In., U.S. G5 121
Muscatatuck, Vernon Fork, stm., In., U.S. G6 121
Muscatine, Ia., U.S. C6 122
Muscatine, co., Ia., U.S. C6 122
Muscat see Masqat, Oman C11 47
Mus-Chaja, gora, mtn., Russia E20 28
Muscle Shoals, Al., U.S. A2 108
Musclow, Mount, mtn., B.C., Can. C4 99
Muscoda, Wi., U.S. E3 156
Muscogee, co., Ga., U.S. D2 117
Musconetcong, stm., N.J., U.S. B4 137
Musconetcong Mountain, mtn., N.J., U.S. B2 137
Muscooten Bay, l., Il., U.S. C3 120
Muscotah, Ks., U.S. C8 123
Muse, Ok., U.S. C7 143
Muse, Pa., U.S. F1 145
Müsgebi, Tur. L11 20
Musgrave, Austl. B8 68
Musgrave Harbour, Newf., Can. D5 102
Musgravetown, Newf., Can. D5 102
Mushandike Sanctuary, Zimb. C10 66
Mushie, Zaire B3 58
Mushin, Nig. H11 64
Muskeg Bay, b., Mn., U.S. B3 130
Muskeget Channel, strt., Ma., U.S. D7 128
Muskeget Island, i., Ma., U.S. D7 128
Muskego, Wi., U.S. F5 156
Muskego Lake, l., Wi., U.S. n11 156
Muskegon, Mi., U.S. E4 129
Muskegon, co., Mi., U.S. E4 129
Muskegon, stm., Mi., U.S. E4 129
Muskegon Heights, Mi., U.S. E4 129
Muskegon Lake, l., Mi., U.S. E4 129
Muskingum, co., Oh., U.S. B4 142
Muskingum, stm., Oh., U.S. C4 142
Muskogee, Ok., U.S. B6 143
Muskogee, co., Ok., U.S. B6 143
Muslimbāgh, Pak. E2 44
Musoma, Tan. B6 58
Musquacook Lakes, l., Me., U.S. B3 126
Musquash, N.B., Can. D3 101
Musquash Mountain, mtn., Me., U.S. C5 126
Musquodoboit Harbour, N.S., Can. E6 101
Musselshell, Mt., U.S. D9 133
Musselshell, co., Mt., U.S. D8 133
Musselshell, stm., Mt., U.S. D9 133
Mussomeli, Italy L8 18
Mussuma, Ang. D4 58
Mustafakemalpaşa, Tur. I12 20
Mustang, Ok., U.S. B4 143
Mustinka, stm., Mn., U.S. E2 130
Mustla, Est. C8 22
Mustvee, Est. C9 22
Muswellbrook, Austl. I9 70
Mūt, Egypt E5 60
Mut, Tur. C2 48
Mutá, Ponta do, c., Braz. B9 79
Mutambara, Zimb. B11 66
Mutare, Zimb. B11 66
Mutlu (Rezovska), stm., Eur. H11 20
Mutsamudu, Com. I16 67a
Mutsu, Japan F16 36
Mutsu-wan, b., Japan F15 36
Muttaburra, Austl. D6 70
Muttenz, Switz. C8 13
Mutton Mountains, mts., Or., U.S. C5 144
Mutuípe, Braz. B9 79
Mutum, Braz. E8 79
Mutum, stm., Braz. J8 84
Mutunópolis, Braz. B4 79
Muxima, Ang. C2 58
Muymano, stm., S.A. D7 82
Muy Muy, Nic. E9 92
Muyua Island, i., Pap. N. Gui. A10 68
Muyua Island, i., Pap. N. Gui. m17 68a
Muyumba, Zaire C5 58
Muzaffarābād, Pak. C5 44
Muzaffarnagar, India F7 44
Muzaffarpur, India G11 44
Muzat, stm., China C3 30
Muzon, Cape, c., Ak., U.S. n23 109
Muztag, mtn., China B12 44
Muztag, mtn., China B9 44
Mvolo, Sud. N5 60
Mvuma, Zimb. B10 66
Mwali (Mohéli), i., Com. I15 67a
Mwanza, Tan. B6 58
Mweka, Zaire B4 58
Mwenezi, Zimb. C10 66
Mweru, Lake, l., Afr. C5 58
Mwinilunga, Zam. D4 58
Myaing, Burma D3 40
Myakka, stm., Fl., U.S. E4 116
Myanaung, Burma E3 40
Myanmar see Burma, ctry., Asia A2 38
Myaungmya, Burma F3 40
Myebon, Burma D2 40
Myerstown, Pa., U.S. F9 145
Myersville, Md., U.S. A2 127
Myingyan, Burma D3 40
Myitkyinā, Burma B4 40
Myittha, Burma D4 40
Myjava, Slov. G17 10
Myllymäki, Fin. J19 6
Mymensingh, Bngl. H14 44
Mynämäki, Fin. K18 6
Mynard, Ne., U.S. h13 134
Mynfontein, S. Afr. H6 66
Myrnam, Alta., Can. C5 98
Myrskylä (Mörskom), Fin. K19 6
Myrtle, Ms., U.S. A4 131
Myrtle Beach, S.C., U.S. D10 147
Myrtle Beach Air Force Base, mil., S.C., U.S. D10 147
Myrtle Grove, Fl., U.S. u14 116
Myrtle Point, Or., U.S. D2 144
Myrtlewood, Al., U.S. C2 108
Myski, Russia G9 28
Myškino, Russia D21 22
Myślenice, Pol. F19 10
Mysłowice, Pol. E19 10
Mysore, India F4 46
Mystic, Ct., U.S. D8 114
Mystic, Ga., U.S. E3 117
Mystic, Ia., U.S. D5 122
Mystic Lakes, l., Ma., U.S. g11 128
Myszków, Pol. E19 10
Myt, Russia E25 22
My Tho, Viet. I9 40
Mytišči, Russia F20 22
Myton, Ut., U.S. C5 151
Mzimba, Mwi. D6 58
Mzimvubu, stm., Afr. H9 66
Mzuzu, Mwi. D6 58

N

Na (Tengtiao), stm., Asia C7 40
Naalehu, Hi., U.S. D6 118
Naas, Ire. H7 8
Nabā, Jabal an- (Mount Nebo), mtn., Jord. E5 50
Nabalat Al-Hajanah, Sud. K5 60
Nabburg, Ger. F12 10
Naberežnyje Čelny, Russia F8 26
Nabeul, Tun. M5 18
Nābha, India E7 44
Nabileque, stm., Braz. I13 82
Nabī Shu'ayb, Jabal an-, mtn., Yemen G3 47
Nabnasset, Ma., U.S. A5 128
Nabogame, Mex. D6 90
Naboomspruit, S. Afr. E9 66
Nabq, Egypt C8 60
Nābulus, Isr. Occ. D4 50
Nacala-Velha, Moz. D8 58
Nacaome, Hond. D7 92
Naches, Wa., U.S. C5 154
Naches, stm., Wa., U.S. C5 154
Nachičevan', Azer. J7 26
Náchod, Czech. E16 10
Nachodka, Russia I18 28
Nacimiento, Chile I2 80
Nacimiento, Lake, res., Ca., U.S. E3 112
Nacmine, Alta., Can. D4 98
Naco, Mex. B5 90
Naco, Az., U.S. F6 110
Nacogdoches, Tx., U.S. D5 150
Nacogdoches, co., Tx., U.S. D5 150
Nácori Chico, Mex. C5 90
Nacozari de García, Mex. B5 90
Ñacunday, Para. D11 80
Nadiād, India I5 44
Nădlac, Rom. C4 20
Nador, Mor. C9 62
Nadvoicy, Russia J24 6
Nadvornaja, Ukr. A8 20
Nadym, Russia D12 26
Nadym, stm., Russia D12 26
Nafadji, Sen. E4 64
Näfels, Switz. D11 13
Nafī, Sau. Ar. I7 48
Naga, Phil. o20 39b
Nâga, Kreb en, clf, Afr. I7 62
Naga Hills, mts., Asia B3 40
Nāgāland, state, India H16 44
Nagano, Japan K13 36
Nagaoka, Japan J13 36
Nagaon, India G15 44
Nāgappattinam, India G5 46
Nāgārjuna Sāgar, res., India D5 46
Nagarote, Nic. E8 92
Nagar Pārkar, Pak. H4 44
Nagasaki, Japan O4 36
Nāgaur, India G5 44
Nagda, India I6 44
Nāgercoil, India H4 46
Nagīna, India F8 44
Nagog Pond, l., Ma., U.S. f10 128
Nagold, Ger. G8 10
Nagornoje, Ukr. D12 20
Nagornyj, Russia F16 28
Nagoya, Japan L11 36
Nāgpur, India J8 44
Nagqu, China E5 30
Nags Head, N.C., U.S. B7 140
Nagua, Dom. Rep. E10 94
Nagyatád, Hung. I17 10
Nagybajom, Hung. I17 10
Nagyecsed, Hung. H22 10
Nagykálló, Hung. H21 10
Nagykanizsa, Hung. I17 10
Nagykőrös, Hung. H19 10
Naha, Japan u2 37b
Nāhan, India E7 44
Nahang (Nihing), stm., Asia H17 48
Nahant, Ma., U.S. g12 128
Nahariyya, Isr. B4 50
Nahāvand, Iran D10 48
Nahe, China B11 30
Nahmakanta Lake, l., Me., U.S. C3 126
Nahualate, stm., Guat. C3 92
Nahuel Huapí, Lago, l., Arg. E2 78
Nahunta, Ga., U.S. E5 117
Naica, Mex. D7 90
Naicam, Sask., Can. E3 105
Nailin, China B7 32
Nain, Newf., Can. g9 102
Nā'īn, Iran E12 48
Naini Tāl, India F8 44
Nairn, La., U.S. E6 125
Nairobi, Kenya B7 58
Naissaar, i., Est. B7 22
Naivasha, Kenya B7 58
Najafābād, Iran E11 48
Najasa, stm., Cuba D6 94
Nájera, Spain C9 16
Naj'Hammādī, Egypt D7 60
Najībābād, India F8 44
Najin, N. Kor. A18 32
Najstenjarvi, Russia J23 6
Naju, S. Kor. H14 32
Nakadōri-shima, i., Japan O4 36
Nakaminato, Japan K15 36
Nakano-shima, i., Japan r4 37b
Nakape, Sud. O5 60
Nakatsu, Japan N6 36
Nakfa, Erit. I10 60
Nakhon Nayok, Thai. G6 40
Nakhon Pathom, Thai. H6 40
Nakhon Phanom, Thai. F8 40
Nakhon Ratchasima, Thai. G7 40
Nakhon Sawan, Thai. G6 40
Nakhon Si Thammarat, Thai. J5 40
Nakina, Ont., Can. o18 103
Nakło nad Notecią, Pol. B17 10
Naknek, Ak., U.S. D8 109
Naknek Lake, l., Ak., U.S. D8 109
Nakskov, Den. N12 6
Nakuru, Kenya B7 58
Nakusp, B.C., Can. D9 99
Nalajch, Mong. B8 30
Nālanda, India D12 42
Nal'čik, Russia I6 26
Nalgonda, India D5 46
Nallen, W.V., U.S. m14 155
Nālūt, Libya E16 62
Nam, stm., Asia D5 40
Namaacha, Moz. E11 66
Namak, Daryācheh-ye, l., Iran D11 48
Namaka, Alta., Can. D4 98
Namaksār, Kowl-e, l., Asia D18 48
Namangan, Uzb. I12 26
Namanock Island, i., N.J., U.S. A3 137
Namapa, Moz. D7 58
Namatanai, Pap. N. Gui. k17 68a
Nambe, N.M., U.S. B4 138
Nambour, Austl. F10 70
Nambucca Heads, Austl. H10 70
Nam Can, Viet. J8 40
Nam Co, l., China E14 44
Nam Dinh, Viet. D9 40
Namekagon, stm., Wi., U.S. B2 156
Namekagon Lake, l., Wi., U.S. B2 156
Namen (Namur), Bel. H6 12
Namhkam, Burma C4 40
Namib Desert, des., Afr. D2 66
Namibe, Ang. E2 58
Namibia, ctry., Afr. F3 58
Namjagbarwa Feng, mtn., China F16 44
Namoi, stm., Austl. H8 70
Namounou, Burkina F10 64
Nampa, Alta., Can. A2 98
Nampa, Id., U.S. F2 119
Namp'awng, Burma C4 40
Namp'o, N. Kor. E13 32
Nampula, Moz. E7 58
Namsang, Burma D4 40
Namsos, Nor. I12 6
Namtu, Burma A2 38
Namur (Namen), Bel. H6 12
Namur, prov., Bel. H6 12
Namutoni, Nmb. B3 66
Namwŏn, S. Kor. H15 32
Namyang, N. Kor. A17 32
Namyit Island, i., Asia C5 38
Namysłów, Pol. D17 10
Nan, Thai. E6 40
Nan, stm., Thai. F6 40
Nanafalia, Al., U.S. C2 108
Nanaimo, B.C., Can. E5 99
Nanakuli, Hi., U.S. B3 118
Nanam, N. Kor. B17 32
Nanango, Austl. F10 70
Nanao, Japan J11 36
Nanay, stm., Peru I6 84
Nance, co., Ne., U.S. C7 134
Nanchang, China G4 34
Nancheng, China H5 34
Nanchong, China E8 30
Nancowry Island, i., India K2 40
Nancun, China G8 32
Nancy, Fr. D13 14
Nancy, Ky., U.S. C5 124
Nancy Creek, stm., Ga., U.S. h8 117
Nanda Devi, mtn., India E8 44
Nandaime, Nic. F8 92
Nānded, India C4 46
N'andoma, Russia E6 26
Nandu, stm., China E11 40
Nandurbār, India J6 44
Nandyāl, India E5 46
Nanga Parbat, mtn., Pak. C6 44
Nangin, Burma I5 40
Nangnim, N. Kor. C15 32
Nangola, Mali E6 64
Nang Rong, Thai. G7 40
Nanjangūd, India F4 46
Nanjiang, China C9 34
Nanjing (Nanking), China C7 34
Nankang, China J3 34
Nanking see Nanjing, China C7 34
Nankou, China I6 34
Nan Ling, mts., China J2 34
Nanlinqiao, China F3 34
Nannine, Austl. E3 68
Nanning, China C10 40
Nanoose Bay, B.C., Can. f11 99
Nanpi, China E4 32
Nanping, China I7 34
Nanpu, China D6 32
Nansa, stm., Spain B7 16
Nansei-shotō (Ryukyu Islands), is., Japan s4 37b
Nansemond, stm., Va., U.S. k14 153
Nanshan Island, i., Asia C6 38
Nanshan see Qilian Shan, mts., China D6 30
Nant, Fr. H10 14
Nantang, China I4 34
Nantes, Fr. E5 14
Nanticoke, Ont., Can. E4 103
Nanticoke, Md., U.S. D6 127
Nanticoke, Pa., U.S. D10 145
Nanticoke, stm., U.S. D6 127
Nanton, Alta., Can. D4 98
Nantong, China C9 34
Nant'ou, Tai. L9 34
Nantua, Fr. F12 14
Nantucket, Ma., U.S. D7 128
Nantucket, co., Ma., U.S. D7 128
Nantucket Island, i., Ma., U.S. D7 128
Nantucket Sound, strt., Ma., U.S. C7 128
Nantuxent Point, c., N.J., U.S. E2 137
Nanty Glo, Pa., U.S. F4 145
Nanuet, N.Y., U.S. g12 139
Nanuque, Braz. D8 79
Nanwan, China C2 34
Nanxiang, China D10 34
Nanxiong, China J3 34
Nanyang, China B1 34
Nanzhao, China B1 34
Naoma, W.V., U.S. n13 155
Não-me-Toque, Braz. E12 80
Naomi Peak, mtn., Ut., U.S. B4 151
Náousa, Grc. I6 20
Napa, Ca., U.S. C2 112
Napa, co., Ca., U.S. C2 112
Napadogan, N.B., Can. C3 101
Napaktok Bay, b., Newf., Can. f9 102
Napanee, Ont., Can. C8 103
Napanoch, N.Y., U.S. D6 139
Napaskiak, Ak., U.S. C7 109
Napatree Point, c., R.I., U.S. G1 146
Napavine, Wa., U.S. C3 154
Napè, Laos E8 40
Napenay, Arg. D8 80
Naper, Ne., U.S. B6 134
Naperville, Il., U.S. B5 120
Napier, N.Z. C6 72
Napier, S. Afr. J4 66
Napier Mountains, mts., Ant. B4 73
Napierville, Que., Can. D4 104
Napinka, Man., Can. E1 100
Naplate, Il., U.S. B5 120
Naples, Fl., U.S. F5 116
Naples, Id., U.S. A2 119
Naples, Me., U.S. E2 126
Naples, N.Y., U.S. C3 139
Naples, Tx., U.S. C5 150
Naples, Ut., U.S. C6 151
Naples see Napoli, Italy I9 18
Napo, prov., Ec. H4 84
Napo, stm., S.A. I6 84
Napoleon, In., U.S. F7 121
Napoleon, Mo., U.S. B3 132
Napoleon, N.D., U.S. C6 141
Napoleon, Oh., U.S. A1 142
Napoleonville, La., U.S. E4 125
Napoli (Naples), Italy I9 18
Nappanee, In., U.S. B5 121
Naqādah, Egypt E7 60
Naqadeh, Iran C8 48
Nara, Japan M10 36
Nara, Mali D6 64
Naracoorte, Austl. K4 70
Naradhan, Austl. I7 70
Naramata, B.C., Can. E8 99
Naranja, Fl., U.S. G6 116
Naranjal, Ec. I3 84
Naranjito, Hond. C6 92
Naranjo, C.R. G10 92
Naranjo, stm., Guat. C3 92
Narasapur, India D6 46
Narasaraopet, India D6 46
Narathiwat, Thai. K6 40
Nara Visa, N.M., U.S. B6 138
Nārāyanganj, Bngl. I14 44
Nārāyani (Gandak), stm., Asia G11 44
Nārāyanpet, India D4 46
Narberth, Pa., U.S. p20 145
Narbonne, Fr. I10 14
Nardò, Italy I13 18
Nare, stm., Col. D5 84
Nares Strait, strt., N.A. A13 86
Narew, stm., Eur. C21 10
Narinda, Baie de, b., Madag. o22 67b
Nariño, dept., Col. G3 84
Narita, Japan L15 36
Nar'jan-Mar, Russia D8 26
Narka, Ks., U.S. C6 123
Narmada, stm., India J5 44
Nārnaul, India F7 44
Narni, Italy G7 18
Naro, Italy L8 18
Narodnaja, gora, mtn., Russia D10 26
Naro-Fominsk, Russia F19 22
Narol, Man., Can. D3 100
Narol, Pol. E23 10
Narooma, Austl. K9 70
Narrabri, Austl. H8 70
Narragansett, R.I., U.S. F4 146
Narragansett Bay, b., R.I., U.S. E5 146
Narraguagus, stm., Me., U.S. D5 126
Narran, stm., Austl. G7 70
Narrandera, Austl. J7 70
Narrogin, Austl. F3 68
Narromine, Austl. I8 70
Narrows, Va., U.S. C2 153
Narsimhapur, India I8 44
Narsīpatnam, India D7 46
Naruna, Va., U.S. C3 153
Narva, Est. B11 22
Narva, stm., Eur. B10 22
Narva laht (Narvskij zaliv), b., Eur. B10 22
Narvik, Nor. G15 6
Narvskij zaliv (Narva laht), b., Eur. B10 22
Narvskoje vodochranilišče, res., Eur. B11 22
Naryn, Kyrg. I13 26
Naryn, stm., Asia I12 26
Naryškino, Russia I18 22
Na San, Thai. J5 40
Nasarawa, Nig. G13 64
Naschel, Arg. G6 80
Naselle, Wa., U.S. C2 154
Nash, Ok., U.S. A3 143
Nash, Tx., U.S. C5 150
Nash, co., N.C., U.S. A4 140
Nashawena Island, i., Ma., U.S. D6 128
Nash Creek, N.B., Can. B3 101
Nāshik, India C2 46
Nashoba Hill, hill, Ma., U.S. f10 128
Nash Stream, stm., N.H., U.S. A4 136
Nashua, Ia., U.S. B5 122
Nashua, Mt., U.S. B10 133
Nashua, N.H., U.S. E4 136
Nashua, stm., U.S. E3 136
Nashville, Ar., U.S. D2 111
Nashville, Ga., U.S. E3 117
Nashville, Il., U.S. E4 120
Nashville, In., U.S. F5 121
Nashville, Ks., U.S. E5 123
Nashville, Mi., U.S. F5 129
Nashville, N.C., U.S. B5 140
Nashville, Tn., U.S. A5 149
Nashwaaksis, N.B., Can. D3 101
Nashwauk, Mn., U.S. C5 130
Nasielsk, Pol. C20 10
Näsijärvi, l., Fin. K18 6
Nāṣir, Sud. M7 60
Nāṣir, Buhayrat, res., Afr. D7 56
Nasīrābād, India G6 44
Nasīrābād, Pak. F3 44
Naskaupi, stm., Newf., Can. g9 102
Nason, Il., U.S. E5 120
Nassau, Bah. B6 94
Nassau, De., U.S. E5 115
Nassau, N.Y., U.S. C7 139
Nassau, co., Fl., U.S. B5 116
Nassau, co., N.Y., U.S. E7 139
Nassau, stm., Fl., U.S. k8 116
Nassau Sound, b., Fl., U.S. B5 116
Nassawadox, Va., U.S. C7 153
Nassawango Creek, stm., Md., U.S. D7 127
Nasser, Lake see Nāṣir, Buhayrat, res., Afr. D7 56
Nassereith, Aus. H10 10
Nässjö, Swe. M14 6
Nastapoka Islands, is., N.W. Ter., Can. E17 96
Nasukoin Mountain, mtn., Mt., U.S. B2 133
Nasva, Russia E13 22
Nata, Bots. C8 66
Natá, Pan. C2 84
Nata, stm., Afr. B8 66
Natagaima, Col. F5 84
Natal, Braz. E11 76
Natal, Indon. E2 38
Natalbany, La., U.S. D5 125
Natalia, Tx., U.S. E3 150
Natanes Plateau, plat., Az., U.S. D5 110
Natash, Wādī, val., Egypt I2 48
Natashquan, Que., Can. h9 102
Natashquan, stm., Can. h9 102
Natchaug, stm., Ct., U.S. B7 114
Natchez, La., U.S. C2 125
Natchez, Ms., U.S. D2 131
Natchitoches, La., U.S. C2 125
Natchitoches, co., La., U.S. C2 125
Nathrop, Co., U.S. C4 113
Natick, Ma., U.S. B5 128
Natimuk, Austl. K4 70
Nation, stm., B.C., Can. B6 99
National City, Ca., U.S. F5 112
Natitingou, Benin F10 64
Nativity, Church of the, Isr. Occ. E4 50
Natl, Jord. E5 50
Natoma, Ks., U.S. C4 123
Natong, China C9 40
Natron, Lake, l., Afr. B7 58
Natrona, co., Wy., U.S. D5 157
Natrona Heights, Pa., U.S. E2 145
Natuna Besar, i., Indon. L10 40
Natuna Besar, Kepulauan, is., Indon. L10 40
Natural Bridge, Al., U.S. A2 108
Natural Bridge, Va., U.S. C3 153
Natural Bridge, Ut., U.S. F3 151
Natural Bridge, Va., U.S. C3 153
Natural Bridges National Monument, Ut., U.S. F6 151
Naturaliste, Cape, c., Austl. F3 68
Naturaliste Channel, strt., Austl. E2 68
Naturita, Co., U.S. C2 113
Nau, Cap de la, c., Spain G12 16
Nauders, Aus. I10 10
Nauen, Ger. C12 10
Naugatuck, Ct., U.S. D3 114
Naugatuck, stm., Ct., U.S. D3 114
Naujamiestis, Lith. F7 22
Naujoji Akmenė, Lith. E5 22
Naumburg, Ger. D11 10
Naungpale, Burma E4 40
Nauroz Kalāt, Pak. F1 44
Nauru, ctry., Oc. G24 2
Naushon Island, i., Ma., U.S. D6 128
Nauta, Peru J6 84
Nautilus Park, Ct., U.S. D7 114
Nautla, Mex. G11 90
Nauvoo, Al., U.S. B2 108
Nauvoo, Il., U.S. C2 120
Nauwigewauk, N.B., Can. D4 101
Nava, Mex. C9 90
Navadwīp, India I13 44
Navahermosa, Spain F7 16
Navajo, Az., U.S. B6 110
Navajo, N.M., U.S. B1 138
Navajo, co., Az., U.S. B5 110
Navajo Dam, N.M., U.S. A2 138
Navajo Indian Reservation, U.S. A4 110
Navajo Mountain, mtn., Ut., U.S. F5 151
Navajo National Monument, Az., U.S. A5 110
Navajo Reservoir, res., U.S. A2 138
Navalmoral de la Mata, Spain F6 16
Navan, Ont., Can. B9 103
Navarin, mys, c., Russia E27 28
Navarino, Isla, i., Chile H3 78
Navarra, prov., Spain C10 16
Navarre, Oh., U.S. B4 142
Navarro, Arg. H9 80
Navarro, co., Tx., U.S. D4 150
Navašino, Russia F25 22
Navasota, Tx., U.S. D4 150
Navassa, N.C., U.S. C4 140
Navassa Island, i., N.A. E7 94
Navesink, N.J., U.S. C4 137
Navia, Arg. H5 80
Navidad, Chile G3 80
Naviraí, Braz. G1 79
Navl'a, Russia I17 22
Năvodari, Rom. E12 20
Navoi, Uzb. I11 26
Navojoa, Mex. D5 90
Navolato, Mex. E6 90
Navoloki, Russia D24 22
Návpaktos, Grc. K5 20
Návplion, Grc. L6 20
Navsāri, India J5 44
Nawābganj, Bngl. H13 44
Nawābshāh, Pak. G3 44
Nāwah, Afg. D2 44
Nawalgarh, India G6 44
Nawiliwili Bay, b., Hi., U.S. B2 118
Náxos, Grc. L9 20
Náxos, i., Grc. L9 20
Nayarit, state, Mex. F7 90
Nāy Band, Iran E14 48
Naylor, Ga., U.S. F3 117
Naylor, Mo., U.S. E7 132
Nayoro, Japan c17 36a
Nazaré, Braz. B9 79
Nazaré, Port. F2 16
Nazaré da Mata, Braz. E11 76
Nazareth, Ky., U.S. C4 124
Nazareth, Pa., U.S. E11 145
Nazareth see Nazerat, Isr. C4 50
Nazário, Braz. D4 79
Nazarovo, Russia F10 28
Nazas, Mex. E7 90
Nazas, stm., Mex. E7 90
Nazca, Peru F4 82
Naze, Japan s4 37b
N'azepetrovsk, Russia F9 26
Nazerat (Nazareth), Isr. C4 50
Nazerat 'Illit, Isr. C4 50
Nazija, Russia B14 22
Nazilli, Tur. L12 20
Nazko, stm., B.C., Can. C6 99
Nazlini, Az., U.S. B6 110
Nazret, Eth. M10 60
Nazyvajevsk, Russia F12 26
N'dalatando, Ang. C2 58
Ndali, Benin G11 64
Ndélé, Cen. Afr. Rep. G5 56
Ndendé, Gabon B2 58
N'Djamena, Chad F4 56
Ndjolé, Gabon B2 58
Ndola, Zam. D5 58
Neagh, Lough, l., N. Ire., U.K. G7 8
Neah Bay, Wa., U.S. A1 154
Neamt, co., Rom. C10 20
Néa Páfos (Paphos), Cyp. D2 48
Near Islands, is., Ak., U.S. E2 109
Nebaj, Guat. B3 92
Nebit-Dag, Turk. J8 26
Neblina, Pico da, mtn., S.A. G9 84
Nebo, Il., U.S. D3 120
Nebo, Ky., U.S. C2 124
Nebo, Mount, mtn., Ut., U.S. D4 151
Nebolči, Russia B16 22
Nebraska, state, U.S. C6 134
Nebraska City, Ne., U.S. D10 134

Name | Map Ref. | Page

Necedah, Wi., U.S. D3 156
Nechako, stm., B.C., Can. C5 99
Nechako Range, mts., B.C., Can. C5 99
Neche, N.D., U.S. A8 141
Neches, stm., Tx., U.S. D5 150
Nechí, Col. C5 84
Nechí, stm., Col. D5 84
Nechmeya, Alg. M2 18
Neckar, stm., Ger. F9 10
Neckarsulm, Ger. F9 10
Necker Island, i., Hi., U.S. m15 118
Necochea, Arg. J9 80
Nederland, Co., U.S. B5 113
Nederland, Tx., U.S. E6 150
Neder Rijn, mth., Neth. E8 12
Nêdong, China F5 30
Nédroma, Alg. C10 62
Nedrow, N.Y., U.S. C4 139
Needham, Ma., U.S. g11 128
Needle Mountain, mtn., Wy., U.S. B3 157
Needles, Ca., U.S. E6 112
Needmore, In., U.S. G4 121
Needville, Tx., U.S. r14 150
Neels Gap, Ga., U.S. B3 117
Neely, Ms., U.S. D5 131
Neelyville, Mo., U.S. E7 132
Ñeembucú, dept., Para. D9 80
Neenah, Wi., U.S. D5 156
Neepawa, Man., Can. D2 100
Neeses, S.C., U.S. D5 147
Neffs, Oh., U.S. B5 142
Neffsville, Pa., U.S. F9 145
Nefta, Tun. D14 62
Nefza, Tun. M4 18
Negage, Ang. C3 58
Négala, Mali E5 64
Negaunee, Mi., U.S. B3 129
Negele, Eth. G8 56
Negev Desert see HaNegev, reg., Isr. G3 50
Negley, Oh., U.S. B5 142
Negombo, Sri L. I5 46
Negoreloje, Bela. H10 22
Negotin, Yugo. E6 20
Negra, Laguna, l., Ur. H12 80
Negra, Punta, c., Belize A6 92
Negra, Punta, c., Peru B1 82
Negreira, Spain C3 16
Negreşti, Rom. C11 20
Negrine, Alg. C14 62
Negritos, Peru J2 84
Negro, stm., Arg. E4 78
Negro, stm., Bol. D9 82
Negro, stm., Bol. F10 82
Negro, stm., Braz. C13 80
Negro, stm., Braz. A6 82
Negro, stm., Braz. H13 82
Negro, stm., Col. E5 84
Negro, stm., N.A. E7 92
Negro, stm., Para. C10 80
Negro, stm., S.A. G10 80
Negro, stm., S.A. H13 84
Negro Mountain, mtn., Md., U.S. k12 127
Negros, i., Phil. C7 38
Neguac, N.B., Can. B4 101
Nehalem, stm., Or., U.S. A3 144
Nehawka, Ne., U.S. D10 134
Nehbandān, Iran F16 48
Neiba, Dom. Rep. E9 94
Neiges, Piton des, mtn., Reu. v17 67c
Neihuang, China H2 32
Neijiang, China F8 30
Neilburg, Sask., Can. E1 105
Neill Point, c., Wa., U.S. f11 154
Neillsville, Wi., U.S. D3 156
Nei Monggol Zizhiqu (Inner Mongolia), prov., China C10 30
Neira, Col. E5 84
Neisse (Nysa Łużycka) (Nisa), stm., Eur. D14 10
Neiva, Col. F5 84
Neixpa, stm., Mex. H8 90
Neja, Russia C26 22
Nejapa de Madero, Mex. I12 90
Nejdek, Czech. E12 10
Nejo, Eth. M8 60
Nekemte, Eth. M9 60
Nekoosa, Wi., U.S. D4 156
Nekrasovskoje, Russia D23 22
Neksø, Den. N14 6
Nelidovo, Russia E15 22
Neligh, Ne., U.S. B7 134
Nellikuppam, India G5 46
Nellis Air Force Base, mil., Nv., U.S. G6 135
Nellore, India E5 46
Nel'ma, Russia H19 28
Nelson, B.C., Can. E9 99
Nelson, N.Z. D4 72
Nelson, Ga., U.S. B2 117
Nelson, Il., U.S. B4 120
Nelson, Mn., U.S. E3 130
Nelson, Mo., U.S. B4 132
Nelson, Ne., U.S. D7 134
Nelson, N.H., U.S. E2 136
Nelson, Wi., U.S. D2 156
Nelson, co., Ky., U.S. C4 124
Nelson, co., N.D., U.S. B7 141
Nelson, co., Va., U.S. C4 153
Nelson, stm., Man., Can. A4 100
Nelson, Cape, c., Austl. L4 70
Nelsonville, Oh., U.S. C3 142
Nelspoort, S. Afr. I6 66
Nelspruit, S. Afr. E10 66
Néma, Maur. C6 64
Nemacolin, Pa., U.S. G2 145
Nemadji, stm., U.S. B1 156
Nemaha, Ne., U.S. D10 134
Nemaha, co., Ks., U.S. C7 123
Nemaha, co., Ne., U.S. D10 134
Neman, Russia F5 22
Neman (Nemunas), stm., Eur. F5 22
Nemeiben Lake, l., Sask., Can. B3 105
Nemenčinė, Lith. G8 22
Nemiscau, Que., Can. h11 104
Nemours, Fr. D9 14
Nemuna, Bjeshkët e, mts., Eur. G3 20
Nemunas (Neman), stm., Eur. F6 22
Nemuro, Japan d20 36a
Nemuro Strait, strt., Asia c20 36a
Nen, stm., China B11 30
Nenagh, Ire. I5 8
Nenana, Ak., U.S. C10 109
Nenaševo, Russia G20 22
Neneckij, state, Russia D9 26
Nentón, stm., N.A. B3 92
Neodesha, Ks., U.S. E8 123
Neoga, Il., U.S. D5 120
Neola, Ia., U.S. C2 122
Neola, Ut., U.S. C5 151
Neopit, Wi., U.S. D5 156
Neosho, Mo., U.S. E3 132
Neosho, Wi., U.S. E5 156
Neosho, co., Ks., U.S. E8 123
Neosho, stm., Ok., U.S. A6 143
Neosho Falls, Ks., U.S. D8 123
Neosho Rapids, Ks., U.S. D8 123
Neotsu, Or., U.S. B3 144
Nepa, stm., Russia F13 28
Nepal (Nepāl), ctry., Asia D11 42
Nepālganj, Nepal F9 44
Nepaug Reservoir, res., Ct., U.S. B3 114
Nepean, Ont., Can. h12 103
Nepeña, Peru C2 82
Nepewassi Lake, l., Ont., Can. A4 103
Nephi, Ut., U.S. D4 151
Nephton, Ont., Can. C7 103
Nepisiguit, stm., N.B., Can. B3 101
Nepisiguit Bay, b., N.B., Can. B4 101
Neponset, Il., U.S. B4 120
Neponset, stm., Ma., U.S. h11 128
Nepton, Ky., U.S. B6 124
Neptune, N.J., U.S. C4 137
Neptune Beach, Fl., U.S. B5 116
Neptune City, N.J., U.S. C4 137
Nera, stm., Eur. E5 20
Nerča, stm., Russia G15 28
Nerčinsk, Russia G15 28
Nerčinskij Zavod, Russia G15 28
Nerechta, Russia D23 22
Nereta, Lat. E8 22
Neriquinha, Ang. E4 58
Nerja, Spain I8 16
Nerl', Russia E23 22
Nerl', stm., Russia E23 22
Nerópolis, Braz. D4 79
Nerussa, stm., Russia I17 22
Nerva, Spain H5 16
Nesbit, Ms., U.S. A3 131
Nesbitt, Man., Can. E2 100
Nescopeck, Pa., U.S. D9 145
Neshanic, stm., N.J., U.S. C3 137
Nesher, Isr. C4 50
Neshkoro, Wi., U.S. E4 156
Neshoba, Ms., U.S. C4 131
Neshoba, co., Ms., U.S. C4 131
Nesika Beach, Or., U.S. E2 144
Nesle, Fr. C9 14
Nesowadnehunk, l., Me., U.S. B3 126
Nesquehoning, Pa., U.S. E10 145
Ness, co., Ks., U.S. D4 123
Ness, Loch, l., Scot., U.K. D9 8
Ness City, Ks., U.S. D4 123
Nesselwang, Ger. H10 10
Nesslau, Switz. D11 13
Nesterov, Russia G5 22
Nestoita, Ukr. B13 20
Néstos (Mesta), stm., Eur. H8 20
Nesvíž, Bela. H9 22
Nes Ẕiyyona, Isr. E3 50
Netanya, Isr. D3 50
Netawaka, Ks., U.S. C8 123
Netcong, N.J., U.S. B3 137
Netherdale, Austl. C8 70
Netherhill, Sask., Can. F1 105
Netherlands (Nederland), ctry., Eur. E9 4
Netherlands Antilles (Nederlandse Antillen), dep., N.A. H10 94
Netrakona, Bngl. H14 44
Nettie, W.V., U.S. C4 155
Nettilling Lake, l., N.W. Ter., Can. C18 96
Nett Lake, Mn., U.S. B5 130
Nett Lake, l., Mn., U.S. B5 130
Nett Lake Indian Reservation, Mn., U.S. B6 130
Nettleton, Ms., U.S. A5 131
Nettuno, Italy H7 18
Neubrandenburg, Ger. B13 10
Neuburg an der Donau, Ger. G11 10
Neuchâtel, Switz. E6 13
Neuchâtel, state, Switz. D6 13
Neuchâtel, Lac de, l., Switz. E6 13
Neudorf, Sask., Can. G4 105
Neuenhagen, Ger. C13 10
Neuf-Brisach, Fr. D14 14
Neufchâteau, Bel. I7 12
Neufchâteau, Fr. D12 14
Neufchâtel-en-Bray, Fr. C8 14
Neuhausen, Switz. C10 13
Neu-Isenburg, Ger. E8 10
Neumarkt [im Hausruckkreis], Aus. G13 10
Neumarkt in der Oberpfalz, Ger. F11 10
Neumarkt in Steiermark, Aus. H14 10
Neumarkt-Sankt Veit, Ger. G12 10
Neumünster, Ger. A9 10
Neunburg vorm Wald, Ger. F12 10
Neunkirchen/Saar, Ger. F7 10
Neuquén, Arg. J4 80
Neuquén, prov., Arg. J4 80
Neuquén, stm., Arg. J4 80
Neurara, Chile C4 80
Neuruppin, Ger. C12 10
Neuschwanstein, Schloss, Ger. C14 13
Neuse, stm., N.C., U.S. B6 140
Neusiedl am See, Aus. H16 10
Neusiedler See, l., Eur. H16 10
Neustadt, Ont., Can. C4 103
Neustadt [an der Aisch], Ger. F10 10
Neustadt an der Waldnaab, Ger. F12 10
Neustadt an der Weinstrasse, Ger. F8 10
Neustadt bei Coburg, Ger. E11 10
Neustadt in Holstein, Ger. A10 10
Neustrelitz, Ger. B13 10
Neu-Ulm, Ger. G10 10
Neuville, Que., Can. C6 104
Neuville-sur-Saône, Fr. G11 14
Neuwied, Ger. E7 10
Neva, stm., Russia B13 22
Nevada, Ia., U.S. B4 122
Nevada, Mo., U.S. D3 132
Nevada, Oh., U.S. B2 142
Nevada, co., Ar., U.S. D2 111
Nevada, co., Ca., U.S. C3 112
Nevada, state, U.S. D5 135
Nevada, Sierra, mts., Spain H8 16
Nevada, Sierra, mts., Ca., U.S. D4 112
Nevada City, Ca., U.S. C3 112
Nevado, Cerro, mtn., Arg. H4 80
Nevado, Cerro, mtn., Col. C4 76
Nevado, Cerro, mtn., Col. F5 84
Nevado de Colima, Parque Nacional del, Mex. H8 90
Nevado de Toluca, Parque Nacional, Mex. H9 90
Nevel', Russia E12 22
Nevel'sk, Russia H20 28
Never, Russia G16 28
Nevers, Fr. E10 14
Neversink, stm., N.Y., U.S. D6 139
Nevertire, Austl. H7 70
Nevesinje, Bos. F2 20
Neville, Sask., Can. H2 105
Nevils, Ga., U.S. D5 117
Nevinnomyssk, Russia I6 26
Nevis, Mn., U.S. D4 130
Nevis, i., St. K./N. F13 94
Nevis, Ben, mtn., Scot., U.K. E9 8
Nevjansk, Russia F10 26
Nevşehir, Tur. B3 48
New, stm., Belize H15 90
New, stm., Guy. F14 84
New, stm., U.S. C3 155
New, stm., Az., U.S. k8 110
New, stm., N.C., U.S. C5 140
New Albany, In., U.S. H6 121
New Albany, Ms., U.S. A4 131
New Albany, Oh., U.S. k11 142
New Albin, Ia., U.S. A6 122
New Alfa, Sud. J8 60
New Alsace, In., U.S. F8 121
New Amsterdam, Guy. D14 84
Newark, Ar., U.S. B4 111
Newark, Ca., U.S. h8 112
Newark, De., U.S. B3 115
Newark, Il., U.S. B5 120
Newark, N.J., U.S. B4 137
Newark, N.Y., U.S. B3 139
Newark, Oh., U.S. B3 142
Newark, Tx., U.S. m9 150
Newark Bay, b., N.J., U.S. k8 137
Newark Lake, l., Nv., U.S. D6 135
Newark-on-Trent, Eng., U.K. H13 8
Newark Valley, N.Y., U.S. C4 139
New Athens, Il., U.S. E4 120
New Auburn, Mn., U.S. F4 130
New Auburn, Wi., U.S. C2 156
New Augusta, Ms., U.S. D4 131
Newaygo, Mi., U.S. E5 129
Newaygo, co., Mi., U.S. E5 129
New Baden, Il., U.S. E4 120
New Baltimore, Mi., U.S. F8 129
New Baltimore, N.Y., U.S. C7 139
New Bedford, Ma., U.S. C6 128
New Bedford, Pa., U.S. D1 145
Newberg, Or., U.S. B4 144
New Berlin, Il., U.S. D4 120
New Berlin, N.Y., U.S. C5 139
New Berlin, Pa., U.S. E7 145
New Berlin, Wi., U.S. n11 156
Newbern, Al., U.S. C2 108
New Bern, N.C., U.S. B5 140
Newbern, Tn., U.S. A2 149
Newberry, Fl., U.S. C4 116
Newberry, In., U.S. G3 121
Newberry, Mi., U.S. B5 129
Newberry, S.C., U.S. C4 147
Newberry, co., S.C., U.S. C4 147
Newberry Springs, Ca., U.S. E5 112
New Bethlehem, Pa., U.S. D3 145
New Bight, Bah. B7 94
New Blaine, Ar., U.S. B2 111
New Bloomfield, Mo., U.S. C5 132
New Bloomfield, Pa., U.S. F7 145
Newborn, Ga., U.S. C3 117
Newboro, Ont., Can. C8 103
New Boston, Il., U.S. B3 120
New Boston, Mi., U.S. p15 129
New Boston, N.H., U.S. E3 136
New Boston, Oh., U.S. D3 142
New Boston, Tx., U.S. C5 150
New Braunfels, Tx., U.S. E3 150
New Bremen, Oh., U.S. B1 142
New Brighton, Mn., U.S. m12 130
New Brighton, Pa., U.S. E1 145
New Britain, Ct., U.S. C4 114
New Britain, i., Pap. N. Gui. m17 68a
New Brockton, Al., U.S. D4 108
Newbrook, Alta., Can. B4 98
New Brunswick, N.J., U.S. C4 137
New Brunswick, prov., Can. C3 101
New Buffalo, Mi., U.S. G4 129
Newburg, Md., U.S. D4 127
Newburg, Mo., U.S. D6 132
Newburg, N.D., U.S. A5 141
Newburg, W.V., U.S. B5 155
Newburg, Wi., U.S. E5 156
Newburgh, Ont., Can. C8 103
Newburgh, In., U.S. I3 121
Newburgh, Me., U.S. D4 126
Newburgh, N.Y., U.S. D6 139
Newburgh Heights, Oh., U.S. h9 142
New Burnside, Il., U.S. F5 120
Newbury, Ont., Can. E3 103
Newbury, Eng., U.K. J12 8
Newbury, Ma., U.S. A6 128
Newbury, N.H., U.S. D2 136
Newbury, Vt., U.S. C4 152
Newburyport, Ma., U.S. A6 128
New Caledonia, dep., Oc. H24 2
New Cambria, Ks., U.S. D6 123
New Cambria, Mo., U.S. B5 132
New Canaan, Ct., U.S. E2 114
New Canton, Il., U.S. D2 120
New Carlisle, In., U.S. A4 121
New Carlisle, Oh., U.S. C1 142
New Carrollton, Md., U.S. C4 127
Newcastle, Austl. I9 70
Newcastle, N.B., Can. C4 101
Newcastle, Ont., Can. D6 103
Newcastle, S. Afr. F9 66
New Castle, Al., U.S. B3 108
New Castle, Co., U.S. B3 113
New Castle, De., U.S. B3 115
New Castle, In., U.S. E7 121
New Castle, Ky., U.S. B4 124
Newcastle, Me., U.S. D3 126
Newcastle, Ne., U.S. B9 134
New Castle, N.H., U.S. D5 136
Newcastle, Ok., U.S. B4 143
New Castle, Pa., U.S. D1 145
Newcastle, Tx., U.S. C3 150
Newcastle, Ut., U.S. F2 151
Newcastle, Wy., U.S. C8 157
New Castle, co., De., U.S. B3 115
Newcastle Creek, N.B., Can. C3 101
Newcastle-under-Lyme, Eng., U.K. H11 8
Newcastle upon Tyne, Eng., U.K. G12 8
Newcastle Waters, Austl. C6 68
New City, N.Y., U.S. D6 139
Newcomb, N.M., U.S. A1 138
Newcomb, Tn., U.S. A7 149
Newcomerstown, Oh., U.S. B4 142
New Concord, Oh., U.S. C4 142
New Cumberland, Pa., U.S. F8 145
New Cumberland, W.V., U.S. A4 155
Newdale, Man., Can. D1 100
Newdale, Id., U.S. F7 119
New Dayton, Alta., Can. E4 98
Newdegate, Austl. F3 68
New Delhi, India F7 44
New Denmark, N.B., Can. C2 101
New Denver, B.C., Can. D9 99
New Durham, N.H., U.S. D4 136
New Edinburg, Ar., U.S. D3 111
New Effington, S.D., U.S. B9 148
New Egypt, N.J., U.S. C3 137
Newell, Ia., U.S. B2 122
Newell, S.D., U.S. C2 148
Newell, W.V., U.S. A4 155
New Ellenton, S.C., U.S. E4 147
Newellton, La., U.S. B4 125
New England, N.D., U.S. C3 141
New England Range, mts., Austl. H9 70
Newenham, Cape, c., Ak., U.S. D7 109
New Era, Mi., U.S. E4 129
New Fairfield, Ct., U.S. D2 114
Newfane, N.Y., U.S. B2 139
Newfane, Vt., U.S. F3 152
Newfield, Me., U.S. E2 126
Newfield, N.J., U.S. D2 137
Newfields, N.H., U.S. D5 136
New Florence, Mo., U.S. C6 132
New Florence, Pa., U.S. F3 145
Newfolden, Mn., U.S. B2 130
Newfound Gap, U.S. f9 140
Newfound Lake, l., N.H., U.S. C3 136
Newfoundland, N.J., U.S. A4 137
Newfoundland, Pa., U.S. D11 145
Newfoundland, prov., Can. D4 102
Newfoundland, i., Newf., Can. D3 102
Newfoundland Mountains, mts., Ut., U.S. B2 151
New Franklin, Mo., U.S. B5 132
New Freedom, Pa., U.S. G8 145
New Galloway, Scot., U.K. F9 8
New Georgia, i., Sol.Is. A11 68
New Germany, N.S., Can. E5 101
New Glarus, Wi., U.S. F4 156
New Glasgow, N.S., Can. D7 101
New Gloucester, Me., U.S. E2 126
New Goshen, In., U.S. E3 121
New Guinea, i. m15 68a
Newhalem, Wa., U.S. A4 154
Newhall, Ia., U.S. C6 122
Newhall, Me., U.S. g7 126
Newhall, W.V., U.S. D3 155
New Hampshire, state, U.S. C3 136
New Hampton, Ia., U.S. A5 122
New Hampton, Mo., U.S. A3 132
New Hampton, N.H., U.S. C3 136
New Hanover, co., N.C., U.S. C5 140
New Hanover, i., Pap. N. Gui. k17 68a
New Harbor, Me., U.S. E3 126
New Harbour, Newf., Can. E5 102
New Harmony, In., U.S. H2 121
New Hartford, Ct., U.S. B4 114
New Hartford, Ia., U.S. B5 122
Newhaven, Eng., U.K. K14 8
New Haven, Ct., U.S. D4 114
New Haven, Il., U.S. F5 120
New Haven, In., U.S. B7 121
New Haven, Ky., U.S. C4 124
New Haven, Mi., U.S. F8 129
New Haven, Mo., U.S. C6 132
New Haven, W.V., U.S. C3 155
New Haven, co., Ct., U.S. D4 114
New Haven, stm., Vt., U.S. C2 152
New Haven Harbor, b., Ct., U.S. E4 114
New Hazelton, B.C., Can. B4 99
New Hebrides Trench K21 158
New Hebrides see Vanuatu, ctry., Oc. H24 2
Newhebron, Ms., U.S. D4 131
New Holland, Ga., U.S. B3 117
New Holland, Il., U.S. C4 120
New Holland, Oh., U.S. C2 142
New Holland, Pa., U.S. F9 145
New Holland, S.D., U.S. D7 148
New Holstein, Wi., U.S. E5 156
New Hope, Al., U.S. A3 108
Newhope, Ar., U.S. C2 111
New Hope, Ky., U.S. C4 124
New Hope, Mn., U.S. m12 130
New Hope, Pa., U.S. F12 145
New Hope, Tn., U.S. D8 149
New Hope Mountain, mtn., Al., U.S. g7 108
New Hudson, Mi., U.S. o14 129
New Iberia, La., U.S. D4 125
Newington, Ct., U.S. C5 114
Newington, Ga., U.S. D5 117
New Inlet, b., N.C., U.S. D5 140
New Ipswich, N.H., U.S. E3 136
New Ireland, i., Pap. N. Gui. k17 68a
New Jersey, state, U.S. C4 137
New Johnsonville, Tn., U.S. A4 149
New Kensington, Pa., U.S. E2 145
New Kent, co., Va., U.S. C5 153
Newkirk, Ok., U.S. A4 143
New Knoxville, Oh., U.S. B1 142
New Kowloon, H.K. M3 34
New Laguna, N.M., U.S. B2 138
New Lake, l., N.C., U.S. B6 140
Newland, N.C., U.S. A1 140
Newlands, Austl. C7 70
New Lebanon, In., U.S. F3 121
New Lebanon, N.Y., U.S. C7 139
New Leipzig, N.D., U.S. C4 141
New Lenox, Il., U.S. B6 120
New Lexington, Oh., U.S. C3 142
New Liberty, Ky., U.S. B5 124
New Lisbon, In., U.S. E7 121
New Lisbon, Wi., U.S. E3 156
New Liskeard, Ont., Can. p20 103
Newllano, La., U.S. C2 125
New London, Ct., U.S. D7 114
New London, In., U.S. D5 121
New London, Ia., U.S. D6 122
New London, Mn., U.S. E4 130
New London, Mo., U.S. B6 132
New London, N.H., U.S. D3 136
New London, N.C., U.S. B2 140
New London, Oh., U.S. A3 142
New London, Wi., U.S. D5 156
New London, co., Ct., U.S. C7 114
New London Submarine Base, mil., Ct., U.S. D7 114
New Lothrop, Mi., U.S. E7 129
New Lowell, Ont., Can. C5 103
New Madison, Oh., U.S. C1 142
New Madrid, Mo., U.S. E8 132
New Madrid, co., Mo., U.S. E8 132
Newman, Austl. D3 68
Newman, Ca., U.S. D3 112
Newman, Il., U.S. D6 120
New Manchester, W.V., U.S. e8 155
Newman Grove, Ne., U.S. C8 134
Newman Lake, l., Wa., U.S. B8 154
Newmanstown, Pa., U.S. F9 145
Newmarket, Ont., Can. C5 103
Newmarket, Ire. I4 8
Newmarket, Eng., U.K. I14 8
New Market, Al., U.S. A3 108
New Market, In., U.S. E4 121
New Market, Ia., U.S. D3 122
Newmarket, N.H., U.S. D5 136
New Market, Tn., U.S. C10 149
New Market, Va., U.S. B4 153
New Martinsville, W.V., U.S. B4 155
New Matamoras, Oh., U.S. C4 142
New Meadows, Id., U.S. D2 119
New Melle, Mo., U.S. C7 132
New Mexico, state, U.S. C3 138
New Miami, Oh., U.S. C1 142
New Milford, Ct., U.S. C2 114
New Milford, N.J., U.S. h8 137
New Milford, Pa., U.S. C10 145
New Mills, N.B., Can. B3 101
New Minden, Il., U.S. E4 120
New Munich, Mn., U.S. E4 130
New Munster, Wi., U.S. n11 156
Newnan, Ga., U.S. C2 117
Newnans Lake, l., Fl., U.S. C4 116
New Norfolk, Austl. N7 70
New Norway, Alta., Can. C4 98
New Offenburg, Mo., U.S. D7 132
New Orleans, La., U.S. E5 125
New Orleans Naval Air Station, mil., La., U.S. k11 125
New Oxford, Pa., U.S. G7 145
New Palestine, In., U.S. E6 121
New Paltz, N.Y., U.S. D6 139
New Paris, In., U.S. B6 121
New Paris, Oh., U.S. C1 142
New Perlican, Newf., Can. E5 102
New Philadelphia, Oh., U.S. B4 142
New Philadelphia, Pa., U.S. E9 145
New Plymouth, N.Z. C5 72
New Plymouth, Id., U.S. F2 119
New Point, In., U.S. F7 121
New Point Comfort, c., Va., U.S. C6 153
Newport, Wales, U.K. I9 8
Newport, Ar., U.S. B4 111
Newport, De., U.S. B3 115
Newport, In., U.S. E3 121
Newport, Ky., U.S. A5 124
Newport, Me., U.S. D3 126
Newport, Mi., U.S. G7 129
Newport, Mn., U.S. n13 130
Newport, Ne., U.S. B6 134
Newport, N.H., U.S. D2 136
Newport, N.C., U.S. C6 140
Newport, Oh., U.S. C4 142
Newport, Or., U.S. C2 144
Newport, Pa., U.S. F7 145
Newport, R.I., U.S. F5 146
Newport, Tn., U.S. D10 149
Newport, Vt., U.S. B4 152
Newport, Wa., U.S. A8 154
Newport, co., R.I., U.S. E5 146
Newport Beach, Ca., U.S. n13 112
New Portland, Me., U.S. D2 126
Newport News, Va., U.S. D6 153
Newport [-on-Tay], Scot., U.K. E11 8
New Port Richey, Fl., U.S. D4 116
Newport Station, N.S., Can. E5 101
New Prague, Mn., U.S. F5 130
New Preston, Ct., U.S. C2 114
New Providence, Ia., U.S. B4 122
New Providence, N.J., U.S. B4 137
New Providence, i., Bah. B6 94
New Richland, Mn., U.S. G5 130
New Richmond, Que., Can. A4 101
New Richmond, In., U.S. D4 121
New Richmond, Oh., U.S. D1 142
New Richmond, Wi., U.S. C1 156
New River, Az., U.S. D3 110
New River, Tn., U.S. C9 149
New River Gorge, val., W.V., U.S. m13 155
New River Inlet, b., N.C., U.S. C5 140
New Roads, La., U.S. D4 125
New Rochelle, N.Y., U.S. E7 139
New Rockford, N.D., U.S. B6 141
New Ross, N.S., Can. E5 101
New Ross, Ire. I7 8
New Ross, In., U.S. E4 121
Newry, N. Ire., U.K. G7 8
Newry, Me., U.S. D2 126
Newry, S.C., U.S. B2 147
New Salem, Il., U.S. D3 120
New Salem, In., U.S. E7 121
New Salem, N.D., U.S. C4 141
New Salisbury, In., U.S. H5 121
New Sarepta, Alta., Can. C4 98
New Sarpy, La., U.S. k11 125
New Schwabenland, reg., Ant. C2 73
New Sharon, Ia., U.S. C5 122
New Sharon, Me., U.S. D2 126
New Siberian Islands see Novosibirskoje ostrova, is., Russia B20 28
New Site, Al., U.S. B4 108
New Site, Ms., U.S. A5 131
New Smyrna Beach, Fl., U.S. C6 116
Newsoms, Va., U.S. D5 153
New South Wales, state, Austl. F9 68
New Straitsville, Oh., U.S. C3 142
New Tazewell, Tn., U.S. C10 149
Newtok, Ak., U.S. C6 109
Newton, Al., U.S. D4 108
Newton, Ga., U.S. E2 117
Newton, Il., U.S. E5 120
Newton, Ia., U.S. C4 122
Newton, Ks., U.S. D6 123
Newton, Ma., U.S. B5 128
Newton, Ms., U.S. C4 131
Newton, N.H., U.S. E4 136
Newton, N.J., U.S. A3 137
Newton, N.C., U.S. B1 140
Newton, Tx., U.S. D6 150
Newton, Ut., U.S. B4 151
Newton, co., Ar., U.S. B2 111
Newton, co., Ga., U.S. C3 117
Newton, co., In., U.S. B3 121
Newton, co., Ms., U.S. C4 131
Newton, co., Mo., U.S. E3 132
Newton, co., Tx., U.S. D6 150
Newton Abbot, Eng., U.K. K10 8
Newton Falls, Oh., U.S. A5 142
Newton Grove, N.C., U.S. B4 140
Newton Junction, N.H., U.S. E4 136
Newton Lake, res., Il., U.S. E5 120
Newton Stewart, Scot., U.K. G9 8
Newtonville, N.J., U.S. D3 137
Newtown, Newf., Can. D5 102
Newtown, Ct., U.S. D2 114
Newtown, In., U.S. D3 121
New Town, N.D., U.S. B3 141
Newtown, Oh., U.S. C1 142
Newtownabbey, N. Ire., U.K. G8 8
Newtown Square, Pa., U.S. p20 145
New Trenton, In., U.S. F8 121
New Ulm, Mn., U.S. F4 130
New Underwood, S.D., U.S. C3 148
New Vienna, Ia., U.S. B6 122
New Vienna, Oh., U.S. C2 142
Newville, Al., U.S. D4 108
Newville, Pa., U.S. F7 145
New Vineyard, Me., U.S. D2 126
New Virginia, Ia., U.S. C4 122
New Washington, In., U.S. G6 121
New Washington, Oh., U.S. B3 142
New Waterford, N.S., Can. C9 101
New Waterford, Oh., U.S. B5 142
New Waverly, Tx., U.S. D5 150
New Westminster, B.C., Can. E6 99
New Whiteland, In., U.S. E5 121
New Wilmington, Pa., U.S. D1 145
New Windsor, Il., U.S. B3 120
New Windsor, Md., U.S. A3 127
New Windsor, N.Y., U.S. D6 139
New World Island, i., Newf., Can. D4 102
New York, N.Y., U.S. E7 139
New York, co., N.Y., U.S. k13 139
New York, state, U.S. C6 139
New York Mills, Mn., U.S. D3 130
New Zealand, ctry., Oc. D4 72
Neyrīz, Iran G13 48
Neyshābūr, Iran C15 48
Nezahualcóyotl, Mex. H10 90
Nezahualcóyotl, Presa, res., Mex. I13 90
Nežin, Ukr. G4 26
Neznanovo, Russia G23 22
Nez Perce, co., Id., U.S. C2 119
Nez Perce Indian Reservation, Id., U.S. C2 119
Nezpique, Bayou, stm., La., U.S. D3 125
Ngami, Lake, l., Bots. C6 66
Ngamiland, dept., Bots. B6 66
Ngamo, Zimb. B8 66
Ngangla Ringco, l., China E10 44
Nganglong Kangri, mts., China D10 44
Ngaoundéré, Cam. G9 54
Ngezi Recreational Park, Zimb. B10 66
Ngoko, stm., Afr. A3 58
Ngolo, Cen. Afr. Rep. M2 60
Ngoring Hu, l., China E6 30
Ngotwane, stm., Afr. E8 66
Nguigmi, Niger F9 54
Nguiroungou, Cen. Afr. Rep. N2 60
Nguru, Nig. F9 54
Nhamundá, Braz. I14 84
Nhamundá, stm., Braz. H14 84
Nhandeara, Braz. F3 79
Nha Trang, Viet. H10 40
Nhill, Austl. K4 70
Niafounké, Mali D7 64
Niagara, Wi., U.S. C6 156
Niagara, co., N.Y., U.S. B2 139
Niagara Falls, Ont., Can. D5 103
Niagara Falls, N.Y., U.S. B1 139
Niagara-on-the-Lake, Ont., Can. D5 103
Niamey, Niger E11 64
Niangara, Zaire H6 56
Niangoloko, Burkina F7 64
Niangua, Mo., U.S. D5 132
Niangua, stm., Mo., U.S. D5 132

Nort-Offe

Name — Map Ref. — Page

North Thompson, stm., B.C., Can. D8 99
North Tonawanda, N.Y., U.S. B2 139
North Troy, Vt., U.S. B4 152
North Tunica, Ms., U.S. A3 131
North Turner Mountain, mtn., Me., U.S. C4 126
North Twin Lake, l., Wi., U.S. B4 156
North Uist, i., Scot., U.K. D6 8
Northumberland, Pa., U.S. E8 145
Northumberland, co., Eng., U.K. F11 8
Northumberland, co., Pa., U.S. D8 145
Northumberland, co., Va., U.S. C6 153
Northumberland Isles, is., Austl. C9 70
Northumberland Strait, strt., Can. C6 101
North Umpqua, stm., Or., U.S. D3 144
North Uxbridge, Ma., U.S. B4 128
Northvale, N.J., U.S. g9 137
North Vancouver, B.C., Can. E6 99
North Vassalboro, Me., U.S. D3 126
North Vernon, In., U.S. F6 121
Northview, Mo., U.S. D4 132
Northville, Ct., U.S. C2 114
Northville, Mi., U.S. p15 129
Northville, N.Y., U.S. B6 139
Northville, S.D., U.S. B7 148
North Waldoboro, Me., U.S. D3 126
North Wales, Pa., U.S. F11 145
North Walpole, N.H., U.S. D2 136
North Warren, Pa., U.S. C3 145
North Waterford, Me., U.S. D2 126
Northway, Ak., U.S. C11 109
North Webster, In., U.S. B6 121
North West Cape, c., Austl. D2 68
North Westchester, Ct., U.S. C6 114
North Westminster, Vt., U.S. E4 152
Northwest Miramichi, stm., N.B., Can. B3 101
Northwest Providence Channel, strt., Bah. A5 94
North West River, Newf., Can. B1 102
Northwest Territories, prov., Can. C12 96
North Wildwood, N.J., U.S. E3 137
North Wilkesboro, N.C., U.S. A1 140
North Windham, Ct., U.S. C7 114
North Windham, Me., U.S. E2 126
Northwood, Ia., U.S. A4 122
Northwood, N.H., U.S. D4 136
Northwood, N.D., U.S. B8 141
Northwood Center, N.H., U.S. D4 136
Northwood Ridge, N.H., U.S. D4 136
North Woodstock, N.H., U.S. B3 136
North York, Ont., Can. D5 103
North York, Pa., U.S. G8 145
North Yorkshire, co., Eng., U.K. G12 8
North Zulch, Tx., U.S. D4 150
Norton, N.B., Can. D4 101
Norton, Ks., U.S. C4 123
Norton, Ma., U.S. C5 128
Norton, Oh., U.S. A4 142
Norton, Va., U.S. f9 153
Norton, W.V., U.S. C5 155
Norton, co., Ks., U.S. C4 123
Norton Air Force Base, mil., Ca., U.S. E5 112
Norton Bay, b., Ak., U.S. C7 109
Norton Creek, stm., Al., U.S. B1 108
Norton Pond, l., Vt., U.S. B5 152
Norton Reservoir, res., Ks., U.S. C3 123
Nortons Corner, Az., U.S. D4 110
Norton Shores, Mi., U.S. E4 129
Norton Sound, strt., Ak., U.S. C6 109
Nortonville, Ks., U.S. C8 123
Nortonville, Ky., U.S. C2 124
Nortorf, Ger. A9 10
Norvegia, Cape, c., Ant. C2 73
Norwalk, Ca., U.S. n12 112
Norwalk, Ct., U.S. E2 114
Norwalk, Ia., U.S. C4 122
Norwalk, Oh., U.S. A3 142
Norwalk, Wi., U.S. E3 156
Norwalk, stm., Ct., U.S. E2 114
Norwalk Islands, is., Ct., U.S. E2 114
Norway, In., U.S. C4 121
Norway, Ia., U.S. C6 122
Norway, Me., U.S. D2 126
Norway, Mi., U.S. C3 129
Norway, S.C., U.S. E5 147
Norway (Norge), ctry., Eur. C10 4
Norway House, Man., Can. C3 100
Norway Lake, l., Mn., U.S. E3 130
Norwegian Sea, Eur. C1 24
Norwell, Ma., U.S. h12 128
Norwich, Eng., U.K. I15 8
Norwich, Ct., U.S. C7 114
Norwich, Ks., U.S. E6 123
Norwich, N.Y., U.S. C5 139
Norwich, N.D., U.S. A5 141
Norwich, Vt., U.S. D4 152
Norwood, Ont., Can. C7 103
Norwood, Co., U.S. C2 113
Norwood, Ga., U.S. C4 117
Norwood, La., U.S. D4 125
Norwood, Ma., U.S. B5 128
Norwood, Mn., U.S. F5 130
Norwood, Mo., U.S. D5 132
Norwood, N.J., U.S. h9 137
Norwood, N.Y., U.S. f10 139
Norwood, N.C., U.S. B2 140
Norwood, Oh., U.S. o13 142
Norwood, Pa., U.S. p20 145
Norwoodville, Ia., U.S. e8 122
Norwottock, Mount, mtn., Ma., U.S. B3 128
Noshiro, Japan G15 36
Nosop (Nossob), stm., Afr. E5 66
Nossa Senhora do Livramento, Braz. F13 82
Nossob (Nosop), stm., Afr. E5 66
Nosy Varika, Madag. r23 67b
Notasulga, Al., U.S. C4 108
Notch Mountain, mtn., Ma., U.S. A3 128
Notch Peak, mtn., Ut., U.S. D2 151
Noteć, stm., Pol. C15 10
Notikewin, Alta., Can. A2 98
Noto, Italy M10 18
Notodden, Nor. L11 6
Noto-hantō, pen., Japan J11 36
Notozero, ozero, l., Russia H23 6
Notre Dame, Monts, mts., Que., Can. k13 104
Notre Dame Bay, b., Newf., Can. D4 102
Notre Dame de Lourdes, Man., Can. E2 100
Notre-Dame-des-Bois, Que., Can. D6 104
Notre-Dame-du-Lac, Que., Can. B9 104
Notre-Dame-du-Laus, Que., Can. C2 104
Nottawa, Ont., Can. C4 103
Nottawasaga Bay, b., Ont., Can. C4 103
Nottaway, stm., Que., Can. h11 104
Nottely Lake, res., Ga., U.S. B2 117
Nottingham, Eng., U.K. I12 8
Nottingham, N.H., U.S. D4 136
Nottingham Island, i., N.W. Ter., Can. D17 96
Nottinghamshire, co., Eng., U.K. H12 8
Nottoway, co., Va., U.S. C4 153
Nottoway, stm., Va., U.S. D5 153
Notus, Id., U.S. F2 119
Nouâdhibou, Maur. J2 62
Nouâdhibou, Râs, c., Afr. J2 62
Nouakchott, Maur. B2 64
Nouâmghâr, Maur. B1 64
Nouméa, N. Cal. H24 2
Nouna, Burkina E8 64
Noupoort, S. Afr. H7 66
Nova América, Braz. C4 79
Nova Andradina, Braz. G2 79
Nova Caipemba, Ang. C2 58
Nova Era, Braz. E7 79
Nova Esperança, Braz. G2 79
Nova Friburgo, Braz. G7 79
Nova Gradiška, Cro. D12 18
Nova Granada, Braz. F4 79
Nova Iguaçu, Braz. G7 79
Novaja Ivanovka, Ukr. D13 20
Novaja Kachovka, Ukr. H4 26
Novaja Kazanka, Kaz. H7 26
Novaja Ladoga, Russia A15 22
Novaja Sibir', ostrov, i., Russia B21 28
Novaja Zeml'a, is., Russia C9 26
Nova Lamego, Gui.-B. E2 64
Nova Lima, Braz. E7 79
Nova Mambone, Moz. C12 66
Nova Olinda do Norte, Braz. I13 84
Nova Ponte, Braz. E5 79
Nova Prata, Braz. E13 80
Novar, Ont., Can. B5 103
Novara, Italy D3 18
Nova Roma, Braz. B5 79
Nova Scotia, prov., Can. D6 101
Nova Sofala, Moz. C12 66
Novato, Ca., U.S. C2 112
Nova Varoš, Yugo. F3 20
Nova Venécia, Braz. E8 79
Nova Vida, Braz. D10 82
Nova Vida, Cachoeira, wtfl, Braz. C10 82
Nova Zagora, Bul. G10 20
Novelda, Spain G11 16
Nové Zámky, Slov. H18 10
Novgorod, Russia C14 22
Novi, Mi., U.S. p15 129
Novi Bečej, Yugo. D4 20
Novigrad, Cro. E10 18
Novi Ligure, Italy E3 18
Novinger, Mo., U.S. A5 132
Novi Pazar, Bul. F11 20
Novi Pazar, Yugo. F4 20
Novi Sad, Yugo. D3 20
Novki, Russia E24 22
Novl'anka, Russia F24 22
Novlenskoje, Russia B22 22
Novo, stm., Braz. A6 82
Nôvo Acôrdo, Braz. B5 79
Novoaltajsk, Russia G8 28
Novoanninskij, Russia G6 26
Novo Aripuanã, Braz. J12 84
Novo Brasil, Braz. D3 79
Novočerkassk, Russia H6 26
Novo Cruzeiro, Braz. D8 79
Novodugino, Russia F17 22
Novodvinsk, Russia E6 26
Novograd-Volynskij, Ukr. G3 26
Novogrudok, Bela. H8 22
Novo Hamburgo, Braz. E13 80
Novo Horizonte, Braz. F4 79
Novoizborsk, Russia D10 22
Novoje Leušino, Russia E23 22
Novojel'n'a, Bela. H8 22
Novokaširsk, Russia G21 22
Novokazalinsk, Kaz. H10 26
Novokujbyševsk, Russia G7 26
Novokuzneck, Russia G9 28
Novol'vovsk, Russia H21 22
Novo Mesto, Slo. D10 18
Novomoskovsk, Russia G21 22
Novomoskovsk, Ukr. H5 26
Novopetrovskoje, Russia F19 22
Novopiscovo, Russia D24 22
Novopolock, Bela. F11 22
Novorossijsk, Russia I5 26
Novorybnoje, Russia C13 28
Novoržev, Russia D12 22
Novošachtinsk, Russia H5 26
Novoselica, Ukr. A10 20
Novosel'skoje, Ukr. D12 20
Novosibirsk, Russia F8 28
Novosibirskije ostrova, is., Russia B20 28
Novosibirskoje vodochranilišče, res., Russia G14 26
Novosil', Russia I20 22
Novosokol'niki, Russia E13 22
Novos'olki, Russia G22 22
Novotroick, Russia G9 26
Novouzensk, Russia G7 26
Novov'atsk, Russia F7 26
Novov'azniki, Russia E25 22
Novovolynsk, Ukr. G2 26
Novozavidovskij, Russia E19 22
Novozybkov, Russia I14 22
Novska, Cro. D11 18
Nový Bohumín, Czech. F18 10
Nový Jičín, Czech. F18 10
Novyj Nekouz, Russia D21 22
Novyj Ropsk, Russia I15 22
Nowa Ruda, Pol. E16 10
Nowa Sól (Neusalz), Pol. D15 10
Nowata, Ok., U.S. A6 143
Nowata, co., Ok., U.S. A6 143
Nowogród, Pol. H4 22
Nowogrodziec, Pol. D15 10
Nowood, stm., Wy., U.S. B5 157
Nowra, Austl. J9 70
Nowshāk, mtn., Asia B4 44
Nowshera, Pak. C4 44
Nowy Dwór Mazowiecki, Pol. C20 10
Nowy Sącz, Pol. F20 10
Nowy Targ, Pol. F20 10
Noxapater, Ms., U.S. C4 131
Noxen, Pa., U.S. D9 145
Noxon, Mt., U.S. C1 133
Noxon Reservoir, res., Mt., U.S. C1 133
Noxontown Lake, res., De., U.S. C3 115
Noxubee, co., Ms., U.S. B5 131
Noxubee, stm., U.S. B5 131
Noyes Island, i., Ak., U.S. n22 109
Noyon, Fr. C10 14
Nsanje, Mwi. E7 58
Nsawam, Ghana I9 64
Nsukka, Nig. H13 64
Ntakat, Maur. C4 64
Ntem, stm., Afr. H9 54
N'Tsaoueni, Com. k15 67a
Ntwetwe Pan, pl., Bots. C7 66
Nuanetsi, stm., Afr. C10 66
Nuanli, China C6 40
Nūbah, Jibāl an-, mts., Sud. L6 60
Nubanusit Lake, l., N.H., U.S. E2 136
Nuberg, Ga., U.S. B4 117
Nubian Desert, des., Sud. G8 60
Ñuble, stm., Chile I3 80
Nucet, Rom. C6 20
N'uchča, Russia E7 26
Nuckolls, co., Ne., U.S. D7 134
Nucla, Co., U.S. C2 113
Nucuray, stm., Peru J5 84
Nueces, co., Tx., U.S. F4 150
Nueces, stm., Tx., U.S. E3 150
Nueltin Lake, l., Can. D13 96
Nuestra Señora de Talavera, Arg. C7 80
Nueva, Isla, i., Chile H3 78
Nueva Antioquia, Col. D8 84
Nueva Asunción, dept., Para. I11 82
Nueva Ciudad Guerrero, Mex. D10 90
Nueva Concepción, El Sal. C5 92
Nueva Esparta, state, Ven. B10 84
Nueva Francia, Arg. E6 80
Nueva Galia, Arg. H6 80
Nueva Germania, Para. B10 80
Nueva Gerona, Cuba D3 94
Nueva Helvecia, Ur. H10 80
Nueva Imperial, Chile J2 80
Nueva Italia de Ruiz, Mex. H8 90
Nueva Ocotepeque, Hond. C5 92
Nueva Palmira, Ur. G9 80
Nueva Rosita, Mex. D9 90
Nueva San Salvador, El Sal. D5 92
Nueva Segovia, dept., Nic. D8 92
Nueva Venecia, Guat. C3 92
Nueve, Canal Numero, Arg. I9 80
Nueve de Julio, Arg. H8 80
Nuevitas, Cuba D6 94
Nuevo, Bajo, Col. G5 94
Nuevo, Cayo, i., Mex. G13 90
Nuevo Berlín, Ur. G9 80
Nuevo Casas Grandes, Mex. B6 90
Nuevo Chagres, Pan. H14 92
Nuevo Delicias, Mex. D8 90
Nuevo Laredo, Mex. D10 90
Nuevo León, state, Mex. D9 90
Nuevo Progreso, Mex. H13 90
Nuevo Rocafuerte, Ec. H5 84
Nuia, Est. C8 22
Nuits-Saint-Georges, Fr. E11 14
N'uja, stm., Russia E14 28
N'uk, ozero, l., Russia I22 6
Nukey Bluff, clf, Austl. I1 70
Nukus, Uzb. I9 26
Nulato, Ak., U.S. C8 109
Nulhegan, stm., Vt., U.S. B5 152
Nullagine, Austl. D4 68
Nullarbor National Park, Austl. F6 68
Nullarbor Plain, pl., Austl. F5 68
Numazu, Japan L13 36
Numila, Hi., U.S. B2 118
Numurkah, Austl. K6 70
Nunda, N.Y., U.S. C3 139
Nunez, Ga., U.S. D4 117
Nunica, Mi., U.S. E4 129
Nunivak Island, i., Ak., U.S. D6 109
Nunjiang, China B12 30
Nunkini, Mex. G14 90
Nunn, Co., U.S. A6 113
Nunnelly, Tn., U.S. B4 149
Nuomin, stm., China B11 30
Nuon, stm., Afr. H5 64
Nuoro, Italy I4 18
Nuquí, Col. E4 84
Nura, stm., Kaz. G12 26
N'urba, Russia E15 28
Nürburgring, Ger. H10 12
Nurek, Taj. A3 44
Nuremberg, Pa., U.S. E9 145
Nuremberg see Nürnberg, Ger. F11 10
Nürnberg (Nuremberg), Ger. F11 10
Nurri, Italy J4 18
Nurri, Mount, hill, Austl. H7 70
Nürtingen, Ger. G9 10
Nūsah, Yemen G5 47
Nusaybin, Tur. C6 48
Nu Shan, mts., China F6 30
Nushki, Pak. F2 44
Nutley, N.J., U.S. B4 137
Nutrioso, Az., U.S. D6 110
Nutter Fort, W.V., U.S. k10 155
Nutting Lake, Ma., U.S. f10 128
Nuuanu Pali, Hi., U.S. g10 118
Nuwaybiʿ al-Muzayyinah, Egypt C8 60
Nuwerus, S. Afr. H4 66
Nxainxai, Bots. B5 66
Nxai Pan National Park, Bots. B7 66
Nxaunxau, Bots. B5 66
Nyaake, Lib. I6 64
Nyabing, Austl. F3 68
Nyack, N.Y., U.S. D7 139
Nyah West, Austl. J5 70
Nyainqêntanglha Shan, mts., China E13 44
Nyakrom, Ghana I9 64
Nyala, Sud. K3 60
Nyamandhlovu, Zimb. B9 66
Nyamina, Mali E6 64
Nyamlell, Sud. M4 60
Nyanza, Rw. B5 58
Nyasa, Lake (Lake Malawi), l., Afr. D6 58
Nyasaland see Malawi, ctry., Afr. D6 58
Nyaunglebin, Burma F4 40
Nybergsund, Nor. K13 6
Nye, co., Nv., U.S. E5 135
Nyiel, Sud. N6 60
Nyíradony, Hung. H21 10
Nyírbátor, Hung. H22 10
Nyíregyháza, Hung. H21 10
Nykøbing, Den. N12 6
Nykøbing, Den. M11 6
Nyköping, Swe. L15 6
Nylstroom, S. Afr. E9 66
Nymburk, Czech. E15 10
Nynäshamn, Swe. L15 6
Nyngan, Austl. H7 70
Nyon, Switz. F5 13
Nyong, stm., Cam. H9 54
Nýrsko, Czech. F13 10
Nysa, Pol. E17 10
Nysa Łużycka (Neisse) (Nisa), stm., Eur. D14 10
Nyssa, Or., U.S. D9 144
Nytva, Russia F9 26
Nzébéla, Gui. G5 64
Nzérékoré, Gui. H5 64
N'zeto, Ang. C2 58
Nzi, stm., I.C. H7 64
Nzwani (Anjouan), i., Com. I16 67a

O

Oacoma, S.D., U.S. D6 148
Oahe, Lake, res., U.S. B6 106
Oahe Dam, S.D., U.S. C5 148
Oahu, i., Hi., U.S. B4 118
Oakbank, Austl. I4 70
Oak Bay, B.C., Can. h12 99
Oak Bay, N.B., Can. D2 101
Oak Bluffs, Ma., U.S. D6 128
Oakboro, N.C., U.S. B2 140
Oakburn, Man., Can. D1 100
Oak City, Ut., U.S. D3 151
Oak Creek, Co., U.S. A4 113
Oak Creek, Wi., U.S. n12 156
Oakdale, Ca., U.S. D3 112
Oakdale, Ct., U.S. D7 114
Oakdale, Ga., U.S. h8 117
Oakdale, La., U.S. D3 125
Oakdale, Ne., U.S. B8 134
Oakdale, Pa., U.S. k13 145
Oakdale, Tn., U.S. D9 149
Oakes, N.D., U.S. C7 141
Oakesdale, Wa., U.S. B8 154
Oakey, Austl. F9 70
Oakfield, Ga., U.S. E3 117
Oakfield, Me., U.S. B4 126
Oakfield, N.Y., U.S. B2 139
Oakfield, Wi., U.S. E5 156
Oakford, Il., U.S. C4 120
Oakford, In., U.S. D5 121
Oak Forest, Il., U.S. k9 120
Oak Grove, Ar., U.S. A2 111
Oak Grove, Ky., U.S. D2 124
Oak Grove, La., U.S. B4 125
Oak Grove, Mo., U.S. B3 132
Oak Grove, Or., U.S. B4 144
Oak Grove Heights, Ar., U.S. A5 111
Oak Harbor, Oh., U.S. A2 142
Oak Harbor, Wa., U.S. A3 154
Oak Hill, Fl., U.S. D6 116
Oak Hill, Mi., U.S. D4 129
Oak Hill, Oh., U.S. D3 142
Oak Hill, Tn., U.S. A5 149
Oak Hill, W.V., U.S. D3 155
Oak Hill, mtn., Ma., U.S. f9 128
Oakhurst, N.J., U.S. C4 137
Oakhurst, Ok., U.S. A5 143
Oak Island, i., Wi., U.S. B3 156
Oak Lake, Man., Can. E1 100
Oak Lake, l., Man., Can. E1 100
Oakland, Ont., Can. D4 103
Oakland, Al., U.S. A2 108
Oakland, Ca., U.S. D2 112
Oakland, Il., U.S. D5 120
Oakland, Ia., U.S. C2 122
Oakland, Ky., U.S. C3 124
Oakland, Me., U.S. D3 126
Oakland, Md., U.S. m12 127
Oakland, Ms., U.S. A4 131
Oakland, Ne., U.S. C9 134
Oakland, N.J., U.S. A4 137
Oakland, Ok., U.S. C5 143
Oakland, Or., U.S. D3 144
Oakland, Pa., U.S. C10 145
Oakland, R.I., U.S. B2 146
Oakland, Tn., U.S. B2 149
Oakland, co., Mi., U.S. F7 129
Oakland City, In., U.S. H3 121
Oakland Park, Fl., U.S. r13 116
Oak Lawn, Il., U.S. B6 120
Oaklawn, Ks., U.S. g12 123
Oaklawn, La., U.S. h12 125
Oakley, Id., U.S. G5 119
Oakley, Ks., U.S. C3 123
Oakley, Mi., U.S. E6 129
Oakley, Ms., U.S. C3 131
Oakley, Ut., U.S. C4 151
Oakman, Al., U.S. B2 108
Oakman, Ga., U.S. B2 117
Oakmont, Pa., U.S. E2 145
Oak Mountain, mtn., Ga., U.S. D2 117
Oak Mountain, mtn., Tn., U.S. h11 149
Oak Orchard, De., U.S. F5 115
Oak Park, Ga., U.S. D4 117
Oak Park, Il., U.S. B6 120
Oak Park, Mi., U.S. p15 129
Oak Point, Man., Can. D3 100
Oak Ridge, Mo., U.S. D8 132
Oak Ridge, N.C., U.S. A3 140
Oakridge, Or., U.S. D4 144
Oak Ridge, Tn., U.S. C9 149
Oak Ridge Reservoir, res., N.J., U.S. A3 137
Oak River, Man., Can. D1 100
Oaks, Ok., U.S. A7 143
Oaks, Pa., U.S. o20 145
Oakton, Ky., U.S. f8 124
Oakton, Va., U.S. g12 153
Oaktown, In., U.S. G3 121
Oak Vale, Ms., U.S. D4 131
Oak Valley, N.J., U.S. D2 137
Oakville, Man., Can. E2 100
Oakville, Ont., Can. D5 103
Oakville, Ct., U.S. C3 114
Oakville, In., U.S. D7 121
Oakville, Ia., U.S. C6 122
Oakville, Mo., U.S. g13 132
Oakville, Wa., U.S. C2 154
Oakwood, Ga., U.S. B3 117
Oakwood, Il., U.S. C6 120
Oakwood, N.D., U.S. A8 141
Oakwood, Oh., U.S. A1 142
Oakwood, Oh., U.S. C1 142
Oakwood, Tx., U.S. D5 150
Oakwood, Va., U.S. e10 153
Oamaru, N.Z. F3 72
Oancea, Rom. D12 20
Oark, Ar., U.S. B2 111
Oatlands, Austl. N7 70
Oatman, Az., U.S. C1 110
Oaxaca, state, Mex. I11 90
Oaxaca [de Juárez], Mex. I11 90
Ob', stm., Russia D11 26
Obama, Japan L10 36
Oban, Austl. C3 70
Oban, Nig. I14 64
Oban, Scot., U.K. E8 8
Obed, Alta., Can. C2 98
Obed, stm., Tn., U.S. C9 149
Obeliai, Lith. F8 22
Oberá, Arg. D11 80
Oberdrauburg, Aus. I12 10
Obergurgl, Aus. I11 10
Oberhausen, Ger. D6 10
Oberlin, Ks., U.S. C3 123
Oberlin, La., U.S. D3 125
Oberlin, Oh., U.S. A3 142
Obernai, Fr. D14 14
Obernburg am Main, Ger. F9 10
Oberon, Austl. I8 70
Oberon, N.D., U.S. B6 141
Oberösterreich, state, Aus. G13 10
Oberpullendorf, Aus. H16 10
Obertin, Ukr. A9 20
Oberursel, Ger. E8 10
Obervellach, Aus. I13 10
Oberwart, Aus. H16 10
Obetz, Oh., U.S. C3 142
Obi, Nig. G14 64
Obi, Kepulauan, is., Indon. F8 38
Obiaruku, Nig. I13 64
Óbidos, Braz. D7 76
Obihiro, Japan e18 36a
Obilatu, Pulau, i., Indon. F8 38
Obing, Ger. G12 10
Obion, Tn., U.S. A2 149
Obion, co., Tn., U.S. A2 149
Obion, stm., Tn., U.S. A2 149
Obion, Middle Fork, stm., Tn., U.S. A3 149
Obion, Rutherford Fork, stm., Tn., U.S. A3 149
Obion, South Fork, stm., Tn., U.S. A3 149
Obion Creek, stm., Ky., U.S. f9 124
Oblong, Il., U.S. D6 120
Oblučje, Russia H18 28
Obninsk, Russia F19 22
Obock, Dji. F9 56
Obol', Bela. F12 22
Oborniki, Pol. C16 10
Oboz'orskij, Russia J27 6
O'Brien, Or., U.S. E3 144
O'Brien, co., Ia., U.S. A2 122
Obščij Syrt, mtn., Asia G8 26
Observation Peak, mtn., Ca., U.S. B3 112
Obskaja guba, b., Russia D12 26
Obuasi, Ghana H9 64
Obuchova, Russia E15 22
Obžericha, Russia D25 22
Ocala, Fl., U.S. C4 116
Ocallí, Peru B2 82
Ocamo, stm., Ven. F10 84
Ocampo, Mex. C5 90
Ocampo, Mex. D8 90
Ocaña, Col. C6 84
Occidental, Cordillera, mts., Col. E4 84
Occidental, Cordillera, mts., Peru C3 82
Occoquan, Va., U.S. B5 153
Ocean, co., N.J., U.S. D4 137
Oceana, W.V., U.S. D3 155
Oceana, co., Mi., U.S. E4 129
Oceana Naval Air Station, mil., Va., U.S. k15 153
Ocean Bluff, Ma., U.S. B6 128
Ocean City, Fl., U.S. u15 116
Ocean City, Md., U.S. D7 127
Ocean City, N.J., U.S. E3 137
Ocean City, Wa., U.S. B1 154
Ocean Gate, N.J., U.S. D4 137
Ocean Grove, Ma., U.S. C5 128
Ocean Grove, N.J., U.S. C4 137
Ocean Park, Wa., U.S. C1 154
Ocean Pines, Md., U.S. D7 127
Oceanport, N.J., U.S. C4 137
Oceanside, Ca., U.S. F5 112
Ocean Springs, Ms., U.S. E5 131
Ocean [Township], N.J., U.S. C4 137
Ocean View, De., U.S. F5 115
Oceanville, N.J., U.S. E4 137
Ocha, Russia G20 28
Ocheda Lake, l., Mn., U.S. G3 130
Ochelata, Ok., U.S. A6 143
Ocheyedan, Ia., U.S. A2 122
Ocheyedan, stm., Ia., U.S. A2 122
Ochiltree, co., Tx., U.S. A2 150
Ochlocknee, Ga., U.S. F2 117
Ochlockonee, stm., Fl., U.S. B2 116
Ochoco Lake, res., Or., U.S. C6 144
Ochopee, Fl., U.S. G5 116
Ocho Rios, Jam. E6 94
Ochota, stm., Russia F20 28
Ochotsk, Russia F20 28
Ochre River, Man., Can. D2 100
Ochsenfurt, Ger. F10 10
Ochvat, Russia E15 22
Ocilla, Ga., U.S. E3 117
Ocmulgee, stm., Ga., U.S. D3 117
Ocmulgee National Monument, Ga., U.S. D3 117
Ocoa, Bahía de, b., Dom. Rep. E9 94
Ocoee, Fl., U.S. D5 116
Ocoee, Tn., U.S. D9 149
Ocoee, Lake, res., Tn., U.S. D9 149
Ocoña, Peru G5 82
Ocoña, stm., Peru G5 82
Oconee, Ga., U.S. D4 117
Oconee, Il., U.S. D4 120
Oconee, co., Ga., U.S. C3 117
Oconee, co., S.C., U.S. B1 147
Oconee, stm., Ga., U.S. C3 117
Oconee, Lake, res., Ga., U.S. C3 117
Ocongate, Peru E6 82
Oconomowoc, Wi., U.S. E5 156
Oconto, Ne., U.S. C6 134
Oconto, Wi., U.S. D6 156
Oconto, co., Wi., U.S. D5 156
Oconto, stm., Wi., U.S. D5 156
Oconto Falls, Wi., U.S. D5 156
Ocós, Guat. C2 92
Ocosingo, Mex. I13 90
Ocotal, Nic. D8 92
Ocotepeque, dept., Hond. C5 92
Ocotillo, Az., U.S. m9 110
Ocotlán, Mex. G8 90
Ocotlán de Morelos, Mex. I11 90
Ocozocoautla [de Espinosa], Mex. I13 90
Ocracoke, N.C., U.S. B7 140
Ocracoke Inlet, b., N.C., U.S. B6 140
Ocracoke Island, i., N.C., U.S. B7 140
Ocros, Peru D3 82
Octavia, Ne., U.S. C8 134
Octoraro Creek, stm., U.S. A5 127
Ocú, Pan. J14 92
Ocumare del Tuy, Ven. B9 84
Ocuri, Bol. H9 82
Ocussi, Indon. A4 68
Oda, Ghana I9 64
Oda, Jabal, mtn., Sud. G9 60
Odanakumadona, Bots. C7 66
Ōdate, Japan G15 36
Odawara, Japan L14 36
Odda, Nor. K10 6
Odebolt, Ia., U.S. B2 122
Odei, stm., Man., Can. A3 100
Odell, Il., U.S. B5 120
Odell, Ne., U.S. D9 134
Odell, Or., U.S. B5 144
Odell Lake, l., Or., U.S. E5 144
Odem, Tx., U.S. F4 150
Ödemiş, Tur. K11 20
Oden, Ar., U.S. C2 111
Odendaalsrus, S. Afr. F8 66
Odense, Den. N12 6
Odenton, Md., U.S. B4 127
Odenville, Al., U.S. B3 108
Oder (Odra), stm., Eur. C14 10
Oderberg, Ger. C14 10
Oderhaff (Zalew Szczeciński), b., Eur. B14 10
Oderzo, Italy D7 18
Odessa, Ont., Can. C8 103
Odessa, Sask., Can. G4 105
Odessa, Ukr. H4 26
Odessa, De., U.S. C3 115
Odessa, Mn., U.S. E2 130
Odessa, Mo., U.S. C4 132
Odessa, Ne., U.S. D6 134
Odessa, N.Y., U.S. C4 139
Odessa, Tx., U.S. D1 150
Odessa, Wa., U.S. B7 154
Odesskoje, Russia G12 26
Odiakwe, Bots. C7 66
Odib, Wādī, val., Afr. F9 60
Odienné, I.C. G6 64
Odin, Il., U.S. E4 120
Odin, Ks., U.S. D5 123
Odincovo, Russia F20 22
Odojev, Russia H19 22
Odon, In., U.S. G4 121
O'Donnell, Tx., U.S. C2 150
Odorheiu Secuiesc, Rom. C9 20
Odum, Ga., U.S. E4 117
Odzi, Zimb. B11 66
Oebisfelde, Ger. C10 10
Oeiras, Braz. E10 76
Oelde, Ger. D8 10
Oelrichs, S.D., U.S. D2 148
Oelsnitz, Ger. E12 10
Oelwein, Ia., U.S. B6 122
Oesterdam, Neth. F5 12
Oettingen in Bayern, Ger. G10 10
Oetz, Aus. H10 10
Ofahoma, Ms., U.S. C4 131
O'Fallon, Il., U.S. E4 120
O'Fallon, Mo., U.S. f12 132
O'Fallon Creek, stm., Mt., U.S. D12 133
Ofaqim, Isr. F3 50
Offa, Nig. G12 64
Offaly, co., Ire. H6 8
Offenbach, Ger. E8 10
Offenburg, Ger. G7 10
Offerle, Ks., U.S. E4 123

Name	Map Ref.	Page

Name — Map Ref. — Page

Paxton, Ma., U.S. B4 128
Paxton, Ne., U.S. C4 134
Paya, Hond. B9 92
Payakumbuh, Indon. O6 40
Payas, Cerro, mtn., Hond. B9 92
Payerne, Switz. E6 13
Payette, Id., U.S. E2 119
Payette, co., Id., U.S. E2 119
Payette, North Fork, stm., Id., U.S. E2 119
Payette, South Fork, stm., Id., U.S. E3 119
Payette Lake, res., Id., U.S. E3 119
Payne, Ga., U.S. D3 117
Payne, Oh., U.S. A1 142
Payne, co., Ok., U.S. A4 143
Payne, Lac, l., Que., Can. g12 104
Payne Bay, b., Can. D19 96
Paynesville, Mn., U.S. E4 130
Payneville, Ky., U.S. C3 124
Paynton, Sask., Can. D1 105
Paysandú, Ur. H9 74
Paysandú, Ur. G9 80
Payson, Az., U.S. C4 110
Payson, Il., U.S. D2 120
Payson, Ut., U.S. C4 151
Payún, Cerro, mtn., Arg. I4 80
Paz, stm., N.A. D4 92
Pazardžik, Bul. G8 20
Pazarköy, Tur. J11 20
Paz de Ariporo, Col. E7 84
Paz de Río, Col. E6 84
P'ažijeva Sel'ga, Russia K24 6
Pazin, Cro. D8 18
Pazña, Bol. H8 82
Pea, stm., Al., U.S. D3 108
Peabody, Ks., U.S. D6 123
Peabody, Ma., U.S. A6 128
Peabody, stm., N.H., U.S. B4 136
Peace, stm., Can. E10 96
Peace, stm., Fl., U.S. E5 116
Peace Dale, R.I., U.S. F3 146
Peace River, Alta., Can. A2 98
Peach, co., Ga., U.S. D3 117
Peacham, Vt., U.S. C4 152
Peacham Pond, res., Vt., U.S. C4 152
Peach Creek, W.V., U.S. D5 155
Peach Orchard, Ar., U.S. A5 111
Peach Orchard Knob, mtn., Ky., U.S. C3 124
Peach Point, c., Ma., U.S. f12 128
Peach Springs, Az., U.S. B2 110
Peaked Mountain, mtn., Me., U.S. B4 126
Peak Hill, Austl. E3 68
Peak Hill, Austl. I8 70
Peaks Island, i., Me., U.S. g7 126
Peale, Mount, mtn., Ut., U.S. E6 151
Pea Patch Island, i., De., U.S. B3 115
Pearcy, Ar., U.S. C2 111
Pea Ridge, Ar., U.S. A1 111
Pea Ridge National Military Park, Ar., U.S. A1 111
Pearisburg, Va., U.S. C2 153
Pearl, Ms., U.S. C3 131
Pearl, stm., U.S. D3 131
Pearland, Tx., U.S. r14 150
Pearl and Hermes Reef, rf., Hi., U.S. k12 118
Pearl City, Hi., U.S. B4 118
Pearl City, Il., U.S. A4 120
Pearl Harbor, b., Hi., U.S. B3 118
Pearl Harbor Naval Station, mil., Hi., U.S. g10 118
Pearlington, Ms., U.S. E4 131
Pearl River, La., U.S. D6 125
Pearl River, N.Y., U.S. g12 139
Pearl River, co., Ms., U.S. E4 131
Pearsall, Tx., U.S. E3 150
Pearsoll Peak, mtn., Or., U.S. E3 144
Pearson, Ga., U.S. E4 117
Pearston, S. Afr. I7 66
Peary Land, reg., Grnld. A16 86
Pease, Mn., U.S. E5 130
Pease, stm., Tx., U.S. B3 150
Pease Air Force Base, mil., N.H., U.S. D5 136
Pebane, Moz. E7 58
Pebas, Peru I7 84
Peć, Yugo. G4 20
Peçanha, Braz. E7 79
Peças, Ilha das, i., Braz. C14 80
Pecatonica, Il., U.S. A4 120
Pecatonica, stm., U.S. A4 120
Pecatonica, East Branch, stm., Wi., U.S. F4 156
Pečenežin, Ukr. A8 20
Pečenga, Russia D4 26
Pechora see Pečora, stm., Russia D8 26
Pecica, Rom. C5 20
Peck, Id., U.S. C2 119
Peck, Ks., U.S. E6 123
Peck, Mi., U.S. E8 129
Peckerwood Lake, res., Ar., U.S. C4 111
Pečora, Russia D9 26
Pečora, stm., Russia D8 26
Pečorskaja guba, b., Russia D8 26
Pečorskoje more, Russia D8 26
Pečory, Russia D10 22
Pecos, N.M., U.S. B4 138
Pecos, Tx., U.S. D1 150
Pecos, co., Tx., U.S. D1 150
Pecos, stm., U.S. E6 106
Pecos National Monument, N.M., U.S. B4 138
Pécs, Hung. I18 10
Peculiar, Mo., U.S. C3 132
Pedasí, Pan. D2 84
Peddāpuram, India D7 46
Pedder, Lake, res., Austl. N7 70
Peddocks Island, i., Ma., U.S. g12 128
Pedernales, Arg. H9 80
Pedernales, Dom. Rep. E9 94
Pedernales, Ven. C11 84
Pedernales, Salar de, pl., Chile D4 80
Pedra Azul, Braz. D8 79
Pedra Grande, Recifes da, rf., Braz. D9 79
Pedra Lume, C.V. k17 64a
Pedras, Braz. I14 84
Pedras Negras, Braz. E10 82
Pedraza, Col. B5 84
Pedregal, Pan. C1 84
Pedregal, Ven. B7 84
Pedregulho, Braz. F5 79
Pedreiras, Braz. D10 76
Pedriceña, Mex. E8 90
Pedricktown, N.J., U.S. D2 137
Pedro Afonso, Braz. E9 76
Pedro Cays, is., Jam. F6 94
Pedrógão Grande, Port. F3 16
Pedro Gomes, Braz. E1 79
Pedro II, Braz. D10 76
Pedro II, Ilha, i., S.A. G9 84
Pedro Juan Caballero, Para. B11 80
Pedro Leopoldo, Braz. E6 79
Pedro Luro, Arg. J7 80
Pedro Muñoz, Spain F9 16
Pedro Osório, Braz. F12 80
Pedro R. Fernández, Arg. E9 80
Peebinga, Austl. J4 70
Peebles, Oh., U.S. D2 142
Peekaboo Mountain, hill, Me., U.S. C5 126
Peekskill, N.Y., U.S. D7 139
Peel, N.B., Can. C2 101
Peel, I. of Man G9 8
Peel, stm., Can. C5 96
Pe Ell, Wa., U.S. C2 154
Peel Point, c., N.W. Ter., Can. B10 96
Peel Sound, strt., N.W. Ter., Can. B13 96
Peene, stm., Ger. B13 10
Peerless, Mt., U.S. B11 133
Peers, Alta., Can. C3 98
Peetz, Co., U.S. A7 113
Peever, S.D., U.S. B9 148
Pegan Hill, hill, Ma., U.S. g10 128
Pegasus Bay, b., N.Z. E4 72
Pegnitz, Ger. F11 10
Pegnitz, stm., Ger. F11 10
Pego, Spain G11 16
Pegram, Tn., U.S. A4 149
Pegu see Bago, Burma F4 40
Pegu Yoma, mts., Burma E3 40
Pehčevo, Mac. H6 20
Pehuajó, Arg. H8 80
Peikang, Tai. L9 34
Peine, Ger. C10 10
Peipus, Lake see Čudskoje ozero, l., Eur. C10 22
Peissenberg, Ger. H11 10
Peixe, Braz. B4 79
Peixe, Rio do, stm., Braz. C3 79
Peixe, Rio do, stm., Braz. G3 79
Peixian, China E10 30
Peiziyan, China H3 32
Pejepscot, Me., U.S. E2 126
Pekalongan, Indon. j14 39a
Pekanbaru, Indon. N6 40
Pekin, Il., U.S. C4 120
Pekin, In., U.S. G5 121
Pekin, N.D., U.S. B7 141
Peking see Beijing, China D4 32
Peklino, Russia H16 22
Pelabuhan Kelang, Malay. M6 40
Pelagie, Isole, is., Italy N7 18
Pelahatchie, Ms., U.S. C4 131
Pełczyce, Pol. B15 10
Peleaga, Vîrful, mtn., Rom. D6 20
Pelechuco, Bol. F7 82
Pelée, Montagne, mtn., Mart. G14 94
Pelee Island, i., Ont., Can. F2 103
Pelham, Ont., Can. D5 103
Pelham, Al., U.S. B3 108
Pelham, Ga., U.S. E2 117
Pelham, N.H., U.S. E4 136
Pelham, S.C., U.S. B3 147
Pelham, Tn., U.S. D8 149
Pelham Manor, N.Y., U.S. h13 139
Pelhřimov, Czech. F15 10
Pelican, Ak., U.S. m21 109
Pelican Bay, b., Man., Can. C1 100
Pelican Lake, l., Man., Can. C1 100
Pelican Lake, l., Mn., U.S. D4 130
Pelican Lake, l., Mn., U.S. D3 130
Pelican Lake, l., Mn., U.S. B6 130
Pelican Lake, l., Mn., U.S. E5 130
Pelican Lake, l., Wi., U.S. C4 156
Pelican Mountain, mtn., Alta., Can. B4 98
Pelican Narrows, Sask., Can. B4 105
Pelican Rapids, Man., Can. C1 100
Pelican Rapids, Mn., U.S. D2 130
Pelileo, Ec. H3 84
Pelion, S.C., U.S. D5 147
Pelister, mtn., Mac. H5 20
Pelkosenniemi, Fin. H20 6
Pella, Ia., U.S. C5 122
Pell City, Al., U.S. B3 108
Pellegrini, Arg. I7 80
Pellegrini, Lago, l., Arg. J4 80
Pell Lake, Wi., U.S. n11 156
Pello, Fin. H19 6
Pellston, Mi., U.S. C6 129
Pelly, Sask., Can. F5 105
Pelly, stm., Yukon, Can. D6 96
Pelly Bay, b., N.W. Ter., Can. C14 96
Pelly Crossing, Yukon, Can. D5 96
Pelly Mountains, mts., Yukon, Can. D6 96
Pelón, Cerro, mtn., Mex. G10 90
Peloncillo Mountains, mts., U.S. E1 138
Peloponnesos see Pelopónnisos, pen., Grc. L6 20
Pelopónnisos, pen., Grc. L6 20
Pelotas, Braz. F12 80
Pelotas, stm., Braz. D13 80
Pelton, Lake, l., La., U.S. E5 125
Pel'ušn'a, Russia C15 22
Pemadumcook Lake, l., Me., U.S. C3 126
Pemalang, Indon. j14 39a
Pematangsiantar, Indon. M5 40
Pemba, Moz. D8 58
Pemba, i., Tan. C7 58
Pemberton, Austl. F3 68
Pemberton, B.C., Can. D6 99
Pemberton, N.J., U.S. D3 137
Pemberville, Oh., U.S. A2 142
Pembina, N.D., U.S. A8 141
Pembina, co., N.D., U.S. A8 141
Pembina, stm., Alta., Can. C3 98
Pembine, Wi., U.S. C6 156
Pembroke, Ont., Can. B7 103
Pembroke, Wales, U.K. J9 8
Pembroke, Ga., U.S. D5 117
Pembroke, Ky., U.S. D2 124
Pembroke, Me., U.S. D5 126
Pembroke, Ma., U.S. B6 128
Pembroke, N.C., U.S. C3 140
Pembroke, Va., U.S. C2 153
Pembroke, Cape, c., N.W. Ter., Can. D16 96
Pembroke Pines, Fl., U.S. r13 116
Pemigewasset, stm., N.H., U.S. C3 136
Pemigewasset, East Branch, stm., N.H., U.S. B3 136
Pemiscot, co., Mo., U.S. E8 132
Pemmican Portage, Sask., Can. D4 105
Pemuco, Chile I2 80
Peña Barroza, Bol. J8 82
Peña Blanca, Pan. I13 92
Pena Blanca, N.M., U.S. B3 138
Penafiel, Port. D3 16
Peña Gorda, Cerro, mtn., Mex. G7 90
Penápolis, Braz. F3 79
Peñaranda de Bracamonte, Spain E6 16
Pen Argyl, Pa., U.S. E11 145
Peñarroya-Pueblonuevo, Spain G6 16
Penas, Golfo de, b., Chile F2 78
Penasco, N.M., U.S. A4 138
Peñasco, Rio, stm., N.M., U.S. E4 138
Penbrook, Pa., U.S. F8 145
Pencahue, Chile H3 80
Pendembu, S.L. G3 64
Pender, Ne., U.S. B9 134
Pender, co., N.C., U.S. C4 140
Pendergrass, Ga., U.S. B3 117
Pendjari, stm., Afr. F7 54
Pendleton, In., U.S. E6 121
Pendleton, Or., U.S. B8 144
Pendleton, S.C., U.S. B2 147
Pendleton, co., Ky., U.S. B5 124
Pendleton, co., W.V., U.S. C5 155
Pendley Hills, Ga., U.S. *h8 117
Pend Oreille, co., Wa., U.S. A8 154
Pend Oreille, Lake, l., Id., U.S. A2 119
Pend Oreille, Mount, mtn., Id., U.S. A2 119
Penedo, Braz. F11 76
Penedono, Port. E4 16
Penetanguishene, Ont., Can. C5 103
Penfield, Ga., U.S. C3 117
Penfield, Il., U.S. C6 120
Penfield, Pa., U.S. D4 145
Penganga, stm., India C5 46
Penge, S. Afr. E10 66
P'enghu Ch'üntao (Pescadores), is., Tai. L8 34
P'enghu Shuitao, strt., Tai. L8 34
Pengkou, China J5 34
Penglai (Dengzhou), China F8 32
Pengshui, China F8 30
Penguin, Austl. M7 70
Pengxian, China E7 30
Penha, Braz. D14 80
Penhold, Alta., Can. C4 98
Peniche, Port. F2 16
Peninsula, Oh., U.S. A4 142
Penitentiary Mountain, hill, Al., U.S. A2 108
Penjamillo [de Degollado], Mex. G9 90
Pennant Point, c., N.S., Can. E6 101
Pennant Station, Sask., Can. G1 105
Pennask Mountain, mtn., B.C., Can. E7 99
Penne, Italy G8 18
Pennell, Mount, mtn., Ut., U.S. F5 151
Penney Farms, Fl., U.S. C5 116
Pennfield, N.B., Can. D3 101
Penn Hills, Pa., U.S. k14 145
Penniac, N.B., Can. C3 101
Pennines, mts., Eng., U.K. G11 8
Pennines, Alpes, mts., Eur. C2 18
Pennington, Al., U.S. C1 108
Pennington, N.J., U.S. C3 137
Pennington, co., Mn., U.S. B2 130
Pennington, co., S.D., U.S. D2 148
Pennington Gap, Va., U.S. f8 153
Pennock, Mn., U.S. E3 130
Pennsauken, N.J., U.S. D2 137
Pennsboro, W.V., U.S. B4 155
Pennsburg, Pa., U.S. F11 145
Penns Grove, N.J., U.S. D2 137
Pennsville, N.J., U.S. D1 137
Pennsylvania, state, U.S. E7 145
Pennville, In., U.S. D7 121
Penny, B.C., Can. C7 99
Penn Yan, N.Y., U.S. C3 139
Pennycutaway, stm., Man., Can. A5 100
Penny Ice Cap, N.W. Ter., Can. C19 96
Penny Strait, strt., N.W. Ter., Can. A13 96
Peno, Russia E15 22
Penobscot, co., Me., U.S. C4 126
Penobscot, stm., Me., U.S. C4 126
Penobscot, East Branch, stm., Me., U.S. C4 126
Penobscot, North Branch, stm., Me., U.S. B2 126
Penobscot, West Branch, stm., Me., U.S. C3 126
Penobscot Bay, b., Me., U.S. D3 126
Penobscot Lake, l., Me., U.S. C2 126
Penokee, Ks., U.S. C4 123
Penola, Austl. K4 70
Peñón Blanco, Mex. E7 90
Penong, Austl. F6 68
Penonomé, Pan. C2 84
Penrith, Austl. I9 70
Pensacola, Fl., U.S. u14 116
Pensacola Bay, b., Fl., U.S. u14 116
Pensacola Dam, Ok., U.S. A6 143
Pensacola Mountains, mts., Ant. D1 73
Pensacola Naval Air Station, mil., Fl., U.S. u14 116
Pense, Sask., Can. G3 105
Pensilvania, Col. E5 84
Pentagon Mountain, mtn., Mt., U.S. C3 133
Penticton, B.C., Can. E8 99
Pentland, Austl. C6 70
Pentland Firth, strt., Scot., U.K. C10 8
Pentwater, Mi., U.S. E4 129
Pênwègon, Burma E4 40
Penza, Russia G7 26
Penzance, Sask., Can. F3 105
Penzance, Eng., U.K. K8 8
Penzberg, Ger. H11 10
Penžina, stm., Russia E25 28
Penžinskaja guba, b., Russia E24 28
Peonan Point, c., Man., Can. D2 100
Peoria, Az., U.S. D3 110
Peoria, Il., U.S. C4 120
Peoria, co., Il., U.S. C4 120
Peoria Heights, Il., U.S. C4 120
Peotone, Il., U.S. B6 120
Pepacton Reservoir, res., N.Y., U.S. C6 139
Pepeekeo, Hi., U.S. D6 118
Pepel, S.L. G3 64
Peper, Sud. N7 60
Pepin, Wi., U.S. D1 156
Pepin, co., Wi., U.S. D2 156
Pepin, Lake, l., U.S. D1 156
Pepper Creek, stm., De., U.S. F5 115
Pepperell, Ma., U.S. A4 128
Pequannock, N.J., U.S. B4 137
Pequest, stm., N.J., U.S. B2 137
Pequop Mountains, mts., Nv., U.S. C7 135
Pequot Lakes, Mn., U.S. D4 130
Perabumulih, Indon. F3 38
Perak, stm., Malay. L6 40
Peralillo, Chile H3 80
Perämeri (Bottenviken), b., Eur. I18 6
Perchtoldsdorf, Aus. G16 10
Percy, Il., U.S. E4 120
Percy Isles, is., Austl. C9 70
Perdeberg, S. Afr. G7 66
Perdido, Al., U.S. D2 108
Perdido, stm., Braz. I13 82
Perdido, stm., U.S. E2 108
Perdido, Monte, mtn., Spain C12 16
Perdido Bay, b., Al., U.S. E2 108
Perdizes, Braz. E5 79
Perdue, Sask., Can. E2 105
Perečin, Ukr. G22 10
Peregonovka, Ukr. A14 20
Pereira, Col. E5 84
Pereira Barreto, Braz. F3 79
Pere Marquette, stm., Mi., U.S. E4 129
Peremyšl', Russia G19 22
Perené, stm., Peru D4 82
Pereslavl'-Zalesskij, Russia E21 22
Peresypkino Pervoje, Russia I25 22
Pérez, Arg. G8 80
Perg, Aus. G14 10
Pergamino, Arg. G8 80
Pergine Valsugana, Italy C6 18
Pergola, Italy F7 18
Perham, Mn., U.S. D3 130
Perico, Arg. C6 80
Pericos, Mex. E6 90
Peridot, Az., U.S. D5 110
Périers, Fr. C5 14
Périgord, hist. reg., Fr. G7 14
Périgueux, Fr. G7 14
Perijá, Serranía De, mts., S.A. B6 84
Periyakulam, India G4 46
Perkasie, Pa., U.S. F11 145
Perkins, Que., Can. D2 104
Perkins, Ga., U.S. D5 117
Perkins, Mi., U.S. C3 129
Perkins, Ok., U.S. B4 143
Perkins, co., Ne., U.S. D4 134
Perkins, co., S.D., U.S. B3 148
Perkinston, Ms., U.S. E4 131
Perla, Ar., U.S. C3 111
Perlas, Archipiélago de las, is., Pan. C3 84
Perlas, Laguna de, b., Nic. E11 92
Perlas, Punta de, c., Nic. E11 92
Perleberg, Ger. B11 10
Perm', Russia F9 26
Pernatty Lagoon, l., Austl. H2 70
Pernell, Ok., U.S. C4 143
Pernik, Bul. G7 20
Péronne, Fr. C9 14
Perot, Bayou, stm., La., U.S. k11 125
Perote, Mex. H11 90
Peroto, Bol. F9 82
Perpignan, Fr. J9 14
Perquimans, co., N.C., U.S. A6 140
Perrine, Fl., U.S. G6 116
Perris, Ca., U.S. F5 112
Perro, Laguna del, l., N.M., U.S. C4 138
Perros, Bahía de, b., Cuba C5 94
Perrot, Île, i., Que., Can. q19 104
Perry, Ar., U.S. B3 111
Perry, Fl., U.S. B3 116
Perry, Ga., U.S. D3 117
Perry, Il., U.S. D3 120
Perry, Ia., U.S. C3 122
Perry, Ks., U.S. C8 123
Perry, Mi., U.S. F6 129
Perry, Mo., U.S. B6 132
Perry, N.Y., U.S. C2 139
Perry, Oh., U.S. A4 142
Perry, Ok., U.S. A4 143
Perry, Ut., U.S. B3 151
Perry, co., Al., U.S. C2 108
Perry, co., Ar., U.S. C3 111
Perry, co., Il., U.S. E4 120
Perry, co., In., U.S. H4 121
Perry, co., Ky., U.S. C6 124
Perry, co., Ms., U.S. D4 131
Perry, co., Mo., U.S. D8 132
Perry, co., Oh., U.S. C3 142
Perry, co., Pa., U.S. F7 145
Perry, co., Tn., U.S. B4 149
Perry Hall, Md., U.S. B5 127
Perry Lake, res., Ks., U.S. C8 123
Perryman, Md., U.S. B5 127
Perry Peak, mtn., Ma., U.S. B1 128
Perry Point, Md., U.S. A5 127
Perrysburg, Oh., U.S. A2 142
Perrysburg Heights, Oh., U.S. e6 142
Perry Stream, stm., N.H., U.S. f7 136
Perry's Victory and International Peace Memorial, hist., Oh., U.S. A2 142
Perrysville, In., U.S. D3 121
Perrysville, Oh., U.S. B3 142
Perryton, Tx., U.S. A2 150
Perryville, Ak., U.S. D8 109
Perryville, Ar., U.S. B3 111
Perryville, Ky., U.S. C5 124
Perryville, Md., U.S. A5 127
Perryville, Mo., U.S. D8 132
Perryville, Tn., U.S. B3 149
Peršaj, Bela. G9 22
Perseverancia, Bol. F10 82
Pershing, In., U.S. E7 121
Pershing, Ia., U.S. C4 122
Pershing, co., Nv., U.S. C3 135
Persia, Ia., U.S. C2 122
Persia see Iran, ctry., Asia C5 42
Persian Gulf (Arabian Gulf), b., Asia H11 48
Persimmon Grove, Ky., U.S. k14 124
Person, co., N.C., U.S. A3 140
Pertek, Tur. B5 48
Perth, Austl. F3 68
Perth, Ont., Can. C8 103
Perth, Scot., U.K. E10 8
Perth Amboy, N.J., U.S. B4 137
Perth-Andover, N.B., Can. D10 101
Pertokar, Erit. I9 60
Peru, Il., U.S. B4 120
Peru, In., U.S. C5 121
Peru, Ks., U.S. E7 123
Peru, Ne., U.S. D10 134
Peru, N.Y., U.S. f11 139
Peru, Vt., U.S. E3 152
Peru (Perú), ctry., S.A. E3 76
Peruaçu, stm., Braz. C6 79
Peru-Chile Trench G7 74
Perugia, Italy F7 18
Perugorría, Arg. E9 80
Peruíbe, Braz. C15 80
Peruípe, stm., Braz. D9 79
Pervoavgustovskij, Russia I18 22
Pervomajsk, Ukr. H4 26
Pervomajskij, Bela. H8 22
Pervomajskij, Russia H23 22
Pervoural'sk, Russia F9 26
Pervyj Kuril'skij proliv, strt., Russia G23 28
Pes', Russia C17 22
Pesaro, Italy F7 18
Pesca, Col. E6 84
Pescadero, Ca., U.S. D2 112
Pescadores, Punta, c., Mex. F5 90
Pescadores, Punta, c., Peru G5 82
Pescadores see P'enghu Ch'üntao, is., Tai. L8 34
Pesčanaja, Ukr. A13 20
Pesčanka, Ukr. A12 20
Pesčanoje, Russia J24 6
Pescara, Italy G9 18
Pescia, Italy F5 18
Pesé, Pan. D2 84
Peseux, Switz. E6 13
Peshastin, Wa., U.S. B5 154
Peshāwar, Pak. C4 44
Peshtigo, Wi., U.S. C6 156
Peshtigo, stm., Wi., U.S. C5 156
Peski, Russia F21 22
Pesmes, Fr. E12 14
Pesočenskij, Russia G19 22
Pesočnoje, Russia C22 22
Pesočnyj, Russia A13 22
Peso da Régua, Port. D4 16
Pesotum, Il., U.S. D5 120
Pespire, Hond. D7 92
Pesqueira, Braz. E11 76
Pessac, Fr. H6 14
Pest, co., Hung. H19 10
Pest'aki, Russia E25 22
Peštera, Bul. G8 20
Pestovo, Russia C18 22
Petacalco, Bahía, b., Mex. I8 90
Petah Tiqwa, Isr. D3 50
Petal, Ms., U.S. D4 131
Petalcingo, Mex. I13 90
Petalión, Kólpos, b., Grc. L8 20
Petaluma, Ca., U.S. C2 112
Pétange, Lux. I8 12
Petare, Ven. B9 84
Petatlán, Mex. I9 90
Petawawa, Ont., Can. B7 103
Petawawa, stm., Ont., Can. A6 103
Petén, dept., Guat. A5 92
Petén Itzá, Lago, l., Guat. I15 90
Petenwell Lake, res., Wi., U.S. D4 156
Peterborough, Austl. I3 70
Peterborough, Ont., Can. C6 103
Peterborough, Eng., U.K. I13 8
Peterborough, N.H., U.S. E3 136
Peterculter, Scot., U.K. D11 8
Peter Dana Point, Me., U.S. C5 126
Peterhead, Scot., U.K. D12 8
Peter I Island, i., Ant. B11 73
Peterman, Al., U.S. D2 108
Peter Pond Lake, l., Sask., Can. m7 105
Petersburg, Ak., U.S. D13 109
Petersburg, De., U.S. D3 115
Petersburg, Il., U.S. C4 120
Petersburg, In., U.S. H3 121
Petersburg, Ky., U.S. h13 124
Petersburg, Mi., U.S. G7 129
Petersburg, Ne., U.S. C7 134
Petersburg, N.D., U.S. A8 141
Petersburg, Oh., U.S. B5 142
Petersburg, Tn., U.S. B5 149
Petersburg, Tx., U.S. C2 150
Petersburg, Va., U.S. C5 153
Petersburg, W.V., U.S. B5 155
Peters Creek, stm., W.V., U.S. m14 155
Petersfield, Man., Can. D3 100
Peters Mountain, mtn., U.S. D4 155
Peterson, Al., U.S. B2 108
Peterson, Ia., U.S. B2 122
Peterson, Mn., U.S. G7 130
Peterson Field, mil., Co., U.S. C6 113
Peterstown, W.V., U.S. D4 155
Petersville, Al., U.S. A2 108
Pétervására, Hung. G20 10
Petilia Policastro, Italy J11 18
Pétionville, Haiti E8 94
Petit Bois Island, i., Ms., U.S. E5 131
Petitcodiac, N.B., Can. D4 101
Petitcodiac, stm., N.B., Can. C5 101
Petit-de-Grat, N.S., Can. D9 101
Petite Amite, stm., La., U.S. h10 125
Petite Rivière, N.S., Can. E5 101
Petite-Rivière-de-l'Île, N.B., Can. B5 101
Petite Rivière Noire, Piton de la, mtn., Mrts. v18 67c
Petit-Étang, N.S., Can. C9 101
Petit-Goâve, Haiti E8 94
Petit Jean, stm., Ar., U.S. B2 111
Petit Lac Des Allemands, l., La., U.S. k11 125
Petit Lake, l., La., U.S. k12 125
Petitot, stm., Can. E8 96
Petit-Rocher, N.B., Can. B4 101
Petit-Saint-Bernard, Col du, Eur. G13 14
Petitsikapau Lake, l., Newf., Can. g8 102
Petlād, India I5 44
Petlalcingo, Mex. H11 90
Peto, Mex. G15 90
Petorca, Chile G3 80
Petoskey, Mi., U.S. C6 129
Petra see Batrā, hist., Jord. H4 50
Petra Velikogo, zaliv, b., Russia I18 28
Petrified Forest National Park, Az., U.S. B6 110
Petrikov, Bela. I11 22
Petrila, Rom. D7 20
Petrinja, Cro. D11 18
Petrodvorec, Russia B12 22
Petrólea, Col. C6 84
Petroleum, In., U.S. C7 121
Petroleum, co., Mt., U.S. C8 133
Petrolia, Ont., Can. E2 103
Petrolia, Ks., U.S. E8 123
Petrolia, Tx., U.S. B3 150
Petrolina, Braz. E10 76
Petrolina de Goiás, Braz. D4 79
Petropavlovsk, Kaz. G11 26
Petropavlovsk-Kamčatskij, Russia G23 28
Petrópolis, Braz. G7 79
Petros, Tn., U.S. C9 149
Petroșani, Rom. D7 20
Petrovsk, Russia G7 26
Petrovskoje, Russia I23 22
Petrovskoje, Russia D22 22
Petrovsk-Zabajkal'skij, Russia G13 28
Petrozavodsk, Russia E4 26
Petrusburg, S. Afr. G7 66
Petrus Steyn, S. Afr. F9 66
Petrusville, S. Afr. H7 66
Pettaquamscutt Lake Shores, R.I., U.S. F4 146
Petten, Neth. C6 12
Pettibone, N.D., U.S. B6 141
Pettigrew, Ar., U.S. B2 111
Pettingell Peak, mtn., Co., U.S. B5 113
Pettis, co., Mo., U.S. C4 132
Pettisville, Oh., U.S. A1 142
Pettus, Tx., U.S. E4 150
Petuchovo, Russia F11 26
Petuški, Russia F22 22
Peuerbach, Aus. G13 10
Pevek, Russia D26 28
Pevely, Mo., U.S. g13 132
Pewamo, Mi., U.S. E6 129
Pewaukee, Wi., U.S. E5 156
Pewaukee Lake, l., Wi., U.S. m11 156
Pewee Valley, Ky., U.S. B4 124
Peykjahlíð, Ice. B5 6a
Peyton, Co., U.S. B6 113
Pézenas, Fr. I10 14
Pezinok, Slov. G17 10
Pfäffikon, Switz. D10 13
Pfarrkirchen, Ger. G12 10
Pfeifer, Ks., U.S. D4 123
Pforzheim, Ger. G8 10
Pfronten, Ger. H10 10
Pfungstadt, Ger. F8 10
Pha-an, Burma F4 40
Phagwāra, India E6 44
Phala, Bots. D8 66
Phalaborwa, S. Afr. D10 66
Phalodi, India G5 44
Phalsbourg, Fr. D14 14
Phaltan, India D3 46
Phan, Thai. E5 40
Phangan, Ko, i., Thai. J6 40
Phangnga, Thai. J5 40
Phanom Dongrak, Thiu Khao, mts., Asia G7 40
Phan Rang, Viet. I10 40
Phan Thiet, Viet. I10 40
Phariāro, Pak. G3 44
Pharr, Tx., U.S. F3 150
Phatthalung, Thai. K6 40
Phayao, Thai. E5 40
Pheba, Ms., U.S. B5 131
Phelps, Ky., U.S. C7 124
Phelps, N.Y., U.S. C3 139
Phelps, Wi., U.S. B4 156
Phelps, co., Mo., U.S. D6 132
Phelps, co., Ne., U.S. D6 134
Phelps Lake, l., N.C., U.S. B6 140
Phenix, Va., U.S. C4 153
Phenix City, Al., U.S. C4 108
Phepane, stm., Afr. E6 66
Phetchabun, Thai. F6 40
Phetchabun, Thiu Khao, mts., Thai. F6 40
Phetchaburi, Thai. H5 40
Phichit, Thai. F6 40

227

Name	Map Ref.	Page
Puerto Pilón, Pan.	H15	92
Puerto Pinasco, Para.	B10	80
Puerto Piray, Arg.	D11	80
Puerto Píritu, Ven.	B10	84
Puerto Plata, Dom. Rep.	E9	94
Puerto Portillo, Peru	C5	82
Puerto Princesa, Phil.	D6	38
Puerto Real, Spain	I5	16
Puerto Rico, Arg.	D11	80
Puerto Rico, Bol.	D8	82
Puerto Rico, Col.	G5	84
Puerto Rico, dep., N.A.	E11	94
Puerto Rico Trench	G13	86
Puerto Rondón, Col.	D7	84
Puerto Saavedra, Chile	J2	80
Puerto Salgar, Col.	E5	84
Puerto Sandino, Nic.	E8	92
Puerto San José, Guat.	D4	92
Puerto San Julián, Arg.	F3	78
Puerto Santa Cruz, Arg.	G3	78
Puerto Sastre, Para.	B10	80
Puerto Siles, Bol.	E9	82
Puerto Suarez, Bol.	H13	82
Puerto Supe, Peru	D3	82
Puerto Tejada, Col.	F4	84
Puerto Tolosa, Col.	H5	84
Puerto Umbría, Col.	G4	84
Puerto Vallarta, Mex.	G7	90
Puerto Varas, Chile	E2	78
Puerto Victoria, Arg.	D11	80
Puerto Victoria, Peru	C4	82
Puerto Viejo, C.R.	G11	92
Puerto Viejo, C.R.	H12	92
Puerto Villamizar, Col.	C6	84
Puerto Villarroel, Bol.	G9	82
Puerto Wilches, Col.	D6	84
Puerto Ybapobó, Para.	B10	80
Pueyrredón, Lago (Lago Cochrane), l., S.A.	F2	78
Pugačov, Russia	G7	26
Puget Sound, strt., Wa., U.S.	B3	154
Puget Sound Naval Shipyard, mil., Wa., U.S.	e10	154
Puget-Théniers, Fr.	I13	14
Puglia, prov., Italy	I11	18
Pugwash, N.S., Can.	D6	101
Puhi, Hi., U.S.	B2	118
Puica, Peru	F5	82
Puigcerdá, Spain	C13	16
Puigmal, mtn., Eur.	C14	16
Puinahua, Canal de, mth., Peru	A4	82
Pujehun, S.L.	H4	64
Pujiang, China	F8	34
Pujilí, Ec.	H3	84
Pukalani, Hi., U.S.	C5	118
Pukaskwa National Park, Ont., Can.	o18	103
Pukch'ang, N. Kor.	D14	32
Pukch'ŏng, N. Kor.	C16	32
Pukeashun Mountain, mtn., B.C., Can.	D8	99
Pukekohe, N.Z.	B5	72
Pukhan-gang, stm., Asia	F15	32
Pukou, China	C7	34
Puksoozero, Russia	J27	6
Pukwana, S.D., U.S.	D6	148
Pula, Cro.	E8	18
Pulacayo, Bol.	I8	82
Púlar, Cerro, mtn., Chile	C4	80
Pulaski, Ga., U.S.	D5	117
Pulaski, Il., U.S.	F4	120
Pulaski, In., U.S.	C4	121
Pulaski, Ia., U.S.	D5	122
Pulaski, N.Y., U.S.	B4	139
Pulaski, Tn., U.S.	B4	149
Pulaski, Va., U.S.	C2	153
Pulaski, Wi., U.S.	D5	156
Pulaski, co., Ar., U.S.	C3	111
Pulaski, co., Ga., U.S.	D3	117
Pulaski, co., Il., U.S.	F4	120
Pulaski, co., In., U.S.	B4	121
Pulaski, co., Ky., U.S.	C5	124
Pulaski, co., Mo., U.S.	D5	132
Pulaski, co., Va., U.S.	C2	153
Puławy, Pol.	D21	10
Pulgaon, India	B5	46
Puli, Tai.	L9	34
Puliyangudi, India	H4	46
Pullman, Mi., U.S.	F4	129
Pullman, Wa., U.S.	C8	154
Púllo, Peru	F5	82
Pully, Switz.	E6	13
Pulog, Mount, mtn., Phil.	m19	39b
Pulsano, Italy	I12	18
Pułtusk, Pol.	C21	10
Pumphrey, Md., U.S.	h11	127
Pumpkin Buttes, mtn., Wy., U.S.	C7	157
Pumpkin Creek, stm., Mt., U.S.	E11	133
Pumpkin Creek, stm., Ne., U.S.	C2	134
Puná, Isla, i., Ec.	I2	84
Punakha, Bhu.	G13	44
Punata, Bol.	G9	82
Pūnch, India	D6	44
Punduga, Russia	A23	22
Pune (Poona), India	C2	46
Púngoè, stm., Afr.	B11	66
Pungo Lake, l., N.C., U.S.	B6	140
P'ungsan, N. Kor.	C16	32
Punia, Zaire	B5	58
Punilla, Sierra de la, mts., Arg.	E4	80
Puning, China	L5	34
Punitaqui, Chile	C2	78
Punitaqui, Chile	F3	80
Punjab, state, India	E6	44
Punnichy, Sask., Can.	F3	105
Puno, Peru	F6	82
Puno, dept., Peru	F6	82
Punta, Cerro de, mtn., P.R.	E11	94
Punta Alta, Arg.	J7	80
Punta Arenas, Chile	G2	78
Punta Banda, Cabo, c., Mex.	B1	90
Punta Cardón, Ven.	B7	84
Punta Colnett, Mex.	B1	90
Punta de Bombón, Peru	G6	82
Punta de Díaz, Chile	E3	80
Punta del Cobre, Chile	D3	80
Punta del Este, Ur.	H11	80
Punta de los Llanos, Arg.	F5	80
Punta de Mata, Ven.	C11	84
Punta de Piedras, Ven.	B10	84
Punta Gorda, Belize	I15	90
Punta Gorda, Nic.	F11	92
Punta Gorda, Fl., U.S.	F4	116
Punta Gorda, stm., Nic.	F11	92
Punta Gorda, Bahía de, b., Nic.	F11	92
Punta Negra, Salar de, pl., Chile	C4	80
Punta Prieta, Mex.	C2	90
Puntarenas, C.R.	H10	92
Puntarenas, prov., C.R.	I11	92
Puntas del Sauce, Ur.	G10	80
Punto Fijo, Ven.	B7	84
Punxsutawney, Pa., U.S.	E4	145
Puolanka, Fin.	I20	6
Puqi, China	F9	30
Puquio, Peru	F4	82
Pur, stm., Russia	D7	28
Puracé, Volcán, vol., Col.	F4	84
Purcell, Mo., U.S.	D3	132
Purcell, Ok., U.S.	B4	143
Purcellville, Va., U.S.	A5	153
Purdham Hill, mtn., Ar., U.S.	h10	111
Purdin, Mo., U.S.	B4	132
Purdy, Mo., U.S.	E4	132
Purgatoire, stm., Co., U.S.	D7	113
Purgatoire Peak, mtn., Co., U.S.	D5	113
Puri, India	K11	44
Purificación, Col.	F5	84
Purificación, Mex.	H7	90
Purificación, stm., Mex.	E10	90
Purikari neem, c., Est.	B8	22
Purmerend, Neth.	C6	12
Pūrnia, India	H12	44
Purple Springs, Alta., Can.	E5	98
Purros, Nmb.	B1	66
Pursglove, W.V., U.S.	B4	155
Puruí, stm., Braz.	H8	84
Puruliya, India	I12	44
Puruni, stm., Guy.	D13	84
Purus (Purús), stm., S.A.	D6	76
Purvis, Ms., U.S.	D4	131
Purwakarta, Indon.	j13	39a
Purwokerto, Indon.	j14	39a
Puryear, Tn., U.S.	A3	149
Pusan, S. Kor.	H17	32
Pushaw Lake, l., Me., U.S.	D4	126
Pushkar, India	G6	44
Pushmataha, Al., U.S.	C1	108
Pushmataha, co., Ok., U.S.	C6	143
Puškin, Russia	B13	22
Puškino, Russia	E20	22
Puškinskije Gory, Russia	D11	22
Püspökladány, Hung.	H21	10
Püssi, Est.	B10	22
Pustoška, Russia	E12	22
Putaendo, Chile	G3	80
Putao, Burma	G17	44
Put'atino, Russia	G24	22
Putian, China	J8	34
Putila, Ukr.	A9	20
Putina, Peru	F7	82
Puting, Tanjung, c., Indon.	F5	38
Putnam, Al., U.S.	C1	108
Putnam, Ct., U.S.	B8	114
Putnam, co., Fl., U.S.	C5	116
Putnam, co., Ga., U.S.	C3	117
Putnam, co., Il., U.S.	B4	120
Putnam, co., In., U.S.	E4	121
Putnam, co., Mo., U.S.	A4	132
Putnam, co., N.Y., U.S.	D7	139
Putnam, co., Oh., U.S.	B1	142
Putnam, co., Tn., U.S.	C8	149
Putnam, co., W.V., U.S.	C3	155
Putnamville, In., U.S.	E4	121
Putney, Ga., U.S.	E2	117
Putney, Vt., U.S.	F3	152
Putorana, plato, plat., Russia	D17	26
Putre, Chile	H7	82
Puttalam, Sri L.	H5	46
Puttgarden, Ger.	A11	10
Putú, Chile	H2	80
Putumayo, ter., Col.	G4	84
Putumayo (Içá), stm., S.A.	I7	84
Putuo, China	F11	34
Puukohola Heiau National Historic Site, hist., Hi., U.S.	D6	118
Puukolii, Hi., U.S.	C5	118
Puula, l., Fin.	K20	6
Puumala, Fin.	K21	6
Puunene, Hi., U.S.	C5	118
Puurmani, Est.	C9	22
Puxi, China	J8	34
Puxico, Mo., U.S.	E7	132
Puyallup, Wa., U.S.	B3	154
Puyallup, stm., Wa., U.S.	C3	154
Puyang, China	H2	32
Puyango (Tumbes), stm., S.A.	I3	84
Puy-de-Dôme, dept., Fr.	G10	14
Puylaurens, Fr.	I9	14
Puyo, Ec.	H4	84
Puyŏ, S. Kor.	G14	32
Pweto, Zaire	C5	58
Pyapon, Burma	F3	40
Pyatt, Ar., U.S.	A3	111
Pyaye, Burma	E3	40
Pyhäjoki, Fin.	I19	6
Pyhäselkä, l., Fin.	J21	6
Pyinmana, Burma	E4	40
Pyles Fork, stm., W.V., U.S.	h10	155
Pymatuning Reservoir, res., U.S.	C1	145
Pyŏktong, N. Kor.	C13	32
Pyŏlch'ang-ni, N. Kor.	D14	32
P'yŏngch'ang, S. Kor.	F16	32
P'yŏngsan, N. Kor.	E14	32
P'yŏngt'aek, S. Kor.	F15	32
P'yŏngyang, N. Kor.	D13	32
Pyramid Lake, l., Nv., U.S.	C2	135
Pyramid Lake Indian Reservation, Nv., U.S.	D2	135
Pyramid Mountains, mts., N.M., U.S.	E1	138
Pyramid Peak, mtn., N.M., U.S.	E1	138
Pyramid Peak, mtn., Wy., U.S.	C2	157
Pyrenees, mts., Eur.	C13	16
Pyrénées-Atlantiques, dept., Fr.	I6	14
Pyrénées-Orientales, dept., Fr.	J9	14
Pyrmont, In., U.S.	D4	121
Pyrzyce, Pol.	B14	10
Pytalovo, Russia	D10	22
Pyu, Burma	E4	40
Pyuntaza, Burma	F4	40

Q

Name	Map Ref.	Page
Qacentina (Constantine), Alg.	B14	62
Qā'emshahr, Iran	C12	48
Qā'en, Iran	E15	48
Qaidam Pendi, China	B16	44
Qalāt, Afg.	D2	44
Qal'at ash-Shaqīf (Beaufort Castle), hist., Leb.	B5	50
Qal'at Bīshah, Sau. Ar.	D3	47
Qal'at Ṣāliḥ, Iraq	F9	48
Qal'at Sukkar, Iraq	F9	48
Qal'eh-ye Now, Afg.	C2	44
Qallābāt, Sud.	K9	60
Qalqīlya, Isr. Occ.	D3	50
Qamar, Ghubbat al-, b., Yemen	F8	47
Qamdo, China	E6	30
Qānā, Leb.	B4	50
Qanā, Sau. Ar.	H6	48
Qandahār, Afg.	E1	44
Qandala, Som.	F10	56
Qantur, Sud.	M3	60
Qārah, Sau. Ar.	G6	48
Qardho, Som.	G10	56
Qarqan, stm., China	D4	30
Qārūn, Birkat, l., Egypt	C6	60
Qāsh, Nahr al- (Gash), stm., Afr.	E8	56
Qaṣr al-Farāfirah, Egypt	D4	60
Qasr el-Boukhari, Alg.	C12	62
Qaṣr-e Shīrīn, Iran	D8	48
Qa'ṭabah, Yemen	H4	47
Qaṭanā, Syria	B6	50
Qatar (Qaṭar), ctry., Asia	D5	42
Qattara Depression see Qaṭṭārah, Munkhafaḍ al-, depr., Egypt	B4	60
Qaṭṭārah, Munkhafaḍ al- (Qattara Depression), depr., Egypt	B4	60
Qazvīn, Iran	C11	48
Qesari, Ḥorbat (Cæsarea), hist., Isr.	C3	50
Qeshm, Iran	H14	48
Qeshm, Jazīreh-ye, i., Iran	H13	48
Qetura, Isr.	I4	50
Qezel Owzan, stm., Iran	C10	48
Qianfang, China	G5	34
Qianqi, China	H9	34
Qianyang, China	F9	30
Qiaogou, China	C4	34
Qiddīsah Kātrīnā, Dayr al- (Monastery of Saint Catherine), Egypt	G3	48
Qidong, China	D10	34
Qidu, China	E6	34
Qiemo, China	A11	44
Qifṭ (Coptos), Egypt	D7	60
Qijiang, China	F8	30
Qijiawan, China	E3	34
Qila Lādgasht, Pak.	H17	48
Qilian Shan, mtn., China	D6	30
Qilian Shan, mts., China	D6	30
Qimen, China	J2	34
Qinā, Egypt	D7	60
Qinā, Wādī, val., Egypt	H2	48
Qingchengzi, China	C11	32
Qingdao (Tsingtao), China	G8	32
Qinghai (Tsinghai), prov., China	D6	30
Qinghai Hu, l., China	D7	30
Qinghezhen, China	F5	32
Qingjiang, China	B8	34
Qingjiang, China	G4	34
Qinglian, China	K1	34
Qinglong, China	B8	40
Qingpu, China	D10	34
Qingshan, China	E3	34
Qingshui, stm., China	D8	30
Qingshui, stm., China	F8	30
Qingtang, China	K2	34
Qingyang, China	D8	30
Qingyangzhen, China	D9	34
Qingyuan, China	G8	30
Qingyuan, China	L2	34
Qingzhou, China	L5	34
Qinhuangdao (Chinwangtao), China	D7	32
Qin Ling, mts., China	E8	30
Qinzhou, China	D10	40
Qionglai, China	E7	30
Qiongzhong, China	E10	40
Qiongzhou Haixia, strt., China	D11	40
Qipanshan, China	A5	32
Qiqian, China	A11	30
Qiqihar (Tsitsihar), China	B11	30
Qiryat Ata, Isr.	C4	50
Qiryat Bialik, Isr.	C4	50
Qiryat Gat, Isr.	E3	50
Qiryat Mal'akhi, Isr.	E3	50
Qiryat Motzkin, Isr.	C4	50
Qiryat Ono, Isr.	D3	50
Qiryat Shemona, Isr.	B5	50
Qiryat Yam, Isr.	C4	50
Qishn, Yemen	G7	47
Qishon, stm., Asia	C4	50
Qishuyan, China	D9	34
Qitai, China	C4	30
Qiyang, China	A11	40
Qnadsa, Alg.	E9	62
Qogir Feng (K2), mtn., Asia	C7	44
Qom, Iran	D11	48
Qomsheh, Iran	E11	48
Qondūz, Afg.	J11	26
Qondūz, stm., Afg.	B3	44
Qonggyai, China	F5	30
Qorveh, Iran	D9	48
Quabbin Reservoir, res., Ma., U.S.	B3	128
Quaco Head, c., N.B., Can.	D4	101
Quaddick, Ct., U.S.	B8	114
Quaddick Reservoir, res., Ct., U.S.	B8	114
Quadros, Lagoa dos, b., Braz.	E13	80
Quail Oaks, Va., U.S.	n18	153
Quakenbrück, Ger.	C7	10
Quaker City, Oh., U.S.	C4	142
Quaker Hill, Ct., U.S.	D7	114
Quakertown, Pa., U.S.	F11	145
Qualicum Beach, B.C., Can.	E5	99
Quanah, Tx., U.S.	B3	150
Quangang, China	G4	34
Quang Ngai, Viet.	G10	40
Quang Trach, Viet.	F9	40
Quannapowitt, Lake, l., Ma., U.S.	f11	128
Quantico, Va., U.S.	B5	153
Quantico Marine Corps Air Station, mil., Va., U.S.	B5	153
Quanzhou (Chuanchou), China	K7	34
Quapaw, Ok., U.S.	A7	143
Qu'Appelle, Sask., Can.	G4	105
Qu'Appelle, stm., Can.	G4	105
Quaraí, Braz.	F10	80
Quaraí, stm., S.A.	F10	80
Quarryville, N.B., Can.	C4	101
Quarryville, Ct., U.S.	B6	114
Quarryville, Pa., U.S.	G9	145
Quartu Sant'Elena, Italy	J4	18
Quartz Mountain, mtn., Or., U.S.	D4	144
Quartzsite, Az., U.S.	D1	110
Quasqueton, Ia., U.S.	B6	122
Quassapaug, Lake, l., Ct., U.S.	C3	114
Quatsino Sound, strt., B.C., Can.	D3	99
Quay, co., N.M., U.S.	C6	138
Qūchān, Iran	C15	48
Queanbeyan, Austl.	J8	70
Québec, Que., Can.	C6	104
Quebec, prov., Can.	C5	104
Quebra-Anzol, stm., Braz.	E5	79
Quebracho, Ur.	F10	80
Quechee, Vt., U.S.	D4	152
Quechee Gorge, val., Vt., U.S.	D4	152
Quedas, Moz.	B11	66
Quedlinburg, Ger.	D11	10
Queen, stm., R.I., U.S.	E3	146
Queen Alexandra Range, mts., Ant.	D8	73
Queen Annes, co., Md., U.S.	B5	127
Queen Bess, Mount, mtn., B.C., Can.	D5	99
Queen Charlotte, B.C., Can.	C1	99
Queen Charlotte Islands, is., B.C., Can.	C1	99
Queen Charlotte Mountains, mts., B.C., Can.	C1	99
Queen Charlotte Sound, strt., B.C., Can.	n17	99
Queen Charlotte Strait, strt., B.C., Can.	D4	99
Queen City, Mo., U.S.	A5	132
Queen City, Tx., U.S.	C5	150
Queen Creek, Az., U.S.	m9	110
Queen Elizabeth Islands, is., N.W. Ter., Can.	B9	86
Queen Mary Coast, Ant.	B6	73
Queen Maud Gulf, b., N.W. Ter., Can.	C12	96
Queen Maud Land, reg., Ant.	C3	73
Queen Maud Mountains, mts., Ant.	D9	73
Queens, co., N.Y., U.S.	E7	139
Queensborough, Ont., Can.	C7	103
Queenscliff, Austl.	L6	70
Queensland, Ga., U.S.	E3	117
Queensland, state, Austl.	D9	68
Queenstown, Austl.	N6	70
Queenstown, N.B., Can.	D3	101
Queenstown, Guy.	D13	84
Queenstown, N.Z.	F2	72
Queenstown, S. Afr.	H8	66
Queenstown, Md., U.S.	C5	127
Queets, Wa., U.S.	B1	154
Queguay Grande, stm., Ur.	G10	80
Queimados, Braz.	G7	79
Quelimane, Moz.	A13	66
Quemado, N.M., U.S.	C1	138
Quemado, Tx., U.S.	E2	150
Quemado, Punta de, c., Cuba	D7	94
Quemado de Güines, Cuba	C4	94
Quemoy see Chinmen Tao, i., Tai.	K7	34
Quemú Quemú, Arg.	I7	80
Quenemo, Ks., U.S.	D8	123
Quepos, C.R.	H10	92
Quequén, Arg.	J9	80
Querary, stm., Col.	G7	84
Quercy, hist. reg., Fr.	H8	14
Querecotillo, Peru	A1	82
Querétaro, Mex.	G9	90
Querétaro, state, Mex.	G10	90
Querobabi, Mex.	B4	90
Quesada, C.R.	G10	92
Quesada, Spain	H8	16
Queshan, China	C3	34
Quesnel, B.C., Can.	C6	99
Quesnel, stm., B.C., Can.	C6	99
Quesnel Lake, l., B.C., Can.	C7	99
Questa, N.M., U.S.	A4	138
Quetico Provincial Park, Ont., Can.	o17	103
Quetta, Pak.	E2	44
Quettehou, Fr.	C5	14
Quetzaltenango, Guat.	C3	92
Quetzaltenango, dept., Guat.	C3	92
Quevedo, Ec.	H3	84
Quezaltepeque, El Sal.	D5	92
Quezaltepeque, Guat.	C5	92
Quezon City, Phil.	n19	39b
Qufu, China	H5	32
Quibdó, Col.	E4	84
Quiberon, Fr.	E3	14
Quíbor, Ven.	C8	84
Quiches, Peru	C3	82
Quicksand Pond, l., R.I., U.S.	E6	146
Quidnessett, R.I., U.S.	E4	146
Quidnick, R.I., U.S.	D3	146
Quidnick Reservoir, res., R.I., U.S.	D2	146
Quiindy, Para.	C10	80
Quila, Mex.	E6	90
Quilalí, Nic.	D8	92
Quilcene, Wa., U.S.	B3	154
Quileute Indian Reservation, Wa., U.S.	B1	154
Quilimarí, Chile	G3	80
Quilino, Arg.	F6	80
Quillabamba, Peru	E5	82
Quillacollo, Bol.	G8	82
Quillagua, Chile	I7	82
Quillan, Fr.	J9	14
Quill Lake, Sask., Can.	E3	105
Quillota, Chile	G3	80
Quilon, India	H4	46
Quilpie, Austl.	F6	70
Quilpué, Chile	G3	80
Quimarí, Alto de, mtn., Col.	C4	84
Quimbaya, Col.	E5	84
Quimby, Ia., U.S.	B2	122
Quime, Bol.	G8	82
Quimilí, Arg.	D7	80
Quimper, Fr.	D2	14
Quimperlé, Fr.	E3	14
Quinault, Wa., U.S.	B2	154
Quinault, stm., Wa., U.S.	B1	154
Quinault, Lake, l., Wa., U.S.	B2	154
Quinault Indian Reservation, Wa., U.S.	B1	154
Quince Mil, Peru	E6	82
Quinches, Peru	E3	82
Quincy, Ca., U.S.	C3	112
Quincy, Fl., U.S.	B2	116
Quincy, Il., U.S.	D2	120
Quincy, In., U.S.	F4	121
Quincy, Ky., U.S.	B6	124
Quincy, Ma., U.S.	B5	128
Quincy, Mi., U.S.	G6	129
Quincy, Ms., U.S.	B5	131
Quincy, Oh., U.S.	B2	142
Quincy, Wa., U.S.	B6	154
Quincy Bay, b., Ma., U.S.	g12	128
Quindío, dept., Col.	E5	84
Quinebaug, Ct., U.S.	A8	114
Quinebaug, stm., Ct., U.S.	C8	114
Quines, Arg.	G6	80
Quinga, Moz.	E8	58
Quinhagak, Ak., U.S.	D7	109
Qui Nhon, Viet.	H10	40
Quinlan, Tx., U.S.	C4	150
Quinn, stm., Nv., U.S.	B3	135
Quinn Canyon Range, mts., Nv., U.S.	F6	135
Quinnesec, Mi., U.S.	C3	129
Quinnipiac, stm., Ct., U.S.	D4	114
Quintanar de la Orden, Spain	F8	16
Quintana Roo, state, Mex.	H15	90
Quinter, Ks., U.S.	C3	123
Quintero, Chile	G3	80
Quintin, Fr.	D4	14
Quinto, stm., Arg.	H6	80
Quinto de Noviembre, Presa, El Sal.	D6	92
Quinton, Sask., Can.	F3	105
Quinton, Ok., U.S.	B6	143
Quinwood, W.V., U.S.	C4	155
Quirauk Mountain, mtn., Md., U.S.	A2	127
Quiriguá, hist., Guat.	B5	92
Quirihue, Chile	I2	80
Quirindi, Austl.	H9	70
Quirinópolis, Braz.	E3	79
Quiriquire, Ven.	C11	84
Quiroga, Mex.	H9	90
Quiroga, Spain	C4	16
Quirós, Arg.	E6	80
Quissanga, Moz.	D8	58
Quitaque, Tx., U.S.	B2	150
Quitilipi, Arg.	D8	80
Quitman, Ar., U.S.	B3	111
Quitman, Ga., U.S.	F3	117
Quitman, Ms., U.S.	C5	131
Quitman, Tx., U.S.	C5	150
Quitman, co., Ga., U.S.	E1	117
Quitman, co., Ms., U.S.	A3	131
Quitman Mountains, mts., Tx., U.S.	o12	150
Quito, Ec.	H3	84
Quivilla, Peru	C3	82
Quixadá, Braz.	D11	76
Quixito, stm., Braz.	J7	84
Qujiang, China	K2	34
Qujing, China	B7	40
Qulin, Mo., U.S.	E7	132
Qumar, stm., China	D5	30
Qumarlêb, China	E6	30
Quonnipaug Lake, l., Ct., U.S.	D5	114
Quonochontaug, R.I., U.S.	G2	146
Quonochontaug Pond, l., R.I., U.S.	G2	146
Quonset Point, c., R.I., U.S.	E4	146
Quorn, Austl.	I3	70
Qurayyāt, Oman	C11	47
Qurdūd, Sud.	L5	60
Qūṣ, Egypt	E7	60
Quthing, Leso.	H8	66
Quxi, China	L5	34
Quxian, China	G7	34
Quyquyó, Para.	D10	80
Quzhou, China	G2	32

R

Name	Map Ref.	Page
Raab (Rába), stm., Eur.	H15	10
Raahe, Fin.	I19	6
Raalte, Neth.	D9	12
Ra'anana, Isr.	D3	50
Raasiku, Est.	B8	22
Raba, Indon.	G6	38
Rába (Raab), stm., Eur.	H17	10
Rabak, Sud.	K7	60
Rabat (Victoria), Malta	M9	18
Rabat, Mor.	C7	62
Rabaul, Pap. N. Gui.	k17	68a
Rabbit Creek, stm., S.D., U.S.	B3	148
Rabbit Ears Pass, Co., U.S.	A4	113
Rabbit Lake, Sask., Can.	D2	105
Rābigh, Sau. Ar.	C1	47
Rābigh, Sau. Ar.	J5	48
Rabinal, Guat.	B4	92
Rabka, Pol.	F19	10
Rabkavi Banhatti, India	D3	46
Rabočeostrovsk, Russia	I24	6
Rabun, Al., U.S.	D2	108
Rabun, co., Ga., U.S.	B3	117
Rabun Bald, mtn., Ga., U.S.	B3	117
Rabyānah, Ṣaḥrā', des., Libya	D5	56
Raccoon Creek, stm., Oh., U.S.	D3	142
Raccourci Island, i., La., U.S.	D4	125
Race, Cape, c., Newf., Can.	E5	102
Raceland, Ky., U.S.	B7	124
Raceland, La., U.S.	E5	125
Race Point, c., Ma., U.S.	B7	128
Race Pond, Ga., U.S.	F4	117
Rach'a, Russia	A13	22
Rach Gia, Viet.	I8	40
Rachov, Ukr.	A8	20
Racibórz (Ratibor), Pol.	E18	10
Racine, Mn., U.S.	G6	130
Racine, Mo., U.S.	E3	132
Racine, Oh., U.S.	D4	142
Racine, W.V., U.S.	C3	155
Racine, Wi., U.S.	F6	156
Racine, co., Wi., U.S.	F5	156
Racine Dam, U.S.	C3	155
Ráckeve, Hung.	H18	10
Rădăuți, Rom.	B9	20
Radcliff, Ky., U.S.	C4	124
Radcliffe, Ia., U.S.	B4	122
Radeberg, Ger.	D13	10
Radebeul, Ger.	D13	10
Rades, Tun.	B16	62
Radford, Va., U.S.	C2	153
Rādhanpur, India	I4	44
Radisson, Sask., Can.	E2	105
Radium Hot Springs, B.C., Can.	D9	99
Radium Springs, N.M., U.S.	E3	138
Radofinnikovo, Russia	B13	22
Radolfzell, Ger.	H8	10
Radom, Pol.	D21	10
Radomsko, Pol.	D19	10
Radoškoviči, Bela.	G10	22
Radoviš, Mac.	H6	20
Radun', Bela.	G8	22
Radviliškis, Lith.	F6	22
Radville, Sask., Can.	H3	105
Raḍwā, Jabal, mtn., Sau. Ar.	E10	60
Radway, Alta., Can.	B4	98
Rae, N.W. Ter., Can.	D9	96
Rāe Bareli, India	G9	44
Raeford, N.C., U.S.	C3	140
Rae Isthmus, N.W. Ter., Can.	C15	96
Rae Strait, strt., N.W. Ter., Can.	C13	96
Raetihi, N.Z.	C5	72
Rafaela, Arg.	F8	80
Rafaḥ, Isr. Occ.	F2	50
Raffadali, Italy	L8	18
Rafḥā', Sau. Ar.	G7	48
Rafsanjān, Iran	F14	48
Raft, stm., Id., U.S.	G5	119
Raft River Mountains, mts., Ut., U.S.	B2	151
Rafz, Switz.	C10	13
Raga, Sud.	M3	60
Ragged Island, i., Bah.	C7	94
Ragged Island, i., Me., U.S.	E4	126
Ragged Island Range, is., Bah.	C7	94
Ragged Lake, l., Me., U.S.	C3	126
Ragged Top Mountain, mtn., Wy., U.S.	E7	157
Ragland, Al., U.S.	B3	108
Ragusa, Italy	M9	18
Raguva, Lith.	F7	22
Rahad, Nahr ar-, stm., Afr.	F8	56
Rahad al-Bardī, Sud.	L2	60
Rahīmyār Khān, Pak.	F4	44
Rahway, N.J., U.S.	B4	137
Rahway, stm., N.J., U.S.	k7	137
Rāichūr, India	D4	46
Raiganj, India	H13	44
Raigarh, India	J10	44
Railroad Valley, val., Nv., U.S.	E6	135
Railton, Austl.	M7	70
Rainbow Bridge National Monument, Ut., U.S.	F5	151
Rainbow City, Al., U.S.	*A3	108
Rainbow Falls, wtfl, Tn., U.S.	D10	149
Rainbow Flowage, res., Wi., U.S.	C4	156
Rainbow Lake, l., Me., U.S.	C3	126
Rainelle, W.V., U.S.	D4	155
Rainier, Or., U.S.	A4	144
Rainier, Wa., U.S.	C3	154
Rainier, Mount, mtn., Wa., U.S.	C4	154
Rains, co., Tx., U.S.	C5	150
Rainsville, Al., U.S.	A4	108
Rainy Lake, l., Mn., U.S.	B5	130
Rainy River, Ont., Can.	o16	103
Raipur, India	J9	44
Ra'īs, Sau. Ar.	C1	47
Raití, Nic.	C9	92
Rājahmundry, India	D6	46
Rajāj, Sud.	L3	60
Rajang, stm., Malay.	E5	38
Rājapālaiyam, India	H4	46
Rājasthān, state, India	G5	44
Rajčichinsk, Russia	H17	28
Rajka, Hung.	G17	10
Rājkot, India	I4	44
Rāj Nāndgaon, India	J9	44
Rājpipla, India	B2	46
Rājshāhi, Bngl.	H13	44
Rakamaz, Hung.	G21	10
Rakaposhi, mtn., Pak.	B6	44
Rakata, Pulau, i., Indon.	j12	39a
Rake, Ia., U.S.	A4	122
Rakops, Bots.	C7	66
Rakovník, Czech.	E13	10
Rakvere, Est.	B9	22
Raleigh, Newf., Can.	C4	102
Raleigh, Il., U.S.	F5	120
Raleigh, Ms., U.S.	C4	131
Raleigh, N.C., U.S.	B4	140
Raleigh, W.V., U.S.	n13	155
Raleigh, co., W.V., U.S.	D3	155
Raleigh Bay, b., N.C., U.S.	C6	140
Ralls, Tx., U.S.	C2	150
Ralls, co., Mo., U.S.	B6	132
Ralph, Al., U.S.	B2	108
Ralston, Ne., U.S.	g12	134
Ralston, Ok., U.S.	A5	143
Ralston, Wy., U.S.	B4	157

Name Map Ref. Page

Rheda-Wiedenbrück, Ger. D8 10
Rheims see Reims, Fr. C11 14
Rhein, Sask., Can. F4 105
Rheine, Ger. C7 10
Rheinfelden, Ger. H7 10
Rheinland-Pfalz, state, Ger. E6 10
Rhein see Rhine, stm., Eur. D6 10
Rhine, Ga., U.S. E3 117
Rhine (Rhein) (Rhin), stm., Eur. D6 10
Rhinebeck, N.Y., U.S. D7 139
Rhineland, Mo., U.S. C6 132
Rhinelander, Wi., U.S. C4 156
Rhir, Cap, c., Mor. E6 62
Rho, Italy D4 18
Rhode Island, state, U.S. D3 146
Rhode Island, i., R.I., U.S. E5 146
Rhode Island Sound, strt., U.S. F5 146
Rhodell, W.V., U.S. D3 155
Rhodesia see Zimbabwe, ctry., Afr. E5 58
Rhodes Peak, mtn., Id., U.S. C4 119
Rhodes see Ródhos, i., Grc. M12 20
Rhodhiss, N.C., U.S. B1 140
Rhodope Mountains (Rodopi) (Orosirá Rodhópis), mts., Eur. H8 20
Rhome, Tx., U.S. m9 150
Rhön, mts., Ger. E9 10
Rhône, dept., Fr. G11 14
Rhône, stm., Eur. H11 14
Rhône au Rhin, Canal du, Fr. H7 10
Rhourde-El-Baguel, Alg. E14 62
Riaba, Eq. Gui. J14 64
Riachão, Braz. E9 76
Riacho de Santana, Braz. B7 79
Rialma, Braz. C4 79
Rialto, Ca., U.S. m14 112
Rianápolis, Braz. C4 79
Riangnom, Sud. M6 60
Riaño, Spain C6 16
Riau, Kepulauan, is., Indon. N8 40
Ribas do Rio Pardo, Braz. F2 79
Ribeauvillé, Fr. D14 14
Ribeira, Braz. C14 80
Ribeira do Iguape, stm., Braz. C14 80
Ribeira Grande, C.V. k16 64a
Ribeirão do Pinhal, Braz. G3 79
Ribeirão Preto, Braz. F5 79
Ribeirão Vermelho, Braz. F6 79
Ribeirãozinho, Braz. D2 79
Ribemont, Fr. C10 14
Ribera, Italy L8 18
Ribera, N.M., U.S. B4 138
Riberalta, Bol. D8 82
Rib Lake, Wi., U.S. C3 156
Rib Mountain, mtn., Wi., U.S. D4 156
Ribnica, Slo. D9 18
Ribnitz-Damgarten, Ger. A12 10
Ribstone, Alta., Can. C5 98
Ricardo Flores Magón, Mex. C6 90
Ricaurte, Col. G4 84
Riccia, Italy H9 18
Riccione, Italy F7 18
Rice, Mn., U.S. E4 130
Rice, Va., U.S. C4 153
Rice, co., Ks., U.S. D5 123
Rice, co., Mn., U.S. F5 130
Riceboro, Ga., U.S. E5 117
Rice Creek, stm., Mn., U.S. m12 130
Rice Lake, Wi., U.S. C2 156
Rice Lake, l., Ont., Can. C6 103
Rice Lake, l., Mn., U.S. D5 130
Riceton, Sask., Can. G3 105
Riceville, Ia., U.S. A5 122
Riceville, Tn., U.S. D9 149
Rich, co., Ut., U.S. B4 151
Rich, Cape, c., Ont., Can. C4 103
Richard Collinson Inlet, b., N.W. Ter., Can. B10 96
Richard's Bay, S. Afr. G11 66
Richard's Bay, b., S. Afr. G11 66
Richards-Gebaur Air Force Base, mil., Mo., U.S. C3 132
Richards Island, i., N.W. Ter., Can. C6 96
Richardson, Tx., U.S. n10 150
Richardson, co., Ne., U.S. D10 134
Richardson, stm., Can. E10 96
Richardson Lakes, l., Me., U.S. D2 126
Richardson Mountains, mts., Can. C5 96
Richardton, N.D., U.S. C3 141
Richburg, S.C., U.S. B5 147
Rich Creek, Va., U.S. C2 153
Riche, Pointe, c., Newf., Can. C3 102
Richelieu, Fr. E7 14
Richer, Man., Can. E3 100
Richey, Mt., U.S. C11 133
Richfield, Id., U.S. F4 119
Richfield, Mn., U.S. F5 130
Richfield, N.C., U.S. B2 140
Richfield, Pa., U.S. E7 145
Richfield, Ut., U.S. E3 151
Richfield, Wi., U.S. m11 156
Richfield Springs, N.Y., U.S. C5 139
Richford, Vt., U.S. B3 152
Rich Fountain, Mo., U.S. C6 132
Rich Hill, Mo., U.S. C3 132
Richibucto, N.B., Can. C5 101
Richisau, Switz. D10 13
Richland, Ga., U.S. D2 117
Richland, In., U.S. I3 121
Richland, Ia., U.S. C6 122
Richland, Mi., U.S. F5 129
Richland, Mo., U.S. D5 132
Richland, N.J., U.S. D3 137
Richland, Wa., U.S. C6 154
Richland, co., Il., U.S. E5 120
Richland, co., La., U.S. B4 125
Richland, co., Mt., U.S. C12 133
Richland, co., N.D., U.S. C8 141
Richland, co., Oh., U.S. B3 142
Richland, co., S.C., U.S. D6 147
Richland, co., Wi., U.S. E3 156
Richland Balsam, mtn., N.C., U.S. f10 140
Richland Center, Wi., U.S. E3 156
Richland Creek, stm., Tn., U.S. B5 149
Richlands, N.C., U.S. C5 140
Richlands, Va., U.S. e10 153
Richlandtown, Pa., U.S. F11 145
Richmond, Austl. I9 70
Richmond, Austl. C5 70
Richmond, B.C., Can. E6 99
Richmond, P.E.I., Can. C6 101
Richmond, Que., Can. D5 104
Richmond, N.Z. D4 72
Richmond, S. Afr. H6 66
Richmond, S. Afr. G10 66
Richmond, Ca., U.S. D2 112
Richmond, Il., U.S. A5 120
Richmond, In., U.S. E8 121
Richmond, Ks., U.S. D8 123
Richmond, Ky., U.S. C5 124
Richmond, Me., U.S. D3 126
Richmond, Mi., U.S. F8 129
Richmond, Mn., U.S. E4 130
Richmond, Mo., U.S. B4 132
Richmond, Tx., U.S. E5 150
Richmond, Ut., U.S. B4 151
Richmond, Vt., U.S. C3 152
Richmond, Va., U.S. C5 153
Richmond, co., Ga., U.S. C4 117
Richmond, co., N.Y., U.S. E6 139
Richmond, co., N.C., U.S. B3 140
Richmond, co., Va., U.S. C6 153
Richmond Beach, Wa., U.S. B3 154
Richmond Dale, Oh., U.S. C3 142
Richmond Heights, Fl., U.S. s13 116
Richmond Heights, Mo., U.S. f13 132
Richmond Highlands, Wa., U.S. B3 154
Richmond Hill, Ont., Can. D5 103
Richmond Hill, Ga., U.S. E5 117
Richmond National Battlefield Park, Va., U.S. n18 153
Richmondville, N.Y., U.S. C6 139
Richmound, Sask., Can. G1 105
Rich Mountain, mtn., U.S. C1 111
Rich Mountain, mtn., Va., U.S. C1 153
Rich Mountain, mtn., W.V., U.S. C5 155
Rich Square, N.C., U.S. A5 140
Richthofen, Mount, mtn., Co., U.S. A5 113
Richton, Ms., U.S. D5 131
Richview, Il., U.S. E4 120
Richville, Mi., U.S. E7 129
Richwood, La., U.S. B3 125
Richwood, Oh., U.S. B2 142
Richwood, Tx., U.S. r14 150
Richwood, W.V., U.S. C4 155
Richwoods, Mo., U.S. C7 132
Rickenbacker Air Force Base, mil., Oh., U.S. m11 142
Rickman, Tn., U.S. C8 149
Riddle, Or., U.S. E3 144
Riddle Mountain, mtn., Or., U.S. D8 144
Rideau, stm., Ont., Can. B9 103
Riderwood, Al., U.S. C1 108
Ridgecrest, Ca., U.S. E5 112
Ridgecrest, La., U.S. C4 125
Ridgecrest, N.C., U.S. f10 140
Ridgedale, Sask., Can. D3 105
Ridgedale, Mo., U.S. E4 132
Ridge Farm, Il., U.S. D6 120
Ridgefield, Ct., U.S. D2 114
Ridgefield, N.J., U.S. h8 137
Ridgefield, Wa., U.S. D3 154
Ridgefield Park, N.J., U.S. B4 137
Ridgeland, Ms., U.S. C3 131
Ridgeland, S.C., U.S. G6 147
Ridgeley, W.V., U.S. B6 155
Ridgely, Md., U.S. C6 127
Ridgely, Tn., U.S. A2 149
Ridgeside, Tn., U.S. h11 149
Ridge Spring, S.C., U.S. D4 147
Ridgetop, Tn., U.S. A5 149
Ridgetown, Ont., Can. E3 103
Ridgeview, W.V., U.S. C3 155
Ridgeville, Man., Can. E3 100
Ridgeville, Ga., U.S. E5 117
Ridgeville, In., U.S. D7 121
Ridgeville, S.C., U.S. E7 147
Ridgeville Corners, Oh., U.S. A1 142
Ridgeway, Ia., U.S. A6 122
Ridgeway, Mo., U.S. A4 132
Ridgeway, S.C., U.S. C6 147
Ridgeway, Va., U.S. D3 153
Ridgeway, Wi., U.S. E4 156
Ridgewood, N.J., U.S. B4 137
Ridgewood Park, Ct., U.S. D7 114
Ridgway, Co., U.S. C3 113
Ridgway, Il., U.S. F5 120
Ridgway, Pa., U.S. D4 145
Riding Mountain, hills, Man., Can. D1 100
Riding Mountain National Park, Man., Can. D1 100
Ridley Park, Pa., U.S. p20 145
Ried im Innkreis, Aus. G13 10
Rienzi, Ms., U.S. A5 131
Riesa, Ger. D13 10
Riesco, Isla, i., Chile G2 78
Riesi, Italy L9 18
Rietavas, Lith. F4 22
Rietfontein, Nmb. C5 66
Rieti, Italy G7 18
Rif, mts., Mor. C8 62
Riffe Lake, res., Wa., U.S. C3 154
Rifle, Co., U.S. B3 113
Rifle, stm., Mi., U.S. D6 129
Rift Valley, val., Afr. I9 52
Rīga, Lat. E7 22
Riga, Gulf of (Rīgas jūras līcis) (Riia laht), b., Eur. D6 22
Rigacikun, Nig. F13 64
Rīgān, Iran G15 48
Rigaud, Que., Can. D3 104
Rigby, Id., U.S. F7 119
Rīgestān, reg., Afg. E1 44
Riggins, Id., U.S. D2 119
Rigi, mtn., Switz. D10 13
Rigo, Pap. N. Gui. A9 68
Rigolet, Newf., Can. A2 102
Riiser-Larsen Peninsula, pen., Ant. B4 73
Rijeka, Cro. D9 18
Rijswijk, Neth. D5 12
Riley, In., U.S. F3 121
Riley, Ks., U.S. C7 123
Riley, co., Ks., U.S. C7 123
Riley, Mount, mtn., N.M., U.S. F2 138
Rillito, Az., U.S. E4 110
Rima, stm., Nig. E12 64
Rímac, stm., Peru D3 82
Rimachi, Laguna, l., Peru J4 84
Rimavská Sobota, Slov. G20 10
Rimbey, Alta., Can. C3 98
Rimersburg, Pa., U.S. D3 145
Rimi, Nig. E13 64
Rimini, Italy E7 18
Rîmnicu Sărat, Rom. D11 20
Rîmnicu Vîlcea, Rom. D8 20
Rimouski, Que., Can. A9 104
Rimouski, stm., Que., Can. A9 104
Rimouski-Est, Que., Can. A9 104
Rimrock, Az., U.S. C4 110
Rimrock Lake, res., Wa., U.S. C4 154
Rincón, C.R. I11 92
Rincon, Ga., U.S. D5 117
Rincon, N.M., U.S. E2 138
Rinconada, Arg. B5 80
Rincón de la Vieja, Parque Nacional, C.R. G9 92
Rincón del Bonete, Lago Artificial de, res., Ur. G11 80
Rincón del Ocote, Cerro, mtn., Hond. D7 92
Rincón de Romos, Mex. F8 90
Rincon Mountains, mts., Az., U.S. E5 110
Rindal, Nor. J11 6
Rindge, N.H., U.S. E2 136
Riner, Va., U.S. C2 153
Rineyville, Ky., U.S. C4 124
Ringebu, Nor. K12 6
Ringgold, Ga., U.S. B1 117
Ringgold, La., U.S. B2 125
Ringgold, Va., U.S. D3 153
Ringgold, co., Ia., U.S. D3 122
Ringim, Nig. E14 64
Ringling, Ok., U.S. C4 143
Ringoes, N.J., U.S. C3 137
Ringsted, Ia., U.S. A3 122
Ringwood, N.J., U.S. A4 137
Ringwood, Ok., U.S. A3 143
Rinjani, Gunung, mtn., Indon. G6 38
Rinteln, Ger. C9 10
Rio, Fl., U.S. E6 116
Rio, Il., U.S. B3 120
Rio, Wi., U.S. E4 156
Rio Arriba, co., N.M., U.S. A2 138
Rio Azul, Braz. C13 80
Riobamba, Ec. H3 84
Río Blanco, Chile G3 80
Rio Blanco, co., Co., U.S. B2 113
Rio Branco, Braz. C8 82
Río Branco, Ur. G12 80
Río Bravo, Mex. E10 90
Rio Brilhante, Braz. F1 79
Río Caribe, Ven. B11 84
Rio Casca, Braz. F7 79
Río Ceballos, Arg. F6 80
Río Chico, Ven. B10 84
Rio Claro, Braz. G5 79
Río Claro, Trin. I14 94
Río Colorado, Arg. J6 80
Río Cuarto, Arg. G6 80
Rio de Contas, Braz. B8 79
Rio de Janeiro, Braz. G7 79
Rio de Janeiro, state, Braz. G7 79
Río de Jesús, Pan. J13 92
Rio Dell, Ca., U.S. B1 112
Río de Oro, Col. C6 84
Rio do Prado, Braz. D8 79
Rio do Sul, Braz. D14 80
Rio Espera, Braz. F7 79
Río Gallegos, Arg. G3 78
Rio Grande, Braz. G12 80
Río Grande, Mex. F8 90
Río Grande, Nic. E8 92
Rio Grande, N.J., U.S. E3 137
Rio Grande, Oh., U.S. D3 142
Rio Grande, co., Co., U.S. D4 113
Rio Grande City, Tx., U.S. F3 150
Rio Grande do Sul, state, Braz. E11 80
Rio Grande see Grande, Río, stm., N.A. F7 106
Rio Grande Reservoir, res., Co., U.S. D3 113
Ríohacha, Col. B6 84
Río Hato, Pan. C2 84
Rio Hondo, Tx., U.S. F4 150
Rioja, Peru B3 82
Río Lagartos, Mex. G15 90
Riolândia, Braz. E4 79
Rio Largo, Braz. E11 76
Riom, Fr. G10 14
Rio Mulatos, Bol. H8 82
Riondel, B.C., Can. E9 99
Rio Negro, Braz. E1 79
Rio Negro, Braz. D14 80
Ríonegro, Col. D5 84
Ríonegro, Col. D6 84
Río Negro, prov., Arg. J6 80
Rio Negro, Pantanal do, sw., Braz. H13 82
Rionero in Vulture, Italy I10 18
Rio Novo do Sul, Braz. F8 79
Rio Pardo, Braz. E12 80
Rio Pardo de Minas, Braz. C7 79
Río Piedras, Arg. C6 80
Río Pilcomayo, Parque Nacional, Arg. C9 80
Rio Piracicaba, Braz. E7 79
Rio Pomba, Braz. F7 79
Rio Preto, Braz. G7 79
Rio Rancho, N.M., U.S. B3 138
Río San Juan, dept., Nic. F10 92
Río Segundo, Arg. F7 80
Ríosucio, Col. E5 84
Ríosucio, Col. D4 84
Río Tercero, Arg. G6 80
Rio Tinto, Braz. E11 76
Rio Verde, Braz. D3 79
Ríoverde, Mex. G10 90
Rio Verde de Mato Grosso, Braz. E1 79
Rio Vermelho, Braz. E7 79
Rio Vista, Ca., U.S. C3 112
Rioz, Fr. E13 14
Riozinho, stm., Braz. I9 84
Ripley, Ont., Can. C3 103
Ripley, Ca., U.S. F6 112
Ripley, Ms., U.S. A5 131
Ripley, N.Y., U.S. C1 139
Ripley, Oh., U.S. D2 142
Ripley, Ok., U.S. A5 143
Ripley, Tn., U.S. B2 149
Ripley, W.V., U.S. C3 155
Ripley, co., In., U.S. F7 121
Ripley, co., Mo., U.S. E7 132
Ripogenus Pond, l., Me., U.S. C3 126
Ripoll, Spain C14 16
Ripon, Que., Can. D2 104
Ripon, Eng., U.K. G12 8
Ripon, Wi., U.S. E5 156
Riposto, Italy L10 18
Rippey, Ia., U.S. C3 122
Ripples, N.B., Can. D3 101
Rippowam, stm., Ct., U.S. E1 114
Ririe, Id., U.S. F7 119
Ririe Lake, res., Id., U.S. F7 119
Risaralda, dept., Col. E4 84
Riscle, Fr. I6 14
Risco, Mo., U.S. E8 132
Risco, Ilha do, i., Braz. I13 84
Rishiri-tō, i., Japan b16 36a
Rishmayyā, Leb. A5 50
Rishon LeẔiyyon, Isr. E3 50
Rising City, Ne., U.S. C8 134
Rising Star, Tx., U.S. C3 150
Rising Sun, De., U.S. D3 115
Rising Sun, In., U.S. G8 121
Rising Sun, Md., U.S. A5 127
Risingsun, Oh., U.S. A2 142
Rison, Ar., U.S. D3 111
Rison, Md., U.S. C3 127
Risør, Nor. L11 6
Rissani, Mor. E8 62
Risti, Est. C7 22
Ritchie, co., W.V., U.S. B3 155
Ritter, Mount, mtn., Ca., U.S. D4 112
Rittman, Oh., U.S. B4 142
Ritzville, Wa., U.S. B7 154
Riva, Italy D5 18
Rivadavia, Arg. H7 80
Rivadavia, Arg. G4 80
Rivadavia, Arg. C7 80
Rivadavia, Arg. F4 80
Rivadavia, Chile E3 80
Rivanna, stm., Va., U.S. C4 153
Rivas, Nic. F9 92
Rivas, dept., Nic. F8 92
Rive-de-Gier, Fr. G11 14
Rivera, Arg. I7 80
Rivera, Col. F5 84
Rivera, Ur. F11 80
Riverbank, Ca., U.S. D3 112
River Bourgeois, N.S., Can. D9 101
River Cess, Lib. I5 64
Riverdale, Ca., U.S. D4 112
Riverdale, Il., U.S. k9 120
Riverdale, Ia., U.S. g11 122
Riverdale, Md., U.S. C4 127
Riverdale, Ne., U.S. D6 134
Riverdale, N.J., U.S. B4 137
Riverdale, N.D., U.S. B4 141
Riverdale, Va., U.S. D4 153
River Edge, N.J., U.S. h8 137
River Falls, Al., U.S. D3 108
River Falls, Wi., U.S. D1 156
River Forest, Il., U.S. k9 120
Rivergaro, Italy E4 18
River Grove, Il., U.S. k9 120
Riverhaven, In., U.S. B7 121
Riverhead, N.Y., U.S. n16 139
River Hebert, N.S., Can. D5 101
River Heights, Ut., U.S. B4 151
River Hills, Wi., U.S. m12 156
Riverhurst, Sask., Can. G2 105
Riverina, reg., Austl. J6 70
River John, N.S., Can. D6 101
River Jordan, B.C., Can. h11 99
River of Ponds, Newf., Can. C3 102
River Pines, Ma., U.S. f10 128
Riverport, N.S., Can. E5 101
River Ridge, La., U.S. k11 125
River Road, Or., U.S. C3 144
River Rouge, Mi., U.S. p15 129
Rivers, Man., Can. D1 100
Riversdale, S. Afr. J5 66
Riverside, Al., U.S. B3 108
Riverside, Ca., U.S. F5 112
Riverside, Il., U.S. k9 120
Riverside, Ia., U.S. C6 122
Riverside, N.J., U.S. C3 137
Riverside, Pa., U.S. E8 145
Riverside, Ut., U.S. B3 151
Riverside, Wa., U.S. A6 154
Riverside, Wy., U.S. E6 157
Riverside, co., Ca., U.S. F5 112
Riverside-Albert, N.B., Can. D5 101
Riverside Reservoir, res., Co., U.S. A6 113
Riverton, Man., Can. D3 100
Riverton, N.Z. G2 72
Riverton, Ct., U.S. B3 114
Riverton, Il., U.S. D4 120
Riverton, Ia., U.S. D2 122
Riverton, Ks., U.S. E9 123
Riverton, Ne., U.S. D7 134
Riverton, N.J., U.S. C3 137
Riverton, Ut., U.S. C4 151
Riverton, Vt., U.S. C3 152
Riverton, Va., U.S. B4 153
Riverton, Wy., U.S. C4 157
Riverton Heights, Wa., U.S. f11 154
River Vale, N.J., U.S. h8 137
Riverview, Fl., U.S. p11 116
Riverview, Mi., U.S. p15 129
Rives, Tn., U.S. A2 149
Rivesaltes, Fr. J9 14
Rives Junction, Mi., U.S. F6 129
Rivesville, W.V., U.S. B4 155
Riviera, Tx., U.S. F4 150
Riviera Beach, Fl., U.S. F6 116
Riviera Beach, Md., U.S. B4 127
Rivière-à-Pierre, Que., Can. B5 104
Rivière-du-Loup, Que., Can. B8 104
Rivière-Trois-Pistoles, Que., Can. A8 104
Rivière-Verte, N.B., Can. B1 101
Riviersonderend, S. Afr. J4 66
Rivoli, Italy D2 18
Riyadh see Ar-Riyāḍ, Sau. Ar. B5 47
Rize, Tur. G16 4
Rizhao, China H7 32
Roa, Nor. K12 6
Roachdale, In., U.S. E4 121
Road Town, Br. Vir. Is. E12 94
Roan Cliffs, clf, U.S. B1 113
Roan Creek, stm., Co., U.S. B2 113
Roane, co., Tn., U.S. D9 149
Roane, co., W.V., U.S. C3 155
Roan High Knob, mtn., U.S. C11 149
Roan Mountain, Tn., U.S. C11 149
Roann, In., U.S. C6 121
Roanne, Fr. F11 14
Roanoke, Al., U.S. B4 108
Roanoke, Il., U.S. C4 120
Roanoke, In., U.S. C7 121
Roanoke, La., U.S. D3 125
Roanoke, Tx., U.S. m9 150
Roanoke, Va., U.S. C3 153
Roanoke, co., Va., U.S. C2 153
Roanoke, stm., U.S. A5 140
Roanoke Island, i., N.C., U.S. B7 140
Roanoke Rapids, N.C., U.S. A5 140
Roanoke Rapids Lake, res., U.S. A5 140
Roan Plateau, plat., U.S. B2 113
Roaring Fork, stm., Co., U.S. C4 113
Roaring Spring, Pa., U.S. F5 145
Roark, Ky., U.S. C6 124
Roatán, Hond. A8 92
Roatán, Isla de, i., Hond. A8 92
Robâ Oued Yahia, Tun. M4 18
Robards, Ky., U.S. C2 124
Robāṭ Karīm, Iran D11 48
Robb, Alta., Can. C2 98
Robbins, Il., U.S. k9 120
Robbins, N.C., U.S. B3 140
Robbins, Tn., U.S. C9 149
Robbinsdale, Mn., U.S. m12 130
Robbins Island, i., Austl. M6 70
Robbinston, Me., U.S. C5 126
Robbinsville, N.C., U.S. f9 140
Röbel, Ger. B12 10
Robersonville, N.C., U.S. B5 140
Roberta, Ga., U.S. D2 117
Robert Lee, Tx., U.S. D2 150
Roberts, Id., U.S. F6 119
Roberts, Il., U.S. C5 120
Roberts, Mt., U.S. E7 133
Roberts, Wi., U.S. C1 156
Roberts, co., S.D., U.S. B8 148
Roberts, co., Tx., U.S. B2 150
Roberts, Point, c., Wa., U.S. A2 154
Robert's Arm, Newf., Can. D4 102
Roberts Creek Mountain, mtn., Nv., U.S. D5 135
Robertsdale, Al., U.S. E2 108
Robertsdale, Pa., U.S. F5 145
Robertsfield, Lib. H4 64
Robert S. Kerr Reservoir, res., Ok., U.S. B6 143
Roberts Mountain, mtn., Ak., U.S. C6 109
Roberts Mountain, mtn., Wy., U.S. D3 157
Robertson, S. Afr. I4 66
Robertson, co., Ky., U.S. B5 124
Robertson, co., Tn., U.S. A5 149
Robertson, co., Tx., U.S. D4 150
Robertsonville, Que., Can. C6 104
Robertsport, Lib. H4 64
Robertstown, Ga., U.S. B3 117
Robertville, N.B., Can. B4 101
Roberval, Que., Can. A5 104
Robeson, co., N.C., U.S. C3 140
Robins, Ia., U.S. B6 122
Robins Air Force Base, mil., Ga., U.S. D3 117
Robinson, Il., U.S. D6 120
Robinson, Ks., U.S. C8 123
Robinson, Me., U.S. B5 126
Robinson, N.D., U.S. B6 141
Robinson, Pa., U.S. F3 145
Róbinson Crusoe, Isla, i., Chile H7 74
Robinson Fork, stm., W.V., U.S. k9 155
Robinson Fork, stm., W.V., U.S. m14 155
Robinson Mountain, mtn., Ar., U.S. A1 111
Robinson Range, mts., Austl. E3 68
Robinsons, Newf., Can. D2 102
Robinsonville, Ms., U.S. A3 131
Robinvale, Austl. J5 70
Roblin, Man., Can. D1 100
Roboré, Bol. H12 82
Robson, Mount, mtn., B.C., Can. C8 99
Robstown, Tx., U.S. F4 150
Roby, Tx., U.S. C2 150
Roca, Cabo da, c., Port. G2 16
Rocafuerte, Ec. H2 84
Rocanville, Sask., Can. G5 105
Roca Partida, Isla, i., Mex. H3 90
Roca Partida, Punta, c., Mex. H12 90
Rocas, Atol das, atoll, Braz. D12 76
Roccastrada, Italy F6 18
Rocciamelone, mtn., Italy D2 18
Rocha, Ur. H9 74
Rocha, Ur. H11 80
Rochdale, Ma., U.S. B4 128
Rochedinho, Braz. F1 79
Rochedinho, Braz. I14 82
Rochedo, Braz. E1 79
Rochefort, Bel. H7 12
Rochefort, Fr. G6 14
Roche Harbor, Wa., U.S. A2 154
Rochelle, Ga., U.S. E3 117
Rochelle, Il., U.S. B4 120
Rochelle Park, N.J., U.S. h8 137
Roche-Percée, Sask., Can. H4 105
Rocheport, Mo., U.S. C5 132
Rochester, Austl. K6 70
Rochester, Alta., Can. B4 98
Rochester, Il., U.S. D4 120
Rochester, In., U.S. B5 121
Rochester, Ky., U.S. C3 124
Rochester, Mi., U.S. F7 129
Rochester, Mn., U.S. F6 130
Rochester, N.H., U.S. D5 136
Rochester, N.Y., U.S. B3 139
Rochester, Pa., U.S. E1 145
Rochester, Vt., U.S. D3 152
Rochester, Wa., U.S. C2 154
Rochester, Wi., U.S. n11 156
Rochester Mountain, mtn., Vt., U.S. D3 152
Rochfort Bridge, Alta., Can. C3 98
Rochlitz, Ger. D12 10
Rock, Mi., U.S. B3 129
Rock, co., Mn., U.S. G2 130
Rock, co., Ne., U.S. B6 134
Rock, co., Wi., U.S. F4 156
Rock, stm., U.S. B3 120
Rock, stm., U.S. A1 122
Rockall, i., Scot., U.K. D5 4
Rockaway, N.J., U.S. B3 137
Rockaway, Or., U.S. B3 144
Rockaway Beach, Mo., U.S. E4 132
Rockbridge, Il., U.S. D3 120
Rockbridge, co., Va., U.S. C3 153
Rockcastle, co., Ky., U.S. C5 124
Rockcastle, stm., Ky., U.S. C5 124
Rockcliffe Park, Ont., Can. h12 103
Rock Creek, B.C., Can. E8 99
Rock Creek, Mn., U.S. E6 130
Rock Creek, Oh., U.S. A5 142
Rock Creek, stm., U.S. B3 127
Rock Creek, stm., U.S. h14 154
Rock Creek, stm., Il., U.S. B4 120
Rock Creek, stm., Ks., U.S. g10 123
Rock Creek, stm., Ne., U.S. g11 134
Rock Creek, stm., Nv., U.S. C5 135
Rock Creek, stm., Or., U.S. B6 144
Rock Creek, stm., Wa., U.S. B8 154
Rock Creek, stm., Wa., U.S. D5 154
Rock Creek, stm., Wy., U.S. E6 157
Rock Creek Butte, mtn., Or., U.S. C8 144
Rockdale, Il., U.S. B5 120
Rockdale, Md., U.S. B4 127
Rockdale, Tx., U.S. D4 150
Rockdale, co., Ga., U.S. C3 117
Rockefeller Plateau, plat., Ant. D10 73
Rockenhausen, Ger. F7 10
Rockfall, Ct., U.S. C5 114
Rock Falls, Il., U.S. B4 120
Rockfield, In., U.S. C4 121
Rockfield, Ky., U.S. D3 124
Rockford, Al., U.S. C3 108
Rockford, Il., U.S. A4 120
Rockford, Ia., U.S. A5 122
Rockford, Mi., U.S. E5 129
Rockford, Mn., U.S. E5 130
Rockford, Oh., U.S. B1 142
Rockford, Tn., U.S. D10 149
Rockford, Wa., U.S. B8 154
Rockglen, Sask., Can. H3 105
Rock Hall, Md., U.S. B5 127
Rockhampton, Austl. D9 70
Rock Hill, S.C., U.S. B5 147
Rockholds, Ky., U.S. D5 124
Rockingham, N.C., U.S. C3 140
Rockingham, co., N.H., U.S. D4 136
Rockingham, co., N.C., U.S. A3 140
Rockingham, co., Va., U.S. B4 153
Rockingham Bay, b., Austl. B7 70
Rock Island, Que., Can. D5 104
Rock Island, Il., U.S. B3 120
Rock Island, Ok., U.S. B7 143
Rock Island, Wa., U.S. B5 154
Rock Island, co., Il., U.S. B3 120
Rock Island, i., Fl., U.S. C3 116
Rock Island, i., Wi., U.S. C7 156
Rocklake, N.D., U.S. A6 141
Rock Lake, l., Man., Can. E2 100
Rock Lake, l., Wa., U.S. B8 154
Rockland, Ont., Can. B9 103
Rockland, Id., U.S. G6 119
Rockland, Me., U.S. D3 126
Rockland, Ma., U.S. B6 128
Rockland, Mi., U.S. m12 129
Rockland, co., N.Y., U.S. D6 139
Rocklands Reservoir, res., Austl. K5 70
Rockledge, Fl., U.S. D6 116
Rockledge, Ga., U.S. D4 117
Rockledge, Pa., U.S. o20 145
Rocklin, Ca., U.S. C3 112
Rockmart, Ga., U.S. B1 117
Rock Mountain, mtn., Al., U.S. B2 108
Rock Mountain, mtn., Co., U.S. D3 113
Rock Point, Az., U.S. A6 110
Rockport, Ar., U.S. g8 111
Rockport, Il., U.S. D2 120
Rockport, In., U.S. I3 121
Rockport, Ky., U.S. C3 124
Rockport, Me., U.S. D3 126
Rockport, Ma., U.S. A6 128
Rock Port, Mo., U.S. A2 132
Rockport, Tx., U.S. F4 150
Rockport, Wa., U.S. A4 154
Rock Rapids, Ia., U.S. A1 122
Rock River, Wy., U.S. E7 157
Rock Run, Al., U.S. A4 108
Rock Sound, Bah. B6 94
Rocksprings, Tx., U.S. D2 150
Rock Springs, Wi., U.S. E4 156
Rock Springs, Wy., U.S. E3 157
Rockstone, Guy. E13 84
Rockton, Il., U.S. A4 120
Rockvale, Co., U.S. C5 113
Rockvale, Tn., U.S. B5 149
Rock Valley, Ia., U.S. A1 122
Rockville, In., U.S. E3 121
Rockville, Md., U.S. B3 127
Rockville, Mn., U.S. E4 130
Rockville, Mo., U.S. C3 132
Rockville Centre, N.Y., U.S. n15 139
Rockwall, Tx., U.S. C4 150
Rockwall, co., Tx., U.S. C4 150
Rockwell, Ia., U.S. B4 122
Rockwell, N.C., U.S. B2 140
Rockwell City, Ia., U.S. B3 122
Rockwell Park, N.C., U.S. B2 140
Rockwood, Me., U.S. C3 126
Rockwood, Mi., U.S. F7 129
Rockwood, Pa., U.S. G3 145
Rockwood, Tn., U.S. D9 149
Rocky, stm., N.C., U.S. B2 140

Name / Map Ref. / Page

Sainte-Marie, Que., Can. C6 104
Sainte Marie, Il., U.S. E5 120
Sainte-Marie, Cap, c., Madag. t21 67b
Sainte-Marie-aux-Mines, Fr. D14 14
Saint Maries, Id., U.S. B2 119
Sainte Marie-sur-Mer [-Saint Raphaël-sur-Mer], N.B., Can. B5 101
Saint Mark, Ks., U.S. g11 123
Sainte-Marthe, Que., Can. D3 104
Saint Martin, co., La., U.S. D4 125
Saint-Martin (Sint Maarten), i., N.A. E13 94
Saint Martin, Lake, l., Man., Can. D2 100
Saint Martin Island, i., Mi., U.S. C4 129
Saint Martins, N.B., Can. D4 101
Saint Martin Station, Man., Can. D2 100
Saint Martinville, La., U.S. D4 125
Saint Mary, Ky., U.S. C4 124
Saint Mary, Mo., U.S. D8 132
Saint Mary, co., La., U.S. E4 125
Saint Mary-of-the-Woods, In., U.S. E3 121
Saint Mary Peak, mtn., Austl. H3 70
Saint Mary Reservoir, res., Alta., Can. E4 98
Saint Marys, Austl. M8 70
Saint Mary's, Newf., Can. E5 102
Saint Mary's, Ont., Can. D3 103
Saint Marys, Ak., U.S. C7 109
Saint Marys, Ga., U.S. F5 117
Saint Marys, In., U.S. A5 121
Saint Marys, Ks., U.S. C7 123
Saint Marys, Oh., U.S. B1 142
Saint Marys, Pa., U.S. D4 145
Saint Marys, W.V., U.S. B3 155
Saint Marys, co., Md., U.S. D4 127
Saint Marys, stm., N.S., Can. D8 101
Saint Marys, stm., U.S. F5 117
Saint Marys, stm., U.S. C8 121
Saint Marys, stm., Md., U.S. D5 127
Saint Mary's, Cape, c., Newf., Can. E4 102
Saint Mary's Bay, b., Newf., Can. E5 102
Saint Marys Bay, b., N.S., Can. E3 101
Saint Marys City, Md., U.S. D5 127
Saint Marys Entrance, strt., Ga., U.S. F5 117
Saint-Mathieu, Fr. G7 14
Saint Matthew Island, i., Ak., U.S. C5 109
Saint Matthews, Ky., U.S. B4 124
Saint Matthews, S.C., U.S. D6 147
Saint-Maur [-des-Fossés], Fr. D9 14
Saint-Maurice, Que., Can. C5 104
Saint-Maurice, stm., Que., Can. C5 104
Sainte-Maxime, Fr. I13 14
Saint-Méen-le-Grand, Fr. D4 14
Saint Meinrad, In., U.S. H4 121
Sainte-Menehould, Fr. C11 14
Sainte-Mère-Église, Fr. C5 14
Saint-Méthode [-de-Frontenac], Que., Can. C6 104
Saint Michael, Alta., Can. C4 98
Saint Michael, Ak., U.S. C7 109
Saint Michael, Mn., U.S. E5 130
Saint Michaels, Az., U.S. B6 110
Saint Michaels, Md., U.S. C5 127
Saint-Michel [-de-Bellechasse], Que., Can. C7 104
Saint-Mihiel, Fr. D12 14
Sainte-Monique [-de-Nicolet], Que., Can. C5 104
Saint-Moritz see Sankt Moritz, Switz. F16 14
Saint-Nazaire, Fr. E4 14
Saint-Nazaire [-de-Buckland], Que., Can. C7 104
Saint Nazianz, Wi., U.S. D6 156
Saint-Nicolas, Que., Can. o17 104
Saint-Nicolas see Sint-Niklaas, Bel. F5 12
Saint-Odilon, Que., Can. C7 104
Saint-Omer, Fr. B9 14
Saint Onge, S.D., U.S. C2 148
Saintonge, hist. reg., Fr. G6 14
Saint-Ours, Que., Can. D4 104
Saint-Pacôme, Que., Can. B8 104
Saint-Pamphile, Que., Can. C8 104
Saint Paris, Oh., U.S. B2 142
Saint-Pascal, Que., Can. B8 104
Saint Paul, Alta., Can. B5 98
Saint-Paul, Fr. I14 14
Saint-Paul, Reu. v17 67c
Saint Paul, Ak., U.S. D5 109
Saint Paul, In., U.S. F6 121
Saint Paul, Ks., U.S. E8 123
Saint Paul, Mn., U.S. F5 130
Saint Paul, Mo., U.S. f12 132
Saint Paul, Ne., U.S. C7 134
Saint Paul, Or., U.S. h12 144
Saint Paul, Va., U.S. f9 153
Saint Paul, stm., Lib. H4 64
Saint-Paul, Île, i., F.S.A.T. L11 158
Saint-Paulin, Que., Can. C4 104
Saint Paul Island, i., Ak., U.S. D5 109
Saint Paul Park, Mn., U.S. n12 130
Saint Pauls, N.C., U.S. C4 140
Sainte-Perpétue-de-L'Islet, Que., Can. B8 104
Saint Peter, Il., U.S. E5 120
Saint Peter, Mn., U.S. F5 130
Saint Peter Island, i., Austl. F6 68
Saint Peter Port, Guernsey C4 14
Saint Peters, N.S., Can. D9 101
Saint Peters, Mo., U.S. C7 132
Saint Petersburg, Fl., U.S. E4 116
Saint Petersburg Beach, Fl., U.S. p10 116
Saint Petersburg see Sankt-Peterburg, Russia B13 22
Saint-Philémon, Que., Can. C7 104
Saint Philip, In., U.S. I2 121
Saint Phillips Island, i., S.C., U.S. G6 147
Saint-Pie, Que., Can. D5 104
Saint-Pierre, Mart. G14 94
Saint-Pierre, Reu. v17 67c
Saint-Pierre, St. P./M. E3 102
Saint-Pierre, Lac, l., Que., Can. C5 104
Saint Pierre and Miquelon, dep., N.A. E3 102
Saint-Pierre-Église, Fr. C5 14
Saint Pierre Island, i., Sey. C10 58
Saint-Pierre-Jolys, Man., Can. E3 100
Saint-Pierre-Montmagny, Que., Can. C7 104
Saint-Placide, Que., Can. p18 104
Saint-Pol-de-Léon, Fr. D3 14
Saint-Pol-sur-Ternoise, Fr. B9 14
Saint-Pons, Fr. I9 14
Saint-Prime, Que., Can. A5 104
Saint Quentin, N.B., Can. B2 101
Saint-Quentin, Fr. C10 14
Saint-Raphaël, Que., Can. C7 104
Saint-Raphaël, Fr. I13 14
Saint-Raphaël-sur-Mer (part of Sainte Marie-sur-Mer-Saint Raphaël-sur-Mer), N.B., Can. B5 101
Saint-Raymond, Que., Can. C6 104
Saint-Rédempteur, Que., Can. o17 104
Saint Regis, Mt., U.S. C1 133
Saint Regis, West Branch, stm., N.Y., U.S. f10 139
Saint Regis Falls, N.Y., U.S. f10 139
Saint-Rémi, Que., Can. D4 104
Saint-Rémy-de-Provence, Fr. I11 14
Saint-Romuald, Que., Can. C6 104
Saint Rose, La., U.S. k11 125
Sainte Rose du Lac, Man., Can. D2 100
Saintes, Fr. G6 14
Sainte-Sabine-de-Bellechasse, Que., Can. C7 104
Saint Samuel, Que., Can. D7 104
Saint-Sauveur, N.B., Can. B4 101
Saint-Sauveur-des-Monts, Que., Can. D3 104
Saint-Seine-l'Abbaye, Fr. E11 14
Saint-Séverin-de-Beauce, Que., Can. C6 104
Saint Shotts, Newf., Can. E5 102
Saint-Siméon, Que., Can. B8 104
Saint Simons Island, Ga., U.S. E5 117
Saint Simons Island, i., Ga., U.S. E5 117
Saint Simons Sound, strt., Ga., U.S. E5 117
Saintes-Maries-de-la-Mer, Fr. I11 14
Sainte-Sophie [-de-Lévrard], Que., Can. C5 104
Sainte-Sophie [-de-Mégantic], Que., Can. C6 104
Saint Stephen, N.B., Can. D2 101
Saint Stephen, S.C., U.S. E8 147
Saint Stephens, Al., U.S. D1 108
Saint-Sylvestre, Que., Can. C6 104
Saint Tammany, co., La., U.S. D5 125
Sainte-Thècle, Que., Can. C5 104
Saint-Théophile, Que., Can. D7 104
Sainte-Thérèse, Que., Can. D4 104
Saint Thomas, Ont., Can. E3 103
Saint Thomas, Mo., U.S. C5 132
Saint Thomas, N.D., U.S. A8 141
Saint Thomas, Pa., U.S. G6 145
Saint Thomas, i., V.I.U.S. E12 94
Saint Timothée, Que., Can. q18 104
Saint-Tite, Que., Can. C5 104
Saint-Trond see Sint-Truiden, Bel. G7 12
Saint-Tropez, Fr. I13 14
Saint-Valéry-en-Caux, Fr. C7 14
Saint-Valéry-sur-Somme, Fr. B8 14
Saint-Vallier, Que., Can. C7 104
Saint-Vallier-de-Thiey, Fr. I13 14
Sainte-Véronique, Que., Can. C3 104
Saint-Victor, Que., Can. C7 104
Saint Vincent, i., St. Vin. H14 94
Saint Vincent, Cape see São Vicente, Cabo de, c., Port. H2 16
Saint Vincent, Gulf, b., Austl. J3 70
Saint Vincent and the Grenadines, ctry., N.A. H14 94
Saint-Vincent-de-Tyrosse, Fr. I5 14
Saint Vincent Island, i., Fl., U.S. C1 116
Saint Vincent Passage, strt., N.A. H14 94
Saint Vincent's [-Saint Stephens-Peter's River], Newf., Can. E5 102
Saint-Vith (Sankt Vith), Bel. H9 12
Saint Walburg, Sask., Can. D1 105
Saint Wendells, In., U.S. H2 121
Saint Williams, Ont., Can. E4 103
Saint Xavier, Mt., U.S. E9 133
Saint-Zacharie, Que., Can. C7 104
Saitula, China D2 30
Sai Yok, Thai. G5 40
Sajama, Bol. H7 82
Sajama, Nevado, mtn., Bol. H7 82
Sajano-Sušenskoje vodochranilišče, res., Russia G16 26
Şajat, Turk. B17 48
Šajmak', Taj. B6 44
Sajnšand, Mong. C9 30
Sajó (Slaná), stm., Eur. G20 10
Sajószentpéter, Hung. G20 10
Sa Kaeo, Thai. H7 40
Sakai, Japan M10 36
Sakaiminato, Japan L8 36
Sakākah, Sau. Ar. G6 48
Sakakawea, Lake, res., N.D., U.S. B3 141
Sakania, Zaire D5 58
Sakaraha, Madag. s21 67b
Sakarya, stm., Tur. G14 4
Sakata, Japan I14 36
Sakchu, N. Kor. C13 32
Sakété, Benin H11 64
Sakhalin see Sachalin, ostrov, i., Russia G20 28
Şakhrīyāt, Jabal aṣ-, mtn., Jord. F6 50
Sakht Sar, Iran C11 48
Šakiai, Lith. G6 22
Sakiet Sidi Youssef, Tun. M3 18
Sakon Nakhon, Thai. F8 40
Sakonnet, stm., R.I., U.S. E6 146
Sakonnet Point, c., R.I., U.S. F6 146
Sakrand, Pak. G3 44
Sakrivier, S. Afr. H5 66
Sal, i., C.V. k17 64a
Sal, stm., Russia H6 26
Sal, Cay, i., Bah. C4 94
Sal, Point, c., Ca., U.S. E3 112
Sal, Punta, c., Hond. B7 92
Sala, Swe. L15 6
Salaberry-de-Valleyfield, Que., Can. D3 104
Salacgrīva, Lat. D7 22
Salada, Laguna, l., Mex. A2 90
Saladas, Arg. E9 80
Saladillo, Arg. H9 80
Saladillo, stm., Arg. G7 80
Saladillo, stm., Arg. E7 80
Saladillo Dulce, Arroyo, stm., Arg. F8 80
Salado, Arg. E5 80
Salado, stm., Arg. H5 80
Salado, stm., Arg. F8 80
Salado, stm., Arg. E5 80
Salado, stm., Arg. H9 80
Salado, stm., Cuba D6 94
Salado, stm., Mex. D10 90
Salado, Rio, stm., N.M., U.S. C2 138
Sălaj, co., Rom. B7 20
Šalakuša, Russia J27 6
Salala, Chile F3 80
Salala, Lib. H4 64
Salālah, Oman F9 47
Salamá, Guat. B4 92
Salamá, Hond. C8 92
Salamanca, Chile F3 80
Salamanca, Mex. G9 90
Salamanca, Peru F5 82
Salamanca, Spain E6 16
Salamanca, N.Y., U.S. C2 139
Salamat, Bahr, stm., Chad F4 56
Salamina, Col. E5 84
Salamís, Grc. L7 20
Salamís, i., Grc. L7 20
Salamonie, stm., In., U.S. C6 121
Salamonie Lake, res., In., U.S. C6 121
Salantai, Lith. E4 22
Salaquí, Col. D4 84
Salaquí, stm., Col. D4 84
Salas, Peru B2 82
Salatiga, Indon. j15 39a
Salavat, Russia G9 26
Salaverry, Peru C2 82
Salavina, Arg. E7 80
Sala y Gómez, Isla, i., Chile K29 158
Salcajá, Guat. C3 92
Salcantay, Nevado, mtn., Peru E5 82
Salcedo, Dom. Rep. E9 94
Šalčininkai, Lith. G8 22
Saldaña, stm., Col. F5 84
Saldanha, S. Afr. I3 66
Saldungaray, Arg. J8 80
Saldus, Lat. E5 22
Sale, Austl. L7 70
Salé, Mor. C7 62
Salebabu, Pulau, i., Indon. E8 38
Salechard, Russia D5 28
Sale City, Ga., U.S. E2 117
Sale Creek, Tn., U.S. D8 149
Salem, India G5 46
Salem, Al., U.S. C4 108
Salem, Ar., U.S. A4 111
Salem, Il., U.S. E5 120
Salem, In., U.S. G5 121
Salem, Ia., U.S. D6 122
Salem, Ky., U.S. e9 124
Salem, Ma., U.S. A6 128
Salem, Mi., U.S. p14 129
Salem, Mo., U.S. D6 132
Salem, Ne., U.S. D10 134
Salem, N.H., U.S. E4 136
Salem, N.J., U.S. D2 137
Salem, N.M., U.S. E2 138
Salem, N.Y., U.S. B7 139
Salem, Oh., U.S. B5 142
Salem, Or., U.S. C4 144
Salem, S.D., U.S. D8 148
Salem, Ut., U.S. C4 151
Salem, Va., U.S. C2 153
Salem, W.V., U.S. B4 155
Salem, Wi., U.S. n11 156
Salem, co., N.J., U.S. D2 137
Salem, stm., N.J., U.S. D2 137
Salem, Lake, l., Vt., U.S. B4 152
Salemburg, N.C., U.S. B4 140
Salemi, Italy L7 18
Salentina, Penisola, pen., Italy I13 18
Salerno, Italy I9 18
Salerno, Golfo di, b., Italy I9 18
Salesville, Ar., U.S. A3 111
Salgar, Col. E5 84
Salgótarján, Hung. G19 10
Sali, Alg. G10 62
Salí, stm., Arg. D6 80
Salida, Co., U.S. C5 113
Salies-de-Béarn, Fr. I6 14
Salihli, Tur. K12 20
Salim, Sud. K5 60
Salima, Mwi. D6 58
Salimani, Com. k15 67a
Salina, Az., U.S. A6 110
Salina, Ks., U.S. D6 123
Salina, Ok., U.S. A6 143
Salina, Ut., U.S. E4 151
Salina Cruz, Mex. I12 90
Salina Point, c., Bah. C7 94
Salinas, Braz. D7 79
Salinas, Ec. I2 84
Salinas, Ca., U.S. D3 112
Salinas, stm., Braz. D7 79
Salinas, stm., Ca., U.S. D3 112
Salinas, Pampa de las, pl., Arg. G5 80
Salinas de Garci Mendoza, Bol. H8 82
Salinas de Hidalgo, Mex. F9 90
Salinas Peak, mtn., N.M., U.S. D3 138
Salinas Pueblo Missions National Monument, N.M., U.S. C3 138
Saline, La., U.S. B3 125
Saline, Mi., U.S. F7 129
Saline, co., Ar., U.S. C3 111
Saline, co., Il., U.S. F5 120
Saline, co., Ks., U.S. D6 123
Saline, co., Mo., U.S. B4 132
Saline, co., Ne., U.S. D8 134
Saline, stm., Ar., U.S. C1 111
Saline, stm., Ar., U.S. D4 111
Saline, stm., Ks., U.S. C3 123
Saline, North Fork, stm., Il., U.S. F5 120
Saline, South Fork, stm., Ar., U.S. f8 111
Saline Bayou, stm., La., U.S. B3 125
Saline Lake, res., La., U.S. C3 125
Salineville, Oh., U.S. B5 142
Salingyi, Burma D3 40
Salisbury, Austl. J3 70
Salisbury, N.B., Can. C4 101
Salisbury, Eng., U.K. J12 8
Salisbury, Ct., U.S. B2 114
Salisbury, Md., U.S. D6 127
Salisbury, Ma., U.S. A6 128
Salisbury, Mo., U.S. B5 125
Salisbury, N.H., U.S. D3 136
Salisbury, N.C., U.S. B2 140
Salisbury, Pa., U.S. G3 145
Salisbury, Vt., U.S. D2 152
Salisbury see Harare, Zimb. A10 66
Salisbury Island, i., N.W. Ter., Can. D17 96
Salisbury Plain, pl., Eng., U.K. J12 8
Salish Mountains, mts., Mt., U.S. B2 133
Salitpa, Al., U.S. D1 108
Salix, Ia., U.S. B1 122
Saljany, Azer. J7 26
Salkehatchie, stm., S.C., U.S. E5 147
Salkhad, Syria D7 50
Salkum, Wa., U.S. C3 154
Sallanches, Fr. G13 14
Salley, S.C., U.S. D5 147
Salliqueló, Arg. I7 80
Sallisaw, Ok., U.S. B7 143
Salluit, Que., Can. f11 104
Sallūm, Khalīj as-, b., Afr. B3 60
Salmās, Iran B8 48
Salmi, Russia K22 6
Salmo, B.C., Can. E9 99
Salmon, Id., U.S. D5 119
Salmon, stm., N.B., Can. C4 101
Salmon, stm., Id., U.S. D3 119
Salmon, Middle Fork, stm., Id., U.S. E4 119
Salmon, South Fork, stm., Id., U.S. E3 119
Salmon Creek, Wa., U.S. D3 154
Salmon Creek Reservoir, res., Id., U.S. G4 119
Salmon Falls, stm., U.S. D5 136
Salmon Falls Creek, stm., U.S. G4 119
Salmon Mountain, mtn., N.H., U.S. f7 136
Salmon Mountains, mts., Ca., U.S. B2 112
Salmon Peak, mtn., Tx., U.S. E2 150
Salmon Point, c., Ont., Can. D7 103
Salmon River Mountains, mts., Id., U.S. E3 119
Salmon River Reservoir, res., N.Y., U.S. B5 139
Salo, Fin. K18 6
Salò, Italy D5 18
Salobra, stm., Braz. I13 82
Salome, Az., U.S. D2 110
Salon-de-Provence, Fr. I12 14
Salonika see Thessaloníki, Grc. I6 20
Salonta, Rom. C5 20
Saloum, stm., Sen. D2 64
Sal Rei, C.V. k17 64a
Salsacate, Arg. F6 80
Salsilgo, Qawz, dunes, Afr. L2 60
Salsipuedes, Canal, strt., Mex. C3 90
Salsipuedes, Punta, c., C.R. I11 92
Salsipuedes, Punta, c., Mex. A1 90
Sal'sk, Russia H6 26
Salsomaggiore Terme, Italy E4 18
Salt, stm., Az., U.S. D4 110
Salt, stm., Ky., U.S. C4 124
Salt, stm., Mo., U.S. B6 132
Salt, Middle Fork, stm., Mo., U.S. B5 132
Salt, North Fork, stm., Mo., U.S. B5 132
Salt, South Fork, stm., Mo., U.S. B5 132
Salta, Arg. C6 80
Salta, prov., Arg. C5 80
Saltcoats, Sask., Can. F4 105
Salt Creek, stm., Il., U.S. C4 120
Salt Creek, stm., Ks., U.S. f10 123
Salt Creek, stm., Ne., U.S. h11 134
Salt Creek, stm., N.M., U.S. D5 138
Salt Creek, stm., Oh., U.S. C3 142
Salt Creek, stm., Wy., U.S. C6 157
Salter Path, N.C., U.S. C6 140
Salt Fork Lake, res., Oh., U.S. B4 142
Saltillo, Mex. E9 90
Saltillo, Ms., U.S. A5 131
Saltillo, Tn., U.S. B3 149
Salt Lake, co., Ut., U.S. C3 151
Salt Lake, l., Hi., U.S. g10 118
Salt Lake, l., N.M., U.S. E6 138
Salt Lake City, Ut., U.S. C4 151
Salt Lick, Ky., U.S. B6 124
Salto, Arg. H8 80
Salto, Ur. F10 80
Salto da Divisa, Braz. D9 79
Salto de las Rosas, Arg. H4 80
Salto del Guairá, Para. A6 78
Salto del Guairá, Para. C11 80
Salto Grande, Braz. G4 79
Salto Grande, Embalse, res., S.A. F9 80
Salton Sea, l., Ca., U.S. F5 112
Saltonstall, Lake, l., Ct., U.S. D4 114
Salt Point, c., Ca., U.S. C2 112
Salt River Indian Reservation, Az., U.S. k9 110
Salt River Range, mts., Wy., U.S. D2 157
Salt Rock, W.V., U.S. C2 155
Saltsburg, Pa., U.S. F3 145
Saltspring Island, i., B.C., Can. E6 99
Salt Springs, Fl., U.S. C5 116
Saltville, Va., U.S. f10 153
Salt Wells Creek, stm., Wy., U.S. E4 157
Saluda, N.C., U.S. f10 140
Saluda, S.C., U.S. C4 147
Saluda, Va., U.S. C6 153
Saluda, co., S.C., U.S. C4 147
Saluda, stm., S.C., U.S. C4 147
Saluda Dam, S.C., U.S. C5 147
Sālūr, India C7 46
Saluzzo, Italy E2 18
Salvador, Braz. B9 79
Salvador, Sask., Can. E1 105
Salvador, El see El Salvador, ctry., N.A. D6 92
Salvador, Lake, l., La., U.S. E5 125
Salvador Mazza, Arg. B7 80
Salvage, Newf., Can. D5 102
Salvaterra de Magos, Port. F3 16
Salvatierra, Mex. G9 90
Salvisa, Ky., U.S. C5 124
Salwā, Dawhat, b., Asia I11 48
Salwā Baḥrī, Egypt E7 60
Salween (Nu) (Thanlwin), stm., Asia D5 40
Salyān, Nepal F10 44
Salyer, Ca., U.S. B2 112
Salyersville, Ky., U.S. C6 124
Salzach, stm., Eur. G12 10
Salzburg, Aus. H13 10
Salzburg, state, Aus. H13 10
Salzgitter, Ger. C10 10
Salzkammergut, reg., Aus. H13 10
Salzwedel, Ger. C11 10
Samā, Jord. D6 50
Sama, stm., Peru G6 82
Samacá, Col. E6 84
Sama [de Langreo], Spain B6 16
Samaipata, Bol. H10 82
Samalá, stm., Guat. C3 92
Sāmalkot, India D7 46
Samālūṭ, Egypt C6 60
Samambaia, stm., Braz. G2 79
Samaná, Dom. Rep. E10 94
Samaná, Bahía de, b., Dom. Rep. E10 94
Samaná, Cabo, c., Dom. Rep. E10 94
Samana Cay, i., Bah. C8 94
Samandağı, Tur. C3 48
Samaniego, Col. G4 84
Samar, Isr. I4 50
Samara (Kujbyšev), Russia G8 26
Samara, stm., Russia G8 26
Samarai, Pap. N. Gui. n17 68a
Samaria, Id., U.S. G6 119
Samariapo, Ven. E9 84
Samarinda, Indon. F6 38
Samarkand, Uzb. J11 26
Sāmarrā', Iraq D7 48
Samastīpur, India H11 44
Samaúna, Braz. B11 82
Sambalpur, India J10 44
Sambas, Indon. N10 40
Sambava, Madag. o24 67b
Sambawizi, Zimb. B8 66
Sambhal, India F8 44
Sāmbhar, India G6 44
Sâmbor, Camb. H8 40
Sambor, Ukr. F23 10
Samborombón, stm., Arg. H10 80
Samborombón, Bahía, b., Arg. I10 80
Samborondón, Ec. H3 84
Sambre, stm., Eur. B11 14
Sambú, stm., Pan. C3 84
Samburg, Tn., U.S. A2 149
Sambusu, Nmb. A4 66
Samch'ŏk, S. Kor. F17 32
Samch'ŏnp'o, S. Kor. I16 32
Samedan, Switz. E12 13
Samho, N. Kor. D15 32
Samiria, stm., Peru J5 84
Sammamish Lake, l., Wa., U.S. e11 154
Samnaungruppe, mts., Eur. D13 13
Samnye, S. Kor. H15 32
Samoa, Ca., U.S. B1 112
Samoa Islands, is., Oc. J22 158
Samo Alto, Chile F3 80
Samoded, Russia E6 26
Sámos, Grc. L11 20
Sámos, i., Grc. L10 20
Samoset, Fl., U.S. q10 116
Samosir, Pulau, i., Indon. M5 40
Samothrace see Samothráki, i., Grc. I9 20
Samothráki, i., Grc. I9 20
S'amozero, Russia K23 6
Sampacho, Arg. G6 80
Sampit, Indon. F5 38
Sampit, stm., S.C., U.S. E9 147
Sampson, co., N.C., U.S. B4 140
Sampués, Col. C5 84
Sampur, Russia I24 22
Sam Rayburn Reservoir, res., Tx., U.S. D5 150
Samre, Eth. K10 60
Samreboi, Ghana I8 64
Samson, Al., U.S. D3 108
Samsun, Tur. G15 4
Samtown, La., U.S. C3 125
Samuels, Id., U.S. A2 119
Samuhú, Arg. D8 80
Samui, Ko, i., Thai. J6 40
Samut Prakan, Thai. H6 40
Samut Sakhon, Thai. H6 40
Samut Songkhram, Thai. H6 40
S'amža, Russia A24 22
San, Mali E7 64
San (Xan), stm., Asia H9 40
San, stm., Eur. E22 10
Saña, Peru B2 82
Şan'ā', Yemen G4 47
Sanaba, stm., Afr. D4 64
San Acacia, N.M., U.S. C3 138
Sanaga, stm., Cam. J14 64
San Agustín, Arg. J9 80
San Agustín, Arg. F6 80
San Agustín, Col. G4 84
San Agustin, Plains of, pl., N.M., U.S. C2 138
San Agustín de Valle Fértil, Arg. F5 80
Sanak Islands, is., Ak., U.S. E7 109
San Alejo, El Sal. D7 92
Sanalona, Presa, res., Mex. E6 90
San Ambrosio, Isla, i., Chile B1 78
Sanana, Pulau, i., Indon. F8 38
Sanandaj, Iran D9 48
Sanandita, Bol. I10 82
San Andreas, Ca., U.S. C3 112
San Andrés, Col. H4 94
San Andrés, Mex. D2 90
San Andrés, Pan. I12 92
San Andrés, Isla de, i., Col. H4 94
San Andrés de Giles, Arg. H9 80
San Andres Mountains, mts., N.M., U.S. E3 138
San Andres Peak, mtn., N.M., U.S. E3 138
San Andrés Sajcabajá, Guat. B4 92
San Andrés Tuxtla, Mex. H12 90
San Andrés y Providencia, ter., Col. H4 94
Sananduva, Braz. D13 80
San Angelo, Tx., U.S. D2 150
San Anselmo, Ca., U.S. h7 112
San Antero, Col. C5 84
San Antonio, Arg. C6 80
San Antonio, Arg. E6 80
San Antonio, Belize A5 92
San Antonio, Chile D3 80
San Antonio, Chile G3 80
San Antonio, Col. F5 84
San Antonio, C.R. G9 92
San Antonio, Peru B3 82
San Antonio, Fl., U.S. D4 116
San Antonio, N.M., U.S. D3 138
San Antonio, Tx., U.S. E3 150
San Antonio, Ur. F10 80
San Antonio, stm., Mex. B2 90
San Antonio, Cabo, c., Arg. I10 80
San Antonio, Cabo de, c., Cuba D2 94
San Antonio, Punta, c., Mex. C2 90
San Antonio, Punta, c., Mex. D4 90
San Antonio Bay, b., Tx., U.S. E4 150
San Antonio de Areco, Arg. H9 80
San Antonio de los Baños, Cuba C3 94
San Antonio de los Cobres, Arg. C5 80
San Antonio del Táchira, Ven. D6 84
San Antonio de Tamanaco, Ven. C9 84
San Antonio El Bravo, Mex. B7 90
San Antonio Mountain, mtn., N.M., U.S. A3 138
San Antonio Suchitepéquez, Guat. C3 92
San Ardo, Ca., U.S. D3 112
Sanatorium, Ms., U.S. D4 131
San Augustine, Tx., U.S. D5 150
San Augustine, co., Tx., U.S. D5 150
San Bartolomé, Spain n27 17b
San Benedetto del Tronto, Italy G8 18
San Benedicto, Isla, i., Mex. H4 90
San Benito, Bol. G9 82
San Benito, Guat. I15 90
San Benito, Peru B2 82
San Benito, Tx., U.S. F4 150
San Benito, co., Ca., U.S. D3 112
San Benito Mountain, mtn., Ca., U.S. D3 112
San Bernardino, Switz. F11 13
San Bernardino, Ca., U.S. E5 112
San Bernardino, co., Ca., U.S. E5 112
San Bernardo, Arg. D8 80
San Bernardo, Chile G3 80
San Bernardo, Mex. E7 90
San Bernardo, Isla, i., Nic. F9 92
San Bernardo, Islas de, is., Col. C4 84
San Bernardo del Viento, Col. C5 84
San Blas, Mex. G7 90
San Blas, Mex. D5 90
San Blas, Cape, c., Fl., U.S. v16 116
San Blas, Golfo de, b., Pan. C3 84
San Blas, Serranía De, mts., Pan. C3 84
San Blas de los Sauces, Arg. E5 80
San Borja, Bol. F8 82
Sanborn, Ia., U.S. A2 122
Sanborn, Mn., U.S. F3 130
Sanborn, N.D., U.S. C7 141
Sanborn, co., S.D., U.S. D7 148
Sanbornton, N.H., U.S. D3 136
Sanbornville, N.H., U.S. C4 136
San Bruno, Ca., U.S. D2 112
San Buenaventura, Bol. F8 82
San Buenaventura, Mex. D9 90
Sancang, China C9 34
San Carlos, Arg. G4 80
San Carlos, Arg. C6 80
San Carlos, Arg. D11 80
San Carlos, Chile I3 80
San Carlos, Mex. C9 90
San Carlos, Mex. E10 90
San Carlos, Nic. F10 92
San Carlos, Pan. C3 84
San Carlos, Para. B10 80
San Carlos, Phil. C7 38
San Carlos, Phil. n19 39b
San Carlos, Az., U.S. D5 110
San Carlos, Ca., U.S. k8 112

Name	Map Ref.	Page
San Carlos, Ur.	H11	80
San Carlos, Ven.	C8	84
San Carlos, stm., C.R.	G10	92
San Carlos, stm., Ven.	C8	84
San Carlos, Riacho, stm., Para.	B9	80
San Carlos Centro, Arg.	F8	80
San Carlos de Bariloche, Arg.	E2	78
San Carlos de Bolívar, Arg.	I8	80
San Carlos de Guaroa, Col.	F6	84
San Carlos del Zulia, Ven.	C7	84
San Carlos de Río Negro, Ven.	G9	84
San Carlos Indian Reservation, Az., U.S.	D5	110
San Carlos Lake, res., Az., U.S.	D5	110
San Cataldo, Italy	L8	18
San Cayetano, Arg.	J9	80
Sancerre, Fr.	E9	14
Sánchez, Dom. Rep.	E10	94
Sanch'ŏng, S. Kor.	H15	32
San Ciro de Acosta, Mex.	G10	90
San Clemente, Spain	F9	16
San Clemente, Ca., U.S.	F5	112
San Clemente, Cerro, mtn., Chile	F2	78
San Clemente Island, i., Ca., U.S.	F4	112
San Cosme, Arg.	D9	80
San Cristóbal, Arg.	F8	80
San Cristóbal, Dom. Rep.	E9	94
San Cristobal, N.M., U.S.	A4	138
San Cristóbal, Ven.	D6	84
San Cristóbal, Bahía, b., Mex.	D2	90
San Cristóbal, Volcán, vol., Nic.	E7	92
San Cristóbal de la Laguna, Spain	o24	17b
San Cristóbal de las Casas, Mex.	I13	90
San Cristóbal Totonicapán, Guat.	C3	92
San Cristóbal Verapaz, Guat.	B4	92
Sancti Spíritus, Cuba	D5	94
Sancy, Puy de, mtn., Fr.	G9	14
Sand, stm., Alta., Can.	B5	98
San Damián, Peru	E3	82
Sandaré, Mali	D4	64
Sandborn, In., U.S.	G3	121
Sand Coulee, Mt., U.S.	C5	133
Sand Creek, stm., In., U.S.	F6	121
Sand Creek, stm., Ks., U.S.	g12	123
Sand Creek, stm., Wy., U.S.	C7	157
Sanders, Az., U.S.	B6	110
Sanders, Ky., U.S.	B5	124
Sanders, co., Mt., U.S.	C1	133
Sanderson, Tx., U.S.	D1	150
Sandersville, Ga., U.S.	D4	117
Sandersville, Ms., U.S.	D4	131
Sandfly Lake, l., Sask., Can.	B2	105
Sandford, In., U.S.	E2	121
Sandgate, Austl.	F10	70
Sand Hill, Ma., U.S.	h13	128
Sand Hill, Ms., U.S.	D5	131
Sandhill, Ms., U.S.	C4	131
Sand Hill, stm., Newf., Can.	B3	102
Sand Hill, stm., Mn., U.S.	C2	130
Sandia, Peru	F7	82
Sandia Crest, mtn., N.M., U.S.	k8	138
Sandia Indian Reservation, N.M., U.S.	k7	138
Sandia Mountains, mts., N.M., U.S.	k8	138
Sandia Park, N.M., U.S.	k8	138
San Diego, Ca., U.S.	F5	112
San Diego, Tx., U.S.	F3	150
San Diego, co., Ca., U.S.	F5	112
San Diego, stm., Ca., U.S.	o15	112
San Diego, Cabo, c., Arg.	G3	78
San Diego de la Unión, Mex.	G9	90
San Diego Naval Station, mil., Ca., U.S.	o15	112
San Diego Naval Training Center, mil., Ca., U.S.	o15	112
Sandilands, Man., Can.	E3	100
San Dionisio, Nic.	E9	92
Sand Island, i., Hi., U.S.	g10	118
Sand Island, i., Wi., U.S.	B3	156
Sand Key, i., Fl., U.S.	E4	116
Sand Lake, Mi., U.S.	E5	129
Sandlick Creek, stm., W.V., U.S.	n13	155
Sand Mountain, mtn., U.S.	A3	108
Sandoa, Zaire	C4	58
Sandomierz, Pol.	E21	10
Sandoná, Col.	G4	84
San Donà di Piave, Italy	D7	18
Sandoval, Il., U.S.	E4	120
Sandoval, co., N.M., U.S.	B2	138
Sandovalina, Braz.	G3	79
Sandovo, Russia	C19	22
Sandoway, Burma	E3	40
Sandown, N.H., U.S.	E4	136
Sand Point, Ont., Can.	B8	103
Sand Point, Ak., U.S.	D7	109
Sandpoint, Id., U.S.	A2	119
Sandringham, Eng., U.K.	I13	8
Sands Key, i., Fl., U.S.	s3	116
Sandspit, B.C., Can.	C2	99
Sand Springs, Ok., U.S.	A5	143
Sandston, Va., U.S.	m18	153
Sandstone, Austl.	E3	68
Sandstone, Mn., U.S.	D6	130
Sandstone, W.V., U.S.	D4	155
Sandtown, De., U.S.	D3	115
Sandu Ao, b., China	I8	34
Sandusky, Mi., U.S.	E8	129
Sandusky, Oh., U.S.	A3	142
Sandusky, co., Oh., U.S.	A2	142
Sandusky, stm., Oh., U.S.	B2	142
Sandusky Bay, b., Oh., U.S.	A3	142
Sandvika, Nor.	L12	6
Sandviken, Swe.	K15	6
Sandwich, Il., U.S.	B5	120
Sandwich, Ma., U.S.	C7	128
Sandwich Bay, b., Newf., Can.	B3	102
Sandwich Range, mts., N.H., U.S.	C3	136
Sandwīp Island, i., Bngl.	I14	44
Sandy, Or., U.S.	B4	144
Sandy, Ut., U.S.	C4	151
Sandy, stm., Me., U.S.	D2	126
Sandy Bay, b., Nic.	C11	92
Sandy Bay Mountain, mtn., Me., U.S.	C2	126
Sandy Brook, stm., Ct., U.S.	A3	114
Sandy Cape, c., Austl.	E10	70
Sandy Creek, stm., Oh., U.S.	B4	142
Sandy Creek, stm., Ok., U.S.	C2	143
Sandy Hook, Ct., U.S.	D2	114
Sandy Hook, Ky., U.S.	B6	124
Sandy Hook, spit, N.J., U.S.	C5	137
Sandy Island, i., S.C., U.S.	D9	147
Sandykači, Turk.	J10	26
Sandy Lake, Man., Can.	D1	100
Sandy Lake, l., Newf., Can.	D3	102
Sandy Lake, l., Ont., Can.	n16	103
Sandy Lake, l., Sask., Can.	B2	105
Sandy Neck, pen., Ma., U.S.	C7	128
Sandy Point, c., R.I., U.S.	h7	146
Sandy Point Town, St. K./N.	F13	94
Sandy Pond, l., Ma., U.S.	g10	128
Sandy Ridge, Al., U.S.	C3	108
Sandy Ridge, mtn., Va., U.S.	e9	153
Sandy Springs, Ga., U.S.	h8	117
Sandy Springs, S.C., U.S.	B2	147
Sandyville, Md., U.S.	A4	127
Sandyville, W.V., U.S.	C3	155
San Enrique, Arg.	H8	80
San Estanislao, Para.	C10	80
San Esteban, Hond.	B9	92
San Esteban, Isla, i., Mex.	C3	90
San Felipe, Chile	G3	80
San Felipe, Col.	G9	84
San Felipe, Mex.	B2	90
San Felipe, Mex.	G9	90
San Felipe, Phil.	n19	39b
San Felipe, Ven.	B8	84
San Felipe, Castillo de, hist., Guat.	B5	92
San Felipe, Cayos de, is., Cuba	D3	94
San Felipe de Vichayal, Peru	A1	82
San Felipe Indian Reservation, N.M., U.S.	k8	138
San Felipe Nuevo Mercurio, Mex.	E8	90
San Felipe Pueblo, N.M., U.S.	B3	138
San Félix, stm., Pan.	I13	92
San Félix, Isla, i., Chile	K31	158
San Fernando, Chile	H3	80
San Fernando, Mex.	E10	90
San Fernando, Phil.	m19	39b
San Fernando, Phil.	n19	39b
San Fernando, Spain	I5	16
San Fernando, Trin.	I14	94
San Fernando, Ca., U.S.	m12	112
San Fernando, Ven.	D9	84
San Fernando de Atabapo, Ven.	E9	84
San Fernando del Valle de Catamarca, Arg.	E6	80
Sanford, Co., U.S.	D5	113
Sanford, Fl., U.S.	D5	116
Sanford, Me., U.S.	E2	126
Sanford, Mi., U.S.	E6	129
Sanford, N.C., U.S.	B3	140
Sanford, Mount, mtn., Ak., U.S.	C11	109
San Francisco, Arg.	F7	80
San Francisco, Col.	G4	84
San Francisco, C.R.	H9	92
San Francisco, El Sal.	D6	92
San Francisco, Pan.	I14	92
San Francisco, Ca., U.S.	D2	112
San Francisco, co., Ca., U.S.	D2	112
San Francisco, stm., Arg.	B6	80
San Francisco, stm., U.S.	D6	110
San Francisco, Paso de, S.A.	D4	80
San Francisco Bay, b., Ca., U.S.	h8	112
San Francisco de Borja, Mex.	D6	90
San Francisco de la Paz, Hond.	C8	92
San Francisco del Chañar, Arg.	E7	80
San Francisco del Monte de Oro, Arg.	G5	80
San Francisco del Oro, Mex.	D7	90
San Francisco del Rincón, Mex.	G9	90
San Francisco de Macorís, Dom. Rep.	E9	94
San Francisco de Mostazal, Chile	G3	80
San Francisco Libre, Nic.	E8	92
San Francisco Mountains, mts., Ut., U.S.	E2	151
San Franco, Cerro, mtn., Hond.	B7	92
San Gabriel, Ec.	G4	84
San Gabriel, Ca., U.S.	*m12	112
San Gabriel Chilac, Mex.	H11	90
San Gabriel Mountains, mts., Ca., U.S.	m12	112
Sangamner, India	C3	46
Sangamon, co., Il., U.S.	D4	120
Sangamon, stm., Il., U.S.	C3	120
Sanga Puitã, Braz.	G1	79
Sangay, vol., Ec.	H3	84
Sangayán, Isla, i., Peru	E3	82
Sangchungshih, Tai.	J10	34
Sang-e Māsheh, Afg.	D2	44
Sanger, Ca., U.S.	D4	112
Sanger, Tx., U.S.	C4	150
Sangerhausen, Ger.	D11	10
San Germán, Cuba	D6	94
San Germán, P.R.	E11	94
Sangerville, Me., U.S.	C3	126
Sanggan, stm., China	C9	30
Sangha, stm., Afr.	A3	58
Sangihe, Kepulauan, is., Indon.	E8	38
Sangihe, Pulau, i., Indon.	E8	38
San Gil, Col.	D6	84
San Gimignano, Italy	F6	18
San Giovanni in Fiore, Italy	J11	18
San Giovanni in Persiceto, Italy	E6	18
San Giovanni Rotondo, Italy	H10	18
San Giovanni Valdarno, Italy	F6	18
Sangju, S. Kor.	G16	32
Sāngli, India	D3	46
Sangolquí, Ec.	H3	84
San Gorgonio Mountain, mtn., Ca., U.S.	E5	112
San Gottardo, Passo del, Switz.	E10	13
San Gregorio, Arg.	H7	80
San Gregorio, Ur.	G11	80
Sangre Grande, Trin.	I14	94
Sangrūr, India	E6	44
Sanguandian, China	D7	34
Sangudo, Alta., Can.	C3	98
Sangue, Rio do, stm., Braz.	D12	82
Sanhecun, China	A17	32
San Hipólito, Punta, c., Mex.	D3	90
Sanibel, Fl., U.S.	F4	116
Sanibel Island, i., Fl., U.S.	F4	116
San Ignacio, Arg.	D11	80
San Ignacio, C.R.	H10	92
San Ignacio, Hond.	C7	92
San Ignacio, Mex.	D3	90
San Ignacio, Mex.	F9	90
San Ignacio, Para.	D10	80
San Ignacio, Isla, i., Mex.	E5	90
San Ignacio, Laguna, l., Mex.	D3	90
San Ignacio de Moxo, Bol.	F9	82
San Ignacio de Velasco, Bol.	G11	82
Sanilac, co., Mi., U.S.	E8	129
San Ildefonso, Cerro, mtn., Hond	B6	92
San Isidro, Arg.	H9	80
San Isidro, Arg.	E6	80
San Isidro, C.R.	H11	92
San Isidro, Nic.	E8	92
San Isidro, Tx., U.S.	F3	150
San Jacinto, Col.	C5	84
San Jacinto, Ca., U.S.	F5	112
San Jacinto, co., Tx., U.S.	D5	150
San Jacinto, stm., Tx., U.S.	r14	150
San Javier, Arg.	D11	80
San Javier, Arg.	F9	80
San Javier, Bol.	F9	82
San Javier, Bol.	G10	82
San Javier, Ur.	G9	80
San Javier, stm., Arg.	E9	80
San Javier de Loncomilla, Chile	H3	80
Sanjāwi, Pak.	E3	44
San Jerónimo, Guat.	B4	92
San Jerónimo Norte, Arg.	F8	80
Sanjō, Japan	J13	36
San Joaquín, Bol.	E9	82
San Joaquín, Para.	C10	80
San Joaquin, Ca., U.S.	D3	112
San Joaquin, co., Ca., U.S.	D3	112
San Joaquín, stm., Bol.	E10	82
San Joaquin, stm., Ca., U.S.	D3	112
San Joaquin Valley, val., Ca., U.S.	D3	112
San Jon, N.M., U.S.	B6	138
San Jorge, Arg.	F8	80
San Jorge, El Sal.	D6	92
San Jorge, Nic.	F9	92
San Jorge, stm., Col.	C5	84
San Jorge, Bahía, b., Mex.	B3	90
San Jorge, Golfo, b., Arg.	F3	78
San José, Arg.	D11	80
San José, C.R.	H10	92
San José, Para.	C10	80
San Jose, Phil.	n19	39b
San Jose, Az., U.S.	E6	110
San Jose, Ca., U.S.	D3	112
San Jose, Il., U.S.	C4	120
San Jose, N.M., U.S.	B4	138
San José, prov., C.R.	H11	92
San José, Isla, i., Mex.	E4	90
San José, Isla, i., Pan.	C3	84
San José Batuc, Mex.	C5	90
San José Buena Vista, Guat.	D4	92
San José de Bácum, Mex.	D4	90
San José de Chiquitos, Bol.	G11	82
San José de Copán, Hond.	C6	92
San José de Feliciano, Arg.	F9	80
San José de Guanipa, Ven.	C10	84
San José de Guaribe, Ven.	C10	84
San José de Jáchal, Arg.	F4	80
San José de la Esquina, Arg.	G8	80
San José de las Lajas, Cuba	C3	94
San José de las Raíces, Mex.	E9	90
San José del Cabo, Mex.	F5	90
San José del Guaviare, Col.	F6	84
San José de los Molinos, Peru	E4	82
San José de Mayo, Ur.	H10	80
San José de Ocuné, Col.	E7	84
San José de Sisa, Peru	B3	82
San José de Tiznados, Ven.	C9	84
San Jose Island, i., Tx., U.S.	E4	150
San Juan, Arg.	F4	80
San Juan, Guat.	B6	92
San Juan, Peru	F4	82
San Juan, P.R.	E11	94
San Juan, Tx., U.S.	F3	150
San Juan, prov., Arg.	F4	80
San Juan, co., Co., U.S.	D3	113
San Juan, co., N.M., U.S.	A1	138
San Juan, co., Ut., U.S.	F5	151
San Juan, co., Wa., U.S.	A2	154
San Juan, stm., Arg.	G5	80
San Juan, stm., Col.	E4	84
San Juan, stm., Mex.	E10	90
San Juan, stm., N.A.	G10	92
San Juan, stm., Peru	E4	82
San Juan, stm., S.A.	G3	84
San Juan, stm., U.S.	D5	106
San Juan, stm., Ven.	B11	84
San Juan, Pico, mtn., Cuba	D4	94
San Juan Bautista, Para.	D10	80
San Juan Capistrano, Ca., U.S.	F5	112
San Juan Cotzal, Guat.	B3	92
San Juan de Abajo, Mex.	G7	90
San Juan de Colón, Ven.	C6	84
San Juan de Guadalupe, Mex.	E8	90
San Juan [de la Maguana], Dom. Rep.	E9	94
San Juan del César, Col.	B6	84
San Juan del Norte, Nic.	G11	92
San Juan del Oro, stm., Bol.	I9	82
San Juan de los Cayos, Ven.	B8	84
San Juan de los Morros, Ven.	C9	84
San Juan del Río, Mex.	E7	90
San Juan del Río, Mex.	G9	90
San Juan del Sur, Nic.	F9	92
San Juan de Micay, stm., Col.	F4	84
San Juan de Payara, Ven.	D9	84
San Juan Evangelista, Mex.	I12	90
San Juanico, Mex.	D3	90
San Juanillo, C.R.	G9	92
San Juan Island, i., Wa., U.S.	A2	154
San Juanito, Isla, i., Mex.	G6	90
San Juan Mountains, mts., Co., U.S.	D3	113
San Juan Nepomuceno, Col.	C5	84
San Juan Nepomuceno, Para.	D11	80
San Juan Sacatepéquez, Guat.	C4	92
San Juan Teotihuacán, Mex.	H10	90
San Justo, Arg.	F8	80
Sankarani, stm., Afr.	F5	64
Sankosh, stm., Asia	G14	44
Sankt Aegyd am Neuwalde, Aus.	H15	10
Sankt Anton [am Arlberg], Aus.	H10	10
Sankt Gallen, Aus.	H14	10
Sankt Gallen, Switz.	D11	13
Sankt Gallen, state, Switz.	D11	13
Sankt Gilgen, Aus.	H13	10
Sankt Goar, Ger.	E7	10
Sankt Goarshausen, Ger.	E7	10
Sankt Ingbert, Ger.	F7	10
Sankt Johann im Pongau, Aus.	H13	10
Sankt Johann in Tirol, Aus.	H12	10
Sankt Moritz, Switz.	E12	13
Sankt Niklaus, Switz.	F8	13
Sankt Paul [im Lavanttal], Aus.	I14	10
Sankt Peter, Ger.	A8	10
Sankt-Peterburg (Saint Petersburg), Russia	B13	22
Sankt Pölten, Aus.	G15	10
Sankt Valentin, Aus.	G14	10
Sankt Veit an der Glan, Aus.	I14	10
Sankt Vith (Saint-Vith), Bel.	H9	12
Sankt Wendel, Ger.	F7	10
San Lázaro, Para.	B10	80
San Lázaro, Cabo, c., Mex.	E3	90
San Leandro, Ca., U.S.	h8	112
Sanlicheng, China	D3	34
Şanlıurfa, Tur.	C5	48
San Lope, Col.	D7	84
San Lorenzo, Arg.	E9	80
San Lorenzo, Arg.	G8	80
San Lorenzo, Bol.	I9	82
San Lorenzo, Ec.	G3	84
San Lorenzo, Hond.	D7	92
San Lorenzo, Mex.	E8	90
San Lorenzo, Nic.	E9	92
San Lorenzo, N.M., U.S.	E2	138
San Lorenzo, Ven.	C7	84
San Lorenzo, stm., Mex.	E6	90
San Lorenzo, Bahía de, b., Hond.	D7	92
San Lorenzo, Cabo, c., Ec.	H2	84
San Lorenzo, Isla, i., Mex.	C3	90
San Lorenzo, Isla, i., Peru	E3	82
San Lorenzo de El Escorial, Spain	E7	16
Sanlúcar de Barrameda, Spain	I5	16
Sanlúcar la Mayor, Spain	H5	16
San Lucas, Bol.	I9	82
San Lucas, Ec.	I3	84
San Lucas, Mex.	F5	90
San Lucas, Cabo, c., Mex.	F5	90
San Luis, Arg.	G5	80
San Luis, Cuba	D7	94
San Luis, Guat.	A5	92
San Luis, Az., U.S.	E1	110
San Luis, Co., U.S.	D5	113
San Luis, Ven.	B8	84
San Luis, prov., Arg.	H5	80
San Luís, Laguna, l., Bol.	E9	82
San Luis, Point, c., Ca., U.S.	E3	112
San Luis, Sierra de, mts., Arg.	G6	80
San Luis Creek, stm., Co., U.S.	C5	113
San Luis de la Paz, Mex.	G9	90
San Luis del Cordero, Mex.	E7	90
San Luis del Palmar, Arg.	D9	80
San Luis Gonzaga, Mex.	E4	90
San Luis Gonzaga, Bahía, b., Mex.	C2	90
San Luis Jilotepeque, Guat.	C5	92
San Luis Obispo, Ca., U.S.	E3	112
San Luis Obispo, co., Ca., U.S.	E3	112
San Luis Pass, strt., Tx., U.S.	r14	150
San Luis Peak, mtn., Co., U.S.	D4	113
San Luis Potosí, Mex.	F9	90
San Luis Potosí, state, Mex.	F9	90
San Luis Río Colorado, Mex.	A2	90
San Luis Valley, val., Co., U.S.	D4	113
Sanluri, Italy	J3	18
San Manuel, Arg.	I9	80
San Manuel, Az., U.S.	E5	110
San Marcial, stm., Mex.	C4	90
San Marcos, Chile	F3	80
San Marcos, Col.	C5	84
San Marcos, C.R.	H10	92
San Marcos, El Sal.	D5	92
San Marcos, Guat.	C3	92
San Marcos, Hond.	C6	92
San Marcos, Hond.	B6	92
San Marcos, Mex.	I10	90
San Marcos, Tx., U.S.	E4	150
San Marcos, dept., Guat.	B3	92
San Marcos, stm., Tx., U.S.	h8	150
San Marcos, Isla, i., Mex.	D3	90
San Marcos de Colón, Hond.	D8	92
San Marino, S. Mar.	F7	18
San Marino, Ca., U.S.	m12	112
San Marino, ctry., Eur.	G10	4
San Martín, Arg.	E6	80
San Martín, Arg.	G4	80
San Martín, Col.	F6	84
San Martín, dept., Peru	B3	82
San Martín, stm., Bol.	D8	82
San Martín, stm., Bol.	E10	82
San Martín, Lago (Lago O'Higgins), l., S.A.	F2	78
San Martín de los Andes, Arg.	E2	78
San Martín Texmelucan, Mex.	H10	90
San Mateo, Ca., U.S.	D2	112
San Mateo, Fl., U.S.	C5	116
San Mateo, N.M., U.S.	B2	138
San Mateo, Ven.	C10	84
San Mateo, co., Ca., U.S.	D2	112
San Mateo Ixtatán, Guat.	B3	92
San Mateo Mountains, mts., N.M., U.S.	B2	138
San Mateo Mountains, mts., N.M., U.S.	D2	138
San Matías, Bol.	G12	82
San Matías, Golfo, b., Arg.	E4	78
Sanmenxia, China	E9	30
San Miguel, Arg.	E10	80
San Miguel, Bol.	G11	82
San Miguel, Ec.	H3	84
San Miguel, El Sal.	D6	92
San Miguel, Mex.	C9	90
San Miguel, Pan.	C3	84
San Miguel, Peru	E5	82
San Miguel, Spain	o24	17b
San Miguel, Ca., U.S.	E3	112
San Miguel, N.M., U.S.	E3	138
San Miguel, co., Co., U.S.	D2	113
San Miguel, co., N.M., U.S.	B5	138
San Miguel, stm., Bol.	F10	82
San Miguel (Cuilco), stm., N.A.	B2	92
San Miguel, stm., S.A.	H11	82
San Miguel, stm., Co., U.S.	C2	113
San Miguel, Cerro, hill, Bol.	H11	82
San Miguel, Golfo de, b., Pan.	C3	84
San Miguel, Volcán de, vol., El Sal.	D6	92
San Miguel de Allende, Mex.	G9	90
San Miguel de Cruces, Mex.	E7	90
San Miguel del Monte, Arg.	H9	80
San Miguel de Pallaques, Peru	B2	82
San Miguel de Salcedo, Ec.	H3	84
San Miguel de Tucumán, Arg.	D6	80
San Miguel el Alto, Mex.	G8	90
San Miguel Island, i., Ca., U.S.	E3	112
San Miguelito, Nic.	F10	92
San Miguel Ixtahuacán, Guat.	B3	92
San Miguel Mountains, mts., Co., U.S.	D2	113
San Miniato, Italy	F5	18
Sannār, Sud.	K7	60
Sannicandro Garganico, Italy	H10	18
San Nicolás, Hond.	B6	92
San Nicolás, Peru	F4	82
San Nicolás, Spain	p25	17b
San Nicolás, stm., Mex.	H7	90
San Nicolás de los Arroyos, Arg.	G8	80
San Nicolás de los Garza, Mex.	E9	90
San Nicolas Island, i., Ca., U.S.	F4	112
Sannikova, proliv, strt., Russia	C20	28
Sanniquellie, Lib.	H5	64
Sano, Japan	K14	36
Sañogasta, Arg.	E5	80
Sanok, Pol.	F22	10
San Onofre, Col.	C5	84
San Pablo, Col.	G4	84
San Pablo, Phil.	n19	39b
San Pablo, Ca., U.S.	h8	112
San Pablo, Co., U.S.	D5	113
San Pablo, stm., Bol.	F10	82
San Pablo, stm., Pan.	I13	92
San Pablo Bay, b., Ca., U.S.	g8	112
San Patricio, N.M., U.S.	D4	138
San Patricio, co., Tx., U.S.	E4	150
San Patricio, Bayou, stm., La., U.S.	C2	125
San Pedro, Arg.	G9	80
San Pedro, Arg.	C6	80
San Pedro, Arg.	D6	80
San Pedro, Chile	A4	80
San Pedro, Chile	G3	80
San Pedro, Col.	C5	84
San Pedro, C.R.	H10	92
San Pédro, I.C.	I6	64
San Pedro, Para.	C10	80
San Pedro, Ven.	C7	84
San Pedro, dept., Para.	C10	80
San Pedro, stm., Mex.	B5	90
San Pedro, stm., N.A.	I14	90
San Pedro, stm., Az., U.S.	E5	110
San Pedro, Punta, c., Chile	C3	80
San Pedro, Volcán, vol., Chile	A4	80
San Pedro Ayampuc, Guat.	C4	92
San Pedro Bay, b., Ca., U.S.	n12	112
San Pedro Carchá, Guat.	B4	92
San Pedro de Atacama, Chile	B4	80
San Pedro de Buena Vista, Bol.	H9	82
San Pedro de Curahuara, Bol.	G7	82
San Pedro de la Cueva, Mex.	C5	90
San Pedro de las Colonias, Mex.	E8	90
San Pedro del Gallo, Mex.	E7	90
San Pedro de Lloc, Peru	B2	82
San Pedro del Norte, Nic.	D10	92
San Pedro del Paraná, Para.	D10	80
San Pedro de Macorís, Dom. Rep.	E10	94
San Pedro Peaks, mts., N.M., U.S.	A3	138
San Pedro Pinula, Guat.	C5	92
San Pedro Pochutla, Mex.	J11	90
San Pedro Sacatepéquez, Guat.	C3	92
San Pedro Sula, Hond.	B6	92
San Pedro Tabasco, Mex.	I14	90
San Pelayo, Col.	C5	84
Sanpete, co., Ut., U.S.	D4	151
San Pierre, In., U.S.	B4	121
San Pitch Mountains, mts., Ut., U.S.	D4	151
Sanpoil, stm., Wa., U.S.	A7	154
Sanpoil, West Fork, stm., Wa., U.S.	A7	154
San Quintín, Cabo, c., Mex.	B1	90
San Rafael, Arg.	H4	80
San Rafael, Chile	H3	80
San Rafael, Mex.	E9	90
San Rafael, Ca., U.S.	D2	112
San Rafael, N.M., U.S.	B2	138
San Rafael, Ven.	B7	84
San Rafael, stm., Bol.	H12	82
San Rafael, stm., Ut., U.S.	D5	151
San Rafael del Norte, Nic.	D8	92
San Rafael del Sur, Nic.	F8	92
San Rafael Desert, des., Ut., U.S.	E5	151
San Rafael Knob, mtn., Ut., U.S.	E5	151
San Rafael Mountains, mts., Ca., U.S.	E4	112
San Rafael Oriente, El Sal.	D6	92
San Rafael Swell, plat., Ut., U.S.	E5	151
San Rafael Tasajera, El Sal.	D6	92
San Ramón, Arg.	D6	80
San Ramón, Bol.	E9	82
San Ramón, C.R.	G10	92
San Ramón, Hond.	C10	92
San Ramón, Peru	D4	82
San Ramon, Ca., U.S.	h9	112
San Ramón, Ur.	H11	80
San Ramón de la Nueva Orán, Arg.	B6	80
Sanrao, China	L5	34
San Remo, Italy	F2	18
San Román, stm., Guat.	A4	92
San Román, Cabo, c., Ven.	A7	84
San Roque, Arg.	E9	80
San Roque, Arg.	F4	80
San Roque, Spain	I6	16
San Roque, Punta, c., Mex.	D2	90
San Rosendo, Chile	I2	80
San Saba, Tx., U.S.	D3	150
San Saba, co., Tx., U.S.	D3	150
San Salvador, Arg.	F9	80
San Salvador, Arg.	E10	80
San Salvador, El Sal.	D5	92
San Salvador (Watling Island), i., Bah.	B7	94
San Salvador, Volcán de, vol., El Sal.	D5	92
San Salvador de Jujuy, Arg.	C6	80
Sansanné-Mango, Togo	F10	64
Sans Bois Mountains, mts., Ok., U.S.	B6	143
San Sebastián, El Sal.	D6	92
San Sebastián, Guat.	C3	92
San Sebastián, Hond.	C6	92
San Sebastián de la Gomera, Spain	o23	17b
San Sebastián de Yalí, Nic.	D8	92
Sansepolcro, Italy	F7	18
San Severo, Italy	H10	18
Sanshui, China	L1	34
San Simon, Az., U.S.	E6	110
San Simón, stm., Bol.	E10	82
San Simon, stm., Az., U.S.	E6	110
Sanso, Mali	F6	64
San Solano, Arg.	F6	80
Sans-Souci, hist., Haiti	E8	94
Santa, Peru	C2	82
Santa, Id., U.S.	B2	119
Santa, stm., Peru	C2	82
Santa, Isla del, i., Peru	C2	82
Santa Adélia, Braz.	F4	79
Santa Albertina, Braz.	F3	79
Santa Ana, Arg.	D11	80
Santa Ana, Bol.	E9	82
Santa Ana, Bol.	H12	82
Santa Ana, Col.	C5	84
Santa Ana, Ec.	H2	84
Santa Ana, El Sal.	D5	92
Santa Ana, Mex.	E9	90
Santa Ana, Mex.	B4	90
Santa Ana, Ca., U.S.	F5	112
Santa Ana, Ven.	C10	84
Santa Ana, stm., Ca., U.S.	n13	112
Santa Ana, Volcán de, vol., El Sal.	D5	92
Santa Ana del Alto Beni, Bol.	F8	82
Santa Ana Indian Reservation, N.M., U.S.	h7	138
Santa Ana Mountains, mts., Ca., U.S.	n13	112
Santa Ana Pueblo, N.M., U.S.	B3	138
Santa Anna, Tx., U.S.	D3	150
Santa Bárbara, Chile	I2	80
Santa Bárbara, Col.	E5	84
Santa Bárbara, Hond.	C6	92
Santa Bárbara, Mex.	D7	90
Santa Barbara, Ca., U.S.	E4	112
Santa Bárbara, Ven.	F9	84
Santa Bárbara, Ven.	D7	84
Santa Bárbara, dept., Hond.	B6	92
Santa Barbara, co., Ca., U.S.	E3	112
Santa Bárbara, stm., Bol.	G11	82

Name — Map Ref. — Page

Saugatucket, stm., R.I., U.S. F4 146
Saugatuck Reservoir, res., Ct., U.S. D2 114
Saugerties, N.Y., U.S. C7 139
Saugus, Ma., U.S. B5 128
Saugus, stm., Ma., U.S. g11 128
Saujil, Arg. E5 80
Sauk, co., Wi., U.S. E4 156
Sauk, stm., Mn., U.S. E4 130
Sauk, stm., Wa., U.S. A4 154
Sauk Centre, Mn., U.S. E4 130
Sauk City, Wi., U.S. E4 156
Sauk Rapids, Mn., U.S. E4 130
Saukville, Wi., U.S. E6 156
Saül, Fr. Gu. C8 76
Saulgau, Ger. G9 10
Saulieu, Fr. E11 14
Saulkrasti, Lat. D7 22
Saulnierville, N.S., Can. E3 101
Sault-au-Mouton, Que., Can. A8 104
Sault Sainte Marie, Ont., Can. p18 103
Sault Sainte Marie, Mi., U.S. B6 129
Saumarez Reef, rf., Austl. C10 70
Saumur, Fr. E6 14
Saunders, co., Ne., U.S. C9 134
Saunders Island, i., S. Geor. A2 73
Saunders Island, i., S. Geor. J12 74
Saunderstown, R.I., U.S. E4 146
Saunemin, Il., U.S. C5 120
Saurimo, Ang. C4 58
Sausalito, Ca., U.S. D2 112
Sauveterre-de-Béarn, Fr. I6 14
Sauvo, Fin. K18 6
Sava, Italy I12 18
Sava, stm., Eur. F11 4
Savage, Md., U.S. B4 127
Savage, Ms., U.S. A3 131
Savage, Mt., U.S. C12 133
Savage, stm., Md., U.S. k12 127
Savage River Reservoir, res., Md., U.S. k12 127
Savai'i, i., W. Sam. J22 158
Savalou, Benin H10 64
Savanna, Il., U.S. A3 120
Savanna, Ok., U.S. C6 143
Savannah, Ga., U.S. D5 117
Savannah, Mo., U.S. B3 132
Savannah, Tn., U.S. B3 149
Savannah, stm., U.S. F5 147
Savannah River Plant, sci., S.C., U.S. E4 147
Savannakhét, Laos F8 40
Savanna Lake, l., Md., U.S. D6 127
Savanna-la-Mar, Jam. E5 94
Ṣavé, Benin G11 64
Save (Sabi), stm., Afr. C12 66
Sāveh, Iran D11 48
Savelli, Italy J11 18
Saverdun, Fr. I8 14
Saverne, Fr. D14 14
Savigliano, Italy E2 18
Saville Dam, Ct., U.S. B4 114
Savino, Russia E24 22
Savinskij, Russia J27 6
Šavnik, Yugo. G3 20
Savognin, Switz. E12 13
Savoie, dept., Fr. G13 14
Savona, B.C., Can. D7 99
Savona, Italy E3 18
Savona, N.Y., U.S. C3 139
Savoonga, Ak., U.S. C5 109
Savoy, Il., U.S. C5 120
Savran', Ukr. A14 20
Savu Sea see Sawu, Laut, Indon. G7 38
Sawahlunto, Indon. O6 40
Sawāi Mādhopur, India H7 44
Sawākin, Sud. H9 60
Sawankhalok, Thai. F5 40
Sawatch Range, mts., Co., U.S. B4 113
Sawdā', Jabal, mtn., Sau. Ar. E3 47
Sawdā', Jabal as-, hills, Libya C4 56
Sawdā', Qurnat as-, mtn., Leb. D4 48
Sawdirī, Sud. J5 60
Sawhāj, Egypt D6 60
Sawknah, Libya C4 56
Sawmill, Az., U.S. B6 110
Sawnee Mountain, mtn., Ga., U.S. B2 117
Ṣawqirah, Ghubbat, b., Oman E10 47
Sawtooth Mountains, mts., Id., U.S. F4 119
Sawtooth National Recreation Area, Id., U.S. E3 119
Sawtooth Ridge, mtn., Wa., U.S. A5 154
Sawu, Laut (Savu Sea), Indon. G7 38
Sawu, Pulau, i., Indon. H7 38
Sawyer, Ks., U.S. E5 123
Sawyer, Mi., U.S. G4 129
Sawyer, Mn., U.S. D6 130
Sawyer, N.D., U.S. A4 141
Sawyer, co., Wi., U.S. C2 156
Sawyerville, Que., Can. D6 104
Saxapahaw, N.C., U.S. B3 140
Saxby, stm., Austl. B4 70
Saxis, Va., U.S. C7 153
Saxman, Ak., U.S. n24 109
Saxon, Switz. F7 13
Saxonburg, Pa., U.S. E2 145
Saxony see Sachsen, state, Ger. C9 10
Saxton, Pa., U.S. F5 145
Saxtons, stm., Vt., U.S. E3 152
Saxtons River, Vt., U.S. E3 152
Say, Niger E11 64
Sayán, Peru D3 82
Sayan Mountains (Sajany), mts., Asia G11 28
Sayaxché, Guat. I14 90
Saybrook, Il., U.S. C5 120
Saybrook Manor, Ct., U.S. D6 114
Saybrook Point, Ct., U.S. D6 114
Ṣaydā (Sidon), Leb. A4 50
Saydel, Ia., U.S. e8 122
Sayhūt, Yemen G7 47
Sayil, hist., Mex. G15 90
Saylesville, R.I., U.S. B4 146
Saylorsburg, Pa., U.S. E11 145
Saylorville, Ia., U.S. e8 122
Saylorville Lake, res., Ia., U.S. C4 122
Saylūn, Khirbat (Shiloh), hist., Isr. Occ. D4 50
Sayner, Wi., U.S. B4 156
Sayre, Al., U.S. B3 108
Sayre, Ok., U.S. B2 143
Sayre, Pa., U.S. C8 145
Sayreville, N.J., U.S. C4 137
Sayula, Mex. H8 90
Sayville, N.Y., U.S. n15 139
Sayward, B.C., Can. D5 99
Saywūn, Yemen G6 47
Sazonovo, Russia B18 22
Šazud, Taj. B5 44
Sba, Alg. F10 62
Sbeïtla, Tun. N4 18
Sbiba, Tun. N4 18
Scafell Pikes, mtn., Eng., U.K. G10 8
Scalea, Italy J10 18
Scales Mound, Il., U.S. A3 120
Scalp Level, Pa., U.S. F4 145
Scaly Mountain, N.C., U.S. f9 140
Scammon, Ks., U.S. E9 123
Scammon Bay, Ak., U.S. C6 109
Scandia, Alta., Can. D4 98
Scandia, Ks., U.S. C6 123
Scanlon, Mn., U.S. D6 130
Scanterbury, Man., Can. D3 100
Scantic, Ct., U.S. B5 114
Scapa Flow, b., Scot., U.K. C10 8
Scapegoat Mountain, mtn., Mt., U.S. C3 133
Ščapino, Russia F23 28
Scappoose, Or., U.S. B4 144
Scarborough, Ont., Can. m15 103
Scarborough, Trin. I14 94
Scarborough, Eng., U.K. G13 8
Scarborough, Me., U.S. E2 126
Scarbro, W.V., U.S. n13 155
Scarsdale, N.Y., U.S. h13 139
Scawfell Island, i., Austl. C8 70
Ščelkovo, Russia F21 22
Scenic, S.D., U.S. D3 148
Sceptre, Sask., Can. G1 105
Ščerbinka, Russia F20 22
Schaefferstown, Pa., U.S. F9 145
Schaerbeek (Schaarbeek), Bel. G5 12
Schaffhausen, Switz. C10 13
Schaffhausen, state, Switz. C10 13
Schaller, Ia., U.S. B2 122
Schärding, Aus. G13 10
Schaumburg, Il., U.S. h8 120
Schefferville, Que., Can. h13 104
Scheibbs, Aus. G15 10
Scheinfeld, Ger. F10 10
Schelde (Escaut), stm., Eur. D4 10
Schell City, Mo., U.S. C3 132
Schell Creek Range, mts., Nv., U.S. D7 135
Schenectady, N.Y., U.S. C7 139
Schenectady, co., N.Y., U.S. C6 139
Scherer, Lake, res., Ga., U.S. C3 117
Schererville, In., U.S. B3 121
Schertz, Tx., U.S. h7 150
Schesslitz, Ger. F11 10
Scheveningen, Neth. E5 12
Schiedam, Neth. E5 12
Schiermonnikoog, Neth. B9 12
Schiermonnikoog, i., Neth. B9 12
Schiller Park, Il., U.S. k9 120
Schiltigheim, Fr. D14 14
Schio, Italy D6 18
Schipbeek, stm., Eur. D9 12
Schkeuditz, Ger. D12 10
Schladming, Aus. H13 10
Schlater, Ms., U.S. B3 131
Schleicher, co., Tx., U.S. D2 150
Schleswig, Ger. A9 10
Schleswig, Ia., U.S. B2 122
Schleswig-Holstein, state, Ger. A9 10
Schleusingen, Ger. E10 10
Schley, co., Ga., U.S. D2 117
Schlieren, Switz. D9 13
Schlitz, Ger. E9 10
Schlüchtern, Ger. E9 10
Schmalkalden, Ger. E10 10
Schmidmühlen, Ger. F11 10
Schmölln, Ger. E12 10
Schneider, In., U.S. B3 121
Schneverdingen, Ger. B9 10
Schodn'a, Russia F20 22
Schoenchen, Ks., U.S. D4 123
Schofield, Wi., U.S. D4 156
Schofield Barracks, mil., Hi., U.S. g9 118
Schoharie, N.Y., U.S. C6 139
Schoharie, co., N.Y., U.S. C6 139
Schoharie Creek, stm., N.Y., U.S. C6 139
Schönebeck, Ger. C11 10
Schongau, Ger. H10 10
Schoodic Lake, l., Me., U.S. C4 126
Schoolcraft, Mi., U.S. F5 129
Schoolcraft, co., Mi., U.S. B4 129
Schooleys Mountain, mtn., N.J., U.S. B3 137
Schopfheim, Ger. H7 10
Schorndorf, Ger. G9 10
Schouten Island, i., Austl. N8 70
Schouwen, i., Neth. E4 12
Schramberg, Ger. G8 10
Schram City, Il., U.S. D4 120
Schriever, La., U.S. E5 125
Schroeder, Mn., U.S. C8 130
Schroffenstein, mtn., Nmb. F4 66
Schroon Lake, N.Y., U.S. B7 139
Schroon Lake, l., N.Y., U.S. B7 139
Schulenburg, Tx., U.S. E4 150
Schuler, Alta., Can. D5 98
Schulter, Ok., U.S. B6 143
Schultz Lake, l., N.W. Ter., Can. D13 96
Schüpfheim, Switz. E9 13
Schurz, Nv., U.S. E3 135
Schuyler, Ne., U.S. C8 134
Schuyler, Va., U.S. C4 153
Schuyler, co., Il., U.S. C3 120
Schuyler, co., Mo., U.S. A5 132
Schuyler, co., N.Y., U.S. C4 139
Schuylerville, N.Y., U.S. B7 139
Schuylkill, co., Pa., U.S. E9 145
Schuylkill, stm., Pa., U.S. F10 145
Schuylkill Haven, Pa., U.S. E9 145
Schwabach, Ger. F11 10
Schwaben, hist. reg., Ger. G10 10
Schwäbische Alb, mts., Ger. G9 10
Schwäbisch Gmünd, Ger. G9 10
Schwäbisch Hall, Ger. F9 10
Schwabmünchen, Ger. G10 10
Schwanden, Switz. D11 13
Schwandorf, Ger. F12 10
Schwaner, Pegunungan, mts., Indon. F5 38
Schwarza, Ger. E11 10
Schwarzach im Pongau, Aus. H13 10
Schwarzenburg, Switz. E7 13
Schwarzwald (Black Forest), mts., Ger. G8 10
Schwaz, Aus. H11 10
Schwedt, Ger. B14 10
Schweinfurt, Ger. E10 10
Schweizer Nationalpark, Switz. E13 13
Schwerin, Ger. B11 10
Schwyz, Switz. D10 13
Schwyz, state, Switz. D10 13
Sciacca, Italy L8 18
Scicli, Italy M9 18
Science Hill, Ky., U.S. C5 124
Scilla, Italy K10 18
Scilly, Isles of, is., Eng., U.K. L7 8
Scio, Oh., U.S. B4 142
Scio, Or., U.S. C4 144
Scioto, co., Oh., U.S. D3 142
Scioto, stm., Oh., U.S. B2 142
Scipio, In., U.S. F6 121
Scipio, Ut., U.S. D3 151
Scircleville, In., U.S. D5 121
Scituate, Ma., U.S. B6 128
Scituate Reservoir, res., R.I., U.S. C3 146
Scobey, Mt., U.S. B11 133
Scofield Reservoir, res., Ut., U.S. D4 151
Ščokino, Russia G20 22
Scone, Austl. I9 70
Scooba, Ms., U.S. C5 131
Scordia, Italy L9 18
Scotch Plains, N.J., U.S. B4 137
Scotia, Ont., Can. B5 103
Scotia, Ca., U.S. B1 112
Scotia, Ne., U.S. C7 134
Scotia, N.Y., U.S. C7 139
Scotia Sea, S.A. A1 73
Scotland, Ont., Can. D4 103
Scotland, Ar., U.S. B3 111
Scotland, Ct., U.S. C7 114
Scotland, Ga., U.S. D4 117
Scotland, In., U.S. G4 121
Scotland, Pa., U.S. G6 145
Scotland, S.D., U.S. D8 148
Scotland, co., Mo., U.S. A5 132
Scotland, co., N.C., U.S. C3 140
Scotland, ter., U.K. D9 8
Scotland Neck, N.C., U.S. A5 140
Scotlandville, La., U.S. D4 125
Scotrun, Pa., U.S. D11 145
Scotsburn, N.S., Can. D7 101
Scotstown, Que., Can. D6 104
Scott, Sask., Can. E1 105
Scott, Ar., U.S. C3 111
Scott, Ga., U.S. D4 117
Scott, La., U.S. D3 125
Scott, Ms., U.S. B2 131
Scott, co., Ar., U.S. C1 111
Scott, co., Il., U.S. D3 120
Scott, co., In., U.S. G6 121
Scott, co., Ia., U.S. C7 122
Scott, co., Ks., U.S. D3 123
Scott, co., Ky., U.S. B5 124
Scott, co., Mn., U.S. F5 130
Scott, co., Ms., U.S. C4 131
Scott, co., Mo., U.S. D8 132
Scott, co., Tn., U.S. C9 149
Scott, co., Va., U.S. f9 153
Scott, Cape, c., B.C., Can. D3 99
Scott, Mount, mtn., Ok., U.S. C3 143
Scott, Mount, mtn., Or., U.S. E4 144
Scott Air Force Base, mil., Il., U.S. E4 120
Scott Base, sci., Ant. C8 73
Scottburgh, S. Afr. H10 66
Scott City, Ks., U.S. D3 123
Scott City, Mo., U.S. D8 132
Scottdale, Ga., U.S. h8 117
Scottdale, Pa., U.S. F2 145
Scott Islands, is., B.C., Can. D3 99
Scott Mountain, mtn., Id., U.S. E3 119
Scott Peak, mtn., Id., U.S. E6 119
Scott Reef, rf., Austl. B4 68
Scott Reservoir, res., N.C., U.S. A1 140
Scotts, Mi., U.S. F5 129
Scottsbluff, Ne., U.S. C2 134
Scotts Bluff, co., Ne., U.S. C2 134
Scotts Bluff National Monument, Ne., U.S. C2 134
Scottsboro, Al., U.S. A3 108
Scottsburg, In., U.S. G6 121
Scottsdale, Austl. M7 70
Scottsdale, Az., U.S. D4 110
Scotts Hill, Tn., U.S. B3 149
Scotts Mills, Or., U.S. B4 144
Scotts Mountain, mtn., N.J., U.S. B2 137
Scottsville, Ky., U.S. D3 124
Scottsville, N.Y., U.S. B3 139
Scottsville, Va., U.S. C4 153
Scottville, Mi., U.S. E4 129
Scow Bay, Ak., U.S. m23 109
Scraggly Lake, l., Me., U.S. B4 126
Scranton, Ar., U.S. B2 111
Scranton, Ia., U.S. B3 122
Scranton, Ks., U.S. D8 123
Scranton, N.D., U.S. C2 141
Scranton, Pa., U.S. D10 145
Scranton, S.C., U.S. D8 147
Screven, Ga., U.S. E4 117
Screven, co., Ga., U.S. D5 117
Scribner, Ne., U.S. C9 134
Ščučin, Bela. H7 22
Ščučinsk, Kaz. G12 26
Scugog, Lake, l., Ont., Can. C6 103
Scuol (Schuls), Switz. E13 13
Scurry, co., Tx., U.S. C2 150
Scutari, Lake, l., Eur. G3 20
Seaboard, N.C., U.S. A5 140
Seabreeze, De., U.S. F5 115
Sea Bright, N.J., U.S. C5 137
Seabrook, N.H., U.S. E5 136
Seabrook, N.J., U.S. E2 137
Seabrook, Tx., U.S. r14 150
Seabrook Island, i., S.C., U.S. F7 147
Seadrift, Tx., U.S. E4 150
Seaford, De., U.S. F3 115
Seaford, Va., U.S. h15 153
Seaforth, Ont., Can. D3 103
Sea Girt, N.J., U.S. C4 137
Seagoville, Tx., U.S. n10 150
Seagrave, Ont., Can. C6 103
Seagraves, Tx., U.S. C1 150
Seahorse Point, c., N.W. Ter., Can. D16 96
Sea Islands, is., U.S. E10 106
Sea Isle City, N.J., U.S. E3 137
Seal, stm., Man., Can. f8 100
Sea Lake, Austl. J5 70
Seal Cays, is., T./C. Is. D9 94
Seal Cove, N.B., Can. E3 101
Seal Cove, Newf., Can. D3 102
Seale, Al., U.S. C4 108
Seal Harbor, Me., U.S. D4 126
Seal Point, c., P.E.I., Can. C5 101
Seal Rock, Or., U.S. C2 144
Sealy, Tx., U.S. E4 150
Seama, N.M., U.S. B2 138
Seaman, Oh., U.S. D2 142
Seaman Range, mts., Nv., U.S. F6 135
Seara, Braz. D12 80
Searchlight, Nv., U.S. H7 135
Searcy, Ar., U.S. B4 111
Searcy, co., Ar., U.S. B3 111
Searles, Al., U.S. B2 108
Searles, Mn., U.S. F4 130
Searles Lake, l., Ca., U.S. E5 112
Sears Falls, wtfl, Ne., U.S. B5 134
Searsmont, Me., U.S. D3 126
Searsport, Me., U.S. D4 126
Searston, Newf., Can. E2 102
Seaside, Or., U.S. B3 144
Seaside Heights, N.J., U.S. D4 137
Seaside Park, N.J., U.S. D4 137
Seaton, Il., U.S. B3 120
Seat Pleasant, Md., U.S. C4 127
Seattle, Wa., U.S. B3 154
Seattle-Tacoma International Airport, Wa., U.S. f11 154
Seaview, Wa., U.S. C1 154
Seaville, N.J., U.S. E3 137
Seba Beach, Alta., Can. C3 98
Sébaco, Nic. E8 92
Sebago Lake, Me., U.S. E2 126
Sebakwe Recreational Area, Zimb. B10 66
Šebalino, Russia G15 26
Sebasco Estates, Me., U.S. g8 126
Sebastian, Fl., U.S. E6 116
Sebastian, co., Ar., U.S. B1 111
Sebastian, Cape, c., Or., U.S. E2 144
Sebastian Inlet, b., Fl., U.S. E6 116
Sebastián Vizcaíno, Bahía, b., Mex. C2 90
Sebasticook Lake, l., Me., U.S. D3 126
Sebastopol, Ms., U.S. C4 131
Sebderat, Erit. J9 60
Sebec Lake, l., Me., U.S. C3 126
Sebeka, Mn., U.S. D3 130
Seberi, Braz. D12 80
Sebeș, Rom. D7 20
Sebes Körös (Crișul Repede), stm., Eur. B5 20
Sebewaing, Mi., U.S. E7 129
Sebež, Russia E11 22
Şebinkarahisar, Tur. A5 48
Sebiș, Rom. C6 20
Sebnitz, Ger. E14 10
Seboeis, stm., Me., U.S. B4 126
Seboeis Lake, l., Me., U.S. C4 126
Seboomook Lake, l., Me., U.S. C3 126
Seboyeta, N.M., U.S. B2 138
Sebree, Ky., U.S. C2 124
Sebring, Fl., U.S. E5 116
Sebring, Oh., U.S. B4 142
Sebringville, Ont., Can. D3 103
Secas, Islas, is., Pan. J12 92
Secaucus, N.J., U.S. h8 137
Sechelt, B.C., Can. E6 99
Sechura, Peru A1 82
Sechura, Bahía de, b., Peru A1 82
Sechura, Desierto de, des., Peru A1 82
Seclantas, Arg. C5 80
Seco, Ky., U.S. C7 124
Seco, stm., Arg. B7 80
Second Lake, l., N.H., U.S. f7 136
Second Mesa, Az., U.S. B5 110
Secor, Il., U.S. C4 120
Sečovce, Slov. G21 10
Secretary, Md., U.S. C6 127
Secret Lake, l., R.I., U.S. E4 146
Section, Al., U.S. A4 108
Sécure, stm., Bol. F9 82
Security, Co., U.S. C6 113
Seda, China E7 30
Seda, Lat. D8 22
Seda, Lith. E5 22
Sedalia, Co., U.S. B6 113
Sedalia, Ky., U.S. f9 124
Sedalia, Mo., U.S. C4 132
Sedan, Fr. C11 14
Sedan, Ks., U.S. E7 123
Sedano, Spain C8 16
Sedel'nikovo, Russia F13 26
Sederot, Isr. E3 50
Sedgewick, Alta., Can. C5 98
Sedgewick, Mount, mtn., N.M., U.S. B1 138
Sedgwick, Co., U.S. A8 113
Sedgwick, Ks., U.S. E6 123
Sedgwick, Me., U.S. D4 126
Sedgwick, co., Co., U.S. A8 113
Sedgwick, co., Ks., U.S. E6 123
Sedini, Italy I3 18
Sedlčany, Czech. F14 10
Sedley, Sask., Can. G3 105
Sedley, Va., U.S. D6 153
Sedom (Sodom), hist., Isr. F4 50
Sedona, Az., U.S. C4 110
Sedot Yam, Isr. D3 50
Sedova, pik, mtn., Russia C8 26
Sedrata, Alg. M2 18
Sedro Woolley, Wa., U.S. A3 154
Šeduva, Lith. F6 22
Seebe, Alta., Can. D3 98
Seeberg, Switz. D8 13
Seefeld in Tirol, Aus. H11 10
Seehausen, Ger. C11 10
Seeheim, Nmb. F3 66
Seeis, Nmb. D3 66
Seekonk, Ma., U.S. C5 128
Seekonk, stm., R.I., U.S. C4 146
Seeley, Ca., U.S. F6 112
Seeley Lake, Mt., U.S. C3 133
Seeleys Bay, Ont., Can. C8 103
Seelow, Ger. C14 10
Seelyville, In., U.S. F3 121
Seengen, Switz. D9 13
Sées, Fr. D7 14
Seesen, Ger. D10 10
Sefadu, S.L. G4 64
Sefar, hist., Alg. H15 62
Sefare, Bots. D8 66
Sefīd Ābeh, Iran F16 48
Sefrou, Mor. D8 62
Segamat, Malay. M7 40
Şegarcea, Rom. E7 20
Segbana, Benin F11 64
Segbwema, S.L. G4 64
Segeža, Russia E4 26
Segni, Italy H8 18
Segorbe, Spain F11 16
Ségou, Mali E6 64
Segovia, Col. D5 84
Segovia, Spain E7 16
Segozero, ozero, l., Russia J23 6
Segre, stm., Eur. D12 16
Seguam Island, i., Ak., U.S. E5 109
Seguam Pass, strt., Ak., U.S. E5 109
Séguédine, Niger D9 54
Séguéla, I.C. H6 64
Séguéla, Mali D6 64
Seguí, Arg. F8 80
Seguin, Tx., U.S. E4 150
Segundo, Co., U.S. D6 113
Segundo, stm., Arg. F7 80
Segura, Port. F5 16
Segura, stm., Spain G11 16
Sehithwa, Bots. C6 66
Seia, Port. E4 16
Seibert, Co., U.S. B8 113
Seiling, Ok., U.S. A3 143
Seilo, Sud. K2 60
Sein, Île de, i., Fr. D2 14
Seinäjoki, Fin. J18 6
Seine, stm., Fr. C7 14
Seine, Baie de la, b., Fr. C6 14
Seine-et-Marne, dept., Fr. D10 14
Seine-Maritime, dept., Fr. C8 14
Seixal, Port. G2 16
Sejm, stm., Eur. G4 26
Sejmčan, Russia E22 28
Šeke, Eth. M10 60
Seki (Nucha), Azer. I7 26
Seki, Japan L11 36
Seki, Tur. M13 20
Sekiu, Wa., U.S. A1 154
Sekoma, Bots. E6 66
Sekondi-Takoradi, Ghana I9 64
Sek'ota, Eth. K10 60
Šeksna, Russia B21 22
Šelagskij, mys, c., Russia C26 28
Selah, Wa., U.S. C5 154
Selaru, Pulau, i., Indon. G9 38
Selatan, Tanjung, c., Indon. F5 38
Selawik, Ak., U.S. B7 109
Selawik Lake, l., Ak., U.S. B7 109
Selayar, Pulau, i., Indon. G7 38
Selb, Ger. E12 10
Selbu, Nor. J12 6
Selby, S.D., U.S. B5 148
Selbyville, De., U.S. G5 115
Sel'co, Russia H17 22
Selden, Ks., U.S. C3 123
Seldovia, Ak., U.S. D9 109
Selebi Phikwe, Bots. D8 66
Selenga (Selenge), stm., Asia G19 26
Selenge (Selenga), stm., Asia B7 30
Selenn'ach, stm., Russia D20 28
Sélestat, Fr. D14 14
Selezn'ovo, Russia A11 22
Selfridge, N.D., U.S. C5 141
Sélibaby, Maur. D3 64
Šelichova, zaliv, b., Russia F23 28
Seliger, ozero, l., Russia D16 22
Seligman, Az., U.S. B3 110
Seligman, Mo., U.S. E4 132
Selinsgrove, Pa., U.S. E8 145
Selišče, Russia E16 22
Seližarovo, Russia E16 22
Selje, Nor. J9 6
Seljord, Nor. L11 6
Selkirk, Man., Can. D3 100
Selkirk, Scot., U.K. F11 8
Selleck, Wa., U.S. B4 154
Sellers, Al., U.S. C3 108
Sellers, S.C., U.S. C9 147
Sellersburg, In., U.S. H6 121
Sellersville, Pa., U.S. F11 145
Sells, Az., U.S. F4 110
Selm, Ger. D7 10
Selma, Al., U.S. C2 108
Selma, Ca., U.S. D4 112
Selma, In., U.S. D7 121
Selma, N.C., U.S. B4 140
Selmer, Tn., U.S. B3 149
Seltz, Fr. D15 14
Selva, Arg. E7 80
Selvas, for., Braz. E6 76
Selvin, In., U.S. H3 121
Selway, stm., Id., U.S. C3 119
Selwyn, Austl. C4 70
Selwyn Mountains, mts., Can. D6 96
Selwyn Range, mts., Austl. C4 70
Selz, N.D., U.S. B6 141
Šemacha, Azer. A10 48
Seman, stm., Alb. I3 20
Semans, Sask., Can. F3 105
Semarang, Indon. j15 39a
Semeru, Gunung, mtn., Indon. k16 39a
Semeževo, Bela. I10 22
Semibratovo, Russia D22 22
Seminary, Ms., U.S. D4 131
Seminoe Mountains, mts., Wy., U.S. D6 157
Seminoe Reservoir, res., Wy., U.S. D6 157
Seminole, Al., U.S. E2 108
Seminole, Ok., U.S. B5 143
Seminole, Tx., U.S. C1 150
Seminole, co., Fl., U.S. D5 116
Seminole, co., Ga., U.S. F2 117
Seminole, co., Ok., U.S. B5 143
Seminole, Lake, res., U.S. F2 117
Semipalatinsk, Kaz. G8 28
Semisopochnoi Island, i., Ak., U.S. E3 109
Semmes, Al., U.S. E1 108
Semnān, Iran D12 48
Semois, stm., Eur. I7 12
Šemonaicha, Kaz. G14 26
Sem'onov, Russia F6 26
Sem'onovka, Ukr. I15 22
Semporna, Malay. E6 38
Semuliki, stm., Afr. A5 58
Semur-en-Auxois, Fr. E11 14
Sena, Bol. D8 82
Sena, Moz. E7 58
Sena, N.M., U.S. B4 138
Senachwine Lake, l., Il., U.S. B4 120
Senador Canedo, Braz. D4 79
Senador Firmino, Braz. F7 79
Senador Pompeu, Braz. E11 76
Senahú, Guat. B5 92
Sena Madureira, Braz. C7 82
Senanga, Zam. E4 58
Senath, Mo., U.S. E7 132
Senatobia, Ms., U.S. A4 131
Sendafa, Eth. M10 60
Sendai, Japan I15 36
Sêndo, China E15 44
Seneca, Il., U.S. B5 120
Seneca, Ks., U.S. C7 123
Seneca, Mo., U.S. E3 132
Seneca, Pa., U.S. D2 145
Seneca, S.C., U.S. B2 147
Seneca, S.D., U.S. B6 148
Seneca, co., N.Y., U.S. C4 139
Seneca, co., Oh., U.S. A2 142
Seneca Falls, N.Y., U.S. C4 139
Seneca Lake, l., N.Y., U.S. C4 139
Senecaville Lake, res., Oh., U.S. C4 142
Senegal (Sénégal), ctry., Afr. F4 54
Sénégal, stm., Afr. E4 54
Senekal, S. Afr. G8 66
Senftenberg, Ger. D14 10
Sengés, Braz. H4 79
Senhor do Bonfim, Braz. F10 76
Senica, Slov. G17 10
Senigallia, Italy F8 18
Senise, Italy I11 18
Senj, Cro. E9 18
Senja, i., Nor. G15 6
Šenkursk, Russia E6 26
Senlac, Sask., Can. E1 105
Senlis, Fr. C9 14
Senmonorom, Camb. H9 40
Senneterre, Que., Can. k11 104
Sennori, Italy I3 18
Senoia, Ga., U.S. C2 117
Senqu see Orange, stm., Afr. G4 66
Sens, Fr. D10 14
Sensuntepeque, El Sal. D6 92
Senta, Yugo. D4 20
Sentinel, Ok., U.S. B2 143
Sentinel Butte, N.D., U.S. C2 141
Sentinel Butte, mtn., N.D., U.S. C2 141
Seo de Urgel, Spain C13 16
Seoni, India I8 44
Seoul see Sŏul, S. Kor. F14 32
Sepatini, stm., Braz. B9 82
Sepetiba, Baía de, b., Braz. G7 79
Šepetovka, Ukr. G3 26
Sepik, stm., Pap. N. Gui. k15 68a
Sępólno Krajeńskie, Pol. B17 10
Sepopa, Bots. B6 66
Sepoti, stm., Braz. B11 82
Sepotuba, stm., Braz. F13 82
Sept-Îles (Seven Islands), Que., Can. h13 104
Sepulga, stm., Al., U.S. D3 108
Sequatchie, Tn., U.S. D8 149
Sequatchie, co., Tn., U.S. D8 149
Sequatchie, stm., Tn., U.S. D8 149
Sequeros, Spain E5 16
Sequim, Wa., U.S. A2 154
Sequoia National Park, Ca., U.S. D4 112
Sequoyah, co., Ok., U.S. B7 143
Šerabad, Uzb. B2 44
Serachs, Turk. C16 48
Šerafimovič, Russia H6 26
Seraidi, Alg. M2 18
Seraing, Bel. G7 12
Seram (Ceram), i., Indon. F8 38
Seram, Laut (Ceram Sea), Indon. F8 38
Serang, Indon. j13 39a
Serbia see Srbija, state, Yugo. F4 20
Serdobsk, Russia G6 26
Serebr'anyje Prudy, Russia G21 22
Sered', Slov. G17 10
Seredejskij, Russia G18 22
Seredina-Buda, Ukr. I17 22
Seredžius, Lith. F6 22
Seremban, Malay. M6 40
Serengeti Plain, pl., Tan. B6 58
Serenje, Zam. D6 58
Šereševo, Bela. I7 22
Sergeant Bluff, Ia., U.S. B1 122
Sergeja Kirova, ostrova, is., Russia B15 26
Sergejevka, Russia I18 28
Sergijev Posad, Russia E21 22

Name | Map Ref. | Page

South Walpole, Ma., U.S. h10 128
South Waverly, Pa., U.S. C8 145
South Wayne, Wi., U.S. F4 156
South Webster, Oh., U.S. D3 142
South Wellfleet, Ma., U.S. C8 128
South Wellington, B.C., Can. f12 99
Southwest, Pa., U.S. F3 145
South West Africa see Namibia, ctry., Afr. F3 58
South Westbury, N.Y., U.S. *n15 139
South West Cape, c., Austl. N7 70
Southwest Channel, strt., Fl., U.S. E4 116
South West City, Mo., U.S. E3 132
Southwest Harbor, Me., U.S. D4 126
Southwest Head, c., N.B., Can. E3 101
Southwest Miramichi, stm., N.B., Can. C3 101
Southwest Mountains, mts., Va., U.S. B4 153
Southwest National Park, Austl. N7 70
Southwest Pass, strt., La., U.S. F6 125
Southwest Pass, strt., La., U.S. E3 125
Southwest Point, c., Bah. B6 94
Southwest Point, c., R.I., U.S. h7 146
South Weymouth Naval Air Station, mil., Ma., U.S. h12 128
South Whitley, In., U.S. B6 121
Southwick, Ma., U.S. B2 128
South Williamson, Ky., U.S. C7 124
South Williamsport, Pa., U.S. D7 145
South Wilmington, Il., U.S. B5 120
South Windham, Ct., U.S. C7 114
South Windham, Me., U.S. E2 126
South Windsor, Ct., U.S. B5 114
South Wolfeboro, N.H., U.S. C4 136
Southwood, Co., U.S. *B6 113
Southwood Acres, Ct., U.S. A5 114
South Woodstock, Ct., U.S. B8 114
South Yarmouth, Ma., U.S. C7 128
South Zanesville, Oh., U.S. C3 142
Soutpan, S. Afr. G8 66
Soutpansberg, mts., Afr. D9 66
Souvigny, Fr. F10 14
Sovereign, Sask., Can. F2 105
Sovetsk, Russia H20 22
Sovetsk, Russia F2 26
Sovetsk, Russia F7 26
Sovetskaja Gavan', Russia H20 28
Sovetskij, Russia A11 22
Søvik, Nor. J10 6
Soweto, S. Afr. F8 66
Soyapango, El Sal. D5 92
Soyo, Ang. C2 58
Spa, Bel. G8 12
Spadra, Ar., U.S. B2 111
Spain (España), ctry., Eur. G7 4
Spakenburg, Neth. D7 12
Spalding, Sask., Can. E3 105
Spalding, Eng., U.K. I13 8
Spalding, Id., U.S. C2 119
Spalding, Ne., U.S. C7 134
Spalding, co., Ga., U.S. C2 117
Spanaway, Wa., U.S. B3 154
Spangle, Wa., U.S. B8 154
Spangler, Pa., U.S. E4 145
Spaniard's Bay, Newf., Can. E5 102
Spanishburg, W.V., U.S. D3 155
Spanish Fork, Ut., U.S. C4 151
Spanish Fort, Al., U.S. E2 108
Spanish Lake, Mo., U.S. f13 132
Spanish North Africa, dep., Afr. J6 16
Spanish Peak, mtn., Or., U.S. C7 144
Spanish Sahara see Western Sahara, dep., Afr. D4 54
Spanish Town, Jam. F6 94
Sparkman, Ar., U.S. D3 111
Sparks, Ga., U.S. E3 117
Sparks, Nv., U.S. D2 135
Sparks, Ok., U.S. B5 143
Sparland, Il., U.S. B4 120
Sparr, Fl., U.S. C4 116
Sparrows Point, Md., U.S. B5 127
Sparta, Ga., U.S. C4 117
Sparta, Il., U.S. E4 120
Sparta, Mi., U.S. E5 129
Sparta, Mo., U.S. D4 132
Sparta (Lake Mohawk), N.J., U.S. A3 137
Sparta, N.C., U.S. A1 140
Sparta, Tn., U.S. D8 149
Sparta, Wi., U.S. E3 156
Sparta Mountains, mts., N.J., U.S. B3 137
Spartanburg, In., U.S. D8 121
Spartanburg, S.C., U.S. B4 147
Spartanburg, co., S.C., U.S. B3 147
Sparta see Spárti, Grc. L6 20
Spárti (Sparta), Grc. L6 20
Spartivento, Capo, c., Italy K3 18
Sparwood, B.C., Can. E10 99
Spas-Demensk, Russia G17 22
Spas-Klepiki, Russia F23 22
Spassk-Dal'nij, Russia I18 28
Spátha, Ákra, c., Grc. N7 20
Spavinaw, Ok., U.S. A6 143
Spavinaw Creek, stm., Ok., U.S. A7 143
Spear, Cape, c., Newf., Can. E5 102
Spearfish, S.D., U.S. C2 148
Spearman, Tx., U.S. A2 150
Spearville, Ks., U.S. E4 123
Spectacle Pond, l., Me., U.S. D4 126
Spedden, Alta., Can. B5 98
Speed, In., U.S. H6 121
Speedway, In., U.S. E5 121
Speedwell, Va., U.S. D1 153
Speers, Sask., Can. E2 105
Speigener, Al., U.S. C3 108
Speight, Ky., U.S. C7 124
Speightstown, Barb. H15 94
Spello, Italy G7 18
Spelter, W.V., U.S. k10 155
Spence Bay, N.W. Ter., Can. C14 96
Spencer, In., U.S. F4 121
Spencer, Ia., U.S. A2 122
Spencer, Ma., U.S. B4 128
Spencer, Ne., U.S. B7 134
Spencer, N.Y., U.S. C4 139
Spencer, N.C., U.S. B2 140
Spencer, Oh., U.S. A3 142
Spencer, S.D., U.S. D8 148
Spencer, Tn., U.S. D8 149
Spencer, W.V., U.S. C3 155
Spencer, Wi., U.S. D3 156
Spencer, co., In., U.S. H4 121
Spencer, co., Ky., U.S. B4 124
Spencer, Cape, c., Austl. J2 70
Spencer, Cape, c., Ak., U.S. k21 109
Spencer Gulf, b., Austl. J2 70
Spencer Lake, l., Me., U.S. C2 126
Spencerport, N.Y., U.S. B3 139
Spencers Island, N.S., Can. D5 101
Spencerville, In., U.S. B8 121
Spencerville, Md., U.S. B4 127
Spencerville, Oh., U.S. B1 142
Spences Bridge, B.C., Can. D7 99
Spenser Mountains, mts., N.Z. E4 72
Sperling, Man., Can. E3 100
Sperry, Ok., U.S. A6 143
Sperryville, Va., U.S. B4 153
Spesutie Island, i., Md., U.S. B5 127
Speyer, Ger. F8 10
Speyside, Trin. I14 94
Spezia see La Spezia, Italy E4 18
Spiceland, In., U.S. E7 121
Spicer, Mn., U.S. E4 130
Spickard, Mo., U.S. A4 132
Spider Lake, l., Wi., U.S. B2 156
Spiez, Switz. E8 13
Spijkenisse, Neth. F5 12
Spillville, Ia., U.S. A6 122
Spinazzola, Italy I11 18
Spincourt, Fr. C12 14
Spindale, N.C., U.S. B1 140
Spink, co., S.D., U.S. C7 148
Spink Colony, S.D., U.S. C7 148
Spirit Lake, Id., U.S. B2 119
Spirit Lake, Ia., U.S. A2 122
Spirit Lake, l., Ia., U.S. A2 122
Spirit Lake, l., Wa., U.S. C3 154
Spirit River, Alta., Can. B1 98
Spirit River Flowage, res., Wi., U.S. C4 156
Spiritwood, Sask., Can. D2 105
Spiro, Ok., U.S. B7 143
Spirovo, Russia D17 22
Spišská Nová Ves, Slov. G20 10
Spitsbergen, i., Sval. B2 24
Spittal an der Drau, Aus. I13 10
Spitz, Aus. G15 10
Split, Cro. F11 18
Split, Cape, c., N.S., Can. D5 101
Split Lake, l., Man., Can. A4 100
Split Rock Creek, stm., U.S. G2 130
Spluga, Passo della (Splügenpass), Eur. E11 13
Splügen, Switz. E11 13
Spofford, N.H., U.S. E2 136
Spofford Lake, l., N.H., U.S. E2 136
Špogi, Lat. E9 22
Spokane, Wa., U.S. B8 154
Spokane, co., Wa., U.S. B8 154
Spokane, stm., U.S. B8 154
Spokane, Mount, mtn., Wa., U.S. B8 154
Spokane Indian Reservation, Wa., U.S. B8 154
Spoleto, Italy G7 18
Spoon, stm., Il., U.S. C3 120
Spooner, Wi., U.S. C2 156
Spooner Lake, l., Wi., U.S. C2 156
Spornoje, Russia E22 28
Spotswood, N.J., U.S. C4 137
Spotsylvania, Va., U.S. B5 153
Spotsylvania, co., Va., U.S. B5 153
Spottsville, Ky., U.S. C2 124
Spragge, Ont., Can. A2 103
Sprague, Man., Can. E4 100
Sprague, Al., U.S. C3 108
Sprague, Ne., U.S. D9 134
Sprague, Wa., U.S. B8 154
Sprague, W.V., U.S. n13 155
Sprague, stm., Or., U.S. E5 144
Sprague Lake, l., Wa., U.S. B7 154
Sprague River, Or., U.S. E5 144
Spratly Islands, is., Asia D5 38
Spremberg, Ger. D14 10
Sprigg, W.V., U.S. D2 155
Spring, Tx., U.S. q14 150
Spring, stm., Ar., U.S. A4 111
Spring, South Fork, stm., U.S. A4 111
Spring, South Fork, stm., U.S. E6 132
Spring Arbor, Mi., U.S. F6 129
Spring Bay, b., Ut., U.S. B3 151
Springbok, S. Afr. G3 66
Springboro, Oh., U.S. C1 142
Springbrook, Ont., Can. C7 103
Spring Brook, stm., Pa., U.S. n18 145
Spring City, Pa., U.S. F10 145
Spring City, Tn., U.S. D9 149
Spring City, Ut., U.S. D4 151
Spring Coulee, Alta., Can. E4 98
Spring Creek, Tn., U.S. B3 149
Spring Creek, stm., U.S. D4 134
Spring Creek, stm., Co., U.S. B8 113
Spring Creek, stm., Ga., U.S. F2 117
Spring Creek, stm., Nv., U.S. C4 135
Spring Creek, stm., N.D., U.S. B3 141
Springdale, Newf., Can. D3 102
Springdale, Ar., U.S. A1 111
Springdale, Oh., U.S. n13 142
Springdale, Or., U.S. B4 144
Springdale, Pa., U.S. E2 145
Springdale, S.C., U.S. D5 147
Springdale, Ut., U.S. F3 151
Springdale, Wa., U.S. A8 154
Spring Dale, W.V., U.S. D4 155
Springe, Ger. C9 10
Springer, N.M., U.S. A5 138
Springer, Ok., U.S. C4 143
Springerville, Az., U.S. C6 110
Springfield, N.B., Can. D4 101
Springfield, N.S., Can. E5 101
Springfield, Ont., Can. E4 103
Springfield, Ar., U.S. B3 111
Springfield, Co., U.S. D8 113
Springfield, Fl., U.S. u16 116
Springfield, Ga., U.S. D5 117
Springfield, Id., U.S. F6 119
Springfield, Il., U.S. D4 120
Springfield, Ky., U.S. C4 124
Springfield, La., U.S. D5 125
Springfield, Ma., U.S. B2 128
Springfield, Mn., U.S. F4 130
Springfield, Mo., U.S. D4 132
Springfield, Ne., U.S. C9 134
Springfield, N.J., U.S. B4 137
Springfield, Oh., U.S. C2 142
Springfield, Or., U.S. C4 144
Springfield, Pa., U.S. p20 145
Springfield, S.C., U.S. E5 147
Springfield, S.D., U.S. E8 148
Springfield, Tn., U.S. A5 149
Springfield, Vt., U.S. E4 152
Springfield, Va., U.S. g12 153
Springfield, W.V., U.S. B6 155
Springfield, Lake, res., Il., U.S. D4 120
Springfontein, S. Afr. H7 66
Spring Garden, Guy. D13 84
Spring Garden, Al., U.S. B4 108
Spring Glen, Ut., U.S. D5 151
Spring Green, Wi., U.S. E3 156
Spring Grove, Il., U.S. h8 120
Spring Grove, In., U.S. E8 121
Spring Grove, Mn., U.S. G7 130
Spring Grove, Pa., U.S. G8 145
Springhill, N.S., Can. D5 101
Spring Hill, Ar., U.S. D2 111
Spring Hill, Fl., U.S. D4 116
Spring Hill, Ks., U.S. D9 123
Springhill, La., U.S. A2 125
Spring Hill, Tn., U.S. B5 149
Springhill Junction, N.S., Can. D5 101
Spring Hope, N.C., U.S. B4 140
Springhouse, B.C., Can. D6 99
Spring Island, i., S.C., U.S. G6 147
Spring Lake, Mi., U.S. E4 129
Spring Lake, N.J., U.S. C4 137
Spring Lake, N.C., U.S. B4 140
Spring Lake, Ut., U.S. C4 151
Spring Lake, l., Me., U.S. C2 126
Spring Lake, res., U.S. B3 120
Spring Lake Heights, N.J., U.S. C4 137
Spring Mills, Pa., U.S. E6 145
Spring Mountains, mts., Nv., U.S. G6 135
Spring Place, Ga., U.S. B2 117
Springport, In., U.S. D7 121
Springport, Mi., U.S. F6 129
Springs, S. Afr. F9 66
Springside, Sask., Can. F4 105
Springsure, Austl. E8 70
Springvale, Austl. D4 70
Springvale, Me., U.S. E2 126
Spring Valley, Al., U.S. A2 108
Spring Valley, Ca., U.S. F5 112
Spring Valley, Ca., U.S. o16 112
Spring Valley, Il., U.S. B4 120
Spring Valley, Mn., U.S. G6 130
Spring Valley, N.Y., U.S. g12 139
Spring Valley, Oh., U.S. C1 142
Spring Valley, Wi., U.S. D1 156
Springview, Ne., U.S. B6 134
Springville, Al., U.S. B3 108
Springville, In., U.S. G4 121
Springville, Ia., U.S. B6 122
Springville, N.Y., U.S. C2 139
Springville, Ut., U.S. C4 151
Sprucedale, Ont., Can. B5 103
Spruce Fork, stm., W.V., U.S. m12 155
Spruce Grove, Alta., Can. C4 98
Spruce Knob, mtn., W.V., U.S. C6 155
Spruce Knob-Seneca Rocks National Recreation Area, W.V., U.S. C5 155
Spruce Lake, Sask., Can. D1 105
Spruce Mountain, mtn., Az., U.S. C3 110
Spruce Mountain, mtn., Nv., U.S. C7 135
Spruce Pine, Al., U.S. A2 108
Spruce Pine, N.C., U.S. f10 140
Spruce Run Reservoir, res., N.J., U.S. B3 137
Spur, Tx., U.S. C2 150
Spurr, Mount, mtn., Ak., U.S. g15 109
Spy Hill, Sask., Can. G5 105
Squam Lake, l., N.H., U.S. C4 136
Squam Mountains, mts., N.H., U.S. C3 136
Squapan Lake, l., Me., U.S. B4 126
Square Lake, l., Me., U.S. A4 126
Squatec, Que., Can. B9 104
Squaw Cap Mountain, mtn., N.B., Can. B3 101
Squaw Hill, mtn., Wy., U.S. E7 157
Squaw Peak, mtn., Mt., U.S. C2 133
Squibnocket Point, c., Ma., U.S. D6 128
Squinzano, Italy I13 18
Squire, W.V., U.S. D3 155
Srbija (Serbia), state, Yugo. F4 20
Srbobran, Yugo. D3 20
Sredinnyj chrebet, mts., Russia F24 28
Sredna Gora, mts., Bul. G8 20
Sredneje Kujto, ozero, l., Russia I22 6
Srednekolymsk, Russia D22 28
Srednerusskaja vozvyšennost', plat., Russia G5 26
Srednesibirskoje ploskogorje, plat., Russia D13 28
Śrem, Pol. C17 10
Srê Moât, Camb. H9 40
Sremska Mitrovica, Yugo. E3 20
Sremski Karlovci, Yugo. D3 20
Sretensk, Russia G15 28
Sri Jayawardenepura (Kotte), Sri L. I5 46
Srīkākulam, India C7 46
Sri Kālahasti, India F5 46
Sri Lanka, ctry., Asia H11 42
Srīnagar, India C6 44
Srīrampur, India C3 46
Srīrangam, India G5 46
Srīvilliputtūr, India H4 46
Środa Wielkopolski, Pol. C17 10
Staaten, stm., Austl. C8 68
Staaten River National Park, Austl. C8 68
Staatsburg, N.Y., U.S. D7 139
Stachanov, Ukr. H5 26
Stack Reservoir, res., R.I., U.S. C3 146
Stacyville, Ia., U.S. A5 122
Stade, Ger. B9 10
Staden, Bel. G3 12
Stadl-Paura, Aus. G13 10
Stadskanaal, Neth. B10 12
Staffelstein, Ger. E11 10
Stafford, Eng., U.K. I11 8
Stafford, Ct., U.S. B6 114
Stafford, Ks., U.S. E5 123
Stafford, Va., U.S. B5 153
Stafford, co., Ks., U.S. D5 123
Stafford, co., Va., U.S. B5 153
Stafford Pond, l., R.I., U.S. D6 146
Staffordshire, co., Eng., U.K. I11 8
Stafford Springs, Ct., U.S. B6 114
Staffordsville, Ky., U.S. C7 124
Staffordville, Ct., U.S. B6 114
Staicele, Lat. D7 22
Staines, Eng., U.K. J13 8
Stairs Mountain, mtn., N.H., U.S. B4 136
Stalden, Switz. F8 13
Stalheim, Nor. K10 6
Stalingrad see Volgograd, Russia H6 26
Stalowa Wola, Pol. E22 10
Stambaugh, Mi., U.S. B2 129
Stamford, Austl. C5 70
Stamford, Ct., U.S. E1 114
Stamford, Ne., U.S. D6 134
Stamford, N.Y., U.S. C6 139
Stamford, Tx., U.S. C3 150
Stamford, Vt., U.S. F2 152
Stamford, Lake, res., Tx., U.S. C3 150
Stamping Ground, Ky., U.S. B5 124
Stamps, Ar., U.S. D2 111
Stanaford, W.V., U.S. D3 155
Stanardsville, Va., U.S. B4 153
Stanberry, Mo., U.S. A3 132
Stanchfield, Mn., U.S. E5 130
Standard, Alta., Can. D4 98
Standard, Il., U.S. B4 120
Standerton, S. Afr. F9 66
Standing Rock, Al., U.S. B4 108
Standing Rock Indian Reservation, U.S. B4 148
Standish, Me., U.S. E2 126
Standish, Mi., U.S. E7 129
Stanfield, Az., U.S. E3 110
Stanfield, Or., U.S. B7 144
Stanford, Il., U.S. C4 120
Stanford, Ky., U.S. C5 124
Stanford, Mt., U.S. C6 133
Stanhope, Ia., U.S. B4 122
Stanhope, N.J., U.S. B3 137
Stanislaus, co., Ca., U.S. D3 112
Stanke Dimitrov, Bul. G7 20
Stanley, N.B., Can. C3 101
Stanley, Falk. Is. G5 78
Stanley, Ks., U.S. D9 123
Stanley, Ky., U.S. C2 124
Stanley, N.M., U.S. B4 138
Stanley, N.C., U.S. B1 140
Stanley, N.D., U.S. A3 141
Stanley, Va., U.S. B4 153
Stanley, Wi., U.S. D3 156
Stanley, co., S.D., U.S. C5 148
Stanley Reservoir, res., India G4 46
Stanleytown, Va., U.S. D3 153
Stanleyville, N.C., U.S. A2 140
Stanleyville see Kisangani, Zaire A5 58
Stanly, co., N.C., U.S. B2 140
Stanovoj chrebet, mts., Russia F17 28
Stanovoje nagorje (Stanovoy Mountains), mts., Russia F14 28
Stans, Switz. E9 13
Stansbury Mountains, mts., Ut., U.S. C3 151
Stanstead, Que., Can. D5 104
Stanthorpe, Austl. G9 70
Stanton, Al., U.S. C3 108
Stanton, Ia., U.S. D2 122
Stanton, Ky., U.S. C6 124
Stanton, Mi., U.S. E5 129
Stanton, Mo., U.S. C6 132
Stanton, Ne., U.S. C8 134
Stanton, N.D., U.S. B4 141
Stanton, Tn., U.S. B2 149
Stanton, Tx., U.S. C2 150
Stanton, co., Ks., U.S. E2 123
Stanton, co., Ne., U.S. C8 134
Stantonsburg, N.C., U.S. B5 140
Stantonville, Tn., U.S. B3 149
Stanwood, Ia., U.S. C6 122
Stanwood, Wa., U.S. A3 154
Staplehurst, Ne., U.S. D8 134
Staples, Mn., U.S. D4 130
Stapleton, Al., U.S. E2 108
Stapleton, Ga., U.S. C4 117
Stapleton, Ne., U.S. C5 134
Star, Id., U.S. F2 119
Star, Ms., U.S. C3 131
Star, N.C., U.S. B3 140
Stará Boleslav, Czech. E14 10
Starachowice, Pol. D21 10
Staraja Russa, Russia C14 22
Staraja Toropa, Russia E14 22
Staraja Ušica, Ukr. A11 20
Staraja Vičuga, Russia D24 22
Stara Pazova, Yugo. E4 20
Stara Planina (Balkan Mountains), mts., Eur. G8 20
Stara Zagora, Bul. G9 20
Starbuck, Man., Can. E3 100
Starbuck, Mn., U.S. E3 130
Star City, Sask., Can. E3 105
Star City, Ar., U.S. D4 111
Star City, In., U.S. C4 121
Star City, W.V., U.S. B5 155
Stargard Szczeciński (Stargard in Pommern), Pol. B15 10
Stargo, Az., U.S. D6 110
Starica, Russia E17 22
Stark, N.H., U.S. A4 136
Stark, co., Il., U.S. B4 120
Stark, co., N.D., U.S. C3 141
Stark, co., Oh., U.S. B4 142
Starke, Fl., U.S. C4 116
Starke, co., In., U.S. B4 121
Starks, La., U.S. D2 125
Starkville, Co., U.S. D6 113
Starkville, Ms., U.S. B5 131
Starkweather, N.D., U.S. A7 141
Star Lake, l., Mn., U.S. D3 130
Starnberg, Ger. G11 10
Starnberger See, l., Ger. H11 10
Starobin, Bela. I10 22
Starodub, Russia I15 22
Starogard Gdański, Pol. B18 10
Staroje Selo, Bela. F12 22
Staroje Ustje, Russia H24 22
Starokazačje, Ukr. C13 20
Staroseslavino, Russia H23 22
Starožilovo, Russia G22 22
Star Peak, mtn., Nv., U.S. C3 135
Star Prairie, Wi., U.S. C1 156
Starr, co., Tx., U.S. F3 150
Starr Mountain, mtn., Tn., U.S. D9 149
Startex, S.C., U.S. B3 147
Startup, Wa., U.S. B4 154
Staryje Dorogi, Bela. H11 22
Staryje Popel'uchi, Ukr. A12 20
Staryj Oskol, Russia G5 26
Staryj Sambor, Ukr. F22 10
Stassfurt, Ger. D11 10
Staszów, Pol. E21 10
State Center, Ia., U.S. B4 122
State College, Pa., U.S. E6 145
State Line, In., U.S. D2 121
State Line, Ms., U.S. D5 131
Stateline, Nv., U.S. E2 135
State Line, Pa., U.S. G6 145
Staten Island, i., N.Y., U.S. k12 139
Statenville, Ga., U.S. F4 117
State Road, N.C., U.S. A2 140
Statesboro, Ga., U.S. D5 117
Statesville, N.C., U.S. B2 140
Statham, Ga., U.S. C3 117
Statue of Liberty National Monument, N.J., U.S. k8 137
Staunton, Il., U.S. D4 120
Staunton, In., U.S. F3 121
Staunton, Va., U.S. B3 153
Stavanger, Nor. L9 6
Stavely, Alta., Can. D4 98
Stavnoje, Ukr. G22 10
Stavropol', Russia H6 26
Stawell, Austl. K5 70
Stawell, stm., Austl. C5 70
Stawiszyn, Pol. D18 10
Stayner, Ont., Can. C4 103
Stayton, Or., U.S. C4 144
Steamboat, Nv., U.S. D2 135
Steamboat Canyon, Az., U.S. B6 110
Steamboat Mountain, mtn., Mt., U.S. C4 133
Steamboat Mountain, mtn., Wy., U.S. E4 157
Steamboat Rock, Ia., U.S. B4 122
Steamboat Springs, Co., U.S. A4 113
Stearns, Ky., U.S. D5 124
Stearns, co., Mn., U.S. E4 130
Stearns Brook, stm., N.H., U.S. A4 136
Stebbins, Ak., U.S. C7 109
Steckborn, Switz. C10 13
Steele, Al., U.S. B3 108
Steele, Mo., U.S. E8 132
Steele, N.D., U.S. C6 141
Steele, co., Mn., U.S. F5 130
Steele, co., N.D., U.S. B8 141
Steele, Mount, mtn., Wy., U.S. E6 157
Steele City, Ne., U.S. D8 134
Steeleville, Il., U.S. E4 120
Steelton, Pa., U.S. F8 145
Steelville, Mo., U.S. D6 132
Steen, Mn., U.S. G2 130
Steens, Ms., U.S. B5 131
Steens Mountain, mts., Or., U.S. E8 144
Steep Falls, Me., U.S. E2 126
Steep Rock, Man., Can. D2 100
Stefansson Island, i., N.W. Ter., Can. B11 96
Steffisburg, Switz. E8 13
Steger, Il., U.S. B6 120
Steiermark, state, Aus. H15 10
Steilacoom, Wa., U.S. f10 154
Stein, Switz. C8 13
Steinach, Aus. H11 10
Steinbach, Man., Can. E3 100
Steinhatchee, Fl., U.S. C3 116
Steinhatchee, stm., Fl., U.S. C3 116
Steinhausen, Nmb. C4 66
Steinkjer, Nor. I12 6
Steksovo, Russia F26 22
Stella, Ont., Can. C8 103
Stella, Ky., U.S. f9 124
Stella, Ne., U.S. D10 134
Stellarton, N.S., Can. D7 101
Stellenbosch, S. Afr. I4 66
Stenay, Fr. C12 14
Stendal, Ger. C11 10
Stendal, In., U.S. H3 121
Stende, Lat. D5 22
Stenen, Sask., Can. F4 105
Stepanakert, Azer. J7 26
Stephen, Mn., U.S. B2 130
Stephens, Ar., U.S. D2 111
Stephens, co., Ga., U.S. B3 117
Stephens, co., Ok., U.S. C4 143
Stephens, co., Tx., U.S. C3 150
Stephens, Port, b., Austl. I10 70
Stephens City, Va., U.S. A4 153
Stephens Knob, hill, Ky., U.S. D5 124
Stephens Lake, res., Man., Can. A4 100
Stephenson, Mi., U.S. C3 129
Stephenson, co., Il., U.S. A4 120
Stephens Passage, strt., Ak., U.S. m23 109
Stephensport, Ky., U.S. C3 124
Stephenville, Newf., Can. D2 102
Stephenville, Tx., U.S. C3 150
Stephenville Crossing, Newf., Can. D2 102
Stepn'ak, Kaz. G12 26
Sterkstroom, S. Afr. H8 66
Sterling, Ak., U.S. g16 109
Sterling, Co., U.S. A7 113
Sterling, Ct., U.S. C8 114
Sterling, Ga., U.S. E5 117
Sterling, Il., U.S. B4 120
Sterling, Ks., U.S. D5 123
Sterling, Ma., U.S. B4 128
Sterling, Mi., U.S. D6 129
Sterling, Ne., U.S. D9 134
Sterling, N.D., U.S. C5 141
Sterling, Ok., U.S. C3 143
Sterling, Va., U.S. A5 153
Sterling, co., Tx., U.S. D2 150
Sterling City, Tx., U.S. D2 150
Sterling Heights, Mi., U.S. o15 129
Sterling Reservoir, res., Co., U.S. A7 113
Sterlington, La., U.S. B3 125
Sterlitamak, Russia G9 26
Sterrett, Al., U.S. B3 108
Stetson Mountain, mtn., Me., U.S. C4 126
Stetsonville, Wi., U.S. C3 156
Stettin see Szczecin, Pol. B14 10
Stettler, Alta., Can. C4 98
Steuben, co., In., U.S. A7 121
Steuben, co., N.Y., U.S. C3 139
Steubenville, Oh., U.S. B5 142
Stevens, co., Ks., U.S. E2 123
Stevens, co., Mn., U.S. E3 130
Stevens, co., Wa., U.S. A7 154
Stevens Creek Dam, U.S. C4 117
Stevenson, Al., U.S. A4 108
Stevenson, Ct., U.S. D3 114
Stevenson, Wa., U.S. D4 154
Stevenson Lake, l., Man., Can. C4 100
Stevenson Mountain, mtn., Ar., U.S. B1 111
Stevens Pass, Wa., U.S. B4 154
Stevens Peak, mtn., Id., U.S. B3 119
Stevens Point, Wi., U.S. D4 156
Stevens Pottery, Ga., U.S. D3 117
Stevens Village, Ak., U.S. B10 109
Stevensville, Md., U.S. C5 127
Stevensville, Mi., U.S. F4 129
Stevensville, Mt., U.S. D2 133
Steward, Il., U.S. B4 120
Stewardson, Il., U.S. D5 120
Stewart, B.C., Can. B3 99
Stewart, Mn., U.S. F4 130
Stewart, Ms., U.S. B4 131
Stewart, Tn., U.S. A4 149
Stewart, co., Ga., U.S. D2 117
Stewart, co., Tn., U.S. A4 149
Stewart, stm., Yukon, Can. D5 96
Stewart Island, i., N.Z. G1 72
Stewart Mountain, mtn., Az., U.S. k9 110
Stewarton, Scot., U.K. F9 8
Stewarts Point, Nv., U.S. G7 135
Stewartstown, N.H., U.S. f6 136
Stewartstown, Pa., U.S. G8 145
Stewartsville, Al., U.S. B3 108
Stewartsville, In., U.S. H2 121
Stewartsville, Mo., U.S. B3 132
Stewart Valley, Sask., Can. G2 105
Stewartville, Mn., U.S. G6 130
Stewiacke, N.S., Can. D6 101
Steynsburg, S. Afr. H7 66
Steyr, Aus. G14 10
Steytlerville, S. Afr. I7 66
Stickney, S.D., U.S. D7 148
Stif, Alg. B13 62
Stigler, Ok., U.S. B6 143
Stikine, stm., Ak., U.S. D13 109
Stilbaai, S. Afr. J5 66
Stilesville, In., U.S. E4 121
Stilfontein, S. Afr. F8 66
Stilís, Grc. K6 20
Still, Alg. C13 62
Still, stm., Ct., U.S. B3 114
Stillaguamish, North Fork, stm., Wa., U.S. A4 154
Stillaguamish, South Fork, stm., Wa., U.S. A4 154
Stillhouse Hollow Lake, res., Tx., U.S. D4 150
Stillman Valley, Il., U.S. A4 120
Stillmore, Ga., U.S. D4 117
Stillwater, Mn., U.S. E6 130
Stillwater, N.Y., U.S. C7 139
Stillwater, Ok., U.S. A4 143
Stillwater, co., Mt., U.S. E7 133
Stillwater Range, mts., Nv., U.S. D3 135
Stillwater Reservoir, res., N.Y., U.S. B5 139
Stillwater Reservoir, res., R.I., U.S. B3 146
Stillwell, In., U.S. A4 121
Stilson, Ga., U.S. D5 117
Stilwell, Ks., U.S. D9 123
Stilwell, Ok., U.S. B7 143
Stimson, Mount, mtn., Mt., U.S. B3 133
Stînca-Costeşti, Lacul (vodochranilišče Kostešty-Stynka), res., Eur. B11 20
Stine Mountain, mtn., Mt., U.S. E3 133
Stinesville, In., U.S. F4 121
Stinking Lake, l., N.M., U.S. A3 138
Stinnett, Tx., U.S. B2 150
Štip, Mac. H6 20
Stirling, Alta., Can. E4 98
Stirling, Ont., Can. C7 103
Stirling, Scot., U.K. E10 8
Stirling, N.J., U.S. B4 137
Stites, Id., U.S. C3 119
Stockach, Ger. H9 10
Stöckalp, Switz. E9 13
Stockbridge, Ga., U.S. C2 117

Name Map Ref. Page

Tula, Russia G20 22
Tulalip Indian Reservation, Wa., U.S. A3 154
Tulancingo, Mex. G10 90
Tulare, Ca., U.S. D4 112
Tulare, S.D., U.S. C7 148
Tulare, co., Ca., U.S. D4 112
Tulare Lake, l., Ca., U.S. D4 112
Tularosa, N.M., U.S. D3 138
Tularosa Mountains, mts., N.M., U.S. D1 138
Tularosa Valley, val., N.M., U.S. E3 138
Tulbagh, S. Afr. I4 66
Tulcán, Ec. G4 84
Tulcea, Rom. D12 20
Tulcea, co., Rom. D12 20
Tule, stm., Nic. F10 92
Tulelake, Ca., U.S. B3 112
Tule Lake, sw., Ca., U.S. B3 112
Tule River Indian Reservation, Ca., U.S. E4 112
Tule Valley, val., Ut., U.S. D2 151
T'ul'gan, Russia G9 26
Tuli, Zimb. C9 66
Tulia, Tx., U.S. B2 150
Tuling, China J7 34
Tūlkarm, Isr. Occ. D4 50
Tullahoma, Tn., U.S. B5 149
Tullamore, Austl. I7 70
Tullamore, Ire. H6 8
Tulle, Fr. G8 14
Tullibigeal, Austl. I7 70
Tulln, Aus. G16 10
Tullos, La., U.S. C3 125
Tullus, Sud. L3 60
Tully, Austl. A6 70
Tuloma, stm., Russia G23 6
Tulsa, Ok., U.S. A6 143
Tulsa, co., Ok., U.S. B6 143
Tuluá, Col. E4 84
Tulum, Mex. G16 90
Tulum, hist., Mex. G16 90
Tulumayo, stm., Peru D4 82
Tulun, Russia G12 28
Tulungagung, Indon. k15 39a
Tuma, Russia F23 22
Tuma, stm., Nic. D10 92
Tumacacori, Az., U.S. F4 110
Tumacacori National Monument, Az., U.S. F4 110
Tumaco, Col. G3 84
Tumaco, Rada de, b., Col. G3 84
Tumalo, Or., U.S. C5 144
Tumatumari, Guy. E13 84
Tumba, Lac, l., Zaire B3 58
Tumbarumba, Austl. J8 70
Tumbes, Peru I2 84
Tumbes, dept., Peru F2 84
Tumbes (Puyango), stm., S.A. I2 84
Tumble Mountain, mtn., Mt., U.S. E7 133
Tumbler Ridge, B.C., Can. B7 99
Tumbling Shoals, Ar., U.S. B3 111
Tumbotino, Russia F26 22
Tumby Bay, Austl. J2 70
Tumča, stm., Eur. H21 6
Tumen, China A17 32
T'umen', Russia F11 26
Tumen (Tuman-gang), stm., Asia A18 32
Tumeremo, Ven. D12 84
Tumiritinga, Braz. E8 79
Tumkūr, India F4 46
Tummo, Libya D3 56
Tumos, stm., Afr. D2 66
Tumpat, Malay. K7 40
Tumsar, India B5 46
Tumtum, Wa., U.S. B8 154
Tumuc-Humac Mountains, mts., S.A. C7 76
Tumut, Austl. J8 70
Tumwater, Wa., U.S. B3 154
Tunari, Cerro, mtn., Bol. G8 82
Tunas de Zaza, Cuba D5 94
Tunaydah, Egypt E5 60
Tunçbilek, Tur. J13 20
Tunduru, Tan. D7 58
Tundža, stm., Eur. G10 20
T'ung, stm., Russia E16 28
Tungabhadra Reservoir, res., India E4 46
Tungaru, Sud. L6 60
Tungkang, Tai. M9 34
Tungla, Nic. D10 92
Tungsha Tao (Pratas Island), i., Tai. G10 30
Tungshih, Tai. K9 34
Tungurahua, prov., Ec. H3 84
Tuni, India D7 46
Tunia, stm., Col. G6 84
Tunica, Ms., U.S. A3 131
Tunica, co., Ms., U.S. A3 131
Tunis, Tun. M5 18
Tunis, Golfe de, b., Tun. L5 18
Tunisia (Tunisie), ctry., Afr. B8 54
Tunja, Col. E6 84
Tunkás, Mex. G15 90
Tunkhannock, Pa., U.S. C10 145
Tunk Lake, l., Me., U.S. D4 126
Tunnel Hill, Ga., U.S. B1 117
Tunnel Springs, Al., U.S. D2 108
Tunnelton, In., U.S. G5 121
Tunnelton, W.V., U.S. B5 155
Tunp Range, mts., Wy., U.S. D2 157
Tununak, Ak., U.S. C6 109
Tunungayualok Island, i., Newf., Can. g9 102
Tunuyán, Arg. G4 80
Tunuyán, stm., Arg. G5 80
Tunxi, China F7 34
Tuo, stm., China E7 30
Tuocheng, China K4 34
Tuokusidawan Ling, mtn., China B11 44
Tuolumne, Ca., U.S. D3 112
Tuolumne, co., Ca., U.S. C4 112
Tuolumne, stm., Ca., U.S. D3 112
Tupã, Braz. F3 79
Tupaciguara, Braz. E4 79
Tupana, stm., Braz. J12 84
Tupanciretã, Braz. E12 80
Tuparro, stm., Col. E8 84
Tupelo, Ar., U.S. B4 111
Tupelo, Ms., U.S. A5 131
Tupelo, Ok., U.S. C5 143
Tupinambarana, Ilha, i., Braz. I14 84
Tupi Paulista, Braz. F3 79
Tupiraçaba, Braz. C4 79
Tupiza, Bol. I9 82
Tupper, B.C., Can. B7 99
Tupper Lake, N.Y., U.S. A6 139
Tupper Lake, l., N.Y., U.S. A6 139
Tupperville, Ont., Can. E2 103
Tupungato, Arg. G4 80
Tupungato, Cerro, mtn., S.A. G4 80
Túquerres, Col. G4 84
Tura, India H14 44
Tura, stm., Russia F10 26
Turabah, Sau. Ar. D2 47
Turayf, Sau. Ar. F5 48
Turbaco, Col. B5 84
Turbacz, mtn., Pol. F20 10
Turbat, Pak. I17 48
Turbeville, S.C., U.S. D7 147
Turbo, Col. C4 84
Turbotville, Pa., U.S. D8 145
Turda, Rom. C7 20
Turdej, Russia H21 22
Turek, Pol. C18 10
Turfan Depression see Turpan Pendi, depr., China C4 30
Turfan see Turpan, China C4 30
Turgaj, Kaz. H10 26
Turgaj, stm., Kaz. H10 26
Turgajskaja ložbina, val., Kaz. G10 26
Turgajskoje plato, plat., Kaz. G10 26
Turginovo, Russia E19 22
Turgoš, Russia B18 22
Turgutlu, Tur. K11 20
Türi, Est. C8 22
Turia, stm., Spain F11 16
Turimiquire, Cerro, mtn., Ven. B11 84
Turin, Alta., Can. E4 98
Turin, Ga., U.S. C2 117
Turinsk, Russia F10 26
Turin see Torino, Italy D2 18
Turka, Ukr. F23 10
Turkestan, Kaz. I11 26
Túrkeve, Hung. H20 10
Turkey, Tx., U.S. B2 150
Turkey (Türkiye), ctry., Asia H15 4
Turkey, stm., Ia., U.S. B6 122
Turkey Creek, La., U.S. D3 125
Turkey Creek, stm., Ne., U.S. D8 134
Turkey Creek, stm., Ok., U.S. A3 143
Turkey Point, c., Md., U.S. B5 127
Turkish Republic of Northern Cyprus see Cyprus, North, ctry., Asia H14 4
Turkmenistan, ctry., Asia I9 26
Turkmenija see Turkmenistan, ctry., Asia I9 26
Turks and Caicos Islands, dep., N.A. D9 94
Turks Island Passage, strt., T./C. Is. D9 94
Turks Islands, is., T./C. Is. D9 94
Turku (Åbo), Fin. K18 6
Turley, Ok., U.S. A6 143
Turlock, Ca., U.S. D3 112
Turmalina, Braz. D7 79
Turnbull, Mount, mtn., Az., U.S. D5 110
Turneffe Islands, is., Belize I16 90
Turner, Me., U.S. D2 126
Turner, Mt., U.S. B8 133
Turner, Or., U.S. C4 144
Turner, co., Ga., U.S. E3 117
Turner, co., S.D., U.S. D8 148
Turner Mountain, hill, Ct., U.S. C1 114
Turners Falls, Ma., U.S. A2 128
Turner Valley, Alta., Can. D3 98
Turney, Mo., U.S. B3 132
Turnhout, Bel. F6 12
Türnitz, Aus. H15 10
Turnor Lake, l., Sask., Can. m7 105
Turnu-Măgurele, Rom. F8 20
Turon, Ks., U.S. E5 123
Turpan, China C4 30
Turpan Pendi, depr., China C4 30
Turpin, Ok., U.S. e10 143
Turquino, Pico, mtn., Cuba E6 94
Turrell, Ar., U.S. B5 111
Turret Peak, mtn., Az., U.S. C4 110
Turrialba, C.R. H11 92
Turrialba, Volcán, vol., C.R. G11 92
Turriff, Scot., U.K. D11 8
Turrubares, Cerro, mtn., C.R. H10 92
Turtle Creek, N.B., Can. D5 101
Turtle Creek, Pa., U.S. k14 145
Turtle Flambeau Flowage, res., Wi., U.S. B3 156
Turtleford, Sask., Can. D1 105
Turtle Lake, N.D., U.S. B5 141
Turtle Lake, Wi., U.S. C1 156
Turtle Lake, l., Sask., Can. D1 105
Turtle Mountain Indian Reservation, N.D., U.S. A6 141
Turton, S.D., U.S. B7 148
Turu, stm., Russia D12 28
Turuchan, stm., Russia D9 28
Turvo, Braz. E14 80
Turvo, stm., Braz. D3 79
Turvo, stm., Braz. F4 79
Tuscaloosa, Al., U.S. B2 108
Tuscaloosa, co., Al., U.S. B2 108
Tuscany see Toscana, prov., Italy F5 18
Tuscarawas, co., Oh., U.S. B4 142
Tuscarawas, stm., Oh., U.S. B4 142
Tuscarora, Nv., U.S. B5 135
Tuscarora Indian Reservation, N.Y., U.S. B2 139
Tuscarora Mountain, mtn., Pa., U.S. F6 145
Tuscarora Mountains, mts., Nv., U.S. B5 135
Tuscola, Il., U.S. D5 120
Tuscola, Tx., U.S. C3 150
Tuscola, co., Mi., U.S. E7 129
Tusculum College, Tn., U.S. C11 149
Tuscumbia, Al., U.S. A2 108
Tushka, Ok., U.S. C5 143
Tuskegee, Al., U.S. C4 108
Tusket, N.S., Can. F4 101
Tusket, stm., N.S., Can. E4 101
Tustumena Lake, l., Ak., U.S. g16 109
Tutajev, Russia D22 22
Tutang, China F5 34
Tuticorin, India H5 46
Tutóia, Braz. D10 76
Tutrakan, Bul. E10 20
Tuttle, N.D., U.S. B6 141
Tuttle, Ok., U.S. B4 143
Tuttle Creek Dam, Ks., U.S. C7 123
Tuttle Creek Lake, res., Ks., U.S. C7 123
Tutupaca, Volcán, vol., Peru G6 82
Tututalak Mountain, mtn., Ak., U.S. B7 109
Tutwiler, Ms., U.S. A3 131
Tuurun-Poorin lääni, prov., Fin. K18 6
Tuva, state, Russia G16 26
Tuvalu, ctry., Oc. G24 2
Ṭuwayq, Jabal, mts., Sau. Ar. D4 47
Tuxedo, N.C., U.S. f10 140
Tuxedo Park, De., U.S. i7 115
Tuxford, Sask., Can. G3 105
Tuxpan, Mex. G7 90
Tuxpan, Mex. G11 90
Tuxtepec, Mex. H11 90
Tuxtla Gutiérrez, Mex. I13 90
Tuy, stm., Ven. B9 84
Tuy An, Viet. H10 40
Tuyen Quang, Viet. D8 40
Tuy Hoa, Viet. H10 40
Tuz Gölü, l., Tur. H14 4
Tuzigoot National Monument, Az., U.S. C4 110
Ṭūz Khurmātū, Iraq D8 48
Tuzla, Bos. E2 20
Tuzly, Ukr. D14 20
Tver' (Kalinin), Russia E18 22
Tweed, Ont., Can. C7 103
Tweed, stm., U.K. F11 8
Tweed Heads, Austl. G10 70
Tweedsmuir Provincial Park, B.C., Can. C4 99
Tweedy Mountain, mtn., Mt., U.S. E4 133
Twee Rivieren, S. Afr. F5 66
Twelve Mile, In., U.S. C5 121
Twelvepole Creek, stm., W.V., U.S. C2 155
Twelvepole Creek, East Fork, stm., W.V., U.S. D2 155
Twelvepole Creek, West Fork, stm., W.V., U.S. D2 155
Twentymile Creek, stm., W.V., U.S. C3 155
Twentynine Palms, Ca., U.S. E5 112
Twentynine Palms Marine Corps Base, mil., Ca., U.S. E5 112
Twiggs, co., Ga., U.S. D3 117
Twillingate, Newf., Can. D4 102
Twin Bridges, Mt., U.S. E4 133
Twin Buttes, mtn., Or., U.S. C4 144
Twin Buttes Reservoir, res., Tx., U.S. D2 150
Twin City, Ga., U.S. D4 117
Twin Creek, stm., Oh., U.S. C1 142
Twin Falls, Id., U.S. G4 119
Twin Falls, co., Id., U.S. G4 119
Twin Knolls, Az., U.S. m9 110
Twin Lakes, Ga., U.S. F3 117
Twin Lakes, In., U.S. B5 121
Twin Lakes, Wi., U.S. F5 156
Twin Lakes, l., Ct., U.S. A2 114
Twin Lakes, l., Ia., U.S. B3 122
Twin Lakes, l., Me., U.S. C4 126
Twin Lakes Mountain, mtn., N.Y., U.S. B6 139
Twin Mountain, N.H., U.S. B3 136
Twin Mountains, mts., Wy., U.S. E7 157
Twin Peaks, mts., Id., U.S. E4 119
Twin Rivers, N.J., U.S. C4 137
Twin Rocks, Pa., U.S. F4 145
Twinsburg, Oh., U.S. A4 142
Twin Valley, Mn., U.S. C2 130
Twisp, Wa., U.S. A5 154
Two Butte Creek, stm., Co., U.S. D8 113
Twofold Bay, b., Austl. K8 70
Twoforks, stm., Sask., Can. C2 105
Two Harbors, Mn., U.S. C7 130
Two Hills, Alta., Can. C5 98
Two Mile Beach, N.J., U.S. F3 137
Two Prairie, Bayou, stm., Ar., U.S. h11 111
Two Rivers, Wi., U.S. D6 156
Two Rivers, North Branch, stm., Mn., U.S. B2 130
Two Rivers, South Branch, stm., Mn., U.S. B2 130
Tybee Island, Ga., U.S. D6 117
Tychy, Pol. E18 10
Tygart Lake, res., W.V., U.S. B5 155
Tygart River, Falls of the, wtfl, W.V., U.S. k10 155
Tygarts Creek, stm., Ky., U.S. B7 124
Tygart Valley, stm., W.V., U.S. B4 155
Tyger, stm., S.C., U.S. B4 147
Tygh Valley, Or., U.S. B5 144
Tyler, Al., U.S. C3 108
Tyler, Mn., U.S. F2 130
Tyler, Tx., U.S. C5 150
Tyler, co., Tx., U.S. D5 150
Tyler, co., W.V., U.S. B4 155
Tyler, Lake, res., Tx., U.S. C5 150
Tyler Branch, stm., Vt., U.S. B3 152
Tyler Heights, W.V., U.S. C3 155
Tylertown, Ms., U.S. D3 131
Tym, stm., Russia E8 28
Tymochtee Creek, stm., Oh., U.S. B2 142
Tyndall, Man., Can. D3 100
Tyndall, S.D., U.S. E8 148
Tyndall Air Force Base, mil., Fl., U.S. u16 116
Tyndinskij, Russia F16 28
Tyne, stm., Eng., U.K. G11 8
Tynemouth, Eng., U.K. F12 8
Tyner, In., U.S. B5 121
Tyner, Ky., U.S. C6 124
Tyne Valley, P.E.I., Can. C6 101
Týn nad Vltavou, Czech. F14 10
Tyonek, Ak., U.S. C9 109
Tyre see Ṣūr, Leb. B4 50
Tyrma, Russia G18 28
Tyro, Ks., U.S. E8 123
Tyrone, Ky., U.S. B5 124
Tyrone, N.M., U.S. E1 138
Tyrone, Ok., U.S. e9 143
Tyrone, Pa., U.S. E5 145
Tyronza, Ar., U.S. B5 111
Tyrrell, co., N.C., U.S. B6 140
Tyrrell, Lake, l., Austl. J5 70
Tyrrhenian Sea (Mare Tirreno), Eur. I7 18
Tytuvėnai, Lith. F6 22
Ty Ty, Ga., U.S. E3 117
Ty Ty Creek, stm., Ga., U.S. E3 117
Tyvan, Sask., Can. G4 105
Tzaneen, S. Afr. D10 66
Tzucacab, Mex. G15 90

U

Uatumã, stm., Braz. I13 84
Uaupés (Vaupés), stm., S.A. G9 84
Uaxactún, hist., Guat. I15 90
Ubá, Braz. F7 79
Ubaitaba, Braz. C9 79
Ubangi (Oubangui), stm., Afr. H10 54
Ubatã, Braz. C9 79
Ubaté, Col. E6 84
Ubatuba, Braz. G6 79
Ubayyiḍ, Wādī al-, val., Asia B11 60
Ube, Japan N6 36
Úbeda, Spain G8 16
Uberaba, Braz. E5 79
Uberaba, stm., Braz. E4 79
Uberaba, Lagoa, l., S.A. G13 82
Uberlândia, Braz. E4 79
Ubiaja, Nig. H13 64
Ubly, Mi., U.S. E8 129
Ubon Ratchathani, Thai. G8 40
Ubundu, Zaire B5 58
Ucacha, Arg. G7 80
Uč-Adži, Turk. B17 48
Ucayali, dept., Peru C4 82
Ucayali, stm., Peru A4 82
Uchiura-wan, b., Japan e15 36a
Uchiza, Peru C3 82
Uchoa, Braz. F4 79
Ucholovo, Russia H23 22
Uchta, Russia E8 26
Uchtoma, Russia A21 22
Uckermark, reg., Ger. B13 10
Ucluelet, B.C., Can. E5 99
Ucon, Id., U.S. F7 119
Uda, stm., Russia G18 28
Udagamandalam, India G4 46
Udaipur, India H5 44
Udall, Ks., U.S. E6 123
Udamalpet, India G4 46
Udaquiola, Arg. I9 80
Udaypur, Nepal G12 44
Udbina, Cro. E10 18
Uddevalla, Swe. L12 6
Udgīr, India C4 46
Udine, Italy C8 18
Udmurtija, state, Russia F8 26
Udoml'a, Russia D18 22
Udon Thani, Thai. F7 40
Udskaja guba, b., Russia G19 28
Udupi, India F3 46
Udžary, Azer. A9 48
Ueckermünde, Ger. B14 10
Ueda, Japan K13 36
Uehling, Ne., U.S. C9 134
Uelzen, Ger. C10 10
Ueno, Japan M11 36
Uetersen, Ger. B9 10
Ufa, Russia G9 26
Uffenheim, Ger. F10 10
Ufra, Turk. A12 48
Ugab, stm., Nmb. C1 66
Ugāle, Lat. D5 22
Uganda, ctry., Afr. A6 58
Ugashik Lakes, l., Ak., U.S. D8 109
Ughaybish, Sud. L6 60
Ugie, S. Afr. H9 66
Uglegorsk, Russia H20 28
Uglič, Russia D21 22
Uglovka, Russia C16 22
Ugodskij Zavod, Russia F19 22
Ugoma, mtn., Zaire B5 58
Ugra, Russia G17 22
Uh (Už), stm., Eur. G22 10
Uha-dong, N. Kor. C13 32
Uherské Hradiště, Czech. F17 10
Uherský Brod, Czech. F17 10
Uhlenhorst, Nmb. D3 66
Uhlman Lake, l., Man., Can. A2 100
Uhrichsville, Oh., U.S. B4 142
Uíge, Ang. C3 58
Ŭijŏngbu, S. Kor. F15 32
Ŭiju, N. Kor. C12 32
Uil, stm., Kaz. H8 26
Uinebona, stm., Ven. E11 84
Uinkaret Plateau, plat., Az., U.S. A2 110
Uinta, co., Wy., U.S. E2 157
Uinta, stm., Ut., U.S. C5 151
Uintah, co., Ut., U.S. D6 151
Uintah and Ouray Indian Reservation, Ut., U.S. C5 151
Uinta Mountains, mts., Ut., U.S. C5 151
Ŭisŏng, S. Kor. G16 32
Uitenhage, S. Afr. I7 66
Uithoorn, Neth. D6 12
Uivak, Cape, c., Newf., Can. f9 102
Uj, stm., Asia G10 26
Ujandina, stm., Russia D20 28
Ujar, Russia F16 26
Ujarrás, hist., C.R. H11 92
Ujmenskij, Russia I27 6
Újfehértó, Hung. H21 10
Uji-guntō, is., Japan p4 37b
Ujiji, Tan. B5 58
Ujjain, India I6 44
'Ujmān, U.A.E. B9 47
Ujungkulon National Park, Indon. j12 39a
Ujungpandang, Indon. G6 38
Ukiah, Ca., U.S. C2 112
Ukiah, Or., U.S. B8 144
Ukmergė, Lith. F7 22
Ukraine, ctry., Eur. H3 26
Ulaanbaatar, Mong. B8 30
Ulaangom, Mong. B5 30
Ulak Island, i., Ak., U.S. E4 109
Ulan, Austl. I8 70
Ulan Bator see Ulaanbaatar, Mong. B8 30
Ulang, stm., Nic. C11 92
Ulan-Ude, Russia G13 28
Ułazów, Pol. E23 10
Ulchin, S. Kor. G17 32
Ulcinj, Yugo. H3 20
Ulco, S. Afr. G7 66
Ulcumayo, Peru D4 82
Uldz, stm., Asia H14 28
Ulen, Mn., U.S. C2 130
Ulhāsnagar, India C2 46
Uliastaj, Mong. B6 30
Uljanovka, Russia B13 22
Uljanovka, Ukr. A14 20
Uljanovsk, Russia G7 26
Ulla, Bela. F12 22
Ulladulla, Austl. J9 70
Ullapool, Scot., U.K. D8 8
Ullin, Il., U.S. F4 120
Ulm, Ger. G10 10
Ulm, Ar., U.S. C4 111
Ulm, Mt., U.S. C5 133
Ulmarra, Austl. G10 70
Ulongué, Moz. D6 58
Ulrum, Neth. B9 12
Ulsan, S. Kor. H17 32
Ulster, co., N.Y., U.S. D6 139
Ulster, hist. reg., Eur. G6 8
Ultraoriental, Cordillera (Serra do Divisor), mts., S.A. C5 82
Ulu, Russia E17 28
Ulúa, stm., Hond. B6 92
Ulubey, Tur. K13 20
Ulukışla, Tur. C3 48
Ulungur, stm., China B4 30
Ulungur Hu, l., China B4 30
Uluru National Park, Austl. E6 68
Ulverstone, Austl. M7 70
Ulysses, Ks., U.S. E2 123
Ulysses, Ne., U.S. C8 134
Ulysses, Pa., U.S. C6 145
Ulzë, Alb. H3 20
Umán, Mex. G15 90
Uman', Ukr. H4 26
Umari, stm., Braz. B9 82
Umarkot, Pak. H3 44
Umatilla, Fl., U.S. D5 116
Umatilla, Or., U.S. B7 144
Umatilla, co., Or., U.S. B8 144
Umatilla, stm., Or., U.S. B7 144
Umatilla Indian Reservation, Or., U.S. B8 144
Umbagog Lake, l., U.S. A4 136
Umbertide, Italy F7 18
Umboi Island, i., Pap. N. Gui. m16 68a
Umbrail, Pass, Eur. E13 13
Umbria, prov., Italy G7 18
Umbuzero, ozero, l., Russia H24 6
Umcolcus Lake, l., Me., U.S. B4 126
Umeå, Swe. J17 6
Umfuli, stm., Zimb. A9 66
Umhlanga Rocks, S. Afr. G10 66
Umkomaas, S. Afr. H10 66
Umm al-Birak, Sau. Ar. C1 47
Umm al-Qaywayn, U.A.E. B9 47
Umm al-Qiṭṭayn, Jord. D7 50
Umm Badr, Sud. J4 60
Umm Dabbī, Sud. J6 60
Umm Dhibbān, Sud. J5 60
Umm Digulgulaya, Sud. L3 60
Umm Durmān (Omdurman), Sud. J7 60
Umm el Faḥm, Isr. C4 50
Umm Jamālah, Sud. L5 60
Umm Kaddādah, Sud. K4 60
Umm Kuwaykah, Sud. K7 60
Umm Lajj, Sau. Ar. I4 48
Umm Mirdi, Sud. H7 60
Umm Qantur, Sud. J6 60
Umm Qaṣr, Iraq F9 48
Umm Quṣayr, Jord. E5 50
Umm Ruwābah, Sud. K6 60
Umm Sayyālah, Sud. J6 60
Umm Shallī, Sud. L2 60
Umm Shuṭūr, Sud. N7 60
Umm Walad, Syria C6 50
Umnak Island, i., Ak., U.S. E6 109
Um'ot, Russia G25 22
Um'ot, Russia I25 22
Umpire, Ar., U.S. C1 111
Umpqua, stm., Or., U.S. D3 144
Umred, India B5 46
Umreth, India I5 44
Umsaskis Lake, l., Me., U.S. B3 126
Ŭmsŏng, S. Kor. G15 32
Umtanum Ridge, mtn., Wa., U.S. C5 154
Umtata, Transkei H9 66
Umtentweni, S. Afr. H10 66
Umuahia, Nig. I13 64
Umuarama, Braz. G2 79
Umzinto, S. Afr. H10 66
Una, Braz. C9 79
Unadilla, Ga., U.S. D3 117
Unadilla, Ne., U.S. h12 134
Unadilla, N.Y., U.S. C5 139
Unadilla, stm., N.Y., U.S. C5 139
Unaí, Braz. D5 79
Unaka Mountains, mts., U.S. C11 149
Unalakleet, Ak., U.S. C7 109
Unalaska, Ak., U.S. E6 109
Unalaska Island, i., Ak., U.S. E6 109
Unare, stm., Ven. C10 84
'Unayzah, Sau. Ar. H7 48
'Unayzah, Jabal, mts., Asia E5 48
'Unayzah, Jabal, mtn., Jord. G5 50
Uncasville, Ct., U.S. D7 114
Uncia, Bol. H8 82
Uncompahgre, stm., Co., U.S. C3 113
Uncompahgre Butte, mtn., Co., U.S. C2 113
Uncompahgre Mountains, mts., Co., U.S. C3 113
Uncompahgre Peak, mtn., Co., U.S. C3 113
Uncompahgre Plateau, plat., Co., U.S. C2 113
Underhill, Vt., U.S. B3 152
Underhill Center, Vt., U.S. B3 152
Underwood, Al., U.S. B3 108
Underwood, In., U.S. G6 121
Underwood, Ia., U.S. C2 122
Underwood, Mn., U.S. D3 130
Underwood, N.D., U.S. B4 141
Underwood, Wa., U.S. D4 154
Undva nina, c., Est. C4 22
Uneča, Russia I15 22
Uneiuxi, stm., Braz. H10 84
Ungarie, Austl. I7 70
Ungava, Péninsule d', pen., Que., Can. g12 104
Ungava Bay, b., Can. E19 96
Unggi, N. Kor. A18 32
União, Braz. D10 76
União da Vitória, Braz. D13 80
União dos Palmares, Braz. E11 76
Unicoi, Tn., U.S. C11 149
Unicoi, co., Tn., U.S. C11 149
Unicoi Mountains, mts., U.S. D9 149
Unimak Island, i., Ak., U.S. D7 109
Unimak Pass, strt., Ak., U.S. E6 109
Unini, stm., Braz. H12 84
Unión, Arg. H6 80
Unión, C.R. I11 92
Unión, Para. C10 80
Union, Il., U.S. A5 120
Union, Ia., U.S. B4 122
Union, Ky., U.S. k13 124
Union, La., U.S. D5 125
Union, Me., U.S. D3 126
Union, Ms., U.S. C4 131
Union, Mo., U.S. C6 132
Union, Ne., U.S. D10 134
Union, N.H., U.S. D4 136
Union, Or., U.S. B9 144
Union, S.C., U.S. B4 147
Union, Wa., U.S. B2 154
Union, W.V., U.S. D4 155
Union, co., Ar., U.S. D3 111
Union, co., Fl., U.S. B4 116
Union, co., Ga., U.S. B2 117
Union, co., Il., U.S. F4 120
Union, co., In., U.S. E8 121
Union, co., Ia., U.S. C3 122
Union, co., Ky., U.S. C2 124
Union, co., La., U.S. B3 125
Union, co., Ms., U.S. A4 131
Union, co., N.J., U.S. B4 137
Union, co., N.M., U.S. A6 138
Union, co., N.C., U.S. B2 140
Union, co., Oh., U.S. B2 142
Union, co., Or., U.S. B8 144
Union, co., Pa., U.S. E7 145
Union, co., S.C., U.S. B4 147
Union, co., S.D., U.S. E9 148
Union, co., Tn., U.S. C10 149
Union, West Branch, stm., Me., U.S. D4 126
Union Bay, B.C., Can. E5 99
Union Beach, N.J., U.S. C4 137
Union Bridge, Md., U.S. A3 127
Union City, Ca., U.S. h8 112
Union City, Ga., U.S. C2 117
Union City, In., U.S. D8 121
Union City, Mi., U.S. F5 129
Union City, N.J., U.S. h8 137
Union City, Oh., U.S. B1 142
Union City, Ok., U.S. B4 143
Union City, Pa., U.S. C2 145
Union City, Tn., U.S. A2 149
Uniondale, In., U.S. C7 121
Unión de Reyes, Cuba C4 94
Unión de Tula, Mex. H7 90
Union Flat Creek, stm., Wa., U.S. C8 154
Union Gap, Wa., U.S. C5 154
Union Grove, Wi., U.S. F5 156
Union Lake, l., N.J., U.S. E2 137
Union Mill, Hi., U.S. C6 118
Union Mills, In., U.S. B4 121
Union Pier, Mi., U.S. G4 129
Union Point, Ga., U.S. C3 117
Union Springs, Al., U.S. C4 108
Union Springs, N.Y., U.S. C4 139
Union Star, Mo., U.S. B3 132
Uniontown, Al., U.S. C2 108
Uniontown, Ks., U.S. E9 123
Uniontown, Ky., U.S. C2 124
Uniontown, Oh., U.S. B4 142
Uniontown, Pa., U.S. G2 145
Uniontown, Wa., U.S. C8 154
Union Village, R.I., U.S. B3 146
Union Village Reservoir, res., Vt., U.S. D4 152
Unionville, Ct., U.S. B4 114
Unionville, In., U.S. F5 121
Unionville, Mi., U.S. E7 129
Unionville, Mo., U.S. A4 132
Unionville, Oh., U.S. A5 142
Unionville, Tn., U.S. B5 149
United, Pa., U.S. F3 145
United Arab Emirates (Al-Imārāt al-'Arabīyah al-Muttaḥidah), ctry., Asia E5 42
United Arab Republic see Egypt, ctry., Afr. C7 56
United Kingdom, ctry., Eur. E7 4
United Nations Headquarters, N.Y., U.S. h12 139
United States, ctry., N.A. D7 106
United States Air Force Academy, mil., Co., U.S. B6 113
United States Military Academy, mil., N.Y., U.S. C6 139
United States Naval Academy, mil., Md., U.S. C4 127
Unity, Sask., Can. E1 105
Unity, Il., U.S. F4 120
Unity, Me., U.S. D3 126
Unity Pond, l., Me., U.S. D3 126

Name — Map Ref. — Page

Unity Reservoir, res., Or., U.S. C8 144
Universal, In., U.S. E3 121
University City, Mo., U.S. C7 132
University Heights, Ia., U.S. C6 122
University Heights, Oh., U.S. h9 142
University Park, Ia., U.S. C5 122
University Park, N.M., U.S. E3 138
University Park, Tx., U.S. n10 150
University Place, Wa., U.S. f10 154
Unjha, India I5 44
Unna, Ger. D7 10
Uno, Canal Numero, Arg. I10 80
Ŭnp'a, N. Kor. E13 32
Unquillo, Arg. F6 80
Ŭnsan, N. Kor. D14 32
Unterterzen, Switz. D11 13
Unterwalden, state, Switz. E9 13
Unuli Horog, China C14 44
Unža, Russia C27 22
Unža, stm., Russia D26 22
Uozu, Japan K12 36
Upala, C.R. G9 92
Upano, stm., Ec. I3 84
Upata, Ven. C11 84
Upatoi Creek, stm., Ga., U.S. D2 117
Upemba, Lac, l., Zaire C5 58
Upham, N.D., U.S. A5 141
Upía, stm., Col. E6 84
Upington, S. Afr. G5 66
Upire, stm., Ven. B8 84
Upland, Ca., U.S. E5 112
Upland, In., U.S. D7 121
Upland, Ne., U.S. D7 134
Upleta, India J4 44
Upolu, i., W. Sam. J22 158
Upolu Point, c., Hi., U.S. C6 118
Upper Ammonoosuc, stm., N.H., U.S. A4 136
Upper Arlington, Oh., U.S. B2 142
Upper Arrow Lake, res., B.C., Can. D9 99
Upper Blackville, N.B., Can. C4 101
Upperco, Md., U.S. A4 127
Upper Darby, Pa., U.S. G11 145
Upper Demerara-Berbice, prov., Guy. D13 84
Upper Fairmount, Md., U.S. D6 127
Upper Fraser, B.C., Can. B7 99
Upper Frenchville, Me., U.S. A4 126
Upper Gagetown, N.B., Can. D3 101
Upper Gloucester, Me., U.S. E2 126
Upper Graniteville, Vt., U.S. C4 152
Upper Greenwood Lake, N.J., U.S. A4 137
Upper Humber, stm., Newf., Can. D3 102
Upper Iowa, stm., Ia., U.S. A5 122
Upper Island Cove, Newf., Can. E5 102
Upper Kent, N.B., Can. C2 101
Upper Klamath Lake, l., Or., U.S. E4 144
Upper Marlboro, Md., U.S. C4 127
Upper Musquodoboit, N.S., Can. D7 101
Upper New York Bay, b., U.S. k8 137
Upper Red Lake, l., Mn., U.S. B4 130
Upper Saddle River, N.J., U.S. A4 137
Upper Sandusky, Oh., U.S. B2 142
Upper Sheila [Haut Sheila], N.B., Can. B5 101
Upper Takutu-Upper Essequibo, prov., Guy. F13 84
Upperville, Va., U.S. B5 153
Upper Wilson Pond, l., Me., U.S. C3 126
Uppsala, Swe. L15 6
Upright, Cape, c., Ak., U.S. C5 109
Upsala, Mn., U.S. E4 130
Upsala see Uppsala, Swe. L15 6
Upsalquitch, N.B., Can. B3 101
Upshur, co., Tx., U.S. C5 150
Upshur, co., W.V., U.S. C4 155
Upson, co., Ga., U.S. D2 117
Upstart, Cape, c., Austl. B7 70
Upton, Que., Can. D5 104
Upton, Ky., U.S. C4 124
Upton, Ma., U.S. B4 128
Upton, Wy., U.S. B8 157
Upton, co., Tx., U.S. D2 150
Uquía, Cerro, mtn., Ven. E11 84
Urabá, Golfo de, b., Col. C4 84
Uracoa, Ven. C11 84
Uraj, Russia E10 26
Ural, stm., Asia H8 26
Uralla, Austl. H9 70
Ural Mountains see Ural'skije gory, mts., Russia E9 26
Ural'sk, Kaz. G8 26
Ural'skije gory (Ural Mountains), mts., Russia E9 26
Urana, Austl. J7 70
Urandangi, Austl. C3 70
Urandi, Braz. C7 79
Urangan, Austl. E10 70
Urania, La., U.S. C3 125
Urariá, Paraná, mth., Braz. I14 84
Uraricaá, stm., Braz. F11 84
Uraricoera, Braz. F12 84
Uraricoera, stm., Braz. F12 84
Ura-T'ube, Taj. J11 26
Uravan, Co., U.S. C2 113
Urawa, Japan L14 36
Urbana, Ar., U.S. D3 111
Urbana, Il., U.S. C5 120
Urbana, In., U.S. C6 121
Urbana, Ia., U.S. B6 122
Urbana, Mo., U.S. D4 132
Urbana, Oh., U.S. B2 142
Urbancrest, Oh., U.S. m10 142
Urbandale, Ia., U.S. C4 122
Urbania, Italy F7 18
Urbanna, Va., U.S. C6 153
Urbino, Italy F7 18
Urcos, Peru E6 82
Urdinarrain, Arg. G9 80
Uré, Col. D5 84
Urečje, Bela. I10 22
Urén, stm., C.R. H11 92
Ureña, Ven. D6 84
Ures, Mex. C4 90
Urgenč, Uzb. I10 26
Ürgüp, Tur. B3 48
Uri, state, Switz. E10 13
Uriah, Al., U.S. D2 108
Uriah, Mount, mtn., N.Z. E3 72
Uribante, stm., Ven. D7 84
Uribe, Col. F5 84
Uribia, Col. B6 84
Urich, Mo., U.S. C4 132
Urique, Mex. D6 90
Urique, stm., Mex. D6 90
Urituyacu, stm., Peru J5 84
Urla, Tur. K10 20
Urmia see Orūmīyeh, Iran C8 48
Uroševac, Yugo. G5 20
Urrao, Col. D4 84
Ursa, Il., U.S. C2 120
Uršel'skij, Russia F23 22
Urtigueira, Braz. C13 80
Uru, stm., Braz. C4 79
Uruaçu, Braz. C4 79
Uruana, Braz. C4 79
Uruapan del Progreso, Mex. H8 90
Urubamba, Peru E5 82
Urubamba, stm., Peru D5 82
Urubaxi, stm., Braz. H10 84
Urubu, stm., Braz. I13 84
Urucará, Braz. I14 84
Urucu, stm., Braz. J10 84
Uruçuca, Braz. C9 79
Urucuia, stm., Braz. D6 79
Urucurituba, Braz. I14 84
Uruguaiana, Braz. E10 80
Uruguay, ctry., S.A. C5 78
Uruguay (Uruguai), stm., S.A. G9 80
Urumchi see Ürümqi, China C4 30
Ürümqi, China C4 30
Urundel, Arg. B6 80
Urup, ostrov, i., Russia H22 28
Urupá, stm., Braz. D10 82
Urupadi, stm., Braz. J14 84
Urupês, Braz. F4 79
Ur'upinsk, Russia G6 26
Urussanga, Braz. E14 80
Urutaí, Braz. D4 79
Urutaú, Arg. C7 80
Uržum, Russia F8 26
Usa, Japan N6 36
Usa, stm., Russia D9 26
Ušači, Bela. F11 22
Uşak, Tur. K13 20
Ušaki, Russia B13 22
Usakos, Nmb. D2 66
Usborne, Mount, mtn., Falk. Is. G5 78
Usedom, i., Eur. A14 10
'Usfān, Sau. Ar. D1 47
Ushant see Ouessant, Île d', i., Fr. D1 14
'Ushayrah, Sau. Ar. D2 47
Ushuaia, Arg. G3 78
Usingen, Ger. E8 10
Usk, B.C., Can. B3 99
Usk, Wa., U.S. A8 154
Uslar, Ger. D9 10
Usman', Russia I22 22
Usolje-Sibirskoje, Russia G12 28
Usoro, Nig. I13 64
Uspallata, Arg. G4 80
Uspanapa, stm., Mex. I12 90
Usquepaug, R.I., U.S. F3 146
Ussuri (Wusuli), stm., Asia B13 30
Ussurijsk, Russia I18 28
Ustaritz, Fr. I5 14
Ust'-Barguzin, Russia G13 28
Ust'-Cil'ma, Russia D8 26
Ust'-Čorna, Ukr. A7 20
Ust'-Dolyssy, Russia E12 22
Uster, Switz. D10 13
Ust'-Ilimskoje vodochranilišče, res., Russia F18 26
Ústí nad Labem, Czech. E14 10
Ústí nad Orlicí, Czech. F16 10
Ust'-Išim, Russia F12 26
Ustje, Russia D22 22
Ustka, Pol. A16 10
Ust'-Kamčatsk, Russia F24 28
Ust'-Kamenogorsk, Kaz. H8 28
Ust'-Katav, Russia G9 26
Ust'-Koksa, Russia G15 26
Ust'-Kut, Russia F13 28
Ust'-Luga, Russia B11 22
Ust'-Nera, Russia E20 28
Uštobe, Kaz. H13 26
Ust'-Omčug, Russia E21 28
Ust'-Ordynskij, Russia G12 28
Ust'uckoje, Russia C18 22
Ust'urt, plato, plat., Asia I9 26
Ust'-Usa, Russia D9 26
Ust'užna, Russia C19 22
Usu, China C3 30
Usulután, El Sal. D6 92
Usumacinta, stm., N.A. I14 90
Ušumun, Russia G17 28
Utah, co., Ut., U.S. C4 151
Utah, state, U.S. D4 151
Utah Lake, l., Ut., U.S. C4 151
Utapi, Nmb. A2 66
Utashinai, Japan d17 36a
Ute, Ia., U.S. B2 122
Ute Creek, stm., N.M., U.S. A6 138
Utembo, stm., Ang. E4 58
Ute Mountain Indian Reservation, U.S. D2 113
Utena, Lith. F8 22
Ute Reservoir, res., N.M., U.S. B6 138
Utete, Tan. C7 58
Uthai Thani, Thai. G6 40
Utiariti, Braz. E12 82
Utica, Il., U.S. B5 120
Utica, In., U.S. H6 121
Utica, Ks., U.S. D3 123
Utica, Ky., U.S. C2 124
Utica, Mi., U.S. F7 129
Utica, Ms., U.S. C3 131
Utica, Mo., U.S. B4 132
Utica, Ne., U.S. D8 134
Utica, N.Y., U.S. B5 139
Utica, Oh., U.S. B3 142
Utica, S.D., U.S. E8 148
Utiel, Spain F10 16
Utikuma Lake, l., Alta., Can. B3 98
Utila, Hond. A8 92
Utila, Isla de, i., Hond. A8 92
Utinga, stm., Braz. B8 79
Utique, Tun. L5 18
Uto, Japan O5 36
Utopia, Lake, l., N.B., Can. D3 101
Utorgoš, Russia C13 22
Utrecht, Neth. D7 12
Utrecht, S. Afr. F10 66
Utrecht, prov., Neth. D7 12
Utrera, Spain H6 16
Utsunomiya, Japan K14 36
Uttaradit, Thai. F6 40
Uttar Pradesh, state, India G9 44
Utuado, P.R. E11 94
Uudenmaan lääni, prov., Fin. K19 6
Uusikaupunki (Nystad), Fin. K17 6
Uvá, Braz. C3 79
Uvá, stm., Col. F8 84
Uvalda, Ga., U.S. D4 117
Uvalde, Tx., U.S. E3 150
Uvalde, co., Tx., U.S. E3 150
Uvaroviči, Bela. I13 22
Uvarovka, Russia F18 22
Uvarovo, Russia J25 22
Uvat, Russia F11 26
Uvinza, Tan. C6 58
Uvira, Zaire B5 58
Uvs nuur, l., Asia A5 30
Uwajima, Japan N7 36
Uwayl, Sud. M4 60
'Uwaynāt, Jabal al-, mtn., Afr. D5 56
Uwharrie, stm., N.C., U.S. B3 140
Uxbridge, Ma., U.S. B4 128
Uxmal, hist., Mex. G15 90
Uyuni, Bol. I8 82
Uyuni, Salar de, pl., Bol. I8 82
Už (Uh), stm., Eur. G22 10
Užava, Lat. D4 22
Uzbekistan, ctry., Asia I10 26
Uzboj, stm., Turk. B13 48
Uzda, Bela. H10 22
Uzdin, Yugo. D4 20
Užgorod, Ukr. H2 26
Užice, Yugo. F3 20
Uzlovaja, Russia H21 22
Uzunköprü, Tur. H10 20
Užur, Russia F9 28
Užventis, Lith. F5 22

V

Vääksy, Fin. K19 6
Vaala, Fin. I20 6
Vaalserberg, mtn., Neth. G9 12
Vaalwater, S. Afr. E9 66
Vaanta (Vanda), Fin. K19 6
Vaasa (Vasa), Fin. J17 6
Vaasan lääni, prov., Fin. J18 6
Vabalninkas, Lith. F7 22
Vabkent, Uzb. A18 48
Vác, Hung. H19 10
Vaca, Bol. H10 82
Vača, Russia F25 22
Vacacaí, stm., Braz. F11 80
Vaca Key, i., Fl., U.S. H5 116
Vacaria, Braz. E13 80
Vacaria, stm., Braz. D7 79
Vacaria, stm., Braz. F1 79
Vacaville, Ca., U.S. C3 112
Vaccarès, Étang de, b., Fr. I11 14
Vach, stm., Russia E7 28
Vache, Île à, i., Haiti E8 94
Vacherie, La., U.S. h10 125
Vachš, stm., Taj. J11 26
Vacoas, Mrts. v18 67c
Vader, Wa., U.S. C3 154
Vadino, Russia F16 22
Vadito, N.M., U.S. A4 138
Vado, N.M., U.S. E3 138
Vadodara, India I5 44
Vado Ligure, Italy E3 18
Vaduz, Liech. E16 14
Vaga, stm., Russia E6 26
Vagaj, Russia F11 26
Vågåmo, Nor. K11 6
Vágar, i., Faer. Is. D8 6b
Váh, stm., Slov. G17 10
Vaiden, Ms., U.S. B4 131
Vaihingen, Ger. G8 10
Väike-Maarja, Est. B9 22
Vail, Az., U.S. E5 110
Vail, Co., U.S. B4 113
Vail, Ia., U.S. B2 122
Vailly-sur-Aisne, Fr. C10 14
Vaiņode, Lat. E4 22
Vajgač, ostrov, i., Russia C9 26
Valais (Wallis), state, Switz. F7 13
Valašské Meziříčí, Czech. F17 10
Valatie, N.Y., U.S. C7 139
Val-Barrette, Que., Can. C2 104
Val-Bélair, Que., Can. n17 104
Valcheta, Arg. E3 78
Valcourt, Que., Can. D5 104
Valdagno, Italy D6 18
Valdai Hills see Valdajskaja vozvyšennost', hills, Russia D15 22
Valdaj, Russia D16 22
Valdajskaja vozvyšennost', hills, Russia D16 22
Val-David, Que., Can. C3 104
Valdelândia, Braz. C3 79
Valdemārpils, Lat. D5 22
Valdepeñas, Spain G8 16
Valders, Wi., U.S. D6 156
Valdés, Península, pen., Arg. E4 78
Valdese, N.C., U.S. B1 140
Valdéz, Ec. G3 84
Valdez, Ak., U.S. C10 109
Valdez, N.M., U.S. A4 138
Val-d'Isère, Fr. G13 14
Valdivia, Chile D2 78
Valdivia, Col. D5 84
Valdobbiadene, Italy D7 18
Val-d'Oise, dept., Fr. C9 14
Val-d'Or, Que., Can. k11 104
Valdosta, Ga., U.S. F3 117
Vale, Or., U.S. D9 144
Vale, S.D., U.S. C2 148
Valeene, In., U.S. H5 121
Valemount, B.C., Can. C8 99
Valença, Braz. B9 79
Valença, Braz. G7 79
Valença, Port. C3 16
Valençay, Fr. E8 14
Valence, Fr. H11 14
Valencia, Hond. C9 92
València, Spain F11 16
Valencia, Az., U.S. m7 110
Valencia, Ven. B8 84
València, prov., Spain F11 16
Valencia, co., N.M., U.S. C3 138
València, Golf de, b., Spain F12 16
Valencia, Lago de, l., Ven. B9 84
Valencia de Alcántata, Spain F4 16
Valencia Heights, S.C., U.S. D6 147
Valenciennes, Fr. B10 14
Valentine, Ne., U.S. B5 134
Valenza, Italy D3 18
Valera, Ven. C7 84
Valga, Est. D9 22
Valhalla, N.Y., U.S. D7 139
Valhermoso Springs, Al., U.S. A3 108
Valiente, Península, pen., Pan. C2 84
Valiente, Punta, c., Pan. H13 92
Valier, Il., U.S. E4 120
Valier, Mt., U.S. B4 133
Valjevo, Yugo. E3 20
Valka, Lat. D9 22
Valkininkas, Lith. G7 22
Valladolid, Ec. J3 84
Valladolid, Mex. G15 90
Valladolid, Spain D7 16
Vallauris, Fr. I14 14
Valldal, Nor. J10 6
Valle, Lat. E7 22
Valle, Spain B7 16
Valle, dept., Hond. D7 92
Vallecito, Co., U.S. D3 113
Vallecito Reservoir, res., Co., U.S. D3 113
Vallecitos, N.M., U.S. A3 138
Valle d'Aosta, prov., Italy D2 18
Valle de Guanape, Ven. C10 84
Valle de la Pascua, Ven. C9 84
Valle del Cauca, dept., Col. F4 84
Valle de Olivos, Mex. D6 90
Valle de Santiago, Mex. G9 90
Valle de Zaragoza, Mex. D7 90
Valledupar, Col. B6 84
Valle Edén, Ur. F10 80
Vallée-Jonction, Que., Can. C7 104
Vallegrande, Bol. H9 82
Valle Hermoso, Arg. F6 80
Valle Hermoso, Mex. E11 90
Vallehermoso, Spain o23 17b
Vallejo, Ca., U.S. C2 112
Vallenar, Chile E3 80
Valles Mines, Mo., U.S. C7 132
Valletta, Malta N9 18
Valley, Al., U.S. *C4 108
Valley, Ne., U.S. C9 134
Valley, Wa., U.S. A8 154
Valley, co., Id., U.S. E3 119
Valley, co., Mt., U.S. B10 133
Valley, co., Ne., U.S. C6 134
Valley, stm., Man., Can. D1 100
Valley Bend, W.V., U.S. C5 155
Valley Center, Ks., U.S. E6 123
Valley City, N.D., U.S. C8 141
Valley Cottage, N.Y., U.S. g13 139
Valley Creek, stm., Al., U.S. g6 108
Valley East, Ont., Can. p19 103
Valley Falls, Ks., U.S. C8 123
Valley Falls, R.I., U.S. B4 146
Valley Farms, Az., U.S. E4 110
Valleyford, Wa., U.S. B8 154
Valley Forge, Pa., U.S. o20 145
Valley Grove, W.V., U.S. A4 155
Valley Head, Al., U.S. A4 108
Valley Head, W.V., U.S. C4 155
Valley Mills, Tx., U.S. D4 150
Valley of the Kings, hist., Egypt E7 60
Valley Park, Ms., U.S. C3 131
Valley Park, Mo., U.S. f12 132
Valley Springs, Ar., U.S. A3 111
Valley Springs, S.D., U.S. D9 148
Valley Station, Ky., U.S. g11 124
Valley Stream, N.Y., U.S. n15 139
Valleyview, Alta., Can. B2 98
Valley View, Ky., U.S. C5 124
Valley View, Pa., U.S. E8 145
Valley View, Tx., U.S. C4 150
Valliant, Ok., U.S. D6 143
Vallimanca, Arroyo, stm., Arg. H8 80
Vallonia, In., U.S. G5 121
Vallorbe, Switz. E5 13
Valls, Spain D13 16
Vallscreek, W.V., U.S. D3 155
Val Marie, Sask., Can. H2 105
Valmaseda, Spain B8 16
Valmeyer, Il., U.S. E3 120
Valmiera, Lat. D8 22
Valmont, Que., Can. C5 104
Valmy, Nv., U.S. C4 135
Valognes, Fr. C5 14
Valongo, Port. D3 16
Vālpārai, India G4 46
Valparaíso, Braz. F3 79
Valparaíso, Chile G3 80
Valparaiso, Fl., U.S. u15 116
Valparaiso, In., U.S. B3 121
Valparaiso, Ne., U.S. C9 134
Valparaíso, prov., Chile G3 80
Valréas, Fr. H11 14
Vals, Tanjung, c., Indon. G10 38
Valsbaai, b., S. Afr. J4 66
Valsetz, Or., U.S. C3 144
Valtimo, Fin. J21 6
Valujki, Russia G5 26
Val Verda, Ut., U.S. C4 151
Val Verde, co., Tx., U.S. E2 150
Valverde del Camino, Spain H5 16
Van, Tur. B7 48
Van, Tx., U.S. C5 150
Van, W.V., U.S. n12 155
Vanadium, N.M., U.S. E1 138
Van Alstyne, Tx., U.S. C4 150
Vananda, B.C., Can. E5 99
Van Buren, Ar., U.S. B1 111
Van Buren, In., U.S. C6 121
Van Buren, Me., U.S. A5 126
Van Buren, Mo., U.S. E6 132
Van Buren, co., Ar., U.S. B3 111
Van Buren, co., Ia., U.S. D6 122
Van Buren, co., Mi., U.S. F4 129
Van Buren, co., Tn., U.S. D8 149
Vanč, Taj. J12 26
Vance, Ms., U.S. A3 131
Vance, co., N.C., U.S. A4 140
Vance Air Force Base, mil., Ok., U.S. A3 143
Vanceboro, Me., U.S. C5 126
Vanceboro, N.C., U.S. B5 140
Vanceburg, Ky., U.S. B6 124
Vancleave, Ms., U.S. E5 131
Vancouver, B.C., Can. E6 99
Vancouver, Wa., U.S. D3 154
Vancouver, Cape, c., Austl. G3 68
Vancouver Island, i., B.C., Can. E4 99
Vancouver Island Ranges, mts., B.C., Can. D4 99
Vandalia, Il., U.S. E4 120
Vandalia, Mo., U.S. B6 132
Vandenberg Air Force Base, mil., Ca., U.S. E3 112
Vander, N.C., U.S. B4 140
Vanderbijlpark, S. Afr. F8 66
Vanderbilt, Tx., U.S. E4 150
Vanderbilt Peak, mtn., N.M., U.S. E1 138
Vanderburgh, co., In., U.S. H2 121
Vandergrift, Pa., U.S. E2 145
Vanderhoof, B.C., Can. C5 99
Vanderlin Island, i., Austl. C7 68
Vandervoort, Ar., U.S. C1 111
Vanderwagen, N.M., U.S. B1 138
Van Diemen Gulf, b., Austl. B6 68
Vandiver, Al., U.S. B3 108
Vandling, Pa., U.S. C11 145
Vändra, Est. C8 22
Vanduser, Mo., U.S. E8 132
Vandyne, Wi., U.S. k9 156
Vanegas, Mex. F9 90
Vänern, l., Swe. L13 6
Vänersborg, Swe. L13 6
Vangaindrano, Madag. s22 67b
Van Gölü, l., Tur. B7 48
Vangsnes, Nor. K10 6
Vanguard, Sask., Can. H2 105
Van Horn, Tx., U.S. o12 150
Van Horne, Ia., U.S. B5 122
Vanier, Ont., Can. h12 103
Vanimo, Pap. N. Gui. F11 38
Vanino, Russia H20 28
Vāniyambādi, India F5 46
Vankleek Hill, Ont., Can. B10 103
Van Kull, Kill, stm., N.J., U.S. k8 137
Van Lear, Ky., U.S. C7 124
Vanleer, Tn., U.S. A4 149
Van Meter, Ia., U.S. C4 122
Vanna, Ga., U.S. B3 117
Vanndale, Ar., U.S. B5 111
Vannes, Fr. E4 14
Van Ninh, Viet. H10 40
Van Rees, Pegunungan, mts., Indon. F10 38
Vanrhynsdorp, S. Afr. H4 66
Vansant, Va., U.S. e9 153
Vanscoy, Sask., Can. E2 105
Vanskoje, Russia C19 22
Vanstadensrus, S. Afr. G8 66
Vanua Levu, i., Fiji J21 158
Vanuatu, ctry., Oc. H24 2
Van Vleck, Tx., U.S. r14 150
Van Vleet, Ms., U.S. B5 131
Van Wert, Ga., U.S. C1 117
Van Wert, Ia., U.S. D4 122
Van Wert, Oh., U.S. B1 142
Van Wert, co., Oh., U.S. B1 142
Van Wyck, S.C., U.S. B6 147
Van Zandt, co., Tx., U.S. C5 150
Vanzylsrus, S. Afr. F6 66
Vapn'arka, Ukr. A12 20
Var, dept., Fr. I13 14
Var, stm., Fr. I13 14
Varakļāni, Lat. E9 22
Varallo, Italy D3 18
Vārānasi (Benares), India H10 44
Varangerfjorden, Nor. G22 6
Varangerhalvøya, pen., Nor. F21 6
Varaždin, Cro. C11 18
Varazze, Italy E3 18
Varberg, Swe. M13 6
Vardaman, Ms., U.S. B4 131
Vardar (Axiós), stm., Eur. H6 20
Vardø, Nor. F22 6
Varegovo, Russia D22 22
Varel, Ger. B8 10
Varela, Arg. H5 80
Varėna, Lith. G7 22
Varennes, Que., Can. D4 104
Vareš, Bos. E2 20
Varese, Italy D3 18
Varginha, Braz. F6 79
Varina, Va., U.S. C5 153
Varjão, Braz. D4 79
Varkaus, Fin. J20 6
Värmlands Län, co., Swe. L13 6
Varna, Bul. F11 20
Varna, Ont., Can. D3 103
Varna, Il., U.S. B4 120
Varnado, La., U.S. D6 125
Värnamo, Swe. M14 6
Varney, Ont., Can. C4 103
Varnsdorf, Czech. E14 10
Varnville, S.C., U.S. F5 147
Várpalota, Hung. H18 10
Vars, Ont., Can. h13 103
Värska, Est. D10 22
Várzea, Rio da, stm., Braz. D12 80
Várzea da Palma, Braz. D6 79
Várzea Grande, Braz. F13 82
Varzeão, Braz. C14 80
Vas, co., Hung. H16 10
Vasalemma, Est. B7 22
Vashon, Wa., U.S. B3 154
Vashon, Point, c., Wa., U.S. e11 154
Vashon Island, i., Wa., U.S. f11 154
Vasilevičі, Bela. I12 22
Vasiliká, Grc. I7 20
Vasiljevskij Moch, Russia D18 22
Vasiljevskoje, Russia E24 22
Vaskelovo, Russia A13 22
Vaškovci, Ukr. A11 20
Vaškovcy, Ukr. A9 20
Vaslui, Rom. C11 20
Vaslui, co., Rom. C11 20
Vass, N.C., U.S. B3 140
Vassar, Man., Can. E4 100
Vassar, Ks., U.S. D8 123
Vassar, Mi., U.S. E7 129
Västerås, Swe. L15 6
Västerbottens Län, co., Swe. I15 6
Västernorrlands Län, co., Swe. J15 6
Västervik, Swe. M15 6
Västmanlands Län, co., Swe. L15 6
Vasto, Italy G9 18
Vas'ugan, stm., Russia F13 26
Vas'uganje, sw., Russia F7 28
Vasvár, Hung. H16 10
Vatan, Fr. E8 14
Vathí, Grc. L10 20
Vatican City (Città del Vaticano), ctry., Eur. H7 18
V'atka, stm., Russia F8 26
Vatnajökull, Ice. B5 6a
Vatneyri, Ice. B2 6a
Vatomandry, Madag. q23 67b
Vatra Dornei, Rom. B9 20
V'atskije Pol'any, Russia F8 26
Vättern, l., Swe. L14 6
Vaucluse, S.C., U.S. D4 147
Vaucluse, dept., Fr. I12 14
Vaucouleurs, Fr. D12 14
Vaud, state, Switz. E6 13
Vaudreuil, Que., Can. D3 104
Vaughan, Ont., Can. D5 103
Vaughan, Ms., U.S. C3 131
Vaughn, Mt., U.S. C5 133
Vaughn, N.M., U.S. C4 138
Vaupés, ter., Col. G7 84
Vaupés (Uaupés), stm., S.A. G7 84
Vauvert, Fr. I11 14
Vauxhall, Alta., Can. D4 98
Vavatenina, Madag. p23 67b
Vavoua, I.C. H6 64
Vawn, Sask., Can. D1 105
Växjö, Swe. M14 6
Vazante, Braz. E5 79
Vazante Grande, stm., Braz. H13 82
V'azemskij, Russia H18 28
V'az'ma, Russia F17 22
V'azniki, Russia E25 22
Veazie, Me., U.S. D4 126
Veblen, S.D., U.S. B8 148
Vecht, stm., Eur. C9 12
Vechta, Ger. C8 10
Vecsés, Hung. H19 10
Vedea, Rom. E8 20
Vedia, Arg. H8 80
Veedersburg, In., U.S. D3 121
Veendam, Neth. B10 12
Veenendaal, Neth. D8 12
Vega, Tx., U.S. B1 150
Veghel, Neth. E8 12
Vegreville, Alta., Can. C4 98
Veguita, N.M., U.S. C3 138
Veinticinco de Mayo, Arg. H8 80
Veinticinco de Mayo, Arg. H4 80
Veinticinco de Mayo, Ur. H10 80
Veintiocho de Mayo, Ec. I3 84
Veintisiete de Abril, C.R. G9 92
Veisiejai, Lith. G6 22
Vejer de la Frontera, Spain I6 16
Vejle, Den. N11 6
Velarde, N.M., U.S. A4 138
Velardeña, Mex. E8 90
Velas, Cabo, c., C.R. G9 92
Velázquez, Ur. H11 80
Velbert, Ger. D7 10
Velda Rose Estates, Az., U.S. *D4 110
Velddrif, S. Afr. I4 66
Velden, Ger. G12 10
Veldhoven, Neth. F7 12
Velet'ma, Russia F25 22
Vélez, Col. D6 84
Velez de la Gomera, Peñón de, i., Sp. N. Afr. J7 16
Vélez-Málaga, Spain I7 16
Vel'gija, Russia C16 22
Velhas, Rio das, stm., Braz. D6 79
Velikaja, stm., Russia E26 28
Velikaja Kosnica, Ukr. A12 20
Velikaja Michajlovka, Ukr. B13 20
Velika Morava, stm., Yugo. E5 20
Velika Plana, Yugo. E5 20
Velikij Ber'oznyj, Ukr. G22 10
Velikij Byčkov, Ukr. B8 20
Velikije Lučki, Ukr. A6 20
Velikije Luki, Russia E13 22
Velikij Ust'ug, Russia E7 26
Velikodvorskij, Russia F23 22
Veliko Gradište, Yugo. E5 20
Velikoje, Russia D22 22
Velikoploskoje, Ukr. B13 20
Veliko Târnovo, Bul. F9 20
Vélingara, Sen. F4 54
Velíž, Russia F14 22
Velletri, Italy H7 18
Vellore, India F5 46
Velma, Ok., U.S. C4 143
Velp, Neth. D8 12
Velpen, In., U.S. H3 121
Vel'sk, Russia E6 26
Velten, Ger. C13 10
Velva, N.D., U.S. A5 141
Venaco, Fr. I24 15a
Venadillo, Col. E5 84
Venado, Isla del, i., Nic. F11 92
Venado Tuerto, Arg. G8 80
Venâncio Aires, Braz. E12 80
Venango, Ne., U.S. D3 134
Venango, co., Pa., U.S. D2 145
Vence, Fr. I14 14
Venceslau Braz, Braz. G4 79
Venda, ctry., Afr. D10 66
Venda Nova, Port. D4 16
Vendas Novas, Port. G3 16
Vendée, dept., Fr. F5 14
Vendeuvre-sur-Barse, Fr. D11 14
Vendičany, Ukr. A11 20
Vendôme, Fr. E8 14
Venecia, C.R. G10 92
Veneta, Or., U.S. C3 144
Venetie, Ak., U.S. B10 109
Veneto, prov., Italy G18 14
Venev, Russia G21 22
Venezia (Venice), Italy D7 18
Venezuela, ctry., S.A. B5 76

Name	Map Ref.	Page
Venezuela, Golfo de, b., S.A.	B7	84
Vengerovo, Russia	F13	26
Veniaminof, Mount, mtn., Ak., U.S.	D8	109
Venice, Fl., U.S.	E4	116
Venice, Il., U.S.	E3	120
Venice, La., U.S.	E6	125
Venice, Ne., U.S.	g12	134
Venice, Ut., U.S.	E4	151
Venice, Gulf of, b., Eur.	D8	18
Venice see Venezia, Italy	D7	18
Vénissieux, Fr.	G11	14
Venlo, Neth.	F9	12
Venosa, Italy	I10	18
Vent, Aus.	I10	10
Ventanas, Ec.	H3	84
Ventersdorp, S. Afr.	F8	66
Venterstad, S. Afr.	H7	66
Ventimiglia, Italy	F2	18
Ventnor, Ont., Can.	C9	103
Ventnor City, N.J., U.S.	E4	137
Ventspils, Lat.	D4	22
Ventuari, stm., Ven.	E9	84
Ventura (San Buenaventura), Ca., U.S.	E4	112
Ventura, Ia., U.S.	A4	122
Ventura, co., Ca., U.S.	E4	112
Venus, Tx., U.S.	n9	150
Venustiano Carranza, Mex.	I13	90
Venustiano Carranza, Mex.	H8	90
Venustiano Carranza, Bahía, b., Mex.	H16	90
Venustiano Carranza, Presa, res., Mex.	D9	90
Vera, Arg.	E8	80
Veracruz, state, Mex.	H12	90
Veracruz [Llave], Mex.	H11	90
Veraguas, prov., Pan.	I13	92
Veranópolis, Braz.	E13	80
Verāval, India	J4	44
Verbania, Italy	D3	18
Verbena, Al., U.S.	C3	108
Verbilki, Russia	E20	22
Verbovskij, Russia	F25	22
Vercelli, Italy	D3	18
Vercel [-Villedieu-le-Camp], Fr.	E13	14
Verchères, Que., Can.	D4	104
Verchn'aja Inta, Russia	D10	26
Verchn'aja Salda, Russia	F10	26
Verchn'aja Tajmyra, stm., Russia	C11	28
Verchn'aja Troica, Russia	D20	22
Verchn'aja Tura, Russia	F9	26
Verchnedneprovskij, Russia	G16	22
Verchnedvinsk, Bela.	F10	22
Verchnemulomskoje vodochranilišče, res., Russia	G22	6
Verchnevil'ujsk, Russia	E16	28
Verchnij Baskunčak, Russia	H7	26
Verchnij Ufalej, Russia	F10	26
Verchojansk, Russia	D18	28
Verchojanskij chrebet, mts., Russia	D17	28
Verchoturje, Russia	F10	26
Verchovje, Russia	I20	22
Vercors, reg., Fr.	H12	14
Verda, Ky., U.S.	D6	124
Verde, stm., Braz.	D5	79
Verde, stm., Braz.	C4	79
Verde, stm., Braz.	D3	79
Verde, stm., Braz.	E3	79
Verde, stm., Braz.	E4	79
Verde, stm., Braz.	F2	79
Verde, stm., Braz.	E12	82
Verde, stm., Braz.	E13	82
Verde, stm., Mex.	G8	90
Verde, stm., Para.	B9	80
Verde, stm., S.A.	F11	82
Verde, stm., Az., U.S.	C4	110
Verde, Arroyo, stm., Bol.	E8	82
Verde, Cape, c., Bah.	C7	94
Verde Grande, stm., Braz.	C7	79
Verden, Ger.	C9	10
Verden, Ok., U.S.	B3	143
Verde Pequeno, stm., Braz.	C7	79
Verdi, Nv., U.S.	D2	135
Verdigre, Ne., U.S.	B7	134
Verdigris, Ok., U.S.	A6	143
Verdigris, stm., U.S.	A6	143
Verdinho, stm., Braz.	D3	79
Verdi Peak, mtn., Nv., U.S.	C6	135
Verdon, Ne., U.S.	D10	134
Verdun, Que., Can.	q19	104
Verdun, Fr.	I8	14
Verdun-sur-le-Doubs, Fr.	F12	14
Verdun-sur-Meuse, Fr.	C12	14
Vereeniging, S. Afr.	F8	66
Vereja, Russia	F19	22
Veremejki, Bela.	H14	22
Vereščagino, Russia	F8	26
Vergara, Ur.	G12	80
Vergas, Mn., U.S.	D3	130
Vergennes, Il., U.S.	F4	120
Vergennes, Vt., U.S.	C2	152
Verigo, Sask., Can.	F4	105
Verín, Spain	D4	16
Veriora, Est.	C10	22
Veríssimo, Braz.	E4	79
Verkhoyansk see Verchojansk, Russia	D18	28
Vermelho, stm., Braz.	C3	79
Vermilion, Alta., Can.	C5	98
Vermilion, Il., U.S.	D6	120
Vermilion, Oh., U.S.	A3	142
Vermilion, co., Il., U.S.	C6	120
Vermilion, co., La., U.S.	E3	125
Vermilion, stm., Alta., Can.	C5	98
Vermilion, stm., Il., U.S.	C5	120
Vermilion, stm., La., U.S.	E3	125
Vermilion, stm., Mn., U.S.	B6	130
Vermilion, stm., Oh., U.S.	A3	142
Vermilion Bay, Ont., Can.	E5	100
Vermilion Bay, b., La., U.S.	E3	125
Vermilion Lake, l., Mn., U.S.	C6	130
Vermilion Pass, Can.	D2	98
Vermilion Range, hills, Mn., U.S.	C7	130
Vermillion, Ks., U.S.	C7	123
Vermillion, S.D., U.S.	E9	148
Vermillion, co., In., U.S.	E2	121
Vermillion, East Fork, stm., S.D., U.S.	D8	148
Vermillion Bluffs, clf, Co., U.S.	A2	113
Vermillion Creek, stm., Co., U.S.	A2	113
Vermillon, stm., Que., Can.	B4	104
Vermont, Il., U.S.	C3	120
Vermont, state, U.S.	D3	152
Vermontville, Mi., U.S.	F5	129
Vernal, Ut., U.S.	C6	151
Vernayaz, Switz.	F7	13
Verndale, Mn., U.S.	D3	130
Verneuil, Fr.	D7	14
Vernon, B.C., Can.	D8	99
Vernon, Fr.	C8	14
Vernon, Al., U.S.	B1	108
Vernon, Az., U.S.	C6	110
Vernon, Fl., U.S.	u16	116
Vernon, Il., U.S.	E4	120
Vernon, In., U.S.	G6	121
Vernon, Tx., U.S.	B3	150
Vernon, Vt., U.S.	F3	152
Vernon, co., La., U.S.	C2	125
Vernon, co., Mo., U.S.	D3	132
Vernon, co., Wi., U.S.	E3	156
Vernon Bridge, P.E.I., Can.	C7	101
Vernon Center, Mn., U.S.	G4	130
Vernon Hills, Il., U.S.	h9	120
Vernonia, Or., U.S.	B3	144
Vernon River, P.E.I., Can.	C7	101
Verny, Fr.	C13	14
Vero Beach, Fl., U.S.	E6	116
Véroia, Grc.	I6	20
Verona, Ont., Can.	C8	103
Verona, Italy	D6	18
Verona, Il., U.S.	B5	120
Verona, Ky., U.S.	k13	124
Verona, Ms., U.S.	A5	131
Verona, Mo., U.S.	E4	132
Verona, N.J., U.S.	B4	137
Verona, N.C., U.S.	C5	140
Verona, N.D., U.S.	C7	141
Verona, Pa., U.S.	k14	145
Verona, Wi., U.S.	E4	156
Verónica, Arg.	H10	80
Verret, N.B., Can.	B1	101
Verret, Lake, l., La., U.S.	E4	125
Verrettes, Haiti	E8	94
Versailles, Fr.	D9	14
Versailles, Ct., U.S.	C7	114
Versailles, Il., U.S.	D3	120
Versailles, In., U.S.	F7	121
Versailles, Ky., U.S.	B5	124
Versailles, Mo., U.S.	C5	132
Versailles, Oh., U.S.	B1	142
Veršino-Darasunskij, Russia	G15	28
Vert, Cap, c., Sen.	D1	64
Vertientes, Cuba	D5	94
Vertou, Fr.	E5	14
Verviers, Bel.	G8	12
Vervins, Fr.	C10	14
Vescovato, Fr.	I24	15a
Vesjegonsk, Russia	C20	22
Vesoul, Fr.	E13	14
Vespasiano, Braz.	E7	79
Vesper, Wi., U.S.	D4	156
Vesta, C.R.	H11	92
Vesta, Mn., U.S.	F3	130
Vestaburg, Mi., U.S.	E6	129
Vest-Agder, co., Nor.	L10	6
Vestal, N.Y., U.S.	C4	139
Vestal Center, N.Y., U.S.	C4	139
Vestavia Hills, Al., U.S.	g7	108
Vesterålen, is., Nor.	G14	6
Vestfjorden, Nor.	H14	6
Vestfold, co., Nor.	L12	6
Vestmannaeyjar, Ice.	C3	6a
Vesuvio, vol., Italy	I9	18
Vesuvius, Va., U.S.	C3	153
Vesuvius see Vesuvio, vol., Italy	I9	18
Veszprém, Hung.	H17	10
Veszprém, co., Hung.	H17	10
Vésztő, Hung.	I21	10
Veteran, Alta., Can.	C5	98
Veteran, Wy., U.S.	E8	157
Vetluga, Russia	F7	26
Vetralla, Italy	G7	18
Vetrino, Bela.	F11	22
Vetrişoaia, Rom.	C12	20
Vetschau, Ger.	D14	10
Vevay, In., U.S.	G7	121
Vevey, Switz.	F6	13
Vézelise, Fr.	D13	14
Viacha, Bol.	G7	82
Viadana, Italy	E5	18
Viaduto, Braz.	D12	80
Viale, Arg.	F8	80
Viamão, Braz.	F13	80
Viamonte, Arg.	G7	80
Vian, Ok., U.S.	B7	143
Viana, Braz.	D9	76
Viana do Alentejo, Port.	G3	16
Viana do Castelo, Port.	D3	16
Viangchan (Vientiane), Laos	F7	40
Viangphoukha, Laos	D6	40
Viareggio, Italy	F5	18
Vibank, Sask., Can.	G4	105
Viborg, Den.	M11	6
Viborg, S.D., U.S.	D8	148
Vibo Valentia, Italy	K11	18
Vibraye, Fr.	D7	14
Viburnum, Mo., U.S.	D6	132
Vic (Vich), Spain	D14	16
Vícam, Mex.	D4	90
Vicco, Ky., U.S.	C6	124
Vic-en-Bigorre, Fr.	I7	14
Vicente, Point, c., Ca., U.S.	n12	112
Vicente Guerrero, Mex.	F8	90
Vicente López, Arg.	H9	80
Vicente Noble, Dom. Rep.	E9	94
Vicenza, Italy	D6	18
Vichada, dept., Col.	E8	84
Vichada, stm., Col.	E8	84
Vichadero, Ur.	F11	80
Vichigasta, Arg.	E5	80
Vichuquén, Chile	H2	80
Vichy, Fr.	F10	14
Vichy, Mo., U.S.	C6	132
Vici, Ok., U.S.	A2	143
Vicksburg, In., U.S.	F3	121
Vicksburg, Mi., U.S.	F5	129
Vicksburg, Ms., U.S.	C3	131
Vicksburg National Military Park, Ms., U.S.	C3	131
Vico, Fr.	I23	15a
Viçosa, Braz.	F7	79
Victor, Co., U.S.	C5	113
Victor, Id., U.S.	F7	119
Victor, Ia., U.S.	C5	122
Victor, Mt., U.S.	D2	133
Victor, N.Y., U.S.	C3	139
Victor Harbor, Austl.	J3	70
Victoria, Arg.	G8	80
Victoria, Cam.	I14	64
Victoria, B.C., Can.	E6	99
Victoria, Newf., Can.	E5	102
Victoria, P.E.I., Can.	C6	101
Victoria, Chile	J2	80
Victoria, Gren.	H14	94
Victoria (Xianggang), H.K.	M3	34
Victoria, Malay.	D6	38
Victoria, Sey.	B11	58
Victoria, Ar., U.S.	B5	111
Victoria, Il., U.S.	B3	120
Victoria, Ks., U.S.	D4	123
Victoria, Ms., U.S.	A4	131
Victoria, Mo., U.S.	C7	132
Victoria, Tx., U.S.	E4	150
Victoria, Va., U.S.	*C4	153
Victoria, state, Austl.	G9	68
Victoria, co., Tx., U.S.	E4	150
Victoria, stm., Austl.	C6	68
Victoria, Lake, l., Afr.	B6	58
Victoria, Lake, l., Austl.	I4	70
Victoria, Mount, mtn., Burma	D2	40
Victoria, Mount, mtn., Pap. N. Gui.	A9	68
Victoria Beach, Man., Can.	D3	100
Victoria Falls, Zimb.	A7	66
Victoria Falls, wtfl, Afr.	A7	66
Victoria Harbour, Ont., Can.	C5	103
Victoria Island, i., N.W. Ter., Can.	B10	96
Victoria Lake, res., Newf., Can.	D3	102
Victoria Land, reg., Ant.	C8	73
Victoria Nile, stm., Ug.	H7	56
Victoria Peak, mtn., Belize	I15	90
Victoria River Downs, Austl.	C6	68
Victoria Road, Ont., Can.	C6	103
Victoria Strait, strt., N.W. Ter., Can.	C12	96
Victoriaville, Que., Can.	C6	104
Victoria West, S. Afr.	H6	66
Victorica, Arg.	I6	80
Victorino, Ven.	F9	84
Victorino de la Plaza, Arg.	I7	80
Victorville, Ca., U.S.	E5	112
Vičuga, Russia	D24	22
Vicuña, Chile	F3	80
Vicuña Mackenna, Arg.	G6	80
Vidalia, Ga., U.S.	D4	117
Vidalia, La., U.S.	C4	125
Vidal Ramos, Braz.	D14	80
Vidauban, Fr.	I13	14
Videira, Braz.	D13	80
Vidette, Ga., U.S.	C4	117
Vidigueira, Port.	G4	16
Vidin, Bul.	F6	20
Vidisha, India	I7	44
Vidlica, Russia	K23	6
Vidor, Tx., U.S.	D5	150
Vidzeme, hist. reg., Lat.	D8	22
Vidzy, Bela.	F9	22
Viechtach, Ger.	F12	10
Viedma, Arg.	E4	78
Viedma, Lago, l., Arg.	F2	78
Vieja, Sierra, mts., Tx., U.S.	o12	150
Viejo, Cerro, mtn., Peru	J3	84
Viekšniai, Lith.	E5	22
Viella, Spain	C12	16
Vienna, Ont., Can.	E4	103
Vienna, Ga., U.S.	D3	117
Vienna, Il., U.S.	F5	120
Vienna, La., U.S.	B3	125
Vienna, Mo., U.S.	C6	132
Vienna, S.D., U.S.	C8	148
Vienna, Va., U.S.	B5	153
Vienna, W.V., U.S.	B3	155
Vienna see Wien, Aus.	G16	10
Vienne, Fr.	G11	14
Vienne, dept., Fr.	F7	14
Vienne, stm., Fr.	E7	14
Vientiane see Viangchan, Laos	F7	40
Vieques, P.R.	E12	94
Vieques, Isla de, i., P.R.	E12	94
Vierfontein, S. Afr.	F8	66
Viersen, Ger.	D6	10
Vierwaldstättersee, l., Switz.	D9	13
Vierzon, Fr.	E9	14
Viesca, Mex.	E8	90
Viesīte, Lat.	E8	22
Vieste, Italy	H11	18
Vietnam, ctry., Asia	B4	38
Viet Tri, Viet.	D8	40
Vieux Desert, Lac, l., Wi., U.S.	B4	156
Vieux Fort, St. Luc.	H14	94
Vievis, Lith.	G7	22
Vieytes, Arg.	H10	80
Vigan, Phil.	m19	39b
Vigeland, Nor.	L10	6
Vigevano, Italy	D3	18
Vigneulles-lès-Hattonchâtel, Fr.	D12	14
Vignola, Italy	E6	18
Vigo, Spain	C3	16
Vigo, co., In., U.S.	F3	121
Vihowa, Pak.	E4	44
Viitasaari, Fin.	J19	6
Vijāpur, India	I5	44
Vijayawāda, India	D6	46
Vijosë (Aóös), stm., Eur.	I4	20
Viking, Alta., Can.	C5	98
Vikna, i., Nor.	C10	4
Vikramasingapuram, India	H4	46
Vila da Ribeira Brava, C.V.	k16	64a
Vila de Manica, Moz.	B11	66
Vila do Bispo, Port.	H3	16
Vila Fontes, Moz.	A12	66
Vilafranca del Penedès, Spain	D13	16
Vila Gomes da Costa, Moz.	E11	66
Viļaka, Lat.	D10	22
Vilama, Laguna de, l., Arg.	B5	80
Vila Machado, Moz.	B12	66
Vilanculos, Moz.	D12	66
Viļāni, Lat.	E9	22
Vila Nova de Foz Côa, Port.	D4	16
Vila Nova de Gaia, Port.	D3	16
Vilanova i la Geltrú, Spain	D13	16
Vila Novo de Ourém, Port.	F3	16
Vila Paiva de Andrada, Moz.	B12	66
Vila Real, Port.	D4	16
Vila Real de Santo António, Port.	H4	16
Vilar Formoso, Port.	E5	16
Vilas, Co., U.S.	D8	113
Vilas, co., Wi., U.S.	B4	156
Vila Velha, Braz.	F8	79
Vila Velha de Ródão, Port.	F4	16
Vila Verde, Port.	D3	16
Vilcabamba, Cordillera de, mts., Peru	E5	82
Vîlcea, co., Rom.	E8	20
Vilejka, Bela.	G9	22
Vilelas, Arg.	D7	80
Vilhelmina, Swe.	I15	6
Vilhena, Braz.	E11	82
Viljandi, Est.	C8	22
Viljoenskroon, S. Afr.	F8	66
Vilkaviškis, Lith.	G6	22
Vil'kickogo, ostrov, i., Russia	C13	26
Vil'kickogo, proliv, strt., Russia	B18	26
Vilkija, Lith.	F6	22
Vilkovo, Ukr.	D13	20
Villa Abecia, Bol.	I9	82
Villa Aberastain, Arg.	F4	80
Villa Alemana, Chile	G3	80
Villa Ana, Arg.	E9	80
Villa Ángela, Arg.	D8	80
Villa Atamisqui, Arg.	E7	80
Villa Atuel, Arg.	H5	80
Villa Bella, Bol.	D9	82
Villa Berthet, Arg.	D8	80
Villa Bruzual, Ven.	C8	84
Villa Cañás, Arg.	H8	80
Villacañas, Spain	F8	16
Villa Carlos Paz, Arg.	F6	80
Villacarrillo, Spain	G8	16
Villa Castelli, Arg.	E4	80
Villach, Aus.	I13	10
Villacidro, Italy	J3	18
Villa Comaltitlan, Mex.	B2	92
Villa Concepción del Tío, Arg.	F7	80
Villa Constitución, Arg.	G8	80
Villada, Spain	C7	16
Villa de Arista, Mex.	F9	90
Villa de Arriaga, Mex.	G9	90
Villa de Cos, Mex.	F8	90
Villa de Cura, Ven.	B9	84
Villa del Carmen, Arg.	G6	80
Villa del Rosario, Arg.	F7	80
Villa del Rosario, Arg.	F10	80
Villa de María, Arg.	E7	80
Villa de Nova Sintra, C.V.	m16	64a
Villa de San Antonio, Hond.	C7	92
Villa de San Francisco, Hond.	C8	92
Villa de Soto, Arg.	F6	80
Villadiego, Spain	C7	16
Villa Dolores, Arg.	F6	80
Villa Elisa, Arg.	G9	80
Villa Flores, Mex.	I13	90
Villa Florida, Para.	D10	80
Villafranca de los Barros, Spain	G5	16
Villafranca di Verona, Italy	D5	18
Village, Ar., U.S.	D2	111
Village Creek, stm., Al., U.S.	f7	108
Villa General Roca, Arg.	G5	80
Village Springs, Al., U.S.	B3	108
Villagrán, Mex.	E10	90
Villa Grove, Il., U.S.	D5	120
Villaguay, Arg.	F9	80
Villa Guerrero, Mex.	H10	90
Villa Guillermina, Arg.	E9	80
Villa Hayes, Para.	C10	80
Villahermosa, Mex.	I13	90
Villa Hernandarias, Arg.	F9	80
Villa Hidalgo, Mex.	G8	90
Villa Huidobro, Arg.	H6	80
Villaines-la-Juhel, Fr.	D6	14
Villa Insurgentes, Mex.	E4	90
Villa Iris, Arg.	J7	80
Villa Juárez, Mex.	D5	90
Villa Krause, Arg.	F4	80
Villa Larca, Arg.	G6	80
Villaldama, Mex.	D9	90
Villalonga, Arg.	D4	78
Villa Mainero, Mex.	E10	90
Villa María, Arg.	G7	80
Villa María Grande, Arg.	F9	80
Villa Martín, Bol.	I8	82
Villa Matoque, Arg.	C7	80
Villa Mazán, Arg.	E5	80
Villa Media Agua, Arg.	F4	80
Villa Mercedes, Arg.	F4	80
Villamontes, Bol.	I10	82
Villa Nueva, Arg.	G7	80
Villa Nueva, Arg.	G4	80
Villanueva, Col.	B6	84
Villa Nueva, Guat.	C4	92
Villanueva, Hond.	B6	92
Villanueva, Mex.	F8	90
Villa Nueva, Nic.	E8	92
Villanueva, N.M., U.S.	B4	138
Villanueva de Córdoba, Spain	G7	16
Villanueva de la Serena, Spain	G6	16
Villanueva del Río y Minas, Spain	H6	16
Villa Ocampo, Arg.	E9	80
Villa Ojo de Agua, Arg.	E7	80
Villa Oliva, Para.	D10	80
Villa Oropeza, Bol.	H9	82
Villa Park, Il., U.S.	k8	120
Villapinzón, Col.	E6	84
Villa Quinteros, Arg.	D6	80
Villa Ramírez, Arg.	G8	80
Villarcayo, Spain	C8	16
Villa Regina, Arg.	J5	80
Villa Reynolds, Arg.	G6	80
Villa Rica, Ga., U.S.	C2	117
Villa Ridge, Il., U.S.	F4	120
Villa Ridge, Mo., U.S.	C7	132
Villa Rivero, Bol.	G9	82
Villarrica, Chile	D2	78
Villarrica, Col.	F5	84
Villarrica, Para.	C10	80
Villarrobledo, Spain	F9	16
Villas, N.J., U.S.	E3	137
Villa Sandino, Nic.	E10	92
Villa San José, Arg.	G9	80
Villa San Martín, Arg.	E6	80
Villa Santa, Montaña, mtn., Hond.	C8	92
Villa Santo Domingo, Mex.	F9	90
Villasayas, Spain	D9	16
Villa Serrano, Bol.	H9	82
Villasimius, Italy	J4	18
Villasor, Italy	J3	18
Villa Tunari, Bol.	G9	82
Villa Unión, Arg.	E7	80
Villa Unión, Arg.	E4	80
Villa Unión, Mex.	F6	90
Villa Unión, Mex.	C9	90
Villa Valeria, Arg.	H6	80
Villavicencio, Col.	E6	84
Villaviciosa, Spain	B6	16
Villa Viscarra, Bol.	G9	82
Villazón, Bol.	J9	82
Villa Zorraquín, Arg.	F9	80
Villé, Fr.	D14	14
Villedieu, Fr.	D5	14
Villefort, Fr.	H10	14
Villefranche, Fr.	G11	14
Villena, Spain	G11	16
Villeneuve-d'Aveyron, Fr.	H9	14
Villeneuve-Saint-Georges, Fr.	D9	14
Villeneuve-sur-Lot, Fr.	H7	14
Ville Platte, La., U.S.	D3	125
Villers-Bocage, Fr.	C9	14
Villers-Bocage, Fr.	C6	14
Villersexel, Fr.	E13	14
Villerupt, Fr.	C12	14
Ville Saint-Georges, Que., Can.	C7	104
Villeta, Col.	E5	84
Villeurbanne, Fr.	G11	14
Villiers, S. Afr.	F9	66
Villingen-Schwenningen, Ger.	G8	10
Villisca, Ia., U.S.	D3	122
Vilna, Alta., Can.	B5	98
Vilnius, Lith.	G8	22
Vilonia, Ar., U.S.	B3	111
Vilshofen, Ger.	G13	10
Vil'uj, stm., Russia	E16	28
Vil'ujsk, Russia	E16	28
Vil'ujskoje vodochranilišče, res., Russia	E20	26
Vimianzo, Spain	B2	16
Vimoutiers, Fr.	D7	14
Vimperk, Czech.	F13	10
Vina, Al., U.S.	A1	108
Vina, Ca., U.S.	C2	112
Vina, stm., Cam.	G9	54
Viñac, Peru	E4	82
Viña del Mar, Chile	G3	80
Vinalhaven, Me., U.S.	D4	126
Vinalhaven Island, i., Me., U.S.	D4	126
Vinaròs, Spain	E12	16
Vincennes, In., U.S.	G2	121
Vincennes Bay, b., Ant.	B6	73
Vincent, Al., U.S.	B3	108
Vincentown, N.J., U.S.	D3	137
Vinces, Ec.	H3	84
Vinchina, Arg.	E4	80
Vinchos, Peru	E4	82
Vindhya Range, mts., India	I7	44
Vine Brook, stm., Ma., U.S.	g11	128
Vinegar Hill, mtn., Or., U.S.	C8	144
Vine Grove, Ky., U.S.	C4	124
Vineland, N.J., U.S.	E2	137
Vinemont, Al., U.S.	A3	108
Vineyard Haven, Ma., U.S.	D6	128
Vineyard Sound, strt., Ma., U.S.	D6	128
Ving Ngün, Burma	C5	40
Vinh, Viet.	E8	40
Vinh Long, Viet.	I8	40
Vinita, Ok., U.S.	A6	143
Vinkovci, Cro.	D2	20
Vinnica, Ukr.	H3	26
Vinogradov, Ukr.	A7	20
Vinson Massif, mtn., Ant.	C12	73
Vinton, Ia., U.S.	B5	122
Vinton, La., U.S.	D2	125
Vinton, Va., U.S.	C3	153
Vinton, co., Oh., U.S.	C3	142
Viny, Russia	C15	22
Viola, Ar., U.S.	A4	111
Viola, De., U.S.	D3	115
Viola, Id., U.S.	C1	119
Viola, Il., U.S.	B3	120
Viola, Ks., U.S.	E6	123
Viola, Wi., U.S.	E3	156
Violet, La., U.S.	k12	125
Violín, Isla, i., C.R.	I11	92
Vipiteno, Italy	C6	18
Vipos, Arg.	D6	80
Virac, Phil.	C7	38
Virac, Phil.	m19	39b
Viradouro, Braz.	F4	79
Viramgām, India	I5	44
Viranşehir, Tur.	C5	48
Virbalis, Lith.	G5	22
Virden, Man., Can.	E1	100
Virden, Il., U.S.	D4	120
Virden, N.M., U.S.	E1	138
Vire, Fr.	D6	14
Virelles, Bel.	H5	12
Vîrfurile, Rom.	C6	20
Virgem da Lapa, Braz.	D7	79
Virgin, Ut., U.S.	F2	151
Virgin, stm., U.S.	G8	135
Virgin Gorda, i., Br. Vir. Is.	E12	94
Virginia, S. Afr.	G8	66
Virginia, Al., U.S.	g6	108
Virginia, Il., U.S.	D3	120
Virginia, Mn., U.S.	C6	130
Virginia, state, U.S.	C4	153
Virginia Beach, Va., U.S.	D7	153
Virginia City, Mt., U.S.	E5	133
Virginia City, Nv., U.S.	D2	135
Virginia Falls, wtfl, N.W. Ter., Can.	D7	96
Virginia Peak, mtn., Nv., U.S.	D2	135
Virgin Islands, dep., N.A.	E12	94
Virgin Mountains, mts., U.S.	A1	110
Virginópolis, Braz.	E7	79
Virgolândia, Braz.	E7	79
Virôchey, Camb.	H9	40
Virojoki, Fin.	K20	6
Viroqua, Wi., U.S.	E3	156
Virovitica, Cro.	D12	18
Virrat, Fin.	J18	6
Virtaniemi, Fin.	G21	6
Vîrtopu, Rom.	E7	20
Virtsu, Est.	C6	22
Virú, Peru	C2	82
Virudunagar, India	H4	46
Virunga, Zaire	C5	58
Viru-Nigula, Est.	B9	22
Vis, Cro.	F11	18
Vis (Fish), stm., Nmb.	E3	66
Vis, Otok, i., Cro.	F11	18
Visalia, Ca., U.S.	D4	112
Visalia, Ky., U.S.	k14	124
Visayan Sea, Phil.	C7	38
Visby, Swe.	M16	6
Viscount, Sask., Can.	F3	105
Viscount Melville Sound, strt., N.W. Ter., Can.	B11	96
Visé (Wezet), Bel.	G8	12
Višegrad, Bos.	F3	20
Viseu, Port.	E4	16
Vishākhapatnam, India	D7	46
Vislinskij zaliv, b., Eur.	A19	10
Visnagar, India	I5	44
Viso, Monte, mtn., Italy	E2	18
Visoko, Bos.	F2	20
Visokoi Island, i., S. Geor.	A2	73
Visp, Switz.	F8	13
Visselhövede, Ger.	C9	10
Vista, Man., Can.	D1	100
Vista, Ca., U.S.	F5	112
Vista Alegre, Arg.	J4	80
Vista Flores, Arg.	G4	80
Vistula see Wisła, stm., Pol.	A18	10
Vita, Man., Can.	E3	100
Vita, stm., Col.	E8	84
Vitarte, Peru	E3	82
Vitebsk, Bela.	F13	22
Viterbo, Italy	G7	18
Vitichi, Bol.	I9	82
Viti Levu, i., Fiji	J21	158
Vitim, stm., Russia	F14	28
Vitor, Peru	G6	82
Vitor, stm., Peru	G5	82
Vitória, Braz.	G10	74
Vitória, Braz.	F8	79
Vitoria (Gasteiz), Spain	C9	16
Vitória da Conquista, Braz.	C8	79
Vitré, Fr.	D5	14
Vitry-le-François, Fr.	D11	14
Vittangi, Swe.	H17	6
Vitteaux, Fr.	E11	14
Vittel, Fr.	D12	14
Vittoria, Ont., Can.	E4	103
Vittoria, Italy	M9	18
Vittorio Veneto, Italy	D7	18
Viver, Spain	F11	16
Vivi, stm., Russia	D17	26
Vivian, La., U.S.	B2	125
Vivian, S.D., U.S.	D5	148
Vivoratá, Arg.	I10	80
Vivorillo, Cayos, is., Hond.	B11	92
Vizcaíno, Desierto de, des., Mex.	D3	90
Vize, Tur.	H11	20
Vize, ostrov, i., Russia	B13	26
Vizianagaram, India	C7	46
Vižnica, Ukr.	A9	20
Vizzini, Italy	L9	18
Vlaardingen, Neth.	E5	12
Vladikavkaz, Russia	I6	26
Vladimir, Russia	E23	22
Vladimirskij Tupik, Russia	F16	22
Vladivostok, Russia	I18	28
Vlasenica, Bos.	E2	20
Vlasotince, Yugo.	G6	20
Vlieland, i., Neth.	B7	12
Vlissingen (Flushing), Neth.	F4	12
Vlonë see Vlorë, Alb.	I3	20
Vlorë, Alb.	I3	20
Vlorës, Gji i, b., Alb.	I3	20
Vltava, stm., Czech.	F14	10
Vnukovo, Russia	F20	22
Vochtoga, Russia	C24	22
Vodlozero, ozero, l., Russia	J25	6
Vodňany, Czech.	F14	10
Vogelsberg, mts., Ger.	E9	10
Voghera, Italy	E4	18
Vohenstrauss, Ger.	F12	10
Vohibinany, Madag.	q23	67b
Vohilava, Madag.	r23	67b
Vohimarina, Madag.	n24	67b
Vohipeno, Madag.	s22	67b
Võhma, Est.	C8	22
Void, Fr.	D12	14
Voinjama, Lib.	G5	64
Voiron, Fr.	G12	14
Voitsberg, Aus.	H15	10
Voj-Vož, Russia	E8	26
Volary, Czech.	G13	10
Volcán, Arg.	B6	80
Volcán, Pan.	C1	84
Volcán Isluga, Parque Nacional, Chile	H7	82
Volcano, Hi., U.S.	D6	118
Volcán Poás, Parque Nacional, C.R.	G10	92
Volchov, Russia	B15	22
Volchov, stm., Russia	B15	22
Volčje, Ukr.	F22	10
Volga, Russia	D21	22
Volga, Ia., U.S.	B6	122
Volga, S.D., U.S.	C9	148
Volga, stm., Russia	H7	26
Volgino, Russia	C16	22
Volgo-Baltijskij kanal, Russia	L26	6
Volgodonsk, Russia	H6	26
Volgograd (Stalingrad), Russia	H6	26
Volgogradskoje vodochranilišče, res., Russia	H7	26
Volin, S.D., U.S.	E8	148
Volkach, Ger.	F10	10
Völkermarkt, Aus.	I14	10
Völklingen, Ger.	F6	10
Volkovysk, Bela.	H7	22
Volksrust, S. Afr.	F9	66
Volockaja, Russia	A25	22
Volodarsk, Russia	E26	22
Volodarskoje, Kaz.	G11	26
Vologda, Russia	B22	22
Vologda, stm., Russia	B22	22
Volokolamsk, Russia	E18	22
Volontirovka, Mol.	C13	20
Vólos, Grc.	J6	20

World Political Information

This table lists the area, population, population density, form of government, political status, and capital for every country in the world.

The populations are estimates for January 1, 1993 made by Rand McNally on the basis of official data, United Nations estimates, and other available information. Area figures include inland water.

The political units listed in the table are categorized by political status, as follows: A–independent countries; B–internally independent political entities which are under the protection of other countries in matters of defense and foreign affairs; C–colonies and other dependent political units; D–the major administrative subdivisions of Australia, Canada, China, the United Kingdom, and the United States. For comparison, the table also includes the continents and the world.

All footnotes to this table appear on page 260.

Country, Division or Region English (Conventional)	Area in sq. mi.	Area in sq. km.	Estimated Population 1/1/93	Pop. per sq. mi.	Pop. per sq. km.	Form of Government and Political Status	Capital
† Afghanistan	251,826	*652,225*	16,290,000	65	*25*	Islamic republic A	Kābol
Africa	11,700,000	*30,300,000*	668,700,000	57	*22*	...	...
Alabama	52,423	*135,775*	4,128,000	79	*30*	State (U.S.) D	Montgomery
Alaska	656,424	*1,700,139*	564,000	0.9	*0.3*	State (U.S.) D	Juneau
† Albania	11,100	*28,748*	3,305,000	298	*115*	Republic A	Tiranë
Alberta	255,287	*661,190*	2,839,000	11	*4.3*	Province (Canada) D	Edmonton
† Algeria	919,595	*2,381,741*	26,925,000	29	*11*	Provisional military government A	El Djazaïr (Algiers)
American Samoa	77	*199*	52,000	675	*261*	Unincorporated territory (U.S.) C	Pago Pago
Andorra	175	*453*	56,000	320	*124*	Coprincipality (Spanish and French protection) B	Andorra
† Angola	481,354	*1,246,700*	10,735,000	22	*8.6*	Republic A	Luanda
Anguilla	35	*91*	7,000	200	*77*	Dependent territory (U.K. protection) B	The Valley
Anhwei (Anhui)	53,668	*139,000*	58,440,000	1,089	*420*	Province (China) D	Hefei
Antarctica	5,400,000	*14,000,000*	(1)	...	...	...	...
† Antigua and Barbuda	171	*442*	77,000	450	*174*	Parliamentary state A	St. John's
† Argentina	1,073,519	*2,780,400*	32,950,000	31	*12*	Republic A	Buenos Aires and Viedma (6)
Arizona	114,006	*295,276*	3,872,000	34	*13*	State (U.S.) D	Phoenix
Arkansas	53,182	*137,742*	2,410,000	45	*17*	State (U.S.) D	Little Rock
† Armenia	11,506	*29,800*	3,429,000	298	*115*	Republic A	Jerevan
Aruba	75	*193*	65,000	867	*337*	Self-governing territory (Netherlands protection) B	Oranjestad
Asia	17,300,000	*44,900,000*	3,337,800,000	193	*74*	...	...
† Australia	2,966,155	*7,682,300*	16,965,000	5.7	*2.2*	Federal parliamentary state A	Canberra
Australian Capital Territory	927	*2,400*	282,000	304	*118*	Territory (Australia) D	Canberra
† Austria	32,377	*83,856*	7,899,000	244	*94*	Federal republic A	Wien (Vienna)
† Azerbaijan	33,436	*86,600*	7,510,000	225	*87*	Republic A	Baku (Baky)
† Bahamas	5,382	*13,939*	265,000	49	*19*	Parliamentary state A	Nassau
† Bahrain	267	*691*	561,000	2,101	*812*	Monarchy A	Al-Manāmah
† Bangladesh	55,598	*143,998*	120,850,000	2,174	*839*	Republic A	Dhaka (Dacca)
† Barbados	166	*430*	258,000	1,554	*600*	Parliamentary state A	Bridgetown
† Belarus	80,155	*207,600*	10,400,000	130	*50*	Republic A	Minsk
† Belgium	11,783	*30,518*	10,030,000	851	*329*	Constitutional monarchy A	Bruxelles (Brussels)
† Belize	8,866	*22,963*	186,000	21	*8.1*	Parliamentary state A	Belmopan
† Benin	43,475	*112,600*	5,083,000	117	*45*	Republic A	Porto-Novo and Cotonou
Bermuda	21	*54*	60,000	2,857	*1,111*	Dependent territory (U.K.) C	Hamilton
† Bhutan	17,954	*46,500*	1,680,000	94	*36*	Monarchy (Indian protection) B	Thimphu
† Bolivia	424,165	*1,098,581*	7,411,000	17	*6.7*	Republic A	La Paz and Sucre
Bophuthatswana (2)	15,641	*40,509*	2,525,000	161	*62*	National state (South African protection) B	Mmabatho
† Bosnia and Herzegovina	19,741	*51,129*	4,375,000	222	*86*	Republic A	Sarajevo
† Botswana	224,711	*582,000*	1,379,000	6.1	*2.4*	Republic A	Gaborone
† Brazil	3,286,500	*8,511,996*	159,630,000	49	*19*	Federal republic A	Brasília
British Columbia	365,948	*947,800*	3,665,000	10	*3.9*	Province (Canada) D	Victoria
British Indian Ocean Territory	23	*60*	(1)	...	...	Dependent territory (U.K.) C	...
British Virgin Islands	59	*153*	13,000	220	*85*	Dependent territory (U.K.) C	Road Town
† Brunei	2,226	*5,765*	273,000	123	*47*	Monarchy A	Bandar Seri Begawan
† Bulgaria	42,823	*110,912*	8,842,000	206	*80*	Republic A	Sofija (Sofia)
† Burkina Faso	105,869	*274,200*	9,808,000	93	*36*	Provisional military government A	Ouagadougou
† Burma (Myanmar)	261,228	*676,577*	43,070,000	165	*64*	Provisional military government A	Yangon (Rangoon)
† Burundi	10,745	*27,830*	6,118,000	569	*220*	Republic A	Bujumbura
California	163,707	*424,002*	31,310,000	191	*74*	State (U.S.) D	Sacramento
† Cambodia	69,898	*181,035*	8,928,000	128	*49*	Transitional government A	Phnum Pénh (Phnom Penh)
† Cameroon	183,569	*475,442*	12,875,000	70	*27*	Republic A	Yaoundé
† Canada	3,849,674	*9,970,610*	30,530,000	7.9	*3.1*	Federal parliamentary state A	Ottawa
† Cape Verde	1,557	*4,033*	404,000	259	*100*	Republic A	Praia
Cayman Islands	100	*259*	29,000	290	*112*	Dependent territory (U.K.) C	George Town
† Central African Republic	240,535	*622,984*	3,068,000	13	*4.9*	Republic A	Bangui
† Chad	495,755	*1,284,000*	5,297,000	11	*4.1*	Republic A	N'Djamena
Chekiang (Zhejiang)	39,305	*101,800*	43,150,000	1,098	*424*	Province (China) D	Hangzhou
† Chile	292,135	*756,626*	13,635,000	47	*18*	Republic A	Santiago
† China (excl. Taiwan)	3,689,631	*9,556,100*	1,179,030,000	320	*123*	Socialist republic A	Beijing (Peking)
Christmas Island	52	*135*	900	17	*6.7*	External territory (Australia) C	...
Ciskei (2)	2,996	*7,760*	1,105,000	369	*142*	National state (South African protection) B	Bisho
Cocos (Keeling) Islands	5.4	*14*	500	93	*36*	Territory (Australia) C	...
† Colombia	440,831	*1,141,748*	34,640,000	79	*30*	Republic A	Santa Fe de Bogotá
Colorado	104,100	*269,620*	3,410,000	33	*13*	State (U.S.) D	Denver
† Comoros	863	*2,235*	503,000	583	*225*	Federal Islamic republic A	Moroni
† Congo	132,047	*342,000*	2,413,000	18	*7.1*	Republic A	Brazzaville
Connecticut	5,544	*14,358*	3,358,000	606	*234*	State (U.S.) D	Hartford
Cook Islands	91	*236*	18,000	198	*76*	Self-governing territory (New Zealand protection) B	Avarua
† Costa Rica	19,730	*51,100*	3,225,000	163	*63*	Republic A	San José
Côte d'Ivoire, see Ivory Coast	...	...	...	...	...	...	...
† Croatia	21,829	*56,538*	4,793,000	220	*85*	Republic A	Zagreb
† Cuba	42,804	*110,861*	10,900,000	255	*98*	Socialist republic A	La Habana (Havana)
† Cyprus (excl. North Cyprus)	2,276	*5,896*	527,000	232	*89*	Republic A	Nicosia (Levkosía)
Cyprus, North (3)	1,295	*3,355*	193,000	149	*58*	Republic A	Nicosia (Lefkoşa)
† Czech Republic	30,450	*78,864*	10,335,000	339	*131*	Republic A	Praha (Prague)
Delaware	2,489	*6,447*	692,000	278	*107*	State (U.S.) D	Dover
† Denmark	16,638	*43,093*	5,169,000	311	*120*	Constitutional monarchy A	København (Copenhagen)
District of Columbia	68	*177*	590,000	8,676	*3,333*	Federal district (U.S.) D	Washington
† Djibouti	8,958	*23,200*	396,000	44	*17*	Republic A	Djibouti
† Dominica	305	*790*	88,000	289	*111*	Republic A	Roseau
† Dominican Republic	18,704	*48,442*	7,591,000	406	*157*	Republic A	Santo Domingo
† Ecuador	109,484	*283,561*	11,055,000	101	*39*	Republic A	Quito
† Egypt	386,662	*1,001,449*	57,050,000	148	*57*	Socialist republic A	Al-Qāhirah (Cairo)
† El Salvador	8,124	*21,041*	5,635,000	694	*268*	Republic A	San Salvador
England	50,378	*130,478*	48,235,000	957	*370*	Administrative division (U.K.) D	London
† Equatorial Guinea	10,831	*28,051*	394,000	36	*14*	Republic A	Malabo
Eritrea	36,170	*93,679*	3,425,000	95	*37*	Republic A	Asmera
† Estonia	17,413	*45,100*	1,613,000	93	*36*	Republic A	Tallinn
† Ethiopia	446,953	*1,157,603*	51,715,000	116	*45*	Transitional military government A	Adis Abeba
Europe	3,800,000	*9,900,000*	694,900,000	183	*70*	...	...
Faeroe Islands	540	*1,399*	49,000	91	*35*	Self-governing territory (Danish protection) B	Tórshavn
Falkland Islands (4)	4,700	*12,173*	2,100	0.4	*0.2*	Dependent territory (U.K.) C	Stanley

World Political Information

Country, Division or Region English (Conventional)	Area in sq. mi.	Area in sq. km.	Estimated Population 1/1/93	Pop. per sq. mi.	Pop. per sq. km.	Form of Government and Political Status	Capital
† Fiji	7,056	18,274	754,000	107	41	Republic ....A	Suva
† Finland	130,559	338,145	5,074,000	39	15	Republic ....A	Helsinki (Helsingfors)
Florida	65,758	170,313	13,630,000	207	80	State (U.S.) ....D	Tallahassee
† France (excl. Overseas Departments)	211,208	547,026	57,570,000	273	105	Republic ....A	Paris
French Guiana	35,135	91,000	131,000	3.7	1.4	Overseas department (France) C	Cayenne
French Polynesia	1,359	3,521	208,000	153	59	Overseas territory (France) C	Papeete
Fukien (Fujian)	46,332	120,000	31,160,000	673	260	Province (China)	Fuzhou
† Gabon	103,347	267,667	1,115,000	11	4.2	Republic ....A	Libreville
† Gambia	4,127	10,689	916,000	222	86	Republic ....A	Banjul
Georgia	59,441	153,953	6,795,000	114	44	State (U.S.) ....D	Atlanta
Georgia (Sakartvelo)	26,911	69,700	5,593,000	208	80	Provisional military government ....A	Tbilisi
† Germany	137,822	356,955	80,590,000	585	226	Federal republic ....A	Berlin and Bonn
† Ghana	92,098	238,533	16,445,000	179	69	Provisional military government ....A	Accra
Gibraltar	2.3	6.0	32,000	13,913	5,333	Dependent territory (U.K.) C	Gibraltar
† Greece	50,949	131,957	10,075,000	198	76	Republic ....A	Athínai (Athens)
Greenland	840,004	2,175,600	57,000	0.1	...	Self-governing territory (Danish protection) .B	Godthåb (Nuuk)
† Grenada	133	344	97,000	729	282	Parliamentary state	St. George's
Guadeloupe (incl. Dependencies)	687	1,780	413,000	601	232	Overseas department (France) C	Basse-Terre
Guam	209	541	143,000	684	264	Unincorporated territory (U.S.) ....A	Agana
† Guatemala	42,042	108,889	9,705,000	231	89	Republic ....A	Guatemala
Guernsey (incl. Dependencies)	30	78	58,000	1,933	744	Crown dependency (U.K. protection) ..B	St. Peter Port
† Guinea	94,926	245,857	7,726,000	81	31	Provisional military government ....A	Conakry
† Guinea-Bissau	13,948	36,125	1,060,000	76	29	Republic ....A	Bissau
† Guyana	83,000	214,969	737,000	8.9	3.4	Republic ....A	Georgetown
Hainan	13,127	34,000	6,820,000	520	201	Province (China)	Haikou
† Haiti	10,714	27,750	6,509,000	608	235	Provisional military government ....A	Port-au-Prince
Hawaii	10,932	28,313	1,159,000	106	41	State (U.S.) ....D	Honolulu
Heilungkiang (Heilongjiang)	181,082	469,000	36,685,000	203	78	Province (China)	Harbin
Honan (Henan)	64,479	167,000	88,890,000	1,379	532	Province (China)	Zhengzhou
† Honduras	43,277	112,088	5,164,000	119	46	Republic ....A	Tegucigalpa
Hong Kong	414	1,072	5,580,000	13,478	5,205	Chinese territory under British administration .. C	Hong Kong (Victoria)
Hopeh (Hebei)	73,359	190,000	63,500,000	866	334	Province (China)	Shijiazhuang
Hunan	81,081	210,000	63,140,000	779	301	Province (China)	Changsha
† Hungary	35,920	93,033	10,305,000	287	111	Republic ....A	Budapest
Hupeh (Hubei)	72,356	187,400	56,090,000	775	299	Province (China)	Wuhan
† Iceland	39,769	103,000	260,000	6.5	2.5	Republic ....A	Reykjavík
Idaho	83,574	216,456	1,026,000	12	4.7	State (U.S.) ....D	Boise
Illinois	57,918	150,007	11,640,000	201	78	State (U.S.) ....D	Springfield
† India (incl. part of Jammu and Kashmir)	1,237,062	3,203,975	873,850,000	706	273	Federal republic ....A	New Delhi
Indiana	36,420	94,328	5,667,000	156	60	State (U.S.) ....D	Indianapolis
† Indonesia	752,410	1,948,732	186,180,000	247	96	Republic ....A	Jakarta
Inner Mongolia (Nei Monggol)	456,759	1,183,000	22,340,000	49	19	Autonomous region (China) ....D	Hohhot
Iowa	56,276	145,754	2,821,000	50	19	State (U.S.) ....D	Des Moines
† Iran	632,457	1,638,057	60,500,000	96	37	Islamic republic ....A	Tehrān
† Iraq	169,235	438,317	18,815,000	111	43	Republic ....A	Baghdād
† Ireland	27,137	70,285	3,525,000	130	50	Republic ....A	Dublin (Baile Átha Cliath)
Isle of Man	221	572	70,000	317	122	Crown dependency (U.K. protection) ..B	Douglas
† Israel	8,019	20,770	4,593,000	573	221	Republic ....A	Yerushalayim (Jerusalem)
Israeli Occupied Areas [5]	2,947	7,632	2,461,000	835	322	....	....
† Italy	116,324	301,277	56,550,000	486	188	Republic ....A	Roma (Rome)
† Ivory Coast	124,518	322,500	13,765,000	111	43	Republic ....A	Abidjan and Yamoussoukro [6]
† Jamaica	4,244	10,991	2,412,000	568	219	Parliamentary state ....A	Kingston
† Japan	145,870	377,801	124,710,000	855	330	Constitutional monarchy ....A	Tōkyō
Jersey	45	116	85,000	1,889	733	Crown dependency (U.K. protection) ..B	St. Helier
† Jordan	35,135	91,000	3,632,000	103	40	Constitutional monarchy ....A	'Ammān
Kansas	82,282	213,110	2,539,000	31	12	State (U.S.) ....D	Topeka
Kansu (Gansu)	173,746	450,000	23,280,000	134	52	Province (China)	Lanzhou
† Kazakhstan	1,049,156	2,717,300	17,190,000	16	6.3	Republic ....A	Alma-Ata (Almaty)
Kentucky	40,411	104,665	3,745,000	93	36	State (U.S.) ....D	Frankfort
† Kenya	224,961	582,646	26,635,000	118	46	Republic ....A	Nairobi
Kiangsi (Jiangxi)	64,325	166,600	39,270,000	610	236	Province (China)	Nanchang
Kiangsu (Jiangsu)	39,614	102,600	69,730,000	1,760	680	Province (China)	Nanjing (Nanking)
Kiribati	313	811	76,000	243	94	Republic ....A	Bairiki
Kirin (Jilin)	72,201	187,000	25,630,000	355	137	Province (China)	Changchun
† Korea, North	46,540	120,538	22,450,000	482	186	Socialist republic ....A	P'yŏngyang
† Korea, South	38,230	99,016	43,660,000	1,142	441	Republic ....A	Sŏul (Seoul)
† Kuwait	6,880	17,818	2,388,000	347	134	Constitutional monarchy ....A	Al-Kuwayt (Kuwait)
Kwangsi Chuang (Guangxi Zhuangzu)	91,236	236,300	43,975,000	482	186	Autonomous region (China) ....D	Nanning
Kwangtung (Guangdong)	68,726	178,000	65,380,000	951	367	Province (China)	Guangzhou (Canton)
Kweichow (Guizhou)	65,637	170,000	33,745,000	514	199	Province (China)	Guiyang
† Kyrgyzstan	76,641	198,500	4,613,000	60	23	Republic ....A	Biškek
† Laos	91,429	236,800	4,507,000	49	19	Socialist republic ....A	Viangchan (Vientiane)
† Latvia	24,595	63,700	2,737,000	111	43	Republic ....A	Rīga
† Lebanon	4,015	10,400	3,467,000	864	333	Republic ....A	Bayrūt (Beirut)
† Lesotho	11,720	30,355	1,873,000	160	62	Constitutional monarchy under military rule ..A	Maseru
Liaoning	56,255	145,700	41,035,000	729	282	Province (China)	Shenyang (Mukden)
† Liberia	38,250	99,067	2,869,000	75	29	Republic ....A	Monrovia
† Libya	679,362	1,759,540	4,552,000	6.7	2.6	Socialist republic ....A	Ţarābulus (Tripoli)
† Liechtenstein	62	160	30,000	484	188	Constitutional monarchy ....A	Vaduz
† Lithuania	25,174	65,200	3,804,000	151	58	Republic ....A	Vilnius
Louisiana	51,843	134,275	4,282,000	83	32	State (U.S.) ....D	Baton Rouge
† Luxembourg	998	2,586	392,000	393	152	Constitutional monarchy ....A	Luxembourg
Macau	6.6	17	477,000	72,273	28,059	Chinese territory under Portuguese administration C	Macau
Macedonia	9,928	25,713	2,179,000	219	85	Republic ....A	Skopje
† Madagascar	226,658	587,041	12,800,000	56	22	Republic ....A	Antananarivo
Maine	35,387	91,653	1,257,000	36	14	State (U.S.) ....D	Augusta
† Malawi	45,747	118,484	9,691,000	212	82	Republic ....A	Lilongwe
† Malaysia	129,251	334,758	18,630,000	144	56	Federal constitutional monarchy ....A	Kuala Lumpur
† Maldives	115	298	235,000	2,043	789	Republic ....A	Male'
† Mali	482,077	1,248,574	8,754,000	18	7.0	Republic ....A	Bamako
† Malta	122	316	360,000	2,951	1,139	Republic ....A	Valletta
Manitoba	250,947	649,950	1,221,000	4.9	1.9	Province (Canada) ....D	Winnipeg
† Marshall Islands	70	181	51,000	729	282	Republic (U.S. protection) ....A	Majuro (island)
Martinique	425	1,100	372,000	875	338	Overseas department (France) C	Fort-de-France
Maryland	12,407	32,135	4,975,000	401	155	State (U.S.) ....D	Annapolis
Massachusetts	10,555	27,337	6,103,000	578	223	State (U.S.) ....D	Boston
† Mauritania	395,956	1,025,520	2,092,000	5.3	2.0	Republic ....A	Nouakchott

Country, Division or Region English (Conventional)	Area in sq. mi.	Area in sq. km.	Estimated Population 1/1/93	Pop. per sq. mi.	Pop. per sq. km.	Form of Government and Political Status	Capital
† Mauritius (incl. Dependencies)	788	*2,040*	1,096,000	1,391	*537*	Republic A	Port Louis
Mayotte [7]	144	*374*	89,000	618	*238*	Territorial collectivity (France) C	Dzaoudzi and Mamoudzou [6]
† Mexico	759,534	*1,967,183*	86,170,000	113	*44*	Federal republic A	Ciudad de México (Mexico City)
Michigan	96,810	*250,738*	9,488,000	98	*38*	State (U.S.) D	Lansing
† Micronesia, Federated States of	271	*702*	117,000	432	*167*	Republic (U.S. protection) A	Kolonia and Paliker [6]
Midway Islands	2.0	*5.2*	500	250	*96*	Unincorporated territory (U.S.) C	...
Minnesota	86,943	*225,182*	4,513,000	52	*20*	State (U.S.) D	St. Paul
Mississippi	48,434	*125,443*	2,616,000	54	*21*	State (U.S.) D	Jackson
Missouri	69,709	*180,546*	5,231,000	75	*29*	State (U.S.) D	Jefferson City
† Moldova	13,012	*33,700*	4,474,000	344	*133*	Republic A	Kišin'ov (Chişinău)
Monaco	0.7	*1.9*	31,000	44,286	*16,316*	Constitutional monarchy A	Monaco
† Mongolia	604,829	*1,566,500*	2,336,000	3.9	*1.5*	Republic A	Ulaanbaatar (Ulan Bator)
Montana	147,046	*380,850*	821,000	5.6	*2.2*	State (U.S.) D	Helena
Montserrat	39	*102*	13,000	333	*127*	Dependent territory (U.K.) C	Plymouth
† Morocco (excl. Western Sahara)	172,414	*446,550*	27,005,000	157	*60*	Constitutional monarchy A	Rabat
† Mozambique	308,642	*799,380*	15,795,000	51	*20*	Republic A	Maputo
† Myanmar, see Burma	...	...	...	...	...	...	...
† Namibia (excl. Walvis Bay)	317,818	*823,144*	1,603,000	5.0	*1.9*	Republic A	Windhoek
Nauru	8.1	*21*	10,000	1,235	*476*	Republic A	Yaren District
Nebraska	77,358	*200,358*	1,615,000	21	*8.1*	State (U.S.) D	Lincoln
† Nepal	56,827	*147,181*	20,325,000	358	*138*	Constitutional monarchy A	Kāthmāṇḍau
† Netherlands	16,164	*41,864*	15,190,000	940	*363*	Constitutional monarchy A	Amsterdam and 's-Gravenhage (The Hague)
Netherlands Antilles	309	*800*	191,000	618	*239*	Self-governing territory (Netherlands protection) B	Willemstad
Nevada	110,567	*286,368*	1,308,000	12	*4.6*	State (U.S.) D	Carson City
New Brunswick	28,355	*73,440*	824,000	29	*11*	Province (Canada) D	Fredericton
New Caledonia	7,358	*19,058*	177,000	24	*9.3*	Overseas territory (France) C	Nouméa
Newfoundland	156,649	*405,720*	641,000	4.1	*1.6*	Province (Canada) D	St. John's
New Hampshire	9,351	*24,219*	1,154,000	123	*48*	State (U.S.) D	Concord
New Jersey	8,722	*22,590*	7,898,000	906	*350*	State (U.S.) D	Trenton
New Mexico	121,598	*314,939*	1,590,000	13	*5.0*	State (U.S.) D	Santa Fe
New South Wales	309,500	*801,600*	5,770,000	19	*7.2*	State (Australia) D	Sydney
New York	54,475	*141,089*	18,350,000	337	*130*	State (U.S.) D	Albany
† New Zealand	104,454	*270,534*	3,477,000	33	*13*	Parliamentary state A	Wellington
† Nicaragua	50,054	*129,640*	3,932,000	79	*30*	Republic A	Managua
† Niger	489,191	*1,267,000*	8,198,000	17	*6.5*	Provisional military government A	Niamey
† Nigeria	356,669	*923,768*	91,700,000	257	*99*	Provisional military government A	Lagos and Abuja
Ningsia Hui (Ningxia Huizu)	25,637	*66,400*	4,820,000	188	*73*	Autonomous region (China) D	Yinchuan
Niue	100	*258*	1,700	17	*6.6*	Self-governing territory (New Zealand protection) B	Alofi
Norfolk Island	14	*36*	2,600	186	*72*	External territory (Australia) C	Kingston
North America	9,500,000	*24,700,000*	438,200,000	46	*18*	...	...
North Carolina	53,821	*139,397*	6,846,000	127	*49*	State (U.S.) D	Raleigh
North Dakota	70,704	*183,123*	632,000	8.9	*3.5*	State (U.S.) D	Bismarck
Northern Ireland	5,452	*14,121*	1,604,000	294	*114*	Administrative division (U.K.) D	Belfast
Northern Mariana Islands	184	*477*	48,000	261	*101*	Commonwealth (U.S. protection) B	Saipan (island)
Northern Territory	519,771	*1,346,200*	176,000	0.3	*0.1*	Territory (Australia) D	Darwin
Northwest Territories	1,322,910	*3,426,320*	61,000			Territory (Canada) D	Yellowknife
† Norway (incl. Svalbard and Jan Mayen)	149,412	*386,975*	4,308,000	29	*11*	Constitutional monarchy A	Oslo
Nova Scotia	21,425	*55,490*	1,007,000	47	*18*	Province (Canada) D	Halifax
Oceania (incl. Australia)	3,300,000	*8,500,000*	26,700,000	8.1	*3.1*	...	...
Ohio	44,828	*116,103*	11,025,000	246	*95*	State (U.S.) D	Columbus
Oklahoma	69,903	*181,049*	3,205,000	46	*18*	State (U.S.) D	Oklahoma City
† Oman	82,030	*212,457*	1,617,000	20	*7.6*	Monarchy A	Masqaṭ (Muscat)
Ontario	412,581	*1,068,580*	11,265,000	27	*11*	Province (Canada) D	Toronto
Oregon	98,386	*254,819*	2,949,000	30	*12*	State (U.S.) D	Salem
Pacific Islands, Trust Territory of the, see Palau	...	...	...	...	...	...	...
† Pakistan (incl. part of Jammu and Kashmir)	879,902	*339,732*	123,490,000	363	*140*	Federal Islamic republic A	Islāmābād
Palau (Belau)	196	*508*	16,000	82	*31*	Under U.S. administration B	Koror and Melekeok [6]
† Panama	29,157	*75,517*	2,555,000	88	*34*	Republic A	Panamá
† Papua New Guinea	178,704	*462,840*	3,737,000	21	*8.1*	Parliamentary state A	Port Moresby
† Paraguay	157,048	*406,752*	5,003,000	32	*12*	Republic A	Asunción
Peking (Beijing)	6,487	*16,800*	11,290,000	1,740	*672*	Autonomous city (China) D	Beijing (Peking)
Pennsylvania	46,058	*119,291*	12,105,000	263	*101*	State (U.S.) D	Harrisburg
† Peru	496,225	*1,285,216*	22,995,000	46	*18*	Republic A	Lima
† Philippines	115,831	*300,000*	65,500,000	565	*218*	Republic A	Manila
Pitcairn (incl. Dependencies)	19	*49*	50	2.6	*1.0*	Dependent territory (U.K.) C	Adamstown
† Poland	120,728	*312,683*	38,330,000	317	*123*	Republic A	Warszawa (Warsaw)
† Portugal	35,516	*91,985*	10,660,000	300	*116*	Republic A	Lisboa (Lisbon)
Prince Edward Island	2,185	*5,660*	152,000	70	*27*	Province (Canada) D	Charlottetown
Puerto Rico	3,515	*9,104*	3,594,000	1,022	*395*	Commonwealth (U.S. protection) B	San Juan
† Qatar	4,412	*11,427*	492,000	112	*43*	Monarchy A	Ad-Dawḥah (Doha)
Quebec	594,860	*1,540,680*	7,725,000	13	*5.0*	Province (Canada) D	Québec
Queensland	666,876	*1,727,200*	3,000,000	4.5	*1.7*	State (Australia) D	Brisbane
Reunion	969	*2,510*	633,000	653	*252*	Overseas department (France) C	Saint-Denis
Rhode Island	1,545	*4,002*	1,026,000	664	*256*	State (U.S.) D	Providence
† Romania	91,699	*237,500*	23,200,000	253	*98*	Republic A	Bucureşti (Bucharest)
† Russia	6,592,849	*17,075,400*	150,500,000	23	*8.8*	Republic A	Moskva (Moscow)
† Rwanda	10,169	*26,338*	7,573,000	745	*288*	Provisional military government A	Kigali
St. Helena (incl. Dependencies)	121	*314*	7,000	58	*22*	Dependent territory (U.K.) C	Jamestown
† St. Kitts and Nevis	104	*269*	40,000	385	*149*	Parliamentary state A	Basseterre
† St. Lucia	238	*616*	153,000	643	*248*	Parliamentary state A	Castries
St. Pierre and Miquelon	93	*242*	7,000	75	*29*	Territorial collectivity (France) C	Saint-Pierre
† St. Vincent and the Grenadines	150	*388*	116,000	773	*299*	Parliamentary state A	Kingstown
† San Marino	24	*61*	23,000	958	*377*	Republic A	San Marino
† Sao Tome and Principe	372	*964*	134,000	360	*139*	Republic A	São Tomé
Saskatchewan	251,866	*652,330*	1,099,000	4.4	*1.7*	Province (Canada) D	Regina
† Saudi Arabia	830,000	*2,149,690*	15,985,000	19	*7.4*	Monarchy A	Ar-Riyāḍ (Riyadh)
Scotland	30,421	*78,789*	5,145,000	169	*65*	Administrative division (U.K.) D	Edinburgh
† Senegal	75,951	*196,712*	7,849,000	103	*40*	Republic A	Dakar
† Seychelles	175	*453*	70,000	400	*155*	Republic A	Victoria
Shanghai	2,394	*6,200*	13,875,000	5,796	*2,238*	Autonomous city (China) D	Shanghai
Shansi (Shanxi)	60,232	*156,000*	29,865,000	496	*191*	Province (China) D	Taiyuan
Shantung (Shandong)	59,074	*153,000*	87,840,000	1,487	*574*	Province (China) D	Jinan
Shensi (Shaanxi)	79,151	*205,000*	34,215,000	432	*167*	Province (China) D	Xi'an (Sian)
† Sierra Leone	27,925	*72,325*	4,424,000	158	*61*	Transitional military government A	Freetown

World Political Information

Country, Division or Region English (Conventional)	Area in sq. mi.	Area in sq. km.	Estimated Population 1/1/93	Pop. per sq. mi.	Pop. per sq. km.	Form of Government and Political Status	Capital
† Singapore..............	246	636	2,812,000	11,431	4,421	Republic ....A	Singapore
Sinkiang Uighur (Xinjiang Uygur) .	617,764	1,600,000	15,755,000	26	9.8	Autonomous region (China) ....D	Ürümqi
† Slovakia..................	18,933	49,035	5,287,000	279	108	Republic ....A	Bratislava
† Slovenia.................	7,819	20,251	1,965,000	251	97	Republic ....A	Ljubljana
† Solomon Islands	10,954	28,370	366,000	33	13	Parliamentary state ....A	Honiara
† Somalia..................	246,201	637,657	6,000,000	24	9.4	None ....A	Muqdisho (Mogadishu)
† South Africa (incl. Walvis Bay).....	433,680	1,123,226	33,040,000	76	29	Republic ....A	Pretoria, Cape Town, and Bloemfontein
South America	6,900,000	17,800,000	310,700,000	45	17	....	
South Australia	379,925	984,000	1,410,000	3.7	1.4	State (Australia) ....D	Adelaide
South Carolina	32,007	82,898	3,616,000	113	44	State (U.S.) ....D	Columbia
South Dakota.............................	77,121	199,745	718,000	9.3	3.6	State (U.S.) ....D	Pierre
South Georgia and the South Sandwich Islands	1,450	3,755	(1)	. . .	. . .	Dependent territory (U.K.) C	
† Spain...................	194,885	504,750	39,155,000	201	78	Constitutional monarchy ....A	Madrid
Spanish North Africa (8)...............	12	32	144,000	12,000	4,500	Five possessions (Spain) C	
† Sri Lanka	24,962	64,652	17,740,000	711	274	Socialist republic ....A	Colombo and Sri Jayawardenepura
† Sudan...................	967,500	2,505,813	28,760,000	30	11	Provisional military government ....A	Al-Khartūm (Khartoum)
† Suriname................	63,251	163,820	413,000	6.5	2.5	Republic ....A	Paramaribo
† Swaziland...............	6,704	17,364	925,000	138	53	Monarchy ....A	Mbabane and Lobamba
† Sweden..................	173,732	449,964	8,619,000	50	19	Constitutional monarchy ....A	Stockholm
Switzerland	15,943	41,293	6,848,000	430	166	Federal republic ....A	Bern (Berne)
† Syria....................	71,498	185,180	14,070,000	197	76	Socialist republic ....A	Dimashq (Damascus)
Szechwan (Sichuan)	220,078	570,000	111,470,000	507	196	Province (China) ....D	Chengdu
Taiwan	13,900	36,002	20,985,000	1,510	583	Republic ....A	T'aipei
† Tajikstan................	55,251	143,100	5,765,000	104	40	Republic ....A	Dušanbe
† Tanzania................	364,900	945,087	28,265,000	77	30	Republic ....A	Dar es Salaam and Dodoma (6)
Tasmania	26,178	67,800	456,000	17	6.7	State (Australia) ....D	Hobart
Tennessee	42,146	109,158	5,026,000	119	46	State (U.S.) ....D	Nashville
Texas	268,601	695,676	17,610,000	66	25	State (U.S.) ....D	Austin
† Thailand.................	198,115	513,115	58,030,000	293	113	Constitutional monarchy ....A	Krung Thep (Bangkok)
Tibet (Xizang)..............	471,045	1,220,000	2,235,000	4.7	1.8	Autonomous region (China) ....D	Lhasa
Tientsin (Tianjin)..........	4,363	11,300	9,170,000	2,102	812	Autonomous city (China) ....D	Tianjin (Tientsin)
† Togo....................	21,925	56,785	4,030,000	184	71	Provisional military government ....A	Lomé
Tokelau	4.6	12	1,800	391	150	Island territory (New Zealand) C	
† Tonga...................	288	747	103,000	358	138	Constitutional monarchy ....A	Nuku'alofa
Transkei (2)...............	16,816	43,553	4,845,000	288	111	National state (South African protection) ....B	Umtata
† Trinidad and Tobago	1,980	5,128	1,307,000	660	255	Republic ....A	Port of Spain
Tsinghai (Qinghai)	277,994	720,000	4,585,000	16	6.4	Province (China) ....D	Xining
† Tunisia..................	63,170	163,610	8,495,000	134	52	Republic ....A	Tunis
† Turkey...................	300,948	779,452	58,620,000	195	75	Republic ....A	Ankara
† Turkmenistan............	188,456	488,100	3,884,000	21	8.0	Republic ....A	Ašchabad (Ashgabat)
Turks and Caicos Islands	193	500	13,000	67	26	Dependent territory (U.K.) C	Grand Turk
Tuvalu	10	26	10,000	1,000	385	Parliamentary state ....A	Funafuti
† Uganda..................	93,104	241,139	17,410,000	187	72	Republic ....A	Kampala
† Ukraine..................	233,090	603,700	51,990,000	223	86	Republic ....A	Kijev (Kiev)
† United Arab Emirates...............	32,278	83,600	2,590,000	80	31	Federation of monarchs ....A	Abū Ẓaby (Abu Dhabi)
† United Kingdom...........	94,269	244,154	57,890,000	614	237	Constitutional monarchy ....A	London
† United States............	3,787,425	9,809,431	256,420,000	68	26	Federal republic ....A	Washington
† Uruguay.................	68,500	177,414	3,151,000	46	18	Republic ....A	Montevideo
Utah	84,904	219,902	1,795,000	21	8.2	State (U.S.) ....D	Salt Lake City
† Uzbekistan..............	172,742	447,400	21,885,000	127	49	Republic ....A	Taškent (Toshkent)
† Vanuatu.................	4,707	12,190	157,000	33	13	Republic ....A	Port Vila
Vatican City	0.2	0.4	800	4,000	2,000	Monarchical-sacerdotal state ....A	Città del Vaticano (Vatican City)
Venda (2).................	2,393	6,198	732,000	306	118	National state (South African protection) ....B	Thohoyandou
† Venezuela...............	352,145	912,050	19,085,000	54	21	Federal republic ....A	Caracas
Vermont	9,615	24,903	590,000	61	24	State (U.S.) ....D	Montpelier
Victoria	87,877	227,600	4,273,000	49	19	State (Australia) ....D	Melbourne
† Vietnam.................	127,428	330,036	69,650,000	547	211	Socialist republic ....A	Ha Noi
Virginia	42,769	110,771	6,411,000	150	58	State (U.S.) ....D	Richmond
Virgin Islands	133	344	104,000	782	302	Unincorporated territory (U.S.) C	Charlotte Amalie
Wake Island	3.0	7.8	200	67	26	Unincorporated territory (U.S.) C	
Wales	8,018	20,766	2,906,000	362	140	Administrative division (U.K.) ....D	Cardiff
Wallis and Futuna	98	255	17,000	173	67	Overseas territory (France) C	Mata-Utu
Washington	71,303	184,674	5,052,000	71	27	State (U.S.) ....D	Olympia
Western Australia	975,101	2,525,500	1,598,000	1.6	0.6	State (Australia) ....D	Perth
Western Sahara	102,703	266,000	200,000	1.9	0.8	Occupied by Morocco	El Aaiún (Laayone)
† Western Samoa	1,093	2,831	197,000	180	70	Constitutional monarchy ....A	Apia
West Virginia	24,231	62,759	1,795,000	74	29	State (U.S.) ....D	Charleston
Wisconsin	65,503	169,653	5,000,000	76	29	State (U.S.) ....D	Madison
Wyoming	97,818	253,349	462,000	4.7	1.8	State (U.S.) ....D	Cheyenne
† Yemen..................	203,850	527,968	12,215,000	60	23	Republic ....A	San'ā'
Yugoslavia	39,449	102,173	10,670,000	270	104	Republic ....A	Beograd (Belgrade)
Yukon Territory...........................	186,661	483,450	31,000	0.2	0.1	Territory (Canada) ....D	Whitehorse
Yunnan	152,124	394,000	38,450,000	253	98	Province (China) ....D	Kunming
† Zaire...................	905,446	2,345,095	39,750,000	44	17	Republic ....A	Kinshasa
† Zambia..................	290,586	752,614	8,475,000	29	11	Republic ....A	Lusaka
† Zimbabwe...............	150,873	390,759	10,000,000	66	26	Republic ....A	Harare (Salisbury)
WORLD	57,900,000	150,100,000	5,477,000,000	95	36	....	

† Member of the United Nations (1992).
(1) No permanent population.
(2) Bophuthatswana, Ciskei, Transkei, and Venda are not recognized by the United Nations.
(3) North Cyprus unilaterally declared its independence from Cyprus in 1983.
(4) Claimed by Argentina.
(5) Includes West Bank, Golan Heights, and Gaza Strip.
(6) Future capital.
(7) Claimed by Comoros.
(8) Comprises Ceuta, Melilla, and several small islands.

General Information

MOVEMENTS OF THE EARTH

The earth makes one complete revolution around the sun every 365 days, 5 hours, 48 minutes, and 46 seconds.

The earth makes one complete rotation on its axis in 23 hours, 56 minutes and 4 seconds.

The earth revolves in its orbit around the sun at a speed of 66,700 miles per hour (107,343 kilometers per hour).

The earth rotates on its axis at an equatorial speed of more than 1,000 miles per hour (1,600 kilometers per hour).

MEASUREMENTS OF THE EARTH

Estimated age of the earth, at least 4.6 billion years.

Equatorial diameter of the earth, 7,926.38 miles (12,756.27 kilometers).

Polar diameter of the earth, 7,899.80 miles (12,713.50 kilometers).

Mean diameter of the earth, 7,917.52 miles (12,742.01 kilometers).

Equatorial circumference of the earth, 24,901.46 miles (40,075.02 kilometers).

Polar circumference of the earth, 24,855.34 miles (40,000.79 kilometers).

Difference between equatorial and polar circumferences of the earth, 46.12 miles (74.23 kilometers).

Weight of the earth, 6,600,000,000,000,000,000,000 tons, or 6,600 billion billion tons (6,000 billion billion metric tons).

THE EARTH'S SURFACE

Total area of the earth, 197,000,000 square miles (510,000,000 square kilometers).

Total land area of the earth (including inland water and Antarctica, 57,900,000 square miles (149,700,000 square kilometers).

Highest point on the earth's surface, Mt. Everest, Asia, 29,028 feet (8,848 meters).

Lowest point on the earth's land surface, shores of the Dead Sea, Asia, 1,322 feet (403 meters) below sea level.

Greatest known depth of the ocean, the Mariana Trench, southwest of Guam, Pacific Ocean, 35,810 feet (10,915 meters).

THE EARTH'S INHABITANTS

Population of the earth is estimated to be 5,477,000,000 (January 1, 1993).

Estimated population density of the earth, 95 per square mile (36 per square kilometer).

EXTREMES OF TEMPERATURE AND RAINFALL OF THE EARTH

Highest temperature ever recorded, 136° F. (58° C.) at Al-'Azīzīyah, Libya, Africa, on September 13, 1922.

Lowest temperature ever recorded, -129° F. (-89° C.) at Vostok, Antarctica on July 21, 1983.

Highest mean annual temperature, 94° F. (34° C.) at Dalol, Ethiopia.

Lowest mean annual temperature, -70° F. (-50° C.) at Plateau Station, Antarctica.

The greatest local average annual rainfall is at Waialeale, Kauai, Hawaii, 460 inches (11,680 millimeters).

The greatest 24-hour rainfall, 74 inches (1,880 millimeters), is at Cilaos, Reunion Island, March 15-16, 1952.

The lowest local average annual rainfall is at Arica, Chile, .03 inches (8 millimeters).

The longest dry period, over 14 years, is at Arica, Chile, October 1903 to January 1918.

The Continents

CONTINENT	Area (sq. mi.) (sq. km.)	Estimated Population Jan. 1, 1993	Population per sq. mi. (sq. km.)	Mean Elevation (feet) (m.)	Highest Elevation (Feet) (m.)	Lowest Elevation (Feet) (m.)	Highest Recorded Temperature	Lowest Recorded Temperature
North America	9,500,000 (24,700,000)	438,200,000	46 (18)	2,000 (610)	Mt. McKinley, Alaska, United States 20,320 (6,194)	Death Valley, California, United States 282 (84) below sea level	Death Valley, California 134° F (57° C)	Northice, Greenland -87° F (-66° C)
South America	6,900,000 (17,800,000)	310,700,000	45 (17)	1,800 (550)	Cerro Aconcagua, Argentina 22,831 (6,959)	Salinas Chicas, Argentina 138 (42) below sea level	Rivadavia, Argentina 120° F (49° C)	Sarmiento, Argentina -27° F (-33° C)
Europe	3,800,000 (9,900,000)	694,700,000	183 (70)	980 (300)	Gora El'brus, Russia 18,510 (5,642)	Caspian Sea, Europe-Asia 92 (28) below sea level	Sevilla, Spain 122° F (50° C)	Ust' Ščugor, Russia -67° F (-55° C)
Asia	17,300,000 (44,900,000)	3,337,800,000	193 (74)	3,000 (910)	Mt. Everest, China-Nepal 29,028 (8,848)	Dead Sea, Israel-Jordan 1,322 (403) below sea level	Tirat Zevi, Israel 129° F (54° C)	Ojm'akon and Verchojansk, Russia -90° F (-68° C)
Africa	11,700,000 (30,300,000)	668,700,000	57 (22)	1,900 (580)	Kilimanjaro, Tanzania 19,340 (5,895)	Lac Assal, Djibouti 509 (155) below sea level	Al-'Azīzīyah, Libya 136° F (58° C)	Ifrane, Morocco -11° F (-24° C)
Oceania, incl. Australia	3,300,000 (8,500,000)	26,700,000	8.1 (3.1)	....	Mt. Wilhelm, Papua New Guinea 14,793 (4,509)	Lake Eyre, South Australia, Australia 52 (16) below sea level	Cloncurry, Queensland, Australia 128° F (53° C)	Charlottes Pass, New South Wales, Australia -8° F (-22° C)
Australia	2,966,155 (7,682,300)	16,965,000	5.7 (2.2)	1,000 (300)	Mt. Kosciusko, New South Wales 7,310 (2,228)	Lake Eyre, South Australia 52 (16) below sea level	Cloncurry, Queensland 128° F (53° C)	Charlottes Pass, New South Wales -8° F (-22° C)
Antarctica	5,400,000 (14,000,000)	....	....	6,000 (1830)	Vinson Massif 16,066 (4,897)	sea level	Vanda Station 59° F (15° C)	Vostok -129° F (-89° C)
World	57,900,000 (150,100,000)	5,477,000,000	95 (36)	....	Mt. Everest, China-Nepal 29,028 (8,848)	Dead Sea, Israel-Jordan 1,322 (403) below sea level	Al-'Azīzīyah, Libya 136° F (58° C)	Vostok, Antarctica -129° F (-89° C)

Historical Populations *

AREA	1650	1750	1800	1850	1900	1920	1950	1970	1980	1990
North America	5,000,000	5,000,000	13,000,000	39,000,000	106,000,000	147,000,000	219,000,000	316,600,000	365,000,000	423,600,000
South America	8,000,000	7,000,000	12,000,000	20,000,000	38,000,000	61,000,000	111,000,000	187,400,000	239,000,000	293,700,000
Europe	100,000,000	140,000,000	190,000,000	265,000,000	400,000,000	453,000,000	530,000,000	623,700,000	660,300,000	688,000,000
Asia	335,000,000	476,000,000	593,000,000	754,000,000	932,000,000	1,000,000,000	1,418,000,000	2,086,200,000	2,581,000,000	3,156,100,000
Africa	100,000,000	95,000,000	90,000,000	95,000,000	118,000,000	140,000,000	199,000,000	346,900,000	463,800,000	648,300,000
Oceania, incl. Australia	2,000,000	2,000,000	2,000,000	2,000,000	6,000,000	9,000,000	13,000,000	19,200,000	22,700,000	26,300,000
Australia	*	*	*	*	4,000,000	6,000,000	8,000,000	12,460,000	14,510,000	16,950,000
World	550,000,000	725,000,000	900,000,000	1,175,000,000	1,600,000,000	1,810,000,000	2,490,000,000	3,580,000,000	4,332,000,000	5,236,000,000

* Figures prior to 1970 are rounded to the nearest million. Figures in italics represent very rough estimates.

Largest Countries : Population

		Population 1/1/93				Population 1/1/93
1	China	1,179,030,000	16	Turkey		58,620,000
2	India	873,850,000	17	Thailand		58,030,000
3	United States	256,420,000	18	United Kingdom		57,890,000
4	Indonesia	186,180,000	19	France		57,570,000
5	Brazil	159,630,000	20	Egypt		57,050,000
6	Russia	150,500,000	21	Italy		56,550,000
7	Japan	124,710,000	22	Ukraine		51,990,000
8	Pakistan	123,490,000	23	Ethiopia		51,715,000
9	Bangladesh	120,850,000	24	South Korea		43,660,000
10	Nigeria	91,700,000	25	Burma		43,070,000
11	Mexico	86,170,000	26	Zaire		39,750,000
12	Germany	80,590,000	27	Spain		39,155,000
13	Vietnam	69,650,000	28	Poland		38,330,000
14	Philippines	65,500,000	29	Colombia		34,640,000
15	Iran	60,500,000	30	South Africa		33,040,000

Largest Countries : Area

		Area (sq. mi.)	Area (sq. km.)			Area (sq. mi.)	Area (sq. km.)
1	Russia	6,592,849	17,075,400	17	Libya	679,362	1,759,540
2	Canada	3,849,674	9,970,610	18	Iran	632,457	1,638,057
3	United States	3,787,425	9,809,431	19	Mongolia	604,829	1,566,500
4	China	3,689,631	9,556,100	20	Peru	496,225	1,285,216
5	Brazil	3,286,500	8,511,996	21	Chad	495,755	1,284,000
6	Australia	2,966,155	7,682,300	22	Niger	489,191	1,267,000
7	India	1,237,062	3,203,975	23	Mali	482,077	1,248,574
8	Argentina	1,073,519	2,780,400	24	Angola	481,354	1,246,700
9	Kazakhstan	1,049,156	2,717,300	25	Ethiopia	446,953	1,157,603
10	Sudan	967,500	2,505,813	26	Colombia	440,831	1,141,748
11	Algeria	919,595	2,381,741	27	South Africa	433,680	1,123,226
12	Zaire	905,446	2,345,095	28	Bolivia	424,165	1,098,581
13	Greenland	840,004	2,175,600	29	Mauritania	395,956	1,025,520
14	Saudi Arabia	830,000	2,149,690	30	Egypt	386,662	1,001,449
15	Mexico	759,534	1,967,183				
16	Indonesia	752,410	1,948,732				

Principal Mountains

North America

	Height (feet)	Height (meters)
McKinley, Mt., Δ Alaska (Δ United States; Δ North America)	20,320	6,194
Logan, Mt., Δ Canada (Δ Yukon; Δ St. Elias Mts.)	19,524	5,951
Orizaba, Pico de, Δ Mexico	18,406	5,610
St. Elias, Mt., Alaska-Canada	18,008	5,489
Popocatépetl, Volcán, Mexico	17,930	5,465
Foraker, Mt., Alaska	17,400	5,304
Iztaccíhuatl, Mexico	17,159	5,230
Lucania, Mt., Canada	17,147	5,226
Fairweather, Mt., Alaska-Canada (Δ British Columbia)	15,300	4,663
Whitney, Mt., Δ California,	14,494	4,418
Elbert, Mt., Δ Colorado (Δ Rocky Mts.)	14,433	4,399
Massive, Mt., Colorado	14,421	4,396
Harvard, Mt., Colorado	14,420	4,395
Rainier, Mt., Δ Washington (Δ Cascade Range)	14,410	4,392
Williamson, Mt., California	14,375	4,382
Blanca Pk., Colorado (Δ Sangre de Cristo Mts.)	14,345	4,372
La Plata Pk., Colorado	14,336	4,370
Uncompahgre Pk., Colorado (Δ San Juan Mts.)	14,309	4,361
Grays Pk., Colorado (Δ Front Range)	14,270	4,349
Evans, Mt., Colorado	14,264	4,348
Longs Pk., Colorado	14,255	4,345
Wrangell, Mt., Alaska	14,163	4,317
Shasta, Mt., California	14,162	4,317
Pikes Pk., Colorado	14,110	4,301
Colima, Nevado de, Mexico	13,991	4,240
Tajumulco, Volcán, Δ Guatemala (Δ Central America)	13,846	4,220
Gannett Pk., Δ Wyoming	13,804	4,207
Mauna Kea, Δ Hawaii	13,796	4,205
Grand Teton, Wyoming	13,770	4,197
Mauna Loa, Hawaii	13,679	4,169
Kings Pk., Δ Utah	13,528	4,123
Cloud Pk., Wyoming (Δ Bighorn Mts.)	13,167	4,013
Wheeler Pk., Δ New Mexico	13,161	4,011
Boundary Pk., Δ Nevada	13,143	4,006
Waddington, Mt., Canada (Δ Coast Mts.)	13,104	3,994
Robson, Mt., Canada (Δ Canadian Rockies)	12,972	3,954
Granite Pk., Δ Montana	12,799	3,901
Borah Pk., Δ Idaho	12,662	3,859
Humphreys Pk., Δ Arizona	12,633	3,851
Chirripó, Cerro, Δ Costa Rica	12,533	3,819
Columbia, Mt., Canada (Δ Alberta)	12,294	3,747
Adams, Mt., Washington	12,276	3,742
Gunnbjørn Fjeld, Δ Greenland	12,139	3,700
San Gorgonio Mtn., California	11,499	3,505
Barú, Volcán, Δ Panama	11,411	3,475
Hood, Mt., Δ Oregon	11,235	3,424
Lassen Pk., California	10,457	3,187
Duarte, Pico, Δ Dominican Rep. (Δ West Indies)	10,417	3,175
Haleakala Crater, Hawaii (Δ Maui)	10,023	3,055
Paricutín, Mexico	9,186	2,800
El Pital, Cerro, Δ El Salvador-Honduras	8,957	2,730
La Selle, Morne, Δ Haiti	8,773	2,674
Guadalupe Pk., Δ Texas	8,749	2,667
Olympus, Mt., Washington (Δ Olympic Mts.)	7,965	2,428
Blue Mountain Pk., Δ Jamaica	7,402	2,256
Harney Pk., Δ South Dakota (Δ Black Hills)	7,242	2,207
Mitchell, Mt., Δ North Carolina (Δ Appalachian Mts.)	6,684	2,037
Clingmans Dome, North Carolina-Δ Tennessee (Δ Great Smoky Mts.)	6,643	2,025
Turquino, Pico, Δ Cuba	6,470	1,972
Washington, Mt., Δ New Hampshire (Δ White Mts.)	6,288	1,917
Rogers, Mt., Δ Virginia	5,729	1,746
Marcy, Mt., Δ New York (Δ Adirondack Mts.)	5,344	1,629
Katahdin, Mt., Δ Maine	5,268	1,606
Kawaikini, Hawaii (Δ Kauai)	5,243	1,598
Spruce Knob, Δ West Virginia	4,862	1,482
Pelée, Montagne, Δ Martinique	4,583	1,397
Mansfield, Mt., Δ Vermont (Δ Green Mts.)	4,393	1,339
Punta, Cerro de, Δ Puerto Rico	4,389	1,338
Black Mtn., Δ Kentucky-Virginia	4,145	1,263
Kaala, Hawaii (Δ Oahu)	4,040	1,231

South America

Aconcagua, Cerro, Δ Argentina; Δ Andes; (Δ South America)	22,831	6,959
Ojos del Salado, Nevado, Argentina-Δ Chile	22,572	6,880
Bonete, Cerro, Argentina	22,546	6,872
Huascarán, Nevado, Δ Peru	22,204	6,768
Llullaillaco, Volcán, Argentina-Chile	22,110	6,739
Yerupaja, Nevado, Peru	21,765	6,634
Tupungato, Cerro, Argentina-Chile	21,489	6,550
Sajama, Nevado, Bolivia	21,463	6,542
Illimani, Nevado, Δ Bolivia	21,004	6,402
Illampu, Nevado, Bolivia	20,873	6,362
Chimborazo, Δ Ecuador	20,702	6,310
Antofalla, Volcán, Argentina	20,013	6,100
Cotopaxi, Ecuador	19,347	5,897
Misti, Volcán, Peru	19,098	5,821
Huila, Nevado del, Colombia (Δ Cordillera Central)	16,896	5,150
Bolívar, Pico, Δ Venezuela	16,427	5,007
Fitzroy, Monte (Cerro Chaltel), Argentina-Chile	11,073	3,375
Neblina, Pico da, Δ Brazil-Venezuela	9,888	3,014

Europe

El'brus, gora, Δ Russia (Δ Caucasus; Δ Europe)	18,510	5,642
Dychtau, gora, Russia	17,073	5,204
Blanc, Mont (Monte Bianco), Δ France-Δ Italy (Δ Alps)	15,771	4,807
Dufourspitze, Italy-Δ Switzerland	15,203	4,634
Weisshorn, Switzerland	14,783	4,506
Matterhorn, Italy-Switzerland	14,692	4,478
Finsteraarhorn, Switzerland	14,022	4,274
Jungfrau, Switzerland	13,642	4,158
Écrins, Barre des, France	13,458	4,102
Viso, Monte, Italy (Δ Alpes Cottiennes)	12,602	3,841
Grossglockner, Δ Austria	12,457	3,797
Teide, Pico de, Δ Spain (Δ Canary Is.)	12,188	3,715
Mulhacén, Δ Spain (continental)	11,423	3,482
Aneto, Pico de, Spain (Δ Pyrenees)	11,168	3,404
Perdido, Monte, Spain	11,007	3,355
Etna, Monte, Italy (Δ Sicily)	10,902	3,323
Zugspitze, Austria-Δ Germany	9,721	2,963
Musala, Δ Bulgaria	9,596	2,925
Ólimbos (Mount Olympus), Δ Greece	9,570	2,917
Corno Grande, Italy (Δ Apennines)	9,554	2,912
Triglav, Δ Slovenia	9,396	2,864
Korab, Δ Albania-Macedonia	9,026	2,751
Cinto, Monte, France (Δ Corsica)	8,891	2,710
Gerlachovský Štít, Δ Slovakia (Δ Carpathian Mts.)	8,711	2,655
Moldoveanu, Δ Romania	8,346	2,544
Rysy, Czechoslovakia-Δ Poland	8,199	2,499
Galdhøpiggen, Δ Norway (Δ Scandinavia)	8,100	2,469
Parnassos, Greece	8,061	2,457
Ídhi, Óros, Greece (Δ Crete)	8,047	2,453
Pico, Ponta do, Δ Portugal (Δ Azores Is.)	7,713	2,351
Hvannadalshnúkur, Δ Iceland	6,952	2,119
Kebnekaise, Δ Sweden	6,926	2,111
Estrela, Δ Portugal (continental)	6,539	1,993
Narodnaja, gora, Russia (Δ Ural Mts.)	6,217	1,895
Sancy, Puy de, France (Δ Massif Central)	6,184	1,885
La Marmora, Punta, Italy (Δ Sardinia)	6,017	1,834
Hekla, Iceland	4,892	1,491
Nevis, Ben, Δ United Kingdom (Δ Scotland)	4,406	1,343
Haltiatunturi, Δ Finland-Norway	4,357	1,328
Vesuvio, Italy	4,190	1,277
Snowdon, United Kingdom (Δ Wales)	3,560	1,085
Carrauntoohil, Δ Ireland	3,406	1,038
Kékes, Δ Hungary	3,330	1,015
Scafell Pikes, United Kingdom (Δ England)	3,210	978

Asia

Everest, Mount, Δ China-Δ Nepal (Δ Tibet; Δ Himalayas; Δ Asia; Δ World)	29,028	8,848
K2 (Qogir Feng), China-Δ Pakistan (Δ Kashmir; Δ Karakoram Range)	28,250	8,611
Kānchenjunga, Δ India-Nepal	28,208	8,598
Makālu, China-Nepal	27,825	8,481
Dhawlagiri, Nepal	26,810	8,172
Nānga Parbat, Pakistan	26,660	8,126
Annapūrna, Nepal	26,504	8,078
Gasherbrum, China-Pakistan	26,470	8,068
Xixabangma Feng, China	26,286	8,012
Nanda Devi, India	25,645	7,817
Kamet, China-India	25,447	7,756
Namjagbarwa Feng, China	25,446	7,756
Muztag, China (Δ Kunlun Shan)	25,338	7,723
Tirich Mir, Pakistan (Δ Hindu Kush)	25,230	7,690
Gongga Shan, China	24,790	7,556
Kula Kangri, Δ Bhutan	24,784	7,554
Kommunizma, pik, Δ Tajikistan (Δ Pamir)	24,590	7,495
Nowshāk, Δ Afghanistan-Pakistan	24,557	7,485
Pobedy, pik, China-Russia	24,406	7,439
Chomo Lhari, Bhutan-China	23,997	7,314
Muztag, China	23,891	7,282
Lenina, pik, Δ Kyrgyzstan-Tajikistan	23,406	7,134
Api, Nepal	23,399	7,132
Kangrinboqê Feng, China	22,028	6,714
Hkakabo Razi, Δ Burma	19,296	5,881
Damāvend, Qollah-ye, Δ Iran	18,386	5,604
Fūlādī, Kūh-e, Afghanistan	16,847	5,135
Ağrı Dağı (Mount Ararat), Δ Turkey	16,804	5,122
Jaya, Puncak, Δ Indonesia (Δ New Guinea)	16,503	5,030
Kl'učevskaja Sopka, vulkan, Russia (Δ Puluostrov Kamčatka)	15,584	4,750
Trikora, Puncak, Indonesia	15,584	4,750
Belucha, gora, Kazakhstan-Russia	14,783	4,506
Turgen, Mount, Mongolia	14,311	4,362
Kinabalu, Gunong, Δ Malaysia (Δ Borneo)	13,455	4,101
Yü Shan, Δ Taiwan	13,114	3,997
Erciyes Dağı, Turkey	12,851	3,917
Kerinci, Gunung, Indonesia (Δ Sumatra)	12,467	3,800
Fuji-san, Δ Japan (Δ Honshu)	12,388	3,776
Nabī Shu'ayb, Jabal an-, Δ Yemen (Δ Arabian Peninsula)	12,335	3,760
Rinjani, Gunung, Indonesia (Δ Lombok)	12,224	3,726
Semeru, Gunung, Indonesia (Δ Java)	12,060	3,676
Rantekombola, Bulu, Indonesia (Δ Celebes)	11,335	3,455
Slamet, Gunung, Indonesia	11,247	3,428
Fan Si Pan, Δ Vietnam	10,312	3,143
Shām, Jabal ash-, Δ Oman	9,957	3,035
Apo, Mount, Δ Philippines (Δ Mindanao)	9,692	2,954
Pulog, Mount, Philippines (Δ Luzon)	9,626	2,934
Bia, Phou, Δ Laos	9,249	2,819
Shaykh, Jabal ash-, Lebanon-Δ Syria	9,232	2,814
Paektu-san, Δ North Korea-China	9,003	2,744
Inthanon, Doi, Δ Thailand	8,530	2,600
Pidurutalagala, Δ Sri Lanka	8,281	2,524
Mayon Volcano, Philippines	8,077	2,462
Asahi-dake, Japan (Δ Hokkaidō)	7,513	2,290
Tahan, Gunung, Malaysia (Δ Malaya)	7,174	2,187
Ólimbos, Δ Cyprus	6,401	1,951
Halla-san, Δ South Korea	6,398	1,950
Aôral, Phnum, Δ Cambodia	5,948	1,813
Kujū-san, Japan (Δ Kyūshū)	5,863	1,787
Ramm, Jabal, Δ Jordan	5,755	1,754
Meron, Hare, Δ Israel	3,963	1,208
Karmel, Har (Mount Carmel), Israel	1,791	546

Africa

Kilimanjaro, Δ Tanzania (Δ Africa)	19,340	5,895
Kirinyaga (Mount Kenya), Δ Kenya	17,058	5,199
Margherita Peak, Δ Uganda-Δ Zaire	16,763	5,109
Ras Dashen Terara, Δ Ethiopia	15,158	4,620
Meru, Mount, Tanzania	14,978	4,565
Karisimbi, Volcan, Δ Rwanda-Zaire	14,787	4,507
Elgon, Mount, Kenya-Uganda	14,178	4,321
Toubkal, Jebel, Δ Morocco (Δ Atlas Mts.)	13,665	4,165
Cameroon Mountain, Δ Cameroon	13,451	4,100
Ntlenyana, Thabana, Δ Lesotho	11,425	3,482
eNjesuthi, Δ South Africa	11,306	3,446
Koussi, Emi, Δ Chad (Δ Tibesti)	11,204	3,415
Kinyeti, Δ Sudan	10,456	3,187
Santa Isabel, Pico de, Δ Equatorial Guinea (Δ Bioko)	9,869	3,008
Tahat, Δ Algeria (Δ Ahaggar)	9,541	2,908
Maromokotro, Δ Madagascar	9,436	2,876
Kātrīnā, Jabal, Δ Egypt	8,668	2,642
São Tome, Pico de, Δ Sao Tome	6,640	2,024

Oceania

Wilhelm, Mount, Δ Papua New Guinea	14,793	4,509
Giluwe, Mount, Papua New Guinea	14,330	4,368
Bangeta, Mt., Papua New Guinea	13,520	4,121
Victoria, Mount, Papua New Guinea (Δ Owen Stanley Range)	13,238	4,035
Cook, Mount, Δ New Zealand (Δ South Island)	12,349	3,764
Ruapehu, New Zealand (Δ North Island)	9,177	2,797
Balbi, Papua New Guinea (Δ Solomon Is.)	9,000	2,743
Taranaki, Mount, New Zealand	8,260	2,518
Orohena, Mont, Δ French Polynesia (Δ Tahiti)	7,352	2,241
Kosciusko, Mount, Δ Australia (Δ New South Wales)	7,277	2,218
Silisili, Mauga, Δ Western Samoa	6,096	1,858
Panié, Mont, Δ New Caledonia	5,341	1,628
Bartle Frere, Australia (Δ Queensland)	5,322	1,622
Ossa, Mount, Australia (Δ Tasmania)	5,305	1,617
Woodroffe, Mount, Australia (Δ South Australia)	4,724	1,440
Sinewit, Mt., Papua New Guinea	4,462	1,360
Tomanivi, Δ Fiji (Δ Viti Levu)	4,341	1,323
Meharry, Mt., Australia (Δ Western Australia)	4,104	1,251
Ayers Rock, Australia	2,844	867

Antarctica

Vinson Massif, Δ Antarctica	16,066	4,897
Kirkpatrick, Mount, Antarctica	14,856	4,528
Markham, Mount, Antarctica	14,272	4,350
Jackson, Mount, Antarctica	13,747	4,190
Sidley, Mount, Antarctica	13,717	4,181
Wade, Mount, Antarctica	13,396	4,083

Δ *Highest mountain in state, country, range, or region named.*

World Oceans, Seas, Gulfs, Lakes, Rivers and Islands

Oceans, Seas and Gulfs

	Area (sq. mi.)	Area (sq. km.)		Area (sq. mi.)	Area (sq. km.)		Area (sq. mi.)	Area (sq. km.)
Pacific Ocean	63,800,000	165,200,000	South China Sea	1,331,000	3,447,000	Okhotsk, Sea of	619,000	1,603,000
Atlantic Ocean	31,800,000	82,400,000	Caribbean Sea	1,063,000	2,753,000	Norwegian Sea	597,000	1,546,000
Indian Ocean	28,900,000	74,900,000	Mediterranean Sea	967,000	2,505,000	Mexico, Gulf of	596,000	1,544,000
Arctic Ocean	5,400,000	14,000,000	Bering Sea	876,000	2,269,000	Hudson Bay	475,000	1,230,000
Arabian Sea	1,492,000	3,864,000	Bengal, Bay of	839,000	2,173,000	Greenland Sea	465,000	1,204,000

Principal Lakes

	Area (sq. mi.)	Area (sq. km.)		Area (sq. mi.)	Area (sq. km.)		Area (sq. mi.)	Area (sq. km.)
Caspian Sea, Asia—Europe. (Salt)	143,240	370,990	Ontario, Lake, Canada—U.S.	7,540	19,529	Issyk-Kul', ozero, Kyrgyzstan (Salt)	2,425	6,280
Superior, Lake, Canada—U.S.	31,700	82,100	Balchaš, ozero, Kazakhstan	Δ 7,100	18,300	Torrens, Lake, Australia (Salt)	2,300	5,900
Victoria, Lake, Kenya—Tanzania—Uganda	26,820	69,463	Ladožskoje ozero, Russia	6,833	17,700	Albert, Lake, Uganda—Zaire	2,160	5,594
Aral Sea, Kazakhstan—Uzbekistan (Salt)	24,700	64,100	Chad, Lake (Lac Tchad), Cameroon—Chad—Nigeria	6,300	16,300	Vänern, Sweden	2,156	5,584
Huron, Lake, Canada—U.S.	23,000	60,000	Onežskoje ozero, Russia	3,753	9,720	Nettilling Lake, Canada	2,140	5,542
Michigan, Lake, U.S.	22,300	57,800	Eyre, Lake, Australia (Salt)	Δ 3,700	9,500	Winnipegosis, Lake, Canada	2,075	5,374
Tanganyika, Lake, Africa	12,350	31,986	Titicaca, Lago, Bolivia—Peru	3,200	8,300	Bangweulu, Lake, Zambia	1,930	4,999
Bajkal, ozero, Russia	12,200	31,500	Nicaragua, Lago de, Nicaragua	3,150	8,158	Nipigon, Lake, Canada	1,872	4,848
Great Bear Lake, Canada	12,095	31,326	Mai-Ndombe, Lac, Zaire	Δ 3,100	8,000	Orūmīyeh, Daryācheh-ye, Iran (Salt)	Δ 1,815	4,701
Malawi, Lake (Lake Nyasa), Malawi—Mozambique—Tanzania	11,150	28,878	Athabasca, Lake, Canada	3,064	7,935	Manitoba, Lake, Canada	1,785	4,624
Great Slave Lake, Canada	11,030	28,568	Reindeer Lake, Canada	2,568	6,650	Woods, Lake of the, Canada—U.S.	1,727	4,472
Erie, Lake, Canada—U.S.	9,910	25,667	Tônlé Sab, Bœng, Cambodia	Δ 2,500	6,500	Kyoga, Lake, Uganda	1,710	4,429
Winnipeg, Lake, Canada	9,416	24,387	Rudolf, Lake, Ethiopia—Kenya (Salt)	2,473	6,405	Great Salt Lake, U.S. (Salt)	1,680	4,351

Δ Due to seasonal fluctuations in water level, areas of these lakes vary considerably.

Principal Rivers

	Length (miles)	Length (km.)		Length (miles)	Length (km.)		Length (miles)	Length (km.)
Nile, Africa	4,145	6,671	Euphrates, Asia	1,510	2,430	Canadian, North America	906	1,458
Amazon-Ucayali, South America	4,000	6,400	Ural, Asia	1,509	2,428	Brazos, North America	900	1,400
Chang (Yangtze), Asia	3,900	6,300	Arkansas, North America	1,459	2,348	Salado, South America	900	1,400
Mississippi-Missouri, North America	3,740	6,019	Colorado, North America (U.S.-Mexico)	1,450	2,334	Darling, Australia	864	1,390
Huang (Yellow), Asia	3,395	5,464	Aldan, Asia	1,412	2,273	Fraser, North America	851	1,370
Ob'-Irtyš, Asia	3,362	5,410	Syrdarja, Asia	1,370	2,205	Parnaíba, South America	850	1,368
Río de la Plata-Paraná, South America	3,030	4,876	Dnepr, Europe	1,400	2,200	Colorado, North America (Texas)	840	1,352
Congo (Zaïre), Africa	2,900	4,700	Araguaia, South America	1,400	2,200	Dnestr, Europe	840	1,352
Paraná, South America	2,800	4,500	Kasai (Cassai), Africa	1,338	2,153	Rhine, Europe	820	1,320
Amur-Argun', Asia	2,761	4,444	Tarim, Asia	1,328	2,137	Narmada, Asia	800	1,300
Amur (Heilong), Asia	2,744	4,416	Kolyma, Asia	1,323	2,129	St. Lawrence, North America	800	1,300
Lena, Asia	2,700	4,400	Orange, Africa	1,300	2,100	Ottawa, North America	790	1,271
Mackenzie, North America	2,635	4,241	Negro, South America	1,300	2,100	Athabasca, North America	765	1,231
Mekong, Asia	2,600	4,200	Ayeyarwady (Irrawaddy), Asia	1,300	2,100	Pecos, North America	735	1,183
Niger, Africa	2,600	4,200	Red, North America	1,270	2,044	Severskij Donec, Europe	735	1,183
Jenisej, Asia	2,543	4,092	Juruá, South America	1,250	2,012	Green, North America	730	1,175
Missouri-Red Rock, North America	2,533	4,076	Columbia, North America	1,200	2,000	White, North America (Ar.-Mo.)	720	1,159
Mississippi, North America	2,348	3,779	Xingu, South America	1,230	1,979	Cumberland, North America	720	1,159
Murray-Darling, Australia	2,330	3,750	Ucayali, South America	1,220	1,963	Elbe (Labe), Europe	720	1,159
Missouri, North America	2,315	3,726	Saskatchewan-Bow, North America	1,205	1,939	James, North America (N./S. Dakota)	710	1,143
Volga, Europe	2,194	3,531	Peace, North America	1,195	1,923	Gambia, Africa	680	1,094
Madeira, South America	2,013	3,240	Tigris, Asia	1,180	1,899	Yellowstone, North America	671	1,080
São Francisco, South America	1,988	3,199	Don, Europe	1,162	1,870	Tennessee, North America	652	1,049
Grande, Rio (Río Bravo), North America	1,885	3,034	Songhua, Asia	1,140	1,835	Gila, North America	630	1,014
Purús, South America	1,860	2,993	Pečora, Europe	1,124	1,809	Wisła (Vistula), Europe	630	1,014
Indus, Asia	1,800	2,900	Kama, Europe	1,122	1,805	Tagus (Tejo) (Tajo), Europe	625	1,006
Danube, Europe	1,776	2,858	Limpopo, Africa	1,100	1,800	Loire, Europe	625	1,006
Brahmaputra, Asia	1,770	2,849	Angara, Asia	1,105	1,779	Cimarron, North America	600	1,000
Yukon, North America	1,770	2,849	Snake, North America	1,038	1,670	North Platte, North America	618	995
Salween (Nu), Asia	1,750	2,816	Uruguay, South America	1,025	1,650	Albany, North America	610	982
Zambezi, Africa	1,700	2,700	Churchill, North America	1,000	1,600	Tisza (Tisa), Europe	607	977
Vil'uj, Asia	1,647	2,650	Marañón, South America	1,000	1,600	Back, North America	605	974
Tocantins, South America	1,640	2,639	Tobol, Asia	989	1,591	Ouachita, North America	605	974
Orinoco South America,	1,600	2,600	Ohio, North America	981	1,579	Sava, Europe	585	941
Paraguay, South America	1,610	2,591	Magdalena, South America	950	1,529	Nemunas (Neman), Europe	582	937
Amu Darya, Asia	1,578	2,540	Roosevelt, South America	950	1,529	Branco, South America	580	933
Murray, Australia	1,566	2,520	Oka, Europe	900	1,500	Meuse (Maas), Europe	575	925
Ganges, Asia	1,560	2,511	Xiang, Asia	930	1,497	Oder (Odra), Europe	565	909
Pilcomayo, South America	1,550	2,494	Godāvari, Asia	930	1,497	Rhône, Europe	500	800

Principal Islands

	Area (sq. mi.)	Area (sq. km.)		Area (sq. mi.)	Area (sq. km.)		Area (sq. mi.)	Area (sq. km.)
Grønland (Greenland), North America	840,000	2,175,600	Hispaniola, North America	29,400	76,200	New Caledonia, Oceania	6,252	16,192
New Guinea, Asia—Oceania	309,000	800,000	Banks Island, Canada	27,038	70,028	Timor, Indonesia	5,743	14,874
Borneo (Kalimantan), Asia	287,300	744,100	Tasmania, Australia	26,200	67,800	Flores, Indonesia	5,502	14,250
Madagascar, Africa	226,500	587,000	Sri Lanka, Asia	24,900	64,600	Samar, Philippines	5,100	13,080
Baffin Island, Canada	195,928	507,451	Devon Island, Canada	21,331	55,247	Negros, Philippines	4,907	12,710
Sumatera (Sumatra), Indonesia	182,860	473,606	Tierra del Fuego, Isla Grande de, South America	18,600	48,200	Palawan, Philippines	4,550	11,785
Honshū, Japan	89,176	230,966	Kyūshū, Japan	17,129	44,363	Panay, Philippines	4,446	11,515
Great Britain, United Kingdom	88,795	229,978	Melville Island, Canada	16,274	42,149	Jamaica, North America	4,200	11,000
Victoria Island, Canada	83,897	217,291	Southampton Island, Canada	15,913	41,214	Hawaii, United States	4,034	10,448
Ellesmere Island, Canada	75,767	196,236	Spitsbergen, Norway	15,260	39,523	Cape Breton Island, Canada	3,981	10,311
Sulawesi (Celebes), Indonesia	73,057	189,216	New Britain, Papua New Guinea	14,093	36,500	Mindoro, Philippines	3,759	9,735
South Island, New Zealand	57,708	149,463	T'aiwan, Asia	13,900	36,000	Kodiak Island, United States	3,670	9,505
Jawa (Java), Indonesia	51,038	132,187	Hainan Dao, China	13,100	34,000	Bougainville, Papua New Guinea	3,600	9,300
North Island, New Zealand	44,332	114,821	Prince of Wales Island, Canada	12,872	33,339	Cyprus, Asia	3,572	9,251
Cuba, North America	42,800	110,800	Vancouver Island, Canada	12,079	31,285	Puerto Rico, North America	3,500	9,100
Newfoundland, Canada	42,031	108,860	Sicilia (Sicily), Italy	9,926	25,709	New Ireland, Papua New Guinea	3,500	9,000
Luzon, Philippines	40,420	104,688	Somerset Island, Canada	9,570	24,786	Corse (Corsica), France	3,367	8,720
Ísland (Iceland), Europe	39,800	103,000	Sardegna (Sardinia), Italy	9,301	24,090	Krít (Crete), Greece	3,189	8,259
Mindanao, Philippines	36,537	94,630	Shikoku, Japan	7,258	18,799	Vrangel'a, ostrov (Wrangel Island), Russia	2,800	7,300
Ireland, Europe	32,600	84,400	Seram (Ceram), Indonesia	7,191	18,625	Leyte, Philippines	2,785	7,214
Hokkaidō, Japan	32,245	83,515	Nordaustlandet (North East Land), Norway	6,350	16,446	Guadalcanal, Solomon Islands	2,060	5,336
Novaja Zeml'a (Novaya Zemlya), Russia	31,900	82,600				Long Island, United States	1,377	3,566
Sachalin, ostrov (Sakhalin), Russia	29,500	76,400						

World Populations

This table includes every urban center of 50,000 or more population in the world as well as many other important or well-known cities and towns.

The population figures are all from recent censuses (designated C) or official estimates (designated E), except for a few cities for which only unofficial estimates are available (designated U). The date of the census or estimate is specified for each country. Individual exceptions are dated in parentheses.

For many cities, a second population figure is given accompanied by a star (★). The starred population refers to the city's entire metropolitan area, including suburbs. These metropolitan areas have been defined by Rand McNally, following consistent rules to facilitate comparisons among the urban centers of various countries. Where a place is part of the metropolitan area of another city, that city's name is specified in parentheses preceded by (★). A population preceded by a triangle (▲) refers to an entire municipality, commune, or other district, which includes rural areas in addition to the urban center itself. The names of capital cities appear in CAPITALS; the largest city in each country is designated by the symbol (•).

For more recent population totals for countries, see the Rand McNally population estimates in the World Political Information table.

AFGHANISTAN / Afghānestān

1988 E	17,672,000
Herāt	177,300
Jalālābād (1982 E)	58,000
• KĀBOL	1,424,400
Kondūz (1982 E)	57,000
Mazār-e Sharīf	130,600
Qandahār	225,500

ALBANIA / Shqipëri

1989 C	3,182,400
Durrës	82,700
Elbasan	80,700
Korçë	63,600
Shkodër	79,900
• TIRANË	238,100
Vlorë	71,700

ALGERIA / Algérie / Djazaïr

1987 C	23,038,942
Aïn el Beïda	61,997
Aïn Oussera	44,270
Aïn Témouchent	47,479
Annaba (Bône)	305,526
Bab Ezzouar (★ El Djazaïr)	55,211
Barika	56,488
Batna	181,601
Béchar	107,311
Bejaïa (Bougie)	114,534
Beskra	128,281
Bordj Bou Arrerid	84,264
Bordj el Kiffan (★ El Djazaïr)	61,035
Boufarik	41,305
Bou Saâda	66,688
Ech Cheliff (Orléansville)	129,976
El Boulaïda	170,935
• EL DJAZAÏR (ALGIERS) (★ 2,547,983)	1,507,241
El Djelfa	84,207
El Eulma	67,933
El Wad	70,073
Ghardaïa	89,415
Ghilizane	80,091
Guelma	77,821
Jijel	62,793
Khemis	55,335
Khenchla	69,743
Laghouat	67,214
Lemdiyya	85,195
Maghniyya	52,275
Messaad	47,460
Mestghanem	114,037
Mouaskar	64,691
M'Sila	65,805
Qacentina	440,842
Saïda	80,825
Sidi bel Abbès	152,778
Skikda	128,747
Souq Ahras	83,015
Stif	170,182
Tbessa	107,559
Tihert	95,821
Tilimsen	126,882
Tizi-Ouzou	61,163
Touggourt	70,645
Wahran	628,558
Wargla	81,721

AMERICAN SAMOA / Amerika Samoa

1980 C	32,279
• PAGO PAGO	3,075

ANDORRA

1991 E	54,507
• ANDORRA	20,437

ANGOLA

1989 E	9,739,100
Benguela (1983 E)	155,000
Huambo (Nova Lisboa) (1983 E)	203,000
Lobito (1983 E)	150,000
• LUANDA	1,459,900
Lubango (1984 E)	95,915
Namibe (1981 E)	100,000

ANGUILLA

1984 C	6,680
South Hill	961
• THE VALLEY	1,042

ANTIGUA AND BARBUDA

1977 E	72,000
• SAINT JOHN'S	24,359

ARGENTINA

1991 C	32,608,687
Almirante Brown (★ Buenos Aires)	449,105
Avellaneda (★ Buenos Aires)	346,620
Bahía Blanca (1980 C)	223,818
Berazategui (★ Buenos Aires)	243,690
Berisso (★ Buenos Aires)	74,012
• BUENOS AIRES (★ 10,800,000)	2,960,976
Campana (★ Buenos Aires) (1980 C)	54,832
Caseros (Tres de Febrero) (★ Buenos Aires)	349,221
Comodoro Rivadavia (1980 C)	96,817
Concordia (1980 C)	94,222
Córdoba (★ 1,260,000)	1,179,067
Corrientes (1980 C)	180,612
Ensenada (★ Buenos Aires)	48,524
Esteban Echeverría (★ Buenos Aires)	276,017
Florencio Varela (★ Buenos Aires)	253,554
Formosa (1980 C)	93,603
General San Martín (★ Buenos Aires)	407,506
General Sarmiento (San Miguel) (★ Buenos Aires)	646,891
Godoy Cruz (★ Mendoza)	179,502
Gualeguaychú (1980 C)	51,400
Junín (1980 C)	62,458
Lanús (★ Buenos Aires)	466,755
La Plata (★ Buenos Aires)	542,567
La Rioja (1980 C)	67,043
Las Heras (★ Mendoza) (1980 C)	101,579
Lomas de Zamora (★ Buenos Aires)	572,769
Mar del Plata (1980 C)	414,696
Mendoza (★ 650,000)	121,696
Mercedes (1980 C)	50,992
Merlo (★ Buenos Aires)	390,031
Moreno (★ Buenos Aires)	287,188
Morón (★ Buenos Aires)	641,541
Necochea (1980 C)	51,069
Neuquén (1980 C)	90,089
Olavarría (1980 C)	64,097
Paraná (1980 C)	161,638
Pergamino (1980 C)	68,612
Pilar (★ Buenos Aires)	130,177
Posadas (1980 C)	143,889
Presidencia Roque Sáenz Peña (1980 C)	49,341
Punta Alta (1980 C)	56,620
Quilmes (★ Buenos Aires)	509,445
Rafaela (1980 C)	53,273
Resistencia (1980 C)	220,104
Río Cuarto (1980 C)	110,254
Rosario (★ 1,190,000)	1,078,374
Salta (1980 C)	260,744
San Carlos de Bariloche (1980 C)	48,980
San Fernando (★ Buenos Aires)	144,761
San Fernando del Valle de Catamarca (★ 90,000) (1980 C)	78,799
San Francisco (★ 58,536) (1980 C)	51,932
San Isidro (★ Buenos Aires)	299,022
San Juan (★ 300,000)	119,399
San Justo (★ Buenos Aires)	1,121,164
San Lorenzo (★ Rosario) (1980 C)	96,891
San Luis (1980 C)	70,999
San Miguel de Tucumán (★ 525,000) (1980 C)	392,888
San Nicolás de los Arroyos (1980 C)	98,495
San Rafael (1980 C)	70,959
San Salvador de Jujuy (1980 C)	124,950
Santa Fe (1980 C)	292,165
Santiago del Estero (★ 200,000) (1980 C)	148,758
San Vincente (★ Buenos Aires)	74,890
Tandil (1980 C)	79,429
Tigre (★ Buenos Aires)	256,005
Trelew (1980 C)	52,372
Vicente López (★ Buenos Aires)	289,142
Villa Krause (★ San Juan) (1980 C)	66,693
Villa María (1980 C)	67,560
Villa Nueva (★ Mendoza)	222,081
Zárate (1980 C)	67,143

ARMENIA / Hayastan

1989 C	3,283,000
Abovjan (1987 E)	53,000
Ečmiadzin (★ Jerevan) (1987 E)	53,000
• JEREVAN (★ 1,315,000)	1,199,000
Kirovakan (1987 E)	169,000
Kumajri	120,000
Razdan (1987 E)	56,000

ARUBA

1987 E	64,763
• ORANJESTAD	19,800

AUSTRALIA

1989 E	16,833,100
Adelaide (★ 1,036,747)	12,340
Albury (★ 66,530)	40,730
Auburn (★ Sydney)	49,950
Ballarat (★ 80,090)	36,680
Bankstown (★ Sydney)	158,750
Bayswater (★ Perth)	46,426
Bendigo (★ 67,920)	32,050
Berwick (★ Melbourne)	64,100
Blacktown (★ Sydney)	210,900
Blue Mountains (★ Sydney)	70,800
Box Hill (★ Melbourne)	47,700
Brisbane (★ 1,273,511)	744,828
Broadmeadows (★ Melbourne)	105,500
Brunswick (★ Melbourne)	41,100
Camberwell (★ Melbourne)	87,700
Campbelltown (★ Sydney)	139,500
CANBERRA (★ 271,362) (1986 C)	247,194
Canning (★ Perth)	69,104
Canterbury (★ Sydney)	135,200
Caulfield (★ Melbourne)	70,100
Coburg (★ Melbourne)	54,500
Cockburn (★ Perth)	49,802
Coffs Harbour	47,890
Dandenong (★ Melbourne)	59,400
Darwin (★ 73,300)	63,900
Doncaster (★ Melbourne)	107,300
Enfield (★ Adelaide)	64,058
Essendon (★ Melbourne)	55,300
Fairfield (★ Sydney)	176,350
Footscray (★ Melbourne)	48,700
Frankston (★ Melbourne)	90,500
Geelong (★ 148,980)	13,190
Gosford	126,600
Gosnells (★ Perth)	71,862
Heidelberg (★ Melbourne)	63,500
Hobart (★ 181,210)	47,280
Holroyd (★ Sydney)	82,500
Hurstville (★ Sydney)	66,350
Ipswich (★ Brisbane)	75,283
Keilor (★ Melbourne)	103,700
Knox (★ Melbourne)	121,300
Kogarah (★ Sydney)	47,850
Lake Macquarie (★ Newcastle)	161,700
Launceston (★ 92,350)	32,150
Leichhardt (★ Sydney)	58,950
Liverpool (★ Sydney)	99,750
Logan (★ Brisbane)	142,222
Mackay (★ 50,885)	22,583
Malvern (★ Melbourne)	43,400
Marion (★ Adelaide)	74,631
Marrickville (★ Sydney)	84,650
Melbourne (★ 3,039,100)	55,300
Melville (★ Perth)	85,590
Mitcham (★ Adelaide)	63,301
Moorabbin (★ Melbourne)	98,900
Newcastle (★ 425,610)	130,940
Noarlunga (★ Adelaide)	77,352
Northcote (★ Melbourne)	49,100
North Sydney (★ Sydney)	53,400
Nunawading (★ Melbourne)	96,400
Oakleigh (★ Melbourne)	57,600
Parramatta (★ Sydney)	134,600
Penrith (★ Sydney)	152,650
Perth (★ 1,158,387)	82,413
Prahran (★ Melbourne)	43,900
Preston (★ Melbourne)	82,000
Randwick (★ Sydney)	119,200
Redcliffe (★ Brisbane)	48,123
Rockdale (★ Sydney)	88,200
Rockhampton (★ 61,694)	58,890
Ryde (★ Sydney)	94,400
Saint Kilda (★ Melbourne)	46,400
Salisbury (★ Adelaide)	106,129
Shoalhaven	64,070
Southport (★ 254,861)	135,408
South Sydney (★ Sydney)	74,100
Springvale (★ Melbourne)	88,700
Stirling (★ Perth)	181,556
Sunshine (★ Melbourne)	97,700
• Sydney (★ 3,623,550)	9,800
Tea Tree Gully (★ Adelaide)	82,324
Toowoomba	81,071
Townsville (★ 111,972)	83,339
Wagga Wagga	52,180
Wanneroo (★ Perth)	163,324
Waverley (★ Melbourne)	126,300
Waverley (★ Sydney)	61,850
West Torrens (★ Adelaide)	44,711
Willoughby (★ Sydney)	53,950
Wollongong (★ 236,690)	174,770
Woodville (★ Adelaide)	82,590
Woollahra (★ Sydney)	53,850

AUSTRIA / Österreich

1991 C	7,812,100
Bruck an der Mur (★ 52,000)	14,155
Graz (★ 325,000)	232,155
Innsbruck (★ 185,000)	114,996
Klagenfurt (★ 115,000)	89,502
Leoben (★ 52,000)	28,504
Linz (★ 335,000)	202,855
Neunkirchen (★ 45,000)	10,334
Salzburg (★ 220,000)	143,971
Sankt Pölten (★ 67,000)	49,805
Steyr (★ 65,000)	39,542
Villach (★ 65,000)	55,165
Wels (★ 76,000)	53,042
• WIEN (VIENNA) (★ 1,875,000)	1,533,176

AZERBAIJAN

1991 E	7,136,600
Ali-Bajramly	61,500
• BAKU (BAKY) (★ 2,020,000)	1,080,500
Gjandža	282,200
Mingečaur	90,900
Nachičevan'	61,700
Šeki (Nucha)	63,200
Stepanakert	55,200
Sumgait (★ Baku)	236,200

BAHAMAS

1990 C	254,685
Freeport (▲ 171,542)	28,200
• NASSAU	141,000

BAHRAIN / Al-Baḥrayn

1988 E	473,000
• AL-MANĀMAH (★ 273,000) (1986 E)	82,700
Al-Muḥarraq (★ Al-Manāmah)	78,000
Jidd Ḥafṣ (★ Al-Manāmah)	48,000

BANGLADESH

1981 C	87,119,965
Barisāl	172,905
Begamganj	69,623
Bhairab Bāzār	63,563
Bogra	68,749
Brāhmanbāria	87,570
Chāndpur	85,656
Chittagong (★ 1,391,877)	980,000
Chuādanga	76,000
Comilla	184,132
• DHAKA (DACCA) (★ 3,430,312)	2,365,695
Dinājpur	96,718
Farīdpur	66,579
Gopālpur	31,725
Gulshan (★ Dhaka)	215,444
Jamālpur	91,815
Jessore	148,927
Jhenida	47,953
Khulna	648,359
Kishorganj	52,302
Kurīgrām	47,641
Kushtia	74,892
Mādārīpur	63,917
Mīrpur (★ Dhaka)	349,031
Mymensingh	190,991
Naogaon	52,975
Nārāyanganj (★ Dhaka)	405,562
Narsinghdi	76,841
Nawābganj	87,724
Noākhāli	59,065
Pābna	109,065
Patuākhāli	48,121
Rājshāhi	253,740
Rangpur	153,174
Saidpur	126,608
Sātkhira	52,156
Sherpur	48,214
Sirājganj	106,774
Sītākunda (★ Chittagong)	237,520
Sylhet	168,371
Tangail	77,518
Tongi (★ Dhaka)	94,580

BARBADOS

1980 C	244,228
• BRIDGETOWN (★ 115,000)	7,466

BELARUS

1991 E	10,260,400
Baranoviči	166,700
Bobrujsk	223,000
Borisov	150,200
Brest	277,000
Gomel'	503,300
Grodno	284,800
Lida	95,000
• MINSK (★ 1,694,000)	1,633,600
Mogil'ov	363,000
Molodečno	93,500
Mozyr'	103,000
Novopolock	96,600
Orša	125,300
Pinsk	123,800
Polock	78,700
Rečica	69,400
Sluck	60,100
Soligorsk	96,000
Vitebsk	361,500
Žlobin	60,800
Žodino	56,000

BELGIUM / België / Belgique

1987 E	9,864,751
Aalst (Alost) (★ Bruxelles)	77,113
Anderlecht (★ Bruxelles)	88,849
Antwerpen (★ 1,100,000)	479,748
Bastogne (▲ 11,699)	6,900
Brugge (Bruges) (★ 223,000)	117,755
• BRUXELLES (★ 2,385,000)	136,920
Charleroi (★ 480,000)	209,395
Etterbeek (★ Bruxelles)	44,240
Forest (★ Bruxelles)	48,266
Genk (★ Hasselt)	61,391
Gent (Gand) (★ 465,000)	233,856
Hasselt (★ 290,000)	65,563
Ixelles (★ Bruxelles)	76,241
Kortrijk (Courtrai) (★ 202,000)	76,216
La Louvière (★ 147,000)	76,340
Leuven (Louvain) (★ 173,000)	84,583
Liège (Luik) (★ 750,000)	200,891
Mechelen (Malines) (★ 121,000)	75,808
Molenbeek-St.-Jean (★ Bruxelles)	69,764
Mons (Bergen) (★ 242,000)	89,697
Mouscron (★ Lille, France)	53,713
Namur (★ 147,000)	102,670
Oostende (Ostende) (★ 122,000)	68,318
Roeselare (Roulers)	51,963
Saint-Gilles (★ Bruxelles)	42,482
Schaerbeek (★ Bruxelles)	104,919
Seraing (★ Liège)	61,731
Sint-Niklaas (Saint-Nicolas)	68,082
Spa	9,645
Tournai (Doornik) (▲ 66,998)	44,900
Uccle (★ Bruxelles)	75,876
Verviers (★ 101,000)	53,498
Waterloo (★ Bruxelles)	25,232
Woluwe-Saint-Lambert (Sint-Lambrechts-Woluwe) (★ Bruxelles)	47,887

BELIZE

1990 C	184,340
• Belize City	43,621
BELMOPAN	5,256

BENIN / Bénin

1984 E	3,825,000
Abomey	53,000
• COTONOU	478,000
Parakou	92,000
PORTO-NOVO	164,000

C Census. E Official estimate. U Unofficial estimate.
• Largest city in country.

★ Population or designation of metropolitan area, including suburbs (see headnote).
▲ Population of an entire municipality, commune, or district, including rural area.

BERMUDA

1985 E 56,000
• HAMILTON (★ 15,000) 1,676

BHUTAN / Druk-Yul

1982 E 1,333,000
• THIMPHU 12,000

BOLIVIA

1990 E 7,314,000
Cochabamba 413,300
• LA PAZ 1,125,600
Montero
Oruro 207,700
Potosí 120,100
Santa Cruz de la Sierra 696,100
SUCRE 101,400
Tarija 74,600
Trinidad 51,900

BOPHUTHATSWANA

1987 E 1,819,242
• Ga-Rankuwa (1980 C) 48,300
Mafikeng (★ 16,000) (1980 C) 6,500
MMABATHO (★ Mafikeng) (1977 E) 9,062

BOSNIA AND HERZEGOVINA / Bosna i Hercegovina

1987 E 4,400,464
Banja Luka (▲ 193,890) 130,900
• SARAJEVO (▲ 479,688) 341,200
Tuzla (▲ 129,967) 67,300
Zenica (▲ 144,869) 67,500

BOTSWANA

1991 C 1,325,291
Francistown 65,026
• GABORONE 133,791
Selebi Phikwe 39,769

BRAZIL / Brasil

1985 E 135,564,395
Alagoinhas (▲ 116,959) 87,500
Alegrete (▲ 71,898) 56,700
Alvorada (★ Porto Alegre) (1989 E) 115,465
Americana 156,030
Anápolis 225,840
Apucarana (▲ 92,812) 73,700
Aracaju 360,013
Araçatuba 129,304
Araguari (▲ 96,035) 84,300
Arapiraca (▲ 147,879) 91,400
Araraquara (▲ 145,042) 87,500
Araras (▲ 71,652) 59,900
Araxá 61,418
Assis (▲ 74,238) 63,100
Atibaia (▲ 81,263) (1989 E) 64,200
Bacabal (▲ 97,633) (1989 E) 51,600
Bagé (▲ 106,155) 70,800
Barbacena (▲ 99,337) 80,200
Barra do Piraí (▲ 78,189) 55,700
Barra Mansa (★ Volta Redonda) 149,200
Barretos 80,202
Bauru 220,105
Bayeux (★ João Pessoa) 67,182
Belém (★ 1,200,000) 1,116,578
Belford Roxo (★ Rio de Janeiro) 340,700
Belo Horizonte (★ 2,950,000) 2,114,429
Betim (★ Belo Horizonte) 96,810
Birigui (▲ 71,527) (1989 E) 63,660
Blumenau 192,074
Boa Vista (▲ 74,493) (1989 E) 48,700
Botucatu (▲ 71,139) 62,600
Bragança Paulista (▲ 105,099) 76,300
BRASÍLIA 1,567,709
Cabo (▲ 134,748) (1989 E) 62,000
Caçapava (▲ 64,213) 56,600
Cáceres (▲ 92,370) (1989 E) 51,700
Cachoeira do Sul (▲ 91,492) 58,900
Cachoeirinha (★ Porto Alegre) 73,117
Cachoeiro de Itapemirim (▲ 138,156) 95,000
Campina Grande 279,929
Campinas (★ 1,125,000) 841,016
Campo Grande 384,398
Campos (▲ 366,716) 187,900
Campos Elísios (★ Rio de Janeiro) 188,200
Canoas (★ Porto Alegre) 261,222
Carapicuíba (★ São Paulo) 265,856
Carazinho (▲ 62,108) 48,500
Cariacica (★ Vitória) 74,300
Carpina (▲ 71,753) (1989 E) 48,000
Caruaru (▲ 190,794) 152,100
Cascavel (▲ 200,485) 123,100
Castanhal (▲ 89,703) 71,200
Cataguases (▲ 62,080) (1989 E) 50,900
Catanduva (▲ 80,309) 71,400
Caucaia (★ Fortaleza) 78,500
Cavaleiro (★ Recife) 106,600
Caxias (▲ 148,230) 66,300
Caxias do Sul 266,809
Chapecó (▲ 100,997) 64,200
Coelho da Rocha (★ Rio de Janeiro) 164,400
Colatina (▲ 106,260) 58,600
Colombo (★ Curitiba) 65,900
Conselheiro Lafaiete 77,958
Contagem (★ Belo Horizonte) 152,700
Corumbá (▲ 80,666) 65,800
Crato (▲ 86,371) 52,700
Criciúma (▲ 128,410) 85,900
Cruz Alta (▲ 71,817) 58,300
Cruzeiro 63,918
Cubatão (★ Santos) 98,322
Cuiabá (▲ 279,651) 220,400
Curitiba (★ 1,700,000) 1,279,205
Diadema (★ São Paulo) 320,187
Divinópolis 139,940
Dourados (▲ 123,757) 89,200
Duque de Caxias (★ Rio de Janeiro) 353,200
Embu (★ São Paulo) 119,791
Erechim (▲ 70,709) 54,300
Esteio (★ Porto Alegre) 58,964
Feira de Santana (▲ 355,201) 278,600
Ferraz de Vasconcelos (★ São Paulo) 68,831
Florianópolis (★ 365,000) 178,400
Fortaleza (★ 1,825,000) 1,582,414
Foz do Iguaçu (▲ 182,101) 124,900
Franca 182,820
Garanhuns 73,100
Goiânia (★ 1,130,000) (1989 E) 1,038,187
Governador Valadares (▲ 216,957) 192,300
Guaratinguetá (▲ 93,534) 80,400
Guarujá (★ Santos) 83,500
Guarulhos (★ São Paulo) 571,700
Ijuí (▲ 82,064) 64,400
Ilhéus (▲ 145,810) 79,400
Imperatriz (▲ 235,453) 119,500
Ipatinga (★ 270,000) 149,100
Ipiíba (★ Rio de Janeiro) 116,200
Itabira (▲ 81,771) 66,300
Itabuna (▲ 167,543) 142,200
Itajaí 104,232
Itajubá (▲ 69,675) 61,500
Itapecerica da Serra (★ São Paulo) 65,500
Itapetininga (▲ 105,512) 76,700
Itapeva (▲ 92,122) (1989 E) 51,400
Itapevi (★ São Paulo) 66,825
Itaquaquecetuba (★ São Paulo) 91,366
Itaquari (★ Vitória) 163,900
Itatiba (▲ 58,508) (1989 E) 49,700
Itaúna 61,446
Itú (▲ 92,786) 77,900
Ituiutaba (▲ 85,365) 74,900
Itumbiara (▲ 78,844) 57,200
Jaboatão (★ Recife) 82,900
Jaboatão (★ Recife) (1989 E) 94,000
Jacareí 149,061
Jataí (▲ 65,383) (1989 E) 49,700
Jaú (▲ 92,547) 74,500
Jequié (▲ 127,070) 92,100
João Monlevade (1989 E) 60,731
João Pessoa (★ 550,000) 348,500
Joinvile 302,877
Juàzeiro (★ Petrolina) 78,600
Juazeiro do Norte 159,806
Juiz de Fora 349,720
Jundiaí (▲ 313,652) 268,900
Lajes (▲ 143,246) 103,600
Lavras 52,100
Leme (▲ 65,006) (1989 E) 55,900
Limeira 186,986
Linhares (▲ 122,453) 53,400
Lins (▲ 59,479) (1989 E) 51,700
Londrina (▲ 346,676) 296,400
Lorena 63,230
Luziânia (▲ 98,408) 71,400
Macapá (▲ 168,839) 109,400
Maceió 482,195
Majé (▲ 225,398) (1989 E) 49,600
Manaus 809,914
Marabá (▲ 133,559) 92,700
Marília (▲ 136,187) 116,100
Maringá 196,871
Mauá (★ São Paulo) 269,321
Mesquita (★ Rio de Janeiro) 161,300
Mogi das Cruzes (▲ 255,636) (★São Paulo) (1989 E) 155,900
Mojiguaçu (▲ 91,994) 81,800
Mojimirim (▲ 63,313) 52,300
Monjolo (★ Rio de Janeiro) 113,900
Montes Claros (▲ 214,472) 183,500
Mossoró (▲ 158,723) 128,300
Muriaé (▲ 80,466) 57,600
Muribeca dos Guararapes (★ Recife) (1989 E) 196,000
Natal 510,106
Neves (★ Rio de Janeiro) 163,600
Nilópolis (★ Rio de Janeiro) 112,800
Niterói (★ Rio de Janeiro) 441,684
Nova Friburgo (▲ 143,529) 103,500
Nova Iguaçu (★ Rio de Janeiro) 592,800
Novo Hamburgo (★ Porto Alegre) 167,744
Olinda (★ Recife) 316,600
Osasco (★ São Paulo) 591,568
Ourinhos (▲ 65,841) 58,100
Paranaguá (▲ 94,809) 82,300
Paranavaí (▲ 75,511) 60,900
Parnaíba (▲ 116,206) 90,200
Parque Industrial (★ Belo Horizonte) 228,400
Passo Fundo (▲ 137,843) 117,500
Passos (▲ 79,393) 65,500
Patos 74,298
Patos de Minas (▲ 99,027) 69,000
Paulo Afonso (▲ 86,182) 75,300
Pelotas (▲ 277,730) 210,300
Petrolina (★ 225,000) 92,100
Petrópolis (▲ 284,535) (★Rio de Janeiro) (1989 E) 173,600
Pindamonhangaba (▲ 86,990) 64,100
Pinheirinho (★ Curitiba) 51,600
Piracicaba (▲ 252,079) 211,000
Poá (★ São Paulo) 66,006
Poços de Caldas 100,004
Ponta Grossa 223,154
Porto Alegre (★ 2,600,000) 1,272,121
Porto Velho (▲ 202,011) 152,700
Pouso Alegre (▲ 65,958) 58,300
Praia Grande (★ Santos) 67,800
Presidente Prudente 155,883
Queimados (★ Rio de Janeiro) 113,700
Recife (★ 2,625,000) 1,287,623
Ribeirão Preto 383,125
Rio Branco (▲ 145,486) 109,800
Rio Claro 129,859
Rio de Janeiro (★ 10,150,000) 5,603,388
Rio do Sul (1989 E) 48,860
Rio Grande 164,221
Rio Verde (▲ 92,954) 59,400
Rondonópolis (▲ 101,642) 65,500
Salto (1989 E) 59,561
Salvador (★ 2,050,000) 1,804,438
Santa Bárbara d'Oeste 95,818
Santa Cruz do Sul (▲ 115,288) 60,300
Santa Maria (▲ 196,827) 163,900
Santana do Livramento (▲ 70,489) 60,100
Santarém (▲ 226,618) 120,800
Santa Rita (★ João Pessoa) 60,100
Santa Rosa (▲ 66,925) (1989 E) 51,500
Santo André (★ São Paulo) 635,129
Santo Angelo (▲ 107,559) 57,700
Santos (★ 1,065,000) 460,100
São Bernardo do Campo (★ São Paulo) 562,485
São Borja (▲ 71,317) (1989 E) 50,600
São Caetano do Sul (★ São Paulo) 171,005
São Carlos 140,383
São Gonçalo (★ Rio de Janeiro) 262,400
São João da Boa Vista (▲ 61,653) 50,400
São João del-Rei (▲ 74,385) 61,400
São João de Meriti (★ Rio de Janeiro) 241,700
São José do Rio Preto 229,221
São José dos Campos 372,578
São José dos Pinhais (★ Curitiba) 64,100
São Leopoldo (★ Porto Alegre) 114,065
São Lourenco da Mata (★ Recife) 65,936
São Luís (★ 600,000) 227,900
• São Paulo (★ 15,175,000) 10,063,110
São Vicente (★ Santos) 239,778
Sapucaia do Sul (★ Porto Alegre) 91,820
Sertãozinho (▲ 72,441) (1989 E) 60,100
Sete Lagoas 121,418
Sete Pontes (★ Rio de Janeiro) 72,300
Sobral (▲ 112,275) 69,400
Sorocaba 327,468
Susano (★ São Paulo) 128,924
Taboão da Serra (★ São Paulo) 122,112
Tatuí (▲ 69,358) 56,000
Taubaté 205,120
Teófilo Otoni (▲ 126,265) 82,700
Teresina (★ 525,000) 425,300
Teresópolis (▲ 115,859) 92,600
Timon (★ Teresina) 68,300
Três Rios (▲ 93,902) (1989 E) 61,900
Tubarão (▲ 82,082) 70,400
Tupã (▲ 65,867) (1989 E) 51,400
Ubá (▲ 67,166) (1989 E) 53,700
Uberaba 244,875
Uberlândia 312,024
Uruguaiana (▲ 105,862) 91,500
Varginha 74,630
Várzea Grande (▲ 124,188) (1989 E) 64,600
Vicente de Carvalho (★ Santos) 102,700
Vila Velha (★ Vitória) 91,900
Vitória (★ 735,000) 201,500
Vitória da Conquista (▲ 198,150) 145,800
Vitória de Santo Antão (▲ 100,450) 67,800
Volta Redonda (★ 375,000) 219,267

BRITISH VIRGIN ISLANDS

1980 C 12,034
• ROAD TOWN 2,479

BRUNEI

1981 C 192,832
• BANDAR SERI BEGAWAN (★ 64,000) 22,777
Seria 23,415

BULGARIA / Bâlgarija

1989 E 8,986,636
Asenovgrad
Blagoevgrad 74,236
Burgas 200,464
Dimitrovgrad 57,102
Dobrič 112,582
Gabrovo 80,930
Haskovo 93,609
Jambol 97,414
Kârdžali 58,995
Kazanlâk 63,776
Kjustendil 55,620
Loveč 50,872
Mihajlovgrad 55,203
Pazardžik 83,451
Pernik 97,930
Pleven 136,287
Plovdiv 364,162
Razgrad 56,494
Ruse 190,720
Silistra 56,907
Sliven 109,432
• SOFIJA (★ 1,205,000) 1,136,875
Stara Zagora 158,151
Šumen 107,973
Varna 306,300
Veliko Târnovo 71,709
Vidin 65,892
Vraca 81,992

BURKINA FASO

1985 C 7,964,705
Bobo Dioulasso 228,668
Koudougou 51,926
• OUAGADOUGOU 441,514
Ouahigouya 38,902

BURMA / Myanmar

1983 C 34,124,908
Bago (Pegu) 150,528
Chauk 51,437
Dawei (Tavoy) 69,882
Henzada 82,005
Kale 52,628
Lashio 88,590
Magway 54,881
Mandalay 532,949
Mawlamyine (Moulmein) 219,961
Maymyo 63,782
Meiktila 96,496
Mergui (Myeik) 88,600
Mogok 49,392
Monywa 106,843
Myingyan 77,060
Myitkyinā 56,427
Nyaunglebin 55,194
Pakokku 71,860
Pathein (Bassein) 144,096
Prome (Pyè) 83,332
Pyinmana 52,962
Sagaing 46,212
Shwebo 52,185
Sittwe (Akyab) 107,621
Taunggyi 108,231
Thaton 61,790
Toungoo 65,861
• YANGON (RANGOON) (★ 2,800,000) 2,705,039
Yenangyaung 62,582

BURUNDI

1990 C 5,356,266
• BUJUMBURA 226,628

CAMBODIA / Kâmpŭchéa

1990 E 8,567,582
Bătdâmbâng 94,412
Kâmpóng Saôm 67,452
• PHNUM PENH 477,874
Prey Vêng 41,456
Siĕmréab 76,434
Sisŏphŏn 67,041
Ta Khmau 34,947

CAMEROON / Cameroun

1986 E 10,446,409
Bafoussam (1985 E) 89,000
Bamenda (1985 E) 72,000
• Douala 1,029,731
Foumban (1985 E) 50,000
Garoua (1985 E) 96,000
Kumba (1985 E) 67,000
Maroua 103,653
Ngaoundéré (1985 E) 61,000
Nkongsamba 123,149
YAOUNDE 653,670

CANADA

1986 C 25,354,064

CANADA: ALBERTA

1986 C 2,375,278
Calgary (★ 671,326) 636,104
Edmonton (★ 785,465) 573,982
Lethbridge 58,841
Medicine Hat (★ 50,734) 41,804
Red Deer 54,425

CANADA: BRITISH COLUMBIA

1986 C 2,889,207
Burnaby (★ Vancouver) 145,161
Coquitlam (★ Vancouver) (1991 C) 84,021
Delta (★ Vancouver) (1991 C) 88,978
Kamloops 61,773
Kelowna (★ 89,730) 61,213
Matsqui (★ 88,420) 51,449
Nanaimo (★ 60,420) 49,029
Prince George 67,621
Richmond (★ Vancouver) 108,492
Saanich (★ Victoria) (1991 C) 95,577
Surrey (★ Vancouver) (1991 C) 245,173
Vancouver (★ 1,380,729) 431,147
Victoria (★ 255,547) 66,303

CANADA: MANITOBA

1986 C 1,071,232
Winnipeg (★ 625,304) 594,551

CANADA: NEW BRUNSWICK

1986 C 710,422
Fredericton (★ 65,768) 44,352
Moncton (★ 102,084) 55,468
Saint John (★ 121,265) 76,381

CANADA: NEWFOUNDLAND

1986 C 568,349
Saint John's (★ 161,901) 96,216

CANADA: NORTHWEST TERRITORIES

1986 C 52,238
Yellowknife 11,753

CANADA: NOVA SCOTIA

1986 C 873,199
Dartmouth (★ Halifax) 65,243
Halifax (★ 295,990) 113,577
Sydney (★ 119,470) 27,754

CANADA: ONTARIO

1986 C 9,113,515
Barrie (★ 67,703) 48,287
Brampton (★ Toronto) 188,498
Brantford (★ 90,521) 76,146
Burlington (★ Hamilton) 116,675
Cambridge (Galt) (★ Kitchener) 79,920
Cornwall (★ 51,719) 46,425
East York (★ Toronto) 101,085
Etobicoke (★ Toronto) 302,973
Gloucester (★ Ottawa) 89,810
Guelph (★ 85,962) 78,235
Hamilton (★ 557,029) 306,728
Kingston (★ 122,350) 55,050
Kitchener (★ 311,195) 150,604
London (★ 342,302) 269,140
Markham (★ Toronto) 114,597
Mississauga (★ Toronto) 374,005
Nepean (★ Ottawa) 95,490
Niagara Falls (★ Saint Catharines) 72,107
North Bay (★ 57,422) 50,623
North York (★ Toronto) 556,297
Oakville (★ Toronto) 87,107
Oshawa (★ 203,543) 123,651
OTTAWA (★ 819,263) 300,763
Peterborough (★ 87,083) 61,049
Saint Catharines (★ 343,258) 123,455
Sarnia (★ 85,700) 49,033
Sault Sainte Marie (★ 101,800) (1991 C) 81,476
Scarborough (★ Toronto) 484,676

C Census. E Official estimate. U Unofficial estimate.
• Largest city in country.
★ Population or designation of metropolitan area, including suburbs (see headnote).
▲ Population of an entire municipality, commune, or district, including rural area.

Sudbury (★ 148,877) 88,717
Thunder Bay (★ 122,217) 112,272
• Toronto (★ 3,427,168) 612,289
Vaughan (★ Toronto) 65,058
Waterloo (★ Kitchener) 58,718
Windsor (★ 253,988) 193,111
York (★ Toronto) 135,401

CANADA: PRINCE EDWARD ISLAND

1986 C 126,646

Charlottetown (★ 53,868) 15,776

CANADA: QUÉBEC

1986 C 6,540,276

Beauport (★ Québec) 62,869
Brossard (★ Montréal) 57,441
Charlesbourg (★ Québec) 68,996
Chicoutimi (★ 158,468) 61,083
Drummondville (★ 56,283) 36,020
Gatineau (★ Ottawa) 81,244
Hull (★ Ottawa) 58,722
Jonquière (★ Chicoutimi) 58,467
La Salle (★ Montréal) 75,621
Laval (★ Montréal) 284,164
Longueuil (★ Montréal) 125,441
Montréal (★ 2,921,357) 1,015,420
Montréal-Nord (★ Montréal) 90,303
Québec (★ 603,267) 164,580
Sainte-Foy (★ Québec) 69,615
Saint-Hubert (★ Montréal) 66,218
Saint-Jean-sur-Richelieu (★ 59,958) 34,745
Saint-Laurent (★ Montréal) 67,002
Saint-Léonard (★ Montréal) 75,947
Shawinigan (★ 61,965) 21,470
Sherbrooke (★ 129,960) 74,438
Trois-Rivières (★ 128,888) 50,122
Verdun (★ Montréal) 60,246

CANADA: SASKATCHEWAN

1986 C 1,010,198

Regina (★ 186,521) 175,064
Saskatoon (★ 200,665) 177,641

CANADA: YUKON

1986 C 23,504

Whitehorse 15,199

CAPE VERDE / Cabo Verde

1990 C 341,491

Mindelo 47,109
• PRAIA 61,644

CAYMAN ISLANDS

1988 E 25,900

• GEORGE TOWN 13,700

CENTRAL AFRICAN REPUBLIC / République centrafricaine

1984 E 2,517,000

• BANGUI 473,817
Bouar (1982 E) 48,000

CHAD / Tchad

1988 E 5,428,000

Abéché 40,000
Moundou 100,000
• N'DJAMENA 500,000
Sarh 76,835

CHILE

1982 C 11,329,736

Antofagasta (1990 E) 218,800
Apoquindo (★ Santiago) 175,735
Arica (1990 E) 177,300
Calama 81,684
Cerrillos (★ Santiago) 67,013
Cerro Navia (★ Santiago) 137,777
Chillán (1990 E) 146,000
Concepción (★ 710,000) (1990 E) 306,500
Conchalí (★ Santiago) 157,884
Copiapó 69,045
Coquimbo 62,186
Coronel (★ Concepción) 65,918
Curicó 60,550
El Bosque (★ Santiago) 143,717
Huechuraba (★ Santiago) 56,313
Independencia (★ Santiago) 86,724
Iquique (1990 E) 148,500
La Cisterna (★ Santiago) 95,863
La Florida (★ Santiago) 191,883
La Granja (★ Santiago) 109,168
La Pintana (★ Santiago) 73,932
La Reina (★ Santiago) 80,452
La Serena (1990 E) 105,600
Las Rejas (★ Santiago) 147,918
Linares 46,433
Lo Espejo (★ Santiago) 124,462
Lo Prado (★ Santiago) 103,575
Los Ángeles 70,529
Lota (★ Concepción) 47,133
Macul (★ Santiago) 113,100
Maipú (★ Santiago) 114,117
Ñuñoa (★ Santiago) 168,919
Osorno (1990 E) 117,400
Ovalle 43,023
Pedro Aguirre Cerda (★ Santiago) 145,207
Peñalolén (★ Santiago) 137,298
Providencia (★ Santiago) 115,449
Pudahuel (★ Santiago) 97,578
Puente Alto (★ Santiago) (1990 E) 187,400
Puerto Montt (1990 E) 106,500
Punta Arenas (1990 E) 120,000
Quilpué (★ Valparaíso) (1990 E) 107,400
Quinta Normal (★ Santiago) 128,989
Rancagua (1990 E) 190,400
Recoleta (★ Santiago) 164,292
Renca (★ Santiago) 93,928
San Antonio 61,486
San Bernardo (★ Santiago) (1990 E) 188,200
San Joaquín (★ Santiago) 123,904
San Miguel (★ Santiago) 88,764
San Ramón (★ Santiago) 99,410
• SANTIAGO (★ 4,100,000) 232,667
Talca (1990 E) 164,500
Talcahuano (★ Concepción) (1990 E) 246,900
Temuco (1990 E) 211,700
Valdivia (1990 E) 113,500
Vallenar 38,375
Valparaíso (★ 690,000) (1990 E) 276,800
Villa Alemana (★ Valparaíso) 55,766
Viña del Mar (★ Valparaíso) (1990 E) 281,100
Vitacura (★ Santiago) 72,038

CHINA / Zhongguo

1988 E 1,103,983,000

Abagnar Qi (▲ 100,700) (1986 E) 71,700
Acheng (1985 E) 100,304
Aihui (▲ 135,000) (1986 E) 76,700
Aksu (▲ 345,900) (1986 E) 143,100
Altay (▲ 141,700) (1986 E) 62,800
Anci (Langfang) (▲ 522,800) (1986 E) 122,100
Anda (▲ 425,500) (1986 E) 130,200
Ankang (1985 E) 89,188
Anqing (▲ 433,900) (1986 E) 213,200
Anshan 1,330,000
Anshun (▲ 214,700) (1986 E) 128,800
Anyang (▲ 541,900) (1986 E) 361,200
Baicheng (▲ 282,000) (1986 E) 198,600
Baiquan (1985 E) 50,996
Baiyin (▲ 301,900) (1986 E) 157,100
Baoding (▲ 535,100) (1986 E) 423,200
Baoji (▲ 359,500) (1986 E) 286,200
Baoshan (▲ 688,400) (1986 E) 52,300
Baotou (Paotow) 1,130,000
Baoying (1985 E) 50,479
Bei'an (▲ 440,500) (1986 E) 199,500
Beihai (▲ 175,900) (1986 E) 119,000
BEIJING (PEKING) (★ 7,200,000) 6,710,000
Beipiao (▲ 603,700) (1986 E) 180,900
Bengbu (▲ 612,600) (1986 E) 403,900
Benxi (Penhsi) 860,000
Bijie (1985 E) 54,871
Binxian (▲ 177,900) (1986 E) 86,700
Binxian (1982 C) 127,326
Boli (1985 E) 61,990
Bose (▲ 271,400) (1986 E) 82,000
Boshan (1975 U) 100,000
Boxian (1985 E) 63,222
Boxing (1982 C) 57,554
Boyang (1985 E) 60,688
Butha Qi (Zalantun) (▲ 389,500) (1986 E) 111,300
Cangshan (Bianzhuang) (1982 C) 79,334
Cangzhou (▲ 293,600) (1986 E) 196,700
Changchun (▲ 2,000,000) 1,822,000
Changde (▲ 220,800) (1986 E) 178,200
Changge (1982 C) 67,002
Changji (▲ 233,400) (1986 E) 110,500
Changqing (1982 C) 65,094
Changsha 1,230,000
Changshou (1985 E) 51,923
Changshu (▲ 998,000) (1986 E) 281,300
Changtu (1985 E) 49,937
Changyi (1982 C) 64,513
Changzhi (▲ 463,400) (1986 E) 273,000
Changzhou (Changchow) (1986 E) 522,700
Chao'an (▲ 1,214,500) (1986 E) 265,400
Chaoxian (▲ 739,500) (1986 E) 116,800
Chaoyang, Guangdong prov. (1985 E) 85,968
Chaoyang, Liaoning prov. (▲ 318,900) (1986 E) 180,300
Chengde (▲ 330,400) (1986 E) 226,600
Chengdu (Chengtu) (▲ 2,960,000) 1,884,000
Chenghai (1985 E) 50,631
Chenxian (▲ 191,900) (1986 E) 143,500
Chifeng (Ulanhad) (▲ 882,900) (1986 E) 299,000
Chongqing (Chungking) (▲ 2,890,000) 2,502,000
Chuxian (▲ 365,000) (1986 E) 113,300
Chuxiong (▲ 379,400) (1986 E) 67,700
Da'an (1985 E) 70,552
Dachangzhen (1975 U) 50,000
Dalian (Dairen) 2,280,000
Dandong (1986 E) 579,800
Daqing (▲ 880,000) 640,000
Dashiqiao (1985 E) 68,898
Datong (▲ 1,040,000) 810,000
Datong (1985 E) 55,529
Dawa (1985 E) 142,581
Daxian (▲ 209,400) (1986 E) 142,000
Dehui (1985 E) 60,247
Dengfeng (1982 C) 49,746
Deqing (1982 C) 48,726
Deyang (▲ 753,400) (1986 E) 184,800
Dezhou (▲ 276,200) (1986 E) 161,300
Didao (1975 U) 50,000
Dinghai (1985 E) 50,161
Dongchuan (Xincun) (▲ 275,100) (1986 E) 67,400
Dongguan (▲ 1,208,500) (1986 E) 254,900
Dongsheng (▲ 121,300) (1986 E) 57,500
Dongtai (1985 E) 65,788
Dongying (▲ 514,400) (1986 E) 178,100
Dukou (▲ 551,200) (1986 E) 380,200
Dunhua (▲ 448,000) (1986 E) 217,100
Duyun (▲ 386,600) (1986 E) 123,800
Echeng (▲ 938,000) (1986 E) 217,400
Enshi (▲ 679,000) (1986 E) 84,300
Erenhot (1986 E) 7,200
Ergun Zuoqi (1985 E) 55,970
Feixian (1982 C) 73,246
Fengcheng (1985 E) 66,745
Foshan (▲ 312,700) (1986 E) 243,500
Fujin (1985 E) 60,948
Fuling (▲ 973,500) (1986 E) 166,300
Fushun (Funan) 1,290,000
Fuxian (Wafangdian) (▲ 960,700) (1986 E) 246,200
Fuxin 700,000
Fuyang (▲ 195,200) (1986 E) 143,400
Fuyu, Heilongjiang prov. (1985 E) 48,670
Fuyu, Jilin prov. (1985 E) 98,373
Fuzhou, Fujian prov. (▲ 1,240,000) 910,000
Fuzhou, Jiangxi prov. (▲ 171,800) (1986 E) 106,700
Gaixian (1985 E) 67,587
Ganhe (1985 E) 48,128
Ganzhou (▲ 346,000) (1986 E) 191,600
Gaoqing (Tianzhen) (1982 C) 70,411
Gaoyou (1985 E) 57,844
Gejiu (Kokiu) (▲ 341,700) (1986 E) 193,600
Golmud (1986 E) 60,300
Gongchangling (1982 C) 49,281
Guanghua (▲ 420,000) (1986 E) 104,400
Guangyuan (▲ 805,500) (1986 E) 162,200
Guangzhou (Canton) (▲ 3,420,000) 3,100,000
Guanxian, Shandong prov. (1982 C) 49,782
Guanxian, Sichuan prov. (1985 E) 65,039
Guilin (Kweilin) (▲ 457,500) (1986 E) 324,200
Guixian (1985 E) 61,970
Guiyang (Kweiyang) (▲ 1,430,000) 1,030,000
Haicheng (▲ 984,800) (1986 E) 210,700
Haifeng (1985 E) 50,401
Haikou (▲ 289,600) (1986 E) 209,200
Hailar (▲ 163,549) (1986 E) 180,000
Hailin (1985 E) 58,909
Hailong (Meihekou) (▲ 534,200) (1986 E) 117,500
Hailun (1985 E) 83,448
Haiyang (Dongcun) (1982 C) 77,098
Hami (Kumul) (▲ 270,300) (1986 E) 146,400
Hancheng (▲ 304,200) (1986 E) 66,600
Handan (▲ 1,030,000) 870,000
Hangu (1975 U) 100,000
Hangzhou (Hangchow) 1,290,000
Hanzhong (▲ 415,000) (1986 E) 151,700
Harbin 2,710,000
Hebi (▲ 321,600) (1986 E) 158,500
Hechi (▲ 266,800) (1986 E) 74,400
Hechuan (1985 E) 65,237
Hefei (▲ 930,000) 740,000
Hegang (1986 E) 588,300
Helong (1985 E) 62,665
Hengshui (▲ 286,500) (1986 E) 83,100
Hengyang (▲ 601,300) (1986 E) 419,200
Heshan (▲ 109,600) (1986 E) 42,000
Heze (Caozhou) (▲ 1,001,500) (1986 E) 115,400
Hohhot (▲ 830,000) 670,000
Hongjiang (▲ 67,000) (1986 E) 54,300
Horqin Youyi Qianqi (Ulan Hot) (▲ 192,100) (1986 E) 129,100
Hotan (▲ 122,800) (1986 E) 71,700
Houma (▲ 158,500) (1986 E) 67,000
Huadian (1985 E) 75,183
Huai'an (1985 E) 65,673
Huaibei (▲ 447,200) (1986 E) 252,100
Huaide (▲ 899,400) (1986 E) 187,600
Huaihua (▲ 427,100) (1986 E) 102,000
Huainan (▲ 1,110,000) 700,000
Huaiyin (Wangying) (▲ 382,500) (1986 E) 201,700
Huanan (1985 E) 66,596
Huanggang (1982 C) 65,961
Huangshi (▲ 431,713) (1986 E) 451,900
Huayun (Huarong) (▲ 313,500) (1986 E) 81,000
Huinan (Chaoyang) (1985 E) 52,429
Huizhou (▲ 182,100) (1986 E) 117,000
Hulan (1985 E) 74,989
Hunjiang (Badaojiang) (▲ 687,700) (1986 E) 442,600
Huzhou (▲ 964,400) (1986 E) 208,500
Jiading (1985 E) 60,718
Jiamusi (Kiamusze) (▲ 557,700) (1986 E) 429,800
Ji'an (▲ 184,300) (1986 E) 132,200
Jiangling (1985 E) 77,887
Jiangmen (▲ 231,700) (1986 E) 168,800
Jiangyin (1985 E) 66,476
Jiangyou (1985 E) 72,663
Jian'ou (1985 E) 55,180
Jiaohe (1985 E) 51,504
Jiaojiang (▲ 385,200) (1986 E) 82,300
Jiaoxian (1985 E) 51,869
Jiaozuo (▲ 509,900) (1986 E) 335,400
Jiawang (1975 U) 50,000
Jiaxing (▲ 686,500) (1986 E) 210,200
Jiayuguan (▲ 102,100) (1986 E) 73,800
Jiexiu (1985 E) 51,300
Jieyang (1985 E) 98,531
Jilin (Kirin) 1,200,000
Jinan (Tsinan) (▲ 2,140,000) 1,546,000
Jinchang (Baijiazui) (▲ 136,000) (1986 E) 90,500
Jincheng (▲ 612,700) (1986 E) 99,900
Jingdezhen (Kingtechen) (▲ 569,700) (1986 E) 304,000
Jingmen (▲ 946,500) (1986 E) 227,000
Jinhua (▲ 799,900) (1986 E) 147,800
Jining, Nei Monggol prov. (1986 E) 163,300
Jining, Shandong prov. (▲ 765,700) (1986 E) 222,600
Jinshi (▲ 219,700) (1986 E) 73,700
Jinxi (▲ 634,300) (1986 E) 223,100
Jinxian (1985 E) 95,761
Jinzhou (Chinchou) (▲ 810,000) 710,000
Jishou (▲ 194,500) (1986 E) 59,500
Jishu (1985 E) 75,587
Jiujiang (▲ 382,300) (1986 E) 248,500
Jiuquan (Suzhou) (▲ 269,900) (1986 E) 56,300
Jiutai (1985 E) 63,021
Jixi (▲ 820,000) 700,000
Jixian (1985 E) 59,725
Juancheng (1982 C) 54,110
Junan (Shizilu) (1982 C) 90,222
Junxian (▲ 423,400) (1986 E) 97,000
Juxian (1982 C) 51,666
Kaifeng (▲ 629,100) (1986 E) 458,800
Kaili (▲ 342,100) (1986 E) 96,600
Kaiping (1985 E) 54,145
Kaiyuan (▲ 342,100) (1986 E) 96,600
Kaiyuan (1985 E) 85,762
Karamay (▲ 168,868) (1986 E) 185,300
Kashi (▲ 194,500) (1986 E) 146,300
Keshan (1985 E) 65,088
Korla (▲ 219,000) (1986 E) 129,400
Kunming (▲ 1,550,000) 1,310,000
Kunshan (1985 E) 44,645
Kuqa (1985 E) 63,847
Kuytun (1986 E) 60,200
Laiwu (▲ 1,041,800) (1986 E) 143,500
Langxiang (1985 E) 64,658
Lanxi (1985 E) 53,236
Lanxi (▲ 606,800) (1986 E) 70,500
Lanzhou (Lanchow) (▲ 1,420,000) 1,297,000
Lechang (1986 E) 56,913
Lengshuijiang (▲ 277,600) (1986 E) 101,700
Lengshuitan (▲ 362,000) (1986 E) 60,900
Leshan (▲ 972,300) (1986 E) 307,300
Lhasa (▲ 107,700) (1986 E) 84,400
Lianyungang (Xinpu) (▲ 459,400) (1986 E) 288,000
Liaocheng (▲ 724,300) (1986 E) 119,000
Liaoyang (▲ 576,900) (1986 E) 442,600
Liaoyuan (▲ 771,577) (1986 E) 370,400
Liling (▲ 856,300) (1986 E) 107,100
Linfen (▲ 530,100) (1986 E) 157,600
Lingling (▲ 515,300) (1986 E) 72,700
Lingyuan (1985 E) 66,825
Linhai (1985 E) 52,653
Linhe (▲ 365,900) (1986 E) 99,800
Linkou (1985 E) 52,936
Linqing (▲ 603,000) (1986 E) 87,000
Linqu (1982 C) 84,196
Linxia (▲ 150,200) (1986 E) 72,900
Linyi (▲ 1,365,000) (1986 E) 190,000
Liuzhou 680,000
Longjiang (1985 E) 51,156
Longyan (▲ 378,500) (1986 E) 114,500
Loudi (▲ 254,300) (1986 E) 84,200
Lu'an (▲ 163,400) (1986 E) 122,600
Lufeng (1985 E) 53,015
Luohe (▲ 159,100) (1986 E) 102,300
Luoyang (Loyang) (▲ 1,090,000) 760,000
Luzhou (▲ 360,300) (1986 E) 237,800
Ma'anshan (▲ 367,000) (1986 E) 258,900
Manzhouli (1986 E) 116,600
Maoming (▲ 434,900) (1986 E) 118,600
Meixian (▲ 740,600) (1986 E) 169,100
Mengyin (1982 C) 70,602
Mianyang, Sichuan prov. (▲ 848,500) (1986 E) 233,900
Minhang (1975 U) 60,000
Mishan (1985 E) 54,919
Mixian (1982 C) 64,776
Mudanjiang (▲ 580,982) 650,000
Nahe (1985 E) 49,725
N'aizishen (1985 E) 51,982
Nancha (1975 U) 50,000
Nanchang (▲ 1,260,000) 1,090,000
Nanchong (▲ 238,100) (1986 E) 158,000
Nanjing (Nanking) 2,390,000
Nanning (▲ 1,000,000) 720,000
Nanpiao (1982 C) 67,274
Nanping (▲ 420,800) (1986 E) 157,100
Nantong (▲ 411,000) (1986 E) 308,800
Nanyang (▲ 294,800) (1986 E) 199,400
Neihuang (1982 C) 56,039
Neijiang (▲ 298,500) (1986 E) 191,100
Ning'an (1985 E) 49,334
Ningbo (▲ 1,050,000) 570,000
Ningyang (1982 C) 55,424
Nong'an (1985 E) 55,966
Nunjiang (1985 E) 59,276
Orogen Zizhiqi (1985 E) 48,042
Panshan (▲ 343,100) (1986 E) 248,100
Panshi (1985 E) 59,270
Pingdingshan (▲ 819,900) (1986 E) 363,200
Pingliang (▲ 362,500) (1986 E) 85,400
Pingxiang, Jiangxi prov. (▲ 1,286,700) (1986 E) 368,700
Pingyi (1982 C) 89,373
Pingyin (1982 C) 62,827
Potou (▲ 456,100) (1986 E) 59,000
Puqi (1985 E) 65,239
Putian (▲ 265,400) (1986 E) 64,600
Putuo (1985 E) 50,962
Puyang (▲ 1,086,100) (1986 E) 131,000
Qian Gorlos (1985 E) 79,494
Qingdao (Tsingtao) 1,300,000
Qinggang (1985 E) 43,075
Qingjiang, Jiangsu prov. (▲ 246,617) (1982 C) 150,000
Qingjiang, Jiangxi prov. (1985 E) 42,698
Qingyuan (1985 E) 51,756

C Census. E Official estimate. U Unofficial estimate.
• Largest city in country.
★ Population or designation of metropolitan area, including suburbs (see headnote).
▲ Population of an entire municipality, commune, or district, including rural area.

Qinhuangdao (Chinwangtao) (▲ 436,000) (1986 E) 307,500
Qinzhou (▲ 923,400) (1986 E) 97,100
Qiqihar (Tsitsihar) (▲ 1,330,000) 1,180,000
Qitaihe (▲ 309,900) (1986 E) 166,400
Qixia (1982 C) 54,158
Qixian (1982 C) 53,041
Quanzhou (Chuanchou) (▲ 436,000) (1986 E) 157,000
Qujing (▲ 758,000) (1986 E) 135,000
Quxian (▲ 704,800) (1986 E) 124,000
Raoping (1985 E) 54,831
Rizhao (▲ 970,300) (1986 E) 93,300
Rongcheng (1982 C) 52,878
Rugao (1985 E) 50,643
Rui'an (1985 E) 57,993
Sanmenxia (Shanxian) (▲ 150,000) (1986 E) 79,000
Sanming (▲ 214,300) (1986 E) 144,900
• Shanghai (★ 9,300,000) ... 7,220,000
Shangqiu (Zhuji) (▲ 199,400) (1986 E) 135,400
Shangrao (▲ 142,500) (1986 E) 113,000
Shangshui (1982 C) 50,191
Shantou (Swatow) (▲ 790,000) 560,000
Shanwei (1985 E) 61,234
Shaoguan (▲ 344,892) (1986 E) 363,100
Shaowu (▲ 266,700) (1986 E) 81,400
Shaoxing (▲ 250,900) (1986 E) 167,100
Shaoyang (▲ 465,900) (1986 E) 218,600
Shashi (1986 E) 253,700
Shenxian (1982 C) 50,208
Shenyang (Mukden) (▲ 4,370,000) 3,910,000
Shenzhen (▲ 231,900) (1986 E) 189,600
Shiguaigou (1975 U) 50,000
Shihezi (▲ 549,300) (1987 E) 304,700
Shijiazhuang 1,220,000
Shiyan (▲ 332,600) (1986 E) 227,300
Shizuishan (▲ 317,400) (1986 E) 225,500
Shouguang (1982 C) 83,400
Shuangcheng (1985 E) 91,163
Shuangliao (1985 E) 67,326
Shuangyashan (1986 E) 427,300
Shuicheng (▲ 2,216,500) (1986 E) 363,500
Shulan (1986 E) 50,582
Shunde (1985 E) 50,262
Siping (▲ 357,800) (1986 E) 280,100
Sishui (1982 C) 82,990
Songjiang (1985 E) 71,864
Songjianghe (1985 E) 53,023
Suifenhe (▲ 21,700) (1986 E) 13,900
Suihua (▲ 732,100) (1986 E) 200,400
Suileng (1985 E) 68,399
Suining (▲ 1,174,900) (1986 E) 118,500
Suixian (▲ 1,281,600) (1986 E) 187,700
Suqian (1985 E) 50,742
Suxian (▲ 218,600) (1986 E) 123,300
Suzhou (Soochow) 740,000
Tai'an (▲ 1,325,400) (1986 E) 215,900
Taiyuan (▲ 1,980,000) 1,700,000
Taizhou (▲ 210,800) (1987 E) 143,200
Tancheng (1982 C) 61,857
Tangshan (▲ 1,440,000) ... 1,080,000
Tao'an (1985 E) 76,269
Tengxian (1985 E) 53,254
Tianjin (Tientsin) (▲ 5,540,000) 4,950,000
Tianshui (▲ 953,200) (1986 E) 209,500
Tiefa (▲ 146,367) (1982 C) 60,000
Tieli (1985 E) 102,527
Tieling (▲ 454,100) (1986 E) 326,100
Tongchuan (▲ 393,200) (1986 E) 268,900
Tonghua (▲ 367,400) (1986 E) 290,200
Tongliao (▲ 253,100) (1986 E) 190,100
Tongling (▲ 216,400) (1986 E) 182,900
Tongren (1985 E) 50,307
Tongxian (1985 E) 97,168
Tumen (▲ 99,700) (1986 E) 77,600
Tunxi (▲ 104,500) (1986 E) 61,800
Turpan (▲ 196,800) (1986 E) 52,300
Ürümqi (▲ 1,147,300) 1,060,000
Wangkui (1985 E) 52,021
Wangqing (1985 E) 61,237
Wanxian (▲ 280,800) (1986 E) 138,700
Weifang (▲ 1,042,200) (1986 E) 312,500
Weihai (▲ 220,800) (1986 E) 83,000
Weinan (▲ 699,400) (1986 E) 111,300
Weishan (Xiazhen) (1982 C) 57,932
Weixian (Hanting) (1982 C) 50,180
Wenzhou (▲ 530,600) (1986 E) 372,200
Wuchang (1985 E) 64,403
Wuhai (1986 E) 266,000
Wuhan 3,570,000
Wuhu (▲ 502,200) (1986 E) 396,000
Wulian (Hongning) (1982 C) 51,718
Wusong (1982 C) 64,017
Wuwei (Liangzhou) (▲ 804,000) (1986 E) 115,500
Wuxi (Wuhsi) 880,000
Wuzhong (▲ 402,400) (1986 E) 48,600
Wuzhou (Wuchow) (▲ 261,500) (1986 E) 194,800
Xiaguan (▲ 395,800) (1986 E) 112,100
Xiamen (Amoy) (▲ 546,400) (1986 E) 343,700
Xi'an (Sian) (▲ 2,580,000) ... 2,210,000
Xiangfan (▲ 421,200) (1986 E) 314,900
Xiangtan (▲ 511,100) (1986 E) 389,500
Xianning (▲ 402,200) (1986 E) 122,200
Xianyang (▲ 641,800) (1986 E) 285,900
Xiaogan (▲ 1,204,400) (1986 E) 125,500
Xiaoshan (1985 E) 63,074
Xichang (▲ 161,000) (1986 E) 105,000
Xinghua (1985 E) 75,573
Xinglongzhen (1982 C) 52,961
Xingtai (▲ 350,800) (1986 E) 265,600
Xinhui (1985 E) 77,381
Xining (Sining) 620,000
Xinmin (1985 E) 47,900
Xintai (▲ 1,157,300) (1986 E) 171,400
Xinwen (Suncun) (1975 U) 50,000
Xinxian (▲ 398,600) (1986 E) 74,200
Xinxiang (▲ 540,500) (1986 E) 411,000
Xinyang (▲ 234,200) (1986 E) 169,100
Xinyu (▲ 610,600) (1986 E) 140,200
Xuancheng (1985 E) 52,387
Xuanhua (1975 U) 140,000
Xuanwei (1982 C) 70,081
Xuchang (▲ 247,200) (1986 E) 167,800
Xuguit Qi (Yakeshi) (1986 E) 390,000
Xuzhou (Süchow) 860,000
Yaan (▲ 277,600) (1986 E) 89,200
Yan'an (▲ 259,800) (1986 E) 86,700
Yancheng (▲ 1,251,400) (1986 E) 258,400
Yangcheng (1982 C) 57,255
Yangjiang (1986 E) 91,433
Yangquan (▲ 478,900) (1986 E) 295,100
Yangzhou (▲ 417,300) (1986 E) 321,500
Yanji (▲ 216,900) (1986 E) 175,000
Yanji (Longjing) (1985 E) 55,035
Yanling (1982 C) 52,679
Yantai (Chefoo) (▲ 717,300) (1986 E) 327,000
Yanzhou (1985 E) 48,972
Yaxian (Sanya) (▲ 321,700) (1986 E) 70,500
Yi'an (1986 E) 54,253
Yibin (Ipin) (▲ 636,500) (1986 E) 218,800
Yichang (Ichang) (1986 E) 410,500
Yichuan (1982 C) 58,914
Yichun, Heilongjiang prov. 840,000
Yichun, Jiangxi prov. (▲ 770,200) (1986 E) 132,600
Yidu (1985 E) 54,838
Yilan (1985 E) 50,436
Yima (▲ 84,800) (1986 E) 53,700
Yinan (Jiehu) (1982 C) 67,803
Yinchuan (▲ 396,900) (1986 E) 268,200
Yingchengzi (1985 E) 59,072
Yingkou (▲ 480,000) (1986 E) 366,900
Yingtan (▲ 116,200) (1986 E) 64,500
Yining (Kuldja) (▲ 232,000) (1986 E) 153,200
Yiyang (▲ 365,000) (1986 E) 155,300
Yiyuan (Nanma) (1982 C) 53,800
Yong'an (▲ 269,000) (1986 E) 105,100
Yongchuan (1985 E) 70,444
Yuci (▲ 420,700) (1986 E) 171,000
Yueyang (▲ 411,300) (1986 E) 239,500
Yulin, Guangxi Zhuangzu prov. (▲ 1,228,800) (1986 E) 115,600
Yulin, Shaanxi prov. (1985 E) 51,610
Yumen (Laojunmiao) (▲ 160,100) (1986 E) 84,300
Yuncheng, Shandong prov. (1982 C) 54,262
Yuncheng, Shansi prov. (▲ 434,900) (1986 E) 87,000
Yunyang (1982 C) 54,903
Yushu (1985 E) 57,222
Yuyao (▲ 772,700) (1986 E) 169,700
Zaozhuang (▲ 1,592,000) (1986 E) 292,200
Zhangjiakou (Kalgan) (▲ 640,000) 500,000
Zhangye (▲ 394,200) (1986 E) 73,000
Zhangzhou (Longxi) (▲ 310,400) (1986 E) 159,400
Zhanjiang (▲ 920,900) (1986 E) 335,500
Zhaodong (1985 E) 99,836
Zhaoqing (Gaoyao) (▲ 187,600) (1986 E) 145,700
Zhaotong (▲ 546,600) (1986 E) 77,500
Zhaoyuan (1985 E) 42,426
Zhaoyuan (1982 C) 56,389
Zhengzhou (Chengchow) (▲ 1,580,000) 1,150,000
Zhenjiang (1986 E) 412,400
Zhongshan (Shiqizhen) (▲ 1,059,700) (1986 E) 238,700
Zhoucun (1975 U) 50,000
Zhoukouzhen (▲ 220,400) (1986 E) 110,500
Zhuhai (▲ 155,000) (1986 E) 88,800
Zhumadian (▲ 149,500) (1986 E) 99,400
Zhuoxian (1985 E) 54,523
Zhuzhou (Chuchow) (▲ 499,600) (1986 E) 344,800
Zibo (Zhangdian) (▲ 2,370,000) 840,000
Zigong (Tzukung) (▲ 909,300) (1986 E) 361,700
Zixing (▲ 334,300) (1986 E) 97,100
Ziyang (1985 E) 57,349
Zouping (1982 C) 49,274
Zouxian (1985 E) 61,578
Zunyi (▲ 347,600) (1986 E) 236,600

CISKEI

1986 E 882,200
BISHO 2,850
• Mdantsane (★ East London, S. Afr.) 242,823

COLOMBIA

1985 C 27,867,326
Armenia 187,130
Barrancabermeja 137,406
Barranquilla (★ 1,140,000) 899,781
Bello (★ Medellín) 212,861
Bucaramanga (★ 550,000) 352,326
Buenaventura 160,342
Buga 82,992
Cali (★ 1,400,000) 1,350,565
Cartagena 531,426
Cartago 97,791
Ciénaga 56,860
Cúcuta (★ 445,000) 379,478
Dos Quebradas (★ Pereira) 101,480
Duitama 56,390
Envigado (★ Medellín) 91,391
Florencia 66,430
Floridablanca (★ Bucaramanga) 143,824
Girardot 70,078
Ibagué 292,965
Itagüí (★ Medellín) 137,623
Magangué 49,160
Maicao 46,033
Malambo (★ Barranquilla) 52,584
Manizales (★ 330,000) 299,352
Medellín (★ 2,095,000) 1,468,089
Montería 157,466
Neiva 194,556
Ocaña 51,443
Palmira 175,186
Pasto 197,407
Pereira (★ 390,000) 233,271
Popayán 141,964
• SANTA FE DE BOGOTÁ (★ 4,260,000) 3,982,941
Santa Marta 177,922
Sincelejo 120,537
Soacha (★ Santa Fe de Bogotá) 109,051
Sogamoso 64,437
Soledad (★ Barranquilla) 165,791
Tuluá 99,721
Tunja 93,792
Valledupar 142,771
Villa Rosario (★ Cúcuta) 63,615
Villavicencio 178,685
Zipaquirá 45,676

COMOROS / Al-Qumur / Comores

1990 E 452,742
• MORONI 23,432

CONGO

1989 C 2,188,367
• BRAZZAVILLE 693,712
Dolisie 57,991
Pointe-Noire 350,139

COOK ISLANDS

1986 C 18,155
• AVARUA 9,678

COSTA RICA

1988 E 2,851,000
Alajuela (▲ 34,556) (1984 C) 29,273
Desamparados (★ San José) (1984 C) 43,352
Puerto Limón (▲ 62,600) 40,400
Puntarenas (1984 C) 29,224
• SAN JOSÉ (★ 670,000) 278,600

CROATIA / Hrvatska

1987 E 4,673,517
Osijek (▲ 162,490) 106,800
Rijeka (▲ 199,282) 166,400
Split 191,074
• ZAGREB 697,925

CUBA

1991 E 10,694,465
Bayamo 139,061
Camagüey 286,404
Cárdenas (▲ 84,590) 69,800
Cárdenas (1981 C) 59,352
Ciego de Ávila 101,620
Cienfuegos 136,233
Florida 51,442
Guantánamo 215,864
Holguín 236,967
• LA HABANA (HAVANA) (★ 2,210,000) 2,119,059
Las Tunas 126,678
Manzanillo 108,668
Matanzas 119,510
Morón 49,793
Palma Soriano (▲ 124,543) 66,600
Pinar del Río 136,303
Sancti Spíritus 97,522
Santa Clara 203,753
Santiago de Cuba 434,541

CYPRUS / Kıbrıs / Kípros

1982 C 512,097
Lárnax (Larnaca) (★ 48,330) 35,823
Lemesós (Limassol) (★ 107,161) 74,782
• NICOSIA (LEVKOSÍA) (★ 185,000) 48,221

CYPRUS, NORTH / Kuzey Kıbrıs

1985 E 160,287
Gazimağusa (Famagusta) 19,428
• NICOSIA (LEFKOŞA) 37,400

CZECH REPUBLIC / Česká Republika

1991 C 10,298,731
Brno (★ 450,000) 387,986
Česká Lípa 39,667
České Budějovice (★ 114,000) 97,283
Český Těšín (★ Třinec) 28,737
Cheb 31,847
Chomutov (★ 80,000) 53,191
Děčín (★ 72,000) 55,112
Frýdek-Místek (★ Ostrava) 65,067
Havířov (★ Ostrava) 86,267
Hodonín 30,736
Hradec Králové (★ 113,000) 99,889
Jablonec nad Nisou (★ Liberec) 45,918
Jihlava 52,271
Karlovy Vary (Carlsbad) 56,291
Karviná (★ Ostrava) 68,368
Kladno (★ 88,500) 71,735
Kolín 31,582
Kroměříž (★ 38,500) 28,962
Liberec (★ 175,000) 101,934
Litvínov (★ Most) 29,085
Mladá Boleslav 44,471
Most (★ 135,000) 70,675
Nový Jičín 29,028
Olomouc (★ 126,000) 105,690
Opava (★ 78,000) 63,601
Orlová (★ Ostrava) 36,307
Ostrava (★ 760,000) 327,553
Pardubice 94,857
Písek 29,542
Plzeň (★ 210,000) 173,129
• PRAHA (★ 1,328,000) 1,212,010
Přerov 51,341
Příbram 36,869
Prostějov 50,102
Šumperk 30,446
Tábor (★ 55,500) 36,329
Teplice (★ 94,000) 53,039
Třebíč 39,348
Třinec (★ 87,500) 45,189
Trutnov 31,957
Ústí nad Labem (★ 115,000) 99,739
Valašské Meziříčí 28,153
Vsetín 31,584
Zlín (★ 124,000) 84,634
Znojmo 39,910

DENMARK / Danmark

1992 E 5,162,126
Ålborg (▲ 156,614) 115,200
Århus (▲ 267,873) 207,300
Ballerup (★ København) 45,476
Esbjerg (▲ 81,843) 72,200
Fredericia (▲ 46,617) 28,700
Frederiksberg (★ København) 86,372
Gentofte (★ København) 66,077
Gladsakse (★ København) 60,604
Helsingør (Elsinore) (★ København) 56,794
Horsens (▲ 55,123) 47,200
Hvidovre (★ København) 48,754
• KØBENHAVN (★ 1,670,000) 464,566
Kolding (▲ 57,982) 42,700
Kongens Lyngby (★ København) 49,612
Odense (▲ 179,487) 142,800
Randers 61,440
Rønne 15,236
Roskilde (▲ 50,158) (★København) 40,700
Vejle (▲ 51,845) 45,700

DJIBOUTI

1976 E 226,000
• DJIBOUTI 120,000

DOMINICA

1984 E 77,000
• ROSEAU 9,348

DOMINICAN REPUBLIC / República Dominicana

1990 E 7,169,800
Barahona 80,400
La Romana 147,800
La Vega 192,300
Mao 58,400
Puerto Plata 94,900
San Cristóbal 137,500
San Francisco de Macorís 165,300
San Juan [de la Maguana] 129,700
San Pedro de Macorís 144,300
Santiago [de los Caballeros] 489,500
• SANTO DOMINGO 2,411,900

ECUADOR

1990 C 9,648,189
Ambato 124,166
Babahoyo 50,285
Cuenca 194,981
Eloy Alfaro (★ Guayaquil) 82,359
Esmeraldas 98,558
• Guayaquil (★ 1,508,444) ... 1,508,444
Ibarra 80,991
La Libertad 53,108
Loja 94,305
Machala 144,197
Manta 125,505
Milagro 93,637
Portoviejo 132,937
Quevedo 86,910
QUITO (★ 1,300,000) 1,100,847
Riobamba 94,505
Santo Domingo de los Colorados 114,422

EGYPT / Mişr

1986 C 48,205,049
Abnūb 48,519
Abū Kabīr 69,509
Abū Tīj 48,711
Akhmīm 70,602
Al-'Arīsh 67,638
Al-Fayyūm 212,523
Al-Hawāmidīyah (★ Al-Qāhirah) 73,060
Al-Iskandarīyah (Alexandria) (★ 3,350,000) 2,917,327
Al-Ismā'īlīyah (★ 235,000) 212,567
Al-Jīzah (Giza) (★ Al-Qāhirah) 1,870,508
Al-Maḥallah al-Kubrā 358,844
Al-Manṣūrah (★ 375,000) 316,870
Al-Manzilah 55,090
Al-Maṭarīyah 74,754
Al-Minyā 179,136
• AL-QĀHIRAH (CAIRO) (★ 9,300,000) 6,052,836
Al-Qanāṭir al-Khayrīyah 48,909
Al-Uqṣur (Luxor) 125,404
Armant 54,650
Ashmūn 54,450
As-Sinbillāwayn 60,285
As-Suways (Suez) 326,820
Aswān 191,461
Asyūṭ 273,191

C Census. E Official estimate. U Unofficial estimate.
• Largest city in country.

★ Population or designation of metropolitan area, including suburbs (see headnote).
▲ Population of an entire municipality, commune, or district, including rural area.

Az-Zaqāzīq 245,496
Bahtīm (★ Al-Qāhirah) 275,807
Banhā 115,571
Banī Mazār 47,964
Banī Suwayf 151,813
Bilbays 96,540
Bilqās Qism Awwal 73,162
Biyalā 47,781
Būlāq ad-Dakrūr (★ Al-Qāhirah) 148,787
Būr Sa'īd (Port Said) 399,793
Būsh 54,482
Damanhūr 190,840
Disūq 78,119
Dumyāṭ (Damietta) 89,498
Fāqūs 48,625
Hawsh 'Īsā (1980 C) 53,619
Idkū 70,729
Jirjā 70,899
Kafr ad-Dawwār (★ Al-Iskandarīyah) 195,102
Kafr ash-Shaykh 102,910
Kafr az-Zayyāt 58,061
Kawm Umbū 52,131
Maghāghah 50,807
Mallawī 99,062
Manfalūt 52,644
Marsā Maṭrūḥ 43,192
Minūf 69,883
Mīt Ghamr (★ 100,000) 92,253
Qalyūb 86,684
Qinā 119,794
Rashīd (Rosetta) 52,014
Rummānah 50,014
Samālūṭ 62,404
Sāqiyat Makkī 51,062
Sawhāj 132,965
Shibīn al-Kawm 132,751
Shubrā al-Khaymah (★ Al-Qāhirah) 710,794
Sinnūris 55,323
Ṭahṭā 58,516
Ṭalkhā (★ Al-Manṣūrah) 55,757
Ṭanṭā 334,505
Ṭimā 47,223
Warrāq al-'Arab (★ Al-Qāhirah) 127,108
Ziftā (★ Mīt Ghamr) 69,050

EL SALVADOR

1985 E 5,337,896

Delgado (★ San Salvador) 67,684
Mejicanos (★ San Salvador) 91,465
Nueva San Salvador (★ San Salvador) 53,688
San Miguel 88,520
• SAN SALVADOR (★ 920,000) 462,652
Santa Ana 137,879
Soyapango (★ San Salvador) 60,000

EQUATORIAL GUINEA / Guinea Ecuatorial

1983 C 300,000

• MALABO 31,630

ERITREA

1987 2,951,000

• ASMERA (1988 E) 319,353
Mitsiwa (1984 C) 15,441

ESTONIA / Eesti

1991 E 1,581,800

Kohtla-Järve 74,700
Narva 83,000
Pärnu 54,200
• TALLINN 481,500
Tartu 115,300

ETHIOPIA / Ityopiya

1986 E 44,927,000

• ADIS ABEBA (★ 1,760,000) (1988 E) 1,686,300
Akaki Beseka (★ Adis Abeba) 59,000
Awasa (1984 C) 36,169
Bahir Dar 60,000
Debre Zeyit 56,000
Dese 77,000
Dire Dawa 107,000
Gonder 88,000
Harer 68,000
Jima 67,000
Mekele 66,000
Nazret 83,000

FAEROE ISLANDS / Føroyar

1990 E 47,946

• TÓRSHAVN 14,767

FALKLAND ISLANDS

1986 C 1,916

• STANLEY 1,200

FIJI

1986 C 715,375

Lautoka (★ 39,057) 28,728
• SUVA (★ 141,273) 69,665

FINLAND / Suomi

1992 E 5,029,002

Espoo (Esbo) (★ Helsinki) 175,670
• HELSINKI (HELSINGFORS) (★ 1,040,000) 497,542
Joensuu 48,182
Jyväskylä (★ 93,000) (1990 E) 67,026
Kotka 56,515
Kouvola (★ 53,821) 32,066
Kuopio 81,593
Lahti (★ 108,000) 93,414
Lappeenranta 55,358
Oulu (★ 121,000) (1990 E) 102,280
Pori 76,432
Tampere (★ 241,000) 173,797
Turku (Åbo) (★ 228,000) 159,403
Vaasa (Vasa) 53,764
Vantaa (Vanda) (★ Helsinki) 157,274

FRANCE

1990 C 56,614,493

Aix-en-Provence (★ Marseille) 123,842
Ajaccio 58,315
Albi (★ 54,359) 46,579
Alès (★ 76,856) 41,037
Amiens (★ 156,120) 131,872
Angers (★ 208,282) 141,404
Angoulême (★ 102,908) 42,876
Annecy (★ 126,729) 49,644
Antibes (★ Cannes) 63,248
Antony (★ Paris) 57,771
Argenteuil (★ Paris) 93,096
Arles (★ 54,309) 39,000
Armentières (★ 57,738) 25,219
Arras (★ 79,607) 38,983
Asnières [-sur-Seine] (★ Paris) 71,850
Aubervilliers (★ Paris) 67,557
Aulnay-sous-Bois (★ Paris) 82,314
Avignon (★ 181,136) 86,939
Bastia (★ 52,446) 37,845
Bayonne (★ 164,378) 40,051
Beauvais (★ 57,704) 54,190
Belfort (★ 77,844) 50,125
Besançon (★ 122,623) 113,828
Béthune (★ 261,535) 24,556
Béziers (★ 76,304) 70,996
Blois (★ 65,132) 49,318
Bondy (★ Paris) 46,676
Bordeaux (★ 760,000) 210,336
Boulogne-Billancourt (★ Paris) 101,743
Boulogne-sur-Mer (★ 91,249) 43,678
Bourg-en-Bresse (★ 55,784) 40,972
Bourges (★ 94,731) 75,609
Brest (★ 201,480) 147,956
Brive-la-Gaillarde (★ 64,379) 49,765
Bruay-en-Artois (★ Béthune) 24,927
Caen (★ 191,490) 112,846
Calais (★ 101,768) 75,309
Cambrai (★ 48,133) 33,092
Cannes (★ 335,647) 68,676
Carcassonne 43,470
Castres (★ 46,482) 44,812
Châlons-sur-Marne (★ 61,452) 48,423
Chalon-sur-Saône (★ 77,764) 54,575
Chambéry (★ 103,283) 54,120
Champigny-sur-Marne (★ Paris) 79,486
Charleville-Mézières (★ 67,213) 57,008
Chartres (★ 85,933) 39,595
Châteauroux (★ 67,090) 50,969
Châtellerault (★ 36,298) 34,678
Cherbourg (★ 92,045) 27,121
Cholet 55,132
Clamart (★ Paris) 47,227
Clermont-Ferrand (★ 254,416) 136,181
Clichy (★ Paris) 48,030
Cognac (★ 27,468) 19,528
Colmar (★ 83,816) 63,498
Colombes (★ Paris) 78,513
Compiègne (★ 67,057) 41,896
Courbevoie (★ Paris) 65,389
Creil (★ 97,119) 31,956
Créteil (★ Paris) 82,088
Denain (★ Valenciennes) 19,544
Dieppe (★ 43,348) 35,894
Dijon (★ 230,451) 146,703
Douai (★ 199,562) 42,175
Drancy (★ Paris) 60,707
Dunkerque (★ 190,879) 70,331
Elbeuf (★ 53,886) 16,604
Épinal (★ 62,140) 36,732
Épinay-sur-Seine (★ Paris) 48,762
Évreux (★ 57,968) 49,103
Évry (★ Paris) 45,531
Fontainebleau (★ 35,706) 15,714
Fontenay-sous-Bois (★ Paris) 51,868
Forbach (★ 98,758) 27,076
Fréjus (★ 73,967) 41,486
Gennevilliers (★ Paris) 44,818
Grenoble (★ 404,733) 150,758
Hagondange (★ 112,061) 8,222
Hayange (★ Thionville) 15,638
Issy-les-Moulineaux (★ Paris) 46,127
Ivry-sur-Seine (★ Paris) 53,619
La Rochelle (★ 100,264) 71,094
La Seyne-sur-Mer (★ Toulon) 59,968
Laval (★ 56,855) 50,473
Le Blanc-Mesnil (★ Paris) 46,956
Le Havre (★ 253,627) 195,854
Le Mans (★ 189,107) 145,502
Lens (★ 323,174) 35,017
Le Puy (★ 43,499) 21,743
Levallois-Perret (★ Paris) 47,548
Lille (★ 1,050,000) 172,142
Limoges (★ 170,065) 133,464
Longwy (★ 41,300) 15,439
Lorient (★ 115,488) 59,271
Lourdes 16,300
Lyon (★ 1,335,000) 415,487
Mâcon (★ 46,714) 37,275
Maisons-Alfort (★ Paris) 53,375
Mantes-la-Jolie (★ Paris) 45,087
Marseille (★ 1,225,000) 800,550
Martigues (★ Marseille) 31,300
Maubeuge (★ 102,772) 34,989
Meaux (★ 63,006) 48,305
Melun (★ 107,705) 35,319
Menton (★ Monaco, Monaco) 29,141
Mérignac (★ Bordeaux) 57,273
Metz (★ 193,117) 119,594
Meudon (★ Paris) 45,339
Montargis (★ 52,804) 15,020
Montbéliard (★ 117,510) 29,005
Montceau-les-Mines (★ 47,283) 22,999
Montluçon (★ 63,018) 44,248
Montpellier (★ 248,303) 207,996
Montreuil-sous-Bois (★ Paris) 94,754
Moulins (★ 41,715) 22,799
Moyeuvre-Grande (★ Hagondange) 9,203
Mulhouse (Mülhausen) (★ 223,856) 108,357
Nancy (★ 329,447) 99,351
Nanterre (★ Paris) 84,565
Nantes (★ 496,078) 244,995
Neuilly-sur-Seine (★ Paris) 61,768
Nevers (★ 58,915) 41,968
Nice (★ 516,740) 342,439
Nîmes (★ 138,527) 128,471
Niort (★ 65,792) 57,012
Noisy-le-Grand (★ Paris) 54,032
Noisy-le-Sec (★ Paris) 36,309
Orléans (★ 243,153) 105,111
Orly (★ Paris) 21,646
Pantin (★ Paris) 47,303
• PARIS (★ 10,275,000) 2,152,423
Pau (★ 144,674) 82,157
Périgueux (★ 63,322) 30,280
Perpignan (★ 157,873) 105,983
Pessac (★ Bordeaux) 51,055
Poissy (★ Paris) 36,745
Poitiers (★ 107,625) 78,894
Quimper (★ 65,954) 59,437
Reims (★ 206,437) 180,620
Rennes (★ 245,065) 197,536
Roanne (★ 77,160) 41,756
Rodez (★ 39,017) 24,701
Romans-sur-Isère (★ 49,212) 32,734
Roubaix (★ Lille) 97,746
Rouen (★ 380,161) 102,723
Rueil-Malmaison (★ Paris) 66,401
Saint-Brieuc (★ 83,861) 44,752
Saint-Chamond (★ 81,795) 38,878
Saint-Denis (★ Paris) 89,988
Saint-Dizier (★ 40,097) 33,552
Saint-Étienne (★ 313,338) 199,396
Saint-Lô (★ 2,760) 21,546
Saint-Malo 48,057
Saint-Maur-des-Fossés (★ Paris) 77,206
Saint-Nazaire (★ 131,511) 64,812
Saint-Ouen (★ Paris) 42,343
Saint-Quentin (★ 71,113) 60,644
Sarcelles (★ Paris) 56,833
Sartrouville (★ Paris) 50,329
Sevran 48,478
Soissons (★ 46,168) 29,829
Strasbourg (★ 415,000) 252,338
Suresnes (★ Paris) 35,998
Tarbes (★ 77,787) 47,566
Thionville (★ 132,413) 39,712
Toulon (★ 437,553) 167,619
Toulouse (★ 650,000) 358,688
Tourcoing (★ Lille) 93,765
Tours (★ 282,152) 129,509
Troyes (★ 122,763) 59,255
Valence (★ 107,965) 63,437
Valenciennes (★ 338,392) 38,441
Vénissieux (★ Lyon) 60,444
Verdun-sur-Meuse (★ 26,711) 20,753
Versailles (★ Paris) 87,789
Vichy (★ 61,566) 27,714
Villefranche (★ 55,249) 29,542
Villejuif (★ Paris) 48,405
Villeneuve-d'Ascq (★ Lille) 65,320
Villeurbanne (★ Lyon) 116,872
Vitry-sur-Seine (★ Paris) 82,400
Wattrelos (★ Lille) 43,675

FRENCH GUIANA / Guyane française

1982 C 73,022

• CAYENNE 38,091

FRENCH POLYNESIA / Polynésie française

1988 C 188,814

• PAPEETE (★ 80,000) 23,555

GABON

1985 E 1,312,000

Franceville 58,800
Lambaréné 49,500
• LIBREVILLE 235,700
Port Gentil 124,400

GAMBIA

1983 C 687,817

• BANJUL (★ 160,000) 44,188
Brikama 19,624

GEORGIA

1991 E 5,464,200

Batumi 137,500
Gori 70,100
Kutaisi 238,200
Poti (1979 C) 51,100
Rustavi (★ Tbilisi) 161,900
Suchumi 120,000
• TBILISI (★ 1,460,000) 1,279,000
Zugdidi 50,600

GERMANY / Deutschland

1991 E 79,753,227

Aachen (★ 540,000) 241,861
Aalen (★ 78,000) 64,781
Ahlen 54,169
Albstadt 49,021
Alsdorf (★ Aachen) 46,935
Altenburg 48,926
Amberg 43,111
Arnsberg 75,864
Aschaffenburg (★ 150,000) 34,098
Augsburg (★ 420,000) 256,877
Baden-Baden 51,849
Bad Homburg (★ Frankfurt am Main) 51,820
Bad Oeynhausen 46,475
Bad Salzuflen (★ Herford) 53,771
Bamberg (★ 122,000) 70,521
Bautzen 48,588
Bayreuth (★ 87,000) 72,345
Bergheim (★ Köln) 58,146
Bergisch Gladbach (★ Köln) 104,037
Bergkamen (★ Essen) 49,761
BERLIN (★ 4,150,000) 3,433,695
Bielefeld (★ 535,000) 319,037
Bitterfeld (★ 105,000) 17,988
Bocholt 68,936
Bochum (★ Essen) 396,486
BONN (★ 575,000) 292,234
Bottrop (★ Essen) 118,936
Brandenburg 89,889
Braunschweig (★ 320,000) 258,833
Bremen (★ 790,000) 551,219
Bremerhaven (★ 180,000) 130,446
Castrop-Rauxel (★ Essen) 79,037
Celle 72,260
Chemnitz (★ 500,000) 294,244
Coburg 44,246
Cottbus 125,891
Cuxhaven 56,090
Dachau (★ München) 35,387
Darmstadt (★ 315,000) 138,920
Delmenhorst (★ Bremen) 75,154
Dessau (★ 138,000) 96,754
Detmold 70,074
Dinslaken (★ Essen) 65,313
Dormagen (★ Köln) 58,260
Dorsten (★ Essen) 78,035
Dortmund (★ Essen) 599,055
Dresden (★ 870,000) 490,571
Duisburg (★ Essen) 535,447
Düren (★ 108,000) 86,508
Düsseldorf (★ 1,225,000) 575,794
Eberswalde 52,586
Eisenach 45,220
Eisenhüttenstadt 50,216
Emden 50,735
Erfurt 208,989
Erlangen (★ Nürnberg) 102,440
Eschweiler (★ Aachen) 54,675
• Essen (★ 5,050,000) 626,973
Esslingen (★ Stuttgart) 91,685
Euskirchen 49,654
Flensburg (★ 98,000) 86,977
Frankenthal (★ Mannheim) 46,966
Frankfurt am Main (★ 1,935,000) 644,865
Frankfurt an der Oder 86,131
Freiberg 48,609
Freiburg (★ 235,000) 191,029
Friedrichshafen 54,129
Fulda (★ 74,000) 56,289
Fürth (★ Nürnberg) 103,362
Garbsen (★ Hannover) 60,776
Garmisch-Partenkirchen 26,837
Gelsenkirchen (★ Essen) 293,714
Gera 129,037
Giessen (★ 155,000) 74,497
Gladbeck (★ Essen) 80,267
Göppingen (★ 155,000) 54,957
Görlitz 72,237
Goslar (★ 72,000) 46,251
Gotha 54,525
Göttingen 121,831
Greifswald 66,251
Grevenbroich (★ Düsseldorf) 60,835
Gummersbach 50,965
Gütersloh (★ Bielefeld) 86,807
Hagen (★ Essen) 214,449
Halberstadt 45,364
Halle (★ 455,000) 310,234
Hamburg (★ 2,385,000) 1,652,363
Hameln (★ 65,000) 58,539
Hamm 179,639
Hanau (★ Frankfurt am Main) 86,913
Hannover (★ 1,000,000) 513,010
Hattingen (★ Essen) 58,241
Heidelberg (★ Mannheim) 136,796
Heidenheim (★ 80,000) 50,532
Heilbronn (★ 245,000) 115,843
Herford (★ 120,000) 63,893
Herne (★ Essen) 178,132
Herten (★ Essen) 69,245
Hilden (★ Düsseldorf) 54,782
Hildesheim (★ 126,000) 105,291
Hof 52,913
Hoyerswerda 64,888
Hürth (★ Köln) 50,808
Ingolstadt (★ 145,000) 105,489
Iserlohn 96,314
Jena 102,518
Kaiserslautern (★ 130,000) 99,351
Kamen (★ Essen) 46,160
Karlsruhe (★ 505,000) 275,061
Kassel (★ 375,000) 194,268
Kempten (Allgäu) 61,906
Kerpen (★ Köln) 57,337
Kiel (★ 325,000) 245,567
Kleve 45,963
Koblenz (★ 170,000) 108,733
Köln (★ 1,810,000) 953,551
Konstanz 75,089
Krefeld (★ Essen) 244,020
Landshut 59,066
Langenfeld (★ Düsseldorf) 53,455
Langenhagen (★ Hannover) 47,432
Leipzig (★ 720,000) 511,079
Leverkusen (★ Köln) 160,919
Lingen 49,137
Lippstadt 62,345
Lübeck (★ 250,000) 214,758
Lüdenscheid 79,401
Ludwigsburg (★ Stuttgart) 82,343
Ludwigshafen (★ Mannheim) 162,173
Lüneburg 61,870
Lünen (★ Essen) 87,845
Magdeburg (★ 400,000) 278,807
Mainz (★ Wiesbaden) 179,486
Mannheim (★ 1,525,000) 310,411
Marburg 74,146
Marl (★ Essen) 91,467
Meerbusch (★ Düsseldorf) 52,104
Menden 56,527
Merseburg (★ Halle) 42,905
Minden (★ 121,000) 78,145
Moers (★ Essen) 104,595
Mönchengladbach (★ 410,000) 259,436
Mülheim an der Ruhr (★ Essen) 177,681
München (Munich) (★ 1,900,000) 1,229,026
Münster 259,438
Neubrandenburg 89,284
Neumünster 80,743
Neunkirchen/Saar (★ 125,000) 51,536
Neuss (★ Düsseldorf) 147,019
Neustadt an der Weinstrasse 51,988
Neu-Ulm (★ Ulm) 46,264
Neuwied (★ 157,000) 62,075
Norderstedt (★ Hamburg) 68,450
Nordhausen 46,422
Nordhorn 49,359
Nürnberg (★ 1,065,000) 493,692
Oberhausen (★ Essen) 223,840
Offenbach (★ Frankfurt am Main) 114,992
Offenburg 52,964
Oldenburg 143,131
Osnabrück (★ 270,000) 163,168
Paderborn 120,680
Passau 50,328
Peine 46,654
Pforzheim (★ 230,000) 112,944
Pirmasens 47,680
Pirna (★ Dresden) 41,798
Plauen 71,774
Potsdam (★ Berlin) 139,794
Ratingen (★ Düsseldorf) 91,007
Ravensburg (★ 75,000) 45,650
Recklinghausen (★ Essen) 125,060
Regensburg (★ 180,000) 121,691
Remscheid (★ Wuppertal) 123,155
Reutlingen (★ 170,000) 103,687
Rheine 70,452
Riesa 45,440
Rosenheim 56,340
Rostock 248,088
Rüsselsheim (★ Wiesbaden) 59,430
Saarbrücken (★ 365,000) 191,694
Saarlouis (★ 115,000) 38,160
Salzgitter 114,355
Sankt Augustin (★ Bonn) 51,886
Schwäbisch Gmünd 60,081
Schwedt 50,633
Schweinfurt (★ 105,000) 54,483
Schwerin 127,447
Schwerte (★ Essen) 50,696
Siegburg (★ 175,000) 35,441
Siegen (★ 192,000) 109,174
Sindelfingen (★ Stuttgart) 58,805
Solingen (★ Wuppertal) 165,401
Speyer 46,553
Stendal 48,532
Stolberg (★ Aachen) 57,231
Stralsund 72,780
Stuttgart (★ 2,005,000) 579,988

C Census. E Official estimate. U Unofficial estimate.
• Largest city in country.

★ Population or designation of metropolitan area, including suburbs (see headnote).
▲ Population of an entire municipality, commune, or district, including rural area.

Suhl 54,731
Trier (★ 122,000) 97,835
Troisdorf (★ Siegburg) 64,430
Tübingen 80,372
Ulm (★ 215,000) 110,529
Unna (★ Essen) 61,552
Velbert (★ Essen) 89,253
Viersen (★ Mönchengladbach) 77,453
Villingen-Schwenningen 78,218
Weimar 60,326
Wesel 59,631
Wetzlar (★ 96,000) 51,737
Wiesbaden (★ 790,000) 260,301
Wilhelmshaven (★ 122,000) 90,561
Wismar 55,509
Witten (★ Essen) 105,403
Wittenberg 49,682
Wolfenbüttel (★ Braunschweig) 52,032
Wolfsburg 128,510
Worms (★ Mannheim) 76,503
Wuppertal (★ 845,000) 383,660
Würzburg (★ 195,000) 127,777
Zweibrücken (★ 100,000) 33,918
Zwickau (★ 180,000) 114,632

GHANA

1987 E 13,577,538

• ACCRA (★ 1,390,000) 949,113
Ashiaman (★ Accra) (1984 C) 49,427
Cape Coast (1984 C) 86,620
Koforidua (1984 C) 54,400
Kumasi (★ 540,000) 385,192
Obuasi (1984 C) 60,146
Sekondi (★ 175,352) (1984 C) 32,355
Tafo (★ Kumasi) (1984 C) 50,432
Takoradi (★ Sekondi) (1984 C) 61,527
Tamale (★ 168,091) 151,069
Tema (★ Accra) 109,975
Teshie (★ Accra) (1984 C) 62,954

GIBRALTAR

1988 E 30,077

• GIBRALTAR 30,077

GREECE / Ellás

1981 C 9,740,417

Aiyáleo (★ Athínai) (1991 C) 79,560
Akharnaí (1991 C) 60,062
Amaroúsion (★ Athínai) (1991 C) 63,619
Ampelókipoi (★ Thessaloníki) 40,033
• ATHÍNAI (ATHENS) (★ 3,096,775) (1991 E) 748,110
Áyios Dhimítrios (★ Athínai) (1991 C) 57,387
Ermoúpolis (★ 16,595) 13,876
Galátsion (★ Athínai) (1991 C) 56,972
Glifádha (★ Athínai) (1991 C) 62,310
Ilioúpolis (★ Athínai) (1991 C) 72,623
Ioánnina (1991 C) 56,496
Iráklion (★ 110,958) 102,398
Kalámai (★ 43,235) 42,075
Kalamariá (★ Thessaloníki) 51,676
Kallithéa (★ Athínai) (1991 C) 110,738
Kardhítsa (1991 C) 30,451
Kateríni (★ 39,895) 38,404
Kavála (1991 C) 58,576
Keratsínion (★ Athínai) (1991 C) 71,845
Khalándrion (★ Athínai) (1991 C) 72,286
Khalkís (1991 C) 51,482
Khaniá (★ 61,976) 47,451
Khíos (★ 29,742) 24,070
Koridhallós (★ Athínai) (1991 C) 63,033
Kórinthos (Corinth) (1991 C) 28,903
Lárisa (★ 125,623) (1991 C) 113,426
Návplion (1991 C) 11,453
Néa Ionía (★ Athínai) (1991 C) 60,364
Néa Liósia (★ Athínai) (1991 C) 78,029
Neápolis (★ Thessaloníki) 31,464
Néa Smírni (★ Athínai) (1991 C) 69,319
Níkaia (★ Athínai) (1991 C) 87,924
Palaión Fáliron (★ Athínai) (1991 C) 60,974
Pátrai (★ 154,596) 142,163
Peristérion (★ Athínai) (1991 C) 145,854
Piraiévs (Piraeus) (★ Athínai) (1991 C) 169,622
Ródhos (Rhodes) (1991 C) 43,619
Sérrai (1991 C) 50,875
Spárti (Sparta) (★ 14,388) 12,975
Thessaloníki (Salonika) (★ 706,180) 406,413
Tríkala (1991 C) 48,810
Trípolis (1991 C) 21,772
Véroia (1991 C) 38,871
Víron (★ Athínai) (1991 C) 57,149
Vólos (★ 107,407) 71,378
Zográfos (★ Athínai) (1991 C) 78,570

GREENLAND / Grønland / Kalaallit Nunaat

1990 E 55,558

Egedesminde (Aasiaat) 3,308
• GODTHÅB (NUUK) 12,217
Holsteinsborg (Sisimiut) 4,871

GRENADA

1991 C 90,691

• SAINT GEORGE'S (★ 25,000) 4,439

GUADELOUPE

1982 C 328,400

BASSE-TERRE (★ 26,600) 13,656
Les Abymes (★ Pointe-à-Pitre) 56,165
• Pointe-à-Pitre (★ 83,000) 25,310

GUAM

1990 C 133,152

• AGANA (★ 50,000) 1,139

GUATEMALA

1989 E 8,935,395

Escuintla 60,673
• GUATEMALA (★ 1,400,000) 1,057,210
Quetzaltenango 88,769

GUERNSEY

1991 C 58,867

• SAINT PETER PORT (★ 36,000) 16,648

GUINEA / Guinée

1986 E 6,225,000

• CONAKRY 800,000
Kankan 100,000
Kindia 80,000
Labé 110,000
Nzérékoré (1983 C) 55,356

GUINEA-BISSAU / Guiné-Bissau

1988 E 945,000

• BISSAU 125,000

GUYANA

1983 E 918,000

• GEORGETOWN (★ 188,000) 78,500

HAITI / Haïti

1987 E 5,531,802

Cap-Haïtien 72,161
Gonaïves 37,034
• PORT-AU-PRINCE (★ 880,000) 797,000

HONDURAS

1988 C 4,376,839

Choluteca 53,799
El Progreso 55,523
La Ceiba 68,289
San Pedro Sula 279,356
• TEGUCIGALPA 551,606

HONG KONG

1986 C 5,395,997

Kowloon (Jiulong) (★ Victoria) 774,781
Kwai Chung (★ Victoria) 131,362
New Kowloon (Xinjiulong) (★ Victoria) 1,526,910
Sha Tin (★ Victoria) 355,810
Sheung Shui 87,206
Tai Po 119,679
Tsuen Wan (Quanwan) (★ Victoria) 514,241
Tuen Mun (★ Victoria) 262,458
• VICTORIA (★ 4,770,000) (1991 C) 1,250,993
Yuen Long 75,740

HUNGARY / Magyarország

1991 C 10,354,842

Békéscsaba (▲ 67,691) 58,900
• BUDAPEST (★ 2,515,000) 2,018,035
Debrecen 213,927
Dunaújváros 58,874
Eger 62,474
Győr 129,598
Hódmezővásárhely (▲ 51,180) 42,800
Kaposvár 71,368
Kecskemét (▲ 103,568) 82,000
Miskolc 194,033
Nagykanizsa 53,700
Nyíregyháza (▲ 114,596) 88,800
Ózd 43,020
Pécs 170,023
Salgótarján 47,500
Sopron 55,140
Szeged 176,135
Székesfehérvár 109,106
Szolnok 78,661
Szombathely 85,702
Tatabánya 73,854
Vác 33,858
Veszprém 64,277
Zalaegerszeg 62,357

ICELAND / Ísland

1991 E 259,577

Akureyri 14,436
• REYKJAVÍK (★ 149,482) 99,623

INDIA / Bharat

1991 C 844,324,222

Abohar 107,016
Achalpur 96,216
Ādilābād 84,233
Adītyapur (★ Jamshedpur) 78,184
Ādoni 135,718
Agartala 157,636
Āgra (★ 955,684) 899,195
Āgra Cantonment (★ Āgra) 49,975
Ahmadābād (★ 3,297,655) 2,872,865
Ahmadnagar (★ 221,710) 181,015
Āīzawl 154,343
Ajmer 401,930
Akola 327,946
Akot 65,670
Alandur (★ Madras) 125,009
Alīgarh 479,978
Ālīpur Duār (★ 103,512) 65,945
Allahābād (★ 858,213) 806,447
Alleppey (★ 264,887) 174,606
Alwal (★ Hyderābād) 66,064
Alwar (★ 211,162) 206,107
Amalner 76,406
Ambājogāi 57,054
Ambāla 119,535
Ambāla Cantonment (★ Ambāla Sadar) 48,903
Ambāla Sadar (★ 139,615) 90,712
Ambāsamudram (★ 59,527) 33,860
Ambattur (★ Madras) 223,332
Ambikāpur (★ 53,228) 50,278
Āmbūr 75,728
Amrāvati 433,746
Amreli (★ 69,279) 67,740
Amritsar 709,456
Amroha 136,893
Anakāpalle 84,362
Ānand (★ 168,776) 110,144
Anantapur 174,792
Anjār 51,207
Ankleshwar (★ 78,064) 51,708
Ara 156,871
Arakkonam 71,500
Arcot (★ 114,884) 45,193
Arni 54,881
Aruppukkottai 78,184
Asansol (★ 763,845) 261,836
Ashoknagar-Kalyangarh (★ Hābra) 96,315
Āttūr 55,529
Auraiya 50,771
Aurangābād (★ 592,052) 572,034
Avadi (★ Madras) 180,291
Āzamgarh 78,382
Badagara (★ 102,429) 72,441
Bagaha 64,574
Bāgalkot 76,819
Bahādurgarh (★ 57,195) 56,484
Baharampur (★ 126,303) 115,036
Bahraich 135,352
Baidyabāti (★ Calcutta) 90,601
Bālāghāt (★ 67,113) 62,164
Balāngīr 70,014
Bāleshwar (★ 102,504) 86,116
Ballarpur (★ 92,438) 83,511
Ballia 84,758
Bālly (★ Calcutta) 73,265
Bālly (★ Calcutta) 181,978
Balrāmpur 60,077
Bālurghāt (★ 126,199) 119,829
Bānda 97,227
Bangalore (★ 4,086,548) 2,650,659
Bangaon 79,433
Bānkura 114,927
Bansberia (★ Calcutta) 93,447
Bānswāra (★ 67,952) 66,676
Banūr 55,660
Bāpatla 62,688
Bārākpur (★ Calcutta) 133,429
Bārān 57,703
Baranagar (★ Calcutta) 223,770
Bārāsat (★ Calcutta) 102,648
Baraut 67,673
Barddhamān 244,789
Bareilly (★ 607,652) 583,473
Bargarh 51,135
Bāripada (★ 68,895) 49,569
Bārmer 69,385
Barnāla 75,387
Bārsi 88,774
Basīrhāt 101,652
Basti 87,512
Batala (★ 106,062) 88,896
Bathinda 159,114
Beāwar (★ 106,715) 105,357
Begusarai (★ 83,907) 71,362
Bela 66,845
Belampalli 66,608
Belgaum (★ 401,619) 325,639
Bellary 245,758
Bettiah 92,583
Betūl 63,489
Bhadohi 63,590
Bhadrak 76,390
Bhadrāvati (★ 149,131) 55,413
Bhadrāvati New Town (★ Bhadrāvati) 74,864
Bhadreswar (★ Calcutta) 72,414
Bhāgalpur (★ 261,855) 254,993
Bhandāra 71,762
Bharatpur (★ 156,844) 148,506
Bharūch (★ 138,246) 132,312
Bhātpāra (★ Calcutta) 304,298
Bhavāni (★ 97,020) 35,202
Bhāvnagar (★ 403,521) 400,636
Bhawānipatna 51,014
Bhilai (★ 688,670) 389,601
Bhīlwāra 183,791
Bhīmavaram 125,495
Bhind 109,731
Bhiwandi (★ 391,670) 378,546
Bhiwāni 121,449
Bhopāl 1,063,662
Bhubaneshwar 411,542
Bhuj (★ 110,734) 91,901
Bhusāwal (★ 159,459) 144,804
Bīd 112,351
Bīdar (★ 130,804) 107,542
Bihār 200,976
Bijāpur (★ 193,038) 186,846
Bijnor (★ 73,570) 66,156
Bīkāner 415,355
Bilāspur (★ 233,570) 190,911
Bīlīmora (★ 50,940) 46,366
Birlapur (★ 65,333) 20,239
Birnagar (★ 92,108) 20,014
Bishnupur 56,119
Bodhan 64,386
Bodināyakkanūr 66,028
Bokāro Steel City (★ 415,686) 350,540
Bolpur 52,866
Bombay (★ 12,571,720) 9,909,547
Botād 64,491
Brahmapur 210,585
Brajrajnagar 69,548
Budaun 116,706
Budge Budge (★ Calcutta) 73,361
Bulandshahr 126,737
Buldāna 52,738
Bulsār (★ 111,759) 57,903
Būndi 65,016
Burhānpur 172,809
• Calcutta (★ 11,605,833) 4,388,262
Calicut (★ 800,913) 419,531
Cannanore (★ Tellicherry) 65,233
Chāībāsa 56,657
Chākdaha 74,780
Chakradharpur (★ 48,329) 33,263
Chālisgaon 77,346
Champdāni (★ Calcutta) 98,818
Chandannagar (★ Calcutta) 122,351
Chandausi 82,733
Chandīgarh (★ 574,646) 502,992
Chāndpur 55,829
Chandrapur 225,841
Changanācheri 52,448
Channapatna 55,210
Chāpra 136,824
Chās 65,146
Chhatarpur (★ 75,515) 72,745
Chhindwāra (★ 96,852) 93,731
Chidambaram (★ 68,819) 58,927
Chikmagalūr 60,814
Chilakalūrupet 79,081
Chingleput 53,784
Chintāmani 50,376
Chīrāla (★ 142,654) 80,837
Chitradurga (★ 103,345) 87,053
Chittaranjan (★ 58,338) 47,148
Chittaurgarh 71,566
Chittoor 133,233
Chopda 49,112
Chūru (★ 82,818) 82,430
Cochin (★ 1,139,543) 564,038
Coimbatore (★ 1,135,549) 853,402
Contai 53,425
Coonoor (★ 99,615) 47,100
Cuddalore 143,774
Cuddapah (★ 215,545) 121,422
Cuttack (★ 439,273) 402,390
Dabgram 146,917
Dabhoi 50,619
Dāhod (★ 96,568) 66,444
Dāltenganj 56,408
Damoh (★ 105,032) 95,553
Dānāpur (★ Patna) 84,104
Dandeli 52,699
Darbhanga 218,274
Darjiling 73,088
Datia 65,565
Dāvangere (★ 287,114) 265,971
Dehra Dūn (★ 367,411) 270,028
Dehri 94,526
Delhi (★ 8,375,188) 7,174,755
Delhi Cantonment (★ Delhi) 94,326
Deoband 62,461
Deoghar (★ 85,846) 76,322
Deolāli Cantonment (★ Nāsik) 51,115
Deoria 81,943
Dewās 163,699
Dhamtari 69,273
Dhanbad (★ 817,549) 151,334
Dhār 59,089
Dhārāpuram 48,392
Dharmapuri 59,070
Dharmavaram 78,747
Dhaulpur 68,524
Dholka (★ 54,351) 49,855
Dhorāji (★ 79,414) 77,683
Dhrāngadhra 54,281
Dhuburi 65,861
Dhule 277,957
Dibrugarh (★ 123,885) 118,374
Dimāpur 56,918
Dindigul 182,293
Dīsa 61,888
Dod Ballāpur 54,468
Dum Dum (★ Calcutta) 40,942
Durg (★ Bhilai) 150,513
Durgāpur 415,986
Elūru 212,918
Erode (★ 357,427) 158,774
Etah 78,424
Etāwah 124,032
Faizābād (★ 177,505) 125,012
Farīdābad New Township (★ Delhi) 613,828
Farīdkot 56,038
Farrukhābād (★ 207,783) 193,624
Fatehpur 117,203
Fathpur 66,398
Fāzilka 57,386
Fīrozābād (★ 270,534) 215,089
Fīrozpur 77,505
Fīrozpur Cantonment 53,691
Gadag 133,918
Gandhidham 104,392
Gāndhinagar 121,746
Ganga Ghat 50,520
Gangānagar 161,377
Gangāpur (★ 68,982) 53,784
Gangāwati (★ 81,108) 64,807
Gangtok 24,971
Gārulia (★ Calcutta) 80,872
Gaya (★ 293,971) 291,220
Ghāziābād (★ 519,508) 460,949
Ghāzīpur 77,069
Girīdīh 77,912
Godhra (★ 100,363) 96,514
Gokāk 52,037
Gonda 106,078
Gondal (★ 81,533) 80,506
Gondia 109,271
Gopichettipālaiyam 48,349
Gorakhpur 489,850
Gudivāda 101,635
Gudiyāttam (★ 89,966) 82,652
Gūdūr 55,962
Gulbarga (★ 309,962) 303,139
Guna (★ 100,389
Guntakal 107,560
Guntūr 471,020
Gurdāspur 54,575
Gurgaon (★ 134,639) 120,790
Guruvayur (★ 118,626) 20,209
Guwāhāti 577,591
Gwalior (★ 720,068) 692,982
Hābra (★ 196,457) 100,142
Hājīpur 87,669
Haldwāni 102,744
Hālisahar (★ Calcutta) 113,670
Hānsi 59,638
Hanumāngarh (★ 82,717) 78,504
Hāora (★ Calcutta) 946,732
Hāpur 146,591
Hardoi 88,632
Haridwār (★ 188,961) 148,882
Harihar 66,660
Hassan (★ 108,458) 90,719
Hāthras 113,653
Hazārībāg 97,712
Himatnagar 50,929
Hindaun 60,761
Hindupur 104,635
Hinganghāt 78,709
Hingoli 54,444
Hisār (★ 180,774) 172,873
Hoshangābād 70,820
Hoshiārpur 122,528
Hospet (★ 134,935) 96,499
Hubli-Dhārwār 647,640
Hugli-Chinsurah (★ Calcutta) 142,388
Hyderābād (★ 4,280,261) 2,991,884
Ichaikaronji (★ 235,854) 214,835
Imphāl (★ 200,615) 196,268
Indore (★ 1,104,065) 1,086,673
Ingrāj Bāzār (★ 176,991) 139,018
Itānagar 17,320
Itārsi (★ 85,706) 78,700
Jabalpur (★ 887,188) 739,961
Jabalpur Cantonment (★ Jabalpur) 56,742
Jagādhri (★ Yamunānagar) 67,371
Jagdalpur (★ 84,553) 65,544
Jagtiāl 67,965
Jahānābād 51,846
Jaipur (★ 1,514,425) 1,454,678
Jalandhar 519,530
Jālgaon 241,603
Jālna 174,958
Jalpāiguri 67,495
Jamālpur 86,123
Jamkhandi 48,111
Jammu (★ 223,361) (1981 C) 206,135
Jamnagar (★ 365,464) 325,475
Jamshedpur (★ 834,535) 461,212
Jaora (★ 55,986) 54,960
Jaunpur 136,287
Jaypur 65,582
Jetpur (★ 95,290) 73,556
Jhānsi (★ 368,590) 301,304
Jharia (★ Dhanbād) 69,542
Jhārsuguda 65,022

C Census. E Official estimate. U Unofficial estimate.
• Largest city in country.

★ Population or designation of metropolitan area, including suburbs (see headnote).
▲ Population of an entire municipality, commune, or district, including rural area.

Jhunjhunūn 71,972
Jīnd 85,307
Jodhpur 648,621
Jorhāt (★ 111,584) 57,998
Jūnāgadh (★ 166,755) 130,132
Kadaiyanallūr 68,805
Kadiri 63,428
Kagaznagar 57,653
Kairāna 56,083
Kaithal 71,294
Kākināda (★ 327,407) 279,875
Kalamassery (★ Cochin) 54,313
Kālol (★ 92,320) 81,916
Kalyān (★ Bombay) 1,014,062
Kāmāreddi 48,641
Kāmārhāti (★ Calcutta) 266,625
Kambam 51,987
Kāmthi (★ 131,837) 78,586
Kānchipuram (★ 169,813) 145,028
Kānchrāpāra (★ Calcutta) 100,059
Kānnangād (★ 118,180) 57,133
Kannauj 59,650
Kānpur (★ 2,111,284) 1,958,282
Kānpur Cantonment
(★ Kānpur) 93,109
Kapra (★ Hyderābād) 87,607
Kapūrthala (1981 C) 63,083
Karād 56,705
Kāraikāl 61,875
Kāraikkudi (★ 110,473) 71,599
Kāranja 48,857
Karauli 48,961
Karīmnagar 148,349
Karnāl (★ 176,120) 173,742
Karūr (★ 110,605) 73,428
Kārwār 51,011
Kāsaragod 50,123
Kāsganj 75,610
Kāshīpur 69,889
Katihār (★ 154,101) 135,348
Kātwa 55,535
Kāvali 65,804
Kāyankulam 67,170
Keshod 50,164
Khadki Cantonment
(★ Pune) 78,046
Khambhāt (★ 89,813) 76,724
Khāmgaon 73,705
Khammam (★ 148,646) 127,812
Khandwa 145,111
Khanna 72,140
Kharagpur (★ 279,736) 189,101
Kharagpur Railway Settlement
(★ Kharagpur) 881,253
Khardaha 88,278
Khargone 66,776
Khurja 80,384
Kishanganj 64,462
Kishangarh Bās 81,944
Koch Bihār (★ 92,628) 71,028
Kodarma 53,560
Kohīma 53,122
Kolār 83,219
Kolār Gold Fields
(★ 156,398) 72,481
Kolhāpur (★ 417,286) 405,118
Konnagar (★ Calcutta) 62,214
Korba 124,365
Kota 536,444
Kot Kapūra 62,403
Kottagūdem (★ 102,061) 80,420
Kottayam (★ 166,178) 62,829
Kovilpatti 77,967
Krishnagiri 60,252
Krishnanagar 120,918
Kukatpalle (★ Hyderābād) 185,378
Kulti (★ Asansol) 108,930
Kumārapālaiyam
(★ Bhavāni) 57,532
Kumbakonam
(★ 150,502) 139,449
Kundla (★ 65,732) 64,762
Kurasia (★ 71,638) 15,828
Kurichi (★ Coimbatore) 63,688
Kurnool (★ 274,795) 236,313
Lādnūn 48,174
Lakhīmpur 79,549
Lalitpur (1981 C) 55,756
Lalitpur 79,891
Lātūr 197,164
Luckeesarai 53,198
Lucknow (★ 1,642,134) 1,592,010
Lucknow Cantonment
(★ Lucknow) 50,124
Ludhiāna 1,012,062
Machilīpatnam (Bandar) 159,007
Madanapalle 73,729
Madgaon (Margao)
(★ 72,070) 58,745
Mādhavaram (★ Madras) 49,005
Madhubani 53,543
Madras (★ 5,361,468) 3,795,028
Madurai (★ 1,093,702) 951,696
Mahbūbnagar 116,775
Mahesāna (★ 109,540) 87,889
Mahoba 56,152
Mahuva (★ 63,837) 59,675
Mainpuri 76,696
Makrāna (★ 66,654) 59,648
Malappuram (★ 142,203) 49,690
Malaut 56,856
Mālegaon 342,431
Māler Kotla 88,587
Malkajgiri (★ Hyderābād) 126,066
Malkāpur 51,302
Mancheriyal 52,626
Mandsaur 95,758
Mandya 119,970
Mangalagiri 59,276
Mangalore (★ 425,785) 272,819
Mango (★ Jamshedpur) 110,024
Manjeri 69,335
Manmād 61,257
Mannārgudi 56,563
Mānsa 55,088
Mathura (★ 233,235) 226,850
Maunath Bhanjan 136,447
Mawāna 51,644
Māyūram 77,042
Medinīpur 125,098
Meerut (★ 846,954) 752,078
Meerut Cantonment
(★ Meerut) 94,876
Melappālaiyam
(★ Tirunelveli) 68,318
Mettuppālaiyam 63,217
Mhow (★ 83,649) 74,852
Mira Bhayandar
(★ Bombay) 175,372
Miraj (★ Sāngli) 121,564
Miryalaguda 65,836
Mirzāpur 169,368
Modinagar (★ 124,197) 102,307
Moga (★ 110,867) 108,213
Mokāma 59,519
Morādābād (★ 432,434) 416,836
Morbi (★ 120,107) 90,349
Morena 147,095
Mormugao (★ 91,285) 83,209
Motihāri (★ 82,965) 77,440
Mubārakpur (★ 62,721) 45,388
Muktsar 66,377
Munger 150,042
Murwāra 163,390
Muzaffarnagar
(★ 247,729) 240,057
Muzaffarpur 240,450
Mysore (★ 652,246) 480,006
Nābha 54,079
Nadiād (★ 170,018) 166,852
Nagaon 93,324
Nāgappattinam
(★ 99,024) 86,155
Nāgaur 68,088
Nagda 79,405
Nāgercoil 189,482
Nagīna 58,494
Nāgpur (★ 1,661,409) 1,622,225
Naihāti (★ Calcutta) 132,032
Najībābād 66,842
Nalasopara (★ Bombay) 67,548
Nalgonda 84,674
Nānded (★ 308,853) 274,626
Nandurbār 78,364
Nandyāl 120,171
Nangi (★ Calcutta) 52,909
Narasapur 56,358
Narasaraopet 88,766
Nārnaul 51,880
Nāshik (★ 722,139) 646,896
Navadwīp (★ 156,117) 125,247
Navsāri (★ 190,019) 125,980
Nawābganj (★ 77,613) 64,719
Nawāda 53,075
Nawalgarh 51,168
Nedumangād 49,864
Neemuch (★ 90,460) 81,397
Nellore 316,445
New Bārākpur
(★ Calcutta) 63,857
New Bombay
(★ Bombay) 307,297
NEW DELHI (★ Delhi) 294,149
Neyveli (★ 126,494) 117,471
Nipāni 51,622
Nirmal 57,777
Nizāmābād 240,924
North Bārākpur
(★ Calcutta) 100,513
North Dum Dum
(★ Calcutta) 151,298
Ongole (★ 128,128) 100,544
Orai 98,640
Osmānābād 67,980
Pālakodu 56,972
Palani (★ 75,948) 68,747
Pālanpur (★ 90,231) 80,620
Pālayankottai
(★ Tirunelveli) 97,662
Pālghāt (★ 179,695) 122,964
Pāli 136,797
Pallavaram (★ Madras) 111,194
Palwal 59,127
Palwancha 52,892
Panaji (Panjim) (★ 85,199) 42,915
Pandharpur 79,798
Pānihāti (★ Calcutta) 275,359
Pānīpat 191,010
Panruti 51,424
Panvel 58,845
Paramakkudi 72,105
Parbhani 190,235
Parli 72,573
Pātan (★ 97,025) 96,109
Pathānkot (★ 147,130) 142,862
Patiāla (★ 268,521) 253,341
Patna (★ 1,098,572) 916,980
Pattukkottai 57,909
Payyannūr 64,011
Periyakulam 46,739
Petlād 48,546
Phagwāra (★ 88,855) 83,702
Pīlībhīt 106,329
Pilkhua 50,218
Pimpri-Chinchwad
(★ Pune) 515,962
Pollāchi (★ 127,180) 87,012
Pondicherry (★ 401,337) 202,648
Ponmalai
(★ Tiruchchirāppalli) 70,196
Ponnāni 51,754
Ponnūru Nidubrolu 54,352
Porbandar (★ 160,043) 116,546
Port Blair 74,810
Proddatūr 133,860
Pudukkottai 98,619
Puliyangudi 53,206
Pune (Poona)
(★ 2,485,014) 1,559,558
Pune Cantonment
(★ Pune) 81,978
Puri 124,835
Pūrnia (★ 135,995) 114,189
Puruliya 92,574
Pusad 55,919
Quilon (★ 362,402) 139,717
Qutubullapur
(★ Hyderābād) 105,380
Rabkavi Banhatti 60,607
Rāe Bareli 130,101
Rāichūr (★ 170,500) 157,477
Raiganj (★ 159,675) 151,454
Raigarh (★ 92,569) 89,166
Raipur (★ 461,851) 437,887
Rājahmundry (★ 403,781) 326,071
Rājapālaiyam 114,042
Rajendranagar
(★ Hyderābād) 83,849
Rajhara-Jharandalli 55,928
Rājkot (★ 651,007) 556,137
Rāj Nāndgaon 125,394
Rājpur (★ 86,390) 61,121
Rājpura 70,886
Rāmanagaram 50,411
Rāmanāthapuram 52,654
Rāmgarh (★ 82,186) 51,138
Rāmpur 242,752
Rānāghāt (★ 126,611) 64,244
Rānchi (★ 614,454) 598,498
Rānībennur 67,419
Rānīganj (★ 155,644) 62,014
Ratangarh 55,078
Ratlām (★ 195,752) 183,370
Ratnāgiri 56,512
Raurkela (★ 398,692) 215,489
Raurkela Civil Township
(★ Raurkela) 140,192
Rāyagāda 48,352
Rewa 128,918
Rewāri 75,294
Rishīkesh (★ 71,510) 44,399
Rishra (★ Calcutta) 102,649
Robertson Pet (★ Kolār Gold Fields) 67,900
Rohtak 215,844
Roorkee (★ 90,116) 80,236
Rudrapur 61,067
Sāgar (★ 256,878) 195,106
Sahāranpur 373,904
Saharsa 80,071
Sahaswān 51,067
Sāhibganj 49,133
Salem (★ 573,685) 363,934
Sāmalkot 48,727
Sambalpur (★ 192,917) 130,766
Sambhal 150,012
Sangamner 48,895
Sangareddi 50,098
Sāngli (★ 363,728) 193,181
Sangrūr 56,374
Sankarankovil 48,739
Sardārshahr 67,969
Sarni 84,201
Sāsarām 98,220
Sātāra 95,133
Satna (★ 160,191) 156,321
Sawāi Mādhopur
(★ 77,561) 72,037
Secunderābād Cantonment
(★ Hyderābād) 167,461
Sehore 71,437
Seoni 64,302
Serampore (★ Calcutta) 137,087
Serilungampalle
(★ Hyderābād) 72,648
Shahdol (★ 60,572) 55,554
Shāhjahānpur
(★ 260,260) 237,663
Shāmli 70,347
Shāntipur 109,911
Shikohābād 63,240
Shiliguri 226,677
Shillong (★ 222,273) 130,691
Shimoga (★ 192,647) 178,882
Shivpuri 108,271
Shrirampur (★ 79,042) 71,356
Siddhapur (★ 51,586) 50,858
Siddipet 54,020
Sikandarābād 61,035
Sīkar 148,235
Silchar 115,045
Silvassa 11,720
Simla (★ 109,860) 81,463
Sindri (★ Dhānbād) 72,349
Sircilla 50,012
Sirsa 112,542
Sītāmarhi (★ 67,320) 44,910
Sītāpur 120,595
Siuri 54,274
Sivakāsi (★ 102,139) 65,556
Siwān 81,092
Solāpur (★ 620,499) 603,870
Sonīpat 142,992
South Dum Dum
(★ Calcutta) 230,507
Srīkākulam 88,684
Srikalahasti 61,575
Srīnagar (★ 606,002)
(1981 C) 594,775
Srīrangam
(★ Tiruchchirāppalli) 69,928
Srīvilliputtūr 68,543
Sujāngarh 70,393
Sultānpur 76,567
Sūrat (★ 1,517,076) 149,643
Surendranagar
(★ 166,309) 105,973
Suriāpet 60,563
Tādepallegūdem 88,979
Tādpatri 71,043
Talipparamba 60,242
Tāmbaram (★ Madras) 106,590
Tānda 69,989
Tanuku 62,877
Tellicherry (★ 463,951) 103,577
Tenāli 143,836
Tenkāsi 55,044
Tezpur 54,999
Thāna (★ Bombay) 796,620
Thānesar 81,275
Thanjāvūr 200,216
Theni-Allinagaram 65,958
Thiruvārūr 49,194
Thrippunithura (★ Cochin) 51,032
Tīkamgarh 54,130
Tindivanam 61,715
Tinsukia 73,760
Tiruchchirāppalli
(★ 711,120) 386,628
Tiruchengodu 62,903
Tirunelveli (★ 365,932) 135,762
Tirupati (★ 189,030) 174,393
Tiruppattūr 54,884
Tiruppur (★ 305,546) 235,076
Tirūr 49,450
Tiruvalla 54,745
Tiruvannāmalai 108,291
Tirūvottiyūr (★ Madras) 167,851
Tītāgarh (★ Calcutta) 113,831
Tonk 100,020
Trichūr (★ 274,898) 73,849
Trivandrum (★ 825,682) 523,733
Ttruchchendūr (★ 75,400) 27,363
Tumkūr (★ 179,497) 138,598
Tuticorin (★ 284,193) 205,105
Udagamandalam 81,726
Udaipur 307,682
Udamalpet 58,643
Udgīr 70,409
Ujjain 366,787
Ulhāsnagar (★ Bombay) 368,822
Ulubāria 155,188
Unjha 50,947
Unnāo 107,246
Upleta 51,553
Uppal Kalan
(★ Hyderābād) 75,039
Uttarpara-Kotrung
(★ Calcutta) 100,867
Vadodara (★ 1,115,390) 1,021,084
Vālpārai 106,289
Vāniyambādi (★ 92,097) 72,282
Vārānasi (Benares)
(★ 1,026,467) 925,962
Vasai (Bassein)
(★ 83,572) 39,741
Veerappanchattiram
(★ Erode) 61,598
Vejalpur (★ Ahmadābād) 89,053
Vellore (★ 304,713) 172,467
Verāval (★ 119,995) 93,826
Vidisha 92,917
Vijayawāda (★ 845,305) 701,351
Vikramasingapuram 49,034
Viluppuram 88,916
Viramgām 51,089
Virār (★ Bombay) 57,581
Virudunagar 70,951
Vishākhapatnam
(★ 1,051,918) 750,024
Visnagar (★ 59,693) 57,834
Vizianagaram
(★ 176,125) 159,461
Vriddhāchalam 52,763
Wadhwan
(★ Surendranager) 49,773
Warangal (★ 466,877) 446,760
Wardha 102,974
Wāshīm 49,133
Yamunānagar
(★ 219,642) 144,250
Yavatmāl (★ 121,834) 108,591
Yemmiganur 65,118

INDONESIA

1990 C 179,378,946

Ambon (▲ 275,888) 205,193
Balikpapan 344,147
Banda Aceh (Kuturaja)
(▲ 184,650) 143,360
Bandung (★ 2,220,000) 2,058,122
Banjarmasin 480,737
Banyuwangi (1980 C) 90,378
Batang (1980 C) 49,328
Bekasi (★ Jakarta)
(1980 C) 144,290
Bengkulu 170,183
Binjai (▲ 181,866) 127,184
Blitar (★ 150,000) 118,933
Bogor (★ 560,000) 271,341
Bojonegoro (1980 C) 57,483
Bukittinggi 83,753
Cianjur (1980 C) 105,655
Cibinong (1980 C) 87,580
Cilacap (1980 C) 127,017
Cimahi (★ Bandung)
(1971 C) 72,367
Ciparay (1980 C) 66,854
Cirebon (★ 275,000) 254,477
Denpasar (1980 C) 159,233
Depok (★ Jakarta)
(1980 C) 126,693
Dili (▲ 123,475) 10,900
Garut (1980 C) 145,624
Genteng (1980 C) 59,481
Gorontalo (▲ 119,745) 94,058
Gresik (1980 C) 86,418
• JAKARTA (★ 10,000,000) 8,227,746
Jambi 339,786
Jayapura (Sukarnapura)
(1980 C) 60,641
Jember (1980 C) 171,284
Jombang (1980 C) 58,800
Karawang (1980 C) 72,195
Kediri 249,538
Kisaran (1980 C) 58,129
Klangenang (1980 C) 64,013
Klaten (1980 C) 117,560
Kudus (1980 C) 154,478
Kupang (1980 C) 84,587
Lumajang (1980 C) 58,495
Madiun (★ 200,000) 170,050
Magelang (★ 160,000) 123,156
Majalaya (1980 C) 87,474
Malang 695,089
Manado 320,600
Mataram (1980 C) 210,485
Medan 1,730,052
Mojokerto 99,707
Muncar (1980 C) 47,009
Padang (▲ 631,263) 477,064
Padangsidempuan
(1980 C) 56,984
Palangkaraya 112,511
Palembang 1,144,047
Pangkalpinang 113,129
Pare (1980 C) 47,262
Parepare (▲ 101,421) 84,093
Pasuruan (★ 190,000) 152,075
Pati (1980 C) 50,159
Payakumbuh (▲ 90,838) 50,475
Pekalongan (★ 380,000) 242,714
Pekanbaru 398,621
Pemalang (1980 C) 72,663
Pematangsiantar
(★ 250,000) 219,316
Ponorogo (1980 C) 55,523
Pontianak 396,658
Pringsewu (1980 C) 56,115
Probolinggo (▲ 176,906) 131,077
Purwakarta (1980 C) 61,995
Purwokerto (1980 C) 143,787
Salatiga 98,012
Samarinda (▲ 407,174) 334,851
Semarang 1,249,230
Serang (1980 C) 78,209
Sibolga 71,559
Sidoarjo (1980 C) 56,090
Singaraja (1980 C) 53,368
Singkawang (1980 C) 58,693
Situbondo (1980 C) 58,299
Sorong (1980 C) 52,041
Subang (1980 C) 52,041
Sukabumi (★ 225,000) 119,938
Surabaya 2,473,272
Surakarta (★ 590,000) 503,827
Taman (1980 C) 64,358
Tangerang (1980 C) 97,091
Tanjungbalai 107,751
Tanjungkarang-Telukbetung
(▲ 636,418) 457,927
Tanjungpinang 105,820
Tarakan (1980 C) 46,657
Tasikmalaya (1980 C) 192,267
Tebingtinggi 116,749
Tegal (★ 450,000) 229,553
Tembilahan (1980 C) 52,140
Tuban (1980 C) 48,558
Tulungagung (1980 C) 91,585
Ujungpandang (Makasar) 944,372
Yogyakarta (★ 510,000) 412,059

IRAN / Īrān

1986 C 49,445,010

Ābādān (1976 C) 296,081
Āghā Jārī (1982 E) 64,000
Ahar (1982 E) 52,000
Ahvāz 579,826
Alīgūdarz 53,843
Āmol 118,242
Andīmeshk (1982 E) 53,000
Arāk 265,349
Ardabīl 281,973
Bābol 115,320
Bākhtarān (Kermānshāh) 560,514
Bandar-e 'Abbās 201,642
Bandar-e Anzalī (Bandar-e Pahlavī)
(1982 E) 83,000
Bandar-e Būshehr 120,787
Bandar-e Māh Shahr
(1982 E) 88,000
Behbahān (1982 E) 84,000
Bīrjand (1982 E) 68,000
Bojnūrd (1982 E) 82,000
Borāzjān (1982 E) 53,000
Borūjerd 183,879
Dezfūl 151,420
Do Rūd (1982 E) 52,000
Emāmshahr (Shāhrūd)
(1982 E) 68,000
Eşfahān (★ 1,175,000) 986,753
Eslāmābād (1982 E) 71,000
Eslāmshahr (★ Tehrān) 215,129
Fasā (1982 E) 67,000
Gonbad-e Qābūs
(1982 E) 75,000
Gorgān 139,430
Hamadān 272,499
Īlām (1982 E) 75,000
Jahrom (1982 E) 68,000
Karaj (★ Tehrān) 275,100
Kāshān 138,599
Kāzerūn (1982 E) 63,000
Kermān 257,284
Khomeynīshahr
(★ Eşfahān) 104,647
Khorramābād 208,592
Khorramshahr (1976 C) 146,706
Khvorāsgān 51,155
Khvoy 115,343
Mahābād (1982 E) 63,000
Malāyer 103,640
Marāgheh 100,679
Marand (1982 E) 59,000
Marv Dasht (1982 E) 72,000
Mashhad 1,463,508
Masjed-e Soleymān 104,787
Mehr Shānī 57,477
Mīāndoāb (1982 E) 52,000
Mīāneh (1982 E) 57,000
Najafābād 129,058
Naqadeh 52,275
Neyshābūr 109,258
Orūmīyeh (Reẕā'īyeh) 300,746
Qā'emshahr 109,288
Qarchaqah 77,957
Qazvīn 248,591
Qom 543,139
Qomsheh (1982 E) 67,000
Qūchān (1982 E) 61,000
Rafsanjān (1982 E) 61,000
Rāmhormoz (1982 E) 53,000
Rasht 290,897
Sabzevār 129,103
Sanandaj 204,537
Saqqez (1982 E) 76,000
Sārī 141,020
Semnān (1982 E) 54,000
Shahr-e Kord (1982 E) 63,000
Shīrāz 848,289
Shīrvān 48,688
Shūshtar 65,840
Sīrjān (1982 E) 67,000
Tabrīz 971,482
• TEHRĀN (★ 7,500,000) 6,042,584
Torbat-e Heydarīyeh
(1982 E) 62,000
Varāmīn (1982 E) 51,000

C Census. E Official estimate. U Unofficial estimate.
• Largest city in country.

★ Population or designation of metropolitan area, including suburbs (see headnote).
▲ Population of an entire municipality, commune, or district, including rural area.

Yazd 230,483
Zābol (1982 E) 58,000
Zāhedān 281,923
Zanjān 215,261
Zarrīn Shahr (1982 E) 69,000

IRAQ / Al 'Irāq

1985 E 15,584,987

Ad-Dīwānīyah (1970 E) 62,300
Al-'Amārah 131,785
Al-Baṣrah 616,700
Al-Hillah 215,249
Al-Kūt 73,022
Al-Mawṣil 570,926
An-Najaf 242,603
An-Nāṣirīyah 138,842
Ar-Ramādī 137,388
As-Samāwah 75,293
As-Sulaymānīyah 279,424
• BAGHDAD (1987 C) 3,841,268
Ba'qūbah 114,516
Irbīl 333,903
Karbalā' 184,574
Kirkūk (1970 E) 207,900

IRELAND / Éire

1986 C 3,540,643

Cork (★ 173,694) 133,271
• DUBLIN (BAILE ÁTHA CLIATH) (★ 1,140,000) 502,749
Dún Laoghaire (★ Dublin) 54,715
Galway 47,104
Limerick (★ 76,557) 56,279
Waterford (★ 41,054) 39,529

ISLE OF MAN

1991 C 69,788

• DOUGLAS (★ 30,000) 22,214

ISRAEL / Isrā'īl / Yisra'el

1991 E 4,713,800

Ashdod 83,900
Ashqelon 59,700
Bat Yam (★ Tel Aviv-Yafo) 141,300
Be'ér Sheva (Beersheba) 122,000
Bene Beraq (★ Tel Aviv-Yafo) 116,700
Elat 26,300
Giv'atayim (★ Tel Aviv-Yafo) 46,600
Hefa (★ 450,000) 245,900
Herzliyya (★ Tel Aviv-Yafo) 77,200
Holon (★ Tel Aviv-Yafo) 156,700
Kefar Sava (★ Tel Aviv-Yafo) 61,100
Lod (Lydda) (★ Tel Aviv-Yafo) 43,300
Nazerat (Nazareth) (★ 77,000) 53,600
Netanya (★ Tel Aviv-Yafo) 132,200
Petah Tiqwa (★ Tel Aviv-Yafo) 144,000
Ra'ananna (★ Tel Aviv-Yafo) 53,600
Ramat Gan (★ Tel Aviv-Yafo) 119,500
Rehovot (★ Tel Aviv-Yafo) 80,300
Rishon LeZiyyon (★ Tel Aviv-Yafo) 139,500
• Tel Aviv-Yafo (★ 1,735,000) 339,400
YERUSHALAYIM (AL-QUDS) (JERUSALEM) (★ 560,000) 524,500

ISRAELI OCCUPIED TERRITORIES

1991 E 1,704,900

Al-Quds (Jerusalem) (★ Yerushalayim) (1976 E) 90,000
Arīhā (Jericho) (1967 C) 6,829
Bayt Lahm (Bethlehem) (1971 E) 25,000
• Ghazzah (1967 C) 118,272
Khān Yūnis (1967 C) 52,997
Nābulus (1971 E) 64,000
Rafah (1967 C) 49,812

ITALY / Italia

1991 C 56,411,290

Afragola (★ Napoli) 59,940
Alessandria (▲ 93,351) (1990 E) 74,000
Altamura 57,462
Ancona (1990 E) 103,268
Andria 82,556
Arezzo (▲ 91,623) (1990 E) 74,200
Asti (▲ 74,497) (1990 E) 62,800
Avellino 54,343
Aversa (★ Napoli) 50,361
Bari (★ 475,000) 341,273
Barletta 86,215
Benevento (▲ 62,683) 51,900
Bergamo (★ 345,000) 115,655
Biella (1990 E) 50,993
Bitonto 49,792
Bologna (★ 525,000) (1990 E) 411,803
Bolzano (1990 E) 100,380
Brescia (1990 E) 196,766
Brindisi 91,778
Busto Arsizio (★ Milano) 77,001
Cagliari (★ 305,000) (1990 E) 211,719
Caltanissetta (1990 E) 62,853
Campobasso (▲ 51,307) (1990 E) 44,400
Carpi (▲ 60,794) (1990 E) 49,600
Carrara (★ Massa) (1990 E) 68,480
Caserta 68,811
Casoria (▲ 79,315) (★Napoli) 57,800
Castellammare di Stabia (★ Napoli) 68,720
Catania (★ 550,000) 330,037
Catanzaro (1990 E) 103,802
Cava de'Tirreni (★ Salerno) 52,610
Cerignola 54,971
Cesena (▲ 89,497) (1990 E) 72,200
Chieti (1990 E) 57,535
Cinisello Balsamo (★ Milano) 75,606
Civitavecchia 50,856
Collegno (★ Torino) 47,192
Cologno Monzese (★ Milano) 50,853
Como (★ 165,000) 85,955
Cosenza (★ 150,000) (1990 E) 104,483
Cremona (1990 E) 75,160
Crotone (▲ 61,813) (1990 E) 54,300
Cuneo (▲ 55,838) (1990 E) 47,900
Empoli (▲ 42,790) 32,300
Ercolano (★ Napoli) 60,869
Ferrara (▲ 140,600) (1990 E) 110,700
Firenze (★ 640,000) 402,316
Foggia 155,042
Foligno (▲ 53,518) (1990 E) 42,500
Forlì (▲ 109,755) (1990 E) 90,600
Gela (1990 E) 79,718
Genova (Genoa) (★ 805,000) 675,639
Giugliano in Campania (★ Napoli) 59,091
Grosseto (▲ 71,373) (1990 E) 57,000
Imola (▲ 62,352) (1990 E) 48,800
Imperia (1990 E) 41,278
L'Aquila (▲ 67,818) (1990 E) 43,100
La Spezia (★ 185,000) 101,701
Latina (▲ 105,543) 72,700
Lecce (1990 E) 102,344
Lecco 45,859
Legnano (★ Milano) 50,068
Livorno (1990 E) 171,265
Lucca (1990 E) 86,437
Manfredonia 58,157
Mantova (▲ 54,228) (1990 E) 46,800
Marsala 77,218
Massa (★ 145,000) (1990 E) 67,779
Matera (1990 E) 54,872
Messina (1990 E) 274,846
Mestre (▲ 317,837) (★Venezia) (1990 E) 181,900
• Milano (Milan) (★ 3,750,000) 1,371,008
Modena (1990 E) 177,501
Molfetta 66,658
Moncalieri (★ Torino) 58,433
• MONOPOLI (▲ 43,019) 33,100
Monza (★ Milano) 121,151
Napoli (Naples) (★ 2,875,000) 1,024,601
Nicastro (▲ 69,660) (1990 E) 53,700
Nocera Inferiore 49,021
Novara (1990 E) 103,349
Padova (★ 270,000) (1990 E) 218,186
Palermo 697,162
Parma (1990 E) 173,991
Pavia (1990 E) 80,073
Perugia (▲ 150,576) (1990 E) 109,500
Pesaro (▲ 90,341) (1990 E) 78,700
Pescara (1990 E) 128,553
Piacenza 102,252
Pisa (1990 E) 101,500
Pistoia (▲ 87,275) 73,900
Pordenone (1990 E) 50,222
Portici (★ Napoli) 67,824
Potenza (▲ 68,499) (1990 E) 58,800
Pozzuoli (▲ 75,706) (★Napoli) 67,100
Prato (★ 215,000) 165,364
Quartu Sant'Elena (1990 E) 60,852
Ragusa (1990 E) 69,423
Ravenna (▲ 136,724) (1990 E) 87,000
Reggio di Calabria (1990 E) 178,496
Reggio nell'Emilia (▲ 131,880) (1990 E) 108,800
Rho (★ Milano) 51,646
Rimini (▲ 130,896) (1990 E) 114,800
Rivoli (★ Torino) 51,884
ROMA (★ 3,175,000) 2,693,383
Salerno (★ 250,000) 153,436
San Benedetto del Tronto (1990 E) 45,220
San Giorgio a Cremano (★ Napoli) 62,168
San Remo (1990 E) 59,247
San Severo 55,376
Sassari (1990 E) 120,011
Savona (★ 112,000) (1990 E) 68,997
Scandicci (★ Firenze) 53,264
Sesto Fiorentino (★ Firenze) 46,899
Sesto San Giovanni (★ Milano) 85,175
Siena (1990 E) 57,745
Siracusa (1990 E) 125,444
Taranto 232,200
Teramo (▲ 52,490) (1990 E) 36,100
Terni (▲ 109,809) (1990 E) 93,400
Torino (★ 1,550,000) 961,916
Torre Annunziata (★ Napoli) 50,346
Torre del Greco (★ Napoli) 101,456
Trani 49,337
Trapani (▲ 69,273) 59,700
Trento (▲ 102,124) (1990 E) 83,100
Treviso (1990 E) 83,886
Trieste (Triest) (1990 E) 231,047
Udine (★ 126,000) (1990 E) 98,322
Varese 85,461
Venezia (Venice) (★ 420,000) (1990 E) 85,100
Vercelli (1990 E) 50,207
Verona (1990 E) 258,946
Viareggio (▲ 60,559) (1990 E) 51,500
Vicenza (1990 E) 109,333
Vigevano (1990 E) 61,380
Viterbo (▲ 60,213) (1990 E) 48,700
Vittoria (1990 E) 56,970

IVORY COAST / Côte d'Ivoire

1983 E 9,300,000

• ABIDJAN 1,950,000
Bouaké 275,000
Daloa (1986 E) 120,000
Korhogo 125,000
Man (1986 E) 59,000
YAMOUSSOUKRO 80,000

JAMAICA

1990 E 2,392,000

• KINGSTON (★ 820,000) 661,600
Montego Bay (▲ 155,700) 80,500
Portmore (★ Kingston) (1982 C) 73,426
Spanish Town (▲ 358,600) (★Kingston) 96,100

JAPAN / Nihon

1990 C 123,611,541

Abiko (★ Tōkyō) 120,629
Ageo (★ Tōkyō) 194,952
Aizu-wakamatsu 119,084
Akashi (★ Ōsaka) 270,728
Akigawa (★ Tōkyō) 50,388
Akishima (★ Tōkyō) 105,375
Akita 302,359
Akō 51,131
Amagasaki (★ Ōsaka) 498,998
Anan (▲ 59,045) 47,000
Anjō 142,217
Aomori 287,813
Arao (★ Ōmuta) 59,508
Asahikawa 359,069
Asaka (★ Tōkyō) 103,621
Ashikaga 167,687
Ashiya (★ Ōsaka) 87,528
Atami 47,290
Atsugi (★ Tōkyō) 197,292
Ayase (★ Tōkyō) 77,926
Beppu 130,323
Bisai (★ Nagoya) 55,881
Chiba (★ Tōkyō) 829,467
Chichibu 60,916
Chigasaki (★ Tōkyō) 201,672
Chikushino (★ Fukuoka) 70,303
Chiryū (★ Nagoya) 54,061
Chita (★ Nagoya) 75,434
Chitose 78,947
Chōfu (★ Tōkyō) 197,680
Chōshi 85,138
Daitō (★ Ōsaka) 126,460
Dazaifu (★ Fukuoka) 62,408
Ebetsu (★ Sapporo) 97,201
Ebina (★ Tōkyō) 105,816
Eniwa 55,613
Fuchū (★ Tōkyō) 209,419
Fuchū 45,738
Fuchū 50,061
Fuji (★ 370,000) 222,500
Fujieda (★ Shizuoka) 119,815
Fujiidera (★ Ōsaka) 65,924
Fujimi (★ Tōkyō) 94,858
Fujinomiya (★ Fuji) 117,093
Fujioka (▲ 60,983) 50,100
Fujisawa (★ Tōkyō) 350,335
Fuji-yoshida 54,802
Fukaya (▲ 94,023) 75,600
Fukuchiyama (▲ 66,506) 56,700
Fukui 252,750
Fukuoka (★ 1,750,000) 1,237,107
Fukushima 277,526
Fukuyama 365,615
Funabashi (★ Tōkyō) 533,273
Furukawa (▲ 64,227) 51,200
Fussa (★ Tōkyō) 58,053
Gamagōri 84,819
Gifu 410,318
Ginowan (1985 C) 69,206
Ginowan 75,899
Gotemba 79,560
Gushikawa 54,026
Gyōda 83,181
Habikino (★ Ōsaka) 115,035
Hachinohe 241,065
Hachiōji (★ Tōkyō) 466,373
Hadano (★ Tōkyō) 155,619
Hagi 50,619
Hakodate 307,251
Hamada 49,139
Hamakita 81,159
Hamamatsu 534,624
Hanamaki (▲ 70,514) 55,000
Handa (★ Nagoya) 99,550
Hannō (★ Tōkyō) 73,216
Hashima 61,460
Hasuda (★ Tōkyō) 59,703
Hatogaya (★ Tōkyō) 56,441
Hatsukaichi (★ Hiroshima) 63,441
Hekinan 65,901
Higashihiroshima (★ Hiroshima) 94,206
Higashikurume (★ Tōkyō) 113,800
Higashimatsuyama 84,395
Higashimurayama (★ Tōkyō) 134,002
Higashiōsaka (★ Ōsaka) 518,251
Higashiyamato (★ Tōkyō) 75,124
Hikari (★ Tokuyama) 47,613
Hikone 99,518
Himeji (★ 660,000) 454,360
Himi (▲ 60,768) 51,400
Hino (★ Tōkyō) 165,935
Hirakata (★ Ōsaka) 390,790
Hiratsuka (★ Tōkyō) 245,944
Hirosaki (▲ 174,710) 133,800
Hiroshima (★ 1,575,000) 1,085,677
Hita (▲ 64,694) 57,100
Hitachi 202,145
Hōfu 117,639
Honjō 59,094
Hōya (★ Tōkyō) 95,148
Hyūga 58,448
Ibaraki (★ Ōsaka) 254,080
Ichihara (★ Tōkyō) 257,717
Ichikawa (★ Tōkyō) 436,597
Ichinomiya (★ Nagoya) 262,434
Ichinoseki (▲ 61,971) 50,100
Iida (▲ 91,859) 64,700
Iizuka (★ 110,000) 83,133
Ikeda (★ Ōsaka) 104,219
Ikoma (★ Ōsaka) 99,598
Imabari 123,114
Imari (▲ 60,887) 50,000
Ina (▲ 60,063) 49,500
Inagi (★ Tōkyō) 58,593
Inazawa (★ Nagoya) 96,277
Inuyama (★ Nagoya) 69,803
Iruma (★ Tōkyō) 137,585
Isahaya 90,678
Ise (Uji-yamada) 104,162
Isehara (★ Tōkyō) 89,568
Isesaki 115,939
Ishinomaki 121,980
Itami (★ Ōsaka) 186,132
Itō 71,223
Iwaki (Taira) 355,817
Iwakuni 109,534
Iwamizawa 80,423
Iwata 83,521
Iwatsuki (★ Tōkyō) 106,462
Izumi (★ Sendai) 124,216
Izumi (★ Ōsaka) 146,105
Izumi-ōtsu (★ Ōsaka) 67,037
Izumi-sano (★ Ōsaka) 88,862
Izumo (▲ 82,680) 69,600
Jōetsu 130,114
Jōyō (★ Ōsaka) 84,770
Kadoma (★ Ōsaka) 142,288
Kaga 69,199
Kagoshima 536,685
Kainan (★ Wakayama) 48,598
Kaizuka (★ Ōsaka) 79,236
Kakamigahara 129,682
Kakegawa (▲ 72,795) 59,000
Kakogawa (★ Ōsaka) 239,803
Kamagaya (★ Tōkyō) 95,052
Kamaishi 52,483
Kamakura (★ Tōkyō) 174,299
Kameoka 85,283
Kamifukuoka (★ Tōkyō) 58,753
Kanazawa 442,872
Kani (★ Nagoya) 80,012
Kanoya (▲ 77,652) 61,500
Kanuma (▲ 90,044) 74,900
Karatsu (▲ 79,206) 70,500
Kariya (★ Nagoya) 120,121
Kasai 51,789
Kasaoka (▲ 59,618) 52,700
Kashihara (★ Ōsaka) 115,556
Kashiwa (★ Tōkyō) 305,060
Kashiwara (★ Ōsaka) 76,819
Kashiwazaki (▲ 88,309) 75,300
Kasuga (★ Fukuoka) 88,703
Kasugai (★ Nagoya) 266,599
Kasukabe (★ Tōkyō) 188,809
Katano (★ Ōsaka) 65,311
Katsuta 109,826
Kawachi-nagano (★ Ōsaka) 108,770
Kawagoe (★ Tōkyō) 304,860
Kawaguchi (★ Tōkyō) 438,667
Kawanishi (★ Ōsaka) 141,254
Kawasaki (★ Tōkyō) 1,173,606
Kesennuma 65,578
Kimitsu (▲ 89,243) 76,100
Kiryū 126,443
Kisarazu 123,434
Kishiwada (★ Ōsaka) 188,553
Kitaibaraki 51,092
Kitakyūshū (★ 1,525,000) 1,026,467
Kitami 107,247
Kitamoto (★ Tōkyō) 63,933
Kiyose (★ Tōkyō) 67,540
Kōbe (★ Ōsaka) 1,477,423
Kōchi 317,090
Kodaira (★ Tōkyō) 164,021
Kōfu 200,630
Koga (★ Tōkyō) 58,227
Koganei (★ Tōkyō) 105,888
Kokubunji (★ Tōkyō) 100,958
Komae (★ Tōkyō) 74,197
Komaki (★ Nagoya) 124,441
Komatsu 106,072
Kōnan (★ Nagoya) 93,836
Kōnosu (★ Tōkyō) 72,436
Kōriyama 314,651
Koshigaya (★ Tōkyō) 285,280
Kudamatsu (★ Tokuyama) 53,029
Kuki (★ Tōkyō) 66,852
Kumagaya 152,122
Kumamoto 579,305
Kunitachi (★ Tōkyō) 65,830
Kurashiki 414,692
Kure (★ Hiroshima) 216,717
Kuroiso (▲ 52,346) 41,900
Kurume 228,350
Kusatsu (★ Ōsaka) 94,766
Kushiro 205,640
Kuwana (★ Nagoya) 97,911
Kyōto (★ Ōsaka) 1,461,140
Machida (★ Tōkyō) 349,030
Maebashi 286,261
Maizuru 96,329
Marugame 75,607
Matsubara (★ Ōsaka) 135,921
Matsudo (★ Tōkyō) 456,211
Matsue 142,931
Matsumoto 200,723
Matsusaka 118,727
Matsuyama 443,317
Mihara 85,518
Miki (★ Ōsaka) 76,509
Minō (★ Ōsaka) 122,133
Misato (★ Tōkyō) 128,377
Mishima (★ Numazu) 105,419
Mitaka (★ Tōkyō) 165,555
Mito 234,970
Miura (★ Tōkyō) 52,441
Miyako 58,505
Miyakonojō (▲ 130,155) 106,200
Miyazaki 287,367
Mobara 83,437
Moriguchi (★ Ōsaka) 157,365
Morioka 235,440
Moriyama 58,561
Mukō (★ Ōsaka) 52,932
Munakata 68,267
Muroran (★ 195,000) 117,852
Musashimurayama (★ Tōkyō) 65,555
Musashino (★ Tōkyō) 139,069
Mutsu 48,470
Nabari 68,933
Nagahama 55,482
Nagano 347,036
Nagaoka 185,938
Nagaokakyō (★ Ōsaka) 77,193
Nagareyama (★ Tōkyō) 140,059
Nagasaki 444,616
Nagoya (★ 4,800,000) 2,154,664
Naha 304,896
Nakama (★ Kitakyūshū) 49,216
Nakatsu 66,383
Nakatsugawa 53,722
Nanao 50,101
Nara (★ Ōsaka) 349,356
Narashino (★ Tōkyō) 151,472
Narita 86,708
Naruto 64,577
Naze 46,309
Neyagawa (★ Ōsaka) 256,521
Niigata 486,087
Niihama 129,151
Niitsu (▲ 64,005) 55,700
Niiza (★ Tōkyō) 138,919
Nishinomiya (★ Ōsaka) 426,919
Nishio 95,198
Nobeoka 130,615
Noboribetsu (★ Muroran) 55,575
Noda (★ Tōkyō) 114,476
Nōgata 62,532
Noshiro (▲ 55,915) 47,800
Numazu (★ 495,000) 211,731
Obihiro 167,389
Ōbu (★ Nagoya) 69,721
Ōdate (▲ 68,196) 58,500
Odawara 193,415
Ōgaki 148,281
Ōita 408,502
Ōkawa 45,705
Okaya 59,854
Okayama 593,742
Okazaki 306,821
Okegawa (★ Tōkyō) 69,030
Okinawa (1985 C) 101,210
Okinawa 105,852
Ōme (★ Tōkyō) 125,945
Ōmi-hachiman (★ Ōsaka) 66,068
Ōmiya (★ Tōkyō) 403,779
Ōmura 73,437
Ōmuta (★ 225,000) 150,461
Ōnojō (★ Fukuoka) 75,217
Onomichi 97,104
Ōsaka (★ 16,900,000) 2,623,831
Ōta 139,801
Otaru (★ Sapporo) 163,215
Ōtsu (★ Ōsaka) 260,004
Owariasahi (★ Nagoya) 65,676
Oyama (▲ 142,263) 120,000
Sabae 62,284
Saga 169,964
Sagamihara (★ Tōkyō) 531,562
Saijō 56,823
Saiki 52,325
Sakado (★ Tōkyō) 95,736
Sakai (★ Ōsaka) 807,859
Sakaide 63,878
Sakata 100,808
Saku (▲ 62,005) 50,000
Sakura (★ Tōkyō) 144,688
Sakurai 60,261
Sanda (▲ 64,560) Ōsaka) 54,500
Sanjō 85,824
Sano 83,484
Sapporo (★ 1,900,000) 1,671,765

C Census. E Official estimate. U Unofficial estimate.
• Largest city in country.

★ Population or designation of metropolitan area, including suburbs (see headnote).
▲ Population of an entire municipality, commune, or district, including rural area.

Sasebo 244,693
Satte 54,339
Sayama (★ Tōkyō) 157,307
Sayama (★ Ōsaka) 54,323
Seki 68,386
Sendai, Kagoshima pref. (▲ 71,736) 58,000
Sendai, Miyagi pref. (★ 1,175,000) 918,378
Sennan (★ Ōsaka) 60,054
Seto 126,343
Settsu (★ Ōsaka) 87,465
Shibata (▲ 78,168) 63,600
Shijōnawate (★ Ōsaka) 50,036
Shiki (★ Tōkyō) 63,492
Shimada (▲ 73,809) 64,500
Shimizu (★ Shizuoka) 241,524
Shimodate (▲ 66,030) 54,100
Shimonoseki (★ Kitakyūshū) 262,643
Shiogama (★ Sendai) 62,025
Shizuoka (★ 975,000) 472,199
Sōka (★ Tōkyō) 206,129
Suita (★ Ōsaka) 345,187
Suwa 52,465
Suzuka 174,103
Tachikawa (★ Tōkyō) 152,817
Tagajō (★ Sendai) 58,456
Tagawa 57,701
Tajimi (★ Nagoya) 94,036
Takaishi (★ Ōsaka) 65,084
Takamatsu 329,695
Takaoka (★ 220,000) 175,469
Takarazuka (★ Ōsaka) 201,863
Takasago (★ Ōsaka) 93,267
Takasaki 236,463
Takatsuki (★ Ōsaka) 359,867
Takayama 65,245
Takefu 70,188
Takikawa 49,591
Tama (★ Tōkyō) 144,490
Tamano 73,240
Tanabe (▲ 69,861) 59,100
Tanashi (★ Tōkyō) 75,141
Tatebayashi 76,223
Tenri 68,818
Tochigi 86,216
Toda (★ Tōkyō) 87,600
Tōkai (★ Nagoya) 97,359
Toki 64,946
Tokoname (★ Nagoya) 51,784
Tokorozawa (★ Tōkyō) 303,047
Tokushima 263,356
Tokuyama (★ 250,000) 110,900
• TŌKYŌ (★ 30,300,000) 8,163,127
Tomakomai 160,116
Tondabayashi (★ Ōsaka) 110,444
Toride (★ Tōkyō) 81,667
Tosu 55,878
Tottori 142,477
Toyama 321,459
Toyoake (★ Nagoya) 62,156
Toyohashi 337,988
Toyokawa 111,731
Toyonaka (★ Ōsaka) 409,843
Toyota 332,336
Tsu 157,178
Tsuchiura 127,470
Tsuruga 68,039
Tsuruoka 99,891
Tsushima (★ Nagoya) 59,345
Tsuyama 89,405
Ube (★ 230,000) 175,052
Ueda 119,435
Ueno (▲ 60,239) 51,400
Uji (★ Ōsaka) 177,018
Uozu 49,516
Urasoe 89,993
Urawa (★ Tōkyō) 418,267
Urayasu (★ Tōkyō) 115,675
Usa (▲ 50,830) 38,600
Ushiku 60,698
Utsunomiya 426,809
Uwajima 68,034
Wakayama (★ 495,000) 396,554
Wakkanai 48,232
Wakō (★ Tōkyō) 56,891
Warabi (★ Tōkyō) 73,620
Yachiyo (★ Tōkyō) 148,615
Yaizu (★ Shizuoka) 112,188
Yamagata 249,493
Yamaguchi 129,467
Yamato (★ Tōkyō) 194,870
Yamato-kōriyama (★ Ōsaka) 92,948
Yamato-takada (★ Ōsaka) 68,236
Yao (★ Ōsaka) 277,724
Yashio (★ Tōkyō) 72,474
Yatsushiro (▲ 108,135) 88,300
Yawata (★ Ōsaka) 75,761
Yokkaichi 274,184
Yokohama (★ Tōkyō) 3,220,350
Yokosuka (★ Tōkyō) 433,361
Yonago 131,453
Yonezawa 94,763
Yono (★ Tōkyō) 79,058
Yotsukaidō (★ Tōkyō) 72,157
Yukuhashi 65,713
Zama (★ Tōkyō) 112,100
Zushi (★ Tōkyō) 56,705

JERSEY

1991 C 84,082
• SAINT HELIER (★ 46,500) 28,123

JORDAN / Al-Urdun

1989 E 3,111,000
Al-Baq'ah (★ 'Ammān) 63,985
• 'AMMĀN (★ 1,625,000) 936,300
Ar-Ruṣayfah (★ 'Ammān) 72,580
As-Salt 47,585
Az-Zarqā' (★ 'Ammān) 318,055
Irbid 167,785

KAZAKHSTAN

1991 E 16,793,100
Aktau 169,000
Akt'ubinsk 266,600
• ALMA-ATA (ALMATY) (★ 1,190,000) 1,156,200
Arkalyk 64,900
Aterau 156,700
Balchaš 87,600
Çelinograd 286,000
Čimkent 438,800
Džambul 312,300
Džetygara 48,900
Džezkazgan 111,100
Ekibastuz 138,900
Karaganda 608,600
Kentau 65,100
Kokčetav 143,300
Kustanaj 233,900
Kzyl-Orda 158,200
Leninogorsk 69,500
Leninsk 73,000
Pavlodar 342,500
Petropavlovsk 248,300
Rudnyj 128,800
Šachtinsk 65,300
Saptajev 61,400
Šaran' 62,600
Ščučinsk 56,000
Semipalatinsk 344,700
Taldy-Kurgan 136,100
Turkestan 81,200
Ural'sk 214,000
Ust'-Kamenogorsk 332,900
Žanatas 53,000
Zyr'anovsk 53,800

KENYA

1990 E 24,870,000
Eldoret (1979 C) 50,503
Kisumu (1984 E) 167,100
Machakos (1983 E) 92,300
Meru (1979 C) 72,049
Mombasa 537,000
• NAIROBI 1,505,000
Nakuru (1984 E) 101,700

KIRIBATI

1990 C 72,298
BAIRIKI 2,226
• Bikenibeu 5,055

KOREA, NORTH / Chosŏn-minjujuŭi-inmīn-konghwaguk

1981 E 18,317,000
Ch'ŏngjin 490,000
Haeju (1983 E) 213,000
Hamhŭng (1970 E) 150,000
Hŭngnam (1976 E) 260,000
Kaesŏng 259,000
Kanggye (1967 E) 130,000
Kimch'aek (Sŏngjin) (1967 E) 265,000
Namp'o 241,000
• P'YŎNGYANG (★ 1,600,000) 1,283,000
Sinŭiju 305,000
Songnim (1944 C) 53,035
Wŏnsan 398,000

KOREA, SOUTH / Taehan-min'guk

1990 C 43,520,199
Andong 116,932
Ansan (★ Sŏul) 252,157
Anyang (★ Sŏul) 480,668
Bucheon (★ Sŏul) 667,777
Changsŭngp'o 48,614
Changwŏn (★ Masan) 323,138
Chech'ŏn 102,037
Cheju 232,687
Chinhae 120,207
Chinju 258,365
Chŏmch'ŏn 47,802
Ch'ŏnan 211,382
Ch'ŏngju 497,429
Chŏnju 86,850
Chŏnju, Chŏlla Pukdo prov. 517,104
Ch'unch'ŏn 174,153
Ch'ungju 129,994
Ch'ungmu 92,159
Hanam (★ Sŏul) 101,278
Inch'ŏn (★ Sŏul) 1,818,293
Iri 203,401
Kangnŭng 152,605
Kimch'ŏn 81,349
Kimhae 106,166
Kimje 55,136
Kongju 65,195
Kumi 206,101
Kŭmsŏng (1985 C) 58,897
Kunp'o (★ Sŏul) 99,956
Kunsan 218,216
Kwachŏn (★ Sŏul) 72,328
Kwangju 1,144,695
Kwangmyŏng (★ Sŏul) 328,803
Kyŏngju 141,895
Kyŏngsan 60,524
Masan (★ 625,000) 496,639
Mikŭm (★ Sŏul) 74,688
Miryang 52,995
Mokp'o 253,423
Naju 55,306
Namwŏn 63,121
Ŏnyang 66,379
Osan 59,492
P'ohang 318,595
Pusan (★ 3,800,000) 3,797,566
P'yŏngt'aek 79,238
Samch'ŏnp'o 62,824
Sangju 51,875
Shihŭng (★ Sŏul) 107,190
Sŏgwipo 88,292
Sŏkch'o 73,796
Sŏngnam (★ Sŏul) 540,764
Songtan 77,460
Sŏsan 55,930
• SŎUL (★ 15,850,000) 10,627,790
Sunch'ŏn 167,209
Suwŏn (★ Sŏul) 644,968
T'aebaek 89,770
Taech'ŏn 56,922
Taegu 2,228,834
Taejŏn 1,062,084
Tongduch'ŏn 71,448
Tonghae 89,162
Tongkwang 70,118
Ŭijŏngbu (★ Sŏul) 212,368
Ŭiwang 96,892
Ulsan 682,978
Wŏnju 173,013
Yŏch'ŏn 63,802
Yŏngch'ŏn 48,890
Yŏngju 84,335
Yŏsu 173,164

KUWAIT / Al-Kuwayt

1985 C 1,697,301
Abraq Khīṭān (★ Al-Kuwayt) 45,120
Al-Aḥmadī (★ 285,000) 26,899
Al-Farwānīyah (★ Al-Kuwayt) 68,701
Al-Fuḥayḥīl (★ Al-Aḥmadī) 50,081
Al-Jahrah (★ Al-Kuwayt) 111,222
• AL-KUWAYT (★ 1,375,000) 44,335
As-Sālimīyah (★ Al-Kuwayt) 153,359
Aṣ-Ṣulaybīyah (★ Al-Kuwayt) 51,314
Hawallī (★ Al-Kuwayt) 145,126
Qalīb ash-Shuyūkh (★ Al-Kuwayt) 114,771
South Khīṭān (★ Al-Kuwayt) 69,256
Subahiya (★ Al-Aḥmadī) 60,787

KYRGYZSTAN

1991 E 4,422,200
• BIŠKEK 631,300
Džalal-Abad 79,900
Kara-Balta 55,000
Karakol (Prževal'sk) 64,300
Oš 238,200
Tokmak 71,200

LAOS / Lao

1985 C 3,584,803
Savannakhét (1975 E) 53,000
• VIANGCHAN (VIENTIANE) 377,409

LATVIA / Latvija

1991 E 2,680,500
Daugavpils 129,000
Jelgava 74,500
Jūrmala (★ Rīga) 66,500
Liepāja 114,900
• RĪGA (★ 1,005,000) 910,200
Ventspils 50,400

LEBANON / Lubnān

1982 E 2,637,000
• BAYRŪT (★ 1,675,000) 509,000
Saydā 105,000
Şūr (Tyre) (1970 E) 12,500
Tarābulus (Tripoli) (★ 950,000) 198,000

LESOTHO

1986 C 1,577,536
• MASERU 109,382

LIBERIA

1986 E 2,221,000
• MONROVIA 465,000

LIBYA / Lībiyā

1988 E 3,772,500
Al-Bayḍā (Beida) (1984 C) 67,120
Banghāzī 446,250
Darnah (1984 C) 62,179
Misrātah 121,669
• TARABULUS (TRIPOLI) 591,062
Tubruq (Tobruk) (1984 C) 75,282

LIECHTENSTEIN

1992 E 29,386
• VADUZ 4,887

LITHUANIA / Lietuva

1989 C 3,690,000
Alytus (1987 E) 71,000
Kaunas 423,000
Klaipėda (Memel) 204,000
Panevėžys 126,000
Šiauliai 145,000
• VILNIUS 582,000

LUXEMBOURG

1991 C 384,062
Esch-sur-Alzette (★ 83,000) 24,012
• LUXEMBOURG (★ 136,000) 75,377

MACAU

1989 E 452,300
• MACAU 452,300

MACEDONIA / Makedonija

1987 E 2,064,581
Bitola (▲ 143,090) 76,200
• SKOPJE (▲ 547,214) 444,900

MADAGASCAR / Madagasikara

1988 E 11,238,000
• ANTANANARIVO 1,250,000
Antsirabe (▲ 100,000) 52,700
Antsiranana 220,000
Fianarantsoa 300,000
Mahajanga 200,000
Toamasina 230,000
Toliara 150,000

MALAWI / Malaŵi

1987 C 7,982,607
• Blantyre 331,588
LILONGWE 233,973

MALAYSIA

1980 C 13,136,109
Alor Setar 69,435
Batu Pahat 64,727
Butterworth (★ George Town) 77,982
George Town (Pinang) (★ 495,000) 248,241
Ipoh 293,849
Johor Baharu (★ Singapore) 246,395
Kelang 192,080
Keluang 50,315
Kota Baharu 167,872
Kota Kinabalu (Jesselton) 55,997
• KUALA LUMPUR (★ 1,475,000) 919,610
Kuala Terengganu 180,296
Kuantan 131,547
Kuching 72,555
Melaka 87,494
Miri 52,125
Muar (Bandar Maharani) 65,151
Petaling Jaya (★ Kuala Lumpur) 207,805
Sandakan 70,420
Seremban 132,911
Sibu 85,231
Taiping 146,000
Telok Anson 49,148

MALDIVES

1990 C 213,215
• MALE' 55,130

MALI

1987 C 7,696,348
• BAMAKO 658,275
Gao 54,874
Kayes 48,216
Koutiala 48,010
Mopti 73,979
Ségou 88,877
Sikasso 73,050
Tombouctou (Timbuktu) 31,925

MALTA

1991 E 355,910
• VALLETTA (★ 215,000) 9,199

MARSHALL ISLANDS

1980 C 30,873
• Jarej-Uliga-Delap 8,583

MARTINIQUE

1982 C 328,566
• FORT-DE-FRANCE (★ 116,017) 99,844

MAURITANIA / Mauritanie / Mūrītāniyā

1987 E 2,007,000
• NOUAKCHOTT 285,000

MAURITIUS

1989 E 1,081,669
Beau Bassin-Rose Hill (★ Port Louis) 94,236
Curepipe (★ Port Louis) 66,704
• PORT LOUIS (★ 420,000) 141,870
Quatre Bornes (★ Port Louis) 65,759
Vacoas-Phoenix (★ Port Louis) 56,335

MAYOTTE

1985 E 67,205
• DZAOUDZI (★ 6,979) 5,865

MEXICO / México

1990 C 81,249,645
Acámbaro 52,248
Acapulco [de Juárez] 515,374
Aguascalientes 440,425
Apatzingán de la Constitución 76,643
Apodaca 103,364
Atlixco 74,233
Buenavista 114,653
Campeche 150,518
Cancún 167,730
Cárdenas 61,017
Celaya 214,856
Chalco (★ Ciudad de México) 224,190
Chetumal 94,158
Chicoloapan de Juárz 57,306
Chihuahua 516,153
Chilpancingo de los Bravo 97,165
Chimalhuacán 235,587
Cholula [de Rivadabia] (★ Puebla) 53,673
Ciudad Acuña 52,983
Ciudad del Carmen 83,806
• CIUDAD DE MÉXICO (★ 14,100,000) 8,235,744
Ciudad Guzmán 72,619
Ciudad Hidalgo 48,476
Ciudad Juárez (★ El Paso, Tex., U.S.A.) 789,522
Ciudad Lerdo (★ Torreón) 46,593
Ciudad López Mateos 315,059
Ciudad Madero (★ Tampico) 160,331
Ciudad Mante 76,799
Ciudad Obregón 219,980
Ciudad Valles 91,402
Ciudad Victoria 194,996
Coacalco 151,255
Coatzacoalcos 198,817
Colima 106,967
Comitan de Dominguez 48,299
Comondú 74,346
Córdoba 130,695
Cortazar 45,579
Cuauhtémoc 69,895
Cuautitlán Izcalli (★ Ciudad de México) 313,238
Cuernavaca 279,187
Culiacán 415,046
Delicias 87,412
Durango 348,036
Ecatepec (★ Ciudad de México) 1,218,135
Ensenada 169,426
Fresnillo 75,118
Garza García (★ Monterrey) 113,017
Gómez Palacio (★ Torreón) 164,092
Guadalajara (★ 2,325,000) 1,650,042
Guadalupe 46,433
Guadalupe (★ Monterrey) 535,332
Guamúchil 49,635
Guanajuato 73,108
Guasave 49,338
Guaymas 87,484
Hermosillo 406,417
Heroica Zitácuaro 66,983
Hidalgo del Parral 88,197
Iguala 83,412

C Census. E Official estimate. U Unofficial estimate.
• Largest city in country.

★ Population or designation of metropolitan area, including suburbs (see headnote).
▲ Population of an entire municipality, commune, or district, including rural area.

Irapuato 265,042
Ixtapaluca 115,711
Jiutepec 82,845
Juchitán de Zaragoza 53,666
Lagos de Moreno 63,646
La Paz 137,641
La Piedad de Cabadas 62,625
Las Choapas 43,868
Las Truchas 53,581
León 758,279
Los Mochis 162,659
Los Reyes la Paz 134,544
Manzanillo 67,697
Matamoros (★ Brownsville, Tex., U.S.A.) 266,055
Matehuala 54,713
Mazatlán 262,705
Mérida 523,422
Metepec 116,203
Mexicali (★ 460,000) 438,377
Minatitlán 142,060
Monclova 177,792
Monterrey (★ 2,015,000) 1,068,996
Morelia 428,486
Naucalpan de Juárez (★ Ciudad de México) 845,960
Navojoa 82,618
Nezahualcóyotl (★ Ciudad de México) 1,255,456
Nogales 105,873
Nuevo Laredo (★ Laredo, Tex., U.S.A.) 218,413
Oaxaca [de Juárez] 212,818
Ocotlán 62,595
Orizaba (★ 215,000) 114,216
Pachuca 174,013
Papantla [de Olarte] 46,075
Piedras Negras 96,178
Poza Rica 151,739
Puebla (★ 1,200,000) 1,007,170
Puerto Vallarta 93,503
Querétaro 385,503
Reynosa 265,663
Río Bravo 67,092
Sahuayo de José María Morelos 50,463
Salamanca 123,190
Salina Cruz 61,656
Saltillo 420,947
San Andrés Tuxtla 49,658
San Cristóbal de las Casas 73,388
San Francisco del Rincón 52,291
San Juan del Río 61,652
San Luis Potosí (★ 600,000) 489,238
San Luis Río Colorado 95,461
San Martín Texmelucan 57,519
San Miguel de Allende 48,935
San Nicolás de los Garza (★ Monterrey) 436,603
San Pablo de las Salinas 84,217
Santa Catarina (★ Monterrey) 162,707
Silao 50,828
Soledad de Graciano Sanchez 123,943
Tampico (★ 440,000) 272,690
Tapachula 138,858
Tecomán 60,938
Tehuacán 139,450
Temixco 65,058
Tepatitlán de Morelos 54,036
Tepic 206,967
Texcoco [de Mora] (★ Ciudad de México) 74,194
Tijuana (★ San Diego, Calif., U.S.A.) 698,752
Tlalnepantla (★ Ciudad de México) 702,270
Tlaquepaque (★ Guadalajara) 328,031
Tlaxcala [de Xicoténcatl] 50,486
Toluca [de Lerdo] 327,865
Tonalá 151,190
Torreón (★ 690,000) 439,436
Tulancingo 75,477
Tuxpan 69,224
Tuxtepec 62,788
Tuxtla Gutiérrez 289,626
Uruapan del Progreso 187,623
Valle de Santiago 56,009
Veracruz [Llave] (★ 540,000) 438,821
Villa Frontera 58,216
Villahermosa 261,231
Villa Nicolás Romero 148,342
Xalapa 279,451
Zacatecas 100,051
Zamora de Hidalgo 109,751
Zapopan (★ Guadalajara) 668,323

MICRONESIA, FEDERATED STATES OF

1985 E 94,534

• KOLONIA 6,306

MOLDOVA

1991 E 4,366,300

Bel'c' 164,900
Bendery 141,500
Kišin'ov 676,700
Rybnica 62,900
Tiraspol' 186,000

MONACO

1990 C 29,972

• MONACO (★ 87,000) 29,972

MONGOLIA / Mongol Ard Uls

1989 E 2,040,000

Darchan (1985 E) 69,800
• ULAANBAATAR 548,400

MONTSERRAT

1980 C 11,606

• PLYMOUTH 1,568

MOROCCO / Al-Magreb

1982 C 20,419,555

Agadir 110,479
Beni-Mellal 95,003
Berkane 60,490
• Casablanca (Dar-el-Beida) (★ 2,475,000) 2,139,204
El-Jadida (Mazagan) 81,455
Fès (★ 535,000) 448,823
Kenitra 188,194
Khemisset 58,925
Khouribga 127,181
Ksar-el-Kebir 73,541
Larache 63,893
Marrakech (★ 535,000) 439,728
Meknès (★ 375,000) 319,783
Mohammedia (Fedala) (★ Casablanca) 105,120
Nador 62,040
Oued-Zem 58,744
Oujda 260,082
RABAT (★ 980,000) 518,616
Safi 197,309
Salé (★ Rabat) 289,391
Settat 65,203
Sidi Kacem 55,833
Sidi Slimane 50,457
Tanger (Tangier) (★ 370,000) 266,346
Tan-Tan 41,451
Taza 77,216
Temera (★ Rabat) 48,644
Tétouan 199,615

MOZAMBIQUE / Moçambique

1989 E 15,326,476

Beira 291,604
Chimoio (1986 E) 86,928
Inhambane (1986 E) 64,274
• MAPUTO 1,069,727
Nacala 101,615
Nampula 197,379
Pemba (1986 E) 50,215
Quelimane 78,520
Tete (1986 E) 56,178
Xai-Xai (1986 E) 51,620

NAMIBIA

1988 E 1,760,000

• WINDHOEK 114,500

NAURU / Naoero

1987 E 8,000

NEPAL / Nepāl

1981 C 15,022,839

Bhaktapur 48,472
• KĀTHMĀNDAU (★ 320,000) 235,160
Wirāṭnagar 93,544

NETHERLANDS / Nederland

1991 E 15,010,000

Alkmaar (★ 124,000) 90,767
Almelo 62,664
Alphen aan den Rijn 62,404
Amersfoort 101,966
Amstelveen (★ Amsterdam) 70,337
• AMSTERDAM (★ 1,875,000) 702,686
Apeldoorn 148,195
Arnhem (★ 305,000) 131,707
Assen 50,353
Bergen op Zoom 46,897
Breda (★ 163,000) 124,792
Delft (★ 's-Gravenhage) 89,369
Den Helder 61,463
Deventer 67,473
Dordrecht (★ 209,000) 110,472
Ede (▲ 94,721) 50,000
Eindhoven (★ 384,000) 192,810
Emmen (▲ 92,896) 36,900
Enschede (★ 252,000) 146,509
Geleen (★ 179,000) 33,833
Gouda 65,918
Groningen (★ 208,000) 168,701
Haarlem (★ Amsterdam) 149,464
Haarlemmermeer (▲ 98,070) (★Amsterdam) 13,600
Heerlen (★ 267,500) 94,304
Helmond 69,968
Hengelo (★ Enschede) 76,377
Hilversum (★ Amsterdam) 84,662
Hoorn 58,202
IJmuiden (★ Amsterdam) 60,129
Kerkrade (★ Heerlen) 53,276
Leeuwarden 85,697
Leiden (★ 190,000) 111,927
Maastricht (★ 163,000) 117,398
Nieuwegein (★ Utrecht) 58,912
Nijmegen (★ 242,000) 145,646
Oss 51,688
Purmerend (★ Amsterdam) 61,056
Ridderkerk (★ Rotterdam) 45,990
Rijswijk (★ 's-Gravenhage) 47,709
Roosendaal 60,732
Rotterdam (★ 1,120,000) 582,238
Schiedam (★ Rotterdam) 70,206
'S-GRAVENHAGE (THE HAGUE) (★ 772,000) 444,256
's-Hertogenbosch (★ 200,000) 92,052
Soest (★ Amersfoort) 41,415
Spijkenisse (★ Rotterdam) 69,103
Tilburg (★ 233,000) 158,839
Utrecht (★ 527,000) 231,232
Veenendaal 49,689
Venlo (★ 87,000) 64,386
Vlaardingen (★ Rotterdam) 73,711
Vlissingen (Flushing) (▲ 43,799) 25,100
Zaanstad (★ Amsterdam) 130,684
Zeist (★ Utrecht) 59,363
Zoetermeer (★ 's-Gravenhage) 99,094
Zwolle 95,574

NETHERLANDS ANTILLES / Nederlandse Antillen

1990 E 189,687

• WILLEMSTAD (★ 130,000) (1981 C) 31,883

NEW CALEDONIA / Nouvelle-Calédonie

1989 C 164,173

• NOUMÉA (★ 97,581) 65,110

NEW ZEALAND

1991 C 3,434,950

• Auckland (★ 855,571) 315,668
Christchurch (★ 307,179) 292,858
Dunedin 116,577
Hamilton (★ 148,625) 101,448
Invercargill 56,148
Lower Hutt (★ Wellington) 94,540
Manukau (★ Auckland) 226,147
Napier (★ 110,216) 51,645
Palmerston North (★ 70,951) 70,318
Rotorua (★ 53,702) 45,144
Takapuna (★ Auckland) 74,360
Tauranga (★ 70,803) 46,308
Waitemata (★ Auckland) 136,716
WELLINGTON (★ 350,000) 150,301
Whangarei (★ 44,183) 40,101

NICARAGUA

1985 E 3,272,100

Chinandega 75,000
Granada (1981 E) 64,642
León 101,000
• MANAGUA 682,000
Masaya 75,000
Matagalpa 68,000

NIGER

1988 C 7,250,383

Agadez 50,164
Maradi 112,965
• NIAMEY 398,265
Tahoua 51,607
Zinder 120,892

NIGERIA

1987 E 101,907,000

Aba 239,800
Abakaliki 56,800
Abeokuta 341,300
Ado-Ekiti 287,000
Afikpo 65,790
Agege 83,810
Akure 129,600
Amaigbo 53,690
Apomu 49,570
Aramoko 48,280
Asaba 47,410
Awka 88,800
Azare 50,020
Bauchi 68,840
Benin City 183,200
Bida 100,200
Calabar 139,800
Deba 110,600
Duku 52,880
Ede 245,200
Effon-Alaiye 122,300
Ejigbo 84,570
Emure-Ekiti 58,750
Enugu 252,500
Epe 80,560
Erin-Oshogbo 59,940
Eruwa 49,140
Fiditi 49,440
Gboko 49,390
Gbongan 53,990
Gombe 86,120
Gusau 126,200
Ibadan 1,144,000
Idah 50,550
Idanre 56,080
Ife 237,000
Ifon-Oshogbo 65,980
Igbasa-Odo 48,040
Igboho 85,230
Igbo-Ora 68,060
Igede-Ekiti 56,570
Ihiala 73,240
Ijebu-Igbo 78,680
Ijebu-Ode 124,900
Ijero-Ekiti 76,420
Ikare 112,500
Ikerre 195,400
Ikire 94,450
Ikirun 144,900
Ikole 71,860
Ikorodu 147,700
Ikot Ekpene 69,440
Ila 210,800
Ilawe-Ekiti 147,300
Ilesha 302,100
Ilobu 159,000
Ilorin 380,000
Inisa 95,630
Ipoti-Ekiti 53,220
Ise-Ekiti 82,580
Iseyin 173,500
Iwo 289,100
Jega (1985 E) 47,000
Jimeta 66,130
Jos 164,700
Kaduna 273,200
Kano 538,300
Katsina 165,000
Kaura Namoda 52,910
Keffi 57,790
Kishi 77,210
Kumo 118,200
Lafia 97,810
Lafiagi 57,580
• LAGOS (★ 3,800,000) 1,213,000
Lalupon 56,130
Lere 49,670
Maiduguri 255,100
Makurdi 98,350
Minna 109,300
Mubi 51,190
Mushin (★ Lagos) 266,100
Nguru 78,770
Nsukka 47,760
Ode-Ekiti 48,910
Offa 157,500
Ogbomosho 582,900
Oka 114,400
Oke-Mesi 55,040
Okwe 52,550
Olupona 65,720
Ondo 135,300
Onitsha 298,200
Opobo 64,620
Oron 62,260
Oshogbo 380,800
Owerri (1985 E) 37,000
Owo 146,600
Oyan 50,930
Oyo 204,700
Pindiga 64,130
Port Harcourt 327,300
Potiskum 56,490
Sapele 111,200
Shagamu 93,610
Shaki 139,000
Shomolu (★ Lagos) 120,700
Sokoto 163,700
Ugep 81,910
Umuahia 52,550
Uyo 60,500
Warri 100,700
Zaria 302,800

NIUE

1989 C 2,267

• ALOFI 706

NORTHERN MARIANA ISLANDS

1980 C 16,780

• Chalan Kanoa 2,678
Garapan 2,063

NORWAY / Norge

1987 E 4,190,000

Bærum (★ Oslo) (1985 E) 83,000
Bergen (★ 239,000) 209,320
Drammen (★ 73,000) (1985 E) 50,700
Fredrikstad (★ 52,000) (1983 E) 27,618
Hammerfest (1983 E) 7,208
Kristiansand (1985 E) 62,200
Narvik (1983 E) 19,080
• OSLO (★ 720,000) 452,415
Skien (★ 77,981) (1985 E) 46,700
Stavanger (★ 132,000) (1985 E) 94,200
Tromsø (1985 E) 47,800
Trondheim 135,010
Louga (1988 C) 52,763

OMAN / ʻUmān

1983 E 1,131,000

• MASQAT (MUSCAT) 30,000
Maṭraḥ (1971 E) 14,000
Ṣūr 30,000

PAKISTAN / Pākistān

1981 C 84,253,644

Abbottābād (★ 65,996) 32,188
Ahmadpur East 56,979
Attock (★ 39,986) 26,233
Bahāwalnagar 74,533
Bahāwalpur (★ 180,263) 152,009
Bannu (★ 43,210) 35,170
Bhakkar 41,934
Chārsadda 62,530
Chīchāwatni 50,241
Chiniot 105,559
Chishtiān Mandi 61,959
Daska 55,555
Dera Ghāzi Khān 102,007
Dera Ismāīl Khān (★ 68,145) 64,358
Drigh Road Cantonment (★ Karāchi) 56,742
Faisalabad (Lyallpur) 1,104,209
Gojra 68,000
Gujrānwāla (★ 658,753) 600,993
Gujrānwāla Cantonment (★ Gujrānwāla) 57,760
Gujrāt 155,058
Hāfizābād 83,464
Hyderābād (★ 800,000) 702,539
Hyderābād Cantonment (★ Hyderābād) 48,990
ISLAMABAD (★ Rāwalpindi) 204,364
Jacobābād 79,365
Jarānwāla 69,459
Jhang Sadar 195,558
Jhelum (★ 106,462) 92,646
Kamālia 61,107
Kāmoke 71,097
• Karāchi (★ 5,300,000) 4,901,627
Karāchi Cantonment (★ Karāchi) 181,981
Kasūr 155,523
Khairpur 61,447
Khānewāl 89,090
Khānpur 70,589
Khāriān Cantonment (★ 51,506) 16,042
Khushāb 56,274
Kohāt (★ 77,604) 55,832
Lahore (★ 3,025,000) 2,707,215
Lahore Cantonment (★ Lahore) 245,474
Lārkāna 123,890
Leiah 51,482
Malir Cantonment (★ Karāchi) 47,588
Mandi Būrewāla 86,311
Mardān (★ 147,977) 141,842
Miānwāli 59,159
Mingāora 88,078
Mīrpur Khās 124,371
Multān (★ 732,070) 696,316
Muzaffargarh 53,000
Nawābshāh 102,139
Nowshera (★ 74,913) 38,875
Okāra (★ 153,483) 127,455
Pākpattan 69,820
Peshāwar (★ 566,248) 506,896
Peshāwar Cantonment (★ Peshāwar) 59,352
Quetta (★ 285,719) 244,842
Rahīmyār Khān (★ 132,635) 119,036
Rāwalpindi (★ 1,040,000) 457,091
Rāwalpindi Cantonment (★ Rāwalpindi) 337,752
Sādiqābād 63,935
Sāhīwal 150,954
Sargodha (★ 291,362) 231,895
Sargodha Cantonment (★ Sargodha) 59,467
Shekhūpura 141,168
Shikārpur 88,138
Shorkot (★ 50,568) 18,533
Siālkot (★ 302,009) 258,147
Sukkur 190,551
Tando Ādam 62,744
Turbat 52,337
Vihāri 53,799
Wāh Cantonment 122,335
Wazīrābād 62,725

PALAU / Belau

1986 C 13,873

• KOROR 8,629

PANAMA / Panamá

1990 C 2,315,047

Balboa (★ Panamá) 1,214
Colón (★ 96,000) 54,469
David 65,635
• PANAMÁ (★ 770,000) 411,549
San Miguelito (★ Panamá) 242,529

PAPUA NEW GUINEA

1990 C 3,534,038

Lae 78,265
• PORT MORESBY 193,242
Rabaul 16,883

C Census. E Official estimate. U Unofficial estimate.
• Largest city in country.

★ Population or designation of metropolitan area, including suburbs (see headnote).
▲ Population of an entire municipality, commune, or district, including rural area.

PARAGUAY

1992 C ... 4,123,550

- • ASUNCIÓN (★ 700,000) ... 502,426
- Caaguazú ... 38,200
- Capiatá ... 83,189
- Ciudad del Este ... 133,896
- Encarnación ... 55,359
- Fernando de la Mora (★ Asunción) ... 95,287
- Lambaré (★ Asunción) ... 99,681
- Mariano Roque Alonso ... 39,240
- Pedro Juan Caballero ... 53,601
- San Lorenzo (★ Asunción) ... 133,311

PERU / Perú

1981 C ... 17,031,221

- Arequipa (★ 446,942) ... 108,023
- Ayacucho (★ 69,533) ... 57,432
- Barranco (★ Lima) ... 46,478
- Breña (★ Lima) ... 112,398
- Cajamarca ... 62,259
- Callao (★ Lima) ... 264,133
- Cerro de Pasco (★ 66,373) ... 55,597
- Chiclayo (★ 279,527) ... 213,095
- Chimbote ... 223,341
- Chorrillos (★ Lima) ... 141,881
- Chosica ... 65,139
- Cuzco (★ 184,550) ... 89,563
- Huacho ... 43,398
- Huancayo (★ 164,954) ... 84,845
- Huánuco ... 61,812
- Ica ... 114,786
- Iquitos ... 178,738
- Jesús María (★ Lima) ... 83,179
- Juliaca ... 87,651
- La Victoria (★ Lima) ... 270,778
- • LIMA (★ 4,608,010) ... 371,122
- Lince (★ Lima) ... 80,456
- Magdalena (★ Lima) ... 55,535
- Miraflores (★ Lima) ... 103,453
- Pisco ... 55,604
- Piura (★ 207,934) ... 144,609
- Pucallpa ... 112,263
- Pueblo Libre (★ Lima) ... 83,985
- Puno ... 67,397
- Rímac (★ Lima) ... 184,484
- San Isidro (★ Lima) ... 71,203
- San Martín de Porras (★ Lima) ... 404,856
- Santiago de Surco (★ Lima) ... 146,636
- Sullana ... 89,037
- Surquillo (★ Lima) ... 134,158
- Tacna ... 97,173
- Talara ... 57,351
- Trujillo (★ 354,301) ... 202,469
- Tumbes ... 47,936
- Vitarte (★ Lima) ... 145,504

PHILIPPINES / Pilipinas

1990 C ... 60,477,000

- Angeles ... 236,000
- Antipolo (▲ 68,912) (1980 C) ... 54,117
- Bacolod ... 364,000
- Bacoor (★ Manila) (1980 C) ... 90,364
- Baguio ... 183,000
- Baliuag (1980 C) ... 70,555
- Biñan (★ Manila) (1980 C) ... 83,684
- Binangonan (1980 C) ... 80,980
- Bislig (▲ 81,615) (1980 C) ... 49,498
- Bocaue (1980 C) ... 49,693
- Butuan (▲ 228,000) ... 99,000
- Cabanatuan (▲ 173,000) ... 75,700
- Cagayan de Oro (▲ 340,000) ... 255,000
- Cainta (★ Manila) (1980 C) ... 59,025
- Calamba (▲ 121,175) (1980 C) ... 72,359
- Caloocan (★ Manila) ... 746,000
- Carmona (★ Manila) (1980 C) ... 65,014
- Cavite (★ 195,000) ... 92,000
- Cebu (★ 825,000) ... 610,000
- Cotabato ... 127,000
- Dagupan ... 122,000
- Davao (▲ 850,000) ... 569,300
- Dumaguete ... 80,000
- General Santos (Dadiangas) (▲ 250,000) ... 157,600
- Guagua (1980 C) ... 72,609
- Iloilo ... 311,000
- Isabela (Basilan) (▲ 49,891) (1980 C) ... 11,491
- Jolo (1980 C) ... 52,429
- Lapu-Lapu (Opon) ... 146,000
- Las Piñas (★ Manila) (1984 E) ... 190,364
- Legaspi (▲ 121,000) ... 63,000
- Lucena ... 151,000
- Mabalacat (▲ 80,966) (1980 C) ... 54,988
- Makati (★ Manila) (1984 E) ... 408,991
- Malabon (★ Manila) (1984 E) ... 212,930
- Malolos (1980 C) ... 95,699
- Mandaluyong (★ Manila) (1984 E) ... 226,670
- Mandaue (★ Cebu) ... 180,000
- Mangaldan (1980 C) ... 50,434
- • MANILA (★ 9,650,000) ... 1,587,000
- Marawi ... 92,000
- Marikina (★ Manila) (1984 E) ... 248,183
- Meycauayan (★ Manila) (1980 C) ... 83,579
- Muntinglupa (★ Manila) (1984 E) ... 172,421
- Naga ... 115,000
- Navotas (★ Manila) (1984 E) ... 146,899
- Olongapo ... 192,000
- Pagadian (▲ 107,000) ... 52,400
- Parañaque (★ Manila) (1984 E) ... 252,791
- Pasay (★ Manila) ... 354,000
- Pasig (★ Manila) (1984 E) ... 318,853
- Puerto Princesa (▲ 92,000) ... 52,000
- Quezon City (★ Manila) ... 1,632,000
- San Fernando (1980 C) ... 110,891
- San Juan del Monte (★ Manila) (1984 E) ... 139,126
- San Pablo (▲ 161,000) ... 83,900
- San Pedro (1980 C) ... 74,556
- Santa Cruz (1980 C) ... 60,620
- Santa Rosa (★ Manila) (1980 C) ... 64,325
- Tacloban ... 138,000
- Tagbilaran ... 56,000
- Tagig (★ Manila) (1984 E) ... 130,719
- Taytay (★ Manila) (1980 C) ... 75,328
- Valenzuela (★ Manila) (1984 E) ... 275,725
- Zamboanga (▲ 444,000) ... 107,000

PITCAIRN

1988 C ... 59

- • ADAMSTOWN ... 59

POLAND / Polska

1991 E ... 38,183,200

- Będzin (★ Katowice) ... 76,200
- Bełchatów ... 57,400
- Biała Podlaska ... 53,100
- Białystok ... 270,600
- Bielsko-Biała ... 181,300
- Bydgoszcz ... 381,500
- Bytom (Beuthen) (★ Katowice) ... 231,200
- Chełm ... 66,400
- Chorzów (★ Katowice) ... 131,900
- Częstochowa ... 258,000
- Dąbrowa Górnicza (★ Katowice) ... 136,900
- Dzierżoniów (Reichenbach) (★ 89,000) ... 38,000
- Elbląg (Elbing) ... 126,100
- Ełk ... 52,400
- Gdańsk (Danzig) (★ 909,000) ... 465,100
- Gdynia (★ Gdańsk) ... 251,500
- Gliwice (Gleiwitz) (★ Katowice) ... 214,200
- Głogów ... 73,300
- Gniezno ... 70,400
- Gorzów Wielkopolski (Landsberg an der Warthe) ... 124,300
- Grudziądz ... 102,300
- Inowrocław ... 77,700
- Jastrzębie-Zdrój ... 103,700
- Jaworzno (★ Katowice) ... 99,500
- Jelenia Góra (Hirschberg) ... 93,400
- Kalisz ... 106,200
- • Katowice (★ 2,778,000) ... 366,800
- Kędzierzyn Kozle ... 71,700
- Kielce ... 214,200
- Konin ... 80,300
- Koszalin (Köslin) ... 108,700
- Kraków (★ 828,000) ... 750,500
- Krosno ... 49,700
- Kutno ... 50,400
- Legionowo (★ Warszawa) ... 50,800
- Legnica (Liegnitz) ... 105,200
- Leszno ... 58,300
- Łódź (★ 1,061,000) ... 848,200
- Łomża ... 59,300
- Lubin ... 82,300
- Lublin (★ 389,000) ... 351,400
- Mielec ... 61,800
- Mysłowice (★ Katowice) ... 93,800
- Nowy Sącz ... 78,200
- Olsztyn (Allenstein) ... 162,900
- Opole (Oppeln) ... 128,400
- Ostrołęka ... 50,700
- Ostrowiec Świętokrzyski ... 78,600
- Ostrów Wielkopolski ... 73,300
- Pabianice (★ Łódź) ... 75,200
- Piekary Śląskie (★ Katowice) ... 68,500
- Piła (Schneidemühl) ... 72,300
- Piotrków Trybunalski ... 81,000
- Płock ... 123,400
- Poznań (★ 672,000) ... 590,100
- Pruszków (★ Warszawa) ... 53,700
- Przemyśl ... 68,500
- Puławy ... 85,700
- Racibórz (Ratibor) ... 64,400
- Radom ... 228,500
- Radomsko ... 50,400
- Ruda Śląska (★ Katowice) ... 171,000
- Rybnik ... 144,000
- Rzeszów ... 153,000
- Siedlce ... 72,000
- Siemianowice Śląskie (★ Katowice) ... 81,100
- Skarżysko-Kamienna ... 50,900
- Słupsk (Stolp) ... 101,200
- Sopot (★ Gdańsk) ... 46,700
- Sosnowiec (★ Katowice) ... 259,400
- Stalowa Wola ... 70,000
- Starachowice ... 56,600
- Stargard Szczeciński (Stargard in Pommern) ... 71,000
- Starogard Gdański ... 49,500
- Suwałki ... 61,300
- Świdnica (Schweidnitz) ... 63,300
- Świętochłowice (★ Katowice) ... 60,500
- Świnoujście (Swinemünde) ... 43,300
- Szczecin (Stettin) (★ 449,000) ... 413,400
- Tarnów ... 121,200
- Tarnowskie Góry (★ Katowice) ... 74,100
- Tczew ... 59,500
- Tomaszów Mazowiecki ... 69,900
- Toruń ... 202,300
- Tychy (★ Katowice) ... 191,700
- Wałbrzych (Waldenburg) (★ 207,000) ... 141,000
- WARSZAWA (★ 2,323,000) ... 1,655,700
- Włocławek ... 122,200
- Wodzisław Śląski ... 111,800
- Wrocław (Breslau) ... 643,200
- Zabrze (Hindenburg) (★ Katowice) ... 205,000
- Zamość ... 61,800
- Zawiercie ... 56,600
- Zgierz (★ Łódź) ... 59,000
- Zielona Góra (Grünberg) ... 114,100
- Zory ... 67,000

PORTUGAL

1981 C ... 9,833,014

- Amadora (★ Lisboa) ... 95,518
- Barreiro (★ Lisboa) ... 50,863
- Braga ... 63,033
- Coimbra ... 74,616
- • LISBOA (★ 2,250,000) ... 807,167
- Ponta Delgada ... 21,187
- Porto (★ 1,225,000) ... 327,368
- Setúbal ... 77,885
- Vila Nova de Gaia (★ Porto) ... 62,469

PUERTO RICO

1990 C ... 3,522,037

- Arecibo (★ 160,500) ... 49,545
- Bayamón (▲ 220,262) (★San Juan) ... 202,103
- Caguas (▲ 133,447) (★San Juan) ... 92,429
- Carolina (▲ 177,806) (★San Juan) ... 162,404
- Guaynabo (▲ 92,886) (★San Juan) ... 73,385
- Mayagüez (★ 200,600) ... 83,010
- Ponce (★ 232,700) ... 159,151
- • SAN JUAN (★ 1,877,000) ... 426,832

QATAR / Qaṭar

1986 C ... 369,079

- • AD-DAWḤAH (DOHA) (★ 310,000) ... 217,294
- Ar-Rayyān (★ Ad-Dawḥah) ... 91,996

REUNION / Réunion

1982 C ... 515,814

- • SAINT-DENIS (▲ 109,072) ... 84,400

ROMANIA / România

1992 C ... 22,760,449

- Alba Iulia ... 71,254
- Alexandria ... 58,582
- Arad ... 190,088
- Bacău ... 204,495
- Baia Mare ... 148,815
- Bîrlad ... 77,009
- Bistriţa ... 87,793
- Botoşani ... 126,204
- Brăila ... 234,706
- Braşov ... 323,835
- • BUCUREŞTI (BUCHAREST) (★ 2,300,000) ... 2,064,474
- Buzău ... 148,247
- Călăraşi ... 76,886
- Cluj-Napoca ... 328,008
- Constanţa ... 350,476
- Craiova ... 303,520
- Deva ... 78,366
- Drobeta-Turnu Severin ... 115,526
- Focşani ... 101,296
- Galaţi ... 325,788
- Giurgiu ... 74,236
- Hunedoara ... 81,198
- Iaşi ... 342,994
- Lugoj ... 50,983
- Medgidia ... 46,586
- Mediaş ... 64,488
- Miercurea-Ciuc ... 46,029
- Oneşti ... 59,008
- Oradea ... 220,848
- Petroşani (★ 76,000) ... 52,532
- Piatra Neamţ ... 123,175
- Piteşti ... 179,479
- Ploieşti (★ 310,000) ... 252,073
- Reşiţa ... 96,798
- Rîmnicu Vîlcea ... 113,356
- Roman ... 80,192
- Satu Mare ... 131,859
- Sfîntu-Gheorghe ... 68,070
- Sibiu ... 169,696
- Slatina ... 85,336
- Slobozia ... 55,614
- Suceava ... 114,355
- Tecuci ... 46,735
- Timişoara ... 334,278
- Tîrgovişte ... 97,876
- Tîrgu Jiu ... 98,267
- Tîrgu-Mureş ... 163,625
- Tulcea ... 97,500
- Turda ... 61,135
- Vaslui ... 80,151
- Zalău ... 68,322

RUSSIA

1991 E ... 148,542,700

- Abakan ... 157,300
- Achtubinsk ... 50,800
- Ačinsk ... 122,000
- Alapajevsk ... 50,300
- Alatyr' ... 47,700
- Aleksandrov ... 68,600
- Aleksin ... 74,200
- Al'metjevsk ... 132,700
- Amursk ... 59,600
- Anapa ... 55,900
- Angarsk ... 268,500
- Anžero-Sudžensk ... 107,000
- Apatity ... 88,600
- Archangel'sk ... 420,400
- Armavir ... 162,200
- Arsenjev ... 71,200
- Art'om ... 70,100
- Arzamas ... 111,800
- Asbest ... 84,900
- Astrachan' ... 511,900
- Azov ... 80,700
- Balakovo ... 201,300
- Balašicha (★ Moskva) ... 137,600
- Balašov ... 97,300
- Barnaul (★ 673,000) ... 606,800
- Batajsk (★ Rostov-na-Donu) ... 93,300
- Belebej ... 54,500
- Belgorod ... 311,400
- Belogorsk ... 74,300
- Beloreč'ensk ... 51,900
- Beloreck ... 73,100
- Belovo ... 92,900
- Berdsk (★ Novosibirsk) ... 80,400
- Berezniki ... 199,700
- Berezovskiy ... 51,900
- Bijsk ... 234,600
- Birobidžan ... 86,300
- Blagoveščensk ... 211,000
- Bor (★ Nižnij Novgorod) ... 64,500
- Borisoglebsk ... 72,100
- Boroviči ... 62,800
- Br'ansk ... 458,900
- Bratsk ... 259,400
- Bud'onnovsk ... 57,500
- Bugul'ma ... 91,100
- Buguruslan ... 54,100
- Buj ... 62,900
- Bujnaksk ... 57,900
- Buzuluk ... 85,100
- Čajkovskij ... 88,300
- Čapajevsk ... 96,000
- Čebarkul' ... 50,700
- Čeboksary ... 436,000
- Čechov ... 60,200
- Čel'abinsk (★ 1,325,000) ... 1,148,300
- Čeremchovo ... 73,600
- Čerepovec ... 315,900
- Čerkessk ... 117,000
- Černogorsk ... 79,700
- Chabarovsk ... 613,300
- Chasavjurt ... 72,800
- Chimki (★ Moskva) ... 135,500
- Cholmsk ... 51,800
- Čistopol' ... 66,600
- Čita ... 376,300
- Čusovoj ... 58,000
- Derbent ... 81,500
- Dimitrovgrad ... 127,000
- Dmitrov ... 65,600
- Dolgoprudnyj (★ Moskva) ... 71,100
- Domodedovo (★ Moskva) ... 56,300
- Doneck ... 48,900
- Dubna ... 67,200
- Dzeržinsk (★ Nižnij Novgorod) ... 286,700
- Elektrostal' ... 153,000
- Elista ... 92,700
- Engel's (★ Saratov) ... 183,600
- Fr'azino (★ Moskva) ... 54,000
- Furmanov ... 45,900
- Gatčina (★ Sankt-Peterburg) ... 80,600
- Gelendžik ... 48,600
- Georgijevsk ... 63,700
- Georgiu-Dež ... 54,600
- Glazov ... 106,000
- Gorno-Altajsk ... 47,500
- Gr'azi ... 47,700
- Groznyj ... 401,400
- Gubkin ... 76,400
- Gukovo ... 67,700
- Gus'-Chrustal'nyj ... 77,000
- Inta ... 60,900
- Irbit ... 51,300
- Irkutsk ... 640,500
- Išim ... 65,900
- Išimbaj ... 71,000
- Iskitim ... 68,700
- Ivanovo ... 482,200
- Ivantejevka (★ Moskva) ... 53,200
- Iževsk ... 646,800
- Jakutsk ... 193,300
- Jarcevo ... 54,000
- Jaroslavl' ... 638,100
- Jefremov ... 56,600
- Jegorjevsk ... 74,200
- Jejsk ... 79,400
- Jelec ... 121,300
- Jelizovo ... 48,700
- Jermolajevo ... 65,600
- Jessentuki ... 86,300
- Joškar-Ola ... 247,800
- Jurga ... 94,000
- Južno-Sachalinsk ... 164,000
- Kaliningrad (Königsberg) ... 408,100
- Kaliningrad (★ Moskva) ... 161,500
- Kaluga ... 315,500
- Kamensk-Šachtinskij ... 73,100
- Kamensk-Ural'skij ... 208,700
- Kamyšin ... 124,400
- Kanaš ... 56,100
- Kandalakša ... 54,300
- Kansk ... 109,900
- Kaspijsk ... 61,900
- Kazan' (★ 1,165,000) ... 1,107,300
- Kemerovo ... 520,700
- Kimry ... 62,000
- Kinel' ... 33,800
- Kinešma ... 104,900
- Kingisepp ... 50,600
- Kiriši ... 53,100
- Kirov ... 491,200
- Kirovo-Čepeck ... 95,600
- Kisel'ovsk (★ Prokopjevsk) ... 126,900
- Kislovodsk ... 116,800
- Kizel ... 36,600
- Klimovsk (★ Moskva) ... 57,600
- Klin ... 95,100
- Klincy ... 71,200
- Kogalym ... 48,200
- Kol'čugino ... 45,600
- Kolomna ... 163,500
- Kolpino (★ Sankt-Peterburg) ... 144,500
- Komsomol'sk-na-Amure ... 318,800
- Kopejsk (★ Čel'abinsk) ... 78,300
- Korkino ... 44,800
- Korsakov ... 45,300
- Kostroma ... 281,800
- Kotlas ... 68,900
- Kovrov ... 161,900
- Krasnodar ... 631,200
- Krasnogorsk (★ Moskva) ... 91,700
- Krasnojarsk ... 924,400
- Krasnokamensk ... 57,800
- Krasnokamsk ... 67,000
- Krasnoturjinsk ... 67,200
- Krasnoufimsk ... 46,100
- Krasnoural'sk ... 34,800
- Krasnyj Sulin ... 43,200
- Kropotkin ... 76,600
- Krymsk ... 51,100
- Kstovo (★ Nižnij Novgorod) ... 65,300
- Kujbyšev ... 51,600
- Kungur ... 81,800
- Kurgan ... 363,800
- Kursk ... 433,300
- Kušva ... 43,300
- Kuzneck ... 100,000
- Kyzyl ... 88,000
- Labinsk ... 58,600
- Leninogorsk ... 63,300
- Leninsk-Kuzneckij ... 133,400
- Lesosibirsk ... 69,300
- Lipeck ... 460,100
- Livny ... 52,600
- Lobn'a (★ Moskva) ... 61,000
- L'ubercy (★ Moskva) ... 164,900
- Lys'va ... 77,800
- Lytkarino (★ Moskva) ... 51,700
- Machačkala ... 333,500
- Magadan ... 154,900
- Magnitogorsk ... 443,900
- Majkop ... 152,500
- Mcensk ... 49,200
- Meleuz ... 55,200
- Meždurečensk ... 107,500
- Miass ... 169,700
- Michajlovka ... 58,700
- Mičurinsk ... 109,400
- Mineral'nyje Vody ... 72,500
- Minusinsk ... 74,200
- Mončegorsk ... 68,100
- Moršansk ... 50,500
- • MOSKVA (MOSCOW) (★ 13,150,000) ... 8,801,500
- Murmansk ... 472,900
- Murom ... 126,000
- Mytišči (★ Moskva) ... 153,900
- Naberežnyje Čelny ... 510,100
- Nachodka ... 164,500
- Nadym ... 52,200
- Nal'čik ... 240,600
- Naro-Fominsk ... 58,800
- Nazarovo ... 65,200
- Neftejugansk ... 65,500
- Ner'ungri ... 77,200
- Nevinnomyssk ... 123,300
- Nikolo-Berjozovka ... 110,500
- Nižnekamsk ... 196,200
- Nižnevartovsk ... 247,400
- Nižnij Novgorod (Gorky) (★ 2,025,000) ... 1,445,000
- Nižnij Tagil ... 439,200
- Njagan ... 59,800
- Noginsk ... 122,700
- Nojabr'sk ... 88,900
- Noril'sk ... 169,000
- Novgorod ... 233,800
- Novoaltajsk (★ Barnaul) ... 55,200
- Novočeboksarsk ... 119,300
- Novočerkassk ... 188,500
- Novodvinsk ... 50,300
- Novokujbyševsk (★ Samara) ... 113,200
- Novokuzneck ... 601,900
- Novomoskovsk, Tula oblast' (★ 365,000) ... 145,800
- Novorossijsk ... 188,600
- Novošachtinsk ... 107,300
- Novosibirsk (★ 1,600,000) ... 1,446,300
- Novotroick ... 107,600
- Novyj Urengoj ... 93,600
- Obninsk ... 103,700
- Odincovo (★ Moskva) ... 128,400
- Okt'abr'skij ... 106,700
- Omsk (★ 1,190,000) ... 1,166,800
- Orechovo-Zujevo (★ 205,000) ... 136,800

C Census. E Official estimate. U Unofficial estimate.
• Largest city in country.

★ Population or designation of metropolitan area, including suburbs (see headnote).
▲ Population of an entire municipality, commune, or district, including rural area.

Orel	345,200
Orenburg	556,500
Orsk	272,200
Osinniki	63,200
Otradnyj	49,600
Partizansk	50,000
P'atigorsk	131,100
Pavlovo	72,200
Pavlovskij Posad	70,800
Pečora	65,500
Penza	551,100
Perm' (★ 1,180,000)	1,110,400
Pervoural'sk	143,700
Petrodvorec (★ Sankt-Peterburg)	83,800
Petropavlovsk-Kamčatskij	272,900
Petrozavodsk	277,400
Podol'sk (★ Moskva)	208,500
Polevskoj	71,900
Prochladnyj	58,500
Prokopjevsk (★ 410,000)	272,600
Pskov	207,500
Puškin (★ Sankt-Peterburg)	95,300
Puškino (★ Moskva)	75,800
Ramenskoje	88,800
Rasskazovo	49,800
R'azan'	527,200
Reutov (★ Moskva)	68,900
Revda	66,000
Roslavl'	60,700
Rossoš'	58,900
Rostov-na-Donu (★ 1,165,000)	1,027,600
Rubcovsk	172,500
Ruzajevka	52,100
Rybinsk	252,600
Ržev	70,900
Šachty	227,700
Šadrinsk	87,500
Safonovo	56,300
Sajanogorsk	53,000
Salavat	151,400
Sal'sk	61,700
Samara (★ 1,505,000)	1,257,300
Sankt-Peterburg (Saint Petersburg) (★ 5,525,000)	4,466,800
Saransk	319,600
Sarapul	110,600
Saratov (★ 1,155,000)	911,100
Šatka	51,100
Ščelkovo (★ Moskva)	109,600
Ščokino	68,800
Šelechov	48,600
Sergijev Posad (Zagorsk)	115,600
Serov	103,800
Serpuchov	141,200
Severodvinsk	251,500
Severomorsk	66,200
Slav'ansk-Na-Kubani	58,500
Smolensk	349,800
Soči	341,500
Sokol	46,700
Solikamsk	110,200
Solnečnogorsk (★ Moskva)	56,700
Sosnovyj Bor	56,700
Spassk-Dal'nij	61,100
Staryj Oskol	181,900
Stavropol'	328,300
Sterlitamak	252,200
Stupino	74,600
Šuja	69,000
Surgut	261,100
Sverdlovsk, Sverdlovsk oblast' (★ 1,620,000)	1,375,400
Svetlogorsk	71,600
Svobodnyj	80,900
Syktyvkar	224,000
Syzran'	174,900
Taganrog	293,600
Talnach	65,600
Tambov	309,600
Temirtau	213,100
Tichoreck	67,600
Tichvin	71,800
Tobol'sk	96,800
Toljatti	654,700
Tomsk	505,600
Toržok	50,500
Troick	89,800
Tuapse	63,800
Tujmazy	59,800
Tula (★ 640,000)	543,600
Tulun	53,700
T'umen'	494,200
Tver'	455,300
Tyndinskij	64,700
Uchta	112,100
Ufa (★ 1,118,000)	1,097,000
Uglič	40,000
Ulan-Ude	362,400
Uljanovsk	648,300
Usinsk	52,300
Usolje-Sibirskoje	106,800
Ussurijsk	160,200
Ust'-Ilimsk	112,200
Ust'-Kut	61,800
Uzlovaja (★ Novomoskovsk)	34,000
V'az'ma	59,900
Velikije Luki	115,400
Verchn'aja Pyšma (★ Sverdlovsk)	53,500
Verchn'aja Salda	55,100
Vičuga	49,700
Vidnoje (★ Moskva)	56,900
Vladikavkaz	306,000
Vladimir	355,600
Vladivostok	648,000
Volchov	50,100
Volgodonsk	180,700
Volgograd (Stalingrad) (★ 1,360,000)	1,007,300
Vologda	289,200
Vol'sk	65,500
Volžsk	62,000
Volžskij (★ Volgograd)	278,400
Vorkuta	117,400
Voronež	900,000
Voskresensk	81,400
Votkinsk	104,500
Vyborg	81,100
Vyksa	62,200
Vyšnij Voločok	64,600
Zarinsk	51,800
Zelenograd (★ Moskva)	162,700
Železnodorožnyj (★ Moskva)	99,300
Železnogorsk	89,200
Zel'onodol'sk	97,000
Žigulevsk	45,000
Zlatoust	208,200
Žukovskij	101,300

RWANDA

1991 C	6,762,145
• KIGALI (1990 C)	232,733

SAINT HELENA

1987 C	5,644
• JAMESTOWN	1,413

SAINT KITTS AND NEVIS

1980 C	44,404
• BASSETERRE	14,725
Charlestown	1,771

SAINT LUCIA

1987 E	142,342
• CASTRIES	53,933

SAINT PIERRE AND MIQUELON / Saint-Pierre-et-Miquelon

1982 C	6,041
• SAINT-PIERRE	5,371

SAINT VINCENT AND THE GRENADINES

1987 E	112,589
• KINGSTOWN (★ 28,936)	19,028

SAN MARINO

1988 E	22,304
• SAN MARINO	2,777

SAO TOME AND PRINCIPE / São Tomé e Príncipe

1970 C	73,631
• SÃO TOMÉ	17,380

SAUDI ARABIA / Al-'Arabīyah as-Su'ūdīyah

1980 E	9,229,000
Abhā (1974 C)	30,150
Ad-Dammām	200,000
Al-Hufūf (1974 C)	101,271
Al-Khubar (1974 C)	48,817
Al-Madīnah (Medina)	290,000
Al-Mubarraz (1974 C)	54,325
AR-RIYĀD (RIYADH)	1,250,000
Aṭ-Ṭā'if	300,000
Buraydah (1974 C)	69,940
Hā'il (1974 C)	40,502
• Jiddah (Jeddah)	1,300,000
Khamīs Mushayṭ (1974 C)	49,581
Makkah (Mecca)	550,000
Najran (1974 C)	47,501
Tabūk (1974 C)	74,825

SENEGAL / Sénégal

1988 C	6,892,720
• DAKAR	1,490,450
Diourbel	77,548
Kaolack	152,007
Saint-Louis	160,689
Thiès	184,902
Ziguinchor	124,283

SEYCHELLES

1984 E	64,718
• VICTORIA	23,000

SIERRA LEONE

1985 C	3,515,812
Bo	59,768
• FREETOWN (★ 525,000)	469,776
Kenema	52,473
Koidu	82,474
Makeni	49,038

SINGAPORE

1990 C	2,690,100
• SINGAPORE (★ 3,025,000)	2,690,100

SLOVAKIA / Slovenská Republika

1991 C	5,268,935
Banská Bystrica	85,007
• BRATISLAVA	441,453
Komárno	37,370
Košice	234,840
Martin	58,338
Michalovce	38,866
Nitra	89,888
Nové Zámky	42,851
Poprad	52,878
Považská Bystrica	39,801
Prešov	87,788
Prievidza	53,393
Spišská Nová Ves	39,187
Trenčín	56,733
Trnava	71,641
Žilina	83,853
Zvolen	41,935

SLOVENIA / Slovenija

1987 E	1,936,606
• LJUBLJANA (▲ 316,607)	233,200
Maribor (▲ 187,651)	107,400

SOLOMON ISLANDS

1986 C	285,176
• HONIARA	30,413

SOMALIA / Somaliya

1984 E	5,423,000
Berbera	65,000
Hargeysa	70,000
Kismaayo	70,000
Marka	60,000
• MUQDISHO	600,000

SOUTH AFRICA / Suid-Afrika

1985 C	23,385,645
Alberton (★ Johannesburg)	66,155
Alexandra (★ Johannesburg)	67,276
Atteridgeville (★ Pretoria)	73,439
Bellville (★ Cape Town)	68,915
Benoni (★ Johannesburg)	94,926
Bloemfontein (★ 235,000)	104,381
Boksburg (★ Johannesburg)	110,832
Botshabelo (★ Bloemfontein)	95,625
Brakpan (★ Johannesburg)	46,416
CAPE TOWN (KAAPSTAD) (★ 1,790,000)	776,617
Carletonville (★ 120,499)	97,874
Daveyton (★ Johannesburg)	99,056
Diepmeadow (★ Johannesburg)	192,682
Durban (★ 1,550,000)	634,301
East London (Oos-Londen) (★ 320,000)	85,699
Edendale (★ Pietermaritzburg)	47,001
Elsies River (★ Cape Town)	70,067
Empumalanga (★ Durban)	47,938
Evaton (★ Vereeniging)	52,559
Galeshewe (★ Kimberley)	63,238
Germiston (★ Johannesburg)	116,718
Grassy Park (★ Cape Town)	50,193
Guguleto (★ Cape Town)	63,893
• Johannesburg (★ 3,650,000)	632,369
Kagiso (★ Johannesburg)	50,647
Katlehong (★ Johannesburg)	137,745
Kayamnandi (★ Port Elizabeth)	220,548
Kempton Park (★ Johannesburg)	87,721
Kimberley (★ 145,000)	74,061
Klerksdorp (★ 205,000)	48,947
Krugersdorp (★ Johannesburg)	73,767
Kwa Makuta (★ Durban)	71,378
Kwa Mashu (★ Durban)	111,593
Kwanobuhle (★ Port Elizabeth)	52,376
Kwa-Thema (★ Johannesburg)	78,640
Ladysmith (★ 31,670)	25,102
Lekoa (Shapeville) (★ Vereeniging)	218,392
Madadeni (★ Newcastle)	65,832
Mamelodi (★ Pretoria)	127,033
Mangaung (★ Bloemfontein)	79,851
Ntuzuma (★ Durban)	61,834
Nyanga (★ Cape Town)	148,882
Ozisweni (★ Newcastle)	51,934
Paarl (★ Cape Town)	63,671
Parow (★ Cape Town)	60,294
Pietermaritzburg (★ 230,000)	133,809
Pinetown (★ Durban)	55,770
Port Elizabeth (★ 690,000)	272,844
PRETORIA (★ 960,000)	443,059
Randburg (★ Johannesburg)	74,347
Randfontein (★ Johannesburg)	43,763
Roodepoort-Maraisburg (★ Johannesburg)	141,764
Sandton (★ Johannesburg)	86,089
Soshanguve (★ Pretoria)	68,598
Soweto (★ Johannesburg)	521,948
Springs (★ Johannesburg)	68,235
Tembisa (★ Johannesburg)	149,282
Thabong (★ Welkom)	43,470
Uitenhage (★ Port Elizabeth)	54,987
Umlazi (★ Durban)	194,933
Vanderbijlpark (★ Vereeniging)	59,865
Vereeniging (★ 525,000)	60,584
Verwoerdburg (★ Pretoria)	49,891
Vosloosrus (★ Johannesburg)	52,061
Walvisbaai (Walvis Bay) (★ 16,607)	9,687
Welkom (★ 215,000)	54,488
Westonaria (★ Johannesburg)	46,523

SPAIN / España

1988 E	39,217,804
Alacant (Alicante)	261,051
Albacete	125,997
Alcalá de Guadaira	50,935
Alcalá de Henares (★ Madrid)	150,021
Alcobendas (★ Madrid)	73,455
Alcoi (Alcoy)	66,074
Alcorcón (★ Madrid)	139,796
Algeciras	99,528
Almería	157,644
Avilés (★ 131,000)	87,811
Badajoz (▲ 122,407)	106,400
Badalona (★ Barcelona)	225,229
Baracaldo (★ Bilbao)	113,502
Barcelona (★ 4,040,000)	1,714,355
Bilbao (★ 985,000)	384,733
Burgos	160,561
Cáceres	71,598
Cádiz (★ 240,000)	156,591
Cartagena (▲ 172,710)	70,000
Castelló de la Plana	131,809
Ciudad Real	56,300
Córdoba	302,301
Cornellà de Llobregat (★ Barcelona)	86,866
Coslada (★ Madrid)	68,765
Donostia (San Sebastián) (★ 285,000)	177,622
Dos Hermanas (▲ 68,456)	60,600
Elda	56,756
El Ferrol del Caudillo (★ 129,000)	86,503
El Prat de Llobregat (★ Barcelona)	64,193
El Puerto de Santa María (▲ 62,285)	49,900
Elx (Elche) (▲ 180,256)	158,300
Fuenlabrada (★ Madrid)	128,872
Gernika-Lumo (Guernica y Luno) (▲ 17,836) (1981 C)	12,214
Getafe (★ Madrid)	135,367
Gijón	262,156
Granada	263,334
Granollers (★ Barcelona)	49,045
Guadalajara	61,309
Huelva	137,826
Irún	54,886
Jaén	106,435
Jerez de la Frontera (▲ 183,007)	156,200
La Coruña	248,862
La Línea	60,956
Las Palmas de Gran Canaria (▲ 366,347)	319,000
Leganés (★ Madrid)	168,403
León (★ 159,000)	136,558
L'Hospitalet de Llobregat (★ Barcelona)	278,449
Linares	58,622
Lleida (Lérida) (▲ 109,795)	91,500
Logroño	119,038
Lugo (▲ 78,795)	68,700
• MADRID (★ 4,650,000)	3,102,846
Málaga	574,456
Manresa	65,607
Mataró	100,817
Mérida	52,368
Móstoles (★ Madrid)	181,648
Murcia (▲ 314,124)	149,800
Orense	106,042
Oviedo (▲ 190,073)	168,900
Palencia	76,692
Palma (▲ 314,608)	249,000
Pamplona	180,598
Parla (★ Madrid)	66,253
Portugalete (★ Bilbao)	57,813
Puertollano	52,284
Reus	83,800
Rubí (★ Barcelona)	48,807
Sabadell (★ Barcelona)	189,489
Salamanca	159,342
San Baudilio de Llobrega (★ Barcelona)	77,502
San Cristóbal de la Laguna (▲ 111,533)	25,900
San Fernando (★ Cádiz)	81,975
San Sebastián de los Reyes (★ Madrid)	51,653
Santa Coloma de Gramanet (★ Barcelona)	136,042
Santa Cruz de Tenerife	215,228
Santander (▲ 190,795)	166,800
Santiago de Compostela (▲ 88,110)	68,800
Santurce-Antiguo (★ Bilbao)	52,334
Segovia	54,402
Sevilla (★ 945,000)	663,132
Talavera de la Reina	68,158
Tarragona (▲ 109,586)	63,500
Tarrasa (★ Barcelona)	161,410
Toledo	59,551
Torrejón de Ardoz (★ Madrid)	83,267
Torrent (★ València)	55,751
València (★ 1,270,000)	743,933
Valladolid	331,461
Vigo (▲ 271,128)	179,500
Vitoria (Gasteiz)	204,264
Zamora	62,047
Zaragoza	582,239

SPANISH NORTH AFRICA / Plazas de Soberanía en el Norte de África

1988 E	122,905
• Ceuta	67,188
Melilla	55,717

SRI LANKA

1989 E	16,806,000
Battaramulla (★ Colombo) (1981 C)	56,535
Batticaloa	50,000
• COLOMBO (★ 2,050,000)	612,000
Dehiwala-Mount Lavinia (★ Colombo)	193,000
Galle	83,000
Jaffna	128,000
Kandy	103,000
Moratuwa (★ Colombo)	166,000
Negombo	64,000
SRI JAYAWARDENEPURA (KOTTE) (★ Colombo)	108,000
Trincomalee	49,000

SUDAN / As-Sūdān

1983 C	20,594,197
Al-Fāshir	84,298
• AL-KHARṬŪM (★ 1,450,000)	473,597
Al-Kharṭūm Baḥrī (★ Al-Kharṭūm)	340,857
Al-Qaḍārif	116,876
Al-Ubayyiḍ	137,582
'Aṭbarah	72,836
Būr Sūdān (Port Sudan)	206,038
Jūbā	84,377
Kassalā	141,429
Kūstī	89,135
Nyala	111,693
Umm Durmān (Omdurman) (★ Al-Kharṭūm)	526,192
Wad Madanī	145,015
Wāw	90,960

SURINAME

1988 E	392,000
• PARAMARIBO (★ 296,000)	241,000
Wanica (★ Paramaribo)	55,000

SWAZILAND

1986 C	712,131
LOBAMBA	
Manzini (★ 30,000)	18,084
• MBABANE	38,290

SWEDEN / Sverige

1991 E	8,590,630
Borås	101,766
Eskilstuna	89,765
Gävle (▲ 88,568)	67,900
Göteborg (★ 710,894)	433,042
Halmstad (▲ 80,061)	51,300
Helsingborg	109,267
Huddinge (★ Stockholm)	73,829
Järfälla (★ Stockholm)	56,359
Jönköping	111,486
Karlstad	76,467
Linköping	122,268
Luleå	68,412
Lund (★ Malmö)	87,681
Malmö (★ 445,000)	233,887

C Census. E Official estimate. U Unofficial estimate.
• Largest city in country.
★ Population or designation of metropolitan area, including suburbs (see headnote).
▲ Population of an entire municipality, commune, or district, including rural area.

Mölndal (★ Göteborg) 52,028
Nacka (★ Stockholm) 64,056
Norrköping 120,522
Örebro 120,944
Södertälje (★ Stockholm) 81,786
Sollentuna (★ Stockholm) 51,377
Solna (★ Stockholm) 51,841
• STOCKHOLM (★ 1,449,972) 674,452
Sundsvall (▲ 93,808) 50,800
Täby (★ Stockholm) 56,714
Trollhättan 51,047
Tumba (★ Stockholm) 68,542
Umeå (▲ 91,258) 59,500
Uppsala 167,508
Västerås 119,761
Växjö (▲ 69,547) 46,000

SWITZERLAND / Schweiz / Suisse / Svizzera

1990 E 6,673,850

Aarau (★ 58,903) 15,881
Arbon (★ 41,639) 12,284
Baden (★ 71,769) 14,545
Basel (Bâle) (★ 575,000) 169,587
BERN (BERNE) (★ 298,363) 134,393
Biel (Bienne) (★ 83,133) 52,023
Fribourg (Freiburg) (★ 59,141) 33,962
Genève (Geneva) (★ 470,000) 165,404
Lausanne (★ 263,442) 122,600
Locarno (★ 42,350) 14,149
Lugano (★ 94,800) 26,055
Luzern (★ 163,026) 59,115
Neuchâtel (★ 66,457) 32,509
Sankt Gallen (★ 126,845) 73,191
Schaffhausen (★ 53,501) 33,956
Thun (★ 78,978) 37,707
Vevey (★ 65,074) 15,207
Winterthur (★ 110,000) (1991 E) 86,496
Zug (★ 68,698) 21,467
• Zürich (★ 870,000) (1991 E) 347,634

SYRIA / Sūrīyah

1988 E 11,338,000

Al-Ḥasakah (1981 C) 73,426
Al-Lādhiqīyah (Latakia) 249,000
Al-Qāmishlī 126,236
Ar-Raqqah 113,000
Dar'ā (1981 C) 49,534
Dārayyā (★ Dimashq) 53,204
Dayr az-Zawr 112,000
• DIMASHQ (DAMASCUS) (★ 2,000,000) 1,326,000
Dūmā (★ Dimashq) 66,130
Ḥalab (Aleppo) (★ 1,335,000) 1,261,000
Ḥamāh 222,000
Ḥimṣ 447,000
Idlib (1981 C) 51,682
Jaramānah (★ Dimashq) 96,681
Kābir aṣ Ṣaghīr 47,728
Madīnat ath Thawrah 58,151
Salamīyah 46,844
Ṭarṭūs (1981 C) 52,589

TAIWAN / T'aiwan

1991 E 20,352,966

Changhua (▲ 215,224) 165,000
Chiai (1992 E) 258,713
Chilung (1992 E) 357,000
Chungho (★ T'aipei) 374,339
Chungli 269,804
Chutung (1988 E) 104,797
Fangshan (★ Kaohsiung) 290,777
Fengyüan (▲ 151,642) 121,100
Hsichih (★ T'aipei) (1980 C) 70,031
Hsinchu (1992 E) 330,576
Hsinchuang (★ T'aipei) 299,174
Hsintien (★ T'aipei) 225,517
Hualien 107,552
Ilan (▲ 81,751) (1980 C) 70,900
Kangshan (1980 C) 78,049
Kaohsiung (★ 1,845,000) (1992 E) 1,401,239
Lotung (1980 C) 57,925
Lukang (1980 C) 72,019
Miaoli (1980 C) 81,500
Nant'ou (1980 C) 84,038
P'ingchen (★ T'aipei) 147,030
P'ingtung (▲ 210,801) 172,400
Sanchung (★ T'aipei) 375,996
Shulin (★ T'aipei) 111,993
Tach'i (1980 C) 67,209
T'aichung (1992 E) 785,182
T'ainan (1992 E) 692,116
• T'AIPEI (★ 6,130,000) (1992) 2,706,453
T'aipeihsien (★ T'aipei) 538,954
T'aitung (▲ 108,196) 79,100
Taoyüan 241,263
T'oufen (1980 C) 66,536
T'uch'eng (▲ 136,928) T'aipei) 80,300
Yangmei (1980 C) 84,353
Yüanlin (▲ 121,251) 53,200
Yungho (★ T'aipei) 249,736
Yungkang (▲ 136,705) 70,900

TAJIKISTAN

1991 E 5,358,300

Chudžand (Leninabad) 164,500
• DUŠANBE 582,400
Kul'ab 79,300
Kurgan-T'ube 58,400

TANZANIA

1984 E 21,062,000

Arusha 69,000
• DAR ES SALAAM 1,300,000
Dodoma 54,000
Iringa 67,000
Kigoma (1978 C) 50,044
Mbeya 93,000
Morogoro 72,000
Moshi 62,000
Mtwara (1978 C) 48,510
Mwanza (1978 C) 110,611
Tabora 87,000
Tanga 121,000
Ujiji (1967 C) 21,369
Zanzibar (1985 E) 133,000

THAILAND / Prathet Thai

1988 E 54,960,917

Chiang Mai 164,030
Chon Buri 47,286
Hat Yai 138,046
Khon Kaen 131,340
• KRUNG THEP (BANGKOK) (★ 7,025,000) (1989 E) ... 5,845,152
Nakhon Ratchasima 204,982
Nakhon Sawan 105,220
Nakhon Si Thammarat 72,407
Nonthaburi (★ Krung Thep) 218,354
Pattaya 56,402
Phitsanulok 77,675
Phra Nakhon Si Ayutthaya 60,847
Sakon Nakhon 25,110
Samut Prakan (★ Krung Thep) 73,327
Samut Sakhon 53,984
Saraburi 61,206
Songkhla 84,433
Trang 48,042
Ubon Ratchathani 100,374
Udon Thani 81,202
Yala 67,383

TOGO

1987 E 3,148,000

• LOMÉ 500,000
Sokodé 55,000

TOKELAU

1986 C 1,690

TONGA

1986 C 94,535

• NUKU'ALOFA 21,265

TRANSKEI

1987 E 3,081,770

• UMTATA (1978 E) 30,000

TRINIDAD AND TOBAGO

1990 C 1,234,388

• PORT OF SPAIN (★ 370,000) 50,878
San Fernando (★ 75,000) 30,092

TUNISIA / Tunis / Tunisie

1984 C 6,975,450

Ariana (★ Tunis) 98,655
Bardo (★ Tunis) 65,669
Ben Arous (★ Tunis) 52,105
Bizerte 94,509
Gabès 92,258
Gafsa 60,970
Hammam Lif (★ Tunis) 47,009
Houmt Essouk 92,269
Kairouan 72,254
Kasserine 47,606
La Goulette (★ Tunis) 61,609
Menzel Bourguiba 51,399
Sfax (★ 310,000) 231,911
Sousse (★ 160,000) 83,509
• TUNIS (★ 1,225,000) 596,654
Zarzis 49,063

TURKEY / Türkiye

1990 C 56,473,035

Adana 916,150
Adapazarı 171,225
Adıyaman 100,045
Afyon 95,643
Ağrı 58,038
Akhisar 73,944
Aksaray 90,698
Akşehir 51,746
Alanya 52,460
Amasya 57,288
ANKARA (★ 2,650,000) ... 2,559,471
Antakya (Antioch) 123,871
Antalya 378,208
Aydın 107,011
Bafra 65,600
Balıkesir 170,589
Bandırma 77,444
Batman 147,347
Bilecik 23,273
Bolu 60,789
Burdur 56,432
Bursa 834,576
Çanakkale 53,995
Ceyhan 85,308
Cizre 50,023
Çorlu 74,681
Çorum 116,810
Darıca 53,560
Denizli 204,118
Diyarbakır 381,144
Düzce 61,878
Edirne 102,345
Elazığ 204,603
Elbistan 54,741
Ereğli, Konya prov. 74,283
Ereğli, Zonguldak prov. 63,987
Erzincan 91,772
Erzurum 242,391
Esenyurt (★ İstanbul) 70,280
Eskişehir 413,082
Gaziantep 603,434
Gebze (★ İstanbul) 159,116
Gelibolu 18,670
Gemlik 50,237
Giresun 67,604
Gölcük 64,911
Gümüşhane 26,014
Hakkâri 30,407
İçel (Mersin) 422,357
İnegöl 71,120
İskenderun 154,807
Isparta 112,117
• İstanbul (★ 7,550,000) 6,620,241
İzmir (★ 1,900,000) 1,757,414
İzmit 256,882
Kadirli 55,061
Kahramanmaraş 228,129
Karabük 105,373
Karaman 76,525
Kars 78,455
Kastamonu 51,560
Kayseri 421,362
Kilis 82,882
Kırıkhan 68,601
Kırıkkale 185,431
Kırşehir 73,538
Kızıltepe 60,134
Konya 513,346
Körfez 65,786
Kozan 54,451
Kütahya 130,994
Lüleburgaz 52,384
Malatya 281,776
Manisa 158,928
Mardin 53,005
Muş 44,019
Nazilli 80,277
Nevşehir 52,719
Niğde 55,035
Nizip 58,604
Nusaybin 49,671
Ödemiş 51,620
Ordu 102,107
Osmaniye 123,307
Polatlı 60,158
Rize 52,031
Salihli 70,861
Samsun 303,979
Şanlıurfa 276,528
Siirt 68,320
Silvan (Miyafarkin) 59,865
Sinop 25,537
Sivas 221,512
Siverek 63,049
Söke 50,866
Soma 49,977
Sultanbeyli (★ İstanbul) 82,298
Tarsus 187,508
Tatvan 54,071
Tekirdağ 80,442
Tokat 83,058
Trabzon 143,941
Tunceli 24,513
Turgutlu 73,634
Turhal 68,384
Uşak 105,270
Van 153,111
Viranşehir 57,461
Yalova (★ İstanbul) 65,823
Yozgat 50,335
Zonguldak (★ 220,000) 116,725

TURKMENISTAN

1991 E 3,714,100

• AŠCHABAD (ASHGABAT) 412,200
Čardžou 166,400
Krasnovodsk 59,500
Mary 94,900
Nebit-Dag 89,100
Tašauz 117,000

TURKS AND CAICOS ISLANDS

1990 C 11,465

• GRAND TURK 3,691

TUVALU

1979 C 7,349

• FUNAFUTI 2,191

UGANDA

1991 C 16,582,700

Jinja 60,979
• KAMPALA 773,463
Masaka 49,070
Mbale 53,634

UKRAINE / Ukrayina

1991 E 5,194,440

Achtyrka 52,300
Alčevsk (★ Stachanov) 126,000
Aleksandrija 104,900
Antracit (★ Krasnyj Luč) 72,800
Art'omovsk 90,800
Belaja Cerkov' 204,400
Belgorod-Dnestrovskij 56,800
Berd'ansk 138,700
Berdičev 93,400
Borispol' (★ Kijev) 52,700
Br'anka (★ Stachanov) 64,500
Brovary (★ Kijev) 84,800
Čerkassy 302,200
Černigov 305,700
Černovcy 258,800
Červonograd 74,000
Charcyzsk (★ Doneck) 69,300
Char'kov (★ 2,050,000) ... 1,622,800
Cherson 365,400
Chmel'nickij 244,500
Dimitrov (★ Krasnoarmejsk) 371,800
Dneprodzeržinsk (★ Dnepropetrovsk) 284,400
Dnepropetrovsk (★ 1,600,000) 1,189,300
Doneck (★ 2,125,000) 1,121,300
Drogobyč 79,200
Druzkovka (★ Kramatorsk) 74,400
Džankoj 54,500
Dzeržinsk (★ Gorlovka) 50,500
Energodar 51,500
Fastov 54,400
Feodosija 85,600
Gorlovka (★ 700,000) 336,600
Iljičovsk (★ Odessa) 56,000
Ivano-Frankovsk 241,000
Izmail 95,100
Iz'um 64,800
Jalta 89,300
Jenakijevo (★ Gorlovka) 120,100
Jevpatorija 110,500
Kaluš 69,400
Kamenec-Podol'skij 104,900
Kerč' 178,300
• KIJEV (★ 3,250,000) 263,500
Kirovograd 277,900
Kolomyja 66,200
Komsomol'sk 56,000
Konotop 97,700
Konstantinovka 107,800
Korosten' 67,500
Kovel' 69,700
Kramatorsk (★ 515,000) 201,300
Krasnoarmejsk (★ 180,000) 73,300
Krasnodon (★ 165,000) 54,800
Krasnyj Luč (★ 320,000) 113,400
Kremenčug 240,600
Krivoj Rog 724,000
Lisičansk (★ 415,000) 126,400
Lozovaja 74,100
Lubny 60,300
Luck 209,500
Lugansk (Vorošilovgrad) (★ 650,000) 503,900
L'vov 802,200
Makejevka (★ Doneck) 423,900
Marganec 54,700
Mariupol' (Ždanov) 521,800
Melitopol' 176,900
Mukačevo 88,000
Nežin 82,000
Nikolajev 511,600
Nikopol' 159,000
Novaja Kachovka 59,000
Novograd-Volynskij 56,100
Novomoskovsk, Dnepropetrovsk oblast' 76,600
Novovolynsk 56,400
Odessa (★ 1,185,000) 1,100,700
Pavlograd 134,300
Pervomajsk 83,800
Pervomajsk (★ Stachanov) 52,000
Poltava 320,100
Priluki 72,900
Romny 57,700
Roven'ki 58,500
Rovno 239,300
Rubežnoje (★ Lisičansk) 75,100
Šacht'orsk (★ Torez) 73,100
Šepetovka 51,900
Sevastopol' 366,200
Severodoneck (★ Lisičansk) 133,300
Simferopol' 352,600
Slav'ansk (★ Kramatorsk) 137,100
Smela 81,200
Šnežnoje (★ Torez) 68,900
Šostka 95,200
Stachanov (★ 700,000) 112,700
Stryj 68,200
Sumy 303,300
Sverdlovsk, Vorosilovgrad oblast' (★ 145,000) 83,700
Svetlovodsk 57,900
Ternopol' 219,200
Torez (★ 320,000) 88,100
Uman' 97,700
Užgorod 122,600
Vinnica 380,900
Zaporožje 896,600
Žitomir 297,500
Žoltyje Vody 64,900

UNITED ARAB EMIRATES / Al-Imārāt al-'Arabīyah al-Muttaḥidah

1980 C 980,000

ABŪ ẒABY (ABU DHABI) 242,975
Al-'Ayn 101,663
Ash-Shāriqah 125,149
• Dubayy 265,702
Ra's al-Khaymah 42,000

UNITED KINGDOM

1981 C 55,678,079

UNITED KINGDOM: ENGLAND

1981 C 46,220,955

Aldershot (★ London) 53,665
Ashton-under-Lyne (★ Manchester) 43,605
Aylesbury 51,999
Barnsley 76,783
Barrow-in-Furness 50,174
Basildon (★ London) 94,800
Basingstoke 73,027
Bath 84,283
Bebington (★ Liverpool) 62,618
Bedford 75,632
Beeston and Stapleford (★ Nottingham) 64,785
Benfleet (★ London) 50,783
Birkenhead (★ Liverpool) 99,075
Birmingham (★ 2,675,000) 1,013,995
Blackburn (★ 221,900) 109,564
Blackpool (★ 280,000) 146,297
Bognor Regis 50,323
Bolton (★ Manchester) 143,960
Bootle 70,860
Bournemouth (★ 315,000) 142,829
Bracknell (★ London) 52,257
Bradford (★ Leeds) 293,336
Brentwood (★ London) 51,212
Brighton (★ 420,000) 134,581
Bristol (★ 630,000) 413,861
Burnley (★ 160,000) 76,365
Burton upon Trent 59,040
Bury (★ Manchester) 61,785
Bury Saint Edmunds 30,563
Camberley see Frimley and Camberley
Cambridge 87,111
Cannock (★ Birmingham) 54,503
Canterbury 34,546
Carlisle 72,206
Carlton (★ Nottingham) 46,053
Chatham (★ London) 65,835
Cheadle and Gatley (★ Manchester) 59,478
Chelmsford (★ London) 91,109
Cheltenham 87,188
Cheshunt (★ London) 49,616
Chester 80,154
Chesterfield (★ 127,000) 73,352
Clacton-on-Sea 39,618
Colchester 87,476
Corby 48,704
Coventry (★ 645,000) 318,718
Crawley (★ London) 80,113
Crewe 59,097
Crosby (★ Liverpool) 54,103
Darlington 85,519
Dartford (★ London) 62,032
Derby (★ 275,000) 218,026
Dewsbury (★ Leeds) 49,612
Doncaster 74,727
Dover 33,461
Dudley (★ Birmingham) 186,513
Dunstable (★ Luton) 48,436
Durham 38,105
Eastbourne 86,715
Eastleigh (★ Southampton) 58,585
Ellesmere Port (★ Liverpool) 65,829
Epsom and Ewell (★ London) 65,830
Esher / Molesey (★ London) 46,688
Exeter 88,235
Fareham / Portchester (★ Portsmouth) 55,563
Farnborough (★ London) 48,063
Folkestone 42,949
Frimley and Camberley (★ London) 45,108
Gateshead (★ Newcastle) 91,429
Gillingham (★ London) 92,531
Gloucester (★ 115,000) 106,526
Gosport (★ Portsmouth) 69,664
Gravesend (★ London) 53,450
Grays (★ London) 45,881
Greasby / Moreton (★ Liverpool) 56,410
Great Yarmouth 54,777
Grimsby (★ 145,000) 91,532
Guildford (★ London) 61,509
Halesowen (★ Birmingham) 57,533
Halifax 76,675
Harlow (★ London) 79,150
Harrogate 63,637
Hartlepool (★ Middlesbrough) 91,749
Hastings 74,979
Havant (★ Portsmouth) 50,098

C Census. E Official estimate. U Unofficial estimate.
• Largest city in country.
★ Population or designation of metropolitan area, including suburbs (see headnote).
▲ Population of an entire municipality, commune, or district, including rural area.

Hemel Hempstead (★ London) ... 80,110
Hereford ... 48,277
Hertford (★ London) ... 21,350
High Wycombe (▲ 156,800) ... 69,575
Hove (★ Brighton) ... 65,587
Huddersfield (▲ 377,400) ... 147,825
Huyton-with-Roby (★ Liverpool) ... 62,011
Ipswich ... 129,661
Keighley (★ Leeds) ... 49,188
Kidderminster ... 50,385
Kingston upon Hull (★ 350,000) ... 322,144
Kingswood (★ Bristol) ... 54,736
Kirkby (★ Liverpool) ... 52,825
Lancaster ... 43,902
Leeds (★ 1,540,000) ... 445,242
Leicester (★ 495,000) ... 324,394
Lincoln ... 79,980
Littlehampton ... 46,028
Liverpool (★ 1,525,000) ... 538,809
• LONDON (★ 11,100,000) ... 6,574,009
Loughborough ... 44,895
Lowestoft ... 59,430
Luton (★ 220,000) ... 163,209
Macclesfield ... 47,525
Maidenhead (★ London) ... 59,809
Maidstone ... 86,067
Manchester (★ 2,775,000) ... 437,612
Mansfield (★ 198,000) ... 71,325
Margate ... 53,137
Middlesbrough (★ 580,000) ... 158,516
Middleton (★ Manchester) ... 51,373
Milton Keynes ... 36,886
Newcastle-under-Lyme (★ Stoke-on-Trent) ... 73,208
Newcastle upon Tyne (★ 1,300,000) ... 199,064
Northampton ... 154,172
Norwich (★ 230,000) ... 169,814
Nottingham (★ 655,000) ... 273,300
Nuneaton (★ Coventry) ... 60,337
Oldbury / Smethwick (★ Birmingham) ... 153,268
Oldham (★ Manchester) ... 107,095
Oxford (★ 230,000) ... 113,847
Penzance ... 18,501
Peterborough ... 113,404
Plymouth (★ 290,000) ... 238,583
Poole (★ Bournemouth) ... 122,815
Portsmouth (★ 485,000) ... 174,218
Preston (★ 250,000) ... 166,675
Ramsgate ... 36,678
Reading (★ 200,000) ... 194,727
Redditch (★ Birmingham) ... 61,639
Reigate / Redhill (★ London) ... 48,241
Rochdale (★ Manchester) ... 97,292
Rotherham (★ Sheffield) ... 122,374
Royal Leamington Spa (★ Coventry) ... 56,552
Royal Tunbridge Wells ... 57,699
Rugby ... 59,039
Runcorn (★ Liverpool) ... 63,995
Saint Albans (★ London) ... 76,709
Saint Helens ... 114,397
Sale (★ Manchester) ... 57,872
Salford (★ Manchester) ... 96,525
Salisbury ... 36,890
Scarborough ... 36,665
Scunthorpe ... 79,043
Sheffield (★ 710,000) ... 470,685
Shrewsbury ... 57,731
Slough (★ London) ... 106,341
Solihull (★ Birmingham) ... 93,940
Southampton (★ 415,000) ... 211,321
Southend-on-Sea (★ London) ... 155,720
Southport (★ Liverpool) ... 88,596
South Shields (★ Newcastle) ... 86,488
Stafford ... 60,915
Staines (★ London) ... 51,949
Stapleford see Beeston and Stapleford
Stevenage ... 74,757
Stockport (★ Manchester) ... 135,489
Stockton-on-Tees (★ Middlesbrough) ... 86,699
Stoke-on-Trent (★ 440,000) ... 272,446
Stourbridge (★ Birmingham) ... 55,136
Stratford-upon-Avon ... 20,941
Stretford (★ Manchester) ... 47,522
Sunderland (★ Newcastle) ... 195,064
Sutton Coldfield (★ Birmingham) ... 102,572
Swindon ... 127,348
Tanworth ... 63,260
Taunton ... 47,793
Torquay (★ 112,400) ... 54,430
Wakefield (★ Leeds) ... 74,764
Wallasey (★ Liverpool) ... 62,465
Walsall (★ Birmingham) ... 177,923
Walton and Weybridge (★ London) ... 50,031
Warrington ... 81,366
Washington (★ Newcastle) ... 48,856
Waterlooville (★ Portsmouth) ... 57,296
Watford (★ London) ... 109,503
West Bromwich (★ Birmingham) ... 153,725
Weston-super-Mare ... 60,821
Weybridge see Walton and Weybridge
Widnes ... 55,973
Wigan (★ Manchester) ... 88,725
Woking (★ London) ... 92,667
Wolverhampton (★ Birmingham) ... 263,501
Worcester ... 75,466
Worthing (★ Brighton) ... 90,687
York (★ 145,000) ... 123,126

UNITED KINGDOM: NORTHERN IRELAND

1990 E ... 1,589,400
Bangor (★ Belfast) ... 72,600
Belfast (★ 685,000) ... 295,100
Castlereagh (★ Belfast) ... 58,100
Londonderry (Derry) ... 100,500
Lurgan (★ 63,000) ... 20,991
Newtownabbey (★ Belfast) ... 72,900

UNITED KINGDOM: SCOTLAND

1990 E ... 5,102,400
Aberdeen ... 211,080
Ayr (★ 100,000) (1981 C) ... 48,493
Clydebank (★ Glasgow) (1981 C) ... 51,832
Coatbridge (1981 C) ... 50,831
Cumbernauld (★ Glasgow) ... 50,700
Dundee ... 172,860
Dunfermline (★ 125,817) (1981 C) ... 52,105
East Kilbride (★ Glasgow) ... 70,500
Edinburgh (★ 630,000) ... 434,520
Falkirk (★ 148,171) (1981 C) ... 36,372
Glasgow (★ 1,800,000) ... 689,210
Greenock (★ 101,000) (1981 C) ... 58,436
Hamilton (★ Glasgow) (1981 C) ... 51,666
Irvine (★ 94,000) ... 56,000
Kilmarnock (★ 84,000) (1981 C) ... 51,799
Kirkcaldy (★ 148,171) (1981 C) ... 46,356
Motherwell (★ Glasgow) (1981 C) ... 30,616
Paisley (★ Glasgow) (1981 C) ... 84,330
Perth (1981 C) ... 41,916
Stirling (★ 61,000) (1981 C) ... 36,640

UNITED KINGDOM: WALES

1981 C ... 2,790,462
Cardiff (★ 625,000) ... 262,313
Cwmbran (★ Newport) ... 44,592
Llanelli ... 45,336
Merthyr Tydfil ... 38,893
Neath (★ Swansea) ... 48,687
Newport (★ 310,000) ... 115,896
Pontypool (★ Newport) ... 36,064
Port Talbot (★ 130,000) ... 40,078
Rhondda (★ Cardiff) ... 70,980
Swansea (★ 275,000) ... 172,433
Wrexham ... 39,929

UNITED STATES

1990 C ... 248,709,873

UNITED STATES: ALABAMA

1990 C ... 4,040,587
Anniston (★ 116,034) ... 26,623
Auburn (★ 61,100) ... 33,830
Birmingham (★ 907,810) ... 265,968
Decatur (★ 131,556) ... 48,761
Dothan (★ 130,964) ... 53,589
Florence (★ 131,327) ... 36,426
Gadsden (★ 99,840) ... 42,523
Huntsville (★ 238,912) ... 159,789
Mobile (★ 476,923) ... 196,278
Montgomery (★ 292,517) ... 187,106
Tuscaloosa (★ 150,522) ... 77,759

UNITED STATES: ALASKA

1990 C ... 550,043
Anchorage (★ 248,400) ... 226,338
Fairbanks (★ 59,500) ... 30,843
Juneau ... 26,751

UNITED STATES: ARIZONA

1990 C ... 3,665,228
Chandler (★ Phoenix) ... 90,533
Glendale (★ Phoenix) ... 148,134
Mesa (★ Phoenix) ... 288,091
Nogales (★ Nogales, Mexico) ... 19,489
Phoenix (★ 2,122,101) ... 900,013
Scottsdale (★ Phoenix) ... 130,069
Tempe (★ Phoenix) ... 141,865
Tucson (★ 666,880) ... 405,390
Yuma (★ 106,895) ... 54,923

UNITED STATES: ARKANSAS

1990 C ... 2,350,725
Fayetteville (★ 113,409) ... 42,099
Fort Smith (★ 175,911) ... 72,798
Hot Springs National Park (★ 56,500) ... 32,462
Jonesboro (★ 49,300) ... 46,535
Little Rock (★ 513,117) ... 175,795

North Little Rock (★ Little Rock) ... 61,741
Pine Bluff (★ 85,487) ... 57,140

UNITED STATES: CALIFORNIA

1990 C ... 29,760,021
Alameda (★ Oakland) ... 76,459
Alhambra (★ Los Angeles) ... 82,106
Anaheim (★ 2,410,556) (★Los Angeles) ... 266,406
Antioch (★ Oakland) ... 62,195
Arden (★ Sacramento) ... 62,900
Bakersfield (★ 543,477) ... 174,820
Baldwin Park (★ Los Angeles) ... 69,330
Bellflower (★ Los Angeles) ... 61,815
Berkeley (★ Oakland) ... 102,724
Buena Park (★ Anaheim) ... 68,784
Burbank (★ Los Angeles) ... 93,643
Calexico (★ Mexicali, Mexico) ... 18,633
Camarillo (★ Oxnard) ... 52,303
Carlsbad (★ San Diego) ... 63,126
Carmichael (★ Sacramento) ... 48,702
Carson (★ Los Angeles) ... 83,995
Cerritos (★ Los Angeles) ... 53,240
Chico (★ 182,120) ... 40,079
Chino (★ Riverside) ... 59,682
Chula Vista (★ San Diego) ... 135,163
Citrus Heights (★ Sacramento) ... 112,800
Clovis (★ Fresno) ... 50,323
Compton (★ Los Angeles) ... 90,454
Concord (★ Oakland) ... 111,348
Corona (★ Riverside) ... 76,095
Costa Mesa (★ Anaheim) ... 96,357
Cucamonga (★ Riverside) ... 101,409
Daly City (★ San Francisco) ... 92,311
Diamond Bar (★ Los Angeles) ... 53,672
Downey (★ Los Angeles) ... 91,444
East Los Angeles (★ Los Angeles) ... 126,379
El Cajon (★ San Diego) ... 88,693
El Monte (★ Los Angeles) ... 106,209
El Toro (★ Anaheim) ... 62,685
Escondido (★ San Diego) ... 108,635
Eureka (★ 89,800) ... 27,025
Fairfield (★ Vallejo) ... 77,211
Fontana (★ Riverside) ... 87,535
Fountain Valley (★ Anaheim) ... 53,691
Fremont (★ Oakland) ... 173,339
Fresno (★ 667,490) ... 354,202
Fullerton (★ Anaheim) ... 114,144
Gardena (★ Los Angeles) ... 49,847
Garden Grove (★ Anaheim) ... 143,050
Glendale (★ Los Angeles) ... 180,038
Hacienda Heights (★ Los Angeles) ... 58,200
Hawthorne (★ Los Angeles) ... 71,349
Hayward (★ Oakland) ... 111,498
Hemet (★ Riverside) ... 36,094
Huntington Beach (★ Anaheim) ... 181,519
Huntington Park (★ Los Angeles) ... 56,065
Inglewood (★ Los Angeles) ... 109,602
Irvine (★ Anaheim) ... 110,330
La Habra (★ Anaheim) ... 51,266
Lakewood (★ Los Angeles) ... 73,557
La Mesa (★ San Diego) ... 52,931
Lancaster (★ 189,300) (★Los Angeles) ... 97,291
Livermore (★ Oakland) ... 56,741
Lodi (★ Stockton) ... 51,874
Lompoc (★ Santa Barbara) ... 37,649
Long Beach (★ Los Angeles) ... 429,433
Los Angeles (★ 14,531,529) ... 3,485,398
Lynwood (★ Los Angeles) ... 61,945
Merced (★ 178,403) ... 56,216
Milpitas (★ San Jose) ... 50,686
Mission Viejo (★ Anaheim) ... 72,820
Modesto (★ 370,522) ... 164,730
Montebello (★ Los Angeles) ... 59,564
Monterey (★ Salinas) ... 31,954
Monterey Park (★ Los Angeles) ... 60,738
Mountain View (★ San Jose) ... 67,460
Napa (★ Vallejo) ... 61,842
National City (★ San Diego) ... 54,249
Newport Beach (★ Anaheim) ... 66,643
Norwalk (★ Los Angeles) ... 94,279
Oakland (★ 2,082,914) (★San Francisco) ... 372,242
Oceanside (★ San Diego) ... 128,398
Ontario (★ Riverside) ... 133,179
Orange (★ Anaheim) ... 110,658
Oxnard (★ 669,016) (★Los Angeles) ... 142,216
Palm Springs (★ Riverside) ... 40,181
Palo Alto (★ San Jose) ... 55,900
Pasadena (★ Los Angeles) ... 131,591
Pico Rivera (★ Los Angeles) ... 59,177

Pleasanton (★ Oakland) ... 50,553
Pomona (★ Los Angeles) ... 131,723
Porterville (★ Visalia) ... 29,563
Rancho Cordova (★ Sacramento) ... 48,731
Redding (★ 147,036) ... 66,462
Redlands (★ Riverside) ... 60,394
Redondo Beach (★ Los Angeles) ... 60,167
Redwood City (★ San Francisco) ... 66,072
Rialto (★ Riverside) ... 72,388
Richmond (★ Oakland) ... 87,425
Riverside (★ 2,588,793) (★Los Angeles) ... 226,505
Rosemead (★ Los Angeles) ... 51,638
Sacramento (★ 1,481,102) ... 369,365
Salinas (★ 355,660) ... 108,777
San Bernardino (★ Riverside) ... 164,164
San Diego (★ 2,949,000) ... 1,110,549
San Francisco (★ 6,253,311) ... 723,959
San Jose (★ 1,497,577) (★San Francisco) ... 782,248
San Leandro (★ Oakland) ... 68,223
San Mateo (★ San Francisco) ... 85,486
Santa Ana (★ Anaheim) ... 293,742
Santa Barbara (★ 369,608) ... 85,571
Santa Clara (★ San Jose) ... 93,613
Santa Cruz (★ 229,734) (★San Francisco) ... 49,040
Santa Maria (★ Santa Barbara) ... 61,284
Santa Monica (★ Los Angeles) ... 86,905
Santa Rosa (★ 388,222) (★San Francisco) ... 113,313
Santee (★ San Diego) ... 52,902
Simi Valley (★ Oxnard) ... 100,217
South Gate (★ Los Angeles) ... 86,284
South San Francisco (★ San Francisco) ... 54,312
South Whittier (★ Los Angeles) ... 51,100
Spring Valley (★ San Diego) ... 54,600
Stockton (★ 480,628) ... 210,943
Sunnyvale (★ San Jose) ... 117,229
Thousand Oaks (★ Oxnard) ... 104,352
Torrance (★ Los Angeles) ... 133,107
Tustin (★ Anaheim) ... 50,689
Union City (★ Oakland) ... 53,762
Upland (★ Riverside) ... 63,374
Vacaville (★ Vallejo) ... 71,479
Vallejo (★ 451,186) (★San Francisco) ... 109,199
Ventura (San Buenaventura) (★ Oxnard) ... 92,575
Visalia (★ 311,921) ... 75,636
Vista (★ San Diego) ... 71,872
Walnut Creek (★ Oakland) ... 60,569
Watsonville (★ Santa Cruz) ... 31,099
West Covina (★ Los Angeles) ... 96,086
Westminster (★ Anaheim) ... 78,118
Whittier (★ Los Angeles) ... 77,671
Yorba Linda (★ Anaheim) ... 52,422
Yuba City (★ 122,643) ... 27,437

UNITED STATES: COLORADO

1990 C ... 3,294,394
Arvada (★ Denver) ... 89,235
Aurora (★ Denver) ... 222,103
Boulder (★ 225,339) (★Denver) ... 83,312
Colorado Springs (★ 397,014) ... 281,140
Denver (★ 1,848,319) ... 467,610
Fort Collins (★ 186,136) ... 87,758
Grand Junction (★ 85,200) ... 29,034
Greeley (★ 131,821) ... 60,536
Lakewood (★ Denver) ... 126,481
Longmont (★ Boulder) ... 51,555
Loveland (★ Fort Collins) ... 37,352
Pueblo (★ 123,051) ... 98,640
Thornton (★ Denver) ... 55,031
Westminster (★ Denver) ... 74,625

UNITED STATES: CONNECTICUT

1990 C ... 3,287,116
Bridgeport (★ 443,722) (★New York, N.Y.) ... 141,686
Bristol (★ 79,488) (★Hartford) ... 60,640
Danbury (★ 187,867) (★New York, N.Y.) ... 65,585
East Hartford (★ Hartford) ... 50,452
Fairfield (★ Bridgeport) ... 53,418
Greenwich (★ Stamford) ... 58,441
Hamden (★ New Haven) ... 53,100
Hartford (★ 1,085,837) ... 139,739
Manchester (★ Hartford) ... 51,000
Meriden (★ New Haven) ... 59,479
Milford (★ Bridgeport) ... 48,168

New Britain (★ 148,188) (★Hartford) ... 75,491
New Haven (★ 530,180) ... 130,474
New London (★ 266,819) ... 28,540
Norwalk (★ 127,378) (★New York, N.Y.) ... 78,331
Stamford (★ 202,557) (★New York, N.Y.) ... 108,056
Stratford (★ Bridgeport) ... 49,389
Torrington (★ 58,800) ... 33,687
Waterbury (★ 221,629) ... 108,961
West Hartford (★ Hartford) ... 59,100
West Haven (★ New Haven) ... 54,021

UNITED STATES: DELAWARE

1990 C ... 666,168
Dover (★ 78,900) ... 27,630
Wilmington (★ Philadelphia, Pa.) ... 71,529

UNITED STATES: DISTRICT OF COLUMBIA

1990 C ... 606,900
WASHINGTON (★ 3,923,574) ... 606,900

UNITED STATES: FLORIDA

1990 C ... 12,937,926
Boca Raton (★ West Palm Beach) ... 61,492
Brandon (★ Tampa) ... 57,985
Cape Coral (★ Fort Myers) ... 74,991
Carol City (★ Miami) ... 52,800
City of Sunrise (★ Fort Lauderdale) ... 64,407
Clearwater (★ Tampa) ... 98,784
Daytona Beach (★ 370,712) ... 61,921
De Land (★ Daytona Beach) ... 16,491
Fort Lauderdale (★ 1,255,488) (★Miami) ... 149,377
Fort Myers (★ 335,113) ... 45,206
Fort Pierce (★ 251,071) ... 36,830
Fort Walton Beach (★ 143,776) ... 21,471
Gainesville (★ 204,111) ... 84,770
Hialeah (★ Miami) ... 188,004
Hollywood (★ Fort Lauderdale) ... 121,697
Jacksonville (★ 906,727) ... 635,230
Kendall (★ Miami) ... 53,100
Lakeland (★ 405,382) ... 70,576
Largo (★ Tampa) ... 65,674
Melbourne (★ 398,978) ... 59,646
Miami (★ 3,192,582) ... 358,548
Miami Beach (★ Miami) ... 92,639
Naples (★ 152,099) ... 19,505
Ocala (★ 194,833) ... 42,045
Orlando (★ 1,072,748) ... 164,693
Panama City (★ 126,994) ... 34,378
Pembroke Pines (★ Fort Lauderdale) ... 65,452
Pensacola (★ 344,406) ... 58,165
Plantation (★ Fort Lauderdale) ... 66,692
Pompano Beach (★ Fort Lauderdale) ... 72,411
Saint Petersburg (★ Tampa) ... 238,629
Sarasota (★ 277,776) ... 50,961
Tallahassee (★ 233,598) ... 124,773
Tampa (★ 2,067,959) ... 280,015
Venice (★ Sarasota) ... 16,922
West Palm Beach (★ 863,518) ... 67,643
Winter Haven (★ Lakeland) ... 24,725

UNITED STATES: GEORGIA

1990 C ... 6,478,216
Albany (★ 112,561) ... 78,122
Athens (★ 156,267) ... 45,734
Atlanta (★ 2,833,511) ... 394,017
Augusta (★ 396,809) ... 44,639
Columbus (★ 243,072) ... 178,681
Macon (★ 281,103) ... 106,612
Rome (★ 74,900) ... 30,326
Savannah (★ 242,622) ... 137,560
Valdosta (★ 64,000) ... 39,806
Warner Robins (★ Macon) ... 43,726

UNITED STATES: HAWAII

1990 C ... 1,108,229
Hilo (★ 47,600) ... 37,808
Honolulu (★ 836,231) ... 365,272

UNITED STATES: IDAHO

1990 C ... 1,006,749
Boise (★ 205,775) ... 125,738
Idaho Falls (★ 72,700) ... 43,929
Lewiston (★ 44,300) ... 28,082
Nampa (★ 70,500) ... 28,365

C Census.   E Official estimate.   U Unofficial estimate.
• Largest city in country.

★ Population or designation of metropolitan area, including suburbs (see headnote).
▲ Population of an entire municipality, commune, or district, including rural area.

Pocatello (★ 56,700) 46,080

UNITED STATES: ILLINOIS

1990 C 11,430,602

Arlington Heights (★ Chicago) 75,460
Aurora (★ 356,884) (★Chicago) 99,581
Bloomington (★ 129,180) 51,972
Champaign (★ 173,025) 63,502
Chicago (★ 8,065,633) 2,783,726
Cicero (★ Chicago) 67,436
Danville (★ 68,000) 33,828
Decatur (★ 117,206) 83,885
De Kalb (★ 52,200) 34,925
Des Plaines (★ Chicago) 53,223
East Saint Louis (★ Saint Louis, Mo.) 40,944
Elgin (★ Aurora) 77,010
Evanston (★ Chicago) 73,233
Galesburg (★ 40,600) 33,530
Joliet (★ 389,650) (★Chicago) 76,836
Kankakee (★ 96,255) 27,575
Mount Prospect (★ Chicago) 53,170
Naperville (★ Chicago) 85,351
Oak Lawn (★ Chicago) 56,182
Oak Park (★ Chicago) 53,648
Peoria (★ 339,172) 113,504
Quincy (★ 50,600) 39,681
Rockford (★ 283,719) 139,426
Schaumburg (★ Chicago) 68,586
Skokie (★ Chicago) 59,432
Springfield (★ 189,550) 105,227
Waukegan (★ Chicago) 69,392
Wheaton (★ Chicago) 51,464

UNITED STATES: INDIANA

1990 C 5,544,159

Anderson (★ 130,669) 59,459
Bloomington (★ 108,978) 60,633
Columbus (★ 59,000) 31,802
Elkhart (★ 156,198) 43,627
Evansville (★ 278,990) 126,272
Fort Wayne (★ 363,811) 173,072
Gary (★ 604,526) (★Chicago, Il.) 116,646
Hammond (★ Gary) 84,236
Indianapolis (★ 1,249,822) 731,327
Kokomo (★ 96,946) 44,962
Lafayette (★ 130,598) 43,764
Marion (★ 76,900) 32,618
Michigan City (★ 55,600) 33,822
Muncie (★ 119,659) 71,035
Richmond (★ 64,100) 38,705
South Bend (★ 247,052) 105,511
Terre Haute (★ 130,812) 57,483

UNITED STATES: IOWA

1990 C 2,776,755

Ames (★ 65,400) 47,198
Cedar Rapids (★ 168,767) 108,751
Clinton (★ 39,600) 29,201
Council Bluffs (★ Omaha, Ne.) 54,315
Davenport (★ 350,861) 95,333
Des Moines (★ 392,928) 193,187
Dubuque (★ 86,403) 57,546
Iowa City (★ 96,119) 59,738
Mason City 29,040
Sioux City (★ 115,018) 80,505
Waterloo (★ 146,611) 66,467

UNITED STATES: KANSAS

1990 C 2,477,574

Hutchinson (★ 46,800) 39,308
Kansas City (★ Kansas City, Mo.) 149,767
Lawrence (★ 81,798) 65,608
Manhattan (★ 47,400) 37,712
Olathe (★ Kansas City, Mo.) 63,352
Overland Park (★ Kansas City, Mo.) 111,790
Salina (★ 42,700) 42,303
Topeka (★ 160,976) 119,883
Wichita (★ 485,270) 304,011

UNITED STATES: KENTUCKY

1990 C 3,685,296

Bowling Green (★ 59,100) 40,641
Covington (★ Cincinnati, Oh.) 43,264
Frankfort 25,968
Lexington (★ 348,428) 225,366
Louisville (★ 952,662) 269,063
Owensboro (★ 87,189) 53,549
Paducah (★ 63,000) 27,256

UNITED STATES: LOUISIANA

1990 C 4,219,973

Alexandria (★ 131,556) 49,188
Baton Rouge (★ 528,264) 219,531
Bossier City (★ Shreveport) 52,721
Houma (★ 182,842) 96,982
Kenner (★ New Orleans) 72,033
Lafayette (★ 208,740) 94,440
Lake Charles (★ 168,134) 70,580
Metairie (★ New Orleans) 149,428
Monroe (★ 142,191) 54,909
New Iberia (★ 49,000) 31,828
New Orleans (★ 1,238,816) 496,938
Shreveport (★ 334,341) 198,525

UNITED STATES: MAINE

1990 C 1,227,928

Augusta (★ 56,700) 21,325
Bangor (★ 88,745) 33,181
Lewiston (★ 88,141) 39,757
Portland (★ 215,281) 64,358

UNITED STATES: MARYLAND

1990 C 4,781,468

Annapolis (★ Baltimore) 33,187
Baltimore (★ 2,382,172) 736,014
Bethesda (★ Washington, D.C.) 62,936
Columbia (★ Baltimore) 75,883
Cumberland (★ 101,643) 23,706
Dundalk (★ Baltimore) 65,800
Hagerstown (★ 121,393) 35,445
Salisbury (★ 72,400) 20,592
Silver Spring (★ Washington, D.C.) 76,046
Towson (★ Baltimore) 49,445
Wheaton (★ Washington, D.C.) (1989) 58,300

UNITED STATES: MASSACHUSETTS

1990 C 6,016,425

Amherst (★ 44,700) 17,824
Boston (★ 4,171,643) 574,283
Brockton (★ 189,478) (★Boston) 92,788
Brookline (★ Boston) 54,718
Cambridge (★ Boston) 95,802
Chicopee (★ Springfield) 56,632
Fall River (★ 157,272) (★Providence, R.I.) 92,703
Fitchburg (★ 102,797) 41,194
Framingham (★ Boston) 64,989
Haverhill (★ Lawrence) 51,418
Lawrence (★ 393,516) (★Boston) 70,207
Lowell (★ 273,067) (★Boston) 103,439
Lynn (★ Salem) 81,245
Malden (★ Boston) 53,884
Medford (★ Boston) 57,407
New Bedford (★ 175,641) 99,922
Newton (★ Boston) 82,585
Northampton (★ Springfield) 29,289
Pittsfield (★ 79,250) 48,622
Quincy (★ Boston) 84,985
Somerville (★ Boston) 76,210
Springfield (★ 529,519) 156,983
Taunton (★ 59,700) 49,832
Waltham (★ Boston) 57,878
Weymouth (★ Boston) 54,063
Worcester (★ 436,905) 169,759

UNITED STATES: MICHIGAN

1990 C 9,295,297

Ann Arbor (★ 282,937) (★Detroit) 109,592
Battle Creek (★ 135,982) 53,540
Benton Harbor (★ 161,378) 12,818
Clinton Township (★ Detroit) 77,900
Dearborn (★ Detroit) 89,286
Dearborn Heights (★ Detroit) 60,838
Detroit (★ 4,665,236) 1,027,974
East Lansing (★ Lansing) 50,677
Farmington Hills (★ Detroit) 74,652
Flint (★ 430,459) 140,761
Grand Rapids (★ 688,399) 189,126
Holland (★ Grand Rapids) 30,745
Jackson (★ 149,756) 37,446
Kalamazoo (★ 223,411) 80,277
Lansing (★ 432,674) 127,321
Livonia (★ Detroit) 100,850
Monroe (★ 62,600) (★Detroit) 22,902
Muskegon (★ 158,983) 40,283
Pontiac (★ Detroit) 71,166
Port Huron (★ Sarnia, Canada) 33,694
Redford Township (★ Detroit) 54,387
Roseville (★ Detroit) 51,412
Royal Oak (★ Detroit) 65,410
Saginaw (★ 399,320) 69,512
Saint Clair Shores (★ Detroit) 68,107
Sault Sainte Marie 14,689
Southfield (★ Detroit) 75,728
Sterling Heights (★ Detroit) 117,810
Taylor (★ Detroit) 70,811
Troy (★ Detroit) 72,884
Warren (★ Detroit) 144,864
Westland (★ Detroit) 84,724
Wyoming (★ Grand Rapids) 63,891

UNITED STATES: MINNESOTA

1990 C 4,375,099

Bloomington (★ Minneapolis) 86,335
Brooklyn Park (★ Minneapolis) 56,381
Burnsville (★ Minneapolis) 51,288
Coon Rapids (★ Minneapolis) 52,978
Duluth (★ 239,971) 85,493
Mankato (★ 48,400) 31,477
Minneapolis (★ 2,464,124) 368,383
Plymouth (★ Minneapolis) 50,889
Rochester (★ 106,470) 70,745
Saint Cloud (★ 190,921) 48,812
Saint Paul (★ Minneapolis) 272,235

UNITED STATES: MISSISSIPPI

1990 C 2,573,216

Biloxi (★ 197,125) 46,319
Columbus (★ 52,100) 23,799
Greenville (★ 48,500) 45,226
Gulfport (★ Biloxi) 40,775
Hattiesburg (★ 71,600) 41,882
Jackson (★ 395,396) 196,637
Laurel (★ 47,300) 18,827
Meridian (★ 60,600) 41,036
Natchez (★ 45,700) 19,460
Pascagoula (★ 115,243) 25,899
Vicksburg (★ 43,500) 20,908

UNITED STATES: MISSOURI

1990 C 5,117,073

Cape Girardeau (★ 59,100) 34,438
Columbia (★ 112,379) 69,101
Florissant (★ Saint Louis) 51,206
Independence (★ Kansas City) 112,301
Jefferson City (★ 60,100) 35,481
Joplin (★ 134,910) 40,961
Kansas City (★ 1,566,280) 435,146
Saint Charles (★ Saint Louis) 54,555
Saint Joseph (★ 83,083) 71,852
Saint Louis (★ 2,444,099) 396,685
Springfield (★ 240,593) 140,494

UNITED STATES: MONTANA

1990 C 799,065

Billings (★ 113,419) 81,151
Butte (★ 33,900) 33,336
Great Falls (★ 77,691) 55,097
Helena 24,569
Missoula (★ 65,700) 42,918

UNITED STATES: NEBRASKA

1990 C 1,578,385

Grand Island (★ 42,200) 39,386
Lincoln (★ 213,641) 191,972
Omaha (★ 618,262) 335,795

UNITED STATES: NEVADA

1990 C 1,201,833

Carson City 40,443
Henderson (★ Las Vegas) 64,942
Las Vegas (★ 741,459) 258,295
Paradise (★ Las Vegas) 124,682
Reno (★ 254,667) 133,850
Sparks (★ Reno) 53,367
Sunrise Manor (★ Las Vegas) 95,362

UNITED STATES: NEW HAMPSHIRE

1990 C 1,109,252

Concord (★ 73,300) 36,006
Manchester (★ 147,809) 99,567
Nashua (★ 180,557) (★Boston, Ma.) 79,662
Portsmouth (★ 223,578) 25,925

UNITED STATES: NEW JERSEY

1990 C 7,730,188

Atlantic City (★ 319,416) 37,986
Bayonne (★ Jersey City) 61,444
Bloomfield (★ Newark) 45,061
Brick Township (★ New York, N.Y.) 66,473
Camden (★ Philadelphia, Pa.) 87,492
Cherry Hill (★ Philadelphia, Pa.) 69,319
Clifton (★ New York, N.Y.) 71,742
East Orange (★ Newark) 73,552
Edison (★ New York, N.Y.) 88,680
Elizabeth (★ Newark) 110,002
Irvington (★ Newark) 59,774
Jersey City (★ 553,099) (★New York, N.Y.) 228,537
Middletown (★ New York, N.Y.) 62,298
Newark (★ 1,824,321) (★New York, N.Y.) 275,221
Passaic (★ New York, N.Y.) 58,041
Paterson (★ New York, N.Y.) 140,891
Trenton (★ 325,824) (★Philadelphia, Pa.) 88,675
Union (★ Newark) 50,024
Union City (★ Jersey City) 58,012
Vineland (★ 138,053) (★Philadelphia, Pa.) 54,780

UNITED STATES: NEW MEXICO

1990 C 1,515,069

Albuquerque (★ 480,577) 384,736
Farmington (★ 50,300) 33,997
Las Cruces (★ 135,510) 62,126
Roswell (★ 50,600) 44,654
Santa Fe (★ 117,043) 55,859

UNITED STATES: NEW YORK

1990 C 17,990,455

Albany (★ 874,304) 101,082
Auburn (★ 52,900) 31,258
Binghamton (★ 264,497) 53,008
Buffalo (★ 1,189,288) 328,123
Cheektowaga (★ Buffalo) 84,387
Elmira (★ 95,195) 33,724
Glens Falls (★ 118,539) 15,023
Hempstead (★ New York) 49,453
Irondequoit (★ Rochester) 52,322
Ithaca (★ 82,700) 29,541
Jamestown (★ 141,895) 34,681
Kingston (★ 88,200) 23,095
Levittown (★ New York) 53,286
Lockport (★ 57,500) (★Buffalo) 24,426
Mount Vernon (★ New York) 67,153
Newburgh (★ 102,300) (★New York) 26,454
New Rochelle (★ New York) 67,265
• New York (★ 18,087,251) 7,322,564
Niagara Falls (★ 220,756) (★Buffalo) 61,840
Poughkeepsie (★ 259,462) 28,844
Rochester (★ 1,002,410) 231,636
Schenectady (★ Albany) 65,566
Syracuse (★ 659,864) 163,860
Troy (★ Albany) 54,269
Utica (★ 316,633) 68,637
West Seneca (★ Buffalo) 47,866
Yonkers (★ New York) 188,082

UNITED STATES: NORTH CAROLINA

1990 C 6,628,637

Asheville (★ 174,821) 61,607
Burlington (★ 108,213) 39,498
Charlotte (★ 1,162,093) 395,934
Durham (★ Raleigh) 136,611
Fayetteville (★ 274,566) 75,695
Gastonia (★ Charlotte) 54,732
Goldsboro (★ 94,200) 40,709
Greensboro (★ 942,091) 183,521
Hickory (★ 221,700) 28,301
High Point (★ Greensboro) 69,496
Jacksonville (★ 149,838) 30,013
Kannapolis (★ Charlotte) 29,696
Raleigh (★ 735,480) 207,951
Rocky Mount (★ 83,400) 48,997
Salisbury (★ Charlotte) 23,087
Wilmington (★ 120,284) 55,530
Winston-Salem (★ Greenboro) 143,485

UNITED STATES: NORTH DAKOTA

1990 C 638,800

Bismarck (★ 83,831) 49,256
Fargo (★ 153,296) 74,111
Grand Forks (★ 70,683) 49,425
Minot (★ 39,800) 34,544

UNITED STATES: OHIO

1990 C 10,347,115

Akron (★ 657,575) (★Cleveland) 223,019
Alliance (★ Canton) 23,376
Ashtabula (★ 40,900) 21,633
Brunswick (★ Cleveland) 28,230
Canton (★ 394,106) 84,161
Cincinnati (★ 1,744,124) 364,040
Cleveland (★ 2,759,823) 505,616
Cleveland Heights (★ Cleveland) 54,052
Columbus (★ 1,377,419) 632,910
Dayton (★ 951,270) 182,044
East Liverpool (★ 44,400) 13,654
Elyria (★ Lorain) 56,746
Euclid (★ Cleveland) 54,875
Hamilton (★ 291,479) (★Cincinnati) 61,368
Kettering (★ Dayton) 60,569
Lakewood (★ Cleveland) 59,718
Lancaster (★ Columbus) 34,507
Lima (★ 154,340) 45,549
Lorain (★ 271,126) (★Cleveland) 71,245
Mansfield (★ 126,137) 50,627
Marion (★ 53,900) 34,075
Middletown (★ 107,200) (★Cincinnati) 46,022
Newark (★ Columbus) 44,389
Parma (★ Cleveland) 87,876
Portsmouth (★ 64,300) 22,676
Sandusky (★ 79,800) 29,764
Springfield (★ Dayton) 70,487
Steubenville (★ 142,523) 22,125
Toledo (★ 614,128) 332,943
Warren (★ Youngstown) 50,793
Youngstown (★ 492,619) 95,732
Zanesville (★ 67,800) 26,778

UNITED STATES: OKLAHOMA

1990 C 3,145,585

Broken Arrow (★ Tulsa) 58,043
Edmond (★ Oklahoma City) 52,315
Enid (★ 56,735) 45,309
Lawton (★ 111,486) 80,561
Midwest City (★ Oklahoma City) 52,267
Muskogee (★ 49,500) 37,708
Norman (★ Oklahoma City) 80,071
Oklahoma City (★ 958,839) 444,719
Tulsa (★ 708,954) 367,302

UNITED STATES: OREGON

1990 C 2,842,321

Beaverton (★ Portland) 53,310
Corvallis (★ 98,700) 44,757
Eugene (★ 282,912) 112,669
Gresham (★ Portland) 68,235
Medford (★ 146,389) 46,951
Portland (★ 1,477,895) 437,319
Salem (★ 278,024) 107,786

UNITED STATES: PENNSYLVANIA

1990 C 11,881,643

Abington (★ Philadelphia) 59,300
Allentown (★ 686,688) 105,090
Altoona (★ 130,542) 51,881
Bensalem (★ Philadelphia) 56,788
Bethlehem (★ Allentown) 71,428
Bristol (★ Philadelphia) 57,129
Butler (★ 86,500) 15,714
Coatesville (★ 93,400) (★Philadelphia) 11,038
Erie (★ 275,572) 108,718
Hanover (★ York) 14,399
Harrisburg (★ 587,986) 52,376
Haverford (★ Philadelphia) 49,848
Hazleton (★ Scranton) 24,730
Johnstown (★ 241,247) 28,134
Lancaster (★ 422,822) 55,551
Lebanon (★ Harrisburg) 24,800
Lower Merion Township (★ Philadelphia) 58,003
New Castle (★ 68,400) 28,334
Oil City (★ 42,000) 11,949
Penn Hills (★ Pittsburgh) 51,430
Philadelphia (★ 5,899,345) 1,585,577
Pittsburgh (★ 2,242,798) 369,879
Pottstown (★ 88,300) (★Philadelphia) 21,831
Pottsville (★ 54,200) 16,603
Reading (★ 336,523) 78,380
Scranton (★ 734,175) 81,805
Sharon (★ 121,003) 17,493
State College (★ 123,786) 38,923
Uniontown (★ 53,200) (★Pittsburgh) 12,034
Upper Darby (★ Philadelphia) 84,054
Washington (★ 66,000) (★Pittsburgh) 15,864
Wilkes-Barre (★ Scranton) 47,523
Williamsport (★ 118,710) 31,933
York (★ 417,848) 42,192

UNITED STATES: RHODE ISLAND

1990 C 1,003,464

Cranston (★ Providence) 76,060
East Providence (★ Providence) 50,380
Newport (★ 64,500) 28,227
Pawtucket (★ 329,384) (★Providence) 72,644
Providence (★ 1,141,510) 160,728
Warwick (★ Providence) 85,427

C Census. E Official estimate. U Unofficial estimate.
• Largest city in country.
★ Population or designation of metropolitan area, including suburbs (see headnote).
▲ Population of an entire municipality, commune, or district, including rural area.

UNITED STATES: SOUTH CAROLINA

1990 C	3,486,703
Anderson (★ 145,196)	26,184
Charleston (★ 506,875)	80,414
Columbia (★ 453,331)	98,052
Florence (★ 114,344)	29,813
Greenville (★ 640,861)	58,282
North Charleston (★ Charleston)	70,218
Rock Hill (★ Charlotte, N.C.)	41,643
Spartanburg (★ Greenville)	43,467
Sumter (★ 90,300)	41,943

UNITED STATES: SOUTH DAKOTA

1990 C	696,004
Pierre	12,906
Rapid City (★ 81,343)	54,523
Sioux Falls (★ 123,809)	100,814

UNITED STATES: TENNESSEE

1990 C	4,877,185
Bristol (★ Johnson City)	23,421
Chattanooga (★ 433,210)	152,466
Clarksville (★ 169,439)	75,494
Jackson (★ 77,982)	48,949
Johnson City (★ 436,047)	49,381
Kingsport (★ Johnson City)	36,365
Knoxville (★ 604,816)	165,121
Memphis (★ 981,747)	610,337
Murfreesboro (★ Nashville)	44,922
Nashville (★ 985,026)	487,969

UNITED STATES: TEXAS

1990 C	16,986,510
Abilene (★ 119,655)	106,654
Amarillo (★ 187,547)	157,615
Arlington (★ Fort Worth)	261,721
Austin (★ 781,572)	465,622
Baytown (★ Houston)	63,850
Beaumont (★ 361,226)	114,323
Brownsville (★ 460,000)	98,962
Bryan (★ 121,862)	55,002
Carrollton (★ Dallas)	82,169
College Station (★ Bryan)	52,456
Corpus Christi (★ 349,894)	257,453
Dallas (★ 3,885,415)	1,006,877
Denton (★ Dallas)	66,270
El Paso (★ 650,000)	515,342
Fort Worth (★ 1,332,053) (★Dallas)	447,619
Freeport (★ 88,600) (★Houston)	11,389
Galveston (★ 217,399) (★Houston)	59,070
Garland (★ Dallas)	180,650
Grand Prairie (★ Dallas)	99,616
Harlingen (★ Brownsville)	48,735
Houston (★ 3,711,043)	1,630,553
Irving (★ Dallas)	155,037
Killeen (★ 255,301)	63,535
Laredo (★ 354,000)	122,899
Longview (★ 162,431)	70,311
Lubbock (★ 222,636)	186,206
Lufkin (★ 56,000)	30,206
McAllen (★ 383,545)	84,021
Mesquite (★ Dallas)	101,484
Midland (★ 106,611)	89,443
Odessa (★ 118,934)	89,699
Pasadena (★ Houston)	119,363
Plano (★ Dallas)	128,713
Port Arthur (★ Beaumont)	58,724
Richardson (★ Dallas)	74,840
San Angelo (★ 98,458)	84,474
San Antonio (★ 1,302,099)	935,933
Sherman (★ 95,021)	31,601
Temple (★ Killeen)	46,109
Texarkana (★ 120,132)	31,656
Tyler (★ 151,309)	75,450
Victoria (★ 74,361)	55,076
Waco (★ 189,123)	103,590
Wichita Falls (★ 122,378)	96,259

UNITED STATES: UTAH

1990 C	1,722,850
Logan (★ 60,300)	32,762
Ogden (★ Salt Lake City)	63,909
Orem (★ Provo)	67,561
Provo (★ 263,590)	86,835
Salt Lake City (★ 1,072,227)	159,936
Sandy (★ Salt Lake City)	75,058
West Valley City (★ Salt Lake City)	86,976

UNITED STATES: VERMONT

1990 C	562,758
Burlington (★ 131,439)	39,127
Montpelier (★ 52,800)	8,247
Rutland (★ 53,000)	18,230

UNITED STATES: VIRGINIA

1990 C	6,187,358
Alexandria (★ Washington, D.C.)	111,183
Annandale (★ Washington, D.C.)	50,975
Arlington (★ Washington, D.C.)	170,936
Charlottesville (★ 131,107)	40,341
Chesapeake (★ Norfolk)	151,976
Danville (★ 108,711)	53,056
Hampton (★ Norfolk)	133,793
Lynchburg (★ 142,199)	66,049
Martinsville (★ 67,100)	16,162
Newport News (★ Norfolk)	170,045
Norfolk (★ 1,396,107)	261,229
Portsmouth (★ Norfolk)	103,907
Richmond (★ 865,640)	203,056
Roanoke (★ 224,477)	96,397
Suffolk (★ Norfolk)	52,141
Virginia Beach (★ Norfolk)	393,069

UNITED STATES: WASHINGTON

1990 C	4,866,692
Bellevue (★ Seattle)	86,874
Bellingham (★ 127,780)	52,179
Bremerton (★ 189,731)	38,142
Everett (★ Seattle)	69,961
Lakes District (★ Tacoma)	58,412
Longview (★ 67,100)	31,499
Olympia (★ 161,238)	33,840
Pasco (★ Richland)	20,337
Seattle (★ 2,559,164)	516,259
Spokane (★ 361,364)	177,196
Tacoma (★ 586,203) (★Seattle)	176,664
Yakima (★ 188,823)	54,827

UNITED STATES: WEST VIRGINIA

1990 C	1,793,477
Beckley (★ 64,300)	18,296
Charleston (★ 250,454)	57,287
Clarksburg (★ 53,800)	18,059
Fairmont (★ 53,700)	20,210
Huntington (★ 312,529)	54,844
Morgantown (★ 71,500)	25,879
Parkersburg (★ 149,169)	33,862
Wheeling (★ 159,301)	34,882

UNITED STATES: WISCONSIN

1990 C	4,891,769
Appleton (★ 315,121)	65,695
Beloit (★ Janesville)	35,573
Eau Claire (★ 137,543)	56,856
Fond du Lac (★ 52,400)	37,757
Green Bay (★ 194,594)	96,466
Janesville (★ 139,510)	52,133
Kenosha (★ 128,181) (★Chicago, Il.)	80,352
La Crosse (★ 97,904)	51,003
Madison (★ 367,085)	191,262
Manitowoc (★ 57,300)	32,520
Milwaukee (★ 1,607,183)	628,088
Oshkosh (★ Appleton)	55,006
Racine (★ 175,034) (★Milwaukee)	84,298
Sheboygan (★ 103,877)	49,676
Waukesha (★ Milwaukee)	56,958
Wausau (★ 115,400)	37,060
Wauwatosa (★ Milwaukee)	49,366
West Allis (★ Milwaukee)	63,221

UNITED STATES: WYOMING

1990 C	453,588
Casper (★ 61,226)	46,742
Cheyenne (★ 73,142)	50,008

URUGUAY

1985 C	2,955,241
Las Piedras (★ Montevideo)	58,288
Melo	42,615
Mercedes	36,702
Minas	34,661
• MONTEVIDEO (★ 1,550,000)	1,251,647
Paysandú	76,191
Rivera	57,316
Salto	80,823

UZBEKISTAN

1991 E	20,708,200
Almalyk	116,400
Andižan	298,300
Angren	132,600
Bekabad	82,800
Buchara	249,600
Chodžejli	61,200
Čirčik (★ Taškent)	158,400
Denau	49,300
Džizak	110,900
Fergana	226,500
Gulistan	56,900
Jangijul'	56,900
Kagan	49,800
Karši	168,000
Kattakurgan	59,600
Kokand	175,000
Margilan	124,900
Namangan	319,200
Navoi	111,600
Nukus	179,600
Šachrisabz	53,200
Samarkand	370,500
• TAŠKENT (TASHKENT) (★ 2,325,000)	2,113,300
Termez	90,400
Urgenč	130,400

VANUATU

1989 C	142,944
• PORT VILA (★ 23,000)	19,311

VATICAN CITY / Città del Vaticano

1988 E	766

VENDA

1985 C	459,819
Makwarela	3,712
• Shayandima	4,853
THOHOYANDOU	3,641

VENEZUELA

1990 C	18,105,265
Acarigua (1981 C)	91,662
Barcelona	109,061
Barinas	152,853
Barquisimeto	602,622
Baruta (★ Caracas) (1981 C)	200,063
Cabimas (1981 C)	140,435
Cagua (1981 C)	53,704
Calabozo (1981 C)	61,995
• CARACAS (★ 3,600,000)	18,245,892
Carora (1981 C)	58,694
Carúpano (1981 C)	64,579
Catia La Mar (★ Caracas) (1981 C)	87,916
Chacao (★ Caracas) (1981 C)	72,703
Ciudad Bolívar	225,846
Ciudad Guayana (1981 C)	314,497
Ciudad Ojeda (Lagunillas) (1981 C)	83,565
Coro	124,616
Cumaná	212,492
El Limón (1981 C)	65,122
El Tigre (1981 C)	73,595
Guacara (1981 C)	72,727
Guanare	83,380
Guarenas (★ Caracas) (1981 C)	101,742
La Asunción	16,585
La Victoria (1981 C)	70,828
Los Dos Caminos (★ Caracas) (1981 C)	63,346
Los Teques (★ Caracas)	143,519
Maiquetía (★ Caracas) (1981 C)	66,056
Maracaibo	1,207,513
Maracay	354,428
Mariara (1981 C)	47,242
Maturín	207,382
Mérida	167,992
Petare (★ Caracas) (1981 C)	395,715
Porlamar (1981 C)	51,079
Pozuelos (1981 C)	80,342
Puerto Ayacucho	35,865
Puerto Cabello (1981 C)	71,759
Puerto la Cruz (1981 C)	53,881
Punto Fijo (1981 C)	71,114
San Carlos	50,339
San Cristóbal	220,697
San Felipe	65,793
San Fernando	72,733
San Juan de los Morros	67,645
Trujillo	32,683
Tucupita	40,946
Turmero (1981 C)	111,186
Valencia	903,076
Valera (1981 C)	102,068
Valle de la Pascua (1981 C)	55,761

VIETNAM / Viet Nam

1989 C	64,411,668
Bac Giang	50,879
Bac Lieu	83,483
Bien Hoa	273,879
Buon Me Thuot	97,044
Ca Mau	81,901
Cam Pha	105,336
Can Tho (1978 C)	208,078
Chau Doc	50,935
Da Lat	102,583
Da Nang	369,734
Hai Duong	53,370
Hai Phong (▲ 1,447,523)	351,919
HA NOI (★ 1,275,000)	905,939
Hoa Binh	69,323
Hon Gai	123,102
Hue	211,718
Long Xuyen	128,814
Minh Hai (1979 C)	72,517
My Tho	104,724
Nam Dinh	165,629
Nha Trang	213,460
Phan Rang	71,111
Phan Thiet	114,236
Play Cu	76,991
Qui Nhon	159,852
Rach Gia	137,784
Sa Dec	50,733
Soc Trang (1979 C)	74,967
Soc Trang	87,899
Tan An	50,288
Thai Binh	57,640
Thai Nguyen	124,871
Thanh Hoa	84,951
• Thanh Pho Ho Chi Minh (Saigon) (★ 3,300,000)	2,796,229
Tra Vinh	47,785
Tuy Hoa	54,081
Uong Bi	49,595
Viet Tri	73,347
Vinh	110,793
Vinh Long	81,620
Vung Tau	123,528
Yen Bai	58,645

VIRGIN ISLANDS OF THE UNITED STATES

1990 C	101,809
• CHARLOTTE AMALIE (★ 32,000)	12,331

WALLIS AND FUTUNA / Wallis et Futuna

1983 E	12,408
• MATÂ'UTU	815
Ono (1976 C)	624

WESTERN SAHARA

1982 E	142,000
• EL AAIÚN	93,875

WESTERN SAMOA / Samoa i Sisifo

1981 C	156,349
• APIA	33,170

YEMEN / Al-Yaman

1990 E	15,267,000
'Adan (★ 318,000) (1984 E)	176,100
Al-Ḥudaydah (1986 C)	155,110
Al-Mukallā (1984 E)	58,000
• ṢAN'Ā' (1986 C)	427,150
Ta'izz (1986 C)	178,043

YUGOSLAVIA / Jugoslavija

1987 E	10,342,020
• BEOGRAD (★ 1,400,000)	1,130,000
Kragujevac (▲ 171,609)	94,800
Niš (▲ 240,219)	168,400
Novi Sad (▲ 266,772)	176,000
Pančevo (★ Beograd)	62,700
Podgorica (▲ 145,163)	82,500
Priština (▲ 244,830)	125,400
Subotica (▲ 153,306)	100,500
Zrenjanin (▲ 140,009)	65,400

ZAIRE / Zaïre

1984 C	30,729,443
Bandundu	63,642
Beni	44,141
Boma	197,617
Bukavu	167,950
Bumba	51,197
Bunia	59,598
Butembo	73,312
Gandajika	64,878
Gemena	63,052
Goma	77,908
Ilebo (Port-Francqui)	53,877
Isiro	78,268
Kalemie (Albertville)	73,528
Kamina	62,789
Kananga (Luluabourg)	298,693
Kikwit	149,296
Kindu	66,812
• KINSHASA (LÉOPOLDVILLE) (1986 E)	3,000,000
Kipushi	53,207
Kisangani (Stanleyville)	317,581
Kolwezi	416,122
Likasi (Jadotville)	213,862
Lubumbashi (Élisabethville)	564,830
Matadi	138,798
Mbandaka (Coquilhatville)	137,291
Mbuji-Mayi (Bakwanga)	486,235
Mwene-Ditu	94,560
Tshikapa	116,016
Uvira	74,432

ZAMBIA

1990 C	7,818,447
Chililabombwe (Bancroft) (★ 76,848)	35,200
Chingola	167,954
Kabwe (Broken Hill)	166,519
Kalulushi	75,197
Kitwe (★ 338,207)	247,100
Livingstone	82,218
Luanshya (★ 146,275)	79,500
• LUSAKA	982,362
Mufulira (★ 152,944)	85,000
Ndola	376,311

ZIMBABWE

1983 E	7,740,000
Bulawayo (1982 C)	495,317
Chitungwiza (★ Harare)	202,000
Gweru (1982 C)	78,940
• HARARE (★ 890,000)	681,000
Mutare (1982 C)	75,358

C Census. E Official estimate. U Unofficial estimate.
• Largest city in country.

★ Population or designation of metropolitan area, including suburbs (see headnote).
▲ Population of an entire municipality, commune, or district, including rural area.

United States General Information

Geographical Facts

ELEVATION

The highest elevation in the United States is Mount McKinley, Alaska, 20,320 feet.

The lowest elevation in the United States is in Death Valley, California, 282 feet below sea level.

The average elevation of the United States is 2,500 feet.

EXTREMITIES

Direction	Location	Latitude	Longitude
North	Point Barrow, Ak.	71° 23'N.	156° 29'W.
South	Ka Lae (point) Hi.	18° 56'N.	155° 41'W.
East	West Quoddy Head, Me.	44° 49'N.	66° 57'W.
West	Cape Wrangell, Ak.	52° 55'N.	172° 27'E.

LENGTH OF BOUNDARIES

The total length of the Canadian boundary of the United States is 5,525 miles.

The total length of the Mexican boundary of the United States is 1,933 miles.

The total length of the Atlantic coastline of the United States is 2,069 miles.

The total length of the Pacific and Arctic coastline of the United States is 8,683 miles.

The total length of the Gulf of Mexico coastline of the United States is 1,631 miles.

The total length of all coastlines and land boundaries of the United States is 19,841 miles.

The total length of the tidal shoreline and land boundaries of the United States is 96,091 miles.

GEOGRAPHIC CENTERS

The geographic center of the United States (including Alaska and Hawaii) is in Butte County, South Dakota at 44° 58'N., 103° 46'W.

The geographic center of North America is in North Dakota, a few miles west of Devils Lake, at 48° 10'N., 100° 10'W.

EXTREMES OF TEMPERATURE

The highest temperature ever recorded in the United States was 134° F., at Greenland Ranch, Death Valley, California, on July 10, 1913.

The lowest temperature ever recorded in the United States was -80° F., at Prospect Creek, Alaska, on January 23, 1971.

Historical Facts

TERRITORIAL ACQUISITIONS

Accession	Date	Area (sq. mi.)	Cost in Dollars
Original territory of the Thirteen States	1790	888,685	
Purchase of Louisiana Territory, from France	1803	827,192	$11,250,000
By treaty with Spain: Florida	1819	58,560	5,000,000
Other areas	1819	13,443	
Annexation of Texas	1845	390,144	
Oregon Territory, by treaty with Great Britain	1846	285,580	
Mexican Cession	1848	529,017	$15,000,000
Gadsden Purchase, from Mexico	1853	29,640	$10,000,000
Purchase of Alaska, from Russia	1867	586,412	7,200,000
Annexation of Hawaiian Islands	1898	6,450	
Puerto Rico, by treaty with Spain	1899	3,435	
Guam, by treaty with Spain	1899	212	
American Samoa, by treaty with Great Britain and Germany	1900	76	
Virgin Islands, by purchase from Denmark	1917	133	$25,000,000

Note: The Philippines, ceded by Spain in 1898 for $20,000,000 were a territorial possession of the United States from 1898 to 1946. On July 4, 1946 they became the independent Republic of the Philippines.

Note: The Canal Zone, ceded by Panama in 1903 for $10,000,000 was a territory of the United States from 1903 to 1979. As a result of treaties signed in 1977, sovereignty over the Canal Zone reverted to Panama in 1979.

WESTWARD MOVEMENT OF CENTER OF POPULATION

Year	U.S.Population Total at Census	Approximate Location
1790	3,929,214	23 miles east of Baltimore, Md.
1800	5,308,483	18 miles west of Baltimore, Md.
1810	7,239,881	40 miles northwest of Washington, D.C.
1820	9,638,453	16 miles east of Moorefield, W. Va.
1830	12,866,020	19 miles southwest of Moorefield, W. Va.
1840	17,069,453	16 miles south of Clarksburg, W. Va.
1850	23,191,876	23 miles southeast of Parkersburg, W. Va.
1860	31,443,321	20 miles southeast of Chillicothe, Ohio
1870	39,818,449	48 miles northeast of Cincinnati, Ohio
1880	50,155,783	8 miles southwest of Cincinnati, Ohio
1890	62,947,714	20 miles east of Columbus, Ind.
1900	75,994,575	6 miles southeast of Columbus, Ind.
1910	91,972,266	Bloomington, Ind.
1920	105,710,620	8 miles southeast of Spencer, Ind.
1930	122,775,046	3 miles northeast of Linton, Ind.
1940	131,669,275	2 miles southeast of Carlisle, Ind.
1950	150,697,361	8 miles northwest of Olney, Ill.
1960	179,323,175	6 miles northwest of Centralia, Ill.
1970	204,816,296	5 miles southeast of Mascoutah, Ill.
1980	226,549,010	1/4 mile west of DeSoto, Mo.
1990	248,709,873	10 miles southeast of Steelville, Mo.

State Areas and Populations

STATE	Land Area* square miles	Water Area* square miles	Total Area* square miles	Area Rank land area	1990 Population	1990 Population per square mile	1980 Population	1970 Population	1960 Population	Pop. Rank 1990	Pop. Rank 1980	Pop. Rank 1970
Alabama	50,750	1,673	52,423	28	4,040,587	80	3,894,046	3,444,354	3,266,740	22	22	21
Alaska	570,374	86,051	656,424	1	550,043	1.0	401,851	302,583	226,167	49	50	50
Arizona	113,642	364	114,006	6	3,665,228	32	2,716,756	1,775,399	1,302,161	24	29	33
Arkansas	52,075	1,107	53,182	27	2,350,725	45	2,286,357	1,923,322	1,786,272	33	33	32
California	155,973	7,734	163,707	3	29,760,021	191	23,667,372	19,971,069	15,717,204	1	1	1
Colorado	103,730	371	104,100	8	3,294,394	32	2,889,735	2,209,596	1,753,947	26	28	30
Connecticut	4,845	698	5,544	48	3,287,116	678	3,107,576	3,032,217	2,535,234	27	25	24
Delaware	1,955	535	2,489	49	666,168	341	594,317	548,104	446,292	46	47	41
District of Columbia	61	7	68	.....	606,900	9,949	638,432	756,668	763,956	.....	.....	.....
Florida	53,997	11,761	65,758	26	12,937,926	240	9,747,015	6,791,418	4,951,560	4	7	9
Georgia	57,919	1,522	59,441	21	6,478,216	112	5,462,982	4,587,930	3,943,116	11	13	15
Hawaii	6,423	4,508	10,932	47	1,108,229	173	964,691	769,913	632,772	41	39	40
Idaho	82,751	823	83,574	11	1,006,749	12	944,127	713,015	667,191	42	41	43
Illinois	55,593	2,325	57,918	24	11,430,602	206	11,427,414	11,110,285	10,081,158	6	5	5
Indiana	35,870	550	36,420	38	5,544,159	155	5,490,212	5,195,392	4,662,498	14	12	11
Iowa	55,875	401	56,276	23	2,776,755	50	2,913,808	2,825,368	2,757,537	30	27	25
Kansas	81,823	459	82,282	13	2,477,574	30	2,364,236	2,249,071	2,178,611	32	32	28
Kentucky	39,732	679	40,411	36	3,685,296	93	3,660,324	3,220,711	3,038,156	23	23	23
Louisiana	43,566	8,277	51,843	33	4,219,973	97	4,206,098	3,644,637	3,257,022	21	19	20
Maine	30,865	4,523	35,387	39	1,227,928	40	1,125,043	993,722	969,265	38	38	38
Maryland	9,775	2,633	12,407	42	4,781,468	489	4,216,933	3,923,897	3,100,689	19	18	18
Massachusetts	7,838	2,717	10,555	45	6,016,425	768	5,737,093	5,689,170	5,148,578	13	11	10
Michigan	56,809	40,001	96,810	22	9,295,297	164	9,262,044	8,881,826	7,823,194	8	8	7
Minnesota	79,617	7,326	86,943	14	4,375,099	55	4,075,970	3,806,103	3,413,864	20	21	19
Mississippi	46,914	1,520	48,434	31	2,573,216	55	2,520,698	2,216,994	2,178,141	31	31	29
Missouri	68,898	811	69,709	18	5,117,073	74	4,916,759	4,677,623	4,319,813	15	15	13
Montana	145,556	1,490	147,046	4	799,065	5.5	786,690	694,409	674,767	44	44	44
Nebraska	76,878	481	77,358	15	1,578,385	21	1,569,825	1,485,333	1,411,330	36	35	35
Nevada	109,806	761	110,567	7	1,201,833	11	800,508	488,738	285,278	39	43	47
New Hampshire	8,969	382	9,351	44	1,109,252	124	920,610	737,681	606,921	40	42	42
New Jersey	7,419	1,303	8,722	46	7,730,188	1,042	7,365,011	7,171,112	6,066,782	9	9	8
New Mexico	121,365	234	121,598	5	1,515,069	12	1,303,542	1,017,055	951,023	37	37	37
New York	47,224	7,251	54,475	30	17,990,455	381	17,558,165	18,241,391	16,782,304	2	2	2
North Carolina	48,718	5,103	53,821	29	6,628,637	136	5,880,415	5,084,411	4,556,155	10	10	12
North Dakota	68,994	1,710	70,704	17	638,800	9.3	652,717	617,792	632,446	47	46	46
Ohio	40,953	3,875	44,828	35	10,847,115	265	10,797,603	10,657,423	9,706,397	7	6	6
Oklahoma	68,679	1,224	69,903	19	3,145,585	46	3,025,487	2,559,463	2,328,284	28	26	27
Oregon	96,003	2,383	98,386	10	2,842,321	30	2,633,156	2,091,533	1,768,687	29	30	31
Pennsylvania	44,820	1,239	46,058	32	11,881,643	265	11,864,751	11,800,766	11,319,366	5	4	3
Rhode Island	1,045	500	1,545	50	1,003,464	960	947,154	949,723	859,488	43	40	39
South Carolina	30,111	1,896	32,007	40	3,486,703	116	3,120,730	2,590,713	2,382,594	25	24	26
South Dakota	75,898	1,224	77,121	16	696,004	9.2	690,768	666,257	680,514	45	45	45
Tennessee	41,220	926	42,146	34	4,877,185	118	4,591,023	3,926,018	3,567,089	17	17	17
Texas	261,914	6,687	268,601	2	16,986,510	65	14,225,288	11,198,655	9,579,677	3	3	4
Utah	82,168	2,736	84,904	12	1,722,850	21	1,461,037	1,059,273	890,627	35	36	36
Vermont	9,249	366	9,615	43	562,758	61	511,456	444,732	389,881	48	48	48
Virginia	39,598	3,171	42,769	37	6,187,358	156	5,346,797	4,651,448	3,966,949	12	14	14
Washington	66,582	4,721	71,303	20	4,866,692	73	4,132,353	3,413,244	2,853,214	18	20	22
West Virginia	24,087	145	24,231	41	1,793,477	74	1,950,186	1,744,237	1,860,421	34	34	34
Wisconsin	54,314	11,190	65,503	25	4,891,769	90	4,705,642	4,417,821	3,951,777	16	16	16
Wyoming	97,105	714	97,818	9	453,588	4.7	469,557	332,416	330,066	50	49	49
United States	3,536,342	251,083	3,787,425	.....	248,709,873	70	226,542,360	203,302,031	179,323,175	.....	.....	.....

*The sum of the area figures for all states does not equal U.S. total due to rounding.

United States 1990 Populations and Zip Codes

The following alphabetical list shows populations for all counties and over 15,000 selected cities and towns in the United States. ZIP codes are shown for all of the cities listed in the table. The state abbreviation following each name is that used by the United States Postal Service.

ZIP codes are listed for cities and towns after the state abbreviations. For each city with more than one ZIP code, the range of numbers assigned to the city is shown: For example, the ZIP code range for Chicago is 60601–99, and this indicates that the numbers between 60601 and 60699 are valid Chicago ZIP codes. ZIP codes are not listed for counties.

Populations for cities and towns appear as *italics* after the ZIP codes, and populations for counties appear after the state abbreviations. These populations are either 1990 census figures or, where census data are not available, estimates created by Rand McNally. City populations are for central cities, not metropolitan areas. For New England, 1990 census populations are given for incorporated cities. Estimates are used for unincorporated places that are not treated separately by the census. 'Town' (or 'township') populations are not included unless the town is considered to be primarily urban and contains only one commonly used placename.

Counties are identified by a square symbol (□).

Abbreviations for State Names

AK	Alaska	**IA**	Iowa	**MS**	Mississippi	**PA**	Pennsylvania
AL	Alabama	**ID**	Idaho	**MT**	Montana	**RI**	Rhode Island
AR	Arkansas	**IL**	Illinois	**NC**	North Carolina	**SC**	South Carolina
AZ	Arizona	**IN**	Indiana	**ND**	North Dakota	**SD**	South Dakota
CA	California	**KS**	Kansas	**NE**	Nebraska	**TN**	Tennessee
CO	Colorado	**KY**	Kentucky	**NH**	New Hampshire	**TX**	Texas
CT	Connecticut	**LA**	Louisiana	**NJ**	New Jersey	**UT**	Utah
DC	District of Columbia	**MA**	Massachusetts	**NM**	New Mexico	**VA**	Virginia
		MD	Maryland	**NV**	Nevada	**VT**	Vermont
DE	Delaware	**ME**	Maine	**NY**	New York	**WA**	Washington
FL	Florida	**MI**	Michigan	**OH**	Ohio	**WI**	Wisconsin
GA	Georgia	**MN**	Minnesota	**OK**	Oklahoma	**WV**	West Virginia
HI	Hawaii	**MO**	Missouri	**OR**	Oregon	**WY**	Wyoming

A

Abbeville, AL 36310 • *3,173*
Abbeville, LA 70510–11 • *11,187*
Abbeville, SC 29620 • *5,778*
Abbeville □, SC • 23,862
Abbotsford, WI 54405 • *1,916*
Abbott Run Valley, RI 02864 • *1,050*
Aberdeen, ID 83210 • *1,406*
Aberdeen, MD 21001 • *13,087*
Aberdeen, MS 39730 • *6,837*
Aberdeen, NC 28315 • *2,700*
Aberdeen, OH 45101 • *1,329*
Aberdeen, SD 57401–02 • *24,927*
Aberdeen, WA 98520 • *16,565*
Abernathy, TX 79311 • *2,720*
Abilene, KS 67410 • *6,242*
Abilene, TX 79601–08 • *106,654*
Abingdon, IL 61410 • *3,597*
Abingdon, VA 24210 • *7,003*
Abington, MA 02351 • *13,817*
Abington [Township], PA 19001 • *59,084*
Abita Springs, LA 70420 • *1,296*
Absarokee, MT 59001 • *1,067*
Absecon, NJ 08201 • *7,298*
Academia, OH 43050 • *1,447*
Acadia □, LA • 55,882
Accomack □, VA • 31,703
Ackerman, MS 39735 • *1,573*
Ackley, IA 50601 • *1,696*
Acton, CA 93510 • *1,471*
Acton, MA 01720 • *2,300*
Acushnet, MA 02743 • *6,030*
Acworth, GA 30101 • *4,519*
Ada, MN 56510 • *1,708*
Ada, OH 45810 • *5,413*
Ada, OK 74820–21 • *15,820*
Ada □, ID • 205,775
Adair □, IA • 8,409
Adair □, KY • 15,360
Adair □, MO • 24,577
Adair □, OK • 18,421
Adairsville, GA 30103 • *2,131*
Adams, CO 80022 • *2,200*
Adams, MA 01220 • *6,356*
Adams, NY 13605 • *1,753*
Adams, WI 53910 • *1,715*
Adams □, CO • 265,038
Adams □, ID • 3,254
Adams □, IL • 66,090
Adams □, IN • 31,095
Adams □, IA • 4,866
Adams □, MS • 35,356
Adams □, NE • 29,625
Adams □, ND • 3,174
Adams □, OH • 25,371
Adams □, PA • 78,274
Adams □, WA • 13,603
Adams □, WI • 15,682
Adams Center, NY 13606 • *1,675*
Adamstown, PA 19501 • *1,108*
Adamsville, AL 35005 • *4,161*
Adamsville, RI 02801 • *600*
Adamsville, TN 38310 • *1,745*
Addis, LA 70710 • *1,222*
Addison, CT 06033 • *2,460*
Addison, IL 60101 • *32,058*
Addison, NY 14801 • *1,842*
Addison, TX 75001 • *8,783*
Addison □, VT • 32,953
Addyston, OH 45001 • *1,198*
Adel, GA 31620 • *5,093*
Adel, IA 50003 • *3,304*
Adelanto, CA 92301 • *8,517*
Adelphi, MD 20783 • *13,524*
Adobe Acres, NM 87105 • *2,400*
Adrian, MI 49221 • *22,097*
Adrian, MN 56110 • *1,141*
Adrian, MO 64720 • *1,582*
Advance, MO 63730 • *1,139*
Affton, MO 63123 • *21,106*
Afton, DE 19810 • *1,200*
Afton, MN 55001 • *2,645*
Afton, WY 83110 • *1,394*
Agawam, MA 01001 • *10,190*
Agoura Hills, CA 91301 • *20,390*
Ahoskie, NC 27910 • *4,391*
Aiea, HI 96701 • *8,906*
Aiken, SC 29801–03 • *19,872*
Aiken □, SC • 120,940
Ainsworth, NE 69210 • *1,870*
Air Park West, NE 68524 • *3,100*
Aitkin, MN 56431 • *1,698*
Aitkin □, MN • 12,425
Ajo, AZ 85321 • *2,919*
Akiachak, AK 99551 • *400*
Akron, CO 80720 • *1,599*
Akron, IA 51001 • *1,450*
Akron, NY 14001 • *2,906*
Akron, OH 44301–98 • *223,019*
Akron, PA 17501 • *3,869*
Alabaster, AL 35007 • *14,732*
Alachua, FL 32615 • *4,529*
Alachua □, FL • 181,596
Alakanuk, AK 99554 • *544*
Alamance □, NC • 108,213
Alameda, CA 94501 • *76,459*
Alameda, NM 87114 • *5,900*
Alameda □, CA • 1,279,182
Alamo, CA 94507 • *12,277*
Alamo, NV 89001 • *400*
Alamo, TN 38001 • *2,426*
Alamo, TX 78516 • *8,210*
Alamogordo, NM 88310–11 • *27,596*
Alamo Heights, TX 78208 • *6,502*
Alamosa, CO 81101–02 • *7,579*
Alamosa □, CO • 13,617
Alamosa East, CO 81101 • *1,389*
Albany, CA 94706 • *16,327*
Albany, GA 31701–07 • *78,122*
Albany, IN 47320 • *2,357*
Albany, KY 42602 • *2,062*
Albany, MN 56307 • *1,548*
Albany, MO 64402 • *1,958*
Albany, NY 12201–60 • *101,082*
Albany, OR 97321 • *29,462*
Albany, TX 76430 • *1,962*
Albany, WI 53502 • *1,140*
Albany □, NY • 292,594
Albany □, WY • 30,797
Albemarle, NC 28001–02 • *14,939*
Albemarle □, VA • 68,040
Albert Lea, MN 56007 • *18,310*
Albertson, NY 11507 • *5,166*
Albertville, AL 35950 • *14,507*
Albertville, MN 55301 • *1,251*
Albia, IA 52531 • *3,870*
Albion, IL 62806 • *2,116*
Albion, IN 46701 • *1,823*
Albion, MI 49224 • *10,066*
Albion, NE 68620 • *1,916*
Albion, NY 14411 • *5,863*
Albion, PA 16401 • *1,575*
Albion, RI 02802 • *1,600*
Albuquerque, NM 87101–99 • *384,736*
Alburtis, PA 18011 • *1,415*
Alcester, SD 57001 • *843*
Alcoa, TN 37701 • *6,400*
Alcona □, MI • 10,145
Alcorn □, MS • 31,722
Alden, NY 14004 • *2,457*
Alderson, WV 24910 • *1,152*
Alderwood Manor, WA 98011 • *16,524*
Aledo, IL 61231 • *3,681*
Alexander □, IL • 10,626
Alexander □, NC • 27,544
Alexander City, AL 35010 • *14,917*
Alexandria, IN 46001 • *5,709*
Alexandria, KY 41001 • *5,592*
Alexandria, LA 71301–15 • *49,188*
Alexandria, MN 56308 • *7,838*
Alexandria, VA 22301–20 • *111,183*
Alexandria Bay, NY 13607 • *1,194*
Alfalfa □, OK • 6,416
Alfred, NY 14802 • *4,559*
Alger □, MI • 8,972
Algoma, WI 54201 • *3,353*
Algona, IA 50511 • *6,015*
Algona, WA 98001 • *1,694*
Algonac, MI 48001 • *4,551*
Algonquin, IL 60102 • *11,663*
Algood, TN 38501 • *2,399*
Alhambra, CA 91801–99 • *82,106*
Alice, TX 78332–33 • *19,788*
Aliceville, AL 35442 • *3,009*
Aliquippa, PA 15001 • *13,374*
Allamakee □, IA • 13,855
Allegan, MI 49010 • *4,547*
Allegan □, MI • 90,509
Allegany, NY 14706 • *1,980*
Allegany □, MD • 74,946
Allegany □, NY • 50,470
Alleghany □, NC • 9,590
Alleghany □, VA • 13,176
Allegheny □, PA • 1,336,449
Allen, TX 75002 • *18,309*
Allen, TX 75002 • *18,309*
Allen □, IN • 300,836
Allen □, KS • 14,638
Allen □, KY • 14,628
Allen □, LA • 21,226
Allen □, OH • 109,755
Allendale, NJ 07401 • *5,900*
Allendale, SC 29810 • *4,410*
Allendale □, SC • 11,722
Allen Park, MI 48101 • *31,092*
Allenton, RI 02852 • *600*
Allentown, NJ 08501 • *1,828*
Allentown, PA 18101–95 • *105,090*
Alliance, NE 69301 • *9,765*
Alliance, OH 44601 • *23,376*
Allison, IA 50602 • *1,000*
Allison Park, PA 15101 • *5,600*
Allouez, WI 54301 • *14,431*
Alloway, NJ 08001 • *1,371*
Allyn, WA 98524 • *1,100*
Alma, AR 72921 • *2,959*
Alma, GA 31510 • *3,663*
Alma, MI 48801 • *9,034*
Alma, NE 68920 • *1,226*
Almont, MI 48003 • *2,354*
Aloha, OR 97006 • *34,284*
Alondra Park, CA 90249 • *12,215*
Alpena, MI 49707 • *11,354*
Alpena □, MI • 30,605
Alpha, NJ 08865 • *2,530*
Alpharetta, GA 30201–02 • *13,002*
Alpine, CA 91901 • *9,695*
Alpine, NJ 07620 • *1,716*
Alpine, TX 79830–31 • *5,637*
Alpine, UT 84003 • *3,492*
Alpine □, CA • 1,113
Alsip, IL 60658 • *18,227*
Alta, IA 51002 • *1,820*
Altadena, CA 91001–02 • *42,658*
Altamont, IL 62411 • *2,296*
Altamont, KS 67330 • *1,048*
Altamont, NY 12009 • *1,519*
Altamont, OR 97601 • *18,591*
Altamonte Springs, FL 32701 • *34,879*
Alta Sierra, CA 95949 • *5,709*
Altavista, VA 24517 • *3,686*
Alto, TX 75925 • *1,027*
Alton, IL 62002 • *32,905*
Alton, IA 51003 • *1,063*
Alton, NH 03809 • *975*
Alton Bay, NH 03810 • *1,000*
Altoona, FL 32702 • *1,300*
Altoona, IA 50009 • *7,191*
Altoona, PA 16601–03 • *51,881*
Altoona, WI 54720 • *5,889*
Alturas, CA 96101 • *3,231*
Altus, OK 73521–23 • *21,910*
Alva, FL 33920 • *1,200*
Alva, OK 73717 • *5,495*
Alvarado, TX 76009 • *2,918*
Alvin, TX 77511–12 • *19,220*
Amador □, CA • 30,039
Amagansett, NY 11930 • *2,188*
Amana, IA 52203 • *540*
Amarillo, TX 79101–76 • *157,615*
Ambler, PA 19002 • *6,609*
Amboy, IL 61310 • *2,377*
Ambridge, PA 15003 • *8,133*
Amelia, LA 70340 • *2,447*
Amelia, OH 45102 • *1,837*
Amelia □, VA • 8,787
Amenia, NY 12501 • *1,057*
American Canyon, CA 94589 • *7,706*
American Falls, ID 83211 • *3,757*
American Fork, UT 84003–04 • *15,696*
Americus, GA 31709 • *16,512*
Amery, WI 54001 • *2,657*
Ames, IA 50010 • *47,198*
Amesbury, MA 01913 • *12,109*
Amherst, MA 01002–04 • *17,824*
Amherst, NH 03031 • *850*
Amherst, NY 14226 • *45,600*
Amherst, OH 44001 • *10,332*
Amherst, VA 24521 • *1,060*
Amherst □, VA • 28,578
Amherstdale, WV 25607 • *1,200*
Amite, LA 70422 • *4,236*
Amite □, MS • 13,328
Amity, OR 97101 • *1,175*
Amityville, NY 11701 • *9,286*
Ammon, ID 83401 • *5,002*
Amory, MS 38821 • *7,093*
Amsterdam, NY 12010 • *20,714*
Anaconda, MT 59711 • *10,278*
Anacortes, WA 98221 • *11,451*
Anadarko, OK 73005 • *6,586*
Anaheim, CA 92801–25 • *266,406*
Anahola, HI 96703 • *1,181*
Anahuac, TX 77514 • *1,993*
Anamosa, IA 52205 • *5,100*
Anandale, LA 71301 • *2,000*
Anchorage, AK 99501–40 • *226,338*
Anchorage, KY 40223 • *2,082*
Andalusia, AL 36420 • *9,269*
Anderson, AK 99744 • *628*
Anderson, CA 96007 • *8,299*
Anderson, IN 46011–18 • *59,459*
Anderson, MO 64831 • *1,432*
Anderson, SC 29621–25 • *26,184*
Anderson □, KS • 7,803
Anderson □, KY • 14,571
Anderson □, SC • 145,196
Anderson □, TN • 68,250
Anderson □, TX • 48,024
Andover, KS 67002 • *4,047*
Andover, MA 01810 • *8,242*
Andover, MN 55304 • *15,216*
Andover, NY 14806 • *1,125*
Andover, OH 44003 • *1,216*
Andrew □, MO • 14,632
Andrews, IN 46702 • *1,118*
Andrews, NC 28901 • *2,551*
Andrews, SC 29510 • *3,050*
Andrews, TX 79714 • *10,678*
Andrews □, TX • 14,338
Androscoggin □, ME • 105,259
Angelina □, TX • 69,884
Angels Camp, CA 95222 • *2,409*
Angier, NC 27501 • *2,235*
Angle Lake, WA 98188 • *5,000*
Angleton, TX 77515–16 • *17,140*
Angola, IN 46703 • *5,824*
Angola, NY 14006 • *2,231*
Angoon, AK 99820 • *638*
Aniak, AK 99557 • *540*
Anita, IA 50020 • *1,068*
Ankeny, IA 50021 • *18,482*
Anna, IL 62906 • *4,805*
Anna, OH 45302 • *1,164*
Annalee Heights, VA 22042 • *1,750*
Anna Maria, FL 34216 • *1,744*
Annandale, MN 55302 • *2,054*
Annandale, VA 22003 • *50,975*
Annapolis, MD 21401–05 • *33,187*
Ann Arbor, MI 48103–08 • *109,592*
Anne Arundel □, MD • 427,239
Anniston, AL 36201–06 • *26,623*
Annville, PA 17003 • *4,294*
Anoka, MN 55303–04 • *17,192*
Anoka □, MN • 243,641
Anson, TX 79501 • *2,644*
Anson □, NC • 23,474
Ansonia, CT 06401 • *18,403*
Ansonia, OH 45303 • *1,279*
Ansted, WV 25812 • *1,643*
Antelope □, NE • 7,965
Anthony, FL 32617 • *1,200*
Anthony, KS 67003 • *2,516*
Anthony, NM 88021 • *5,160*
Anthony, RI 02816 • *2,980*
Anthony, TX 88021 • *3,328*
Antigo, WI 54409 • *8,276*
Antioch, CA 94509 • *62,195*
Antioch, IL 60002 • *6,105*
Antlers, OK 74523 • *2,524*
Anton, TX 79313 • *1,212*
Antrim, NH 03440 • *1,325*
Antrim □, MI • 18,185
Antwerp, OH 45813 • *1,677*
Apache, OK 73006 • *1,591*
Apache □, AZ • 61,591
Apache Junction, AZ 85217–20 • *18,100*
Apalachicola, FL 32320 • *2,602*
Apalachin, NY 13732 • *1,208*
Apex, NC 27502 • *4,968*
Aplington, IA 50604 • *1,034*
Apollo, PA 15613 • *1,895*
Apollo Beach, FL 33572 • *6,025*
Apopka, FL 32703–04 • *13,512*
Appalachia, VA 24216 • *1,994*
Appanoose □, IA • 13,743
Appleton, MN 56208 • *1,552*
Appleton, WI 54911–15 • *65,695*
Appleton City, MO 64724 • *1,280*
Apple Valley, CA 92307–08 • *46,079*
Apple Valley, MN 55124 • *34,598*
Applewood, CO 80401 • *11,069*
Appleyard, WA 98801 • *1,207*
Appling □, GA • 15,744
Appomattox, VA 24522 • *1,707*
Appomattox □, VA • 12,298
Aptos, CA 95003 • *9,061*
Aquia Harbour, VA 22554 • *6,308*
Arab, AL 35016 • *6,321*
Arabi, LA 70032 • *8,787*
Aransas □, TX • 17,892
Aransas Pass, TX 78336 • *7,180*
Arapahoe, NE 68922 • *1,001*
Arapahoe □, CO • 391,511
Arbuckle, CA 95912 • *1,912*
Arcade, CA 95821 • *47,900*
Arcade, NY 14009 • *2,081*
Arcadia, CA 91006–07 • *48,290*
Arcadia, FL 33821 • *6,488*
Arcadia, IN 46030 • *1,468*
Arcadia, LA 71001 • *3,079*
Arcadia, SC 29320 • *2,088*
Arcadia, WI 54612 • *2,166*
Arcanum, OH 45304 • *1,953*
Arcata, CA 95521 • *15,197*
Archbald, PA 18403 • *6,291*
Archbold, OH 43502 • *3,440*
Archdale, NC 27263 • *6,913*
Archer, FL 32618 • *1,372*
Archer □, TX • 7,973
Archer City, TX 76351 • *1,748*
Archuleta □, CO • 5,345
Arco, ID 83213 • *1,016*
Arcola, IL 61910 • *2,678*
Arden, CA 95825 • *62,900*
Arden Hills, MN 55112 • *9,199*
Ardmore, AL 35739 • *1,090*
Ardmore, IN 46628 • *2,250*
Ardmore, OK 73401–03 • *23,079*
Ardsley, NY 10502 • *4,272*
Arenac □, MI • 14,931
Argos, IN 46501 • *1,642*
Arizona Sunsites, AZ 85625 • *1,100*
Arkadelphia, AR 71923 • *10,014*
Arkansas □, AR • 21,653
Arkansas City, KS 67005 • *12,762*
Arkoma, OK 74901 • *2,393*
Arlington, GA 31713 • *1,513*
Arlington, MA 02174 • *44,630*
Arlington, MN 55307 • *1,886*
Arlington, NE 68002 • *1,178*
Arlington, NY 12603 • *11,948*
Arlington, OH 45814 • *1,267*
Arlington, SD 57212 • *908*
Arlington, TN 38002 • *1,541*
Arlington, TX 76010–18 • *261,721*
Arlington, VT 05250 • *1,311*
Arlington, VA 22201–19 • *170,936*
Arlington, WA 98223 • *4,037*
Arlington □, VA • 170,936
Arlington Heights, IL 60004–07 • *75,460*
Arma, KS 66712 • *1,542*
Armada, MI 48005 • *1,548*
Armijo, NM 87105 • *14,600*
Armonk, NY 10504 • *2,745*
Armour, SD 57313 • *854*
Armstrong, IA 50514 • *1,025*
Armstrong □, PA • 73,478
Armstrong □, TX • 2,021
Arnaudville, LA 70512 • *1,444*
Arnold, MD 21012 • *20,261*
Arnold, MN 55803 • *1,500*
Arnold, MO 63010 • *18,828*
Arnold, PA 15068 • *6,113*
Arnold Mills, RI 02864 • *600*
Aroostook □, ME • 86,936
Arroyo Grande, CA 93420–21 • *14,378*
Artesia, CA 90701–03 • *15,464*
Artesia, NM 88210–11 • *10,610*
Arthur, IL 61911 • *2,112*
Arthur □, NE • 462
Arundel Village, MD 21225 • *3,370*
Arvada, CO 80001–06 • *89,235*
Arvin, CA 93203 • *9,286*
Asbury Park, NJ 07712 • *16,799*
Ascension □, LA • 58,214
Ashaway, RI 02804 • *1,584*
Ashburn, GA 31714 • *4,827*
Ashburnham, MA 01430 • *1,300*
Ashdown, AR 71822 • *5,150*
Ashe □, NC • 22,209
Asheboro, NC 27203 • *16,362*
Asherton, TX 78827 • *1,608*
Asheville, NC 28801–16 • *61,607*
Ashford, AL 36312 • *1,926*
Ash Grove, MO 65604 • *1,128*
Ashland, AL 36251 • *2,034*
Ashland, CA 94541 • *16,590*
Ashland, IL 62612 • *1,257*
Ashland, KS 67831 • *1,032*
Ashland, KY 41101–05 • *23,622*
Ashland, MA 01721 • *9,165*
Ashland, MO 65010 • *1,252*
Ashland, NE 68003 • *2,136*
Ashland, NH 03217 • *1,915*
Ashland, OH 44805 • *20,079*
Ashland, OR 97520 • *16,234*
Ashland, PA 17921 • *3,859*
Ashland, VA 23005 • *5,864*
Ashland, WI 54806 • *8,695*
Ashland □, OH • 47,507
Ashland □, WI • 16,307
Ashland City, TN 37015 • *2,552*
Ashley, ND 58413 • *1,052*
Ashley, OH 43003 • *1,059*
Ashley, PA 18706 • *3,291*
Ashley □, AR • 24,319
Ashtabula, OH 44004 • *21,633*
Ashtabula □, OH • 99,821
Ashton, ID 83420 • *1,114*
Ashton, IL 61006 • *1,042*
Ashton, MD 20861 • *1,800*
Ashton, RI 02864 • *820*
Ashville, AL 35953 • *1,494*
Ashville, OH 43103 • *2,254*
Ashwaubenon, WI 54304 • *16,376*
Asotin □, WA • 17,605
Aspen, CO 81611–15 • *5,049*
Aspen Hill, MD 20906 • *45,494*
Aspermont, TX 79502 • *1,214*
Aspinwall, PA 15215 • *2,880*
Assinippi, MA 02339 • *1,400*
Assonet, MA 02702 • *1,200*
Assumption, IL 62510 • *1,244*
Assumption □, LA • 22,753
Astoria, IL 61501 • *1,205*
Astoria, OR 97103 • *10,069*
Atascadero, CA 93422–23 • *23,138*
Atascosa □, TX • 30,533
Atchison, KS 66002 • *10,656*
Atchison □, KS • 16,932
Atchison □, MO • 7,457
Atco, NJ 08004 • *2,020*
Athens, AL 35611 • *16,901*
Athens, GA 30601–13 • *45,734*
Athens, IL 62613 • *1,404*
Athens, NY 12015 • *1,708*
Athens, OH 45701 • *21,265*
Athens, PA 18810 • *3,468*
Athens, TN 37303 • *12,054*
Athens, TX 75751 • *10,967*
Athens □, OH • 59,549
Atherton, CA 94027 • *7,163*
Athol, MA 01331 • *8,732*
Atkins, AR 72823 • *2,834*
Atkins, VA 24311 • *1,130*
Atkinson, NE 68713 • *1,380*
Atkinson □, GA • 613
Atlanta, GA 30301–83 • *394,017*
Atlanta, IL 61723 • *1,616*
Atlanta, TX 75551 • *6,118*
Atlantic, IA 50022 • *7,432*
Atlantic □, NJ • 224,327
Atlantic Beach, FL 32233 • *11,636*
Atlantic City, NJ 08401–06 • *37,986*
Atlantic Highlands, NJ 07716 • *4,629*
Atmore, AL 36502 • *8,046*
Atoka, OK 74525 • *3,298*
Atoka □, OK • 12,778
Attala □, MS • 18,481
Attalla, AL 35954 • *6,859*
Attica, IN 47918 • *3,457*
Attica, NY 14011 • *2,630*
Attleboro, MA 02703 • *38,383*
Atwater, CA 95301 • *22,282*
Atwater, MN 56209 • *1,053*
Atwood, IL 61913 • *1,253*
Atwood, KS 67730 • *1,388*
Atwood, TN 38220 • *1,066*
Auberry, CA 93602 • *1,866*
Auburn, AL 36830–49 • *33,830*
Auburn, CA 95603–04 • *10,592*
Auburn, GA 30203 • *3,139*
Auburn, IL 62615 • *3,724*

Auburn, IN 46706 • 9,379
Auburn, KY 42206 • 1,273
Auburn, ME 04210–12 • 24,309
Auburn, MA 01501 • 14,845
Auburn, MI 48611 • 1,855
Auburn, NE 68305 • 3,443
Auburn, NY 13021–24 • 31,258
Auburn, WA 98001–02 • 33,102
Auburndale, FL 33823 • 8,858
Auburn Heights, MI 48321 • 17,076
Audrain □, MO • 23,599
Audubon, IA 50025 • 2,524
Audubon, NJ 08106 • 9,205
Audubon, PA 19407 • 6,328
Audubon □, IA • 7,334
Auglaize □, OH • 44,585
August, CA 95201 • 6,376
Augusta, AR 72006 • 2,759
Augusta, GA 30901–19 • 44,639
Augusta, KS 67010 • 7,876
Augusta, KY 41002 • 1,336
Augusta, ME 04330–38 • 21,325
Augusta, WI 54722 • 1,510
Augusta □, VA • 54,677
Aulander, NC 27805 • 1,209
Ault, CO 80610 • 1,107
Aumsville, OR 97325 • 1,650
Aurora, CO 80010–19 • 222,103
Aurora, IL 60504–07 • 99,581
Aurora, IN 47001 • 3,825
Aurora, MN 55705 • 1,965
Aurora, MO 65605 • 6,459
Aurora, NE 68818 • 3,810
Aurora, OH 44202 • 9,192
Aurora □, SD • 3,135
Au Sable, MI 48750 • 1,542
Au Sable Forks, NY 12912 • 2,100
Austell, GA 30001 • 4,173
Austin, IN 47102 • 4,310
Austin, MN 55912 • 21,907
Austin, NV 89310 • 370
Austin, TX 78701–89 • 465,622
Austin □, TX • 19,832
Austintown, OH 44512 • 32,371
Autauga □, AL • 34,222
Ava, MO 65608 • 2,938
Avalon, CA 90704 • 2,918
Avalon, NJ 08202 • 1,809
Avalon, PA 15202 • 5,784
Avella, PA 15312 • 1,200
Avenal, CA 93204 • 9,770
Avenel, MD • 5,600
Avenel, NJ 07001 • 15,504
Aventura, FL 33180 • 14,914
Averill Park, NY 12018 • 1,656
Avery □, NC • 14,867
Avilla, IN 46710 • 1,366
Avis, PA 17721 • 1,506
Avoca, IA 51521 • 1,497
Avoca, NY 14809 • 1,033
Avoca, PA 18641 • 2,897
Avocado Heights, CA 91746 • 14,232
Avon, CT 06001 • 13,937
Avon, MA 02322 • 5,026
Avon, NY 14414 • 2,995
Avon, OH 44011 • 7,337
Avon by the Sea, NJ 07717 • 2,165
Avondale, AZ 85323 • 16,169
Avondale, LA 70094 • 5,813
Avondale, OH 45404 • 5,000
Avondale Estates, GA 30002 • 2,209
Avon Lake, OH 44012 • 15,066
Avonmore, PA 15618 • 1,089
Avon Park, FL 33825 • 8,042
Avoyelles □, LA • 39,159
Ayden, NC 28513 • 4,740
Ayer, MA 01432 • 2,889
Azalea Park, FL 32807 • 8,926
Azle, TX 76020 • 8,868
Aztec, NM 87410 • 5,479
Azusa, CA 91702 • 41,333

B

Babbitt, MN 55706 • 1,562
Babbitt, NV • 1,800
Babylon, NY 11702–04 • 12,249
Baca □, CO • 4,556
Bacliff, TX 77518 • 5,549
Bacon □, GA • 9,566
Bad Axe, MI 48413 • 3,484
Baden, PA 15005 • 5,074
Badin, NC 28009 • 1,481
Bagdad, AZ 86321 • 1,858
Bagdad, FL 32530 • 1,457
Baggs, WY 82321 • 272
Bagley, MN 56621 • 1,388
Bailey □, TX • 7,064
Baileys Crossroads, VA 22041 • 19,507
Bainbridge, GA 31717 • 10,712
Bainbridge, NY 13733 • 1,550
Baird, TX 79504 • 1,658
Bairdford, PA 15006 • 1,200
Baker, LA 70714 • 13,233
Baker, MT 59313 • 1,818
Baker, OR 97814 • 9,140
Baker □, FL • 18,486
Baker □, GA • 3,615
Baker □, OR • 15,317
Bakersfield, CA 93301–89 • 174,820
Balch Springs, TX 75180 • 17,406
Bald Knob, AR 72010 • 2,653
Baldwin, FL 32234 • 1,450
Baldwin, GA 30511 • 1,439
Baldwin, LA 70514 • 2,379
Baldwin, NY 11510 • 22,719
Baldwin, PA 15234 • 21,923
Baldwin, WI 54002 • 2,022
Baldwin □, AL • 98,280
Baldwin □, GA • 39,530
Baldwin City, KS 66006 • 2,961
Baldwin Park, CA 91706 • 69,330
Baldwinsville, NY 13027 • 6,591
Baldwinville, MA 01436 • 1,795
Baldwyn, MS 38824 • 3,204
Balfour, NC 28706 • 1,118
Ball, LA 71405 • 3,305
Ballard □, KY • 7,902
Ballardvale, MA 01810 • 1,270
Ballinger, TX 76821 • 3,975
Ballston Spa, NY 12020 • 4,937
Ballwin, MO 63011 • 21,816
Balmville, NY 12550 • 2,963
Baltic, CT 06330 • 2,000
Baltimore, MD 21201–99 • 736,014
Baltimore, OH 43105 • 2,971
Baltimore □, MD • 692,134
Baltimore Highlands, MD 21227 • 7,300
Bamberg, SC 29003 • 3,843
Bamberg □, SC • 16,902
Bandera □, TX • 10,562
Bandon, OR 97411 • 2,215
Bangor, ME 04401–02 • 33,181
Bangor, MI 49013 • 1,922
Bangor, PA 18013 • 5,383
Bangor, WI 54614 • 1,076
Bangor Township, MI 48706 • 17,494
Bangs, TX 76823 • 1,555
Banks □, GA • 10,308
Banner □, NE • 852
Banning, CA 92220 • 20,570
Bannock □, ID • 66,026
Baraboo, WI 53913 • 9,203
Baraga, MI 49908 • 1,231
Baraga □, MI • 7,954
Barataria, LA 70036 • 1,160
Barber □, KS • 5,874
Barberton, OH 44203 • 27,623
Barbour □, AL • 25,417
Barbour □, WV • 15,699
Barboursville, WV 25504 • 2,774
Barbourville, KY 40906 • 3,658
Bardstown, KY 40004 • 6,801
Bargersville, IN 46106 • 1,681
Bar Harbor, ME 04609 • 2,768
Barker Heights, NC 28739 • 1,137
Barling, AR 72923 • 4,078
Barnegat, NJ 08005 • 1,160
Barnes □, ND • 12,545
Barnesboro, PA 15714 • 2,530
Barnesville, GA 30204 • 4,747
Barnesville, MN 56514 • 2,066
Barnesville, OH 43713 • 4,326
Barnsdall, OK 74002 • 1,316
Barnstable, MA 02630 • 2,790
Barnstable □, MA • 186,605
Barnwell, SC 29812 • 5,255
Barnwell □, SC • 20,293
Barrackville, WV 26559 • 1,443
Barre, MA 01005 • 1,094
Barre, VT 05641 • 9,482
Barren □, KY • 34,001
Barrington, IL 60010–11 • 9,504
Barrington, NJ 08007 • 6,774
Barrington, RI 02806 • 15,849
Barron, WI 54812 • 2,986
Barron □, WI • 40,750
Barron Lake, MI 49120 • 1,600
Barrow, AK 99723 • 3,469
Barrow □, GA • 29,721
Barry, IL 62312 • 1,391
Barry □, MI • 50,057
Barry □, MO • 27,547
Barstow, CA 92310–12 • 21,472
Bartholomew □, IN • 63,657
Bartlesville, OK 74003–06 • 34,256
Bartlett, IL 60103 • 19,373
Bartlett, TN 38134 • 26,989
Bartlett, TX 76511 • 1,439
Barton, OH 43905 • 1,039
Barton, VT 05822 • 908
Barton □, KS • 29,382
Barton □, MO • 11,312
Bartonville, IL 61607 • 5,643
Bartow, FL 33830 • 14,716
Bartow □, GA • 55,911
Barview, OR 97420 • 1,402
Basalt, CO 81621 • 1,128
Basehor, KS 66007 • 1,591
Basile, LA 70515 • 1,808
Basin, WY 82410 • 1,180
Basking Ridge, NJ 07920 • 3,060
Bassett, VA 24055 • 1,579
Bass Lake, IN 46534 • 1,500
Bastrop, LA 71220–21 • 13,916
Bastrop, TX 78602 • 4,044
Bastrop □, TX • 38,263
Batavia, IL 60510 • 17,076
Batavia, NY 14020–21 • 16,310
Batavia, OH 45103 • 1,700
Bates □, MO • 15,025
Batesburg, SC 29006 • 4,082
Batesville, AR 72501–03 • 9,187
Batesville, IN 47006 • 4,720
Batesville, MS 38606 • 6,403
Bath, ME 04530 • 9,799
Bath, NY 14810 • 5,801
Bath, PA 18014 • 2,358
Bath, SC 29816 • 2,242
Bath □, KY • 9,692
Bath □, VA • 4,799
Baton Rouge, LA 70801–98 • 219,531
Battle Creek, MI 49015–17 • 53,540
Battle Ground, WA 98604 • 3,758
Battle Mountain, NV 89820 • 3,542
Baudette, MN 56623 • 1,146
Bawcomville, LA 71291 • 2,250
Baxley, GA 31513 • 3,841
Baxter, MN 56425 • 3,695
Baxter, TN 38544 • 1,289
Baxter □, AR • 31,186
Baxter Springs, KS 66713 • 4,351
Bay, AR 72411 • 1,660
Bay □, FL • 126,994
Bay □, MI • 111,723
Bayard, NE 69334 • 1,196
Bayard, NM 88023 • 2,598
Bayberry, NY 13088 • 6,710
Bay City, MI 48706–08 • 38,936
Bay City, OR 97107 • 1,027
Bay City, TX 77414 • 18,170
Bayfield, CO 81122 • 1,090
Bayfield □, WI • 14,008
Bay Head, NJ 08742 • 1,226
Baylor □, TX • 4,385
Bay Minette, AL 36507 • 7,168
Bayonet Point, FL 34667 • 21,860
Bayonne, NJ 07002 • 61,444
Bayou Cane, LA 70359 • 15,876
Bayou George, FL 32401 • 1,500
Bayou La Batre, AL 36509 • 2,456
Bay Pines, FL 33504 • 4,171
Bayport, MN 55003 • 3,200
Bayport, NY 11705 • 7,702
Bay Ridge, MD 21403 • 1,989
Bay Saint Louis, MS 39520–21 • 8,063
Bay Shore, NY 11706 • 21,279
Bayshore Gardens, FL 34207 • 17,062
Bayside, WI 53217 • 4,789
Bay Springs, MS 39422 • 1,729
Baytown, TX 77520–22 • 63,850
Bay Village, OH 44140 • 17,000
Bayville, NY 11709 • 7,193
Beach, IL 60085 • 9,513
Beach, ND 58621 • 1,205
Beach Haven, NJ 08008 • 1,475
Beachwood, NJ 08722 • 9,324
Beachwood, OH 44122 • 10,677
Beacon, NY 12508 • 13,243
Beacon Falls, CT 06403 • 1,285
Beacon Square, FL 34652 • 6,265
Beadle □, SD • 18,253
Bear, DE 19701 • 1,200
Bearden, AR 71720 • 1,021
Beardstown, IL 62618 • 5,270
Bear Lake □, ID • 6,084
Bear Town, MS 39648 • 1,277
Beatrice, NE 68310 • 12,354
Beatty, NV 89003 • 1,623
Beattyville, KY 41311 • 1,131
Beaufort, NC 28516 • 3,808
Beaufort, SC 29901–03 • 9,576
Beaufort □, NC • 42,283
Beaufort □, SC • 86,425
Beaumont, CA 92223 • 9,685
Beaumont, MS 39423 • 1,054
Beaumont, TX 77701–26 • 114,323
Beauregard □, LA • 30,083
Beaver, OK 73932 • 1,584
Beaver, PA 15009 • 5,028
Beaver, UT 84713 • 1,998
Beaver, WV 25813 • 1,244
Beaver □, OK • 6,023
Beaver □, PA • 186,093
Beaver □, UT • 4,765
Beavercreek, OH 45385 • 33,626
Beaverdale, PA 15921 • 1,000
Beaver Dam, KY 42320 • 2,904
Beaver Dam, WI 53916 • 14,196
Beaver Falls, PA 15010 • 10,687
Beaverhead □, MT • 8,424
Beaverton, MI 48612 • 1,150
Beaverton, OR 97005–07 • 53,310
Beckemeyer, IL 62219 • 1,070
Becker □, MN • 27,881
Beckham □, OK • 18,812
Beckley, WV 25801–02 • 18,296
Bedford, IN 47421 • 13,817
Bedford, IA 50833 • 1,528
Bedford, MA 01730 • 13,067
Bedford, NH 03102 • 1,400
Bedford, OH 44146 • 14,822
Bedford, PA 15522 • 3,137
Bedford, TX 76021–22 • 43,762
Bedford, VA 24523 • 6,073
Bedford □, PA • 47,919
Bedford □, TN • 30,411
Bedford □, VA • 45,656
Bedford Heights, OH 44146 • 12,131
Bedford Hills, NY 10507 • 3,140
Bee □, TX • 25,135
Beebe, AR 72012 • 4,455
Beecher, IL 60401 • 2,032
Beecher, MI 48458 • 14,465
Beech Grove, IN 46107 • 13,383
Beech Island, SC 29842 • 1,500
Bee Ridge, FL 34233 • 6,406
Beeville, TX 78102–04 • 13,547
Beggs, OK 74421 • 1,150
Bel Air, MD 21014 • 8,860
Bel Aire, KS 67220 • 3,695
Belchertown, MA 01007 • 2,339
Belcourt, ND 58316 • 2,458
Belding, MI 48809 • 5,969
Belen, NM 87002 • 6,547
Belfast, ME 04915 • 6,355
Belfast, NY 14711 • 1,100
Belfield, ND 58622 • 887
Belford, NJ 07718 • 6,300
Belgrade, MT 59714 • 3,411
Belhaven, NC 27810 • 2,269
Belington, WV 26250 • 1,850
Belknap □, NH • 49,216
Bell, CA 90201 • 34,365
Bell □, KY • 31,506
Bell □, TX • 191,088
Bellair, FL 32073 • 5,200
Bellaire, MI 49615 • 1,104
Bellaire, OH 43906 • 6,028
Bellaire, TX 77401–02 • 13,842
Bella Vista, AR 72712 • 9,083
Bellbrook, OH 45305 • 6,511
Belle, MO 65013 • 1,218
Belle, WV 25015 • 1,421
Belleair, FL 34616 • 3,968
Belle Chasse, LA 70037 • 8,512
Bellefontaine, OH 43311 • 12,142
Bellefontaine Neighbors, MO 63137 • 10,922
Bellefonte, DE 19809 • 1,243
Bellefonte, PA 16823 • 6,358
Belle Fourche, SD 57717 • 4,335
Belle Glade, FL 33430 • 16,177
Belle Isle, FL 32809 • 5,272
Belle Meade, TN 37205 • 2,839
Bellemoor, DE 19802 • 1,040
Belle Plaine, IA 52208 • 2,834
Belle Plaine, KS 67013 • 1,649
Belle Plaine, MN 56011 • 3,149
Belle Vernon, PA 15012 • 1,213
Belleview, FL 32506 • 8,000
Belleview, FL 32620 • 2,666
Belle View, VA 22307 • 3,500
Belleville, IL 62220–25 • 42,785
Belleville, KS 66935 • 2,517
Belleville, MI 48111–12 • 3,270
Belleville, NJ 07109 • 34,213
Belleville, PA 17004 • 1,589
Belleville, WI 53508 • 1,456
Bellevue, ID 83313 • 1,275
Bellevue, IA 52031 • 2,239
Bellevue, KY 41073 • 6,997
Bellevue, MI 49021 • 1,401
Bellevue, NE 68005 • 30,982
Bellevue, OH 44811 • 8,146
Bellevue, PA 15202 • 9,126
Bellevue, WA 98004–09 • 86,874
Bellflower, CA 90706–07 • 61,815
Bell Gardens, CA 90201 • 42,355
Bellingham, MA 02019 • 4,535
Bellingham, WA 98225–27 • 52,179
Bellmawr, NJ 08031 • 12,603
Bellmead, TX 76705 • 8,336
Bellmore, NY 11710 • 16,438
Bellows Falls, VT 05101 • 3,313
Bellport, NY 11713 • 2,572
Bells, TN 38006 • 1,643
Bellville, OH 44813 • 1,568
Bellville, TX 77418 • 3,378
Bellwood, IL 60104 • 20,241
Bellwood, PA 16617 • 1,976
Bellwood, VA 23234 • 6,178
Belmar, NJ 07719 • 5,877
Belmond, IA 50421 • 2,500
Belmont, CA 94002 • 24,127
Belmont, MA 02178 • 24,720
Belmont, MS 38827 • 1,554
Belmont, NY 14813 • 1,006
Belmont, NC 28012 • 8,434
Belmont □, OH • 71,074
Bel-Nor, MO 63133 • 2,935
Beloit, KS 67420 • 4,066
Beloit, OH 44609 • 1,037
Beloit, WI 53511–12 • 35,573
Beloit North, WI 53511 • 5,457
Belpre, OH 45714 • 6,796
Belt, MT 59412 • 571
Belton, MO 64012 • 18,150
Belton, SC 29627 • 4,646
Belton, TX 76513 • 12,476
Beltrami □, MN • 34,384
Beltsville, MD 20705 • 14,476
Belvedere, GA 30032 • 6,100
Belvedere, SC 29841 • 6,133
Belvedere Park, GA 30032 • 18,089
Belvidere, IL 61008 • 15,958
Belvidere, NJ 07823 • 2,669
Belzoni, MS 39038 • 2,536
Bement, IL 61813 • 1,668
Bemidji, MN 56601–19 • 11,245
Benavides, TX 78341 • 1,788
Benbrook, TX 76126 • 19,564
Bend, OR 97701–09 • 20,469
Benewah □, ID • 7,937
Ben Hill □, GA • 16,245
Benicia, CA 94510 • 24,437
Benkelman, NE 69021 • 1,193
Benld, IL 62009 • 1,604
Ben Lomond, CA 95005 • 7,884
Bennett, CO 80102 • 1,757
Bennett □, SD • 3,206
Bennettsville, SC 29512 • 9,345
Bennington, VT 05201 • 9,532
Bennington □, VT • 35,845
Bennion, UT 84118 • 9,575
Bensalem, PA 19020–21 • 52,368
Bensenville, IL 60106 • 17,767
Bensley, VA 23234 • 5,093
Benson, AZ 85602 • 3,824
Benson, MN 56215 • 3,235
Benson, NC 27504 • 2,810
Benson □, ND • 7,198
Bent □, CO • 5,048
Bentleyville, PA 15314 • 2,673
Benton, AR 72015 • 18,177
Benton, IL 62812 • 7,216
Benton, KY 42025 • 3,899
Benton, LA 71006 • 2,047
Benton □, AR • 97,499
Benton □, IN • 9,441
Benton □, IA • 22,429
Benton □, MN • 30,185
Benton □, MS • 8,046
Benton □, MO • 13,859
Benton □, OR • 70,811
Benton □, TN • 14,524
Benton □, WA • 112,560
Benton City, WA 99320 • 1,806
Benton Harbor, MI 49022–23 • 12,818
Benton Heights, MI 49022 • 5,465
Bentonville, AR 72712–14 • 11,257
Benwood, WV 26031 • 1,669
Benzie □, MI • 12,200
Beowawe, NV 89821 • 250
Berea, KY 40403 • 9,126
Berea, OH 44017 • 19,051
Berea, SC 29611 • 13,535
Beresford, SD 57004 • 1,849
Bergen, NY 14416 • 1,103
Bergen □, NJ • 825,380
Bergenfield, NJ 07621 • 24,458
Berkeley, CA 94701–10 • 102,724
Berkeley, IL 60163 • 5,137
Berkeley, MO 63134 • 12,450
Berkeley, RI 02864 • 830
Berkeley □, SC • 128,776
Berkeley □, WV • 59,253
Berkeley Heights, NJ 07922 • 11,980
Berkley, MI 48072 • 16,960
Berks □, PA • 336,523
Berkshire □, MA • 139,352
Berlin, CT 06037 • 1,040
Berlin, MD 21811 • 2,616
Berlin, NH 03570 • 11,824
Berlin, NJ 08009 • 5,672
Berlin, NY 12022 • 1,200
Berlin, PA 15530 • 2,064
Berlin, WI 54923 • 5,371
Bernalillo, NM 87004 • 5,960
Bernalillo □, NM • 480,577
Bernardsville, NJ 07924 • 6,597
Berne, IN 46711 • 3,559
Bernice, LA 71222 • 1,543
Bernie, MO 63822 • 1,847
Berrien □, GA • 14,153
Berrien □, MI • 161,378
Berrien Springs, MI 49103 • 1,927
Berry, AL 35546 • 1,218
Berryville, AR 72616 • 3,212
Berryville, VA 22611 • 3,097
Berthoud, CO 80513 • 2,990
Bertie □, NC • 20,388
Bertrand, MI 49120 • 5,500
Berwick, LA 70342 • 4,375
Berwick, ME 03901 • 2,378
Berwick, PA 18603 • 10,976
Berwyn, IL 60402 • 45,426
Berwyn, PA 19312 • 8,150
Bessemer, AL 35020–23 • 33,497
Bessemer, MI 49911 • 2,272
Bessemer, PA 16112 • 1,196
Bessemer City, NC 28016 • 4,698
Bethalto, IL 62010 • 9,507
Bethany, CT 06525 • 1,170
Bethany, IL 61914 • 1,369
Bethany, MO 64424 • 3,005
Bethany, OK 73008 • 20,075
Bethany, WV 26032 • 1,139
Bethany Beach, DE 19930 • 326
Bethel, AK 99559 • 4,674
Bethel, CT 06801 • 8,835
Bethel, ME 04217 • 1,225
Bethel, NC 27812 • 1,842
Bethel, OH 45106 • 2,407
Bethel, VT 05032 • 1,866
Bethel Acres, OK 74801 • 2,505
Bethel Park, PA 15102 • 33,823
Bethesda, MD 20813–17 • 62,936
Bethesda, OH 43719 • 1,161
Bethlehem, CT 06751 • 1,976
Bethlehem, PA 18015–18 • 71,428
Bethpage, NY 11714 • 15,761
Bettendorf, IA 52722 • 28,132
Beulah, ND 58523 • 3,363
Beverly, MA 01915 • 38,195
Beverly, NJ 08010 • 2,973
Beverly, OH 45715 • 1,444
Beverly Hills, CA 90209–13 • 31,971
Beverly Hills, FL 32665 • 6,163
Beverly Hills, MI 48009 • 10,610
Bexar □, TX • 1,185,394
Bexley, OH 43209 • 13,088
Bibb □, AL • 16,576
Bibb □, GA • 149,967
Bicknell, IN 47512 • 3,357
Biddeford, ME 04005 • 20,710
Bienville □, LA • 15,979
Big Bear City, CA 92314 • 3,500
Big Bend, WI 53103 • 1,299
Big Delta, AK 99737 • 400
Big Flats, NY 14814 • 2,658
Bigfork, MT 59911 • 1,080
Biggs, CA 95917 • 1,581
Big Horn □, MT • 11,337
Big Horn □, WY • 10,525
Big Lake, MN 55309 • 3,113
Big Lake, TX 76932 • 3,672
Big Pine, CA 93513 • 1,158
Big Piney, WY 83113 • 454
Big Rapids, MI 49307 • 12,603
Big Sandy, MT 59520 • 740
Big Sandy, TX 75755 • 1,185
Big Spring, TX 79720–21 • 23,093
Big Stone □, MN • 6,285
Big Stone Gap, VA 24219 • 4,748
Big Timber, MT 59011 • 1,557
Billerica, MA 01821–22 • 6,840
Billings, MT 59101–08 • 81,151
Billings □, ND • 1,108
Billings Heights, MT 59105 • 8,480
Biloxi, MS 39530–35 • 46,319
Biltmore Forest, NC 28803 • 1,327
Bingham, ME 04920 • 1,071
Bingham □, ID • 37,583
Binghamton, NY 13901–05 • 53,008
Birchwood City, MD 20745 • 4,870
Birchwood Park, DE 19711 • 2,250
Bird Island, MN 55310 • 1,326
Birdsboro, PA 19508 • 4,222
Birmingham, AL 35201–61 • 265,968
Birmingham, MI 48009–12 • 19,997
Bisbee, AZ 85603 • 6,288
Biscayne Gardens, FL 33168 • 13,000
Biscayne Park, FL 33161 • 3,068
Biscoe, NC 27209 • 1,484
Bishop, CA 93514–15 • 3,475
Bishop, TX 78343 • 3,337
Bishopville, SC 29010 • 3,560
Bismarck, MO 63624 • 1,579
Bismarck, ND 58501–07 • 49,256
Biwabik, MN 55708 • 1,097
Bixby, OK 74008 • 9,502
Black Canyon City, AZ 85324 • 1,811
Black Creek, WI 54106 • 1,152
Black Diamond, WA 98010 • 1,422
Black Earth, WI 53515 • 1,248
Blackfoot, ID 83221 • 9,646
Blackford □, IN • 14,067
Black Forest, CO 80908 • 8,143
Black Hawk, SD 57718 • 1,955
Black Hawk □, IA • 123,798
Black Jack, MO 63031 • 6,128
Black Lick, PA 15716 • 1,100
Blacklick Estates, OH 43227 • 10,080
Black Mountain, NC 28711 • 5,418
Black Point Beach Club, CT 06357 • 1,200
Black River, NY 13612 • 1,349
Black River Falls, WI 54615 • 3,490
Blacksburg, SC 29702 • 1,907
Blacksburg, VA 24060–63 • 34,590
Blackshear, GA 31516 • 3,263
Blackstone, MA 01504 • 4,460
Blackstone, VA 23824 • 3,497
Blackville, SC 29817 • 2,688
Blackwell, OK 74631 • 7,538
Blackwood, NJ 08012 • 5,120
Bladen □, NC • 28,663
Bladenboro, NC 28320 • 1,821
Bladensburg, MD 20710 • 8,064
Blades, DE 19973 • 834
Blaine, MN 55433 • 38,975
Blaine, TN 37709 • 1,326
Blaine, WA 98230 • 2,489
Blaine □, ID • 13,552
Blaine □, MT • 6,728
Blaine □, NE • 675
Blaine □, OK • 11,470
Blair, NE 68008 • 6,860
Blair, WI 54616 • 1,126
Blair □, PA • 130,542
Blairsville, PA 15717 • 3,595
Blakely, GA 31723 • 5,595
Blakely, PA 18447 • 7,222
Blanchard, LA 71009 • 1,175
Blanchard, OK 73010 • 1,922
Blanchester, OH 45107 • 4,206
Blanco, TX 78606 • 1,238
Blanco □, TX • 5,972
Bland □, VA • 6,514
Blanding, UT 84511 • 3,162
Blasdell, NY 14219 • 2,900
Blauvelt, NY 10913 • 4,470
Blawnox, PA 15238 • 1,626
Bleckley □, GA • 10,430
Bledsoe □, TN • 9,669

Blende, CO 81006 • 1,330
Blennerhassett, WV 26101 • 2,924
Blissfield, MI 49228 • 3,172
Block Island, RI 02807 • 620
Bloomer, WI 54724 • 3,085
Bloomfield, CT 06002 • 7,120
Bloomfield, IN 47424 • 2,592
Bloomfield, IA 52537 • 2,580
Bloomfield, MO 63825 • 1,800
Bloomfield, NE 68718 • 1,181
Bloomfield, NJ 07003 • 45,061
Bloomfield, NM 87413 • 5,214
Bloomfield Hills, MI 48302–04 • 4,288
Bloomfield Township, MI 48302 • 42,137
Bloomingdale, GA 31302 • 2,271
Bloomingdale, IL 60108 • 16,614
Bloomingdale, NJ 07403 • 7,530
Bloomingdale, TN 37660 • 10,953
Blooming Prairie, MN 55917 • 2,043
Bloomington, CA 92316 • 15,116
Bloomington, IL 61701–04 • 51,972
Bloomington, IN 47401–08 • 60,633
Bloomington, MN 55420 • 86,335
Bloomington, TX 77951 • 1,888
Bloomsburg, PA 17815 • 12,439
Blossburg, PA 16912 • 1,571
Blossom, TX 75416 • 1,440
Blount □, AL • 39,248
Blount □, TN • 85,969
Blountstown, FL 32424 • 2,404
Blountsville, AL 35031 • 1,527
Blountville, TN 37617 • 2,605
Blowing Rock, NC 28605 • 1,257
Blue Ash, OH 45242 • 11,860
Blue Diamond, NV 89004 • 420
Blue Earth, MN 56013 • 3,745
Blue Earth □, MN • 54,044
Bluefield, VA 24605 • 5,363
Bluefield, WV 24701 • 12,756
Blue Grass, IA 52726 • 1,214
Blue Hills, CT 06002 • 3,206
Blue Island, IL 60406 • 21,203
Blue Lake, CA 95525 • 1,235
Blue Mound, IL 62513 • 1,161
Blue Rapids, KS 66411 • 1,131
Blue Ridge, GA 30513 • 1,336
Blue Ridge, VA 24064 • 2,840
Blue Ridge Summit, PA 17214 • 1,800
Blue Springs, MO 64014–15 • 40,153
Bluewell, WV 24701 • 2,752
Bluff City, TN 37618 • 1,390
Bluffdale, UT 84065 • 2,152
Bluff Park, AL 35226 • 8,000
Bluffton, IN 46714 • 9,020
Bluffton, OH 45817 • 3,367
Blythe, CA 92225–26 • 8,428
Blytheville, AR 72315–19 • 22,906
Boalsburg, PA 16827 • 2,206
Boardman, OH 44512 • 38,596
Boardman, OR 97818 • 1,387
Boaz, AL 35957 • 6,928
Boca Grande, FL 33921 • 1,200
Boca Raton, FL 33431–34 • 61,492
Boerne, TX 78006 • 4,274
Bogalusa, LA 70427–29 • 14,280
Bogart, GA 30622 • 1,018
Bogata, TX 75417 • 1,421
Boger City, NC 28092 • 1,373
Bogota, NJ 07603 • 7,824
Bohemia, NY 11716 • 9,556
Boiling Springs, NC 28017 • 2,445
Boiling Springs, PA 17007 • 1,978
Boise, ID 83701–15 • 125,738
Boise □, ID • 3,509
Boise City, OK 73933 • 1,509
Bolingbrook, IL 60440 • 40,843
Bolivar, MO 65613 • 6,845
Bolivar, NY 14715 • 1,261
Bolivar, TN 38008 • 5,969
Bolivar □, MS • 41,875
Bollinger □, MO • 10,619
Bolton Landing, NY 12814 • 1,600
Bon Air, VA 23235 • 16,413
Bonaventure, FL 33317 • 6,000
Bond □, IL • 14,991
Bondsville, MA 01009 • 1,992
Bonduel, WI 54107 • 1,210
Bondurant, IA 50035 • 1,584
Bonham, TX 75418 • 6,686
Bon Homme □, SD • 7,089
Bonifay, FL 32425 • 2,612
Bonita, CA 91903 • 12,542
Bonita Springs, FL 33923 • 13,600
Bonneauville, PA 17325 • 1,282
Bonner □, ID • 26,622
Bonners Ferry, ID 83805 • 2,193
Bonner Springs, KS 66012 • 6,413
Bonne Terre, MO 63628 • 3,871
Bonneville □, ID • 72,207
Bonney Lake, WA 98390 • 7,494
Bonnie Doone, NC 28303 • 3,893
Bono, AR 72416 • 1,220
Booker, TX 79005 • 1,236
Boomer, WV 25031 • 1,051
Boone, IA 50036 • 12,392
Boone, NC 28607 • 12,915
Boone □, AR • 28,297
Boone □, IL • 30,806
Boone □, IN • 38,147
Boone □, IA • 25,186
Boone □, KY • 57,589
Boone □, MO • 112,379
Boone □, NE • 6,667
Boone □, WV • 25,870
Booneville, AR 72927 • 3,804
Booneville, MS 38829 • 7,955
Boonsboro, MD 21713 • 2,445
Boonton, NJ 07005 • 8,343
Boonville, CA 95415 • 1,000
Boonville, IN 47601 • 6,724
Boonville, MO 65233 • 7,095
Boonville, NY 13309 • 2,220
Boonville, NC 27011 • 1,009
Boothbay Harbor, ME 04538 • 1,267
Borden □, TX • 799
Bordentown, NJ 08505 • 4,341
Borger, TX 79007–08 • 15,675
Boron, CA 93516 • 2,101
Borrego Springs, CA 92004 • 2,244
Boscobel, WI 53805 • 2,706
Bosque □, TX • 15,125
Bossert Estates, NJ 08505 • 1,830
Bossier □, LA • 86,088
Bossier City, LA 71111–13 • 52,721
Boston, GA 31626 • 1,395
Boston, MA 02101–99 • 574,283
Boswell, PA 15531 • 1,485
Botetourt □, VA • 24,992
Bothell, WA 98011–12 • 12,345
Botkins, OH 45306 • 1,340
Bottineau, ND 58318 • 2,598
Bottineau □, ND • 8,011
Boulder, CO 80301–08 • 83,312
Boulder, MT 59632 • 1,316
Boulder □, CO • 225,339
Boulder City, NV 89005–06 • 12,567
Boulder Creek, CA 95006 • 6,725
Boulder Hill, IL 60538 • 8,894
Boulevard Heights, MD 20743 • 1,820
Boundary □, ID • 8,332
Bound Brook, NJ 08805 • 9,487
Bountiful, UT 84010–11 • 36,659
Bourbon, IN 46504 • 1,672
Bourbon, MO 65441 • 1,188
Bourbon □, KS • 14,966
Bourbon □, KY • 19,236
Bourbonnais, IL 60914 • 13,934
Bourg, LA 70343 • 2,073
Bourne, MA 02532 • 1,284
Boutte, LA 70039 • 1,200
Bovina, TX 79009 • 1,549
Bowdon, GA 30108 • 1,981
Bowie, MD 20715–21 • 37,589
Bowie, TX 76230 • 4,990
Bowie □, TX • 81,665
Bowling Green, FL 33834 • 1,836
Bowling Green, KY 42101–04 • 40,641
Bowling Green, MO 63334 • 2,976
Bowling Green, OH 43402 • 28,176
Bowman, ND 58623 • 1,741
Bowman, SC 29018 • 1,063
Bowman □, ND • 3,596
Box Butte □, NE • 13,130
Box Elder, SD 57719 • 2,680
Box Elder □, UT • 36,485
Boxford, MA 01921 • 2,072
Boyce, LA 71409 • 1,361
Boyd □, KY • 51,150
Boyd □, NE • 2,835
Boyertown, PA 19512 • 3,759
Boyes Hot Springs, CA 95416 • 5,973
Boyle □, KY • 25,641
Boyne City, MI 49712 • 3,478
Boynton Beach, FL 33435–37 • 46,194
Bozeman, MT 59715 • 22,660
Bracken □, KY • 7,766
Brackenridge, PA 15014 • 3,784
Brackettville, TX 78832 • 1,740
Braddock, PA 15104 • 4,682
Braddock Heights, MD 21714 • 4,778
Bradenton, FL 34201–10 • 43,779
Bradenville, PA 15620 • 1,100
Bradford, OH 45308 • 2,005
Bradford, PA 16701 • 9,625
Bradford, RI 02808 • 1,604
Bradford, TN 38316 • 1,154
Bradford, VT 05033 • 672
Bradford □, FL • 22,515
Bradford □, PA • 60,967
Bradfordwoods, PA 15015 • 1,329
Bradley, FL 33835 • 1,108
Bradley, IL 60915 • 10,792
Bradley, WV 25818 • 2,144
Bradley □, AR • 11,793
Bradley □, TN • 73,712
Bradley Beach, NJ 07720 • 4,475
Bradner, OH 43406 • 1,093
Brady, TX 76825 • 5,946
Braham, MN 55006 • 1,139
Braidwood, IL 60408 • 3,584
Brainerd, MN 56401 • 12,353
Braintree, MA 02184 • 33,836
Branch □, MI • 41,502
Branch Village, RI 02895 • 400
Branchville, SC 29432 • 1,107
Brandenburg, KY 40108 • 1,857
Brandon, FL 33510 • 57,985
Brandon, MS 39042–43 • 11,077
Brandon, SC 29611 • 2,170
Brandon, SD 57005 • 3,543
Brandon, VT 05733 • 1,902
Brandywine, MD 20613 • 1,406
Branford, CT 06405 • 27,603
Branford Hills, CT 06405 • 3,460
Branson, MO 65616 • 3,706
Brantley, AL 36009 • 1,015
Brantley □, GA • 11,077
Brant Rock, MA 02020 • 1,850
Bratenahl, OH 44108 • 1,356
Brattleboro, VT 05301–04 • 8,612
Brawley, CA 92227 • 18,923
Braxton □, WV • 12,998
Brazil, IN 47834 • 7,640
Brazoria, TX 77422 • 2,717
Brazoria □, TX • 191,707
Brazos □, TX • 121,862
Brea, CA 92621–22 • 32,873
Breathitt □, KY • 15,703
Breaux Bridge, LA 70517 • 6,515
Breckenridge, CO 80424 • 1,285
Breckenridge, MI 48615 • 1,301
Breckenridge, MN 56520 • 3,708
Breckenridge, TX 76024 • 5,665
Breckenridge Hills, MO 63114 • 5,404
Breckinridge □, KY • 16,312
Brecksville, OH 44141 • 11,818
Breese, IL 62230 • 3,567
Bremen, GA 30110 • 4,356
Bremen, IN 46506 • 4,725
Bremen, OH 43107 • 1,386
Bremer □, IA • 22,813
Bremerton, WA 98310–15 • 38,142
Bremond, TX 76629 • 1,110
Brenham, TX 77833–34 • 11,952
Brent, AL 35034 • 2,776
Brent, FL 32503 • 21,624
Brentwood, CA 94513 • 7,563
Brentwood, MD 20722 • 3,005
Brentwood, MO 63144 • 8,150
Brentwood, NY 11717 • 45,218
Brentwood, NY • 45,218
Brentwood, OH 45231 • 3,568
Brentwood, PA 15227 • 10,823
Brentwood, SC 29405 • 2,000
Brentwood, TN 37027 • 16,392
Brevard, NC 28712 • 5,388
Brevard □, FL • 398,978
Brewer, ME 04412 • 9,021
Brewster, MA 02631 • 1,818
Brewster, NY 10509 • 1,566
Brewster, OH 44613 • 2,307
Brewster, WA 98812 • 1,633
Brewster □, TX • 8,681
Brewton, AL 36426–27 • 5,885
Briarcliff Manor, NY 10510 • 7,070
Brick [Township], NJ 08723 • 55,473
Bridge City, LA 70094 • 8,327
Bridge City, TX 77611 • 8,034
Bridgehampton, NY 11932 • 1,997
Bridgeport, AL 35740 • 2,936
Bridgeport, CT 06601–50 • 141,686
Bridgeport, IL 62417 • 2,118
Bridgeport, MI 48722 • 8,569
Bridgeport, NE 69336 • 1,581
Bridgeport, OH 43912 • 2,318
Bridgeport, PA 19405 • 4,292
Bridgeport, TX 76026 • 3,581
Bridgeport, WA 98813 • 1,498
Bridgeport, WV 26330 • 6,739
Bridger, MT 59014 • 692
Bridgeton, MO 63044 • 17,779
Bridgeton, NJ 08302 • 18,942
Bridgetown, OH 45211 • 11,460
Bridgeview, IL 60455 • 14,402
Bridgeville, DE 19933 • 1,210
Bridgeville, PA 15017 • 5,445
Bridgewater, MA 02324 • 7,242
Bridgewater, NJ 08807 • 5,630
Bridgewater, VA 22812 • 3,918
Bridgman, MI 49106 • 2,140
Bridgton, ME 04009 • 2,195
Brielle, NJ 08730 • 4,406
Brigantine, NJ 08203 • 11,354
Brigham City, UT 84302 • 15,644
Brighton, AL 35020 • 4,518
Brighton, CO 80601 • 14,203
Brighton, IL 62012 • 2,270
Brighton, MI 48116 • 5,686
Brighton, NY 14610 • 34,455
Brilliant, OH 43913 • 1,672
Brillion, WI 54110 • 2,840
Brinkley, AR 72021 • 4,234
Briscoe □, TX • 1,971
Bristol, CT 06010–11 • 60,640
Bristol, IN 46507 • 1,133
Bristol, NH 03222 • 1,483
Bristol, RI 02809 • 21,625
Bristol, TN 37620–25 • 23,421
Bristol, VT 05443 • 1,801
Bristol, VA 24201–03 • 18,426
Bristol □, MA • 506,325
Bristol □, RI • 48,859
Bristol [Township], PA 19007 • 58,773
Bristow, OK 74010 • 4,062
Britt, IA 50423 • 2,133
Britton, SD 57430 • 1,394
Broadalbin, NY 12025 • 1,397
Broad Brook, CT 06016 • 1,280
Broadkill Beach, DE 19968 • 390
Broadus, MT 59317 • 572
Broadview, IL 60153 • 8,713
Broadview Heights, OH 44141 • 12,219
Broadview Park, FL 33314 • 6,109
Broadwater □, MT • 3,318
Broadway, VA 22815 • 1,209
Brockport, NY 14420 • 8,749
Brockton, MA 02401–05 • 92,788
Brockway, PA 15824 • 2,207
Brocton, NY 14716 • 1,387
Brodhead, KY 40409 • 1,140
Brodhead, WI 53520 • 3,165
Brodheadsville, PA 18322 • 1,500
Broken Arrow, OK 74011–14 • 58,043
Broken Bow, NE 68822 • 3,778
Broken Bow, OK 74728 • 3,961
Bronson, MI 49028 • 2,342
Bronx □, NY • 1,203,789
Bronxville, NY 10708 • 6,028
Brooke □, WV • 26,992
Brookfield, CT 06804 • 1,500
Brookfield, IL 60513 • 18,876
Brookfield, MA 01506 • 2,968
Brookfield, MO 64628 • 4,888
Brookfield, VA 22021 • 2,100
Brookfield, WI 53005 • 35,184
Brookfield Center, CT 06804 • 1,400
Brookhaven, MS 39601 • 10,243
Brookhaven, PA 19015 • 8,567
Brookhaven, WV 26505 • 3,836
Brookings, OR 97415 • 4,400
Brookings, SD 57006 • 16,270
Brookings □, SD • 25,207
Brooklawn, NJ 08030 • 1,805
Brookline, MA 02146 • 54,718
Brooklyn, CT 06234 • 1,400
Brooklyn, IN 46111 • 1,162
Brooklyn, IA 52211 • 1,439
Brooklyn, OH 44144 • 11,706
Brooklyn, SC 29210 • 1,850
Brooklyn Center, MN 55429 • 28,887
Brooklyn Park, MD 21225 • 10,987
Brooklyn Park, MN 55443 • 56,381
Brookneal, VA 24528 • 1,344
Brook Park, OH 44142 • 22,865
Brookport, IL 62910 • 1,070
Brooks, KY 40109 • 2,464
Brooks □, GA • 15,398
Brooks □, TX • 8,204
Brookshire, TX 77423 • 2,922
Brookside, AL 35036 • 1,365
Brookside, DE 19713 • 15,307
Brookston, IN 47923 • 1,804
Brooksville, FL 34601–14 • 7,440
Brooksville, MS 39739 • 1,098
Brookville, IN 47012 • 2,529
Brookville, NY 11545 • 3,716
Brookville, OH 45309 • 4,621
Brookville, PA 15825 • 4,184
Brookwood, NJ 08527 • 5,500
Broomall, PA 19008 • 10,930
Broome □, NY • 212,160
Broomfield, CO 80020–21 • 24,638
Broussard, LA 70518 • 3,213
Broward □, FL • 1,255,488
Browardale, FL 33311 • 6,257
Brown □, IL • 5,836
Brown □, IN • 14,080
Brown □, KS • 11,128
Brown □, MN • 26,984
Brown □, NE • 3,657
Brown □, OH • 34,966
Brown □, SD • 35,580
Brown □, TX • 34,371
Brown □, WI • 194,594
Brown City, MI 48416 • 1,244
Brown Deer, WI 53209 • 12,236
Brownfield, TX 79316 • 9,560
Brownfields, LA 70811 • 5,229
Browning, MT 59417 • 1,170
Brownsburg, IN 46112 • 7,628
Browns Mills, NJ 08015 • 11,429
Brownstown, IN 47220 • 2,872
Brownsville, FL 33142 • 15,607
Brownsville, OR 97327 • 1,281
Brownsville, PA 15417 • 3,164
Brownsville, TN 38012 • 10,019
Brownsville, TX 78520–26 • 98,962
Brownville, LA 71291 • 1,700
Brownville, NY 13615 • 1,138
Brownwood, TX 76803–04 • 18,387
Broxton, GA 31519 • 1,211
Broyhill Park, VA 22042 • 3,600
Bruce, MS 38915 • 2,127
Bruceton, TN 38317 • 1,586
Brule □, SD • 5,485
Brundidge, AL 36010 • 2,472
Brunswick, GA 31520–22 • 16,433
Brunswick, ME 04011 • 14,683
Brunswick, MD 21716 • 5,117
Brunswick, MO 65236 • 1,074
Brunswick, OH 44212 • 28,230
Brunswick □, NC • 50,985
Brunswick □, VA • 15,987
Brush, CO 80723 • 4,165
Brusly, LA 70719 • 1,824
Bryan, OH 43506 • 8,348
Bryan, TX 77801–06 • 55,002
Bryan □, GA • 15,438
Bryan □, OK • 32,089
Bryans Road, MD 20616 • 3,809
Bryant, AR 72022 • 5,269
Bryantville, MA 02327 • 1,800
Bryn Mawr, WA 98178 • 1,500
Bryson City, NC 28713 • 1,145
Buchanan, GA 30113 • 1,009
Buchanan, MI 49107 • 4,992
Buchanan, VA 24066 • 1,222
Buchanan □, IA • 20,844
Buchanan □, MO • 83,083
Buchanan □, VA • 31,333
Buckeye, AZ 85326 • 5,038
Buckeye Lake, OH 43008 • 2,986
Buckhannon, WV 26201 • 5,909
Buckingham □, VA • 12,873
Buckley, WA 98321 • 3,516
Bucknell Manor, VA 22307 • 2,300
Buckner, MO 64016 • 2,873
Bucks □, PA • 541,174
Bucksport, ME 04416 • 2,989
Bucksport, SC 29527 • 1,022
Bucyrus, OH 44820 • 13,496
Buda, TX 78610 • 1,795
Budd Lake 0L, NJ • 7,272
Buechel, KY 40218 • 7,081
Buena, NJ 08310 • 4,441
Buena Park, CA 90620–24 • 68,784
Buena Vista, CO 81211 • 1,752
Buena Vista, FL 34691 • 3,000
Buena Vista, GA 31803 • 1,472
Buena Vista, VA 24416 • 6,406
Buena Vista □, IA • 19,965
Buffalo, IA 52728 • 1,260
Buffalo, MN 55313 • 6,856
Buffalo, MO 65622 • 2,414
Buffalo, NY 14201–40 • 328,123
Buffalo, OK 73834 • 1,312
Buffalo, SC 29321 • 1,569
Buffalo, TX 75831 • 1,555
Buffalo, WY 82834 • 3,302
Buffalo □, NE • 37,447
Buffalo □, SD • 1,759
Buffalo □, WI • 13,584
Buffalo Center, IA 50424 • 1,081
Buffalo Grove, IL 60089 • 36,427
Buford, GA 30518 • 8,771
Buhl, ID 83316 • 3,516
Buhler, KS 67522 • 1,277
Buies Creek, NC 27506 • 2,085
Bullhead City, AZ 86430 • 21,951
Bullitt □, KY • 47,567
Bulloch □, GA • 43,125
Bullock □, AL • 11,042
Bull Shoals, AR 72619 • 1,534
Buna, TX 77612 • 1,900
Bunche Park, FL 33054 • 4,000
Buncombe □, NC • 174,821
Bunker Hill, IL 62014 • 1,722
Bunker Hill, OR 97420 • 1,242
Bunkerville, NV 89007 • 300
Bunkie, LA 71322 • 5,044
Bunnell, FL 32110 • 1,873
Buras, LA 70041 • 1,600
Burbank, CA 91501–10 • 93,643
Burbank, IL 60459 • 27,600
Burdickville, RI 02808 • 500
Bureau □, IL • 35,688
Burgaw, NC 28425 • 1,807
Burgettstown, PA 15021 • 1,634
Burgin, KY 40310 • 1,009
Burien, WA 98062 • 25,089
Burkburnett, TX 76354 • 10,145
Burke, SD 57523 • 756
Burke, VA 22015 • 57,734
Burke □, GA • 20,579
Burke □, NC • 75,744
Burke □, ND • 3,002
Burkesville, KY 42717 • 1,815
Burleigh □, ND • 60,131
Burleson, TX 76028 • 16,113
Burleson □, TX • 13,625
Burley, ID 83318 • 8,702
Burlingame, CA 94010–11 • 26,801
Burlingame, KS 66413 • 1,074
Burlington, CO 80807 • 2,941
Burlington, IA 52601 • 27,208
Burlington, KS 66839 • 2,735
Burlington, KY 41005 • 6,070
Burlington, MA 01803 • 23,302
Burlington, NJ 08016 • 9,835
Burlington, NC 27215–17 • 39,498
Burlington, ND 58722 • 995
Burlington, VT 05401–04 • 39,127
Burlington, WA 98233 • 4,349
Burlington, WI 53105 • 8,855
Burlington □, NJ • 395,066
Burnet, TX 78611 • 3,423
Burnet □, TX • 22,677
Burnett □, WI • 13,084
Burney, CA 96013 • 3,423
Burnham, PA 17009 • 2,197
Burns, OR 97720 • 2,913
Burns, TN 37029 • 1,127
Burns, WY 82053 • 254
Burns Flat, OK 73624 • 1,027
Burnsville, MN 55337 • 51,288
Burnsville, NC 28714 • 1,482
Burnt Hills, NY 12027 • 1,550
Burr Ridge, IL 60521 • 7,669
Burt □, NE • 7,868
Burton, MI 48509 • 27,617
Burton, OH 44021 • 1,349
Burton, SC 29902 • 6,917
Burtonsville, MD 20866 • 5,853
Burwell, NE 68823 • 1,278
Bushnell, FL 33513 • 1,998
Bushnell, IL 61422 • 3,288
Butler, AL 36904 • 1,872
Butler, GA 31006 • 1,673
Butler, IN 46721 • 2,601
Butler, MO 64730 • 4,099
Butler, NJ 07405 • 7,392
Butler, PA 16001–03 • 15,714
Butler, WI 53007 • 2,079
Butler □, AL • 21,892
Butler □, IA • 15,731
Butler □, KS • 50,580
Butler □, KY • 11,245
Butler □, MO • 38,765
Butler □, NE • 8,601
Butler □, OH • 291,479
Butler □, PA • 152,013
Butner, NC 27509 • 4,679
Butte, MT 59701–03 • 33,336
Butte □, CA • 182,120
Butte □, ID • 2,918
Butte □, SD • 7,914
Buttonwillow, CA 93206 • 1,301
Butts □, GA • 15,326
Buxton, NC 27920 • 1,300
Buzzards Bay, MA 02532 • 3,250
Byers, CO 80103 • 1,065
Byesville, OH 43723 • 2,435
Byfield, MA 01922 • 1,200
Bylas, AZ 85530 • 1,219
Byron, GA 31008 • 2,276
Byron, IL 61010 • 2,284
Byron, MN 55920 • 2,441
Byron, WY 82412 • 470

C

Cabarrus □, NC • 98,935
Cabell □, WV • 96,827
Cabin Creek, WV 25035 • 1,300
Cabin John, MD 20818 • 1,690
Cabool, MO 65689 • 2,006
Cabot, AR 72023 • 8,319
Cache, OK 73527 • 2,251
Cache □, UT • 70,183
Caddo □, LA • 248,253
Caddo □, OK • 29,550
Cadillac, MI 49601 • 10,104
Cadiz, KY 42211 • 2,148
Cadiz, OH 43907 • 3,439
Cadott, WI 54727 • 1,328
Cahaba Heights, AL 35243 • 4,778
Cahokia, IL 62206 • 17,550
Cairnbrook, PA 15924 • 1,081
Cairo, GA 31728 • 9,035
Cairo, IL 62914 • 4,846
Cairo, NY 12413 • 1,273
Calais, ME 04619 • 3,963
Calaveras □, CA • 31,998
Calavo Gardens, CA 91941 • 6,100
Calcasieu □, LA • 168,134
Calcutta, OH 43920 • 1,212
Caldwell, ID 83605–06 • 18,400
Caldwell, KS 67022 • 1,351
Caldwell, NJ 07006 • 7,549
Caldwell, OH 43724 • 1,786
Caldwell, TX 77836 • 3,181
Caldwell □, KY • 13,232
Caldwell □, LA • 9,810
Caldwell □, MO • 8,380
Caldwell □, NC • 70,709
Caldwell □, TX • 26,392
Caledonia, MN 55921 • 2,846
Caledonia, NY 14423 • 2,262
Caledonia □, VT • 27,846
Calera, AL 35040 • 2,136
Calera, OK 74730 • 1,536
Calexico, CA 92231–32 • 18,633
Calhoun, GA 30701 • 7,135
Calhoun □, AL • 116,034
Calhoun □, AR • 5,826
Calhoun □, FL • 11,011
Calhoun □, GA • 5,013
Calhoun □, IL • 5,322
Calhoun □, IA • 11,508
Calhoun □, MI • 135,982
Calhoun □, MS • 14,908
Calhoun □, SC • 12,753
Calhoun □, TX • 19,053
Calhoun □, WV • 7,885
Calhoun City, MS 38916 • 1,838
Calhoun Falls, SC 29628 • 2,328
Caliente, NV 89008 • 1,111
Califon, NJ 07830 • 1,073
California, MD 20619 • 7,626
California, MO 65018 • 3,465
California, PA 15419 • 5,748
Calipatria, CA 92233 • 2,690
Calistoga, CA 94515 • 4,468
Callahan □, TX • 11,859
Callaway, FL 32401 • 12,253
Callaway □, MO • 32,809
Calloway □, KY • 30,735
Calmar, IA 52132 • 1,026
Calumet □, WI • 34,291
Calumet City, IL 60409 • 37,840
Calumet Park, IL 60643 • 8,418
Calvert, TX 77837 • 1,536
Calvert □, MD • 51,372
Calvert City, KY 42029 • 2,531
Calverton, MD 20705 • 12,046

United States Populations and ZIP Codes

Calverton Park, MO 63136 • *1,404*
Camanche, IA 52730 • *4,436*
Camarillo, CA 93010–11 • *52,303*
Camas, WA 98607 • *6,442*
Camas □, ID • *727*
Cambria, CA 93428 • *5,382*
Cambria □, PA • *163,029*
Cambrian Park, CA 95124 • *2,998*
Cambridge, IL 61238 • *2,124*
Cambridge, MD 21613 • *11,514*
Cambridge, MA 02138 • *95,802*
Cambridge, MN 55008 • *5,094*
Cambridge, NE 69022 • *1,107*
Cambridge, NY 12816 • *1,906*
Cambridge, OH 43725 • *11,748*
Cambridge City, IN 47327 • *2,091*
Cambridge Springs, PA 16403 • *1,837*
Camden, AL 36726 • *2,414*
Camden, AR 71701 • *14,380*
Camden, DE 19934 • *1,899*
Camden, ME 04843 • *4,022*
Camden, NJ 08101–10 • *87,492*
Camden, NY 13316 • *2,552*
Camden, OH 45311 • *2,210*
Camden, SC 29020 • *6,696*
Camden, TN 38320 • *3,643*
Camden □, GA • *30,167*
Camden □, MO • *27,495*
Camden □, NJ • *502,824*
Camden □, NC • *5,904*
Camdenton, MO 65020 • *2,561*
Camelot, WA 98002 • *4,900*
Cameron, LA 70631 • *2,041*
Cameron, MO 64429 • *4,831*
Cameron, TX 76520 • *5,580*
Cameron, WV 26033 • *1,177*
Cameron, WI 54822 • *1,273*
Cameron □, LA • *9,260*
Cameron □, PA • *5,913*
Cameron □, TX • *260,120*
Cameron Park, CA 95682 • *11,897*
Camilla, GA 31730 • *5,008*
Camino, CA 95709 • *1,500*
Camp □, TX • *9,904*
Campbell, CA 95008–09 • *36,048*
Campbell, FL 34746 • *3,884*
Campbell, MO 63933 • *2,165*
Campbell, OH 44405 • *10,038*
Campbell □, KY • *83,866*
Campbell □, SD • *1,965*
Campbell □, TN • *35,079*
Campbell □, VA • *47,572*
Campbell □, WY • *29,370*
Campbellsport, WI 53010 • *1,732*
Campbellsville, KY 42718–19 • *9,577*
Camp Hill, AL 36850 • *1,415*
Camp Hill, PA 17011 • *7,831*
Camp Point, IL 62320 • *1,230*
Camp Springs, MD 20748 • *16,392*
Camp Verde, AZ 86322 • *6,243*
Canaan, CT 06018 • *1,194*
Canadensis, PA 18325 • *1,200*
Canadian, TX 79014 • *2,417*
Canadian □, OK • *74,409*
Canajoharie, NY 13317 • *2,278*
Canal Fulton, OH 44614 • *4,157*
Canal Winchester, OH 43110 • *2,617*
Canandaigua, NY 14424–25 • *10,725*
Canastota, NY 13032 • *4,673*
Canby, MN 56220 • *1,826*
Canby, OR 97013 • *8,983*
Candler □, GA • *7,744*
Candlewood Isle, CT 06812 • *1,100*
Candlewood Shores, CT 06804 • *1,620*
Cando, ND 58324 • *1,564*
Caney, KS 67333 • *2,062*
Canfield, OH 44406 • *5,409*
Canisteo, NY 14823 • *2,421*
Cannelton, IN 47520 • *1,786*
Cannon □, TN • *10,467*
Cannon Beach, OR 97110 • *1,221*
Cannondale, CT 06897 • *1,500*
Cannon Falls, MN 55009 • *3,232*
Canon City, CO 81212 • *12,687*
Canonsburg, PA 15317 • *9,200*
Canterbury, DE 19943 • *500*
Canton, CT 06019 • *1,563*
Canton, GA 30114 • *4,817*
Canton, IL 61520 • *13,922*
Canton, MA 02021 • *18,182*
Canton, MI 48187 • *57,047*
Canton, MS 39046 • *10,062*
Canton, MO 63435 • *2,623*
Canton, NY 13617 • *6,379*
Canton, NC 28716 • *3,790*
Canton, OH 44701–99 • *84,161*
Canton, PA 17724 • *1,966*
Canton, SD 57013 • *2,787*
Canton, TX 75103 • *2,949*
Cantonment, FL 32533 • *3,200*
Canutillo, TX 79835 • *4,500*
Canyon, TX 79015 • *11,365*
Canyon □, ID • *90,076*
Canyon Lake, CA 92380 • *7,938*
Canyon Lake, TX 78130 • *9,975*
Canyonville, OR 97417 • *1,219*
Capac, MI 48014 • *1,583*
Cape Canaveral, FL 32920 • *8,014*
Cape Charles, VA 23310 • *1,398*
Cape Coral, FL 33904 • *74,991*
Cape Elizabeth, ME 04107 • *8,854*
Cape Girardeau, MO 63701–02 • *34,438*
Cape Girardeau □, MO • *61,633*
Cape May, NJ 08204 • *4,668*
Cape May □, NJ • *95,089*
Cape May Court House, NJ 08210 • *4,426*
Cape Saint Claire, MD 21401 • *7,878*
Capitola, CA 95010 • *10,171*
Capitol Heights, MD 20743 • *3,633*
Capitol View, SC 29209 • *10,456*
Captain Cook, HI 96704 • *2,595*
Captiva, FL 33924 • *1,200*
Caraway, AR 72419 • *1,178*
Carbon □, MT • *8,080*
Carbon □, PA • *56,846*
Carbon □, UT • *20,228*
Carbon □, WY • *16,659*
Carbondale, CO 81623 • *3,004*
Carbondale, IL 62901–03 • *27,033*
Carbondale, KS 66414 • *1,526*
Carbondale, PA 18407 • *10,664*
Carbon Hill, AL 35549 • *2,115*
Cardington, OH 43315 • *1,770*
Carencro, LA 70520 • *5,429*
Carey, OH 43316 • *3,684*
Caribou, ME 04736 • *9,415*
Caribou □, ID • *6,963*
Carle Place, NY 11514 • *5,107*
Carleton, MI 48117 • *2,770*
Carlin, NV 89822 • *2,220*
Carlinville, IL 62626 • *5,416*
Carlisle, AR 72024 • *2,253*
Carlisle, IA 50047 • *3,241*
Carlisle, KY 40311 • *1,639*
Carlisle, OH 45005 • *4,872*
Carlisle, PA 17013 • *18,419*
Carlisle □, KY • *5,238*
Carl Junction, MO 64834 • *4,123*
Carlsbad, CA 92008–09 • *63,126*
Carlsbad, NM 88220–21 • *24,952*
Carlstadt, NJ 07072 • *5,510*
Carlton, OR 97111 • *1,289*
Carlton □, MN • *29,259*
Carlyle, IL 62231 • *3,474*
Carmel, CA 93921–23 • *4,239*
Carmel, IN 46032 • *25,380*
Carmel, NY 10512 • *3,395*
Carmi, IL 62821 • *5,564*
Carmichael, CA 95608–09 • *48,702*
Carnation, WA 98014 • *1,243*
Carnegie, OK 73015 • *1,593*
Carnegie, PA 15106 • *9,278*
Carney, MD 21234 • *25,578*
Carneys Point, NJ 08069 • *7,686*
Carnot, PA 15108 • *4,750*
Caro, MI 48723 • *4,054*
Carol City, FL 33055 • *53,331*
Caroleen, NC 28019 • *1,100*
Carolina Beach, NC 28428 • *3,630*
Caroline □, MD • *27,035*
Caroline □, VA • *19,217*
Carol Stream, IL 60188 • *31,716*
Carpentersville, IL 60110 • *23,049*
Carpinteria, CA 93013–14 • *13,747*
Carrabelle, FL 32322 • *1,200*
Carrboro, NC 27510 • *11,553*
Carrier Mills, IL 62917 • *1,991*
Carrington, ND 58421 • *2,267*
Carrizo Springs, TX 78834 • *5,745*
Carrizozo, NM 88301 • *1,075*
Carroll, IA 51401 • *9,579*
Carroll □, AR • *18,654*
Carroll □, GA • *71,422*
Carroll □, IL • *16,805*
Carroll □, IN • *18,809*
Carroll □, IA • *21,423*
Carroll □, KY • *9,292*
Carroll □, MD • *123,372*
Carroll □, MS • *9,237*
Carroll □, MO • *10,748*
Carroll □, NH • *35,410*
Carroll □, OH • *26,521*
Carroll □, TN • *27,514*
Carroll □, VA • *26,594*
Carrollton, AL 35447 • *1,170*
Carrollton, GA 30117 • *16,029*
Carrollton, IL 62016 • *2,507*
Carrollton, KY 41008 • *3,715*
Carrollton, MI 48724 • *6,521*
Carrollton, MO 64633 • *4,406*
Carrollton, OH 44615 • *3,042*
Carrollton, TX 75006–08 • *82,169*
Carrolltown, PA 15722 • *1,286*
Carrollwood, FL 33618 • *11,400*
Carson, CA 90749 • *83,995*
Carson □, TX • *6,576*
Carson City, MI 48811 • *1,158*
Carson City, NV 89701–21 • *40,443*
Carter □, KY • *24,340*
Carter □, MO • *5,515*
Carter □, MT • *1,503*
Carter □, OK • *42,919*
Carter □, TN • *51,505*
Carteret, NJ 07008 • *19,025*
Carteret □, NC • *52,556*
Carter Lake, IA 51510 • *3,200*
Cartersville, GA 30120 • *12,035*
Carterville, IL 62918 • *3,630*
Carterville, MO 64835 • *2,013*
Carthage, IL 62321 • *2,657*
Carthage, MS 39051 • *3,819*
Carthage, MO 64836 • *10,747*
Carthage, NY 13619 • *4,344*
Carthage, TN 37030 • *2,386*
Carthage, TX 75633 • *6,496*
Caruthersville, MO 63830 • *7,389*
Carver, MA 02330 • *1,500*
Carver □, MN • *47,915*
Carver Ranch Estates, FL 33023 • *5,600*
Carville, LA 70721 • *1,108*
Cary, IL 60013 • *10,043*
Cary, NC 27511 • *43,858*
Caryville, TN 37714 • *1,751*
Casa de Oro, CA 92077 • *9,500*
Casa Grande, AZ 85222 • *19,082*
Casas Adobes, AZ 85704 • *12,155*
Cascade, CO 80809 • *1,000*
Cascade, ID 83611 • *877*
Cascade, IA 52033 • *1,812*
Cascade, MT 59421 • *729*
Cascade □, MT • *77,691*
Cascade Vista, WA 98058 • *7,800*
Casey, IL 62420 • *2,914*
Casey □, KY • *14,211*
Cashion, AZ 85329 • *3,014*
Cashmere, WA 98815 • *2,544*
Casper, WY 82601–15 • *46,742*
Caspian, MI 49915 • *1,031*
Cass □, IL • *13,437*
Cass □, IN • *38,413*
Cass □, IA • *15,128*
Cass □, MI • *49,477*
Cass □, MN • *21,791*
Cass □, MO • *63,808*
Cass □, NE • *21,318*
Cass □, ND • *102,874*
Cass □, TX • *29,982*
Cass City, MI 48726 • *2,276*
Casselberry, FL 32707–08 • *18,911*
Casselton, ND 58012 • *1,601*
Cassia □, ID • *19,532*
Cassopolis, MI 49031 • *1,822*
Cassville, MO 65625 • *2,371*
Cassville, WI 53806 • *1,144*
Castanea, PA 17726 • *1,123*
Castile, NY 14427 • *1,078*
Castle Dale, UT 84513 • *1,704*
Castle Hayne, NC 28429 • *1,182*
Castle Hills, DE 19720 • *1,475*
Castle Park, CA 92011 • *6,300*
Castle Point, MO 63136 • *7,800*
Castle Rock, CO 80104 • *8,708*
Castle Rock, WA 98611 • *2,067*
Castle Shannon, PA 15234 • *9,135*
Castleton, VT 05735 • *600*
Castleton on Hudson, NY 12033 • *1,491*
Castlewood, VA 24224 • *2,110*
Castro □, TX • *9,070*
Castro Valley, CA 94546 • *48,619*
Castroville, TX 78009 • *2,159*
Caswell □, NC • *20,693*
Catahoula □, LA • *11,065*
Catalina Foothills, AZ 85718 • *1,470*
Catasauqua, PA 18032 • *6,662*
Cataumet, MA 02534 • *1,500*
Catawba □, NC • *118,412*
Catawissa, PA 17820 • *1,683*
Cathedral City, CA 92234–35 • *30,085*
Catlettsburg, KY 41129 • *2,231*
Catlin, IL 61817 • *2,173*
Catonsville, MD 21228 • *35,233*
Catoosa, OK 74015 • *2,954*
Catoosa □, GA • *42,464*
Catron □, NM • *2,563*
Catskill, NY 12414 • *4,690*
Cattaraugus, NY 14719 • *1,100*
Cattaraugus □, NY • *84,234*
Cavalier, ND 58220 • *1,508*
Cavalier □, ND • *6,064*
Cave City, AR 72521 • *1,503*
Cave City, KY 42127 • *1,953*
Cave Creek, AZ 85331 • *2,925*
Cave Junction, OR 97523 • *1,126*
Cave Spring, VA 24018 • *24,053*
Cavetown, MD 21720 • *1,533*
Cayce, SC 29033 • *11,163*
Cayuga, IN 47928 • *1,083*
Cayuga □, NY • *82,313*
Cayuga Heights, NY 14850 • *3,457*
Cazenovia, NY 13035 • *3,007*
Cecil □, MD • *71,347*
Cedar □, IA • *17,381*
Cedar □, MO • *12,093*
Cedar □, NE • *10,131*
Cedar Bluff, AL 35959 • *1,174*
Cedar Bluff Two, TN 37722 • *2,000*
Cedarburg, WI 53012 • *9,895*
Cedar City, UT 84720–22 • *13,443*
Cedar Crest, NM 87008 • *1,200*
Cedaredge, CO 81413 • *1,380*
Cedar Falls, IA 50613 • *34,298*
Cedar Grove, NJ 07009 • *12,053*
Cedar Grove, WV 25039 • *1,213*
Cedar Grove, WI 53013 • *1,521*
Cedar Hill, MO 63016 • *1,966*
Cedar Hill, TX 75104 • *19,976*
Cedar Hills, OR 97005 • *9,294*
Cedarhurst, NY 11516 • *5,716*
Cedar Lake, IN 46303 • *8,885*
Cedar Rapids, IA 52401–10 • *108,751*
Cedar Springs, MI 49319 • *2,600*
Cedartown, GA 30125 • *7,978*
Cedarville, NJ 08311 • *1,100*
Cedarville, OH 45314 • *3,210*
Celina, OH 45822 • *9,650*
Celina, TN 38551 • *1,493*
Celina, TX 75009 • *1,737*
Celoron, NY 14720 • *1,232*
Cementon, PA 18052 • *1,050*
Center, CO 81125 • *1,963*
Center, ND 58530 • *826*
Center, TX 75935 • *4,950*
Centerburg, OH 43011 • *1,323*
Centereach, NY 11720 • *26,720*
Center Line, MI 48015 • *9,026*
Center Moriches, NY 11934 • *5,987*
Center Point, AL 35215 • *22,657*
Center Point, IA 52213 • *1,693*
Centerville, IN 47330 • *2,398*
Centerville, IA 52544 • *5,936*
Centerville, MA 02632 • *9,190*
Centerville, OH 45459 • *21,082*
Centerville, PA 15417 • *3,842*
Centerville, SD 57014 • *887*
Centerville, TN 37033 • *3,616*
Centerville, UT 84014 • *11,500*
Central, NM 88026 • *1,835*
Central, SC 29630 • *2,438*
Central City, CO 80427 • *335*
Central City, IL 62801 • *1,390*
Central City, IA 52214 • *1,063*
Central City, KY 42330 • *4,979*
Central City, NE 68826 • *2,868*
Central City, PA 15926 • *1,246*
Central Falls, RI 02863 • *17,637*
Central Heights, AZ 85501 • *1,500*
Centralia, IL 62801 • *14,274*
Centralia, MO 65240 • *3,414*
Centralia, WA 98531 • *12,101*
Central Islip, NY 11722 • *26,028*
Central Park, WA 98520 • *2,669*
Central Point, OR 97502 • *7,509*
Central Square, NY 13036 • *1,671*
Central Valley, CA 96019 • *4,340*
Central Valley, NY 10917 • *1,929*
Central Village, CT 06332 • *1,600*
Centre, AL 35960 • *2,893*
Centre □, PA • *123,786*
Centre City, NJ 08051 • *2,070*
Centre Hall, PA 16828 • *1,203*
Centreville, AL 35042 • *2,508*
Centreville, IL 62207 • *7,489*
Centreville, MD 21617 • *2,097*
Centreville, MI 49032 • *1,516*
Centreville, MS 39631 • *1,771*
Centreville, VA 22020 • *26,585*
Century, FL 32535 • *1,989*
Century Village, FL 33409 • *8,363*
Ceredo, WV 25507 • *1,916*
Ceres, CA 95307 • *26,314*
Cerritos, CA 90703 • *53,240*
Cerro Gordo, IL 61818 • *1,436*
Cerro Gordo □, IA • *46,733*
Chadbourn, NC 28431 • *2,005*
Chadds Ford, PA 19317 • *1,200*
Chadron, NE 69337 • *5,588*
Chadwicks, NY 13319 • *2,000*
Chaffee, MO 63740 • *3,059*
Chaffee □, CO • *12,684*
Chaffin, MA 01520 • *3,980*
Chagrin Falls, OH 44022 • *4,146*
Chalfonte, DE 19810 • *1,740*
Challis, ID 83226 • *1,073*
Chalmette, LA 70043–44 • *31,860*
Chama, NM 87520 • *1,048*
Chamberlain, SD 57325 • *2,347*
Chambers □, AL • *36,876*
Chambers □, TX • *20,088*
Chambersburg, PA 17201 • *16,647*
Chamblee, GA 30341 • *7,668*
Champaign, IL 61820–21 • *63,502*
Champaign □, IL • *173,025*
Champaign □, OH • *36,019*
Champion, OH 44481 • *5,270*
Champlain, NY 12919 • *1,273*
Champlin, MN 55316 • *16,849*
Chandler, AZ 85224–27 • *90,533*
Chandler, IN 47610 • *3,099*
Chandler, OK 74834 • *2,596*
Chandler, TX 75758 • *1,630*
Chandler Heights, AZ 85227 • *1,000*
Chanhassen, MN 55317 • *11,732*
Channahon, IL 60410 • *4,266*
Channel Lake, IL 60002 • *1,660*
Channelview, TX 77530 • *25,564*
Chantilly, VA 22021–22 • *29,337*
Chanute, KS 66720 • *9,488*
Chapel Hill, NC 27514–16 • *38,719*
Chapel Square, VA 22003 • *2,400*
Chapman, KS 67431 • *1,264*
Chapmanville, WV 25508 • *1,110*
Chappaqua, NY 10514 • *6,380*
Chardon, OH 44024 • *4,446*
Chariton, IA 50049 • *4,616*
Chariton □, MO • *9,202*
Charleroi, PA 15022 • *5,014*
Charles □, MD • *101,154*
Charles City, IA 50616 • *7,878*
Charles City □, VA • *6,282*
Charles Mix □, SD • *9,131*
Charleston, AR 72933 • *2,128*
Charleston, IL 61920 • *20,398*
Charleston, MS 38921 • *2,328*
Charleston, MO 63834 • *5,085*
Charleston, SC 29401–22 • *80,414*
Charleston, WV 25301–75 • *57,287*
Charleston □, SC • *295,039*
Charlestown, IN 47111 • *5,889*
Charlestown, NH 03603 • *1,173*
Charlestown, RI 02813 • *1,500*
Charles Town, WV 25414 • *3,122*
Charlevoix, MI 49720 • *3,116*
Charlevoix □, MI • *21,468*
Charlotte, MI 48813 • *8,083*
Charlotte, NC 28201–41 • *395,934*
Charlotte, TX 78011 • *1,475*
Charlotte □, FL • *110,975*
Charlotte □, VA • *11,688*
Charlotte Hall, MD 20622 • *1,992*
Charlotte Harbor, FL 33980 • *3,327*
Charlottesville, VA 22901–08 • *40,341*
Charlton □, GA • *8,496*
Charlton City, MA 01508 • *1,400*
Charter Oak, CA 91724 • *8,858*
Chase □, KS • *3,021*
Chase □, NE • *4,381*
Chase City, VA 23924 • *2,442*
Chaska, MN 55318 • *11,339*
Chatfield, MN 55923 • *2,226*
Chatham, IL 62629 • *6,074*
Chatham, MA 02633 • *1,916*
Chatham, NJ 07928 • *8,007*
Chatham, NY 12037 • *1,920*
Chatham, VA 24531 • *1,354*
Chatham □, GA • *216,935*
Chatham □, NC • *38,759*
Chatom, AL 36518 • *1,094*
Chatsworth, GA 30705 • *2,865*
Chatsworth, IL 60921 • *1,186*
Chattahoochee, FL 32324 • *4,382*
Chattahoochee □, GA • *16,934*
Chattanooga, TN 37401–22 • *152,466*
Chattaroy, WV 25667 • *1,182*
Chattooga □, GA • *22,242*
Chautauqua □, KS • *4,407*
Chautauqua □, NY • *141,895*
Chauvin, LA 70344 • *3,375*
Chaves □, NM • *57,849*
Chazy, NY 12921 • *1,000*
Cheatham □, TN • *27,140*
Cheboygan, MI 49721 • *4,999*
Cheboygan □, MI • *21,398*
Checotah, OK 74426 • *3,290*
Cheektowaga, NY 14225 • *84,387*
Chehalis, WA 98532 • *6,527*
Chelan, WA 98816 • *2,969*
Chelan □, WA • *52,250*
Chelmsford, MA 01824 • *32,388*
Chelsea, MA 02150 • *28,710*
Chelsea, MI 48118 • *3,772*
Chelsea, OK 74016 • *1,620*
Chelsea Estates, DE 19720 • *1,320*
Cheltenham Township, PA 19012 • *35,509*
Chemung □, NY • *95,195*
Chenango □, NY • *51,768*
Chenango Bridge, NY 13745 • *2,890*
Cheney, KS 67025 • *1,560*
Cheney, WA 99004 • *7,723*
Cheneyville, LA 71325 • *1,005*
Chenoa, IL 61726 • *1,732*
Chenoweth, OR 97058 • *3,246*
Chepachet, RI 02814 • *900*
Cheraw, SC 29520 • *5,505*
Cherokee, AL 35616 • *1,479*
Cherokee, IA 51012 • *6,026*
Cherokee, OK 73728 • *1,787*
Cherokee □, AL • *19,543*
Cherokee □, GA • *90,204*
Cherokee □, IA • *14,098*
Cherokee □, KS • *21,374*
Cherokee □, NC • *20,170*
Cherokee □, OK • *34,049*
Cherokee □, SC • *44,506*
Cherokee □, TX • *41,049*
Cherokee Village, AR 72525 • *3,200*
Cherry □, NE • *6,307*
Cherry Hill, NJ 08002–03 • *69,319*
Cherry Hills Village, CO 80110 • *5,245*
Cherryland, CA 94541 • *11,088*
Cherryvale, KS 67335 • *2,464*
Cherry Valley, CA 92223 • *5,945*
Cherry Valley, IL 61016 • *1,615*
Cherry Valley, MA 01611 • *1,120*
Cherryville, NC 28021 • *4,756*
Chesaning, MI 48616 • *2,567*
Chesapeake, OH 45619 • *1,073*
Chesapeake, VA 23320–28 • *151,976*
Chesapeake, WV 25315 • *1,896*
Chesapeake Beach, MD 20732 • *2,403*
Cheshire, CT 06410 • *25,684*
Cheshire, MA 01225 • *1,100*
Cheshire □, NH • *70,121*
Chesilhurst, NJ 08089 • *1,526*
Chesnee, SC 29323 • *1,280*
Chester, CA 96020 • *2,082*
Chester, CT 06412 • *1,563*
Chester, IL 62233 • *8,194*
Chester, MT 59522 • *942*
Chester, NJ 07930 • *1,214*
Chester, NY 10918 • *3,270*
Chester, PA 19013–16 • *41,856*
Chester, SC 29706 • *7,158*
Chester, VT 05143 • *550*
Chester, VA 23831 • *14,896*
Chester, WV 26034 • *2,905*
Chester □, PA • *376,396*
Chester □, SC • *32,170*
Chester □, TN • *12,819*
Chester Depot, VT 05144 • *500*
Chesterfield, IN 46017 • *2,730*
Chesterfield, SC 29709 • *1,373*
Chesterfield □, SC • *38,577*
Chesterfield □, VA • *209,274*
Chesterton, IN 46304 • *9,124*
Chestertown, MD 21620 • *4,005*
Chester Township, PA 19013 • *5,399*
Chestnut Hill Estates, DE 19713 • *1,730*
Chestnut Ridge, NY 10952 • *7,517*
Cheswick, PA 15024 • *1,971*
Cheswold, DE 19936 • *321*
Chetek, WI 54728 • *1,953*
Chetopa, KS 67336 • *1,357*
Chevak, AK 99563 • *598*
Cheverly, MD 20785 • *6,023*
Cheviot, OH 45211 • *9,616*
Chevy Chase, MD 20815 • *8,559*
Chewelah, WA 99109 • *1,945*
Cheyenne, WY 82001–09 • *50,008*
Cheyenne □, CO • *2,397*
Cheyenne □, KS • *3,243*
Cheyenne □, NE • *9,494*
Cheyenne Wells, CO 80810 • *1,128*
Chicago, IL 60601–66 • *2,783,726*
Chicago Heights, IL 60411 • *33,072*
Chicago Ridge, IL 60415 • *13,643*
Chickamauga, GA 30707 • *2,149*
Chickasaw, AL 36611 • *6,649*
Chickasaw □, IA • *13,295*
Chickasaw □, MS • *18,085*
Chickasha, OK 73018 • *14,988*
Chico, CA 95926–28 • *40,079*
Chicopee, MA 01013–22 • *56,632*
Chicora, PA 16025 • *1,058*
Chiefland, FL 32626 • *1,917*
Childersburg, AL 35044 • *4,579*
Childress, TX 79201 • *5,055*
Childress □, TX • *5,953*
Chilhowie, VA 24319 • *1,971*
Chili Center, NY 14624 • *4,360*
Chillicothe, IL 61523 • *5,959*
Chillicothe, MO 64601 • *8,804*
Chillicothe, OH 45601 • *21,923*
Chillum, MD 20783 • *31,309*
Chilton, WI 53014 • *3,240*
Chilton □, AL • *32,458*
Chimayo, NM 87522 • *2,789*
China Grove, NC 28023 • *2,732*
Chincoteague, VA 23336 • *3,572*
Chinle, AZ 86503 • *5,059*
Chino, CA 91708–10 • *59,682*
Chinook, MT 59523 • *1,512*
Chino Valley, AZ 86323 • *4,837*
Chipley, FL 32428 • *3,866*
Chippewa □, MI • *34,604*
Chippewa □, MN • *13,228*
Chippewa □, WI • *52,360*
Chippewa Falls, WI 54729 • *12,727*
Chisago □, MN • *30,521*
Chisago City, MN 55013 • *2,009*
Chisholm, ME 04239 • *1,653*
Chisholm, MN 55719 • *5,290*
Chittenango, NY 13037 • *4,734*
Chittenden □, VT • *131,761*
Choctaw, OK 73020 • *8,545*
Choctaw □, AL • *16,018*
Choctaw □, MS • *9,071*
Choctaw □, OK • *15,302*
Choteau, MT 59422 • *1,741*
Chouteau, OK 74337 • *1,771*
Chouteau □, MT • *5,452*
Chowan □, NC • *13,506*
Chowchilla, CA 93610 • *5,930*
Chrisman, IL 61924 • *1,136*
Christian □, IL • *34,418*
Christian □, KY • *68,941*
Christian □, MO • *32,644*
Christiana, DE 19702 • *500*
Christiana, PA 17509 • *1,045*
Christiansburg, VA 24073 • *15,004*
Christmas, FL 32709 • *1,200*
Christopher, IL 62822 • *2,774*
Chubbuck, ID 83202 • *7,791*
Chugwater, WY 82210 • *192*
Chula Vista, CA 91909–15 • *135,163*
Church Hill, TN 37642 • *4,834*
Churchill, OH 44505 • *7,700*
Churchill □, NV • *17,938*
Church Point, LA 70525 • *4,677*
Churchville, NY 14428 • *1,731*
Churubusco, IN 46723 • *1,781*
Cibola □, NM • *23,794*
Cicero, IL 60650 • *67,436*
Cicero, IN 46034 • *3,268*
Cimarron, KS 67835 • *1,626*
Cimarron □, OK • *3,301*
Cimarron Hills, CO 80906 • *11,160*
Cincinnati, OH 45201–75 • *364,040*
Cinnaminson, NJ 08077 • *14,583*
Circle, MT 59215 • *805*
Circle Pines, MN 55014 • *4,704*
Circleville, OH 43113 • *11,666*
Cisco, TX 76437 • *3,813*
Citra, FL 32113 • *1,500*
Citronelle, AL 36522 • *3,671*
Citrus, CA 91702 • *9,481*

Citrus □, FL • 93,515
Citrus Heights, CA 95610–11 • 107,439
City Of Sunrise, FL 33313 • 64,407
City View, SC 29611 • 1,490
Clackamas, OR 97015 • 2,578
Clackamas □, OR • 278,850
Claiborne, LA 71291 • 8,300
Claiborne □, LA • 17,405
Claiborne □, MS • 11,370
Claiborne □, TN • 26,137
Clair-Mel City, FL 33619 • 7,000
Clairton, PA 15025 • 9,656
Clallam □, WA • 56,464
Clanton, AL 35045 • 7,669
Clara City, MN 56222 • 1,307
Clare, MI 48617 • 3,021
Clare □, MI • 24,952
Claremont, CA 91711 • 32,503
Claremont, NH 03743 • 13,902
Claremore, OK 74017–18 • 13,280
Clarence, MO 63437 • 1,026
Clarendon, AR 72029 • 2,072
Clarendon, TX 79226 • 2,067
Clarendon □, SC • 28,450
Clarendon Hills, IL 60514 • 6,994
Claridge, PA 15623 • 1,200
Clarinda, IA 51632 • 5,104
Clarion, IA 50525 • 2,703
Clarion, PA 16214 • 6,457
Clarion □, PA • 41,699
Clark, NJ 07066 • 14,629
Clark, SD 57225 • 1,292
Clark □, AR • 21,437
Clark □, ID • 762
Clark □, IL • 15,921
Clark □, IN • 87,777
Clark □, KS • 2,418
Clark □, KY • 29,496
Clark □, MO • 7,547
Clark □, NV • 741,459
Clark □, OH • 147,548
Clark □, SD • 4,403
Clark □, WA • 238,053
Clark □, WI • 31,647
Clarkdale, AZ 86324 • 2,144
Clarke □, AL • 27,240
Clarke □, GA • 87,594
Clarke □, IA • 8,287
Clarke □, MS • 17,313
Clarke □, VA • 12,101
Clarkesville, GA 30523 • 1,151
Clarksburg, WV 26301–02 • 18,059
Clarksdale, MS 38614 • 19,717
Clarks Summit, PA 18411 • 5,433
Clarkston, GA 30021 • 5,385
Clarkston, MI 48346–48 • 1,005
Clarkston, WA 99403 • 6,753
Clarksville, AR 72830 • 5,833
Clarksville, DE 19970 • 500
Clarksville, IN 47129 • 19,833
Clarksville, IA 50619 • 1,382
Clarksville, TN 37040–43 • 75,494
Clarksville, TX 75426 • 4,311
Clarksville, VA 23927 • 1,243
Clarkton, MO 63837 • 1,113
Clatskanie, OR 97016 • 1,629
Clatsop □, OR • 33,301
Claude, TX 79019 • 1,199
Clawson, MI 48017 • 13,874
Claxton, GA 30417 • 2,464
Clay, KY 42404 • 1,173
Clay □, AL • 13,252
Clay □, AR • 18,107
Clay □, FL • 105,986
Clay □, GA • 3,364
Clay □, IL • 14,460
Clay □, IN • 24,705
Clay □, IA • 17,585
Clay □, KS • 9,158
Clay □, KY • 21,746
Clay □, MN • 50,422
Clay □, MS • 21,120
Clay □, MO • 153,411
Clay □, NE • 7,123
Clay □, NC • 7,155
Clay □, SD • 13,186
Clay □, TN • 7,238
Clay □, TX • 10,024
Clay □, WV • 9,983
Clay Center, KS 67432 • 4,613
Clay City, KY 40312 • 1,258
Claymont, DE 19702 • 9,800
Claypool, AZ 85532 • 1,942
Claysburg, PA 16625 • 1,399
Clayton, AL 36016 • 1,564
Clayton, DE 19938 • 1,163
Clayton, GA 30525 • 1,613
Clayton, MO 63105 • 13,874
Clayton, NJ 08312 • 6,155
Clayton, NM 88415 • 2,484
Clayton, NY 13624 • 2,160
Clayton, NC 27520 • 4,756
Clayton □, GA • 182,052
Clayton □, IA • 19,054
Clear Creek □, CO • 7,619
Clearfield, KY 40313 • 1,250
Clearfield, PA 16830 • 6,633
Clearfield, UT 84015 • 21,435
Clearfield □, PA • 78,097
Clearlake, CA 95422 • 11,804
Clear Lake, IA 50428 • 8,183
Clear Lake, SD 57226 • 1,247
Clearlake, WA 98235 • 1,100
Clear Lake Shores, TX 77565 • 1,096
Clearwater, FL 34615–30 • 98,784
Clearwater, KS 67026 • 1,875
Clearwater, SC 29822 • 4,731
Clearwater □, ID • 8,505
Clearwater □, MN • 8,309
Cleburne, TX 76031–33 • 22,205
Cleburne □, AL • 12,730
Cleburne □, AR • 19,411
Cle Elum, WA 98922 • 1,778
Cleland Heights, DE 19805 • 1,120
Clementon, NJ 08021 • 5,601
Clemmons, NC 27012 • 6,020
Clemson, SC 29631–33 • 11,096
Clendenin, WV 25045 • 1,203
Cleona, PA 17042 • 2,322
Clermont, FL 34711–12 • 6,910
Clermont □, OH • 150,187
Cleveland, GA 30528 • 1,653
Cleveland, MS 38732–33 • 15,384
Cleveland, OH 44101–99 • 505,616
Cleveland, OK 74020 • 3,156
Cleveland, TN 37311–12 • 30,354
Cleveland, TX 77327–28 • 7,124
Cleveland, WI 53015 • 1,398
Cleveland □, AR • 7,781
Cleveland □, NC • 84,714
Cleveland □, OK • 174,253
Cleveland Heights, OH 44118 • 54,052
Cleves, OH 45002 • 2,208
Clewiston, FL 33440 • 6,085
Cliffside Park, NJ 07010 • 20,393
Clifton, AZ 85533 • 2,840
Clifton, CO 81520 • 12,671
Clifton, IL 60927 • 1,347
Clifton, NJ 07011–15 • 71,742
Clifton, TX 76634 • 3,195
Clifton Forge, VA 24422 • 4,679
Clifton Heights, PA 19018 • 7,111
Clifton Knolls, NY 12065 • 5,636
Clifton Springs, NY 14432 • 2,175
Clinch □, GA • 6,160
Clint, TX 79836 • 1,035
Clinton, AR 72031 • 2,213
Clinton, CT 06413 • 3,439
Clinton, IL 61727 • 7,437
Clinton, IN 47842 • 5,040
Clinton, IA 52732–33 • 29,201
Clinton, KY 42031 • 1,547
Clinton, LA 70722 • 1,904
Clinton, ME 04927 • 1,485
Clinton, MD 20735 • 19,987
Clinton, MA 01510 • 7,943
Clinton, MI 49236 • 2,475
Clinton, MS 39056 • 21,847
Clinton, MO 64735 • 8,703
Clinton, NJ 08809 • 2,054
Clinton, NY 13323 • 2,238
Clinton, NC 28328 • 8,204
Clinton, OK 73601 • 9,298
Clinton, SC 29325 • 7,987
Clinton, TN 37716 • 8,972
Clinton, UT 84015 • 7,945
Clinton, WA 98236 • 2,000
Clinton, WI 53525 • 1,849
Clinton □, IL • 33,944
Clinton □, IN • 30,974
Clinton □, IA • 51,040
Clinton □, KY • 9,135
Clinton □, MI • 57,883
Clinton □, MO • 16,595
Clinton □, NY • 85,969
Clinton □, OH • 35,415
Clinton □, PA • 37,182
Clinton Township, MI 48043 • 85,866
Clintonville, WI 54929 • 4,351
Clintwood, VA 24228 • 1,542
Clio, AL 36017 • 1,365
Clio, MI 48420 • 2,629
Clive, IA 50322 • 7,462
Cloquet, MN 55720 • 10,885
Closter, NJ 07624 • 8,094
Cloud □, KS • 11,023
Clover, SC 29710 • 3,422
Cloverdale, CA 95425 • 4,924
Cloverdale, IN 46120 • 1,681
Cloverleaf, TX 77015 • 18,230
Cloverport, KY 40111 • 1,207
Clovis, CA 93612–13 • 50,323
Clovis, NM 88101–03 • 30,954
Clute, TX 77531 • 8,910
Clyde, NY 14433 • 2,409
Clyde, NC 28721 • 1,041
Clyde, OH 43410 • 5,776
Clyde, TX 79510 • 3,002
Clymer, PA 15728 • 1,499
Coachella, CA 92236 • 16,896
Coahoma, TX 79511 • 1,133
Coahoma □, MS • 31,665
Coal □, OK • 5,780
Coal City, IL 60416 • 3,907
Coal Fork, WV 25306 • 2,100
Coalgate, OK 74538 • 1,895
Coal Grove, OH 45638 • 2,251
Coalinga, CA 93210 • 8,212
Coalville, UT 84017 • 1,065
Coatesville, PA 19320 • 11,038
Coats, NC 27521 • 1,493
Cobb □, GA • 447,745
Cobden, IL 62920 • 1,090
Cobleskill, NY 12043 • 5,268
Cochise □, AZ • 97,624
Cochituate, MA 01778 • 6,046
Cochran, GA 31014 • 4,390
Cochran □, TX • 4,377
Cochranton, PA 16314 • 1,174
Cocke □, TN • 29,141
Cockeysville, MD 21030 • 18,668
Cockrell Hill, TX 75211 • 3,746
Cocoa, FL 32922–27 • 17,722
Cocoa Beach, FL 32931–32 • 12,123
Coconino □, AZ • 96,591
Coconut Creek, FL 33060 • 27,485
Codington □, SD • 22,698
Cody, WY 82414 • 7,897
Coeburn, VA 24230 • 2,165
Coeur d'Alene, ID 83814 • 24,563
Coffee □, AL • 40,240
Coffee □, GA • 29,592
Coffee □, TN • 40,339
Coffey □, KS • 8,404
Coffeyville, KS 67337 • 12,917
Cohasset, MA 02025 • 6,800
Cohoes, NY 12047 • 16,825
Cokato, MN 55321 • 2,180
Coke □, TX • 3,424
Cokeville, WY 83114 • 493
Colbert, OK 74733 • 1,043
Colbert □, AL • 51,666
Colby, KS 67701 • 5,396
Colby, WI 54421 • 1,532
Colchester, CT 06415 • 3,212
Colchester, IL 62326 • 1,645
Cold Bay, AK 99571 • 148
Cold Spring, KY 41076 • 2,880
Cold Spring, MN 56320 • 2,459
Cold Spring Harbor, NY 11724 • 4,789
Coldwater, MI 49036 • 9,607
Coldwater, MS 38618 • 1,502
Coldwater, OH 45828 • 4,335
Cole □, MO • 63,579
Colebrook, NH 03576 • 2,444
Cole Camp, MO 65325 • 1,054
Coleman, MI 48618 • 1,237
Coleman, TX 76834 • 5,410
Coleman □, TX • 9,710
Coleraine, MN 55722 • 1,041
Coles □, IL • 51,644
Colfax, CA 95713 • 1,306
Colfax, IA 50054 • 2,462
Colfax, LA 71417 • 1,696
Colfax, WA 99111 • 2,713
Colfax, WI 54730 • 1,110
Colfax □, NE • 9,139
Colfax □, NM • 12,925
College, AK 99701 • 11,249
Collegedale, TN 37315 • 5,048
College Park, GA 30337 • 20,457
College Park, MD 20740–41 • 21,927
College Place, WA 99324 • 6,308
College Station, AR 72053 • 3,800
College Station, TX 77840–45 • 52,456
Collegeville, PA 19426 • 4,227
Colleton □, SC • 34,377
Colleyville, TX 76034 • 12,724
Collier □, FL • 152,099
Collierville, TN 38017 • 14,427
Collin □, TX • 264,036
Collingdale, PA 19023 • 9,175
Collingswood, NJ 08108 • 15,289
Collingsworth □, TX • 3,573
Collins, MS 39428 • 2,541
Collins Park, DE 19720 • 2,100
Collinsville, AL 35961 • 1,429
Collinsville, CT 06022 • 2,591
Collinsville, IL 62234 • 22,446
Collinsville, OK 74021 • 3,612
Collinsville, VA 24078 • 7,280
Collinwood, TN 38450 • 1,014
Colmar Manor, MD 20722 • 1,249
Coloma, MI 49038 • 1,679
Colon, MI 49040 • 1,224
Colonia, NJ 07067 • 18,238
Colonial Beach, VA 22443 • 3,132
Colonial Heights, TN 37663 • 6,716
Colonial Heights, VA 23834 • 16,064
Colonial Park, PA 17109 • 13,777
Colonie, NY 12212 • 8,019
Colorado □, TX • 18,383
Colorado City, AZ 86021 • 2,426
Colorado City, CO 81019 • 1,149
Colorado City, TX 79512 • 4,749
Colorado Springs, CO 80901–99 • 281,140
Colquitt, GA 31737 • 1,991
Colquitt □, GA • 36,645
Colstrip, MT 59323 • 3,035
Colton, CA 92324 • 40,213
Columbia, CA 95310 • 1,799
Columbia, IL 62236 • 5,524
Columbia, KY 42728 • 3,845
Columbia, MD 21044–46 • 75,883
Columbia, MS 39429 • 6,815
Columbia, MO 65201–05 • 69,101
Columbia, PA 17512 • 10,701
Columbia, SC 29201–92 • 98,052
Columbia, TN 38401–02 • 28,583
Columbia □, AR • 25,691
Columbia □, FL • 42,613
Columbia □, GA • 66,031
Columbia □, NY • 62,982
Columbia □, OR • 37,557
Columbia □, PA • 63,202
Columbia □, WA • 4,024
Columbia □, WI • 45,088
Columbia City, IN 46725 • 5,706
Columbia City, OR 97018 • 1,003
Columbia Falls, MT 59912 • 2,942
Columbia Heights, MN 55421 • 18,910
Columbiana, AL 35051 • 2,968
Columbiana, OH 44408 • 4,961
Columbiana □, OH • 108,276
Columbine, CO 80123 • 23,969
Columbus, GA 31901–09 • 178,681
Columbus, IN 47201–03 • 31,802
Columbus, KS 66725 • 3,268
Columbus, MS 39701–05 • 23,799
Columbus, MT 59019 • 1,573
Columbus, NE 68601 • 19,480
Columbus, OH 43201–91 • 632,910
Columbus, TX 78934 • 3,367
Columbus, WI 53925 • 4,093
Columbus □, NC • 49,587
Columbus Grove, OH 45830 • 2,231
Columbus Junction, IA 52738 • 1,616
Colusa, CA 95932 • 4,934
Colusa □, CA • 16,275
Colver, PA 15927 • 1,024
Colville, WA 99114 • 4,360
Colwich, KS 67030 • 1,091
Comal □, TX • 51,832
Comanche, OK 73529 • 1,695
Comanche, TX 76442 • 4,087
Comanche □, KS • 2,313
Comanche □, OK • 111,486
Comanche □, TX • 13,381
Combee Settlement, FL 33801 • 5,463
Combined Locks, WI 54113 • 2,190
Comfort, TX 78013 • 1,477
Commack, NY 11725 • 36,124
Commerce, CA 90040 • 12,135
Commerce, GA 30529 • 4,108
Commerce, OK 74339 • 2,426
Commerce, TX 75428 • 6,825
Commerce City, CO 80022 • 16,466
Common Fence Point, RI 02871 • 860
Como, MS 38619 • 1,387
Compton, CA 90220–24 • 90,454
Comstock, MI 49041 • 5,600
Comstock Park, MI 49321 • 6,530
Concho □, TX • 3,044
Concord, CA 94518–24 • 111,348
Concord, MA 01742 • 4,680
Concord, MO 63128 • 19,859
Concord, NH 03301–03 • 36,006
Concord, NC 28025–27 • 27,347
Concord, TN 37901 • 3,420
Concordia, KS 66901 • 6,167
Concordia, MO 64020 • 2,160
Concordia □, LA • 20,828
Conecuh □, AL • 14,054
Conejos □, CO • 7,453
Conemaugh, PA 15909 • 1,470
Congers, NY 10920 • 8,003
Conklin, NY 13748 • 1,800
Conley, GA 30027 • 5,528
Conneaut, OH 44030 • 13,241
Connell, WA 99326 • 2,005
Connellsville, PA 15425 • 9,229
Connersville, IN 47331 • 15,550
Conover, NC 28613 • 5,465
Conrad, MT 59425 • 2,891
Conroe, TX 77301–05 • 27,610
Conshohocken, PA 19428 • 8,064
Constantia, NY 13044 • 1,140
Constantine, MI 49042 • 2,032
Continental, OH 45831 • 1,214
Contoocook, NH 03229 • 1,334
Contra Costa □, CA • 803,732
Converse, IN 46919 • 1,144
Converse, SC 29329 • 1,173
Converse, TX 78109 • 8,887
Converse □, WY • 11,128
Convoy, OH 45832 • 1,200
Conway, AR 72032 • 26,481
Conway, FL 32809 • 13,159
Conway, NH 03818 • 1,604
Conway, PA 15027 • 2,424
Conway, SC 29526–27 • 9,819
Conway □, AR • 19,151
Conway Springs, KS 67031 • 1,384
Conyers, GA 30207–08 • 7,380
Cook □, GA • 13,456
Cook □, IL • 5,105,067
Cook □, MN • 3,868
Cooke □, TX • 30,777
Cookeville, TN 38501–02 • 21,744
Coolidge, AZ 85228 • 6,927
Coon Rapids, IA 50058 • 1,266
Coon Rapids, MN 55433 • 52,978
Cooper, TX 75432 • 2,153
Cooper □, MO • 14,835
Cooper City, FL 33328 • 20,791
Cooper Road, LA 71107 • 11,050
Coopersburg, PA 18036 • 2,599
Cooperstown, NY 13326 • 2,180
Cooperstown, ND 58425 • 1,247
Coopersville, MI 49404 • 3,421
Coos □, NH • 34,828
Coos □, OR • 60,273
Coosa □, AL • 11,063
Coos Bay, OR 97420 • 15,076
Copake, NY 12516 • 1,200
Copiague, NY 11726 • 20,769
Copiah □, MS • 27,592
Coplay, PA 18037 • 3,267
Copperas Cove, TX 76522 • 24,079
Coquille, OR 97423 • 4,121
Coral Gables, FL 33134 • 40,091
Coral Hills, MD 20743 • 11,032
Coral Springs, FL 33065 • 79,443
Coral Terrace, FL 33157 • 23,255
Coralville, IA 52241 • 10,347
Coral Way Village, FL 33155 • 9,000
Coram, NY 11727 • 30,111
Coraopolis, PA 15108 • 6,747
Corbin, KY 40701–02 • 7,419
Corcoran, CA 93212 • 13,364
Corcoran, MN 55340 • 5,199
Cordaville, MA 01772 • 1,530
Cordele, GA 31015 • 10,321
Cordell, OK 73632 • 2,903
Cordova, AL 35550 • 2,623
Cordova, AK 99574 • 2,110
Cordova, NC 28330 • 1,200
Corinth, MS 38834 • 11,820
Corinth, NY 12822 • 2,760
Cornelia, GA 30531 • 3,219
Cornelius, NC 28031 • 2,581
Cornelius, OR 97113 • 6,148
Cornell, WI 54732 • 1,541
Corning, AR 72422 • 3,323
Corning, CA 96021 • 5,870
Corning, IA 50841 • 1,806
Corning, NY 14830 • 11,938
Cornville, AZ 86325 • 1,200
Cornwall, PA 17016 • 3,231
Cornwall on Hudson, NY 12520 • 3,093
Corona, CA 91718–20 • 76,095
Coronado, CA 92118 • 26,540
Coronado, CO 80229 • 6,890
Corpus Christi, TX 78401–82 • 257,453
Corrigan, TX 75939 • 1,764
Corriganville, MD 21524 • 1,020
Corry, PA 16407 • 7,216
Corsicana, TX 75110 • 22,911
Corson □, SD • 4,195
Corte Madera, CA 94925 • 8,272
Cortez, CO 81321 • 7,284
Cortez, FL 34215 • 4,509
Cortland, NY 13045 • 19,801
Cortland, OH 44410 • 5,666
Cortland □, NY • 48,963
Corunna, MI 48817 • 3,091
Corvallis, OR 97330–33 • 44,757
Corydon, IN 47112 • 2,661
Corydon, IA 50060 • 1,675
Coryell □, TX • 64,213
Coshocton, OH 43812 • 12,193
Coshocton □, OH • 35,427
Cosmopolis, WA 98537 • 1,372
Costa Mesa, CA 92626–28 • 96,357
Costilla □, CO • 3,190
Cottage Grove, MN 55016 • 22,935
Cottage Grove, OR 97424 • 7,402
Cottle □, TX • 2,247
Cottleville, MO 63338 • 2,936
Cotton □, OK • 6,651
Cottondale, AL 35453 • 1,960
Cotton Plant, AR 72036 • 1,150
Cottonport, LA 71327 • 2,600
Cotton Valley, LA 71018 • 1,130
Cottonwood, AL 36320 • 1,385
Cottonwood, AZ 86326 • 5,918
Cottonwood, CA 96022 • 1,747
Cottonwood, ID 83522 • 822
Cottonwood, UT 84121 • 11,554
Cottonwood □, MN • 12,694
Cottonwood Heights, UT 84121 • 28,766
Cotuit, MA 02635 • 1,750
Cotulla, TX 78014 • 3,694
Coudersport, PA 16915 • 2,854
Coulee Dam, WA 99116 • 1,087
Council, ID 83612 • 831
Council Bluffs, IA 51501–03 • 54,315
Council Grove, KS 66846 • 2,228
Country Club Hills, IL 60478 • 15,431
Country Homes, WA 99218 • 5,126
Countryside, IL 60525 • 5,716
Coupeville, WA 98239 • 1,377
Coushatta, LA 71019 • 1,845
Covedale, OH 45238 • 6,669
Covelo, CA 95428 • 1,057
Coventry, CT 06238 • 10,063
Coventry, DE 19720 • 1,165
Coventry, RI 02816 • 6,980
Covina, CA 91722–24 • 43,207
Covington, GA 30209 • 10,026
Covington, IN 47932 • 2,747
Covington, KY 41011–18 • 43,264
Covington, LA 70433–34 • 7,691
Covington, OH 45318 • 2,603
Covington, TN 38019 • 7,487
Covington, VA 24426 • 6,991
Covington □, AL • 36,478
Covington □, MS • 16,527
Cowan, TN 37318 • 1,738
Cowarts, AL 36321 • 1,400
Coweta, OK 74429 • 6,159
Coweta □, GA • 53,853
Cowley, WY 82420 • 477
Cowley □, KS • 36,915
Cowlitz □, WA • 82,119
Cowpens, SC 29330 • 2,176
Coxsackie, NY 12051 • 2,789
Cozad, NE 69130 • 3,823
Crab Orchard, WV 25827 • 2,919
Crabtree, PA 15624 • 1,000
Crafton, PA 15205 • 7,188
Craig, AK 99921 • 1,260
Craig, CO 81625–26 • 8,091
Craig □, OK • 14,104
Craig □, VA • 4,372
Craighead □, AR • 68,956
Craigsville, WV 26205 • 1,955
Cramerton, NC 28032 • 2,371
Cranbury, NJ 08512 • 1,255
Crandall, TX 75114 • 1,652
Crandon, WI 54520 • 1,958
Crane, AZ 85365 • 2,650
Crane, MO 65633 • 1,218
Crane, TX 79731 • 3,533
Crane □, TX • 4,652
Cranford, NJ 07016 • 22,624
Cranston, RI 02910 • 76,060
Craven □, NC • 81,613
Crawford, NE 69339 • 1,115
Crawford □, AR • 42,493
Crawford □, GA • 8,991
Crawford □, IL • 19,464
Crawford □, IN • 9,914
Crawford □, IA • 16,775
Crawford □, KS • 35,568
Crawford □, MI • 12,260
Crawford □, MO • 19,173
Crawford □, OH • 47,870
Crawford □, PA • 86,169
Crawford □, WI • 15,940
Crawfordsville, IN 47933 • 13,584
Crawfordville, FL 32327 • 1,110
Creedmoor, NC 27522 • 1,504
Creek □, OK • 60,915
Creighton, NE 68729 • 1,223
Creighton, PA 15030 • 1,658
Crenshaw □, AL • 13,635
Creola, AL 36525 • 1,896
Cresaptown, MD 21502 • 4,645
Crescent, OK 73028 • 1,236
Crescent City, CA 95531 • 4,380
Crescent City, FL 32112 • 1,859
Crescent Springs, KY 41016 • 2,179
Cresco, IA 52136 • 3,669
Cresskill, NJ 07626 • 7,558
Cresson, PA 16630 • 1,784
Cressona, PA 17929 • 1,694
Cresthaven, FL 33064 • 2,400
Crest Hill, IL 60435 • 10,643
Crestline, CA 92325 • 8,594
Crestline, OH 44827 • 4,934
Creston, IA 50801 • 7,911
Creston, OH 44217 • 1,848
Crestview, FL 32536 • 9,886
Crestview, HI 96797 • 1,000
Crestwood, IL 60445 • 10,823
Crestwood, KY 40014 • 1,435
Crestwood, MO 63126 • 11,234
Crestwood Village, NJ 08759 • 8,030
Creswell, OR 97426 • 2,431
Crete, IL 60417 • 6,773
Crete, NE 68333 • 4,841
Creve Coeur, IL 61611 • 5,938
Creve Coeur, MO 63141 • 12,304
Crewe, VA 23930 • 2,276
Cricket, NC 28659 • 2,015
Cridersville, OH 45806 • 1,885
Crisfield, MD 21817 • 2,880
Crisp □, GA • 20,011
Crittenden □, AR • 49,939
Crittenden □, KY • 9,196
Crocker, MO 65452 • 1,077
Crockett, CA 94525 • 3,228
Crockett, TX 75835 • 7,024
Crockett □, TN • 13,378
Crockett □, TX • 4,078
Crofton, MD 21114 • 12,781
Cromwell, CT 06416 • 1,100
Crook □, OR • 14,111
Crook □, WY • 5,294
Crookston, MN 56716 • 8,119
Crooksville, OH 43731 • 2,601
Crosby, MN 56441 • 2,073
Crosby, ND 58730 • 1,312
Crosby, TX 77532 • 1,811
Crosby □, TX • 7,304
Crosbyton, TX 79322 • 2,026
Cross □, AR • 19,225
Cross City, FL 32628 • 2,041
Crossett, AR 71635 • 6,282
Crosslake, MN 56442 • 1,132
Cross Lanes, WV 25313 • 10,878
Cross Plains, TN 37049 • 1,025
Cross Plains, TX 76443 • 1,063
Cross Plains, WI 53528 • 2,098
Crossville, AL 35962 • 1,350
Crossville, TN 38555 • 6,930
Croswell, MI 48422 • 2,174
Crothersville, IN 47229 • 1,687
Croton-on-Hudson, NY 10520 • 7,018
Crow Agency, MT 59022 • 1,446
Crowell, TX 79227 • 1,230
Crowley, LA 70526–27 • 13,983
Crowley, TX 76036 • 6,974

United States Populations and ZIP Codes

Crowley □, CO • *3,946*
Crown Point, IN 46307 • *17,728*
Crownpoint, NM 87313 • *2,108*
Crow Wing □, MN • *44,249*
Crozet, VA 22932 • *2,256*
Crystal, MN 55428 • *23,788*
Crystal Bay, NV 89402 • *1,200*
Crystal Beach, FL 34681 • *1,450*
Crystal City, MO 63019 • *4,088*
Crystal City, TX 78839 • *8,263*
Crystal Falls, MI 49920 • *1,922*
Crystal Lake, CT 06029 • *1,200*
Crystal Lake, FL 33803 • *5,300*
Crystal Lake, IL 60014 • *24,512*
Crystal Lawns, IL 60435 • *1,660*
Crystal River, FL 32629 • *4,044*
Crystal Springs, MS 39059 • *5,643*
Cuba, IL 61427 • *1,440*
Cuba, MO 65453 • *2,537*
Cuba, NY 14727 • *1,690*
Cuba City, WI 53807 • *2,024*
Cucamonga, CA 91730 • *101,409*
Cudahy, CA 90201 • *22,817*
Cudahy, WI 53110 • *18,659*
Cuero, TX 77954 • *6,700*
Culberson □, TX • *3,407*
Culbertson, MT 59218 • *796*
Cullen, LA 71021 • *1,642*
Cullman, AL 35055–56 • *13,367*
Cullman □, AL • *67,613*
Culloden, WV 25510 • *2,907*
Cullowhee, NC 28723 • *1,200*
Culpeper, VA 22701 • *8,581*
Culpeper □, VA • *27,791*
Culver, IN 46511 • *1,404*
Culver City, CA 90230–33 • *38,793*
Cumberland, KY 40823 • *3,112*
Cumberland, MD 21501–05 • *23,706*
Cumberland, WI 54829 • *2,163*
Cumberland □, IL • *10,670*
Cumberland □, KY • *6,784*
Cumberland □, ME • *243,135*
Cumberland □, NJ • *138,053*
Cumberland □, NC • *274,566*
Cumberland □, PA • *195,257*
Cumberland □, TN • *34,736*
Cumberland □, VA • *7,825*
Cumberland Center, ME 04021 • *1,890*
Cumberland Foreside, ME 04110 • *1,000*
Cumberland Hill, RI 02864 • *6,379*
Cuming □, NE • *10,117*
Cumming, GA 30130 • *2,828*
Cupertino, CA 95014–16 • *40,263*
Currituck □, NC • *13,736*
Curry □, NM • *42,207*
Curry □, OR • *19,327*
Curtisville, PA 15032 • *1,285*
Curwensville, PA 16833 • *2,924*
Cushing, OK 74023 • *7,218*
Cusseta, GA 31805 • *1,107*
Custer, SD 57730 • *1,741*
Custer □, CO • *1,926*
Custer □, ID • *4,133*
Custer □, MT • *11,697*
Custer □, NE • *12,270*
Custer □, OK • *26,897*
Custer □, SD • *6,179*
Cut Bank, MT 59427 • *3,329*
Cutchogue, NY 11935 • *1,730*
Cuthbert, GA 31740 • *3,730*
Cutler, FL 33157 • *16,201*
Cutler Ridge, FL 33157 • *21,268*
Cutlerville, MI 49508 • *11,228*
Cut Off, LA 70345 • *5,325*
Cuyahoga □, OH • *1,412,140*
Cuyahoga Falls, OH 44221–24 • *48,950*
Cynthiana, KY 41031 • *6,497*
Cypress, CA 90630 • *42,655*
Cypress Lake, FL 33919 • *10,491*
Cypress Quarters, FL 34972 • *1,343*
Cyril, OK 73029 • *1,072*

D

Dacono, CO 80514 • *2,228*
Dacula, GA 30211 • *2,217*
Dade □, FL • *1,937,094*
Dade □, GA • *13,147*
Dade □, MO • *7,449*
Dade City, FL 33525–26 • *5,633*
Dadeville, AL 36853 • *3,276*
Daggett □, UT • *690*
Dagsboro, DE 19939 • *398*
Dahlonega, GA 30533 • *3,086*
Daingerfield, TX 75638 • *2,572*
Dakota □, MN • *275,227*
Dakota □, NE • *16,742*
Dakota City, IA 50529 • *1,024*
Dakota City, NE 68731 • *1,470*
Dale, IN 47523 • *1,553*
Dale □, AL • *49,633*
Dale City, VA 22193 • *47,170*
Daleville, AL 36322 • *5,117*
Daleville, IN 47334 • *1,681*
Dalhart, TX 79022 • *6,246*
Dallam □, TX • *5,461*
Dallas, GA 30132 • *2,810*
Dallas, NC 28034 • *3,012*
Dallas, OR 97338 • *9,422*
Dallas, PA 18612 • *2,567*
Dallas, TX 75201–99 • *1,006,877*
Dallas □, AL • *48,130*
Dallas □, AR • *9,614*
Dallas □, IA • *29,755*
Dallas □, MO • *12,646*
Dallas □, TX • *1,852,810*
Dallas Center, IA 50063 • *1,454*
Dallas City, IL 62330 • *1,037*
Dallastown, PA 17313 • *3,974*
Dalton, GA 30720–22 • *21,761*
Dalton, MA 01226–27 • *6,797*
Dalton, OH 44618 • *1,377*
Dalton, PA 18414 • *1,369*
Dalton Gardens, ID 83814 • *1,951*
Daly City, CA 94014–17 • *92,311*
Damascus, MD 20872 • *9,817*
Dana Point, CA 92629 • *31,896*
Danbury, CT 06810–13 • *65,585*
Danbury, TX 77534 • *1,447*
Dandridge, TN 37725 • *1,540*
Dane □, WI • *367,085*
Dania, FL 33004 • *13,024*
Daniels □, MT • *2,266*
Danielson, CT 06239 • *4,441*
Dannemora, NY 12929 • *4,005*
Dansville, NY 14437 • *5,002*
Dante, VA 24237 • *1,083*
Danvers, MA 01923 • *24,174*
Danville, AR 72833 • *1,585*
Danville, CA 94526 • *31,306*
Danville, IL 61832–34 • *33,828*
Danville, IN 46122 • *4,345*
Danville, KY 40422–23 • *12,420*
Danville, OH 43014 • *1,001*
Danville, PA 17821 • *5,165*
Danville, VA 24540–43 • *53,056*
Daphne, AL 36526 • *11,290*
Darby, PA 19023 • *11,140*
Darby Township, PA 19036 • *10,955*
Dardanelle, AR 72834 • *3,722*
Dare □, NC • *22,746*
Darien, CT 06820 • *18,130*
Darien, GA 31305 • *1,783*
Darien, IL 60559 • *18,341*
Darien, WI 53114 • *1,158*
Darke □, OH • *53,619*
Darley Woods, DE 19810 • *1,220*
Darlington, SC 29532 • *7,311*
Darlington, WI 53530 • *2,235*
Darlington □, SC • *61,851*
Darrington, WA 98241 • *1,042*
Dartmouth Woods, DE 19810 • *1,970*
Dassel, MN 55325 • *1,082*
Dauphin □, PA • *237,813*
Davenport, FL 33837 • *1,529*
Davenport, IA 52801–09 • *95,333*
Davenport, WA 99122 • *1,502*
David City, NE 68632 • *2,522*
Davidson, NC 28036 • *4,046*
Davidson □, NC • *126,677*
Davidson □, TN • *510,784*
Davidsville, PA 15928 • *1,167*
Davie, FL 33328 • *47,217*
Davie □, NC • *27,859*
Daviess □, IN • *27,533*
Daviess □, KY • *87,189*
Daviess □, MO • *7,865*
Davis, CA 95616–17 • *46,209*
Davis, OK 73030 • *2,543*
Davis □, IA • *8,312*
Davis □, UT • *187,941*
Davison, MI 48423 • *5,693*
Davison □, SD • *17,503*
Davisville, RI 02852 • *500*
Dawes □, NE • *9,021*
Dawson, GA 31742 • *5,295*
Dawson, MN 56232 • *1,626*
Dawson □, GA • *9,429*
Dawson □, MT • *9,505*
Dawson □, NE • *19,940*
Dawson □, TX • *14,349*
Dawson Springs, KY 42408 • *3,129*
Day □, SD • *6,978*
Dayton, KY 41074 • *6,576*
Dayton, MN 55327 • *4,443*
Dayton, NV 89403 • *2,217*
Dayton, NJ 08810 • *1,200*
Dayton, OH 45401–90 • *182,044*
Dayton, OR 97114 • *1,526*
Dayton, TN 37321 • *5,671*
Dayton, TX 77535 • *5,151*
Dayton, WA 99328 • *2,468*
Dayton, WY 82836 • *565*
Daytona Beach, FL 32114–25 • *61,921*
Dayville, CT 06241 • *1,500*
Deadwood, SD 57732 • *1,830*
Deaf Smith □, TX • *19,153*
Deal, NJ 07723 • *1,179*
Deale, MD 20751 • *4,151*
Dearborn, MI 48120–26 • *89,286*
Dearborn □, IN • *38,835*
Dearborn Heights, MI 48127 • *60,838*
De Baca □, NM • *2,252*
De Bary, FL 32713 • *7,176*
Decatur, AL 35601–03 • *48,761*
Decatur, GA 30030–37 • *17,336*
Decatur, IL 62521–26 • *83,885*
Decatur, IN 46733 • *8,644*
Decatur, MI 49045 • *1,760*
Decatur, MS 39327 • *1,248*
Decatur, TN 37322 • *1,361*
Decatur, TX 76234 • *4,252*
Decatur □, GA • *25,511*
Decatur □, IN • *23,645*
Decatur □, IA • *8,338*
Decatur □, KS • *4,021*
Decatur □, TN • *10,472*
Decherd, TN 37324 • *2,196*
Deckerville, MI 48427 • *1,015*
Decorah, IA 52101 • *8,063*
Dedham, MA 02026 • *23,782*
Deep River, CT 06417 • *2,520*
Deerfield, IL 60015 • *17,327*
Deerfield, WI 53531 • *1,617*
Deerfield Beach, FL 33441–43 • *46,325*
Deer Lodge, MT 59722 • *3,378*
Deer Lodge □, MT • *10,278*
Deer Park, NY 11729 • *28,840*
Deer Park, OH 45236 • *6,181*
Deer Park, TX 77536 • *27,652*
Deer Park, WA 99006 • *2,278*
Defiance, OH 43512 • *16,768*
Defiance □, OH • *39,350*
De Forest, WI 53532 • *4,882*
De Funiak Springs, FL 32433 • *5,120*
De Graff, OH 43318 • *1,331*
De Kalb, IL 60115 • *34,925*
De Kalb, MS 39328 • *1,073*
De Kalb, TX 75559 • *1,976*
De Kalb □, AL • *54,651*
De Kalb □, GA • *545,837*
De Kalb □, IL • *77,932*
De Kalb □, IN • *35,324*
De Kalb □, MO • *9,967*
De Kalb □, TN • *14,360*
Delafield, WI 53018 • *5,347*
Del Aire, CA 90250 • *8,040*
Delanco, NJ 08075 • *3,316*
De Land, FL 32720–24 • *16,491*
Delano, CA 93215–16 • *22,762*
Delano, MN 55328 • *2,709*
Delavan, IL 61734 • *1,642*
Delavan, WI 53115 • *6,073*
Delavan Lake, WI 53115 • *2,177*
Delaware, OH 43015 • *20,030*
Delaware □, IN • *119,659*
Delaware □, IA • *18,035*
Delaware □, NY • *47,225*
Delaware □, OH • *66,929*
Delaware □, OK • *28,070*
Delaware □, PA • *547,651*
Delaware City, DE 19706 • *1,682*
Delcambre, LA 70528 • *1,978*
Del City, OK 73115 • *23,928*
De Leon, TX 76444 • *2,190*
De Leon Springs, FL 32130 • *1,481*
Delevan, NY 14042 • *1,214*
Delhi, LA 71232 • *3,169*
Delhi, NY 13753 • *3,064*
Delhi Hills, OH 45238 • *27,647*
Dell Rapids, SD 57022 • *2,484*
Dellwood, MO 63136 • *5,245*
Del Mar, CA 92014 • *4,860*
Delmar, DE 19940 • *962*
Delmar, MD 21875 • *1,430*
Delmar, NY 12054 • *8,360*
Del Norte, CO 81132 • *1,674*
Del Norte □, CA • *23,460*
Del Park Manor, DE 19808 • *1,550*
Delphi, IN 46923 • *2,531*
Delphos, OH 45833 • *7,093*
Delran, NJ 08075 • *14,811*
Delray Beach, FL 33444–47 • *47,181*
Del Rio, FL 33617 • *8,248*
Del Rio, TX 78840–42 • *30,705*
Delta, CO 81416 • *3,789*
Delta, OH 43515 • *2,849*
Delta, UT 84624 • *2,998*
Delta □, CO • *20,980*
Delta □, MI • *37,780*
Delta □, TX • *4,857*
Delta Junction, AK 99737 • *652*
Deltaville, VA 23043 • *1,082*
Deltona, FL 32725 • *50,828*
Demarest, NJ 07627 • *4,800*
Deming, NM 88030–31 • *10,970*
Demopolis, AL 36732 • *7,512*
Demorest, GA 30535 • *1,088*
Demotte, IN 46310 • *2,482*
Denham Springs, LA 70726–27 • *8,381*
Denison, IA 51442 • *6,604*
Denison, TX 75020–21 • *21,505*
Denmark, SC 29042 • *3,762*
Denmark, WI 54208 • *1,612*
Dennis, MA 02638 • *2,500*
Dennison, OH 44621 • *3,282*
Dennis Port, MA 02639 • *2,775*
Denny Terrace, SC 29203 • *1,885*
Dent □, MO • *13,702*
Denton, MD 21629 • *2,977*
Denton, NC 27239 • *1,292*
Denton, TX 76201–06 • *66,270*
Denton □, TX • *273,525*
Dentsville, SC 29204 • *11,839*
Denver, CO 80201–95 • *467,610*
Denver, IA 50622 • *1,600*
Denver, PA 17517 • *2,861*
Denver □, CO • *467,610*
Denver City, TX 79323 • *5,145*
Denville, NJ 07834 • *14,380*
De Pere, WI 54115 • *16,569*
Depew, NY 14043 • *17,673*
Deposit, NY 13754 • *1,936*
Depue, IL 61322 • *1,729*
De Queen, AR 71832 • *4,633*
De Quincy, LA 70633 • *3,474*
Derby, CT 06418 • *12,199*
Derby, KS 67037 • *14,699*
Derby, NY 14047 • *1,200*
Derby Line, VT 05830 • *855*
De Ridder, LA 70634 • *9,868*
Dermott, AR 71638 • *4,715*
Derry, NH 03038 • *20,446*
Derry, PA 15627 • *2,950*
Derwood, MD 20855 • *1,500*
Des Allemands, LA 70030 • *2,504*
Des Arc, AR 72040 • *2,001*
Deschutes □, OR • *74,958*
Desert Hot Springs, CA 92240 • *11,668*
Desha □, AR • *16,798*
Deshler, OH 43516 • *1,876*
Desloge, MO 63601 • *4,150*
De Smet, SD 57231 • *1,172*
Des Moines, IA 50301–95 • *193,187*
Des Moines, WA 98188 • *17,283*
Des Moines □, IA • *42,614*
De Soto, IL 62924 • *1,500*
De Soto, IA 50069 • *1,033*
De Soto, KS 66018 • *2,291*
De Soto, MO 63020 • *5,993*
De Soto, TX 75115 • *30,544*
De Soto □, FL • *23,865*
De Soto □, LA • *25,346*
De Soto □, MS • *67,910*
Despard, WV 26301 • *1,018*
Des Peres, MO 63131 • *8,395*
Des Plaines, IL 60016–19 • *53,223*
Destin, FL 32540–41 • *8,080*
Destrehan, LA 70047 • *8,031*
Detroit, MI 48201–44 • *1,027,974*
Detroit Lakes, MN 56501–02 • *6,635*
Deuel □, NE • *2,237*
Deuel □, SD • *4,522*
Devils Lake, ND 58301 • *7,782*
Devine, TX 78016 • *3,928*
Devola, OH 45750 • *2,736*
Devon, PA 19333 • *6,620*
Devonshire, DE 19810 • *2,120*
Dewey, OK 74029 • *3,326*
Dewey □, OK • *5,551*
Dewey □, SD • *5,523*
Dewey Beach, DE 19971 • *204*
Deweyville, TX 77614 • *1,218*
De Witt, AR 72042 • *3,553*
De Witt, IA 52742 • *4,514*
De Witt, MI 48820 • *3,964*
De Witt, NY 13214 • *8,244*
De Witt □, IL • *16,516*
De Witt □, TX • *18,840*
Dexter, ME 04930 • *2,650*
Dexter, MI 48130 • *1,497*
Dexter, MO 63841 • *7,559*
Dexter, NY 13634 • *1,030*
Diamond Bar, CA 91765 • *53,672*
Diamond Hill, RI 02864 • *810*
Diamond Lake, IL 60060 • *1,500*
Diamond Springs, CA 95619 • *2,872*
Diamondville, WY 83116 • *864*
Diaz, AR 72043 • *1,363*
D'Iberville, MS 39532 • *6,566*
Diboll, TX 75941 • *4,341*
Dickens □, TX • *2,571*
Dickenson □, VA • *17,620*
Dickey □, ND • *6,107*
Dickinson, ND 58601–02 • *16,097*
Dickinson, TX 77539 • *9,497*
Dickinson □, IA • *14,909*
Dickinson □, KS • *18,958*
Dickinson □, MI • *26,831*
Dickson, TN 37055 • *8,791*
Dickson □, TN • *35,061*
Dickson City, PA 18519 • *6,276*
Dierks, AR 71833 • *1,263*
Dighton, KS 67839 • *1,361*
Dighton, MA 02715 • *1,100*
Dillard, OR 97432 • *1,000*
Dilley, TX 78017 • *2,632*
Dillingham, AK 99576 • *2,017*
Dillon, MT 59725 • *3,991*
Dillon, SC 29536 • *6,829*
Dillon □, SC • *29,114*
Dillsboro, IN 47018 • *1,200*
Dillsburg, PA 17019 • *1,925*
Dilworth, MN 56529 • *2,562*
Dimmit □, TX • *10,433*
Dimmitt, TX 79027 • *4,408*
Dimondale, MI 48821 • *1,247*
Dingmans Ferry, PA 18328 • *1,200*
Dinuba, CA 93618 • *12,743*
Dinwiddie □, VA • *20,960*
Dishman, WA 99213 • *9,671*
District Heights-Forestville, MD 20747 • *6,704*
Divernon, IL 62530 • *1,178*
Divide □, ND • *2,899*
Dixfield, ME 04224 • *1,300*
Dix Hills, NY 11746 • *25,849*
Dixie □, FL • *10,585*
Dixon, CA 95620 • *10,401*
Dixon, IL 61021 • *15,144*
Dixon, MO 65459 • *1,585*
Dixon □, NE • *6,143*
Dixonville, PA 15734 • *1,000*
Dobbs Ferry, NY 10522 • *9,940*
Dobson, NC 27017 • *1,195*
Docena, AL 35060 • *1,000*
Dock Junction, GA 31520 • *7,094*
Doddridge □, WV • *6,994*
Dodge □, GA • *17,607*
Dodge □, MN • *15,731*
Dodge □, NE • *34,500*
Dodge □, WI • *76,559*
Dodge Center, MN 55927 • *1,954*
Dodge City, KS 67801 • *21,129*
Dodge Park, MD 20785 • *4,842*
Dodgeville, WI 53533 • *3,882*
Dolgeville, NY 13329 • *2,452*
Dolomite, AL 35061 • *2,590*
Dolores □, CO • *1,504*
Dolton, IL 60419 • *23,930*
Dona Ana, NM 88032 • *950*
Dona Ana □, NM • *135,510*
Donaldsonville, LA 70346 • *7,949*
Donalsonville, GA 31745 • *2,761*
Doneraile, SC 29532 • *1,276*
Doniphan, MO 63935 • *1,713*
Doniphan □, KS • *8,134*
Donley □, TX • *3,696*
Donna, TX 78537 • *12,652*
Donora, PA 15033 • *5,928*
Dooly □, GA • *9,901*
Door □, WI • *25,690*
Dora, AL 35062 • *2,214*
Doraville, GA 30340 • *7,626*
Dorchester □, MD • *30,236*
Dorchester □, SC • *83,060*
Dormont, PA 15216 • *9,772*
Dorothy Pond, MA 01527 • *1,670*
Dorr, MI 49323 • *1,450*
Dorset, VT 05251 • *550*
Dorsey, MD 21227 • *1,186*
Dothan, AL 36301–04 • *53,589*
Double Springs, AL 35553 • *1,138*
Dougherty □, GA • *96,311*
Douglas, AZ 85607–08 • *12,822*
Douglas, GA 31533 • *10,464*
Douglas, MI 49406 • *1,040*
Douglas, WY 82633 • *5,076*
Douglas □, CO • *60,391*
Douglas □, GA • *71,120*
Douglas □, IL • *19,464*
Douglas □, KS • *81,798*
Douglas □, MN • *28,674*
Douglas □, MO • *11,876*
Douglas □, NE • *416,444*
Douglas □, NV • *27,637*
Douglas □, OR • *94,649*
Douglas □, SD • *3,746*
Douglas □, WA • *26,205*
Douglas □, WI • *41,758*
Douglass, KS 67039 • *1,722*
Douglasville, GA 30133–35 • *11,635*
Dousman, WI 53118 • *1,277*
Dover, AR 72837 • *1,055*
Dover, DE 19901–03 • *27,630*
Dover, FL 33527 • *2,606*
Dover, MA 02030 • *2,163*
Dover, NH 03820 • *25,042*
Dover, NJ 07801 • *15,115*
Dover, OH 44622 • *11,329*
Dover, PA 17315 • *1,884*
Dover, TN 37058 • *1,341*
Dover-Foxcroft, ME 04426 • *3,077*
Dover Plains, NY 12522 • *1,847*
Dowagiac, MI 49047 • *6,409*
Downers Grove, IL 60515–17 • *46,858*
Downey, CA 90239–42 • *91,444*
Downingtown, PA 19335 • *7,749*
Downs, KS 67437 • *1,119*
Downsville, NY 13755 • *1,100*
Doylestown, OH 44230 • *2,668*
Doylestown, PA 18901 • *8,575*
Dracut, MA 01826 • *25,594*
Drain, OR 97435 • *1,011*
Draper, UT 84020 • *7,257*
Drayton, ND 58225 • *961*
Drayton, SC 29333 • *1,443*
Drayton Plains, MI 48330 • *18,000*
Dreamland Villa, AZ 85205 • *3,400*
Dresden, OH 43821 • *1,581*
Dresden, TN 38225 • *2,488*
Dresslerville, NV 89410 • *180*
Drew, MS 38737 • *2,349*
Drew □, AR • *17,369*
Drexel, NC 28619 • *1,746*
Drexel, OH 45427 • *5,143*
Drexel Hill, PA 19026 • *29,744*
Dripping Springs, TX 78620 • *1,033*
Druid Hills, GA 30333 • *12,174*
Drumright, OK 74030 • *2,799*
Dryden, NY 13053 • *1,908*
Dry Ridge, KY 41035 • *1,601*
Duarte, CA 91010 • *20,688*
Dublin, CA 94568 • *23,229*
Dublin, GA 31021 • *16,312*
Dublin, OH 43017 • *16,366*
Dublin, PA 18917 • *1,985*
Dublin, TX 76446 • *3,190*
Dublin, VA 24084 • *2,012*
Du Bois, PA 15801 • *8,286*
Dubois, WY 82513 • *895*
Dubois □, IN • *36,616*
Duboistown, PA 17701 • *1,201*
Dubuque, IA 52001–04 • *57,546*
Dubuque □, IA • *86,403*
Duchesne, UT 84021 • *1,308*
Duchesne □, UT • *12,645*
Dudley, MA 01570–71 • *3,700*
Due West, SC 29639 • *1,220*
Dukes □, MA • *11,639*
Dulce, NM 87528 • *2,438*
Duluth, GA 30136 • *9,029*
Duluth, MN 55801–16 • *85,493*
Dumas, AR 71639 • *5,520*
Dumas, TX 79029 • *12,871*
Dumfries, VA 22026 • *4,282*
Dumont, NJ 07628 • *17,187*
Dunaire, GA 30032 • *7,170*
Dunbar, PA 15431 • *1,213*
Dunbar, WV 25064 • *8,697*
Duncan, OK 73533–34 • *21,732*
Duncan, SC 29334 • *2,152*
Duncan Falls, OH 43734 • *1,200*
Duncannon, PA 17020 • *1,450*
Duncansville, PA 16635 • *1,309*
Duncanville, TX 75116 • *35,748*
Dundalk, MD 21222 • *65,800*
Dundee, FL 33838 • *2,335*
Dundee, IL 60118 • *3,728*
Dundee, MI 48131 • *2,664*
Dundee, NY 14837 • *1,588*
Dundee, OR 97115 • *1,663*
Dundy □, NE • *2,582*
Dunedin, FL 34697–98 • *34,012*
Dunellen, NJ 08812 • *6,528*
Dunkirk, IN 47336 • *2,739*
Dunkirk, NY 14048 • *13,989*
Dunklin □, MO • *33,112*
Dunlap, IN 46514 • *5,705*
Dunlap, IA 51529 • *1,251*
Dunlap, TN 37327 • *3,731*
Dunleith, DE 19801 • *2,600*
Dunmore, PA 18512 • *15,403*
Dunn, NC 28334–35 • *8,336*
Dunn □, ND • *4,005*
Dunn □, WI • *35,909*
Dunnellon, FL 32630 • *1,624*
Dunn Loring Woods, VA 22180 • *2,800*
Dunseith, ND 58329 • *723*
Dunsmuir, CA 96025 • *2,129*
Dunwoody, GA 30338 • *26,302*
Du Page □, IL • *781,666*
Duplin □, NC • *39,995*
Dupont, CO 80024 • *5,200*
Dupont, PA 18641 • *2,984*
Dupont Manor, DE 19901 • *1,059*
Duquesne, PA 15110 • *8,525*
Du Quoin, IL 62832 • *6,697*
Durand, IL 61024 • *1,100*
Durand, MI 48429 • *4,283*
Durand, WI 54736 • *2,003*
Durango, CO 81301–02 • *12,430*
Durant, IA 52747 • *1,549*
Durant, MS 39063 • *2,838*
Durant, OK 74701–02 • *12,823*
Durham, CA 95938 • *1,500*
Durham, CT 06422 • *2,650*
Durham, NH 03824 • *9,236*
Durham, NC 27701–22 • *136,611*
Durham □, NC • *181,835*
Duryea, PA 18642 • *4,869*
Duson, LA 70529 • *1,465*
Dutchess □, NY • *259,462*
Duval □, FL • *672,971*
Duval □, TX • *12,918*
Duxbury, MA 02331–32 • *1,637*
Dwight, IL 60420 • *4,230*
Dyer, IN 46311 • *10,923*
Dyer, TN 38330 • *2,204*
Dyer □, TN • *34,854*
Dyersburg, TN 38024–25 • *16,317*
Dyersville, IA 52040 • *3,703*
Dysart, IA 52224 • *1,230*

E

Eagan, MN 55121 • *47,409*
Eagar, AZ 85925 • *4,025*
Eagle, CO 81631 • *1,580*
Eagle, ID 83616 • *3,327*
Eagle, NE 68347 • *1,047*
Eagle, WI 53119 • *1,182*
Eagle □, CO • *21,928*
Eagle Grove, IA 50533 • *3,671*
Eagle Lake, MN 56024 • *1,703*
Eagle Lake, TX 77434 • *3,551*
Eagle Lake, WI 53139 • *1,000*
Eagle Pass, TX 78852–53 • *20,651*
Eagle Point, OR 97524 • *3,008*
Eagle River, WI 54521 • *1,374*
Eagleton Village, TN 37801 • *5,331*
Earle, AR 72331 • *3,393*
Earlham, IA 50072 • *1,157*
Earlimart, CA 93219 • *5,881*
Earlington, KY 42410 • *1,833*
Earlville, IL 60518 • *1,435*
Early □, GA • *11,854*
Earth, TX 79031 • *1,228*
Easley, SC 29640–42 • *15,195*
East Alton, IL 62024 • *7,063*
East Arlington, VT 05252 • *600*
East Aurora, NY 14052 • *6,647*
East Bangor, PA 18013 • *1,006*
East Barre, VT 05649 • *700*
East Baton Rouge □, LA • *380,105*

East Berlin, PA 17316 • *1,175*
East Bernard, TX 77435 • *1,544*
East Bethel, MN 55005 • *8,050*
East Billerica, MA 01821 • *3,830*
East Brady, PA 16028 • *1,047*
East Brewton, AL 36426 • *2,579*
East Bridgewater, MA 02333 • *3,270*
East Brookfield, MA 01515 • *1,396*
East Brooklyn, CT 06239 • *1,481*
East Brunswick, NJ 08816 • *43,548*
East Carbon, UT 84520 • *1,270*
East Carroll □, LA • *9,709*
Eastchester, NY 10709 • *18,537*
East Chicago, IN 46312 • *33,892*
East Cleveland, OH 44112 • *33,096*
East Compton, CA 90221 • *7,967*
East Dennis, MA 02641 • *1,500*
East Detroit, MI 48021 • *35,283*
East Douglas, MA 01516 • *1,945*
East Dubuque, IL 61025 • *1,914*
East Falmouth, MA 02536 • *5,577*
East Farmingdale, NY 11735 • *4,510*
East Feliciana □, LA • *19,211*
East Flat Rock, NC 28726 • *3,218*
East Gaffney, SC 29340 • *3,278*
Eastgate, WA 98007 • *4,434*
East Glenville, NY 12302 • *6,518*
East Granby, CT 06026 • *1,200*
East Grand Forks, MN 56721 • *8,658*
East Grand Rapids, MI 49506 • *10,807*
East Greenville, PA 18041 • *3,117*
East Greenwich, RI 02818 • *11,865*
East Half Hollow Hills, NY 11746 • *7,010*
Eastham, MA 02642 • *1,150*
East Hampton, CT 06424 • *2,167*
Easthampton, MA 01027 • *15,580*
East Hampton, NY 11937 • *1,402*
East Hanover, NJ • *9,926*
East Hartford, CT 06128 • *50,452*
East Haven, CT 06512 • *26,144*
East Helena, MT 59635 • *1,538*
East Hemet, CA 92343 • *17,611*
East Hills, NY 11576 • *6,746*
East Islip, NY 11730 • *14,325*
East Jordan, MI 49727 • *2,240*
Eastlake, OH 44094 • *21,161*
East La Mirada, CA 90638 • *9,367*
Eastland, TX 76448 • *3,690*
Eastland □, TX • *18,488*
East Lansing, MI 48823–26 • *50,677*
East Las Vegas, NV 89112 • *11,087*
East Liverpool, OH 43920 • *13,654*
East Longmeadow, MA 01028 • *12,905*
East Los Angeles, CA 90022 • *126,379*
East Lyme, CT 06333 • *1,200*
Eastman, GA 31023 • *5,153*
East Marietta, GA 30062 • *11,900*
East Marion, NY 11939 • *1,500*
East Matunuck, RI 02879 • *500*
East Meadow, NY 11554 • *36,609*
East Middlebury, VT 05740 • *500*
East Midvale, UT 84047 • *3,800*
East Millinocket, ME 04430 • *2,075*
East Moline, IL 61244 • *20,147*
East Montpelier, VT 05651 • *600*
East Naples, FL 33962 • *22,951*
East Newark, NJ 07029 • *2,157*
East Newnan, GA 30263 • *1,173*
East Norriton, PA 19401 • *13,324*
East Northport, NY 11731 • *20,411*
Easton, MD 21601 • *9,372*
Easton, PA 18042–44 • *26,276*
East Orange, NJ 07017–19 • *73,552*
East Orleans, MA 02643 • *1,850*
Eastover, SC 29044 • *1,044*
East Palatka, FL 32131 • *1,989*
East Palestine, OH 44413 • *5,168*
East Palo Alto, CA 94303 • *23,451*
East Patchogue, NY 11772 • *20,195*
East Pea Ridge, WV 25705 • *4,980*
East Peoria, IL 61611 • *21,378*
East Pepperell, MA 01463 • *2,296*
East Petersburg, PA 17520 • *4,197*
East Pittsburgh, PA 15112 • *2,160*
Eastpoint, FL 32328 • *1,577*
East Point, GA 30344 • *34,402*
Eastport, ME 04631 • *1,965*
Eastport, NY 11941 • *1,500*
East Porterville, CA 93257 • *5,790*
East Port Orchard, WA 98366 • *5,409*
East Prairie, MO 63845 • *3,416*
East Providence, RI 02914 • *50,380*
East Quogue, NY 11942 • *4,372*
East Richmond, CA 94805 • *5,100*
East Ridge, TN 37412 • *21,101*
East River, CT 06443 • *3,440*
East Rochester, NY 14445 • *6,932*
East Rockaway, NY 11518 • *10,152*
East Rockingham, NC 28379 • *4,158*
East Rutherford, NJ 07073 • *7,902*
East Saint Louis, IL 62201–08 • *40,944*
Eastsound, WA 98245 • *1,100*
East Spencer, NC 28039 • *2,055*
East Stroudsburg, PA 18301 • *8,781*
East Tawas, MI 48730 • *2,887*
East Templeton, MA 01438 • *1,300*
East Troy, WI 53120 • *2,664*
East Tustin, CA 92705 • *10,000*
East Vestal, NY 13902 • *6,310*
East View, WV 26301 • *1,222*
East Walpole, MA 02032 • *3,760*
East Wareham, MA 02538 • *1,500*
East Washington, PA 15301 • *2,126*
East Wenatchee, WA 98802 • *2,701*
East Windsor, NJ 08520 • *15,000*
Eastwood, MI 49001 • *6,340*
Eastwood Hills, UT 84106 • *1,200*
Eaton, CO 80615 • *1,959*
Eaton, IN 47338 • *1,614*
Eaton, OH 45320 • *7,396*
Eaton □, MI • *92,879*
Eaton Rapids, MI 48827 • *4,695*
Eatonton, GA 31024 • *4,737*
Eatontown, NJ 07724 • *13,800*
Eatonville, WA 98328 • *1,374*
Eau Claire, WI 54701–03 • *56,856*
Eau Claire □, WI • *85,183*
Ebensburg, PA 15931 • *3,872*
Eccles, WV 25836 • *1,162*
Echo Bay, NV 89040 • *120*
Echols □, GA • *2,334*
Eckhart Mines, MD 21528 • *1,333*
Eclectic, AL 36024 • *1,087*

Economy, PA 15005 • *9,519*
Ecorse, MI 48229 • *12,180*
Ector □, TX • *118,934*
Edcouch, TX 78538 • *2,878*
Eddy □, NM • *48,605*
Eddy □, ND • *2,951*
Eddystone, PA 19013 • *2,446*
Eddyville, IA 52553 • *1,010*
Eddyville, KY 42038 • *1,889*
Eden, NY 14057 • *3,088*
Eden, NC 27288 • *15,238*
Eden, TX 76837 • *1,567*
Eden Prairie, MN 55344 • *39,311*
Edenton, NC 27932 • *5,268*
Edgar, WI 54426 • *1,318*
Edgar □, IL • *19,595*
Edgartown, MA 02539 • *3,062*
Edgecombe □, NC • *56,558*
Edgefield, SC 29824 • *2,563*
Edgefield □, SC • *18,375*
Edgeley, ND 58433 • *680*
Edgemere, MD 21221 • *9,226*
Edgemont, SD 57735 • *906*
Edgemoor, DE 19802 • *5,853*
Edgerton, KS 66021 • *1,244*
Edgerton, MN 56128 • *1,106*
Edgerton, OH 43517 • *1,896*
Edgerton, WI 53534 • *4,254*
Edgerton, WY 82635 • *247*
Edgewater, AL 35224 • *1,120*
Edgewater, CO 80214 • *4,613*
Edgewater, FL 32132 • *15,337*
Edgewater, MD 21037 • *1,600*
Edgewater, NJ 07020 • *5,001*
Edgewater Park, NJ 08010 • *8,388*
Edgewood, IN 46011 • *2,057*
Edgewood, KY 41017 • *8,143*
Edgewood, MD • *3,470*
Edgewood, MD 21040 • *23,903*
Edgewood, OH 44004 • *5,189*
Edgewood, PA 15218 • *3,581*
Edgewood, WA 98372 • *2,650*
Edgeworth, PA 15143 • *1,670*
Edina, MN 55410 • *46,070*
Edina, MO 63537 • *1,283*
Edinboro, PA 16412 • *7,736*
Edinburg, TX 78539–40 • *29,885*
Edinburgh, IN 46124 • *4,536*
Edison, GA 31746 • *1,182*
Edison, NJ 08817–20 • *88,680*
Edmond, OK 73034 • *52,315*
Edmonds, WA 98020 • *30,744*
Edmondson Heights, MD 21207 • *4,750*
Edmonson □, KY • *10,357*
Edmonton, KY 42129 • *1,477*
Edmore, MI 48829 • *1,126*
Edmunds □, SD • *4,356*
Edna, TX 77957 • *5,343*
Edwards, MS 39066 • *1,279*
Edwards □, IL • *7,440*
Edwards □, KS • *3,787*
Edwards □, TX • *2,266*
Edwardsburg, MI 49112 • *1,142*
Edwardsville, IL 62025 • *14,579*
Edwardsville, KS 66113 • *3,979*
Edwardsville, PA 18704 • *5,399*
Effingham, IL 62401 • *11,851*
Effingham □, GA • *25,687*
Effingham □, IL • *31,704*
Egg Harbor City, NJ 08215 • *4,583*
Egypt, MA 02066 • *1,100*
Egypt Lake, FL 33614 • *14,580*
Ehrenberg, AZ 85334 • *1,500*
Elba, AL 36323 • *4,011*
Elbert □, CO • *9,646*
Elbert □, GA • *18,949*
Elberta, GA 31093 • *1,559*
Elberton, GA 30635 • *5,682*
Elbow Lake, MN 56531 • *1,186*
Elburn, IL 60119 • *1,275*
El Cajon, CA 92019–22 • *88,693*
El Campo, TX 77437 • *10,511*
El Centro, CA 92243–44 • *31,384*
El Cerrito, CA 94530 • *22,869*
Eldersburg, MD 21784 • *9,720*
Eldon, IA 52554 • *1,070*
Eldon, MO 65026 • *4,419*
Eldora, IA 50627 • *3,038*
El Dorado, AR 71730–31 • *23,146*
Eldorado, IL 62930 • *4,536*
El Dorado, KS 67042 • *11,504*
Eldorado, TX 76936 • *2,019*
El Dorado □, CA • *125,995*
El Dorado Hills, CA 95630 • *6,395*
El Dorado Springs, MO 64744 • *3,830*
Eldridge, IA 52748 • *3,378*
Eleanor, WV 25070 • *1,256*
Electra, TX 76360 • *3,113*
Eleele, HI 96705 • *1,489*
El Encanto Heights, CA 93117 • *7,700*
Elfers, FL 34680 • *12,356*
Elgin, IL 60120–23 • *77,010*
Elgin, ND 58533 • *765*
Elgin, OR 97827 • *1,586*
Elgin, TX 78621 • *4,846*
Elida, OH 45807 • *1,486*
Elizabeth, NJ 07201–08 • *110,002*
Elizabeth City, NC 27906–09 • *14,292*
Elizabethton, TN 37643–44 • *11,931*
Elizabethtown, KY 42701–02 • *18,167*
Elizabethtown, NC 28337 • *3,704*
Elizabethtown, PA 17022 • *9,952*
Elizabethville, PA 17023 • *1,467*
Elk □, KS • *3,327*
Elk □, PA • *34,878*
Elkader, IA 52043 • *1,510*
Elk City, OK 73644 • *10,428*
Elk Grove, CA 95624 • *17,483*
Elk Grove Village, IL 60009 • *33,429*
Elkhart, IN 46514–17 • *43,627*
Elkhart, KS 67950 • *2,318*
Elkhart, TX 75839 • *1,076*
Elkhart □, IN • *156,198*
Elkhart Lake, WI 53020 • *1,019*
Elkhorn, NE 68022 • *1,398*
Elkhorn, WI 53121 • *5,337*
Elkin, NC 28621 • *3,790*
Elkins, WV 26241 • *7,420*
Elkland, PA 16920 • *1,849*
Elk Mountain, WY 82324 • *174*
Elko, NV 89801–02 • *14,736*
Elko □, NV • *33,530*
Elk Point, SD 57025 • *1,423*

Elk Rapids, MI 49629 • *1,626*
Elkridge, MD 21227 • *12,953*
Elk River, MN 55330 • *11,143*
Elkton, KY 42220 • *1,789*
Elkton, MD 21921–22 • *9,073*
Elkton, VA 22827 • *1,935*
Elkview, WV 25071 • *1,047*
Ellaville, GA 31806 • *1,724*
Ellendale, DE 19941 • *313*
Ellendale, ND 58436 • *1,798*
Ellensburg, WA 98926 • *12,361*
Ellenton, FL 34222 • *2,573*
Ellenville, NY 12428 • *4,243*
Ellerbe, NC 28338 • *1,132*
Ellerslie, MD 21529 • *1,500*
Ellettsville, IN 47429 • *3,275*
Ellicott City, MD 21043 • *41,396*
Ellijay, GA 30540 • *1,178*
Ellington, CT 06029 • *1,500*
Ellinwood, KS 67526 • *2,329*
Elliott □, KY • *6,455*
Ellis, KS 67637 • *1,814*
Ellis □, KS • *26,004*
Ellis □, OK • *4,497*
Ellis □, TX • *85,167*
Ellisville, MS 39437 • *3,634*
Ellisville, MO 63011 • *7,545*
Ellport, PA 16117 • *1,243*
Ellsworth, KS 67439 • *2,294*
Ellsworth, ME 04605 • *5,975*
Ellsworth, PA 15331 • *1,048*
Ellsworth, WI 54011 • *2,706*
Ellsworth □, KS • *6,586*
Ellwood City, PA 16117 • *8,894*
Elma, WA 98541 • *3,011*
Elm City, NC 27822 • *1,624*
Elmer, NJ 08318 • *1,571*
Elm Grove, WI 53122 • *6,261*
Elmhurst, IL 60126 • *42,029*
Elmira, NY 14901–05 • *33,724*
El Mirage, AZ 85335 • *5,001*
Elmira Heights, NY 14903 • *4,359*
Elmont, NY 11003 • *28,612*
El Monte, CA 91731–34 • *106,209*
Elmora, PA 15737 • *1,500*
Elmore, OH 43416 • *1,334*
Elmore □, AL • *49,210*
Elmore □, ID • *21,205*
Elmwood, IL 61529 • *1,841*
Elmwood Park, IL 60635 • *23,206*
Elmwood Park, NJ 07407 • *17,623*
Elmwood Place, OH 45216 • *2,937*
Eloise, FL 33880 • *1,408*
Elon College, NC 27244 • *4,394*
Eloy, AZ 85231 • *7,211*
El Paso, IL 61738 • *2,499*
El Paso, TX 79901–99 • *515,342*
El Paso □, CO • *397,014*
El Paso □, TX • *591,610*
El Portal, FL 33138 • *2,457*
El Reno, OK 73036 • *15,414*
Elroy, WI 53929 • *1,533*
Elsa, TX 78543 • *5,242*
Elsberry, MO 63343 • *1,898*
El Segundo, CA 90245 • *15,223*
Elsmere, DE 19805 • *5,935*
Elsmere, KY 41018 • *6,847*
Elsmere, NY 12054 • *4,180*
El Sobrante, CA 94803 • *9,852*
Elton, LA 70532 • *1,277*
El Toro, CA 92630 • *62,685*
Elvins, MO 63601 • *1,391*
Elwood, IN 46036 • *9,494*
Elwood, KS 66024 • *1,079*
Elwood, NJ 08217 • *1,400*
Elwood, NY 11731 • *10,916*
Ely, MN 55731 • *3,968*
Ely, NV 89301 • *4,756*
Elyria, OH 44035–39 • *56,746*
Elysburg, PA 17824 • *1,890*
Emanuel □, GA • *20,546*
Emerson, GA 30137 • *1,201*
Emerson, NJ 07630 • *6,930*
Emery □, UT • *10,332*
Eminence, KY 40019 • *2,055*
Emmaus, PA 18049 • *11,157*
Emmet □, IA • *11,569*
Emmet □, MI • *25,040*
Emmetsburg, IA 50536 • *3,940*
Emmett, ID 83617 • *4,601*
Emmitsburg, MD 21727 • *1,688*
Emmonak, AK 99581 • *642*
Emmons □, ND • *4,830*
Empire, NV 89405 • *300*
Emporia, KS 66801 • *25,512*
Emporia, VA 23847 • *5,306*
Emporium, PA 15834 • *2,513*
Emsworth, PA 15202 • *2,892*
Encampment, WY 82325 • *490*
Encinitas, CA 92023–24 • *55,386*
Enderlin, ND 58027 • *997*
Endicott, NY 13760 • *13,531*
Endwell, NY 13760 • *12,602*
Enfield (Thompsonville), CT 06082–83 • *8,458*
Enfield, NH 03748 • *1,560*
Enfield, NC 27823 • *3,082*
England, AR 72046 • *3,351*
Engleside, VA 22309 • *24,058*
Englewood, CO 80110–12 • *29,387*
Englewood, FL 34223–24 • *15,025*
Englewood, NJ 07631–32 • *24,850*
Englewood, OH 45322 • *11,432*
Englewood, TN 37329 • *1,611*
Englewood Cliffs, NJ 07632 • *5,634*
Englishtown, NJ 07726 • *1,268*
Enid, OK 73701–06 • *45,309*
Enka, NC 28728 • *5,567*
Ennis, MT 59729 • *773*
Ennis, TX 75119–20 • *13,883*
Enoch, UT 84720 • *1,947*
Enola, PA 17025 • *5,961*
Enon, OH 45323 • *2,605*
Enoree, SC 29335 • *1,107*
Enosburg Falls, VT 05450 • *1,350*
Ensley, FL 32504 • *16,362*
Enterprise, AL 36330–31 • *20,123*
Enterprise, OR 97828 • *1,905*
Enterprise, WV 26568 • *1,058*
Enumclaw, WA 98022 • *7,227*
Ephraim, UT 84627 • *3,363*
Ephrata, PA 17522 • *12,133*
Ephrata, WA 98823 • *5,349*

Epping, NH 03042 • *1,384*
Epworth, IA 52045 • *1,297*
Erath, LA 70533 • *2,428*
Erath □, TX • *27,991*
Erial, NJ 08081 • *2,500*
Erick, OK 73645 • *1,083*
Erie, CO 80516 • *1,258*
Erie, IL 61250 • *1,572*
Erie, KS 66733 • *1,276*
Erie, PA 16501–65 • *108,718*
Erie □, NY • *968,532*
Erie □, OH • *76,779*
Erie □, PA • *275,572*
Erin, TN 37061 • *1,586*
Erlanger, KY 41018 • *15,979*
Erma, NJ 08204 • *2,045*
Errol Heights, OR 97266 • *10,487*
Erwin, NC 28339 • *4,061*
Erwin, TN 37650 • *5,015*
Escalon, CA 95320 • *4,437*
Escambia □, AL • *35,518*
Escambia □, FL • *262,798*
Escanaba, MI 49829 • *13,659*
Escatawpa, MS 39552 • *3,902*
Escondido, CA 92025–27 • *108,635*
Esmeralda □, NV • *1,344*
Esmond, RI 02917 • *4,320*
Espanola, NM 87532 • *8,389*
Esparto, CA 95627 • *1,487*
Esperance, WA 98043 • *11,236*
Espy, PA 17815 • *1,430*
Essex, CT 06426 • *2,500*
Essex, MD 21221 • *40,872*
Essex, MA 01929 • *1,507*
Essex, VT 05451 • *800*
Essex □, MA • *670,080*
Essex □, NJ • *778,206*
Essex □, NY • *37,152*
Essex □, VT • *6,405*
Essex □, VA • *8,689*
Essex Fells, NJ 07021 • *2,363*
Essex Junction, VT 05452–53 • *8,396*
Essexville, MI 48732 • *4,088*
Estacada, OR 97023 • *2,016*
Estelle, LA 70072 • *14,091*
Estell Manor, NJ 08319 • *1,404*
Estes Park, CO 80517 • *3,184*
Estherville, IA 51334 • *6,720*
Estill, SC 29918 • *2,387*
Estill □, KY • *14,614*
Estill Springs, TN 37330 • *1,408*
Etna, PA 15223 • *4,200*
Etowah, TN 37331 • *3,815*
Etowah □, AL • *99,840*
Ettrick, VA 23803 • *5,290*
Euclid, OH 44117 • *54,875*
Eudora, AR 71640 • *3,155*
Eudora, KS 66025 • *3,006*
Eufaula, AL 36027 • *13,220*
Eufaula, OK 74432 • *2,652*
Eugene, OR 97401–05 • *112,669*
Euless, TX 76039–40 • *38,149*
Eunice, LA 70535 • *11,162*
Eunice, NM 88231 • *2,676*
Eupora, MS 39744 • *2,145*
Eureka, CA 95501–02 • *27,025*
Eureka, IL 61530 • *4,435*
Eureka, KS 67045 • *2,974*
Eureka, MO 63025 • *4,683*
Eureka, MT 59917 • *1,043*
Eureka, NV 89316 • *650*
Eureka, SC 29706 • *1,738*
Eureka, SD 57437 • *1,197*
Eureka □, NV • *1,547*
Eureka Springs, AR 72632 • *1,900*
Eustis, FL 32726–27 • *12,967*
Eutaw, AL 35462 • *2,281*
Evangeline □, LA • *33,274*
Evans, CO 80620 • *5,877*
Evans, GA 30809 • *2,000*
Evans □, GA • *8,724*
Evans City, PA 16033 • *2,054*
Evansdale, IA 50707 • *4,638*
Evanston, IL 60201–04 • *73,233*
Evanston, WY 82930–31 • *10,903*
Evansville, IN 47701–37 • *126,272*
Evansville, WI 53536 • *3,174*
Evansville, WY 82636 • *1,403*
Evart, MI 49631 • *1,744*
Evarts, KY 40828 • *1,063*
Eveleth, MN 55734 • *4,064*
Everett, MA 02149 • *35,701*
Everett, PA 15537 • *1,777*
Everett, WA 98201–08 • *69,961*
Evergreen, AL 36401 • *3,911*
Evergreen, CO 80439 • *7,582*
Evergreen Park, IL 60642 • *20,874*
Everman, TX 76140 • *5,672*
Everson, WA 98247 • *1,490*
Ewa, HI 96706 • *3,780*
Ewa Beach, HI 96706–07 • *14,315*
Ewing Township, NJ 08618 • *34,185*
Excelsior Springs, MO 64024 • *10,354*
Exeter, CA 93221 • *7,276*
Exeter, NH 03833 • *9,556*
Exeter, PA 18643 • *5,691*
Exmore, VA 23350 • *1,115*
Experiment, GA 30223 • *3,762*
Eyota, MN 55934 • *1,448*

F

Fabens, TX 79838 • *5,599*
Factoryville, PA 18419 • *1,310*
Fairbank, IA 50629 • *1,018*
Fairbanks, AK 99701 • *30,843*
Fair Bluff, NC 28439 • *1,068*
Fairborn, OH 45324 • *31,300*
Fairburn, GA 30213 • *4,013*
Fairbury, IL 61739 • *3,643*
Fairbury, NE 68352 • *4,335*
Fairchance, PA 15436 • *1,918*
Fairdale, KY 40118 • *6,563*
Fairfax, CA 94930 • *6,931*
Fairfax, DE 19803 • *2,075*
Fairfax, MN 55332 • *1,276*
Fairfax, OK 74637 • *1,749*
Fairfax, SC 29827 • *2,317*
Fairfax, VA 22030–39 • *19,622*
Fairfax □, VA • *818,584*
Fairfield, AL 35064 • *12,200*
Fairfield, CA 94533 • *77,211*
Fairfield, CT 06430–32 • *53,418*

Fairfield, IL 62837 • *5,439*
Fairfield, IA 52556 • *9,768*
Fairfield, ME 04937 • *2,794*
Fairfield, NJ 07004 • *7,615*
Fairfield, OH 45014 • *39,729*
Fairfield, TX 75840 • *3,234*
Fairfield □, CT • *827,645*
Fairfield □, OH • *103,461*
Fairfield □, SC • *22,295*
Fairfield Bay, AR 72088 • *2,332*
Fair Grove, NC 27360 • *1,500*
Fairhaven, MA 02719 • *15,759*
Fair Haven, NJ 07704 • *5,270*
Fair Haven, VT 05743 • *2,432*
Fairhope, AL 36532–33 • *8,485*
Fair Lawn, NJ 07410 • *30,548*
Fairlawn, OH 44313 • *5,779*
Fairlawn, VA 24141 • *2,399*
Fairlea, WV 24902 • *1,743*
Fairless Hills, PA 19030 • *9,026*
Fairmont, IL 60441 • *2,260*
Fairmont, MN 56031 • *11,265*
Fairmont, NC 28340 • *2,489*
Fairmont, WV 26554–55 • *20,210*
Fairmount, IN 46928 • *3,130*
Fairmount, NY 13031 • *12,266*
Fairmount Heights, MD 20743 • *1,238*
Fair Oaks, CA 95628 • *26,867*
Fair Oaks, GA 30060 • *6,996*
Fairoaks, PA 15003 • *1,854*
Fair Plain, MI 49022 • *8,051*
Fairport, NY 14450 • *5,943*
Fairport Harbor, OH 44077 • *2,978*
Fairton, NJ 08320 • *1,359*
Fairview, MT 59221 • *869*
Fairview, NJ 07022 • *10,733*
Fairview, OK 73737 • *2,936*
Fairview, OR 97024 • *2,391*
Fairview, PA 16415 • *1,988*
Fairview, TN 37062 • *4,210*
Fairview Heights, IL 62208 • *14,351*
Fairview Park, IN 47842 • *1,446*
Fairview Park, OH 44126 • *18,028*
Fairview Shores, FL 32804 • *13,192*
Fairway, KS 66205 • *4,173*
Fairwood, WA 98058 • *2,000*
Fairwood, WA 99218 • *5,807*
Falconer, NY 14733 • *2,653*
Falcon Heights, MN 55113 • *5,380*
Falfurrias, TX 78355 • *5,788*
Falkville, AL 35622 • *1,337*
Fall Branch, TN 37656 • *1,203*
Fallbrook, CA 92028 • *22,095*
Fall City, WA 98024 • *1,582*
Fall Creek, WI 54742 • *1,034*
Fallon, NV 89406 • *6,438*
Fallon □, MT • *3,103*
Fall River, MA 02720–26 • *92,703*
Fall River □, SD • *7,353*
Falls □, TX • *17,712*
Falls Church, VA 22040–46 • *9,578*
Falls City, NE 68355 • *4,769*
Falls Creek, PA 15840 • *1,087*
Fallston, MD 21047 • *5,730*
Falls Township, PA 19054 • *36,083*
Falmouth, KY 41040 • *2,378*
Falmouth, ME 04105 • *7,610*
Falmouth, MA 02540 • *4,047*
Falmouth, VA 22405 • *3,541*
Fannin □, GA • *15,992*
Fannin □, TX • *24,804*
Fanwood, NJ 07023 • *7,115*
Fargo, ND 58102–09 • *74,111*
Faribault, MN 55021 • *17,085*
Faribault □, MN • *16,937*
Farley, IA 52046 • *1,354*
Farmer City, IL 61842 • *2,114*
Farmers Branch, TX 75234 • *24,250*
Farmersburg, IN 47850 • *1,159*
Farmersville, CA 93223 • *6,235*
Farmerville, LA 71241 • *3,334*
Farmingdale, ME 04345 • *2,070*
Farmingdale, NJ 07727 • *1,462*
Farmingdale, NY 11735 • *8,022*
Farmington, AR 72730 • *1,322*
Farmington, CT 06032 • *2,500*
Farmington, IL 61531 • *2,535*
Farmington, ME 04938 • *4,197*
Farmington, MI 48335–36 • *10,132*
Farmington, MN 55024 • *5,940*
Farmington, MO 63640 • *11,598*
Farmington, NH 03835 • *3,567*
Farmington, NM 87401–02 • *33,997*
Farmington, UT 84025 • *9,028*
Farmington Hills, MI 48331–34 • *74,652*
Farmingville, NY 11738 • *14,842*
Farmland, IN 47340 • *1,412*
Farmville, NC 27828 • *4,392*
Farmville, VA 23901 • *6,046*
Farragut, TN 37922 • *12,793*
Farrell, PA 16121 • *6,841*
Farwell, TX 79325 • *1,373*
Faulk □, SD • *2,744*
Faulkland Heights, DE 19808 • *1,300*
Faulkner □, AR • *60,006*
Faulkton, SD 57438 • *809*
Fauquier □, VA • *48,741*
Fayette, AL 35555 • *4,909*
Fayette, IA 52142 • *1,317*
Fayette, MS 39069 • *1,853*
Fayette, MO 65248 • *2,888*
Fayette, OH 43521 • *1,248*
Fayette □, AL • *17,962*
Fayette □, GA • *62,415*
Fayette □, IL • *20,893*
Fayette □, IN • *26,015*
Fayette □, IA • *21,843*
Fayette □, KY • *225,366*
Fayette □, OH • *27,466*
Fayette □, PA • *145,351*
Fayette □, TN • *25,559*
Fayette □, TX • *20,095*
Fayette □, WV • *47,952*
Fayetteville, AR 72701–03 • *42,099*
Fayetteville, GA 30214 • *5,827*
Fayetteville, NC 28301–14 • *75,695*
Fayetteville, PA 17222 • *3,033*
Fayetteville, TN 37334 • *6,921*
Fayetteville, WV 25840 • *2,182*
Fayville, MA 01745 • *1,000*
Federal Heights, CO 80221 • *9,342*
Federalsburg, MD 21632 • *2,365*
Federal Way, WA 98003 • *67,554*

Feeding Hills, MA 01030 • 5,470
Fellowship, NJ 08057 • 4,250
Fellsmere, FL 32948 • 2,179
Felton, CA 95041 • 5,350
Felton, DE 19943 • 683
Fennimore, WI 53809 • 2,378
Fennville, MI 49408 • 1,023
Fenton, MI 48430 • 8,444
Fentress □, TN • 14,669
Ferdinand, IN 47532 • 2,318
Fergus □, MT • 12,083
Fergus Falls, MN 56537–38 • 12,362
Ferguson, MO 63135 • 22,286
Fernandina Beach, FL 32034 • 8,765
Fern Creek, KY 40291 • 16,406
Ferndale, CA 95536 • 1,331
Ferndale, MD 21061 • 16,355
Ferndale, MI 48220 • 25,084
Ferndale, PA 15905 • 2,020
Ferndale, WA 98248 • 5,398
Fernley, NV 89408 • 5,164
Fern Park, FL 32730 • 8,294
Fernway, PA 16063 • 9,072
Ferriday, LA 71334 • 4,111
Ferris, TX 75125 • 2,212
Ferron, UT 84523 • 1,606
Ferry □, WA • 6,295
Ferry Farms, VA 22405 • 1,600
Fessenden, ND 58438 • 655
Festus, MO 63028 • 8,105
Fieldale, VA 24089 • 1,018
Fig Garden, CA 93704 • 9,000
Filer, ID 83328 • 1,511
Fillmore, CA 93015–16 • 11,992
Fillmore, UT 84631 • 1,956
Fillmore □, MN • 20,777
Fillmore □, NE • 7,103
Findlay, OH 45839–40 • 35,703
Finley, TN 38030 • 1,014
Finney □, KS • 33,070
Fircrest, WA 98466 • 5,258
Firebaugh, CA 93622 • 4,429
Firestone, CO 80520 • 1,358
Fisher, IL 61843 • 1,526
Fisher □, TX • 4,842
Fishers, IN 46038 • 7,508
Fishkill, NY 12524 • 1,957
Fiskdale, MA 01518 • 2,189
Fitchburg, MA 01420 • 41,194
Fitzgerald, GA 31750 • 8,612
Five Points, NM 87105 • 4,200
Flagler □, FL • 28,701
Flagler Beach, FL 32136 • 3,820
Flagstaff, AZ 86001–16 • 45,857
Flanders, NJ 07836 • 3,040
Flandreau, SD 57028 • 2,311
Flathead □, MT • 59,218
Flatonia, TX 78941 • 1,295
Flat River, MO 63601 • 4,823
Flat Rock, MI 48134 • 7,290
Flat Rock, NC 28731 • 1,200
Flatwoods, KY 41139 • 7,799
Fleetwood, PA 19522 • 3,478
Fleming □, KY • 12,292
Flemingsburg, KY 41041 • 3,071
Flemington, NJ 08822 • 4,047
Flemington, PA 17745 • 1,321
Fletcher, NC 28732 • 2,787
Fletcher, OK 73541 • 1,002
Flint, MI 48501–32 • 140,761
Flint City, AL 35601 • 1,033
Flippin, AR 72634 • 1,006
Flomaton, AL 36441 • 1,811
Flora, IL 62839 • 5,054
Flora, IN 46929 • 2,179
Flora, MS 39071 • 1,482
Florala, AL 36442 • 2,075
Floral City, FL 32636 • 2,609
Floral Park, NY 11001–05 • 15,947
Florence, AL 35630–33 • 36,426
Florence, AZ 85232 • 7,510
Florence, CA 90001 • 43,900
Florence, CO 81226 • 2,990
Florence, KY 41042 • 18,624
Florence, MS 39073 • 1,831
Florence, NJ 08518 • 4,203
Florence, OR 97439 • 5,162
Florence, SC 29501–06 • 29,813
Florence □, SC • 114,344
Florence □, WI • 4,590
Floresville, TX 78114 • 5,247
Florham Park, NJ 07932 • 8,521
Florida, NY 10921 • 2,497
Florida City, FL 33034 • 5,806
Florida Ridge, FL 32960 • 12,218
Florin, CA 95828 • 24,330
Florissant, MO 63031–34 • 51,206
Flossmoor, IL 60422 • 8,651
Flower Hill, NY 11050 • 4,490
Flowery Branch, GA 30542 • 1,251
Flowood, MS 39208 • 2,860
Floyd □, GA • 81,251
Floyd □, IN • 64,404
Floyd □, IA • 17,058
Floyd □, KY • 43,586
Floyd □, TX • 8,497
Floyd □, VA • 12,005
Floydada, TX 79235 • 3,896
Flushing, MI 48433 • 8,542
Flushing, OH 43977 • 1,042
Fluvanna □, VA • 12,429
Foard □, TX • 1,794
Folcroft, PA 19032 • 7,506
Foley, AL 36535–36 • 4,937
Foley, MN 56329 • 1,854
Folkston, GA 31537 • 2,285
Follansbee, WV 26037 • 3,339
Folly Beach, SC 29439 • 1,398
Folsom, CA 95630 • 29,802
Folsom, NJ 08037 • 2,181
Fonda, NY 12068 • 1,007
Fond du Lac, WI 54935–36 • 37,757
Fond du Lac □, WI • 90,083
Fontana, CA 92334–36 • 87,535
Fontana, WI 53125 • 1,635
Foothill Farms, CA 95841 • 17,135
Ford □, IL • 14,275
Ford □, KS • 27,463
Ford City, CA 93268 • 3,781
Ford City, PA 16226 • 3,413
Ford Heights, IL 60411 • 4,259
Fords, NJ 08863 • 14,392
Fords Prairie, WA 98531 • 2,480
Fordyce, AR 71742 • 4,729
Foreman, AR 71836 • 1,267
Forest, MS 39074 • 5,060
Forest, OH 45843 • 1,594
Forest □, PA • 4,802
Forest □, WI • 8,776
Forest Acres, SC 29206 • 7,197
Forest City, IA 50436 • 4,430
Forest City, NC 28043 • 7,475
Forest City, PA 18421 • 1,846
Forestdale, AL 35214 • 10,395
Forestdale, RI 02824 • 530
Forest Dale, VT 05745 • 350
Forest Grove, OR 97116 • 13,559
Forest Hill, TX 76119 • 11,482
Forest Hills, PA 15221 • 7,335
Forest Knolls, CA 94933 • 2,000
Forest Lake, MN 55025 • 5,833
Forest Park, GA 30050–51 • 16,925
Forest Park, IL 60130 • 14,918
Forest Park, LA 71291 • 1,400
Forest Park, OH 45240 • 18,609
Forked River, NJ 08731 • 1,950
Forks, WA 98331 • 2,862
Forney, TX 75126 • 4,070
Forrest, IL 61741 • 1,124
Forrest □, MS • 68,314
Forrest City, AR 72335 • 13,364
Forreston, IL 61030 • 1,361
Forsyth, GA 31029 • 4,268
Forsyth, IL 62535 • 1,275
Forsyth, MO 65653 • 1,175
Forsyth, MT 59327 • 2,178
Forsyth □, GA • 44,083
Forsyth □, NC • 265,878
Fort Ashby, WV 26719 • 1,288
Fort Atkinson, WI 53538 • 10,227
Fort Bend □, TX • 225,421
Fort Benton, MT 59442 • 1,660
Fort Bragg, CA 95437 • 6,078
Fort Branch, IN 47648 • 2,447
Fort Collins, CO 80521–26 • 87,758
Fort Covington, NY 12937 • 1,200
Fort Davis, TX 79734 • 1,100
Fort Defiance, AZ 86504 • 4,489
Fort Deposit, AL 36032 • 1,240
Fort Dodge, IA 50501 • 25,894
Fort Edward, NY 12828 • 3,561
Fort Fairfield, ME 04742 • 1,729
Fort Gaines, GA 31751 • 1,248
Fort Gibson, OK 74434 • 3,359
Fort Hall, ID 83203 • 2,681
Fort Kent, ME 04743 • 2,123
Fort Laramie, WY 82212 • 243
Fort Lauderdale, FL 33301–51 • 149,377
Fort Lee, NJ 07024 • 31,997
Fort Loramie, OH 45845 • 1,042
Fort Loudon, PA 17224 • 1,200
Fort Lupton, CO 80621 • 5,159
Fort Madison, IA 52627 • 11,618
Fort McKinley, OH 45426 • 9,740
Fort Meade, FL 33841 • 4,976
Fort Mill, SC 29715 • 4,930
Fort Mitchell, KY 41017 • 7,438
Fort Morgan, CO 80701 • 9,068
Fort Myers, FL 33901–19 • 45,206
Fort Myers Beach, FL 33931–32 • 9,284
Fort Myers Shores, FL 33905 • 5,460
Fort Oglethorpe, GA 30742 • 5,880
Fort Payne, AL 35967 • 11,838
Fort Pierce, FL 34945–54 • 36,830
Fort Pierre, SD 57532 • 1,854
Fort Plain, NY 13339 • 2,416
Fort Recovery, OH 45846 • 1,313
Fort Scott, KS 66701 • 8,362
Fort Shawnee, OH 45806 • 4,128
Fort Smith, AR 72901–17 • 72,798
Fort Stockton, TX 79735 • 8,524
Fort Sumner, NM 88119 • 1,269
Fort Thomas, KY 41075 • 16,032
Fortuna, CA 95540 • 8,788
Fort Valley, GA 31030 • 8,198
Fortville, IN 46040 • 2,690
Fort Walton Beach, FL 32547–48 • 21,471
Fort Washington Forest, MD 20744 • 1,010
Fort Wayne, IN 46801–99 • 173,072
Fort Wingate, NM 87316 • 950
Fort Worth, TX 76101–85 • 447,619
Fort Wright, KY 41011 • 6,570
Forty Fort, PA 18704 • 5,049
Fort Yukon, AK 99740 • 580
Fosston, MN 56542 • 1,529
Foster □, ND • 3,983
Foster City, CA 94404 • 28,176
Foster Village, HI 96818 • 3,700
Fostoria, OH 44830 • 14,983
Fountain, CO 80817 • 9,984
Fountain □, IN • 17,808
Fountain Hill, PA 18015 • 4,637
Fountain Inn, SC 29644 • 4,388
Fountain Place, LA • 9,200
Fountain Valley, CA 92708 • 53,691
Four Corners, OR 97301 • 12,156
Four Oaks, NC 27524 • 1,308
Fowler, CA 93625 • 3,208
Fowler, CO 81039 • 1,154
Fowler, IN 47944 • 2,333
Fowlerville, MI 48836 • 2,648
Foxboro, MA 02035 • 5,706
Fox Chapel, PA 15238 • 5,319
Fox Lake, IL 60020 • 7,478
Fox Lake, WI 53933 • 1,269
Fox Point, WI 53217 • 7,238
Fox River Grove, IL 60021 • 3,551
Frackville, PA 17931 • 4,700
Framingham, MA 01701 • 64,994
Franconia, VA 22310 • 19,882
Frankenmuth, MI 48734 • 4,408
Frankford, DE 19945 • 591
Frankfort, IL 60423 • 7,180
Frankfort, IN 46041 • 14,754
Frankfort, KY 40601–22 • 25,968
Frankfort, MI 49635 • 1,546
Frankfort, NY 13340 • 2,693
Frankfort, OH 45628 • 1,065
Franklin, IN 46131 • 12,907
Franklin, KY 42134–35 • 7,607
Franklin, LA 70538 • 9,004
Franklin, MA 02038 • 9,965
Franklin, NE 68939 • 1,112
Franklin, NH 03235 • 8,304
Franklin, NJ 07416 • 4,977
Franklin, NC 28734 • 2,873
Franklin, OH 45005 • 11,026
Franklin, PA 16323 • 7,329
Franklin, TN 37064–65 • 20,098
Franklin, TX 77856 • 1,336
Franklin, VA 23851 • 7,864
Franklin, WI 53132 • 21,855
Franklin □, AL • 27,814
Franklin □, AR • 14,897
Franklin □, FL • 8,967
Franklin □, GA • 16,650
Franklin □, ID • 9,232
Franklin □, IL • 40,319
Franklin □, IN • 19,580
Franklin □, IA • 11,364
Franklin □, KS • 21,994
Franklin □, KY • 43,781
Franklin □, LA • 22,387
Franklin □, ME • 29,008
Franklin □, MA • 70,092
Franklin □, MS • 8,377
Franklin □, MO • 80,603
Franklin □, NE • 3,938
Franklin □, NY • 46,540
Franklin □, NC • 36,414
Franklin □, OH • 961,437
Franklin □, PA • 121,082
Franklin □, TN • 34,725
Franklin □, TX • 7,802
Franklin □, VT • 39,980
Franklin □, VA • 39,549
Franklin □, WA • 37,473
Franklin Lakes, NJ 07417 • 9,873
Franklin Park, IL 60131 • 18,485
Franklin Park, PA 15143 • 10,109
Franklin Square, NY 11010 • 28,205
Franklinton, LA 70438 • 4,007
Franklinton, NC 27525 • 1,615
Franklinville, NJ 08322 • 1,020
Franklinville, NY 14737 • 1,739
Frankston, TX 75763 • 1,127
Frankton, IN 46044 • 1,736
Fraser, MI 48026 • 13,899
Frazee, MN 56544 • 1,176
Frazeysburg, OH 43822 • 1,165
Frazier Park, CA 93225 • 2,201
Frederic, WI 54837 • 1,124
Frederica, DE 19946 • 761
Frederick, MD 21701–02 • 40,148
Frederick, OK 73542 • 5,221
Frederick □, MD • 150,208
Frederick □, VA • 45,723
Fredericksburg, IA 50630 • 1,011
Fredericksburg, TX 78624 • 6,934
Fredericksburg, VA 22401–08 • 19,027
Fredericktown, MO 63645 • 3,950
Fredericktown, OH 43019 • 2,443
Fredericktown, PA 15333 • 1,052
Fredonia, AZ 86022 • 1,207
Fredonia, KS 66736 • 2,599
Fredonia, NY 14063 • 10,436
Fredonia, WI 53021 • 1,558
Freeborn □, MN • 33,060
Freeburg, IL 62243 • 3,115
Freedom, CA 95019 • 8,361
Freedom, PA 15042 • 1,897
Freedom, WY 83120 • 450
Freehold, NJ 07728 • 10,742
Freeland, MI 48623 • 1,421
Freeland, PA 18224 • 3,909
Freeman, SD 57029 • 1,293
Freemansburg, PA 18017 • 1,946
Freeport, IL 61032 • 25,840
Freeport, ME 04032 • 1,829
Freeport, NY 11520 • 39,894
Freeport, PA 16229 • 1,983
Freeport, TX 77541 • 11,389
Freer, TX 78357 • 3,271
Freestone □, TX • 15,818
Fremont, CA 94536–39 • 173,339
Fremont, IN 46737 • 1,407
Fremont, MI 49412 • 3,875
Fremont, NE 68025 • 23,680
Fremont, NC 27830 • 1,710
Fremont, OH 43420 • 17,648
Fremont □, CO • 32,273
Fremont □, ID • 10,937
Fremont □, IA • 8,226
Fremont □, WY • 33,662
French Island, WI 54601 • 4,478
French Lick, IN 47432 • 2,087
Frenchtown, NJ 08825 • 1,528
Fresno, CA 93701–94 • 354,202
Fresno □, CA • 667,490
Frewsburg, NY 14738 • 1,817
Friars Point, MS 38631 • 1,334
Friday Harbor, WA 98250 • 1,492
Fridley, MN 55432 • 28,335
Friend, NE 68359 • 1,111
Friendship, NY 14739 • 1,423
Friendswood, TX 77546 • 22,814
Frio □, TX • 13,472
Friona, TX 79035 • 3,688
Frisco, CO 80443 • 1,601
Frisco City, AL 36445 • 1,581
Fritch, TX 79036 • 2,335
Frontenac, KS 66762 • 2,588
Frontier □, NE • 3,101
Front Royal, VA 22630 • 11,880
Frostburg, MD 21532 • 8,075
Frostproof, FL 33843 • 2,808
Fruita, CO 81521 • 4,045
Fruit Heights, UT 84037 • 3,900
Fruitland, ID 83619 • 2,400
Fruitland, MD 21826 • 3,511
Fruitland Park, FL 34731 • 2,754
Fruitport, MI 49415 • 1,090
Fruitvale, CO 81504 • 1,070
Fruitvale, WA 98902 • 4,125
Fruitville, FL 34232 • 9,808
Fryeburg, ME 04037 • 1,580
Fulda, MN 56131 • 1,212
Fullerton, CA 92631–35 • 114,144
Fullerton, NE 68638 • 1,452
Fulton, IL 61252 • 3,698
Fulton, KY 42041 • 3,078
Fulton, MS 38843 • 3,387
Fulton, MO 65251 • 10,033
Fulton, NY 13069 • 12,929
Fulton □, AR • 10,037
Fulton □, GA • 648,951
Fulton □, IL • 38,080
Fulton □, IN • 18,840
Fulton □, KY • 8,271
Fulton □, NY • 54,191
Fulton □, OH • 38,498
Fulton □, PA • 13,837
Fultondale, AL 35068 • 6,400
Funkstown, MD 21734 • 1,136
Fuquay-Varina, NC 27526 • 4,562
Furnas □, NE • 5,553
Fyffe, AL 35971 • 1,094

G

Gabbs, NV 89409 • 667
Gadsden, AL 35901–05 • 42,523
Gadsden □, FL • 41,105
Gaffney, SC 29340–42 • 13,145
Gage □, NE • 22,794
Gages Lake, IL 60030 • 8,349
Gahanna, OH 43230 • 27,791
Gaines □, TX • 14,123
Gainesboro, TN 38562 • 1,002
Gainesville, FL 32601–14 • 84,770
Gainesville, GA 30501–07 • 17,885
Gainesville, TX 76240 • 14,256
Gaithersburg, MD 20877–79 • 39,542
Galax, VA 24333 • 6,670
Galena, AK 99741 • 833
Galena, IL 61036 • 3,647
Galena, KS 66739 • 3,308
Galesburg, IL 61401–02 • 33,530
Galesburg, MI 49053 • 1,863
Gales Ferry, CT 06335 • 1,191
Galesville, WI 54630 • 1,278
Galeton, PA 16922 • 1,370
Galeville, NY 13088 • 4,695
Galion, OH 44833 • 11,859
Gallatin, MO 64640 • 1,864
Gallatin, TN 37066 • 18,794
Gallatin □, IL • 6,909
Gallatin □, KY • 5,393
Gallatin □, MT • 50,463
Gallia □, OH • 30,954
Galliano, LA 70354 • 4,294
Gallipolis, OH 45631 • 4,831
Gallitzin, PA 16641 • 2,003
Gallup, NM 87301–05 • 19,154
Galt, CA 95632 • 8,889
Galva, IL 61434 • 2,742
Galveston, IN 46932 • 1,609
Galveston, TX 77550–54 • 59,070
Galveston □, TX • 217,399
Gambell, AK 99742 • 525
Gambier, OH 43022 • 2,073
Gambrills, MD 21054 • 1,200
Ganado, AZ 86505 • 3,400
Ganado, TX 77962 • 1,701
Gang Mills, NY 14870 • 2,738
Gantt, SC 29605 • 13,891
Gap, PA 17527 • 1,200
Garberville, CA 95440 • 1,200
Garden □, NE • 2,460
Gardena, CA 90247–49 • 49,847
Garden City, GA 31408 • 7,410
Garden City, ID 83704 • 6,369
Garden City, KS 67846 • 24,097
Garden City, MI 48135–36 • 31,846
Garden City, MO 64747 • 1,225
Garden City, NY 11530 • 21,686
Garden City Park, NY 11040 • 7,437
Gardendale, AL 35071 • 9,251
Garden Grove, CA 92640–45 • 143,050
Garden Home, OR 97223 • 5,500
Gardiner, ME 04345 • 6,746
Gardner, IL 60424 • 1,237
Gardner, KS 66030 • 3,191
Gardner, MA 01440 • 20,125
Gardnerville, NV 89410 • 2,177
Gardnerville Ranchos, NV 89410 • 7,455
Garfield, NJ 07026 • 26,727
Garfield □, CO • 29,974
Garfield □, MT • 1,589
Garfield □, NE • 2,141
Garfield □, OK • 56,735
Garfield □, UT • 3,980
Garfield □, WA • 2,248
Garfield Heights, OH 44125 • 31,739
Garfield Park, DE 19720 • 1,415
Garland, TX 75040–48 • 180,650
Garland, UT 84312 • 1,637
Garland □, AR • 73,397
Garner, IA 50438 • 2,916
Garner, NC 27529 • 14,967
Garnett, KS 66032 • 3,210
Garrard □, KY • 11,579
Garretson, SD 57030 • 924
Garrett, IN 46738 • 5,349
Garrett □, MD • 28,138
Garrettsville, OH 44231 • 2,014
Garrison, MD 21055 • 5,045
Garrison, ND 58540 • 1,530
Garvin □, OK • 26,605
Garwood, NJ 07027 • 4,227
Gary, IN 46401–11 • 116,646
Gary, WV 24836 • 1,355
Garysburg, NC 27831 • 1,057
Garyville, LA 70051 • 3,181
Garza □, TX • 5,143
Gas City, IN 46933 • 6,296
Gasconade □, MO • 14,006
Gasport, NY 14067 • 1,336
Gassville, AR 72635 • 1,167
Gaston, NC 27832 • 1,003
Gaston □, NC • 175,093
Gastonia, NC 28051–56 • 54,732
Gate City, VA 24251 • 2,214
Gates, NY 14624 • 30,000
Gates □, NC • 9,305
Gatesville, TX 76528 • 11,492
Gatlinburg, TN 37738 • 3,417
Gautier, MS 39553 • 10,088
Gaylord, MI 49735 • 3,256
Gaylord, MN 55334 • 1,935
Gearhart, OR 97138 • 1,027
Geary, OK 73040 • 1,347
Geary □, KS • 30,453
Geauga □, OH • 81,129
Geistown, PA 15904 • 2,749
Gem □, ID • 11,844
Genesee, ID 83832 • 725
Genesee, MI 48437 • 1,400
Genesee □, MI • 430,459
Genesee □, NY • 60,060
Geneseo, IL 61254 • 5,990
Geneseo, NY 14454 • 7,187
Geneva, AL 36340 • 4,681
Geneva, IL 60134 • 12,617
Geneva, IN 46740 • 1,280
Geneva, NE 68361 • 2,310
Geneva, NY 14456 • 14,143
Geneva, OH 44041 • 6,597
Geneva □, AL • 23,647
Geneva-on-the-Lake, OH 44041 • 1,626
Genoa, IL 60135 • 3,083
Genoa, NE 68640 • 1,082
Genoa, NV 89411 • 190
Genoa, OH 43430 • 2,262
Genoa City, WI 53128 • 1,277
Gentry, AR 72734 • 1,726
Gentry □, MO • 6,848
George, IA 51237 • 1,066
George □, MS • 16,673
Georgetown, CA 95634 • 2,000
Georgetown, CT 06829 • 1,694
Georgetown, DE 19947 • 3,732
Georgetown, IL 61846 • 3,678
Georgetown, IN 47122 • 2,092
Georgetown, KY 40324 • 11,414
Georgetown, MA 01833 • 2,100
Georgetown, OH 45121 • 3,627
Georgetown, SC 29440–42 • 9,517
Georgetown, TX 78626–28 • 14,842
Georgetown □, SC • 46,302
George West, TX 78022 • 2,586
Georgiana, AL 36033 • 1,933
Gering, NE 69341 • 7,946
Gerlach, NV 89412 • 200
Germantown, IL 62245 • 1,167
Germantown, MD 20874 • 41,145
Germantown, OH 45327 • 4,916
Germantown, TN 38138 • 32,893
Germantown, WI 53022 • 13,658
Gettysburg, PA 17325 • 7,025
Gettysburg, SD 57442 • 1,510
Giants Neck, CT 06357 • 1,200
Gibbon, NE 68840 • 1,525
Gibbstown, NJ 08027 • 5,404
Gibsland, LA 71028 • 1,224
Gibson □, IN • 31,913
Gibson □, TN • 46,315
Gibsonburg, OH 43431 • 2,579
Gibson City, IL 60936 • 3,396
Gibsonia, FL 33805 • 5,168
Gibsonia, PA 15044 • 3,500
Gibsonton, FL 33534 • 7,706
Gibsonville, NC 27249 • 3,441
Giddings, TX 78942 • 4,093
Gideon, MO 63848 • 1,104
Gifford, FL 32960 • 6,278
Gig Harbor, WA 98335 • 3,236
Gila □, AZ • 40,216
Gila Bend, AZ 85337 • 1,747
Gilbert, AZ 85234 • 29,188
Gilbert, MN 55741 • 1,934
Gilbert, OR 97266 • 4,000
Gilbertsville, PA 19525 • 3,994
Gilbertville, MA 01031 • 1,029
Gilchrist □, FL • 9,667
Gilcrest, CO 80623 • 1,084
Giles □, TN • 25,741
Giles □, VA • 16,366
Gilford Park, NJ 08753 • 8,668
Gillespie, IL 62033 • 3,645
Gillespie □, TX • 17,204
Gillett, WI 54124 • 1,303
Gillette, WY 82716–17 • 17,635
Gilliam □, OR • 1,717
Gilman, IL 60938 • 1,816
Gilman, VT 05904 • 500
Gilmer, TX 75644 • 4,822
Gilmer □, GA • 13,368
Gilmer □, WV • 7,669
Gilpin □, CO • 3,070
Gilroy, CA 95020–21 • 31,487
Girard, IL 62640 • 2,164
Girard, KS 66743 • 2,794
Girard, OH 44420 • 11,304
Girard, PA 16417 • 2,879
Girardville, PA 17935 • 1,889
Glacier □, MT • 12,121
Glades □, FL • 7,591
Glade Spring, VA 24340 • 1,435
Gladeview, FL 33138 • 15,637
Gladewater, TX 75647 • 6,027
Gladstone, MI 49837 • 4,565
Gladstone, MO 64118 • 26,243
Gladstone, NJ 07934 • 2,111
Gladstone, OR 97027 • 10,152
Gladwin, MI 48624 • 2,682
Gladwin □, MI • 21,896
Glasco, NY 12432 • 1,538
Glascock □, GA • 2,357
Glasford, IL 61533 • 1,115
Glasgow, KY 42141–42 • 12,351
Glasgow, MO 65254 • 1,295
Glasgow, MT 59230 • 3,572
Glasgow, VA 24555 • 1,140
Glasgow Village, MO 63137 • 5,199
Glassboro, NJ 08028 • 15,614
Glasscock □, TX • 1,447
Glassport, PA 15045 • 5,582
Glastonbury, CT 06033 • 7,082
Gleason, TN 38229 • 1,402
Glen Allen, VA 23060 • 9,010
Glen Avon, CA • 12,663
Glenbrook, NV 89413 • 400
Glen Burnie, MD 21061 • 37,305
Glen Burnie Park, MD 21061 • 3,260
Glen Carbon, IL 62034 • 7,731
Glencoe, AL 35905 • 4,670
Glencoe, IL 60022 • 8,499
Glencoe, MN 55336 • 4,648
Glen Cove, NY 11542 • 24,149
Glendale, AZ 85301–12 • 148,134
Glendale, CA 91201–14 • 180,038
Glendale, CO 80222 • 2,453
Glendale, MS 39401 • 1,329
Glendale, MO 63122 • 5,945
Glendale, OH 45246 • 2,445
Glendale, RI 02826 • 700
Glendale, SC 29346 • 1,049
Glen Dale, WV 26038 • 1,612
Glendale, WI 53209 • 14,088
Glendale Heights, IL 60139 • 27,973
Glendive, MT 59330 • 4,802
Glendo, WY 82213 • 195

Glendola, NJ 07719 • 2,340
Glendora, CA 91740 • 47,828
Glendora, NJ 08029 • 5,201
Glen Ellyn, IL 60137–38 • 24,944
Glen Gardner, NJ 08826 • 1,665
Glenham, NY 12527 • 2,832
Glen Head, NY 11545 • 6,870
Glen Lyon, PA 18617 • 2,082
Glenmora, LA 71433 • 1,686
Glenn □, CA • 24,798
Glennallen, AK 99588 • 451
Glenn Dale, MD 20769 • 9,689
Glenns Ferry, ID 83623 • 1,304
Glennville, GA 30427 • 3,676
Glenolden, PA 19036 • 7,260
Glenpool, OK 74033 • 6,688
Glen Raven, NC 27215 • 2,616
Glen Ridge, NJ 07028 • 7,076
Glen Rock, NJ 07452 • 10,883
Glen Rock, PA 17327 • 1,688
Glenrock, WY 82637 • 2,153
Glen Rose, TX 76043 • 1,949
Glens Falls, NY 12801 • 15,023
Glenside, PA 19038 • 8,704
Glen Ullin, ND 58631 • 927
Glenview, IL 60025 • 37,093
Glenville, WV 26351 • 1,923
Glenwood, AR 71943 • 1,354
Glenwood, IL 60425 • 9,289
Glenwood, IA 51534 • 4,571
Glenwood, MN 56334 • 2,573
Glenwood, VA 24541 • 2,276
Glenwood City, WI 54013 • 1,026
Glenwood Farms, VA 23223 • 3,200
Glenwood Hills, GA 30032 • 5,240
Glenwood Springs, CO 81601–02 • 6,561
Glidden, IA 51443 • 1,099
Globe, AZ 85501–02 • 6,062
Gloster, MS 39638 • 1,323
Gloucester, MA 01930–31 • 28,716
Gloucester, VA 23061 • 1,200
Gloucester □, NJ • 230,082
Gloucester □, VA • 30,131
Gloucester City, NJ 08030 • 12,649
Gloucester Point, VA 23062 • 8,509
Glouster, OH 45732 • 2,001
Gloversville, NY 12078 • 16,656
Gloverville, SC 29828 • 2,753
Glynn □, GA • 62,496
Gnadenhutten, OH 44629 • 1,226
Goddard, KS 67052 • 1,804
Godfrey, IL 62035 • 5,436
Goffstown, NH 03045 • 2,700
Gogebic □, MI • 18,052
Golconda, NV 89414 • 200
Gold Bar, WA 98251 • 1,078
Gold Beach, OR 97444 • 1,546
Golden, CO 80401–03 • 13,116
Goldendale, WA 98620 • 3,319
Golden Gate, FL 33999 • 14,148
Golden Glades, FL 33055 • 25,474
Golden Meadow, LA 70357 • 2,049
Golden Valley, MN 55427 • 20,971
Golden Valley □, MT • 912
Golden Valley □, ND • 2,108
Goldfield, NV 89013 • 600
Goldsboro, NC 27530–34 • 40,709
Goldthwaite, TX 76844 • 1,658
Goleta, CA 93117 • 28,600
Golf Manor, OH 45237 • 4,154
Goliad, TX 77963 • 1,946
Goliad □, TX • 5,980
Gonzales, CA 93926 • 4,660
Gonzales, LA 70737 • 7,003
Gonzales, TX 78629 • 6,527
Gonzales □, TX • 17,205
Gonzalez, FL 32560 • 7,669
Goochland □, VA • 14,163
Goodhue □, MN • 40,690
Gooding, ID 83330 • 2,820
Gooding □, ID • 11,633
Goodland, FL 33933 • 1,000
Goodland, IN 47948 • 1,033
Goodland, KS 67735 • 4,983
Goodlettsville, TN 37072 • 11,219
Goodman, MS 39079 • 1,256
Goodman, MO 64843 • 1,094
Goodsprings, NV 89019 • 150
Goodview, MN 55987 • 2,878
Goodwater, AL 35072 • 1,840
Goodwell, OK 73939 • 1,065
Goodyear, AZ 85338 • 6,258
Goose Creek, SC 29445 • 24,692
Gordo, AL 35466 • 1,918
Gordon, GA 31031 • 2,468
Gordon, NE 69343 • 1,803
Gordon □, GA • 35,072
Gordonsville, VA 22942 • 1,351
Gorham, ME 04038 • 3,618
Gorham, NH 03581 • 1,910
Gorman, TX 76454 • 1,290
Goshen, IN 46526 • 23,797
Goshen, NY 10924 • 5,255
Goshen, OH 45122 • 1,400
Goshen □, WY • 12,373
Gosnell, AR 72319 • 3,783
Gosper □, NE • 1,928
Gothenburg, NE 69138 • 3,232
Gould, AR 71643 • 1,470
Goulding, FL 32503 • 4,159
Goulds, FL 33170 • 7,284
Gouverneur, NY 13642 • 4,604
Gove □, KS • 3,231
Gowanda, NY 14070 • 2,901
Gower, MO 64454 • 1,249
Gowrie, IA 50543 • 1,028
Grace, ID 83241 • 973
Graceville, FL 32440 • 2,675
Gracewood, GA 30812 • 1,000
Grady □, GA • 20,279
Grady □, OK • 41,747
Grafton, MA 01519 • 1,520
Grafton, ND 58237 • 4,840
Grafton, OH 44044 • 3,344
Grafton, WV 26354 • 5,524
Grafton, WI 53024 • 9,340
Grafton □, NH • 74,929
Graham, CA 90002 • 10,600
Graham, NC 27253 • 10,426
Graham, TX 76046 • 8,986
Graham □, AZ • 26,554
Graham □, KS • 3,543
Graham □, NC • 7,196
Grainger □, TN • 17,095
Grain Valley, MO 64029 • 1,898
Grambling, LA 71245 • 5,484
Gramercy, LA 70052 • 2,412
Granbury, TX 76048–49 • 4,045
Granby, CT 06035 • 9,369
Granby, MA 01033 • 1,327
Granby, MO 64844 • 1,945
Grand □, CO • 7,966
Grand □, UT • 6,620
Grand Bay, AL 36541 • 3,383
Grand Blanc, MI 48439 • 7,760
Grand Caillou, LA 70360 • 1,400
Grand Canyon, AZ 86023 • 1,499
Grand Coteau, LA 70541 • 1,118
Grandfield, OK 73546 • 1,224
Grand Forks, ND 58201–06 • 49,425
Grand Forks □, ND • 70,683
Grand Haven, MI 49417 • 11,951
Grand Island, NE 68801–03 • 39,386
Grand Isle, LA 70358 • 1,455
Grand Isle □, VT • 5,318
Grand Junction, CO 81501–06 • 29,034
Grand Ledge, MI 48837 • 7,579
Grand Marais, MN 55604 • 1,171
Grand Prairie, TX 75050–54 • 99,616
Grand Rapids, MI 49501–99 • 189,126
Grand Rapids, MN 55744 • 7,976
Grand Saline, TX 75140 • 2,630
Grand Terrace, CA 92324 • 10,946
Grand Traverse □, MI • 64,273
Grandview, MO 64030 • 24,967
Grandview, WA 98930 • 7,169
Grandview Heights, OH 43212 • 7,010
Grandville, MI 49418 • 15,624
Granger, IN 46530 • 20,241
Granger, TX 76530 • 1,190
Granger, WA 98932 • 2,053
Grangeville, ID 83530 • 3,226
Granite, OK 73547 • 1,844
Granite □, MT • 2,548
Granite City, IL 62040 • 32,862
Granite Falls, MN 56241 • 3,083
Granite Falls, NC 28630 • 3,253
Granite Falls, WA 98252 • 1,060
Granite Quarry, NC 28072 • 1,646
Graniteville, MA 01886 • 1,010
Graniteville, SC 29829 • 1,158
Graniteville, VT 05654 • 500
Grant, NE 69140 • 1,239
Grant □, AR • 13,948
Grant □, IN • 74,169
Grant □, KS • 7,159
Grant □, KY • 15,737
Grant □, LA • 17,526
Grant □, MN • 6,246
Grant □, NE • 769
Grant □, NM • 27,676
Grant □, ND • 3,549
Grant □, OK • 5,689
Grant □, OR • 7,853
Grant □, SD • 8,372
Grant □, WA • 54,758
Grant □, WV • 10,428
Grant □, WI • 49,264
Grant Park, IL 60940 • 1,024
Grants, NM 87020 • 8,626
Grantsburg, WI 54840 • 1,144
Grants Pass, OR 97526–27 • 17,488
Grantsville, UT 84029 • 4,500
Grantville, GA 30220 • 1,180
Granville, IL 61326 • 1,407
Granville, NY 12832 • 2,646
Granville, OH 43023 • 4,353
Granville □, NC • 38,345
Grapeland, TX 75844 • 1,450
Grapevine, TX 76051 • 29,202
Grasonville, MD 21638 • 2,439
Grass Lake, IL 60002 • 2,191
Grass Valley, CA 95945 • 9,048
Gratiot □, MI • 38,982
Graves □, KY • 33,550
Gravette, AR 72736 • 1,412
Gray, GA 31032 • 2,189
Gray, LA 70359 • 1,500
Gray □, KS • 5,396
Gray □, TX • 23,967
Grayling, MI 49738 • 1,944
Graylyn Crest, DE 19810 • 4,380
Grays Harbor □, WA • 64,175
Grayslake, IL 60030 • 7,388
Grayson, KY 41143 • 3,510
Grayson □, KY • 21,050
Grayson □, TX • 95,021
Grayson □, VA • 16,278
Graysville, AL 35073 • 2,241
Graysville, TN 37338 • 1,301
Grayville, IL 62844 • 2,043
Great Barrington, MA 01230 • 2,810
Great Bend, KS 67530 • 15,427
Great Falls, MT 59401–06 • 55,097
Great Falls, SC 29055 • 2,307
Great Falls, VA 22066 • 6,945
Great Neck, NY 11020–27 • 8,745
Great Neck Estates, NY 11021 • 2,790
Greece, NY 14626 • 15,632
Greece, NY • 15,632
Greeley, CO 80631–34 • 60,536
Greeley □, KS • 1,774
Greeley □, NE • 3,006
Green, OR 97470 • 5,076
Green □, KY • 10,371
Green □, WI • 30,339
Greenacres, CA 93308 • 7,379
Green Acres, DE 19803 • 1,140
Greenacres, WA 99016 • 4,250
Greenacres City, FL 33463 • 18,683
Green Bay, WI 54301–24 • 96,466
Greenbelt, MD 20770 • 21,096
Greenbriar, VA 22033 • 6,200
Greenbrier, AR 72058 • 2,130
Green Brier, TN 37073 • 2,873
Greenbrier □, WV • 34,693
Green Brook, NJ 08812 • 2,380
Greencastle, IN 46135 • 8,984
Greencastle, PA 17225 • 3,600
Green Cove Springs, FL 32043 • 4,497
Greendale, IN 47025 • 3,881
Greendale, WI 53129 • 15,128
Greene, IA 50636 • 1,142
Greene, NY 13778 • 1,812
Greene □, AL • 10,153
Greene □, AR • 31,804
Greene □, GA • 11,793
Greene □, IL • 15,317
Greene □, IN • 30,410
Greene □, IA • 10,045
Greene □, MS • 10,220
Greene □, MO • 207,949
Greene □, NY • 44,739
Greene □, NC • 15,384
Greene □, OH • 136,731
Greene □, PA • 39,550
Greene □, TN • 55,853
Greene □, VA • 10,297
Greeneville, TN 37743–44 • 13,532
Greenfield, CA 93927 • 7,464
Greenfield, IL 62044 • 1,162
Greenfield, IN 46140 • 11,657
Greenfield, IA 50849 • 2,074
Greenfield, MA 01301–02 • 14,016
Greenfield, MO 65661 • 1,416
Greenfield, OH 45123 • 5,172
Greenfield, TN 38230 • 2,105
Greenfield, WI 53220 • 33,403
Greenfield Plaza, IA 50315 • 2,200
Green Forest, AR 72638 • 2,050
Green Harbor, MA 02041 • 1,900
Greenhills, OH 45218 • 4,393
Green Island, NY 12183 • 2,490
Green Lake, WI 54941 • 1,064
Green Lake □, WI • 18,651
Greenlawn, NY 11740 • 13,208
Greenlee □, AZ • 8,008
Greenock, PA 15047 • 2,500
Greenport, NY 11944 • 2,070
Green River, WY 82935 • 12,711
Green Rock, IL 61241 • 2,615
Greensboro, AL 36744 • 3,047
Greensboro, GA 30642 • 2,860
Greensboro, MD 21639 • 1,441
Greensboro, NC 27401–95 • 183,521
Greensburg, IN 47240 • 9,286
Greensburg, KS 67054 • 1,792
Greensburg, KY 42743 • 1,990
Greensburg, PA 15601 • 16,318
Green Springs, OH 44836 • 1,446
Greensville □, VA • 8,853
Greentown, IN 46936 • 2,172
Green Tree, PA 15220 • 4,905
Greenup, IL 62428 • 1,616
Greenup, KY 41144 • 1,158
Greenup □, KY • 36,742
Green Valley, AZ 85614 • 13,231
Green Valley, MD 21771 • 9,424
Greenview, SC 29203 • 5,515
Greenville, AL 36037 • 7,492
Greenville, CA 95947 • 1,396
Greenville, DE 19807 • 800
Greenville, GA 30222 • 1,167
Greenville, IL 62246 • 4,806
Greenville, KY 42345 • 4,689
Greenville, ME 04441 • 1,601
Greenville, MI 48838 • 8,101
Greenville, MS 38701–04 • 45,226
Greenville, NH 03048 • 1,135
Greenville, NY 10583 • 9,528
Greenville, NC 27834–36 • 44,972
Greenville, OH 45331 • 12,863
Greenville, PA 16125 • 6,734
Greenville, RI 02828 • 8,303
Greenville, SC 29601–16 • 58,282
Greenville, TX 75401–03 • 23,071
Greenville □, SC • 320,167
Greenwich, CT 06830–36 • 58,441
Greenwich, NY 12834 • 1,961
Greenwich, OH 44837 • 1,442
Greenwood, AR 72936 • 3,984
Greenwood, DE 19950 • 578
Greenwood, IN 46142 • 26,265
Greenwood, LA 71033 • 2,092
Greenwood, MS 38930 • 18,906
Greenwood, MO 64034 • 1,505
Greenwood, PA 16601 • 1,650
Greenwood, SC 29646–49 • 20,807
Greenwood □, KS • 7,847
Greenwood □, SC • 59,567
Greenwood Lake, NY 10925 • 3,208
Greenwood Village, CO 80111 • 7,589
Greer, SC 29650–52 • 10,322
Greer □, OK • 6,559
Gregg □, TX • 104,948
Gregory, SD 57533 • 1,384
Gregory □, SD • 5,359
Greilickville, MI 49684 • 1,060
Grenada, MS 38901 • 10,864
Grenada □, MS • 21,555
Gresham, OR 97030 • 68,235
Gresham Park, GA 30316 • 9,000
Gretna, FL 32332 • 1,981
Gretna, LA 70053–54 • 17,208
Gretna, NE 68028 • 2,249
Gretna, VA 24557 • 1,339
Greybull, WY 82426 • 1,789
Gridley, CA 95948 • 4,631
Gridley, IL 61744 • 1,304
Griffin, GA 30223–24 • 21,347
Griffith, IN 46319 • 17,916
Grifton, NC 28530 • 2,393
Griggs □, ND • 3,303
Griggsville, IL 62340 • 1,218
Grimes, IA 50111 • 2,653
Grimes □, TX • 18,828
Grindall Creek, VA 23234 • 1,710
Grinnell, IA 50112 • 8,902
Griswold, IA 51535 • 1,049
Groesbeck, OH 45239 • 6,684
Groesbeck, TX 76642 • 3,185
Grosse Ile, MI 48138 • 9,781
Grosse Pointe, MI 48236 • 5,681
Grosse Pointe Farms, MI 48236 • 10,092
Grosse Pointe Park, MI 48230 • 12,857
Grosse Pointe Woods, MI 48225 • 17,715
Grossmont, CA 91941 • 2,600
Groton, CT 06340 • 9,837
Groton, MA 01450 • 1,044
Groton, NY 13073 • 2,398
Groton, SD 57445 • 1,196
Grottoes, VA 24441 • 1,455
Grove, OK 74344 • 4,020
Grove City, FL 34224 • 2,374
Grove City, OH 43123 • 19,661
Grove City, PA 16127 • 8,240
Grove Hill, AL 36451 • 1,551
Groveland, FL 34736 • 2,300
Groveland, MA 01834 • 3,780
Groveport, OH 43125 • 2,948
Grover City, CA 93433 • 11,656
Groves, TX 77619 • 16,513
Groveton, NH 03582 • 1,255
Groveton, TX 75845 • 1,071
Groveton, VA 22303 • 19,997
Groveton Gardens, VA 22303 • 2,600
Grovetown, GA 30813 • 3,596
Groveville, NJ 08620 • 2,900
Gruetli-Laager, TN 37339 • 1,810
Grulla, TX 78548 • 1,335
Grundy, VA 24614 • 1,305
Grundy □, IL • 32,337
Grundy □, IA • 12,029
Grundy □, MO • 10,536
Grundy □, TN • 13,362
Grundy Center, IA 50638 • 2,491
Gruver, TX 79040 • 1,172
Guadalupe, AZ 85283 • 5,458
Guadalupe, CA 93434 • 5,479
Guadalupe □, NM • 4,156
Guadalupe □, TX • 64,873
Guernsey, WY 82214 • 1,155
Guernsey □, OH • 39,024
Gueydan, LA 70542 • 1,611
Guilford, CT 06437 • 2,588
Guilford, ME 04443 • 1,082
Guilford □, NC • 347,420
Guin, AL 35563 • 2,464
Gulf □, FL • 11,504
Gulf Breeze, FL 32561 • 5,530
Gulf Gate Estates, FL 34231 • 11,622
Gulfport, FL 33707 • 11,727
Gulfport, MS 39501–07 • 40,775
Gulf Shores, AL 36542 • 3,261
Gumboro, DE 19945 • 200
Gunnison, CO 81230 • 4,636
Gunnison, UT 84634 • 1,298
Gunnison □, CO • 10,273
Guntersville, AL 35976 • 7,038
Gurdon, AR 71743 • 2,199
Gurley, AL 35748 • 1,007
Gurnee, IL 60031 • 13,701
Gustine, CA 95322 • 3,931
Guthrie, KY 42234 • 1,504
Guthrie, OK 73044 • 10,518
Guthrie □, IA • 10,935
Guthrie Center, IA 50115 • 1,614
Guttenberg, IA 52052 • 2,257
Guttenberg, NJ 07093 • 8,268
Guymon, OK 73942 • 7,803
Gwinhurst, DE 19809 • 1,340
Gwinn, MI 49841 • 2,370
Gwinner, ND 58040 • 585
Gwinnett □, GA • 352,910
Gypsum, CO 81637 • 1,750

H

Haakon □, SD • 2,624
Habersham □, GA • 27,621
Hacienda Heights, CA 91745 • 52,354
Hackensack, NJ 07601–08 • 37,049
Hackettstown, NJ 07840 • 8,120
Hackleburg, AL 35564 • 1,161
Haddam, CT 06438 • 1,200
Haddonfield, NJ 08033 • 11,628
Haddon Heights, NJ 08035 • 7,860
Hadlock, WA 98339 • 1,752
Hagerman, NM 88232 • 961
Hagerstown, IN 47346 • 1,835
Hagerstown, MD 21740 • 35,445
Hahira, GA 31632 • 1,353
Hahnville, LA 70057 • 2,599
Hailey, ID 83333 • 3,687
Haines, AK 99827 • 1,238
Haines City, FL 33844 • 11,683
Hainesport, NJ 08036 • 1,250
Halawa Heights, HI 96701 • 7,000
Hale □, AL • 15,498
Hale □, TX • 34,671
Hale Center, TX 79041 • 2,067
Haledon, NJ 07508 • 6,951
Haleiwa, HI 96712 • 2,442
Hales Corners, WI 53130 • 7,623
Halethorpe, MD 21227 • 19,750
Haleyville, AL 35565 • 4,452
Half Hollow Hills, NY 11746 • 5,110
Half Moon, NC 28540 • 6,306
Half Moon Bay, CA 94019 • 8,886
Halfway, MD 21740 • 8,873
Halifax □, NC • 55,516
Halifax □, VA • 29,033
Haliimaile, HI 96768 • 841
Hall □, GA • 95,428
Hall □, NE • 48,925
Hall □, TX • 3,905
Hallandale, FL 33009 • 30,996
Hallettsville, TX 77964 • 2,718
Hallie, WI 54729 • 1,300
Hallock, MN 56728 • 1,304
Hallowell, ME 04347 • 2,534
Halls, TN 37918 • 6,450
Halls, TN 38040 • 2,431
Halls Crossroads, TN 37918 • 1,900
Hallstead, PA 18822 • 1,274
Hallsville, TX 75650 • 2,288
Halstead, KS 67056 • 2,015
Haltom City, TX 76117 • 32,856
Hamblen □, TN • 50,480
Hamburg, AR 71646 • 3,098
Hamburg, IA 51640 • 1,248
Hamburg, NJ 07419 • 2,566
Hamburg, NY 14075 • 10,442
Hamburg, PA 19526 • 3,987
Hamden, CT 06514 • 52,434
Hamel, MN 55340 • 3,096
Hamilton, AL 35570 • 5,787
Hamilton, IL 62341 • 3,281
Hamilton, MA 01936 • 1,000
Hamilton, MI 49419 • 1,000
Hamilton, MO 64644 • 1,737
Hamilton, MT 59840 • 2,737
Hamilton, NY 13346 • 3,790
Hamilton, OH 45011–18 • 61,368
Hamilton, TX 76531 • 2,937
Hamilton □, FL • 10,930
Hamilton □, IL • 8,499
Hamilton □, IN • 108,936
Hamilton □, IA • 16,071
Hamilton □, KS • 2,388
Hamilton □, NE • 8,862
Hamilton □, NY • 5,279
Hamilton □, OH • 866,228
Hamilton □, TN • 285,536
Hamilton □, TX • 7,733
Hamilton City, CA 95951 • 1,811
Hamilton Square, NJ 08690 • 10,970
Ham Lake, MN 55304 • 8,924
Hamlet, NC 28345 • 6,196
Hamlin, TX 79520 • 2,791
Hamlin, WV 25523 • 1,030
Hamlin □, SD • 4,974
Hammond, IN 46320–27 • 84,236
Hammond, LA 70401–04 • 15,871
Hammond, WI 54015 • 1,097
Hammonton, NJ 08037 • 12,208
Hampden, ME 04444 • 3,895
Hampden □, MA • 456,310
Hampden Highlands, ME 04444 • 1,540
Hampshire, IL 60140 • 1,843
Hampshire □, MA • 146,568
Hampshire □, WV • 16,498
Hampstead, MD 21074 • 2,608
Hampton, AR 71744 • 1,562
Hampton, GA 30228 • 2,694
Hampton, IA 50441 • 4,133
Hampton, NH 03842 • 7,989
Hampton, NJ 08827 • 1,515
Hampton, SC 29924 • 2,997
Hampton, TN 37658 • 2,236
Hampton, VA 23651–70 • 133,793
Hampton □, SC • 18,191
Hampton Bays, NY 11946 • 7,893
Hamtramck, MI 48212 • 18,372
Hana, HI 96713 • 683
Hanahan, SC 29406 • 13,176
Hanamaulu, HI 96715 • 3,611
Hanapepe, HI 96716 • 1,395
Hanceville, AL 35077 • 2,246
Hancock, MD 21750 • 1,926
Hancock, MI 49930 • 4,547
Hancock, NY 13783 • 1,330
Hancock □, GA • 8,908
Hancock □, IL • 21,373
Hancock □, IN • 45,527
Hancock □, IA • 12,638
Hancock □, KY • 7,864
Hancock □, ME • 46,948
Hancock □, MS • 31,760
Hancock □, OH • 65,536
Hancock □, TN • 6,739
Hancock □, WV • 35,233
Hand □, SD • 4,272
Hanford, CA 93230–32 • 30,897
Hankinson, ND 58041 • 1,038
Hanna, WY 82327 • 1,076
Hanna City, IL 61536 • 1,205
Hannibal, MO 63401 • 18,004
Hanover, IN 47243 • 3,610
Hanover, MA 02339 • 2,500
Hanover, NH 03755 • 6,538
Hanover, PA 17331 • 14,399
Hanover □, VA • 63,306
Hanover Center, MA 02339 • 1,000
Hanover Park, IL 60103 • 32,895
Hanover Township, NJ 07981 • 11,538
Hansen, ID 83334 • 848
Hansford □, TX • 5,848
Hanson, MA 02341 • 2,188
Hanson □, SD • 2,994
Hapeville, GA 30354 • 5,483
Happy Valley, OR 97236 • 1,519
Harahan, LA 70123 • 9,927
Haralson □, GA • 21,966
Harbeson, DE 19951 • 500
Harbor, OR 97415 • 2,143
Harbor Beach, MI 48441 • 2,089
Harborcreek, PA 16421 • 1,500
Harbor Springs, MI 49740 • 1,540
Hardee □, FL • 19,499
Hardeeville, SC 29927 • 1,583
Hardeman □, TN • 23,377
Hardeman □, TX • 5,283
Hardin, IL 62047 • 1,071
Hardin, MT 59034 • 2,940
Hardin □, IL • 5,189
Hardin □, IA • 19,094
Hardin □, KY • 89,240
Hardin □, OH • 31,111
Hardin □, TN • 22,633
Hardin □, TX • 41,320
Harding □, NM • 987
Harding □, SD • 1,669
Hardinsburg, KY 40143 • 1,906
Hardwick, GA 31034 • 8,800
Hardwick, VT 05843 • 1,400
Hardy □, WV • 10,977
Harford □, MD • 182,132
Hargill, TX 78549 • 1,030
Harker Heights, TX 76543 • 12,841
Harkers Island, NC 28531 • 1,759
Harlan, IN 46743 • 1,200
Harlan, IA 51537 • 5,148
Harlan, KY 40831 • 2,686
Harlan □, KY • 36,574
Harlan □, NE • 3,810
Harlem, FL 33440 • 2,826
Harlem, GA 30814 • 2,199
Harlem, MT 59526 • 882
Harleysville, PA 19438 • 7,405
Harlingen, TX 78550–52 • 48,735
Harlowton, MT 59036 • 1,049
Harmon □, OK • 3,793
Harmony, MN 55939 • 1,081
Harmony, PA 16037 • 1,054
Harmony, RI 02829 • 820
Harnett □, NC • 67,822
Harney □, OR • 7,060
Harper, KS 67058 • 1,735
Harper □, KS • 7,124
Harper □, OK • 4,063
Harpers Ferry, WV 25425 • 308
Harper Woods, MI 48225 • 14,903
Harrah, OK 73045 • 4,206
Harriman, TN 37748 • 7,119
Harrington, DE 19952 • 2,311
Harrington Park, NJ 07640 • 4,623
Harris, RI 02816 • 1,050
Harris □, GA • 17,788
Harris □, TX • 2,818,199
Harrisburg, AR 72432 • 1,943
Harrisburg, IL 62946 • 9,289
Harrisburg, OR 97446 • 1,939
Harrisburg, PA 17101–13 • 52,376
Harris Hill, NY 14221 • 4,577

United States Populations and ZIP Codes

Harrison, AR 72601–02 • *9,922*
Harrison, MI 48625 • *1,835*
Harrison, NJ 07029 • *13,425*
Harrison, NY 10528 • *23,308*
Harrison, OH 45030 • *7,518*
Harrison, TN 37341 • *7,191*
Harrison □, IN • *29,890*
Harrison □, IA • *14,730*
Harrison □, KY • *16,248*
Harrison □, MS • *165,365*
Harrison □, MO • *8,469*
Harrison □, OH • *16,085*
Harrison □, TX • *57,483*
Harrison □, WV • *69,371*
Harrisonburg, VA 22801 • *30,707*
Harrison Township, MI 48045 • *24,685*
Harrisonville, MO 64701 • *7,683*
Harristown, IL 62537 • *1,319*
Harrisville, RI 02830 • *1,654*
Harrisville, UT 84404 • *3,004*
Harrisville, WV 26362 • *1,839*
Harrodsburg, KY 40330 • *7,335*
Hart, MI 49420 • *1,942*
Hart, TX 79043 • *1,221*
Hart □, GA • *19,712*
Hart □, KY • *14,890*
Hartford, AL 36344 • *2,448*
Hartford, CT 06101–99 • *139,739*
Hartford, IL 62048 • *1,676*
Hartford, KY 42347 • *2,532*
Hartford, MI 49057 • *2,341*
Hartford, SD 57033 • *1,262*
Hartford, VT 05047 • *500*
Hartford, WI 53027 • *8,188*
Hartford □, CT • *851,783*
Hartford City, IN 47348 • *6,960*
Hartington, NE 68739 • *1,583*
Hartland, ME 04943 • *1,038*
Hartland, WI 53029 • *6,906*
Hartley, IA 51346 • *1,632*
Hartley □, TX • *3,634*
Hartsdale, NY 10530 • *9,587*
Hartselle, AL 35640 • *10,795*
Hartshorne, OK 74547 • *2,120*
Hartsville, SC 29550 • *8,372*
Hartsville, TN 37074 • *2,188*
Hartville, OH 44632 • *2,031*
Hartwell, GA 30643 • *4,555*
Harvard, IL 60033 • *5,975*
Harvard, MA 01451 • *1,200*
Harvey, IL 60426 • *29,771*
Harvey, LA 70058 • *21,222*
Harvey, MI 49855 • *1,377*
Harvey, ND 58341 • *2,263*
Harvey □, KS • *31,028*
Harwich, MA 02645 • *4,399*
Harwich Port, MA 02646 • *2,300*
Harwinton, CT 06791 • *5,228*
Harwood Heights, IL 60656 • *7,680*
Hasbrouck Heights, NJ 07604 • *11,488*
Haskell, AR 72015 • *1,342*
Haskell, OK 74436 • *2,143*
Haskell, TX 79521 • *3,362*
Haskell □, KS • *3,886*
Haskell □, OK • *10,940*
Haskell □, TX • *6,820*
Haslett, MI 48840 • *10,230*
Hastings, MI 49058 • *6,549*
Hastings, MN 55033 • *15,445*
Hastings, NE 68901–02 • *22,837*
Hastings, PA 16646 • *1,431*
Hastings-on-Hudson, NY 10706 • *8,000*
Hatboro, PA 19040 • *7,382*
Hatch, NM 87937 • *1,136*
Hatfield, MA 01038 • *1,234*
Hatfield, PA 19440 • *2,650*
Hatteras, NC 27943 • *1,000*
Hattiesburg, MS 39401–07 • *41,882*
Hatton, ND 58240 • *800*
Haubstadt, IN 47639 • *1,455*
Haughton, LA 71037 • *1,664*
Hauppauge, NY 11788 • *19,750*
Hauula, HI 96717 • *3,479*
Havana, FL 32333 • *1,654*
Havana, IL 62644 • *3,610*
Havelock, NC 28532 • *20,268*
Haven, KS 67543 • *1,198*
Haverford [Township], PA 19083 • *52,371*
Haverhill, MA 01830–35 • *51,418*
Haverstraw, NY 10927 • *9,438*
Havre, MT 59501 • *10,201*
Havre de Grace, MD 21078 • *8,952*
Havre North, MT 59501 • *1,110*
Hawaii □, HI • *120,317*
Hawaiian Gardens, CA 90716 • *13,639*
Hawarden, IA 51023 • *2,439*
Hawi, HI 96719 • *924*
Hawkins □, TN • *44,565*
Hawkinsville, GA 31036 • *3,527*
Hawley, MN 56549 • *1,655*
Hawley, PA 18428 • *1,244*
Haworth, NJ 07641 • *3,384*
Haw River, NC 27258 • *1,855*
Hawthorne, CA 90250–51 • *71,349*
Hawthorne, FL 32640 • *1,305*
Hawthorne, NV 89415–16 • *4,162*
Hawthorne, NJ 07506 • *17,084*
Hawthorne, NY 10532 • *4,764*
Hayden, CO 81639 • *1,444*
Hayden, ID 83835 • *3,744*
Hayes □, NE • *1,222*
Hayesville, OR 97303 • *14,318*
Hayfield, MN 55940 • *1,283*
Hayfield, VA 22310 • *2,300*
Hayfork, CA 96041 • *2,605*
Haynesville, LA 71038 • *2,854*
Hays, KS 67601 • *17,767*
Hays □, TX • *65,614*
Haysville, KS 67060 • *8,364*
Hayti, MO 63851 • *3,280*
Hayward, CA 94540–46 • *111,498*
Hayward, WI 54843 • *1,897*
Hayward Addition, SD 57106 • *1,000*
Haywood □, NC • *46,942*
Haywood □, TN • *19,437*
Hazard, KY 41701 • *5,416*
Hazardville, CT 06082 • *5,179*
Hazel Crest, IL 60429 • *13,334*
Hazel Dell, WA 98660 • *15,386*
Hazel Green, AL 35750 • *2,208*
Hazel Green, WI 53811 • *1,171*
Hazel Park, MI 48030 • *20,051*
Hazelwood, MO 63042–45 • *15,324*
Hazelwood, NC 28738 • *1,678*
Hazen, AR 72064 • *1,668*
Hazen, ND 58545 • *2,818*
Hazlehurst, GA 31539 • *4,202*
Hazlehurst, MS 39083 • *4,221*
Hazlet, NJ 07730 • *23,013*
Hazleton, PA 18201 • *24,730*
Headland, AL 36345 • *3,266*
Healdsburg, CA 95448 • *9,469*
Healdton, OK 73438 • *2,872*
Healy, AK 99743 • *487*
Heard □, GA • *8,628*
Hearne, TX 77859 • *5,132*
Heath, OH 43056 • *7,231*
Heavener, OK 74937 • *2,601*
Hebbronville, TX 78361 • *4,465*
Heber City, UT 84032 • *4,782*
Heber Springs, AR 72543 • *5,628*
Hebron, IN 46341 • *3,183*
Hebron, KY 41048 • *1,200*
Hebron, NE 68370 • *1,765*
Hebron, ND 58638 • *888*
Hebron, OH 43025 • *2,076*
Hector, MN 55342 • *1,145*
Heeia, HI 96744 • *5,010*
Heflin, AL 36264 • *2,906*
Hegins, PA 17938 • *1,200*
Helena, AL 35080 • *3,918*
Helena, AR 72342 • *7,491*
Helena, GA 31037 • *1,256*
Helena, MT 59601–26 • *24,569*
Helena, OK 73741 • *1,043*
Hellam, PA 17406 • *1,375*
Hellertown, PA 18055 • *5,662*
Helmetta, NJ 08828 • *1,211*
Helotes, TX 78023 • *1,535*
Helper, UT 84526 • *2,148*
Hemet, CA 92343–44 • *36,094*
Hemlock, MI 48626 • *1,601*
Hemphill, TX 75948 • *1,182*
Hemphill □, TX • *3,720*
Hempstead, NY 11550–54 • *49,453*
Hempstead, TX 77445 • *3,551*
Hempstead □, AR • *21,621*
Henagar, AL 35978 • *1,934*
Henderson, KY 42420 • *25,945*
Henderson, LA 70517 • *1,543*
Henderson, NV 89015–16 • *64,942*
Henderson, NC 27536 • *15,655*
Henderson, TN 38340 • *4,760*
Henderson, TX 75652–53 • *11,139*
Henderson □, IL • *8,096*
Henderson □, KY • *43,044*
Henderson □, NC • *69,285*
Henderson □, TN • *21,844*
Henderson □, TX • *58,543*
Henderson's Point, MS 39571 • *1,114*
Hendersonville, NC 28739 • *7,284*
Hendersonville, TN 37075 • *32,188*
Hendricks □, IN • *75,717*
Hendry □, FL • *25,773*
Hennepin □, MN • *1,032,431*
Hennessey, OK 73742 • *1,902*
Henniker, NH 03242 • *1,693*
Henrico □, VA • *217,881*
Henrietta, NY 14467 • *1,200*
Henrietta, NC 28076 • *1,412*
Henrietta, TX 76365 • *2,896*
Henry, IL 61537 • *2,591*
Henry □, AL • *15,374*
Henry □, GA • *58,741*
Henry □, IL • *51,159*
Henry □, IN • *48,139*
Henry □, IA • *19,226*
Henry □, KY • *12,823*
Henry □, MO • *20,044*
Henry □, OH • *29,108*
Henry □, TN • *27,888*
Henry □, VA • *56,942*
Henryetta, OK 74437 • *5,872*
Henryville, IN 47126 • *1,132*
Hephzibah, GA 30815 • *2,466*
Heppner, OR 97836 • *1,412*
Herculaneum, MO 63048 • *2,263*
Hercules, CA 94547 • *16,829*
Hereford, TX 79045 • *14,745*
Herington, KS 67449 • *2,685*
Heritage Village, CT 06488 • *9,700*
Herkimer, NY 13350 • *7,945*
Herkimer □, NY • *65,797*
Hermann, MO 65041 • *2,754*
Hermantown, MN 55811 • *6,761*
Herminie, PA 15637 • *2,000*
Hermiston, OR 97838 • *10,040*
Hermitage, PA 16148 • *15,300*
Hermosa Beach, CA 90254 • *18,219*
Hernando, FL 32642 • *2,103*
Hernando, MS 38632 • *3,125*
Hernando □, FL • *101,115*
Herndon, VA 22070–71 • *16,139*
Herrin, IL 62948 • *10,857*
Herscher, IL 60941 • *1,278*
Hershey, PA 17033 • *11,860*
Hertford, NC 27944 • *2,105*
Hertford □, NC • *22,523*
Hesperia, CA 92345 • *50,418*
Hesston, KS 67062 • *3,012*
Hettinger, ND 58639 • *1,574*
Hettinger □, ND • *3,445*
Hewitt, TX 76643 • *8,983*
Hewlett, NY 11557 • *6,620*
Heyburn, ID 83336 • *2,714*
Heyworth, IL 61745 • *1,627*
Hialeah, FL 33010–16 • *188,004*
Hiawatha, IA 52233 • *4,986*
Hiawatha, KS 66434 • *3,603*
Hibbing, MN 55746–47 • *18,046*
Hickman, KY 42050 • *2,689*
Hickman, NE 68372 • *1,081*
Hickman □, KY • *5,566*
Hickman □, TN • *16,754*
Hickory, NC 28601–03 • *28,301*
Hickory □, MO • *7,335*
Hickory Hills, IL 60457 • *13,021*
Hicksville, NY 11801–05 • *40,174*
Hicksville, OH 43526 • *3,664*
Hico, TX 76457 • *1,342*
Hidalgo, TX 78557 • *3,292*
Hidalgo □, NM • *5,958*
Hidalgo □, TX • *383,545*
Higganum, CT 06441 • *1,692*
Higginsville, MO 64037 • *4,693*
High Bridge, NJ 08829 • *3,886*
Highland, CA 92346 • *34,439*
Highland, IL 62249 • *7,525*
Highland, IN 46322 • *23,696*
Highland, MI 48356–57 • *750*
Highland, NY 12528 • *4,492*
Highland □, OH • *35,728*
Highland □, VA • *2,635*
Highland Falls, NY 10928 • *3,937*
Highland Heights, OH 44124 • *6,249*
Highland Lakes, NJ 07422 • *4,550*
Highland Park, IL 60035 • *30,575*
Highland Park, MI 48203 • *20,121*
Highland Park, NJ 08904 • *13,279*
Highland Park, TX 75205 • *8,739*
Highlands, NJ 07732 • *4,849*
Highlands, TX 77562 • *6,632*
Highlands □, FL • *68,432*
Highland Springs, VA 23075 • *13,823*
Highmore, SD 57345 • *835*
High Point, NC 27260–65 • *69,496*
High Ridge, MO 63049 • *2,380*
High Spire, PA 17034 • *2,668*
High Springs, FL 32643 • *3,144*
Hightstown, NJ 08520 • *5,126*
Highview, KY 40228 • *14,814*
Highwood, IL 60040 • *5,331*
Hilbert, WI 54129 • *1,211*
Hildale, UT 84784 • *1,325*
Hill □, MT • *17,654*
Hill □, TX • *27,146*
Hill City, KS 67642 • *1,835*
Hillcrest, NY 10977 • *6,447*
Hillcrest Center, CA 93306 • *26,900*
Hillcrest Heights, MD 20748 • *17,136*
Hilliard, FL 32046 • *1,751*
Hilliard, OH 43026 • *11,796*
Hillsboro, IL 62049 • *4,400*
Hillsboro, KS 67063 • *2,704*
Hillsboro, MO 63050 • *1,625*
Hillsboro, NH 03244 • *1,826*
Hillsboro, ND 58045 • *1,488*
Hillsboro, OH 45133 • *6,235*
Hillsboro, OR 97123–24 • *37,520*
Hillsboro, TX 76645 • *7,072*
Hillsboro, WI 54634 • *1,288*
Hillsborough, CA 94010 • *10,667*
Hillsborough, NC 27278 • *4,263*
Hillsborough □, FL • *834,054*
Hillsborough □, NH • *336,073*
Hillsdale, MI 49242 • *8,170*
Hillsdale, NJ 07642 • *9,750*
Hillsdale □, MI • *43,431*
Hillside, IL 60162 • *7,672*
Hillside, NJ 07205 • *21,044*
Hillside Heights, DE 19711 • *1,500*
Hillsville, VA 24343 • *2,008*
Hillview, KY 40229 • *6,119*
Hilo, HI 96720–21 • *37,808*
Hilton, NY 14468 • *5,216*
Hilton Head Island, SC 29928 • *23,694*
Hinckley, IL 60520 • *1,682*
Hinds □, MS • *254,441*
Hines, OR 97738 • *1,452*
Hinesville, GA 31313 • *21,603*
Hingham, MA 02043 • *5,454*
Hinsdale, IL 60521–22 • *16,029*
Hinsdale, NH 03451 • *1,718*
Hinsdale □, CO • *467*
Hinton, OK 73047 • *1,233*
Hinton, WV 25951 • *3,433*
Hiram, GA 30141 • *1,389*
Hiram, OH 44234 • *1,330*
Hitchcock, TX 77563 • *5,868*
Hitchcock □, NE • *3,750*
Hitchcock Lake, CT 06716 • *1,640*
Hobart, IN 46342 • *21,822*
Hobart, OK 73651 • *4,305*
Hobbs, NM 88240–41 • *29,115*
Hobe Sound, FL 33455 • *11,507*
Hoboken, NJ 07030 • *33,397*
Hockessin, DE 19707 • *2,430*
Hocking □, OH • *25,533*
Hockley □, TX • *24,199*
Hodgeman □, KS • *2,177*
Hodgenville, KY 42748 • *2,721*
Hoffman Estates, IL 60194–95 • *46,561*
Hogansville, GA 30230 • *2,976*
Hohenwald, TN 38462 • *3,760*
Ho-Ho-Kus, NJ 07423 • *3,935*
Hoisington, KS 67544 • *3,182*
Hoke □, NC • *22,856*
Hokes Bluff, AL 35903 • *3,739*
Holbrook, AZ 86025–29 • *4,686*
Holbrook, MA 02343 • *11,041*
Holbrook, NY 11741 • *25,273*
Holcomb, KS 67851 • *1,400*
Holden, MA 01520 • *4,040*
Holden, MO 64040 • *2,389*
Holden, WV 25625 • *1,246*
Holden Heights, FL 32805 • *4,387*
Holdenville, OK 74848 • *4,792*
Holdrege, NE 68949 • *5,671*
Holgate, OH 43527 • *1,290*
Holiday, FL 34690 • *19,360*
Holiday City at Berkeley, NJ 08757 • *5,750*
Holladay, UT 84117 • *22,189*
Holland, MI 49422–24 • *30,745*
Holland, NY 14080 • *1,288*
Holland, OH 43528 • *1,210*
Holland, PA 18966 • *5,250*
Holland, TX 76534 • *1,118*
Hollandale, MS 38748 • *3,576*
Holley, NY 14470 • *1,890*
Holliday, TX 76366 • *1,475*
Hollidaysburg, PA 16648 • *5,624*
Hollins, VA 24019 • *13,305*
Hollis, OK 73550 • *2,584*
Hollister, CA 95023–24 • *19,212*
Hollister, MO 65672 • *2,628*
Holliston, MA 01746 • *12,622*
Holly, MI 48442 • *5,595*
Holly Hill, FL 32117 • *11,141*
Holly Hill, SC 29059 • *1,478*
Holly Springs, GA 30142 • *2,406*
Holly Springs, MS 38634–35 • *7,261*
Hollywood, FL 33019–29 • *121,697*
Hollywood, SC 29449 • *2,094*
Holmen, WI 54636 • *3,220*
Holmes □, FL • *15,778*
Holmes □, MS • *21,604*
Holmes □, OH • *32,849*
Holstein, IA 51025 • *1,449*
Holt, AL 35404 • *4,125*
Holt, MI 48842 • *11,744*
Holt □, MO • *6,034*
Holt □, NE • *12,599*
Holton, KS 66436 • *3,196*
Holtsville, NY 11742 • *14,972*
Holtville, CA 92250 • *4,820*
Holualoa, HI 96725 • *3,834*
Holyoke, CO 80734 • *1,931*
Holyoke, MA 01040–41 • *43,704*
Homedale, ID 83628 • *1,963*
Home Gardens, CA 91720 • *7,780*
Homeland Park, SC 29621 • *6,569*
Home Place, IN 46240 • *1,300*
Homer, AK 99603 • *3,660*
Homer, IL 61849 • *1,264*
Homer, LA 71040 • *4,152*
Homer, MI 49245 • *1,758*
Homer, NY 13077 • *3,476*
Homer City, PA 15748 • *1,809*
Homerville, GA 31634 • *2,560*
Homestead, FL 33030–35 • *26,866*
Homestead, PA 15120 • *4,179*
Hometown, IL 60456 • *4,769*
Homewood, AL 35209 • *22,922*
Homewood, IL 60430 • *19,278*
Homewood, OH 45015 • *2,550*
Hominy, OK 74035 • *2,342*
Homosassa, FL 32646 • *2,113*
Hondo, TX 78861 • *6,018*
Honea Path, SC 29654 • *3,841*
Honeoye Falls, NY 14472 • *2,340*
Honesdale, PA 18431 • *4,972*
Honey Brook, PA 19344 • *1,184*
Honey Grove, TX 75446 • *1,681*
Honeypot Glen, CT 06410 • *1,200*
Honeyville, UT 84314 • *1,112*
Honokaa, HI 96727 • *2,186*
Honolulu, HI 96801–50 • *365,272*
Honolulu □, HI • *836,231*
Honomu, HI 96728 • *532*
Hood □, TX • *28,981*
Hood River, OR 97031 • *4,632*
Hood River □, OR • *16,903*
Hoodsport, WA 98548 • *1,100*
Hooker, OK 73945 • *1,551*
Hooker □, NE • *793*
Hooksett, NH 03106 • *2,573*
Hoonah, AK 99829 • *795*
Hooper Bay, AK 99604 • *845*
Hoopeston, IL 60942 • *5,871*
Hoosick Falls, NY 12090 • *3,490*
Hoover, AL 35216 • *39,788*
Hooverson Heights, WV 26037 • *3,056*
Hopatcong, NJ 07843 • *15,586*
Hope, AR 71801 • *9,643*
Hope, IN 47246 • *2,171*
Hope, RI 02831 • *270*
Hopedale, MA 01747 • *3,961*
Hope Mills, NC 28348 • *8,184*
Hope Valley, RI 02832 • *1,446*
Hopewell, NJ 08525 • *1,968*
Hopewell, VA 23860 • *23,101*
Hopewell Junction, NY 12533 • *1,786*
Hopkins, MN 55343–47 • *16,534*
Hopkins, SC 29061 • *1,600*
Hopkins □, KY • *46,126*
Hopkins □, TX • *28,833*
Hopkinsville, KY 42240–41 • *29,809*
Hopkinton, MA 01748 • *2,305*
Hopkinton, RI 02833 • *550*
Hopwood, PA 15445 • *2,021*
Hoquiam, WA 98550 • *8,972*
Horicon, WI 53032 • *3,873*
Hornell, NY 14843 • *9,877*
Horn Lake, MS 38637 • *9,069*
Horry □, SC • *144,053*
Horse Cave, KY 42749 • *2,284*
Horseheads, NY 14844–45 • *6,802*
Horsham, PA 19044 • *15,051*
Horton, KS 66439 • *1,885*
Hortonville, WI 54944 • *2,029*
Hot Spring □, AR • *26,115*
Hot Springs, SD 57747 • *4,325*
Hot Springs □, WY • *4,809*
Hot Springs National Park, AR 71901–14 • *32,462*
Hot Springs Village, AR 71901 • *6,361*
Houghton, MI 49931 • *7,498*
Houghton, NY 14744 • *1,740*
Houghton □, MI • *35,446*
Houghton Lake, MI 48629 • *3,353*
Houghton Lake Heights, MI 48630 • *2,449*
Houlton, ME 04730 • *5,627*
Houma, LA 70360–64 • *96,982*
Housatonic, MA 01236 • *1,184*
Houston, DE 19954 • *487*
Houston, MN 55943 • *1,013*
Houston, MS 38851 • *3,903*
Houston, MO 65483 • *2,118*
Houston, PA 15342 • *1,445*
Houston, TX 77001–99 • *1,630,553*
Houston □, AL • *81,331*
Houston □, GA • *89,208*
Houston □, MN • *18,497*
Houston □, TN • *7,018*
Houston □, TX • *21,375*
Houtzdale, PA 16651 • *1,204*
Howard, SD 57349 • *1,156*
Howard, WI 54303 • *9,874*
Howard □, AR • *13,569*
Howard □, IN • *80,827*
Howard □, IA • *9,809*
Howard □, MD • *187,328*
Howard □, MO • *9,631*
Howard □, NE • *6,055*
Howard □, TX • *32,343*
Howard City, MI 49329 • *1,351*
Howard Lake, MN 55349 • *1,343*
Howards Grove-Millersville, WI 53083 • *2,329*
Howell, MI 48843–44 • *8,184*
Howell □, MO • *31,447*
Howland, ME 04448 • *1,304*
Howland, OH 44484 • *6,732*
Hoxie, AR 72433 • *2,676*
Hoxie, KS 67740 • *1,342*
Hoyt Lakes, MN 55750 • *2,348*
Huachuca City, AZ 85616 • *1,782*
Hubbard, OH 44425 • *8,248*
Hubbard, OR 97032 • *1,881*
Hubbard, TX 76648 • *1,589*
Hubbard □, MN • *14,939*
Hubbell, MI 49934 • *1,174*
Huber Heights, OH 45424 • *38,696*
Huber Ridge, OH 43081 • *5,255*
Huber South, OH 45439 • *4,800*
Hudson, FL 34667 • *7,344*
Hudson, IL 61748 • *1,006*
Hudson, IA 50643 • *2,037*
Hudson, MA 01749 • *14,267*
Hudson, MI 49247 • *2,580*
Hudson, NH 03051 • *7,626*
Hudson, NY 12534 • *8,034*
Hudson, NC 28638 • *2,819*
Hudson, OH 44236 • *5,159*
Hudson, WI 54016 • *6,378*
Hudson, WY 82515 • *392*
Hudson □, NJ • *553,099*
Hudson Falls, NY 12839 • *7,651*
Hudson Lake, IN 46552 • *1,347*
Hudsonville, MI 49426 • *6,170*
Hudspeth □, TX • *2,915*
Huerfano □, CO • *6,009*
Hueytown, AL 35023 • *15,280*
Huffakers, NV 89501 • *150*
Hughes, AR 72348 • *1,810*
Hughes □, OK • *13,023*
Hughes □, SD • *14,817*
Hughesville, MD 20637 • *1,319*
Hughesville, PA 17737 • *2,049*
Hugo, MN 55038 • *4,417*
Hugo, OK 74743 • *5,978*
Hugoton, KS 67951 • *3,179*
Hulett, WY 82720 • *429*
Hull, IA 51239 • *1,724*
Hull, MA 02045 • *10,466*
Humansville, MO 65674 • *1,084*
Humble, TX 77338–39 • *12,060*
Humboldt, IA 50548 • *4,438*
Humboldt, KS 66748 • *2,178*
Humboldt, NE 68376 • *1,003*
Humboldt, TN 38343 • *9,651*
Humboldt □, CA • *119,118*
Humboldt □, IA • *10,756*
Humboldt □, NV • *12,844*
Hummels Wharf, PA 17831 • *1,069*
Humphreys □, MS • *12,134*
Humphreys □, TN • *15,795*
Hunt □, TX • *64,343*
Hunterdon □, NJ • *107,776*
Huntertown, IN 46748 • *1,330*
Huntingburg, IN 47542 • *5,242*
Huntingdon, PA 16652 • *6,843*
Huntingdon, TN 38344 • *4,180*
Huntingdon □, PA • *44,164*
Huntington, IN 46750 • *16,389*
Huntington, MA 01050 • *1,200*
Huntington, NY 11743 • *18,243*
Huntington, TX 75949 • *1,794*
Huntington, UT 84528 • *1,875*
Huntington, VA 22303 • *7,489*
Huntington, WV 25701–79 • *54,844*
Huntington □, IN • *35,427*
Huntington Bay, NY 11743 • *1,521*
Huntington Beach, CA 92646–49 • *181,519*
Huntington Park, CA 90255 • *56,065*
Huntington Station, NY 11746 • *28,247*
Huntington Woods, MI 48070 • *6,419*
Huntley, IL 60142 • *2,453*
Huntsville, AL 35801–24 • *159,789*
Huntsville, AR 72740 • *1,605*
Huntsville, MO 65259 • *1,567*
Huntsville, TX 77340–44 • *27,925*
Hurley, NM 88043 • *1,534*
Hurley, NY 12443 • *4,644*
Hurley, WI 54534 • *1,782*
Hurlock, MD 21643 • *1,706*
Huron, OH 44839 • *7,030*
Huron, SD 57350 • *12,448*
Huron □, MI • *34,951*
Huron □, OH • *56,240*
Hurricane, UT 84737 • *3,915*
Hurricane, WV 25526 • *4,461*
Hurst, TX 76053–54 • *33,574*
Hurt, VA 24563 • *1,294*
Hutchins, TX 75141 • *2,719*
Hutchinson, KS 67501–05 • *39,308*
Hutchinson, MN 55350 • *11,523*
Hutchinson □, SD • *8,262*
Hutchinson □, TX • *25,689*
Huxley, IA 50124 • *2,047*
Hyannis, MA 02601 • *14,120*
Hyannis Port, MA 02647 • *1,100*
Hyattsville, MD 20780–89 • *13,864*
Hybla Valley, VA 22306 • *15,491*
Hydaburg, AK 99922 • *384*
Hyde, PA 16843 • *1,643*
Hyde □, NC • *5,411*
Hyde □, SD • *1,696*
Hyde Park, NY 12538 • *2,550*
Hyde Park, UT 84318 • *2,190*
Hydeville, VT 05750 • *450*
Hyndman, PA 15545 • *1,019*
Hyrum, UT 84319 • *4,829*

I

Iberia □, LA • *68,297*
Iberville □, LA • *31,049*
Ida, MI 48140 • *1,000*
Ida □, IA • *8,365*
Idabel, OK 74745 • *6,957*
Ida Grove, IA 51445 • *2,357*
Idaho □, ID • *13,783*
Idaho Falls, ID 83401–15 • *43,929*
Idaho Springs, CO 80452 • *1,834*
Idalou, TX 79329 • *2,074*
Ilion, NY 13357 • *8,888*
Illmo, MO 63780 • *1,368*
Imlay, NV 89418 • *250*
Imlay City, MI 48444 • *2,921*
Immokalee, FL 33934 • *14,120*
Imperial, CA 92251 • *4,113*
Imperial, NE 69033 • *2,007*
Imperial, PA 15126 • *3,200*
Imperial □, CA • *109,303*
Imperial Beach, CA 91932–33 • *26,512*
Incline Village, NV 89450 • *4,500*
Independence, CA 93526 • *1,000*
Independence, IA 50644 • *5,972*
Independence, KS 67301 • *9,942*
Independence, KY 41051 • *10,444*
Independence, LA 70443 • *1,632*
Independence, MO 64050–58 • *112,301*
Independence, OH 44131 • *6,500*

Independence, OR 97351 • 4,425
Independence, WI 54747 • 1,041
Independence □, AR • 31,192
Indiana, PA 15701 • 15,174
Indiana □, PA • 89,994
Indianapolis, IN 46201–90 • 731,327
Indian Harbour Beach, FL 32937 • 6,933
Indian Head, MD 20640 • 3,531
Indian Heights, IN 46902 • 3,669
Indian Hills, CO 80454 • 2,000
Indian Neck, CT 06405 • 2,430
Indianola, IA 50125 • 11,340
Indianola, MS 38751 • 11,809
Indian Ridge Estates, AZ 85715 • 1,260
Indian River □, FL • 90,208
Indian Rocks Beach, FL 34635 • 3,963
Indian Springs, NV 89018 • 1,164
Indiantown, FL 34956 • 4,794
Indian Trail, NC 28079 • 1,942
Indio, CA 92201–02 • 36,793
Ingalls Park, IL 60431 • 2,730
Ingham □, MI • 281,912
Ingleside, TX 78362 • 5,696
Inglewood, CA 90301–12 • 109,602
Inglewood, TX 98011 • 6,500
Ingram, PA 15205 • 3,901
Inkom, ID 83245 • 769
Inkster, MI 48141 • 30,772
Inman, KS 67546 • 1,035
Inman, SC 29349 • 1,742
Inniswold, LA 70809 • 1,100
Inola, OK 74036 • 1,444
Institute, WV 25112 • 1,400
Interlachen, FL 32148 • 1,160
International Falls, MN 56649 • 8,325
Inver Grove Heights, MN 55076–77 • 22,477
Inverness, CA 94937 • 1,422
Inverness, FL 32650–52 • 5,797
Inverness, IL 60067 • 6,503
Inverness, MS 38753 • 1,174
Inwood, FL 33880 • 6,824
Inwood, NY 11696 • 7,767
Inwood, WV 25428 • 1,360
Inyo □, CA • 18,281
Iola, KS 66749 • 6,351
Iola, WI 54945 • 1,125
Iona, ID 83427 • 1,049
Ione, CA 95640 • 6,516
Ionia, MI 48846 • 5,935
Ionia □, MI • 57,024
Iosco □, MI • 30,209
Iota, LA 70543 • 1,256
Iowa, LA 70647 • 2,588
Iowa □, IA • 14,630
Iowa □, WI • 20,150
Iowa City, IA 52240–46 • 59,738
Iowa Falls, IA 50126 • 5,424
Iowa Park, TX 76367 • 6,072
Ipswich, MA 01938 • 4,132
Ipswich, SD 57451 • 965
Iraan, TX 79744 • 1,322
Iredell □, NC • 92,931
Irion □, TX • 1,629
Irmo, SC 29063 • 11,280
Iron □, MI • 13,175
Iron □, MO • 10,726
Iron □, UT • 20,789
Iron □, WI • 6,153
Irondale, AL 35210 • 9,454
Irondequoit, NY 14617 • 52,322
Ironia, NJ 07845 • 1,110
Iron Mountain, MI 49801 • 8,525
Iron River, MI 49935 • 2,095
Ironton, MO 63650 • 1,539
Ironton, OH 45638 • 12,751
Ironwood, MI 49938 • 6,849
Iroquois □, IL • 30,787
Irvine, CA 92713–20 • 110,330
Irvine, KY 40336 • 2,836
Irving, TX 75060–63 • 155,037
Irvington, KY 40146 • 1,180
Irvington, NJ 07111 • 59,774
Irvington, NY 10533 • 6,348
Irwin, PA 15642 • 4,604
Irwin □, GA • 8,649
Isabella □, MI • 54,624
Isanti, MN 55040 • 1,228
Isanti □, MN • 25,921
Iselin, NJ 08830 • 16,141
Ishpeming, MI 49849 • 7,200
Islamorada, FL 33036 • 1,220
Island □, WA • 60,195
Island Heights, NJ 08732 • 1,470
Island Park, NY 11558 • 4,860
Island Park, RI 02871 • 1,240
Island Pond, VT 05846 • 1,222
Isla Vista, CA 93117 • 20,395
Isle of Palms, SC 29451 • 3,680
Isle of Wight □, VA • 25,053
Isleta, NM 87022 • 1,703
Islington, MA 02090 • 4,920
Islip, NY 11751 • 18,924
Islip Terrace, NY 11752 • 5,530
Issaquah, WA 98027 • 7,786
Issaquena □, MS • 1,909
Italy, TX 76651 • 1,699
Itasca, IL 60143 • 6,947
Itasca, TX 76055 • 1,523
Itasca □, MN • 40,863
Itawamba □, MS • 20,017
Ithaca, MI 48847 • 3,009
Ithaca, NY 14850–52 • 29,541
Itta Bena, MS 38941 • 2,377
Iuka, MS 38852 • 3,122
Iva, SC 29655 • 1,174
Ives Estates, FL 33162 • 13,531
Ivins, UT 84738 • 1,630
Ivoryton, CT 06442 • 2,200
Izard □, AR • 11,364

J

Jacinto City, TX 77029 • 9,343
Jack □, TX • 6,981
Jackpot, NV 89825 • 570
Jacksboro, TN 37757 • 1,568
Jacksboro, TX 76056 • 3,350
Jackson, AL 36545 • 5,819
Jackson, CA 95642 • 3,545
Jackson, GA 30233 • 4,076
Jackson, KY 41339 • 2,466
Jackson, LA 70748 • 3,891
Jackson, MI 49201–04 • 37,446
Jackson, MN 56143 • 3,559
Jackson, MS 39201–98 • 196,637
Jackson, MO 63755 • 9,256
Jackson, OH 45640 • 6,144
Jackson, SC 29831 • 1,681
Jackson, TN 38301–08 • 48,949
Jackson, WI 53037 • 2,486
Jackson, WY 83001–02 • 4,472
Jackson □, AL • 47,796
Jackson □, AR • 18,944
Jackson □, CO • 1,605
Jackson □, FL • 41,375
Jackson □, GA • 30,005
Jackson □, IL • 61,067
Jackson □, IN • 37,730
Jackson □, IA • 19,950
Jackson □, KS • 11,525
Jackson □, KY • 11,955
Jackson □, LA • 15,705
Jackson □, MI • 149,756
Jackson □, MN • 11,677
Jackson □, MS • 115,243
Jackson □, MO • 633,232
Jackson □, NC • 26,846
Jackson □, OH • 30,230
Jackson □, OK • 28,764
Jackson □, OR • 146,389
Jackson □, SD • 2,811
Jackson □, TN • 9,297
Jackson □, TX • 13,039
Jackson □, WV • 25,938
Jackson □, WI • 16,588
Jackson Center, OH 45334 • 1,398
Jacksonville, AL 36265 • 10,283
Jacksonville, AR 72076 • 29,101
Jacksonville, FL 32201–98 • 635,230
Jacksonville, IL 62650–51 • 19,324
Jacksonville, NC 28540–46 • 30,013
Jacksonville, OR 97530 • 1,896
Jacksonville, TX 75766 • 12,765
Jacksonville Beach, FL 32250 • 17,839
Jaffrey, NH 03452 • 2,558
Jal, NM 88252 • 2,156
Jamesburg, NJ 08831 • 5,294
James City, NC 28560 • 4,279
James City □, VA • 34,859
James Island, SC 29412 • 24,124
Jamestown, CA 95327 • 2,178
Jamestown, KY 42629 • 1,641
Jamestown, NY 14701–02 • 34,681
Jamestown, NC 27282 • 2,600
Jamestown, ND 58401–02 • 15,571
Jamestown, OH 45335 • 1,794
Jamestown, RI 02835 • 2,156
Jamestown, TN 38556 • 1,862
James Town, WY 82935 • 280
Janesville, CA 96114 • 1,200
Janesville, MN 56048 • 1,969
Janesville, WI 53545–47 • 52,133
Jarrettsville, MD 21084 • 2,148
Jasmine Estates, FL 34668 • 17,136
Jasonville, IN 47438 • 2,200
Jasper, AL 35501–02 • 13,553
Jasper, FL 32052 • 2,099
Jasper, GA 30143 • 1,772
Jasper, IN 47546–47 • 10,030
Jasper, TN 37347 • 2,780
Jasper, TX 75951 • 6,959
Jasper □, GA • 8,453
Jasper □, IL • 10,609
Jasper □, IN • 24,960
Jasper □, IA • 34,795
Jasper □, MS • 17,114
Jasper □, MO • 90,465
Jasper □, SC • 15,487
Jasper □, TX • 31,102
Jay, OK 74346 • 2,220
Jay □, IN • 21,512
Jean, NV 89019 • 150
Jeanerette, LA 70544 • 6,205
Jeannette, PA 15644 • 11,221
Jeff Davis □, GA • 12,032
Jeff Davis □, TX • 1,946
Jefferson, GA 30549 • 2,763
Jefferson, IA 50129 • 4,292
Jefferson, LA 70121 • 14,521
Jefferson, NC 28640 • 1,300
Jefferson, OH 44047 • 3,331
Jefferson, OR 97352 • 1,805
Jefferson, PA 15025 • 9,533
Jefferson, TX 75657 • 2,199
Jefferson, WI 53549 • 6,078
Jefferson □, AL • 651,525
Jefferson □, AR • 85,487
Jefferson □, CO • 438,430
Jefferson □, FL • 11,296
Jefferson □, GA • 17,408
Jefferson □, ID • 16,543
Jefferson □, IL • 37,020
Jefferson □, IN • 29,797
Jefferson □, IA • 16,310
Jefferson □, KS • 15,905
Jefferson □, KY • 664,937
Jefferson □, LA • 448,306
Jefferson □, MS • 8,653
Jefferson □, MO • 171,380
Jefferson □, MT • 7,939
Jefferson □, NE • 8,759
Jefferson □, NY • 110,943
Jefferson □, OH • 80,298
Jefferson □, OK • 7,010
Jefferson □, OR • 13,676
Jefferson □, PA • 46,083
Jefferson □, TN • 33,016
Jefferson □, TX • 239,397
Jefferson □, WA • 20,146
Jefferson □, WV • 35,926
Jefferson □, WI • 67,783
Jefferson City, MO 65101–10 • 35,481
Jefferson City, TN 37760 • 5,494
Jefferson Davis □, LA • 30,722
Jefferson Davis □, MS • 14,051
Jefferson Farms, DE 19720 • 3,130
Jefferson Manor, VA 22303 • 2,300
Jeffersontown, KY 40299 • 23,221
Jefferson Valley, NY 10535 • 6,420
Jefferson Village, VA 22042 • 2,500
Jeffersonville, GA 31044 • 1,545
Jeffersonville, IN 47129–31 • 21,841
Jeffersonville, KY 40337 • 1,854
Jeffersonville, OH 43128 • 1,281
Jeffrey City, WY 82310 • 1,882
Jellico, TN 37762 • 2,447
Jemez Pueblo, NM 87024 • 1,301
Jemison, AL 35085 • 1,898
Jena, LA 71342 • 2,626
Jenison, MI 49428–29 • 17,882
Jenkins, KY 41537 • 2,751
Jenkins □, GA • 8,247
Jenkintown, PA 19046 • 4,574
Jenks, OK 74037 • 7,493
Jennings, LA 70546 • 11,305
Jennings, MO 63136 • 15,905
Jennings □, IN • 23,661
Jennings Lodge, OR 97222 • 11,480
Jensen Beach, FL 34957–58 • 9,884
Jerauld □, SD • 2,425
Jericho, NY 11753 • 13,141
Jericho, VT 05465 • 1,300
Jermyn, PA 18433 • 2,263
Jerome, ID 83338 • 6,529
Jerome, PA 15937 • 1,074
Jerome □, ID • 15,138
Jersey □, IL • 20,539
Jersey City, NJ 07301–11 • 228,537
Jersey Shore, PA 17740 • 4,353
Jerseyville, IL 62052 • 7,382
Jessamine □, KY • 30,508
Jessup, MD 20794 • 6,537
Jessup, PA 18434 • 4,605
Jesup, GA 31545 • 8,958
Jesup, IA 50648 • 2,121
Jewell, IA 50130 • 1,106
Jewell □, KS • 4,251
Jewett City, CT 06351 • 3,349
Jim Hogg □, TX • 5,109
Jim Thorpe, PA 18229 • 5,048
Jim Wells □, TX • 37,679
Joanna, SC 29351 • 1,735
Jo Daviess □, IL • 21,821
John Day, OR 97845 • 1,836
Johnson, KS 67855 • 1,348
Johnson, VT 05656 • 1,470
Johnson □, AR • 18,221
Johnson □, GA • 8,329
Johnson □, IL • 11,347
Johnson □, IN • 88,109
Johnson □, IA • 96,119
Johnson □, KS • 355,054
Johnson □, KY • 23,248
Johnson □, MO • 42,514
Johnson □, NE • 4,673
Johnson □, TN • 13,766
Johnson □, TX • 97,165
Johnson □, WY • 6,145
Johnsonburg, PA 15845 • 3,350
Johnson City, NY 13790 • 16,890
Johnson City, TN 37601–15 • 49,381
Johnson Creek, WI 53038 • 1,259
Johnsonville, SC 29555 • 1,415
Johnston, IA 50131 • 4,702
Johnston, RI 02919 • 26,542
Johnston, SC 29832 • 2,688
Johnston □, NC • 81,306
Johnston □, OK • 10,032
Johnston City, IL 62951 • 3,706
Johnstown, CO 80534 • 1,579
Johnstown, NY 12095 • 9,058
Johnstown, OH 43031 • 3,237
Johnstown, PA 15901–09 • 28,134
Joliet, IL 60431–36 • 76,836
Jones, OK 73049 • 2,424
Jones □, GA • 20,739
Jones □, IA • 19,444
Jones □, MS • 62,031
Jones □, NC • 9,414
Jones □, SD • 1,324
Jones □, TX • 16,490
Jonesboro, AR 72401–03 • 46,535
Jonesboro, GA 30236–37 • 3,635
Jonesboro, IL 62952 • 1,728
Jonesboro, IN 46938 • 2,073
Jonesboro, LA 71251 • 4,305
Jonesborough, TN 37659 • 3,091
Jones Creek, TX 77541 • 2,160
Jonesport, ME 04649 • 1,525
Jonestown, MS 38639 • 1,467
Jonesville, LA 71343 • 2,720
Jonesville, MI 49250 • 2,283
Jonesville, NC 28642 • 1,549
Jonesville, SC 29353 • 1,205
Joplin, MO 64801–04 • 40,961
Joppatowne, MD 21085 • 11,084
Jordan, MN 55352 • 2,909
Jordan, NY 13080 • 1,325
Joseph, OR 97846 • 1,073
Josephine □, OR • 62,649
Joshua, TX 76058 • 3,828
Joshua Tree, CA 92252 • 3,898
Jourdanton, TX 78026 • 3,220
Juab □, UT • 5,817
Juanita, WA 98033 • 10,500
Judith Basin □, MT • 2,282
Judsonia, AR 72081 • 1,915
Julesburg, CO 80737 • 1,295
Julian, CA 92036 • 1,284
Junction, TX 76849 • 2,654
Junction City, KS 66441 • 20,604
Junction City, KY 40440 • 1,983
Junction City, OR 97448 • 3,670
Juneau, AK 99801–03 • 26,751
Juneau, WI 53039 • 2,157
Juneau □, WI • 21,650
Juniata □, PA • 20,625
Jupiter, FL 33458 • 24,986
Justice, IL 60458 • 11,137
Justin, TX 76247 • 1,234

K

Kaaawa, HI 96730 • 1,138
Kadoka, SD 57543 • 736
Kahaluu, HI 96725 • 380
Kahaluu, HI 96744 • 3,068
Kahoka, MO 63445 • 2,195
Kahuku, HI 96731 • 2,063
Kahului, HI 96732–33 • 16,889
Kailua, HI 96734 • 36,818
Kailua Kona, HI 96739–40 • 9,126
Kake, AK 99830 • 700
Kalaheo, HI 96741 • 3,592
Kalama, WA 98625 • 1,210
Kalamazoo, MI 49001–09 • 80,277
Kalamazoo □, MI • 223,411
Kalawao □, HI • 130
Kalispell, MT 59901 • 11,917
Kalkaska, MI 49646 • 1,952
Kalkaska □, MI • 13,497
Kalona, IA 52247 • 1,942
Kamas, UT 84036 • 1,061
Kamiah, ID 83536 • 1,157
Kamuela (Waimea), HI 96743 • 5,972
Kanab, UT 84741 • 3,289
Kanabec □, MN • 12,802
Kanawha □, WV • 207,619
Kandiyohi □, MN • 38,761
Kane, PA 16735 • 4,590
Kane □, IL • 317,471
Kane □, UT • 5,169
Kaneohe, HI 96744 • 35,448
Kankakee, IL 60901 • 27,575
Kankakee □, IL • 96,255
Kannapolis, NC 28081–83 • 29,696
Kansas City, KS 66101–19 • 149,767
Kansas City, MO 64101–99 • 435,146
Kapaa, HI 96746 • 8,149
Kapaau, HI 96755 • 1,083
Kaplan, LA 70548 • 4,535
Karnes □, TX • 12,455
Karnes City, TX 78118 • 2,916
Karns, TN 37921 • 1,458
Kasson, MN 55944 • 3,514
Kathleen, FL 33849 • 2,743
Katy, TX 77449–50 • 8,005
Kauai □, HI • 51,177
Kaufman, TX 75142 • 5,238
Kaufman □, TX • 52,220
Kaukauna, WI 54130 • 11,982
Kaumakani, HI 96747 • 803
Kaunakakai, HI 96748 • 2,658
Kay □, OK • 48,056
Kaycee, WY 82639 • 256
Kayenta, AZ 86033 • 4,372
Kaysville, UT 84037 • 13,961
Keaau, HI 96749 • 1,584
Kealakekua, HI 96750 • 1,453
Kealia, HI 96751 • 700
Keansburg, NJ 07734 • 11,069
Kearney, MO 64060 • 1,790
Kearney, NE 68847–48 • 24,396
Kearney □, NE • 6,629
Kearns, UT 84118 • 28,374
Kearny, AZ 85237 • 2,262
Kearny, NJ 07031–32 • 34,874
Kearny □, KS • 4,027
Keego Harbor, MI 48320 • 2,932
Keene, NH 03431 • 22,430
Keene, TX 76059 • 3,944
Keeseville, NY 12944 • 1,854
Keewatin, MN 55753 • 1,118
Keith □, NE • 8,584
Keizer, OR 97303 • 21,884
Kekaha, HI 96752 • 3,506
Keller, TX 76248 • 13,683
Kellogg, ID 83837 • 2,591
Kelseyville, CA 95451 • 2,861
Kelso, WA 98626 • 11,820
Kemmerer, WY 83101 • 3,020
Kemp, TX 75143 • 1,184
Kemper □, MS • 10,356
Kenai, AK 99611 • 6,327
Kenbridge, VA 23944 • 1,264
Ken Caryl, CO 80123 • 24,391
Kendall, FL 33156 • 87,271
Kendall □, IL • 39,413
Kendall □, TX • 14,589
Kendall Park, NJ 08824 • 7,127
Kendallville, IN 46755 • 7,773
Kenedy, TX 78119 • 3,763
Kenedy □, TX • 460
Kenilworth, IL 60043 • 2,402
Kenilworth, NJ 07033 • 7,574
Kenly, NC 27542 • 1,549
Kenmare, ND 58746 • 1,214
Kenmore, NY 14217 • 17,180
Kenmore, WA 98028 • 8,917
Kennebec □, ME • 115,904
Kennebunk, ME 04043 • 4,206
Kennebunkport, ME 04046 • 1,100
Kennedy Heights, LA 70094 • 2,000
Kennedy Township, PA 15108 • 7,152
Kenner, LA 70062–65 • 72,033
Kennesaw, GA 30144 • 8,936
Kennett, MO 63857 • 10,941
Kennett Square, PA 19348 • 5,218
Kennewick, WA 99336–37 • 42,155
Kennydale, WA 98056 • 2,000
Kenosha, WI 53140–44 • 80,352
Kenosha □, WI • 128,181
Kenova, WV 25530 • 3,748
Ken Rock, IL 61109 • 3,300
Kensett, AR 72082 • 1,741
Kensington, CA 94707 • 4,974
Kensington, CT 06037 • 8,306
Kensington, MD 20895 • 1,713
Kent, OH 44240 • 28,835
Kent, WA 98031–32 • 37,960
Kent □, DE • 110,993
Kent □, MD • 17,842
Kent □, MI • 500,631
Kent □, RI • 161,135
Kent □, TX • 1,010
Kentfield, CA 94904 • 6,030
Kentland, IN 47951 • 1,798
Kenton, DE 19955 • 232
Kenton, OH 43326 • 8,356
Kenton, TN 38233 • 1,366
Kenton □, KY • 142,031
Kentwood, LA 70444 • 2,468
Kentwood, MI 49508 • 37,826
Kenvil, NJ 07847 • 3,050
Kenwood, OH 45236 • 7,469
Kenyon, MN 55946 • 1,552
Kenyon, RI 02836 • 400
Keokea, HI 96790 • 900
Keokuk, IA 52632 • 12,451
Keokuk □, IA • 11,624
Keosauqua, IA 52565 • 1,020
Keota, IA 52248 • 1,000
Kerens, TX 75144 • 1,702
Kerhonkson, NY 12446 • 1,629
Kermit, TX 79745 • 6,875
Kern □, CA • 543,477
Kernersville, NC 27284–85 • 10,836
Kernville, CA 93238 • 1,656
Kerr □, TX • 36,304
Kerrville, TX 78028–29 • 17,384
Kershaw, SC 29067 • 1,814
Kershaw □, SC • 43,599
Ketchikan, AK 99901 • 8,263
Ketchum, ID 83340 • 2,523
Kettering, MD 20772 • 9,901
Kettering, OH 45429 • 60,569
Kettle Falls, WA 99141 • 1,272
Kewanee, IL 61443 • 12,969
Kewaskum, WI 53040 • 2,515
Kewaunee, WI 54216 • 2,750
Kewaunee □, WI • 18,878
Keweenaw □, MI • 1,701
Keya Paha □, NE • 1,029
Key Biscayne, FL 33149 • 8,854
Key Largo, FL 33037 • 11,336
Keyport, NJ 07735 • 7,586
Keyser, WV 26726 • 5,870
Keystone Heights, FL 32656 • 1,315
Key West, FL 33040–41 • 24,832
Kiana, AK 99749 • 385
Kidder □, ND • 3,332
Kiel, WI 53042 • 2,910
Kihei, HI 96753 • 11,107
Kilauea, HI 96754 • 1,685
Kilgore, TX 75662–63 • 11,066
Killdeer, ND 58640 • 722
Killeen, TX 76540–47 • 63,535
Killen, AL 35645 • 1,047
Kilmarnock, VA 22482 • 1,109
Kimball, NE 69145 • 2,574
Kimball □, NE • 4,108
Kimberly, AL 35091 • 1,096
Kimberly, ID 83341 • 2,367
Kimberly, WI 54136 • 5,406
Kimble □, TX • 4,122
Kincaid, IL 62540 • 1,353
Kinder, LA 70648 • 2,246
Kinderhook, NY 12106 • 1,293
King, NC 27021 • 4,059
King □, TX • 354
King □, WA • 1,507,319
King and Queen □, VA • 6,289
King City, CA 93930 • 7,634
King Cove, AK 99612 • 451
Kingfisher, OK 73750 • 4,095
Kingfisher □, OK • 13,212
King George □, VA • 13,527
Kingman, AZ 86401–02 • 12,722
Kingman, KS 67068 • 3,196
Kingman □, KS • 8,292
King of Prussia, PA 19406 • 18,406
Kings, MS 39180 • 1,165
Kings □, CA • 101,469
Kings □, NY • 2,300,664
King Salmon, AK 99613 • 696
Kingsburg, CA 93631 • 7,205
Kingsbury □, SD • 5,925
Kingsford, MI 49801 • 5,480
Kingsgate, WA 98011 • 14,259
Kingsland, GA 31548 • 4,699
Kingsland, TX 78639 • 2,725
Kingsley, IA 51028 • 1,129
Kings Mountain, NC 28086 • 8,763
Kings Park, NY 11754 • 17,773
Kings Park, VA 22151 • 6,000
Kings Park West, VA 22032 • 6,000
Kings Point, FL 33484 • 12,422
Kings Point, NY 11024 • 4,843
Kingsport, TN 37660–65 • 36,365
Kingston, ID 83839 • 1,000
Kingston, MA 02364 • 4,774
Kingston, NJ 08528 • 1,200
Kingston, NY 12401 • 23,095
Kingston, OH 45644 • 1,153
Kingston, OK 73439 • 1,237
Kingston, PA 18704 • 14,507
Kingston, RI 02881 • 6,504
Kingston, TN 37763 • 4,552
Kingston Springs, TN 37082 • 1,529
Kingstown, MD 21620 • 1,660
Kingstree, SC 29556 • 3,858
Kingsville, MD 21087 • 3,550
Kingsville (North Kingsville), OH 44048 • 1,243
Kingsville, TX 78363–64 • 25,276
King William □, VA • 10,913
Kingwood, TX 77339 • 37,397
Kingwood, WV 26537 • 3,243
Kinloch, MO 63140 • 2,702
Kinnelon, NJ 07405 • 8,470
Kinney □, TX • 3,119
Kinsey, AL 36301 • 1,679
Kinsley, KS 67547 • 1,875
Kinston, NC 28501–03 • 25,295
Kiowa, KS 67070 • 1,160
Kiowa □, CO • 1,688
Kiowa □, KS • 3,660
Kiowa □, OK • 11,347
Kipnuk, AK 99614 • 470
Kirby, TX 78219 • 8,326
Kirbyville, TX 75956 • 1,871
Kirkland, IL 60146 • 1,011
Kirkland, WA 98033–34 • 40,052
Kirksville, MO 63501 • 17,152
Kirkwood, DE 19708 • 350
Kirkwood, MO 63122 • 27,291
Kirtland, NM 87417 • 3,552
Kirtland, OH 44094 • 5,881
Kissimmee, FL 34741–46 • 30,050
Kit Carson □, CO • 7,140
Kitsap □, WA • 189,731
Kittanning, PA 16201 • 5,120
Kittery, ME 03904 • 5,151
Kittery Point, ME 03905 • 1,093
Kittitas □, WA • 26,725
Kittson □, MN • 5,767
Kitty Hawk, NC 27949 • 1,937
Klamath □, OR • 57,702
Klamath Falls, OR 97601–03 • 17,737
Klawock, AK 99925 • 722
Kleberg □, TX • 30,274
Klein, TX 77379 • 12,000
Klickitat □, WA • 16,616
Knightdale, NC 27545 • 1,884
Knights Landing, CA 95645 • 1,000
Knightstown, IN 46148 • 2,048
Knob Noster, MO 65336 • 2,261
Knott □, KY • 17,906
Knox, IN 46534 • 3,705
Knox, PA 16232 • 1,182
Knox □, IL • 56,393
Knox □, IN • 39,884
Knox □, KY • 29,676
Knox □, ME • 36,310

United States Populations and ZIP Codes

Knox □, MO • 4,482
Knox □, NE • 9,534
Knox □, OH • 47,473
Knox □, TN • 335,749
Knox □, TX • 4,837
Knox City, TX 79529 • 1,440
Knoxville, IL 61448 • 3,243
Knoxville, IA 50138 • 8,232
Knoxville, TN 37901–50 • 165,121
Kodiak, AK 99615 • 6,365
Kohler, WI 53044 • 1,817
Kokomo, IN 46901–04 • 44,962
Koloa, HI 96756 • 1,791
Konawa, OK 74849 • 1,508
Koochiching □, MN • 16,299
Koontz Lake, IN 46574 • 1,615
Kootenai □, ID • 69,795
Koppel, PA 16136 • 1,024
Kosciusko, MS 39090 • 6,986
Kosciusko □, IN • 65,294
Kossuth □, IA • 18,591
Kotlik, AK 99620 • 461
Kotzebue, AK 99752 • 2,751
Kountze, TX 77625 • 2,056
Kouts, IN 46347 • 1,603
Krebs, OK 74554 • 1,955
Kremmling, CO 80459 • 1,166
Krotz Springs, LA 70750 • 1,285
Kula, HI 96790 • 1,300
Kulpmont, PA 17834 • 3,233
Kuna, ID 83634 • 1,955
Kurtistown, HI 96760 • 910
Kutztown, PA 19530 • 4,704
Kwethluk, AK 99621 • 558
Kwigillingok, AK 99622 • 278
Kyle, TX 78640 • 2,225

L

Labadieville, LA 70372 • 1,821
La Barge, WY 83123 • 493
La Belle, FL 33935 • 2,703
Labette □, KS • 23,693
La Canada Flintridge, CA 91011 • 19,378
Lac du Flambeau, WI 54538 • 1,180
La Center, KY 42056 • 1,040
Lacey, WA 98503 • 19,279
Lackawanna, NY 14218 • 20,585
Lackawanna □, PA • 219,039
Laclede □, MO • 27,158
Lacombe, LA 70445 • 6,523
Lacon, IL 61540 • 1,986
Laconia, NH 03246–47 • 15,743
Lacoochee, FL 33537 • 2,072
Lac qui Parle □, MN • 8,924
La Crescent, MN 55947 • 4,311
La Crescenta, CA 91214 • 12,500
La Crosse, KS 67548 • 1,427
La Crosse, WI 54601–03 • 51,003
La Crosse □, WI • 97,904
La Cygne, KS 66040 • 1,066
Ladd, IL 61329 • 1,283
Ladera Heights, CA 90045 • 6,316
Ladoga, IN 47954 • 1,124
Ladson, SC 29456 • 13,540
Ladue, MO 63124 • 8,847
Lady Lake, FL 32159 • 8,071
Ladysmith, WI 54848 • 3,938
Lafayette, AL 36862 • 3,151
Lafayette, CA 94549 • 23,501
Lafayette, CO 80026 • 14,548
Lafayette, GA 30728 • 6,313
Lafayette, IN 47901–06 • 43,764
Lafayette, LA 70501–09 • 94,440
Lafayette, NC 28304 • 3,200
Lafayette, OR 97127 • 1,292
La Fayette, RI 02852 • 640
Lafayette, TN 37083 • 3,641
Lafayette □, AR • 9,643
Lafayette □, FL • 5,578
Lafayette □, LA • 164,762
Lafayette □, MS • 31,826
Lafayette □, MO • 31,107
Lafayette □, WI • 16,076
Lafayette Southwest, LA • 5,500
La Feria, TX 78559 • 4,360
Lafitte, LA 70067 • 1,507
La Follette, TN 37766 • 7,192
Lafourche □, LA • 85,860
La Grande, OR 97850 • 11,766
La Grange, GA 30240–41 • 25,597
La Grange, IL 60525 • 15,362
Lagrange, IN 46761 • 2,382
La Grange, KY 40031 • 3,853
La Grange, MO 63448 • 1,102
La Grange, NC 28551 • 2,805
Lagrange, OH 44050 • 1,199
La Grange, TX 78945 • 3,951
Lagrange □, IN • 29,477
La Grange Highlands, IL 60525 • 3,660
La Grange Park, IL 60525 • 12,861
Laguna Beach, CA 92651–54 • 23,170
Laguna Hills, CA 92653 • 46,731
Laguna Niguel, CA 92677 • 44,400
La Habra, CA 90631–33 • 51,266
Lahaina, HI 96761 • 9,073
La Harpe, IL 61450 • 1,407
Laie, HI 96762 • 5,577
Laingsburg, MI 48848 • 1,148
La Junta, CO 81050 • 7,637
Lake □, CA • 50,631
Lake □, CO • 6,007
Lake □, FL • 152,104
Lake □, IL • 516,418
Lake □, IN • 475,594
Lake □, MI • 8,583
Lake □, MN • 10,415
Lake □, MT • 21,041
Lake □, OH • 215,499
Lake □, OR • 7,186
Lake □, SD • 10,550
Lake □, TN • 7,129
Lake Alfred, FL 33850 • 3,622
Lake Andes, SD 57356 • 846
Lake Arrowhead, CA 92317 • 6,539
Lake Arthur, LA 70549 • 3,194
Lake Barcroft, VA 22041 • 8,686
Lake Bluff, IL 60044 • 5,513
Lake Butler, FL 32054 • 2,116
Lake Carmel, NY 10512 • 8,489
Lake Charles, LA 70601–29 • 70,580
Lake City, AR 72437 • 1,833
Lake City, FL 32055–56 • 10,005
Lake City, IA 51449 • 1,841
Lake City, MN 55041 • 4,391
Lake City, PA 16423 • 2,519
Lake City, SC 29560 • 7,153
Lake City, TN 37769 • 2,166
Lake Crystal, MN 56055 • 2,084
Lake Delta, NY 13440 • 1,980
Lake Delton, WI 53940 • 1,470
Lake Elmo, MN 55042 • 5,903
Lake Elsinore, CA 92330–31 • 18,285
Lake Erie Beach, NY 14006 • 4,509
Lakefield, MN 56150 • 1,679
Lake Forest, FL 33023 • 5,400
Lake Forest, IL 60045 • 17,836
Lake Geneva, WI 53147 • 5,979
Lake Grove, NY 11755 • 9,612
Lake Hamilton, AR 71913 • 1,331
Lake Havasu City, AZ 86403–05 • 24,363
Lake Helen, FL 32744 • 2,344
Lakehurst, NJ 08733 • 3,078
Lake in the Hills, IL 60102 • 5,866
Lake Jackson, TX 77566 • 22,776
Lake Katrine, NY 12449 • 1,998
Lakeland, FL 33801–13 • 70,576
Lakeland, GA 31635 • 2,467
Lakeland Highlands, FL 33801 • 9,972
Lakeland Village, CA 92330 • 5,159
Lake Linden, MI 49945 • 1,203
Lake Lorraine, FL 32569 • 6,779
Lake Luzerne, NY 12846 • 1,160
Lake Magdalene, FL 33612 • 15,973
Lake Mary, FL 32746 • 5,929
Lake Mills, IA 50450 • 2,143
Lake Mills, WI 53551 • 4,143
Lakemore, OH 44250 • 2,684
Lake Odessa, MI 48849 • 2,256
Lake Of The Woods □, MN • 4,076
Lake Orion, MI 48360–62 • 3,057
Lake Oswego, OR 97034–35 • 30,576
Lake Park, FL 33403 • 6,704
Lake Placid, FL 33852 • 1,158
Lake Placid, NY 12946 • 2,485
Lakeport, CA 95453 • 4,390
Lake Preston, SD 57249 • 663
Lake Providence, LA 71254 • 5,380
Lake Ridge, VA 22192 • 23,862
Lake Ronkonkoma, NY 11779 • 18,997
Lake Shore, MD 21122 • 13,269
Lakeside, CA 92040 • 39,412
Lakeside, CT 06488 • 1,200
Lakeside, FL 32073 • 29,137
Lakeside, OR 97449 • 1,437
Lakeside, VA 23228 • 12,081
Lakeside Park, KY 41017 • 3,131
Lakeside-Pinetop, AZ 85935 • 2,422
Lake Station, IN 46405 • 13,899
Lake Stevens, WA 98258 • 3,380
Lake Telemark, NJ 07866 • 1,121
Lakeview, GA 30741 • 5,237
Lake View, IA 51450 • 1,303
Lakeview, MI 48850 • 1,108
Lake View, NY 14085 • 1,460
Lakeview, NY 11552 • 5,476
Lakeview, OH 43331 • 1,056
Lakeview, OR 97630 • 2,526
Lake Villa, IL 60046 • 2,857
Lake Village, AR 71653 • 2,791
Lakeville, CT 06039 • 1,800
Lakeville, MA 02346 • 1,948
Lakeville, MN 55044 • 24,854
Lakeville, NY 14480 • 1,000
Lake Wales, FL 33853 • 9,670
Lake Wissota, WI 54729 • 2,175
Lakewood, CA 90711–16 • 73,557
Lakewood, CO 80215 • 126,481
Lakewood, IL 60014 • 1,609
Lakewood, IA 50211 • 1,950
Lakewood, NJ 08701 • 26,095
Lakewood, NY 14750 • 3,564
Lakewood, OH 44107 • 59,718
Lakewood, WA 98259 • 58,412
Lakewood Center, WA 98499 • 58,412
Lakewood Park, FL 34951 • 7,211
Lake Worth, FL 33460–67 • 28,564
Lake Zurich, IL 60047 • 14,947
Lakin, KS 67860 • 2,060
Lakota, ND 58344 • 898
La Luz, NM 88337 • 1,625
Lamar, CO 81052 • 8,343
Lamar, MO 64759 • 4,168
Lamar, PA 16848 • 1,200
Lamar, SC 29069 • 1,125
Lamar □, AL • 15,715
Lamar □, GA • 13,038
Lamar □, MS • 30,424
Lamar □, TX • 43,949
La Marque, TX 77568 • 14,120
Lamb □, TX • 15,072
Lambert, MS 38643 • 1,131
Lambertville, MI 48144 • 7,860
Lambertville, NJ 08530 • 3,927
La Mesa, CA 91941–44 • 52,931
La Mesa, NM 88044 • 900
Lamesa, TX 79331 • 10,809
La Mirada, CA 90637–38 • 40,452
Lamoille, NV 89828 • 110
Lamoille □, VT • 19,735
Lamoni, IA 50140 • 2,319
Lamont, CA 93241 • 11,517
La Moure, ND 58458 • 970
La Moure □, ND • 5,383
Lampasas, TX 76550 • 6,382
Lampasas □, TX • 13,521
Lanai City, HI 96763 • 2,400
Lanark, IL 61046 • 1,382
Lancashire, DE 19810 • 1,175
Lancaster, CA 93534–39 • 97,291
Lancaster, KY 40444 • 3,421
Lancaster, NH 03584 • 1,859
Lancaster, NY 14086 • 11,940
Lancaster, OH 43130 • 34,507
Lancaster, PA 17601–05 • 55,551
Lancaster, SC 29720–21 • 8,914
Lancaster, TX 75146 • 22,117
Lancaster, WI 53813 • 4,192
Lancaster □, NE • 213,641
Lancaster □, PA • 422,822
Lancaster □, SC • 54,516
Lancaster □, VA • 10,896
Lancaster Village, DE 19805 • 1,100
Landen, OH 45040 • 9,263
Lander, WY 82520 • 7,023
Lander □, NV • 6,266
Landess, IN 46944 • 1,500
Landis, NC 28088 • 2,333
Land O' Lakes, FL 34639 • 7,892
Landover, MD 20784 • 5,052
Landrum, SC 29356 • 2,347
Lane □, KS • 2,375
Lane □, OR • 282,912
Lanesboro, MA 01237 • 1,000
Lanett, AL 36863 • 8,985
Langdon, ND 58249 • 2,241
Langeloth, PA 15054 • 1,112
Langhorne, PA 19047 • 1,361
Langlade □, WI • 19,505
Langley, SC 29834 • 1,714
Langley Park, MD 20783 • 17,474
Langston, OK 73050 • 1,471
Lanham, MD 20706 • 5,000
Lanier □, GA • 5,531
Lansdale, PA 19446 • 16,362
Lansdowne, MD 21227 • 9,430
Lansdowne, PA 19050 • 11,712
L'Anse, MI 49946 • 2,151
Lansford, PA 18232 • 4,583
Lansing, IL 60438 • 28,086
Lansing, IA 52151 • 1,007
Lansing, KS 66043 • 7,120
Lansing, MI 48901–33 • 127,321
Lantana, FL 33462 • 8,392
La Palma, CA 90623 • 15,392
La Paz □, AZ • 13,844
Lapeer, MI 48446 • 7,759
Lapeer □, MI • 74,768
Lapel, IN 46051 • 1,742
La Place, LA 70068–69 • 24,194
La Plata, MD 20646 • 5,841
La Plata, MO 63549 • 1,401
La Plata □, CO • 32,284
Laporte, CO 80535 • 1,300
La Porte, IN 46350 • 21,507
La Porte, TX 77571–72 • 27,910
La Porte □, IN • 107,066
La Porte City, IA 50651 • 2,128
La Pryor, TX 78872 • 1,343
La Puente, CA 91744–49 • 36,955
Lapwai, ID 83540 • 932
Laramie, WY 82063–71 • 26,687
Laramie □, WY • 73,142
Larchmont, NY 10538 • 6,181
Larchmont North, NY 10538 • 11,240
Laredo, TX 78040–44 • 122,899
Largo, FL 34640–49 • 65,674
Larimer □, CO • 186,136
Larimore, ND 58251 • 1,464
La Riviera, CA 95826 • 10,986
Larkspur, CA 94939 • 11,070
Larksville, PA 18704 • 4,700
Larned, KS 67550 • 4,490
Larose, LA 70373 • 5,772
Larue □, KY • 11,679
La Salle, CO 80645 • 1,783
La Salle, IL 61301 • 9,717
La Salle □, IL • 106,913
La Salle □, LA • 13,662
La Salle □, TX • 5,254
Las Animas, CO 81054 • 2,481
Las Animas □, CO • 13,765
Las Cruces, NM 88001–08 • 62,126
Lassen □, CA • 27,598
Las Vegas, NV 89101–99 • 258,295
Las Vegas, NM 87701 • 14,753
Latah □, ID • 30,617
Lathrop, MO 64465 • 1,794
Lathrop Wells, NV 89020 • 350
Latimer □, OK • 10,333
Laton, CA 93242 • 1,415
Latrobe, PA 15650 • 9,265
Latta, SC 29565 • 1,565
Lauderdale □, AL • 79,661
Lauderdale □, MS • 75,555
Lauderdale □, TN • 23,491
Lauderdale Lakes, FL 33313 • 27,341
Lauderhill, FL 33313 • 49,708
Laughlin, NV 89028–29 • 140
Laughlintown, PA 15655 • 1,000
Laurel, DE 19956 • 3,226
Laurel, FL 34272 • 8,245
Laurel, MD 20707–09 • 19,438
Laurel, MS 39440–42 • 18,827
Laurel, MT 59044 • 5,686
Laurel, VA 23060 • 13,011
Laurel □, KY • 43,438
Laurel Bay, SC 29902 • 4,972
Laureldale, PA 19605 • 3,726
Laurel Hill, NC 28351 • 2,314
Laurence Harbor, NJ 08879 • 6,361
Laurens, IA 50554 • 1,550
Laurens, SC 29360 • 9,694
Laurens □, GA • 39,988
Laurens □, SC • 58,092
Laurinburg, NC 28352–53 • 11,643
Laurium, MI 49913 • 2,268
Lavaca, AR 72941 • 1,253
Lavaca □, TX • 18,690
La Vale, MD 21502 • 5,000
Lavallette, NJ 08735 • 2,299
La Vergne, TN 37086 • 7,499
La Verkin, UT 84745 • 1,771
La Verne, CA 91750 • 30,897
Laverne, OK 73848 • 1,269
La Vista, GA 30329 • 4,900
La Vista, NE 68128 • 9,840
Lavonia, GA 30553 • 1,840
Lawai, HI 96765 • 1,787
Lawndale, CA 90260–61 • 27,331
Lawnside, NJ 08045 • 2,841
Lawrence, IN 46226 • 26,763
Lawrence, KS 66044–46 • 65,608
Lawrence, MA 01840–45 • 70,207
Lawrence, NY 11559 • 6,513
Lawrence □, AL • 31,513
Lawrence □, AR • 17,457
Lawrence □, IL • 15,972
Lawrence □, IN • 42,836
Lawrence □, KY • 13,998
Lawrence □, MS • 12,458
Lawrence □, MO • 30,236
Lawrence □, OH • 61,834
Lawrence □, PA • 96,246
Lawrence □, TN • 35,303
Lawrenceburg, IN 47025 • 4,375
Lawrenceburg, KY 40342 • 5,911
Lawrenceburg, TN 38464 • 10,412
Lawrence Park, PA 16511 • 4,310
Lawrenceville, GA 30243–46 • 16,848
Lawrenceville, IL 62439 • 4,897
Lawrenceville, NJ 08648 • 6,446
Lawrenceville, VA 23868 • 1,486
Lawson, MO 64062 • 1,876
Lawsonia, MD 21817 • 1,326
Lawtell, LA 70550 • 1,014
Lawton, MI 49065 • 1,685
Lawton, OK 73501–07 • 80,561
Layton, UT 84040–41 • 41,784
Laytonville, CA 95454 • 1,133
Lea □, NM • 55,765
Leachville, AR 72438 • 1,743
Lead, SD 57754 • 3,632
Leadville, CO 80461 • 2,629
Leadwood, MO 63653 • 1,247
League City, TX 77573–74 • 30,159
Leake □, MS • 18,436
Leakesville, MS 39451 • 1,129
Lealman, FL 33714 • 21,748
Leavenworth, KS 66048 • 38,495
Leavenworth, WA 98826 • 1,692
Leavenworth □, KS • 64,371
Leavittsburg, OH 44430 • 2,220
Leawood, KS 66206 • 19,693
Lebanon, DE 19901 • 130
Lebanon, IL 62254 • 3,688
Lebanon, IN 46052 • 12,059
Lebanon, KY 40033 • 5,695
Lebanon, MO 65536 • 9,983
Lebanon, NH 03766 • 12,183
Lebanon, NJ 08833 • 1,036
Lebanon, OH 45036 • 10,453
Lebanon, OR 97355 • 10,950
Lebanon, PA 17042 • 24,800
Lebanon, TN 37087–88 • 15,208
Lebanon, VA 24266 • 3,386
Lebanon □, PA • 113,744
Lebanon Junction, KY 40150 • 1,741
Le Center, MN 56057 • 2,006
Le Claire, IA 52753 • 2,734
Lecompte, LA 71346 • 1,592
Lee, MA 01238 • 2,020
Lee □, AL • 87,146
Lee □, AR • 13,053
Lee □, FL • 335,113
Lee □, GA • 16,250
Lee □, IL • 34,392
Lee □, IA • 38,687
Lee □, KY • 7,422
Lee □, MS • 65,581
Lee □, NC • 41,374
Lee □, SC • 18,437
Lee □, TX • 12,854
Lee □, VA • 24,496
Leechburg, PA 15656 • 2,504
Leedom Estates, DE 19720 • 1,100
Leeds, AL 35094 • 9,946
Leelanau □, MI • 16,527
Lee Park, PA 18702 • 3,800
Leesburg, FL 34748–49 • 14,903
Leesburg, GA 31763 • 1,452
Leesburg, OH 45135 • 1,063
Leesburg, VA 22075 • 16,202
Lees Summit, MO 64063–64 • 46,418
Leesville, LA 71446 • 7,638
Leesville, SC 29070 • 2,025
Leetonia, OH 44431 • 2,070
Leetsdale, PA 15056 • 1,387
Leflore □, MS • 37,341
Le Flore □, OK • 43,270
Le Grand, CA 95333 • 1,205
Lehi, UT 84043 • 8,475
Lehigh □, PA • 291,130
Lehigh Acres, FL 33936 • 13,611
Lehighton, PA 18235 • 5,914
Leicester, MA 01524 • 3,200
Leipsic, DE 19901 • 236
Leipsic, OH 45856 • 2,203
Leisure City, FL 33033 • 19,379
Leitchfield, KY 42754–55 • 4,965
Leland, MS 38756 • 6,366
Le Mars, IA 51031 • 8,454
Lemay, MO 63125 • 18,005
Lemhi □, ID • 6,899
Lemmon, SD 57638 • 1,614
Lemmon Valley, NV 89501 • 4,100
Lemon Grove, CA 91945–46 • 23,984
Lemont, IL 60439 • 7,348
Lemont, PA 16851 • 2,613
Lemoore, CA 93245 • 13,622
Lena, IL 61048 • 2,605
Lenawee □, MI • 91,476
Lenexa, KS 66215 • 34,034
Lennox, CA 90304 • 22,757
Lennox, SD 57039 • 1,767
Lenoir, NC 28645 • 14,192
Lenoir □, NC • 57,274
Lenoir City, TN 37771 • 6,147
Lenox, IA 50851 • 1,303
Lenox, MA 01240 • 1,687
Leo, IN 46765 • 1,200
Leominster, MA 01453 • 38,145
Leon, IA 50144 • 2,047
Leon □, FL • 192,493
Leon □, TX • 12,665
Leonard, TX 75452 • 1,744
Leonardo, NJ 07737 • 3,720
Leonardtown, MD 20650 • 1,475
Leonia, NJ 07605 • 8,365
Leon Valley, TX 78238 • 9,581
Leoti, KS 67861 • 1,738
Lepanto, AR 72354 • 2,033
Le Roy, IL 61752 • 2,777
Le Roy, NY 14482 • 4,974
Leslie, MI 49251 • 1,872
Leslie, SC 29730 • 1,102
Leslie □, KY • 13,642
Lester Prairie, MN 55354 • 1,180
Le Sueur, MN 56058 • 3,714
Le Sueur □, MN • 23,239
Letcher □, KY • 27,000
Levelland, TX 79336–38 • 13,986
Levittown, NY 11756 • 53,286
Levittown, PA 19058 • 55,362
Levy □, FL • 25,923
Lewes, DE 19958 • 2,295
Lewis □, ID • 3,516
Lewis □, KY • 13,029
Lewis □, MO • 10,233
Lewis □, NY • 26,796
Lewis □, TN • 9,247
Lewis □, WA • 59,358
Lewis □, WV • 17,223
Lewis and Clark □, MT • 47,495
Lewisburg, OH 45338 • 1,584
Lewisburg, PA 17837 • 5,785
Lewisburg, TN 37091 • 9,879
Lewisburg, WV 24901 • 3,598
Lewisport, KY 42351 • 1,778
Lewiston, ID 83501 • 28,082
Lewiston, ME 04240–43 • 39,757
Lewiston, MN 55952 • 1,298
Lewiston, NY 14092 • 3,048
Lewiston, UT 84320 • 1,532
Lewistown, IL 61542 • 2,572
Lewistown, MT 59457 • 6,051
Lewistown, PA 17044 • 9,341
Lewisville, AR 71845 • 1,424
Lewisville, TX 75067 • 46,521
Lexington, IL 61753 • 1,809
Lexington, KY 40501–96 • 225,366
Lexington, MA 02173 • 28,974
Lexington, MS 39095 • 2,227
Lexington, MO 64067 • 4,860
Lexington, NE 68850 • 6,601
Lexington, NC 27292–93 • 16,581
Lexington, OH 44904 • 4,124
Lexington, OK 73051 • 1,776
Lexington, SC 29071–73 • 3,289
Lexington, TN 38351 • 5,810
Lexington, VA 24450 • 6,959
Lexington □, SC • 167,611
Lexington Park, MD 20653 • 9,943
Libby, MT 59923 • 2,532
Liberal, KS 67901–05 • 16,573
Liberty, IN 47353 • 2,051
Liberty, KY 42539 • 1,937
Liberty, MO 64068 • 20,459
Liberty, NY 12754 • 4,128
Liberty, NC 27298 • 2,047
Liberty, SC 29657 • 3,228
Liberty, TX 77575 • 7,733
Liberty □, FL • 5,569
Liberty □, GA • 52,745
Liberty □, MT • 2,295
Liberty □, TX • 52,726
Liberty Acres, CA 90250 • 4,700
Liberty Center, OH 43532 • 1,084
Liberty Lake, WA 99019 • 2,015
Libertyville, IL 60048 • 19,174
Licking, MO 65542 • 1,328
Licking □, OH • 128,300
Lidgerwood, ND 58053 • 799
Lighthouse Point, FL 33064 • 10,378
Ligonier, IN 46767 • 3,443
Ligonier, PA 15658 • 1,638
Lihue, HI 96766 • 5,536
Lilbourn, MO 63862 • 1,378
Lilburn, GA 30247 • 9,301
Lillington, NC 27546 • 2,048
Lilly, PA 15938 • 1,162
Lima, NY 14485 • 2,165
Lima, OH 45801–09 • 45,549
Limestone, ME 04750–51 • 1,245
Limestone □, AL • 54,135
Limestone □, TX • 20,946
Limon, CO 80828 • 1,831
Lincoln, AL 35096 • 2,941
Lincoln, AR 72744 • 1,460
Lincoln, CA 95648 • 7,248
Lincoln, DE 19960 • 500
Lincoln, IL 62656 • 15,418
Lincoln, KS 67455 • 1,381
Lincoln, ME 04457 • 3,399
Lincoln, MA 01773 • 2,860
Lincoln, NE 68501–72 • 191,972
Lincoln □, AR • 13,690
Lincoln □, CO • 4,529
Lincoln □, GA • 7,442
Lincoln □, ID • 3,308
Lincoln □, KS • 3,653
Lincoln □, KY • 20,045
Lincoln □, LA • 41,745
Lincoln □, ME • 30,357
Lincoln □, MN • 6,890
Lincoln □, MS • 30,278
Lincoln □, MO • 28,892
Lincoln □, MT • 17,481
Lincoln □, NE • 32,508
Lincoln □, NV • 3,775
Lincoln □, NM • 12,219
Lincoln □, NC • 50,319
Lincoln □, OK • 29,216
Lincoln □, OR • 38,889
Lincoln □, SD • 15,427
Lincoln □, TN • 28,157
Lincoln □, WA • 8,864
Lincoln □, WV • 21,382
Lincoln □, WI • 26,993
Lincoln □, WY • 12,625
Lincoln Acres, CA 91947 • 1,800
Lincoln City, OR 97367 • 5,892
Lincoln Heights, OH 45215 • 4,805
Lincoln Park, CO 81212 • 3,728
Lincoln Park, GA 30286 • 1,755
Lincoln Park, MI 48146 • 41,832
Lincoln Park, NJ 07035 • 10,978
Lincolnshire, IL 60069 • 4,931
Lincolnton, GA 30817 • 1,476
Lincolnton, NC 28092 • 6,847
Lincoln Village, CA 95207 • 4,236
Lincoln Village, OH 43228 • 9,958
Lincolnwood, IL 60645 • 11,365
Lincroft, NJ 07738 • 4,740
Linda, CA 95901 • 13,033
Lindale, GA 30147 • 4,187
Lindale, TX 75771 • 2,428
Linden, AL 36748 • 2,548
Linden, MI 48451 • 2,415
Linden, NJ 07036 • 36,701
Linden, TN 37096 • 1,099
Linden, TX 75563 • 2,375
Lindenhurst, IL 60046 • 8,038
Lindenhurst, NY 11757 • 26,879
Lindenwold, NJ 08021 • 18,734
Lindgren Acres, FL 33177 • 22,290
Lindon, UT 84042 • 3,818
Lindsay, CA 93247 • 8,338
Lindsay, OK 73052 • 2,947
Lindsborg, KS 67456 • 3,076
Lindstrom, MN 55045 • 2,461
Linesville, PA 16424 • 1,166
Lineville, AL 36266 • 2,394
Lingle, WY 82223 • 473
Linglestown, PA 17112 • 3,700

Linn, MO 65051 • 1,148
Linn □, IA • 168,767
Linn □, KS • 8,254
Linn □, MO • 13,885
Linn □, OR • 91,227
Lino Lakes, MN 55014 • 8,807
Linthicum Heights, MD • 2,950
Linthicum Heights, MD 21090 • 7,547
Linton, IN 47441 • 5,814
Linton, ND 58552 • 1,410
Linwood, NJ 08221 • 6,866
Lipscomb, AL 35020 • 2,892
Lipscomb □, TX • 3,143
Lisbon, IA 52253 • 1,452
Lisbon, ME 04250 • 1,240
Lisbon, NH 03585 • 1,246
Lisbon, ND 58054 • 2,177
Lisbon, OH 44432 • 3,037
Lisbon Falls, ME 04252 • 4,674
Lisle, IL 60532 • 19,512
Litchfield, CT 06759 • 1,378
Litchfield, IL 62056 • 6,883
Litchfield, MI 49252 • 1,317
Litchfield, MN 55355 • 6,041
Litchfield □, CT • 174,092
Litchfield Park, AZ 85340 • 3,303
Lithia Springs, GA 30057 • 11,403
Lithonia, GA 30058 • 2,448
Lititz, PA 17543 • 8,280
Little Canada, MN 55110 • 8,971
Little Chute, WI 54140 • 9,207
Little Compton, RI 02837 • 500
Little Creek, DE 19961 • 167
Little Falls, MN 56345 • 7,232
Little Falls, NJ 07424 • 11,294
Little Falls, NY 13365 • 5,829
Little Ferry, NJ 07643 • 9,989
Littlefield, TX 79339 • 6,489
Little River □, AR • 13,966
Little Rock, AR 72201–31 • 175,795
Little Silver, NJ 07739 • 5,721
Littlestown, PA 17340 • 2,974
Littleton, CO 80120–27 • 33,685
Littleton, MA 01460 • 2,867
Littleton, NH 03561 • 4,633
Little Valley, NY 14755 • 1,188
Live Oak, CA 95062 • 15,212
Live Oak, CA 95953 • 4,320
Live Oak, FL 32060 • 6,332
Live Oak, TX 78233 • 10,023
Live Oak □, TX • 9,556
Live Oak Manor, LA 70094 • 2,150
Livermore, CA 94550 • 56,741
Livermore, KY 42352 • 1,534
Livermore Falls, ME 04254 • 1,935
Livingston, AL 35470 • 3,530
Livingston, CA 95334 • 7,317
Livingston, MT 59047 • 6,701
Livingston, NJ 07039 • 26,609
Livingston, TN 38570 • 3,809
Livingston, TX 77351 • 5,019
Livingston □, IL • 39,301
Livingston □, KY • 9,062
Livingston □, LA • 70,526
Livingston □, MI • 115,645
Livingston □, MO • 14,592
Livingston □, NY • 62,372
Livingston Manor, NY 12758 • 1,482
Livonia, MI 48150–54 • 100,850
Livonia, NY 14487 • 1,434
Llangollen Estates, DE 19720 • 1,070
Llano, TX 78643 • 2,962
Llano □, TX • 11,631
Lloyd Harbor, NY 11743 • 3,343
Lochearn, MD 21207 • 25,240
Loch Lomond, VA 22110 • 3,292
Lockhart, FL 32810 • 11,636
Lockhart, TX 78644 • 9,205
Lock Haven, PA 17745 • 9,230
Lockland, OH 45215 • 4,357
Lockney, TX 79241 • 2,207
Lockport, IL 60441 • 9,401
Lockport, LA 70374 • 2,503
Lockport, NY 14094 • 24,426
Lockwood, MO 65682 • 1,041
Lockwood, MT 59101 • 3,967
Locust, NC 28097 • 1,940
Locust Grove, GA 30248 • 1,681
Locust Grove, OK 74352 • 1,326
Lodi, CA 95240–42 • 51,874
Lodi, NJ 07644 • 22,355
Lodi, OH 44254 • 3,042
Lodi, WI 53555 • 2,093
Logan, IA 51546 • 1,401
Logan, OH 43138 • 6,725
Logan, UT 84321 • 32,762
Logan, WV 25601 • 2,206
Logan □, AR • 20,557
Logan □, CO • 17,567
Logan □, IL • 30,798
Logan □, KS • 3,081
Logan □, KY • 24,416
Logan □, NE • 878
Logan □, ND • 2,847
Logan □, OH • 42,310
Logan □, OK • 29,011
Logan □, WV • 43,032
Logandale, NV 89021 • 500
Logansport, IN 46947 • 16,812
Logansport, LA 71049 • 1,390
Loganville, GA 30249 • 3,180
Lolo, MT 59847 • 2,746
Loma Linda, CA 92354 • 17,400
Lombard, IL 60148 • 39,408
Lomira, WI 53048 • 1,542
Lomita, CA 90717 • 19,382
Lompoc, CA 93436 • 37,649
Lonaconing, MD 21539 • 1,122
London, KY 40741 • 5,757
London, OH 43140 • 7,807
Londonderry, NH 03053 • 10,114
Londontown, MD 21037 • 6,992
Lone Grove, OK 73443 • 4,114
Lone Pine, CA 93545 • 1,818
Long □, GA • 6,202
Long Beach, CA 90801–88 • 429,433
Long Beach, IN 46360 • 2,044
Long Beach, MS 39560 • 15,804
Long Beach, NY 11561 • 33,510
Long Beach, WA 98631 • 1,236
Longboat Key, FL 34228 • 5,937
Long Branch, NJ 07740 • 28,658
Long Lake, IL 60041 • 2,888
Longmeadow, MA 01106 • 15,467
Longmont, CO 80501–02 • 51,555
Longport, NJ 08403 • 1,224
Long Prairie, MN 56347 • 2,786
Long Valley, NJ 07853 • 1,744
Long View, NC 28601 • 3,229
Longview, TX 75601–15 • 70,311
Longview, WA 98632 • 31,499
Longwood, FL 32750 • 13,316
Lonoke, AR 72086 • 4,022
Lonoke □, AR • 39,268
Lonsdale, MN 55046 • 1,252
Lonsdale, RI 02865 • 3,850
Loogootee, IN 47553 • 2,884
Lookout Mountain, TN 37350 • 1,901
Lorain, OH 44052–55 • 71,245
Lorain □, OH • 271,126
Lordsburg, NM 88045 • 2,951
Lorenzo, TX 79343 • 1,208
Loretto, PA 15940 • 1,072
Loretto, TN 38469 • 1,515
Loris, SC 29569 • 2,067
Lorton, VA 22079 • 15,385
Los Alamitos, CA 90720–21 • 11,676
Los Alamos, NM 87544 • 11,455
Los Alamos □, NM • 18,115
Los Altos, CA 94022–24 • 26,303
Los Altos Hills, CA 94022 • 7,514
Los Angeles, CA 90001–99 • 3,485,398
Los Angeles □, CA • 8,863,164
Los Banos, CA 93635 • 14,519
Los Fresnos, TX 78566 • 2,473
Los Gatos, CA 95030–32 • 27,357
Los Lunas, NM 87031 • 6,013
Los Molinos, CA 96055 • 1,709
Los Nietos, CA 90606 • 7,100
Los Osos, CA 93402 • 8,000
Los Padillas, NM 87105 • 2,400
Los Ranchos de Albuquerque, NM 87107 • 3,955
Los Serranos, CA 91709 • 7,099
Lost Hills, CA 93249 • 1,212
Loudon, TN 37774 • 4,026
Loudon □, TN • 31,255
Loudonville, NY 12211 • 10,822
Loudonville, OH 44842 • 2,915
Loudoun □, VA • 86,129
Louisa, KY 41230 • 1,990
Louisa, VA 23093 • 1,088
Louisa □, IA • 11,592
Louisa □, VA • 20,325
Louisburg, KS 66053 • 1,964
Louisburg, NC 27549 • 3,037
Louisiana, MO 63353 • 3,967
Louisville, CO 80027 • 12,361
Louisville, GA 30434 • 2,429
Louisville, IL 62858 • 1,098
Louisville, KY 40201–99 • 269,063
Louisville, MS 39339 • 7,169
Louisville, OH 44641 • 8,087
Loup □, NE • 683
Loup City, NE 68853 • 1,104
Love □, OK • 8,157
Loveland, CO 80537–39 • 37,352
Loveland, OH 45140 • 9,990
Loveland Park, OH 45140 • 1,357
Lovell, WY 82431 • 2,131
Lovelock, NV 89419 • 2,069
Loves Park, IL 61111 • 15,462
Loving, NM 88256 • 1,243
Loving □, TX • 107
Lovington, IL 61937 • 1,143
Lovington, NM 88260 • 9,322
Lowell, AR 72745 • 1,224
Lowell, IN 46356 • 6,430
Lowell, MA 01850–54 • 103,439
Lowell, MI 49331 • 3,983
Lowell, NC 28098 • 2,704
Lowellville, OH 44436 • 1,349
Lower Burrell, PA 15068 • 12,251
Lower Merion Township, PA 19003 • 59,629
Lower Paia, HI 96779 • 1,500
Lowndes □, AL • 12,658
Lowndes □, GA • 75,981
Lowndes □, MS • 59,308
Lowville, NY 13367 • 3,632
Loxley, AL 36551 • 1,161
Loyal, WI 54446 • 1,244
Loyall, KY 40854 • 1,100
Lubbock, TX 79401–99 • 186,206
Lubbock □, TX • 222,636
Lucas □, IA • 9,070
Lucas □, OH • 462,361
Lucasville, OH 45648 • 1,575
Luce □, MI • 5,763
Lucedale, MS 39452 • 2,592
Lucerne, CA 95458 • 2,011
Lucernemines, PA 15754 • 1,074
Lucerne Valley, CA 92356 • 1,300
Luck, WI 54853 • 1,022
Ludington, MI 49431 • 8,507
Ludlow, KY 41016 • 4,736
Ludlow, MA 01056 • 18,150
Ludlow, VT 05149 • 1,123
Ludowici, GA 31316 • 1,291
Lufkin, TX 75901–03 • 30,206
Lugoff, SC 29078 • 3,211
Lula, GA 30554 • 1,018
Luling, LA 70070 • 2,803
Luling, TX 78648 • 4,661
Lumber City, GA 31549 • 1,429
Lumberport, WV 26386 • 1,014
Lumberton, MS 39455 • 2,121
Lumberton, NC 28358–59 • 18,601
Lumpkin, GA 31815 • 1,250
Lumpkin □, GA • 14,573
Luna □, NM • 18,110
Luna Pier, MI 48157 • 1,507
Lund, NV 89317 • 330
Lunenburg, MA 01462 • 1,694
Lunenburg □, VA • 11,419
Luray, VA 22835 • 4,587
Lusk, WY 82225 • 1,504
Lutcher, LA 70071 • 3,907
Luther, OK 73054 • 1,560
Lutherville-Timonium, MD 21093 • 16,442
Lutz, FL 33549 • 10,552
Luverne, AL 36049 • 2,555
Luverne, MN 56156 • 4,382
Luxemburg, WI 54217 • 1,151
Luxora, AR 72358 • 1,338
Luzerne, PA 18709 • 3,206
Luzerne □, PA • 328,149
Lycoming □, PA • 118,710
Lyford, TX 78569 • 1,674
Lykens, PA 17048 • 1,986
Lyman, SC 29365 • 2,271
Lyman, WY 82937 • 1,896
Lyman □, SD • 3,638
Lynbrook, NY 11563 • 19,208
Lynch, KY 40855 • 1,166
Lynchburg, OH 45142 • 1,212
Lynchburg, TN 37352 • 4,721
Lynchburg, VA 24501–06 • 66,049
Lyncourt, NY 13208 • 4,516
Lynden, WA 98264 • 5,709
Lyndhurst, NJ 07071 • 18,262
Lyndhurst, OH 44124 • 15,982
Lyndon, KY 40222 • 8,037
Lyndonville, VT 05851 • 1,255
Lyndora, PA 16045 • 3,000
Lynn, IN 47355 • 1,183
Lynn, MA 01901–08 • 81,245
Lynn □, TX • 6,758
Lynne Acres, MD 21207 • 5,910
Lynnfield, MA 01940 • 11,274
Lynn Garden, TN 37665 • 7,213
Lynn Garden, TN 37665 • 3,950
Lynn Haven, FL 32444 • 9,298
Lynnwood, WA 98036–37 • 28,695
Lynwood, CA 90262 • 61,945
Lyon □, IA • 11,952
Lyon □, KS • 34,732
Lyon □, KY • 6,624
Lyon □, MN • 24,789
Lyon □, NV • 20,001
Lyon Mountain, NY 12952 • 1,000
Lyons, CO 80540 • 1,227
Lyons, GA 30436 • 4,502
Lyons, IL 60534 • 9,828
Lyons, KS 67554 • 3,688
Lyons, NE 68038 • 1,144
Lyons, NY 14489 • 4,280
Lytle, TX 78052 • 2,255

M

Mabank, TX 75147 • 1,739
Mableton, GA 30059 • 25,725
Mabscott, WV 25871 • 1,543
Mabton, WA 98935 • 1,482
MacClenny, FL 32063 • 3,966
Macedon, NY 14502 • 1,400
Macedonia, OH 44056 • 7,509
Machesney Park, IL 61111 • 19,033
Machias, ME 04654 • 1,773
Mackinac □, MI • 10,674
Mackinaw, IL 61755 • 1,331
Mackinaw City, MI 49701 • 875
Macomb, IL 61455 • 19,952
Macomb □, MI • 717,400
Macon, GA 31201–95 • 106,612
Macon, IL 62544 • 1,282
Macon, MS 39341 • 2,256
Macon, MO 63552 • 5,571
Macon □, AL • 24,928
Macon □, GA • 13,114
Macon □, IL • 117,206
Macon □, MO • 15,345
Macon □, NC • 23,499
Macon □, TN • 15,906
Macoupin □, IL • 47,679
Macungie, PA 18062 • 2,597
Madawaska, ME 04756 • 3,653
Madeira, OH 45243 • 9,141
Madelia, MN 56062 • 2,237
Madera, CA 93637–39 • 29,281
Madera □, CA • 88,090
Madill, OK 73446 • 3,069
Madison, AL 35758 • 14,904
Madison, AR 72359 • 1,263
Madison, CT 06443 • 2,139
Madison, FL 32340 • 3,345
Madison, GA 30650 • 3,483
Madison, IL 62060 • 4,629
Madison, IN 47250 • 12,006
Madison, ME 04950 • 2,956
Madison, MN 56256 • 1,951
Madison, MS 39110 • 7,471
Madison, NE 68748 • 2,135
Madison, NJ 07940 • 15,850
Madison, NC 27025 • 2,371
Madison, OH 44057 • 2,477
Madison, SD 57042 • 6,257
Madison, WV 25130 • 3,051
Madison, WI 53701–19 • 191,262
Madison □, AL • 238,912
Madison □, AR • 11,618
Madison □, FL • 16,569
Madison □, GA • 21,050
Madison □, ID • 23,674
Madison □, IL • 249,238
Madison □, IN • 130,669
Madison □, IA • 12,483
Madison □, KY • 57,508
Madison □, LA • 12,463
Madison □, MS • 53,794
Madison □, MO • 11,127
Madison □, MT • 5,989
Madison □, NE • 32,655
Madison □, NY • 69,120
Madison □, NC • 16,953
Madison □, OH • 37,068
Madison □, TN • 77,982
Madison □, TX • 10,931
Madison □, VA • 11,949
Madison Heights, MI 48071 • 32,196
Madison Heights, VA 24572 • 11,700
Madisonville, KY 42431 • 16,200
Madisonville, TN 37354 • 3,033
Madisonville, TX 77864 • 3,569
Madras, OR 97741 • 3,443
Madrid, IA 50156 • 2,395
Maeser, UT 84078 • 2,598
Magalia, CA 95954 • 8,987
Magdalena, NM 87825 • 861
Magee, MS 39111 • 3,607
Magna, UT 84044 • 17,829
Magnolia, AR 71753 • 11,151
Magnolia, MS 39652 • 2,245
Magnolia, NJ 08049 • 4,861
Magoffin □, KY • 13,077
Mahanoy City, PA 17948 • 5,209
Mahaska □, IA • 21,522
Mahnomen, MN 56557 • 1,154
Mahnomen □, MN • 5,044
Mahomet, IL 61853 • 3,103
Mahoning □, OH • 264,806
Mahopac, NY 10541 • 7,755
Mahwah, NJ 07430 • 7,500
Maiden, NC 28650 • 2,574
Maili, HI 96792 • 6,059
Maine, NY 13802 • 1,110
Maitland, FL 32751 • 9,110
Maize, KS 67101 • 1,520
Major □, OK • 8,055
Makaha, HI 96792 • 7,990
Makakilo City, HI 96706 • 9,828
Makawao, HI 96768 • 5,405
Makaweli, HI 96769 • 700
Malabar, FL 32950 • 1,977
Malad City, ID 83252 • 1,946
Malaga, NJ 08328 • 2,140
Malakoff, TX 75148 • 2,038
Malden, MA 02148 • 53,884
Malden, MO 63863 • 5,123
Malheur □, OR • 26,038
Malibu, CA 90264–65 • 10,000
Malone, NY 12953 • 6,777
Malta, MT 59538 • 2,340
Malvern, AR 72104 • 9,256
Malvern, IA 51551 • 1,210
Malvern, OH 44644 • 1,112
Malvern, PA 19355 • 2,944
Malverne, NY 11565 • 9,054
Mamaroneck, NY 10543 • 17,325
Mammoth, AZ 85618 • 1,845
Mammoth Lakes, CA 93546 • 4,785
Mammoth Spring, AR 72554 • 1,097
Mamou, LA 70554 • 3,483
Manahawkin, NJ 08050 • 1,594
Manasquan, NJ 08736 • 5,369
Manassas, VA 22110–11 • 27,957
Manassas Park, VA 22111 • 6,734
Manatee □, FL • 211,707
Manawa, WI 54949 • 1,169
Mancelona, MI 49659 • 1,370
Manchaug, MA 01526 • 1,000
Manchester, CT 06040 • 51,618
Manchester, GA 31816 • 4,104
Manchester, IA 52057 • 5,137
Manchester, KY 40962 • 1,634
Manchester, MD 21102 • 2,810
Manchester, MA 01944 • 5,424
Manchester, MI 48158 • 1,753
Manchester, MO 63011 • 6,542
Manchester, NH 03101–10 • 99,567
Manchester, NY 14504 • 1,598
Manchester, OH 45144 • 2,223
Manchester, PA 17345 • 1,830
Manchester, TN 37355 • 7,709
Manchester, VT 05254 • 561
Manchester Center, VT 05255 • 1,574
Mandan, ND 58554 • 15,177
Mandeville, LA 70448 • 7,083
Mangum, OK 73554 • 3,344
Manhasset, NY 11030 • 7,718
Manhattan, KS 66502 • 37,712
Manhattan, MT 59741 • 1,034
Manhattan Beach, CA 90266 • 32,063
Manheim, PA 17545 • 5,011
Manila, AR 72442 • 2,635
Manistee, MI 49660 • 6,734
Manistee □, MI • 21,265
Manistique, MI 49854 • 3,456
Manito, IL 61546 • 1,711
Manitou Springs, CO 80829 • 4,535
Manitowoc, WI 54220–21 • 32,520
Manitowoc □, WI • 80,421
Mankato, KS 66956 • 1,037
Mankato, MN 56001–03 • 31,477
Manlius, NY 13104 • 4,764
Manly, IA 50456 • 1,349
Mannford, OK 74044 • 1,826
Manning, IA 51455 • 1,484
Manning, SC 29102 • 4,428
Mannington, WV 26582 • 2,184
Manokotak, AK 99628 • 385
Manomet, MA 02345 • 1,500
Manor, TX 78653 • 1,041
Manorhaven, NY 11050 • 5,672
Mansfield, AR 72944 • 1,018
Mansfield, LA 71052 • 5,389
Mansfield, MA 02048 • 7,170
Mansfield, MO 65704 • 1,429
Mansfield, OH 44901–07 • 50,627
Mansfield, PA 16933 • 3,538
Mansfield, TX 76063 • 15,607
Mansfield Center, CT 06250 • 1,043
Manson, IA 50563 • 1,844
Mansura, LA 71350 • 1,601
Manteca, CA 95336 • 40,773
Manteno, IL 60950 • 3,488
Manti, UT 84642 • 2,268
Manton, MI 49663 • 1,161
Mantua, NJ 08051 • 1,350
Mantua, OH 44255 • 1,178
Mantua Hills, VA 22031 • 1,600
Manvel, TX 77578 • 3,733
Manville, NJ 08835 • 10,567
Manville, RI 02838 • 3,030
Many, LA 71449 • 3,112
Many Farms, AZ 86538 • 1,294
Maple Bluff, WI 53704 • 1,352
Maple Grove, MN 55369 • 38,736
Maple Heights, OH 44137 • 27,089
Maple Lake, MN 55358 • 1,394
Maple Plain, MN 55359 • 2,005
Maple Shade, NJ 08052 • 19,211
Mapleton, IA 51034 • 1,294
Mapleton, MN 56065 • 1,526
Mapleton, UT 84663 • 3,572
Maple Valley, WA 98038 • 1,211
Mapleville, RI 02839 • 1,300
Maplewood, MN 55109 • 30,954
Maplewood, MO 63143 • 9,962
Maplewood, NJ 07040 • 21,756
Maquoketa, IA 52060 • 6,111
Marana, AZ 85653 • 2,187
Marathon, FL 33050 • 8,857
Marathon, NY 13803 • 1,107
Marathon, WI 54448 • 1,606
Marathon □, WI • 115,400
Marble Falls, TX 78654 • 4,007
Marblehead, MA 01945 • 19,971
Marble Hill, MO 63764 • 1,447
Marbleton, WY 83113 • 634
Marbury, MD 20658 • 1,244
Marceline, MO 64658 • 2,645
Marcellus, MI 49067 • 1,193
Marco, FL 33937 • 9,493
Marcus, IA 51035 • 1,171
Marcus Hook, PA 19061 • 2,546
Marengo, IL 60152 • 4,768
Marengo, IA 52301 • 2,270
Marengo □, AL • 23,084
Marfa, TX 79843 • 2,424
Margate, FL 33063 • 42,985
Margate, MD 21060 • 1,900
Margate City, NJ 08402 • 8,431
Marianna, AR 72360 • 5,910
Marianna, FL 32446 • 6,292
Maricopa, AZ 85239 • 1,600
Maricopa, CA 93252 • 1,193
Maricopa □, AZ • 2,122,101
Mariemont, OH 45227 • 3,118
Marienville, PA 16239 • 1,400
Maries □, MO • 7,976
Marietta, GA 30060–68 • 44,129
Marietta, OH 45750 • 15,026
Marietta, OK 73448 • 2,306
Marin □, CA • 230,096
Marina, CA 93933 • 26,436
Marina del Rey, CA 90292 • 7,431
Marine City, MI 48039 • 4,556
Marinette, WI 54143 • 11,843
Marinette □, WI • 40,548
Maringouin, LA 70757 • 1,149
Marion, AL 36756 • 4,211
Marion, AR 72364 • 4,391
Marion, IL 62959 • 14,545
Marion, IN 46952–53 • 32,618
Marion, IA 52302 • 20,403
Marion, KS 66861 • 1,906
Marion, KY 42064 • 3,320
Marion, MA 02738 • 1,426
Marion, MS 39342 • 1,359
Marion, NY 14505 • 1,080
Marion, NC 28752 • 4,765
Marion, OH 43301–02 • 34,075
Marion, PA 17235 • 1,000
Marion, SC 29571 • 7,658
Marion, SD 57043 • 831
Marion, VA 24354 • 6,630
Marion, WI 54950 • 1,242
Marion □, AL • 29,830
Marion □, AR • 12,001
Marion □, FL • 194,833
Marion □, GA • 5,590
Marion □, IL • 41,561
Marion □, IN • 797,159
Marion □, IA • 30,001
Marion □, KS • 12,888
Marion □, KY • 16,499
Marion □, MS • 25,544
Marion □, MO • 27,682
Marion □, OH • 64,274
Marion □, OR • 228,483
Marion □, SC • 33,899
Marion □, TN • 24,860
Marion □, TX • 9,984
Marion □, WV • 57,249
Marionville, MO 65705 • 1,920
Mariposa, CA 95338 • 1,152
Mariposa □, CA • 14,302
Marissa, IL 62257 • 2,375
Marked Tree, AR 72365 • 3,100
Markesan, WI 53946 • 1,496
Markham, IL 60426 • 13,136
Markham, TX 77456 • 1,206
Markle, IN 46770 • 1,208
Marks, MS 38646 • 1,758
Marksville, LA 71351 • 5,526
Marlboro, NY 12542 • 2,200
Marlboro □, SC • 29,361
Marlborough, CT 06447 • 5,535
Marlborough, MA 01752 • 31,813
Marlborough, NH 03455 • 1,211
Marlene Village, OR 97005 • 1,500
Marlette, MI 48453 • 1,924
Marley, MD 21060 • 7,100
Marlin, TX 76661 • 6,386
Marlinton, WV 24954 • 1,148
Marlow, OK 73055 • 4,416
Marlow Heights, MD 20748 • 5,885
Marlton, NJ 08053 • 10,228
Marmaduke, AR 72443 • 1,164
Marmet, WV 25315 • 1,879
Maroa, IL 61756 • 1,602
Marquette, MI 49855 • 21,977
Marquette □, MI • 70,887
Marquette □, WI • 12,321
Marquette Heights, IL 61554 • 3,077
Marrero, LA 70072–73 • 36,671
Mars, PA 16046 • 1,713
Marseilles, IL 61341 • 4,811
Marshall, AR 72650 • 1,318
Marshall, IL 62441 • 3,555
Marshall, MI 49068 • 6,891
Marshall, MN 56258 • 12,023
Marshall, MO 65340 • 12,711
Marshall, TX 75670–71 • 23,682
Marshall, WI 53559 • 2,329
Marshall □, AL • 70,832
Marshall □, IL • 12,846
Marshall □, IN • 42,182
Marshall □, IA • 38,276
Marshall □, KS • 11,705
Marshall □, KY • 27,205
Marshall □, MN • 10,993
Marshall □, MS • 30,361
Marshall □, OK • 10,829
Marshall □, SD • 4,844
Marshall □, TN • 21,539
Marshall □, WV • 37,356
Marshallton, DE 19808 • 1,765
Marshalltown, IA 50158 • 25,178
Marshallville, GA 31057 • 1,457
Marshfield, MA 02050 • 4,002
Marshfield, MO 65706 • 4,374
Marshfield, WI 54449 • 19,291
Marshfield Hills, MA 02051 • 2,201
Mars Hill, ME 04758 • 1,500
Mars Hill, NC 28754 • 1,611
Marshville, NC 28103 • 2,020
Marsing, ID 83639 • 798
Marstons Mills, MA 02648 • 8,017
Mart, TX 76664 • 2,004
Martha Lake, WA 98012 • 10,155
Martin, SD 57551 • 1,151
Martin, TN 38237 • 8,600

Martin □, FL • *100,900*
Martin □, IN • *10,369*
Martin □, KY • *12,526*
Martin □, MN • *22,914*
Martin □, NC • *25,078*
Martin □, TX • *4,956*
Martinez, CA 94553 • *31,808*
Martinez, GA 30907 • *33,731*
Martinsburg, PA 16662 • *2,119*
Martinsburg, WV 25401 • *14,073*
Martins Ferry, OH 43935 • *7,990*
Martinsville, IL 62442 • *1,161*
Martinsville, IN 46151 • *11,677*
Martinsville, VA 24112–15 • *16,162*
Marvell, AR 72366 • *1,545*
Maryland City, MD 20724 • *6,813*
Maryland Heights, MO 63043 • *25,407*
Marysville, CA 95901 • *12,324*
Marysville, KS 66508 • *3,359*
Marysville, MI 48040 • *8,515*
Marysville, OH 43040 • *9,656*
Marysville, PA 17053 • *2,425*
Marysville, WA 98270 • *10,328*
Maryville, MO 64468 • *10,663*
Maryville, TN 37801–04 • *19,208*
Mascot, TN 37806 • *2,138*
Mascoutah, IL 62258 • *5,511*
Mason, MI 48854 • *6,768*
Mason, NV 89447 • *400*
Mason, OH 45040 • *11,452*
Mason, TX 76856 • *2,041*
Mason, WV 25260 • *1,053*
Mason □, IL • *16,269*
Mason □, KY • *16,666*
Mason □, MI • *25,537*
Mason □, TX • *3,423*
Mason □, WA • *38,341*
Mason □, WV • *25,178*
Masonboro, NC 28403 • *7,010*
Mason City, IL 62664 • *2,323*
Mason City, IA 50401 • *29,040*
Masontown, PA 15461 • *3,759*
Massac □, IL • *14,752*
Massapequa, NY 11758 • *22,018*
Massapequa Park, NY 11762 • *18,044*
Massena, NY 13662 • *11,719*
Massillon, OH 44646–48 • *31,007*
Mastic, NY 11950 • *13,778*
Mastic Beach, NY 11951 • *10,293*
Masury, OH 44438 • *1,836*
Matagorda □, TX • *36,928*
Matamoras, PA 18336 • *1,934*
Matawan, NJ 07747 • *9,270*
Mather, PA 15346 • *1,300*
Mathews □, VA • *8,348*
Mathis, TX 78368 • *5,423*
Matoaca, VA 23803 • *1,967*
Mattapoisett, MA 02739 • *2,949*
Matteson, IL 60443 • *11,378*
Matthews, NC 28105–06 • *13,651*
Mattituck, NY 11952 • *3,902*
Mattoon, IL 61938 • *18,441*
Mattydale, NY 13211 • *6,418*
Matunuck, RI 02879 • *550*
Maud, OK 74854 • *1,204*
Maugansville, MD 21767 • *1,707*
Maui □, HI • *100,374*
Mauldin, SC 29662 • *11,587*
Maumee, OH 43537 • *15,561*
Maunaloa, HI 96770 • *405*
Maunawili, HI 96734 • *4,847*
Maury □, TN • *54,812*
Mauston, WI 53948 • *3,439*
Maverick □, TX • *36,378*
Maxton, NC 28364 • *2,373*
Maxwell Acres, WV 26041 • *1,000*
Mayer, AZ 86333 • *1,800*
Mayes □, OK • *33,366*
Mayfield, KY 42066 • *9,935*
Mayfield, PA 18433 • *1,890*
Mayfield Heights, OH 44124 • *19,847*
Mayflower, AR 72106 • *1,415*
Mayflower Village, CA 91016 • *4,978*
Maynard, MA 01754 • *10,325*
Maynardville, TN 37807 • *1,298*
Mayo, MD 21106 • *2,537*
Mayodan, NC 27027 • *2,471*
Mays Landing, NJ 08330 • *2,090*
Maysville, KY 41056 • *7,169*
Maysville, MO 64469 • *1,176*
Maysville, OK 73057 • *1,203*
Mayville, MI 48744 • *1,010*
Mayville, NY 14757 • *1,636*
Mayville, ND 58257 • *2,092*
Mayville, WI 53050 • *4,374*
Maywood, CA 90270 • *27,850*
Maywood, IL 60153–54 • *27,139*
Maywood, NJ 07607 • *9,473*
Mazomanie, WI 53560 • *1,377*
McAdoo, PA 18237 • *2,459*
McAlester, OK 74501–02 • *16,370*
McAllen, TX 78501–04 • *84,021*
McAlmont, AR 72117 • *1,800*
McAlpine, MD 21043 • *2,230*
McArthur, OH 45651 • *1,541*
McCall, ID 83638 • *2,005*
McCamey, TX 79752 • *2,493*
McCandless, PA 15237 • *28,781*
McCaysville, GA 30555 • *1,065*
McClain □, OK • *22,795*
McCleary, WA 98557 • *1,235*
McCloud, CA 96057 • *1,555*
McClure, PA 17841 • *1,070*
McColl, SC 29570 • *2,685*
McComb, MS 39648 • *11,591*
McComb, OH 45858 • *1,544*
McCone □, MT • *2,276*
McConnellsburg, PA 17233 • *1,106*
McConnelsville, OH 43756 • *1,804*
McCook, NE 69001 • *8,112*
McCook □, SD • *5,688*
McCormick, SC 29835 • *1,659*
McCormick □, SC • *8,868*
McCracken □, KY • *62,879*
McCreary □, KY • *15,603*
McCrory, AR 72101 • *1,971*
McCulloch □, TX • *8,778*
McCurtain □, OK • *33,433*
McDermitt, NV 89421 • *373*
McDonald □, MO • *16,938*
McDonough, GA 30253 • *2,929*
McDonough □, IL • *35,244*
McDowell □, NC • *35,681*
McDowell □, WV • *35,233*
McDuffie □, GA • *20,119*
McEwen, TN 37101 • *1,442*
McFarland, CA 93250 • *7,005*
McFarland, WI 53558 • *5,232*
McGehee, AR 71654 • *4,997*
McGill, NV 89318 • *1,258*
McGrath, AK 99627 • *528*
McGraw, NY 13101 • *1,074*
McGregor, TX 76657 • *4,683*
McHenry, IL 60050–51 • *16,177*
McHenry □, IL • *183,241*
McHenry □, ND • *6,528*
McIntosh □, GA • *8,634*
McIntosh □, ND • *4,021*
McIntosh □, OK • *16,779*
McKean □, PA • *47,131*
McKee City, NJ 08232 • *1,200*
McKeesport, PA 15130–35 • *26,016*
McKees Rocks, PA 15136 • *7,691*
McKenzie, TN 38201 • *5,168*
McKenzie □, ND • *6,383*
McKinley □, NM • *60,686*
McKinleyville, CA 95521 • *10,749*
McKinney, TX 75069–70 • *21,283*
McLaughlin, SD 57642 • *780*
McLean, VA 22101 • *38,168*
McLean □, IL • *129,180*
McLean □, KY • *9,628*
McLean □, ND • *10,457*
McLeansboro, IL 62859 • *2,677*
McLennan □, TX • *189,123*
McLeod □, MN • *32,030*
McLoud, OK 74851 • *2,493*
McMechen, WV 26040 • *2,130*
McMinn □, TN • *42,383*
McMinnville, OR 97128 • *17,894*
McMinnville, TN 37110 • *11,194*
McMullen □, TX • *817*
McNairy □, TN • *22,422*
McPherson, KS 67460 • *12,422*
McPherson □, KS • *27,268*
McPherson □, NE • *546*
McPherson □, SD • *3,228*
McQueeney, TX 78123 • *2,063*
McRae, GA 31055 • *3,007*
McRoberts, KY 41835 • *1,101*
McSherrystown, PA 17344 • *2,769*
Mead, WA 99021 • *2,150*
Meade, KS 67864 • *1,526*
Meade □, KS • *4,247*
Meade □, KY • *24,170*
Meade □, SD • *21,878*
Meadowbrook, FL 32808 • *5,200*
Meadowood, DE 19711 • *2,100*
Meadville, PA 16335 • *14,318*
Meagher □, MT • *1,819*
Mebane, NC 27302 • *4,754*
Mecca, CA 92254 • *1,966*
Mechanic Falls, ME 04256 • *2,388*
Mechanicsburg, OH 43044 • *1,803*
Mechanicsburg, PA 17055 • *9,452*
Mechanicsville, IA 52306 • *1,012*
Mechanicsville, VA 23111 • *22,027*
Mechanicville, NY 12118 • *5,249*
Mecklenburg □, NC • *511,433*
Mecklenburg □, VA • *29,241*
Mecosta □, MI • *37,308*
Medfield, MA 02052 • *5,985*
Medford, MA 02155 • *57,407*
Medford, NJ 08055 • *1,800*
Medford, NY 11763 • *21,274*
Medford, OK 73759 • *1,172*
Medford, OR 97501–04 • *46,951*
Medford, WI 54451 • *4,283*
Medford Lakes, NJ 08055 • *4,462*
Media, PA 19063–65 • *5,957*
Mediapolis, IA 52637 • *1,637*
Medical Lake, WA 99022 • *3,664*
Medicine Bow, WY 82329 • *389*
Medicine Lodge, KS 67104 • *2,453*
Medina, NY 14103 • *6,686*
Medina, OH 44256 • *19,231*
Medina, WA 98039 • *2,981*
Medina □, OH • *122,354*
Medina □, TX • *27,312*
Medway, MA 02053 • *3,890*
Meeker, CO 81641 • *2,098*
Meeker, OK 74855 • *1,003*
Meeker □, MN • *20,846*
Meeteetse, WY 82433 • *368*
Mehlville, MO 63129 • *27,557*
Meigs, GA 31765 • *1,120*
Meigs □, OH • *22,987*
Meigs □, TN • *8,033*
Meiners Oaks, CA 93023 • *3,329*
Melbourne, AR 72556 • *1,562*
Melbourne, FL 32901–10 • *59,646*
Melbourne Beach, FL 32951 • *3,021*
Melcher, IA 50163 • *1,302*
Mellette □, SD • *2,137*
Melrose, FL 32666 • *1,700*
Melrose, MA 02176 • *28,150*
Melrose, MN 56352 • *2,561*
Melrose Park, FL 33312 • *6,477*
Melrose Park, IL 60160–63 • *20,859*
Melville, LA 71353 • *1,562*
Melville, NY 11747 • *12,586*
Melvindale, MI 48122 • *11,216*
Memphis, FL 34221 • *6,760*
Memphis, MI 48041 • *1,221*
Memphis, MO 63555 • *2,094*
Memphis, TN 38101–87 • *610,337*
Memphis, TX 79245 • *2,465*
Mena, AR 71953 • *5,475*
Menahga, MN 56464 • *1,076*
Menands, NY 12204 • *4,333*
Menard, TX 76859 • *1,606*
Menard □, IL • *11,164*
Menard □, TX • *2,252*
Menasha, WI 54952 • *14,711*
Mendenhall, MS 39114 • *2,463*
Mendham, NJ 07945 • *4,890*
Mendocino, CA 95460 • *1,008*
Mendocino □, CA • *80,345*
Mendota, CA 93640 • *6,821*
Mendota, IL 61342 • *7,018*
Mendota Heights, MN 55118 • *9,431*
Menifee □, KY • *5,092*
Menlo Park, CA 94025–28 • *28,040*
Menno, SD 57045 • *768*
Menominee, MI 49858 • *9,398*
Menominee □, MI • *24,920*
Menominee □, WI • *3,890*
Menomonee Falls, WI 53051–52 • *26,840*
Menomonie, WI 54751 • *13,547*
Mentor, OH 44060–61 • *47,358*
Mentor-on-the-Lake, OH 44060 • *8,271*
Mequon, WI 53092 • *18,885*
Meraux, LA 70075 • *8,000*
Merced, CA 95339–44 • *56,216*
Merced □, CA • *178,403*
Mercedes, TX 78570 • *12,694*
Mercer, PA 16137 • *2,444*
Mercer, WI 54547 • *1,300*
Mercer □, IL • *17,290*
Mercer □, KY • *19,148*
Mercer □, MO • *3,723*
Mercer □, NJ • *325,824*
Mercer □, ND • *9,808*
Mercer □, OH • *39,443*
Mercer □, PA • *121,003*
Mercer □, WV • *64,980*
Mercer Island, WA 98040 • *20,816*
Mercersburg, PA 17236 • *1,640*
Mercerville, NJ 08619 • *15,600*
Merchantville, NJ 08109 • *4,095*
Meredith, NH 03253 • *1,654*
Meredosia, IL 62665 • *1,134*
Meriden, CT 06450 • *59,479*
Meridian, ID 83642 • *9,596*
Meridian, MS 39301–09 • *41,036*
Meridian, PA 16001 • *3,473*
Meridian, TX 76665 • *1,390*
Meridian Hills, IN 46260 • *1,728*
Meridianville, AL 35759 • *2,852*
Meriwether □, GA • *22,411*
Merkel, TX 79536 • *2,469*
Merriam, KS 66203 • *11,821*
Merrick, NY 11566 • *23,042*
Merrick □, NE • *8,042*
Merrifield, VA 22031 • *8,399*
Merrill, WI 54452 • *9,860*
Merrillville, IN 46410 • *27,257*
Merrimac, MA 01860 • *2,050*
Merrimack, NH 03054 • *1,300*
Merrimack □, NH • *120,005*
Merritt Island, FL 32952–54 • *32,886*
Merryville, LA 70653 • *1,235*
Merton, WI 53056 • *1,199*
Mesa, AZ 85201–16 • *288,091*
Mesa □, CO • *93,145*
Mescalero, NM 88340 • *1,159*
Mesilla, NM 88046 • *1,975*
Mesquite, NV 89024 • *1,871*
Mesquite, TX 75149–50 • *101,484*
Metairie, LA 70001–11 • *149,428*
Metamora, IL 61548 • *2,520*
Metcalfe, MS 38760 • *1,092*
Metcalfe □, KY • *8,963*
Methuen, MA 01844 • *39,990*
Metlakatla, AK 99926 • *1,407*
Metropolis, IL 62960 • *6,734*
Metter, GA 30439 • *3,707*
Metuchen, NJ 08840 • *12,804*
Metzger, OR 97223 • *3,149*
Mexia, TX 76667 • *6,933*
Mexico, ME 04257 • *2,302*
Mexico, MO 65265 • *11,290*
Mexico, NY 13114 • *1,555*
Meyersdale, PA 15552 • *2,518*
Miami, AZ 85539 • *2,018*
Miami, FL 33101–99 • *358,548*
Miami, OK 74354–55 • *13,142*
Miami □, IN • *36,897*
Miami □, KS • *23,466*
Miami □, OH • *93,182*
Miami Beach, FL 33139 • *92,639*
Miami Lakes, FL 33014 • *12,750*
Miamisburg, OH 45342–43 • *17,834*
Miami Shores, FL 33138 • *10,084*
Miami Springs, FL 33166 • *13,268*
Micco, FL 32958 • *8,757*
Michigan Center, MI 49254 • *4,863*
Michigan City, IN 46360 • *33,822*
Middleboro (Middleborough Center), MA 02346 • *6,837*
Middleburg, FL 32068 • *6,223*
Middleburg, PA 17842 • *1,422*
Middleburgh, NY 12122 • *1,436*
Middleburg Heights, OH 44130 • *14,702*
Middlebury, CT 06762 • *4,140*
Middlebury, IN 46540 • *2,004*
Middlebury, VT 05753 • *6,007*
Middlefield, CT 06455 • *1,200*
Middlefield, OH 44062 • *1,898*
Middle Island, NY 11953 • *7,848*
Middleport, NY 14105 • *1,876*
Middleport, OH 45760 • *2,725*
Middle River, MD 21220 • *24,616*
Middlesboro, KY 40965 • *11,328*
Middlesex, NJ 08846 • *13,055*
Middlesex □, CT • *143,196*
Middlesex □, MA • *1,398,468*
Middlesex □, NJ • *671,780*
Middlesex □, VA • *8,653*
Middleton, ID 83644 • *1,851*
Middleton, MA 01949 • *4,135*
Middleton, WI 53562 • *13,289*
Middletown, CA 95461 • *2,000*
Middletown, CT 06457 • *42,762*
Middletown, DE 19709 • *3,834*
Middletown, IN 47356 • *2,333*
Middletown, KY 40243 • *5,016*
Middletown, MD 21769 • *1,834*
Middletown, NJ 07718 • *62,298*
Middletown, NY 10940 • *24,160*
Middletown, OH 45042–44 • *46,022*
Middletown, PA 17057 • *9,254*
Middletown, RI 02840 • *3,350*
Middletown, VA 22645 • *1,061*
Middletown Township, PA 19037 • *6,866*
Middleville, MI 49333 • *1,966*
Midfield, AL 35228 • *5,559*
Midland, MI 48640–42 • *38,053*
Midland, PA 15059 • *3,321*
Midland, TX 79701–12 • *89,443*
Midland □, MI • *75,651*
Midland □, TX • *106,611*
Midland City, AL 36350 • *1,819*
Midland Park, KS 67216 • *1,200*
Midland Park, NJ 07432 • *7,047*
Midland Park, SC 29405 • *1,300*
Midlothian, IL 60445 • *14,372*
Midlothian, TX 76065 • *5,141*
Midvale, UT 84047 • *11,886*
Midway, DE 19971 • *500*
Midway, KY 40347 • *1,290*
Midway, OR 97233 • *19,000*
Midway, PA 15060 • *1,043*
Midway, UT 84049 • *1,554*
Midwest, WY 82643 • *495*
Midwest City, OK 73110 • *52,267*
Mifflin □, PA • *46,197*
Mifflinburg, PA 17844 • *3,480*
Mifflinville, PA 18631 • *1,329*
Milaca, MN 56353 • *2,182*
Milam □, TX • *22,946*
Milan, GA 31060 • *1,056*
Milan, IL 61264 • *5,831*
Milan, IN 47031 • *1,529*
Milan, MI 48160 • *4,040*
Milan, MO 63556 • *1,767*
Milan, NM 87021 • *1,911*
Milan, OH 44846 • *1,464*
Milan, TN 38358 • *7,512*
Milbank, SD 57252 • *3,879*
Milesburg, PA 16853 • *1,144*
Miles City, MT 59301 • *8,461*
Milford, CT 06460 • *48,168*
Milford, DE 19963 • *6,040*
Milford, IL 60953 • *1,512*
Milford, IN 46542 • *1,388*
Milford, IA 51351 • *2,170*
Milford, ME 04461 • *2,228*
Milford, MA 01757 • *23,339*
Milford, MI 48380–82 • *5,511*
Milford, NE 68405 • *1,886*
Milford, NH 03055 • *8,015*
Milford, NJ 08848 • *1,273*
Milford, OH 45150 • *5,660*
Milford, PA 18337 • *1,064*
Milford, UT 84751 • *1,107*
Mililani Town, HI 96789 • *29,359*
Millard □, UT • *11,333*
Millbrae, CA 94030 • *20,412*
Millbrook, AL 36054 • *6,050*
Millbrook, NY 12545 • *1,339*
Millburn, NJ 07041 • *18,630*
Millbury, MA 01527 • *4,940*
Millbury, OH 43447 • *1,081*
Mill City, OR 97360 • *1,555*
Millcreek, UT 84109 • *32,230*
Millcreek Township, PA 16505 • *46,100*
Milledgeville, GA 31061 • *17,727*
Milledgeville, IL 61051 • *1,076*
Mille Lacs □, MN • *18,670*
Millen, GA 30442 • *3,808*
Miller, SD 57362 • *1,678*
Miller □, AR • *38,467*
Miller □, GA • *6,280*
Miller □, MO • *20,700*
Miller Place, NY 11764 • *9,315*
Millersburg, OH 44654 • *3,051*
Millersburg, PA 17061 • *2,729*
Millers Falls, MA 01349 • *1,084*
Millersport, OH 43046 • *1,010*
Millersville, PA 17551 • *8,099*
Mill Hall, PA 17751 • *1,702*
Milliken, CO 80543 • *1,605*
Millington, MI 48746 • *1,114*
Millington, TN 38053 • *17,866*
Millinocket, ME 04462 • *6,922*
Millis, MA 02054 • *3,777*
Millport, AL 35576 • *1,203*
Mills, WY 82644 • *1,574*
Mills □, IA • *13,202*
Mills □, TX • *4,531*
Millsboro, DE 19966 • *1,643*
Millstadt, IL 62260 • *2,566*
Milltown, NJ 08850 • *6,968*
Millvale, PA 15209 • *4,341*
Mill Valley, CA 94941–42 • *13,038*
Millville, MA 01529 • *1,693*
Millville, NJ 08332 • *25,992*
Millville, UT 84326 • *1,202*
Millwood, WA 99212 • *1,559*
Milnor, ND 58060 • *651*
Milo, ME 04463 • *2,129*
Milpitas, CA 95035–36 • *50,686*
Milroy, PA 17063 • *1,456*
Milstead, GA 30207 • *1,500*
Milton, DE 19968 • *1,417*
Milton, FL 32570–71 • *7,216*
Milton, MA 02186 • *25,725*
Milton, NH 03851 • *1,000*
Milton, NY 12547 • *1,140*
Milton, PA 17847 • *6,746*
Milton, VT 05468 • *1,578*
Milton, WA 98354 • *4,995*
Milton, WV 25541 • *2,242*
Milton, WI 53563 • *4,434*
Milton-Freewater, OR 97862 • *5,533*
Milwaukee, WI 53201–95 • *628,088*
Milwaukee □, WI • *959,275*
Milwaukie, OR 97222 • *18,692*
Mimosa Park, LA 70070 • *4,516*
Mims, FL 32754 • *9,412*
Mina, NV 89422 • *400*
Minco, OK 73059 • *1,411*
Minden, LA 71055 • *13,661*
Minden, NE 68959 • *2,749*
Minden, NV 89423 • *1,441*
Mine Hill, NJ 07801 • *3,250*
Mineola, NY 11501 • *18,994*
Mineola, TX 75773 • *4,321*
Miner, MO 63801 • *1,218*
Miner □, SD • *3,272*
Mineral □, CO • *558*
Mineral □, MT • *3,315*
Mineral □, NV • *6,475*
Mineral □, WV • *26,697*
Mineral Point, WI 53565 • *2,428*
Mineral Springs, AR 71851 • *1,004*
Mineral Wells, TX 76067 • *14,870*
Minersville, PA 17954 • *4,877*
Minerva, OH 44657 • *4,318*
Minetto, NY 13115 • *1,252*
Mineville, NY 12956 • *1,000*
Mingo □, WV • *33,739*
Mingo Junction, OH 43938 • *4,297*
Minidoka □, ID • *19,361*
Minier, IL 61759 • *1,155*
Minneapolis, KS 67467 • *1,983*
Minneapolis, MN 55401–80 • *368,383*
Minnehaha □, SD • *123,809*
Minneota, MN 56264 • *1,417*
Minnetonka, MN 55345 • *48,370*
Minocqua, WI 54548 • *1,280*
Minonk, IL 61760 • *1,982*
Minooka, IL 60447 • *2,561*
Minot, ND 58701–02 • *34,544*
Minquadale, DE 19720 • *790*
Minster, OH 45865 • *2,650*
Mint Hill, NC 28212 • *11,567*
Minturn, CO 81645 • *1,066*
Mio, MI 48647 • *1,500*
Mira Loma, CA 91752 • *15,786*
Miramar, FL 33023 • *40,663*
Misenheimer, NC 28109 • *1,000*
Mishawaka, IN 46544–46 • *42,608*
Mishicot, WI 54228 • *1,296*
Missaukee □, MI • *12,147*
Mission, KS 66205 • *9,504*
Mission, TX 78572 • *28,653*
Mission Hills, KS 66205 • *3,446*
Mission Viejo, CA 92691 • *72,820*
Mississippi □, AR • *57,525*
Mississippi □, MO • *14,442*
Mississippi State, MS 39762 • *12,400*
Missoula, MT 59801–07 • *42,918*
Missoula □, MT • *78,687*
Missouri City, TX 77459 • *36,176*
Missouri Valley, IA 51555 • *2,888*
Mitchell, IL 62040 • *1,320*
Mitchell, IN 47446 • *4,669*
Mitchell, NE 69357 • *1,743*
Mitchell, SD 57301 • *13,798*
Mitchell □, GA • *20,275*
Mitchell □, IA • *10,928*
Mitchell □, KS • *7,203*
Mitchell □, NC • *14,433*
Mitchell □, TX • *8,016*
Mitchellville, IA 50169 • *1,670*
Mizpah, NJ 08342 • *1,000*
Moab, UT 84532 • *3,971*
Moberly, MO 65270 • *12,839*
Mobile, AL 36601–95 • *196,278*
Mobile □, AL • *378,643*
Mobridge, SD 57601 • *3,768*
Mocanaqua, PA 18655 • *1,100*
Mocksville, NC 27028 • *3,399*
Modesto, CA 95350–56 • *164,730*
Modoc □, CA • *9,678*
Moenkopi, AZ 86045 • *1,200*
Moffat □, CO • *11,357*
Mogadore, OH 44260 • *4,008*
Mohall, ND 58761 • *931*
Mohave □, AZ • *93,497*
Mohawk, NY 13407 • *2,986*
Mohnton, PA 19540 • *2,484*
Mojave, CA 93501–02 • *3,763*
Mokena, IL 60448 • *6,128*
Molalla, OR 97038 • *3,651*
Moline, IL 61265 • *43,202*
Molino, FL 32577 • *1,207*
Momence, IL 60954 • *2,968*
Monaca, PA 15061 • *6,739*
Monahans, TX 79756 • *8,101*
Monarch Mills, SC 29379 • *2,214*
Moncks Corner, SC 29461 • *5,607*
Mondovi, WI 54755 • *2,491*
Monee, IL 60449 • *1,044*
Monessen, PA 15062 • *9,901*
Monett, MO 65708 • *6,529*
Monette, AR 72447 • *1,115*
Monfort Heights, OH 45239 • *9,745*
Moniteau □, MO • *12,298*
Monmouth, IL 61462 • *9,489*
Monmouth, OR 97361 • *6,288*
Monmouth □, NJ • *553,124*
Monmouth Beach, NJ 07750 • *3,303*
Monmouth Junction, NJ 08852 • *1,570*
Mono □, CA • *9,956*
Monon, IN 47959 • *1,585*
Monona, IA 52159 • *1,520*
Monona, WI 53716 • *8,637*
Monona □, IA • *10,034*
Monongah, WV 26554 • *1,018*
Monongahela, PA 15063 • *4,928*
Monongalia □, WV • *75,509*
Monroe, GA 30655 • *9,759*
Monroe, IA 50170 • *1,739*
Monroe, LA 71201–13 • *54,909*
Monroe, MI 48161 • *22,902*
Monroe, NY 10950 • *6,672*
Monroe, NC 28110–12 • *16,127*
Monroe, OH 45050 • *4,490*
Monroe, UT 84754 • *1,472*
Monroe, WA 98272 • *4,278*
Monroe, WI 53566 • *10,241*
Monroe □, AL • *23,968*
Monroe □, AR • *11,333*
Monroe □, FL • *78,024*
Monroe □, GA • *17,113*
Monroe □, IL • *22,422*
Monroe □, IN • *108,978*
Monroe □, IA • *8,114*
Monroe □, KY • *11,401*
Monroe □, MI • *133,600*
Monroe □, MS • *36,582*
Monroe □, MO • *9,104*
Monroe □, NY • *713,968*
Monroe □, OH • *15,497*
Monroe □, PA • *95,709*
Monroe □, TN • *30,541*
Monroe □, WV • *12,406*
Monroe □, WI • *36,633*
Monroe Center, CT 06468 • *7,900*
Monroe City, MO 63456 • *2,701*
Monroe Park, DE 19807 • *1,000*
Monroeville, AL 36460–61 • *6,993*
Monroeville, IN 46773 • *1,232*
Monroeville, OH 44847 • *1,381*
Monroeville, PA 15146 • *29,169*
Monrovia, CA 91016 • *35,761*
Monsey, NY 10952 • *13,986*
Monson, MA 01057 • *2,101*
Montague, CA 96064 • *1,415*
Montague, MI 49437 • *2,276*
Montague □, TX • *17,274*
Mont Alto, PA 17237 • *1,395*
Montauk, NY 11954 • *3,001*
Mont Belvieu, TX 77580 • *1,323*
Montcalm □, MI • *53,059*
Montchanin, DE 19710 • *500*
Montclair, CA 91763 • *28,434*
Montclair, NJ 07042–44 • *37,729*
Mont Clare, PA 19453 • *1,800*
Monteagle, TN 37356 • *1,138*
Montebello, CA 90640 • *59,564*
Montecito, CA 93108 • *9,300*

Montello, NV 89830 • 200
Montello, WI 53949 • 1,329
Monterey, CA 93940 • 31,954
Monterey, TN 38574 • 2,559
Monterey □, CA • 355,660
Monterey Park, CA 91754 • 60,738
Montesano, WA 98563 • 3,064
Montevallo, AL 35115 • 4,239
Montevideo, MN 56265 • 5,499
Monte Vista, CO 81144 • 4,324
Montezuma, GA 31063 • 4,506
Montezuma, IN 47862 • 1,134
Montezuma, IA 50171 • 1,651
Montezuma □, CO • 18,672
Montgomery, AL 36101-99 • 187,106
Montgomery, IL 60538 • 4,267
Montgomery, MN 56069 • 2,399
Montgomery, NY 12549 • 2,696
Montgomery, OH 45242 • 9,753
Montgomery, PA 17752 • 1,631
Montgomery, WV 25136 • 2,449
Montgomery □, AL • 209,085
Montgomery □, AR • 7,841
Montgomery □, GA • 7,163
Montgomery □, IL • 30,728
Montgomery □, IN • 34,436
Montgomery □, IA • 12,076
Montgomery □, KS • 38,816
Montgomery □, KY • 19,561
Montgomery □, MD • 757,027
Montgomery □, MS • 12,388
Montgomery □, MO • 11,355
Montgomery □, NY • 51,981
Montgomery □, NC • 23,346
Montgomery □, OH • 573,809
Montgomery □, PA • 678,111
Montgomery □, TN • 100,498
Montgomery □, TX • 182,201
Montgomery □, VA • 73,913
Montgomery City, MO 63361 • 2,281
Montgomery Village, MD 20879 • 32,315
Monticello, AR 71655 • 8,116
Monticello, FL 32344 • 2,573
Monticello, GA 31064 • 2,289
Monticello, IL 61856 • 4,549
Monticello, IN 47960 • 5,237
Monticello, IA 52310 • 3,522
Monticello, KY 42633 • 5,357
Monticello, MN 55362 • 4,941
Monticello, MS 39654 • 1,755
Monticello, NY 12701 • 6,597
Monticello, UT 84535 • 1,806
Monticello, WI 53570 • 1,140
Montmorency □, MI • 8,936
Montour □, PA • 17,735
Montour Falls, NY 14865 • 1,845
Montoursville, PA 17754 • 4,983
Montpelier, ID 83254 • 2,656
Montpelier, IN 47359 • 1,880
Montpelier, OH 43543 • 4,299
Montpelier, VT 05601-02 • 8,247
Montrose, AL 36559 • 1,400
Montrose, CO 81401-02 • 8,854
Montrose, MI 48457 • 1,811
Montrose, PA 18801 • 1,982
Montrose, VA 23231 • 6,405
Montrose □, CO • 24,423
Montvale, NJ 07645 • 6,946
Montville, CT 06353 • 16,673
Montville, NJ 07045 • 2,600
Monument, CO 80132 • 1,020
Monument Beach, MA 02553 • 1,800
Monument Heights, VA 23226 • 2,500
Moodus, CT 06469 • 1,170
Moody, TX 76557 • 1,329
Moody □, SD • 6,507
Moonachie, NJ 07074 • 2,817
Moorcroft, WY 82721 • 768
Moore, OK 73160 • 40,318
Moore □, NC • 59,013
Moore □, TN • 4,721
Moore □, TX • 17,865
Moorefield, WV 26836 • 2,148
Moore Haven, FL 33471 • 1,432
Mooreland, OK 73852 • 1,157
Moorestown, NJ 08057 • 16,500
Mooresville, IN 46158 • 5,541
Mooresville, NC 28115 • 9,317
Moorhead, MN 56560-61 • 32,295
Moorhead, MS 38761 • 2,417
Moorpark, CA 93020-21 • 25,494
Moose Lake, MN 55767 • 1,206
Moosic, PA 18507 • 5,339
Moosup, CT 06354 • 3,289
Mora, MN 55051 • 2,905
Mora, NM 87732 • 1,200
Mora □, NM • 4,264
Moraga, CA 94556 • 15,852
Moraine, OH 45439 • 5,989
Moravia, NY 13118 • 1,559
Morehead, KY 40351 • 8,357
Morehead City, NC 28557 • 6,046
Morehouse, MO 63868 • 1,068
Morehouse □, LA • 31,938
Morenci, AZ 85540 • 1,799
Morenci, MI 49256 • 2,342
Moreno Valley, CA 92387-88 • 118,779
Morgan, UT 84050 • 2,023
Morgan □, AL • 100,043
Morgan □, CO • 21,939
Morgan □, GA • 12,883
Morgan □, IL • 36,397
Morgan □, IN • 55,920
Morgan □, KY • 11,648
Morgan □, MO • 15,574
Morgan □, OH • 14,194
Morgan □, TN • 17,300
Morgan □, UT • 5,528
Morgan □, WV • 12,128
Morgan City, LA 70380-81 • 14,531
Morganfield, KY 42437 • 3,776
Morgan Hill, CA 95037-38 • 23,928
Morganton, NC 28655 • 15,085
Morgantown, KY 42261 • 2,284
Morgantown, MS 39120 • 3,288
Morgantown, WV 26502-07 • 25,879
Moriarty, NM 87035 • 1,399
Morningdale, MA 01505 • 1,130
Morocco, IN 47963 • 1,044
Moroni, UT 84646 • 1,115
Morrill □, NE • 5,423
Morrilton, AR 72110 • 6,551
Morris, AL 35116 • 1,136
Morris, IL 60450 • 10,270
Morris, MN 56267 • 5,613
Morris, OK 74445 • 1,216
Morris □, KS • 6,198
Morris □, NJ • 421,353
Morris □, TX • 13,200
Morrison, IL 61270 • 4,363
Morrison □, MN • 29,604
Morrison City, TN 37660 • 2,032
Morrisonville, IL 62546 • 1,113
Morrisonville, NY 12962 • 1,742
Morris Plains, NJ 07950 • 5,219
Morristown, NJ 07960-63 • 16,189
Morristown, TN 37813-16 • 21,385
Morrisville, NY 13408 • 2,732
Morrisville, PA 19067 • 9,765
Morrisville, VT 05661 • 1,984
Morro Bay, CA 93442-43 • 9,664
Morrow, GA 30260 • 5,168
Morrow, OH 45152 • 1,206
Morrow □, OH • 27,749
Morrow □, OR • 7,625
Morton, IL 61550 • 13,799
Morton, MS 39117 • 3,212
Morton, TX 79346 • 2,597
Morton, WA 98356 • 1,130
Morton □, KS • 3,480
Morton □, ND • 23,700
Morton Grove, IL 60053 • 22,408
Moscow, ID 83843 • 18,519
Moscow, PA 18444 • 1,527
Moses Lake, WA 98837 • 11,235
Mosheim, TN 37818 • 1,451
Mosinee, WI 54455 • 3,820
Moss Bluff, LA 70611 • 8,039
Moss Point, MS 39563 • 17,837
Motley □, TX • 1,532
Mott, ND 58646 • 1,019
Moulton, AL 35650 • 3,248
Moultrie, GA 31768 • 14,865
Moultrie □, IL • 13,930
Mound, MN 55364 • 9,634
Mound Bayou, MS 38762 • 2,222
Mound City, MO 64470 • 1,273
Moundridge, KS 67107 • 1,531
Mounds, IL 62964 • 1,407
Mounds View, MN 55432 • 12,541
Moundsville, WV 26041 • 10,753
Moundville, AL 35474 • 1,348
Mountainair, NM 87036 • 926
Mountain Brook, AL 35223 • 19,810
Mountain City, NV 89831 • 110
Mountain City, TN 37683 • 2,169
Mountain Grove, MO 65711 • 4,182
Mountain Home, AR 72653 • 9,027
Mountain Home, ID 83647 • 7,913
Mountain Iron, MN 55768 • 3,362
Mountain Lake, MN 56159 • 1,906
Mountain Lake Park, MD 21550 • 1,938
Mountain Lakes, NJ 07046 • 3,847
Mountain Park, GA 30087 • 11,025
Mountainside, NJ 07092 • 6,657
Mountain View, AR 72560 • 2,439
Mountain View, CA 94039-43 • 67,460
Mountain View, CO 80521 • 2,100
Mountain View, MO 65548 • 2,036
Mountain View, NM 87105 • 2,300
Mountain View, OK 73062 • 1,086
Mountain View, WY 82604 • 1,200
Mountain View, WY 82939 • 1,189
Mountain Village, AK 99632 • 674
Mount Airy, MD 21771 • 3,730
Mount Airy, NC 27030 • 7,156
Mount Angel, OR 97362 • 2,778
Mount Arlington, NJ 07856 • 3,630
Mount Ayr, IA 50854 • 1,796
Mount Carmel, IL 62863 • 8,287
Mount Carmel, PA 17851 • 7,196
Mount Carroll, IL 61053 • 1,726
Mount Clemens, MI 48043-46 • 18,405
Mount Dora, FL 32757 • 7,196
Mount Ephraim, NJ 08059 • 4,517
Mount Freedom, NJ 07970 • 1,920
Mount Gay, WV 25637 • 1,200
Mount Gilead, NC 27306 • 1,336
Mount Gilead, OH 43338 • 2,846
Mount Healthy, OH 45231 • 7,580
Mount Holly, NJ 08060 • 10,639
Mount Holly, NC 28120 • 7,710
Mount Holly Springs, PA 17065 • 1,925
Mount Hope, WV 25880 • 1,573
Mount Horeb, WI 53572 • 4,182
Mount Jackson, VA 22842 • 1,583
Mount Jewett, PA 16740 • 1,029
Mount Joy, PA 17552 • 6,398
Mount Juliet, TN 37122 • 5,389
Mount Kisco, NY 10549 • 9,108
Mountlake Terrace, WA 98043 • 19,320
Mount Lebanon, PA 15228 • 33,362
Mount Morris, IL 61054 • 2,919
Mount Morris, MI 48458 • 3,292
Mount Morris, NY 14510 • 3,102
Mount Olive, AL 35117 • 2,270
Mount Olive, IL 62069 • 2,126
Mount Olive, NC 28365 • 4,582
Mount Olympus, UT 84117 • 7,413
Mount Orab, OH 45154 • 1,929
Mount Penn, PA 19606 • 2,883
Mount Pleasant, IA 52641 • 8,027
Mount Pleasant, MI 48858-59 • 23,285
Mount Pleasant, NC 28124 • 1,027
Mount Pleasant, PA 15666 • 4,787
Mount Pleasant, SC 29464-65 • 30,108
Mount Pleasant, TN 38474 • 4,278
Mount Pleasant, TX 75455 • 12,291
Mount Pleasant, UT 84647 • 2,092
Mount Pocono, PA 18344 • 1,795
Mount Prospect, IL 60056 • 53,170
Mount Pulaski, IL 62548 • 1,610
Mountrail □, ND • 7,021
Mount Rainier, MD 20712 • 7,954
Mount Savage, MD 21545 • 1,640
Mount Shasta, CA 96067 • 3,460
Mount Sinai, NY 11766 • 8,023
Mount Sterling, IL 62353 • 1,922
Mount Sterling, KY 40353 • 5,362
Mount Sterling, OH 43143 • 1,647
Mount Union, PA 17066 • 2,878
Mount Vernon, GA 30445 • 1,914
Mount Vernon, IL 62864 • 16,988
Mount Vernon, IN 47620 • 7,217
Mount Vernon, IA 52314 • 3,657
Mount Vernon, KY 40456 • 2,654
Mount Vernon, MO 65712 • 3,726
Mount Vernon, NY 10550-53 • 67,153
Mount Vernon, OH 43050 • 14,550
Mount Vernon, TX 75457 • 2,219
Mount Vernon, WA 98273 • 17,647
Mount View, RI 02852 • 610
Mount Washington, KY 40047 • 5,226
Mount Wolf, PA 17347 • 1,365
Mount Zion, IL 62549 • 4,522
Moville, IA 51039 • 1,306
Moweaqua, IL 62550 • 1,785
Mower □, MN • 37,385
Moyock, NC 27958 • 1,400
Muenster, TX 76252 • 1,387
Muhlenberg □, KY • 31,318
Mukilteo, WA 98275 • 7,007
Mukwonago, WI 53149 • 4,457
Mulberry, AR 72947 • 1,448
Mulberry, FL 33860 • 2,988
Mulberry, IN 46058 • 1,262
Mulberry, NC 28659 • 2,339
Muldraugh, KY 40155 • 1,376
Muldrow, OK 74948 • 2,889
Muleshoe, TX 79347 • 4,571
Mullan, ID 83846 • 821
Mullens, WV 25882 • 2,006
Mullica Hill, NJ 08062 • 1,117
Mullins, SC 29574 • 5,910
Multnomah □, OR • 583,887
Mulvane, KS 67110 • 4,674
Muncie, IN 47302-08 • 71,035
Muncy, PA 17756 • 2,702
Munday, TX 76371 • 1,600
Mundelein, IL 60060 • 21,215
Munford, TN 38058 • 2,326
Munfordville, KY 42765 • 1,556
Munhall, PA 15120 • 13,158
Munising, MI 49862 • 2,783
Munster, IN 46321 • 19,949
Murfreesboro, AR 71958 • 1,542
Murfreesboro, NC 27855 • 2,580
Murfreesboro, TN 37129-33 • 44,922
Murphy, MO 63026 • 9,342
Murphy, NC 28906 • 1,575
Murphys, CA 95247 • 1,517
Murphysboro, IL 62966 • 9,176
Murray, KY 42071 • 14,439
Murray, UT 84107 • 31,282
Murray □, GA • 26,147
Murray □, MN • 9,660
Murray □, OK • 12,042
Murrells Inlet, SC 29576 • 3,334
Murrysville, PA 15668 • 17,240
Muscatine, IA 52761 • 22,881
Muscatine □, IA • 39,907
Muscle Shoals, AL 35661 • 9,611
Muscoda, WI 53573 • 1,287
Muscogee □, GA • 179,278
Muscoy, CA 92405 • 7,541
Muse, PA 15350 • 1,250
Muskego, WI 53150 • 16,813
Muskegon, MI 49440-45 • 40,283
Muskegon □, MI • 158,983
Muskegon Heights, MI 49444 • 13,176
Muskingum □, OH • 82,068
Muskogee, OK 74401-03 • 37,708
Muskogee □, OK • 68,078
Musselshell □, MT • 4,106
Mustang, OK 73064 • 10,434
Myerstown, PA 17067 • 3,236
Myrtle Beach, SC 29577-78 • 24,848
Myrtle Grove, FL 32506 • 17,402
Myrtle Point, OR 97458 • 2,712
Mystic, CT 06355 • 2,618
Mystic Island, NJ 08087 • 7,400

N

Naalehu, HI 96772 • 1,027
Naamans Gardens, DE 19810 • 1,500
Nabnasset, MA 01886 • 3,600
Nacogdoches, TX 75961-63 • 30,872
Nacogdoches □, TX • 54,753
Nags Head, NC 27959 • 1,838
Nahant, MA 01908 • 3,828
Nahunta, GA 31553 • 1,049
Nampa, ID 83651-53 • 28,365
Nanakuli, HI 96792 • 9,575
Nance □, NE • 4,275
Nanticoke, PA 18634 • 12,267
Nantucket, MA 02554 • 3,069
Nantucket □, MA • 6,012
Nanty Glo, PA 15943 • 3,190
Nanuet, NY 10954 • 14,065
Napa, CA 94558-59 • 61,842
Napa □, CA • 110,765
Napanoch, NY 12458 • 1,068
Naperville, IL 60540 • 85,351
Naples, FL 33939-42 • 19,505
Naples, NY 14512 • 1,237
Naples, TX 75568 • 1,508
Naples, UT 84078 • 1,334
Naples Park, FL 33963 • 8,002
Napoleon, ND 58561 • 930
Napoleon, OH 43545 • 8,884
Nappanee, IN 46550 • 5,510
Naranja, FL 33032 • 5,790
Narberth, PA 19072 • 4,278
Narragansett, RI 02882 • 3,721
Narrows, VA 24124 • 2,082
Naselle, WA 98638 • 1,000
Nash, TX 75569 • 2,162
Nash □, NC • 76,677
Nashua, IA 50658 • 1,476
Nashua, NH 03060-63 • 79,662
Nashville, AR 71852 • 4,639
Nashville, GA 31639 • 4,782
Nashville, IL 62263 • 3,202
Nashville, MI 49073 • 1,654
Nashville, NC 27856 • 3,617
Nashville, TN 37201-35 • 487,969
Nashwauk, MN 55769 • 1,026
Nassau, NY 12123 • 1,254
Nassau □, FL • 43,941
Nassau □, NY • 1,287,348
Nassau Shores, NY 11758 • 5,110
Natalia, TX 78059 • 1,216
Natchez, MS 39120-22 • 19,460
Natchitoches, LA 71457-58 • 16,609
Natchitoches □, LA • 36,689
Natick, MA 01760 • 30,100
National City, CA 91950-51 • 54,249
National Park, NJ 08063 • 3,413
Natrona □, WY • 61,226
Natrona Heights, PA 15065 • 12,200
Naugatuck, CT 06770 • 30,625
Nautilus Park, CT 06340 • 6,500
Nauvoo, IL 62354 • 1,108
Navajo □, AZ • 77,658
Navarre, OH 44662 • 1,635
Navarro □, TX • 39,926
Navasota, TX 77868-69 • 6,296
Navesink, NJ 07752 • 1,420
Nazareth, PA 18064 • 5,713
Neah Bay, WA 98357 • 1,300
Nebraska City, NE 68410 • 6,547
Nederland, CO 80466 • 1,099
Nederland, TX 77627 • 16,192
Nedrow, NY 13120 • 2,980
Needham, MA 02192 • 27,557
Needles, CA 92363 • 5,191
Needville, TX 77461 • 2,199
Neenah, WI 54956-57 • 23,219
Neffs, OH 43940 • 1,213
Negaunee, MI 49866 • 4,741
Neillsville, WI 54456 • 2,680
Nekoosa, WI 54457 • 2,557
Neligh, NE 68756 • 1,742
Nelson □, KY • 29,710
Nelson □, ND • 4,410
Nelson □, VA • 12,778
Nelsonville, OH 45764 • 4,563
Nemacolin, PA 15351 • 1,097
Nemaha □, KS • 10,446
Nemaha □, NE • 7,980
Nenana, AK 99760 • 393
Neodesha, KS 66757 • 2,837
Neoga, IL 62447 • 1,678
Neosho, MO 64850 • 9,254
Neosho □, KS • 17,035
Nephi, UT 84648 • 3,515
Neptune, NJ 07753 • 28,366
Neptune Beach, FL 32233 • 6,816
Neptune City, NJ 07753 • 4,997
Nesconset, NY 11767 • 10,712
Nescopeck, PA 18635 • 1,651
Neshoba □, MS • 24,800
Nesquehoning, PA 18240 • 3,364
Ness □, KS • 4,033
Ness City, KS 67560 • 1,724
Netcong, NJ 07857 • 3,311
Nether Providence Township, PA 19013 • 13,229
Nettleton, MS 38858 • 2,462
Nevada, IA 50201 • 6,009
Nevada, MO 64772 • 8,597
Nevada □, AR • 10,101
Nevada □, CA • 78,510
Nevada City, CA 95959 • 2,855
New Albany, IN 47150-51 • 36,322
New Albany, MS 38652 • 6,775
New Albany, OH 43054 • 1,621
Newark, AR 72562 • 1,159
Newark, CA 94560 • 37,861
Newark, DE 19711-15 • 25,098
Newark, NJ 07101-75 • 275,221
Newark, NY 14513 • 9,849
Newark, OH 43055-58 • 44,389
Newark Valley, NY 13811 • 1,082
New Athens, IL 62264 • 2,010
Newaygo, MI 49337 • 1,336
Newaygo □, MI • 38,202
New Baden, IL 62265 • 2,602
New Baltimore, MI 48047 • 5,798
New Bedford, MA 02740-48 • 99,922
Newberg, OR 97132 • 13,086
New Berlin, NY 13411 • 1,220
New Berlin, WI 53151 • 33,592
New Bern, NC 28560-64 • 17,363
Newbern, TN 38059 • 2,515
Newberry, FL 32669 • 1,644
Newberry, MI 49868 • 1,873
Newberry, SC 29108 • 10,542
Newberry □, SC • 33,172
New Bethlehem, PA 16242 • 1,151
New Bloomfield, PA 17068 • 1,092
New Boston, MI 48164 • 1,200
New Boston, OH 45662 • 2,717
New Boston, TX 75570 • 5,057
New Braunfels, TX 78130-33 • 27,334
New Bremen, OH 45869 • 2,558
New Brighton, MN 55112 • 22,207
New Brighton, PA 15066 • 6,854
New Britain, CT 06050-53 • 75,491
New Brockton, AL 36351 • 1,184
New Brunswick, NJ 08901-06 • 41,711
New Buffalo, MI 49117 • 2,317
Newburg, KY 40218 • 21,647
Newburgh, IN 47629-30 • 2,880
Newburgh, NY 12550-53 • 26,454
Newburgh Heights, OH 44105 • 2,310
Newburyport, MA 01950-52 • 16,317
New Canaan, CT 06840 • 17,864
New Carlisle, IN 46552 • 1,446
New Carlisle, OH 45344 • 6,049
New Carrollton, MD 20784 • 12,002
New Cassel, NY 11590 • 10,257
New Castle, AL 35119 • 1,100
New Castle, DE 19720 • 4,837
New Castle, IN 47362 • 17,753
Newcastle, OK 73065 • 4,214
New Castle, PA 16101-08 • 28,334
Newcastle, WY 82701 • 3,003
New Castle □, DE • 441,946
New City, NY 10956 • 33,673
Newcomerstown, OH 43832 • 4,012
New Concord, OH 43762 • 2,086
New Cumberland, PA 17070 • 7,665
New Cumberland, WV 26047 • 1,363
New Egypt, NJ 08533 • 2,327
Newell, IA 50568 • 1,089
Newell, WV 26050 • 1,724
New Ellenton, SC 29809 • 2,515
Newellton, LA 71357 • 1,576
New England, ND 58647 • 663
New Fairfield, CT 06812 • 4,600
Newfane, NY 14108 • 3,001
Newfield, NJ 08344 • 1,592
New Franklin, MO 65274 • 1,107
New Freedom, PA 17349 • 2,920
New Glarus, WI 53574 • 1,899
New Hampton, IA 50659 • 3,660
New Hanover □, NC • 120,284
New Hartford, CT 06057 • 1,269
New Haven, CT 06501-36 • 130,474
New Haven, IN 46774 • 9,320
New Haven, MI 48048 • 2,331
New Haven, MO 63068 • 1,757
New Haven, WV 25265 • 1,632
New Haven □, CT • 804,219
New Holland, GA 30501 • 1,200
New Holland, PA 17557 • 4,484
New Holstein, WI 53061 • 3,342
New Hope, AL 35760 • 2,248
New Hope, MN 55428 • 21,853
New Hope, NC 27604 • 5,694
New Hope, PA 18938 • 1,400
New Hyde Park, NY 11040 • 9,728
New Iberia, LA 70560-62 • 31,828
Newington, CT 06131 • 29,208
Newington, VA 22122 • 17,965
New Johnsonville, TN 37134 • 1,643
New Kensington, PA 15068 • 15,894
New Kent □, VA • 10,445
Newkirk, OK 74647 • 2,168
New Lenox, IL 60451 • 9,627
New Lexington, OH 43764 • 5,117
New Lisbon, WI 53950 • 1,491
Newllano, LA 71461 • 2,660
New London, CT 06320 • 28,540
New London, IA 52645 • 1,922
New London, NH 03257 • 3,180
New London, OH 44851 • 2,642
New London, WI 54961 • 6,658
New London □, CT • 254,957
New Madrid, MO 63869 • 3,350
New Madrid □, MO • 20,928
Newman, CA 95360 • 4,151
Newmanstown, PA 17073 • 1,410
Newmarket, NH 03857 • 4,917
New Market, TN 37820 • 1,086
New Market, VA 22844 • 1,435
New Martinsville, WV 26155 • 6,705
New Matamoras, OH 45767 • 1,002
New Miami, OH 45011 • 2,555
New Milford, CT 06776 • 5,775
New Milford, NJ 07646 • 15,990
Newnan, GA 30263-65 • 12,497
New Orleans, LA 70101-95 • 496,938
New Oxford, PA 17350 • 1,617
New Paltz, NY 12561 • 5,463
New Paris, IN 46553 • 1,007
New Paris, OH 45347 • 1,801
New Philadelphia, OH 44663 • 15,698
New Philadelphia, PA 17959 • 1,283
New Plymouth, ID 83655 • 1,313
Newport, AR 72112 • 7,459
Newport, DE 19804 • 1,240
Newport, KY 41071-76 • 18,871
Newport, ME 04953 • 1,843
Newport, MI 48166 • 1,100
Newport, MN 55055 • 3,720
Newport, NH 03773 • 3,772
Newport, NC 28570 • 2,516
Newport, OR 97365 • 8,437
Newport, PA 17074 • 1,568
Newport, RI 02840 • 28,227
Newport, TN 37821 • 7,123
Newport, VT 05855 • 4,434
Newport, WA 99156 • 1,691
Newport □, RI • 87,194
Newport Beach, CA 92657-63 • 66,643
Newport East, RI 02840 • 11,080
Newport Hills, WA 98002 • 14,736
Newport News, VA 23601-09 • 170,045
New Port Richey, FL 34652-56 • 14,044
New Prague, MN 56071 • 3,569
New Preston, CT 06777 • 1,217
New Providence, NJ 07974 • 11,439
New Richland, MN 56072 • 1,237
New Richmond, OH 45157 • 2,408
New Richmond, WI 54017 • 5,106
New River Station, NC 28542 • 9,732
New Roads, LA 70760 • 5,303
New Rochelle, NY 10801-05 • 67,265
New Rockford, ND 58356 • 1,604
New Salem, ND 58563 • 909
New Sarpy, LA 70078 • 2,946
New Sharon, IA 50207 • 1,136
New Smyrna Beach, FL 32168-70 • 16,543
New Tazewell, TN 37825 • 1,864
Newton, AL 36352 • 1,580
Newton, IL 62448 • 3,154
Newton, IA 50208 • 14,789
Newton, KS 67114 • 16,700
Newton, MA 02158 • 82,585
Newton, MS 39345 • 3,701
Newton, NJ 07860 • 7,521
Newton, NC 28658 • 9,304
Newton, TX 75966 • 1,885
Newton □, AR • 7,666
Newton □, GA • 41,808
Newton □, IN • 13,551
Newton □, MS • 20,291
Newton □, MO • 44,445
Newton □, TX • 13,569
Newton Falls, OH 44444 • 4,866
Newtown, CT 06470 • 1,800
New Town, ND 58763 • 1,388
Newtown, OH 45244 • 1,589
Newtown Square, PA 19073 • 11,366
New Ulm, MN 56073 • 13,132
Newville, PA 17241 • 1,349
New Washington, OH 44854 • 1,057
New Washoe City, NV 89701 • 2,875
New Waterford, OH 44445 • 1,278
New Whiteland, IN 46184 • 4,097
New Wilmington, PA 16142 • 2,706
New Windsor, NY 12553 • 8,898
New York, NY 10001-99 • 7,322,564
New York □, NY • 1,487,536
Nez Perce □, ID • 33,754
Niagara, WI 54151 • 1,999
Niagara □, NY • 220,756
Niagara Falls, NY 14301-05 • 61,840
Niantic, CT 06357 • 3,048
Nibley, UT 84321 • 1,167
Niceville, FL 32578 • 10,507
Nicholas □, KY • 6,725
Nicholas □, WV • 26,775
Nicholasville, KY 40356 • 13,603
Nicholls, GA 31554 • 1,003
Nichols Hills, OK 73116 • 4,020
Nickerson, KS 67561 • 1,137
Nicollet □, MN • 28,076
Nicoma Park, OK 73066 • 2,353
Nikiska, AK 99635 • 1,109
Niland, CA 92257 • 1,183

Niles, IL 60648 • *28,284*
Niles, MI 49120 • *12,458*
Niles, OH 44446 • *21,128*
Ninety Six, SC 29666 • *2,099*
Ninilchik, AK 99639 • *456*
Niobrara □, WY • *2,499*
Nipomo, CA 93444 • *7,109*
Niskayuna, NY 12309 • *4,942*
Nisswa, MN 56468 • *1,391*
Nitro, WV 25143 • *6,851*
Niwot, CO 80544 • *2,666*
Nixa, MO 65714 • *4,707*
Nixon, NV 89424 • *150*
Nixon, TX 78140 • *1,995*
Noank, CT 06340 • *1,406*
Noble, OK 73068 • *4,710*
Noble □, IN • *37,877*
Noble □, OH • *11,336*
Noble □, OK • *11,045*
Nobles □, MN • *20,098*
Noblesville, IN 46060 • *17,655*
Nocatee, FL 33864 • *1,300*
Nocona, TX 76255 • *2,870*
Nodaway □, MO • *21,709*
Noel, MO 64854 • *1,169*
Nogales, AZ 85621 • *19,489*
Nokomis, FL 34274–75 • *3,448*
Nokomis, IL 62075 • *2,534*
Nolan □, TX • *16,594*
Nome, AK 99762 • *3,500*
Noorvik, AK 99763 • *531*
Nora Springs, IA 50458 • *1,505*
Norco, CA 91760 • *23,302*
Norco, LA 70079 • *3,385*
Norcross, GA 30071 • *5,947*
Norfolk, CT 06058 • *1,500*
Norfolk, NE 68701 • *21,476*
Norfolk, NY 13667 • *1,412*
Norfolk, VA 23501–93 • *261,229*
Norfolk □, MA • *616,087*
Norland, FL 33169 • *22,109*
Normal, IL 61761 • *40,023*
Norman, OK 73069–72 • *80,071*
Norman □, MN • *7,975*
Normandy, MO 63121 • *4,480*
Norridge, IL 60656 • *14,459*
Norridgewock, ME 04957 • *1,496*
Norris, TN 37828 • *1,303*
Norris City, IL 62869 • *1,341*
Norristown, PA 19401–09 • *30,749*
North Adams, MA 01247 • *16,797*
North Albany, OR 97321 • *4,325*
North Amherst, MA 01059 • *6,239*
North Amityville, NY 11701 • *13,849*
Northampton, MA 01060–61 • *29,289*
Northampton, PA 18067 • *8,717*
Northampton □, NC • *20,798*
Northampton □, PA • *247,105*
Northampton □, VA • *13,061*
North Andover, MA 01845 • *20,129*
North Andrews Gardens, FL 33308 • *9,002*
North Apollo, PA 15673 • *1,391*
North Arlington, NJ 07032 • *13,790*
North Atlanta, GA 30319 • *27,812*
North Attleboro, MA 02760–63 • *16,178*
North Auburn, CA 95603 • *10,301*
North Augusta, SC 29841 • *15,351*
North Aurora, IL 60542 • *5,940*
North Babylon, NY 11703 • *18,081*
North Baltimore, OH 45872 • *3,139*
North Bay Shore, NY 11706 • *12,799*
North Beach, MD 20714 • *1,173*
North Bellmore, NY 11710 • *19,707*
North Bellport, NY 11713 • *8,182*
North Belmont, NC 28012 • *10,762*
North Bend, NE 68649 • *1,249*
North Bend, OR 97459 • *9,614*
North Bend, WA 98045 • *2,578*
North Bennington, VT 05257 • *1,520*
North Bergen, NJ 07047 • *48,414*
North Berwick, ME 03906 • *1,568*
North Billerica, MA 01862 • *5,400*
Northborough, MA 01532 • *5,761*
North Braddock, PA 15104 • *7,036*
North Branch, MI 48461 • *1,023*
North Branch, MN 55056 • *1,867*
North Branch, NJ 08876 • *2,620*
North Branford, CT 06471 • *6,600*
Northbridge, MA 01534 • *3,570*
Northbrook, IL 60062 • *32,308*
Northbrook, OH 45231 • *11,471*
North Brookfield, MA 01535 • *2,635*
North Brunswick, NJ 08902 • *31,287*
North Brunswick Township, NJ 08902 • *31,287*
North Caldwell, NJ 07006 • *5,832*
North Canton, OH 44720 • *14,748*
North Cape May, NJ 08204 • *3,574*
North Charleston, SC 29406 • *70,218*
North Chicago, IL 60064 • *34,978*
North City, WA 98155 • *8,200*
North Cohasset, MA 02025 • *1,045*
North College Hill, OH 45239 • *11,002*
North Collins, NY 14111 • *1,335*
North Conway, NH 03860 • *2,032*
North Corbin, KY 40701 • *1,601*
North Crossett, AR 71635 • *3,358*
North Dartmouth, MA 02747 • *8,080*
North Decatur, GA 30033 • *13,936*
North Dighton, MA 02764 • *1,174*
North Druid Hills, GA 30033 • *14,170*
North Eagle Butte, SD 57625 • *1,423*
North East, MD 21901 • *1,913*
North East, PA 16428 • *4,617*
North Eastham, MA 02651 • *1,570*
Northeast Henrietta, NY 14534 • *10,650*
North Easton, MA 02356 • *4,420*
North Fair Oaks, CA 94025 • *13,912*
North Falmouth, MA 02556 • *3,150*
Northfield, IL 60093 • *4,635*
Northfield, MA 01360 • *1,322*
Northfield, MN 55057 • *14,684*
Northfield, NH 03276 • *1,375*
Northfield, NJ 08225 • *7,305*
Northfield, OH 44067 • *3,624*
Northfield, VT 05663 • *1,889*
Northfield Falls, VT 05664 • *600*
North Fond du Lac, WI 54935 • *4,292*
Northford, CT 06472 • *3,180*
North Fort Myers, FL 33903 • *30,027*
Northglenn, CO 80233 • *27,195*
North Grafton, MA 01536 • *3,050*
North Great River, NY 11722 • *3,964*
North Grosvenordale, CT 06255 • *1,705*
North Gulfport, MS 39501 • *4,966*
North Haledon, NJ 07508 • *7,987*
North Hampton, NH 03862 • *1,000*
North Haven, CT 06473 • *22,249*
North Highlands, CA 95660 • *42,105*
North Hill, WA 98166 • *5,706*
North Houston, TX 77086 • *12,800*
North Hudson, WI 54016 • *3,101*
North Industry, OH 44707 • *3,250*
North Judson, IN 46366 • *1,582*
North Kansas City, MO 64116 • *4,130*
North Kingstown, RI 02852–54 • *2,750*
North Kingsville, OH 44068 • *2,672*
North La Junta, CO 81050 • *1,076*
Northlake, IL 60164 • *12,505*
North Las Vegas, NV 89030–31 • *47,707*
North Lauderdale, FL 33068 • *26,506*
North Lewisburg, OH 43060 • *1,160*
North Liberty, IN 46554 • *1,366*
North Liberty, IA 52317 • *2,926*
North Lindenhurst, NY 11757 • *10,563*
North Little Rock, AR 72114–20 • *61,741*
North Logan, UT 84321 • *3,768*
North Madison, OH 44057 • *8,699*
North Manchester, IN 46962 • *6,383*
North Mankato, MN 56001 • *10,164*
North Massapequa, NY 11758 • *19,365*
North Merrick, NY 11566 • *12,113*
North Merrydale, LA 70812 • *4,000*
North Miami, FL 33161 • *49,998*
North Miami Beach, FL 33162 • *35,359*
North Muskegon, MI 49445 • *3,919*
North Myrtle Beach, SC 29582 • *8,636*
North Naples, FL 33963 • *13,422*
North New Hyde Park, NY 11040 • *14,359*
North Ogden, UT 84404 • *11,668*
North Olmsted, OH 44070 • *34,204*
North Oxford, MA 01537 • *1,250*
North Palm Beach, FL 33408 • *11,343*
North Park, IL 61111 • *15,806*
North Patchogue, NY 11772 • *7,374*
North Pembroke, MA 02358 • *2,485*
North Plainfield, NJ 07060 • *18,820*
North Platte, NE 69101–03 • *22,605*
Northport, AL 35476 • *17,366*
North Port, FL 34287 • *11,973*
Northport, NY 11768 • *7,572*
North Prairie, WI 53153 • *1,322*
North Providence, RI 02911 • *32,090*
North Reading, MA 01864 • *11,455*
North Richland Hills, TX 76118 • *45,895*
Northridge, OH 45502 • *5,939*
Northridge, OH 45414 • *9,448*
North Ridgeville, OH 44039 • *21,564*
North Riverside, IL 60546 • *6,005*
North Royalton, OH 44133 • *23,197*
North Salt Lake, UT 84054 • *6,474*
North Sarasota, FL 34234 • *6,702*
North Scituate, MA 02060 • *4,891*
North Sioux City, SD 57049 • *2,019*
North Springfield, OR 97477 • *5,451*
North Springfield, VT 05150 • *750*
North Springfield, VA 22151 • *8,996*
North Star, DE 19711 • *1,030*
North St. Paul, MN 55109 • *12,376*
North Sudbury, MA 01776 • *2,630*
North Syracuse, NY 13212 • *7,363*
North Tarrytown, NY 10591 • *8,152*
North Terre Haute, IN 47805 • *2,000*
North Tewksbury, MA 01876 • *1,030*
North Tonawanda, NY 14120 • *34,989*
North Troy, VT 05859 • *723*
North Tunica, MS 38676 • *1,314*
Northumberland, PA 17857 • *3,860*
Northumberland □, PA • *96,771*
Northumberland □, VA • *10,524*
North Uxbridge, MA 01538 • *1,500*
Northvale, NJ 07647 • *4,563*
North Valley Stream, NY 11580 • *14,574*
North Vernon, IN 47265 • *5,311*
North Versailles, PA 15137 • *12,302*
Northview, MI 49505 • *13,712*
Northview, OH 45322 • *10,337*
Northville, MI 48167 • *6,226*
Northville, NY 12134 • *1,180*
North Wales, PA 19454 • *3,802*
North Wantagh, NY 11793 • *12,276*
North Warren, PA 16365 • *1,232*
North Wildwood, NJ 08260 • *5,017*
North Wilkesboro, NC 28659 • *3,384*
North Windham, ME 04062 • *4,077*
Northwood, IA 50459 • *1,940*
Northwood, ND 58267 • *1,166*
Northwood, OH 43619 • *5,506*
Northwoods, MO 63121 • *5,106*
North York, PA 17404 • *1,689*
Norton, KS 67654 • *3,017*
Norton, MA 02766 • *1,899*
Norton, OH 44203 • *11,477*
Norton, VA 24273 • *4,247*
Norton □, KS • *5,947*
Norton Shores, MI 49441 • *21,755*
Nortonville, KY 42442 • *1,209*
Norwalk, CA 90650–52 • *94,279*
Norwalk, CT 06850–56 • *78,331*
Norwalk, IA 50211 • *5,726*
Norwalk, OH 44857 • *14,731*
Norway, ME 04268 • *3,023*
Norway, MI 49870 • *2,910*
Norwell, MA 02061 • *1,200*
Norwich, CT 06360 • *37,391*
Norwich, NY 13815 • *7,613*
Norwich, VT 05055 • *1,000*
Norwood, MA 02062 • *28,700*
Norwood, MN 55368 • *1,351*
Norwood, NJ 07648 • *4,858*
Norwood, NY 13668 • *1,841*
Norwood, NC 28128 • *1,617*
Norwood, OH 45212 • *23,674*
Norwood, PA 19074 • *6,162*
Norwoodville, IA 50317 • *1,200*
Nottoway □, VA • *14,993*
Novato, CA 94947–49 • *47,585*
Novi, MI 48374–77 • *32,998*
Nowata, OK 74048 • *3,896*
Nowata □, OK • *9,992*
Noxubee □, MS • *12,604*
Nuckolls □, NE • *5,786*
Nueces □, TX • *291,145*
Nulato, AK 99765 • *359*
Nunda, NY 14517 • *1,347*
Nutley, NJ 07110 • *27,099*
Nutter Fort, WV 26301 • *1,819*
Nutting Lake, MA 01865 • *3,180*
Nyack, NY 10960 • *6,558*
Nye □, NV • *17,781*
Nyssa, OR 97913 • *2,629*

O

Oak Bluffs, MA 02557 • *1,124*
Oak Brook, IL 60521 • *9,178*
Oak Creek, WI 53154 • *19,513*
Oakdale, CA 95361 • *11,961*
Oakdale, GA 30080 • *1,080*
Oakdale, LA 71463 • *6,832*
Oakdale, MN 55128 • *18,374*
Oakdale, NY 11769 • *7,875*
Oakdale, PA 15071 • *1,752*
Oakes, ND 58474 • *1,775*
Oakfield, NY 14125 • *1,818*
Oakfield, WI 53065 • *1,003*
Oak Forest, IL 60452 • *26,203*
Oak Grove, KY 42262 • *2,863*
Oak Grove, LA 71263 • *2,126*
Oak Grove, OR 97267 • *12,576*
Oak Grove, SC 29073 • *7,173*
Oak Harbor, OH 43449 • *2,637*
Oak Harbor, WA 98277 • *17,176*
Oak Hill, MI 49660 • *1,000*
Oak Hill, OH 45656 • *1,831*
Oak Hill, WV 25901 • *6,812*
Oakhurst, OK 74050 • *2,200*
Oakland, CA 94601–62 • *372,242*
Oakland, IA 51560 • *1,496*
Oakland, ME 04963 • *3,510*
Oakland, MD 21550 • *2,078*
Oakland, NE 68045 • *1,279*
Oakland, NJ 07436 • *11,997*
Oakland, RI 02830 • *600*
Oakland □, MI • *1,083,592*
Oakland City, IN 47660 • *2,810*
Oakland Park, FL 33334 • *26,326*
Oak Lawn, IL 60453–59 • *56,182*
Oaklawn, KS 67216 • *4,200*
Oakley, CA 94561 • *18,374*
Oakley, KS 67748 • *2,045*
Oaklyn, NJ 08107 • *4,430*
Oakmont, PA 15139 • *6,961*
Oak Orchard, DE 19966 • *350*
Oak Park, CA 91301 • *5,000*
Oak Park, IL 60301–05 • *53,648*
Oak Park, MI 48237 • *30,462*
Oak Ridge, FL 32809 • *15,388*
Oakridge, OR 97463 • *3,063*
Oak Ridge, TN 37830 • *27,310*
Oakton, VA 22124 • *24,610*
Oak Valley, NJ 08090 • *5,400*
Oakville, CT 06779 • *8,741*
Oakville, MO 63129 • *31,750*
Oakwood, GA 30566 • *1,464*
Oakwood, IL 61858 • *1,533*
Oakwood, OH 45419 • *3,392*
Oberlin, KS 67749 • *2,197*
Oberlin, LA 70655 • *1,808*
Oberlin, OH 44074 • *8,191*
Obetz, OH 43207 • *3,167*
Obion, TN 38240 • *1,241*
Obion □, TN • *31,717*
Oblong, IL 62449 • *1,616*
O'Brien □, IA • *15,444*
Ocala, FL 32670–78 • *42,045*
Ocean □, NJ • *433,203*
Oceana, WV 24870 • *1,791*
Oceana □, MI • *22,454*
Ocean Bluff, MA 02065 • *2,500*
Ocean City, FL 32548 • *5,422*
Ocean City, MD 21842 • *5,146*
Ocean City, NJ 08226 • *15,512*
Ocean Gate, NJ 08740 • *2,078*
Ocean Grove, MA 02777 • *4,560*
Oceano, CA 93445 • *6,169*
Ocean Park, WA 98640 • *1,650*
Ocean Port, NJ 07757 • *6,146*
Oceanside, CA 92054–56 • *128,398*
Oceanside, NY 11572 • *32,423*
Ocean Springs, MS 39564–65 • *14,658*
Ocean [Township], NJ 07712 • *23,570*
Ocean View, DE 19970 • *606*
Oceanville, NJ 08231 • *1,000*
Ochiltree □, TX • *9,128*
Ocilla, GA 31774 • *3,182*
Ocoee, FL 34761 • *12,778*
Oconee □, GA • *17,618*
Oconee □, SC • *57,494*
Oconomowoc, WI 53066 • *10,993*
Oconto, WI 54153 • *4,474*
Oconto □, WI • *30,226*
Oconto Falls, WI 54154 • *2,584*
Odebolt, IA 51458 • *1,158*
Odell, IL 60460 • *1,030*
Odem, TX 78370 • *2,366*
Odenton, MD 21113 • *12,833*
Odessa, DE 19730 • *303*
Odessa, MO 64076 • *3,695*
Odessa, TX 79760–68 • *89,699*
Odin, IL 62870 • *1,150*
Odon, IN 47562 • *1,475*
O'Donnell, TX 79351 • *1,102*
Oelwein, IA 50662 • *6,493*
O'Fallon, IL 62269 • *16,073*
O'Fallon, MO 63366 • *18,698*
Ogallala, NE 69153 • *5,095*
Ogden, IA 50212 • *1,909*
Ogden, KS 66517 • *1,494*
Ogden, UT 84401–14 • *63,909*
Ogdensburg, NJ 07439 • *2,722*
Ogdensburg, NY 13669 • *13,521*
Ogemaw □, MI • *18,681*
Ogle □, IL • *45,957*
Oglesby, IL 61348 • *3,619*
Oglethorpe, GA 31068 • *1,302*
Oglethorpe □, GA • *9,763*
Ogunquit, ME 03907 • *1,492*
Ohatchee, AL 36271 • *1,042*
Ohio □, IN • *5,315*
Ohio □, KY • *21,105*
Ohio □, WV • *50,871*
Ohioville, PA 15059 • *3,865*
Oil City, LA 71061 • *1,282*
Oil City, PA 16301 • *11,949*
Oildale, CA 93308 • *26,553*
Oilton, OK 74052 • *1,060*
Ojai, CA 93023–24 • *7,613*
Okaloosa □, FL • *143,776*
Okanogan, WA 98840 • *2,370*
Okanogan □, WA • *33,350*
Okarche, OK 73762 • *1,160*
Okauchee, WI 53069 • *2,300*
Okauchee Lake, WI 53058 • *3,819*
Okawville, IL 62271 • *1,274*
Okeechobee, FL 34972–74 • *4,943*
Okeechobee □, FL • *29,627*
Okeene, OK 73763 • *1,343*
Okemah, OK 74859 • *3,085*
Okemos, MI 48864 • *20,216*
Okfuskee □, OK • *11,551*
Oklahoma □, OK • *599,611*
Oklahoma City, OK 73101–80 • *444,719*
Oklawaha, FL 32179 • *1,200*
Okmulgee, OK 74447 • *13,441*
Okmulgee □, OK • *36,490*
Okolona, KY 40219 • *18,902*
Okolona, MS 38860 • *3,267*
Oktibbeha □, MS • *38,375*
Ola, AR 72853 • *1,090*
Olathe, CO 81425 • *1,263*
Olathe, KS 66061–62 • *63,352*
Olcott, NY 14126 • *1,432*
Old Bethpage, NY 11804 • *5,610*
Old Bridge, NJ 08857 • *22,151*
Old Forge, NY 13420 • *1,061*
Old Forge, PA 18518 • *8,834*
Oldham □, KY • *33,263*
Oldham □, TX • *2,278*
Old Harbor, AK 99643 • *284*
Old Orchard Beach, ME 04064 • *7,789*
Old Saybrook, CT 06475 • *1,820*
Oldsmar, FL 34677 • *8,361*
Old Tappan, NJ 07675 • *4,254*
Old Town, ME 04468 • *8,317*
Olean, NY 14760 • *16,946*
Olive Branch, MS 38654 • *3,567*
Olive Hill, KY 41164 • *1,809*
Olivehurst, CA 95961 • *9,738*
Oliver, PA 15472 • *3,271*
Oliver □, ND • *2,381*
Oliver Springs, TN 37840 • *3,433*
Olivet, MI 49076 • *1,604*
Olivette, MO 63132 • *7,573*
Olivia, MN 56277 • *2,623*
Olla, LA 71465 • *1,410*
Olmito, TX 78575 • *1,400*
Olmos Park, TX 78212 • *2,161*
Olmsted □, MN • *106,470*
Olmsted Falls, OH 44138 • *6,741*
Olney, IL 62450 • *8,664*
Olney, MD 20832 • *23,019*
Olney, TX 76374 • *3,519*
Olton, TX 79064 • *2,116*
Olympia, WA 98501–07 • *33,840*
Olympia Heights, FL 33175 • *36,900*
Olyphant, PA 18447 • *5,222*
Omaha, NE 68101–72 • *335,795*
Omak, WA 98841 • *4,117*
Omro, WI 54963 • *2,836*
Onalaska, WI 54650 • *11,284*
Onancock, VA 23417 • *1,434*
Onarga, IL 60955 • *1,281*
Onawa, IA 51040 • *2,936*
Onaway, MI 49765 • *1,039*
Oneco, FL 34264 • *6,417*
Oneida, NY 13421 • *10,850*
Oneida, OH 45042 • *1,650*
Oneida, TN 37841 • *3,502*
Oneida □, ID • *3,492*
Oneida □, NY • *250,836*
Oneida □, WI • *31,679*
O'Neill, NE 68763 • *3,852*
Oneonta, AL 35121 • *4,844*
Oneonta, NY 13820 • *13,954*
Onida, SD 57564 • *761*
Onondaga □, NY • *468,973*
Onset, MA 02558 • *1,461*
Onslow □, NC • *149,838*
Ontario, CA 91761–62 • *133,179*
Ontario, OH 44862 • *4,026*
Ontario, OR 97914 • *9,392*
Ontario □, NY • *95,101*
Ontonagon, MI 49953 • *2,040*
Ontonagon □, MI • *8,854*
Oolitic, IN 47451 • *1,424*
Ooltewah, TN 37363 • *1,200*
Oostburg, WI 53070 • *1,931*
Opal Cliffs, CA 95062 • *5,940*
Opa-Locka, FL 33054–56 • *15,283*
Opelika, AL 36801–03 • *22,122*
Opelousas, LA 70570–71 • *18,151*
Opp, AL 36467 • *6,985*
Opportunity, WA 99206 • *22,326*
Oquawka, IL 61469 • *1,442*
Oracle, AZ 85623 • *3,043*
Oradell, NJ 07649 • *8,024*
Oran, MO 63771 • *1,164*
Orange, CA 92664–69 • *110,658*
Orange, CT 06477 • *12,830*
Orange, MA 01364 • *3,791*
Orange, NJ 07050–52 • *29,925*
Orange, TX 77630–31 • *19,381*
Orange, VA 22960 • *2,582*
Orange □, CA • *2,410,556*
Orange □, FL • *677,491*
Orange □, IN • *18,409*
Orange □, NY • *307,647*
Orange □, NC • *93,851*
Orange □, TX • *80,509*
Orange □, VT • *26,149*
Orange □, VA • *21,421*
Orange Beach, AL 36561 • *2,253*
Orangeburg, SC 29115–16 • *13,739*
Orangeburg □, SC • *84,803*
Orange City, FL 32763 • *5,347*
Orange City, IA 51041 • *4,940*
Orange Grove, MS 39503 • *15,676*
Orange Grove, TX 78372 • *1,175*
Orange Lake, FL 32681 • *1,000*
Orange Park, FL 32073 • *9,488*
Orangevale, CA 95662 • *26,266*
Orangeville, UT 84537 • *1,459*
Orchard City, CO 81410 • *2,218*
Orchard Homes, MT 59801 • *10,317*
Orchard Mesa, CO 81501 • *5,977*
Orchard Park, NY 14127 • *3,280*
Orchards, WA 98662 • *8,828*
Orchard Valley, WY 82007 • *3,321*
Orcutt, CA 93455 • *1,500*
Ord, NE 68862 • *2,481*
Ordway, CO 81063 • *1,025*
Oregon, IL 61061 • *3,891*
Oregon, OH 43616 • *18,334*
Oregon, WI 53575 • *4,519*
Oregon □, MO • *9,470*
Oregon City, OR 97045 • *14,698*
Orem, UT 84057–59 • *67,561*
Orfordville, WI 53576 • *1,219*
Orient, NY 11957 • *1,000*
Orinda, CA 94563 • *16,642*
Orion, IL 61273 • *1,821*
Oriskany, NY 13424 • *1,450*
Orland, CA 95963 • *5,052*
Orlando, FL 32801–72 • *164,693*
Orland Park, IL 60462 • *35,720*
Orleans, IN 47452 • *2,083*
Orleans, IN 47452 • *2,161*
Orleans, MA 02653 • *1,699*
Orleans, VT 05860 • *806*
Orleans □, LA • *496,938*
Orleans □, NY • *41,846*
Orleans □, VT • *24,053*
Orlovista, FL 32811 • *5,990*
Ormond Beach, FL 32174–76 • *29,721*
Ormond By The Sea, FL 32174 • *8,157*
Orofino, ID 83544 • *2,868*
Orono, ME 04473 • *9,789*
Orono, MN 55323 • *7,285*
Orosi, CA 93647 • *5,486*
Oroville, CA 95965–66 • *11,960*
Oroville, WA 98844 • *1,505*
Orrville, OH 44667 • *7,712*
Orting, WA 98360 • *2,106*
Ortonville, MI 48462 • *1,252*
Ortonville, MN 56278 • *2,205*
Orwell, OH 44076 • *1,258*
Orwigsburg, PA 17961 • *2,780*
Osage, IA 50461 • *3,439*
Osage, WY 82723 • *350*
Osage □, KS • *15,248*
Osage □, MO • *12,018*
Osage □, OK • *41,645*
Osage Beach, MO 65065 • *2,599*
Osage City, KS 66523 • *2,689*
Osakis, MN 56360 • *1,256*
Osawatomie, KS 66064 • *4,590*
Osborne, KS 67473 • *1,778*
Osborne □, KS • *4,867*
Osburn, ID 83849 • *1,579*
Osceola, AR 72370 • *8,930*
Osceola, IN 46561 • *1,999*
Osceola, IA 50213 • *4,164*
Osceola, WI 54020 • *2,075*
Osceola □, FL • *107,728*
Osceola □, IA • *7,267*
Osceola □, MI • *20,146*
Osceola Mills, PA 16666 • *1,310*
Oscoda, MI 48750 • *1,061*
Oscoda □, MI • *7,842*
Osgood, IN 47037 • *1,688*
Oshkosh, WI 54901–04 • *55,006*
Oskaloosa, IA 52577 • *10,632*
Oskaloosa, KS 66066 • *1,074*
Osprey, FL 34229 • *2,597*
Osseo, MN 55369 • *2,704*
Osseo, WI 54758 • *1,551*
Ossian, IN 46777 • *2,428*
Ossining, NY 10562 • *22,582*
Osterville, MA 02655 • *2,911*
Oswego, IL 60543 • *3,876*
Oswego, KS 67356 • *1,870*
Oswego, NY 13126 • *19,195*
Oswego □, NY • *121,771*
Otay, CA 92010 • *6,400*
Oteen, NC 28805 • *1,400*
Otego, NY 13825 • *1,068*
Otero □, CO • *20,185*
Otero □, NM • *51,928*
Othello, WA 99344 • *4,638*
Otis Orchards, WA 99027 • *3,200*
Otoe □, NE • *14,252*
Otsego, MI 49078 • *3,937*
Otsego □, MI • *17,957*
Otsego □, NY • *60,517*
Ottawa, IL 61350 • *17,451*
Ottawa, KS 66067 • *10,667*
Ottawa, OH 45875 • *3,999*
Ottawa □, KS • *5,634*
Ottawa □, MI • *187,768*
Ottawa □, OH • *40,029*
Ottawa □, OK • *30,561*
Ottawa Hills, OH 43606 • *4,543*
Otterbein, IN 47970 • *1,291*
Otter Tail □, MN • *50,714*
Ottumwa, IA 52501 • *24,488*
Ouachita □, AR • *30,574*
Ouachita □, LA • *142,191*
Ouray, CO 81427 • *644*
Ouray □, CO • *2,295*
Outagamie □, WI • *140,510*
Overland, MO 63114 • *17,987*
Overland Park, KS 66204 • *111,790*
Overlea, MD 21206 • *12,137*
Overlook, OH 45431 • *6,000*
Overton, NV 89040 • *1,111*
Overton, TX 75684 • *2,105*
Overton □, TN • *17,636*
Ovid, MI 48866 • *1,442*
Owasso, OK 74055 • *11,151*
Owatonna, MN 55060 • *19,386*
Owego, NY 13827 • *4,442*
Owen □, IN • *17,281*
Owen □, KY • *9,035*
Owensboro, KY 42301–03 • *53,549*
Owensville, IN 47665 • *1,053*
Owensville, MO 65066 • *2,325*
Owensville, OH 45160 • *1,019*
Owenton, KY 40359 • *1,306*
Owings Mills, MD 21117 • *9,474*
Owingsville, KY 40360 • *1,491*
Owosso, MI 48867 • *16,322*
Owsley □, KY • *5,036*
Owyhee, NV 89832 • *908*
Owyhee □, ID • *8,392*
Oxford, AL 36203 • *9,362*
Oxford, CT 06483 • *1,600*
Oxford, GA 30267 • *1,945*
Oxford, IN 47971 • *1,273*
Oxford, KS 67119 • *1,143*
Oxford, MA 01540 • *5,969*
Oxford, MI 48370–71 • *2,929*
Oxford, MS 38655 • *9,984*
Oxford, NC 27565 • *7,913*
Oxford, NJ 07863 • *1,767*
Oxford, NY 13830 • *1,738*

Oxford, NC 27565 • 7,913
Oxford, OH 45056 • 18,937
Oxford, PA 19363 • 3,769
Oxford □, ME • 52,602
Oxnard, CA 93030–35 • 142,216
Oxon Hill, MD 20745 • 36,267
Oyster Bay, NY 11771 • 6,687
Ozark, AL 36360–61 • 12,922
Ozark, AR 72949 • 3,330
Ozark, MO 65721 • 4,243
Ozark □, MO • 8,598
Ozaukee □, WI • 72,831
Ozona, FL 34660 • 1,500
Ozona, TX 76943 • 3,181

P

Paauilo, HI 96776 • 620
Pace, FL 32571 • 6,277
Pacific, MO 63069 • 4,350
Pacific, WA 98047 • 4,622
Pacific □, WA • 18,882
Pacifica, CA 94044 • 37,670
Pacific Beach, WA 98571 • 1,200
Pacific City, OR 97135 • 1,500
Pacific Grove, CA 93950 • 16,117
Pacific Palisades, HI 96782 • 10,000
Packwood, WA 98361 • 1,010
Pacolet, SC 29372 • 1,736
Paddock Lake, WI 53168 • 2,662
Paden City, WV 26159 • 2,862
Paducah, KY 42001–03 • 27,256
Paducah, TX 79248 • 1,788
Page, AZ 86040 • 6,598
Page □, IA • 16,870
Page □, VA • 21,690
Pageland, SC 29728 • 2,666
Page Manor, OH 45431 • 9,300
Pagosa Springs, CO 81147 • 1,207
Pahala, HI 96777 • 1,520
Pahoa, HI 96778 • 1,027
Pahokee, FL 33476 • 6,822
Pahrump, NV 89041 • 7,424
Paia, HI 96779 • 2,091
Paincourtville, LA 70391 • 1,550
Painesville, OH 44077 • 15,699
Painted Post, NY 14870 • 1,950
Paintsville, KY 41240 • 4,354
Pajarito, NM 87105 • 1,400
Palacios, TX 77465 • 4,418
Palatine, IL 60067 • 39,253
Palatka, FL 32177 • 10,201
Palestine, IL 62451 • 1,619
Palestine, TX 75801–02 • 18,042
Palisade, CO 81526 • 1,871
Palisades Park, NJ 07650 • 14,536
Palm Bay, FL 32905 • 62,632
Palm Beach, FL 33480 • 9,814
Palm Beach □, FL • 863,518
Palm Beach Gardens, FL 33410 • 22,965
Palm Coast, FL 32135 • 14,287
Palmdale, CA 93550–51 • 68,842
Palm Desert, CA 92260–61 • 23,252
Palmer, AK 99645 • 2,866
Palmer, MA 01069 • 4,069
Palmer, MS 39401 • 2,765
Palmer, TX 75152 • 1,659
Palmer Lake, CO 80133 • 1,480
Palmer Park, MD 20785 • 7,019
Palmerton, PA 18071 • 5,394
Palmetto, FL 34220–21 • 9,268
Palmetto, GA 30268 • 2,612
Palmetto Estates, FL 33157 • 12,293
Palm Harbor, FL 34682–85 • 50,256
Palm Springs, CA 92262–64 • 40,181
Palm Springs, FL 33460 • 9,763
Palm Springs North, FL 33015 • 5,300
Palm Valley, FL 32082 • 9,960
Palmyra, MO 63461 • 3,371
Palmyra, NJ 08065 • 7,056
Palmyra, NY 14522 • 3,566
Palmyra, PA 17078 • 6,910
Palmyra, WI 53156 • 1,539
Palo Alto, CA 94301–09 • 55,900
Palo Alto □, IA • 10,669
Palo Pinto □, TX • 25,055
Palos Heights, IL 60463 • 11,478
Palos Hills, IL 60465 • 17,803
Palos Park, IL 60464 • 4,199
Palos Verdes Estates, CA 90274 • 13,512
Pamlico □, NC • 11,372
Pampa, TX 79065–66 • 19,959
Pamplico, SC 29583 • 1,314
Pana, IL 62557 • 5,796
Panaca, NV 89042 • 700
Panama, OK 74951 • 1,528
Panama City, FL 32401–13 • 34,378
Panama City Beach, FL 32407–08 • 4,051
Pandora, OH 45877 • 1,009
Panguitch, UT 84759 • 1,444
Panhandle, TX 79068 • 2,353
Panola □, MS • 29,996
Panola □, TX • 22,035
Panora, IA 50216 • 1,100
Panthersville, GA 30032 • 9,874
Paola, KS 66071 • 4,698
Paoli, IN 47454 • 3,542
Paoli, PA 19301 • 5,603
Paonia, CO 81428 • 1,403
Papaikou, HI 96781 • 1,634
Papillion, NE 68046 • 10,372
Paradise, CA 95969 • 25,408
Paradise, NV 89109 • 124,682
Paradise Hills, NM 87114 • 5,513
Paradise Valley, AZ 85253 • 11,671
Paradise Valley, NV 89426 • 150
Paragould, AR 72450–51 • 18,540
Paramount, CA 90723 • 47,669
Paramount, MD 21740 • 1,878
Paramus, NJ 07652–53 • 25,067
Parchment, MI 49004 • 1,958
Pardeeville, WI 53954 • 1,630
Paris, AR 72855 • 3,674
Paris, IL 61944 • 8,987
Paris, KY 40361–62 • 8,730
Paris, MO 65275 • 1,486
Paris, TN 38242 • 9,332
Paris, TX 75460–61 • 24,699
Park □, CO • 7,174
Park □, MT • 14,562
Park □, WY • 23,178
Park City, KS 67219 • 5,050
Park City, UT 84060 • 4,468
Parke □, IN • 15,410
Parker, AZ 85344 • 2,897
Parker, CO 80134 • 5,450
Parker, FL 32401 • 4,598
Parker, SD 57053 • 984
Parker □, TX • 64,785
Parker City, IN 47368 • 1,323
Parkersburg, IA 50665 • 1,804
Parkersburg, WV 26101–06 • 33,862
Parkesburg, PA 19365 • 2,981
Park Falls, WI 54552 • 3,104
Park Forest, IL 60466 • 24,656
Park Hills, KY 41015 • 3,321
Parkin, AR 72373 • 1,847
Parkland, WA 98444 • 20,882
Park Layne, OH 45344 • 4,895
Park Rapids, MN 56470 • 2,863
Park Ridge, IL 60068 • 36,175
Park Ridge, NJ 07656 • 8,102
Park River, ND 58270 • 1,725
Parkrose, OR 97230 • 21,108
Parkston, SD 57366 • 1,572
Parkville, MD 21234 • 31,617
Parkville, MO 64152 • 2,402
Parkwater, WA 99211 • 4,300
Parkway, CA 95823 • 12,000
Parkwood, NC 27713 • 4,123
Parkwood, WA 98366 • 6,853
Parlier, CA 93648 • 7,938
Parma, ID 83660 • 1,597
Parma, OH 44129 • 87,876
Parma Heights, OH 44130 • 21,448
Parmer □, TX • 9,863
Parole, MD 21401 • 10,054
Parowan, UT 84761 • 1,873
Parrish, AL 35580 • 1,433
Parshall, ND 58770 • 943
Parsons, KS 67357 • 11,924
Parsons, TN 38363 • 2,033
Parsons, WV 26287 • 1,453
Pasadena, CA 91101–09 • 131,591
Pasadena, MD 21122 • 10,012
Pasadena, TX 77501–08 • 119,363
Pascagoula, MS 39567–68 • 25,899
Pasco, WA 99301–02 • 20,337
Pasco □, FL • 281,131
Pascoag, RI 02859 • 5,011
Paso Robles, CA 93446–47 • 18,583
Pasquotank □, NC • 31,298
Passaic, NJ 07055 • 58,041
Passaic □, NJ • 453,060
Pass Christian, MS 39571 • 5,557
Pataskala, OH 43062 • 3,046
Patchogue, NY 11772 • 11,060
Paterson, NJ 07501–44 • 140,891
Patrick □, VA • 17,473
Patten, ME 04765 • 1,256
Patterson, LA 70392 • 4,736
Patterson, NY 12563 • 1,200
Patton, PA 16668 • 2,206
Paul, ID 83347 • 901
Paulding, OH 45879 • 2,605
Paulding □, GA • 41,611
Paulding □, OH • 20,488
Paullina, IA 51046 • 1,134
Paulsboro, NJ 08066 • 6,577
Pauls Valley, OK 73075 • 6,150
Pawcatuck, CT 06379 • 5,289
Paw Creek, NC 28130 • 1,700
Pawhuska, OK 74056 • 3,825
Pawling, NY 12564 • 1,974
Pawnee, IL 62558 • 2,384
Pawnee, OK 74058 • 2,197
Pawnee □, KS • 7,555
Pawnee □, NE • 3,317
Pawnee □, OK • 15,575
Pawnee City, NE 68420 • 1,008
Paw Paw, MI 49079 • 3,169
Pawtucket, RI 02860–65 • 72,644
Paxton, IL 60957 • 4,289
Paxton, MA 01612 • 1,550
Payette, ID 83661 • 5,592
Payette □, ID • 16,434
Payne, OH 45880 • 1,244
Payne □, OK • 61,507
Paynesville, MN 56362 • 2,275
Payson, AZ 85541 • 8,377
Payson, IL 62360 • 1,114
Payson, UT 84651 • 9,510
Peabody, KS 66866 • 1,349
Peabody, MA 01960–61 • 47,039
Peace Dale, RI 02883 • 3,100
Peach □, GA • 21,189
Peach Orchard, GA 30906 • 13,800
Peachtree City, GA 30269 • 19,027
Pea Ridge, AR 72751 • 1,620
Pearisburg, VA 24134 • 2,064
Pearl, MS 39208 • 19,588
Pearland, TX 77581 • 18,697
Pearl City, HI 96782 • 30,993
Pearl River, LA 70452 • 1,507
Pearl River, NY 10965 • 15,314
Pearl River □, MS • 38,714
Pearsall, TX 78061 • 6,924
Pearson, GA 31642 • 1,714
Pecatonica, IL 61063 • 1,760
Pecos, NM 87552 • 1,012
Pecos, TX 79772 • 12,069
Pecos □, TX • 14,675
Peculiar, MO 64078 • 1,777
Pedricktown, NJ 08067 • 1,500
Peebles, OH 45660 • 1,782
Peekskill, NY 10566 • 19,536
Pegram, TN 37143 • 1,371
Pekin, IL 61554–55 • 32,254
Pekin, IN 47165 • 1,095
Pelahatchie, MS 39145 • 1,553
Pelham, AL 35124 • 9,765
Pelham, GA 31779 • 3,869
Pelham, NY 10803 • 6,413
Pelham Manor, NY 10803 • 5,443
Pelican Rapids, MN 56572 • 1,886
Pella, IA 50219 • 9,270
Pell City, AL 35125 • 8,118
Pell Lake, WI 53157 • 2,018
Pemberton, NJ 08068 • 1,367
Pemberville, OH 43450 • 1,279
Pembina □, ND • 9,238
Pembroke, GA 31321 • 1,503
Pembroke, MA 02359 • 2,000
Pembroke, NC 28372 • 2,241
Pembroke, VA 24136 • 1,064
Pembroke Park, FL 33009 • 4,933
Pembroke Pines, FL 33024 • 65,452
Pemiscot □, MO • 21,921
Pen Argyl, PA 18072 • 3,492
Penbrook, PA 17103 • 2,791
Pender, NE 68047 • 1,208
Pender □, NC • 28,855
Pendleton, IN 46064 • 2,309
Pendleton, OR 97801 • 15,126
Pendleton, SC 29670 • 3,314
Pendleton □, KY • 12,036
Pendleton □, WV • 8,054
Pendley Hills, GA 30032 • 5,400
Pend Oreille □, WA • 8,915
Penfield, NY 14526 • 6,260
Penn Acres, DE 19720 • 2,430
Penn Hills, PA 15235 • 51,430
Pennington, NJ 08534 • 2,537
Pennington □, MN • 13,306
Pennington □, SD • 81,343
Pennington Gap, VA 24277 • 1,922
Pennsauken, NJ 08110 • 34,733
Pennsboro, WV 26415 • 1,282
Pennsburg, PA 18073 • 2,460
Penns Grove, NJ 08069 • 5,228
Pennsville, NJ 08070 • 12,218
Penn Yan, NY 14527 • 5,248
Penobscot □, ME • 146,601
Pensacola, FL 32501–26 • 58,165
Pentwater, MI 49449 • 1,050
Peoria, AZ 85345 • 50,618
Peoria, IL 61601–56 • 113,504
Peoria □, IL • 182,827
Peoria Heights, IL 61614 • 6,930
Peotone, IL 60468 • 2,947
Pepeekeo, HI 96783 • 1,813
Pepin □, WI • 7,107
Pepperell, MA 01463 • 2,350
Pepper Pike, OH 44124 • 6,185
Pequannock, NJ 07440 • 12,844
Perdido, AL 36562 • 1,200
Perham, MN 56573 • 2,075
Perkasie, PA 18944 • 7,878
Perkins, OK 74059 • 1,925
Perkins □, NE • 3,367
Perkins □, SD • 3,932
Perquimans □, NC • 10,447
Perrine, FL 33157 • 15,576
Perris, CA 92370 • 21,460
Perry, FL 32347 • 7,151
Perry, GA 31069 • 9,452
Perry, IA 50220 • 6,652
Perry, MI 48872 • 2,163
Perry, NY 14530 • 4,219
Perry, OH 44081 • 1,012
Perry, OK 73077 • 4,978
Perry, UT 84302 • 1,211
Perry □, AL • 12,759
Perry □, AR • 7,969
Perry □, IL • 21,412
Perry □, IN • 19,107
Perry □, KY • 30,283
Perry □, MS • 10,865
Perry □, MO • 16,648
Perry □, OH • 31,557
Perry □, PA • 41,172
Perry □, TN • 6,612
Perry Hall, MD 21128 • 22,723
Perry Heights, OH 44646 • 9,055
Perryman, MD 21130 • 2,160
Perrysburg, OH 43551–52 • 12,551
Perryton, TX 79070 • 7,607
Perryville, AR 72126 • 1,141
Perryville, MD 21903 • 2,456
Perryville, MO 63775 • 6,933
Pershing □, NV • 4,336
Person □, NC • 30,180
Perth Amboy, NJ 08861–63 • 41,967
Peru, IL 61354 • 9,302
Peru, IN 46970 • 12,843
Peru, NE 68421 • 1,110
Peru, NY 12972 • 1,565
Peshtigo, WI 54157 • 3,154
Petal, MS 39465 • 7,883
Petaluma, CA 94952–55 • 43,184
Peterborough, NH 03458 • 2,685
Petersburg, AK 99833 • 3,207
Petersburg, IL 62675 • 2,261
Petersburg, IN 47567 • 2,449
Petersburg, MI 49270 • 1,201
Petersburg, TX 79250 • 1,292
Petersburg, VA 23801–05 • 38,386
Petersburg, WV 26847 • 2,360
Petersville, AL 35633 • 1,730
Petoskey, MI 49770 • 6,056
Petroleum □, MT • 519
Petros, TN 37845 • 1,286
Pettis □, MO • 35,437
Pevely, MO 63070 • 2,831
Pewaukee, WI 53072 • 4,941
Pewee Valley, KY 40056 • 1,283
Pharr, TX 78577 • 32,921
Phelps, KY 41553 • 1,120
Phelps, NY 14532 • 1,978
Phelps □, MO • 35,248
Phelps □, NE • 9,715
Phenix City, AL 36867–69 • 25,312
Philadelphia, MS 39350 • 6,758
Philadelphia, NY 13673 • 1,478
Philadelphia, PA 19101–96 • 1,585,577
Philadelphia □, PA • 1,585,577
Phil Campbell, AL 35581 • 1,317
Philip, SD 57567 • 1,077
Philippi, WV 26416 • 3,132
Philipsburg, MT 59858 • 925
Philipsburg, PA 16866 • 3,048
Phillips, TX 79007 • 1,729
Phillips, WI 54555 • 1,592
Phillips □, AR • 28,838
Phillips □, CO • 4,189
Phillips □, KS • 6,590
Phillips □, MT • 5,163
Phillipsburg, KS 67661 • 2,828
Phillipsburg, NJ 08865 • 15,757
Philmont, NY 12565 • 1,623
Philo, IL 61864 • 1,028
Philomath, OR 97370 • 2,983
Phoenix, AZ 85001–82 • 983,403
Phoenix, IL 60426 • 2,217
Phoenix, NY 13135 • 2,435
Phoenix, OR 97535 • 3,239
Phoenixville, PA 19460 • 15,066
Piatt □, IL • 15,548
Picayune, MS 39466 • 10,633
Picher, OK 74360 • 1,714
Pickaway □, OH • 48,255
Pickens, MS 39146 • 1,285
Pickens, SC 29671 • 3,042
Pickens □, AL • 20,699
Pickens □, GA • 14,432
Pickens □, SC • 93,894
Pickerington, OH 43147 • 5,668
Pickett □, TN • 4,548
Pico Rivera, CA 90660–61 • 59,177
Piedmont, AL 36272 • 5,288
Piedmont, CA 94611 • 10,602
Piedmont, MO 63957 • 2,166
Piedmont, OK 73078 • 2,522
Piedmont, SC 29673 • 4,143
Piedmont, WV 26750 • 1,094
Pierce, ID 83546 • 746
Pierce, NE 68767 • 1,615
Pierce □, GA • 13,328
Pierce □, NE • 7,827
Pierce □, ND • 5,052
Pierce □, WA • 586,203
Pierce □, WI • 32,765
Pierce City, MO 65723 • 1,382
Pierceton, IN 46562 • 1,030
Pierre, SD 57501 • 12,906
Pierre Part, LA 70339 • 3,053
Pierson, FL 32180 • 2,988
Pierz, MN 56364 • 1,014
Pigeon, MI 48755 • 1,207
Pigeon Cove, MA 01966 • 1,660
Pigeon Forge, TN 37863 • 3,027
Piggott, AR 72454 • 3,777
Pike □, AL • 27,595
Pike □, AR • 10,086
Pike □, GA • 10,224
Pike □, IL • 17,577
Pike □, IN • 12,509
Pike □, KY • 72,583
Pike □, MS • 36,882
Pike □, MO • 15,969
Pike □, OH • 24,249
Pike □, PA • 27,966
Pike Lake, MN 55811 • 1,004
Pikesville, MD 21208 • 24,815
Piketon, OH 45661 • 1,717
Pikeville, KY 41501–02 • 6,324
Pikeville, TN 37367 • 1,771
Pilot Mountain, NC 27041 • 1,181
Pilot Point, TX 76258 • 2,538
Pilot Rock, OR 97868 • 1,478
Pilot Station, AK 99650 • 463
Pima, AZ 85543 • 1,725
Pima □, AZ • 666,880
Pimmit Hills, VA 22043 • 6,019
Pinal □, AZ • 116,379
Pinardville, NH 03045 • 4,654
Pinckney, MI 48169 • 1,603
Pinckneyville, IL 62274 • 3,372
Pinconning, MI 48650 • 1,291
Pine □, MN • 21,264
Pine Bluff, AR 71601–13 • 57,140
Pine Bluffs, WY 82082 • 1,054
Pine Bridge, CT 06403 • 1,160
Pine Bush, NY 12566 • 1,445
Pine Castle, FL 32809 • 8,276
Pine City, MN 55063 • 2,613
Pinedale, WY 82941 • 1,181
Pine Grove, PA 17963 • 2,118
Pine Grove Mills, PA 16868 • 1,129
Pine Hill, NJ 08021 • 9,854
Pine Hills, FL 32808 • 35,322
Pinehurst, MA 01866 • 6,614
Pinehurst, NJ 08201 • 1,850
Pinehurst, NC 28374 • 5,103
Pine Island, MN 55963 • 2,125
Pine Island, NY 10969 • 1,200
Pine Knot, KY 42635 • 1,549
Pine Lawn, MO 63120 • 5,092
Pine Level, NC 27568 • 1,217
Pinellas □, FL • 851,659
Pinellas Park, FL 34664–66 • 43,426
Pine Plains, NY 12567 • 1,312
Pine Ridge, SD 57770 • 2,596
Pinetops, NC 27864 • 1,514
Pine Valley, CA 91962 • 1,297
Pineville, KY 40977 • 2,198
Pineville, LA 71360–61 • 12,251
Pineville, NC 28134 • 2,970
Pinewald, NJ 08721 • 1,700
Pinewood, FL 33168 • 15,518
Pinewood Park, FL 33168 • 8,300
Piney Point, MD 20674 • 1,200
Piney View, WV 25906 • 1,085
Pinole, CA 94564 • 17,460
Pinson, AL 35126 • 1,430
Pioche, NV 89043 • 830
Pioneer, OH 43554 • 1,287
Pipestone, MN 56164 • 4,554
Pipestone □, MN • 10,491
Piqua, OH 45356 • 20,612
Pirtleville, AZ 85626 • 1,364
Piscataquis □, ME • 18,653
Piscataway, NJ 08854–55 • 42,223
Pisgah, OH 45069 • 15,660
Pisgah Forest, NC 28768 • 1,899
Pismo Beach, CA 93448–49 • 7,669
Pitcairn, PA 15140 • 4,087
Pitkin □, CO • 12,661
Pitman, NJ 08071 • 9,365
Pitt □, NC • 107,924
Pittsboro, NC 27312 • 1,436
Pittsburg, CA 94565 • 47,564
Pittsburg, KS 66762 • 17,775
Pittsburg, TX 75686 • 4,007
Pittsburg □, OK • 40,581
Pittsburgh, PA 15201–90 • 369,879
Pittsfield, IL 62363 • 4,231
Pittsfield, ME 04967 • 3,222
Pittsfield, MA 01201–03 • 48,622
Pittsfield, NH 03263 • 1,717
Pittsford, VT 05763 • 650
Pittston, PA 18640–44 • 9,389
Pittsylvania □, VA • 55,655
Piute □, UT • 1,277
Pixley, CA 93256 • 2,457
Placentia, CA 92670 • 41,259
Placer □, CA • 172,796
Placerville, CA 95667 • 8,355
Plain City, OH 43064 • 2,278
Plain City, UT 84404 • 2,722
Plain Dealing, LA 71064 • 1,074
Plainedge, NY 11714 • 8,739
Plainfield, CT 06374 • 2,856
Plainfield, IL 60544 • 4,557
Plainfield, IN 46168 • 10,433
Plainfield, NJ 07059–63 • 46,567
Plainfield, VT 05667 • 600
Plainfield Heights, MI 49505 • 5,000
Plains, MT 59859 • 992
Plains, PA 18705 • 4,694
Plains, TX 79355 • 1,422
Plainsboro, NJ 08536 • 1,560
Plainview, MN 55964 • 2,768
Plainview, NE 68769 • 1,333
Plainview, NY 11803 • 26,207
Plainview, TX 79072–73 • 21,700
Plainville, CT 06062 • 17,392
Plainville, KS 67663 • 2,173
Plainville, MA 02762 • 5,857
Plainwell, MI 49080 • 4,057
Plaistow, NH 03865 • 1,850
Plano, IL 60545 • 5,104
Plano, TX 75074–75 • 128,713
Plantation, FL 33317 • 66,692
Plant City, FL 33564–67 • 22,754
Plantersville, MS 38862 • 1,046
Plantsite, AZ 85540 • 1,500
Plantsville, CT 06479 • 7,050
Plaquemine, LA 70764–65 • 7,186
Plaquemines □, LA • 25,575
Platte, SD 57369 • 1,311
Platte □, MO • 57,867
Platte □, NE • 29,820
Platte □, WY • 8,145
Platte City, MO 64079 • 2,947
Platteville, CO 80651 • 1,515
Platteville, WI 53818 • 9,708
Plattsburg, MO 64477 • 2,248
Plattsburgh, NY 12901 • 21,255
Plattsmouth, NE 68048 • 6,412
Pleasant Gap, PA 16823 • 1,699
Pleasant Garden, NC 27313 • 2,228
Pleasant Grove, AL 35127 • 8,458
Pleasant Grove, UT 84062 • 13,476
Pleasant Hill, CA 94523 • 31,585
Pleasant Hill, IL 62366 • 1,030
Pleasant Hill, IA 50301 • 3,671
Pleasant Hill, MO 64080 • 3,827
Pleasant Hill, OH 45359 • 1,066
Pleasant Hills, PA 15236 • 8,884
Pleasanton, CA 94566 • 50,553
Pleasanton, KS 66075 • 1,231
Pleasanton, TX 78064 • 7,678
Pleasant Prairie, WI 53158 • 11,961
Pleasants □, WV • 7,546
Pleasant Valley, MO 64068 • 2,731
Pleasant Valley, NY 12569 • 1,688
Pleasant View, CO 80401 • 3,460
Pleasant View, UT 84404 • 3,603
Pleasantville, IA 50225 • 1,536
Pleasantville, NJ 08232 • 16,027
Pleasantville, NY 10570–72 • 6,592
Pleasure Beach, CT 06385 • 1,356
Pleasure Ridge Park, KY 40258 • 25,131
Plentywood, MT 59254 • 2,136
Plover, WI 54467 • 8,176
Plum, PA 15239 • 25,609
Plumas □, CA • 19,739
Plumsteadville, PA 18949 • 1,200
Plymouth, CT 06782 • 1,070
Plymouth, FL 32768 • 2,700
Plymouth, IN 46563 • 8,303
Plymouth, MA 02360–61 • 7,258
Plymouth, MI 48170 • 9,560
Plymouth, MN 55441 • 50,889
Plymouth, NH 03264 • 3,967
Plymouth, NC 27962 • 4,328
Plymouth, OH 44865 • 1,942
Plymouth, PA 18651 • 7,134
Plymouth, WI 53073 • 6,769
Plymouth □, IA • 23,388
Plymouth □, MA • 435,276
Plymouth Township, PA 19401 • 17,168
Poca, WV 25159 • 1,124
Pocahontas, AR 72455 • 6,151
Pocahontas, IA 50574 • 2,085
Pocahontas □, IA • 9,525
Pocahontas □, WV • 9,008
Pocasset, MA 02559 • 2,200
Pocatalico, WV 25320 • 2,450
Pocatello, ID 83201–06 • 46,080
Pocola, OK 74902 • 3,664
Pocomoke City, MD 21851 • 3,922
Poinsett □, AR • 24,664
Point Clear, AL 36564 • 2,125
Pointe Coupee □, LA • 22,540
Point Hope, AK 99766 • 639
Point Marion, PA 15474 • 1,344
Point Pleasant, NJ 08742 • 18,177
Point Pleasant, WV 25550 • 4,996
Point Pleasant Beach, NJ 08742 • 5,112
Poipu, HI 96756 • 975
Polk, PA 16342 • 1,267
Polk □, AR • 17,347
Polk □, FL • 405,382
Polk □, GA • 33,815
Polk □, IA • 327,140
Polk □, MN • 32,498
Polk □, MO • 21,826
Polk □, NE • 5,675
Polk □, NC • 14,416
Polk □, OR • 49,541
Polk □, TN • 13,643
Polk □, TX • 30,687
Polk □, WI • 34,773
Polk City, FL 33868 • 1,439
Polk City, IA 50226 • 1,908
Polo, IL 61064 • 2,514
Polson, MT 59860 • 3,283
Pomeroy, OH 45769 • 2,259
Pomeroy, WA 99347 • 1,393
Pomona, CA 91765–69 • 131,723
Pomona, NJ 08240 • 2,624
Pompano Beach, FL 33060–69 • 72,411
Pompano Beach Highlands, FL 33060 • 17,915
Pompton Lakes, NJ 07442 • 10,539
Ponca City, OK 74601–04 • 26,359
Ponchatoula, LA 70454 • 5,425
Pondera □, MT • 6,433
Ponte Vedra Beach, FL 32082 • 1,700
Pontiac, IL 61764 • 11,428
Pontiac, MI 48340–43 • 71,166
Pontotoc, MS 38863 • 4,570
Pontotoc □, MS • 22,237

United States Populations and ZIP Codes

Pontotoc □, OK • 34,119
Pooler, GA 31322 • 4,453
Poolesville, MD 20837 • 3,796
Pope □, AR • 45,883
Pope □, IL • 4,373
Pope □, MN • 10,745
Poplar, MT 59255 • 881
Poplar Bluff, MO 63901 • 16,996
Poplarville, MS 39470 • 2,561
Poquonock Bridge, CT 06340 • 2,770
Poquoson, VA 23662 • 11,005
Portage, IN 46368 • 29,060
Portage, MI 49081 • 41,042
Portage, PA 15946 • 3,105
Portage, WI 53901 • 8,640
Portage □, OH • 142,585
Portage □, WI • 61,405
Portage Lakes, OH 44319 • 13,373
Portageville, MO 63873 • 3,401
Portales, NM 88130 • 10,690
Port Allegany, PA 16743 • 2,391
Port Allen, LA 70767 • 6,277
Port Angeles, WA 98362 • 17,710
Port Aransas, TX 78373 • 2,233
Port Arthur, TX 77640–43 • 58,724
Port Barre, LA 70577 • 2,144
Port Bolivar, TX 77650 • 1,600
Port Byron, IL 61275 • 1,002
Port Byron, NY 13140 • 1,359
Port Carbon, PA 17965 • 2,134
Port Charlotte, FL 33952 • 41,535
Port Chester, NY 10573 • 24,728
Port Clinton, OH 43452 • 7,106
Port Dickinson, NY 13901 • 1,785
Port Edwards, WI 54469 • 1,848
Porter, IN 46304 • 3,118
Porter, TX 77365 • 7,000
Porter □, IN • 128,932
Porterdale, GA 30270 • 1,278
Porterville, CA 93257–58 • 29,563
Port Ewen, NY 12466 • 3,444
Port Gibson, MS 39150 • 1,810
Port Henry, NY 12974 • 1,263
Port Hueneme, CA 93041–44 • 20,319
Port Huron, MI 48060–61 • 33,694
Port Isabel, TX 78578 • 4,467
Port Jefferson, NY 11777 • 7,455
Port Jefferson Station, NY 11776 • 7,232
Port Jervis, NY 12771 • 9,060
Portland, CT 06480 • 5,645
Portland, IN 47371 • 6,483
Portland, ME 04101–12 • 64,358
Portland, MI 48875 • 3,889
Portland, OR 97201–99 • 437,319
Portland, TN 37148 • 5,165
Portland, TX 78374 • 12,224
Port Lavaca, TX 77979 • 10,886
Port Monmouth, NJ 07758 • 3,800
Port Neches, TX 77651 • 12,974
Port Norris, NJ 08349 • 1,701
Port O'Connor, TX 77982 • 1,031
Portola, CA 96122 • 2,193
Port Orange, FL 32127 • 35,317
Port Orchard, WA 98366 • 4,984
Port Orford, OR 97465 • 1,025
Port Penn, DE 19731 • 300
Port Richey, FL 34667–74 • 2,523
Port Royal, SC 29935 • 2,985
Port Saint Joe, FL 32456 • 4,044
Port Saint Lucie, FL 34952 • 55,866
Port Salerno, FL 34992 • 7,786
Portsmouth, NH 03801–02 • 25,925
Portsmouth, OH 45662 • 22,676
Portsmouth, RI 02871 • 3,540
Portsmouth, VA 23701–09 • 103,907
Port St. John, FL 32922 • 8,933
Port Sulphur, LA 70083 • 3,523
Port Townsend, WA 98368 • 7,001
Portville, NY 14770 • 1,040
Port Vue, PA 15133 • 4,641
Port Washington, NY 11050 • 15,387
Port Washington, WI 53074 • 9,338
Port Wentworth, GA 31407 • 4,012
Posen, IL 60469 • 4,226
Posey □, IN • 25,968
Poseyville, IN 47633 • 1,089
Post, TX 79356 • 3,768
Post Falls, ID 83854 • 7,349
Postville, IA 52162 • 1,472
Poteau, OK 74953 • 7,210
Poteet, TX 78065 • 3,206
Poth, TX 78147 • 1,642
Potlatch, ID 83855 • 790
Potomac, MD 20851 • 45,634
Potomac Heights, MD 20640 • 1,524
Potomac Park, MD 21502 • 1,800
Potosi, MO 63664 • 2,683
Potsdam, NY 13676 • 10,251
Pottawatomie □, KS • 16,128
Pottawatomie □, OK • 58,760
Pottawattamie □, IA • 82,628
Potter □, PA • 16,717
Potter □, SD • 3,190
Potter □, TX • 97,874
Potter Valley, CA 95469 • 1,500
Pottstown, PA 19464 • 21,831
Pottsville, PA 17901 • 16,603
Poughkeepsie, NY 12601–03 • 28,844
Poulsbo, WA 98370 • 4,848
Poultney, VT 05764 • 1,731
Poway, CA 92064 • 43,516
Powder River □, MT • 2,090
Powder Springs, GA 30073 • 6,893
Powell, OH 43065 • 2,154
Powell, TN 37849 • 7,534
Powell, WY 82435 • 5,292
Powell □, KY • 11,686
Powell □, MT • 6,620
Powellhurst, OR 97236 • 28,756
Powellton, WV 25161 • 1,905
Power □, ID • 7,086
Poweshiek □, IA • 19,033
Powhatan □, VA • 15,328
Powhatan Point, OH 43942 • 1,807
Poydras, LA 70085 • 4,029
Poynette, WI 53955 • 1,662
Prague, OK 74864 • 2,308
Prairie □, AR • 9,518
Prairie □, MT • 1,383
Prairie City, IA 50228 • 1,360
Prairie City, OR 97869 • 1,117
Prairie du Chien, WI 53821 • 5,659
Prairie du Sac, WI 53578 • 2,380
Prairie Grove, AR 72753 • 1,761
Prairie View, TX 77446 • 4,004
Prairie Village, KS 66208 • 23,186
Pratt, KS 67124 • 6,687
Pratt □, KS • 9,702
Prattville, AL 36066–67 • 19,587
Preble □, OH • 40,113
Premont, TX 78375 • 2,914
Prentiss, MS 39474 • 1,487
Prentiss □, MS • 23,278
Prescott, AZ 86301–14 • 26,455
Prescott, AR 71857 • 3,673
Prescott, WI 54021 • 3,243
Presho, SD 57568 • 654
Presidio, TX 79845 • 3,072
Presidio □, TX • 6,637
Presque Isle, ME 04769 • 10,550
Presque Isle □, MI • 13,743
Preston, ID 83263 • 3,710
Preston, IA 52069 • 1,025
Preston, MN 55965 • 1,530
Preston □, WV • 29,037
Prestonsburg, KY 41653 • 3,558
Price, UT 84501 • 8,712
Price □, WI • 15,600
Prichard, AL 36610 • 34,311
Priest River, ID 83856 • 1,560
Primrose, RI 02895 • 500
Prince Edward □, VA • 17,320
Prince Frederick, MD 20678 • 1,885
Prince George □, VA • 27,394
Prince Georges □, MD • 729,268
Princes Lakes, IN 46164 • 1,055
Princess Anne, MD 21853 • 1,666
Princeton, FL 33032 • 7,073
Princeton, IL 61356 • 7,197
Princeton, IN 47670 • 8,127
Princeton, KY 42445 • 6,940
Princeton, MN 55371 • 3,719
Princeton, MO 64673 • 1,021
Princeton, NJ 08540–43 • 12,016
Princeton, NC 27569 • 1,181
Princeton, WV 24740 • 7,043
Princeton, WI 54968 • 1,458
Princeton Junction, NJ 08550 • 2,362
Princeville, IL 61559 • 1,421
Princeville, NC 27886 • 1,652
Prince William □, VA • 215,686
Prineville, OR 97754 • 5,355
Prior Lake, MN 55372 • 11,482
Proctor, MN 55810 • 2,974
Proctor, VT 05765 • 1,979
Proctorsville, VT 05153 • 480
Prophetstown, IL 61277 • 1,749
Prospect, CT 06712 • 6,807
Prospect, KY 40059 • 2,788
Prospect, OH 43342 • 1,148
Prospect, OR 97536 • 1,200
Prospect, PA 16052 • 1,122
Prospect Heights, IL 60070 • 15,239
Prospect Park, NJ 07508 • 5,053
Prospect Park, PA 19076 • 6,764
Prosperity, SC 29127 • 1,116
Prosperity, WV 25909 • 1,322
Prosser, WA 99350 • 4,476
Providence, KY 42450 • 4,123
Providence, RI 02901–40 • 160,728
Providence, UT 84332 • 3,344
Providence □, RI • 596,270
Provincetown, MA 02657 • 3,374
Provo, UT 84601–06 • 86,835
Prowers □, CO • 13,347
Prudenville, MI 48651 • 1,100
Prudhoe Bay, AK 99734 • 47
Pryor, OK 74361–62 • 8,327
Pueblo, CO 81001–19 • 98,640
Pueblo □, CO • 123,051
Puhi, HI 96766 • 1,210
Pukalani, HI 96788 • 5,879
Pulaski, NY 13142 • 2,525
Pulaski, TN 38478 • 7,895
Pulaski, VA 24301 • 9,985
Pulaski, WI 54162 • 2,200
Pulaski □, AR • 349,660
Pulaski □, GA • 8,108
Pulaski □, IL • 7,523
Pulaski □, IN • 12,643
Pulaski □, KY • 49,489
Pulaski □, MO • 41,307
Pulaski □, VA • 34,496
Pullman, WA 99163–65 • 23,478
Pumphrey, MD 21227 • 5,483
Punta Gorda, FL 33948–55 • 10,747
Punxsutawney, PA 15767 • 6,782
Purcell, OK 73080 • 4,784
Purcellville, VA 22132 • 1,744
Purvis, MS 39475 • 2,140
Pushmataha □, OK • 10,997
Putnam, CT 06260 • 6,835
Putnam □, FL • 65,070
Putnam □, GA • 14,137
Putnam □, IL • 5,730
Putnam □, IN • 30,315
Putnam □, MO • 5,079
Putnam □, NY • 83,941
Putnam □, OH • 33,819
Putnam □, TN • 51,373
Putnam □, WV • 42,835
Putney, VT 05346 • 1,100
Puyallup, WA 98371–74 • 23,875

Q

Quail Oaks, VA 23234 • 1,500
Quaker Hill, CT 06375 • 2,052
Quakertown, PA 18951 • 8,982
Quanah, TX 79252 • 3,413
Quarryville, PA 17566 • 1,642
Quartz Hill, CA 93536 • 9,626
Quartzsite, AZ 85346 • 1,876
Quay □, NM • 10,823
Quechee, VT 05059 • 550
Queen Annes □, MD • 33,953
Queen City, TX 75572 • 1,748
Queen Creek, AZ 85242 • 2,667
Queens □, NY • 1,951,598
Queensborough, WA 98021 • 4,850
Questa, NM 87556 • 1,707
Quidnessett, RI 02852 • 3,300
Quidnick, RI 02816 • 2,300
Quilcene, WA 98376 • 1,200
Quincy, CA 95971 • 2,700
Quincy, FL 32351 • 7,444
Quincy, IL 62301–06 • 39,681
Quincy, MA 02169 • 84,985
Quincy, MI 49082 • 1,680
Quincy, WA 98848 • 3,738
Quinebaug, CT 06262 • 1,031
Quinhagak, AK 99655 • 501
Quinlan, TX 75474 • 1,360
Quinton, OK 74561 • 1,133
Quitman, GA 31643 • 5,292
Quitman, MS 39355 • 2,736
Quitman, TX 75783 • 1,684
Quitman □, GA • 2,209
Quitman □, MS • 10,490
Quonochontaug, RI 02813 • 1,500

R

Rabun □, GA • 11,648
Raceland, KY 41169 • 2,256
Raceland, LA 70394 • 5,564
Racine, WI 53401–08 • 84,298
Racine □, WI • 175,034
Radcliff, KY 40159–60 • 19,772
Radford, VA 24141–43 • 15,940
Radnor Township, PA 19087 • 28,705
Raeford, NC 28376 • 3,469
Ragland, AL 35131 • 1,807
Rahway, NJ 07065–67 • 25,325
Rainbow City, AL 35901 • 7,673
Rainelle, WV 25962 • 1,681
Rainier, OR 97048 • 1,674
Rains □, TX • 6,715
Rainsville, AL 35986 • 3,875
Raleigh, MS 39153 • 1,291
Raleigh, NC 27601–61 • 207,951
Raleigh □, WV • 76,819
Raleigh Hills, OR 97225 • 6,066
Ralls, TX 79357 • 2,172
Ralls □, MO • 8,476
Ralston, NE 68127 • 6,236
Rambleton Acres, DE 19720 • 1,700
Ramblewood, NJ 08054 • 6,181
Ramona, CA 92065 • 13,040
Ramsay, MI 49959 • 1,075
Ramseur, NC 27316 • 1,186
Ramsey, MN 55303 • 12,408
Ramsey, NJ 07446 • 13,228
Ramsey □, MN • 485,765
Ramsey □, ND • 12,681
Ranchester, WY 82839 • 676
Rancho Cordova, CA 95670 • 48,731
Rancho Mirage, CA 92270 • 9,778
Rancho Palos Verdes, CA 90274 • 41,659
Rancho Rinconado, CA 95014 • 4,206
Ranchos de Taos, NM 87557 • 1,779
Rancocas Woods, NJ 08060 • 1,250
Rand, WV 25306 • 2,400
Randall □, TX • 89,673
Randallstown, MD 21133 • 26,277
Randleman, NC 27317 • 2,612
Randolph, ME 04345 • 1,949
Randolph, MA 02368 • 30,093
Randolph, NY 14772 • 1,298
Randolph, VT 05060 • 2,200
Randolph, WI 53956 • 1,729
Randolph □, AL • 19,881
Randolph □, AR • 16,558
Randolph □, GA • 8,023
Randolph □, IL • 34,583
Randolph □, IN • 27,148
Randolph □, MO • 24,370
Randolph □, NC • 106,546
Randolph □, WV • 27,803
Randolph Hills, MD 20852 • 4,180
Random Lake, WI 53075 • 1,439
Rangely, CO 81648 • 2,278
Ranger, TX 76470 • 2,803
Rankin, PA 15104 • 2,503
Rankin, TX 79778 • 1,011
Rankin □, MS • 87,161
Ransom □, ND • 5,921
Ransomville, NY 14131 • 1,542
Ranson, WV 25438 • 2,890
Rantoul, IL 61866 • 17,212
Raoul, GA 30510 • 1,400
Rapid City, SD 57701–09 • 54,523
Rapides □, LA • 131,556
Rapid Valley, SD 57701 • 5,968
Rappahannock □, VA • 6,622
Raritan, NJ 08869 • 5,798
Rathdrum, ID 83858 • 2,000
Raton, NM 87740 • 7,372
Ravalli □, MT • 25,010
Raven, VA 24639 • 2,640
Ravena, NY 12143 • 3,547
Ravenel, SC 29470 • 2,165
Ravenna, NE 68869 • 1,317
Ravenna, OH 44266 • 12,069
Ravenswood, WV 26164 • 4,189
Rawlins, WY 82301 • 9,380
Rawlins □, KS • 3,404
Ray, ND 58849 • 603
Ray □, MO • 21,971
Raymond, MS 39154 • 2,275
Raymond, NH 03077 • 2,516
Raymond, WA 98577 • 2,901
Raymondville, TX 78580 • 8,880
Raymore, MO 64083 • 5,592
Rayne, LA 70578 • 8,502
Raynham, MA 02767 • 3,709
Raynham Center, MA 02768 • 3,709
Raytown, MO 64133 • 30,601
Rayville, LA 71269 • 4,411
Reading, MA 01867 • 22,539
Reading, MI 49274 • 1,127
Reading, OH 45215 • 12,038
Reading, PA 19601–12 • 78,380
Reagan □, TX • 4,514
Real □, TX • 2,412
Reamstown, PA 17567 • 2,649
Rector, AR 72461 • 2,268
Red Bank, NJ 07701–04 • 10,636
Red Bank, SC 29073 • 6,112
Red Bank, TN 37415 • 12,322
Red Bay, AL 35582 • 3,451
Redbird, OH 44057 • 1,600
Red Bluff, CA 96080 • 12,363
Red Bud, IL 62278 • 2,918
Red Cloud, NE 68970 • 1,204
Redding, CA 96001–03 • 66,462
Redding, CT 06875 • 1,000
Redfield, AR 72132 • 1,082
Redfield, SD 57469 • 2,770
Redford, MI 48239 • 54,387
Redgranite, WI 54970 • 1,009
Red Hook, NY 12571 • 1,794
Redkey, IN 47373 • 1,383
Red Lake □, MN • 4,525
Red Lake Falls, MN 56750 • 1,481
Redlands, CA 92373–75 • 60,394
Red Lion, PA 17356 • 6,130
Red Lodge, MT 59068 • 1,958
Redmond, OR 97756 • 7,163
Redmond, WA 98052–53 • 35,800
Red Oak, GA 30272 • 2,800
Red Oak, IA 51566 • 6,264
Red Oak, TX 75154 • 3,124
Red Oaks, LA 70815 • 1,600
Red Oaks Mill, NY 12603 • 4,906
Redondo Beach, CA 90277–78 • 60,167
Red River □, LA • 9,387
Red River □, TX • 14,317
Red Springs, NC 28377 • 3,799
Red Willow □, NE • 11,705
Red Wing, MN 55066 • 15,134
Redwood, UT 84119 • 1,850
Redwood □, MN • 17,254
Redwood City, CA 94061–65 • 66,072
Redwood Falls, MN 56283 • 4,859
Redwood Valley, CA 95470 • 1,300
Reed City, MI 49677 • 2,379
Reedley, CA 93654 • 15,791
Reedsburg, WI 53959 • 5,834
Reedsport, OR 97467 • 4,796
Reedsville, PA 17084 • 1,030
Reedsville, WI 54230 • 1,182
Reedurban, OH 44710 • 6,650
Reese, MI 48757 • 1,414
Reeves □, TX • 15,852
Reform, AL 35481 • 2,105
Refugio, TX 78377 • 3,158
Refugio □, TX • 7,976
Rehoboth Beach, DE 19971 • 1,234
Reidland, KY 42001 • 4,054
Reidsville, GA 30453 • 2,469
Reidsville, NC 27320–23 • 12,183
Reinbeck, IA 50669 • 1,605
Reisterstown, MD 21136 • 19,314
Reliance, WY 82943 • 500
Remington, IN 47977 • 1,247
Remsen, IA 51050 • 1,513
Reno, NV 89501–70 • 133,850
Reno □, KS • 62,389
Renovo, PA 17764 • 1,526
Rensselaer, IN 47978 • 5,045
Rensselaer, NY 12144 • 8,255
Rensselaer □, NY • 154,429
Renton, WA 98055–59 • 41,688
Renville, MN 56284 • 1,315
Renville □, MN • 17,673
Renville □, ND • 3,160
Republic, MI 49879 • 1,100
Republic, MO 65738 • 6,292
Republic, PA 15475 • 1,400
Republic □, KS • 6,482
Reserve, LA 70084 • 8,847
Reston, VA 22090 • 48,556
Revere, MA 02151 • 42,786
Rexburg, ID 83440 • 14,302
Reynolds, GA 31076 • 1,166
Reynolds □, MO • 6,661
Reynoldsburg, OH 43068 • 25,748
Reynoldsville, PA 15851 • 2,818
Rhea □, TN • 24,344
Rhinebeck, NY 12572 • 2,725
Rhinelander, WI 54501 • 7,427
Rialto, CA 92376–77 • 72,388
Rice □, KS • 10,610
Rice □, MN • 49,183
Rice Lake, WI 54868 • 7,998
Rich □, UT • 1,725
Richardson, TX 75080–83 • 74,840
Richardson □, NE • 9,937
Richardson Park, DE 19804 • 1,100
Richardton, ND 58652 • 625
Richboro, PA 18954 • 5,332
Richfield, MN 55423 • 35,710
Richfield, UT 84701 • 5,593
Richfield Springs, NY 13439 • 1,565
Richford, VT 05476 • 1,425
Rich Hill, MO 64779 • 1,317
Richland, GA 31825 • 1,668
Richland, MO 65556 • 2,029
Richland, WA 99352 • 32,315
Richland □, IL • 16,545
Richland □, LA • 20,629
Richland □, MT • 10,716
Richland □, ND • 18,148
Richland □, OH • 126,137
Richland □, SC • 285,720
Richland □, WI • 17,521
Richland Center, WI 53581 • 5,018
Richland Hills, TX 76118 • 7,978
Richlands, VA 24641 • 4,456
Richlandtown, PA 18955 • 1,195
Richmond, CA 94801–08 • 87,425
Richmond, IL 60071 • 1,016
Richmond, IN 47374–75 • 38,705
Richmond, KY 40475–76 • 21,155
Richmond, ME 04357 • 1,775
Richmond, MI 48062 • 4,141
Richmond, MO 64085 • 5,738
Richmond, TX 77469 • 9,801
Richmond, UT 84333 • 1,955
Richmond, VT 05477 • 650
Richmond, VA 23201–94 • 203,056
Richmond □, GA • 189,719
Richmond □, NY • 378,977
Richmond □, NC • 44,518
Richmond □, VA • 7,273
Richmond Beach, WA 98160 • 5,000
Richmond Heights, FL 33156 • 8,583
Richmond Heights, MO 63117 • 10,448
Richmond Heights, OH 44143 • 9,611
Richmond Highlands, WA 98133 • 26,037
Richmond Hill, GA 31324 • 2,934
Rich Square, NC 27869 • 1,058
Richton, MS 39476 • 1,034
Richton Park, IL 60471 • 10,523
Richwood, OH 43344 • 2,186
Richwood, WV 26261 • 2,808
Riddle, OR 97469 • 1,143
Ridge, NY 11961 • 11,734
Ridgecrest, CA 93555 • 27,725
Ridgecrest, WA 98155 • 5,500
Ridgefield, CT 06877 • 6,363
Ridgefield, NJ 07657 • 9,996
Ridgefield, WA 98642 • 1,297
Ridgefield Park, NJ 07660 • 12,454
Ridgeland, MS 39157–58 • 11,714
Ridgeland, SC 29936 • 1,071
Ridgely, MD 21660 • 1,034
Ridgely, TN 38080 • 1,775
Ridgetop, TN 37152 • 1,132
Ridgeville, SC 29472 • 1,625
Ridgewood, NJ 07450–52 • 24,152
Ridgway, IL 62979 • 1,103
Ridgway, PA 15853 • 4,793
Ridley Park, PA 19078 • 7,592
Ridley Township, PA 19018 • 33,771
Rifle, CO 81650 • 4,636
Rigby, ID 83442 • 2,681
Riley □, KS • 67,139
Rimersburg, PA 16248 • 1,053
Rincon, GA 31326 • 2,697
Ringgold, GA 30736 • 1,675
Ringgold, LA 71068 • 1,856
Ringgold □, IA • 5,420
Ringling, OK 73456 • 1,250
Ringwood, NJ 07456 • 12,623
Rio, FL 34957 • 1,054
Rio Arriba □, NM • 34,365
Rio Blanco □, CO • 5,972
Rio Dell, CA 95562 • 3,012
Rio Del Mar, CA 95003 • 8,919
Rio Grande, NJ 08242 • 2,505
Rio Grande □, CO • 10,770
Rio Grande City, TX 78582 • 9,891
Rio Hondo, TX 78583 • 1,793
Rio Linda, CA 95673 • 9,481
Rio Rancho, NM 87124 • 32,505
Rio Vista, CA 94571 • 3,316
Ripley, MS 38663 • 5,371
Ripley, NY 14775 • 1,189
Ripley, OH 45167 • 1,816
Ripley, TN 38063 • 6,188
Ripley, WV 25271 • 3,023
Ripley □, IN • 24,616
Ripley □, MO • 12,303
Ripon, WI 54971 • 7,241
Rising Sun, DE 19934 • 540
Rising Sun, IN 47040 • 2,311
Rising Sun, MD 21911 • 1,263
Rison, AR 71665 • 1,258
Ritchie □, WV • 10,233
Rittman, OH 44270 • 6,147
Ritzville, WA 99169 • 1,725
Riverbank, CA 95367 • 8,547
Riverdale, CA 93656 • 1,980
Riverdale, GA 30274 • 9,359
Riverdale, IL 60627 • 13,671
Riverdale, MD 20737–38 • 5,185
Riverdale, NJ 07457 • 2,370
Riverdale, UT 84405 • 6,419
River Edge, NJ 07661 • 10,603
River Falls, WI 54022 • 10,610
River Forest, IL 60305 • 11,669
River Grove, IL 60171 • 9,961
Riverhead, NY 11901 • 8,814
River Heights, UT 84321 • 1,274
River Hills, WI 53217 • 1,612
River Oaks, TX 76114 • 6,580
River Pines, MA 01821 • 3,620
River Ridge, LA 70123 • 14,800
River Road, OR 97404 • 9,443
River Rouge, MI 48218 • 11,314
Riverside, AL 35135 • 1,004
Riverside, CA 92501–19 • 226,505
Riverside, IL 60546 • 8,774
Riverside, NJ 08075 • 7,974
Riverside, PA 17868 • 1,991
Riverside □, CA • 1,170,413
Riverton, IL 62561 • 2,638
Riverton, NJ 08077 • 2,775
Riverton, UT 84065 • 11,261
Riverton, VT 05663 • 150
Riverton, WY 82501 • 9,202
Riverton Heights, WA 98188 • 14,182
River Vale, NJ 07675 • 9,410
Riverview, FL 33569 • 6,478
Riverview, MI 48192 • 13,894
Rivesville, WV 26588 • 1,064
Riviera Beach, FL 33404 • 27,639
Riviera Beach, MD 21122 • 11,376
Roane □, TN • 47,227
Roane □, WV • 15,120
Roan Mountain, TN 37687 • 1,220
Roanoke, AL 36274 • 6,362
Roanoke, IL 61561 • 1,910
Roanoke, IN 46783 • 1,018
Roanoke, TX 76262 • 1,616
Roanoke, VA 24001–38 • 96,397
Roanoke □, VA • 79,332
Roanoke Rapids, NC 27870 • 15,722
Roaring Spring, PA 16673 • 2,615
Robbins, IL 60472 • 7,498
Robbinsdale, MN 55422 • 14,396
Robersonville, NC 27871 • 1,940
Robert Lee, TX 76945 • 1,276
Roberts, WI 54023 • 1,043
Roberts □, SD • 9,914
Roberts □, TX • 1,025
Robertsdale, AL 36567 • 2,401
Robertson □, KY • 2,124
Robertson □, TN • 41,494
Robertson □, TX • 15,511
Robertsville, NJ 07746 • 9,841
Robeson □, NC • 105,179
Robinson, IL 62454 • 6,740
Robinson, TX 76706 • 7,111
Robstown, TX 78380 • 12,849
Rochdale, MA 01542 • 1,105
Rochelle, GA 31079 • 1,510
Rochelle, IL 61068 • 8,769
Rochelle Park, NJ 07662 • 5,587
Rochester, IL 62563 • 2,676
Rochester, IN 46975 • 5,969
Rochester, MI 48306–09 • 7,130
Rochester, MN 55901–06 • 70,745
Rochester, NH 03867–68 • 26,630
Rochester, NY 14601–92 • 231,636
Rochester, PA 15074 • 4,156
Rochester, VT 05767 • 500
Rochester, WA 98579 • 1,150
Rochester Hills, MI 48309 • 61,766
Rock □, MN • 9,806
Rock □, NE • 2,019
Rock □, WI • 139,510
Rockaway, NJ 07866 • 6,243

Rockbridge □, VA • 18,350
Rockcastle □, KY • 14,803
Rock Creek, MN 55067 • 1,040
Rock Creek 0M, OR • 8,282
Rockdale, IL 60436 • 1,709
Rockdale, MD 21207 • 5,885
Rockdale, TX 76567 • 5,235
Rockdale □, GA • 54,091
Rock Falls, IL 61071 • 9,654
Rockford, IL 61101–32 • 139,426
Rockford, MI 49341 • 3,750
Rockford, MN 55373 • 2,665
Rockford, OH 45882 • 1,119
Rock Hall, MD 21661 • 1,584
Rock Hill, MO 63124 • 5,217
Rock Hill, SC 29730–32 • 41,643
Rockingham, NC 28379 • 9,399
Rockingham □, NH • 245,845
Rockingham □, NC • 86,064
Rockingham □, VA • 57,482
Rock Island, IL 61201–04 • 40,552
Rock Island □, IL • 148,723
Rockland, ME 04841 • 7,972
Rockland, MA 02370 • 15,695
Rockland □, NY • 265,475
Rockledge, FL 32955–56 • 16,023
Rockledge, PA 19111 • 2,679
Rocklin, CA 95677 • 19,033
Rockmart, GA 30153 • 3,356
Rockport, IN 47635 • 2,315
Rockport, ME 04856 • 1,100
Rockport, MA 01966 • 4,690
Rock Port, MO 64482 • 1,438
Rockport, TX 78382 • 4,753
Rock Rapids, IA 51246 • 2,601
Rock River, WY 82083 • 190
Rocksprings, TX 78880 • 1,339
Rock Springs, WY 82901–02 • 19,050
Rockton, IL 61072 • 2,928
Rock Valley, IA 51247 • 2,540
Rockville, IN 47872 • 2,706
Rockville, MD 20847–59 • 44,835
Rockville Centre, NY 11570–71 • 24,727
Rockwall, TX 75087 • 10,486
Rockwall □, TX • 25,604
Rockwell, IA 50469 • 1,008
Rockwell, NC 28138 • 1,598
Rockwell City, IA 50579 • 1,981
Rockwell Park, NC 28213 • 2,600
Rockwood, MI 48173 • 3,141
Rockwood, OR 97233 • 11,000
Rockwood, PA 15557 • 1,014
Rockwood, TN 37854 • 5,348
Rocky Creek, FL 33615 • 7,800
Rocky Ford, CO 81067 • 4,162
Rocky Hill, CT 06067 • 14,559
Rocky Mount, NC 27801–04 • 48,997
Rocky Mount, VA 24151 • 4,098
Rocky Point, NY 11778 • 8,596
Rocky River, OH 44116 • 20,410
Rodeo, CA 94572 • 7,589
Roderfield, WV 24881 • 1,200
Rodney Village, DE 19901 • 1,745
Roebling, NJ 08554 • 2,415
Roebuck, SC 29376 • 1,966
Roeland Park, KS 66203 • 7,706
Roessleville, NY 12205 • 10,753
Roger Mills □, OK • 4,147
Rogers, AR 72756–57 • 24,692
Rogers, TX 76569 • 1,131
Rogers □, OK • 55,170
Rogers City, MI 49779 • 3,642
Rogersville, AL 35652 • 1,125
Rogersville, TN 37857 • 4,149
Rogue River, OR 97537 • 1,759
Rohnert Park, CA 94927–28 • 36,326
Roland, IA 50236 • 1,035
Roland, OK 74954 • 2,481
Rolette □, ND • 12,772
Rolla, MO 65401 • 14,090
Rolla, ND 58367 • 1,286
Rolling Fork, MS 39159 • 2,444
Rolling Hills Estates, CA 90274 • 7,789
Rolling Meadows, IL 60008 • 22,591
Rollinsford, NH 03869 • 2,645
Roma, TX 78584 • 8,059
Rome, GA 30161–65 • 30,326
Rome, IL 61562 • 1,902
Rome, NY 13440 • 44,350
Rome City, IN 46784 • 1,138
Romeo, MI 48065 • 3,520
Romeoville, IL 60441 • 14,074
Romney, WV 26757 • 1,966
Romulus, MI 48174 • 22,897
Ronan, MT 59864 • 1,547
Ronceverte, WV 24970 • 1,754
Ronkonkoma, NY 11779 • 20,391
Roodhouse, IL 62082 • 2,139
Rooks □, KS • 6,039
Roosevelt, NY 11575 • 15,030
Roosevelt, UT 84066 • 3,915
Roosevelt □, MT • 10,999
Roosevelt □, NM • 16,702
Roosevelt Park, MI 49441 • 3,885
Rosamond, CA 93560 • 7,430
Roscoe, IL 61073 • 2,079
Roscoe, TX 79545 • 1,446
Roscommon □, MI • 19,776
Roseau, MN 56751 • 2,396
Roseau □, MN • 15,026
Roseboro, NC 28382 • 1,441
Rosebud, TX 76570 • 1,638
Rosebud □, MT • 10,505
Roseburg, OR 97470 • 17,032
Rosedale, MD 21237 • 18,703
Rosedale, MS 38769 • 2,595
Rose Hill, KS 67133 • 2,399
Rose Hill, NC 28458 • 1,287
Rose Hill, VA 22310 • 12,675
Roseland, CA 95407 • 8,779
Roseland, FL 32957 • 1,379
Roseland, LA 70456 • 1,093
Roseland, NJ 07068 • 4,847
Roseland, OH 44906 • 3,000
Roselle, IL 60172 • 20,819
Roselle, NJ 07203 • 20,314
Roselle Park, NJ 07204 • 12,805
Rosemead, CA 91770 • 51,638
Rosemont, CA 95826 • 22,851
Rosemount, MN 55068 • 8,622
Rosenberg, TX 77471 • 20,183
Rosepine, LA 70659 • 1,135
Roseto, PA 18013 • 1,555

Roseville, CA 95678 • 44,685
Roseville, IL 61473 • 1,151
Roseville, MI 48066 • 51,412
Roseville, MN 55113 • 33,485
Roseville, OH 43777 • 1,847
Rosewood Heights, IL 62024 • 4,821
Rosiclare, IL 62982 • 1,378
Roslyn Heights, NY 11577 • 6,405
Ross, OH 45061 • 2,124
Ross □, OH • 69,330
Rossford, OH 43460 • 5,861
Rossmoor, CA 90720 • 9,893
Ross Township, PA 15237 • 33,482
Rossville, GA 30741–42 • 3,601
Rossville, IL 60963 • 1,334
Rossville, IN 46065 • 1,175
Rossville, KS 66533 • 1,052
Roswell, GA 30075–77 • 47,923
Roswell, NM 88201–02 • 44,654
Rotan, TX 79546 • 1,913
Rothschild, WI 54474 • 3,310
Rothsville, PA 17543 • 2,097
Rotterdam, NY 12303 • 21,228
Roulette, PA 16746 • 1,500
Round Lake, IL 60073 • 3,550
Round Lake Beach, IL 60073 • 16,434
Round Mountain, NV 89045 • 210
Round Rock, TX 78664 • 30,923
Roundup, MT 59072 • 1,808
Rouses Point, NY 12979 • 2,377
Routt □, CO • 14,088
Rouzerville, PA 17250 • 1,188
Rowan □, KY • 20,353
Rowan □, NC • 110,605
Rowland, NC 28383 • 1,139
Rowland Heights, CA 91748 • 32,700
Rowlett, TX 75088 • 23,260
Rowley, MA 01969 • 1,144
Roxboro, NC 27573 • 7,332
Roy, UT 84067 • 24,603
Royal Oak, MI 48067–73 • 65,410
Royal Pines, NC 28704 • 1,600
Royalton, IL 62983 • 1,191
Royersford, PA 19468 • 4,458
Royse City, TX 75089 • 2,206
Royston, GA 30662 • 2,758
Rubidoux, CA 92509 • 24,367
Rugby, ND 58368 • 2,909
Ruidoso, NM 88345 • 4,600
Ruidoso Downs, NM 88346 • 920
Ruleville, MS 38771 • 3,245
Rumford, ME 04276 • 5,419
Rumson, NJ 07760 • 6,701
Runge, TX 78151 • 1,139
Runnels □, TX • 11,294
Runnemede, NJ 08078 • 9,042
Rupert, ID 83350 • 5,455
Rupert, WV 25984 • 1,104
Rural Hall, NC 27045 • 1,652
Rush □, IN • 18,129
Rush □, KS • 3,842
Rush City, MN 55069 • 1,497
Rushford, MN 55971 • 1,485
Rushmere, VA 23430 • 1,064
Rush Springs, OK 73082 • 1,229
Rushville, IL 62681 • 3,229
Rushville, IN 46173 • 5,533
Rushville, NE 69360 • 1,127
Rusk, TX 75785 • 4,366
Rusk □, TX • 43,735
Rusk □, WI • 15,079
Ruskin, FL 33570–73 • 6,046
Russell, KS 67665 • 4,781
Russell, KY 41169 • 4,014
Russell, PA 16345 • 1,000
Russell □, AL • 46,860
Russell □, KS • 7,835
Russell □, KY • 14,716
Russell □, VA • 28,667
Russell Springs, KY 42642 • 2,363
Russellville, AL 35653 • 7,812
Russellville, AR 72801 • 21,260
Russellville, KY 42276 • 7,454
Russellville, OR 97216 • 6,500
Russellville, TN 37860 • 1,069
Ruston, LA 71270–73 • 20,027
Ruth, NV 89319 • 550
Rutherford, NJ 07070–75 • 17,790
Rutherford, TN 38369 • 1,303
Rutherford □, NC • 56,918
Rutherford □, TN • 118,570
Rutherfordton, NC 28139 • 3,617
Rutland, MA 01543 • 2,145
Rutland, VT 05701–02 • 18,230
Rutland □, VT • 62,142
Rye, NH 03870 • 835
Rye, NY 10580 • 14,936
Rye Brook, NY 10573 • 7,765

S

Sabattus, ME 04280 • 3,696
Sabetha, KS 66534 • 2,341
Sabina, OH 45169 • 2,662
Sabinal, TX 78881 • 1,584
Sabine □, LA • 22,646
Sabine □, TX • 9,586
Sac □, IA • 12,324
Sacaton, AZ 85221 • 1,452
Sac City, IA 50583 • 2,492
Sachse, TX 75040 • 5,346
Sackets Harbor, NY 13685 • 1,313
Saco, ME 04072 • 15,181
Sacramento, CA 95801–66 • 369,365
Sacramento □, CA • 1,041,219
Saddle Brook, NJ 07662 • 13,296
Saddle River, NJ 07458 • 2,950
Saegertown, PA 16433 • 1,066
Safety Harbor, FL 34695 • 15,124
Safford, AZ 85546 • 7,359
Sagadahoc □, ME • 33,535
Sagamore, MA 02561 • 2,589
Sagamore Hills, OH 44067 • 4,700
Sag Harbor, NY 11963 • 2,134
Saginaw, MI 48601–08 • 69,512
Saginaw, TX 76179 • 8,551
Saginaw □, MI • 211,946
Saguache □, CO • 4,619
Saint Albans, VT 05478 • 7,339
Saint Albans, WV 25177 • 11,194
Saint Andrews, SC 29407 • 9,908
Saint Andrews, SC 29210 • 25,692
Saint Ann, MO 63074 • 14,489

Saint Anne, IL 60964 • 1,153
Saint Ansgar, IA 50472 • 1,063
Saint Anthony, ID 83445 • 3,010
Saint Anthony, MN 55418 • 7,727
Saint Augustine, FL 32084–86 • 11,692
Saint Bernard, OH 45217 • 5,344
Saint Bernard □, LA • 66,631
Saint Charles, IL 60174–75 • 22,501
Saint Charles, MD 20601 • 28,717
Saint Charles, MI 48655 • 2,144
Saint Charles, MN 55972 • 2,642
Saint Charles, MO 63301–03 • 54,555
Saint Charles □, LA • 42,437
Saint Charles □, MO • 212,907
Saint Charles Mesa, CO 81006 • 7,050
Saint Clair, MI 48079 • 5,116
Saint Clair, MO 63077 • 3,917
Saint Clair, PA 17970 • 3,524
Saint Clair □, AL • 50,009
Saint Clair □, IL • 262,852
Saint Clair □, MI • 145,607
Saint Clair □, MO • 8,457
Saint Clair Shores, MI 48080–82 • 68,107
Saint Clairsville, OH 43950 • 5,162
Saint Cloud, FL 34769–73 • 12,453
Saint Cloud, MN 56301–04 • 48,812
Saint Croix □, WI • 50,251
Saint Croix Falls, WI 54024 • 1,640
Saint David, AZ 85630 • 1,500
Saint Elmo, IL 62458 • 1,473
Saint Francis, KS 67756 • 1,495
Saint Francis, MN 55070 • 2,538
Saint Francis, SD 57572 • 815
Saint Francis, WI 53207 • 9,245
Saint Francis □, AR • 28,497
Saint Francisville, LA 70775 • 1,700
Saint Francois □, MO • 48,904
Sainte Genevieve, MO 63670 • 4,411
Sainte Genevieve □, MO • 16,037
Saint George, SC 29477 • 2,077
Saint George, UT 84770–71 • 28,502
Saint Georges, DE 19733 • 500
Saint Helena, CA 94574 • 4,990
Saint Helena □, LA • 9,874
Saint Helens, OR 97051 • 7,535
Saint Henry, OH 45883 • 1,907
Saint Ignace, MI 49781 • 2,568
Saint Ignatius, MT 59865 • 778
Saint James, MN 56081 • 4,364
Saint James, MO 65559 • 3,256
Saint James, NY 11780 • 12,703
Saint James □, LA • 20,879
Saint James City, FL 33956 • 1,094
Saint Jo, TX 76265 • 1,048
Saint John, IN 46373 • 4,921
Saint John, KS 67576 • 1,357
Saint Johns, AZ 85936 • 3,294
Saint Johns, MI 48879 • 7,284
Saint Johns, MO 63114 • 7,466
Saint Johns □, FL • 83,829
Saint Johnsbury, VT 05819 • 6,424
Saint Johnsville, NY 13452 • 1,825
Saint John the Baptist □, LA • 39,996
Saint Joseph, IL 61873 • 2,052
Saint Joseph, LA 71366 • 1,517
Saint Joseph, MI 49085 • 9,214
Saint Joseph, MN 56374 • 3,294
Saint Joseph, MO 64501–08 • 71,852
Saint Joseph □, IN • 247,052
Saint Joseph □, MI • 58,913
Saint Landry □, LA • 80,331
Saint Lawrence □, NY • 111,974
Saint Leo, FL 33574 • 1,009
Saint Louis, MI 48880 • 3,828
Saint Louis, MO 63101–88 • 396,685
Saint Louis □, MN • 198,213
Saint Louis □, MO • 993,529
Saint Louis Park, MN 55426 • 43,787
Saint Lucie □, FL • 150,171
Saint Maries, ID 83861 • 2,442
Saint Martin □, LA • 43,978
Saint Martinville, LA 70582 • 7,137
Saint Mary □, LA • 58,086
Saint Marys, AK 99658 • 441
Saint Marys, GA 31558 • 8,187
Saint Marys, IN 46556 • 1,800
Saint Marys, KS 66536 • 1,791
Saint Marys, OH 45885 • 8,441
Saint Marys, PA 15857 • 5,511
Saint Marys, WV 26170 • 2,148
Saint Marys □, MD • 75,974
Saint Marys City, MD 20686 • 3,200
Saint Matthews, KY 40207 • 15,800
Saint Matthews, SC 29135 • 2,345
Saint Michael, MN 55376 • 2,506
Saint Michaels, MD 21663 • 1,301
Saint Paris, OH 43072 • 1,842
Saint Paul, AK 99660 • 763
Saint Paul, IN 47272 • 1,032
Saint Paul, MN 55101–89 • 272,235
Saint Paul, MO 63366 • 1,192
Saint Paul, NE 68873 • 2,009
Saint Paul, VA 24283 • 1,007
Saint Paul Park, MN 55071 • 4,965
Saint Pauls, NC 28384 • 1,992
Saint Peter, MN 56082 • 9,421
Saint Peters, MO 63376 • 45,779
Saint Petersburg, FL 33701–84 • 238,629
Saint Petersburg Beach, FL 33706 • 9,200
Saint Rose, LA 70087 • 2,800
Saint Simons Island, GA 31522 • 12,026
Saint Stephen, SC 29479 • 1,697
Saint Stephens, NC 28601 • 8,734
Saint Tammany □, LA • 144,508
Salamanca, NY 14779 • 6,566
Sale Creek, TN 37373 • 1,050
Salem, AR 72576 • 1,474
Salem, IL 62881 • 7,470
Salem, IN 47167 • 5,619
Salem, MA 01970–71 • 38,091
Salem, MO 65560 • 4,486
Salem, NH 03079 • 12,000
Salem, NJ 08079 • 6,883
Salem, OH 44460 • 12,233
Salem, OR 97301–14 • 107,786
Salem, SD 57058 • 1,289
Salem, UT 84653 • 2,284
Salem, VA 24153 • 23,756
Salem, WV 26426 • 2,063
Salem, WI 53168 • 1,020
Salem □, NJ • 65,294
Salida, CO 81201 • 4,737
Salina, KS 67401–02 • 42,303

Salina, OK 74365 • 1,153
Salina, UT 84654 • 1,943
Salinas, CA 93901–15 • 108,777
Saline, MI 48176 • 6,660
Saline □, AR • 64,183
Saline □, IL • 26,551
Saline □, KS • 49,301
Saline □, MO • 23,523
Saline □, NE • 12,715
Salineville, OH 43945 • 1,474
Salisbury, CT 06068 • 1,600
Salisbury, MD 21801–03 • 20,592
Salisbury, MA 01952 • 3,729
Salisbury, MO 65281 • 1,881
Salisbury, NC 28144–46 • 23,087
Sallisaw, OK 74955 • 7,122
Salmon, ID 83467 • 2,941
Salmon Creek, WA 98665 • 11,989
Saltillo, MS 38866 • 1,782
Salt Lake □, UT • 725,956
Salt Lake City, UT 84101–90 • 159,936
Salt Springs, FL 32113 • 1,500
Saltville, VA 24370 • 2,300
Saltwater, WA 98188 • 2,200
Saluda, SC 29138 • 2,798
Saluda □, SC • 16,357
Salyersville, KY 41465 • 1,917
Samoset, FL 34208 • 3,119
Sampson □, NC • 47,297
Samson, AL 36477 • 2,190
Samtown, LA 71301 • 3,500
San Andreas, CA 95249 • 2,115
San Angelo, TX 76901–06 • 84,474
San Anselmo, CA 94960 • 11,743
San Antonio, TX 78201–99 • 935,933
Sanatoga, PA 19464 • 5,534
San Augustine, TX 75972 • 2,337
San Augustine □, TX • 7,999
San Benito, TX 78586 • 20,125
San Benito □, CA • 36,697
San Bernardino, CA 92401–27 • 164,164
San Bernardino □, CA • 1,418,380
Sanborn, IA 51248 • 1,345
Sanborn □, SD • 2,833
San Bruno, CA 94066 • 38,961
San Carlos, AZ 85550 • 2,918
San Carlos, CA 94070 • 26,167
San Carlos Park, FL 33912 • 11,785
San Clemente, CA 92672–74 • 41,100
Sandalfoot Cove, FL 33433 • 14,214
Sanders □, MT • 8,669
Sanderson, TX 79848 • 1,128
Sandersville, GA 31082 • 6,290
Sand Hill, MA 02066 • 1,800
Sandia, NM 87047 • 6,742
San Diego, CA 92101–99 • 1,110,549
San Diego, TX 78384 • 4,983
San Diego □, CA • 2,498,016
San Dimas, CA 91773 • 32,397
Sandoval, IL 62882 • 1,535
Sandoval □, NM • 63,319
Sand Point, AK 99661 • 878
Sandpoint, ID 83862–65 • 5,203
Sand Springs, OK 74063 • 15,346
Sandston, VA 23150 • 3,630
Sandstone, MN 55072 • 2,057
Sandusky, MI 48471 • 2,403
Sandusky, OH 44870–71 • 29,764
Sandusky □, OH • 61,963
Sandwich, IL 60548 • 5,567
Sandwich, MA 02563 • 2,998
Sandy, OR 97055 • 4,152
Sandy, UT 84070 • 75,058
Sandy Hook, CT 06482 • 1,100
Sandy Springs, GA 30328 • 67,842
Sandy Springs, SC 29677 • 1,200
San Felipe Pueblo, NM 87001 • 1,557
San Fernando, CA 91340–46 • 22,580
Sanford, FL 32771–73 • 32,387
Sanford, ME 04073 • 10,296
Sanford, NC 27330–31 • 14,475
San Francisco, CA 94101–88 • 723,959
San Francisco □, CA • 723,959
Sangamon □, IL • 178,386
Sanger, CA 93657 • 16,839
Sanger, TX 76266 • 3,508
Sanibel, FL 33957 • 5,468
Sanilac □, MI • 39,928
San Jacinto, CA 92383 • 16,210
San Jacinto □, TX • 16,372
San Joaquin □, CA • 480,628
San Jose, CA 95101–96 • 782,248
San Juan, TX 78589 • 10,815
San Juan □, CO • 745
San Juan □, NM • 91,605
San Juan □, UT • 12,621
San Juan □, WA • 10,035
San Juan Capistrano, CA 92690–93 • 26,183
San Leandro, CA 94577–79 • 68,223
San Lorenzo, CA 94580 • 19,987
San Luis, AZ 85634 • 4,212
San Luis Obispo, CA 93401–12 • 41,958
San Luis Obispo □, CA • 217,162
San Manuel, AZ 85631 • 4,009
San Marcos, CA 92069 • 38,974
San Marcos, TX 78666–67 • 28,743
San Marino, CA 91108 • 12,959
San Mateo, CA 94401–04 • 85,486
San Mateo □, CA • 649,623
San Miguel □, CO • 3,653
San Miguel □, NM • 25,743
San Pablo, CA 94806 • 25,158
San Patricio □, TX • 58,749
Sanpete □, UT • 16,259
San Rafael, CA 94901–15 • 48,404
San Ramon, CA 94583 • 35,303
San Remo, NY 11754 • 7,770
San Saba, TX 76877 • 2,626
San Saba □, TX • 5,401
Sans Souci, SC 29609 • 7,612
Santa Ana, CA 92701–08 • 293,742
Santa Anna, TX 76878 • 1,249
Santa Barbara, CA 93101–90 • 85,571
Santa Barbara □, CA • 369,608
Santa Clara, CA 95050–56 • 93,613
Santa Clara, OR 97404 • 12,834
Santa Clara, UT 84765 • 2,322
Santa Clara □, CA • 1,497,577
Santa Cruz, CA 95060–67 • 49,040
Santa Cruz, NM 87567 • 975
Santa Cruz □, AZ • 29,676
Santa Cruz □, CA • 229,734

Santa Fe, NM 87501–06 • 55,859
Santa Fe, TX 77510 • 8,429
Santa Fe □, NM • 98,928
Santa Fe Springs, CA 90670–71 • 15,520
Santa Margarita, CA 93453 • 1,200
Santa Maria, CA 93454–56 • 61,284
Santa Monica, CA 90401–11 • 86,905
Santa Paula, CA 93060–61 • 25,062
Santaquin, UT 84655 • 2,386
Santa Rosa, CA 95401–09 • 113,313
Santa Rosa, NM 88435 • 2,263
Santa Rosa □, FL • 81,608
Santa Venetia, CA 94901 • 6,000
Santa Ynez, CA 93460 • 4,200
Santee, CA 92071 • 52,902
Santo Domingo Pueblo, NM 87052 • 2,866
San Ygnacio, TX 78067 • 1,000
Sappington, MO 63126 • 10,917
Sapulpa, OK 74066–67 • 18,074
Saraland, AL 36571 • 11,751
Saranac, MI 48881 • 1,461
Saranac Lake, NY 12983 • 5,377
Sarasota, FL 34230–43 • 50,961
Sarasota □, FL • 277,776
Sarasota Springs, FL 34232 • 16,088
Saratoga, CA 95070–71 • 28,061
Saratoga, TX 77585 • 1,200
Saratoga, WY 82331 • 1,969
Saratoga □, NY • 181,276
Saratoga Springs, NY 12866 • 25,001
Sarcoxie, MO 64862 • 1,330
Sardis, GA 30456 • 1,116
Sardis, MS 38666 • 2,128
Sargent □, ND • 4,549
Sarpy □, NE • 102,583
Sartell, MN 56377 • 5,393
Satanta, KS 67870 • 1,073
Satellite Beach, FL 32937 • 9,889
Satsuma, AL 36572 • 5,194
Saugerties, NY 12477 • 3,915
Saugus, MA 01906 • 25,549
Sauk □, WI • 46,975
Sauk Centre, MN 56378 • 3,581
Sauk City, WI 53583 • 3,019
Sauk Rapids, MN 56379 • 7,825
Sauk Village, IL 60411 • 9,926
Saukville, WI 53080 • 3,695
Sault Sainte Marie, MI 49783 • 14,689
Saunders □, NE • 18,285
Saunderstown, RI 02874 • 400
Sausalito, CA 94965–66 • 7,152
Savage, MD 20763 • 2,850
Savage, MN 55378 • 9,906
Savanna, IL 61074 • 3,819
Savannah, GA 31401–20 • 137,560
Savannah, MO 64485 • 4,352
Savannah, TN 38372 • 6,547
Savoonga, AK 99769 • 519
Savoy, IL 61874 • 2,674
Sawyer □, WI • 14,181
Saxonburg, PA 16056 • 1,345
Saxtons River, VT 05154 • 541
Saybrook Manor, CT 06475 • 1,073
Saydel, IA 50313 • 3,500
Saylesville, RI 02865 • 3,510
Saylorsburg, PA 18353 • 1,500
Sayre, OK 73662 • 2,881
Sayre, PA 18840 • 5,791
Sayreville, NJ 08872 • 34,986
Sayville, NY 11782 • 16,550
Scalp Level, PA 15963 • 1,158
Scappoose, OR 97056 • 3,529
Scarborough, ME 04074 • 2,586
Scarsdale, NY 10583 • 16,987
Schaumburg, IL 60192–94 • 68,586
Schenectady, NY 12301–09 • 65,566
Schenectady □, NY • 149,285
Schererville, IN 46375 • 19,926
Schertz, TX 78154 • 10,555
Schiller Park, IL 60176 • 11,189
Schleicher □, TX • 2,990
Schley □, GA • 3,588
Schofield, WI 54476 • 2,415
Schoharie, NY 12157 • 1,045
Schoharie □, NY • 31,859
Schoolcraft, MI 49087 • 1,517
Schoolcraft □, MI • 8,302
Schroon Lake, NY 12870 • 1,100
Schulenburg, TX 78956 • 2,455
Schurz, NV 89427 • 617
Schuyler, NE 68661 • 4,052
Schuyler □, IL • 7,498
Schuyler □, MO • 4,236
Schuyler □, NY • 18,662
Schuylerville, NY 12871 • 1,364
Schuylkill □, PA • 152,585
Schuylkill Haven, PA 17972 • 5,610
Scioto □, OH • 80,327
Scituate, MA 02066 • 5,180
Scobey, MT 59263 • 1,154
Scotch Plains, NJ 07076 • 21,160
Scotchtown, NY 10940 • 8,765
Scotia, CA 95565 • 1,200
Scotia, NY 12302 • 7,359
Scotland, SD 57059 • 968
Scotland □, MO • 4,822
Scotland □, NC • 33,754
Scotland Neck, NC 27874 • 2,575
Scotlandville, LA 70807 • 15,113
Scott, LA 70583 • 4,912
Scott □, AR • 10,205
Scott □, IL • 5,644
Scott □, IN • 20,991
Scott □, IA • 150,979
Scott □, KS • 5,289
Scott □, KY • 23,867
Scott □, MN • 57,846
Scott □, MS • 24,137
Scott □, MO • 39,376
Scott □, TN • 18,358
Scott □, VA • 23,204
Scott City, KS 67871 • 3,785
Scott City, MO 63780 • 4,292
Scottdale, GA 30079 • 8,636
Scottdale, PA 15683 • 5,184
Scott Lake, FL 33055 • 14,588
Scottsbluff, NE 69361–63 • 13,711
Scotts Bluff □, NE • 36,025
Scottsboro, AL 35768 • 13,786
Scottsburg, IN 47170 • 5,334
Scottsdale, AZ 85250–71 • 130,069
Scotts Valley, CA 95066–67 • 8,615
Scottsville, KY 42164 • 4,278

United States Populations and ZIP Codes

Scottsville, NY 14546 • 1,912
Scott Township, PA 15106 • 17,118
Scottville, MI 49454 • 1,287
Scranton, PA 18501–19 • 81,805
Screven □, GA • 13,842
Scurry □, TX • 18,634
Seabreeze, DE 19971 • 350
Sea Bright, NJ 07760 • 1,693
Seabrook, MD 20706 • 7,660
Seabrook, NJ 08302 • 1,457
Seabrook, TX 77586 • 6,685
Sea Cliff, NY 11579 • 5,054
Seadrift, TX 77983 • 1,277
Seaford, DE 19973 • 5,689
Seaford, NY 11783 • 15,597
Seaford, VA 23696 • 2,340
Seagate, NC 28403 • 5,444
Sea Girt, NJ 08750 • 2,099
Seagoville, TX 75159 • 8,969
Seagraves, TX 79359 • 2,398
Sea Isle City, NJ 08243 • 2,692
Seal Beach, CA 90740 • 25,098
Sealy, TX 77474 • 4,541
Seaman, OH 45679 • 1,013
Searchlight, NV 89029 • 430
Searcy, AR 72143 • 15,180
Searcy □, AR • 7,841
Searsport, ME 04974 • 1,151
Seaside, CA 93955 • 38,901
Seaside, OR 97138 • 5,359
Seaside Heights, NJ 08751 • 2,366
Seaside Park, NJ 08752 • 1,871
Seat Pleasant, MD 20743 • 5,359
Seattle, WA 98101–99 • 516,259
Sebastian, FL 32958 • 10,205
Sebastian □, AR • 99,590
Sebewaing, MI 48759 • 1,923
Sebree, KY 42455 • 1,510
Sebring, FL 33870–72 • 8,900
Sebring, OH 44672 • 4,848
Secaucus, NJ 07094 • 14,061
Security, CO 80911 • 6,660
Sedalia, MO 65301–02 • 19,800
Sedan, KS 67361 • 1,306
Sedgwick, KS 67135 • 1,438
Sedgwick □, CO • 2,690
Sedgwick □, KS • 403,662
Sedona, AZ 86336 • 7,720
Sedro Woolley, WA 98284 • 6,031
Seekonk, MA 02771 • 12,269
Seeley, CA 92273 • 1,228
Seelyville, IN 47878 • 1,090
Seguin, TX 78155–56 • 18,853
Seiling, OK 73663 • 1,031
Selah, WA 98942 • 5,113
Selawik, AK 99770 • 596
Selby, SD 57472 • 707
Selbyville, DE 19975 • 1,335
Selden, NY 11784 • 20,608
Seldovia, AK 99663 • 316
Selinsgrove, PA 17870 • 5,384
Sellersburg, IN 47172 • 5,745
Sellersville, PA 18960 • 4,479
Sells, AZ 85634 • 2,750
Selma, AL 36701–02 • 23,755
Selma, CA 93662 • 14,757
Selma, NC 27576 • 4,600
Selmer, TN 38375 • 3,838
Seminole, OK 74868 • 7,071
Seminole, TX 79360 • 6,342
Seminole □, FL • 287,529
Seminole □, GA • 9,010
Seminole □, OK • 25,412
Seminole Park, FL 34647 • 8,000
Semmes, AL 36575 • 2,250
Senath, MO 63876 • 1,622
Senatobia, MS 38668 • 4,772
Seneca, IL 61360 • 1,878
Seneca, KS 66538 • 2,027
Seneca, MO 64865 • 1,885
Seneca, PA 16346 • 1,300
Seneca, SC 29678–79 • 7,726
Seneca □, NY • 33,683
Seneca □, OH • 59,733
Seneca Falls, NY 13148 • 7,370
Sequatchie □, TN • 8,863
Sequim, WA 98382 • 3,616
Sequoyah □, OK • 33,828
Sergeant Bluff, IA 51054 • 2,772
Sesser, IL 62884 • 2,087
Seven Hills, OH 44131 • 12,339
Seven Oaks, SC 29210 • 15,722
Severn, MD 21144 • 24,499
Severna Park, MD 21146 • 25,879
Sevier □, AR • 13,637
Sevier □, TN • 51,043
Sevier □, UT • 15,431
Sevierville, TN 37862 • 7,178
Seville, OH 44273 • 1,810
Sewanee, TN 37375 • 2,128
Seward, AK 99664 • 2,699
Seward, NE 68434 • 5,634
Seward □, KS • 18,743
Seward □, NE • 15,450
Sewell, NJ 08080 • 1,870
Sewickley, PA 15143 • 4,134
Seymour, CT 06483 • 14,288
Seymour, IN 47274 • 15,576
Seymour, MO 65746 • 1,636
Seymour, TN 37865 • 7,026
Seymour, TX 76380 • 3,185
Seymour, WI 54165 • 2,782
Seymourville, LA 70764 • 2,891
Shackelford □, TX • 3,316
Shady Cove, OR 97539 • 1,351
Shady Side, MD 20764 • 4,107
Shadyside, OH 43947 • 3,934
Shady Spring, WV 25918 • 1,929
Shafter, CA 93263 • 8,409
Shaftsbury, VT 05262 • 700
Shaker Heights, OH 44120 • 30,831
Shakopee, MN 55379 • 11,739
Shaler Township, PA 15116 • 30,533
Shallowater, TX 79363 • 1,708
Shamokin, PA 17872 • 9,184
Shamokin Dam, PA 17876 • 1,690
Shamrock, TX 79079 • 2,286
Shannock, RI 02875 • 950
Shannon, GA 30172 • 1,703
Shannon, MS 38868 • 1,419
Shannon □, MO • 7,613
Shannon □, SD • 9,902
Shannontown, SC 29150 • 7,900
Sharkey □, MS • 7,066
Sharon, MA 02067 • 5,893
Sharon, PA 16146 • 17,493
Sharon, TN 38255 • 1,047
Sharon, WI 53585 • 1,250
Sharon Hill, PA 19079 • 5,771
Sharonville, OH 45241 • 13,153
Sharp □, AR • 14,109
Sharpes, FL 32922 • 3,348
Sharpley, DE 19803 • 1,250
Sharpsburg, MD 21782 • 659
Sharpsburg, NC 27878 • 1,536
Sharpsburg, PA 15215 • 3,781
Sharpsville, PA 16150 • 4,729
Shasta □, CA • 147,036
Shattuck, OK 73858 • 1,454
Shaw, MS 38773 • 2,349
Shawano, WI 54166 • 7,598
Shawano □, WI • 37,157
Shawnee, KS 66203 • 37,993
Shawnee, OK 74801–02 • 26,017
Shawnee □, KS • 160,976
Shawneetown, IL 62984 • 1,575
Sheboygan, WI 53081–83 • 49,676
Sheboygan □, WI • 103,877
Sheboygan Falls, WI 53085 • 5,823
Sheffield, AL 35660–62 • 10,380
Sheffield, IA 50475 • 1,174
Sheffield, MA 01257 • 1,100
Sheffield, PA 16347 • 1,294
Sheffield Lake, OH 44054 • 9,825
Shelbina, MO 63468 • 2,172
Shelburn, IN 47879 • 1,147
Shelburne Falls, MA 01370 • 1,996
Shelby, MI 49455 • 48,655
Shelby, MS 38774 • 2,806
Shelby, MT 59474 • 2,763
Shelby, NC 28150–51 • 14,669
Shelby, OH 44875 • 9,564
Shelby □, AL • 99,358
Shelby □, IL • 22,261
Shelby □, IN • 40,307
Shelby □, IA • 13,230
Shelby □, KY • 24,824
Shelby □, MO • 6,942
Shelby □, OH • 44,915
Shelby □, TN • 826,330
Shelby □, TX • 22,034
Shelbyville, IL 62565 • 4,943
Shelbyville, IN 46176 • 15,336
Shelbyville, KY 40065 • 6,238
Shelbyville, TN 37160 • 14,049
Sheldon, IL 60966 • 1,109
Sheldon, IA 51201 • 4,937
Sheldon, TX 77028 • 1,653
Shelley, ID 83274 • 3,536
Shell Lake, WI 54871 • 1,161
Shellman, GA 31786 • 1,162
Shell Rock, IA 50670 • 1,385
Shelter Island, NY 11964 • 1,193
Shelton, CT 06484 • 35,418
Shelton, WA 98584 • 7,241
Shenandoah, IA 51601 • 5,572
Shenandoah, PA 17976 • 6,221
Shenandoah, VA 22849 • 2,213
Shenandoah □, VA • 31,636
Shepherd, MI 48883 • 1,413
Shepherd, TX 77371 • 1,812
Shepherdstown, WV 25443 • 1,287
Shepherdsville, KY 40165 • 4,805
Sherborn, MA 01770 • 1,490
Sherburn, MN 56171 • 1,105
Sherburne, NY 13460 • 1,531
Sherburne □, MN • 41,945
Sheridan, AR 72150 • 3,098
Sheridan, CO 80110 • 4,976
Sheridan, IL 60551 • 1,288
Sheridan, IN 46069 • 2,046
Sheridan, OR 97378 • 3,979
Sheridan, WY 82801 • 13,900
Sheridan □, KS • 3,043
Sheridan □, MT • 4,732
Sheridan □, NE • 6,750
Sheridan □, ND • 2,148
Sheridan □, WY • 23,562
Sheridan Beach, WA 98155 • 6,518
Sherman, TX 75090–91 • 31,601
Sherman □, KS • 6,926
Sherman □, NE • 3,718
Sherman □, OR • 1,918
Sherman □, TX • 2,858
Sherrelwood, CO 80221 • 16,636
Sherrill, NY 13461 • 2,864
Sherwood, AR 72116 • 18,893
Sherwood, OR 97140 • 3,093
Sherwood Manor, CT 06082 • 6,357
Sherwood Park, DE 19808 • 2,000
Shiawassee □, MI • 69,770
Shickshinny, PA 18655 • 1,108
Shillington, PA 19607 • 5,062
Shiloh, OH 44878 • 11,607
Shiloh, PA 17404 • 8,245
Shiner, TX 77984 • 2,074
Shinglehouse, PA 16748 • 1,243
Shinnston, WV 26431 • 2,543
Ship Bottom, NJ 08008 • 1,352
Shippensburg, PA 17257 • 5,331
Shiprock, NM 87420 • 7,687
Shirley, MA 01464 • 1,559
Shirley, NY 11967 • 22,936
Shishmaref, AK 99772 • 456
Shively, KY 40216 • 15,535
Shoemakersville, PA 19555 • 1,443
Shore Acres, MA 02066 • 1,200
Shores Acres, RI 02852 • 410
Shoreview, MN 55112 • 24,587
Shorewood, IL 60435 • 6,264
Shorewood, MN 55331 • 5,917
Shorewood, WI 53211 • 14,116
Shorewood Hills, WI 53705 • 1,680
Short Beach, CT 06405 • 2,500
Shortsville, NY 14548 • 1,485
Shoshone, ID 83352 • 1,249
Shoshone □, ID • 13,931
Shoshoni, WY 82649 • 497
Show Low, AZ 85901 • 5,019
Shreve, OH 44676 • 1,584
Shreveport, LA 71101–10 • 198,525
Shrewsbury, MA 01545 • 23,400
Shrewsbury, MO 63119 • 6,416
Shrewsbury, NJ 07702 • 3,096
Shrewsbury, PA 17361 • 2,672
Shullsburg, WI 53586 • 1,236
Shungnak, AK 99773 • 223
Sibley, IA 51249 • 2,815
Sibley □, MN • 14,366
Sicklerville, NJ 08081 • 1,750
Sidney, IL 61877 • 1,027
Sidney, IA 51652 • 1,253
Sidney, MT 59270 • 5,217
Sidney, NE 69162 • 5,959
Sidney, NY 13838 • 4,720
Sidney, OH 45365 • 18,710
Siegle, LA 71291 • 1,600
Sierra □, CA • 3,318
Sierra □, NM • 9,912
Sierra Madre, CA 91024 • 10,762
Sierra Vista, AZ 85635–36 • 32,983
Siesta Key, FL 34242 • 7,772
Signal Hill, CA 90806 • 8,371
Signal Mountain, TN 37377 • 7,034
Sigourney, IA 52591 • 2,111
Sikeston, MO 63801 • 17,641
Siler City, NC 27344 • 4,808
Siloam Springs, AR 72761 • 8,151
Silsbee, TX 77656 • 6,368
Silt, CO 81652 • 1,095
Silver Bay, MN 55614 • 1,894
Silver Bow □, MT • 33,941
Silver City, NV 89428 • 100
Silver City, NM 88061–62 • 10,683
Silver Creek, NY 14136 • 2,927
Silverdale, WA 98383 • 7,660
Silver Grove, KY 41085 • 1,102
Silver Hill, MD 20746 • 1,580
Silver Lake, KS 66539 • 1,390
Silver Lake, MA 01887 • 2,900
Silver Lake, WI 53170 • 1,801
Silverpeak, NV 89047 • 190
Silver Spring, MD 20901–12 • 76,046
Silver Springs, FL 32688 • 1,082
Silver Springs, NV 89429 • 2,253
Silver Springs Shores, FL 32672 • 6,421
Silverton, NJ 08753 • 9,175
Silverton, OH 45236 • 5,859
Silverton, OR 97381 • 5,635
Silview, DE 19804 • 1,500
Silvis, IL 61282 • 6,926
Simi Valley, CA 93062–65 • 100,217
Simmesport, LA 71369 • 2,092
Simpson, PA 18407 • 1,670
Simpson □, KY • 15,145
Simpson □, MS • 23,953
Simpsonville, SC 29681 • 11,708
Simsbury, CT 06070 • 5,577
Sinclair, WY 82334 • 500
Sinton, TX 78387 • 5,549
Sioux □, IA • 29,903
Sioux □, NE • 1,549
Sioux □, ND • 3,761
Sioux Center, IA 51250 • 5,074
Sioux City, IA 51101–11 • 80,505
Sioux Falls, SD 57101–18 • 100,814
Siskiyou □, CA • 43,531
Sisseton, SD 57262 • 2,181
Sistersville, WV 26175 • 1,797
Sitka, AK 99835 • 8,588
Skagit □, WA • 79,555
Skagway, AK 99840 • 692
Skamania □, WA • 8,289
Skaneateles, NY 13152 • 2,724
Skiatook, OK 74070 • 4,910
Skokie, IL 60076–77 • 59,432
Skowhegan, ME 04976 • 6,990
Sky Lake, FL 32809 • 6,202
Skyland, NV 89448 • 660
Skyland, NC 28776 • 1,100
Skyway, WA 98178 • 8,500
Slackwoods, NJ 08638 • 8,100
Slater, IA 50244 • 1,268
Slater, MO 65349 • 2,186
Slater, SC 29683 • 1,000
Slatersville, RI 02876 • 2,330
Slatington, PA 18080 • 4,678
Slaton, TX 79364 • 6,078
Slayton, MN 56172 • 2,147
Sleepy Eye, MN 56085 • 3,694
Slickville, PA 15684 • 1,178
Slidell, LA 70458–61 • 24,124
Slinger, WI 53086 • 2,340
Slippery Rock, PA 16057 • 3,008
Sloan, NY 14225 • 3,830
Sloatsburg, NY 10974 • 3,035
Slocomb, AL 36375 • 1,906
Slope □, ND • 907
Smackover, AR 71762 • 2,232
Smethport, PA 16749 • 1,734
Smith □, KS • 5,078
Smith □, MS • 14,798
Smith □, TN • 14,143
Smith □, TX • 151,309
Smith Center, KS 66967 • 2,016
Smithers, WV 25186 • 1,162
Smithfield, NC 27577 • 7,540
Smithfield, PA 15478 • 1,000
Smithfield, UT 84335 • 5,566
Smithfield, VA 23430 • 4,686
Smith River, CA 95567 • 1,000
Smiths, AL 36877 • 1,700
Smithsburg, MD 21783 • 1,221
Smithton, IL 62285 • 1,587
Smithtown, NY 11787 • 25,638
Smithville, MO 64089 • 2,525
Smithville, OH 44677 • 1,354
Smithville, TN 37166 • 3,791
Smithville, TX 78957 • 3,196
Smyrna, DE 19977 • 5,231
Smyrna, GA 30080–82 • 30,981
Smyrna, TN 37167 • 13,647
Smyth □, VA • 32,370
Sneads, FL 32460 • 1,746
Sneedville, TN 37869 • 1,446
Snellville, GA 30278 • 12,084
Snohomish, WA 98290 • 6,499
Snohomish □, WA • 465,642
Snoqualmie, WA 98065 • 1,546
Snowflake, AZ 85937 • 3,679
Snow Hill, MD 21863 • 2,217
Snow Hill, NC 28580 • 1,378
Snyder, OK 73566 • 1,619
Snyder, TX 79549 • 12,195
Snyder □, PA • 36,680
Soap Lake, WA 98851 • 1,149
Socastee, SC 29577 • 10,426
Social Circle, GA 30279 • 2,755
Socorro, NM 87801 • 8,159
Socorro □, NM • 14,764
Soda Springs, ID 83276 • 3,111
Soddy-Daisy, TN 37379 • 8,240
Sodus, NY 14551 • 1,904
Sodus Point, NY 14555 • 1,190
Solana, FL 33950 • 1,128
Solana Beach, CA 92075 • 12,962
Solano □, CA • 340,421
Soldotna, AK 99669 • 3,482
Soledad, CA 93960 • 7,146
Solomons, MD 20688 • 1,500
Solon, IA 52333 • 1,050
Solon, OH 44139 • 18,548
Solvay, NY 13209 • 6,717
Somerdale, NJ 08083 • 5,440
Somers, CT 06071 • 9,108
Somerset, KY 42501–02 • 10,733
Somerset, MA 02725 • 17,655
Somerset, NJ 08873–75 • 22,070
Somerset, OH 43783 • 1,390
Somerset, PA 15501 • 6,454
Somerset, TX 78069 • 1,144
Somerset, WI 54025 • 1,065
Somerset □, ME • 49,767
Somerset □, MD • 23,440
Somerset □, NJ • 240,279
Somerset □, PA • 78,218
Somers Point, NJ 08244 • 11,216
Somersville, CT 06072 • 1,200
Somersworth, NH 03878 • 11,249
Somerton, AZ 85350 • 5,282
Somervell □, TX • 5,360
Somerville, MA 02143 • 76,210
Somerville, NJ 08876–77 • 11,632
Somerville, TN 38068 • 2,047
Somerville, TX 77879 • 1,542
Somonauk, IL 60552 • 1,263
Sonoma, CA 95476 • 8,121
Sonoma □, CA • 388,222
Sonora, CA 95370 • 4,153
Sonora, TX 76950 • 2,751
Soperton, GA 30457 • 2,797
Sophia, WV 25921 • 1,182
Soquel, CA 95073 • 9,188
Sorrento, LA 70778 • 1,119
Souderton, PA 18964 • 5,957
Sound Beach, NY 11789 • 9,102
South Acton, MA 01720 • 3,220
South Amboy, NJ 08879 • 7,863
South Amherst, MA 01002 • 5,053
South Amherst, OH 44001 • 1,765
Southampton, NY 11968–69 • 3,980
Southampton □, VA • 17,550
South Ashburnham, MA 01466 • 1,110
Southaven, MS 38671 • 17,949
South Barre, VT 05670 • 1,314
South Bay, FL 33493 • 3,558
South Belmar, NJ 07719 • 1,482
South Beloit, IL 61080 • 4,072
South Bend, IN 46601–80 • 105,511
South Bend, WA 98586 • 1,551
South Berwick, ME 03908 • 5,877
Southborough, MA 01772 • 1,450
South Boston, VA 24592 • 6,997
South Bound Brook, NJ 08880 • 4,185
South Bradenton, FL 34205 • 20,398
Southbridge, MA 01550 • 13,631
South Broadway, WA 98902 • 2,735
South Burlington, VT 05403 • 12,809
Southbury, CT 06488 • 3,000
South Charleston, OH 45368 • 1,626
South Charleston, WV 25303 • 13,645
South Chicago Heights, IL 60411 • 3,597
South Congaree, SC 29169 • 2,406
South Connellsville, PA 15425 • 2,204
South Dartmouth, MA 02748 • 9,850
South Daytona, FL 32121 • 12,482
South Decatur, GA 30034 • 19,350
South Deerfield, MA 01373 • 1,906
South Dennis, MA 02660 • 2,500
South Duxbury, MA 02332 • 3,017
South Easton, MA 02375 • 1,530
South Elgin, IL 60177 • 7,474
South El Monte, CA 91733 • 20,850
Southern Pines, NC 28387–88 • 9,129
South Euclid, OH 44121 • 23,866
South Fallsburg, NY 12779 • 2,115
South Farmingdale, NY 11735 • 15,377
Southfield, MI 48034 • 75,728
South Fork, PA 15956 • 1,197
South Fulton, TN 38257 • 2,688
South Gastonia, NC 28052 • 5,487
South Gate, CA 90280 • 86,284
Southgate, FL 34239 • 7,324
Southgate, KY 41071 • 3,266
South Gate, MD 21061 • 27,564
Southgate, MI 48195 • 30,771
South Glastonbury, CT 06073 • 1,570
Southglenn, CO 80122 • 43,087
South Glens Falls, NY 12801 • 3,506
South Grafton, MA 01560 • 2,610
South Hackensack, NJ 07606 • 2,229
South Hadley, MA 01075 • 5,340
South Hadley Falls, MA 01075 • 5,100
South Hamilton, MA 01982 • 2,720
South Haven, IN 46383 • 6,112
South Haven, MI 49090 • 5,563
South Hill, NY 14850 • 5,423
South Hill, VA 23970 • 4,217
South Hingham, MA 02043 • 4,080
South Holland, IL 60473 • 22,105
South Hooksett, NH 03106 • 3,638
South Hopkinton, RI 02813 • 900
South Houston, TX 77587 • 14,207
South Huntington, NY 11746 • 9,624
South Hutchinson, KS 67505 • 2,444
Southington, CT 06489 • 38,518
South International Falls, MN 56679 • 2,806
South Jacksonville, IL 62650 • 3,187
South Jordan, UT 84065 • 12,220
South Lake Tahoe, CA 95702 • 21,586
South Lancaster, MA 01561 • 1,772
South Laramie, WY 82070 • 1,500
South Laurel, MD 20708 • 18,591
South Lebanon, OH 45065 • 2,696
South Lockport, NY 14094 • 7,112
South Lyon, MI 48178 • 5,857
South Miami, FL 33143 • 10,404
South Miami Heights, FL 33157 • 30,030
South Milwaukee, WI 53172 • 20,958
South Nyack, NY 10960 • 3,352
South Ogden, UT 84403 • 12,105
Southold, NY 11971 • 5,192
South Orange, NJ 07079 • 16,390
South Paris, ME 04281 • 2,320
South Pasadena, CA 91030 • 23,936
South Patrick Shores, FL 32937 • 10,249
South Pekin, IL 61564 • 1,184
South Pittsburg, TN 37380 • 3,295
South Plainfield, NJ 07080 • 20,489
Southport, FL 32409 • 1,992
Southport, IN 46227 • 1,969
Southport, NY 14904 • 7,753
Southport, NC 28461 • 2,369
South Portland, ME 04106 • 23,163
South River, NJ 08882 • 13,692
South Royalton, VT 05068 • 700
South Saint Paul, MN 55075–77 • 20,197
South Salt Lake, UT 84115 • 10,129
South San Francisco, CA 94080–83 • 54,312
South San Gabriel, CA 91770 • 7,700
South San Jose Hills, CA 91744 • 17,814
South Sarasota, FL 34239 • 5,298
South Setauket, NY 11733 • 5,990
Southside, AL 35901 • 5,580
Southside Place, TX 77005 • 1,392
South Sioux City, NE 68776 • 9,677
South Stony Brook, NY 11790 • 6,120
South Streator, IL 61364 • 2,334
South Sumter, SC 29150 • 4,371
South Toms River, NJ 08757 • 3,869
South Torrington, WY 82240 • 300
South Tucson, AZ 85713 • 5,093
South Valley Stream, NY 11581 • 5,328
South Venice, FL 34293 • 11,951
South Walpole, MA 02071 • 1,300
South Waverly, PA 14892 • 1,049
South Wellfleet, MA 02663 • 2,300
South Westbury, NY 11590 • 9,732
Southwest Harbor, ME 04679 • 1,952
South Whitley, IN 46787 • 1,482
South Whittier, CA 90605 • 51,100
Southwick, MA 01077 • 1,170
South Williamsport, PA 17701 • 6,496
South Windham, CT 06266 • 1,644
South Windham, ME 04082 • 1,350
South Windsor, CT 06074 • 10,800
Southwood, CO 80120 • 2,050
Southwood Acres, CT 06082 • 8,963
South Woodstock, CT 06267 • 1,112
South Yarmouth, MA 02664 • 10,358
South Yuba City, CA 95991 • 8,816
South Zanesville, OH 43701 • 1,969
Spalding □, GA • 54,457
Spanaway, WA 98387 • 15,001
Spangler, PA 15775 • 2,068
Spanish Fork, UT 84660 • 11,272
Spanish Fort, AL 36527 • 3,732
Spanish Lake, MO 63138 • 20,322
Sparks, GA 31647 • 1,205
Sparks, NV 89431–36 • 53,367
Sparr, FL 32192 • 1,100
Sparta, GA 31087 • 1,710
Sparta, IL 62286 • 4,853
Sparta, MI 49345 • 3,968
Sparta (Lake Mohawk), NJ 07871 • 8,930
Sparta, NC 28675 • 1,957
Sparta, TN 38583 • 4,681
Sparta, WI 54656 • 7,788
Spartanburg, SC 29301–18 • 43,467
Spartanburg □, SC • 226,800
Spearfish, SD 57783 • 6,966
Spearman, TX 79081 • 3,197
Speedway, IN 46224 • 13,092
Spencer, IN 47460 • 2,609
Spencer, IA 51301 • 11,066
Spencer, MA 01562 • 6,306
Spencer, NC 28159 • 3,219
Spencer, TN 38585 • 1,125
Spencer, WV 25276 • 2,279
Spencer, WI 54479 • 1,757
Spencer □, IN • 19,490
Spencer □, KY • 6,801
Spencerport, NY 14559 • 3,606
Spencerville, MD 20868 • 1,780
Spencerville, OH 45887 • 2,288
Spicer, MN 56288 • 1,020
Spindale, NC 28160 • 4,040
Spink □, SD • 7,981
Spirit Lake, ID 83869 • 790
Spirit Lake, IA 51360 • 3,871
Spiro, OK 74959 • 2,146
Spokane, WA 99201–28 • 177,196
Spokane □, WA • 361,364
Spooner, WI 54801 • 2,464
Spotswood, NJ 08884 • 7,983
Spotsylvania □, VA • 57,403
Sprague, WV 25926 • 2,090
Spring, TX 77373 • 33,111
Spring Arbor, MI 49283 • 2,010
Springboro, OH 45066 • 6,590
Spring City, PA 19475 • 3,433
Spring City, TN 37381 • 2,199
Spring Creek 0M, NV • 5,866
Springdale, AR 72764–66 • 29,941
Springdale, OH 45246 • 10,621
Springdale, PA 15144 • 3,992
Springdale, SC 29169 • 3,226
Springer, NM 87747 • 1,262
Springerville, AZ 85938 • 1,802
Springfield, CO 81073 • 1,475
Springfield, FL 32401 • 8,715
Springfield, GA 31329 • 1,415
Springfield, IL 62701–94 • 105,227
Springfield, KY 40069 • 2,875
Springfield, MA 01101–05 • 156,983
Springfield, MI 49015 • 5,582
Springfield, MN 56087 • 2,173
Springfield, MO 65801–99 • 140,494
Springfield, NE 68059 • 1,426
Springfield, NJ 07081 • 13,240
Springfield, OH 45501–06 • 70,487
Springfield, OR 97477–78 • 44,683
Springfield, PA 19064 • 24,160
Springfield, SD 57062 • 834
Springfield, TN 37172 • 11,227
Springfield, VT 05156 • 4,207
Springfield, VA 22150 • 23,706
Spring Garden, PA 17403 • 11,127
Spring Green, WI 53588 • 1,283
Spring Grove, IL 60081 • 1,066
Spring Grove, MN 55974 • 1,153
Spring Grove, PA 17362 • 1,863
Spring Hill, FL 34606 • 31,117

Spring Hill, KS 66083 • 2,191
Springhill, LA 71075 • 5,668
Spring Hill, TN 37174 • 1,464
Spring Hope, NC 27882 • 1,221
Spring Lake, MI 49456 • 2,537
Spring Lake, NJ 07762 • 3,499
Spring Lake, NC 28390 • 7,524
Spring Lake Heights, NJ 07762 • 5,341
Spring Lake Park, MN 55432 • 6,532
Springvale, ME 04083 • 3,542
Spring Valley, IL 61362 • 5,246
Spring Valley, MN 55975 • 2,461
Spring Valley, NY 10977 • 21,802
Spring Valley, WI 54767 • 1,051
Springville, AL 35146 • 1,910
Springville, IA 52336 • 1,068
Springville, NY 14141 • 4,310
Springville, UT 84663–64 • 13,950
Spruce Pine, NC 28777 • 2,010
Spur, TX 79370 • 1,300
Staatsburg, NY 12580 • 1,100
Stafford, KS 67578 • 1,344
Stafford □, KS • 5,365
Stafford □, VA • 61,236
Stafford Springs, CT 06076 • 4,100
Stambaugh, MI 49964 • 1,281
Stamford, CT 06901–12 • 108,056
Stamford, NY 12167 • 1,211
Stamford, TX 79553 • 3,817
Stamford, VT 05352 • 400
Stamps, AR 71860 • 2,478
Stanaford, WV 25927 • 1,706
Stanberry, MO 64489 • 1,310
Standish, MI 48658 • 1,377
Stanfield, AZ 85272 • 1,700
Stanfield, OR 97875 • 1,568
Stanford, CA 94305 • 18,097
Stanford, KY 40484 • 2,686
Stanhope, NJ 07874 • 3,393
Stanislaus □, CA • 370,522
Stanley, NC 28164 • 2,823
Stanley, ND 58784 • 1,371
Stanley, VA 22851 • 1,186
Stanley, WI 54768 • 2,011
Stanley □, SD • 2,453
Stanleytown, VA 24168 • 1,563
Stanleyville, NC 27045 • 4,779
Stanly □, NC • 51,765
Stanton, CA 90680 • 30,491
Stanton, KY 40380 • 2,795
Stanton, MI 48888 • 1,504
Stanton, NE 68779 • 1,549
Stanton, TX 79782 • 2,576
Stanton □, KS • 2,333
Stanton □, NE • 6,244
Stanwood, WA 98292 • 1,961
Staples, MN 56479 • 2,754
Stapleton, AL 36578 • 1,300
Starbuck, MN 56381 • 1,143
Star City, AR 71667 • 2,138
Star City, WV 26505 • 1,251
Stargo, AZ 85540 • 1,038
Stark □, IL • 6,534
Stark □, ND • 22,832
Stark □, OH • 367,585
Starke, FL 32091 • 5,226
Starke □, IN • 22,747
Starkville, MS 39759 • 18,458
Starr □, TX • 40,518
Startex, SC 29377 • 1,162
State Center, IA 50247 • 1,248
State College, PA 16801–05 • 38,923
Stateline, NV 89449 • 1,379
State Line, PA 17263 • 1,253
Statesboro, GA 30458 • 15,854
Statesville, NC 28677 • 17,567
Statham, GA 30666 • 1,360
Staunton, IL 62088 • 4,806
Staunton, VA 24401 • 24,461
Stayton, OR 97383 • 5,011
Steamboat, NV 89511 • 450
Steamboat Springs, CO 80487 • 6,695
Stearns, KY 42647 • 1,550
Stearns □, MN • 118,791
Stebbins, AK 99671 • 400
Steele, AL 35987 • 1,046
Steele, MO 63877 • 2,395
Steele, ND 58482 • 762
Steele □, MN • 30,729
Steele □, ND • 2,420
Steeleville, IL 62288 • 2,059
Steelton, PA 17113 • 5,152
Steelville, MO 65565 • 1,465
Steger, IL 60475 • 8,584
Steilacoom, WA 98388 • 5,728
Stephens, AR 71764 • 1,137
Stephens □, GA • 23,257
Stephens □, OK • 42,299
Stephens □, TX • 9,010
Stephens City, VA 22655 • 1,186
Stephenson □, IL • 48,052
Stephenville, TX 76401 • 13,502
Sterling, AK 99672 • 3,802
Sterling, CO 80751 • 10,362
Sterling, IL 61081 • 15,132
Sterling, KS 67579 • 2,115
Sterling, MA 01564 • 1,250
Sterling, VA 22170 • 20,512
Sterling □, TX • 1,438
Sterling City, TX 76951 • 1,096
Sterling Heights, MI 48310–14 • 117,810
Sterlington, LA 71280 • 1,140
Steuben □, IN • 27,446
Steuben □, NY • 99,088
Steubenville, OH 43952 • 22,125
Stevens □, KS • 5,048
Stevens □, MN • 10,634
Stevens □, WA • 30,948
Stevenson, AL 35772 • 2,046
Stevenson, WA 98648 • 1,147
Stevens Point, WI 54481 • 23,006
Stevensville, MI 49127 • 1,230
Stevensville, MT 59870 • 1,221
Stewart □, GA • 5,654
Stewart □, TN • 9,479
Stewartstown, PA 17363 • 1,308
Stewartville, MN 55976 • 4,520
Stickney, IL 60402 • 5,678
Stigler, OK 74462 • 2,574
Stillwater, MN 55082–83 • 13,882
Stillwater, NY 12170 • 1,531
Stillwater, OK 74074–76 • 36,676
Stillwater □, MT • 6,536
Stilwell, OK 74960 • 2,663
Stinnett, TX 79083 • 2,166
Stirling, NJ 07980 • 1,800
Stockbridge, GA 30281 • 3,359
Stockbridge, MA 01262 • 2,408
Stockbridge, MI 49285 • 1,202
Stockdale, TX 78160 • 1,268
Stockholm, NJ 07460 • 1,200
Stockton, CA 95201–19 • 210,943
Stockton, IL 61085 • 1,871
Stockton, KS 67669 • 1,507
Stockton, MO 65785 • 1,579
Stoddard □, MO • 28,895
Stokes □, NC • 37,223
Stokesdale, NC 27357 • 2,134
Stollings, WV 25646 • 1,200
Stone □, AR • 9,775
Stone □, MS • 10,750
Stone □, MO • 19,078
Stoneboro, PA 16153 • 1,091
Stoneham, MA 02180 • 22,203
Stone Harbor, NJ 08247 • 1,025
Stone Mountain, GA 30083 • 6,494
Stoneville, NC 27048 • 1,109
Stonewall, LA 71078 • 1,266
Stonewall, MS 39363 • 1,148
Stonewall □, TX • 2,013
Stonewood, WV 26301 • 1,996
Stonington, CT 06378 • 1,100
Stonington, IL 62567 • 1,006
Stony Brook, NY 11790 • 13,726
Stony Point, NY 10980 • 10,587
Stony Point, NC 28678 • 1,286
Storey □, NV • 2,526
Storm Lake, IA 50588 • 8,769
Storrs, CT 06268 • 12,198
Story, WY 82842 • 700
Story □, IA • 74,252
Story City, IA 50248 • 2,959
Stottville, NY 12172 • 1,369
Stoughton, MA 02072 • 26,777
Stoughton, WI 53589 • 8,786
Stow, MA 01775 • 1,200
Stow, OH 44224 • 27,702
Stowe, PA 19464 • 3,598
Stowe, VT 05672 • 450
Stowe Township, PA 15136 • 7,681
Strabane, PA 15363 • 1,200
Strafford, MO 65757 • 1,166
Strafford □, NH • 104,233
Strasburg, CO 80136 • 1,005
Strasburg, OH 44680 • 1,995
Strasburg, PA 17579 • 2,568
Strasburg, VA 22657 • 3,762
Stratford, CT 06497 • 49,389
Stratford, DE 19720 • 1,950
Stratford, NJ 08084 • 7,614
Stratford, OK 74872 • 1,404
Stratford, TX 79084 • 1,781
Stratford, WI 54484 • 1,515
Stratford Landing, VA 22308 • 2,800
Strathmore, CA 93267 • 2,353
Strathmore, NJ 07747 • 7,060
Strawberry Point, IA 52076 • 1,357
Streamwood, IL 60103 • 30,987
Streator, IL 61364 • 14,121
Streetsboro, OH 44241 • 9,932
Stromsburg, NE 68666 • 1,241
Strongsville, OH 44136 • 35,308
Stroud, OK 74079 • 2,666
Stroudsburg, PA 18360 • 5,312
Struthers, OH 44471 • 12,284
Stryker, OH 43557 • 1,468
Stuart, FL 34994–97 • 11,936
Stuart, IA 50250 • 1,522
Stuarts Draft, VA 24477 • 5,087
Sturbridge, MA 01566 • 2,093
Sturgeon Bay, WI 54235 • 9,176
Sturgis, KY 42459 • 2,184
Sturgis, MI 49091 • 10,130
Sturgis, SD 57785 • 5,330
Sturtevant, WI 53177 • 3,803
Stutsman □, ND • 22,241
Stuttgart, AR 72160 • 10,420
Sublette, KS 67877 • 1,378
Sublette □, WY • 4,843
Sublimity, OR 97385 • 1,491
Succasunna, NJ 07876 • 7,750
Sudbury, MA 01776 • 1,860
Sudbury Center, MA 01776 • 2,590
Sudley, VA 22110 • 7,321
Suffern, NY 10901 • 11,055
Suffield, CT 06078 • 1,353
Suffolk, VA 23432–38 • 52,141
Suffolk □, MA • 663,906
Suffolk □, NY • 1,321,864
Sugar City, ID 83448 • 1,275
Sugar Creek, MO 64054 • 3,982
Sugarcreek, PA 16323 • 5,532
Sugar Grove, VA 24375 • 1,027
Sugar Hill, GA 30518 • 4,557
Sugar Land, TX 77478–79 • 24,529
Sugarland Run, VA 22170 • 9,357
Sugar Loaf, VA 24018 • 2,000
Sugar Notch, PA 18706 • 1,044
Suisun City, CA 94585 • 22,686
Suitland, MD 20746 • 35,400
Sulligent, AL 35586 • 1,886
Sullivan, IL 61951 • 4,354
Sullivan, IN 47882 • 4,663
Sullivan, MO 63080 • 5,661
Sullivan □, IN • 18,993
Sullivan □, MO • 6,326
Sullivan □, NH • 38,592
Sullivan □, NY • 69,277
Sullivan □, PA • 6,104
Sullivan □, TN • 143,596
Sullivans Island, SC 29482 • 1,623
Sully □, SD • 1,589
Sulphur, LA 70663–64 • 20,125
Sulphur, OK 73086 • 4,824
Sulphur Springs, TX 75482 • 14,062
Sultan, WA 98294 • 2,236
Sumiton, AL 35148 • 2,604
Summerfield, NC 27358 • 2,051
Summers □, WV • 14,204
Summersville, WV 26651 • 2,906
Summerville, GA 30747 • 5,025
Summerville, SC 29483–85 • 22,519
Summit, IL 60501 • 9,971
Summit, MS 39666 • 1,566
Summit, NJ 07901 • 19,757
Summit, TN 37363 • 8,307
Summit □, CO • 12,881
Summit □, OH • 514,990
Summit □, UT • 15,518
Summit Hill, PA 18250 • 3,332
Sumner, IL 62466 • 1,083
Sumner, IA 50674 • 2,078
Sumner, WA 98390 • 6,281
Sumner □, KS • 25,841
Sumner □, TN • 103,281
Sumter, SC 29150–54 • 41,943
Sumter □, AL • 16,174
Sumter □, FL • 31,577
Sumter □, GA • 30,228
Sumter □, SC • 102,637
Sunbury, OH 43074 • 2,046
Sunbury, PA 17801 • 11,591
Sun City, AZ 85351 • 38,126
Sun City, CA 92381 • 14,930
Sun City Center, FL 33573 • 8,326
Suncook, NH 03275 • 5,214
Sundance, WY 82729 • 1,139
Sundown, TX 79372 • 1,759
Sunflower □, MS • 32,867
Sunland Park, NM 88063 • 8,179
Sunny Isles, FL 33160 • 11,772
Sunnyside, CA 93727 • 5,000
Sunnyside, WA 98944 • 11,238
Sunnyvale, CA 94086–89 • 117,229
Sun Prairie, WI 53590 • 15,333
Sunray, TX 79086 • 1,729
Sunrise Manor, NV 89110 • 95,362
Sunset, FL 33143 • 15,810
Sunset, LA 70584 • 2,201
Sunset, UT 84015 • 5,128
Sunset Beach, HI 96712 • 800
Sun Valley, ID 83353–54 • 938
Sun Valley, NV 89433 • 11,391
Superior, AZ 85273 • 3,468
Superior, MT 59872 • 881
Superior, NE 68978 • 2,397
Superior, WI 54880 • 27,134
Superior, WY 82945 • 273
Suquamish, WA 98392 • 3,105
Surf City, NJ 08008 • 1,375
Surfside, FL 33154 • 4,108
Surfside Beach, SC 29575 • 3,845
Surgoinsville, TN 37873 • 1,499
Surprise, AZ 85374 • 7,122
Surrey, ND 58785 • 856
Surry □, NC • 61,704
Surry □, VA • 6,145
Susanville, CA 96130 • 7,279
Susquehanna, PA 18847 • 1,760
Susquehanna □, PA • 40,380
Sussex, NJ 07461 • 2,201
Sussex, WI 53089 • 5,039
Sussex □, DE • 113,229
Sussex □, NJ • 130,943
Sussex □, VA • 10,248
Sutherland, NE 69165 • 1,032
Sutherlin, OR 97479 • 5,020
Sutter □, CA • 64,415
Sutter Creek, CA 95685 • 1,835
Sutton, NE 68979 • 1,353
Sutton □, TX • 4,135
Suwanee, GA 30174 • 2,412
Suwannee □, FL • 26,780
Swain □, NC • 11,268
Swainsboro, GA 30401 • 7,361
Swampscott, MA 01907 • 13,650
Swannanoa, NC 28778 • 3,538
Swansboro, NC 28584 • 1,165
Swansea, IL 62221 • 8,201
Swanton, OH 43558 • 3,557
Swanton, VT 05488 • 2,360
Swanwyck Estates, DE 19720 • 1,320
Swarthmore, PA 19081 • 6,157
Swartz Creek, MI 48473 • 4,851
Swatara Township, PA 17111 • 19,700
Swayzee, IN 46986 • 1,059
Swedesboro, NJ 08085 • 2,024
Sweeny, TX 77480 • 3,297
Sweet Grass □, MT • 3,154
Sweet Home, OR 97386 • 6,850
Sweet Springs, MO 65351 • 1,595
Sweetwater, FL 33152 • 13,909
Sweetwater, TN 37874 • 5,066
Sweetwater, TX 79556 • 11,967
Sweetwater □, WY • 38,823
Sweetwater Creek, FL 33614 • 18,000
Swift □, MN • 10,724
Swisher □, TX • 8,133
Swissvale, PA 15218 • 10,637
Switzer, WV 25647 • 1,004
Switzerland, FL 32043 • 2,400
Switzerland □, IN • 7,738
Swoyerville, PA • 5,630
Sycamore, AL 35149 • 1,250
Sycamore, IL 60178 • 9,708
Sykesville, MD 21784 • 2,303
Sykesville, PA 15865 • 1,387
Sylacauga, AL 35150 • 12,520
Sylva, NC 28779 • 1,809
Sylvan Beach, NY 13157 • 1,119
Sylvania, GA 30467 • 2,871
Sylvania, OH 43560 • 17,301
Sylvan Lake, MI 48320 • 1,884
Sylvester, GA 31791 • 5,702
Syosset, NY 11791 • 18,967
Syracuse, IN 46567 • 2,729
Syracuse, KS 67878 • 1,606
Syracuse, NE 68446 • 1,646
Syracuse, NY 13201–90 • 163,860
Syracuse, UT 84075 • 4,658

T

Tabor City, NC 28463 • 2,330
Tacoma, WA 98401–99 • 176,664
Taft, CA 93268 • 5,902
Taft, TX 78390 • 3,222
Tahlequah, OK 74464–65 • 10,398
Tahoe City, CA 95730 • 1,300
Tahoka, TX 79373 • 2,868
Takoma Park, MD 20912 • 16,700
Talbot □, GA • 6,524
Talbot □, MD • 30,549
Talbotton, GA 31827 • 1,046
Talent, OR 97540 • 3,274
Taliaferro □, GA • 1,915
Talihina, OK 74571 • 1,297
Talladega, AL 35160 • 18,175
Talladega □, AL • 74,107
Tallahassee, FL 32301–17 • 124,773
Tallahatchie □, MS • 15,210
Tallapoosa, GA 30176 • 2,805
Tallapoosa □, AL • 38,826
Tallassee, AL 36078 • 5,112
Talleyville, DE 19803 • 6,346
Tallmadge, OH 44278 • 14,870
Tallulah, LA 71282–84 • 8,526
Tama, IA 52339 • 2,697
Tama □, IA • 17,419
Tamalpais Valley, CA 94941 • 5,000
Tamaqua, PA 18252 • 7,943
Tamarac, FL 33321 • 44,822
Tamiami, FL 33165 • 33,845
Tampa, FL 33601–97 • 280,015
Tanana, AK 99777 • 345
Taney □, MO • 25,561
Taneytown, MD 21787 • 3,695
Tangipahoa □, LA • 85,709
Taos, NM 87571 • 4,065
Taos □, NM • 23,118
Taos Pueblo, NM 87571 • 1,030
Tappahannock, VA 22560 • 1,550
Tappan, NY 10983 • 6,867
Tara Hills, CA 94564 • 6,000
Tarboro, NC 27886 • 11,037
Tarentum, PA 15084 • 5,674
Tariffville, CT 06081 • 1,477
Tarkio, MO 64491 • 2,243
Tarpey, CA 93727 • 4,000
Tarpon Springs, FL 34688–91 • 17,906
Tarrant, AL 35217 • 8,046
Tarrant □, TX • 1,170,103
Tarrytown, NY 10591 • 10,739
Tate, GA 30177 • 1,000
Tate □, MS • 21,432
Tattnall □, GA • 17,722
Taunton, MA 02780 • 49,832
Tavares, FL 32778 • 7,383
Tavernier, FL 33070 • 2,433
Tawas City, MI 48763–64 • 2,009
Taylor, AZ 85939 • 2,418
Taylor, MI 48180 • 70,811
Taylor, PA 18517 • 6,941
Taylor, TX 76574 • 11,472
Taylor □, FL • 17,111
Taylor □, GA • 7,642
Taylor □, IA • 7,114
Taylor □, KY • 21,146
Taylor □, TX • 119,655
Taylor □, WV • 15,144
Taylor □, WI • 18,901
Taylor Mill, KY 41015 • 5,530
Taylors, SC 29687 • 19,619
Taylorsville, IN 47280 • 1,044
Taylorsville, MS 39168 • 1,412
Taylorsville, NC 28681 • 1,566
Taylorville, IL 62568 • 11,133
Tazewell, TN 37879 • 2,150
Tazewell, VA 24651 • 4,176
Tazewell □, IL • 123,692
Tazewell □, VA • 45,960
Tchula, MS 39169 • 2,186
Teague, TX 75860 • 3,268
Teaneck, NJ 07666 • 37,825
Teaticket, MA 02536 • 2,600
Tecumseh, MI 49286 • 7,462
Tecumseh, NE 68450 • 1,702
Tecumseh, OK 74873 • 5,750
Tehachapi, CA 93561 • 5,791
Tehama □, CA • 49,625
Tekamah, NE 68061 • 1,852
Telfair □, GA • 11,000
Telford, PA 18969 • 4,238
Tell City, IN 47586 • 8,088
Teller □, CO • 12,468
Telluride, CO 81435 • 1,309
Temecula, CA 92390 • 27,099
Tempe, AZ 85280–85 • 141,865
Temperance, MI 48182 • 6,542
Temple, GA 30179 • 1,870
Temple, OK 73568 • 1,223
Temple, PA 19560 • 1,491
Temple, TX 76501–05 • 46,109
Temple City, CA 91780 • 31,100
Temple Terrace, FL 33617 • 16,444
Templeton, MA 01468 • 1,000
Tenafly, NJ 07670 • 13,326
Tenaha, TX 75974 • 1,072
Tenino, WA 98589 • 1,292
Tennessee Ridge, TN 37178 • 1,271
Tennille, GA 31089 • 1,552
Tensas □, LA • 7,103
Ten Sleep, WY 82442 • 311
Terra Alta, WV 26764 • 1,713
Terrebonne □, LA • 96,982
Terre Haute, IN 47801–08 • 57,483
Terre Hill, PA 17581 • 1,282
Terrell, TX 75160 • 12,490
Terrell □, GA • 10,653
Terrell □, TX • 1,410
Terrell Hills, TX 78209 • 4,592
Terry, MT 59349 • 659
Terry □, TX • 13,218
Terrytown, LA 70053 • 23,787
Terryville, CT 06786 • 5,426
Terryville, NY 11776 • 7,380
Tesuque, NM 87574 • 1,490
Teton □, ID • 3,439
Teton □, MT • 6,271
Teton □, WY • 11,172
Teton Village, WY 83025 • 250
Teutopolis, IL 62467 • 1,417
Tewksbury, MA 01876 • 10,540
Texarkana, AR 75502 • 22,631
Texarkana, TX 75501–05 • 31,656
Texas □, MO • 21,476
Texas □, OK • 16,419
Texas City, TX 77590–92 • 40,822
Texico, NM 88135 • 966
Thatcher, AZ 85552 • 3,763
Thayer, MO 65791 • 1,996
Thayer □, NE • 6,635
Thayne, WY 83127 • 267
The Colony, TX 75056 • 22,113
The Dalles, OR 97058 • 11,060
Theodore, AL 36582 • 6,509
The Plains, OH 45780 • 2,644
Thermalito, CA 95965 • 5,646
Thermopolis, WY 82443 • 3,247
The Village, OK 73120 • 10,353
The Village of Indian Hill, OH 45243 • 5,383
The Woodlands, TX 77380 • 29,205
Thibodaux, LA 70301–02 • 14,035
Thief River Falls, MN 56701 • 8,010
Thiensville, WI 53092 • 3,301
Thomas, OK 73669 • 1,246
Thomas □, GA • 38,986
Thomas □, KS • 8,258
Thomas □, NE • 851
Thomasboro, IL 61878 • 1,250
Thomaston, CT 06787 • 3,590
Thomaston, GA 30286 • 9,127
Thomaston, ME 04861 • 2,445
Thomasville, AL 36784 • 4,301
Thomasville, GA 31792 • 17,457
Thomasville, NC 27360–61 • 15,915
Thompson, ND 58278 • 930
Thompson Falls, MT 59873 • 1,319
Thomson, GA 30824 • 6,862
Thonotosassa, FL 33592 • 1,500
Thoreau, NM 87323 • 1,099
Thorndale, TX 76577 • 1,092
Thorndike, MA 01079 • 1,100
Thornton, CO 80229 • 55,031
Thorntown, IN 46071 • 1,506
Thornwood, NY 10594 • 7,025
Thorofare, NJ 08086 • 1,800
Thorp, WI 54771 • 1,657
Thorsby, AL 35171 • 1,465
Thousand Oaks, CA 91359–62 • 104,352
Three Forks, MT 59752 • 1,203
Three Oaks, MI 49128 • 1,786
Three Rivers, MA 01080 • 3,006
Three Rivers, MI 49093 • 7,413
Three Rivers, TX 78071 • 1,889
Throckmorton, TX 76083 • 1,036
Throckmorton □, TX • 1,880
Throop, PA 18512 • 4,070
Thunderbolt, GA 31404 • 2,786
Thurmont, MD 21788 • 3,398
Thurston □, NE • 6,936
Thurston □, WA • 161,238
Tiburon, CA 94920 • 7,532
Tice, FL 33905 • 3,971
Ticonderoga, NY 12883 • 2,770
Tierra Amarilla, NM 87575 • 900
Tiffin, OH 44883 • 18,604
Tift □, GA • 34,998
Tifton, GA 31793–94 • 14,215
Tigard, OR 97223 • 29,344
Tillamook, OR 97141 • 4,001
Tillamook □, OR • 21,570
Tillman □, OK • 10,384
Tillmans Corner, AL 36619 • 17,988
Tillson, NY 12486 • 1,688
Tilton, IL 61833 • 2,729
Tilton, NH 03276 • 1,380
Tiltonsville, OH 43963 • 1,517
Timberlake, VA 24502 • 10,314
Timberville, VA 22853 • 1,596
Timmonsville, SC 29161 • 2,182
Timpson, TX 75975 • 1,029
Tinley Park, IL 60477 • 37,121
Tinton Falls, NJ 07724 • 12,361
Tioga, LA 71477 • 1,200
Tioga, ND 58852 • 1,278
Tioga □, NY • 52,337
Tioga □, PA • 41,126
Tippah □, MS • 19,523
Tipp City, OH 45371 • 6,027
Tippecanoe □, IN • 130,598
Tipton, CA 93272 • 1,383
Tipton, IN 46072 • 4,751
Tipton, IA 52772 • 2,998
Tipton, MO 65081 • 2,026
Tipton, OK 73570 • 1,043
Tipton □, IN • 16,119
Tipton □, TN • 37,568
Tiptonville, TN 38079 • 2,149
Tishomingo, OK 73460 • 3,116
Tishomingo □, MS • 17,683
Titus □, TX • 24,009
Titusville, FL 32780–83 • 39,394
Titusville, PA 16354 • 6,434
Tiverton, RI 02878 • 7,259
Tivoli, NY 12583 • 1,035
Toast, NC 27049 • 2,125
Tobyhanna, PA 18466 • 1,200
Toccoa, GA 30577 • 8,266
Todd □, KY • 10,940
Todd □, MN • 23,363
Todd □, SD • 8,352
Todd Estates, DE 19713 • 2,000
Togiak, AK 99678 • 613
Tohatchi, NM 87325 • 661
Tok, AK 99780 • 935
Toledo, IL 62468 • 1,199
Toledo, IA 52342 • 2,380
Toledo, OH 43601–99 • 332,943
Toledo, OR 97391 • 3,174
Tolland, CT 06084 • 1,200
Tolland □, CT • 128,699
Tolleson, AZ 85353 • 4,434
Tolono, IL 61880 • 2,605
Toluca, IL 61369 • 1,315
Tomah, WI 54660 • 7,570
Tomahawk, WI 54487 • 3,328
Tomball, TX 77375 • 6,370
Tombstone, AZ 85638 • 1,220
Tom Green □, TX • 98,458
Tompkins □, NY • 94,097
Tompkinsville, KY 42167 • 2,861
Toms River, NJ 08753–57 • 7,524
Tonawanda, NY 14150–51 • 17,284
Tonawanda, NY 14223 • 65,284
Tonganoxie, KS 66086 • 2,347
Tonkawa, OK 74653 • 3,127
Tonopah, NV 89049 • 3,616
Tooele, UT 84074 • 13,887
Tooele □, UT • 26,601
Toole □, MT • 5,046
Toombs □, GA • 24,072
Topeka, KS 66601–99 • 119,883
Toppenish, WA 98948 • 7,419
Topsfield, MA 01983 • 2,711
Topsham, ME 04086 • 6,147
Topton, PA 19562 • 1,987
Toronto, OH 43964 • 6,127
Torrance, CA 90501–10 • 133,107
Torrance □, NM • 10,285
Torrington, CT 06790 • 33,687
Torrington, WY 82240 • 5,651
Totowa, NJ 07512 • 10,177
Touisset, MA 02777 • 1,520

United States Populations and ZIP Codes

Toulon, IL 61483 • 1,328
Towaco, NJ 07082 • 1,020
Towanda, KS 67144 • 1,289
Towanda, PA 18848 • 3,242
Tower City, PA 17980 • 1,518
Town and Country, WA 99210 • 4,921
Town Creek, AL 35672 • 1,379
Towner, ND 58788 • 669
Towner □, ND • 3,627
Town 'n Country, FL 33615 • 60,946
Towns □, GA • 6,754
Townsend, DE 19734 • 322
Townsend, MA 01469 • 1,164
Townsend, MT 59644 • 1,635
Towson, MD 21204 • 49,445
Tracy, CA 95376–78 • 33,558
Tracy, MN 56175 • 2,059
Tracy City, TN 37387 • 1,556
Tracyton, WA 98393 • 2,621
Traer, IA 50675 • 1,552
Trafford, PA 15085 • 3,345
Trail Creek, IN 46360 • 2,463
Traill □, ND • 8,752
Transylvania □, NC • 25,520
Travelers Rest, SC 29690 • 3,069
Traverse □, MN • 4,463
Traverse City, MI 49684 • 15,155
Travis □, TX • 576,407
Treasure □, MT • 874
Treasure Island, FL 33706 • 7,266
Trego □, KS • 3,694
Tremont, IL 61568 • 2,088
Tremont, PA 17981 • 1,814
Tremonton, UT 84337 • 4,264
Trempealeau, WI 54661 • 1,039
Trempealeau □, WI • 25,263
Trenton, FL 32693 • 1,287
Trenton, GA 30752 • 1,994
Trenton, IL 62293 • 2,481
Trenton, MI 48183 • 20,586
Trenton, MO 64683 • 6,129
Trenton, NJ 08601–91 • 88,675
Trenton, OH 45067 • 6,189
Trenton, TN 38382 • 4,836
Tresckow, PA 18254 • 1,033
Treutlen □, GA • 5,994
Trevorton, PA 17881 • 2,058
Triangle, VA 22172 • 4,740
Tri City, OR 97457 • 3,585
Trigg □, KY • 10,361
Tri Lakes, IN 46725 • 3,299
Trimble □, KY • 6,090
Trinidad, CO 81082 • 8,580
Trinidad, TX 75163 • 1,056
Trinity, AL 35673 • 1,380
Trinity, NC 27370 • 5,469
Trinity, TX 75862 • 2,648
Trinity □, CA • 13,063
Trinity □, TX • 11,445
Trion, GA 30753 • 1,661
Tripoli, IA 50676 • 1,188
Tripp □, SD • 6,924
Triumph, LA 70041 • 1,200
Trona, CA 93562 • 1,400
Trooper, PA 19401 • 5,137
Trotwood, OH 45426 • 8,816
Troup □, GA • 55,536
Trousdale □, TN • 5,920
Troutdale, OR 97060 • 7,852
Troutman, NC 28166 • 1,493
Troy, AL 36081 • 13,051
Troy, ID 83871 • 699
Troy, IL 62294 • 6,046
Troy, KS 66087 • 1,073
Troy, MI 48083–84 • 72,884
Troy, MO 63379 • 3,811
Troy, MT 59935 • 953
Troy, NH 03465 • 2,097
Troy, NY 12180–83 • 54,269
Troy, NC 27371 • 3,404
Troy, OH 45373 • 19,478
Troy, PA 16947 • 1,262
Troy, TN 38260 • 1,047
Truckee, CA 95734 • 3,484
Truman, MN 56088 • 1,292
Trumann, AR 72472 • 6,304
Trumansburg, NY 14886 • 1,611
Trumbull, CT 06611 • 32,000
Trumbull □, OH • 227,813
Trussville, AL 35173 • 8,266
Truth or Consequences (Hot Springs), NM 87901 • 6,221
Tryon, NC 28782 • 1,680
Tualatin, OR 97062 • 15,013
Tuba City, AZ 86045 • 7,323
Tuckahoe, NY 10707 • 6,302
Tucker, GA 30084 • 25,781
Tucker □, WV • 7,728
Tuckerman, AR 72473 • 2,020
Tuckerton, NJ 08087 • 3,048
Tucson, AZ 85701–51 • 405,390
Tucumcari, NM 88401 • 6,831
Tukwila, WA 98188 • 11,874
Tulare, CA 93274–75 • 33,249
Tulare □, CA • 311,921
Tularosa, NM 88352 • 2,615
Tulelake, CA 96134 • 1,010
Tulia, TX 79088 • 4,699
Tullahoma, TN 37388 • 16,761
Tulsa, OK 74101–94 • 367,302
Tulsa □, OK • 503,341
Tumwater, WA 98502 • 9,976
Tunica, MS 38676 • 1,175
Tunica □, MS • 8,164
Tunkhannock, PA 18657 • 2,251
Tununak, AK 99681 • 316
Tuolumne, CA 95379 • 1,686
Tuolumne □, CA • 48,456
Tupelo, MS 38801–03 • 30,685
Tupper Lake, NY 12986 • 4,087
Turley, OK 74156 • 2,930
Turlock, CA 95380–81 • 42,198
Turner, OR 97392 • 1,281
Turner □, GA • 8,703
Turner □, SD • 8,576
Turners Falls, MA 01376 • 4,731
Turtle Creek, PA 15145 • 6,556
Turtle Lake, ND 58575 • 681
Tuscaloosa, AL 35401–06 • 77,759
Tuscaloosa □, AL • 150,522
Tuscarawas □, OH • 84,090
Tuscola, IL 61953 • 4,155
Tuscola □, MI • 55,498
Tuscumbia, AL 35674 • 8,413
Tuskegee, AL 36083 • 12,257
Tustin, CA 92680–81 • 50,689
Tuttle, OK 73089 • 2,807
Tutwiler, MS 38963 • 1,391
Tuxedo Park, DE 19804 • 1,300
Twentynine Palms, CA 92277–78 • 11,821
Twiggs □, GA • 9,806
Twin City, GA 30471 • 1,466
Twin Falls, ID 83301–03 • 27,591
Twin Falls □, ID • 53,580
Twin Knolls, AZ 85207 • 5,210
Twin Lakes, CA 95060 • 5,379
Twin Lakes, WI 53181 • 3,989
Twin Rivers, NJ 08520 • 7,715
Twinsburg, OH 44087 • 9,606
Two Harbors, MN 55616 • 3,651
Two Rivers, WI 54241 • 13,030
Tybee Island, GA 31328 • 2,842
Tyler, MN 56178 • 1,257
Tyler, TX 75701–13 • 75,450
Tyler □, TX • 16,646
Tyler □, WV • 9,796
Tyler Heights, WV 25312 • 4,070
Tylertown, MS 39667 • 1,938
Tyndall, SD 57066 • 1,201
Tyrone, NM 88065 • 950
Tyrone, PA 16686 • 5,743
Tyrrell □, NC • 3,856
Tysons Corner, VA 22102 • 13,124

U

Ucon, ID 83454 • 895
Uhrichsville, OH 44683 • 5,604
Uinta □, WY • 18,705
Uintah □, UT • 22,211
Ukiah, CA 95482 • 14,599
Uleta, FL 33162 • 10,000
Ulster □, NY • 165,304
Ulysses, KS 67880 • 5,474
Umatilla, FL 32784 • 2,350
Umatilla, OR 97882 • 3,046
Umatilla □, OR • 59,249
Unadilla, GA 31091 • 1,620
Unadilla, NY 13849 • 1,265
Unalakleet, AK 99684 • 714
Unalaska, AK 99685 • 3,089
Uncasville, CT 06382 • 1,597
Underwood, AL 35630 • 1,950
Underwood, ND 58576 • 976
Unicoi □, TN • 16,549
Union, KY 41091 • 1,001
Union, MS 39365 • 1,875
Union, MO 63084 • 5,909
Union, NJ 07083 • 50,024
Union, OH 45322 • 5,501
Union, OR 97883 • 1,847
Union, SC 29379 • 9,836
Union, UT 84047 • 13,684
Union □, AR • 46,719
Union □, FL • 10,252
Union □, GA • 11,993
Union □, IL • 17,619
Union □, IN • 6,976
Union □, IA • 12,750
Union □, KY • 16,557
Union □, LA • 20,690
Union □, MS • 22,085
Union □, NJ • 493,819
Union □, NM • 4,124
Union □, NC • 84,211
Union □, OH • 31,969
Union □, OR • 23,598
Union □, PA • 36,176
Union □, SC • 30,337
Union □, SD • 10,189
Union □, TN • 13,694
Union Beach, NJ 07735 • 6,156
Union City, CA 94587 • 53,762
Union City, GA 30291 • 8,375
Union City, IN 47390 • 3,612
Union City, MI 49094 • 1,767
Union City, NJ 07087 • 58,012
Union City, OH 45390 • 1,984
Union City, OK 73090 • 1,000
Union City, PA 16438 • 3,537
Union City, TN 38261 • 10,513
Uniondale, NY 11553 • 20,328
Union Gap, WA 98903 • 3,120
Union Grove, WI 53182 • 3,669
Union Lake, MI 48386–87 • 8,500
Union Park, FL 32817 • 6,890
Union Pier, MI 49129 • 1,039
Union Point, GA 30669 • 1,753
Union Springs, AL 36089 • 3,975
Union Springs, NY 13160 • 1,142
Uniontown, AL 36786 • 1,730
Uniontown, KY 42461 • 1,008
Uniontown, OH 44685 • 1,500
Uniontown, PA 15401 • 12,034
Union Village, RI 02895 • 2,150
Unionville, CT 06085 • 3,500
Unionville, MO 63565 • 1,989
Universal City, TX 78148 • 13,057
University City, MO 63130 • 40,087
University Gardens, NY 11020 • 4,600
University Heights, IA 52240 • 1,042
University Heights, OH 44118 • 14,790
University Park, IL 60466 • 6,204
University Park, NM 88003 • 4,520
University Park, TX 75205 • 22,259
University Place, WA 98465 • 27,701
Upland, CA 91785–86 • 63,374
Upland, IN 46989 • 3,295
Upper Arlington, OH 43221 • 34,128
Upper Darby, PA 19082–83 • 84,054
Upper Dublin Township, PA 19002 • 22,348
Upper Greenwood Lake, NJ 07421 • 2,734
Upper Merion Township, PA 19406 • 26,138
Upper Moreland Township, PA 19090 • 25,874
Upper Providence Township, PA 19063 • 9,727
Upper Saddle River, NJ 07458 • 7,198
Upper Saint Clair, PA 15241 • 19,692
Upper Sandusky, OH 43351 • 5,906
Upshur □, TX • 31,370
Upshur □, WV • 22,867
Upson □, GA • 26,300
Upton, MA 01568 • 1,500
Upton, WY 82730 • 980
Upton □, TX • 4,447
Urbana, IL 61801 • 36,344
Urbana, OH 43078 • 11,353
Urbandale, IA 50322 • 23,500
Usquepaug, RI 02892 • 400
Utah □, UT • 263,590
Utica, MI 48315–18 • 5,081
Utica, MS 39175 • 1,033
Utica, NY 13501–05 • 68,637
Utica, OH 43080 • 1,997
Uvalde, TX 78801–02 • 14,729
Uvalde □, TX • 23,340
Uxbridge, MA 01569 • 3,340

V

Vacaville, CA 95687–88 • 71,479
Vacherie, LA 70090 • 2,169
Vadnais Heights, MN 55110 • 11,041
Vail, CO 81657–58 • 3,659
Valatie, NY 12184 • 1,487
Valdese, NC 28690 • 3,914
Valdez, AK 99686 • 4,068
Valdosta, GA 31601–04 • 39,806
Vale, OR 97918 • 1,491
Valencia, AZ 85326 • 1,200
Valencia □, NM • 45,235
Valencia Heights, SC 29205 • 4,122
Valentine, NE 69201 • 2,826
Valhalla, NY 10595 • 6,200
Valinda, CA 91744 • 18,735
Vallejo, CA 94589–92 • 109,199
Valle Vista, CA 92343 • 8,751
Valley, AL 36854 • 8,173
Valley, NE 68064 • 1,775
Valley □, ID • 6,109
Valley □, MT • 8,239
Valley □, NE • 5,169
Valley Center, KS 67147 • 3,624
Valley City, ND 58072 • 7,163
Valley Cottage, NY 10989 • 9,007
Valley Falls, KS 66088 • 1,253
Valley Falls, RI 02864 • 11,175
Valley Forge, PA 19481–82 • 1,500
Valley Mills, TX 76689 • 1,085
Valley Park, MO 63088 • 4,165
Valley Ridge, WA 98188 • 6,500
Valley Springs, SD 57068 • 739
Valley Station, KY 40272 • 22,840
Valley Stream, NY 11580–82 • 33,946
Valley View, PA 17983 • 1,749
Valparaiso, FL 32580 • 4,672
Valparaiso, IN 46383–84 • 24,414
Val Verda, UT 84010 • 3,712
Val Verde □, TX • 38,721
Van, TX 75790 • 1,854
Van Alstyne, TX 75095 • 2,090
Van Buren, AR 72956 • 14,979
Van Buren, ME 04785 • 2,759
Van Buren □, AR • 14,008
Van Buren □, IA • 7,676
Van Buren □, MI • 70,060
Van Buren □, TN • 4,846
Vance □, NC • 38,892
Vanceburg, KY 41179 • 1,713
Vancleave, MS 39564 • 3,214
Vancouver, WA 98660–68 • 46,380
Vandalia, IL 62471 • 6,114
Vandalia, MO 63382 • 2,683
Vandalia, OH 45377 • 13,882
Vandenberg Village, CA 93436 • 5,871
Vander, NC 28301 • 1,179
Vanderburgh □, IN • 165,058
Vandergrift, PA 15690 • 5,904
Van Horn, TX 79855 • 2,930
Van Lear, KY 41265 • 1,050
Vansant, VA 24656 • 1,187
Van Vleck, TX 77482 • 1,534
Van Wert, OH 45891 • 10,891
Van Wert □, OH • 30,464
Van Zandt □, TX • 37,944
Varina, VA 23231 • 2,500
Varnville, SC 29944 • 1,970
Vassar, MI 48768 • 2,559
Vaughn, MT 59487 • 2,270
Veazie, ME 04401 • 1,610
Veedersburg, IN 47987 • 2,192
Velda Rose Estates, AZ 85205 • 2,330
Velva, ND 58790 • 968
Venango □, PA • 59,381
Veneta, OR 97487 • 2,519
Venice, FL 34292–93 • 16,922
Venice, IL 62090 • 3,571
Venice Gardens, FL 34293 • 7,701
Ventnor City, NJ 08406 • 11,005
Ventura (San Buenaventura), CA 93001–07 • 92,575
Ventura □, CA • 669,016
Veradale, WA 99037 • 7,836
Verda, KY 40828 • 1,133
Verdi, NV 89439 • 1,140
Vergennes, VT 05491 • 2,578
Vermilion, OH 44089 • 11,127
Vermilion □, IL • 88,257
Vermilion □, LA • 50,055
Vermillion, SD 57069 • 10,034
Vermillion □, IN • 16,773
Vernal, UT 84078–79 • 6,644
Vernon, AL 35592 • 2,247
Vernon, CT 06066 • 30,200
Vernon, TX 76384 • 12,001
Vernon □, LA • 61,961
Vernon □, MO • 19,041
Vernon □, WI • 25,617
Vernon Hills, IL 60061 • 15,319
Vernonia, OR 97064 • 1,808
Vero Beach, FL 32960–68 • 17,350
Verona, MS 38879 • 2,893
Verona, NJ 07044 • 13,597
Verona, PA 15147 • 3,260
Verona, WI 53593 • 5,374
Versailles, IN 47042 • 1,791
Versailles, KY 40383 • 7,269
Versailles, MO 65084 • 2,365
Versailles, OH 45380 • 2,351
Vestal, NY 13850–51 • 5,530
Vestavia Hills, AL 35216 • 19,749
Vevay, IN 47043 • 1,393
Vian, OK 74962 • 1,414
Vicksburg, MI 49097 • 2,216
Vicksburg, MS 39180–82 • 20,908
Victor, NY 14564 • 2,308
Victoria, KS 67671 • 1,157
Victoria, TX 77901–05 • 55,076
Victoria, VA 23974 • 1,830
Victoria □, TX • 74,361
Victorville, CA 92392–93 • 40,674
Vidalia, GA 30474 • 11,078
Vidalia, LA 71373 • 4,953
Vidor, TX 77662 • 10,935
Vienna, GA 31092 • 2,708
Vienna, IL 62995 • 1,446
Vienna, VA 22180–83 • 14,852
Vienna, WV 26105 • 10,862
View Park, CA 90043 • 5,900
Vigo □, IN • 106,107
Vilas □, WI • 17,707
Villa Grove, IL 61956 • 2,734
Villa Hills, KY 41016 • 7,739
Villa Park, CA 92667 • 6,299
Villa Park, IL 60181 • 22,253
Villa Rica, GA 30180 • 6,542
Villas, NJ 08251 • 8,136
Ville Platte, LA 70586 • 9,037
Villisca, IA 50864 • 1,332
Vilonia, AR 72173 • 1,133
Vincennes, IN 47591 • 19,859
Vincent, AL 35178 • 1,767
Vine Grove, KY 40175 • 3,586
Vineland, NJ 08360 • 54,780
Vineyard Haven, MA 02568 • 1,762
Vinita, OK 74301 • 5,804
Vinton, IA 52349 • 5,103
Vinton, LA 70668 • 3,154
Vinton, VA 24179 • 7,665
Vinton □, OH • 11,098
Viola, NY 10952 • 4,504
Violet, LA 70092 • 8,574
Virden, IL 62690 • 3,635
Virginia, IL 62691 • 1,767
Virginia, MN 55792 • 9,410
Virginia Beach, VA 23450–67 • 393,069
Virginia City, NV 89440 • 920
Viroqua, WI 54665 • 3,922
Visalia, CA 93277–79 • 75,636
Vista, CA 92083–84 • 71,872
Vivian, LA 71082 • 4,156
Volcano, HI 96785 • 1,516
Volga, SD 57071 • 1,263
Volusia □, FL • 370,712

W

Wabash, IN 46992 • 12,127
Wabash □, IL • 13,111
Wabash □, IN • 35,069
Wabasha, MN 55981 • 2,384
Wabasha □, MN • 19,744
Wabasso, FL 32970 • 1,145
Wabaunsee □, KS • 6,603
Waco, TX 76701–16 • 103,590
Waconia, MN 55387 • 3,498
Wade Hampton, SC 29607 • 20,014
Wadena, MN 56482 • 4,131
Wadena □, MN • 13,154
Wadesboro, NC 28170 • 3,645
Wading River, NY 11792 • 5,317
Wadley, GA 30477 • 2,473
Wadsworth, IL 60083 • 1,826
Wadsworth, NV 89442 • 640
Wadsworth, OH 44281 • 15,718
Wagner, SD 57380 • 1,462
Wagoner, OK 74467 • 6,894
Wagoner □, OK • 47,883
Wahiawa, HI 96786 • 17,386
Wahkiakum □, WA • 3,327
Wahoo, NE 68066 • 3,681
Wahpeton, ND 58074–75 • 8,751
Waialua, HI 96791 • 3,943
Waianae, HI 96792 • 8,758
Waikapu, HI 96793 • 729
Wailua, HI 96746 • 2,018
Wailuku, HI 96793 • 10,688
Waimanalo, HI 96795 • 3,508
Waimea, HI 96712 • 600
Waimea, HI 96796 • 5,972
Wainwright, AK 99782 • 492
Waipahu, HI 96797 • 31,435
Waipio Acres, HI 96786 • 5,304
Waite Park, MN 56387 • 5,020
Wakarusa, IN 46573 • 1,667
Wake □, NC • 423,380
Wa Keeney, KS 67672 • 2,161
Wakefield, MA 01880 • 24,825
Wakefield, MI 49968 • 2,318
Wakefield, NE 68784 • 1,082
Wakefield, RI 02879–83 • 3,450
Wakefield, VA 23888 • 1,070
Wake Forest, NC 27587–88 • 5,769
Wakulla □, FL • 14,202
Walbridge, OH 43465 • 2,736
Walcott, IA 52773 • 1,356
Walden, NY 12586 • 5,836
Waldo, AR 71770 • 1,495
Waldo, FL 32694 • 1,017
Waldo □, ME • 33,018
Waldoboro, ME 04572 • 1,420
Waldport, OR 97394 • 1,595
Waldron, AR 72958 • 3,024
Waldwick, NJ 07463 • 9,757
Walhalla, ND 58282 • 1,131
Walhalla, SC 29691 • 3,755
Walker, LA 70785 • 3,727
Walker, MI 49504 • 17,279
Walker □, AL • 67,670
Walker □, GA • 58,340
Walker □, TX • 50,917
Walkersville, MD 21793 • 4,145
Walkerton, IN 46574 • 2,061
Walkertown, NC 27051 • 1,200
Walkerville, MT 59701 • 605
Wall, SD 57790 • 834
Wallace, ID 83873 • 1,010
Wallace, NC 28466 • 2,939
Wallace □, KS • 1,821
Walla Walla, WA 99362 • 26,478
Walla Walla □, WA • 48,439
Walled Lake, MI 48390 • 6,278
Wallen, IN 46806 • 1,000
Waller, TX 77484 • 1,493
Waller □, TX • 23,390
Wallingford, CT 06492 • 17,827
Wallingford, VT 05773 • 1,148
Wallington, NJ 07057 • 10,828
Wallis, TX 77485 • 1,001
Wallkill, NY 12589 • 2,125
Wallowa □, OR • 6,911
Walnut, CA 91789 • 29,105
Walnut, IL 61376 • 1,463
Walnut Cove, NC 27052 • 1,088
Walnut Creek, CA 94593–98 • 60,569
Walnut Park, CA 90255 • 14,722
Walnutport, PA 18088 • 2,055
Walnut Ridge, AR 72476 • 4,388
Walpole, MA 02081 • 5,495
Walsenburg, CO 81089 • 3,300
Walsh □, ND • 13,840
Walterboro, SC 29488 • 5,492
Walters, OK 73572 • 2,519
Walthall □, MS • 14,352
Waltham, MA 02154 • 57,878
Walthourville, GA 31333 • 2,024
Walton, IN 46994 • 1,053
Walton, KY 41094 • 2,034
Walton, NY 13856 • 3,326
Walton □, FL • 27,760
Walton □, GA • 38,586
Walworth, WI 53184 • 1,614
Walworth □, SD • 6,087
Walworth □, WI • 75,000
Wamac, IL 62801 • 1,501
Wamego, KS 66547 • 3,706
Wamesit, MA 01876 • 2,700
Wamsutter, WY 82336 • 240
Wanaque, NJ 07465 • 9,711
Wanchese, NC 27981 • 1,380
Wando Woods, SC 29405 • 5,253
Wantagh, NY 11793 • 18,567
Wapakoneta, OH 45895 • 9,214
Wapato, WA 98951 • 3,795
Wapello, IA 52653 • 2,013
Wapello □, IA • 35,687
Wappingers Falls, NY 12590 • 4,605
War, WV 24892 • 1,081
Ward, AR 72176 • 1,269
Ward □, ND • 57,921
Ward □, TX • 13,115
Warden, WA 98857 • 1,639
Ware, MA 01082 • 6,533
Ware □, GA • 35,471
Wareham, MA 02571 • 2,607
Warehouse Point, CT 06088 • 1,880
Ware Shoals, SC 29692 • 2,497
Waretown, NJ 08758 • 1,283
Warminster, PA 18974 • 35,463
Warner, OK 74469 • 1,479
Warner Robins, GA 31088 • 43,726
Warr Acres, OK 73132 • 9,288
Warren, AR 71671 • 6,455
Warren, IL 61087 • 1,550
Warren, IN 46792 • 1,185
Warren, MA 01083 • 1,516
Warren, MI 48089–93 • 144,864
Warren, MN 56762 • 1,813
Warren, OH 44481–85 • 50,793
Warren, PA 16365 • 11,122
Warren, RI 02885 • 11,385
Warren, VT 05674 • 350
Warren □, GA • 6,078
Warren □, IL • 19,181
Warren □, IN • 8,176
Warren □, IA • 36,033
Warren □, KY • 76,673
Warren □, MS • 47,880
Warren □, MO • 19,534
Warren □, NJ • 91,607
Warren □, NY • 59,209
Warren □, NC • 17,265
Warren □, OH • 113,909
Warren □, PA • 45,050
Warren □, TN • 32,992
Warren □, VA • 26,142
Warren Park, IN 46219 • 1,763
Warrensburg, IL 62573 • 1,274
Warrensburg, MO 64093 • 15,244
Warrensburg, NY 12885 • 3,204
Warrensville Heights, OH 44122 • 15,745
Warrenton, GA 30828 • 2,056
Warrenton, MO 63383 • 3,564
Warrenton, OR 97146 • 2,681
Warrenton, VA 22186 • 4,830
Warrenville, IL 60555 • 11,333
Warrenville, SC 29851 • 1,029
Warrick □, IN • 44,920
Warrington, FL 32507 • 16,040
Warrington, PA 18976 • 6,980
Warrior, AL 35180 • 3,280
Warroad, MN 56763 • 1,679
Warsaw, IL 62379 • 1,882
Warsaw, IN 46580–81 • 10,968
Warsaw, KY 41095 • 1,202
Warsaw, MO 65355 • 1,696
Warsaw, NY 14569 • 3,830
Warsaw, NC 28398 • 2,859
Warwick, NY 10990 • 5,984
Warwick, RI 02886–89 • 85,427
Wasatch □, UT • 10,089
Wasco, CA 93280 • 12,412
Wasco □, OR • 21,683
Waseca, MN 56093 • 8,385
Waseca □, MN • 18,079
Washakie □, WY • 8,388
Washburn, IL 61570 • 1,075
Washburn, IA 50706 • 1,400
Washburn, ME 04786 • 1,880
Washburn, ND 58577 • 1,506
Washburn, WI 54891 • 2,285
Washburn □, WI • 13,772
Washington, DC 20001–99 • 606,900
Washington, GA 30673 • 4,279
Washington, IL 61571 • 10,099
Washington, IN 47501 • 10,838
Washington, IA 52353 • 7,074
Washington, KS 66968 • 1,304
Washington, LA 70589 • 1,253
Washington, MO 63090 • 10,704
Washington, NJ 07882 • 6,474
Washington, NC 27889 • 9,075
Washington, PA 15301 • 15,864
Washington, UT 84780 • 4,198
Washington □, AL • 16,694
Washington □, AR • 113,409
Washington □, CO • 4,812
Washington □, FL • 16,919
Washington □, GA • 19,112
Washington □, ID • 8,550
Washington □, IL • 14,965
Washington □, IN • 23,717

Washington □, IA • 19,612
Washington □, KS • 7,073
Washington □, KY • 10,441
Washington □, LA • 43,185
Washington □, ME • 35,308
Washington □, MD • 121,393
Washington □, MN • 145,896
Washington □, MS • 67,935
Washington □, MO • 20,380
Washington □, NE • 16,607
Washington □, NY • 59,330
Washington □, NC • 13,997
Washington □, OH • 62,254
Washington □, OK • 48,066
Washington □, OR • 311,554
Washington □, PA • 204,584
Washington □, RI • 110,006
Washington □, TN • 92,315
Washington □, TX • 26,154
Washington □, UT • 48,560
Washington □, VT • 54,928
Washington □, VA • 45,837
Washington □, WI • 95,328
Washington Court House, OH 43160 • 12,983
Washington Park, FL 33314 • 6,930
Washington Park, IL 62204 • 7,431
Washington Terrace, UT 84403 • 8,189
Washington Township, NJ 07675 • 9,245
Washita □, OK • 11,441
Washoe □, NV • 254,667
Washoe City, NV 89701 • 400
Washougal, WA 98671 • 4,764
Washtenaw □, MI • 282,937
Wasilla, AK 99687 • 4,028
Waskom, TX 75692 • 1,812
Watauga, TX 76148 • 20,009
Watauga □, NC • 36,952
Watchung, NJ 07060 • 5,110
Waterbury, CT 06701–26 • 108,961
Waterbury, VT 05676 • 1,702
Waterbury Center, VT 05677 • 500
Waterford, CT 06385 • 17,930
Waterford, MI 48327–29 • 66,692
Waterford, NY 12188 • 2,370
Waterford, PA 16441 • 1,492
Waterford, WI 53185 • 2,431
Waterford Works, NJ 08089 • 1,200
Waterloo, IL 62298 • 5,072
Waterloo, IN 46793 • 2,040
Waterloo, IA 50701–07 • 66,467
Waterloo, NY 13165 • 5,116
Waterloo, WI 53594 • 2,712
Waterman, IL 60556 • 1,074
Waterproof, LA 71375 • 1,080
Watertown, CT 06795 • 20,456
Watertown, FL 32055 • 3,340
Watertown, MA 02172 • 33,284
Watertown, NY 13601–03 • 29,429
Watertown, SD 57201 • 17,592
Watertown, TN 37184 • 1,250
Watertown, WI 53094 • 19,142
Water Valley, MS 38965 • 3,610
Waterville, ME 04901–03 • 17,173
Waterville, MN 56096 • 1,771
Waterville, NY 13480 • 1,664
Waterville, OH 43566 • 4,517
Watervliet, MI 49098 • 1,867
Watervliet, NY 12189 • 11,061
Watford City, ND 58854 • 1,784
Wathena, KS 66090 • 1,160
Watkins Glen, NY 14891 • 2,207
Watkinsville, GA 30677 • 1,600
Watonga, OK 73772 • 3,408
Watonwan □, MN • 11,682
Watseka, IL 60970 • 5,424
Watsontown, PA 17777 • 2,310
Watsonville, CA 95076–77 • 31,099
Wattsville, SC 29360 • 1,324
Wauchula, FL 33873 • 3,253
Wauconda, IL 60084 • 6,294
Waukee, IA 50263 • 2,512
Waukegan, IL 60085–87 • 69,392
Waukesha, WI 53186–88 • 56,958
Waukesha □, WI • 304,715
Waukomis, OK 73773 • 1,322
Waukon, IA 52172 • 4,019
Waunakee, WI 53597 • 5,897
Waupaca, WI 54981 • 4,957
Waupaca □, WI • 46,104
Waupun, WI 53963 • 8,207
Wauregan, CT 06387 • 1,200
Waurika, OK 73573 • 2,088
Wausau, WI 54401–02 • 37,060
Wauseon, OH 43567 • 6,322
Waushara □, WI • 19,385
Wautoma, WI 54982 • 1,784
Wauwatosa, WI 53213 • 49,366
Waveland, MS 39576 • 5,369
Waverly, IL 62692 • 1,402
Waverly, IA 50677 • 8,539
Waverly, MI 48917 • 15,614
Waverly, NE 68462 • 1,869
Waverly, NY 14892 • 4,787
Waverly, OH 45690 • 4,477
Waverly, TN 37185 • 3,925
Waverly, VA 23890 • 2,223
Waxahachie, TX 75165 • 18,168
Waxhaw, NC 28173 • 1,294
Waycross, GA 31501 • 16,410
Wayland, MA 01778 • 2,550
Wayland, MI 49348 • 2,751
Wayland, NY 14572 • 1,976
Waylyn, SC 29405 • 2,400
Waymart, PA 18472 • 1,337
Wayne, MI 48184–88 • 19,899
Wayne, NE 68787 • 5,142
Wayne, NJ 07470–74 • 47,025
Wayne, WV 25570 • 1,128
Wayne □, GA • 22,356
Wayne □, IL • 17,241
Wayne □, IN • 71,951
Wayne □, IA • 7,067
Wayne □, KY • 17,468
Wayne □, MI • 2,111,687
Wayne □, MS • 19,517
Wayne □, MO • 11,543
Wayne □, NE • 9,364
Wayne □, NY • 89,123
Wayne □, NC • 104,666
Wayne □, OH • 101,461
Wayne □, PA • 39,944
Wayne □, TN • 13,935
Wayne □, UT • 2,177
Wayne □, WV • 41,636
Wayne City, IL 62895 • 1,099
Waynesboro, GA 30830 • 5,701
Waynesboro, MS 39367 • 5,143
Waynesboro, PA 17268 • 9,578
Waynesboro, TN 38485 • 1,824
Waynesboro, VA 22980 • 18,549
Waynesburg, OH 44688 • 1,068
Waynesburg, PA 15370 • 4,270
Waynesville, MO 65583 • 3,207
Waynesville, NC 28786 • 6,758
Waynesville, OH 45068 • 1,949
Waynewood, VA 22308 • 5,000
Wayzata, MN 55391 • 3,806
Weakley □, TN • 31,972
Weatherford, OK 73096 • 10,124
Weatherford, TX 76086–87 • 14,804
Weatherly, PA 18255 • 2,640
Weatogue, CT 06089 • 2,521
Weaver, AL 36277 • 2,715
Weaverville, CA 96093 • 3,370
Weaverville, NC 28787 • 2,107
Webb, AL 36376 • 1,039
Webb □, TX • 133,239
Webb City, MO 64870 • 7,449
Webberville, MI 48892 • 1,698
Weber □, UT • 158,330
Weber City, VA 24251 • 1,377
Webster, MA 01570 • 11,849
Webster, NY 14580 • 5,464
Webster, PA 15087 • 1,000
Webster, SD 57274 • 2,017
Webster □, GA • 2,263
Webster □, IA • 40,342
Webster □, KY • 13,955
Webster □, LA • 41,989
Webster □, MS • 10,222
Webster □, MO • 23,753
Webster □, NE • 4,279
Webster □, WV • 10,729
Webster City, IA 50595 • 7,894
Webster Groves, MO 63119 • 22,987
Websterville, VT 05678 • 600
Wedgewood, MO 63031 • 6,700
Weed, CA 96094 • 3,062
Weed Heights, NV 89447 • 230
Weedsport, NY 13166 • 1,996
Weehawken, NJ 07087 • 12,385
Weeping Water, NE 68463 • 1,008
Weigelstown, PA 17315 • 8,665
Weimar, TX 78962 • 2,052
Weippe, ID 83553 • 532
Weirsdale, FL 32195 • 1,500
Weirton, WV 26062 • 22,124
Weiser, ID 83672 • 4,571
Wekiva Springs, FL 32750 • 23,026
Welch, WV 24801 • 3,028
Welcome, SC 29611 • 6,560
Weld □, CO • 131,821
Weldon, NC 27890 • 1,392
Weleetka, OK 74880 • 1,112
Wellesley, MA 02181 • 26,615
Wellfleet, MA 02667 • 1,200
Wellford, SC 29385 • 2,511
Wellington, CO 80549 • 1,340
Wellington, FL 33414 • 20,670
Wellington, KS 67152 • 8,411
Wellington, NV 89444 • 280
Wellington, OH 44090 • 4,140
Wellington, TX 79095 • 2,456
Wellington, UT 84542 • 1,632
Wellman, IA 52356 • 1,085
Wells, ME 04090 • 1,200
Wells, MI 49894 • 1,150
Wells, MN 56097 • 2,465
Wells, NV 89835 • 1,256
Wells □, IN • 25,948
Wells □, ND • 5,864
Wellsboro, PA 16901 • 3,430
Wellsburg, WV 26070 • 3,385
Wellston, OH 45692 • 6,049
Wellsville, KS 66092 • 1,563
Wellsville, MO 63384 • 1,430
Wellsville, NY 14895 • 5,241
Wellsville, OH 43968 • 4,532
Wellsville, UT 84339 • 2,206
Wellton, AZ 85356 • 1,066
Welsh, LA 70591 • 3,299
Wenatchee, WA 98801–07 • 21,756
Wendell, ID 83355 • 1,963
Wendell, NC 27591 • 2,822
Wendover, UT 84083 • 1,127
Wenham, MA 01984 • 3,897
Wenonah, NJ 08090 • 2,331
Wentzville, MO 63385 • 5,088
Weslaco, TX 78596 • 21,877
Wesleyville, PA 16510 • 3,655
Wessington Springs, SD 57382 • 1,083
Wesson, MS 39191 • 1,510
West, TX 76691 • 2,515
West Acton, MA 01720 • 5,230
West Alexandria, OH 45381 • 1,460
West Allis, WI 53214 • 63,221
West Andover, MA 01810 • 1,970
West Athens, CA 90247 • 8,859
West Babylon, NY 11704 • 42,410
West Barnstable, MA 02668 • 1,000
West Baton Rouge □, LA • 19,419
West Bay Shore, NY 11706 • 4,907
West Bend, WI 53095 • 23,916
West Berlin, NJ 08091 • 2,970
West Billerica, MA 01862 • 1,920
West Blocton, AL 35184 • 1,468
Westborough, MA 01581 • 3,917
West Bountiful, UT 84087 • 4,477
West Boylston, MA 01583 • 3,130
West Bradenton, FL 34205 • 4,528
West Branch, IA 52358 • 1,908
West Branch, MI 48661 • 1,914
West Bridgewater, MA 02379 • 2,140
Westbrook, CT 06498 • 2,060
Westbrook, ME 04092 • 16,121
West Brookfield, MA 01585 • 1,419
West Burlington, IA 52655 • 3,083
Westbury, NY 11590 • 13,060
Westby, WI 54667 • 1,866
West Caldwell, NJ 07004 • 10,422
West Cape May, NJ 08204 • 1,026
West Carroll □, LA • 12,093
West Carrollton, OH 45449 • 14,403
West Carson, CA 90502 • 20,143
West Carthage, NY 13619 • 2,166
West Chatham, MA 02669 • 1,504
Westchester, FL 33136 • 29,883
Westchester, IL 60153 • 17,301
West Chester, PA 19380–82 • 18,041
Westchester □, NY • 874,866
West Chicago, IL 60185–86 • 14,796
West Columbia, SC 29169–72 • 10,588
West Columbia, TX 77486 • 4,372
West Compton, CA 90220 • 5,451
West Concord, MA 01742 • 5,761
West Concord, NC 28027 • 5,859
West Covina, CA 91790–93 • 96,086
West Crossett, AR 71635 • 2,019
West Dennis, MA 02670 • 2,307
West Des Moines, IA 50265 • 31,702
West Elmira, NY 14905 • 5,218
Westerly, RI 02891 • 16,477
Westernport, MD 21562 • 2,454
Western Springs, IL 60558 • 11,984
Westerville, OH 43081–82 • 30,269
West Fairview, PA 17025 • 1,403
West Falmouth, MA 02574 • 1,600
West Fargo, ND 58078 • 12,287
West Feliciana □, LA • 12,915
Westfield, IN 46074 • 3,304
Westfield, MA 01085–86 • 38,372
Westfield, NJ 07090–92 • 28,870
Westfield, NY 14787 • 3,451
Westfield, PA 16950 • 1,119
Westfield, WI 53964 • 1,125
Westford, MA 01886 • 1,200
West Fork, AR 72774 • 1,607
West Frankfort, IL 62896 • 8,526
West Freehold, NJ 07728 • 11,166
Westgate, FL 33401 • 2,100
West Gate, VA 22110 • 6,565
West Gate of Lomond, VA 22110 • 5,400
West Glens Falls, NY 12801 • 5,964
West Goshen, PA 19380 • 8,948
West Grove, PA 19390 • 2,128
Westham, VA 23229 • 3,200
West Hanover, MA 02339 • 1,700
West Hartford, CT 06127 • 60,110
West Haven, CT 06516 • 54,021
West Haven, OR 97225 • 3,400
West Haverstraw, NY 10993 • 9,183
West Hazleton, PA 18201 • 4,136
West Helena, AR 72390 • 9,695
West Hempstead, NY 11552 • 17,689
West Hollywood, CA 90069 • 36,118
Westhope, ND 58793 • 578
West Hyannisport, MA 02672 • 1,200
West Islip, NY 11795 • 28,419
West Jefferson, NC 28694 • 1,002
West Jefferson, OH 43162 • 4,504
West Jordan, UT 84084 • 42,892
West Kingston, RI 02892 • 1,150
West Lafayette, IN 47906–07 • 25,907
West Lafayette, OH 43845 • 2,129
Westlake, LA 70669 • 5,007
Westlake, OH 44145 • 27,018
Westlake Village, CA 91361 • 7,455
Westland, MI 48185 • 84,724
West Lawn, PA 19609 • 1,606
West Liberty, IA 52776 • 2,935
West Liberty, KY 41472 • 1,887
West Liberty, OH 43357 • 1,613
West Liberty, WV 26074 • 1,434
West Linn, OR 97068 • 16,367
West Long Branch, NJ 07764 • 7,690
West Marion, NC 28752 • 1,291
West Medway, MA 02053 • 1,940
West Melbourne, FL 32901 • 8,399
West Memphis, AR 72301 • 28,259
Westmere, NY 12203 • 6,750
West Miami, FL 33174 • 5,727
West Mifflin, PA 15122–23 • 23,644
West Milford, NJ 07480 • 25,430
West Milton, OH 45383 • 4,348
West Milwaukee, WI 53214 • 3,973
Westminster, CA 92683–84 • 78,118
Westminster, CO 80030–31 • 74,625
Westminster, MD 21157 • 13,068
Westminster, SC 29693 • 3,120
West Modesto, CA 95351 • 6,135
West Monroe, LA 71291–94 • 14,096
Westmont, CA 90044 • 31,100
Westmont, IL 60559 • 21,228
Westmont, NJ 08108 • 5,630
Westmont, PA 15905 • 5,789
Westmoreland, TN 37186 • 1,726
Westmoreland □, PA • 370,321
Westmoreland □, VA • 15,480
Westmorland, CA 92281 • 1,380
West Mystic, CT 06388 • 3,595
West Newton, PA 15089 • 3,152
West New York, NJ 07093 • 38,125
West Norriton, PA 19401 • 15,209
West Nyack, NY 10960 • 3,437
Weston, CT 06883 • 1,370
Weston, MA 02193 • 11,169
Weston, MO 64098 • 1,528
Weston, OH 43569 • 1,716
Weston, WV 26452 • 4,994
Weston, WI 54476 • 9,714
Weston □, WY • 6,518
West Orange, NJ 07052 • 39,103
Westover, WV 26505 • 4,201
West Palm Beach, FL 33401–20 • 67,643
West Pasco, WA 99301 • 7,312
West Paterson, NJ 07424 • 10,982
West Pawlet, VT 05775 • 350
West Pensacola, FL 32505 • 22,107
West Peoria, IL 61604 • 5,314
West Pittsburg, CA 94565 • 17,453
West Pittsburg, PA 16160 • 1,133
West Pittston, PA 18643 • 5,590
West Plains, MO 65775 • 8,913
West Point, CA 95255 • 1,500
West Point, GA 31833 • 3,571
West Point, IA 52656 • 1,079
West Point, KY 40177 • 1,216
West Point, MS 39773 • 8,489
West Point, NE 68788 • 3,250
West Point, NY 10996–97 • 8,024
West Point, UT 84015 • 4,258
West Point, VA 23181 • 2,938
Westport, CT 06880–83 • 24,407
Westport, IN 47283 • 1,478
Westport, WA 98595 • 1,892
West Portsmouth, OH 45662 • 3,551
West Puente Valley, CA 91744 • 20,254
West Reading, PA 19611 • 4,142
West Rutland, VT 05777 • 2,246
West Sacramento, CA 95691 • 28,898
West Saint Paul, MN 55118 • 19,248
West Salem, IL 62476 • 1,042
West Salem, OH 44287 • 1,534
West Salem, WI 54669 • 3,611
West Sayville, NY 11796 • 4,680
West Seneca, NY 14224 • 47,866
West Simsbury, CT 06092 • 2,149
West Slope, OR 97225 • 7,959
West Springfield, MA 01089–90 • 27,537
West Springfield, VA 22152 • 28,126
West Swanzey, NH 03469 • 1,055
West Terre Haute, IN 47885 • 2,495
West Union, IA 52175 • 2,490
West Union, OH 45693 • 3,096
West Unity, OH 43570 • 1,677
West University Place, TX 77005 • 12,920
West Upton, MA 01587 • 1,300
Westvale, NY 13219 • 5,952
West Valley City, UT 84120 • 86,976
Westview, FL 33168 • 9,668
West View, PA 15229 • 7,734
Westville, IL 61883 • 3,387
Westville, IN 46391 • 5,255
Westville, NJ 08093 • 4,573
Westville, OK 74965 • 1,374
West Wareham, MA 02576 • 2,059
West Warren, MA 01092 • 1,200
West Warwick, RI 02893 • 29,268
West Webster, NY 14580 • 8,690
Westwego, LA 70094–96 • 11,218
West Whittier, CA 90606 • 13,800
West Willow, MI 48198 • 4,300
Westwood, CA 96137 • 2,017
Westwood, KS 66205 • 1,772
Westwood, KY 41101 • 5,300
Westwood, MA 02090 • 6,500
Westwood, MI 49007 • 8,957
Westwood, NJ 07675 • 10,446
Westwood Lakes, FL 33165 • 11,522
West Wyoming, PA 18644 • 3,117
West Yarmouth, MA 02673 • 5,409
West Yellowstone, MT 59758 • 913
West York, PA 17404 • 4,283
Wethersfield, CT 06129 • 25,651
Wetumka, OK 74883 • 1,427
Wetumpka, AL 36092 • 4,670
Wetzel □, WV • 19,258
Wewahitchka, FL 32465 • 1,779
Wewoka, OK 74884 • 4,050
Wexford □, MI • 26,360
Weyauwega, WI 54983 • 1,665
Weymouth, MA 02188 • 54,063
Whalom, MA 01420 • 1,340
Wharton, NJ 07885 • 5,405
Wharton, TX 77488 • 9,011
Wharton □, TX • 39,955
Whatcom □, WA • 127,780
Wheatland, CA 95692 • 1,631
Wheatland, WY 82201 • 3,271
Wheatland □, MT • 2,246
Wheaton, IL 60187–89 • 51,464
Wheaton, MD 20902 • 58,300
Wheaton, MN 56296 • 1,615
Wheat Ridge, CO 80033–34 • 29,419
Wheeler, TX 79096 • 1,393
Wheeler □, GA • 4,903
Wheeler □, NE • 948
Wheeler □, OR • 1,396
Wheeler □, TX • 5,879
Wheelersburg, OH 45694 • 5,113
Wheeling, IL 60090 • 29,911
Wheeling, WV 26003 • 34,882
Whitacres, CT 06082 • 2,410
White □, AR • 54,676
White □, GA • 13,006
White □, IL • 16,522
White □, IN • 23,265
White □, TN • 20,090
White Bear Lake, MN 55110 • 24,704
White Bluff, TN 37187 • 1,988
White Castle, LA 70788 • 2,102
White Center, WA 98126 • 15,700
White City, OR 97503 • 5,891
White City, UT 84070 • 6,506
White Cloud, MI 49349 • 1,147
White Deer, TX 79097 • 1,125
Whitefield, NH 03598 • 1,041
Whitefish, MT 59937 • 4,368
Whitefish Bay, WI 53217 • 14,272
White Hall, AR 71602 • 3,849
White Hall, IL 62092 • 2,814
Whitehall, MI 49461 • 3,027
Whitehall, MT 59759 • 1,067
Whitehall, NY 12887 • 3,071
Whitehall, OH 43213 • 20,572
Whitehall, PA 15227 • 14,451
Whitehall, WI 54773 • 1,494
White Haven, PA 18661 • 1,132
White Horse, NJ 08610 • 9,397
White Horse Beach, MA 02381 • 1,200
Whitehouse, OH 43571 • 2,528
White House, TN 37188 • 2,987
White House Station, NJ 08889 • 1,400
White Island Shores, MA 02538 • 2,000
White Meadow Lake, NJ 07866 • 8,002
White Oak, MD 20901 • 18,671
White Oak, OH 45239 • 12,430
White Oak, PA 15131 • 8,761
White Pigeon, MI 49099 • 1,458
White Pine, MI 49971 • 1,142
White Pine, TN 37890 • 1,771
White Pine □, NV • 9,264
White Plains, MD 20695 • 3,560
White Plains, NY 10601–07 • 48,718
Whiteriver, AZ 85941 • 3,775
White River Junction, VT 05001 • 2,521
White Rock, NM 87544 • 6,192
White Salmon, WA 98672 • 1,861
Whitesboro, NY 13492 • 4,195
Whitesboro, TX 76273 • 3,209
Whitesburg, KY 41858 • 1,636
White Settlement, TX 76108 • 15,472
Whiteside □, IL • 60,186
White Sulphur Springs, MT 59645 • 963
White Sulphur Springs, WV 24986 • 2,779
Whiteville, NC 28472 • 5,078
Whiteville, TN 38075 • 1,050
Whitewater, WI 53190 • 12,636
Whitewood, SD 57793 • 891
Whitewright, TX 75491 • 1,713
Whitfield □, GA • 72,462
Whitfield Estates, FL 34243 • 3,152
Whiting, IN 46394 • 5,155
Whiting, WI 54481 • 1,838
Whitinsville, MA 01588 • 5,639
Whitley □, IN • 27,651
Whitley □, KY • 33,326
Whitley City, KY 42653 • 1,133
Whitman, MA 02382 • 13,534
Whitman, WV 25652 • 1,651
Whitman □, WA • 38,775
Whitman Square, NJ 08012 • 3,490
Whitmire, SC 29178 • 1,702
Whitmore Lake, MI 48189 • 3,251
Whitmore Village, HI 96786 • 3,373
Whitney, SC 29303 • 4,052
Whitney, TX 76692 • 1,626
Whitney Point, NY 13862 • 1,054
Whittier, AK 99693 • 243
Whittier, CA 90601–12 • 77,671
Whitwell, TN 37397 • 1,622
Wibaux, MT 59353 • 628
Wibaux □, MT • 1,191
Wichita, KS 67201–78 • 304,011
Wichita □, KS • 2,758
Wichita □, TX • 122,378
Wichita Falls, TX 76301–11 • 96,259
Wickenburg, AZ 85358 • 4,515
Wickliffe, OH 44092 • 14,558
Wickliffe, OH 44515 • 7,240
Wicomico □, MD • 74,339
Wiconisco, PA 17097 • 1,321
Widefield, CO 80911 • 12,112
Wiggins, MS 39577 • 3,185
Wilbarger □, TX • 15,121
Wilber, NE 68465 • 1,527
Wilberforce, OH 45384 • 2,639
Wilbraham, MA 01095 • 3,352
Wilburton, OK 74578 • 3,092
Wilcox, PA 15870 • 1,000
Wilcox □, AL • 13,568
Wilcox □, GA • 7,008
Wilder, ID 83676 • 1,232
Wilder, VT 05088 • 1,576
Wildorado, TX 79098 • 2,000
Wildwood, FL 34785 • 3,421
Wildwood, IL 60030 • 2,034
Wildwood, NJ 08260 • 4,484
Wildwood Crest, NJ 08260 • 3,631
Wilkes □, GA • 10,597
Wilkes □, NC • 59,393
Wilkes-Barre, PA 18701–73 • 47,523
Wilkesboro, NC 28697 • 2,573
Wilkin □, MN • 7,516
Wilkinsburg, PA 15221 • 21,080
Wilkinson □, GA • 10,228
Wilkinson □, MS • 9,678
Wilkins Township, PA 15145 • 7,487
Will □, IL • 357,313
Willacoochee, GA 31650 • 1,205
Willacy □, TX • 17,705
Willamina, OR 97396 • 1,717
Willard, MO 65781 • 2,177
Willard, NY 14588 • 1,339
Willard, OH 44890 • 6,210
Willard, UT 84340 • 1,298
Willcox, AZ 85643 • 3,122
Williams, AZ 86046 • 2,532
Williams, CA 95987 • 2,297
Williams □, ND • 21,129
Williams □, OH • 36,956
Williams Bay, WI 53191 • 2,108
Williamsburg, IA 52361 • 2,174
Williamsburg, KY 40769 • 5,493
Williamsburg, MA 01096 • 1,200
Williamsburg, OH 45176 • 2,322
Williamsburg, PA 16693 • 1,456
Williamsburg, VA 23185–88 • 11,530
Williamsburg □, SC • 36,815
Williamson, NY 14589 • 1,768
Williamson, WV 25661 • 4,154
Williamson □, IL • 57,733
Williamson □, TN • 81,021
Williamson □, TX • 139,551
Williamsport, IN 47993 • 1,798
Williamsport, MD 21795 • 2,103
Williamsport, PA 17701–03 • 31,933
Williamston, MI 48895 • 2,922
Williamston, NC 27892 • 5,503
Williamston, SC 29697 • 3,876
Williamstown, KY 41097 • 3,023
Williamstown, MA 01267 • 4,791
Williamstown, NJ 08094 • 10,891
Williamstown, PA 17098 • 1,509
Williamstown, VT 05679 • 650
Williamstown, WV 26187 • 2,774
Williamsville, IL 62693 • 1,140
Williamsville, NY 14221 • 5,583
Willimantic, CT 06226 • 14,746
Willingboro, NJ 08046 • 36,291
Willis, TX 77378 • 2,764
Williston, FL 32696 • 2,179
Williston, ND 58801–02 • 13,131
Williston, SC 29853 • 3,099
Williston Park, NY 11596 • 7,516
Willits, CA 95490 • 5,027
Willmar, MN 56201 • 17,531
Willoughby, OH 44094–95 • 20,510
Willoughby Hills, OH 44092 • 8,427
Willow Brook, CA 90222 • 32,772
Willowbrook, IL 60521 • 8,598
Willow Grove, PA 19090 • 16,325
Willowick, OH 44094 • 15,269
Willow Run, DE 19805 • 1,600
Willow Run, MI 48198 • 7,200
Willows, CA 95988 • 5,988
Willow Springs, IL 60480 • 4,509
Willow Springs, MO 65793 • 2,038
Willston, VA 22044 • 2,000
Wilmerding, PA 15148 • 2,222
Wilmette, IL 60091 • 26,690
Wilmington, DE 19801–99 • 71,529
Wilmington, IL 60481 • 4,743
Wilmington, MA 01887 • 17,654
Wilmington, NC 28401–12 • 55,530
Wilmington, OH 45177 • 11,199
Wilmington, VT 05363 • 550
Wilmington Island, GA 31410 • 11,230
Wilmington Manor, DE 19720 • 8,568
Wilmington Manor Gardens, DE 19720 • 1,500
Wilmore, KY 40390 • 4,215
Wilmot, AR 71676 • 1,067
Wilson, AR 72395 • 1,068